£30

PRINCIPLES OF SCOTTISH
PRIVATE LAW

PRINCIPLES OF
SCOTTISH
PRIVATE
LAW

By
DAVID M. WALKER

M.A., LL.B. (Glas.), LL.D. (Lond.), Ph.D., LL.D., Hon. LL.D. (Edin.),
One of Her Majesty's Counsel in Scotland,
Of the Middle Temple, Barrister,
Regius Professor of Law in the
University of Glasgow

SECOND EDITION

VOLUME I

CLARENDON PRESS · OXFORD

1975

Oxford University Press, Ely House, London W.1

GLASGOW NEW YORK TORONTO MELBOURNE WELLINGTON
CAPE TOWN IBADAN NAIROBI DAR ES SALAAM LUSAKA ADDIS ABABA
DELHI BOMBAY CALCUTTA MADRAS KARACHI LAHORE DACCA
KUALA LUMPUR SINGAPORE HONG KONG TOKYO

ISBN 0 19 825336 2
© *Oxford University Press 1975*

First published 1970

Second Edition 1975

*Printed in Great Britain
by William Clowes & Sons, Limited
London, Beccles and Colchester*

PREFACE

THE purpose of this book is to provide students and practitioners of the law of Scotland with a plain statement, as concise as reasonably practicable, of the leading general principles and rules and the chief detailed rules of the private law of Scotland, and of the main qualifications and exceptions thereto, systematically set out, and supported by references to the main authorities for the propositions stated. It is hoped that this will provide a useful basis for the study of the original sources of the principles and rules in statutes, judicial decisions, and institutional writings, and of the more detailed textbooks on the particular branches and topics of the private law.

The scope of the book covers the whole of the substantive private law, including international private law and remedies, but, save incidentally, excludes the adjective law, namely the subjects of evidence, procedure, pleading and court practice, diligence, representation and legal aid, practical conveyancing and office practice. Even within these limits the private law steadily grows more voluminous and complicated, and it steadily becomes more difficult to discern general principles in the mass of particular enactments and decisions and to state them accurately. Despite this there is continuing value in a general book which tries to set out the principles and rules of the whole private law systematically, so that the different branches of law can be related one to another as parts of a larger whole and that whole be considered as a rational entity. Since the subject-matter of many groups of chapters, and even of some single chapters, has provided material enough for substantial books on those topics alone, it has been impossible, and no attempt has been made, to deal with every point of detail or matter of dispute or difficulty, nor to cite all the authorities. The older authorities may be found in older books, but I have tried to give a subtantial citation of modern authorities. Non-Scottish authorities have been cited only where this seemed necessary. For reasons of space historical, jurisprudential and comparative discussions have necessarily been excluded. In this new edition I have rearranged much of the material, revised the whole text and rewritten many passages.

I am indebted to many secretaries who toiled to convert the manuscript into typescript, particularly Mrs. Simpson, Mrs. McGrane, and Mrs. Buchanan, to Mrs. Jennifer Dick, who prepared the Tables of Cases and of Statutes, to the Delegates and staff of the Oxford University Press, and to the printers who have devoted so much skill and care to the printing.

Many of my academic colleagues in Glasgow and in other Scottish universities have given me the benefit of their views on various points, and to them all I offer my thanks. I am, however, alone responsible for the final state of the whole book.

I have sought to state the law as at 1 January 1975, but where possible have noted some later changes.

Department of Private Law,   D.M.W.
The University of Glasgow,
Glasgow, G12 8QQ.

CONTENTS

CONTENTS

PART 2

THE PARTICULAR CONTRACTS

CONTENTS

PART 3

OBLIGATIONS OF RESTITUTION

PART 4

PARTICULAR OBLIGATIONS OF RESTITUTION

PART 5

OBLIGATIONS OF REPARATION ARISING FROM DELICT GENERALLY

PART 6

THE PARTICULAR DELICTS

PART 3

RIGHTS IN INCORPOREAL HERITABLE OBJECTS
OF PROPERTY

PART 4

RIGHTS IN CORPOREAL MOVEABLE OBJECTS OF
PROPERTY

PART 5

RIGHTS IN INCORPOREAL MOVEABLE OBJECTS OF
PROPERTY

BOOK VI
LAW OF TRUSTS

TABLE OF CASES

TABLE OF CASES

TABLE OF STATUTES

1913—*continued*
Bankruptcy (Sc.) Act—*continued*

AUTHORITIES AND ABBREVIATIONS

A.A.   Act of Adjournal.

A.Ass.   Act of the General Assembly of the Church of Scotland.

A.P.S.   Acts of the Parliaments of Scotland, 1124–1707, ed. Cosmo Innes and Thomas Thomson, 11 vols. in 12, 1814–1875.

A.S.   Act of Sederunt.

Anton.   Professor A. E. Anton, *Private International Law*, 1967.

Balf.   Sir James Balfour of Pittendreich, *Practicks: or a System of the more Ancient Law of Scotland*, 1754 and (Stair Socy.) 1962–3.

Bankt.   Andrew McDouall, Lord Bankton, *Institute of the Laws of Scotland in Civil Rights*, 3 vols., 1751–3.

Begg.   J. Henderson Begg, *Law of Scotland relating to Law Agents*, 2nd ed., 1883.

Bell, *Arb.*   J. M. Bell, *Law of Arbitration in Scotland*, 2nd ed., 1877.

Bell, *Comm.*   Professor G. J. Bell, *Commentaries on the Law of Scotland and the Principles of Mercantile Jurisprudence*, 7th ed., 1870.

Bell, *Conv.*   Professor A. Montgomery Bell, *Lectures on Conveyancing*, 3rd ed., 2 vols., 1882.

Bell, *Dict.*   William Bell, *Dictionary and Digest of the Law of Scotland*, 7th ed., 1890.

Bell, *Prin.*   Professor G. J. Bell, *Principles of the Law of Scotland*, 10th ed., 1899.

Borthwick.   J. Borthwick, *Law of Libel and Slander in Scotland*, 1826.

Broun.   J. C. C. Broun, *Law of Nuisance in Scotland*, 1891.

M. P. Brown.   M. P. Brown, *Law of Sale*, 1821.

Brown.   Richard Brown, *Sale of Goods Act, 1893*, 2nd ed., 1911.

Burn-Murdoch.   H. Burn-Murdoch, *Interdict in the Law of Scotland*, 1933.

Burns.   John Burns, *Conveyancing Practice*, 4th ed., 1957.

C.   Code (Corpus Juris Civilis).

C.L.J.   Cambridge Law Journal.

Cheshire.   G. C. Cheshire, *Private International Law*, 9th ed., 1974.

Clark.   F. W. Clark, *Law of Partnership and Joint Stock Companies*, 2 vols., 1866.

Clive and Wilson.   E. Clive and J. G. Wilson, *Law of Husband and Wife*, 1974.

Cooper.   F. T. Cooper, *Law of Defamation and Verbal Injury*, 2nd ed., 1906.

Craig.   Sir Thomas Craig, *Jus Feudale*, 3rd ed., 1732, and trs. Lord President Clyde, 2 vols., 1934.

D.   Digest (Corpus Juris Civilis).

Dallas.   George Dallas of St. Martin's, *Styles of Writs*, 2nd ed., 1774.

Dicey and Morris.   A. V. Dicey and J. H. C. Morris, *Conflict of Laws*, 9th ed., 1974.

Dickson.   W. G. Dickson, *Law of Evidence in Scotland*, 3rd ed., 2 vols., 1887.

Dirleton.   Sir George Nisbet, Lord Dirleton, *Doubts and Questions in the Law, especially of Scotland*, 1698.

Dobie.   W. J. Dobie, *Manual of the Law of Liferent and Fee in Scotland*, 1941.

Dobie, *Prac.*   W. J. Dobie, *Law and Practice in the Sheriff Court*, 1948.

Duff, *Deeds.*   A. Duff, *Treatise on Deeds, chiefly affecting moveables*, 1840.

Duff, *Feudal.*   A. Duff, *Treatise on Deeds and Forms used in the Constitution Transmission and Extinction of Feudal Rights*, 1838.

Duncan and Dykes.   G. Duncan and D. Oswald Dykes, *Principles of Civil Jurisdiction as applied in the Law of Scotland*, 1911.

Encyc.   *Encyclopaedia of the Laws of Scotland*, 18 vols., 1926–52.

Ersk.   Professor John Erskine of Carnock, *An Institute of the Law of Scotland*, 8th ed., 2 vols., 1871.

Ersk., *Prin.*   Professor John Erskine of Carnock, *Principles of the Law of Scotland*, 21st ed., 1911.

Ferguson, *Roads.*   J. Ferguson, *Law of Roads, Streets, Rights of Way, Bridges and Ferries*, 1904.

Ferguson, *Water.*   J. Ferguson, *Law of Water and Water Rights in Scotland*, 1907.

Forbes.   Professor William Forbes, *Institutes of the Law of Scotland*, 2 vols., 1722–30.

Fraser, *H. & W.*   Patrick, Lord Fraser, *Husband and Wife according to the Law of Scotland*, 2nd ed., 2 vols., 1876–8.

Fraser, *M. & S.*   Patrick, Lord Fraser, *Master and Servant, Employer and Workman, Master and Apprentice*, 3rd ed., 1882.

Fraser, *P. & Ch.*   Patrick, Lord Fraser, *Law of Scotland relative to Parent and Child and Guardian and Ward*, 3rd ed., 1906.

Gibb.   Professor A. Dewar Gibb, *International Law of Jurisdiction in England and Scotland*, 1926.

Gibb and Dalrymple.   *Scottish Judicial Dictionary*, 1946.

Gloag.   Professor W. M. Gloag, *Law of Contract*, 2nd ed., 1929.

Gloag and Henderson.   Professor W. M. Gloag and Professor R. C. Henderson, *Introduction to the Law of Scotland*, 7th ed., 1968.

Gloag and Irvine.   Professor W. M. Gloag and J. M. Irvine, *Law of Rights in Security, Heritable and Moveable, and Cautionary Obligations*, 1897.

Goudy.   Henry Goudy, *Law of Bankruptcy in Scotland*, 4th ed., 1914.

Gow.   J. J. Gow, *Mercantile and Industrial Law of Scotland*, 1964.

Graham Stewart.   J. Graham Stewart, *Law of Diligence*, 1898.

Halsbury.   Laws of England, 3rd ed., 43 vols., 1952–64.

Henderson.   Professor R. C. Henderson, *Principles of Vesting in the Law of Succession*, 2nd ed., 1938.

Hope, *Major Prac.*   Sir Thomas Hope, *Major Practicks*, 1608–33, 2 vols. (Stair Socy.), 1937–8.

Hope, *Minor Prac.*   Sir Thomas Hope, *Minor Practicks*, 1726.

Hume.   Baron David Hume, *Decisions*, 1781–1822, 1839.

Hume, *Comm.*   Baron David Hume, *Commentaries on the Law of Scotland respecting Crimes*, 4th ed., 2 vols., 1844.

Hume, *Lect.*   Baron David Hume, *Lectures on the Law of Scotland*, 6 vols. (Stair Socy.), 1939–58.

Hunter.   R. Hunter, *Law of Landlord and Tenant*, 4th ed., 2 vols., 1876.

I.C.L.Q.   International and Comparative Law Quarterly, 1952–.

Inst.   Institutes (Corpus Juris Civilis).

Irons.   J. Campbell Irons, *Judicial Factors*, 1908.

J.R.   Juridical Review, 1889–.

Kames, *Eluc.*   Henry Home, Lord Kames, *Elucidations respecting the Law of Scotland*, 1777.

Kames, *H.L.T.*   Henry Home, Lord Kames, *Historical Law Tracts*, 4th ed., 1817.

Kames, *Equity.*   Henry Home, Lord Kames, *Principles of Equity*, 5th ed., 1825.

L.Q.R.   Law Quarterly Review, 1886–.

Mor.   W. M. Morison's *Dictionary of Decisions*, 22 vols.

M.L.R.   Modern Law Review, 1937–.

Mackay, *Manual.*   Aeneas J. G. Mackay, *Manual of Practice in the Court of Session*, 1893.

Mackay, *Prac.*   Aeneas J. G. Mackay, *Practice of the Court of Session*, 2 vols., 1877–9.

Mack.   Sir George Mackenzie of Rosehaugh, *Institutions of the Law of Scotland*, 1684.

Mack., *Crim.*   Sir George Mackenzie of Rosehaugh, *Laws and Customs of Scotland in Matters Criminal*, 2nd ed., 1699.

Mackenzie Stuart.   Professor A. Mackenzie Stuart, *Law of Trusts*, 1932.

Maclaren.   J. A. Maclaren, *Court of Session Practice*, 1916.

McLaren.   John, Lord McLaren, *Law of Wills and Succession*, 3rd ed., 1894; Supplement by Dykes, 1934.

Menzies.   Professor Allan Menzies, *Lectures on Conveyancing according to the Law of Scotland*, revised ed., 1900.

Menzies, *Trs.*   A. J. P. Menzies, *Law of Scotland affecting Trustees*, 2nd ed., 1913.

Millar.   J. H. Millar, *Handbook of Prescription according to the Law of Scotland*, 1893.

Miller, *Partnership.*   Professor J. Bennett Miller, *Law of Partnership in Scotland*, 1973.

More, *Lect.*   Professor J. S. More, *Lectures on the Law of Scotland*, ed. McLaren, 2 vols., 1864.

More, *Notes.*   Professor J. S. More, *Notes to Stair's Institutions*, in fifth edition thereof, 1832.

Morris.   J. H. C. Morris, *The Conflict of Laws*, 1971.

Napier.   Mark Napier, *Law of Prescription in Scotland*, 2nd ed., 1854.

N.I.L.Q.   Northern Ireland Legal Quarterly.

Nov.   Novels (Corpus Juris Civilis).

Paton and Cameron.   G. C. H. Paton and J. G. S. Cameron, *Law of Landlord and Tenant*, 1967.

Q.A.   *Quoniam Attachiamenta.*

R.C.   Rules of the Court of Session, 1965.

R.M.   *Regiam Majestatem*, ed. Skene, 1609, and ed. Cooper (Stair Socy.), 1947.

Rankine, *Bar.*   Professor Sir John Rankine, *Law of Personal Bar in Scotland*, 1921.

Rankine, *L.O.*   Professor Sir John Rankine, *Law of Land Ownership in Scotland*, 4th ed., 1909.

Rankine, *Leases.*   Professor Sir John Rankine, *Law of Leases in Scotland*, 3rd ed., 1916.

Ross, *Lect.*   Walter Ross, *Lectures on the History and Practice of* the *Law of Scotland relative to Conveyancing and Legal Diligence*, 2nd ed., 2 vols., 1822.

S.L.R.   Scottish Law Review, 1886–1963.

S.L.T. (News).   Scots Law Times, News portion.

Skene, *D.V.S.*   Sir John Skene, *De Verborum Significatione*, 1597.

Smith, *British Justice*.   Professor T. B. Smith, *British Justice— The Scottish Contribution*, 1961.

Smith, *Precedent*.   Professor T. B. Smith, *Doctrines of Judicial Precedent in Scots Law*, 1952.

Smith, *Studies*.   Professor T. B. Smith, *Studies Critical and Comparative*, 1963.

Smith, *Sh.Comm*.   Professor T. B. Smith, *A Short Commentary on the Law of Scotland*, 1963.

Spotiswoode.   Sir Robert Spotiswoode, *Practicks of the Laws of Scotland*, 1706.

Stair.   Sir James Dalrymple, Viscount Stair, *Institutions of the Law of Scotland*, 5th ed., 2 vols., 1832.

Thoms.   G. H. Thoms, *Judicial Factors*, 2nd ed., 1881.

Steuart.   Sir James Steuart, *Answers to Dirleton's Doubts in the Laws of Scotland*, 1715.

Umpherston.   F. Umpherston, *Master and Servant*, 1904.

Walker, *Civil Remedies*.   Professor D. M. Walker, *Law of Civil Remedies in Scotland*, 1974.

Walker, *Damages*.   Professor D. M. Walker, *Law of Damages in Scotland*, 1955.

Walker, *Delict*.   Professor D. M. Walker, *Law of Delict in Scotland*, 2 vols., 1966.

Walker, *Judicial Factors*.   Sheriff N. M. L. Walker, *Judicial Factors*, 1974.

Walker, *Prescription*.   Professor D. M. Walker, *Law of Prescription and Limitation of Actions in Scotland*, 1973.

Walker, *S.L.S.*   Professor D. M. Walker, *The Scottish Legal System*, 3rd ed., 1969.

Walkers.   A. G. Walker and N. M. L. Walker, *Law of Evidence in Scotland*, 1964.

Wallace.   G. Wallace, *System of the Principles of the Law of Scotland*, 1760.

Walton.   F. P. Walton, *Handbook of the Law of Husband and Wife in Scotland*, 3rd ed., 1951.

Wilson.   W. A. Wilson, *Law of Trusts and Trustees in Scotland*, 1974.

Wood.   Professor J. P. Wood, *Lectures on Conveyancing*, 1903.

BOOK I

INTRODUCTORY AND GENERAL

The Introductory and General Book deals with those matters of an introductory character which are necessarily preliminary to the understanding of the rules of any of the particular branches of the subject, and also those principles of wide general application, not falling wholly within any one branch of private law.

CHAPTER 1

SCOTTISH PRIVATE LAW:
ITS SCOPE, SOURCES, AND LITERATURE

1. SCOPE OF SCOTTISH PRIVATE LAW

THE private law is the branch of the municipal law of Scotland comprising the principles and rules applied in defining and determining the rights and duties of ordinary private persons in their relations with one another, and of the State, and of public and governmental agencies and persons, in respects in which they do not enjoy any special position, right, or immunity, by virtue of any rule of public law.[1] The division between private and public law is not clear or rigid nor is it so familiar as in continental legal systems.

Private law is entirely civil in character, being defined and applied by civil courts under civil procedure, though at many points touching and interacting with principles applied by the criminal courts in dealing, under rules of criminal procedure, with the kinds of conduct legally deemed criminal and punishable, and with principles applied by administrative authorities and tribunals in dealing with disputes arising from matters of public administration, and with the principles applied by courts of special jurisdiction, which are sometimes civil and sometimes criminal in character. Scottish private law has never known the distinguishable, and sometimes conflicting, bodies of rules of common law and of equity, as long did, and to some extent does, English law, nor distinct bodies of civil and of commercial law, applicable respectively to ordinary citizens and to merchants, as do many European systems of law. Equitable principles and rules derived from commercial and maritime customs are woven into the fabric of the private law.

In each of public and private law a distinction exists between rules of substantive law, which state what rights and duties are recognized in various categories of relationships, and what legal remedies exist for infringement thereof, and rules of adjective law

---

[1] See also Inst. I, 1, 4; Stair I, 1, 23; Bankt. I, 1, 54; Ersk. I, 1, 29; Articles of Union, 1707, Art. 18; Markby, *Elements of Law* (6th ed.) 151; Holland, *Jurisprudence* (13th ed.) 128; Salmond, 533; Pollock, *Jurisprudence and Legal Essays*, Ch. 4; Jones, *Historical Introduction on the Theory of Law*, Ch. 5; Paton, *Jurisprudence* (3rd ed.) Ch. 14; Walker, *S.L.S.*, Ch. 4.

which define the means whereby rights can be vindicated, duties enforced and remedies obtained.

Within private law the most satisfactory classification is fundamentally that of the Roman law, into law of persons, law of things, and law of actions,[1] which was generally adopted by the earlier Scottish institutional writers,[2] by the modern Roman law of the German jurists,[3] and by European codifications.[4]

The arrangement herein adopted substantially follows these models. The General Part[5] deals with matters common to many or all branches of the private law, and that on International Private Law[6] with cases where an issue involves a non-Scottish or international element.[7] The Law of Persons[8] deals both with natural living persons and with juristic persons or corporations.[9] The Law of Things is divided into rights of obligation[10] or personal rights availing only against other particular persons,[11] and rights of property[12] or real rights availing against other persons generally.[13] Distinct branches of the law of things deal with the holding of rights in trust,[14] the rules as to the disposal of the estate of a deceased person,[15] and the transfer of the property of an insolvent to his creditors,[16] On the substantive rules are dependent the adjective rules of the forms and methods requisite to create, transfer, and extinguish the recognized kinds of rights of a proprietary kind. The Law of Actions includes the law of civil remedies for breaches of legal duty[17] and the rules of civil procedure, practice, pleading, evidence, and diligence.[18]

Within each of these main divisions are heads and subheads,

---

[1] Gaius I, 8; Inst. I, 2, 12; Dig. I, 5, 1. See further Buckland, 56–9.

[2] Stair I, 1, 23; Mack. I, 2, 1; Bankt. I, 1, 86; Ersk. I, 2, 1. Bell departed from Roman arrangement.

[3] General Part; Special Part—property, obligations, family law, inheritance.

[4] e.g. French Code Civil: Persons; Property Rights; Acquisition of Property (including Obligations). German Burgerliches Gesetzbuch: General Principles; Obligations; Things; Family Law; Inheritance. But these codes do not deal with rules applicable to specifically commercial transactions.

[5] Book I.

[6] Book II.

[7] Stair I, 1, 16; Bankt. I, 1, 76; Ersk. III, 2, 39.

[8] Book III.   [9] Stair I, 4–6; Mack. I, 6–7; Bankt. I, 5–7; Ersk. I, 5–7.

[10] Book IV.

[11] Stair I, 7–18; Mack. III, 1–7; Bankt. I, 4 and 8–24; Ersk. III, 1–7.

[12] Book V.

[13] Stair II, 1–12; Mack. II, 1–13; Bankt. II, 1–12; III, 1–3; Ersk. II, 1–12.

[14] Book VI.

[15] Book VII; Stair III, 4–9; Mack. III, 8–10; Bankt. III, 4–9; Ersk. III, 8–10.

[16] Book VIII.   [17] Book IX.

[18] Stair IV; Mack. IV; Bankt. IV; Ersk. IV; These topics are, save for incidental mentions, excluded from this book.

mostly derived from Roman law, but necessarily modified by indigenous developments and the progress of legal science.

2. SOURCES AND THEIR EVALUATION

The term 'sources' of Scottish Private Law may be used of at least three sets of facts,[1] namely

(1) historical sources, or the facts, events, ideas, and practices which have, down to the present time, influenced the development, content, and form of the principles and rules of the positive law;

(2) philosophical or theoretical sources, or the presuppositions, beliefs, ideals, and doctrines, religious, moral, social, political, and economic, which underlie and explain the character of various legal doctrines accepted and enacted; and

(3) formal or legal sources, or those statements of principles and rules which are recognized by courts and legal advisers as authoritative, and from which rules for the definition of rights and the determination of matters in controversy in particular cases may be discovered. The formal or legal sources alone yield principles and rules which are parts of the positive law and are enforceable. The historical and philosophical sources merely help to explain the form and content of particular rules.

Historical sources

The historical sources of Scottish Private Law are the customary practices of the community, generally accepted as binding and enforceable, ancient statutes and books of law, such as *Regiam Majestatem*, principles of conduct enunciated in the Bible and generally followed in reliance thereon, principles developed in the Civil Law of Rome and accepted in Scotland, usually through the mediation of the writings of French, German, and Dutch jurists from the fourteenth to the eighteenth centuries, the principles of the Canon Law of the Roman Church as developed down to the Reformation and accepted in Scotland, the principles of the feudal law of Western Europe applied in Scottish practice, the principles of the general mercantile and maritime customs of Western Europe, and some principles of the common law and equity of England. Many of these have been adopted in Scots law under

---

[1] Walker, *S.L.S.*, Ch. 8.

the influence of the great systematic writings of the institutional writers.[1]

Philosophical sources

The philosophical sources are difficult to isolate. They include above all the ideas of justice generally held at various times by the legally dominant sections of the community, related to the prevailing religious, moral, social, political, and economic views.

They include such principles as a belief in the equality of individuals before the law, and in the freedom of individuals to act as they please, subject only to specified restrictions; acceptance of the Christian notion of marriage and the family; the acceptance of the belief that individuals should be free to bind themselves legally as they wish, and must take care for their own protection, a principle greatly modified in modern times by statutory intervention for the protection of the presumed weaker partner; the belief that an individual should have to compensate for harm done to others for which he is morally responsible, to which has been added in certain cases in modern times, the obligation to compensate for harm resulting from a risk created by the individual's activities, or for harm resulting from his failure to implement a statutorily-imposed duty; the acceptance of the doctrine of private ownership of property and of the means of production, exchange, and distribution, a principle increasingly qualified, restricted, and subjected to exceptions; the acceptance of the doctrine that, subject to certain limitations, an individual is free to determine the way in which his property will devolve after his death, but that, failing such provision, the law will destine it to certain surviving relatives.[2]

No single body of philosophic thought or beliefs has had a monopoly of influence, but particularly important have been the idea of natural law,[3] and, in modern times, the idea of utility, of serving the greatest good of the greatest number.

Formal or legal sources

The formal or legal sources alone yield authoritative statements of principles and rules for the guidance of legal advisers and for

---

[1] On these sources see the various chapters in (Stair Society) *Sources and Literature* and *Introductory History*. See also Stair I, 1, 6–9, 12–14, 16; Bankt. I, 1, 38–46; Ersk. I, 1, 27–8, 30–6, 41–2.

[2] cf. Stair I, 1, 18; Pound, *Jural Postulates*, in *Outlines of Jurisprudence* (5th ed.), 168.

[3] cf. Stair I, 1, 6; Ersk. I, 1, 7–17.

application by the courts to the resolution of controversies brought before them.[1] They are of six kinds.

(I) LEGISLATION

Legislation comprises (a) the law of the European Communities, both existing at the date of the United Kingdom's entry into the European Communities[2] and made thereafter, which under the Community Treaties is directly enforceable in member states. These comprise provisions of the Community Treaties themselves, regulations, directives and decisions of the Council of Ministers and of the Commission. That part of Community law which has direct effect takes precedence over the domestic law of each member state, and national courts are obliged to apply it and enforce it when called on to do so.[3] Any enactment passed or to be passed by the United Kingdom Parliament must be construed and have effect subject to obligations and restrictions from time to time created or arising by or under the Treaties.[4]

It also comprises (b) the bodies of statutes or Acts enacted by the Parliaments of Scotland down to 1707, of the Parliaments of Great Britain from 1707 to 1800, and of the Parliaments of the United Kingdom since 1801, in all cases so far as amended but not repealed by subsequent legislation,[5] and (c) subordinate or delegated legislation.

Statutes comprise public general statutes, of general application throughout the United Kingdom, or one or more of the countries thereof, and local and personal Acts, applicable only to particular localities or to particular bodies or persons. The former are enactments of public bills introduced by the government of the day, or by a private member; the latter are introduced as private bills and the promoters must satisfy a select committee at a hearing of a judicial nature that the statutory powers or authority sought are necessary for their purposes and may properly be granted. Public authorities and private bodies more frequently now obtain parliamentary powers by obtaining from the Secretary of State for Scotland, if necessary after inquiry, a pro-

---

[1] See generally Craig I, 8, 1–17; Stair I, 1, 16; Mack. I, 1, 6–15; Bankt. I, 1, 58–86; Ersk. I, 1, 30–60.

[2] 1 January 1973.

[3] European Communities Act, 1972, Ss. 2(1), 3(1).

[4] *Ibid.*, S. 2(4).

[5] See further Erskine May, *Parliamentary Practice;* Craies, *Statute Law.* On Scots Acts see Ersk. I, 1, 37–9.

visional order granting the desired powers, which is subsequently confirmed by the passing of a bill brought in by the Secretary of State for Scotland as a Provisional Order Confirmation Act.[1] Private Acts are of the nature of contracts, sanctioned by Parliament, between the promoters and the public.[2] If an undertaking is established by private Act it can be abandoned only under statutory authority.[3]

The Crown still has powers, in limited classes of case, of legislation by authority of the royal prerogative, by way of Orders in Council, Letters Patent, or Proclamations. Such powers are almost confined to actings in wartime and to legislation for colonies. It is incompetent to challenge an Act of Parliament as being *ultra vires* or to inquire into the validity of the procedure whereby it was passed ;[4] the same applies to regulations or bye-laws declared to have effect as if enacted in an Act.

Subordinate or delegated legislation consists of rules, regulations, and orders made by a minister of the Crown or other person or body to whom or which Parliament has delegated power to issue such legislation, and who or which remains, in the exercise of this power, subject to the control of Parliament. Such legislation was formerly known collectively as Statutory Rules and Orders and since 1947 as Statutory Instruments.[5] Unless expressly declared by the empowering Act to have the force of statute, subordinate legislation may be challenged as *ultra vires*.[6] The chief forms of subordinate legislation are Orders in Council, and ministerial or departmental Regulations, Rules, or Orders,[7] and local authority bye-laws.

Certain public authorities and local authorities have delegated statutory powers to make by-laws which have application only within the area of the authority's responsibility. Local authority by-laws normally require the confirmation of an autho-

---

[1] For procedure see Private Legislation Procedure (Scotland) Act, 1936. In certain cases orders made by Ministers may be given Parliamentary authority under the Statutory Orders (Special Procedure) Acts, 1945 and 1965.

[2] *Milligan* v. *Ayr Harbour Trs.*, 1915 S.C. 937.

[3] *Ellice* v. *Invergarry Ry. Co.*, 1913 S.C. 849.

[4] *Hamilton* v. *Fyfe*, 1907 S.C. (J.) 79; *B.R. Board* v. *Pickin* [1974] 1 All E.R. 609.

[5] Statutory Instruments Act, 1946.

[6] *Institute of Patent Agents* v. *Lockwood* (1894) 21 R. (H.L.) 61; *Dunsmore* v. *Lindsay* (1903) 6 F. (J.) 14; *Shepherd* v. *Howman*, 1918 J.C. 78; *Lawson* v. *Torrance*, 1929 J.C. 119; *Sommerville* v. *Langmuir*, 1932 J.C. 55; *Sommerville* v. *Lord Advocate*, 1933 S.L.T. 48. See also *Henderson* v. *Ross*, 1928 J.C. 74, 76.

[7] They are published in annual volumes known down to 1947 as Statutory Rules and Orders and since then as Statutory Instruments.

rity such as the Secretary of State or the sheriff.[1] A by-law is open to challenge as *ultra vires*,[2] as unreasonable, or as contrary to the general law,[4] and even though it has obtained the requisite approval.[5] It falls if the authorizing statute is repealed.[6]

Acts of Sederunt are rules of a legislative kind made by the Court of Session under powers conferred originally at its foundation[7] or, in modern times, under the authority of statute.[8] They are now confined to the regulation of procedure in the civil courts. The extant Acts were collected in the codifying Act of Sederunt, 1913, now almost entirely replaced by the Rules of Court authorized by the Administration of Justice (Scotland) Act, 1933.[9] Acts of Sederunt are now normally statutory instruments.[10]

Acts of Adjournal are Acts passed by the High Court of Justiciary under similar powers for regulating procedural matters in the criminal courts. They also are now normally statutory instruments.[10]

Authority of legislation

Where legislation of any kind is in force in relation to any subject, it is authoritative, in that it is superior to any inconsistent rule of law, however old or well-established, and overrules it,[11] and mandatory, in that it must be implemented, unless it clearly appears to be permissive.

---

[1] See Local Government (Sc.) Act, 1973, Ss. 201–4; *Aldred* v. *Miller*, 1925 J.C. 21; *Baird* v. *Glasgow Corporation*, 1935 S.C. (H.L.) 21. On effect of confirmation see *Crichton* v. *Forfarshire Road Trs.* (1886) 13 R. (J.) 99. On sheriff's function see *Glasgow Corpn.* v. *Glasgow Churches' Council*, 1944 S.C. 97.

[2] *Kerr* v. *Auld* (1890) 18 R. (J.) 12; *Eastburn* v. *Wood* (1892) 19 R. (J.) 100; *Rae* v. *Hamilton* (1904) 6 F. (J.) 42; *Rossi* v. *Edinburgh Mags.* (1904) 7 F. (H. L.) 85; *McGregor* v. *Disselduff*, 1907 S. C. (J.) 21; cf. *Shepherd* v. *Howman*, 1918 J.C. 78; *Aldred, supra*; *Aldred* v. *Langmuir*, 1932 J.C. 22; *Baird, supra*.

[3] *Saunders* v. *S.E. Ry.* (1880) 5 Q.B.D. 456; *Apthorpe* v. *Edinburgh Street Tramway Co.* (1882) 10 R. 344; *Dunsmore* v. *Lindsay* (1903) 6 F. (J.) 14; *Da Prato* v. *Partick Mags.*, 1907 S.C. (H.L.) 5; *Ronaldson* v. *Williamson*, 1911 S.C. (J.) 102. The court is slow to hold unreasonable a by-law passed by a public representative body; *Kruse* v. *Johnson* [1898] 2 Q.B. 91; *Aldred, supra*; *Baird, supra*.

[4] *Dunsmore* v. *Lindsay* (1903) 6 F. (J.) 14; *Aldred, supra*.

[5] *Lawson* v. *Torrance*, 1929 J.C. 119.

[6] *Watson* v. *Winch* [1916] 1 K.B. 688.

[7] Ersk. I, 1, 40.

[8] Hence the power falls if the statute is repealed; *Inglis's Trustees* v. *Macpherson*, 1910 S.C. 46.

[9] See *Rules of Court*, 1965. On whether the Court of Session can entertain an action to determine the validity of one of its own Acts of Sederunt, see *Carron Co.* v. *Hislop*, 1930 S.C. 1050.

[10] Law Reform (Miscellaneous Provisions) (Sc.) Act, 1966, S. 10.

[11] *Gower* v. *Sheriff of Caithness* (1828) 6 S. 650.

Proof of terms of legislation

Courts take official notice of the Community Treaties,[1] the Official Journal of the Communities[2] and of any decision of, or expression of opinion by, the European Court. The Official Journal is admissible as evidence of any instrument or other act of any of the Communities or of any Community institution. Evidence of any instrument issued by a Community institution may be given by a certified true copy, by production of a copy purporting to be printed by the Queen's Printer, or where the instrument is in the custody of a government department by production of a certified true copy. In Scotland evidence given in such a manner is sufficient evidence.[3]

Public general statutes of the U.K. Parliament are judicially noticed and the terms thereof need not be proved to a court. The text of an Act as printed by the Queen's Printer will be accepted as accurate.[4] The text of a Scots Act as printed in the Record edition would probably be accepted.[5]

The terms of Private Acts must be proved to the court, but the Interpretation Act, 1889, s. 9, provides that all Acts passed after 1850 are to be public Acts and judicially noticed as such, unless the contrary is expressly provided by the Act, in which case a copy certified by the Clerk of the Parliaments must be produced unless the Act provides that a Queen's Printer's copy shall be admitted in evidence.

The terms of statutory instruments may be proved by production of a copy of the London or Edinburgh *Gazette* purporting to contain the order or regulation, or of a copy of the order or regulation, purporting to be printed by the Government printer,[6] or of a copy or extract purporting to be certified to be true by one of the

---

[1] i.e. The European Coal and Steel Community Treaty, 1951; The European Economic Community Treaty, 1957; The European Atomic Energy Community Treaty, 1957; The Convention on certain Institutions common to the European Communities, 1957; the Treaty establishing a single Council and single Commission, 1965; the amending Treaty, 1970.

[2] i.e. the *Journal Officiel de la Communauté Européenne de Charbon et de l'Acier*, 1952–58; the *Journal Officiel des Communautés Européennes*, 1958–67, and the latter in two sections, since 1968, containing legislative and other texts respectively.

[3] European Communities Act, 1972, S. 3.

[4] cf. *Aiton* v. *Stephen* (1876) 3 R. (H.L.) 4; *Scottish Drainage Co.* v. *Campbell* (1889) 16 R. (H.L.) 16.

[5] i.e. *The Acts of the Parliaments of Scotland*, ed. Innes and Thomson (12 vols., 1814–75); Scots Acts still in force in 1966 are reprinted in *The Acts of the Parliaments of Scotland* (H.M.S.O., 1966), but see *Kemp* v. *Glasgow Corpn.*, 1920 S.C. (H.L.) 73, 78.

[6] *Macmillan* v. *McConnell*, 1917 J.C. 43; *Herkes* v. *Dickie*, 1958 J.C. 51.

persons statutorily empowered to certify, without proof of the handwriting or official position of any person so certifying.[1]

The production of a copy of a by-law purporting to be made by a local authority under any enactment or by any other authority to whose by-laws the Local Government (Sc.) Act, 1973, S. 201 applies, upon which is endorsed a certificate purporting to be signed by the clerk of the authority stating that the by-law was made by the authority, that the copy is a true copy, that on a specified date the by-law was confirmed by the authority named or was sent to the Secretary of State and has not been disallowed, and the date fixed by the confirming authority for the coming into operation of the by-law, is evidence of the facts stated in the certificate until the contrary is proved, without proof of the handwriting or official position of any person purporting to sign a certificate under this provision.[2] If the empowering statute provides that the by-law is to have the same effect as if it were contained in the Act[3] or to have the effect of an Act,[4] no proof of it is required.[5]

Acts of Sederunt and Acts of Adjournal are statutory instruments[6] and do not require proof.

Application

A statute of the United Kingdom Parliament prima facie applies to the whole United Kingdom.[7] The express exclusion of Ireland suggests the inclusion of Scotland in the area of application.[8] If intended to apply to Scotland only this is stated and the word (Scotland) is included in the title. If intended not to apply to Scotland this may be stated expressly, or it may appear from such facts as that the statute is an amendment of an Act from which Scotland was excluded,[9] or is expressed in English technical

---

[1] Documentary Evidence Acts, 1868 and 1882.

[2] Local Government (Sc.) Act, 1973, S. 204; see also *Herkes* v. *Dickie*, 1958 J.C. 51.

[3] e.g. *Inst. of Patent Agents* v. *Lockwood* (1894) 21 R. (H.L.) 61.

[4] e.g. *Hamilton* v. *Fyfe*, 1907 S.C. (J.) 79.

[5] *Herkes* v. *Dickie*, 1958 J.C. 51.

[6] Statutory Instruments Act, 1946, S. 1(2); Law Reform (Miscellaneous Provisions) (Sc.) Act, 1966, S. 10.

[7] *Bridges* v. *Fordyce* (1844) 6 D. 968; (1847) 6 Bell 1; *H.M.A.* v. *Burns*, 1967 J.C. 15.

[8] *Scottish Drug Depot* v. *Fraser* (1905) 7 F. 646, 648.

[9] *Westminster Fire Office* v. *Glasgow Provident Investment Socy.* (1888) 15 R. (H.L.) 89, 94; *Levy* v. *Jackson* (1903) 5 F. 1170; See also *McLean* v. *Murdoch* (1882) 10 R. (J.) 34; *Bell* v. *Mitchell* (1905) 8 F. (J.) 15.

terms without mention of their Scottish counterparts,[1] or incorporates by reference statutes not applicable to Scotland.[2] If
intended to apply in part to Scotland this may be stated expressly
or may appear from the existence of parts or sections of the Act
applicable in terminology only to Scotland.

Statutes applicable to the United Kingdom are commonly
framed in English technical terms with an 'application to Scotland' section giving the equivalent terms to be used when applying sections to Scottish conditions.[3]

Commencement

An Act of Parliament *prima facie* comes into force on the date
on which it receives the Royal Assent,[4] but an Act may provide for
the date of its coming into force, or provide that a Minister may,
by statutory instrument, bring the Act or parts of it, into force on
a date or dates specified by him. Hence an Act, though passed,
may be only partly in force, or not in force at all. Effect cannot
be given to an Act passed but not yet in force.[5]

Duration

Once passed and brought into force a statute continues in
force, even though not applied, until repealed, unless expressly
enacted for a limited period only, in which case the Act lapses
automatically at the end of the period, unless continued in force
by an Expiring Laws Continuance Act or made permanent.
Alternatively, an Act may provide that its duration may be terminated by Order in Council.

Desuetude

Prior to 1707, and subsequently, but in respect of pre-1707
Scots Acts only, a statute might be held abrogated by desuetude,
by great antiquity together with absence of recent precedent for
the application of the Act, long disregard of it in practice, and its

[1] *Levy, supra; Scottish Drug Depot, supra.* But see *H.M.A.* v. *Holmes and Lockyer* (1869) 1
Coup. 221; *Perth Water Commrs.* v. *McDonald* (1879) 6 R. 1050; *Dunlop* v. *Goudie* (1895)
22 R. (J.) 34; *Murray* v. *Comptroller General of Patents,* 1932 S.C. 726; cf. *Conn* v. *Renfrew
Mags.* (1906) 8 F. 905; *Wilson* v. *Kilmarnock Assessor,* 1913 S.C. 704.

[2] *H.M.A.* v. *Cox* (1872) 2 Coup. 229; *H.M.A.* v. *Davidson* (1872) 2 Coup. 278.

[3] But see *Wan Ping Nam* v. *Federal German Republic Minister of Justice,* 1972 S.L.T.
220.

[4] Acts of Parliament (Commencement) Act, 1793; *Tomlinson* v. *Bullock* (1878) 4 Q.B.D.
230; *R.* v. *Weston* [1910] 1 K.B. 17.

[5] *Wilson* v. *Dagnall* [1972] 2 All E.R. 44.

being obsolete and inappropriate in modern conditions.[1] Since the repeal of much obsolete pre-1707 legislation in 1906 and 1964[2] there is a rebuttable presumption that any Scots Act not thereby repealed is not in desuetude. Desuetude has no application to post-1707 legislation.

Amendment

An Act may be amended in any respect and to any extent by any subsequent Act, either expressly, or by implication arising from the occurrence of an inconsistent provision in a subsequent Act.[3] The whole statute law on one topic must be read together and in case of inconsistency the latest provision is presumed to supersede earlier ones.

Repeal

An Act, or any part thereof, may be repealed by any subsequent Act, either expressly, or impliedly, when a subsequent provision is inconsistent with the earlier one, which is held superseded thereby.[4] The courts are, however, unwilling to imply repeal in this way.[5] An Act may be repealed *quoad* England but be left in force *quoad* Scotland.[6] The repeal of an Act wholly obliterates it, and does not revive anything not in force at the time of the repeal, unless such an intention is disclosed.[7] Nor does the repeal of an Act which had repealed earlier legislation revive that legislation unless such an intention is disclosed.[8] A special Act is not repealed by a general Act unless there is express reference thereto or a necessary inconsistency in allowing both to stand.[9] A public Act is

---

[1] Craig I, 8, 9; Stair I, 1, 16; Mack. I, 1, 10; Bankt. I, 1, 60; Ersk. I, 1, 45; *Gardiner* v. *Kilrenny Mags.* (1826) 4 S. 539; (1828) 6 S. 693; *Bute* v. *More* (1870) 9 M. 180; *Middleton* v. *Tough,* 1908 S.C. (J.) 32; *McAra* v. *Edinburgh Mags.,* 1913 S.C. 1059; *Brown* v. *Edinburgh Mags.,* 1931 S.L.T. 456; *MacCormick* v. *L.A.,* 1953 S.C. 396, 417.

[2] Statute Law Revision (Scotland) Acts, 1906 and 1964.

[3] *Mount* v. *Taylor* (1868) L.R. 3 C.P. 645.

[4] *Kutner* v. *Phillips* [1891] 2 Q.B. 267, 272; *Lang* v. *Munro* (1892) 19 R. (J.) 53; *Ross* v. *Ross* (1894) 22 R. 174; *Melville Coal Co.* v. *Clark* (1904) 6 F. 913; *Hendrie* v. *Caledonian Ry.,* 1909 S.C. 776; *Cowdenbeath Mags.* v. *Cowdenbeath Gas Co.,* 1915 S.C. 323; *Moss' Empires* v. *Glasgow Assessor,* 1917 S.C. (H.L.) 1; *Angus C.C.* v. *Montrose Mags.,* 1933 S.C. 505.

[5] *Bain* v. *Mackay* (1875) 2 R. (J.) 32; *Dobbs* v. *Grand Junction Waterworks Co.* (1882) 9 Q.B.D. 151; *Kutner* v. *Phillips* [1891] 2 Q.B. 267; *Aberdeen Tramways Co.* v. *Aberdeen Mags.,* 1927 S.C. 683.

[6] *Smith's Trs.* v. *Gaydon,* 1931 S.C. 533; *Lindsay's Trs.* v. *L.,* 1931 S.C. 586.

[7] Interpretation Act, 1889, S. 38(2); *Henderson's Trs.* v. *H.,* 1930 S.L.T. 346; *Moray C.C.* v. *Maclean,* 1962 S.C. 601.

[8] Interpretation Act, 1889, S. 11(1). For a case of express revival of a repealed Act by a later Act, see Trade Disputes and Trade Unions Act, 1946, S. 1.

[9] *N.B. Ry.* v. *Wingate,* 1913 S.C. 1092; *Aberdeen Suburban Tramways Co.* v. *Aberdeen Mags.,* 1927 S.C. 683, 689.

not repealed by a private Act unless such clearly appears to be the intention.[1] The repeal of an Act does not affect rights or liabilities acquired or incurred by persons acting under the Act while in force,[2] nor affect any legal proceeding or remedy in respect of any such right or liability, which may be enforced notwithstanding the repeal.[3]

Interpretation of legislation

Interpretation[4] or construction is necessary to ascertain whether a particular statutory provision is applicable to the facts before the court, and, if so, what it prescribes or requires. It is always a question of law for the court, to be determined by consideration of the words used in the light of legal arguments, not one to be determined by evidence, and the question is to ascertain what is the fair meaning and intention of the legislature.[5] A statute cannot be challenged as being *ultra vires* or on the ground that its purpose is illegal.[6]

Literal and liberal interpretation

There may be conflict between the two main judicial approaches to legislation, the literal approach, which stresses attention to the words actually used, and the liberal approach, which stresses the legislative purpose and general intention to remedy defects in the law. The literal meaning ought not to prevail if opposed to the legislative intention appearing in the statute, if the words are sufficiently flexible to admit of another construction by which that intention will be better effectuated.[7] The purpose or spirit of the legislation cannot be given effect to if the words used preclude the court from so doing.[8]

Liberal interpretation is necessary when construing pre-1707 Scots Acts, which were commonly drafted generally, and as to

---

[1] *Russell* v. *Aberdeen Mags.* (1899) 1 F. 792; *Balfour*, 1909 S.C. 358.

[2] Interpretation Act, 1889, S. 38(2); *Smith's Trs.* v. *Irvine and Fullarton Property, etc. Socy.* (1903) 6 F. 99; *Moray County Council* v. *Maclean*, 1962 S.C. 601.

[3] Ibid.

[4] See generally Ersk. I, 1, 49–60; Craies on *Statute Law* (7th ed.); Maxwell on *Interpretation of Statutes* (12th ed.); Walker, *S.L.S.*, Ch. 8; Report of Law Commission and Scottish Law Commission on Interpretation of Statutes (Sc. L. Comm. No. 11, 1969).

[5] *E. Breadalbane* v. *Lord Advocate* (1870) 8 M. 835.

[6] *Cheney* v. *Conn* [1968] 1 All E.R. 779.

[7] *Caledonian Ry.* v. *N.B. Ry.* (1881) 8 R. (H.L.) 23; *Inland Revenue* v. *Luke*, 1963 S.C. (H.L.) 65.

[8] *Campbell's Trs.* v. *O'Neill*, 1911 S.C. 188, 196.

which greater weight must be given to contemporaneous interpretation.[1]

If the meaning of an Act is plain effect must be given to it
without speculation as to Parliament's intention.[2]

Interpretation Act and interpretation sections in Acts

The Interpretation Act, 1889, assigns meanings to a number
of words commonly found in statutes, unless the context of a
particular act gives a contrary indication,[3] and many statutes
contain their own interpretation sections assigning particular
meanings to words for the purposes of that Act. But if defined
expressions are used in a context which the definition does not fit,
the words may be used in their ordinary meaning.[4]

Failing such assigned meanings the usual dictionary meaning of
a word falls to be adopted,[5] and its technical meaning if it has
one.[6] A judge, such as the sheriff of a locality affected, does not
require to be instructed in the meaning of technical terms used in
a local statute.[7]

Relevance of context

A statute must be read as a whole and sections read in the light
of one another. Words and phrases must be read in their context
and may take on a shade of meaning from the context. This
requires that words be interpreted by regard to the whole section
or Act in which they appear[8] and even to the whole course of
legislation,[9] and with regard to the general scope of the Act.[10]

In particular the maxim *noscitur a sociis* expresses the principle

---

[1] *Johnstone* v. *Stotts* (1802) 4 Pat. 274, 283; *Fergusson* v. *Skirving* (1852) 1 Macq. 232;
Thomas v. *Thomson* (1865) 3 M. 1160, 1165; *E. Home* v. *L. Belhaven & Stenton* (1903) 5 F.
(H.L.) 13, 23; *Heriot's Tr.* v. *Paton's Trs.*, 1912 S.C. 1123; *Whatmough's Tr.* v. *B.L. Bank*,
1934 S.C. (H.L.) 51.

[2] *Glasgow Court House Commrs.* v. *Lanarkshire C.C.* (1900) 3 F. 103; *West Highland Ry.*
v. *Inverness C.C.* (1904) 6 F. 1052. But see *Caledonian Ry.* v. *N.B. Ry.* (1881) 8 R. (H.L.) 23,
30; *Bradlaugh* v. *Clarke* (1883) 8 App. Cas. 354, 384.

[3] *Colquhoun* v. *Dumbarton Mags.*, 1907 S.C. (J.) 57; *Griffith* v. *Ferrier*, 1952 J.C. 56.

[4] *Strathern* v. *Padden*, 1926 J.C. 9; *Chernack* v. *Mill*, 1938 J.C. 39.

[5] *Vacher* v. *London Compositors* [1913] A.C. 107; *Lord Advocate* v. *Mirrielees' Trs.*, 1945
S.C. (H.L.) 1.

[6] *Clerical Assurance Co.* v. *Carter* (1889) 22 Q.B.D. 444.

[7] *Oliver* v. *Hislop*, 1946 J.C. 20.

[8] *Edinburgh Street Tramways* v. *Torbain* (1877) 3 App. Cas. 58, 68; *Colquhoun* v. *Brooks*
(1889) 14 App. Cas. 493, 506.

[9] *Tennent* v. *Partick Mags.* (1894) 21 R. 735; *Antrobus* (1896) 23 R. 1032; *Lord Advocate*
v. *Sprot's Trs.* (1901) 3 F. 440; *Barty* v. *Hill*, 1907 S.C. (J.) 36; *Campbell's Trs.* v. *O'Neill*,
1911 S.C. 188; *Hamilton* v. *N.C.B.*, 1960 S.C. (H.L.) 1.

[10] *Hutchison's Trs.* v. *Downie's Trs.*, 1923 S.L.T. 49.

that a word of indefinite meaning takes a shade of meaning from the accompanying words.[1]

The maxim *expressio unius est exclusio alterius* imports that an express mention of one thing or category may be held to imply the exclusion from the statute of the other thing or category of the same kind.[2]

The *ejusdem generis* principle is to the effect that if statute enumerates a number of items or categories belonging to some class or genus of things, any subsequent general words must be held limited to other things of the same class as those enumerated.[3] The principle does not apply if the enumerated items belong to no recognizable genus or have no common factor,[4] nor if the subsequent general words are so general as clearly not to be limited by the context of the items specifically enumerated,[5] nor if the general object of the Act indicates that the general words should not be restricted in meaning by the earlier specific words.[6]

Usage and contemporanea expositio

In construing ancient statutes weight may be attached to the interpretation adopted in practice through a long course of time and to contemporaneous decisions of the courts,[7] but these factors are of little value in construing more modern statutes particularly if unambiguous.[8] Even in modern, but not very recent, statutes, *contemporanea expositio* may impart a shade of meaning to an ambiguous word.[9] Where an Act is silent or doubtful, long continued usage may supply the defect.[10] But no usage can prevail against a plain statutory provision,[11] nor can

---

[1] *Muir* v. *Keay* (1875) L.R. 10 Q.B. 594.

[2] *Stevenson* v. *Hunter* (1903) 5 F. 761; *Inverness C.C.* v. *Inverness Mags.*, 1909 S.C. 386.

[3] *Henretty* v. *Hart* (1885) 13 R. (J.) 9; *Walker* v. *Lamb* (1892) 19 R. (J.) 50; *Caledonian Ry.* v. *Glasgow Corpn.* (1901) 3 F. 526, 531; *Duncan* v. *Jackson* (1905) 8 F. 323; *Admiralty* v. *Burns*, 1910 S.C. 531; *Moss' Empires* v. *Glasgow Assessor*, 1917 S.C. (H.L.) 1; *Baird* v. *Lees*, 1924 S.C. 83; *Benzie* v. *Mickel*, 1945 J.C. 47; *Minister of Pensions* v. *Ballantyne*, 1948 S.C. 176; *Lord Advocate* v. *Glasgow Corpn.*, 1958 S.C. 12; *Mortimer* v. *Allison*, 1959 S.C. (H.L.) 1.

[4] *Crichton Stuart* v. *Ogilvie*, 1914 S.C. 888.

[5] *Skinner* v. *Shew* [1893] 1 Ch. 413.

[6] *Powell* v. *Kempton Park Racecourse Co.* [1899] A.C. 143.

[7] *Clyde Navigation Trs.* v. *Laird* (1883) 10 R. (H.L.) 77; *Graham* v. *Irving* (1899) 2 F. 29; *Middleton* v. *Tough*, 1908 S.C. (J.) 32; *Borthwick-Norton* v. *Gavin Paul*, 1947 S.C. 659, 693–4.

[8] *Walker Trs.* v. *Lord Advocate*, 1912 S.C. (H.L.) 12.

[9] *Scottish Cinema and Variety Theatres* v. *Ritchie*, 1929 S.C. 350.

[10] *Dunbar Mags.* v. *Dunbar Heritors* (1835) 1 S. & McL. 134, 195; *Molleson* v. *Hutchison* (1892) 19 R. 581, 587.

[11] *Dunbar Mags.* v. *Roxburghe* (1835) 3 Cl. & F. 335, 358; *Gorham* v. *Bishop of Exeter* (1850) 15 Q.B. 52, 73; *Walker Trs., supra*, 17.

usage under a repealed Act be used to help construe the repealing Act.[1]

Internal and external aids to construction

Assistance in interpretation may be derived from examination of other parts of the Act in question such as the long title,[2] the preamble,[3] headings prefixed to groups of sections or parts of an Act,[4] and schedules,[5] but not the short title,[6] rubric,[7] marginal notes,[8] or punctuation.[9]

Assistance may also be obtained from sources outside the Act under interpretation, such as the prior state of the law,[10] prior statutes repealed or consolidated by the present Act,[11] subsequent Acts in *pari materia*,[12] prior cases in which the precise words or phrase, or the same, or very similar, words or phrases in another Act on a related subject, have been construed,[13] usage and

---

[1] *Thomson* v. *Bent Colliery Co.*, 1912 S.C. 242.

[2] *Fielding* v. *Morley Corpn.* [1899] 1 Ch. 1, 3; *Fenton* v. *Thorley* [1903] A.C. 443, 447; *Miller & Lang* v. *Macniven and Cameron* (1908) 16 S.L.T. 56; *Vacher* v. *London Socy. of Compositors* [1913] A.C. 107, 128; *Mags. of Buckie* v. *Dowager Countess of Seafield's Trs.*, 1928 S.C. 525.

[3] *Minister of Brydekirk* v. *Minister of Hoddam* (1877) 4 R. 798; *Caledonian Ry.* v. *N.B. Ry.* (1881) 8 R. (H.L.) 23, 25; *Tennent* v. *Partick Mags.* (1894) 21 R. 735; *Renfrewshire C.C.* v. *Orphan Homes of Scotland* (1898) 1 F. 186; *Ellerman Lines* v. *Murray* [1931] A.C. 126; *A. G.* v. *Prince Ernest of Hanover* [1957] A.C. 436; *Anderson* v. *Jenkins*, 1967 S.C. 231.

[4] *Lang* v. *Kerr, Anderson & Co.* (1878) 5 R. (H.L.) 65, 67; *Nelson* v. *McPhee* (1889) 17 R. (J.) 1; *Scott* v. *Alexander* (1890) 17 R. (J.) 35; *Inglis* v. *Robertson & Baxter* (1898) 25 R. (H.L.) 70; *McEwan* v. *Perth Mags.* (1905) 7 F. 714; *Mags. of Buckie, supra*; *Martins* v. *Fowler* [1926] A.C. 746, 750; *Alexander* v. *Mackenzie*, 1947 J.C. 155; *Brodie* v. *Ker*, 1952 S.C. 216, 225; *D.P.P.* v. *Schildkamp* [1969] 3 All E.R. 1640.

[5] *Ellerman Lines* v. *Murray* [1931] A.C. 126; but a schedule cannot extend or overrule a provision in the body of an Act: *Laird* v. *C.N.T.* (1883) 10 R. (H.L.) 77; *Jacobs* v. *Hart* (1900) 2 F. (J.) 33.

[6] *Re Boaler* [1915] 1 K.B. 21.

[7] *Farquharson* v. *Whyte* (1886) 13 R. (J.) 29.

[8] *D. Devonshire* v. *O'Connor* [1890] 24 Q.B.D. 468, 478; *Nixon* v. *A.G.* [1930] 1 Ch. 566, 593; *Chandler* v. *D.P.P.* [1964] A.C. 763.

[9] *I.R.C.* v. *Hinchy* [1960] A.C. 748; but see *Turnbull's Trs.* v. *L.A.*, 1918 S.C. (H.L.) 88; *Alexander* v. *Mackenzie*, 1947 J.C. 155; *D.P.P.* v. *Schildkamp* [1969] 3 All E.R. 1640.

[10] *Bank of England* v. *Vagliano* [1891] A.C. 107, 144; *Eastman Photographic Co.* v. *Comptroller-General of Patents* [1898] A.C. 571, 575; *L.A.* v. *Sprot's Trs.* (1901) 3 F. 440; *Sharp* v. *Morrison*, 1922 S.L.T. 272; *Avery* v. *N. E. Ry.* [1938] A.C. 606, 612, 617.

[11] *Walsh* v. *Pollokshaws Mags.*, 1907 S.C. (H.L.) 1; *Sharp, supra.* But one enactment cannot be controlled by reference to previous legislation if it is plain: *Sandys* v. *Lowden & Rowe* (1874) 2 R. (J.) 7; see also *Couper* v. *Mackenzie* (1906) 8 F. 1202; *Jack* v. *Thom*, 1952 J.C. 41.

[12] *Re Macmanaway* [1951] A.C. 161; *A.G.* v. *Prince Ernest of Hanover* [1957] A.C. 436.

[13] *Barras* v. *Aberdeen Steam Trawling Co.*, 1933 S.C. (H.L.) 21; *Paisner* v. *Goodrich* [1957] A.C. 65; *Inland Revenue* v. *Glasgow Police Athletic Assocn.*, 1953 S.C. (H.L.) 13; *Hamilton* v. *N.C.B.*, 1960 S.C. (H.L.) 1; *Ogden Industries* v. *Lucas* [1970] A.C. 113.

contemporanea expositio,[1] and statements in reputable textbooks on the Act or that general field of law.[2] No reference may be made to Royal Commission or other reports on which the legislation may have been founded[3] nor to Hansard, White Papers, or memoranda circulated to Parliament.[4]

Presumptions

Numerous presumptions may be invoked to assist interpretation, in the absence of clear contrary indications. The most important are: that the Crown, its officials and departments are not bound by statute unless that is expressly stated;[5] that fundamental principles of constitutional law or of common law will not be altered by implication;[6] that a United Kingdom statute is not intended to infringe international law;[7] that a United Kingdom statute is to be interpreted uniformly throughout the United Kingdom;[8] that the existing jurisdiction of the courts is not altered;[9] that an individual may appeal to the ordinary courts if aggrieved;[10] that ordinary procedures may be invoked[11] and are not altered;[12] that a word judicially interpreted and later repeated in a subsequent statute has the meaning originally given it by the court;[13] that statutes imposing a penalty or a tax, encroaching on

[1] *Gorham v. Bishop of Exeter* (1850) 15 Q.B. 52; *Migneault v. Malo* (1872) L.R. 4 P.C. 123; *Welham v. D.P.P.* [1961] A.C. 103.

[2] *Bastin v. Davies* [1950] 1 All E.R. 1095.

[3] *Salkeld v. Johnson* (1846) 2 C.B. 749, 767; *Holme v. Guy* (1877) 5 Ch.D. 901; *R. v. Hertford College* (1878) 3 Q.B.D. 693; But see *McKernan v. United Masons* (1874) 1 R. 453; *Shanks v. United Masons* (1874) 1 R. 823.

[4] *Viscountess Rhondda's Claim* [1922] 2 A.C. 339; *McCormick v. Lord Advocate*, 1953 S.C. 396; *Beswick v. B.* [1968] A.C. 58.

[5] *Schulze v. Steele* (1890) 17 R. (J.) 47; *Somerville v. Lord Advocate* (1893) 20 R. 1050; *Edinburgh Magistrates v. Lord Advocate*, 1912 S.C. 1085; *Salt v. MacKnight*, 1947 J.C. 99; *Tamlin v. Hannaford* [1950] 1 K.B. 18.

[6] *N.B. Ry. v. Mackintosh* (1890) 17 R. 1065; *Nairn v. University Courts of St. Andrews and Edinburgh*, 1909 S.C. (H.L.) 10; *Central Control Board (Liquor Traffic) v. Cannon Brewery Co. Ltd.* [1919] A.C. 744; *Nokes v. Doncaster Amalgamated Collieries* [1940] A.C. 1014; *Hynd's Tr. v. Hynd's Trs.*, 1955 S.C. (H.L.) 1.

[7] *Mortensen v. Peters* (1906) 8 F. (J.) 93.

[8] *E. Breadalbane v. L.A.* (1870) 8 M. 835; *Inland Revenue v. Glasgow Police Athletic Assn.*, 1953 S.C. (H.L.) 13.

[9] *Tennent v. Partick Mags.* (1894) 21 R. 735; *Cameron v. McNiven* (1894) 21 R. (J.) 31; *Dunbar v. Scottish Investment Co.*, 1920 S.C. 210.

[10] *Dunbar, supra*; *Chester v. Bateson* [1920] 1 K.B. 829; *Pyx Granite v. Ministry of Housing* [1960] A.C. 260.

[11] *Portobello Mags. v. Edinburgh Mags.* (1882) 10 R. 130.

[12] *Kinnear v. Whyte* (1868) 6 M. 804.

[13] *Barras v. Aberdeen Steam Trawling Co.*, 1933 S.C. (H.L.) 21. cf. *Nicol's Trs. v. Sutherland*, 1951 S.C. (H.L.) 21.

property rights or restrictive of personal liberty, fall to be strictly construed, as applicable only to cases clearly falling within the circumstances prescribed;[1] that a remedial statute should be given a favourable construction;[2] that an exemption from taxation should be rejected unless clearly conferred;[3] and that where statute creates a crime or offence the commission of the offence requires guilty knowledge or intention and not merely inadvertence; but this presumption is frequently held rebutted by the words used.[4] None of these presumptions is, however, more than an indication of meaning, which may be overcome by indications in the language of the Act.[5]

Private Acts are not construed as conferring any greater powers than are given in plain terms or by necessary inference from the terms used,[6] nor as abrogating general common law rights or public Acts by implication.[7]

Retrospective and prospective operation

Prima facie a statute modifies the law for the future only,[8] but provisions which bear to be declaratory[9] or remedial[10] may be held retrospective also,[11] and any statutory provision may be made retrospective by clear expressions to that effect.[12]

---

[1] *Johnston* v. *Robson* (1868) 6 M. 800; *Scottish Cinema and Variety Theatres* v. *Ritchie*, 1929 S.C. 350; *I.R.C.* v. *Wolfson* [1949] 1 All E.R. 865; *I.R.C.* v. *Hinchy* [1960] A.C. 748; see also *Edinburgh Life Assce. Co.* v. *Inland Revenue* (1875) 2 R. 394; *Ross and Coulter* v. *Inland Revenue*, 1948 S.C. (H.L.) 1.

[2] *Turner* (1869) 8 M. 222; *Robb* v. *Logiealmond School Board* (1875) 2 R. 417.

[3] *Edinburgh Life Assce. Co.* v. *Inland Revenue* (1875) 2 R. 394, 398; *Hogg* v. *Auchtermuchty Parochial Board* (1880) 7 R. 986; *Gillanders* v. *Campbell* (1884) 12 R. 309; *Renfrewshire C.C.* v. *Orphan Homes of Scotland* (1898) 1 F. 186.

[4] *Younghusband* v. *Luftig* [1949] 2 K.B. 354; *Sweet* v. *Parsley* [1970] A.C. 132.

[5] cf. *Edinburgh Life Assurance Co.* v. *Inland Revenue* (1875) 2 R. 394.

[6] *Scottish Drainage and Improvement Co.* v. *Campbell* (1889) 16 R. (H.L.) 16; cf. *Rothes* v. *Kirkcaldy Waterworks Commrs.* (1882) 9 R. (H.L.) 108; *Bruce* v. *Whyte* (1900) 2 F. 823, 829.

[7] *Clyde* v. *Glasgow Ry.* (1885) 12 R. 1315; *Balfour*, 1909 S.C. 358.

[8] *Urquhart* v. *U.* (1853) 1 Macq. 658; *Kerr* v. *M. Ailsa* (1854) 1 Macq. 736; *Brown* v. *Macdonald* (1870) 8 M. 439; *Gardner* v. *Lucas* (1878) 5 R. (H.L.) 105; *Stuart* v. *Jackson* (1889) 17 R. 85; *Callander* v. *Smith* (1900) 2 F. 1140; (1901) 3 F. (H.L.) 28; *Russell* v. *Assoc. Boilermakers* (1907) 15 S.L.T. 118; *N.C.B.* v. *McInnes*, 1968 S.C. 321.

[9] *Scott* v. *Craig's Reps.* (1897) 24 R. 462; *Murray* v. *Inland Revenue*, 1918 S.C. (H.L.) 111.

[10] *Taylor* v. *T.* (1871) 9 M. 893; *Wilson* v. *W.*, 1939 S.C. 102.

[11] See also *Gardner* v. *Lucas* (1878) 5 R. (H.L.) 105.

[12] e.g. War Damage Act, 1965, cancelling decision in *Burmah Oil Co. Ltd.* v. *Lord Advocate*, 1964 S.C. (H.C.) 117.

Imperative, directory or permissive

Prima facie words such as 'must' or 'shall' are imperative,[1] but may be merely directory.[2] Negative and prohibitory words must always be read as imperative.[3] Permissive words normally confer a discretionary power and do not impose an obligation.[4]

But even permissive words may be construed as imperative,[5] where the court holds that the power conferred is coupled with a duty on the person to whom it is given to exercise it.[6]

Provisos and qualifications

When an enacting phrase is followed by a proviso, the latter must be construed with reference to the enactment, and, unless the contrary be explicitly declared, cannot extend the enacting words;[7] but it may be in reality a substantive enactment.[8] A proviso does not necessarily fall to be construed on the principle *expressio unius est exclusio alterius.*[9]

(2) JUDICIAL PRECEDENTS

On matters of European Community law, such as the interpretation of the Community treaties or the validity and interpretation of measures taken by Community institutions or national enterprises judgments of the European Court of Justice are authoritative.

Principles and rules of municipal law of general future application may also be found expressed or implied in the judicial decisions of specific cases heard and determined in the past by the superior courts of Scotland down to date.[10] The bodies of recorded decisions of the superior courts of England and of Ireland are, on certain topics of law, sources of principles having

---

[1] *Pendreigh's Tr.* v. *McLaren & Co.* (1871) 9 M. (H.L.) 49.

[2] *Kinnear* v. *Whyte* (1868) 6 M. 804; *Campbell* v. *Duke of Atholl* (1869) 8 M. 308; *Robertson* v. *Adamson* (1876) 3 R. 978; *Duchess of Sutherland* v. *Reid's Trs.* (1881) 8 R. 514.

[3] *Cowper* v. *Callender* (1872) 10 M. 353.

[4] *Degan* v. *Dundee Corpn.*, 1940 S.C. 457; *Fleming & Ferguson* v. *Paisley Mags.*, 1948 S.C. 547. cf. *Lanark C.C.* v. *East Kilbride*, 1967 S.C. 235.

[5] *Lord Advocate* v. *Sinclair* (1872) 11 M. 137; *Gray* v. *Fife C.C.*, 1911 S.C. 266.

[6] *Walkinshaw* v. *Orr* (1860) 22 D. 627; *Julius* v. *Bishop of Oxford* (1880) 5 App. Cas. 214; *Black* v. *Glasgow Corpn.*, 1958 S.C. 260.

[7] *Forster* v. *F.* (1871) 9 M. 397.

[8] *Davidson* v. *Johnston* (1903) 6 F. 239.

[9] *Stevenson* v. *Hunter* (1903) 5 F. 761.

[10] Gardner, *Judicial Precedent in Scots Law*; Smith, *Judicial Precedent in Scots Law*; Walker, *S.L.S.*, Ch. 8.

similar but lesser authority than have Scottish decisions, and, on certain topics, the recorded decisions of the superior courts of Commonwealth countries, the U.S.A., and other English speaking countries, such as South Africa, which have systems of law having some affinities with Scots law are also of some, but lesser authority.

Formerly a uniform series of decisions of the Court of Session was accounted authoritative, as being evidence of the customary law, but individual decisions created no obligation on subsequent judges to follow them.[1] Since the early nineteenth century, however, largely under English influence, it has been accepted that even single decisions, particularly of the appellate courts, may be held to have established principles which must be followed subsequently.

In addition to recording the manner in which a court decided the previous case, and the opinions expressed therein by the judges regarding the applicable law, a reported decision may be held to contain a statement of legal principle applicable to a case subsequently before a court and decisive of it also. The accepted modern Scottish practice is that even a single decision of a superior court on a legal issue may be held to determine that issue for the future and accordingly to be a precedent to be followed. The actual decision binds only the parties to that case, but the principle on which it was decided or the general rule therein laid down may rule subsequent cases raising the same point for determination, unless the circumstances can fairly be said to be distinguishable, or at least it may have persuasive influence on the decision of subsequent cases.

The authority of a decision does not depend on whether it is reported or not,[2] but unauthenticated,[3] brief or inadequate reports[4] are less trustworthy and valuable than those printed in recognized series of reports or in text books.[5] A decision is not of doubtful validity merely because it was decided by a small majority.[6]

---

[1] Craig I, 8, 13–15; Stair I, 1, 16; Mack. I, 1, 10; Bankt. I, 1, 74; Ersk. I, 1, 47.

[2] *Leighton* v. *Harland & Wolff, Ltd.*, 1953 S.L.T. (Notes) 36; *H.M.A.* v. *Burns*, 1967 J.C. 15.

[3] cf. *Rivoli Hats* v. *Gooch* [1953] 1 W.L.R. 1190; *Birtwistle* v. *Tweedale* [1954] 1 W.L.R. 190; *Perez* v. *C.A.V.* [1959] 2 All E.R. 414.

[4] *Rivoli Hats, supra*; *Birtwistle supra*; *Chapman* v. *C.* [1954] A.C. 429; *Maitland*, 1961 S.C. 291, 294; *McLaughlin*, 1965 S.C. 243.

[5] *Smith* v. *Grayton Estates*, 1960 S.C. 349, 354.

[6] *H.M.A.* v. *Burns, supra*.

Whether precedent 'in point' or not

Before a principle or general rule can be extracted from a prior judicial decision, the court before whom the problem now arises must determine, firstly, whether the prior decision is 'on all fours' or 'in point', that is, deals with the same problem of law, or with a point so closely related as to make a ruling on it decisive, or at least a guide as to the decision, of the case now before the court; and, secondly, where the court which delivered the opinion in the prior case stands in the judicial hierarchy as compared with the court in the instant case, which factor mainly determines whether the precedent, if in point, falls to be treated as binding on the court in the instant case, or only persuasive.

If the precedent is deemed to be not 'in point' it can be ignored; if not directly in point it may be 'distinguished' or set aside on the ground of the existence of some difference in material facts and relevant circumstances from the present case which the present court regards as significant; but if directly in point and indistinguishable on the facts it has an influence on the decision of the instant case depending on the standing in the judicial hierarchy of the court which pronounced the precedent, as superior to the court now considering the matter, or equal, or inferior. It may be a binding precedent which the later court must follow and apply, or a persuasive precedent which influences the later court in its decision.

Precedents binding and persuasive

The principles now accepted are:

(a) Decisions in point of the House of Lords pronounced in Scottish,[1] but not English,[2] appeals (except, probably, English appeals on U.K. statutes[3]) are probably binding on the House itself in future Scottish appeals, though the House now reserves liberty in exceptional cases to reconsider its own precedents,[4] and are binding on all lower Scottish civil courts; though a Court of Session decision which has determined practice for some time will

---

[1] *Houldsworth* v. *City of Glasgow Bank* (1880) 7 R. (H.L.) 53, 62; *London Street Tramways Co.* v. *L.C.C.* [1898] A.C. 375.

[2] *Glasgow Corpn.* v. *Central Land Board,* 1956 S.C. (H.L.) 1; see also *Virtue* v. *Alloa Police Commrs.* (1873) 1 R. 285; *Orr Ewing's Trs.* v. *Orr Ewing* (1885) 13 R. (H.L.) 1; *Blacks* v. *Girdwood* (1885) 13 R. 243; *Primrose* v. *Waterson* (1902) 4 F. 783.

[3] *Rankine* v. *I.R.C.,* 1952 S.C. 177, 186; *I.R.C.* v. *Glasgow Police Athletic Assocn.,* 1953 S.C. (H.L.) 13; *Glasgow Corpn., supra,* 9, 13, 17.

[4] Statement by the Lord Chancellor, 26 July 1966, noted in [1966] 3 All E.R. 77.

not lightly be overruled merely because the House disagrees with it;[1]

(b) Decisions in point of the whole Court of Session,[2] or of a larger bench than either Division[3] are usually regarded as binding on both Divisions of the Inner House and on all inferior civil courts;

(c) Decisions in point of either Division of the Inner House are normally treated as binding on that Division,[4] and on the other Division,[5] and are binding on judges of the Outer House[6] and on all inferior civil courts.

(d) Decisions in point of single judges in the Outer House are not binding on one another[7] but are generally regarded as authoritative in all inferior civil courts.

(e) Decisions in point of a sheriff-principal or sheriff are not binding, but are generally followed in the sheriff court in the absence of reason to the contrary.

(f) Decisions in point of any court standing lower in the hierarchy than the court presently considering the issue have persuasive influence depending in degree on the status of the court, the personal eminence of the judges, and the consistency of the principle of the precedent with reason and settled general principles of the law, but are never binding.

(g) A decision in point may be disregarded if inconsistent with prior authorities not brought to the notice of the court,[8] or depending on social or other views out of keeping with modern views,[9] or if its ratio has been superseded by subsequent legislation.[10]

---

[1] *Kirkpatrick's Trs.* v. *K.* (1874) 1 R. (H.L.) 37. On the binding character of such decisions on lower courts in England see *Cassell* v. *Broome* [1972] 1 All E.R. 801.

[2] e.g. *Hutton's Trs.* v. *H.*, 1916 S.C. 860; *Bell* v. *B.*, 1940 S.C. 229; revd. 1941 S.C. (H.L.) 5; cf. *Sugden* v. *H.M.A.*, 1934 J.C. 103.

[3] *Yuill's Trs.* v. *Thomson* (1902) 4 F. 815; *Cochrane's Exrx.* v. *C.* 1947 S.C. 134; *McElroy* v. *McAllister*, 1949 S.C. 110; *Marshall* v. *Scottish Milk Marketing Board*, 1956 S.C. (H.L.) 37, 39; *Smith* v. *Stewart & Co.*, 1960 S.C. 329.

[4] *Garden's Exor.* v. *More*, 1913 S.C. 285; *Cameron* v. *Glasgow Corpn.*, 1935 S.C. 533; 1936 S.C. (H.L.) 26, 29; *Marshall, supra*; But see *Campbell* v. *West of Scotland Shipbreaking Co.*, 1953 S.C. 173; *Maitland*, 1961 S.C. 291.

[5] But see *Shanks* v. *United Masons* (1874) 1 R. 823, 825; *Earl of Wemyss* v. *Earl of Zetland* (1890) 18 R. 126, 130; *Lord Advocate* v. *Young* (1898) 25 R. 778, where it was indicated that a Division might not be bound by a single previous decision.

[6] e.g. *Fortington* v. *Kinnaird*, 1942 S.C. 239, 244–5.

[7] *Blackwood* v. *Andre*, 1947 S.C. 333, not following *McDaid* v. *C.N.T.*, 1946 S.C. 462.

[8] *Mitchell* v. *Mackersy* (1905) 8 F. 198.

[9] *Bowman* v. *Secular Society* [1917] A.C. 406; *Welldon* v. *Butterley Coal Co.* [1920] 1 Ch. 130; *Beith's Trs.* v. *B.*, 1950 S.C. 66, 70.

[10] *Beith's Trs., supra.*

Overruling power

It is accordingly competent for the House of Lords, a full court, or a Division to overrule as bad law a precedent of the Outer House,[1] and for the House of Lords, a full court or a larger court to overrule a precedent decided by a Division,[2] and possibly for the full court to overrule a precedent decided by seven judges, though this is contrary to practice.[3]

Precedents from other United Kingdom courts

Decisions of the House of Lords on appeal from England or Northern Ireland on matters of law common to Scotland and the other jurisdiction concerned, or on questions of general jurisprudence are persuasive only on Scottish courts, but in a high degree,[4] particularly when dealing with a principle common to Scotland and the other country.[5]

Decisions of the superior courts of England and Northern Ireland (Courts of Appeal and High Courts) are not absolutely binding on any Scottish court but are persuasive in a degree proportionate to the status of the court in the judicial hierarchy of the country in question, particularly in cases where the same statute or a similar principle of common law applies in Scotland to that under consideration in the English or Irish case.

Judgments of the Privy Council are never binding on any Scottish court,[6] though they may be highly persuasive if relevant to Scots law.[7]

Judgments of the superior courts of Commonwealth countries, of the Supreme Court of the U.S.A. and of courts in foreign countries of equivalent status have persuasive force depending on the similarity of the law in question to Scots law on the relevant matter.[8]

---

[1] e.g. *Lennie* v. *L.*, 1950 S.C. (H.L.) 1, overruling *Goold* v. *G.*, 1927 S.C. 177.

[2] e.g. *Fortington* v. *Kinnaird*, 1942 S.C. 239; *McElroy* v. *McAllister*, 1949 S.C. 110; *Smith* v. *Stewart*, 1960 S.C. 329.

[3] *Yuill's Trs.* v. *Thomson* (1902) 4 F. 815.

[4] *Virtue* v. *Alloa Police Commrs.* (1873) 1 R. 285; *Orr Ewing's Trs.* v. *Orr Ewing* (1885) 13 R. (H.L.) 1; *Blacks* v. *Girdwood* (1885) 13 R. 243; *Primrose* v. *Waterston* (1902) 4 F. 783. cf. *Donnelly* v. *Glasgow Corpn.*, 1953 S.C. 107, disapproved by H.L. in *Davie* v. *New Merton Board Mills* [1959] A.C. 604.

[5] cf. *Hamilton* v. *N.C.B.*, 1960 S.C. (H.L.) 1.

[6] *Brown* v. *John Watson, Ltd.*, 1914 S.C. (H.L.) 44; *Duncan* v. *Cammell Laird & Co.* [1942] A.C. 624.

[7] *Leask* v. *Scott* (1877) 2 Q.B.D. 376, 380.

[8] See *Donoghue* v. *Stevenson*, 1932 S.C. (H.L.) 31; *Walsh* v. *L.A.*, 1956 S.C. (H.L.) 126; but see *A/B Karlshamns Oljefabriker* v. *Monarch S.S. Co.*, 1949 S.C. (H.L.) 1.

Practice in other civil courts

In other Scottish civil courts the rules of precedent are less rigidly followed. The Inner House sitting as Court of Exchequer may not have the power of reconsidering precedents before a larger court, the court in this capacity having been established on the English model.[1]

In the Scottish Land Court previous decisions may be not followed.[2] The Lands Valuation Appeal Court may decline to follow its own precedents,[3] but follows decisions of the House of Lords in English cases where those are applicable.[4]

Finding the ratio decidendi

If the court deciding a case considers that a prior decision is directly in point, or at least sufficiently in point to yield a ruling or guidance for the decision of the instant case, and has also decided whether, having regard to what court pronounced the prior decision, its decision is to be treated as binding and decisive, or only persuasive and influential, the later court must determine what was the *ratio decidendi* of the precedent; the *ratio* is the principle of law underlying and justifying the actual decision, or the proposition of law which can be extracted from it, or the legal ground on which it was decided, for which it is authority, and which must, or may, according to circumstances, be applied to the instant case. A precedent, that is, is binding or persuasive, as the case may be, in respect of its containing a principle which justified its disposal in the way it was decided, and which is capable of application to the same, or closely analogous, circumstances now before the later court.[5] It is for the later court to determine what it understands to be the *ratio decidendi* of the precedent.

There are no fixed rules or methods for finding or extracting the *ratio decidendi*; it is not necessarily contained in the rubric of the report, nor expressed in any judgment, but is a proposition of law implicit in the actual decision of the case and consistent with the material facts thereof.[6]

[1] *Drummond* v. *I.R.C.*, 1951 S.C. 482, 488.

[2] *Niven* v. *Cameron*, 1939 S.L.C.R. 23; *Georgeson* v. *Anderston's Trs.*, 1945 S.L.C.R. 44.

[3] *Glasgow Assessor* v. *Watson*, 1920 S.C. 517; *Inverness-shire Assessor* v. *Cameron*, 1938 S.C. 360.

[4] *Aberdeen Assessor* v. *Collie*, 1932 S.C. 304.

[5] *Re Hallett* (1879) 13 Ch.D. 696, 712; *Osborne to Rowlett* (1880) 13 Ch.D. 774, 785; *Fortington* v. *Kinnaird*, 1942 S.C. 239, 269; *Beith's Trs.* v. *B.* 1950 S.C. 66, 70; *Douglas Hamilton* v. *Duke and Duchess of Hamilton's Trs.*, 1961 S.C. 205, 229.

[6] *Walker, S.L.S.*, Ch. 8; see also *Saunders* v. *Anglia Building Socy.* [1970] 3 All E.R. 961, 963.

If the *ratio decidendi* of a precedent has been superseded or invalidated by subsequent legislation or similar cause that *ratio* ceases to be binding.[1]

Obiter dicta

Judicial observations not part of the judge's *ratio decidendi* are called *obiter dicta* and their weight and value varies with their nature and the eminence of the judge who pronounced them. While never binding, they may be invoked or relied on as persuasive precedents in a later case.

Treatment of binding precedent

If the court holds a precedent to be in point and binding on it, it must apply the ratio to the case before the court, or follow it, unless it can 'distinguish' the precedent and hold it not to be in point,[2] or can regard the *ratio* as not binding, having been superseded by later statute or changed social and legal conditions.[3]

Treatment of precedents not binding

If the court holds a precedent in point but not binding in the circumstances the later court may 'not follow' it,[4] or doubt it, or disapprove it,[5] or may treat it as persuasive and follow it.

Other factors affecting evaluation of precedent

Particularly in relation to precedents merely persuasive, a court, in deciding how much weight to attach to a precedent, may consider the age of the precedent,[6] whether it has previously been approved, followed or applied,[7] or distinguished, not followed or criticized,[8] the personal eminence of the judges who decided it,[9] whether other judges were consulted,[10] whether the judges were unanimous or not, whether the case was argued on both sides or not,[11] whether any matters were conceded or not argued, whether

---

[1] *Beith's Trs.* v. *B.*, 1950 S.C. 66.

[2] e.g. *Donoghue* v. *Stevenson*, 1932 S.C. (H.L.) 31, 49–56, 65–9; *Hughes* v. *L.A.*, 1963 S.C. (H.L.) 31, distinguishing *Muir* v. *Glasgow Corpn.*, 1943 S.C. (H.L.) 3.

[3] *Beith's Trs.* v. *B.*, 1950 S.C. 66.

[4] e.g. *McDaid* v. *C.N.T.*, 1946 S.C. 462, not followed in *Blackwood* v. *Andre*, 1947 S.C. 333.

[5] e.g. *Cook* v. *Grubb*, 1963 S.C. 1, disapproving *Torbat* v. *T's Trs.* (1907) 14 S.L.T. 830.

[6] cf. *Donnelly* v. *D.*, 1959 S.C. 97, 102, 103.

[7] cf. *Fortington* v. *Kinnaird*, 1942 S.C. 239, 266; *Baird* v. *B's Trs.*, 1956 S.C. (H.L.) 93, 107–8.

[8] cf. *McElroy* v. *McAllister*, 1949 S.C. 110.

[9] cf. *Stewart* v. *L.M.S. Ry.*, 1943 S.C. (H.L.) 19, 38.

[10] As in *Connell* v. *C.*, 1950 S.C. 505.

[11] cf. *Bell* v. *B.*, 1941 S.C. (H.L.) 5.

any relevant statutes or cases were not considered, and whether the report is satisfactory or not.[1]

(3) INSTITUTIONAL WRITINGS

Principles and rules laid down in those books known as institutional writings and traditionally recognized as having high authority, namely Sir Thomas Craig's *Jus Feudale* (1655); (Sir) James Dalrymple, Viscount Stair's *Institutions of the Law of Scotland* (1681); Sir George Mackenzie's *Institutions of the Law of Scotland* (1684); Andrew McDouall, Lord Bankton's *Institute of the Laws of Scotland* (1751); Henry Home, Lord Kames's *Principles of Equity* (1760); Professor John Erskine's *Institute of the Law of Scotland* (1773); and Professor George Joseph Bell's *Commentaries on the Law of Scotland and the Principles of Mercantile Jurisprudence* (1804) and his *Principles of the Law of Scotland*, (1829), may also be decisive. Of these institutional writers Stair, Erskine, and Bell stand pre-eminent,[2] and it is possibly doubtful whether Mackenzie's *Institutions* and Kames's *Equity* are fully entitled to institutional status.[3]

The authority of a statement in point by any one of the institutional writers is generally accepted as equivalent to that of an Inner House decision to the same effect,[4] but in case of conflict it must yield to any statutory rule or judicial pronouncement. The evaluation of any such statement depends largely on whether the legal context has changed, whether the passage has been approved or criticized, and its consistency with the law on related topics.

Not all the writings of an institutional writer have institutional standing; his lesser works, or works not finally revised or published by him, are of only lesser authority.[5]

---

[1] cf. *Robb* v. *R.*, 1953 S.L.T. 44, criticized in *Hamilton* v. *H.*, 1954 S.L.T. 16.

[2] On the authority of Stair, see *Drew* v. *D.* (1870) 9 M. 163, 167; on Kames see *Kennedy* v. *Stewart* (1889) 16 R. 421, 430; on Bell's *Commentaries* see *Gardner* v. *Cuthbertson* (1824) 2 Sh. App. 291, 298.

[3] In Scottish criminal law Mackenzie's *Laws and Customs of Scotland in Matters Criminal* (1678), Hume's *Commentaries on Crimes* (1797), and, probably, Alison's *Principles* (1832) and *Practice of the Criminal Law of Scotland* (1833) enjoy institutional status. On institutional writers and editions thereof, see Walker, *S.L.S.*, Chs. 8 and 11. There are various other older writings on Scots law which are certainly not institutional.

[4] Lord Normand, *The Scottish Judicature and Legal Procedure* (1941).

[5] *Fortington* v. *Kinnaird*, 1942 S.C. 239; but see *Pettigrew* v. *Harton*, 1956 S.C. 67; *MacLennan* v. *M.*, 1958 S.C. 105; *Thomson* v. *St. Cuthbert's Cooperative Assn.*, 1958 S.C. 380, 394, 398; *N.C.B.* v. *Thomson*, 1959 S.C. 353, 383; *Cole-Hamilton* v. *Boyd*, 1963 S.C. (H.L.) 1.

(4) TREATISES AND TEXTBOOKS

The writings of some later jurists have done much to systematise, rationalise, and explain the law in particular branches and on points of doubt and difficulty their views are entitled to weight, rather less than that accorded to the institutional writers, but still substantial and probably as great as that allowed to the decision of a single judge. This weight attaches only to certain writings, treatises which have repeatedly been regarded as authoritative[1] and not by any means to all textbooks. The standing of, and the weight accorded to statements in, a treatise depends on the regard in which it is held professionally, and may therefore decline with time while newer treatises achieve recognition. Mere textbooks and manuals have no weight.

(5) CUSTOM

Though the common law of the realm declared in the older books and judicial decisions embodies many customs commonly accepted as law throughout the country, and so settled and notorious as not to require evidence, such as the legal rights of spouses and children, a custom not hitherto so recognized may be held in any particular case, if adequately proved, to have been accepted by the parties as binding and be treated as laying down an authoritative rule for them. Customary law derives its binding force from tacit consent presumed from the inveterate usage of the community.[2] Admiralty law is based on the ancient customs of the commercial nations of Europe.[3]

To be given the force of law in an unprecedented case a custom must be proved by evidence,[4] and shown to be a definite and certain practice,[5] habitually observed in the locality[6] or trade in question,[7] fair and reasonable,[8] generally accepted for so long as to justify the inference that it has long been accepted as a binding

---

[1] This class includes Fraser on *Husband and Wife* and on *Parent and Child*; McLaren on *Wills*; Gloag on *Contract*; Candlish Henderson on *Vesting*; Dickson on *Evidence*; Rankine on *Landownership* and on *Leases*.

[2] Stair I, 1, 16; Mack. I, 1, 10; Bankt. I, 1, 58–9; Ersk. I, 1, 43–6.

[3] *Boettcher* v. *Carron Co.* (1861) 23 D. 322, 330; *Currie* v. *McKnight* (1897) 24 R. (H.L.) 1, 3; *Sheaf S.S. Co.* v. *Compania Transmediterranea*, 1930 S.C. 660.

[4] *Mackenzie* v. *Dunlop* (1856) 3 Macq. 22.

[5] *Strathlorne S.S. Co.* v. *Baird*, 1916 S.C. (H.L.) 134.

[6] *M. Queensberry* v. *Wright* (1838) 16 S. 439; *Royal Four Towns Fishing Assoc.* v. *Dumfries Assessor*, 1956 S.C. 379.

[7] *Learmonth* v. *Sinclair's Trs.* (1898) 5 R. 548; *Holman* v. *Peruvian Nitrate Co.* (1878) 5 R. 657; *Clydesdale Bank* v. *Snodgrass*, 1939 S.C. 805.

[8] *Bruce* v. *Smith* (1890) 17 R. 1000; *Cazalet* v. *Morris*, 1916 S.C. 952.

rule,[1] and, though possibly an exception to or qualification of the general rules of law of the country, not contradictory thereof.[2] Custom cannot prevail against statute,[3] nor against express words in a contract.[4]

Apart from custom proven as a general rule of law, mercantile custom may be proved to have been an implied term in a particular contract, where parties knew of and must be held to have contracted subject to, a particular practice or usage of trade.[5]

(6) EQUITY

Principles of equity, of natural justice and right reason, may be resorted to to prevent an unduly rigorous application of strict law from working injustice. Numerous such principles are woven into the fabric of Scots law and are considered as part of the common law.[6] The Scottish courts have always administered an undivided system of law and equity. Apart from many cases where discretion may be exercised and equitable considerations are relevant in the application of rules of strict law, the Court of Session retains an ultimate residuary equitable power, the *nobile officium*, to provide a remedy where justice requires it or to intervene where strict law might work injustice.[7] But this power has come to be much restricted and is now exercised only in circumstances for which there is precedent or analogy.[8]

(7) EXTRANEOUS SOURCES

Failing guidance from any of the foregoing sources the courts may turn to such extraneous sources as legal literature[9] or those other systems of law which have in the past been quarries for the materials of Scots law, such as the Roman law, canon law, feudal

---

[1] Ersk. I, 1, 44; *Learmonth, supra; Macome v. Dickson* (1868) 6 M. 898; *Sturrock v. Murray,* 1952 S.C. 454.

[2] *Dunbar Mags.* v. *Dunbar Heritors* (1835) 1 S. & McL. 134; *Bruce, supra.*

[3] *Walker Trs.* v. *Lord Advocate,* 1912 S.C. (H.L.) 12.

[4] *Tancred Arrol & Co.* v. *Steel Co. of Scotland* (1890) 17 R. (H.L.) 31; *Maclellan v. Peattie's Trs.* (1903) 5 F. 1031.

[5] Bell, *Comm.* I, 465; *Holman v. Peruvian Nitrate Co.* (1878) 5 R. 657; *Strathlorne S.S. Co.* v. *Baird,* 1916 S.C. (H.L.) 134.

[6] Stair I, 1, 16; IV, 3, 1; Ersk. I, 1, 18; I, 3, 22; Kames, *Equity, passim; Historical Law Tracts,* 228; Walker (1954) 66 J.R. 103.

[7] Stair IV, 3, 1; Bankt. IV, 7, 24; Ersk. I, 3, 22; Kames, *H.L.T.,* 231; Walker, *Remedies,* Ch. 65; *Gibson's Trs.,* 1933 S.C. 190, 198.

[8] MacLaren, *Practice,* 100–5; Walker, *Remedies,* Ch. 65.

[9] *Infra.*

law, and the law merchant and maritime, and the leading commentators thereon, other modern systems of law, particularly those founded on similar historical bases, such as the Roman-Dutch, and the French and German Codes, with the commentators thereon, and those developed in countries having a similar social and economic structure, such as England, Northern Ireland, Commonwealth countries, and the U.S.A.[1]

The judgments of dissenting judges, *obiter dicta*, and analogies drawn from principles accepted in other contexts may be prayed in aid.

In the last resort a judge may rely on his own conscience, his idea of what justice, equity, and reason demand in the circumstances and his beliefs as to what is fair and right and reasonable in the circumstances, or consistent with the dictates of morality and public policy.[2]

These formal sources determine the general character of Scottish private law. It is largely but not entirely written law, discoverable from printed materials, but still with scope for the derivation of principles from unwritten law, such as custom or moral beliefs. But it is not a systematic written code of law, established as a piece by a lawgiving authority, but rather the product of growth and development over a long period, a growth influenced by numerous factors of different strengths at different times, not always consistent nor logical.

It is fundamentally a body of common law, based on customs commonly recognized and accepted as binding throughout large parts of the community, recognized and applied by judges in particular cases, and systematized and synthesized with materials from other sources by judges and authoritative text-writers, but increasingly modified, supplemented, and replaced by statements of the presumed general will of the community made by Parliament in the form of statute.[3]

3. LEGAL LITERATURE

Legal literature includes all writings on and about the law other than legislation, reported decisions, and institutional

---

[1] See e.g. *Collins* v. *C.* (1884) 11 R. (H.L.) 19; *Purves' Trs.* v. *P.* (1895) 22 R. 513; *Cantiere San Rocco* v. *Clyde Shipbuilding Co.*, 1923 S.C. (H.L.) 105; *Donoghue* v. *Stevenson*, 1932 S.C. (H.L.) 31; *Sugden* v. *H.M.A.*, 1934 J.C. 1; *Drummond's J.F.* v. *H.M.A.*, 1944 S.C. 298; *A/B Karlshamns Oljefabriker* v. *Monarch S.S. Co.*, 1949 S.C. (H.L.) 1; *Walsh* v. *L.A.*, 1956 S.C. (H.L.) 126.

[2] cf. Stair I, 1, 16. See also *Beresford* v. *Royal Ins. Co.* [1938] A.C. 586; *Steel* v. *Glasgow Iron & Steel Co.*, 1944 S.C. 237.

[3] cf. Ersk. 1, 1, 30.

writings, such as legal dictionaries, encyclopaedias, editorial notes to institutional writings,[1] older non-institutional writings, commentaries, textbooks, academic lectures on law,[2] judge's notes,[3] and periodical literature.

Legal literature is not an authoritative source of rules of law,[4] but merely exposition or criticism of, or commentary on, various principles, or branches of law, but some individual works of legal literature may come to enjoy a reputation and regard falling not far, if at all, short of being authoritative, depending on the personal eminence and reputation of the author, whether or not he held judicial office, the known quality and value of the work, and the extent to which it has received judicial approval.[5] There was formerly an alleged rule that the work of a living author might not be cited in argument, being unauthoritative, while the work of a dead author might be cited, but this rule has now been largely departed from.[6]

Statements in textbooks may assist a judge by reinforcing his view as to a previous decision,[7] but may be disregarded or condemned as incorrect.[8]

[1] See e.g. *Fortington v. Kinnaird*, 1942 S.C. 239, 265, 276.

[2] On the authority of such works see *Kerr v. Martin* (1840) 2 D. 752, 776, 792; *Fortington v. Kinnaird*, 1942 S.C. 239, 253, 265, 276, 277. Reference is also sometimes made by a judge to his own notes of academic lectures: e.g. *Kerr, supra*, 792; *Bute v. More* (1870) 9 M. 180, 190.

[3] See *Hutchison v. H.* (1872) 11 M. 229; *Fortington, supra*, 277.

[4] *Donoghue v. Stevenson*, 1932 S.C. (H.L.) 31, 35.

[5] See under Section 2(4) above.

[6] e.g. citation of Gloag on *Contract*; or Cheshire's *Private International Law*.

[7] cf. *Dempster's Trs. v. D.*, 1949 S.C. 92, 95; *McElroy v. McAllister*, 1949 S.C. 110, 135.

[8] e.g. *Bell v. Blackwood Morton & Sons, Ltd.*, 1960 S.C. 11, 23.

CHAPTER 2

THE CIVIL COURTS AND THEIR JURISDICTION

European Court

IN respect of the topics of European Community Law which have direct internal effect on persons and organisations in Scotland the Court of Justice of the European Communities is supreme. Where questions concerning the interpretation of the Community treaties or the validity or interpretation of measures taken by Community institutions are raised before a national court or tribunal, it may, if it considers that a decision on the question is necessary in order to enable it to give judgment, request the European Court to give a preliminary ruling on the question[1] and if the national court or tribunal is one from whose decisions there is no appeal under national law it is bound to make such a reference.[2]

In other respects the supreme civil court of Scotland is the House of Lords, composed, in modern practice, of at least three of the Lord High Chancellor of Great Britain, the eleven Lords of Appeal in Ordinary, and such other peers of Parliament as hold or have held high judicial office.[3] None of these need be Law Lords who have been appointed from the Scottish Bench or Bar though two usually are. Though formerly sittings for judicial business did not differ from sittings for legislative business, non-legal members of the House have long been excluded, and the House now appoints an Appellate Committee consisting of the statutorily qualified persons to hear appeals and report to the House. It may sit as two committees and when the House is not sitting.

It is not clear whether the House functions as a United Kingdom court or as a Scottish, English, or Northern Irish court depending on the jurisdiction from which the appeal comes, but it has judicial knowledge of the laws of all these systems so that in an appeal from one jurisdiction questions as to the law of another

---

[1] For procedure see A.S. (R.C. Amdt. No. 5) 1972 (S.I. No. 1981, 1972) and R.C. 296 A–E. As to registration of orders of the European Court see A.S. (R.C. Amdt. No. 6) 1972 (S.I. No. 1982, 1972) and R.C. 296 G. See also *Van Duyn* v. *Home Office* [1974] 1 W.L.R. 1107.

[2] E.C.S.C. Treaty, 1951, Art. 41; Treaty of Rome, 1957, Art. 177; *Bulmer* v. *Bollinger* [1974] 2 All E.R. 1226.

[3] Appellate Jurisdiction Acts, 1876–1947; Administration of Justice Act, 1968.

part of the United Kingdom are questions of law before it and not, as in lower courts, questions of fact.[1]

The House exercise appellate jurisdiction only, in respect of any kind of civil case litigated in the Scottish courts, unless such appeal has been excluded by statute,[2] against final judgments of the Inner House of the Court of Session, and against inter-locutory judgments of the Inner House if the Division is not unanimous, or if grants leave to appeal.[3] Where leave is necessary, it is sought by petition to the Inner House.[4]

No appeal is competent directly from the decision of a Lord Ordinary,[5] nor against the verdict of a civil jury,[6] but appeal is competent against an interlocutor allowing or refusing a motion for a new jury trial,[7] against interlocutors allowing or refusing bills of exceptions,[6] interlocutors applying a jury verdict,[8] and interlocutors setting aside a jury verdict and entering judgment for the unsuccessful party.[8]

Service of an order by the House of Lords on a petition for appeal stops all further procedure in the Court of Session even where that Court had refused leave to appeal.[9]

Where evidence has been heard in an inferior court, the find-ings in fact and the law held applicable thereto must be distin-guished,[10] and appeal lies on matters of law only.[11] A remit back may be made to make findings on matters of fact not covered already.[12]

The House is very unwilling to disturb inferences drawn from

---

[1] *Cooper* v. *C.* (1888) 15 R. (H.L.) 21; *Elliot* v. *Joicey*, 1935 S.C. (H.L.) 57.

[2] e.g. Lands Valuation Appeal Court (Valuation of Lands (Sc.) Amdt. Act, 1867, S. 8). No appeal lies from the High Court of Justiciary (*Mackintosh* v. *H.M. Adv.* (1876) 3 R. (H.L.) 34; Criminal Procedure Act, 1887, S. 72).

[3] Court of Session Act, 1808, S. 15; *Girvan* v. *Leng*, 1919, 2 S.L.T. 29; consent of parties will not evade this rule: *Beattie* v. *Glasgow Corpn.*, 1917 S.C. (H.L.) 22. But see *Orr Ewing's Trs.* v. *Orr Ewing* (1885) 13 R. (H.L.) 1.

[4] cf. *Stewart* v. *Kennedy* (1889) 16 R. 521; *Edinburgh Northern Tramways* v. *Mann* (1891) 18 R. 1140, 1152; *Assets Co.* v. *Shirres' Trs.* (1897) 24 R. 418; *D. Portland* v *Wood's Trs.*, 1926 S.C. 640, 653; *Fraser* v. *McNeill*, 1948 S.C. 517, 525.

[5] Court of Session Act, 1808, S. 15.

[6] Jury Trials (Sc.) Act, 1815, Ss. 7 and 9; *Park* v. *Wilsons & Clyde Coal Co.*, 1929 S.C. 679.

[7] Jury Trials (Sc.) Act. 1815, S. 6; Administration of Justice (Sc.) Act, 1972, S. 2.

[8] Jury Trials (Sc.) Act, 1910, S. 2; *Lyal* v. *Henderson*, 1916 S.C. (H.L.) 167. The House may itself exercise this power: 1972 Act, S. 2 (2).

[9] *Edinburgh Northern Tramways*, *supra*.

[10] See *Shepherd* v. *Henderson* (1881) 9 R. (H.L.) 1; *Fleming* v. *Hislop* (1886) 13 R. (H.L.) 43.

[11] Court of Session Act, 1825, S. 40. See also *Strathlorne S.S. Co.* v. *Baird*, 1916 S.C. (H.L.) 134.

[12] *Mackay* v. *Dick & Stevenson* (1881) 8 R. (H.L.) 37; *Gilroy, Sons & Co.* v. *Price* (1892) 20 R. (H.L.) 1; see also *Caird* v. *Sime* (1887) 14 R. (H.L.) 37.

facts by the inferior courts,[1] and will very rarely differ from the view of the judge of first instance on the credibility of the witnesses.[2] The House will not decide hypothetical cases, as where parties agreed not to found on a clause in their contract.[3]

Appeal is taken by petition to the House praying that certain interlocutors of the Court of Session be reviewed and revised, varied or altered. The effect of an appeal is to open to review all interlocutors in the cause, except any repelling preliminary defences which have been acquiesced in.[4]

After judgment is pronounced in the appeal, it is usually necessary, unless the House merely affirms the judgment and dismisses the appeal,[5] to present a petition to the Court of Session to apply the judgment of the House of Lords.[6] At this stage the function of the Court of Session is purely ministerial.[7]

Court of Session

The superior civil court of Scotland is the Court of Session, which sits permanently in Edinburgh.[8] It is a unitary collegiate court composed now of twenty[9] judges, who are styled Senators of the College of Justice or Lords of Council and Session. Formerly the whole Court or at least most of the judges sat

---

[1] *McIntyre* v. *McGavin* (1893) 20 R. (H.L.) 49; *Rixon* v. *Edinburgh Northern Tramways* (1893) 20 R. (H.L.) 53; *Windram* v. *Robertson* (1906) 8 F. (H.L.) 40.

[2] *Montgomerie* v. *Wallace-James* (1903) 6 F. (H.L.) 10, 11; *Kilpatrick* v. *Dunlop*, H.L., 1911, noted at 1916 S.C. 631, note; *Strathlorne S.S. Co.* v. *Baird*, 1916 S.C. (H.L.) 134, 135; *Clarke* v. *Edinburgh & District Tramways Co.*, 1919 S.C. (H.L.) 35, 36; *S.S. Hontestroom* v. *S.S. Sagaporack* [1927] A.C. 37; *Thomas* v. *Thomas*, 1947 S.C. (H.L.) 45. cf. *Dunn* v. *D's Trs.*, 1930 S.C. 131, 144.

[3] *Glasgow Navigation Co.* v. *Iron Ore Co.*, 1910 S.C. (H.L.) 63.

[4] *Alexander* v. *Officers of State* (1868) 6 M. (H.L.) 54.

[5] *Peters* v. *Greenock Mags.* (1893) 20 R. 924; *Reid's Trs.* v. *Dawson*, 1915 S.C. 844.

[6] *Gill* v. *Anderson* (1859) 21 D. 723; *Anstruther* v. *A's Trs.* (1873) 11 M. 955; *Walker* v. *Whitwell*, 1916 S.C. 757.

[7] *Free Church* v. *Lord Overtoun* (1904) 7 F. 202; cf. *Roger* v. *Cochrane*, 1910 S.C. 1. Contrast *Sawers' Exors.* v. *Sawers' Trs.* (1873) 11 M. 451.

[8] See generally Hannay, *College of Justice*; (Stair Society) *Introduction to Scottish Legal History*, Chs. 23–4; Stair IV, 1, 1–69; More's Notes, ccclxvi; Mack. I, 2–4; Bankt. IV, 7, 1–31; Ersk. I, 3, 10–23.

[9] Originally (1532) and for long it was fifteen; the number was reduced to thirteen in 1830 but was restored to fifteen in 1948 (Administration of Justice (Sc.) Act, 1948, S. 1(1)) and raised to nineteen (Restrictive Trade Practices Act, 1956, S. 32; Criminal Justice (Sc.) Act, 1963, S. 49; Resale Prices Act, 1964, S. 9(2), and Administration of Justice Act, 1968, S. 1) with power by Order in Council further to increase the number. An Order was made in 1973. Under the Law Commissions Act, 1965, S. 2, a judge of the Court of Session has been seconded to act as Chairman of the Scottish Law Commission and while so employed does not sit as a judge.

together, one or two judges in turn taking preliminary stages of cases in the Outer House. Since 1808[1] and, as further re-organized in 1825,[2] however, it sits as an Inner House of eight judges, mainly exercising appellate jurisdiction, and an Outer House of twelve judges,[3] wholly concerned with exercising juris-diction at first instance. The Inner House is divided into the First Division, composed of the Lord President of the Court of Session and, normally, three Lords of Session, and the Second Division, composed of the Lord Justice-Clerk and, normally, three Lords of Session. The quorum of each Division is, for most purposes, three. An Extra Division may be established from time to time, composed of any three Lords of Session, the senior presiding, to deal with pressure of business.[4] The Divisions have equal status and authority and there is no fixed allocation of work between them. A larger court of five, seven, or more judges may be convened to dispose of particularly important or difficult points,[5] and the decisions of such sittings enjoy greater weight than those of either Division. The decision of a case heard by a Division or larger court is according to the views of the majority in the Division. The Outer House judges sit singly, alone or, in cases prescribed by statute, with a jury of twelve. A Lord Ordinary may report a case to a Division for guidance on disposal[6] and either Division may consult the other Division.[7] Any Inner House judge may sit as a Lord Ordinary, and a Lord Ordinary may sit to make a quorum in a Division. Parties may not now choose their Lord Ordinary or Division.[8]

The Lord President also holds the office of Lord Justice-General of Scotland, and he, the Lord Justice-Clerk, and the other Lords of Session are also the Lords Commissioners of Justiciary who exercise supreme criminal jurisdiction, both appellate and at first instance, in the High Court of Justiciary, and, on appeal from courts-martial, in the Courts-Martial Appeal Court.

---

[1] Court of Session Act, 1808, Ss. 4, 6.

[2] Court of Session Act, 1825, S. 1.

[3] As at mid-1974 one judge was seconded to the Scottish Law Commission.

[4] Administration of Justice (Sc.) Act, 1933, S. 2.

[5] See e.g. *Houston* v. *Buchanan*, 1937 S.C. 460 (5 judges) (affd. 1940 S.C. (H.L.) 17); *McElroy* v. *McAllister*, 1949 S.C. 110 (7 judges); *Bell* v. *Bell*, 1940 S.C. 229 (whole court—13 judges) (revd. 1941 S.C. (H.L.) 5). See also *Haldane's Trs.* v. *Murphy* (1881) 9 R. 269.

[6] e.g. *Goold* v. *G.*, 1927 S.C. 177; *Macomish's Exors* v. *Jones*, 1932 S.C. 108; *Kerr* v. *Brown*, 1965 S.C. 144. In such a case the Lord Ordinary does not sit with the Division: *F.* v. *F.*, 1945 S.C. 202; *Borland* v. *B.*, 1947 S.C. 432.

[7] e.g. *Bridges* v. *B.*, 1911 S.C. 250; *Connell* v. *C.*, 1950 S.C. 505.

[8] Administration of Justice (Sc.) Act, 1933, S. 5.

Court of Session jurisdiction[1]

In point of area, the Court of Session has jurisdiction over the whole kingdom of Scotland and its territorial waters, and all persons and property therein, and in point of subject-matter, over all kinds of causes connected with Scotland save those expressly excluded from its jurisdiction. The court must in every case be satisfied that it has jurisdiction before granting decree.[2]

It has exclusive jurisdiction in actions relating to personal status, including declarator of marriage, of nullity of marriage, of legitimacy, of bastardy, actions of divorce, and generally actions the main object of which is to determine the personal status of individuals, actions of adherence, and of declarator of putting to silence, certain actions of adjudication, actions of reduction, actions of proving the tenor of a lost document, and in actions against foreigners when they are not subject to the jurisdiction of the Sheriff Court,[3] and in petitions for the winding-up of a company with a paid-up capital exceeding £10,000.

It has concurrent jurisdiction with the sheriff courts in respect of all causes exceeding £250 in value, exclusive of interest and expenses,[4] possessory actions, actions of affiliation and aliment, actions of separation *a mensa et thoro*, and actions of aliment or of adherence and aliment between husband and wife,[5] actions for custody of children,[6] and petitions for the winding up of a company with a paid-up capital of less than £10,000, and generally all actions not reserved exclusively to one court or the other.

The Court of Session's jurisdiction is excluded in respect of all causes not exceeding £250 in value exclusive of interest and expenses.[7]

The Court's jurisdiction is not excluded by implication.[8]

The court probably has jurisdiction to determine the validity of its own Acts of Sederunt.[9]

By various statutes, various kinds of statutory proceedings cannot be originated in the Court of Session, though may sometimes

---

[1] See generally Mackay, *Court of Session Practice* (1877); *Manual of Practice* (1894); MacLaren, *Court of Session Practice* (1917); Thomson and Middleton, *Manual of Court of Session Procedure.*

[2] *Walls' Trs.* v. *Drynan* (1888) 15 R. 359, 363.

[3] *Pagan & Osborne* v. *Haig*, 1910 S.C. 341.

[4] Sheriff Courts (Sc.) Act, 1907, S. 7, amd. Sheriff Courts (Sc.) Act, 1971, S. 31.

[5] Sheriff Courts (Sc.) Act, 1907, S. 5. These actions may be remitted to the Court of Session.

[6] *Murray* v. *Forsyth*, 1917 S.C. 721.

[7] Sheriff Courts (Sc.) Act, 1907, S. 7, amd. Sheriff Courts (Sc.) Act, 1971, S. 31.

[8] *Pagan & Osborne* v. *Haig*, 1910 S.C. 341. cf. *Brodie* v. *Ker*, 1952 S.C. 216, 224.

[9] *Carron Co.* v. *Hislop*, 1930 S.C. 1050.

be appealed thereto. These include certain proceedings under the Heritable Securities (Scotland) Act, 1894, certain applications under the Entail Acts, removings and summary removings of tenants.

Original jurisdiction

In some cases, such as special cases, and petitions relative to companies, procedure must be initiated in the Inner House,[1] but the majority of cases, including all ordinary actions and petitions, are initiated in the Outer House and heard first by a Lord Ordinary alone, or in cases statutorily enumerated,[2] by a Lord Ordinary sitting with a jury of twelve. Where a preliminary defence, such as to the jurisdiction, requires inquiry, this may be taken in a preliminary proof before going into the merits. A judgment of a Lord Ordinary, if not reclaimed, is a judgment of the Court of Session as much as a judgment of a Division or the whole Court.[3] Certain kinds of business are assigned by statute to particular Lords Ordinary. The Court may in any cause on the joint request of the parties summon to its assistance at any hearing a specially qualified assessor.[4]

Parties may on petition have their cause disposed of by a chosen Lord Ordinary by summary trial under such procedure as the parties may agree, from which no appeal lies.[5]

Appellate jurisdiction—Reclaiming motion

The Inner House may hear appeals, brought by way of reclaiming motion, from an interlocutor issued by a Lord Ordinary sitting in the Outer House[6] which disposes of the whole, or any part of the merits, of a cause. Reclaiming opens to review all prior interlocutors pronounced by the Lord Ordinary. The appeal is heard by either Division of the Inner House or an Extra Division, and may be reheard before five or seven judges,[7] or the whole court.[8] Evidence is not reheard but in certain cases further evidence may be heard by one of the judges of the Division.[9] The judges of a

---

[1] Administration of Justice (Sc.) Act, 1933, S. 6(3).

[2] Court of Session Acts, 1825, S. 28 and 1850, S. 49; Evidence (Sc.) Act, 1866, S. 4; *Taylor* v. *Dumbarton Tramways Co.*, 1918 S.C. (H.L.) 96; *Robertson* v. *Bannigan*, 1965 S.C. 20.

[3] *Purves* v. *Carswell* (1905) 8 F. 351, 354; *Macomish's Exrs.* v. *Jones*, 1932 S.C. 108.

[4] Administration of Justice (Sc.) Act, 1933, S. 13; see also Nautical Assessors (Sc.) Act, 1894; and *Rowan* v. *West Camak*, 1923 S.C. 316.

[5] Administration of Justice (Sc.) Act, 1933, S. 10.

[6] Court of Session Act, 1868, Ss. 59–60.   [7] Court of Session Act, 1825, S. 23.

[8] Ibid., S. 24; 1868, S. 60.

[9] Court of Session Act, 1868, Ss. 62, 72; *Pirie* v. *Leask*, 1964 S.C. 103.

Division may consult the other Division before giving a judgment.[1] The Divisions are reluctant to differ on a question of fact from the judge who saw and heard the witnesses.[2]

Appellate jurisdiction—Motion for new trial

In cases tried by a Lord Ordinary and a jury a motion may be made to the Inner House for the allowance of a new trial on specified grounds.[3] When hearing the motion the Lord Ordinary who presided at the trial sits with the Division.[4] Such a motion may be reheard by seven judges.[5] The Division may refuse the motion and apply the jury's verdict, or allow a new trial,[6] or enter judgment for the party unsuccessful at the trial.[7] A third trial may similarly be granted.[8]

Appellate jurisdiction—Appeals from Sheriff Court

An appeal lies to the Inner House from the decision of a sheriff-principal or sheriff exercising the jurisdiction of the sheriff court,[9] unless statute has excluded appeal or provided a special mode of appeal.[10]

Appeal is competent against final judgments, or interlocutors granting interim decree, sisting an action, refusing a reponing note, or for which leave has been granted.[11] No appeal is competent where the value of the cause does not exceed £50,[12] or the cause is being tried as a summary cause,[12] unless the Sheriff after final judgment on appeal certifies the case as suitable for appeal to the Court of Session.[13] There is always right of appeal where the value of the cause is indefinite. An appeal submits to review the

[1] *Connell* v. *C.*, 1950 S.C. 505.

[2] *Dunn* v. *D's Trs.*, 1930 S.C. 131, 144; *Ross* v. *R.*, 1930 S.C. (H.L.) 1; *Jordan* v. *Court Line*, 1947 S.C. 29; cf. *Thomas* v. *T.*, 1947 S.C. (H.L.) 45, 54; *Morrison* v. *Kelly*, 1970 S.L.T. 198; but see *Islip Pedigree Breeding Centre* v. *Abercromby*, 1959 S.L.T. 161.

[3] Jury Trials (Sc.) Act, 1815, S. 6; *Maltman* v. *Tarmac, Ltd.*, 1967 S.C. 177.

[4] Court of Session Act, 1868, Ss. 58, 61; *Bicket* v. *Wood* (1893) 20 R. 874; but see *Park* v. *Wilsons & Clyde Coal Co.*, 1928 S.C. 121.   [5] *Park, supra.*

[6] e.g. *Leadbetter* v. *N.C.B.*, 1952 S.C. 19.

[7] Jury Trials (Sc.) Act, 1910, S. 2; e.g. *Mills* v. *Kelvin & White*, 1913 S.C. 521; *West* v. *Mackenzie*, 1917 S.C. 513; *Moyes* v. *Burntisland Shipbuilding Co.*, 1952 S.C. 429.

[8] e.g. *Flood* v. *Caledonian Ry.* (1889) 27 S.L.R. 127; *Watson* v. *N.B. Ry. Co.* (1904) 7 F. 220; *Mitchell* v. *Caledonian Ry.*, 1910 S.C. 546; *McCallum* v. *Paterson*, 1968 S.C. 280; 1969 S.C. 85. The Court is reluctant to allow a third trial: see *McQuilkin* v. *Glasgow District Subway Co.* (1902) 4 F. 462; *Grant* v. *Baird* (1903) 5 F. 459; *McKnight* v. *General Motor Carrying Co.*, 1936 S.C. 17.

[9] Sheriff Courts (Sc.) Act, 1907, S. 28.

[10] *Lanark C.C.* v. *Airdrie Mags.* (1906) 8 F. 802.

[11] Sheriff Courts (Sc.) Act, 1907, S. 28.

[12] All cases under £250: Sheriff Courts (Civil Jurisdiction and Procedure) Act, 1963, S. 1.

[13] 1907 Act, S. 28.

whole of the interlocutors pronounced in the cause, but does not prevent immediate execution of certain warrants, nor effect the recall of an interim interdict.[1]

The interlocutor of the sheriff applying the verdict in a case tried by jury in the sheriff court may be appealed, if notes of the evidence have been taken, on specified grounds.[2]

Cases brought in the sheriff court may also, in particular circumstances, be removed to the Court of Session for jury trial,[3] or for further procedure, or be remitted by the sheriff.[4]

Other appeals

The Inner House also has jurisdiction in appeals from the Dean of Guild courts in burghs,[5] from the Court of Lord Lyon King of Arms,[6] the Restrictive Practices Court,[7] the Sheriff of Chancery, and under numerous statutes which sometimes provide for the form of appeal. The general right to appeal can be taken away only by express words.[8]

It has also a general power, by way of actions for reduction or suspension, to review the proceedings and decisions of all inferior courts, tribunals, and persons or bodies entrusted with judicial or administrative powers, on complaint that there has been an excess of jurisdiction, a failure to act, or a defect in procedure so serious as to be a denial of natural justice and to render the decision a nullity.[9]

Nobile officium

The Court of Session has an extraordinary equitable power, the *nobile officium*,[10] which is inherent in it as a supreme court by

[1] Sheriff Courts (Sc.) Act, 1907, S. 29.   [2] Sheriff Courts (Sc.) Act, 1907, S. 31.
[3] 1907 Act, S. 30.   [4] 1907 Act, S. 5 and proviso, as amended 1913.
[5] Building (Sc.) Act, 1959, S. 16.
[6] See e.g. *Stewart Mackenzie* v. *Fraser Mackenzie*, 1920 S.C. 764; 1922 S.C. (H.L.) 39.
[7] Restrictive Trade Practices Act, 1956, Sched., para. 7.
[8] *Marr* v. *Lindsay* (1881) 8 R. 784; *Kerr* v. *Hood*, 1907 S.C. 895.
[9] *L.A.* v. *Perth Police Commrs.* (1869) 8 M. 244; *Ashley* v. *Rothesay Mags.* (1873) 11 M. 708; (1874) 1 R. (H.L.) 14; *Dalgleish* v. *Leitch* (1889) 2 White 302; *Moss's Empires* v. *Assessor for Glasgow*, 1917 S.C. 1, 6 per Lord Kinnear; Tribunals and Inquiries Act, 1971, S. 14(2).
[10] Stair IV, 3, 1–2; More's Notes, ccclxxiv; Bankt. IV, 7, 23–28; Ersk. I, 3, 22; Mackay, *Practice*, 1209; *Manual*, 82, 530; Maclaren, *Practice*, 100, 828; see e.g. *Cockburn's Trs.*, 1941 S.C. 187; *Lipton's Trs.*, 1943 S.C. 521; *Sandeman's Trs.*, 1947 S.C. 304; *Dow's Trs.*, 1947 S.C 524; *Fletcher's Trs.*, 1949 S.C. 330; *Registrar General*, 1949 S.L.T. 385; *Fraser*, 1950 S.L.T. (Notes) 34; *Smart* v. *Registrar General*, 1954 S.C. 81; *Mackay*, 1955 S.C. 361; *Bell's Exor.*, 1960 S.L.T. (Notes) 3; *Kippen's Tr.*, 1966 S.L.T. (Notes) 2; *Fraser*, 1967 S.L.T. 178. The High Court of Justiciary has a similar though more limited power: see *Wylie* v. *H.M. Advocate*, 1966 S.L.T. 149; *Wan Ping Nam* v. *Federal German Republic*, 1972 S.L.T. 220. As to the Court of Teinds see *Cumbernauld* v. *Dumbartonshire*, 1920 S.C. 625.

virtue of which it regulates charitable trusts and settles schemes of administration where the original purposes have failed, makes interim appointments to public offices, grants special powers to trustees, gives direction to trustees, grants remedies for exceptional circumstances in bankruptcy proceedings, and permits rectification of mistakes and *casus omissi* in statutory procedure.

Statute has conferred on the Sheriff Court also jurisdiction to dispose of certain matters originally falling under the *nobile officium*, sometimes concurrently with, and sometimes to the exclusion of the Court of Session, in such cases as determination of custody and access to children, the appointment of curators, factors, and trustees, grant of their powers, and their removal, and recall of arrestment and inhibitions.

Inherited jurisdiction

The Court of Session now incorporates, and has assumed the jurisdiction of, the former independent High Court of Admiralty (1681—1830),[1] the Court of Exchequer (1707–1856),[2] and the Jury Court (1815–1830).[3] The inferior Commissary courts (1563) were merged in the sheriff courts in 1876[4] and in 1830 the jurisdiction of the Commissary court of Edinburgh in consistorial matters was transferred to the Court of Session,[5] while it was abolished in 1836.[6] The Bill Chamber was formerly a distinct court within the Court of Session in the hands of the junior Lord Ordinary with responsibilities particularly with regard to diligence, summary remedies, and bankruptcy. It was merged in the Outer House in 1933.[7]

Vacation courts

During vacation the judges, other than the Lord President and Lord Justice-Clerk, act in rotation as vacation judges. The vacation judge can deal with all incidental motions and applications,[8]

---

[1] Court of Session (Sc.) Act, 1830, S. 21. The Sheriff Court also has a limited Admiralty jurisdiction. Between 1681 and 1830 the High Court of Admiralty had exclusive jurisdiction in maritime causes: *Sheaf S.S. Co.* v. *Compania Transmediterranea*, 1930 S.C. 660, 664. For modern Admiralty jurisdiction see Administration of Justice Act, 1956, Ss. 45–50.
[2] Exchequer Court (Sc.) Act, 1856, S. 1; see *Inland Revenue* v. *Barrs*, 1959 S.C. 273; affd. 1961 S.C. (H.L.) 22.
[3] Court of Session (Sc.) Act, 1830, S. 1.
[4] Sheriff Courts (Sc.) Act, 1876, Ss. 35–9.
[5] Court of Session (Sc.) Act, 1830, Ss. 31–3.
[6] Commissary Court of Edinburgh Act, 1836.
[7] Administration of Justice (Sc.) Act, 1933, S. 3.
[8] *Barton* v. *L.M.S. Ry.*, 1932 S.C. 113.

but is not bound to do so if the matter can more conveniently be postponed till the Court resumes.

Special jurisdictions

Judges of the Court of Session also exercise certain special jurisdictions.

The Lands Valuation Appeal Court consists of three judges of the Court of Session and hears appeals by stated case from local Valuation Appeal Committees on the value set on heritable property for local rating purposes.[1] The Court is a supreme court in its own sphere and its proceedings cannot be set aside by the Court of Session.[2] No appeal lies from this court.

The Court of Teinds consists of the Inner House judges and the second junior Lord Ordinary, five being a quorum,[3] and is not a separate court but a function of the Court of Session.[4] The jurisdiction relates to creation and disjunction of parishes, valuation of teinds, augmentation, modification and locality of stipend, but the law and practice have been greatly modified by the Church of Scotland Act, 1921, and the Church of Scotland (Property and Endowments) Act, 1925. An appeal lies to the House of Lords.[5]

The Election Petition Court consists of two judges and hears petitions challenging the validity of the election of persons as members of Parliament.[6] No further appeal lies.

The Registration Appeal Court, of three judges, deals with appeals from the decision of a registration officer taken to the sheriff and brought before the Court by stated case.[7]

The Sheriff Court

The chief inferior Scottish civil court, the Sheriff Court,[8] has jurisdiction in point of area only over its own sheriffdom,[9] and, in point of subject-matter, over all causes save those reserved to the Court of Session or to special courts or tribunals. Neither party

[1] Valuation of Lands (Sc.) Amdt. Act, 1867, S. 8.

[2] *Stirling* v. *Holm* (1873) 11 M. 480.

[3] Court of Session Act, 1839, S. 8; Court of Session Act, 1868, S. 9.

[4] *Presbytery of Stirling* v. *Heritors of Larbert* (1900) 2 F. 562.

[5] *Presbytery of Stirling, supra*; cf. *Galloway* v. *Earl of Minto*, 1922 S.C. (H.L.) 24.

[6] Parliamentary Elections Act, 1868; Representation of the People Act, 1949, Ss. 107–11; *Grieve* v. *Douglas-Home*, 1965 S.C. 315.

[7] Representation of the People Act, 1949, S. 45(8); *Dumfries Electoral Registration Officer* v. *Brydon*, 1964 S.C. 242; *Edinburgh Electoral Registration Officer* v. *Robertson*, 1964 S.C. 448.

[8] See generally (Stair Society) *Introduction to Scottish Legal History*, Chs. 25–6; Bankt. IV, 14, 1–26; Ersk. I, 4, 1–6.

[9] Sheriff Courts (Sc.) Act, 1907, S. 4.

can require a case initiated before the sheriff court to be remitted to the Court of Session, save that actions involving questions of heritable right or title where the value of the subject exceeds £50 per annum or £1,000, succession to moveables exceeding £1000, division of commonty or division or division and sale of common property, where the value in issue exceeds £50 per annum or £1,000, may, within six days of the closing of the record, be required to be remitted,[1] that the sheriff may remit certain actions to the Court of Session,[2] and that certain claims of damages may be required to be remitted for jury trial.[3]

There are excluded from the jurisdiction of the Sheriff Court consistorial causes, but actions relating only incidentally to status are not excluded.[4] Actions of reduction are also excluded from the jurisdiction,[5] though objections to deeds and writings may be maintained *ope exceptionis* in the Sheriff Court, and actions of proving of the tenor.[6] Also excluded are exchequer causes, and ecclesiastical causes.

The Sheriff Court has concurrent jurisdiction[7] with the Court of Session in actions of declarator (except as to status),[8] of separation and aliment, adherence and aliment, or interim aliment between husband and wife, and actions to regulate the custody of children, actions of division of commonty and of division or division and sale of common property, actions relating to questions of heritable right or title[9] (except adjudication and reduction) including declarators of irritancy and removing, and suspension of charges or threatened charges on decrees of the sheriff court or decrees of registration on deeds registered, where the debt does not exceed £50. It has concurrent jurisdiction also in all actions for payment of debt or damages.

It has exclusive jurisdiction in all actions competent in the court where the value of the cause does not exceed £250.[10]

---

[1] 1907 Act, S. 5; *Anderson* v. *McGown*, 1911 S.C. 441.

[2] 1907 Act, S. 5.

[3] 1907 Act, S. 30; *Brown* v. *Glenboig Union Fireclay Co.*, 1911 S.C. 179. The Court of Session may remit such a case back to the sheriff court: *Houston* v. *McIndoe*, 1934 S.C. 362; *Armstrong* v. *Paterson*, 1935 S.C. 464.

[4] *Wright* v. *Sharp* (1880) 7 R. 460; *McDonald* v. *Mackenzie* (1891) 18 R. 502; *Turnbull* v. *Wilsons & Clyde Coal Co.*, 1935 S.C. 580; cf. *Lamont* v. *L.*, 1939 S.C. 484.

[5] *Donald* v. *D.*, 1913 S.C. 274.

[6] *Dunbar* v. *Scottish County Investment Co.*, 1920 S.C. 210.

[7] Sheriff Courts (Sc.) Act, 1907, S. 5.

[8] A question of mental capacity is not a matter of status: *Mears* v. *M.*, 1969 S.L.T. (Sh. Ct.) 21.

[9] See *Pitman* v. *Burnett's Trs.* (1882) 9 R. 444; *Anderson* v. *McGown*, 1911 S.C. 441.

[10] Ibid., S. 7, amd. Sheriff Courts (Sc.) Act, 1971, Ss. 31 and 41; *Dickson & Walker* v. *Mitchell*, 1910 S.C. 139.

Certain classes of actions may be required to be remitted to the Court of Session for jury trial,[1] but may be remitted back by that Court.[2]

The more important cases in the Sheriff court are classed as ordinary actions, proceeding on written pleadings, oral argument, and, where necessary, evidence of disputed facts. Jury trial is competent in limited classes of cases only.[3] A 'summary cause' procedure applies to actions for payment of money not exceeding £250, or which parties consent shall be tried summarily; pleadings may be dispensed with and the evidence is not necessarily recorded.[4] A sheriff has a discretion to determine whether an action shall proceed as an ordinary or a summary cause, no matter in which form it was initiated.[5]

Appeal to Sheriff-Principal

A cause heard by a sheriff may be appealed to the Sheriff-Principal, without leave in the case of final judgments and certain other specified interlocutors,[6] and, in the case of any other interlocutor, if the sheriff grants leave to appeal.[7]

In summary causes appeal against final judgment lies to the Sheriff-Principal on fact and law if the evidence has been recorded, but if not, on law only.[8] Interlocutory judgments may be appealed in the same way as in ordinary causes.

Alternatively to appeal to the Sheriff-Principal, or thereafter, appeal may be taken to the Court of Session.[9]

Appeal to Court of Session

In causes not exceeding £50 in value or tried as a summary cause no appeal lies unless the case has first been appealed to the Sheriff-Principal, and he, after final judgment, certifies the cause as suitable for appeal to the Court of Session.[10]

Appeal is competent in other causes in the case of final judgments, certain specified interlocutors, and any interlocutor against which Sheriff-Principal or Sheriff grants leave to appeal.[10]

[1] 1907 Act, S. 30, amd. Sheriff Courts (Sc.) Act, 1971, S. 39.
[2] *Brown* v. *Campbell*, 1924 S.C. 1048.
[3] 1907 Act, S. 31, amd. 1971 Act, S. 40.
[4] 1907 Act, S. 8; Sheriff Courts (Civil Jurisdiction and Procedure) (Sc.) Act, 1963, S. 1. This is to be replaced by a new 'summary cause' procedure under Sheriff Courts (Sc.) Act, 1971, S. 35.
[5] *Purves* v. *Graham*, 1924 S.C. 477.
[6] Sheriff Courts (Sc.) Act, 1907, S. 27(a)–(e), amended 1913.
[7] Ibid., S. 27(f).   [8] Ibid., S. 8.   [9] Ibid., S. 28.
[10] Sheriff Courts (Sc.) Act, 1907, S. 28.

There is no common law right of appeal to the Court of Session where the sheriff has been acting in an administrative capacity.[1]

Small Debt Causes

Claims of debt not exceeding, or limited to, £50[2] and certain actions of delivery, multiplepoinding and certain other kinds of actions are heard under a special procedure prescribed by the Small Debt Acts.[3] The only writ is the printed form of summons. The whole proceedings are summary and oral, and the only official record is that made in the statutory book of causes.[4] A small debt action may be remitted to the ordinary roll of sheriff court actions[5] but does not thereby become appealable.[6]

A judgment in the Small Debt Court is not appealable to the Sheriff-Principal, nor subject to review at all, save by the High Court of Justiciary, on the ground of corruption or malice and oppression on the part of the sheriff, or such deviations in point of form as took place wilfully or prevented substantial justice being done, or incompetency, including defect of jurisdiction.[7]

The Justice of the Peace Small Debt Court

The Justice of the Peace Small Debt Court has jurisdiction for the recovery of debts not exceeding £5.[8] The court is composed of two or more justices, and no legal practitioner may appear before them.[9] A decree granted in the defender's absence may be recalled and the case reheard at a subsequent court, but a decree granted in foro is final, save that at any time within one year it may be reduced by the Court of Session on the ground of malice or oppression.[10]

[1] *Ross-shire C.C.* v. *Macrae Gilstrap*, 1930 S.C. 808.
[2] Sheriff Courts (Civil Jurisdiction and Procedure) Act, 1963, S. 1.
[3] Small Debt (Sc.) Acts, 1837 to 1889. Under the Sheriff Courts (Sc.) Act, 1971, Ss. 35–38, a new form of 'summary cause' will replace Small Debt Causes and cover all actions not exceeding £250.
[4] 1837 Act, S. 17.
[5] Sheriff Courts (Sc.) Act, 1907, S. 48.
[6] *Price* v. *C.P. Ry.*, 1911 S.C. 631; but see *Allardice* v. *Wallace*, 1957 S.L.T. 225.
[7] 1837 Act, Ss. 30–1. See *Philip* v. *Forfar Building Inv. Co.* (1868) 1 Coup. 87; *Reid* v. *Sinclair* (1894) 22 R. (J.) 12; *Carmichael* v. *Macintyre* (1904) 6 F. (J.) 48. Under the 1971 Act, S. 38 appeal will lie to the Sheriff principal on a point of law, and from the final judgement of the sheriff-principal, if certified to be suitable for appeal, to the Court of Session.
[8] Justices of the Peace Small Debt (Sc.) Act, 1825, S. 2.
[9] Ibid., S. 5.
[10] Ibid., S. 14. See also Wages Arrestment (Sc.) Act, 1845; Justices of the Peace Small Debt (Sc.) Act, 1849; *Wolfe* v. *Robertson* (1906) 8 F. 829.

Restrictive Practices Court

This court is a United Kingdom court consisting of three judges of the High Court in England, nominated by the Lord Chancellor, a judge of the Court of Session nominated by the Lord President, a judge of the Supreme Court of Northern Ireland nominated by the Lord Chief Justice of Northern Ireland and not more than ten laymen, It may sit as a single court or in divisions, the quorum being three, including a judicial member.[1] Its jurisdiction is to determine whether restrictions registered with the Registrar of Restrictive Trading Agreements are not, as they are statutorily presumed to be, contrary to the public interest.[2] Appeal lies, in Scotland, to the Court of Session.[3] It also has jurisdiction to exempt classes of goods from the statutory prohibition of maintenance of resale prices.[4]

The Lyon Court

The Lord Lyon King of Arms is the Queen's principal officer of arms in Scotland. He has extensive ministerial duties, particularly the granting of armorial bearings to persons and corporations, the execution of Royal Proclamations, and the conduct of state ceremonials and solemnities, and appointing and controlling messengers-at-arms. The Court of the Lord Lyon consists of Lyon, three heralds and three pursuivants, but Lyon now always sits alone.[5] Apart from an indefinite common law jurisdiction the court has a statutory jurisdiction to determine entitlement to bear particular arms,[6] but not to determine questions of the chiefship of a clan, or the chieftainship of a branch of a clan.[6] He has no jurisdiction to decide a claim of precedence.[7] Lyon may order the removal of unlawful arms and impose fines.[8] Appeal lies to the Court of Session and to the House of Lords.[9] The Court of Session also has jurisdiction to reduce a decree of the Lyon Court.[10]

The Scottish Land Court

The Land Court was created in 1911[11] and assumed the judicial functions of the Crofters Commission of 1885. It is composed

[1] Restrictive Trade Practices Act, 1956, Ss. 2–5.   [2] Ibid., Ss. 20–23.
[3] Ibid., Sched., paras. 7–8.   [4] Resale Prices Act, 1964, Ss. 5–8.
[5] Lyon King of Arms Act, 1867.
[6] *Maclean of Ardgour* v. *Maclean*, 1941 S.C. 613.
[7] *Royal College of Surgeons* v. *Royal College of Physicians*, 1911 S.C. 1054.
[8] *Macrae's Trs.* v. *Lord Lyon*, 1927 S.L.T. 285.
[9] e.g. *Stewart Mackenzie* v. *Fraser Mackenzie*, 1920 S.C. 764; 1922 S.C. (H.L.) 39.
[10] *Macrae's Trs., supra.*
[11] Small Landholders (Sc.) Act, 1911, S. 3.

of five members,[1] of whom the Chairman has the rank and dignity of a judge of the Court of Session, with a quorum of three,[2] but may delegate its powers to any one member of the court, whose determination may be reviewed by three or more members of the Court.[3] It is a court of law[4] with the usual powers of a court but execution of its decrees requires a decree conform by the sheriff.[5] Its jurisdiction is statutory and includes questions of compensation, grazing rights, succession to crofts, bequest and assignation of crofts, vacant holdings, and questions between landlord and tenant of holdings. An appeal by way of case stated lies from the Court[6] or a member thereof[3] to the Court of Session.

Lands Tribunal for Scotland

The Lands Tribunal for Scotland consists of a legal President and members, some lawyers and some experienced in the valuation of land. Its function is to determine questions of disputed compensation for acquisition of land, variation and discharge of land obligations, and allocation of feuduties.[7] An order of the Tribunal may be recorded for execution in the Books of Council and Session and is enforceable accordingly.[8] The Tribunal may state a case for the opinion of the Court of Session and appeal then lies to the House of Lords.[9]

Buildings authorities

The Secretary of State may provide by regulations for the procedure of local authorities in exercising their jurisdiction and functions as buildings authorities.[10] A person aggrieved by certain decisions of a buildings authority may appeal to the sheriff.[11]

Appeal lay formerly to the Court of Session[12] and now to the sheriff with a further appeal on a question of law to the Court of Session and to the House of Lords.[13]

[1] On their positions see *Mackay and Esslemont* v. *L.A.*, 1937 S.C. 860.
[2] cf. *McCallum* v. *Arthur*, 1955 S.C. 188.
[3] *Strachan* v. *Hunter*, 1916 S.C. 901.
[4] *Matheson* v. *Board of Agriculture*, 1917 S.C. 145. As to contempt of court in the Land Court, see *Milburn*, 1946 S.C. 301.
[5] cf. *D. Argyll* v. *Cameron* (1888) 16 R. 139.
[6] e.g. *Kennedy* v. *Johnstone*, 1956 S.C. 39.
[7] Lands Tribunal Act, 1949, Ss. 1, 2; Land Compensation (Sc.) Act, 1963, Ss. 1 and 8; Conveyancing and Feudal Reform (Sc.) Act, 1970, Ss. 1–7, 50.
[8] 1970 Act, S. 50(2).
[9] Tribunals and Inquiries Act, 1971, S. 13(6).
[10] Buildings (Sc.) Act, 1959, amd. Local Government (Sc.) Act, 1973, Sch. 15.
[11] 1959 Act, S. 16.
[12] cf. *Hall* v. *Sinclair*, 1950 S.L.T. (Notes) 69.
[13] Building (Sc.) Act, 1959, S. 16; *Williamson* v. *Purdie*, 1970 S.C. 240.

Sheriff Court of Chancery

The Sheriff Court of Chancery exists to determine competing claims to be declared heir-at-law of a heritable proprietor. If the deceased had no domicile in Scotland the jurisdiction is exclusive. If he had, the jurisdiction was concurrent with that of the sheriff of the county where the lands lay,[1] but is now exclusive also.[2] The Sheriff of Chancery has exclusive jurisdiction in questions of heirship.[3] Appeal lies to the Court of Session and House of Lords. The office of Sheriff of Chancery was united with that of Sheriff of the Lothians and Peebles on the first vacancy occurring after 1933,[4] and the functions of the court are diminishing in consequence of the reform of the law of succession in 1964.[5]

Church courts

The courts of the Church of Scotland,[6] namely the General Assembly, the Synods, the Presbyteries, and the Kirk Sessions, have a jurisdiction, civil and criminal, supreme in their own sphere and wholly independent of the jurisdictions of the Court of Session and the High Court of Justiciary.[7] But appeal to the civil court lies if a church court acts in excess of jurisdiction or refuses to exercise powers legally conferred on it,[8] and the civil courts may assist the church courts to cite witnesses to attend and give evidence.[9]

The church courts of voluntary churches have no legal status or jurisdiction, but only that conferred by their own constitutions over, and accepted by, their members and adherents,[10] but the civil courts will interfere only so far as the church courts' decisions are unconstitutional or irregular and affect civil or patrimonial rights.[11]

---

[1] Service of Heirs (Sc.) Act, 1847, superseded by Titles to Land Consolidation (Sc.) Act, 1868, Ss. 27–55.

[2] Sheriff of Chancery (Transfer of Jurisdiction) Order, 1971 (S.I. 1971, No. 743).

[3] *Bosville* v. *L. MacDonald*, 1910 S.C. 597; *Menzies* v. *McKenna*, 1914 S.C. 272.

[4] Administration of Justice (Sc.) Act, 1933, S. 31(1).

[5] Succession (Sc.) Act, 1964, Ss. 34(2), 35, and Sched. 3.

[6] See generally (Stair Society) *Introduction to Scottish Legal History*, Ch. 27.

[7] General Assembly Act, 1592; Confession of Faith Ratification Act, 1690; Protestant Religion and Presbyterian Church Act, 1706; Church of Scotland Act, 1921; *Lockhart* v. *Presbytery of Deer* (1851) 13 D. 1296; *Wight* v. *Presbytery of Dunkeld* (1870) 8 M. 921; *Ballantyne* v. *Presbytery of Wigtown*, 1936 S.C. 625.

[8] *Sturrock* v. *Greig* (1849) 11 D. 1220.

[9] *Presbytery of Lews* v. *Fraser* (1874) 1 R. 888.

[10] *McMillan* v. *Free Church General Assembly* (1859) 22 D. 290; 23 D. 1314.

[11] *Smith* v. *Galbraith* (1843) 5 D. 665; *Forbes* v. *Eden* (1867) 5 M. (H.L.) 36; *Wight* v. *Dunkeld* (1870) 8 M. 921; *Brook* v. *Kelly* (1893) 20 R. (H.L.) 104; *Skerret* v. *Oliver* (1896) 23 R. 468; *MacDonald* v. *Burns*, 1940 S.C. 376.

Special tribunals

Some of the many tribunals established for adjudicating on disputes arising in particular relations operate in fields which impinge on private law. These include local tribunals and the National Insurance Commissioner and his deputies,[1] local tribunals and the National Insurance Commissioner and his deputies,[2] industrial tribunals,[3] rent assessment committees,[4] and rent tribunals.[5] Other special tribunals are more directly concerned with issues arising out of public administration. The Tribunals and Inquiries Act, 1971, S. 13 confers on parties to proceedings before certain tribunals a right to appeal to the Court of Session if dissatisfied in point of law.[6]

The Council on Tribunals

The Council on Tribunals, which has a Scottish Committee, exists to keep under review the constitution and working of many tribunals, but does not act as an appellate body from their decisions.[7]

Contempt of Court

Contempt of court may be constituted by rude or disorderly conduct in court, use of improper means to influence the course of justice, conduct which brings the administration of justice into disrepute, and defiance or wilful non-observance of orders of court. Every court has an inherent jurisdiction to punish summarily any conduct amounting to contempt,[8] by admonition, fine or imprisonment. The question of contempt, and the punishment, may be appealed to the Court of Session[9] or House of Lords.[10] A sentence of imprisonment may be appealed to the Court of Session[11] or High Court of Justiciary.[12]

[1] National Insurance Act, 1965, Ss. 70, 77–80.
[2] National Insurance (Industrial Injuries) Act, 1965, Ss. 46, 51–3.
[3] Industrial Training Act, 1964, S. 12; Redundancy Payments Act, 1965, S. 9; Industrial Relations Act, 1971, S. 100.
[4] Rent (Sc.) Act, 1971, Sched. 5.
[5] Rent (Sc.) Act, 1971, S. 84.
[6] cf. *Carron Co.* v. *Robertson,* 1967 S.C. 273.
[7] Tribunals and Inquiries Act, 1971.
[8] Stair IV, 36, 7; Ersk. I, 2, 8.
[9] *Hamilton* v. *Anderson* (1858) 3 Macq. 363; *Munro* v. *Matheson* (1877) 5 R. 308.
[10] *Hamilton* v. *Caledonian Ry.* (1850) 7 Bell 272.
[11] *Maclachlan* v. *Bruce,* 1912 S.C. 440.
[12] *MacLeod* v. *Speirs* (1884) 11 R. (J.) 26; *Graham* v. *Younger,* 1955 J.C. 28.

CHAPTER 3

ARBITRATION

ARBITRATION is the adjudication of a dispute or controversy, on fact or law or both, outside the ordinary civil courts by one or more persons to whom the parties who are at issue refer the matter for decision.[1] It has never been the law of Scotland that an agreement to oust the jurisdiction of the courts was invalid as contrary to public policy.[2]

The submission of certain kinds of disputes to arbitration may be required by statute,[3] or provided for in the parties' contract,[4] or may be adopted by parties when dispute arises in preference to resorting to litigation. In the latter two classes of cases the reference depends on agreement of parties[5] and may raise preliminary questions of the capacity of the parties to refer their disputes.[6] Where the arbitration is prescribed or agreed upon either party may object to the other's attempt to resort instead to the courts,[7] though such an attempt may be necessary to determine, failing agreement, whether or not the matter in controversy is among the kinds of issues prescribed or agreed upon to be determined by arbitration. If parties have agreed to arbitrate, they must arbitrate,[8] unless by common consent they depart from this agreement. The court has no power to release parties from their agreement.[8]

A shadowy distinction exists between an arbitration and a

---

[1] General authorities: Ersk. IV, 3, 29–36; Bell: *Law of Arbitration* (1877); Irons and Melville: *Law of Arbitration in Scotland* (1903).

[2] *Sanderson* v. *Armour*, 1922 S.C. (H.L.) 117, 126.

[3] e.g. Agricultural Holdings (Scotland) Act, 1949, S. 74 ('any question or difference of any kind whatsoever between the landlord and the tenant of an agricultural holding arising out of the tenancy . . .').

[4] e.g. *Hamlyn* v. *Talisker Distillery* (1894) 21 R. (H.L.) 21.

[5] Ersk. IV, 3, 29; *Brakinrig* v. *Menzies* (1841) 4 D. 274.

[6] See e.g. *Thomson's Trs.* v. *Muir* (1867) 6 M. 145; *Aberdeen Town and County Bank* v. *Dean & Son* (1871) 9 M. 842; *McKersies* v. *Mitchell* (1872) 10 M. 861; Bankruptcy (Sc.) Act, 1913, S. 172; Companies Act, 1948, S. 245; Trusts (Sc.) Act, 1921, S. 4.

[7] e.g. *Mauritzen* v. *Baltic Shipping Co.*, 1948 S.C. 646.

[8] *N.B. Ry. Co.* v. *Newburgh, etc. Ry. Co.*, 1911 S.C. 710; *Hegarty & Kelly* v. *Cosmopolitan Ins. Co.*, 1913 S.C. 377, 386; *Sanderson, supra*; *Crawford Bros.* v. *Northern Lighthouses Commrs.*, 1925 S.C. (H.L.) 22.

valuation[1] but the word 'arbitration' in a statute has been held to include a 'valuation'.[2]

Parties to a litigation may be held to have constituted the judge an arbiter, and thereby excluded appeal from him, but only where both parties have agreed and the judge has assented and there has been a complete departure from ordinary procedure.[3]

In course of a litigation a remit or reference may be made to an expert who reports to the court.[4] Consent to a remit does not make him an arbiter and exclude further procedure in court unless the remit is *extra cursum curiae*.[5]

Parties may also by joint minute agree to refer a cause, so far as not disposed of, to a judicial referee, i.e. a person appointed by the court, for decision.[6] A Lord Ordinary or sheriff may thus be made a judicial referee,[7] but a deviation from procedure is not enough to do this.[8]

What matters may be referred to arbitration

Parties may refer to arbitration questions as to any civil right or interest, real or personal, about which they may contract.[9] The questions referred may be questions of fact, or of law,[10] or of discretion, such as as to the proper measure of compensation. Questions of public rights or personal status[11] may not be the subject of arbitration,[12] nor criminal matters,[13] nor any illegal or immoral subject. While a submission should be liberally construed,[14] parties cannot be held to have excluded the jurisdiction of the courts except in so far as they have expressly and clearly agreed to do so.[15]

---

[1] *Nivison* v. *Howat* (1883) 11 R. 182; *Robertson* v. *Boyd & Winans* (1885) 12 R. 429, 430.

[2] *Graham* v. *Mill* (1904) 6 F. 886; *Stewart* v. *Williamson*, 1909 S.C. 1254, 1258; affd. 1910 S.C. (H.L.) 47. In *Gibson* v. *Fotheringham*, 1914 S.C. 987 the matters in issue in an arbitration were entirely matters of valuation.

[3] *White* v. *Morton's Trs.* (1866) 4 M. (H.L.) 53, 58; *Gordon* v. *Bruce* (1897) 24 R. 844. See also *Stark's Trs.* v. *Duncan* (1906) 8 F. 429.

[4] *Steel* v. *S.* (1898) 25 R. 715, 720. [5] *Steel, supra.*

[6] e.g. *Brakinrig, supra*; *Macrae* v. *Edinburgh Street Tramways Co.* (1885) 13 R. 265.

[7] e.g. *Dykes* v. *Merry & Cunninghame* (1869) 7 M. 603.

[8] *Gordon* v. *Bruce* (1897) 24 R. 844. [9] Bankt. I, 23, 17; Bell, *Arbitration*, 120.

[10] *N.B. Ry.* v. *Newburgh Ry.*, 1911 S.C. 710, 719. [11] Bell, 122.

[12] *Ramsay* v. *Hay* (1624) Mor. 16245; but see *E. Kintore* v. *Union Bank* (1863) 1 M. (H.L.) 11. A matter of status may be established, if only incidental to the main issue before the arbiter: *Johnstone* v. *Spencer*, 1908 S.C. 1015; *Turnbull* v. *Wilson & Clyde Coal Co.*, 1935 S.C. 580, but the decision probably applies to that case only.

[13] *Stark's Trs.* v. *Duncan* (1906) 8 F. 429. See also *E. Kintore* v. *Union Bank* (1863) 1 M. (H.L.) 11.

[14] Ersk. IV, 3, 32.

[15] *Calder* v. *Mackay* (1860) 22 D. 741, 744; *Holmes Oil Co.* v. *Pumpherston Oil Co.* (1890) 18 R. (H.L.) 52, 55.

Statutory references

Various statutes provide for the decision of specified issues by arbitration, and provide for the arbiter, his powers, and, some-times, for reference by him to the civil courts on a question of law.[1] Exclusion of the jurisdiction of the courts requires an express provision in, or a clear implication from, the words of the Act.[2] Such a provision is normally imperative and cannot be waived by agreement or conduct of parties but may be merely enabling.[3] It is always, however, a question of law for the court whether the circumstances which have arisen raise a question of the kinds statutorily required to be determined by arbitration,[4] and the courts may determine any questions precedent to the existence of a statutory claim.[5]

Reference under clause in contract

A contract between two parties may include a provision that disputes of specified kinds are to be decided by arbitration. The scope of such an arbitration clause may give rise to difficulty. When incorporated in a contract dealing with particular matters it is presumed confined to the same subject matter.[6] It may further be executorial, confined to the determination of questions which may arise during the execution of the contract, or be general, extending to the decision of any claim which may arise from the

---

[1] e.g. Companies Clauses Consolidation (Sc.) Act, 1845, Ss. 127–41; Lands Clauses Consolidation (Sc.) Act, 1845, Ss. 24, 66; Railways Clauses Consolidation (Sc.) Act, 1845, S. 71; Acquisition of Land (Assessment of Compensation) Act, 1919, S. 1; Friendly Societies Acts, 1896, S. 68; 1948, Ss. 21, 25; Agricultural Holdings (Sc.) Act, 1949, Ss. 68, 74; National Health Service (Sc.) Act, 1947, S. 77; Local Govt. (Sc.) Act, 1973, S. 25.

[2] *Brodie* v. *Ker*, 1952 S.C. 216, 224.

[3] *Houison-Craufurd's Trs.* v. *Davies*, 1951 S.C. 1; *Lanark C.C.* v. *East Kilbride*, 1967 S.C. 235.

[4] e.g. *Caledonian Ry.* v. *Greenock, etc. Ry.* (1874) 1 R. (H.L.) 8; *Mitchell* v. *Caledonian Bldg. Soc.* (1886) 13 R. 918; *Glasgow Mags.* v. *Caledonian Ry.* (1892) 19 R. 874; *Symington's Exor.* v. *Galashiels Co-operative Store Co.* (1894) 21 R. 371; *N.B. Ry.* v. *Lanarkshire and Dumbartonshire Ry.* (1895) 23 R. 76; *Melrose* v. *Edinburgh Savings Bank Trs.* (1897) 24 R. 483; *Lanarkshire Tramways Co.* v. *Motherwell* (1908) 16 S.L.T. 63; *Johnstone* v. *Assoc. Ironmoulders*, 1911, 2 S.L.T. 478; *McGowan* v. *City of Glasgow Friendly Socy.*, 1913 S.C. 991; *Caledonian Ry.* v. *Clyde Shipping Co.*, 1917 S.C. 107; *Picken* v. *P.*, 1934 S.L.T. 75; *Fairholme's Trs.* v. *Graham*, 1943 S.L.T. 158; *Bruce* v. *Muir*, 1944 J.C. 29; *Houison-Craufurd's Trs.* v. *Davies*, 1951 S.C. 1; *Brodie* v. *Ker*, 1952 S.C. 216; *Lanark C.C.* v. *East Kilbride*, 1967 S.C. 235.

[5] *Donaldson's Hospital* v. *Esslemont*, 1925 S.C. 199.

[6] *Lauder* v. *Wingate* (1852) 14 D. 633. See also *Miller* v. *Howie* (1851) 13 D. 608.

contract.[1] The scope of a reference clause is more strictly interpreted in the case of an executorial reference.[2]

The existence and validity of the contract must be established before the arbitration clause can be invoked; if it is doubtful whether the contract exists that is a question for the courts.[3] Similarly whether there is a question to be referred is a question for the courts.[4] Where the clause provides for the appointment of an arbiter by the court, the court will not appoint unless it appears that there is a specific and concrete dispute, *prima facie* falling within the ambit of the arbitration clause.[5] The court also must determine the scope of the reference clause, and whether it applies in the circumstances.[6]

If there is a general arbitration clause its validity is not affected by allegations that the party invoking it has repudiated the contract, or has been in breach of it.[7] Whether either party has repudiated the contract is a question for the arbiter.[8] But if the contract has been justifiably rescinded by either party, the arbitration clause falls with the rest of the contract.[9]

If external circumstances arise which do, or may, have the effect of terminating the contract and releasing both parties from their obligations, on the grounds of supervening impossibility, illegality, or frustration of the adventure,[10] the better view is that

[1] *Mackay* v. *Barry Parochial Board* (1883) 10 R. 1046; *Wright* v. *Greenock Tramways Co.* (1891) 29 S.L.R. 53; *N.B. Ry.* v. *Newburgh & North Fife Ry.*, 1911 S.C. 710; *Sanderson* v. *Armour*, 1922 S.C. (H.L.) 117.
Among references held executorial are: *Kirkwood* v. *Morrison* (1877) 5 R. 79; *Savile St. Foundry Co.* v. *Rothesay Tramways* (1883) 10 R. 821; *Beattie* v. *Macgregor* (1883) 10 R. 1094; *Mackay* v. *Leven Police Commrs.* (1893) 20 R. 1093; *Aviemore Station Hotel Co.* v. *Scott* (1904) 12 S.L.T. 494.
Among references held general are: *Mackay, supra*; *Wright, supra*; *McCosh* v. *Moore* (1905) 8 F. 31; *N.B. Ry., supra*; *Scott* v. *Gerrard*, 1916 S.C. 793.
[2] *Beattie, supra*; *Mackay* v. *Leven, supra*.
[3] *Ransohoff & Wissler* v. *Burrell* (1897) 25 R. 284; *Hoth* v. *Cowan*, 1926 S.C. 58, 64.
[4] *Greenock Parochial Board* v. *Coghill* (1878) 5 R. 732; *Mackay* v. *Leven, supra*; *Woods* v. *Co-operative Ins. Co.*, 1924 S.C. 692.
[5] *Mackay* v. *Leven, supra*; *Allied Airways (Gandar Dower) Ltd.* v. *Secy. of State for Air*, 1950 S.C. 249.
[6] *Crawford Bros.* v. *Northern Lighthouses Commrs.*, 1925 S.C. (H.L.) 22; *Macdonald* v. *Clark*, 1927 S.N. 6.
[7] *N.B. Ry.* v. *Newburgh & North Fife Ry.*, 1911 S.C. 710; *Sanderson* v. *Armour*, 1922 S.C. (H.L.) 117; *Dryburgh* v. *Caledonian Ins. Co.*, 1922 S.N. 85; cf. *Paterson* v. *United Scottish Herring Drifter Ins. Co.*, 1927 S.N. 141.
[8] *Sanderson, supra*.
[9] *Hegarty & Kelly* v. *Cosmopolitan Ins. Corpn.*, 1913 S.C. 377; *Sanderson, supra*, explaining *Municipal Council of Johannesburg* v. *Stewart*, 1909 S.C. (H.L.) 53.
[10] *Scott* v. *Del Sel*, 1923 S.C. (H.L.) 37; *Heyman* v. *Darwins* [1942] A.C. 356; *Mauritzen* v. *Baltic Shipping Co.*, 1948 S.C. 646; *Hirji Mulji* v. *Cheong Yue S.S. Co.* [1926] A.C. 497 is not now followed.

whether the circumstances do terminate the contract or not falls under the arbitration clause also.

If a difference between the parties results in an alleged modification of the contract or an alleged new contract, the question whether this has taken place and has superseded the original contract is probably outwith any arbitration clause in the original contract.[1] A supplementary contract is not governed by an arbitration clause in the main contract unless the intention to incorporate it in the supplementary contract also is evident.

An arbitration clause may bind a person not a party to the contract such as a creditor of one party thereto who has arrested in the hands of the other party thereto and is founding on the contract.[2] An arbitration clause in a principal contract may be held incorporated in a sub-contract between one of the parties and a third party.[3]

Contract to submit

When a dispute has arisen between two parties they may competently agree to submit it to the decision of an arbiter rather than resort to litigation. All parties who may contract may enter into a contract of submission, and statute has empowered many classes of persons to refer disputes to arbitration.[4] Counsel may,[5] but a solicitor may not, save by express authority,[6] submit a claim. Submission may be made verbally, particularly references regarding marches,[7] or in writing,[8] which, if the subject matter be heritable property, must be probative,[9] or improbative supplemented by *rei interventus* or homologation.[10] In general the rules as to constitution, proof and extinction apply to the contract to submit as to any other contract.

A submission falls to be interpreted in the same way as any other contract.[11] The scope of any such reference depends on the

---

[1] *Tough* v. *Dumbarton Waterworks Commrs.* (1872) 11 M. 236; *Hoth* v. *Cowan*, 1926 S.C. 58.

[2] *Palmer* v. *S.E. Lancashire Ins. Co.*, 1932 S.L.T. 68; *Rutherford* v. *Licences and General Ins. Co.*, 1934 S.L.T. 31, 47; see also *Cant* v. *Eagle Star Ins. Co.*, 1937 S.L.T. 444; contrast *McConnell & Reid* v. *Smith*, 1911 S.C. 635.

[3] *Goodwins, Jardine & Co.* v. *Brand* (1905) 7 F. 995.

[4] e.g. Trusts (Sc.) Act, 1921, Ss. 2, 4.

[5] *Forbes* v. *Duffus* (1837) 12 F.C. 321; *MacLaren* v. *Ferrier* (1865) 3 M 833.

[6] *Black* v. *Laidlaw* (1844) 6 D. 1254.

[7] *Otto* v. *Weir* (1871) 9 M. 660.

[8] *Maclellan* v. *Macleod* (1830) 4 W. & S. 157; *Chapman* v. *Edinburgh Prison Board* (1844) 6 D. 1288; *Fraser* v. *L. Lovat* (1850) 7 Bell 171; *Dykes* v. *Roy* (1869) 7 M. 357.

[9] As to what is probative writing, see Ch. 6.

[10] *Brown & Colvill* v. *Gardner* (1739) Mor. 5659.

[11] *Lang* v. *Brown* (1855) 2 Macq. 93; see also Ersk. IV, 3, 32.

terms of the submission. A submission should be liberally construed[1] and if ambiguous may be interpreted in accordance with
the actings of the parties.[2] If doubts arise during the arbitration
the arbiter must form his own opinion thereon,[3] but the ultimate
decision lies with the court,[4] But the court will not readily interfere with an arbitration in progress on this ground.[5]

Submissions are distinguished as general, dealing with all
disputes between the parties existing at the date of the contract,[6]
or special, limited to a particular question, or general-special or
mixed, where there is a general reference of disputes coupled with
the specification of a precise matter in issue. Parties may agree to
submit future disputes.[7]

A submission falls on the death of either party,[8] or of the
arbiter, or oversman,[9] though a judicial reference is not thus
ended,[10] or if by supervening impossibility execution of the arbitration in the mode contemplated is rendered impossible.[11]

Judicial reference

A judicial reference arises when parties to an action in court
agree, voluntarily or at the suggestion of the court, with judicial
authority to refer the matters in issue to an arbiter. A judicial
reference is subject to the same rules as an ordinary submission.[12]
It may be to the Lord Ordinary or sheriff, in which case appeal
from his judgment is precluded,[13] but a mere deviation from
ordinary procedure is not a reference to the judge as arbiter.[14]

[1] Ersk. IV, 3, 32; but see *Calder* v. *Mackay* (1860) 22 D. 741, 744; *Holmes Oil Co.* v.
Pumpherston Oil Co. (1890) 18 R. (H.L.) 52, 55.

[2] *N.B. Ry.* v. *Barr* (1855) 18 D. 102; *Orrell* v. *O.* (1859) 21 D. 554; *Miller* v. *Oliver &*
Boyd (1906) 8 F. 390, 401.

[3] *Bell* v. *Graham*, 1908 S.C. 1060.   [4] *Adams* v. *G.N.S. Ry.* (1890) 18 R. (H.L.) 1, 8.

[5] *Dumbarton Waterworks Commrs.* v. *Blantyre* (1884) 12 R. 115; *Glasgow, Yoker and*
Clydebank Ry. Co. v. *Lidgerwood* (1895) 23 R. 195; *Licenses Ins. Corpn.* v. *Shearer*, 1907
S.C. 10.

[6] Bell, *Arbitration*, 60; *Hood* v. *Baillie* (1832) 11 S. 207; even a general submission does
not put before the arbiter a plea of compensation: *McEwan* v. *Middleton* (1866) 5 M. 159;
or empower him to assess damages: *Blaikie* v. *Aberdeen Ry.* (1852) Paterson's App. 119;
N.B. Ry. v. *Newburgh & North Fife Ry.*, 1911 S.C. 710.

[7] *Robertson* v. *Johnstone* (1835) 13 S. 289.

[8] Ersk. IV, 3, 29; *Ewing* v. *Dewar*, 19 Dec. 1820, F.C.; *Robertson* v. *Cheyne* (1847) 9 D.
599. But the death of one trustee does not have this effect: *Alexander's Trs.* v. *Dymock's Trs.*
(1883) 10 R. 1189.

[9] Ersk. IV, 3, 34.   [10] *Watmore* v. *Burns* (1839) 1 D. 743.

[11] *Graham* v. *Mill* (1904) 6 F. 886.

[12] *Brackenrig* v. *Menzies* (1841) 4 D. 274.

[13] *Dykes* v. *Merry & Cunninghame* (1869) 7 M. 603; *Lindsay* v. *Walker's Trs.* (1877)
4 R. 870.

[14] *Gordon* v. *Bruce* (1897) 24 R. 844; contrast *Steele* v. *Steele* (1898) 5 S.L.T. 466.

The jurisdiction of a judicial referee is determined by the minute referring the action.[1] The referee reports to the court which grants decree in terms thereof.[2]

The Arbiter

The submission is normally to an arbiter, or to two arbiters, with power to them, unless excluded by the reference, to appoint an oversman in case of dispute.[3] The parties may choose whom they will, ignoring physical and legal disabilities,[4] but an arbiter should have no interest in the matter in dispute not known to or disclosed to the parties.[5] A reference to a party,[6] or one party's employee[7] is valid, so long as that employee has not given evidence for his employer or otherwise acted partially.[8] An arbiter is disqualified if he has shown bias before accepting the reference.[9] A reference to a person by name, or to an arbiter to be nominated by another, have always been valid.[10] A reference to a person not named, or to the holder of an office for the time being, was formerly ineffectual,[11] with certain exceptions,[12] but is now valid,[13] as is a reference to arbitration in the customary manner of a particular trade.[14] On the failure of one party to an agreement to refer to concur in nominating a single arbiter, or one of two arbiters, the court

[1] *Mackenzie* v. *Girvan* (1840) 3 D. 318.

[2] *Gillon* v. *Simpson* (1859) 21 D. 243.

[3] Arbitration (Sc.) Act, 1894, S. 4. On method of choice of oversman see *Smith* v. *Liverpool, etc. Insce. Co.* (1887) 14 R. 931.

[4] See *Gordon* v. *E. Errol* (1582) Mor. 8915 (minor); *Fisher* v. *Colquhoun* (1844) 6 D. 1286 (advocate promoted judge); *Bremner* v. *Elder & Elgin Lunacy Board* (1875) 2 R. (H.L.) 136 (indefinite body of persons); *Dixon* v. *Jones, Heard & Ingram* (1884) 11 R. 739 (firm).

[5] *Mackenzie* v. *Clark* (1828) 7 S. 215; *Tennent* v. *Macdonald* (1836) 14 S. 976; *L.N.W. Ry.* v. *Lindsay* (1858) 3 Macq. 99; *Dixon* v. *Jones, Heard & Ingram* (1884) 11 R. 739; *Smith, supra*; *McDougall* v. *Laird* (1894) 22 R. 71; *Peckholtz* v. *Russell* (1900) 7 S.L.T. 160; *Riddell* v. *Lanark Ry.* (1901) 8 S.L.T. 330; *Sellar* v. *Highland Ry.*, 1919 S.C. (H.L.) 19; *Fleming's Trs.* v. *Henderson*, 1962 S.L.T. 401.

[6] *Buchan* v. *Melville* (1902) 4 F. 620.

[7] *Trowsdale* v. *N.B. Ry.* (1864) 2 M. 1334; *Adams* v. *G.N.S. Ry.* (1889) 16 R. 843; 18 R. (H.L.) 1; *Crawford Bros.* v. *Northern Lighthouses Commrs.*, 1925 S.C. (H.L.) 22. But see *Halliday* v. *D. Hamilton's Trs.* (1903) 5 F. 800; *Aviemore Station Hotel Co.* v. *Scott* (1904) 12 S.L.T. 494.

[8] *Dickson* v. *Grant* (1870) 8 M. 566; *McDougall, supra*; *McLauchlan & Brown* v. *Morrison* (1900) 8 S.L.T. 279.

[9] *Dickson, supra*; *Peckholtz, supra*; *McLauchlan & Brown, supra*.

[10] *Murdoch* v. *France* (1894) 2 S.L.T. 320; 1894 Act, S. 1.

[11] *Hendry's Trs.* v. *Renton* (1851) 13 D. 1001; *Tancred Arrol & Co.* v. *Steel Co. of Scotland* (1890) 17 R. (H.L.) 31.

[12] See *Smith* v. *Wharton-Duff* (1843) 5 D. 749; *Caledonian Ins. Co.* v. *Gilmour* (1892) 20 R. (H.L.) 13.

[13] Arbitration (Sc.) Act, 1894, S. 1.

[14] *Douglas* v. *Stiven* (1900) 2 F. 575; *United Creameries Co.* v. *Boyd*, 1912 S.C. 617; *Highgate* v. *British Oil and Grant Co.*, 1914 2 S.L.T. 241.

may appoint.[1] On the failure of two arbiters to agree on an oversman the court may appoint.[2] It has also been held that a party to a contract containing an arbitration clause, notwithstanding that he had left Scotland, had prorogated the jurisdiction of the Scottish court to the effect of entitling it to appoint an arbiter at the instance of the other party, who had claims falling under the arbitration clause.[3]

In commercial arbitrations, in which two arbiters are appointed with power to appoint an oversman, the fact that one arbiter acts as agent for and represents the party appointing him has been recognized and does not invalidate the award.[4]

It is competent for one party to interdict an arbiter before he acts if it is clear that he has no such power as that which he is called on to exercise,[5] or that there is no question for him to decide,[6] or that the arbiter would necessarily be disqualified by bias,[7] or at an early stage if he has taken a step which must render an award bad.[8]

The office of arbiter is gratuitous,[9] unless a fee is stipulated for,[10] but a professional person acting as arbiter is entitled to remuneration,[11] as is the arbiter in a statutory arbitration.[12] Each party is liable for half of the fee.[13] Having accepted office an arbiter cannot resign,[14] but may be ordered by the court at the instance of one or both parties to issue an award.[15]

Where an arbiter under the Agricultural Holdings (Sc.) Act, 1949 has been removed and his award reduced it is competent to appoint a second arbiter.[16]

[1] 1894 Act, Ss. 2–3. cf. *Ross* v. *R.*, 1920 S.C. 530.

[2] 1894 Act, S. 4; *Glasgow P.C.* v. *United Collieries* (1907) 15 S.L.T. 232; *Mackay* v. *Robertson*, 1935 S.L.T. 414.

[3] *D. Fife's Trs.* v. *Taylor*, 1934 S.L.T. 76.

[4] *Scorrier Steamship Coasters* v. *Milne*, 1928 S.N. 109.

[5] *G.S.W. Ry.* v. *Caledonian Ry.* (1871) 44 S. Jur. 29; *Dumbarton Water Commrs.* v. *Blantyre* (1884) 12 R. 115; *McCoard* v. *Glasgow Corpn.*, 1935 S.L.T. 117.

[6] *Greenock Parochial Board* v. *Coghill* (1878) 5 R. 732; *Low & Thomas* v. *Dunbarton C.C.* (1905) 13 S.L.T. 620.

[7] *Caledonian Ry.* v. *Glasgow Corpn.* (1897) 25 R. 74.

[8] *Birkmyre* v. *Moor & Weinberg* (1906) 14 S.L.T. 702.

[9] *Paul* v. *Henderson* (1867) 5 M. 628; *Murray* v. *N.B. Ry.* (1900) 2 F. 460.

[10] *Fraser* v. *Wright* (1838) 16 S. 1049; *Duff* v. *Pirie* (1893) 21 R. 80.

[11] *Macintyre Bros.* v. *Smith*, 1913 S.C. 129. As to amount of fee see *Wilkie* v. *Scottish Aviation Ltd.*, 1956 S.C. 198. As to fee where award inept, see *Rutherford* v. *Findochty Mags.*, 1929 S.N. 130.

[12] *Murray, supra.*

[13] *Macintyre, supra.*   [14] Bell, *Arbitration*, 201.

[15] *Marshall* v. *Edinburgh & Glasgow Ry.* (1853) 15 D. 603. See also *Forbes* v. *Underwood* (1886) 13 R. 465; *Watson* v. *Robertson* (1895) 22 R. 362.

[16] *Dundee Corpn.* v. *Guthrie*, 1969 S.L.T. 93.

The arbiter's powers

The powers of the arbiter are determined primarily by the terms of the statute or the submission to him, which it is for him, subject to review by the court,[1] to interpret.[2] The Court is slow to interfere with an arbitration in progress.[3] If the arbitration clause does not apply to the dispute which has arisen the arbiter has no power to deal with that dispute.[4]

An arbiter cannot assess damages without express power to do so,[5] but has implied power to award expenses[6] though he must hear parties on the matter.[7]

Unless limited by statute, an arbiter's powers under a submission blank as to its endurance continue for a year and a day from the submission to him.[8] If they fall by lapse of time parties are restored to their common law rights of action.[9] A submission, blank as to endurance, may be prorogated or extended in duration by writing by the arbiter, if express power were conferred on him,[10] or by express contract by the parties,[11] or even by actings.[12] If the submission contains no blank and imposes no limit his powers last for forty years.[13] If there is a time-limit the submission falls automatically on its expiry, unless extended by the parties, expressly or by conduct.[14] If there is a reference to two arbiters and an oversman, and power to prorogate was conferred on the arbiters, it will be inferred in the case of the oversman.[15]

---

[1] *Adams* v. *G.N.S. Ry.* (1890) 18 R. (H.L.) 1, 8.

[2] *Calder* v. *Mackay* (1860) 22 D. 741; *Mackay* v. *Leven Police Commrs.* (1893) 20 R. 1093; *Fairholme's Trs.* v. *Graham*, 1943 S.L.T. 158.

[3] *Dumbarton Waterworks Commrs.* v. *L. Blantyre* (1884) 12 R. 115; *Licenses Insce. Corpn.* v. *Shearer*, 1907 S.C. 10.

[4] *Tough* v. *Dumbarton Waterworks Commrs.* (1872) 11 M. 236; *Howden* v. *Dobie* (1882) 9 R. 758; *McAlpine* v. *Lanarkshire and Ayrshire Ry.* (1889) 17 R. 113; *Allan's Tr.* v. *Allan & Sons* (1891) 19 R. 215.

[5] *Aberdeen Ry.* v. *Blaikie Bros.* (1851) 13 D. 527; (1853) Paters. App. 119; *Mackay* v. *Barry Parochial Board* (1883) 10 R. 1046; *McAlpine* v. *Lanarkshire and Ayrshire Ry.* (1889) 17 R. 113; *Mackay* v. *Leven Police Commrs.* (1893) 20 R. 1093.

[6] *Ferrier* v. *Alison* (1845) 4 Bell 161; *Paul* v. *Henderson* (1867) 5 M. 613; *Pollich* v. *Heatley*, 1910 S.C. 469.

[7] *Islay Estates* v. *McCormick*, 1937 S.N. 28.

[8] Ersk. IV, 3, 29; *Dunmore* v. *McInturner* (1829) 7 S. 595; *Graham* v. *Mill* (1904) 6 F. 886.

[9] *Graham, supra.*

[10] Ersk. IV, 3, 29; *Lang* v. *Brown* (1855) 2 Macq. 93; *Graham, supra.*

[11] *Paterson* v. *Sanderson* (1829) 7 S. 616; *Hill, supra.*

[12] *Fleming* v. *Wilson & McLellan* (1827) 5 S. 906; *Paul* v. *Henderson* (1867) 5 M. 613.

[13] Ersk., *supra*; *Fleming* v. *Wilson & McLellan* (1827) 5 S. 906; *Hill* v. *Dundee & Perth Ry.* (1852) 14 D. 1034.

[14] *Hill, supra*; *Paul, supra.*

[15] *Glover* v. *G.* (1805) 4 Pat. 655.

An arbiter in *functus*, the submission discharged and his powers ended once a final award is issued and delivered.[1]

Procedure

The arbiter may fix his own procedure; in informal references no formal procedure is required;[2] he normally orders claims and answers, and hears parties,[3] or their counsel or agents, thereon. A proof,[4] inspection of the subjects in dispute, and the employment of technical assistance may be required. But if skilled assistance is invoked the judgment must be the arbiter's own, though formed after assistance.[5] He has no power to enforce the attendance of witnesses, or obtain production of documents, but the court may, on petition, empower parties to cite witnesses, or to take evidence on commission.[6]

Parties may be barred by failure to do so from objecting to the regularity of proceedings in a statutory arbitration,[7] and an award cannot be set aside for procedural informality if conform to the custom of the place and no substantial injustice has been done.[8]

Once an arbitration has begun the court will interfere with the arbiter proceeding only on strong grounds,[9] but will do so, if it will save parties expense and litigation, if it is plain that the arbiter is going to act *ultra vires*.[10]

The Oversman

Where the submission is to two arbiters, an oversman may be nominated or his nomination may be left to the arbiters. Arbiters

---

[1] Ersk. IV, 3, 32.

[2] *Nivison* v. *Howat* (1883) 11 R. 182; *Holmes Oil Co.* v. *Pumpherston Oil Co.* (1890) 17 R. 624, 656; *Hope* v. *Crookston Bros.* (1890) 17 R. 868; *Paterson* v. *Glasgow Corpn.* (1901) 3 F. (H.L.) 34; *Gibson* v. *Fotheringham*, 1914 S.C. 987.

[3] *Scorrier Steamship Coasters* v. *Milne*, 1928 S.N. 109; he is not always bound to hear parties; *Logan* v. *Leadbetter* (1887) 15 R. 115; *Paterson, supra*; *N.B. Ry.* v. *Wilson*, 1911 S.C. 730. See also *Black* v. *Williams*, 1924 S.C. (H.L.) 22.

[4] *Mackenzie* v. *Girvan* (1840) 3 D. 318; *Caledonian Ry.* v. *Lockhart* (1860) 22 D. (H.L.) 8.

[5] A proof is not essential in a practical matter, so long as the arbiter takes proper means to inform himself of the facts: *Paterson* v. *Glasgow Corpn.* (1901) 3 F. (H.L.) 34; *N.B. Ry.* v. *Wilson*, 1911 S.C. 730; *Henderson* v. *McGown*, 1915, 2 S.L.T. 316; *Cameron* v. *Nicol*, 1930 S.C. 1. In a reference for valuation to a man of skill a proof is unnecessary and incompetent: *Logan* v. *Leadbetter* (1888) 15 R. 115.

[6] *Galloway Water Power Co.* v. *Carmichael*, 1937 S.C. 135; As to witnesses in England, see *Nimmo & Son, Ltd.* (1905) 8 F. 173.

[7] *Cameron* v. *Nicol*, 1930 S.C. 1.

[8] *Hope* v. *Crookston Bros.* (1890) 17 R. 868.

[9] *Fraser* v. *Gordon* (1834) 12 S. 887; *Drew* v. *Leburn* (1853) 18 D. (H.L.) 4; *Farrell* v. *Arnott* (1857) 19 D. 1000; *Wilson* v. *Caledonian Ry.* (1860) 22 D. 697.

[10] *G.S.W. Ry.* v. *Caledonian Ry.* (1871) 44 Sc. Jur. 29; *Sinclair* v. *Clyne's Tr.* (1887) 15 R. 185; Contrast *Trowsdale* v. *Jopp and N.B. Ry.* (1865) 4 M. 31.

have implied power in common law submissions, unless excluded, to nominate an oversman.[1] If they cannot agree the court appoints. Appointment may be made before the submission begins.[2]

If the arbiters fail to agree[3] they should devolve the reference on the oversman, by signed minute,[4] or if the oversman has not yet been appointed, have him appointed.[5] It is sufficient to bring the oversman into active operation that there is a difference of opinion amounting to deadlock.[6] The oversman may hear the evidence led before the arbiters, but this does not invoke his jurisdiction.[7] Arbiters may devolve only part of the submission, issuing their award as to the rest, and may from time to time devolve on the oversman questions on which they disagree while keeping in their own hands the decision of questions not yet considered.[8]

Award

An arbiter is not bound to, but frequently issues notes of his proposed findings, and allows parties to make representations thereon and hears them on their representations.[9] It is questionable whether an arbiter, unless expressly authorized, can make an interim or part award.[10] The decision of the arbiters or oversman is final on both fact and law.[11] The final award or decree-arbitral may be formal or informal, as the submission was,[12] but normally and preferably is attested or holograph.[13] Informal submissions and awards, however, suffice in references *in re mercatoria*,[14] valuations[15] or references at the expiry of an agricultural lease.[16] It

[1] Arbitration (Sc.) Act, 1894, S. 4, overruling *Merry & Cunningham* v. *Brown* (1863) 1 M. (H.L.) 14. As to method of choice see *Smith* v. *Liverpool, London & Globe Ins. Co.* (1887) 14 R. 931.
[2] *Brysson* v. *Mitchell* (1823) 2 S. 382; *Glasgow P.C.* v. *United Collieries, Ltd.* (1907) 15 S.L.T. 232.
[3] e.g. *Sinclair* v. *Fraser* (1884) 11 R. 1139; *Gibson* v. *Fotheringham*, 1914 S.C. 987.
[4] *Kirkaldy* v. *Dalgairn's Trs.*, 16 June 1809, F.C. Nomination at the outset does not amount to devolution: *Brysson, supra*.
[5] *McNair's Trs.* v. *Roxburgh* (1855) 17 D. 445.   [6] *Gibson, supra*.
[7] *Crawford* v. *Paterson* (1858) 20 D. 488.
[8] *Gibson* v. *Fotheringham*, 1914 S.C. 987.
[9] *Baxter* v. *Macarthur* (1836) 14 S. 549; *Islay Estates* v. *McCormick*, 1937 S.N. 28. See also *Wemyss* v. *Ardrossan Harbour Co.* (1893) 20 R. 500.
[10] *Sanderson* v. *Armour*, 1922 S.C. (H.L.) 117.
[11] *Edinburgh & Glasgow Ry.* v. *Hill* (1840) 2 D. 486; *Lyle* v. *Falconer* (1842) 5 D. 236.
[12] *Lang* v. *Brown* (1852) 15 D. 38; *E. Hopetoun* v. *Scots Mines Co.* (1856) 18 D. 739; *Dykes* v. *Roy* (1869) 7 M. 357; *Hope* v. *Crookston Bros.* (1890) 17 R. 868.
[13] *Percy* v. *Meikle*, 25 Nov. 1808, F.C.; *Robertson* v. *Boyd & Winans* (1885) 12 R. 419; *McLaren* v. *Aikman*, 1939 S.C. 222.
[14] *Hope, supra*.   [15] *Robertson, supra*.
[16] *Nivison* v. *Howat* (1883) 11 R. 182; *Cameron* v. *Nicol*, 1930 S.C. 1; *McLaren, supra*.

must be delivered to the parties, or recorded, or delivered to a
third party for communication to the parties.[1] While still un-
delivered it may be altered by the arbiter.[2] It must be final and
exhaustive, deciding all matters submitted for decision, unless
there is express power to make interim or part awards.[3] Once
final award is issued the arbiter's functions are at an end and the
submission is closed. An error, other than a clerical error,[4] cannot
be corrected.

If two arbiters cannot agree they should by minute devolve the
reference on the oversman.[5] In the case of a formal submission the
award must indicate how far it represents agreement between the
arbiters, and how far it is a decision by the oversman of a matter
on which the arbiters could not agree.[6] In informal submissions
an award is not vitiated by failure to distinguish between agreed
elements of award and elements devolved on the oversman
following disagreement.[6]

Where an award is made in an arbitration between parties who
are members of an association, as such members, it ceases to be
binding on a party ceasing to be such a member.[7]

An award excludes subsequent consideration of the issues
between the parties in the same way as does a decree of court.[8]

Case stated on question of law

Subject to express provision to the contrary in an agreement
to refer to arbitration, the arbiter or oversman may, on the
application of a party to the arbitration, and shall, if the Court of
Session on such an application so directs, at any stage in the
arbitration state a case for the opinion of that court on any
question of law arising in the arbitration.[9] In certain cases of
statutory arbitration the arbiter may, or may be required by

[1] *Macrae* v. *Edinburgh Street Tramways Co.* (1885) 13 R. 265.

[2] *Macrae, supra*; *Scott* v. *S.* (1898) 5 S.L.T. 294.

[3] *Mackessock* v. *Drew* (1822) 2 S. 13; *Edinburgh, etc. Ry.* v. *Hill* (1840) 2 D. 486.

[4] *Kerr* v. *Bremner* (1835) 14 S. 180.

[5] *Kirkaldy* v. *Dalgairn's Trs.*, 16 June, 1809, F.C.; *Brysson* v. *Mitchell* (1823) 2 S.
382.

[6] *Cameron* v. *Nicol*, 1930 S.C. 1, 15.

[7] *Bellshill and Mossend Co-operative Socy. Ltd.* v. *Dalziel Co-operative Socy. Ltd.*, 1960
S.C. (H.L.) 64.

[8] *Fraser* v. *Lord Lovat* (1850) 7 Bell 171; *Orrell* v. *O.* (1859) 21 D. 554.

[9] Administration of Justice (Sc.) Act, 1972, S. 3. This does not apply to arbitrations
under statutes conferring power to appeal or to state a case for a court or tribunal, nor to
arbitrations relating to trade disputes within the Industrial Courts Act, 1919, to industrial
disputes within the Industrial Relations Act, 1971, to arbitrations arising from a collective
agreement within the last Act, nor to proceedings before the Industrial Arbitration
Board within S. 124 of the last Act.

either party to, state a case for the opinion of the court on a question of law arising in the course of the arbitration.[1] In such a case the arbiter is bound to apply the law laid down by the court.[2]

If arbitration abortive or not exhaustive

A contractual reference to arbitration does not wholly oust the jurisdiction of the courts; if the arbitration from any cause proves abortive, the court's jurisdiction revives to the effect of enabling it to hear and determine the action on its merits.[3] Similarly if the arbitration cannot exhaust all the matters in issue between the parties, the others must be determined by the court.[4]

Enforcement of decree-arbitral

An arbiter has no power to enforce his award, but a submission may contain a clause consenting to registration of the submission and award for preservation and execution, in which case summary diligence may proceed on an extract from the register. Failing this the award may be enforced by action in court for decree conform.[5] Foreign arbitral awards are, subject to statutory conditions[6] enforceable by action, or, if the agreement for arbitration contains consent to the registration of the award in the Books of Council and Session and the award is so registered, by summary diligence.[7] An award may be unenforceable if it is in unreasonable restraint of trade.[8]

Challenging award

It is not open to appeal to the courts against an arbiter's decision on fact or law, or against his award on the merits, as this would defeat the object of arbitration.[9] A decision on relevancy

---

[1] *Euman* v. *Dalziel*, 1912 S.C. 966; *L.M.S. Ry.* v. *Glasgow Corpn.*, 1940 S.C. 363. It is incompetent by action to have the arbiter ordained to state a case in particular terms: *Forsyth-Grant* v. *Salmon and Gordon*, 1961 S.C. 54.

[2] *Johnston's Trs.* v. *Glasgow Corpn.*, 1912 S.C. 300; *Mitchell-Gill* v. *Buchan*, 1921 S.C. 390.

[3] *Hamlyn* v. *Talisker Distillery* (1894) 21 R. (H.L.) 21, 25; *Mauritzen* v. *Baltic Shipping Co.*, 1948 S.C. 646, 651.

[4] *N.B. Ry.* v. *Newburgh and North Fife Ry.*, 1911 S.C. 710, 721.

[5] *McCosh* v. *Moore* (1905) 8 F. 31. On defences see *Whitehead* v. *Finlay* (1833) 11 S. 170.

[6] Arbitration Act, 1950, Part II, especially S. 37.

[7] Ibid., S. 41.

[8] *Bellshill and Mossend Co-operative Socy. Ltd.* v. *Dalziel Co-op. Socy. Ltd.*, 1958 S.C. 400.

[9] *Mackenzie* v. *Girvan* (1840) 2 Bell 43; *Brakinrig* v. *Menzies* (1841) 4 D. 274 (judicial referee); *Mitchell* v. *Cable* (1848) 10 D. 1297; *Holmes Oil Co.* v. *Pumpherston Oil Co.* (1891) 18 R. (H.L.) 52.

cannot be challenged.[1] The Articles of Regulation, 1695,[2] provided that no award of arbiters pronounced on a subscribed submission might be reduced save on the ground of corruption,[3] bribery, or falsehood. Corruption must be actual. An error in law is not challengeable as 'constructive corruption'.[4]

Apart therefrom, at common law reduction of an award may be sought on the ground that the award is improbative,[5] or *ultra vires*, or the arbiter acted *ultra fines compromissi*,[6] or that the award does not exhaust the submission,[7] or that the arbiter refused proof,[8] or refused to hear parties,[9] or heard only one party,[10] or refused to receive a claim tendered by one party,[11] or that the award is uncertain or ambiguous, or has not been delivered, or has been impetrated by fraud or improper influence,[12] or the arbiter has been misled by the improper and unfair conduct of one party.[13] In mercantile arbitrations the court is slow to reduce an award if substantially just, even though the procedure may not have been wholly regular.[14] In a statutory arbitration it is misconduct on the arbiter's party to have taken the court's opinion on a question of law and not to apply it.[15] An award may be reduced in part, if valid and invalid parts can be severed.[16]

An award must stand on its own and speak for itself. It is not competent in a reduction to examine the arbiter, save to explain an ambiguity in his award or to state whether, in making a valua-

---

[1] *Brown* v. *Associated Fireclay Companies*, 1937 S.C. (H.L.) 42.

[2] A.S. 2 Nov. 1695, S. 25 (issued by Commissioners under Act, 1693, c. 34); see *Adams* v. *G.N.S. Ry.* (1890) 18 R. (H.L.) at 7–8.

[3] *Fraser* v. *Wright* (1838) 16 S. 1055; *Mitchell* v. *Cable* (1848) 10 D 1297; *Miller* v. *Miller* (1855) 17 D. 689; *Ledingham* v. *Elphinstone* (1859) 22 D. 245; *Alexander* v. *Bridge of Allan Water Co.* (1869) 7 M. 492; *Morisons* v. *Thomson's Trs.* (1880) 8 R. 147; *Adams* v. *G.N.S. Ry.* (1890) 18 R. (H.L.) 1.

[4] *Adams, supra*; *Robson* v. *Menzies*, 1913 S.C. (J.) 90, 94.

[5] *McLaren* v. *Aikman*, 1939 S.C. 222. cf. *Dykes* v. *Roy* (1869) 7 M. 357.

[6] *Traill* v. *Coghill* (1885) 22 S.L.R. 616; *Adams, supra*; *Miller* v. *Oliver & Boyd* (1903) 6 F. 77; *McIntyre* v. *Forbes*, 1939 S.L.T. 62.

[7] *Pollich* v. *Heatley*, 1910 S.C. 469; *Donald* v. *Shiell's Exrx.*, 1937 S.C. 52; *Dunlop* v. *Mundell*, 1943 S.L.T. 286.

[8] *Mitchell, supra*; *Brown* v. *Assoc. Fireclay Companies*, 1937 S.C. (H.L.) 42.

[9] *Sharp* v. *Bickerdike* (1815) 3 Dow 102; *Holmes Oil Co.* v. *Pumpherston Oil Co.* (1891) 18 R. (H.L.) 52; *Black* v. *Williams*, 1923 S.C. 510; *Islay Estates Co.* v. *McCormick*, 1937 S.N. 28.

[10] *Sharp, supra*; but see *Black* v. *Williams*, 1924 S.C. (H.L.) 22.

[11] *Drummond* v. *Martin* (1906) 14 S.L.T. 365.

[12] *Logan* v. *Lang*, 15 Nov. 1798, F.C.

[13] *Calder* v. *Gordon* (1837) 15 S. 463.

[14] *Hope* v. *Crookston Bros.* (1890) 17 R. 868.

[15] *Mitchell-Gill* v. *Buchan*, 1921 S.C. 390.

[16] *Cox* v. *Binning* (1867) 6 M. 161; *Adams, supra*; *Islay Estates Co., supra*.

tion, he considered matters not included in the submission to him and accordingly outwith his jurisdiction,[1] but it is competent to take the arbiter's note into consideration.[2]

[1] *Glasgow City Ry.* v. *Macgeorge, Cowan & Galloway* (1886) 13 R. 609; *Clippens Oil Co.* v. *Edinburgh Water Trs.* (1901) 3 F. 1113, 1128; *Donald* v. *Shiell's Exrx.*, 1937 S.C. 52; *Dunlop* v. *Mundell*, 1943 S.L.T. 286.
[2] *Holmes Oil Co.*, *supra*; *Farrans* v. *Roxburgh C.C.*, 1970 S.L.T. 334.

CHAPTER 4

FUNDAMENTAL LEGAL CONCEPTS

T H E principles and rules of Scottish private law are formulated verbally in terms of legal concepts, that is, of general and frequently abstract terms having more or less defined legal connotations, which may and frequently do differ substantially from the connotations of the same words used in non-legal contexts. Some of these concepts require consideration.[1]

The principles and rules of law take the form of statements ascribing to legal persons specified legal rights and legal duties in respect of other persons, conduct or things. Thus the principle: a person must take reasonable care not to harm another person who might foreseeably be injured by his conduct;[2] connotes a legal duty incumbent on the first person, owed to the second person, with regard to certain conduct, vesting the second person with a right not to be harmed by lack of reasonable care in conduct by the first party, and, by implication, with a right to compensation from the first party if he is in fact harmed by the consequences of that party's lack of reasonable care.

Legal persons

The nature, attributes and characteristics of legal persons are discussed subsequently.[3]

Legal rights

'The proper object [of law] is the right itself, whether it concerns persons, things or actions, and according to the several rights and their natural order, ought to be the order of jurisprudence, which may be taken up in a threefold consideration; first, in the constitution and nature of rights; secondly, in their conveyance or translation from one to another, whether it be among the living, or from the dead; thirdly, in their cognition, which comprehends the trial, decision and execution of every right by the legal remedies.'[4] Not every alleged social, moral, political or economic right is recognized as a legal right, and it is

[1] See further Salmond, *Jurisprudence*; Paton, *Jurisprudence*.
[2] cf. *Donoghue* v. *Stevenson*, 1932 S.C. (H.L.) 31.
[3] Ch. 14, *infra*.
[4] Stair I, 1, 23.

only with legal rights that the legal system is concerned. A legal right is a claim vested in a legal person by virtue of some legal title, availing against another legal person (right *in personam*) or other legal persons generally (right *in rem*), giving a claim to performance of some act or to abstention from some kinds of conduct, in relation to some thing, corporeal or incorporeal, and recognized by the courts by virtue of rules of civil law and normally enforceable by them, if need be, by civil procedure and diligence. Some legal rights are imperfect in that they are not directly enforceable, though they may be recognized for certain purposes, such as in defence to a claim.

The legal title which vests a person with a right may be original, such as birth or the attainment of majority, the catching of a fish or the painting of a picture, or the grant of a decree of court in his favour, or the operation of some rule of law; or derivative, such as purchase, or inheritance, or the operation of some rule of law transferring the right to him from another.

A person may be divested of title to a right by alienative or divestitive facts, such as sale, gift, or bequest on death, or the operation of certain rules of law; or by extinctive facts such as consumption, or destruction, or the satisfaction of a decree, or performance of an obligation or the operation of other rules of law. These classes of facts deal respectively with the creation, transfer to or from a person, and extinction of particular rights.

Titles again may be distinguished into acts of the law, operating by force of rules of law themselves, or juristic acts (acts in the law, acts of the party) operating by force of the expressed will of the party, such as agreements or gifts, to which the law normally attributes force.

Rules of law prescribe what rights do come into existence, are transferred, or disappear, on the occurrence of particular investitive or divestitive facts, and what procedures are necessary in various cases validly to invest or divest a person of particular rights.

The thing in relation to which a right exists, or the subject of the right, may be of very many kinds, and the rules of law have to define to what kinds of objects, tangible and intangible, particular rights relate.

Legal duties

A legal duty is a legally required kind and standard of conduct in particular circumstances, incumbent on a legal person, owed to another legal person or persons, requiring particular acts or abstentions, compliance with which is legally obligatory and enforceable, or importing further legal liability, failing compliance. Thus there are legal duties to adhere to one's spouse, to perform one's undertakings, not to harm others unjustifiably, and so on.

A duty may become incumbent by voluntarily undertaking it, or by virtue of a rule of law, but in the latter case persons may sometimes voluntarily, as by entering into a marriage or an employment, put themselves in a position where certain duties are legally incumbent on them, which they could otherwise have avoided.

Rights and duties correlative

The concepts of rights and duties are correlative to each other in that the existence of a right in one person implies a duty on another person or persons with regard to the same subject. Conversely the fact that a duty is incumbent on one person implies that some other person or persons have right to its being implemented. To speak of right or duty is in fact, normally at least, to speak of a right-duty relationship.

Further analysis of rights and duties

The correlative terms 'right' and 'duty' may each be further analysed:[1] rights may be distinguished into (a) claims, or what one may demand or exact from another, such as payment of a debt; (b) liberties or privileges, or what one may do free from legal restraint, such as to criticize a book; (c) powers, what one may do in relation to another, such as to make a will, or raise an action; and (d) immunities, what one may do with legal impunity or freedom from legal retribution, such as to speak what might be slander in the exercise of the judicial office.

Duties may be distinguished into (a) burdens, what one must do to or for another, such as to pay him a debt, or to refrain from injuring him; (b) inabilities,[2] what one is legally unable to do or to prevent, such as to make a man stop smoking; (c) liabilities, what one is legally subjected to perform, such as to pay damages for wrong; and (d) disabilities, what one cannot legally do, such as to sue a foreign diplomat, or prevent, such as the use of legal diligence.

---

[1] See further Hohfeld, *Fundamental Legal Conceptions*, Ch. 1; Kocourek, *Jural Relations*, Chs. 1–3; Salmond, *Jurisprudence*, Ch. 10; Stone, *Legal System and Lawyer's Reasonings*, Ch. 4.

[2] Hohfeld's 'no-right'.

Each of the four kinds of rights is correlative to each of the four kinds of duties, and further logical relationships between the eight terms have been worked out. But in many cases the terms rights and duties are used loosely where one or other of the variants would be more accurate, and the variants are sometimes misused.

Real and personal rights

Rights, including claims, liberties, powers and immunities are distinguishable into real rights or rights *in rem*, available against persons generally, often for the protection or vindication of corporeal things or property, arising by virtue of legal dominion, and personal rights or rights *in personam*, available only against particular persons for the performance of some duty which the latter is bound to implement, arising by virtue of legal obligation.[1] Rights *in rem* are generally negative, being commonly a right not to be interfered with, whereas rights *in personam* are commonly positive.[2]

Rights are also distinguished as proprietary and personal, according as they are part of the person's assets, estate or property, or attach to him as an individual. Hence a right of ownership of land is proprietary, but a right to his reputation, or to custody of his children, is personal.

General and specific duties

Duties similarly may be owed to persons generally, and these are usually negative, such as not to harm anyone else, or to a determinate person only, which are normally positive, such as to perform what one has contractually undertaken to do for that person.

Things

The thing in relation to which a right or duty exists, or the subject-matter of the right, may be of very many kinds and the rules of law have to define to what kinds of things particular rights relate. These things comprise, firstly, relationships of obligation giving rise to mutual rights and duties between

---

[1] See further Stair I, 1, 22; Ersk. III, 1, 2. On the concept of property see Ch. 71, *infra*, and on obligation, see Ch. 29. On the terms right *in rem* and *in personam* see Salmond, *Jurisprudence*, 84.

[2] Rights *in rem* and *in personam*, if violated, do not necessarily give rise to actions *in rem* or *in personam* respectively, that is, to actions for recovery of property or against a determinate person respectively.

persons, including both relationships created voluntarily, such as that of buyer and seller, and relationships occurring by chance, such as that of careless driver and pedestrian, and, secondly, relationships of rights in and to property, comprising objects owned or possessed. Objects of property take many forms and includes both material things, such as buildings and vehicles, and immaterial things having no physical existence, such as copyrights and shares in companies.

Conduct

Conduct includes all human behaviour relevant to the legal issue in question. Conduct may consist of acts, of inactivity or neglect or not-acting, or of omissions or not acting when the person should have acted. In relation to each of these aspects of conduct the person's state of mind is frequently relevant, and the legal results may depend on whether a person's conduct was voluntary or involuntary, and in the former case whether intentional or deliberate, reckless, or merely careless.[1]

Events

Events are happenings not attributable to nor controlled by human powers or conduct, yet having legal significance. They include such happenings as the lapse of time, birth and death, a person's attaining an age, the occurrence of a storm, and the like. Some happenings, however, are attributable at least indirectly to the prior conduct of some person, and must be treated as the consequences of conduct rather than as pure events.

Other concepts

The examination of other concepts will be made in relation to the branches of the law in which those concepts are important; they include legal personality and persons, obligation, contract, delict, negligence, malice, ownership and possession, and so on.

---

[1] These distinctions are analysed in many books on Jurisprudence.

CHAPTER 5

DOCTRINES, PRINCIPLES, AND RULES

THE whole body of the private law consists of verbal statements of what one may or may not, should or should not, do, in various circumstances and of what consequences follow if conduct does not conform to the required standard. It comprises a number of general doctrines and a much large number of principles and rules, which are capable of being classified and arranged in a coherent logical statement and of being stated, exemplified and discussed, and applied to the solution of actual difficulties and controversies.

Doctrines, principles and rules

While there are no fixed meanings for these terms, the word 'doctrine' is usually used of a very general notion which can comprehend many more specific principles and rules, such as the doctrine of personal bar, to the general effect that no person can be allowed to speak or act in contradiction of an attitude he has already asserted by words or actings. A 'principle' of law is a statement in general terms applicable to a large, and frequently uncertain, range of circumstances, such as: an employer must take reasonable care and precautions for the safety of his employees; while a 'rule' is a statement in narrower and more rigid terms applicable to a limited, and possibly very confined, set of circumstances, such as: an employer must take care that dangerous machinery is adequately fenced; To instances of all three kinds of formulations there are frequently exceptions and qualifications, and there are often difficult questions of precisely how a doctrine, principle or rule should be formulated verbally and of whether the circumstances of a particular case fall within or outwith a particular principle or rule. In general doctrines and principles have been formulated inductively by judges and textwriters as generalisations on the basis of prior particular instances; in general rules have been formulated by judges in particular cases and by Parliament in statutes.

Certain doctrines and principles of law are of wide and general application and common to several branches of the law, and underlie numerous specific rules. Their very generality renders them difficult or even incapable of definition and makes it difficult to state categorically in what cases such a principle will apply.

The doctrine of natural justice

The doctrine of natural justice is more commonly invoked in public than in private law, but has important applications in the latter field also. It subsumes three main principles, that a person judging must hear both sides of the case, or at least give both sides equal opportunities of presenting their arguments,[1] that a person should not be, nor even appear to be, judge in a matter where his own interest is, or may be thought to be, involved,[2] and that justice must not only be done, but be seen to be done.[3]

So too a foreign judgment contravening a principle of natural justice cannot be enforced in Scotland. The cases turn on failure to give the litigant notice of the proceedings,[4] or failure to give him an opportunity of presenting his case to the foreign court.[5]

The doctrine of public policy

The doctrine of public policy[6] or public interest or the accepted morality of the community at the time is a limitation which in many contexts is held to justify treating certain conduct as reprehensible and legally unenforceable, though it may not be positively prohibited or otherwise illegal. 'Public policy is that principle of law which holds that no subject can lawfully do that which has a tendency to be injurious to the public or against the public good in which may be termed the policy of the law, or public policy in relation to the law.'[7] The doctrine is necessarily vague and an unsafe basis for decision save where there is precedent,[8] and there is warrant for the view that the courts can no

---

[1] i.e. the principle *audiatur et altera pars*: *Mitchell* v. *Cable* (1848) 10 D. 1297; *Black* v. *Williams*, 1924 S.C. (H.L.) 22; *Barrs* v. *British Wool Marketing Board*, 1957 S.C. 72; *McDonald* v. *Lanarkshire Fire Brigade Joint Cttee.*, 1959 S.C. 141; *St. Johnstone F.C.* v. *S.F.A.*, 1965 S.L.T. 171.

[2] i.e. the principle *nemo judex in causa sua*: *Caledonian Ry.* v. *Ramsay* (1897) 24 R. (J.) 48; *Wildridge* v. *Anderson* (1897) 25 R. (J.) 27; cf. *Palmer* v. *Inverness Hospitals Board*, 1963 S.C. 311.

[3] *Barrs, supra*; cf. *Laughland* v. *Galloway*, 1968 S.L.T. 272.

[4] *Rudd* v. *R.* [1924] P. 72.

[5] *Jacobson* v. *Frachon* (1928) 44 T.L.R. 103.

[6] Generally Lloyd, *Public Policy*; Winfield, 42 H.L.R. 76.

[7] *Egerton* v. *Earl Brownlow* (1853) 4 H.L.C. 1, 196; *E. Caithness* v. *Sinclair*, 1912 S.C. 79.

[8] *Richardson* v. *Mellish* (1824) 2 Bing. 229, 252 ('a very unruly horse'); *Re Mirams* [1891] 1 Q.B. 594, 595; *Janson* v. *Driefontein Consolidated Mines, Ltd.* [1902] A.C. 484, 507.

longer invent new heads of public policy, though they may interpret existing heads in new circumstances.[1]

The doctrine justifies the refusal to enforce agreements to divorce,[2] or collusive agreements,[3] or to recognize promises made *stante matrimonio* to marry another,[4] and the refusal to enforce a will the bequests of which are extravagant or wasteful.[5]

The main applications of the doctrine arise in the field of contract where it is held to justify the judicial refusal to enforce certain kinds of contract,[6] such as one with an alien enemy,[7] one for the obtaining of an honour,[8] or benefit from the government,[9] or for promoting a marriage,[10] contracts unreasonably restricting the party's freedom of action[11] or of marriage,[12] contracts in restraint of trade generally,[13] and a rule wholly excluding the jurisdiction of the courts in case of dispute.[14]

Similarly there is the rule that a person may not benefit from his own crime.[15]

In international private law British courts have sometimes declined to give effect to rights acquired under a foreign system if the rights or the method of obtaining them was deemed contrary to the British concept of public policy.[16] Thus a contract obtained by coercion or objectionable under a British rule of law cannot be enforced though entered into abroad.[17] An action cannot be founded on a foreign judgment deemed contrary to British public policy.[18] But it is difficult to determine what heads of the British concept of public policy are so material as to justify the rejection of rights otherwise validly acquired.

[1] *Janson, supra,* 491; *Fender* v. *Mildmay* [1938] A.C. 1, 23.
[2] *Royle* v. *R.* [1909] P. 24; contrast *Aldridge* v. *A.* (1888) 13 P.D. 210; *L.* v. *L.* [1931] P. 63.
[3] *Lowndes* v. *L.* [1950] P. 223.
[4] *Wilson* v. *Carnley* [1908] 1 K.B. 729; contrast *Fender* v. *Mildmay* [1938] A.C. 1.
[5] *Sutherland's Tr.* v. *Verschoyle,* 1968 S.L.T. 43.
[6] Ch. 33, *infra;* cf. Bell, *Comm.* I, 320.
[7] *Porter* v. *Freudenberg* [1915] 1 K.B. 857; *Rodriguez* v. *Speyer* [1919] A.C. 116.
[8] *Parkinson* v. *College of Ambulance* [1925] 2 K.B. 1.
[9] *Montefiore* v. *Menday Motor Co.* [1918] 2 K.B. 241.
[10] *Hermann* v. *Charlesworth* [1905] 2 K.B. 123.
[11] Ch. 31, *infra.*
[12] *Perris* v. *Lyon* (1807) 9 East 170; cf. *Clayton* v. *Ramsden* [1943] A.C. 320.
[13] Ch. 31, *infra.*
[14] *St. Johnstone F.C.* v. *S.F.A.,* 1965 S.L.T. 171.
[15] *Cleaver* v. *Mutual Life Assocn.* [1892] 1 Q.B. 147; *In re Crippen* [1911] P. 108; *Beresford* v. *Royal Insce. Assocn.* [1938] A.C. 586; contrast *re Houghton* [1915] 2 Ch. 173; *Tinline* v. *White Cross Insce. Assocn.* [1921] 3 K.B. 327.
[16] *Dynamit A/G* v. *Rio Tinto Co. Ltd.* [1918] A.C. 292, 302.
[17] *Hope* v. *H.* (1857) 8 De G. M. & G. 731; *Roussillon* v. *R.* (1880) 14 Ch. D. 351; *Kaufmann* v. *Gerson* [1904] 1 K.B. 591.
[18] *Macartney* v. *M.* [1921] 1 Ch. 522, 527.

The doctrine of good faith

A person acts in good faith when he acts honestly, or does not know, and has no grounds for suspecting, the invalidity or illegality of his conduct or of the rights he claims. The doctrine arises in very many contexts.

Thus in the law of persons, where at least one party to a marriage legally void honestly and *bona fide* believed that it was valid, the marriage is designated 'putative' and the children are deemed legitimate.

In the law of obligations, there is a special requirement of good faith in the case of certain contracts, commonly referred to as contracts *uberrimae fidei*, in which each contracting party must make full disclosure of possibly relevant facts to the other. Such are the contracts of partnership, cautionry, insurance, and contracts between persons in fiduciary relationships.[1]

In the law of property, one who honestly and on reasonable grounds believes himself proprietor of subjects which he possesses is deemed a *bona fide* possessor and, though ejected, has some rights with regard to the gathering and consumption of the fruits of his possession, greater than enjoyed by the squatter or *mala fide* possessor.[2] He has a claim for recompense for improvements executed during his possession.

In negotiable instruments the privileges of being a holder in due course attach only to the person who takes in good faith, for value and without notice of any imperfection in the title of the previous holder. Such a holder acquires a good title even though the instrument was acquired from one who had stolen it.[3]

The doctrine of personal bar

In many circumstances a person may be prevented from exercising what is *prima facie* his legal right by reason of some principle within the general doctrine of personal bar.[4] Stated most generally this doctrine is to the effect that a person cannot be allowed to enforce claims which he has already, expressly or impliedly, repudiated or departed from, or to adopt an attitude inconsistent with his own earlier words or conduct;[5] 'where A has by his words or conduct justified B in believing that a certain state of facts exists, and B has acted upon such belief to his

---

[1] Chs. 38, 45, 46, *infra*.
[2] Ch. 76, *infra*.
[3] cf. *Walker & Watson* v. *Sturrock* (1897) 35 S.L..R. 26.
[4] Generally Rankine on *Personal Bar and Estoppel*.
[5] cf. *Graham* v. *G.* (1881) 9 R. 327; *Baird's Tr.* v. *Murray* (1883) 11 R. 153.

prejudice, A is not permitted to affirm against B that a different state of facts existed at the same time.'[1] Where one or other of the principles which exemplify the doctrine of personal bar applies its effect is conclusively to shut out all pleas and proof contradicting the inference from the earlier conduct.

The general doctrine embraces the principles of *rei interventus*, homologation, ratification, adoption, acquiescence, taciturnity, mora, delay, waiver, standing by, holding out, and similar inference from conduct.

Rei interventus and homologation are normally invoked to prevent a party resiling from a contract which requires to be, but has not been, constituted by probative writings. He may not, however, resile if he has by earlier words or conduct permitted the other party to act on the faith of the contract as if it were perfectly constituted (*rei interventus*[2]), or has himself acted in a manner clearly approbatory of the informal agreement (homologation).[3] Homologation applies also to many circumstances where a party seeks to avoid an obligation which he is held to have approbated.[4]

Ratification of the conduct of an agent, servant or partner by another in the full knowledge that what had been done on his behalf was challengeable is a clear ground for holding him barred from subsequent objection.

Adoption is the acceptance as valid and binding of an obligation which is fundamentally null, such as one constituted by a forged signature.[5] It can be inferred only if the person actually had the knowledge to enable him to repudiate liability, and this knowledge must be actual, and not merely constructive, i.e. attributed to him by law, such as the knowledge of an agent.[6]

Acquiescence consists in intimating, by words or conduct, consent or absence of opposition to what might have been objected to, thereby inducing a person or others to believe that their conduct is being and will be tolerated.[7] It requires knowledge of the contravention.[8] This plea is commonly advanced as a de-

---

[1] *Gatty* v. *Maclaine*, 1921 S.C. (H.L.) 1, 7, per Lord Birkenhead.

[2] Ch. 32, *infra.*   [3] Ch. 32, *infra.*

[4] *Roberts* v. *City of Glasgow Bank* (1879) 6 R. 805; *Westville Shipping Co.* v. *Abram S.S. Co.*, 1923 S.C. (H.L.) 68.

[5] *Urquhart* v. *Bank of Scotland* (1872) 9 S.L.R. 508; cf. *Powrie* v. *Louis* (1881) 18 S.L.R. 533; see also *McKenzie* v. *B.L. Co.* (1881) 8 R. (H.L.) 8; *B.L. Co.* v. *Cowan* (1906) 8 F. 704.

[6] *Muir's Exors.* v. *Craig's Trs.*, 1913 S.C. 349.

[7] *Cairncross* v. *Lorimer* (1860) 3 Macq. 827; *D. Buccleuch* v. *Edinburgh Mags.* (1865) 3 M. 528; *Wylie & Lochhead* v. *McElroy* (1873) 1 R. 41; cf. *Gatty* v. *Maclaine*, 1921 S.C. (H.L.) 1, 7.

[8] *Ben Challum, Ltd.* v. *Buchanan*, 1955 S.C. 348.

fence to an action for nuisance[1] or interference with a servitude right, or for failure to fulfil contractual obligations,[2] but has been pleaded in defence to actions for matrimonial wrong,[3] and in contract where a member might have challenged a building society's rule,[4] where a party continued to accept services under contract after intimation of increased charges therefor,[5] where clauses were added to draft contracts,[6] where a contract was performed after discovery of grounds for rescission,[7] and in many cases of contravention of rights relative to heritage.[8] Save in special circumstances a singular successor is not barred by acquiescence of his predecessor in title from complaining of encroachment.[9]

Taciturnity is mere silence and failure to object. By itself this does not bar any legal claim, as no man is bound at once to voice his objections on pain of otherwise being held barred for the future. But silence may bar a claim if continued and if the other party is thereby induced to act in reliance on non-objection.

Mora, taciturnity and acquiescence are normally linked,[10] in that mere delay to enforce a claim or make objection to an infringement of right short of the period fixed by a prescription statute does not by itself bar a claim unless it is such as to give rise to an inference of non-objection and acquiescence in the *status quo*, or other parties have been prejudiced by the delay and silence.[11]

Waiver consists in conduct which implies acceptance of the other party's conduct and the giving up of any claim to which it might normally have given rise.[12] Thus where A, in breach of contract with B, bought from C who obtained his material from B, and B claimed damages from A, B was held to have waived his rights under the contract to the extent that he had supplied

[1] *Rigby & Beardmore* v. *Downie* (1872) 10 M. 568; *Houldsworth* v. *Wishaw Mags.* (1887) 14 R. 920.

[2] *Johnstone* v. *Hughan* (1894) 21 R. 777; *Eliott's Trs.* v. *E.* (1894) 21 R. 858; *Hamilton* v. *D. Montrose* (1906) 8 F. 1026; *Ben Challum, Ltd., supra*.

[3] *Colvin* v. *Johnstone* (1890) 18 R. 115.

[4] *Sinclair* v. *Mercantile Building Investment Socy.* (1885) 12 R. 1243.

[5] *Caledonian Ry.* v. *Stein & Co.*, 1919 S.C. 324.

[6] *Charles* v. *Shearer* (1900) 8 S.L.T. 273; *Roberts & Cooper* v. *Salvesen*, 1918 S.C. 794.

[7] *Boyd & Forrest* v. *G.S.W. Ry.*, 1915 S.C. (H.L.) 20.

[8] e.g. *Davidson* v. *Thomson* (1890) 17 R. 287; *Fraser* v. *Campbell* (1895) 22 R. 558; *Rankine* v. *Logie Den Land Co.* (1902) 4 F. 1074.

[9] *Brown* v. *Baty*, 1957 S.C. 351.

[10] *Mackenzie* v. *Catton's Trs.* (1877) 5 R. 313. See also *Lees' Trs.* v. *Dun*, 1912 S.C. 50.

[11] *McKenzie* v. *B.L. Co.* (1881) 8 R. (H.L.) 8; see also *Bain* v. *Assets Co.* (1905) 7 F. (H.L.) 104; *B.L. Co.* v. *Cowan* (1906) 8 F. 704; and as to onus of proof *C.B.* v. *A.B.* (1885) 12 R. (H.L.) 36; *Bosville* v. *Macdonald*, 1910 S.C. 597. But see *Cook* v. *N.B. Ry.* (1872) 10 M. 513.

[12] *Shepherd* v. *Reddie* (1870) 8 M. 619; *Callander* v. *Smith* (1900) 8 S.L.T. 109.

materials to C.[1] The inference of waiver is not always to be drawn from failure to reserve a claim of damages for breach of contract on settlement of the contract.[2]

Holding out is the principle which prevents a party from denying that one whom he had allowed to appear to be his agent or partner was in fact such agent or partner.[3]

As a general rule a party pleading that the other is personally barred must have been one with whom the other had a legal relationship, so that the other owed him a duty not to mislead him by his express or implied representation. Thus a customer owes a duty to his bank and is barred from pleading his own carelessness in drawing a cheque so that it could be, and was, fraudulently altered[4] but an acceptor of a bill of exchange does not owe a duty to be careful to a member of the public who may subsequently become an indorsee of the bill.[5] Also, the party pleading personal bar must show that in reliance on the other's words or conduct he has changed his position to his detriment.[6]

The doctrine of res judicata

The doctrine of *res judicata* is recognized to limit vexatious litigation and *ut esset finis litium*.[7] A ground of action heard and determined by a competent court, if rejected, cannot be founded on again. Nor can a second action be brought because the damages in the first one are inadequate.[8] To support a plea of *res judicata* the parties and the subject-matter in the present and the previous decided proceedings must be the same, and the suits must be founded on the same ground of claim, so that the specific point raised in the second has been directly raised and concluded by the judgment in the first suit.[9]

There is no scope for the plea if one of the parties is different,[10]

---

[1] *Steel Co. of Scotland* v. *Tancred Arrol & Co.* (1892) 19 R. 1062. See also *Shepherd* v. *Reddie* (1870) 8 M. 619; *Shiells* v. *Scottish Assce. Corpn.* (1889) 16 R. 1014.

[2] *Clydebank Engineering Co.* v. *Castaneda* (1904) 7 F. (H.L.) 77.

[3] cf. Partnership Act, 1890, S. 14.

[4] *London Joint Stock Bank* v. *Macmillan* [1918] A.C. 777.

[5] *Schofield* v. *L. Londesborough* [1896] A.C. 514.

[6] *Stuart* v. *Potter, Choate & Prentice*, 1911, 1 S.L.T. 377; *Alloa Mags.* v. *Wilson*, 1913 S.C. 6; *Bruce* v. *British Motor Trading Corpn.*, 1924 S.C. 908.

[7] cf. Stair IV, 40, 16–17; Ersk. IV, 3, 1–4; *Macdonald* v. *M.* (1842) 1 Bell 819; *Phosphate Sewage Co.* v. *Molleson* (1879) 6 R. (H.L.) 113; *Edinburgh Water Trs.* v. *Clippens Oil Co.* (1899) 1 F. 899; *G.S.W. Ry.* v. *Boyd and Forrest*, 1918 S.C. (H.L.) 14.

[8] cf. *Balfour* v. *Baird*, 1959 S.C. 64.

[9] *N.B. Ry.* v. *Lanarkshire Ry.* (1897) 24 R. 564; *Glen* v. *Dunlop* (1906) 13 S.L.T. 898.

[10] *Harvie* v. *Stewart* (1870) 9 M. 129; *Scott* v. *Macdonald* (1885) 12 R. 1123; *D. Atholl* v. *Glover Incorporation of Perth* (1899) 1 F. 658; 2 F. (H.L.) 57.

unless the interest of that party were identical with the corresponding party in the earlier action.[1] Nor can the plea be taken if the subject matter of the action is not the same as in the previous action.[2] Nor is the plea open if the later action is based on a different *medium concludendi* or ground of or substantial basis in law,[3] unless the later action is simply raising again in another guise the question decided in the former action.[4] Hence the dismissal of an action on a point of relevancy can never be *res judicata*,[5] nor is a criminal conviction *res judicata* in a subsequent civil action.[6] An action based on statute may or may not be in substance the same claim as a common law action.[7] Nor does the plea prevent a fresh action if new facts have come to light.[8]

A decree in absence can never found a plea of *res judicata* so as to preclude a subsequent action,[9] but a decree based on a compromise between parties may found such a plea,[9] as may a decree by default.[11] A decision in the Sheriff Court may be *res judicata* as regards a later action in the Court of Session,[12] and the decision is an action as regards a later arbitration.[13]

---

[1] *McCaig* v. *Maitland* (1887) 14 R. 295; *Allen* v. *McCombie's Trs.*, 1909 S.C. 710.

[2] *Ryan* v. *McBurnie*, 1940 S.C. 173; *Muir* v. *Jamieson*, 1947 S.C. 314.

[3] *N.B. Ry.* v. *Lanarkshire and Dumbartonshire Ry.* (1897) 24 R. 564; cf. *Grahame* v. *Secretary of State for Scotland*, 1951 S.C. 368.

[4] *Mackintosh* v. *Weir* (1875) 2 R. 877.

[5] *Russel* v. *Gillespie* (1859) 3 Macq. 757; *Menzies* v. *M.* (1893) 20 R. (H.L.) 108; *Cunningham* v. *Skinner* (1902) 4 F. 1124; *Govan Old Victualling Socy.* v. *Wagstaff* (1907) 14 S.L.T. 716.

[6] *Wood* v. *N.B. Ry.* (1899) 1 F. 562; *Faculty of Procurators* v. *Colquhoun* (1900) 2 F. 1192; *Wilson* v. *Bennett* (1904) 6 F. 269.

[7] *Edinburgh Water Trs.* v. *Clippens Oil Co.* (1899) 1 F. 899; *Matuszczyk* v. *N.C.B.*, 1955 S.C. 418.

[8] *G.S.W. Ry.*, *supra*, 31.

[9] *Mackintosh* v. *Smith & Lowe* (1865) 3 M. (H.L.) 6; *Paterson* v. *P.*, 1958 S.C. 141. cf. *Esso Petroleum Co.* v. *Law*, 1956 S.C. 33.

[10] *Young* v. *Y's Trs.*, 1957 S.C. 318; *Hynds* v. *H.*, 1966 S.C. 201; cf. *Boyd & Forrest* v. *G.S.W. Ry.*, 1918 S.C. (H.L.) 14, 26.

[11] *Forrest* v. *Dunlop* (1875) 3 R. 15.

[12] *Brand* v. *Arbroath Police Commrs.* (1890) 17 R. 790; *Hynds* v. *H.*, 1966 S.C. 201.

[13] *G.S.W. Ry.*, *supra*, 31.

CHAPTER 6

AUTHENTICATION OF DEEDS

A DEED or writ is an expression of a party's meaning in words
marked on paper or some similar substance. The words may
be in ink or pencil,[1] written, typewritten,[2] printed or otherwise marked, or partly in one medium, partly in another.[3] The
deed or writ may be intended to constitute an offer or undertaking, a conveyance of property, an expression of testamentary
desire, or any other lawful communication of meaning. The requisites of authentication are prescribed to determine whether or
not the deed can be treated without further evidence as a concluded act or expression of intention by the apparent granter
thereof. For the purposes of authentication writs can be distinguished as solemnly attested deeds, holograph writings,
writings *in re mercatoria* and writings statutorily privileged.[4]

SOLEMNLY ATTESTED DEEDS

The formal authentication of deeds has long been regulated by
statutes which prescribed solemnities of execution. Originally
sealing was necessary,[5] but the Subscription of Deeds Act, 1540
(c. 37) provided that deeds even if sealed should be ineffective
without the subscription of the granter or, if he could not write,
of a notary.[6] The Subscription of Deeds Act, 1579 (c. 18)
(repealed in part) required all 'contracts, obligations, reversions,
assignations and discharges of reversions or eiks thereto, and
generally all writs importing heritable title, or other bonds and
obligations of great importance' to be subscribed and sealed by
the principal parties if they could subscribe, otherwise by two
notaries before four witnesses, designated by their dwelling places
or otherwise that they may be known, present at the time.[7] The

[1] *Muir's Trs.* (1869) 8 M. 53; *Simsons v. S.* (1883) 10 R. 1247; cf. *Hope v. Derwent Rolling Mills* (1905) 7 F. 837.
[2] *Simpson's Trs. v. Macharg* (1902) 9 S.L.T. 398.
[3] Titles to Land Consolidation Act, 1868, S. 149.
[4] See generally Stair IV, 42, 1–19; Mack. III, 2, 4–5; Bankt. I, 11, 24–52; Ersk. III, 2, 6–25; Bell, *Comm.* I, 340–5; *Prin.* §19–21, 2225–32; Duff on *Deeds*; Bell, *Convg.* I, 23–101; Menzies, 77–165; Wood, 66–97; Craigie, *Mov.* 49–97; Dickson I, 399–474; Walkers, 181–217.
[5] Bell, *Convg.* I, 27; Menzies, 82; Craigie, *Mov.* 49.
[6] Bell, *Convg.* I, 28; Menzies, 83; Wood, 68; Craigie, *Mov.* 49.
[7] Bell, *Convg.* I, 29; Menzies, 84; Wood, 68; Craigie, *Mov.* 49.

Act, 1584, c. 11 (later repealed) declared sealing unnecessary in the case of writs agreed to be registered in the Books of Council and Session, and thereafter sealing fell into disuse.[1] The Act, 1593, c. 25 (repealed) required mention of the name and designation of the writer of the deed.[2] The Writs Act, 1672 (c. 16) allowed writs passing the Great or Privy Seals to be written bookwise, each page being signed. The Subscription of Deeds Act, 1681 (c. 5), provided that witnesses must subscribe, that the writer and witnesses must be named and designed in the deed and that these facts could not be supplied by separate condescendence, that no person should subscribe as witness unless he knew the party and saw him subscribe, or saw or heard him give warrant to a notary or notaries to subscribe for him and in evidence thereof touch the notary's pen, or hear him, at the time of the witness's subscription, acknowledge his signature.[3] The Act, 1686, c. 29 (repealed) allowed sasines to be written bookwise, and the Deeds Act, 1696 (c. 15), made it competent to write any deed bookwise, every page to be numbered and signed, and the last page mentioning how many pages are comprised in the writ, and it alone being signed by the witnesses.[4] The requirement of stating of how many pages the deed consisted (Deeds Act, 1696) if written bookwise, was not essential if the deed were on one sheet, even if folded to make four pages,[5] or on sheets battered together to form a roll, in which case it had to be sidescribed at the joins of the sheets.[6] Even where essential, neither an error in stating the number of pages,[7] nor an erasure of part of the word stating the number[8] was fatal to the deed.

The requirement of numbering the pages (Deeds Act, 1696) disappeared with the Form of Deeds (Sc.) Act, 1856.

Mention of the name and designation of the writer under the Act of 1593 and the Subscription of Deeds Act, 1681 (c. 5), continued to be required till 1874, but the requirements were not very strictly interpreted.[9] Mention of the designation of the

[1] Ersk. III, 2, 7; Bell, *Convg.* I, 30; Menzies, 85; Wood, 68; Craigie, *Mov.* 50.

[2] Bell, *Convg.* I, 31; Menzies, 85; Wood, 68; Craigie, *Mov.* 50.

[3] Ersk. III, 2, 13; Bell, *Convg.* I, 31–2; Menzies, 85–6; Wood, 68–9; Craigie, *Mov.* 50.

[4] Bell, *Convg.* I, 32; Menzies, 95; Wood, 69; Craigie, *Mov.* 51.

[5] *Robertson* v. *Ker* (1742) Mor. 16955; *Williamson* v. *W.* (1742) Mor. 16955; *Macdonald* v. *M.* (1778) Mor. 16956; *Smith* v. *B. of Scotland*, 4 July 1816, F.C.

[6] Craigie, *Mov.* 51.   [7] *Smith* v. *N.B. Ins. Co.* (1850) 12 D. 1132.

[8] *Gaywood* v. *McEand* (1828) 6 S. 991; *Cassilis's Trs.* v. *Kennedy* (1831) 9 S. 663.

[9] Bell, *Convg.* I, 59; Menzies, 87–90; *Dronnan* v. *Montgomery* (1716) Mor. 16869; *Ewing* v. *Semple* (1739) Mor. 1352; *Macpherson* v. *M.* (1855) 17 D. 357; *Callender* v. *C's Trs.* (1863) 2 M. 291; *Johnston* v. *Pettigrew* (1865) 3 M. 954; but see *Mitchell* v. *Scott's Trs.* (1874) 2 R. 162.

witnesses also continued to 1874 but this also was interpreted reasonably.[1]

Later reforms of solemnities

The Form of Deeds (Sc.) Act, 1856, abolished the need to number the pages but preserved the need to state of how many pages the deed consisted. The Titles to Land Consolidation (Sc.) Act, 1868, permitted additional sheets to be added to writs (S. 140) and (S. 149) allowed deeds to be partly written and partly printed or engraved or lithographed,[2] provided that in the testing clause the date, the names and designations of the witnesses, the number of pages of the deed, if specified, and the name and designation of the writer of the written portions of the deed were expressed at length, and abolished the need to name the writer of the written portions of the testing clause.

The Conveyancing (Sc.) Act, 1874, S. 38 made it unnecessary to state the name or designation of the printer or writer, the number of pages, or the names and designations of the witnesses in the body or testing clause of the deed, provided that, if not named and designed in the body or testing clause, their designations should be appended to or follow their subscriptions. This section is not retrospective.[3]

Modern essentials

In consequence, since 1874, the essentials of authentication are (1) subscription by the granter[4] at the end, if the deed consists of only one sheet, even if folded to make four pages,[5] or, if written bookwise, at the foot of each page and also at the end,[6] or, if written on more than one sheet joined into a roll, at each junction and also at the end,[7] save that, in the case of conveyances, deeds, instruments or writings, whether relating to land or not, executed after 28 November 1970, but not wills or other testamentary

---

[1] Menzies, 120.

[2] Including typewritten: *Simpson's Trs.* v. *Macharg* (1902) 9 S.L.T. 398.

[3] *Gardner* v. *Lucas* (1878) 5 R. (H.L.) 105. For a form of testing clause see Craigie, *Mov.* 53.

[4] *Foley* v. *Costello* (1904) 6 F. 365; *Taylor's Exces.* v. *Thom*, 1914 S.C. 79; cf. *Bradford* v. *Young* (1884) 11 R. 1135.

[5] *Ferguson*, 1959 S.C. 56; cf. *McLaren* v. *Menzies* (1876) 3 R. 1151.

[6] The requirements of the Deeds Act, 1696, apply only to deeds written on more than one sheet and not to deeds which though written bookwise, are all on one sheet: Menzies, 96; *Smith* v. *Bank of Scotland* (1824) 2 Sh. App. 265; *McCrummen's Trs.* v. *Edinburgh & Glasgow Bank* (1859) 21 D. (H.L.) 3; *Baird's Trs.* v. *B.*, 1955 S.C. 286; *Ferguson, supra*.

[7] Conveyancing and Feudal Reform (Sc.) Act, 1970, S. 44. Plans, inventories, schedules and other appendices to the deed should also be signed, at the foot of each page thereof, subject to the same saving for deeds executed after 28 November 1970.

writings, it is no objection to the probative character of the deed
that it is not subscribed or, if appropriate, signed and sealed, on
every page other than the last page;[1] (2) authentication in the
body of the deed or in the testing clause of deletions, interlineations, marginal additions and erasures; (3) subscription on
the last page by two witnesses who know the granter or have
credible information that the person signing is the granter, and
who see the granter subscribe, or hear him acknowledge his
signature; and (4) mention of the designations of the witnesses in
the body of the deed, or in the testing clause, or appended to their
signatures. The designations may be appended or added at any
time before the deed is recorded in any register for preservation,
or founded on in court, and need not be written by the witnesses
themselves.[1] The essentials are not satisfied by a signature on the
front of a one-page document, signed also and witnessed on the
back, but with no connecting link between front and back.[2] The
requirements of authentication do not apply to Crown writs.[3]

Inessentials

Though usually included, the place of signing[4] and date of
signing[5] are inessential, though the date must be given if the
validity should depend on the specification of the date.[6] A deed
executed on a Sunday is valid.[7] The addition of the word 'witness'
after a witness's signature has never been essential,[8] though
sometimes useful to supplement a defective testing clause.[9] Since
1874 it has not been essential to state the number of pages of
which the deed consists, the name and designation of the writer,
or the names and designations of the witnesses if their designations
are appended to or follow their signatures.

Essential (1)—Subscription by granter

The Sovereign may superscribe; all others must subscribe, at
the end of the last page on which the deed is written,[10] and, in the
case of wills, at the foot of every page.[11] Signature in the margin

---

[1] Conveyancing Act, 1874, S. 38.

[2] *Baird's Trs.* v. *B.*, 1955 S.C. 286; contrast *Russell's Exor.* v. *Duke*, 1946 S.L.T. 242.

[3] *Catton* v. *Mackenzie* (1874) 1 R. 488.   [4] Ersk. III, 2, 18; Bell, *Convg.* I, 64.

[5] Bell, *Convg.* I, 65.   [6] *Elliot* v. *Faulke* (1844) 6 D. 411.   [7] Ibid.

[8] *Morison* v. *L. Salton* (1694) 4 B.S. 163; *L. Blantyre* (1850) 13 D. 40.

[9] *Wemyss* v. *Hay* (1825) 1 W. & S. 140; *McDougall* v. *McD.* (1875) 2 R. 814.

[10] *Taylor's Exces., supra*; *McKillop* v. *Secy. of State for Scotland* (1950) 39 L.C. 17; *McLay*
v. *Farrell*, 1950 S.C. 149. Subscription on a blank page following the last page will not
suffice: *Baird's Trs.* v. *B.*, 1955 S.C. 286.

[11] Conveyancing and Feudal Reform (Sc.) Act, 1970, S. 44.

is not subscription.[1] By the Lyon King of Arms Act, 1672 (c. 47), noblemen and Anglican bishops may subscribe by their titles, but all others do so by their Christian names, or the initial or any abbreviation[2] thereof, and surname, adding, if they wish, the designation of their lands.[3] Peers use their title of honour and peers' eldest sons their courtesy titles.[4]

Married women may use their maiden surname,[5] but commonly use their husband's surname.[6] A deletion of a married name and the substitution of the granter's maiden surname has been held irrelevant, where the granter had later been divorced and resumed her maiden name, and it was admitted that there was no intention to revoke the deed.[7]

The subscription must be complete,[8] by the hand of the granter,[9] which may be supported[10] but not guided in whole[11] or in part,[12] and it must be complete.[13] A signature by mark[14] or stamp[15] or cyclostyle[16] or on a tracing by another[17] or typewritten[18] is valueless, though a granter may follow a copy of his signature by another.[19] A signature may be touched up by the granter, even after attestation and outwith the presence of the witnesses.[20] It is valid though wrongly spelled,[21] or illegible,[22]

---

[1] *Robbie* v. *Carr*, 1959 S.L.T. (Notes) 16.

[2] Bell, *Convg.* I, 37; Menzies, 98; Craigie, *Mov.* 66.

[3] Any discrepancy between the names in the body of the deed and the signature should be mentioned in the testing clause e.g. 'The said A.B.C.D. subscribing A.D.'.

[4] Bell, Menzies, *supra.*

[5] *Dunlop* v. *Greenlees' Trs.* (1863) 2 M. 1. It is not correct to sign both maiden name and married name, or use the initial of the maiden name before the married surname: see *Grieve's Trs.* v. *Japp's Trs.*, 1917, 1 S.L.T. 70.

[6] The surname used should be that under which the granter customarily passed at that time.

[7] *Fotheringham's Tr.* v. *Reid*, 1936 S.C. 831.

[8] *Moncrieff* v. *Monypenny* (1711) Mor. 15936; Rob. App. 26.

[9] *Moncrieff, supra.*

[10] *Noble* v. *N.* (1875) 3 R. 74.

[11] *Ballingall* v. *Robertson* (1806) Hume 916; *Wilson* v. *Pringles* (1814) Hume 923; *Harkness* v. *H.* (1821) 2 Mur. 558.

[12] *Moncrieff, supra.*

[13] *Moncrieff, supra.*

[14] *Crosbie* v. *Witson* (1865) 3 M. 870; *Morton* v. *French*, 1908 S.C. 171; *Donald* v. *McGregor's Exors.*, 1926 S.L.T. 103.

[15] *Stirling-Stuart* v. *Stirling-Crawfurd's Trs.* (1885) 12 R. 610.

[16] *Whyte* v. *Watt* (1893) 21 R. 165.

[17] *Crosbie* v. *Pickens* (1749) Mor. 16814; cf. *Whyte* v. *Watt* (1893) 21 R. 165.

[18] *McBeath's Trs.* v. *McB.*, 1935 S.C. 471, 476.

[19] *Wilson* v. *Raeburn* (1800) Hume 912.

[20] *Stirling-Stuart, supra.*

[21] *Perryman* v. *McClymont* (1852) 14 D. 508.

[22] *Stirling-Stuart, supra.*

or signed by a blind person.[1] If signed on erasure not declared, it has been held that the onus is on the challenger to show that the signature was not genuine or had not been duly tested.[2]

A signature by initials, if recognizably the initial letters of the granter's name,[3] may be sustained if it be proved that the granter did subscribe the deed by initials and was accustomed to subscribe by initials only,[4] but it is not probative *per se*.[5] Similarly a signature of a will by Christian name only has been sustained,[6] though not probative without evidence that such was the granter's normal practice. The designation 'Mr.' or 'Mrs.' or 'Miss' followed by a surname is not a valid signature,[7] but the addition of such a prefix to an otherwise valid signature does not affect it.[8]

Deeds executed by mark are null,[9] but certain documents *in re mercatoria* may be so executed,[10] and statute may permit this,[11] but a mark is not a 'writing under his hand'.[12] The subscription may have preceded the writing of the body of the deed, but the deed is valid if the signature is thereafter acknowledged to the witnesses who then sign.[13] Anything on the deed below the subscription, unless itself subscribed, is not authenticated and invalid.[14] A deed has been held probative though the signature was on erasure not mentioned in the testing clause.[15]

Partnerships sign the firm name, adhibited by one partner, and the signatures of all individual partners. Within the scope of the firm's business the firm name signed by any partner suffices.

Modes of authentication of deeds granted by corporate bodies are prescribed by their constituting Act or charter, or by general legislation.[16]

---

[1] *E. Fife* v. *Fife's Trs.* (1823) 1 Sh. App. 498; *Ker* v. *Hotchkis* (1837) 15 S. 983.

[2] *Brown* v. *Duncan* (1888) 15 R. 511.

[3] *Din* v. *Gillies*, 18 June 1812, F.C.; *Weirs* v. *Ralstons*, 22 June 1813, F.C.

[4] *Weirs* v. *Ralstons*, 22 June 1813, F.C.; *Speirs* v. *Home Speirs* (1879) 6 R. 1359; Bell, *Convg.* I, 49; Menzies, 100. This does not apply to a witness's signature: *Meek* v. *Dunlop* (1707) Mor. 16806.

[5] *Gardner* v. *Lucas* (1878) 5 R. (H.L.) 105.

[6] *Draper* v. *Thomason*, 1954 S.C. 136.

[7] *Allan and Crichton*, 1933 S.L.T. (Sh. Ct.) 2.   [8] cf. *Ferguson*, 1959 S.C. 56.

[9] *Graham* v. *Macleod* (1848) 11 D. 173; *Crosbie* v. *Wilson* (1865) 3 M. 870; *Donald* v. *McGregor's Exors.*, 1926 S.L.T. 103.

[10] Bell, *Comm.* I, 343; *Bryan* v. *Murdoch* (1827) 2 W. & S. 568.

[11] Marriage Notice (Sc.) Act, 1878, S. 16.

[12] *Morton* v. *French*, 1908 S.C. 171.

[13] *Carsewell's Trs.* v. *C.* (1895) 3 S.L.T. 218.

[14] *Taylor's Exces.* v. *Thom*, 1914 S.C. 79; *McLay* v. *Farrell*, 1950 S.C. 149.

[15] *Brown* v. *Duncan* (1888) 15 R. 511.

[16] Local Govt. (Sc.) Act, 1973, S. 193; Companies Act, 1948, S. 32(4).

Essential (2)—Authentication of corrections in deed

At common law deletions, interlineations, marginal additions and words written on erasure had to be authenticated in the deed itself, usually by having corrections of any of these kinds declared in the testing clause and by having marginal additions signed or initialled as well.[1] Corrections not thus authenticated, if material, are held *pro non scriptis*, possibly with the result of vitiating the whole deed.[2]

Words deleted will be treated as cancelled if the deletion is authenticated[3] or intent to delete can be inferred from the circumstances.[4] Interlineations and marginal additions must be authenticated even if apparently holograph,[5] though a holograph addition to a deed, above the signature, has been held valid.[6] Words written on erasures, unless authenticated, will be treated *pro non scriptis*; if the words be essential the deed is vitiated, but if not essential the deed stands but the word on erasure is ignored.[7] Where a deed was *ex facie* probative but the signature was written on erasure it was held that the onus of disproof was on the challenger.[8]

In testamentary writings corrections by the testator not properly authenticated do not invalidate the deed *in toto*, if, as altered, it still contains an effectual expression of final testamentary intention.[9]

By statute[10] no challenge of a notarial instrument by reduction

---

[1] Bell, *Convg.* I, 70; Menzies, 138; Wood, 88; Craigie, *Mov.* 59.

[2] See e.g. *Reid* v. *Kedder* (1840) 1 Rob. 183; *Shepherd* v. *Grant's Trs.* (1847) 6 Bell 153; *Kirkwood* v. *Patrick* (1847) 9 D. 1361; *Boswell* v. *B.* (1852) 14 D. 378; *Fraser* v. *F.* (1854) 16 D. 863; *Gollan* v. *G.* (1863) 1 M. (H.L.) 65; *Munro* v. *Butler Johnstone* (1868) 7 M. 250; *Cattanach's Tr.* v. *Jamieson* (1884) 11 R. 972; *Drummond* v. *Peddie* (1893) 1 S.L.T. 189. In certain cases, e.g. *Milne's Exor.* v. *Waugh*, 1913 S.C. 203; *Allan's Exor.* v. *A.*, 1920 S.C. 732; intention to delete has been inferred from words scored through even though not authenticated. Deletion cannot be effected by pasting a slip of paper over part of a deed: *Dunsire* v. *Bell*, 1909 S.C. (J.) 5.

[3] *Pattison's Trs.* v. *Edinburgh University* (1888) 16 R. 73.

[4] *Milne's Exor.* v. *Waugh*, 1913 S.C. 203; *Allan's Exor.* v. *A.*, 1920 S.C. 732; see also *Gemmell's Exor.* v. *Stirling*, 1923 S.L.T. 384.

[5] *Brown* v. *Maxwell's Exors.* (1884) 11 R. 821.

[6] *Gray's Trs.* v. *Dow* (1900) 3 F. 79.

[7] *Gollan* v. *G.*, *supra*; *McDougall* v. *McD.* (1875) 2 R. 814.

[8] *Brown* v. *Duncan* (1888) 15 R. 511. See also *Dowie* v. *Barclay* (1871) 9 M. 726; *Muir* v. *Thompson* (1876) 3 R. (H.L.) 1.

[9] *Robertson* v. *Ogilvie's Trs.* (1844) 7 D. 236; *Richardson* v. *Biggar* (1845) 8 D. 315; *Grant* v. *Stoddart* (1849) 11 D. 860; *Dundee Mags.* v. *Morris* (1858) 3 Macq. 134; *Parker* v. *Matheson* (1876) 13 S.L.R. 405; *Munro's Exors.* v. *M.* (1890) 18 R. 122; see also *Pattison's Trs.* v. *Edinburgh Univ.* (1888) 16 R. 73.

[10] Titles to Land Consolidation (Sc.) Act, 1868, S. 144, extending Erasures in Deeds (Sc.) Act, 1836, extended to notices of title by Conveyancing (Sc.) Act, 1924, S. 6.

or exception may receive effect, on the ground that any part of the instrument is written on erasure, unless it be proved that such erasures have been made for the purpose of fraud, or the record thereof is not conformable to the instrument as presented for registration. Also[1] no challenge of a deed recorded in the register of sasines may receive effect on the ground that any part of the record thereof is written on erasure unless it be proved to have been made for the purpose of fraud, or the record is not conformable to the deed as presented for registration.

Defects in a testing clause may be rectified at any time before the deed is recorded for preservation or judicially founded upon.[2]

Essentials (3) and (4)—Subscriptions and designations of witnesses

Custom has long established two as the necessary number of witnesses.[3] Pupils,[4] blind persons,[5] and persons mentally defective or mentally incapable[6] may not act as witnesses, nor may one party to a deed witness the signature of another.[7] Any person, male or female, married or unmarried, not being subject to any legal incapacity, aged fourteen or over, may act.[8] Persons may act as witnesses notwithstanding close relationship to the granter,[9] legal infamy,[10] or having an interest, even beneficial, in the deed.[11]

Each witness must either know the granter, or have credible information that the person signing is the person designed as granter of the deed.[12] Each must see the granter subscribe, or hear him acknowledge his signature, before the witness signs.[13] It is competent for the granter to sign in the presence of one witness and acknowledge his signature to the other, or acknowledge it on separate occasions to the two witnesses.[14] It is not essential that

---

[1] Conveyancing (Sc.) Act, 1874, S. 54.

[2] Ibid., S. 38.

[3] Bell, *Convg.* I, 50; Menzies, 113; Wood, 69.

[4] *Davidson* v. *Charteris* (1738) Mor. 16899.

[5] *Cuningham* v. *Spence* (1824) 3 S. 205.

[6] Menzies, 111.

[7] Bell, *Convg.* I, 51; *Miller* v. *Farquharson* (1835) 13 S. 838.

[8] Titles to Land Consolidation (Sc.) Act, 1868, S. 139; *Hannay* (1873) 1 R. 246.

[9] *Falconer* v. *Arnuthnot* (1750) Mor. 16759; *Simsons* v. *S.* (1883) 10 R. 1247; but see *Brownlee* v. *Robb*, 1907 S.C. 1302, 1310.

[10] *Lockhart* v. *Baillie* (1710) Mor. 8433.

[11] *Mitchell* v. *Miller* (1742) Mor. 16900; *Simsons* v. *S.* (1883) 10 R. 1247.

[12] *Walker* v. *Adamson's Reps.* (1716) Mor. 16896; *Brock* v. *B.*, 1908 S.C. 964.

[13] *Geddes* v. *Reid* (1891) R. 1186; *Forrest* v. *Low's Trs.*, 1907 S.C. 1240; *Boyd* v. *Shaw*, 1927 S.C. 414.

[14] *Robertson* v. *McCaig* (1823) 2 S. 544; *Hogg* v. *Campbell* (1864) 2 M. 848.

the granter acknowledges his signature by spoken words.[1] Signature as witness before the granter signs is a nullity.[2] A mutual deed signed by only one party before witnesses may be valid quoad that party only.[3]

The witnesses sign only at the end of the deed. They must have the express or implied authority of the granter to attest, and sign by his request. Two witnesses suffice for any one or more signatures to the same deed, so long as the witnesses saw, or heard acknowledged, each signature, and they need sign only once;[4] if the granters sign at different places or times the witnesses need sign only once if they saw the parties subscribe.[5] They do not need to sign in presence of the granter[6] and may do so at any time before the deed is founded on or registered for preservation,[7] but a long interval should not be allowed to elapse,[8] and they cannot sign after his death.[9] A witness who only hears a signature acknowledged is not entitled to sign *ex intervallo*.[10] If one witness fails to sign the deed is not validly authenticated.[11] A granter may acknowledge his subscription to two witnesses separately at different times.[12]

By their signatures the witnesses attest the execution only; they have no concern with the substance of the deed[13] and the deed may be so folded or covered that they see only the signature which they attest.[14]

The witnesses adhibit their signatures in the same way as do granters, customarily but not necessarily appending the word 'Witness' thereafter. Their designations, included in the testing clause or following their signatures, customarily comprise the occupations and addresses, business or residential, of the witnesses

[1] *Cumming* v. *Skeoch's Trs.* (1879) 6 R. 540, 963; *Sutherland* v. *Low* (1901) 8 S.L.T. 395; 3 F. 972.

[2] *Smyth* v. *S.* (1876) 3 R. 573.

[3] *Millar* v. *Birrell* (1876) 4 R. 87.

[4] *Hardies* v. *H.*, 6 Dec. 1810, F.C.

[5] *Edmonston* v. *E.* (1749) Mor. 16901; but see *Walker* v. *Whitwell*, 1916 S.C. (H.L.) 75; *Hynd's Tr.* v. *Hynd's Trs.*, 1955 S.C. (H.L.) 1.

[6] *Condie* v. *Buchan* (1823) 2 S. 432; *Thomson* v. *Clarkson's Trs.* (1892) 20 R. 59.

[7] *Stewart* v. *Burns* (1877) 4 R. 427; *Murray* (1904) 6 F. 840.

[8] *Frank* v. *F.* (1795) Mor. 16824; affd. (1809) 5 Pat. 278; *Thomson* v. *Clarkson's Trs.* (1892) 20 R. 59; *Stewart* v. *Burns* (1877) 4 R. 427 must now be considered very doubtful.

[9] *Walker* v. *Whitwell*, 1916 S.C. (H.L.) 75, overruling *Tener's Trs.* v. *T's Trs.* (1879) 6 R. 1111; see also *Arnott* v. *Burt* (1872) 11 M. 62; *Beattie* v. *Bain's Trs.* (1899) 6 S.L.T. 277; *Brownlee* v. *Robb*, 1907 S.C. 1302.

[10] *Hogg* v. *Campbell* (1864) 2 M. 848; *Thomson* v. *Clarkson's Trs.* (1892) 20 R. 59.

[11] *Moncrieff* v. *Lowrie* (1896) 23 R. 577.

[12] *Hogg, supra.*

[13] Menzies, 113.

[14] *Lady Ormistoun* v. *Hamilton* (1708) Mor. 16890.

and need only be sufficient to identify them.[1] They may be added by another hand.[2] A discrepancy between a witness's signature and his name in the testing clause is curable as an informality of execution.[3] An erroneous designation does not vitiate, certainly where the meaning is plain from the context.[4] The want of designations may be supplied before the deed is founded on in any court and is in any event curable as an informality of execution.[5]

The onus on a party challenging a deed *ex facie* solemnly executed is heavy,[6] and a granter seeking to reduce his own deed on the ground of defective attestation may be held barred if third parties have acted on the faith of the deed.[7]

Completion of testing clause

The testing clause though customary is not essential; it is part of the deed and any condition or provision therein which might, and should preferably, have been in another clause, is valid, though this is not the function of the testing clause,[8] but words in the testing clause can have no effect in altering or adding to the deed.[9]

The testing clause should be completed at once[10] but may be completed at any time,[11] but not after the death of the granter[12] nor after the deed has been registered for preservation or founded on in court,[13] unless it is not founded on by the party producing it.[14] There should be no material error in it, though a mistake or erasure therein is not necessarily fatal.[15] It need not state the

---

[1] *McDougall* v. *McD.* (1875) 2 R. 814.   [2] Conveyancing (Sc.) Act, 1874, S. 38.
[3] *Richardson's Trs.* (1891) 18 R. 1131.   [4] *Speirs* v. *S's Trs.* (1887) 5 R. 923.
[5] *Thomson's Trs.* v. *Easson* (1878) 6 R. 141; and see *infra*; *Garrett* (1883) 20 S.L.R. 756; *Nisbet* (1897) 24 R. 411.
[6] *Smith* v. *Bank of Scotland* (1824) 2 Sh. App. 265; see also *Condie* v. *Buchan* (1823) 2 S. 432; *Cleland* v. *Paterson* (1837) 15 S. 1246; *Young* v. *Paton*, 1910 S.C. 63; *McArthur* v. *McA's Trs.*, 1931 S.L.T. 463.
[7] *Baird's Tr.* v. *Murray* (1883) 11 R. 153; *National Bank* v. *Campbell* (1892) 19 R. 885; *McLeish* v. *B.L. Bank*, 1911, 2 S.L.T. 168; *Boyd* v. *Shaw*, 1927 S.C. 414; *Sinclair* v. *S.*, 1949 S.L.T. (Notes) 16; *Smellie's Trs.* v. *S.*, 1953 S.L.T. (Notes) 22.
[8] *Dunlop* v. *Greenlees' Trs.* (1865) 3 M. (H.L.) 46; *Chambers' Trs.* v. *Smiths* (1878) 5 R. (H.L.) 151; *Gibson's Trs.* v. *Lamb*, 1931 S.L.T. 22.
[9] *Chambers' Trs.*, *supra*; *Blair* v. *Assets Co.* (1896) 23 R. (H.L.) 36.
[10] Bell, *Convg.* I, 234.
[11] *Blair* v. *E. Galloway* (1827) 6 S. 51 (32 years later); *Stewart* v. *Burns* (1877) 4 R. 427 (4 months later); *sed quaere*.
[12] *Walker* v. *Whitwell*, 1916 S.C. (H.L.) 75; but see *Veasey* v. *Malcolm's Trs.* (1875) 2 R. 748.
[13] Conveyancing (Sc.) Act, 1874, S. 38; *Hill* v. *Arthur* (1870) 9 M. 223; see also *Blair* v. *E. Galloway* (1827) 6 S. 51; *Caldwell* (1871) 10 M. 99.
[14] *Millar* v. *Birrell* (1876) 4 R. 87.   [15] *McDougall* v. *McD.* (1875) 2 R. 814.

names of the witnesses, but only such designations as taken along with their subscriptions, are sufficient for their identification.[1]

Conventional or additional solemnities

Parties may agree or specify that other, greater or less, solemnities than are required by law shall be used in the execution of any deed pursuant to their specification,[2] such as future informal writings supplementary to a will.[3]

Informality of execution

The Conveyancing Act, 1874, S. 39, provides that a deed[4] subscribed by the granter and bearing to be attested by two witnesses subscribing, is not to be deemed invalid or denied effect because of any informality of execution, but the burden of proving that it was subscribed by the granter and by the witnesses lies on the party using or upholding the deed, and proof thereof may be led in any action in which the deed is founded on or objected to, or in a special application to the court to have it declared that such deed was so subscribed. This section is not retrospective.[5] Informalities of execution include signature on the last page only of a deed consisting of more than one sheet;[6] witnesses who only heard acknowledgment of the granter's signature signing *ex intervallo*;[7] a discrepancy between the witness's signature and his name in the testing clause;[8] a deed subscribed and attested but with the testing clause uncompleted;[9] a deed lacking the designations of the attesting witnesses;[10] subscription of granter or witnesses written on erasures;[11] signature with a docquet of attestation carrying over from the first to the third of four pages formed by a single sheet folded;[12] signature at end only before witnesses but no testing clause;[13] a codicil partly on the last sheet of a will and unsigned, but continued on a further sheet and

[1] *McDougall, supra.*

[2] *Campbell's Trs.* v. *C.* (1903) 5 F. 366; cf. *Nasmyth* v. *Hare* (1821) 1 Sh. App. 65.

[3] e.g. *Baird* v. *Jaap* (1856) 18 D. 1246; *Crosbie* v. *Wilson* (1865) 3 M. 870; *Lamont* v. *Glasgow Mags.* (1887) 14 R. 603; *Fraser* v. *Forbes' Trs.* (1899) 1 F. 513; *Waterson's Trs.* v. *St. Giles Boys' Club*, 1943 S.C. 369.

[4] See *McLaren* v. *Menzies* (1876) 3 R. 1151; *Brown* (1883) 11 R. 400.

[5] *Gardner* v. *Lucas* (1878) 5 R. (H.L.) 105; but see *Addison* (1875) 2 R. 457.

[6] *McLaren* v. *Menzies* (1876) 3 R. 1151; *Brown* (1883) 11 R. 400.

[7] *Thomson* v. *Clarkson's Trs.* (1892) 20 R. 59 (within one hour).

[8] *Richardson's Trs.* (1891) 18 R. 1131.   [9] *Addison* (1875) 2 R. 457.

[10] *Thomson's Tr.* v. *Easson* (1878) 6 R. 141; *Garrett* (1883) 20 S.L.R. 756; *Nisbet* (1897) 24 R. 411.

[11] *Brown* v. *Duncan* (1888) 15 R. 511.

[12] *Ferguson*, 1959 S.C. 56. cf. *McNeill* v. *M.*, 1973 S.L.T. (Sh. Ct.) 16.

[13] *Inglis' Trs.* v. *I.* (1901) 4 F. 365.

signed;[1] a will validly executed by the law of the place of execution, but defective by the rules of Scots law,[2] unauthenticated marginal additions, interlineations and erasures;[3] a draft signed as principal.[4]

It is no objection to a petition under S. 39 that the particular informality could previously have been cured under S. 38 of the Act, but which remedy was no longer available in the circumstances.[5]

Defects not curable as informalities

The defect was held not curable but radical where a deed without a testing clause bore to be signed by the granter and witnesses, but the granter denied signing and the witnesses had signed but had not seen him sign nor heard him acknowledge his subscription and the person founding on the deed did not prove that the granter had signed it.[6] Nor does the section assist where the witnesses' signatures were adhibited before the granter signed and they neither saw him sign nor heard him acknowledge his subscription,[7] nor in a case where subscription was lacking,[8] nor where one witness subscribed *ex intervallo*, after the granter's death,[9] nor where a witness did not sign until after the deed had been judicially founded on or registered for preservation,[10] nor, in a case of notarial execution, if the notarial docquet is not holograph,[11] or was completed outwith the presence of the granter and witnesses,[12] or the notary had a disqualifying interest in the deed.[13]

Petitions under S. 39 for declarator that deeds were duly subscribed have been held unnecessary where there were small discrepancies between the granters' signatures and their names as stated in the body of the deeds.[14]

---

[1] *Brown* (1883) 11 R. 400.   [2] *Browne* (1882) 20 S.L.R. 76.

[3] *Veasey* v. *Malcolm's Trs.* (1875) 2 R. 748; *Walker* v. *Whitwell*, 1916 S.C. (H.L.) 75; *Elliot's Exors.*, 1939 S.L.T. 69.

[4] *Shiell*, 1936 S.L.T. 317.   [5] *Thomson's Trs.* v. *Easson* (1878) 6 R. 141.

[6] *Geddes* v. *Reid* (1891) 18 R. 1186.

[7] *Smyth* v. *S.* (1876) 3 R. 573; *Forrest* v. *Low's Trs.*, 1907 S.C. 1240; cf. *Stewart* v. *Burns* (1877) 4 R. 427.

[8] *Baird's Trs.* v. *B.*, 1955 S.C. 286.   [9] *Walker* v. *Whitwell*, 1916 S.C. (H.L.) 75.

[10] *Moncrieff* v. *Lawrie* (1896) 23 R. 577; but see *McLaren* v. *Menzies* (1876) 3 R. 1151, 1158; *Todd* v. *Reid* (1883) 20 S.L.R. 382.

[11] *Irvine* v. *McHardy* (1892) 19 R. 458.

[12] *Hynd's Tr.* v. *Hynd's Trs.*, 1955 S.C. (H.L.) 1.

[13] *Finlay* v. *F's Trs.*, 1948 S.C. 16; *Gorrie's Tr.* v. *Stiven's Exrx.*, 1952 S.C. 1; *Crawfurd's Trs.* v. *Glasgow R.I.*, 1955 S.C. 367.

[14] *Grieve's Trs.* v. *Japp's Trs.*, 1917 1 S.L.T. 70; see also *Dickson's Trs.* v. *Goodall* (1820) Hume 925; *Veasey* v. *Malcolm's Trs.* (1875) 2 R. 748.

If the granter's signature is neither adhibited nor acknowledged in the presence of one of the witnesses it is not an informality but a fatal defect.[1] Similarly, for a witness not to sign till after the granter's death is not an informality but a fundamental nullity,[2] as is a deed registered for preservation or founded on in court before the witnesses have signed,[3] and a single sheet signed, and signed on the reverse before two witnesses, but there being no indication of connection between obverse and reverse.[4] A mutual deed signed and witnessed as to the one part and signed only as to the other may be effectual as to the one part and not the other.[5]

The court will set aside a deed *ex facie* perfectly regular and duly tested only on the clearest possible evidence, and not on the unsupported evidence of one attesting witness that the granter's signature had not been adhibited or acknowledged in her presence,[6] but it may do so in face of both witnesses' evidence if persuaded by other cogent evidence.[7] The granters of onerous deeds have been held barred from challenging their own deeds on the ground that one instrumentary witness had neither seen them sign nor heard them acknowledge their signatures.[8]

Notarial execution

In the case of persons who could not write the Subscription of Deeds Act, 1540 (c. 37), required the subscription of a notary and the Subscription of Deeds Act, 1579 (c. 18), the subscription of two notaries before four witnesses in the case of deeds of great importance, while the Subscription of Deeds Act, 1681 (c. 5), provided that the witnesses should hear the party give warrant to the notaries and in evidence thereof touch their pens.[9] The 1579

---

[1] *Smyth* v. *S.* (1876) 3 R. 573; *Forrest* v. *Low's Trs.,* 1907 S.C. 1240.

[2] *Tener's Trs.* v. *T's Trs.* (1879) 6 R. 1111, overruled by *Walker's Trs.* v. *Whitwell,* 1916 S.C. (H.L.) 75.

[3] *Moncrieff* v. *Lawrie* (1896) 23 R. 577.

[4] *Baird's Trs.* v. *B.,* 1955 S.C. 286; *see also McLaren* v. *Menzies* (1876) 3 R. 1151; *Russell's Exor.* v. *Duke,* 1946 S.L.T. 242; *Ferguson,* 1959 S.C. 56.

[5] *Millar* v. *Birrell* (1876) 4 R. 87.

[6] *Forrests, supra.*

[7] *Young* v. *Paton,* 1910 S.C. 63.

[8] *Baird's Tr.* v. *Murray* (1883) 11 R. 153; *MacLeish* v. *B.L. Co.,* 1911, 2 S.L.T. 168.

[9] Stair III, 8, 34; Ersk. III, 2, 23. For examples of notarial execution under these acts, see *Anderson* v. *Tarbat* (1668) Mor. 16836; *Jack* v. *Jacks* (1671) Mor. 16836; *White* v. *Knox* (1711) Mor. 16841; *Birrel* v. *Moffat* (1745) Mor. 16846; *Rollands* v. *R.* (1767) Mor. 16851; *Stoddart* v. *Arkley* (1799) Mor. 16857; *Russel* v. *Kirk* (1827) 6 S. 133; *Ferrie* v. *Ferrie's Trs.* (1863) 1 M. 291; *Henry* v. *Reid* (1871) 9 M. 503. See also for an account of older law *Atchison's Trs.* v. *A.* (1876) 3 R. 388.

Act was held to apply to persons who could write but were blind.[1] The Disqualification of Ministers Act, 1584 (c. 6), entitled a parish minister to act as notary in the execution of testaments of moveable estate, probably within his own parish only.

The Conveyancing Act, 1874, S. 41, provides that, without prejudice to the previous law and practice, any deed, having been read over to the granter, might be validly executed on his behalf if he were from any cause, permanent or temporary, unable to write, by one notary or justice of the peace subscribing for him, without touching the pen, all before two witnesses, and appending a docquet in the form of Sched. I to the Act or in words to the like effect, setting out that the granter authorized the execution and that the deed had been read over to the granter in presence of the witnesses.[2] The Conveyancing (Sc.) Act, 1924, S. 18,[3] authorizes notarial execution by a law agent[4] or notary public or justice of the peace or, as regards wills or other testamentary writings, by a parish minister acting in his own parish, or any minister of the Church of Scotland appointed to a charge to officiate as minister, in any parish in which part of his charge is situated, or his colleague and successor or assistant and successor so acting, subscribing in presence of the granter and by his authority, all before two witnesses who have heard the deed read over to the granter and heard or seen authority given, and a shorter holograph docquet in the form of Sched. I or in any words to the like effect shall precede the signature of such notary or other person acting.

Essentials of notarial execution

The essentials of notarial execution are accordingly: The granter must from any cause, temporary or permanent, be blind or unable to write.[5] If blind the granter may either sign personally,[6] or have the deed executed notarially.[7] There must be present a notary public, solicitor,[8] justice of the peace or, in the case of testamentary writings, a parish minister in his own parish or his

---

[1] *Reid* v. *Baxter* (1837) 16 S. 273.

[2] The reading over is an essential solemnity, even if the granter is deaf: *Hodges* v. *H's Trs.* (1900) 7 S.L.T. 303; *Watson* v. *Beveridge* (1883) 11 R. 40.

[3] Extended by Church of Scotland (Property and Endowments) Amdt. (Sc.) Act, 1933, S. 13.

[4] So long as enrolled, even though not having a current practising certificate: *Stephen* v. *Scott*, 1927 S.C. 85.

[5] 1874 Act, S. 41; 1924 Act, S. 18.

[6] *E. Fife* v. *Fife's Trs.* (1823) 1 Sh. App. 498.

[7] *Reid* v. *Baxter* (1837) 16 S. 273.

[8] He need not hold a practising certificate: *Stephen* v. *Scott*, 1927 S.C. 85.

colleague and successor. The notary or other person acting must know that the person for whom he acts is the person designed as granter of the deed, or have that fact attested by others.[1] There must be present two other persons to act as instrumentary witnesses.[2] The deed must be read over[3] to the granter by the notary in the presence of the two witnesses.[4] The witnesses have to know the granter or have his identity established to them.[5] The notary or other executant must in the presence of the two witnesses obtain the granter's authority to execute the deed.[6] This may be given in any way which can be 'heard or seen'. The notary must sign the deed in his own name on each page and at the end, as the granter would have done, all in presence of the granter.[6] The notary must add the statutory docquet,[7] or words to the same effect,[8] on the last page of the deed.[9] The docquet must be holograph.[10] The notary signs at the end of the docquet adding his designation by virtue of which he is entitled to act, and the two[11] witnesses also sign there opposite his signature.[12] The witnesses may be designed in the testing clause or have their designations added to their signatures. The completion of the docquet and the signatures of the notary and witnesses must be *unico contextu* with the earlier events and in the presence of the granter, and not *ex intervallo*.[12] The witnesses must see or hear every step of the formalities, reading of the deed, authority to sign, writing of the docquet and signature by the notary, and their signing is part of the formalities.[13] The notary also must not, in his private or other capacity, be a party to the deed,[14] nor act for more than one party, certainly if their interests are or may be

---

[1] A.S. 21 July, 1688.

[2] cf. *Cameron* v. *Holman* (1951) 39 L.C. 14.

[3] cf. *Watson* v. *Beveridge* (1883) 11 R. 40; *Hodges* v. *H's Trs.* (1900) 7 S.L.T. 303.

[4] 1874 Act, S. 41; 1924 Act, S. 18.

[5] Subscription of Deeds Act, 1681 (c. 5).

[6] 1874 Act, S. 41; 1924 Act, S. 18; *Mathieson* v. *Hawthorns* (1899) 1 F. 468. See also *Hynd's Tr.* v. *Hynd's Trs.*, 1955 S.C. (H.L.) 1. If the end of the deed is on the same page as the notarial docquet the signature to the latter will suffice as the signature for that page: *Mathieson, supra*; *Hynd's Tr., supra*.

[7] 1924 Act, Sched. I.

[8] *Atchison's Trs.* v. *A.* (1876) 3 R. 388; *Cameron* v. *Holman* (1951) 39 L.C. 14; see also *Watson* v. *Beveridge* (1883) 11 R. 40; *Hynd's Tr., infra*.

[9] 1924 Act, S. 18.

[10] *Henry* v. *Reid* (1871) 9 M. 503; *Irvine* v. *McHardy* (1892) 19 R. 458; *Campbell* v. *Purdie* (1895) 22 R. 443.

[11] *Cameron, supra*.

[12] *Kissack* v. *Webster's Trs.* (1894) 2 S.L.T. 172; *Hynd's Tr.* v. *H's Trs.*, 1955 S.C. (H.L.) 1.

[13] *Hynd's Tr., supra*.

[14] *Laird of Gormock* v. *The Lady* (1583) Mor. 16874; *Lang* v. *L's Trs.* (1889) 16 R. 590.

opposed.[1] The notary must have no interest, direct or indirect, in the deed. Disqualifying interest includes not only direct benefit under the deed, but being thereby appointed,[2] or having his partner appointed,[3] a trustee or to act as solicitor under the deed, but probably does not include being the employee of solicitors so disqualified,[4] nor being the agent of another party to the deed.[5]

If two parties to a deed need to have it executed notarially, particularly if they have conflicting interests, separate notaries should act for each.[6]

S. 39 of the Conveyancing (Sc.) Act, 1874, did not, prior to the 1924 Act, apply to notarial execution.[7] A defect, such as a non-holograph docquet, cannot be cured after the granter's death.[8]

HOLOGRAPH WRITINGS

Deeds which are holograph, i.e. entirely or in all substantial parts in the handwriting of the granter, are deemed validly executed if signed at the end by the granter, the signatures and designation of witnesses being unnecessary.[9] The authentication statutes do not apply.[10] A wholly typewritten deed signed by the granter with a pen has been held holograph, but only where it was proved or admitted that it had been typed by the granter who had for some time habitually used a typewriter.[11] If a signed holograph deed is witnessed it is the more validly executed, and it remains valid if the witnessing is defective.[12] In the case of a testamentary

[1] *Craig* v. *Richardson* (1610) Mor. 16829; but see *Graeme* v. *G's Trs.* (1868) 7 M. 14.

[2] *Ferrie* v. *F's Trs.* (1863) 1 M. 291; *Newstead* v. *Dansken*, 1918, 1 S.L.T. 136; *Wall's Exors.*, 1939 S.L.T. (Sh. Ct.) 10. See also *Irving* v. *Snow*, 1956 S.C. 257 where notarial execution effected by Scottish notary outside Scotland.

[3] *Finlay* v. *F's Trs.*, 1948 S.C. 16; *Gorrie's Tr.* v. *Stiven's Exrx.*, 1952 S.C. 1; *Crawford's Trs.* v. *Glasgow R.I.*, 1955 S.C. 367.

[4] *Hynd's Tr.* v. *H's Trs.*, 1955 S.C. (H.L.) 1.

[5] *Lang* v. *L's Trs.* (1889) 16 R. 590.

[6] But see *Graeme* v. *G's Trs.* (1868) 7 M. 14.

[7] *Kissack* v. *Webster's Trs.* (1894) 2 S.L.T. 172. See now Conveyancing (Sc.) Act, 1924, S. 18(2).

[8] *Campbell* v. *Purdie* (1895) 22 R. 443. cf. *Walker* v. *Whitwell*, 1916 S.C. (H.L.) 75.

[9] Stair IV, 42, 6; Ersk. III, 2, 22; Bell, *Comm.* I, 341; *Prin.* §20, 2231; *Lawrie* v. *L.* (1859) 21 D. 240; *Callander* v. *C's Trs.* (1863) 2 M. 291; *Christie's Trs.* v. *Muirhead* (1870) 8 M. 461; *Maitland's Trs.* v. *M.* (1871) 10 M. 79; *Skinner* v. *Forbes* (1883) 11 R. 88; *Goldie* v. *Shedden* (1885) 13 R. 138; *Carmichael's Exors.* v. *C.*, 1909 S.C. 1387; *Bridgeford's Exor.* v. *B.*, 1948 S.C. 416; *Tucker* v. *Canch's Tr.*, 1953 S.C. 270; *Gillies* v. *Glasgow R.I.*, 1960 S.C. 438; cf. *Macnaughton* v. *Finlayson's Trs.* (1902) 10 S.L.T. 322. As to whether a telegram can be holograph see *Mowat* v. *Caledonian Banking Co.* (1895) 23 R. 270.

[10] *Macdonald* v. *Cuthbertson* (1891) 18 R. 101.

[11] *McBeath's Trs.* v. *McB.*, 1935 S.C. 471; distinguished in *Chisholm* v. *C.*, 1949 S.C. 434.

[12] *Yeats* v. *Y's Trs.* (1833) 11 S. 915; *Lorimer's Exors.* v. *Hird*, 1959 S.L.T. (Notes) 8; see also *Gunnell's Trs.* v. *Jones*, 1915, 1 S.L.T. 166.

writing in the form of a holograph letter subscription by Christian name only,[1] or by initials,[2] or by the word 'Mum',[3] has been held sufficient, when these were the granters' customary modes of authenticating holograph writings.[4] But a totally unsigned writing, or one superscribed, or one commencing with the granter's name in his own writing, are invalid even though holograph.[5]

A deed or letter written and signed by a partner in the firm name is deemed holograph of the firm.[6] A writ holograph of an authorized agent, and signed in his own name as such agent, is as binding as a writ holograph of the principal.[7] A writ can never be holograph of an incorporated body.

Any holograph deed can be holograph of only one party[8] though it may be holograph of one and adopted as holograph by another. If holograph of only one it will be valid even against him if his being bound does not depend on any other parties also being bound.[9]

A holograph deed of several pages seems not required to be signed on each page.[10]

Holograph deeds superscribed, or merely with the granter's name *in gremio* are invalid, and this informality cannot be cured.[11] But a postscript, though below the signature, may be held authenticated by it, when clearly marked as P.S.[12] Lack of subscription may, however, be cured if the holograph deed is attached to or contained in a signed deed or wrapping.[13]

[1] *Draper* v. *Thomason*, 1954 S.C. 136.   [2] *Speirs* v. *Home Speirs* (1879) 6 R. 1359.

[3] *Rhodes* v. *Peterson*, 1972 S.L.T. 98.

[4] Contrast *Russell's Trs.* v. *Henderson* (1884) 11 R. 283, where there was no such proof.

[5] *Foley* v. *Costello* (1904) 6 F. 365; *Taylor's Exces.* v. *Thom*, 1914 S.C. 79.

[6] *Nisbet* v. *Neil's Trs.* (1869) 7 M. 1097; *McLaren* v. *Law* (1871) 44 S. Jur. 17.

[7] *Whyte* v. *Lee* (1879) 6 R. 699; *Scottish Lands and Bldgs. Co.* v. *Shaw* (1880) 7 R. 756.

[8] *Goldston* v. *Young* (1868) 7 M. 188.

[9] Bell, *Prin.* § 20; *Sproul* v. *Wilson* (1809) Hume 920; *Millar* v. *Farquharson* (1835) 13 S. 838; *McMillan* v. *McM.* (1850) 13 D. 187.

[10] *Cranston* (1890) 17 R. 410; *Campbell's Exors.* v. *Maudslay*, 1934 S.L.T. 420; *Lorimer's Exors.* v. *Hird*, 1959 S.L.T. (Notes) 8.

[11] Stair IV, 42, 6; *Dunlop* v. *D.* (1839) 1 D. 912; *Skinner* v. *Forbes* (1883) 11 R. 88; *Bradford* v. *Young* (1884) 11 R. 1135; *Goldie* v. *Shedden* (1885) 13 R. 138; *Foley* v. *Costello* (1904) 6 F. 365; *Shiell* v. *S.*, 1913, 1 S.L.T. 62; *Taylor's Exces.* v. *Thom*, 1914 S.C. 79; *McKillop* v. *Secy. of State for Scotland* (1951) 39 L.C. 17. As to signature up the side see *Colvin* v. *Hutchison* (1885) 12 R. 947; *Robbie* v. *Carr*, 1959 S.L.T. (Notes) 16. As to some words below signature see *Burnie's Trs.* v. *Lawrie* (1894) 21 R. 1015; *Harvey's Trs.* v. *Carswell*, 1928 S.N. 96; *McLay* v. *Farrell*, 1950 S.C. 149. As to commencing with testator's name, see *Fraser's Exrx., infra.*

[12] *Fraser's Exrx.* v. *Fraser's C.B.*, 1931 S.C. 536.

[13] *Russell's Trs.* v. *Henderson* (1883) 11 R. 283; cf. *Speirs* v. *Home Speirs* (1879) 6 R. 1359; *Murray* v. *Kuffel*, 1910, 2 S.L.T. 388; contrast *France's J.F.* v. *F's Trs.*, 1916, 1 S.L.T. 126; *Stenhouse* v. *S.*, 1922 S.C. 370.

Holograph writings in account books,[1] receipts for partial payments on a bond,[2] and holograph postscripts to a holograph and signed letter[3] have all been held valid though not subscribed.

Corrections in holograph writs

In testamentary holograph writings a marginal addition or interlineation, if holograph of the writer of the main body of the deed, requires no authentication.[4] Deletions are similarly effective though not authenticated.[5] Words written on erasure are similarly effective.[6] The excision of a part of a typewritten will from the copy thereof with a holograph authentication has been held to cancel that part of the principal will,[7] and holograph alterations on a copy will have been held a valid codicil to the principal will.[8]

In *inter vivos* holograph deeds, alterations cannot be presumed made before delivery of the deed even though apparently holograph and require authentication.

Adoption and Incorporation

In some testamentary cases an attested or holograph writ has expressly or by implication incorporated an earlier unauthenticated holograph writing and thereby entitled it also to receive effect.[9] The question is one of intention. Even a docquet on an envelope containing the unauthenticated holograph document may have this effect,[10] and a codicil may adopt and thereby validate a defectively executed will.[11] But a holograph title on the backing sheet of an unsubscribed will has been held inadequate to validate it.[12]

---

[1] Stair IV, 12, 6; *Goldie, supra.*   [2] *Currence v. Hacket* (1688) 2 B.S. 121.

[3] *Wauchope* v. *Niddrie* (1662) Mor. 16965.

[4] *Fraser's Exrx.* v. *Fraser's C.B.*, 1931 S.C. 536, 542; *Reid's Exors.* v. *R.*, 1953 S.L.T. (Notes) 52.

[5] *Milne's Exor.* v. *Waugh*, 1913 S.C. 203; *Allan's Exrx.* v. *A.*, 1920 S.C. 732; *Gemmell's Exor.* v. *Stirling*, 1923 S.L.T. 384.

[6] *Robertson* v. *Ogilvie's Trs.* (1844) 7 D. 236.

[7] *Thomson's Trs.* v. *Bowhill Baptist Church*, 1956 S.C. 217.

[8] *Manson* v. *Edinburgh Royal Institution*, 1948 S.L.T. 196; *Lawson* v. *L.*, 1954 S.L.T. (Notes) 60.

[9] *Baird* v. *Jaap* (1856) 18 D. 1246; *Speirs* v. *Home Speirs* (1879) 6 R. 1359; *Cross's Trs.* v. *C.*, 1921, 1 S.L.T. 244; *Fraser's Exrx.* v. *F's C.B.*, 1931 S.C. 536.

[10] *Maitland's Trs.* v. *M.* (1871) 10 M. 79; *Russell's Trs.* v. *Henderson* (1883) 11 R. 283; *Murray* v. *Kuffel*, 1910, 2 S.L.T. 388; *Shiell* v. *S.*, 1913, 1 S.L.T. 62; *France's J.F.* v. *France's Trs.*, 1916, 1 S.L.T. 126; *Stenhouse* v. *S.*, 1922 S.C. 370; *Macphail's Trs.* v. *M.*, 1940 S.C. 560.

[11] *Liddle* v. *L.* (1898) 6 S.L.T. 218; *Craik's Exrx.* v. *Samson*, 1929 S.L.T. 592.

[12] *Shiell* v. *S.*, 1913, 1 S.L.T. 62; *Stenhouse, supra.*

Sometimes also an authenticated or holograph testamentary writ has sought to adopt or incorporate by anticipation any future codicil, writ or notes, even though not themselves authenticated or informally authenticated.[1] But a future 'writing under my hand' does not include an unsubscribed writing,[2] and a future 'writing' means a probative writing.[3] Nor can a testamentary writ be held to incorporate a later document which is not of a testamentary character.[4]

Incorporation applies also to bilateral contracts[5] and to bonds,[6] and unilateral acknowledgments of debt.[7]

Deeds partly holograph

The category of holograph writs extends to writs partly printed or otherwise produced and partly in the handwriting of the granter and signed by him, if the parts which are holograph are the essentials and sufficient by themselves to convey meaning and capable of receiving effect, the other parts being inessential or merely formal.[8] The deed is, however, invalid if the holograph parts do not, taken by themselves, convey meaning or are incapable of receiving effect, as where they lack executive words.[9] In later cases, concerned with purported wills, the courts have treated the deed as holograph if the holograph parts contained the minimum essentials of a will.[10] Holograph words may also be held to adopt prior non-holograph portions of the document, and validate them as if they were holograph.[11] A deed partly printed and partly holograph is wholly valid if solemnly authenticated.

---

[1] *Crosbie* v. *Wilson* (1865) 3 M. 870; *Pentland* v. *P's. Trs.* (1908) 16 S.L.T. 480; see also *Lamont* v. *Glasgow Mags.* (1887) 14 R. 603.

[2] *Inglis* v. *Harper* (1831) 5 W. & S. 785; *Wilsone's Trs.* v. *Stirling* (1861) 24 D. 163; *Young's Trs.* v. *Ross* (1864) 3 M. 10; *Parker* v. *Matheson* (1876) 13 S.L.R. 405; *Fraser* v. *Forbes' Trs.* (1899) 1 F. 513; *Hamilton's Trs.* v. *H.* (1901) 4 F. 266; *Morton* v. *French*, 1908 S.C. 171; *Waterson's Trs.* v. *St. Giles Boys Club*, 1943 S.C. 369, overruling *Gillespie* v. *Donaldson's Trs.* (1831) 10 S. 174 and *Ronald's Trs.* v. *Lyle*, 1929 S.C. 104.

[3] Bell, *Prin.* §1868; *Dundas* v. *Lowis* (1807) Mor. Appx. Writ. 6; *Morton* v. *French*, 1908 S.C. 171; *Waterson's Trs., supra*, 375.

[4] *Graham's Trs.* v. *Gillies*, 1956 S.C. 437.

[5] *McGinn* v. *Shearer*, 1947 S.C. 334; cf. *Littlejohn* v. *Hadwen* (1882) 20 S.L.R. 5, 7.

[6] *Callender* v. *C's Trs.* (1863) 2 M. 291.

[7] *Christie's Trs.* v. *Muirhead* (1870) 8 M. 461.

[8] *Christie's Trs.* v. *Muirhead* (1870) 8 M. 461; *A's Exors.* v. *B.* (1874) 11 S.L.R. 259; *Murdoch's J.F.* v. *Thomson* (1896) 4 S.L.T. 155; *Carmichael's Exors.* v. *C.*, 1909 S.C. 1387; *Paterson's Trs.* v. *Joy*, 1910 S.C. 1029; *Cameron's Trs.* v. *Mackenzie*, 1915 S.C. 313.

[9] *Macdonald* v. *Cuthbertson* (1840) 18 R. 101; *Tucker* v. *Canch's Tr.*, 1953 S.C. 270.

[10] *Bridgeford's Exor.* v. *B.*, 1948 S.C. 416; *Gillies* v. *Glasgow R.I.*, 1960 S.C. 438.

[11] *Christie's Trs.* v. *Muirhead* (1870) 8 M. 461.

Deeds adopted as holograph

A deed not holograph of a person may be made holograph of him if he writes at the end the words 'adopted as holograph' or equivalent words and signs it.[1] The signature may be above or below the words of adoption but preferably below.[2] The docquet adopting the deed as holograph must itself be holograph.[3] Exceptionally, the words 'accepted as holograph' typewritten and signed have been sustained.[4] Such a deed may be held not binding if the granter establishes that he did not understand the words.[5]

A writ which should by law be holograph or adopted as holograph may have holograph quality imparted to it, if enclosed with and referred to in a holograph writing,[6] or by holograph and signed writing in the margin referring to the rest of the text.[7]

Date

Holograph writings, unless attested, or *in re mercatoria*, do not prove their own dates against third parties,[8] save that a holograph writing of a testamentary character, in the absence of contrary evidence, is deemed to have been made of the date it bears,[9] and holograph acknowledgments of intimations of assignations prove their own dates, even against an arrester of the debt assigned.[10] Any date stated may be of evidential value, but is not conclusive, and the onus of proof of the date is on the party proponing the deed.[11]

Vicennial prescription

Holograph missive letters, bonds,[12] and subscriptions in account books without witnesses, if not pursued for within twenty

---

[1] *Weir* v. *Robertson* (1872) 10 M. 438; *Gavine's Trs.* v. *Lee* (1883) 10 R. 448; cf. *Macdonald* v. *Cuthbertson* (1890) 18 R. 101.

[2] *Gavine's Trs., supra.*

[3] *Maitland's Trs.* v. *M.* (1871) 10 M. 79; *Gavine's Trs.* v. *Lee* (1883) 10 R. 448; *Harvey* v. *Smith* (1904) 6 F. 511.

[4] *McBeath's Trs.* v. *McB.*, 1935 S.C. 471; cf. *Chisholm* v. *C.*, 1949 S.C. 434.

[5] *Harvey* v. *Smith* (1904) 6 F. 511.

[6] *Macphail's Trs.* v. *M.*, 1940 S.C. 560; *McGinn* v. *Shearer*, 1947 S.C. 334.

[7] *Liddle* v. *L.* (1898) 6 S.L.T. 218.

[8] Bell, *Prin.* §20; Dickson, *Evidence*, §775; Menzies, 150.

[9] Conveyancing Act, 1874, S. 40.

[10] *McGill* v. *Hutchison* (1630) Mor. 12605; *E. Selkirk* v. *Gray* (1708) Rob. App. 1.

[11] *Waddel* v. *W's Trs.* (1845) 7 D. 605; *Dyce* v. *Paterson* (1847) 9 D. 1141.

[12] Including all holograph writs on which an obligation can be founded, e.g. a receipt: *Mowat* v. *Banks* (1856) 18 D. 1093; but not an I.O.U.: *Craig* v. *Monteith's Exor.*, 1926 S.C. 123.

years, formerly prescribed unless the pursuer proved the verity of the holograph writing by the defender's oath.[1] After twenty years accordingly such holograph writs established nothing creative of obligation.[2] The prescriptive period runs from the date of the document.[3] They probably now subsist till extinguished by the long negative prescription.[4]

WRITINGS *IN RE MERCATORIA*

By long custom formal execution has been allowed to be dispensed with in the case of writings *in re mercatoria*,[5] which include all the variety of engagements or mandates or acknowledgments which the infinite occasions of trade may require.[6] The category includes bills of exchange, cheques and promissory notes,[7] orders for goods, mandates, procurations, guarantees, offers to buy or sell merchandise or to transport it, and acceptances thereof.[8] It has been held to include a guarantee of payment for goods supplied,[9] an arbiter's award in a mercantile reference,[10] an agreement to buy fittings in premises and take over the tenant's obligations[11] an accession by a creditor to a composition by an insolvent,[12] an acknowledgment that bonds were held on account of a particular person,[13] an agreement to apply for shares in a company,[14] an agreement to take advertising space on walls of buildings,[15] a letter explanatory of a bill,[16] submissions to arbitra-

---

[1] Prescription Act, 1669; *Craig* v. *Monteith's Exor.*, 1926 S.C. 123; *Baird* v. *B's Trs.*, 1954 S.C. 290.

[2] *Bank of Scotland* v. —— (1747) 5 B.S. 748.

[3] *Home* v. *Donaldson* (1773) Mor. 10992; *Macadam* v. *Findlay*, 1911 S.C. 1366; *Dick* v. *Thomson's Trs.*, 1929 S.L.T. 637.

[4] Prescription and Limitation (Sc.) Act, 1973, S. 7.

[5] Ersk. III, 2, 24; Bell, *Comm.* I, 342; *Prin.* §21; Bell, *Convg.* I, 96; Menzies, 159; Wood, 97; Gloag, 185. The expression should receive wide interpretation: *Beardmore* v. *Barry*, 1928 S.C. 101, 110; 1928 S.C. (H.L.) 47.

[6] Bell, *Comm.* I, 342.

[7] Bills of Exchange Act, 1882, Ss. 3, 17 and 32. To warrant summary diligence bills and notes must be dated and signed.

[8] Bell, *supra.*

[9] *Paterson* v. *Wright* (1814) 6 Paton 38.

[10] *Dykes* v. *Roy* (1869) 7 M. 357.

[11] *Kinnimont* v. *Paxton* (1892) 20 R. 128.

[12] Bell, *Comm.* II, 398; *Henry* v. *Strachan & Spence* (1897) 24 R. 1045.

[13] *Stuart* v. *Potter, Choate & Prentice*, 1911 1 S.L.T. 377.

[14] *Beardmore, supra.*

[15] *U.K. Advertising Co.* v. *Glasgow Bag Wash Laundry*, 1926 S.C. 303.

[16] *Thoms* v. *T.* (1867) 6 M. 174.

tions and awards therein in mercantile and agricultural arbitrations.[1]

It has been held not to include a promise to pay an uncertain person,[2] a special document framed to raise money,[3] the engagement of a salesman for longer than a year,[4] an acknowledgment of loan of money,[5] nor a lease of premises.[6]

Docquets of acknowledgment or discharge written on business books or accounts are in the same position as writings *in re mercatoria*.[7] The onus is heavily on the party challenging a docquetted account to prove its inaccuracy.[8]

Doubt exists whether the classes of guarantees within the Mercantile Law Amendment (Sc.) Act, 1856, S. 6, are within the *res mercatoria* category.[9]

A writing *in re mercatoria*, though not attested or holograph, may be authenticated by bare subscription,[10] or even initials[11] or possibly even by cross or mark[12] if that is the party's customary mode of authentication.

Such a writing, if admitted or proved to be signed or initialled by the granter, proves its own date for its mercantile purpose,[13] though not necessarily for any other purpose.[14] Bills and promissory notes, if intended to found summary diligence, must be signed and dated.

WRITINGS STATUTORILY PRIVILEGED

Statutes have in certain case prescribed or permitted special modes of authentication. These include: One witness only: bills of

---

[1] *Nivison* v. *Howat* (1883) 11 R. 182; *Hope* v. *Crookston Bros.* (1890) 17 R. 868; *Cameron* v. *Nicol*, 1930 S.C. 1; *McLaren* v. *Aikman*, 1939 S.C. 222, 228.

[2] *Thomson* v. *Philp* (1867) 5 M. 679.

[3] *Commercial Bank* v. *Kennard* (1859) 21 D. 864.

[4] *Stewart & MacDonald* v. *McCall* (1869) 7 M. 544.

[5] *Paterson* v. *P.* (1897) 25 R. 144.

[6] *Danish Dairy Co.* v. *Gillespie*, 1922 S.C. 656.

[7] *McLaren* v. *Liddell's Trs.* (1860) 22 D. 373; *Fell* v. *Rattray* (1869) 41 Sc. Jur. 236. They may be effective even though not subscribed, if holograph: Stair IV, 42, 6; Dickson, *Evidence* §799. See also *Stephen* v. *Pirie* (1832) 10 S. 279; *Elder* v. *Smith* (1829) 7 S. 656; *Boswell* v. *Montgomerie* (1836) 14 S. 554; *Walker* v. *Drummond* (1836) 14 S. 780; *Laing* v. *L.* (1862) 24 D. 1362. Contrast *Laidlaw* v. *Wilson* (1844) 6 D. 530; *McAdie* v. *McA's Exrx.* (1883) 10 R. 741.

[8] *Laing, supra*; *Struthers* v. *Smith*, 1913 S.C. 1116.

[9] See *Snaddon* v. *London, etc. Assce. Co.* (1902) 5 F. 182.

[10] Bell, *Comm.* I, 342; *Ramsay and Hay* v. *Pyronon* (1632) Mor. 16963.

[11] Bell, *Comm.* I, 343; *Thomson* v. *Crichton* (1676) Mor. 16968.

[12] *Ibid*; *Rose* v. *Johnston* (1878) 5 R. 600.

[13] *Ibid*.

[14] Dickson, *Evidence* §794; cf. *Purvis* v. *Dowie* (1869) 7 M. 764.

sale or mortgages of ships;[1] memorandum and articles of association of companies.[2]

No witness: deeds executed on behalf of a company by the affixing of the seal and subscription by two directors or a director and the secretary;[3] transfer of registered securities;[4] hire-purchase agreements;[5] testamentary nominations under the rules of trade unions, friendly societies and industrial and provident societies.[6]

Authentication by mark: certain testamentary nominations;[7] marriage notices.[8]

THE QUALITY OF BEING PROBATIVE

A probative document is one which, in respect that it complies on the face of it with the prescribed legal formalities, is held to prove the verity of the legal *actus* expressed in it as the genuine *actus* of its author.[9] A deed or writing which is probative proves itself in judicial proceedings, its genuineness is assumed until it is judicially reduced, and the evidence of granter and witnesses that they signed as such is unnecessary.[10] The onus is on a party challenging such a deed to prove that, despite appearances, it was not truly the granter's deed,[11] and it is a heavy onus.[12] A deed or writing which is not probative may be valid and legally effectual

---

[1] Merchant Shipping Act, 1894, S. 24(2).

[2] Companies Act, 1948, Ss. 3, 9(d).

[3] Companies Act, 1948, S. 32(4).

[4] Stock Transfer Act, 1963, S. 1(2).

[5] Hire-Purchase (Sc.) Act, 1965, S. 5(1)(a); *U.D.T. (Commercial) Ltd.* v. *Lindsay*, 1959 S.L.T. (Sh. Ct.) 58.

[6] Friendly Societies Acts, 1896, Ss. 56–7 and 1955, S. 5; Industrial and Provident Societies Act, 1965, S. 23.

[7] e.g. National Savings Bank Regulations, 1966, reg. 46; see also *Morton* v. *French*, 1908 S.C. 171.

[8] Marriage Notice (Sc.) Act, 1878, S. 16.

[9] Bell, *Prin.* §2223; *McBeath's Trs.* v. *McB.*, 1935 S.C. 471, 476.

[10] Menzies, 80; *Reid* v. *Kedder* (1840) 1 Rob. App. 183; *Grant* v. *Shepherd* (1847) 6 Bell 153; *Boswell* v. *B.* (1852) 14 D. 378; *Ferrie* v. *F's Trs.* (1863) 1 M. 291, 298; *Munro* v. *Butler Johnstone* (1868) 7 M. 250; *Hamilton* v. *Lindsay-Bucknall* (1869) 8 M. 323, 327; *McLaren* v. *Menzies* (1876) 3 R. 1151; *Walker* v. *Whitwell*, 1916 S.C. (H.L.) 75, 90; *McBeath's Trs.* v. *McB.*, 1935 S.C. 471, 476; *Irving* v. *Snow*, 1956 S.C. 257, 261.

[11] *Hamilton, supra*; *Boyd* v. *Shaw*, 1927 S.C. 414.

[12] *Smith* v. *Bank of Scotland* (1824) 2 Sh. App. 265; *Cleland* v. *C.* (1838) 1 D. 254; *Donaldson* v. *Stewart* (1842) 4 D. 1215; *Morrison* v. *Maclean's Trs.* (1863) 1 M. 304; *Baird's Trs.* v. *Murray* (1884) 11 R. 153; *Stirling Stuart* v. *Stirling Crawfurd's Trs.* (1885) 12 R. 610; *Young* v. *Paton*, 1910 S.C. 63; *Boyd, supra*; *McArthur* v. *McA's Trs.*, 1931 S.L.T. 463.

but if challenged, the onus is on the party relying on it to establish that it is the granter's deed.[1]

A writing which has been authenticated in accordance with the statutory solemnities is deemed probative,[2] as is a deed notarially executed in accordance with the statutory requirements.[3]

A writing containing blanks not completed before the deed is founded on is not probative but may be effectual as to clauses other than those containing the blanks.[4]

A writing suffering from informality of execution curable under the Conveyancing (Sc.) Act, 1874, S. 39, is not probative but is equally valid and effectual when the defects are cured.

Holograph deeds are not probative,[5] but are equally valid as affording proof of authenticity and of deliberate undertaking if their authenticity is admitted, or established by the person founding on them, frequently *comparatione literarum*. It must be proved not only that text and signature are in the same hand, but that both are in the hand of the granter.[6] In discharging this onus of proof, it is not sufficient to show that the deed has been accepted as holograph by the commissary court for its own purposes, on the strength of affidavits as to handwriting produced to it.[7] Nor does a declaration *in gremio* that the deed is holograph of the granter relieve the proponer of the deed of the onus of proving its validity.[8]

The Conveyancing Amendment (Sc.) Act, 1938, S. 11, however, provided that any writing of a testamentary character on which confirmation of executors nominate had, before its commencement, been granted should be deemed probative as a link in title, but in subsequent cases the validity of the holograph writing had to be established judicially.

The Wills Act, 1963, S. 5,[9] provided that any testamentary instrument should be treated as probative for the conveyance of heritage if confirmation of executors to property disposed of

---

[1] *McIntyre* v. *National Bank*, 1910 S.C. 150.

[2] *Ferrie, supra*; *McLaren* v. *Menzies* (1876) 3 R. 1151.

[3] *Ferrie, supra*; *Hynd's Tr.* v. *H's Trs.*, 1954 S.C. 112.

[4] See *E. Buchan* v. *Scottish Widows Fund* (1857) 19 D. 551; Walkers, 198.

[5] *Cranston* (1890) 17 R. 410, 415. See also Bell, *Prin.* §2231; *Maitland's Trs.* v. *M.* (1871) 10 M. 79.

[6] *Anderson* v. *Gill* (1860) 3 Macq. 180.

[7] *Frederick* v. *Craig*, 1932 S.L.T. 315.

[8] *Anderson* v. *Gill* (1858) 3 Macq. 180; *Harper* v. *Green*, 1938 S.C. 198. Such a declaration was sufficient to justify the grant of confirmation to carry moveable estate: *Cranston* (1890) 17 R. 410.

[9] This section was in force from 1 Jan. 1964 to 9 Sept. 1964, when it was repealed by the Succession (Sc.) Act, 1964.

therein had been issued in Scotland, or a grant of representation made elsewhere had been sealed in Scotland. The Succession (Sc.) Act, 1964, S. 21, now provides that confirmation of an executor to property disposed of in a holograph testamentary disposition is not to be granted unless the court is satisfied by evidence, consisting at least of an affidavit by each of two persons that the writing and signature of the disposition are in the handwriting of the testator. Such a disposition is not accordingly probative. S. 32 substantially re-enacts S. 5 of the 1963 Act but applying it to entitlement to any property, heritable or moveable.

Writings *in re mercatoria* are not probative though valid unless their authenticity is challenged. If challenged, the person founding on the writing must prove its execution and the genuineness of the signature.[1]

Writings statutorily privileged are probably not probative.

---

[1] Ersk. III, 2, 24; Bell, *Comm.* I, 342; *Prin.* §21, 2232; *McIntyre* v. *National Bank*, 1910 S.C. 150.

CHAPTER 7

INTERPRETATION OF DEEDS AND WRITINGS

WRITINGS include not only formally authenticated deeds but all matter of printed documents, holograph writings, writings *in re mercatoria*, and others. They may constitute, or be intended to constitute contracts, copartneries, assignations, dispositions, wills, or to have other legal effect, and interpretation is frequently necessary to determine what, if any, intention is expressed therein, and what legal effect should be given to the words used.[1]

The primary rule is that the granter's intention must be discovered from the expressions used; if the words used are clear and unambiguous they must receive effect, but if they are not, the intention, if discoverable by any reasonable construction, should prevail.[2] In discovering the general intention the deed must be read and interpreted as a whole, so that, if possible, the different parts of the deed are consistent one with another.[3] The words used may be so vague that the court cannot discover any intention with any certainty at all, in which case the deed is unenforceable.[4] A court may find that a writ is a complete nullity.[5]

Words should *prima facie* be given their plain, ordinary and literal meaning,[6] but may be given a special or technical meaning

---

[1] See generally Stair IV, 42, 20–1; Bankt. I, 11, 53; Ersk. III, 3, 87; Bell, *Prin.* §524, 1871, 1879; See also particularly in relation to contracts and wills Chs. 34, 121, *infra*. As to meanings given to words in previous cases see Gibb and Dalrymple, *Scottish Judicial Dictionary*; Stroud, *Judicial Dictionary*; Saunders (ed.), *Words and Phrases Legally Defined*.

[2] cf. Stair IV, 42, 21(4) and (5); *N.B. Oil Co.* v. *Swann* (1868) 6 M. 835; *Burnett* v. *G.N.S. Ry.* (1884) 12 R. (H.L.) 25; *Gore-Brown-Henderson's Trs.* v. *Grenfell*, 1968 S.C. 73, 82.

[3] Ersk. III, 3, 87; Bell, *Prin.* §524; *N.E. Ry.* v. *Hastings* [1900] A.C. 260, 269.

[4] e.g. *McArthur* v. *Lawson* (1877) 4 R. 1134; *Traill* v. *Dewar* (1881) 8 R. 583; *Young* v. *Dougans* (1887) 14 R. 490.

[5] e.g. *Anderson* v. *A.*, 1961 S.C. 59.

[6] *Buchanan* v. *Andrew* (1873) 11 M. (H.L.) 13; *Caledonian Ry.* v. *N.B. Ry.* (1881) 8 R. (H.L.) 23, 30; *Burnett* v. *G.N.S. Ry.* (1884) 12 R. (H.L.) 25; *Crosse* v. *Banks* (1886) 13 R. (H.L.) 40; *Gatty* v. *Maclaine*, 1921 S.C. (H.L.) 1; *Dunbar Mags.* v. *Mackersy*, 1931 S.C. 180.

if used in connection with the usage of some trade or profession.[1] Some words such as 'property' in a will, are so indefinite that only consideration of the whole scheme of the will in relation to the testator's known circumstances can render the word definite.[2] If a plain word appears to bear an unusual meaning, it will be presumed to bear that meaning throughout the deed.[3]

The punctuation of a deed may be considered for the purpose of aiding its construction.[4]

Usage of trade or profession

Professional or trade usage may attach a particular meaning to a word or phrase, or may imply a term into a contract, but not fly in the face of plain words in the contract.[5]

Preference for validity

When in doubt the court will prefer the construction which makes the writing valid and effective to one which renders it ineffective.[6] Similarly, the preference should be given to a construction which gives a meaning to each word and phrase of the deed, though redundant or meaningless words may have been incorporated from a style.

Whether writing deliberative or final

Particularly in relation to wills a question has frequently arisen whether a writing was intended to be a draft, memorandum or jotting, or an expression of concluded intention. The decision depends on consideration of the whole circumstances, including the title and words used.[7]

---

[1] *Thomson* v. *Garioch* (1841) 3 D. 625; *Mackenzie* v. *Dunlop* (1853) 16 D. 129; (1856) 3 Macq. 22; *Hunter* v. *Miller* (1862) 24 D. 1011; *Jack* v. *Roberts* (1865) 3 M. 554; *Fleming* v. *Airdrie Iron Co.* (1882) 9 R. 473. In particular words used in the context of charter-parties, bills of lading or insurance policies must be taken to be used in the sense which such words have long been understood to bear in such contexts: *Salvesen* v. *Guy* (1885) 13 R. 85; *McCowan* v. *Baine & Johnston* (1890) 17 R. 1016; affd. (1891) 18 R. (H.L.) 57; *Lamont, Nisbett & Co.* v. *Hamilton*, 1907 S.C. 628.

[2] e.g. *McLeod's Tr.* v. *McLuckie* (1883) 10 R. 1056; *Oag's Curator* v. *Corner* (1885) 12 R. 1162; *Craw's Trs.* v. *Blacklock*, 1920 S.C. 22.

[3] *Martin* v. *Kelso* (1853) 15 D. 950.

[4] *Turnbull's Trs.* v. *L.A.*, 1918 S.C. (H.L.) 88.

[5] *Tancred Arrol* v. *Steel Co. of Scotland* (1890) 17 R. (H.L.) 31.

[6] Bell, *Prin.* §524(3); *Brown* v. *Sutherland* (1875) 2 R. 615; *Muir* v. *City of Glasgow Bank* (1879) 6 R. (H.L.) 21; *Ainslie's Trs.* v. *Imlach's Exors.*, 1926 S.L.T. 28; *Scottish Farmers Dairy Co.* v. *McGhee*, 1933 S.L.T. 142; cf. *Barr* v. *Waldie* (1893) 21 R. 224, 228.

[7] See Ch. 121, *infra.*

Whether document prepared by lawyer or layman

In deeds or documents professionally prepared words and phrases commonly used in legal contexts are presumed to be used in the sense settled by law, and having their technical legal import. Thus such terms as 'heir at law' and 'next of kin' have settled meanings and will be presumed used with those meanings.[1]

But no such presumption can arise where the document was not professionally prepared, as a word or phrase having a technical connotation may have been used in ignorance thereof and with another intention.[2] Similarly a more liberal construction can be given to documents *inter rusticos*.

Blanks

The effect of a blank in a document varies with the circumstances. Bonds blank as to the name of the creditor, and circulating as negotiable instruments, were declared null by statute.[3] The signature of a bill of exchange blank in any material particular is authority to the person in possession to complete the blank in any way he thinks fit.[4] A signature on blank stamped paper may be authority to the person to whom it is delivered to fill it up as a complete bill of exchange, using the signature for that of the drawer or acceptor or indorser.[4] The onus of proving that the bill was incomplete when delivered, and was completed contrary to his instructions, is on the person who signed the incomplete bill, and it is not for the holder to establish that the bill is in order.[5]

In the case of a feucharter doubts have been expressed as to the competency of filling in from inference from the context a blank in the description of the subjects disponed.[6]

While there is some authority for the view that formal execution of a deed with blanks authorizes its subsequent completion in accordance with the express or implied consent of the granter,[7] it is thought that any part of the deed inserted after the granter's signature can be effective only if the granter is personally barred from challenging its validity. A deed containing blanks is not

---

[1] Stair IV, 42, 21; *Inglis* v. *I.* (1869) 7 M. 435; *Glen* v. *Stewart* (1874) 1 R. (H.L.) 48; *Gregory's Trs.* v. *Alison* (1889) 16 R. (H.L.) 10; *Fulton's Tr.* v. *F.* (1900) 8 S.L.T. 465; *Rutherford's Trs.* v. *Dickie*, 1907 S.C. 1280; *Murray's Factor* v. *Melrose*, 1910 S.C. 924.

[2] cf. Stair IV, 42, 21.

[3] Blank Bonds and Trusts Act, 1696 (c. 25).

[4] Bills of Exchange Act, 1882, S. 20; cf. *Russell* v. *Banknock Coal Co.* (1897) 24 R. 1009.

[5] *Anderson* v. *Somerville, Murray & Co.* (1898) 1 F. 90.

[6] *Musselburgh Mags.* v. *Musselburgh Real Estate Co.* (1904) 7 F. 308.

[7] E. *Buchan* v. *Scottish Widows' Fund* (1857) 19 D. 551; *Carswell's Trs.* v. *C.* (1896) 3 S.L.T. 218.

probative, but may be effectual, depending on the importance of the clause containing the blank. If it is admitted or proved that a deed contained blanks and these have been completed subsequent to execution, the deed is probably not probative unless the completion is mentioned in the testing clause;[1] otherwise the presumption is that the blanks were completed later and the onus is on the party founding on the deed to show that they were completed before execution or with the consent of the granter.[2]

If a deed contains blanks when founded on in court the blank may leave the obligation subsisting[3] or render it wholly ineffectual.[4] If when founded on blanks have been completed the words inserted should be ignored.[5]

The Blank Bonds and Trusts Act, 1696, also provides that all bonds, assignations, dispositions or other deeds, but excepting the bills of exchange or notes of a trading company, subscribed when blank as to the name of the person or persons in whose favour they are conceived, are null, unless the name of the creditor, assignee or disponee is inserted at the time of subscription or before delivery, in the presence of the witnesses who attested the granter's subscription. The onus of proving that the deed was blank as to the name is on the party challenging the deed; the onus is then on the party founding on the deed to establish that the name was inserted before delivery, and in the presence of the witnesses.[6] Despite the Act it has been held that the nullity affects only the names inserted and the clauses affected thereby.[7]

Clerical errors

The court may treat as a mere clerical error, and correct, a word or phrase in a deed, if satisfied that it does not correctly represent the intention of the parties.[8] In one case the court allowed a clerical error in the testing clause of a deed given in for registration in the Books of Council and Session to be corrected, reserving opinions as to the effect of the amendment.[9] In inter-

---

[1] cf. Dickson, *Evidence* 659; Walkers, *Evidence* §184(b).
[2] cf. *E. Buchan* v. *Scottish Widows' Fund* (1857) 19 D. 551.
[3] *Buchanan* v. *Dickie* (1828) 6 S. 986.   [4] *Ewen* v. *E's Trs.* (1830) 4 W. & S. 346.
[5] *Pentland* v. *Hare* (1829) 7 S. 640; *E. Buchan* v. *Scottish Widows' Fund* (1857) 19 D. 551.
[6] *Donaldson* v. *D.* (1749) Mor. 9080.
[7] *Kennedy* v. *Arbuthnot* (1722) Mor. 1681; *Pentland* v. *Hare* (1829) 7 S. 640; *Abernethie* v. *Forbes* (1835) 13 S. 263; cf. *Robertson* v. *Ogilvie's Trs.* (1844) 7 D. 236.
[8] *Glen's Trs.* v. *Lancashire, etc. Ins. Co.* (1906) 8 F. 915; *Krupp* v. *Menzies*, 1907 S.C. 903; cf. *Carricks* v. *Saunders* (1850) 12 D. 812; *McLaren* v. *Liddell's Trs.* (1862) 24 D. 577; *N.B. Ins. Co.* v. *Tunnock & Fraser* (1864) 3 M. 1, 5.
[9] *Caldwell* (1871) 10 M. 99.

preting a will the court has held itself entitled to read one figure for another where this was a manifest error,[1] and to insert, delete or substitute words if satisfied that that is necessary to give effect to the testator's intention.[2] In some cases proof that the document contains a clerical error justifies reduction of the whole document.[3]

The court has, however, no power to make a new bargain for the parties or alter the deed to make it conform to their real intention, or to their prior agreement which it professes to implement; only reduction is competent.[4]

Grammatical error

The court may ignore a grammatical error if it would otherwise nullify the obvious intention of the granter.[5]

Inaccuracy

An inaccurate description does not vitiate if the person or thing designated is recognizable and there is no ambiguity.[6] Similarly an inaccurate enumeration of beneficiaries in a will does not vitiate the gift.[7]

Supplying omission by inference

Where there is an omission or lacuna in a document, the court will rarely supply missing words by inference.[8] But if in the absence of express words the court is judicially convinced that the parties had a particular intention, which by mistake was not expressed, effect may be given to the intention.[9]

---

[1] *Reid's Trs.* v. *Bucher*, 1929 S.C. 615; contrast *Crawford's Trs.* v. *Fleck*, 1910 S.C. 998.

[2] *Crawford's Trs., supra; Scott's Trs.* v. *Bruce*, 1912 S.C. 105; *Robertson's Trs.* v. *R.*, 1969 S.C. 290.

[3] *Glasgow Feuing Co.* v. *Watson's Trs.* (1887) 14 R. 610. In *Anderson* v. *Lambie*, 1954 S.C. (H.L.) 43, the error was not merely clerical, but common error of the solicitors for the parties.

[4] *Steuart's Trs.* v. *Hart* (1875) 3 R. 192, 200; *Anderson, supra.*

[5] *Glen's Trs.* v. *Lancashire and Yorkshire Accident Ins. Co.* (1906) 8 F. 915.

[6] *Wilson's Exors.* v. *Scottish Socy. for Conversion of Israel* (1869) 8 M. 233 (beneficiary); *Speirs* v. *S's Trs.* (1878) 5 R. 923 (designation in testing clause); *Jaffrey's Trs.* v. *S.P.C.A.* (1903) 10 S.L.T. 651; *Allison* v. *Anderson* (1907) 15 S.L.T. 529; *McGrouther's Trs.* v. *L.A.* (1907) 15 S.L.T. 653; cf. *Nasmyth's Trs.* v. *N.S.P.C.C.*, 1914 S.C. (H.L.) 76; *Ormiston's Exor.* v. *Laws*, 1966 S.C. 47.

[7] *Bryce's Tr.* (1878) 5 R. 722; *Lumsden's Trs.* v. *L.*, 1921 1 S.L.T. 155.

[8] *Murdoch* v. *Brass* (1904) 6 F. 841; *Crawford's Trs.* v. *Fleck*, 1910 S.C. 998; contrast *Scott's Trs.* v. *Bruce*, 1912 S.C. 105.

[9] *Dundee Mags.* v. *Duncan* (1883) 11 R. 145.

Liberal interpretation of testamentary writings

A more liberal interpretation may be given to testamentary writings than to deeds *inter vivos,* particularly if not drafted professionally.[1]

Presumption for freedom of property

Words restricting or limiting the ordinary rights of property are narrowly construed, as imposing no greater restriction than they clearly bear.[2]

Construction contra proferentem

Where a bilateral document has been framed entirely by one of the parties, the court resolves ambiguities in a sense unfavourable to the party who framed the deed.[3] Similarly where a contract framed by one party purports to limit or exclude that party's liability in certain circumstances the exception clause is strictly construed.[4] A clause in a contract under which indemnity was sought against claims by third parties has been held not to extend to claims based on the pursuer's own negligence.[5] A bond of caution framed by the creditor is construed in the sense most unfavourable to him.[6] Similarly private Acts of Parliament fall to be construed *contra proferentem.*[7]

Regard to context

Any particular word or phrase must be read in its context.[8]

---

[1] Stair IV, 42, 21(7); Ersk. III, 9, 14.

[2] Stair IV, 42, 21; see *Hood* v. *Traill* (1884) 12 R. 362; *Bainbridge* v. *Campbell,* 1912 S.C. 92; *Anderson* v. *Dickie,* 1914 S.C. 706, affd. 1915 S.C. (H.L.) 79.

[3] Stair IV, 42, 21(2); Ersk. III, 3, 8, 7; *Hutchison* v. *National Loan Assce. Socy.* (1845) 7 D. 467; *Life Assoc.* v. *Foster* (1873) 11 M. 351; *Birrell* v. *Dryer* (1884) 11 R. (H.L.) 41; *Sangster's Trs.* v. *General Accident Corpn.* (1896) 24 R. 56; *Reid* v. *Employer's Accident Ins. Co.* (1899) 1 F. 1031; *Hunter* v. *General Accident Corpn.,* 1909 S.C. 344; 1909 S.C. (H.L.) 30; *Dawsons, Ltd.* v. *Bonnin,* 1922 S.C. (H.L.) 156; *Aitken's Trs.* v. *Bank of Scotland,* 1944 S.C. 270.

[4] *L.N.E. Ry.* v. *Neilson* [1922] 2 A.C. 263; *Ballingall* v. *Dundee Ice Co.,* 1924 S.C. 238; *McCutcheon* v. *Macbrayne,* 1964 S.C. (H.L.) 28.

[5] *N. of S. Hydro-Electric Board* v. *Taylor,* 1956 S.C. 1.

[6] Bell, *Comm.* I, 390; *Prin.* §251; *Napier* v. *Bruce* (1840) 2 D. 556; affd. (1842) 1 Bell 78; *Bayne* v. *Russell* (1869) 7 S.L.R. 101; *Veitch* v. *National Bank,* 1907 S.C. 554; *Harmer* v. *Gibb,* 1911 S.C. 1341; *Aitken's Trs.* v. *Bank of Scotland,* 1944 S.C. 270.

[7] *Scottish Drainage Co.* v. *Campbell* (1889) 16 R. (H.L.) 16; *Colquhoun* v. *Glasgow Procurators' Widows Fund* (1904) 7 F. 345, revd. 1908 S.C. (H.L.) 10.

[8] *N.B. Oil Co.* v. *Swann* (1868) 6 M. 835.

Expressio unius est exclusio alterius

The principle expressed by this maxim applies to contracts as well as to statutes.[1]

Ejusdem generis

The *ejusdem generis* principle[2] applies to deeds and writings as much as to statutes.[3]

Words of reference

Where words are used referring back to a person or subject previously referred to, *prima facie* the words refer to the nearest antecedent capable of sustaining the reference.[4]

Implied terms

In interpreting contracts a common problem is to determine whether or not, and, if so, what terms are to be held implied in the contract by virtue of statute, general rules of common law, custom and usage or the previous actings of parties.[5]

Specialia generalibus derogant

Where there is both a general and a special disposition of property, it is presumed that the property specially mentioned derogates from the general disposition, and to that extent reduces it.[6]

Ambiguity

An ambiguity may be patent, where on the face of the deed there is an uncertainty as to the meaning of word or phrase,[7] or latent, where the deed seems clear, but further information about

---

[1] Ch. 1, *supra*; see also *Chaplin's Trs.* v. *Hoile* (1891) 19 R. 237; *Kilwinning P.C.* v. *Cunninghame Combination Board*, 1909 S.C. 829; *Campbell* v. *McCutcheon*, 1963 S.C. 505.

[2] Ch. 1, *supra*; cf. Ersk. III, 4, 9.

[3] *Lee* v. *Alexander* (1883) 10 R. (H.L.) 91, 93; *Thames & Mersey Ins. Co.* v. *Hamilton* (1887) 12 App. Cas. 484; *Lilly* v. *Stevenson* (1895) 22 R. 278; (charter party); *Gore Booth's Tr.* v. *G.B.* (1898) 25 R. 803 (will); *Glasgow Corpn.* v. *Glasgow Tramways Co.* (1898) 25 R. (H.L.) 77; *Admiralty* v. *Burns*, 1910 S.C. 531 (lease); *Abchurch S.S. Co.* v. *Stinnes*, 1911 S.C. 1010 (charter party); *Arden S.S. Co.* v. *Mathwin*, 1912 S.C. 211 (charter party); *Milne's Trs.* v. *Davidson*, 1956 S.C. 81 (will).

[4] *Shepherd's Trs.* v. *S.*, 1945 S.C. 60 ('children of the said J.S.').

[5] See further Chap. 34, *infra*.

[6] *Nixon* v. *Rogerson's Exor.* (1882) 20 S.L.R. 10; *Montgomery's Trs.* v. *M.* (1895) 22 R. 824; *Alexander* v. *A.* (1896) 23 R. 724.

[7] e.g. *Watcham* v. *A.G. of S.A. Protectorate* [1919] A.C. 533 (land described by boundaries and by acreage, and discrepancy).

the background facts reveals that there is ambiguity.[1] If the ambiguity is patent the court must decide which interpretation should be put on the ambiguous phrase.[2] Extrinsic evidence is, however, admissible as to the background facts to clear up a latent ambiguity.[3] Even in cases of patent ambiguity it has some-times been held necessary and competent to give evidence of surrounding circumstances so that the court has before it all the information available to the parties when they contracted when it is putting a construction on the deed which they entered into.[4]

Ambiguous expressions construed as obligatory

An ambiguous expression will normally be construed as obligatory rather than as giving a party an avenue of escape.[5] Any exception, or exemption, should be expressed.

Party not to be permitted to benefit from own default

Ambiguous terms will not generally be construed in a way which permits a party to take advantage from his own default or breach of duty. If a contract is to be void in certain events, a party cannot make it void by his own action to evade loss or to suit his own convenience.[6] Similarly a party may not derogate from his own grant or undertaking.[7]

Presumption against donation

Where words clearly import donation or gratuitous under-taking they should receive effect; but in doubt, they are not to be understood as obliging gratuitously so that an undertaking to

---

[1] e.g. *Morton v. Hunter* (1830) 4 W. & S. 379; *Logans v. Wright* (1831) 5 W. & S. 242; *Houldsworth v. Gordon Cumming*, 1910 S.C. (H.L.) 49.

[2] Bell, *Prin.* §524; *Logan, supra*; *Lee v. Alexander* (1882) 10 R. 230; (1883) 10 R. (H.L.) 91.

[3] *Macdonald v. Newall* (1898) 1 F. 68; *Houldsworth, supra*; *Robertson's Tr. v. Riddell*, 1911 S.C. 14; *McAdam v. Scott*, 1913, 1 S.L.T. 12; *Hay v. Duthie's Trs.*, 1956 S.C. 511.

[4] *Gray v. G's Trs.* (1878) 5 R. 820; *Welsh's Tr. v. Forbes* (1885) 12 R. 851; *Bank of Scotland v. Stewart* (1891) 18 R. 957; *Stewart v. Shannessy* (1900) 2 F. 1288; *Claddagh S.S. Co. v. Steven*, 1919 S.C. 184; 1919 S.C. (H.L.) 132.

[5] *Menzies v. Barstow* (1840) 2 D. 1317; *Seitz v. Brown* (1872) 10 M. 681; *Ballantine v. Employers Ins. Co.* (1893) 21 R. 305; *Kilmarnock Dist. Cttee. v. Somerwell* (1906) 14 S.L.T. 567; *Nelson v. Dundee E. Coast Shipping Co.*, 1907 S.C. 927; *D/S Danmark v. Poulsen*, 1913 S.C. 1043; *Schele v. Lumsden*, 1916 S.C. 709.

[6] *Kinloch v. Mansfield* (1836) 14 S. 905; *Burns v. Martin* (1885) 12 R. 1343, revd. (1887) 14 R. (H.L.) 20; *Bidoulac v. Sinclair's Tr.* (1889) 17 R. 144; cf. *N.Z. Shipping Co. v. Societe des Ateliers de France* [1919] A.C. 1, 12; *Maritime National Fish v. Ocean Trawlers* [1935] A.C. 524; *Beresford v. Royal Ins.* [1938] A.C. 586.

[7] *Barr v. Lions*, 1956 S.C. 59.

deliver imports loan rather than gift,[1] and an unqualified receipt for money implies loan rather than gift or other ground for payment.[2]

Contemporanea expositio

Where words are ambiguous and equally susceptible of two meanings, if the document has been for long acted on by the parties in a particular sense, such may be held to be the true construction, and may receive effect accordingly.[3] So too where the document is silent as to a matter, it may be interpreted according to the practice of parties under it.[4] Though *contemporanea expositio* is a valuable guide to the interpretation of an old deed[5] it is of little value as to recent contracts.[6]

Demonstrative or taxative

A description in a deed of the subjects of a contract may be demonstrative, i.e. indicating the subjects in question, or taxative, i.e. limiting the subjects to those mentioned. A description limited by the word 'only' is plainly taxative. Thus a description of lands conveyed as being those possessed by the granter or another will usually be held to limit the grant to the lands so possessed.[7] If lands are described by boundaries and their measurements, the latter will normally be held demonstrative only,[8] but otherwise if described by their measurements alone.

[1] Stair IV, 42; 21(6); Ersk. III, 3, 92; cf. *Thomson* v. *Geekie* (1861) 23 D. 693; *Gill* v. *G.*, 1907 S.C. 532.

[2] *Martin* v. *Crawford* (1850) 12 D. 960; *Fraser* v. *Bruce* (1857) 20 D. 115; *Robertson* v. *R.* (1858) 20 D. 371; *Thomson, supra*; *Christie's Trs.* v. *Muirhead* (1870) 8 M. 461; *Duncan's Trs.* v. *Shand* (1873) 11 M. 254; *Gill, supra*. This does not apply to a paid cheque: *Haldane* v. *Speirs* (1872) 10 M. 537; *Scotland* v. *S.*, 1909 S.C. 505.

[3] *Heriot's Hospital* v. *Macdonald* (1830) 4 W. & S. 98; *Pagan* v. *Macrae* (1860) 22 D. 806; *L.A.* v. *Sinclair* (1867) 5 M. (H.L.) 97; *Russell* v. *Cowpar* (1882) 9 R. 660; *Dundee Mags.* v. *Duncan* (1883) 11 R. 145; *Jopp's Trs.* v. *Edmond* (1888) 15 R. 271; cf. *Hunter* v. *Barron's Trs.* (1886) 13 R. 883; *Mackay* v. *Maclachlan* (1899) 7 S.L.T. 48.

[4] *Hewats* v. *Roberton* (1881) 9 R. 175; *Argyllshire Commrs. of Supply* v. *Campbell* (1885) 12 R. 1255; *Shearer* v. *Peddie* (1899) 1 F. 1201; *Macgill* v. *Park* (1899) 2 F. 272; *Boyd* v. *Hamilton*, 1907 S.C. 912.

[5] *N.B. Ry.* v. *Edinburgh Mags.*, 1920 S.C. 409.

[6] *Scott* v. *Howard* (1881) 8 R. (H.L.) 59; *Borthwick-Norton* v. *Gavin Paul*, 1947 S.C. 659, 680.

[7] *Murray* v. *Oliphant's Wife* (1634) Mor. 2262; *Cuninghame* v. *G.S.W. Ry.* (1883) 10 R. 1173; *Millar's Trs.* v. *Rattray* (1891) 18 R. 989; contrast *Gardner* v. *Scott* (1843) 2 Bell 129; *Critchley* v. *Campbell* (1884) 11 R. 475; *Blyth's Trs.* v. *Shaw Stewart* (1883) 11 R. 99; *Currie* v. *Campbell's Trs.* (1888) 16 R. 237.

[8] *Ure* v. *Anderson* (1834) 12 S. 494; *Fleming* v. *Baird* (1841) 3 D. 1015; *Gibson* v. *Bonnington Sugar Co.* (1869) 7 M. 394; *Blyth's Trs.* v. *Shaw Stewart* (1883) 11 R. 99; *Currie* v. *Campbell's Trs.* (1888) 16 R. 237.

Exclusion of prior communings

Where parties after negotiations embody their agreement in a contract or written agreement, the general rule is that it supersedes their prior communings, oral and written, and evidence thereof is incompetent to add to, modify or qualify the written agreement; the contract must be presumed intended to supersede the earlier negotiations and to record the parties' concluded agreement.[1] Similarly a disposition of heritage in implement of a prior contract must be deemed completely to supersede that contract,[2] though it may be otherwise where the deed expressly refers to the prior contract,[3] and parties may agree that this principle shall not apply.[4] Again this rule does not apply where a letter confirming an oral agreement is ambiguous, when evidence as to the original bargain is admissible.[5]

Extrinsic evidence

Extrinsic evidence is admissible, not to help interpret a document,[6] but to inform the court of the meanings which the granter habitually attached to the words in question. Thus translations may be adduced of foreign or dialect words, and explanation of scientific or technical terms,[7] while the meaning of a word or phrase may be shown to have a particular connotation by the custom and usage of a particular trade, or business or place.[8] Similarly extrinsic evidence is admissible to aid in the construction of wills by informing the court of the testator's circumstances and family at the date thereof,[9] or to aid in the construction of a

---

[1] *Forlong* v. *Taylor's Exors.* (1838) 3 S. & McL. 177; *Inglis* v. *Buttery* (1878) 5 R. (H.L.) 87; *Largue* v. *Urquhart* (1881) 18 S.L.R. 491; *Tininver Lime Co.* v. *Coghill* (1881) 19 S.L.R. 7; *Riemann* v. *Young* (1895) 2 S.L.T. 426; *Muller* v. *Weber & Schaer* (1901) 3 F. 401; *Paterson* v. *Inglis* (1902) 10 S.L.T. 449; *McAllister* v. *McGallagley*, 1911 S.C. 112; *Norval* v. *Abbey*, 1939 S.C. 724; *Korner* v. *Shennan*, 1950 S.C. 285.

[2] *Lee* v. *Alexander* (1883) 10 R. (H.L.) 91; *Orr* v. *Mitchell* (1893) 20 R. (H.L.) 27; *Baird* v. *Alexander* (1898) 25 R. (H.L.) 35; *Butter* v. *Foster*, 1912 S.C. 1218; but see *Jamieson* v. *Welsh* (1900) 3 F. 176.

[3] *Inverkeithing Mags.* v. *Ross* (1874) 2 R. 48; *Smith, Laing & Co.* v. *Maitland* (1876) 3 R. 281; see also *Wann* v. *Gray*, 1935 S.N. 8.

[4] *Young* v. *McKellar*, 1909 S.C. 1340; *Fraser* v. *Cox*, 1938 S.C. 506.

[5] *Crondace* v. *Annandale Steamship Co.*, 1925 S.L.T. 449.

[6] cf. *Miller* v. *M.* (1822) 1 Sh. App. 308; *Stewart* v. *S.* (1842) 1 Bell 796; *Davidson* v. *D.* (1906) 14 S.L.T. 337.

[7] *Sutton* v. *Ciceri* (1890) 17 R. (H.L.) 40.

[8] *Von Mehren* v. *Edinburgh Roperie* (1901) 4 F. 232.

[9] *Free Church Trs.* v. *Maitland* (1887) 14 R. 333; *Craw's Trs.* v. *Blacklock*, 1920 S.C. 22; *Ormiston's Exor.* v. *Laws.* 1966 S.C. 47, 51; contrast *Boyd* v. *B's Trs.* (1906) 13 S.L.T. 875; *Devlin's Trs.* v. *Breen*, 1943 S.C. 556; 1945 S.C. (H.L.) 27.

contract by ascertaining the circumstances surrounding the contract.[1]

It is settled that parole evidence is not generally admissible to add to, vary, alter or contradict the terms of a deed or writing.[2] Similarly where a contract is signed apparently as principal, it is not competent to prove by parole evidence that the party was contracting as agent only.[3]

But parole evidence is admissible if a written contract is admitted or alleged not to express the true agreement between the parties,[4] or if the contract is partly oral and partly written,[5] or if the written contract is challenged on the ground of essential error, fraud or illegality,[6] or if it is alleged that the writing was not intended truly to record the contract but to conceal some other transaction.[7]

By what law transaction is regulated

It is frequently material to determine by what system of law the rights and duties of parties are to be determined. If the parties have a common intention on this they may deal with the point expressly, but failing this an inference as to their intention may be drawn from a provision for arbitration in a particular place,[8] from the use of the technical terms of one legal system rather than another,[9] or from other indications of intention. Similarly a will may declare the testator's domicile.

Meanings of particular words and phrases

The Titles to Land Consolidation (Sc.) Act, 1868,[10] and the Conveyancing (Sc.) Act, 1874,[11] authorize the use in conveyan-

---

[1] *Forlong v. Taylor's Exors.* (1838) 3 S. & McL. 177; *Inglis v. Buttery* (1878) 5 R. (H.L.) 87; *Mackenzie v. Liddell* (1883) 10 R. 705.

[2] *Steuart's Trs. v. Hart* (1875) 3 R. 192; *Tancred Arrol & Co. v. Steel Co. of Scotland* (1890) 17 R. (H.L.) 31; *MacLellan v. Peattie's Trs.* (1903) 5 F. 1031; *Forth Collieries v. Hume* (1904) 11 S.L.T. 576; *Lavan v. Aird,* 1919 S.C. 345; *Norval v. Abbey,* 1939 S.C. 724; *Perdikou v. Pattison,* 1958 S.L.T. 153.

[3] *Gibb v. Cunningham & Robertson,* 1925 S.L.T. 608.

[4] *Grant v. Mackenzie* (1899) 1 F. 889; *Krupp v. Menzies,* 1907 S.C. 903.

[5] *Christie v. Hunter* (1880) 7 R. 729.

[6] *Steuart's Trs., supra; Stewart v. Kennedy* (1890) 17 R. (H.L.) 25; *Bell Bros. v. Aitken,* 1939 S.C. 577.

[7] *Maloy v. Macadam* (1885) 12 R. 431; *Imrie v. I.* (1891) 19 R. 185.

[8] *Hamlyn v. Talisker Distillery* (1894) 21 R. (H.L.) 21; *Robertson v. Brandes, Schonwald & Co.* (1906) 8 F. 815.

[9] But see *Mackintosh v. May* (1895) 22 R. 345.

[10] Ss. 5–8 and Sched. B, S. 138.

[11] Ss. 4, 26.

cing deeds of certain short forms of clauses, having prescribed statutory meanings. In many cases the interpretation of particular words and phrases has been considered. In some of these, such as cases of wills, the interpretation may have no application outside the will then construed, but in others, such as cases interpreting words regularly used in common documents, such as charter parties, the interpretation must rule subsequent cases dealing with the same words in another such deed, unless the earlier case is distinguishable on its facts.

CHAPTER 8

THE PUBLIC REGISTERS AND THE REGISTRATION OF DEEDS

N UMEROUS public registers are maintained under various statutes and registration of various deeds, notices and other writs has in many cases important legal conse-quences.[1] Under the Public Registers and Records (Sc.) Act, 1948, separate Keepers are appointed of the Registers and of the Records of Scotland. The former is charged with functions in relation to the General Register of Sasines, the Register of Horn-ings, the Register of Inhibitions and Adjudications, the Register of Entails and the Register of Deeds, and has the powers and duties formerly vested in the Director of Chancery. The latter is charged with the preservation of the public registers, records and rolls of Scotland, as historical documents. The Registers are grouped under the four offices, Chancery Office, Sasine Office, Horning Office and Deeds Office, with which they are historically and administratively connected.

THE REGISTERS

Register of the Great Seal

The Secretary of State for Scotland is now Keeper, and the Keeper of the Registers of Scotland is Deputy Keeper, of the Great Seal of Scotland, under which are authenticated charters and grants of land from the Crown, patents of nobility and com-missions to the principal offices of the Crown. In this register are recorded for preservation only writs passing that seal. Extracts of writs from this register are probative.[2]

Register of the Prince's Seal

Grants of lands forming part of the stewartry or principality of Scotland, destined as provision for the eldest son and heir-apparent of the Crown, pass the Prince's Seal and are recorded in this register.

---

[1] See generally M. Livingstone's *Guide to the Public Records of Scotland* (1905).
[2] Public Records (Sc.) Act, 1809, S. 16.

Register of the Quarter Seal

Under this seal pass royal gifts of forfeiture or of *ultimus haeres*.

Register of the Cachet or Privy Seal

The Privy Seal of Scotland is now in abeyance and its registers, now discontinued, were deposited in 1924 and are now in the custody of the Keeper of the Records of Scotland. Grants formerly authenticated by the Privy Seal, such as of gifts of escheat, feudal casualties, personal rights and presentation to offices in the gift of the Crown, are now made by direct warrant under the Royal Sign Manual.

Register of Crown Writs

By the Titles to Land Consolidation (Sc.) Act, 1868, S. 87, the Director of Chancery[1] is directed to maintain this register and enter in it at full length Crown writs.[2]

Register of Sheriff's Commissions

In this are recorded commissions granted to persons to hold the office of sheriff principal or full-time sheriff.

Record of Service of Heirs

Service was the process whereby an heir to heritage formerly established the fact of his heirship.[3] Decrees therein were recorded by the Director of Chancery[4] in the manner directed by the Lord Clerk Register,[5] in books known as the Record of Services.[6] By virtue of the Succession (Sc.) Act, 1964, service of heirs is now practically obsolete.

Register of Sasines

In 1617 the Registration Act, replacing earlier legislation from 1540 onwards, provided that all instruments of sasine and writs relating to redeemable rights in land were to be recorded in a public general register in Edinburgh within 60 days of the sasine. The Act also established Particular Registers of Sasines through-

---

[1] Office discontinued in 1932 under authority of Reorganization of Offices (Sc.) Act, 1928, S. 7: duties now vested in Keeper of the Registers of Scotland.

[2] As to these see 1868 Act, Ss. 3, 63–79, 83–88, 89, 90, 91.

[3] Titles to Land Consolidation (Sc.) Act, 1868, Ss. 27–35.

[4] Now Keeper of the Registers of Scotland.

[5] Ibid., S. 36.

[6] Ibid., S. 38; The Record of Service was established by the Service of Heirs (Sc.) Act, 1847.

out the country for the sheriffdoms and districts therein specified; writs might be recorded in either the General or Particular Register. An Act of 1693 made the date of recording the criterion of preference, irrespective of actual possession. The Land Registers (Sc.) Act, 1868, discontinued the old General Register of Sasines, instituted a new General Register with separate divisions for each county in Scotland, and abolished all the Particular Registers from dates specified in the Act.

The Act, 1681, c. 11, brought registration of lands held burgage in burghs, or by booking in Paisley, into line by establishing Burgh Registers of Sasines and the Register of Booking in Paisley. In 1926 the Burgh Registers (Sc.) Act provided for the gradual discontinuance of the Burgh Registers of Sasines and the Register of Booking. This is now complete.

The Register of Interruption of Prescriptions, in which had to be registered all summonses used for interrupting prescription of real rights, with executions thereof, ended in 1868, all entries formerly made in it being thereafter made in the Register of Sasines.[1]

The Court of Session has power to make Acts of Sederunt regarding the General Register of Sasines.[2]

Register of Entails

The Entail Act, 1685, empowered landowners to entail their lands[3] subject to certain conditions, of which one was that entails should be recorded in a Register opened for the purpose. Later Acts required other writs relating to entails also to be registered.[4] Since the Entail (Sc.) Act, 1914, which prohibited the creation of new entails, the register is open only for the recording of writs relating to existing entails, such as instruments of disentail.

Register of Hornings

The General and Particular Registers of Hornings recorded applications by a creditor against a debtor under which Letters of Horning were issued under the Signet, in pursuance of which the debtor, on failure to pay, was denounced a rebel with four blasts of the horn by a messenger-at-arms. Letters of Horning had by Act of 1579 to be registered in the Sheriff Court books of the shire in which publication had taken place, but are now in desuetude.

---

[1] Land Registers (Sc.) Act, 1868, S. 15.
[2] Public Registers and Records (Sc.) Act, 1948.
[3] As to this see Ch. 78, *infra*.
[4] See generally Craigie, *Heritable*, 697, 702.

By the Debtors (Sc.) Act, 1838, S. 5, a charge on a decree and its execution might be recorded, within a year and a day after its expiry without payment, in the General Register of Hornings, which registration had the same effect as if the debtor had been denounced rebel in virtue of letters of horning. Extract sheriff court decrees and execution of charges thereon might similarly (S. 10) be recorded in the Particular Register. The Land Registers Act, 1868, S. 18, preserved the Particular Registers of Hornings.

Register of Inhibitions and Adjudications

The Land Registers Act, 1868, Ss. 16, 18, abolished the Particular Registers of Inhibitions and Interdictions,[1] and the Conveyancing (Sc.) Act, 1924, S. 44, amalgamated the General Register of Inhibitions and Interdictions and the Register of Abbreviates of Adjudications[2] into the Register of Inhibitions and Adjudications as the sole register for personal diligences. It contains inhibitions, interdictions, adjudications, reductions, notices of litigiosity,[3] abbreviates of petitions for sequestration, statutorily equivalent to inhibitions, abbreviates of the Acts and Warrants of trustees in bankruptcy, statutorily equivalent to adjudications, and adjudication orders and certificates in bankruptcy under the [English] Bankruptcy Act, 1914.

---

[1] Inhibition is a process whereby a creditor may restrain his debtor from voluntarily alienating or burdening his heritage and follows on Letters of Inhibition passing the Signet. It is ineffective until served on the debtor, and ineffective against persons generally until published at the market cross and pier of Leith, followed by registration within 40 days, formerly in the General Register of Inhibitions (established 1581), in which were recorded notices of inhibitions, letters of inhibition, abbreviates of petitions for sequestration and similar notices, or the appropriate Particular Registers of Inhibitions (established 1600) kept for the counties in which the subjects are situated, and now in the combined Register. The Particular registers were abolished in 1868. Inhibition is still competent and the Letters or Summons of an action containing warrant to inhibit must be registered to have any effect. Inhibition prescribes in five years: Conveyancing Act, 1924, S. 44. See also Ersk. II, 11, 2; Titles to Land Consolidation (Sc.) Act, 1868, Ss. 145, 156.

Interdiction was the process whereby a person of a facile tendency might be disabled, voluntarily by bond of interdiction, or judicially by the Court of Session, from alienating his heritage gratuitously without the consent of the interdicter. To be effective the bond or decree had to be registered in the General Register of Interdictions or the appropriate Particular Register of Interdictions. See Ersk. I, 7, 54. The process is now incompetent: Conveyancing (Sc.) Act, 1924, S. 44.

[2] This had superseded the earlier Register of Apprisings (1636). Adjudication is an action, founded on any decree or liquid document of debt, whereby heritable property may be attached for debt. Service of a summons of adjudication, if followed by registration of a notice in statutory form in the Register renders the lands litigious.

[3] Litigiosity is created by registration of a notice of an action of adjudication or reduction. It prescribes in five years: Conveyancing (Sc.) Act, 1924, S. 44(2).

The Registers of Deeds

Until 1809 it was competent by long standing custom to register writs for preservation or execution in the books of all public courts of record, including the books of the Lord of Council and Session, the books of every sheriff court, commissary courts, and of bailies of royal burghs and burghs of regality. The Public Records (Sc.) Act, 1809, restricted registration to the Books of Council and Session, and Sheriff Court books. In these are registered marriage contracts, bonds, obligations, (since 1824) wills, and a wide variety of other deeds.

Register of Protests

Under various statutes protests of bills of exchange have been recorded in the Books of Council and Session or sheriff court books. Down to 1811 protests were recorded in the Register of Deeds but a separate Register was commenced in 1812. The town clerks of royal burghs still have the right to receive for recording instruments of protest on bills of exchange where all parties are burgesses or domiciled within the burgh when the deeds are presented for registration.[1]

Record of Edictal Citations

The edictal citation of persons furth of Scotland, formerly done at the market cross of Edinburgh and the pier and shore of Leith,[2] was replaced in 1825 by the delivery of a copy of the summons or charge to the keeper of the records of the Court of Session who registered an abstract thereof in books kept for the purpose.[3]

Registers of English and Irish Judgments

By the Judgments Extension Act, 1868, S. 2, a certificate of judgment for debt, damages or costs obtained in the superior courts of England or Northern Ireland may within twelve months be registered in the Register for English and Irish Judgments in the same way as a bond executed according to the law of Scotland, and has the same force and effect as a decree of the Court.[4] The

---

[1] Under Bills of Exchange Acts, 1681 (c. 86), 1696 (c. 38), and 1772, S. 42; see *Sutherland* v. *Gunn* (1854) 16 D. 339. Right preserved by Public Records (Sc.) Act, 1809, S. 1.

[2] See Stair IV, 47, 3; Ersk. I, 2, 18. In certain cases it was also made at the market cross of the county town or head burgh of the county: Act, 1555, c. 6; Ersk. IV, 1, 8.

[3] Court of Session (Sc.) Act, 1825, Ss. 51–52; see also Court of Session (Sc.) Act, 1850, S. 22.

[4] See further Ch. 13, *infra*.

Inferior Courts Judgments Extension Act, 1882, makes similar provision for the judgments of inferior courts being registered by sheriff clerks.

Register of Community Judgments

A Register of Community Judgments has been established in which is registered any Community judgment to which the Secretary of State has appended an order for enforcement or any Euratom inspection order or any order of the European Court that enforcement of a registered Community judgment shall be suspended.[1]

REGISTRATION OF DEEDS

Purposes of Registration

In Scottish practice writs may be recorded for one or more of three purposes, for execution, for preservation, and for publication. Registration for execution is the recording of a deed or probative writ in the Books of Council and Session or Sheriff Court Books so that the grantee may obtain an extract with a warrant for the enforcement by the appropriate diligence of the granters' obligation, the extract and warrant being statutorily equivalent to a decree of court.

Registration for preservation involves the recording of the deed in a public register, the Books of Council and Session or Sheriff Court Books, and its retention in a public office so that it may not be lost or destroyed and an extract may at all times be obtainable by a person requiring one.

The registration for publication of writs relating to land in the Registers of Sasines or, where appropriate, the Register of Entails, is intended to make publicly available to persons interested the state of the title to all pieces of land and the burdens affecting it, and to protect the interest of persons interested therein.[2]

Registration for execution[3]

Where a probative deed, such as a bond or contract, includes a clause stating the granter's consent to the deed being registered for execution, it may be registered in the Books of Council and

---

[1] R.C. 296G added by A.S. 15 December 1972.

[2] Registration in the Register of Inhibitions and Adjudications is not technically known as a register for publication, but it is so in effect.

[3] See generally Bell, *Convg.* I, 220; Menzies, 183; Craigie, *Heritable*, 973; *Moveable*, 470.

Session, if the granter of the obligation resides anywhere in Scotland or is subject to the jurisdiction of the Court of Session, or in the books of a Sheriff Court, if the granter is designed as residing within the jurisdiction of that court. The deed must embody a definite obligation enforceable by decree of court. Certain kinds of writs only, particularly protests of bills of exchange,[1] of promissory notes,[2] exchequer bonds,[3] and certain assignations,[4] may be registered for execution without a clause of consent therein.

The creditor may then at any time obtain an authenticated extract in statutory form[5] which concludes by the Court, or sheriff, granting warrant[6] for all lawful execution thereon. This warrant authorizes diligence against the debtor's property in the same way as if the creditor had obtained a decree of court against the debtor.[7]

Where the original debtor has died it is not possible to do diligence on the extract recorded bond,[8] except in the case where the personal obligation in a bond and disposition in security has transmitted against a person taking the security subjects by succession, gift or bequest from the debtor,[9] provided he has signed an agreement to that effect,[10] or where the obligation has been taken over *in gremio* of a conveyance of the security subjects,[9] provided the purchaser has signed the disposition in his favour.[10] In other cases a decree of constitution of the debt must be obtained.

If a new creditor obtains right from the original creditor and the latter had not obtained decree the new creditor must proceed by letters of horning.

Registration for preservation

Registration of any probative writ for preservation[11] is competent without a clause of consent thereto, but the granter must be subject to the jurisdiction of the court in whose books his writ is

---

[1] Bills of Exchange Act, 1681, and Inland Bills Act, 1696.
[2] Bills of Exchange (Sc.) Act, 1772, S. 41.
[3] Exchequer Court (Sc.) Act, 1856, S. 38.
[4] Under Transmission of Moveable Property (Sc.) Act, 1862, S. 1.
[5] Writs Execution (Sc.) Act, 1877, S. 5.
[6] Ibid., Sched.
[7] Ersk. II, 5, 54; Bell, *Prin.* §68; 1877 Act, S. 3.
[8] *Brown* v. *Binnie* (1635) Mor. 14994.
[9] Conveyancing (Sc.) Act, 1874, S. 47; *Ritchie and Sturrock* v. *Dullatur Feuing Co.* (1881) 9 R. 358.
[10] Conveyancing (Sc.) Act, 1924, S. 15 and Sched. A, Form 2.
[11] See generally Menzies, 136, 189; Craigie, *Heritable*, 231, 394.

registered. An authenticated extract may at any time be obtained, which is equivalent to the principal unless it be challenged on the ground of fraud or forgery.[1] The principal writ is retained and allowed out only by authority of the court and subject to conditions.[2] The court has permitted the correction of a clerical error in the testing clause of a deed given in for registration but not booked,[3] and the chemical examination of a recorded will.[4] There is no power to record only portions of deeds, nor to grant partial extracts only.[5]

Registration for publication[6]

Registration for publication applies to writs affecting land, transferring or burdening or disburdening it. The Registration Act, 1617, which established the Register of Sasines, required Sasines to be registered within 60 days of their dates. The Real Rights Act, 1693 (c. 13) provided that writs should have priority according to the dates of their registration,[7] and the Register of Sasines Act, 1693 (c. 14) required the maintenance of a minute book showing the day and hour of the presentation of writs and the names and designations of presenters. The Titles Act, 1858, sanctioned the direct recording of conveyances of land in the Register of Sasines. Writs to be recorded must have endorsed thereon a warrant of registration,[8] stating on whose behalf the deed is to be registered and in what division of the General Register, signed by the party or his agent, and they may be recorded at any time in the life of the person on whose behalf they are to be registered. Each writ is recorded in the presentment book, which fixes the date and time of entry, the minute book, which contains the names of the parties and a short description of the property and the record volume, and since 1871 a search sheet has been maintained for every unit of property giving an abstract of all deeds affecting that property. After registration,

---

[1] Writs Execution (Sc.) Act, 1877, S. 5.

[2] *Liquidators of Western Bank* (1868) 6 M. 656; *Macdonald* (1877) 5 R. 44; *United Telephone Co.* v. *Maclean* (1882) 9 R. 710; *Inglis* (1882) 9 R. 761; *Walter* (1889) 16 R. 926; *Leigh-Bennett* (1893) 20 R. 787; *Jamieson's Trs.* v. *J.* (1899) 2 F. 96; *Pheysey* (1906) 8 F. 801; *Chevenix-Trench*, 1917 S.C. 168; *Campbell's Trs.*, 1934 S.C. 8.

[3] *Caldwell* (1871) 10 M. 99; *Murray* (1904) 6 F. 840; contrast *Thoms* (1870) 8 M. 857. See also *Mitchell's Trs.*, 1930 S.C. 180.

[4] *Irvine* v. *Powrie's Trs.*, 1915 S.C. 1006.

[5] *B's Exor.* v. *Keeper of the Registers*, 1935 S.C. 745.

[6] See generally Bell, *Convg.* I, 662; Menzies, 555; Wood, 179; Craigie, *Heritable*, 55, 238.

[7] Repeated in Titles to Land Consolidation (Sc.) Act, 1868, S. 142.

[8] Conveyancing (Sc.) Act, 1924, S. 10 and Sched. F.

and being photocopied into the Register, deeds are returned to the presenter for retention, with a certificate of registration endorsed thereon.

Extracts from the Register of Sasines are statutorily declared equivalent to principals, unless the latter should be challenged as forged[1] but conveyancers have always been reluctant to accept them as such. Extracts of a conveyance, deed, instrument or other document bearing to have been recorded in the Register of Sasines are to be accepted for all purposes as sufficient evidence of the contents of the original so recorded and of any matter relating thereto appearing on the extract.[2]

The Keeper has a discretion to refuse to register any deed presented to him; deeds are refused particularly if inappropriate to the Register, or incorrect in legal form.[3]

Registration for combined purposes

Registration for execution and for preservation[4] have a common origin and a largely common development, and a deed may be registered for both purposes if an appropriate clause of consent is contained therein. Statute[5] sanctions a short clause of consent with a statutory meaning.

The conjunction of all three purposes of registration is permitted by the Land Registers Act, 1868, S. 12, which provided that a writ registered in the Sasine Register should be held registered in the Books of Council and Session for preservation, or for preservation and execution, provided it has an appropriate warrant of registration[6] endorsed thereon. Such a writ is retained and only an extract delivered. By the Writs Execution (Sc.) Act, 1877, S. 6, a writ registered in the Register of Sasines for preservation only may be afterwards registered for preservation and execution, provided it contains *in gremio* a clause of registration for preservation and execution.[7]

---

[1] Titles to Land Consolidation (Sc.) Act, 1868, S. 142.

[2] Conveyancing and Feudal Reform (Sc.) Act, 1970, S. 45 (applicable to extracts whether issued before or after that Act).

[3] *Macdonald* v. *Keeper of the General Register of Sasines*, 1914 S.C. 854.

[4] See generally Bell, *Convg.* I, 220.

[5] Titles to Land Consolidation (Sc.) Act, 1868, S. 138.

[6] Form in Conveyancing (Sc.) Act, 1924, S. 10 and Sched. F, No. 2.

[7] See further Craigie, *Heritable*, 240.

CHAPTER 9

TIME, AND THE EFFECT OF LAPSE OF TIME

T IME is a factor constantly arising in legal issues. The interpretation of words and phrases relating to time frequently has to be considered, and the effect of lapse of time on rights is also frequently material.

Computation of time

Time is normally computed in years, months, weeks, and days. Each common year comprises 365 days, but every fourth year is a leap year comprising 366 days. Hundredth years, except every fourth hundred, are common years.[1] In 1752 eleven nominal days were omitted in September to bring the calendar then in use (Julian Calendar) into line with the Gregorian calendar.[2] The calendar year has since 1600 commenced in Scotland on 1st January.[3]

'Month', by common law,[4] mercantile custom[5] and statute[6] is a calendar month, in the absence of contrary indications,[7] and 'week' a calendar week of seven days, from Sunday to Saturday.[8]

A 'day' is *prima facie* the period of twenty four hours between midnight and midnight, but in certain contexts means the period of light within such twenty four hours.[9] The time of day or night referred to is to be held as Greenwich Mean Time,[10] but 'sunrise' and 'sunset' are determined by local time, not the time of sunrise or sunset at Greenwich.[11]

[1] Calendar (New Style) Act, 1750, S. 2 (amd. Calendar Act, 1751).

[2] Ibid., S. 1.

[3] Ibid., S. 1; *Williamson* v. *Hay* (1855) 17 D. 960. In England until 1752 the year commenced on 25 March.

[4] *Smith* v. *Robertson & Jeffray* (1826) 4 S. 442; *Ashley* v. *Rothesay Mags.* (1873) 11 M. 708; *Farquharson* v. *Whyte* (1886) 13 R. (J.) 29; *McNiven* v. *Glasgow Corpn.*, 1920 S.C. 584.

[5] e.g. in relation to bills of exchange: Bills of Exchange Act, 1882, S. 14(4); sale of goods: Sale of Goods Act, 1893, S. 10(2).

[6] Interpretation Act, 1889, S. 3.   [7] *Campbell's Trs.* v. *Cazenove* (1880) 8 R. 21.

[8] *Ferguson* v. *Rodger* (1895) 22 R. 643; *Aberdeen City* v. *Watt* (1901) 3 F. 787; *Roscoe* v. *Mackersy* (1905) 7 F. 761; But see *Fleming* v. *Lochgelly Iron Co.* (1902) 4 F. 890; *McCue* v. *Barclay Curle & Co.* (1902) 4 F. 909.

[9] Night Poaching Act, 1828, S. 12; Day Trespass Act 1832 (Game (Sc.) Act, 1832), S. 3.

[10] Statutes (Definition of Time) Act, 1880, S. 1 (not affected by Summer Time Acts, 1922 to 1947).

[11] *MacKinnon* v. *Nicolson*, 1916 S.C. (J.) 6.

According to *naturalis computatio* time is reckoned *de momento in momentum*,[1] save that if the exact time is unknown, the period is reckoned from the end of the day, month or year in question. It does not matter that certain days of the period were *inutiles*.[2]

According to *civilis computatio*, time is computed *de die in diem*. There are no fractions of a day and the day on which time starts to run is normally excluded from the period to run,[3] particularly if so many 'clear days' are specified.[4] Where a period of time is reckoned in days, months or years it is reckoned *de die in diem*. Thus the prescriptive period runs from midnight on the starting day[5] to midnight on the day having the same number in the same month, the requisite number of years later.[6] Exceptionally the day on which time starts to run is included in the period.[7]

Time normally expires at the earliest moment of the final day of the period,[8] but where the loss of rights is in question, only at the last moment of the final day,[9] and where 'clear days' are specified, it does not expire till the earliest moment of the next day.[10] Where the giving of notice is in question it is sufficient if the notice be sent timeously though not received till outwith the time.[11]

Prescribed dates

When something is required to be done by a prescribed date, *prima facie* the requirement is mandatory.[12]

---

[1] *Drummond* v. *Cunningham-Head* (1624) Mor. 3465 (attainment of majority); *Greig* v. *Anderson* (1883) 20 S.L.R. 421.

[2] Ersk. II, 7, 30; cf. *Hutton* v. *Garland* (1883) 10 R. (J.) 60; *McNiven* v. *Glasgow Corpn.*, 1920 S.C. 584.

[3] *S. Staffs Tramways Co.* v. *Sickness and Accident Corpn.* [1891] 1 Q.B. 402. See also Bills of Exchange Act, 1882, S. 14(2); Bankruptcy (Sc.) Act, 1913, S. 3; *Lindsay* v. *Giles* (1844) 6 D. 771; *Stiven* v. *Reynolds* (1891) 18 R. 422; *Sickness & Accident Assce. Assocn.* v. *General Assce. Corpn.* (1892) 19 R. 977; *Lipman & Co.'s Tr.* (1893) 20 R. 818; *Frew* v. *Morris* (1897) 24 R. (J.) 50; *McLeod & Sons*, 1969 S.C. 16.

[4] *Wilson* (1891) 19 R. 219.

[5] *Simpson* v. *Marshall* (1900) 2 F. 447, 458, 459.

[6] *Simpson*, *supra*; *Cavers Parish Council* v. *Smailholm Parish Council*, 1909 S.C. 195; cf. *Ashley* v. *Rothesay Mags.* (1873) 11 M. 708.

[7] *Hough* v. *Athya* (1879) 6 R. 961; *Mackenzie* v. *Liddell* (1883) 10 R. 705.

[8] The maxim *dies inceptus pro completo habetur*. Bell, *Prin.*, §46, note; *Scott* v. *Rutherford* (1839) 2 D. 206; *Thomson* v. *Kirkcudbright Mags.* (1878) 5 R. 561; cf. *Lawford* v. *Davies* (1878) 4 P.D. 61.

[9] Ersk. III, 7, 30; *Thomson*, *supra*, 563; cf. *Jacobsen* v. *Underwood* (1894) 21 R. 654; *Simpson* v. *Melville* (1899) 6 S.L.T. 355.

[10] *Wilson*, *supra*.

[11] *Charleson* v. *Duffes* (1881) 8 R. (J.) 34.

[12] *Simpson* v. *Selkirk Assessor*, 1948 S.C. 270.

'From' a date

The primary meaning of 'from' a date is after the expiry of that date.[1]

'By' a date

A reply called for 'by' a given date has been held timeously given when posted on that date though not received till later.[2]

'At' or 'on' a date

'At' a date or a time means from the period when that date or time begins to run. 'On' a date or day means at any time within that day.[3]

'Within' so many days or months

When something must be done 'within' a number of days, weeks or months, the number of days runs from the day after the *terminus a quo*, as the first day, to the last moment of the day which completes the prescribed number of days.[4] If the last day is a Sunday and the thing prescribed cannot be done for that day, an extension to the Monday is permissible;[5] similarly the number of months runs from the day after the *terminus a quo* to the day bearing the same number, the prescribed number of months later.[6]

'For' so many weeks or months

Residence 'for' a stated number of weeks, months or years is reckoned from the day when the period begins to the correspondingly numbered day, the requisite number of calendar divisions later.[7]

Term-days

In leases, lettings frequently commence or terminate at the main term days,[8] namely Whitsunday (15th May) or Martinmas

[1] *Ashley* v. *Rothesay Mags.* (1873) 11 M. 708; *Sickness and Accident Assce. Assocn.* v. *General Accident Assce. Corpn.* (1892) 19 R. 977; *Frew* v. *Morris* (1897) 24 R. (J.) 50.

[2] *Jacobsen* v. *Underwood* (1894) 21 R. 654.

[3] *Mackenzie* v. *Liddell* (1883) 10 R. 705, 714.

[4] *Charleson* v. *Duffes* (1881) 8 R. (J.) 34; see also *McDonagh* v. *Maclellan* (1896) 13 R. 1000.

[5] *Russell* v. *R.* (1874) 2 R. 82; *Hutton* v. *Garland* (1883) 10 R. (J.) 60; *Henderson* v. *H.* (1888) 16 R. 5; *McVean* v. *Jamieson* (1896) 23 R. (J.) 25; *Blackburn* v. *Lang's Trs.* (1905) 8 F. 290.

[6] *McNiven* v. *Glasgow Corpn.*, 1920 S.C. 584.

[7] *Cavers Parish Council* v. *Smailholm Parish Council*, 1909 S.C. 195.

[8] The other term (or quarter) days in Scotland are Candlemas (2nd February) and Lammas (1st August). See *Scott Chisholme* v. *Brown* (1893) 20 R. 575.

(11th November),[1] but the Removal Terms (Scotland) Act, 1886, S. 4, provides that, in the absence of express stipulation to the contrary, the tenant shall enter to or remove from the house[2] let at noon on 28th May or 28th November, as the case may be, or on the following day if the 28th be a Sunday. But warning to remove must be given 40 days before 15th May or 11th November. By the Removal Terms (Scotland) Act, 1886, Amendment Act, 1890, S. 2, the terms for a servant hired by the year or half-year similarly, in the absence of express contrary stipulation, run to 28th May or 28th November.

Need for punctuality

A condition of 'punctual payment' in a contract is strictly enforced.[3] It means paid by the due date.[3] But in the absence of an express condition failure to make payment of the price of heritage on the stipulated day is not a material breach of contract justifying rescission.[4] Unless a different intention appears from the terms of the contract stipulations as to time of payment are not deemed to be of the essence of a contract of sale of goods; whether any other stipulation as to time is of the essence of the contract or not depends on the terms of the contract.[5]

EFFECT OF LAPSE OF TIME ON RIGHTS

The lapse of time may affect rights in different ways. A distinction should be drawn between limitations, procedural rules which after the lapse of a time render an obligation unenforceable, sometimes unless it can be established by special methods of proof, and prescriptions, substantive rules which extinguish the obligation completely.[6] But this terminology has not been strictly followed in Scots law and lapse of time must be considered under the following heads: (a) conventional limitations on obligations; (b) the statutory limitations (or prescriptions) which do not extinguish the obligation but alter the mode of proof thereof; (c) statutory limitations on the time within which actions on certain grounds must be raised; (d) the statutory prescriptions which do

[1] *Fraser's Trs.* v. *Maule* (1904) 6 F. 819; *Hunter* v. *Barron's Trs.* (1886) 13 R. 883.

[2] Defined, S. 3.

[3] *Scott Chisholme* v. *Brown, supra*; *Leeds and Hanley Theatre* v. *Broadbent* [1898] 1 Ch. 343; *Gatty* v. *Maclaine* 1921 S.C. (H.L.) 1.

[4] *Rodgers* v. *Fawdry*, 1950 S.C. 483.

[5] Sale of Goods Act, 1893, S. 10(1).

[6] Bell, *Prin.* §586, 605. On prescriptions generally see Napier, *Prescription*; Millar, *Prescription*; Walker, *Prescription*. They are fully considered hereafter in the contexts in which each arises.

extinguish the obligation; (e) the statutory positive prescription which precludes challenges and renders a heritable right un-challengeable; and (f) the effect of *mora* or delay. In relation to the statutory limitations and prescriptions importance attaches to the modes whereby the running of prescription may be in-terrupted, and the effect thereof, and whether prescription runs against persons *non valentes agere*, such as one in minority.

Conventional limitations

A conventional limitation may be created by the will of the parties, by a condition in their obligation, such as a guarantee of a debt for six months.[1]

Statutory limitations (or short prescriptions)

The statutory limitations (or prescriptions) rendered various kinds of obligations unenforceable after the lapse of various periods of time, but did not wholly extinguish the obligation, and in all cases the obligation can still be enforced by resort to different methods of proof of the obligation.

The statutory limitations or prescriptions are:

(1) The triennial prescription of certain kinds of debts not founded on written obligations, after the lapse of which time such a debt must be proved to have been constituted and to be resting owing by the writing, or the admission on oath, of the debtor.[2]

(2) The quinquennial prescription of minister's stipend and multures, and of rents, and of all bargains concerning moveables or sums of money proveable by witnesses.[3]

(3) The sexennial prescription of bills of exchange or notes, except bank notes, by which action must be commenced or diligence raised within six years, failing which the bill or note is extinguished but the debt remains unaffected but its constitution and resting owing must be proved by writ or oath,[4]

(4) The vicennial prescription of holograph missive letters, holograph bonds and subscriptions in account books with-out witnesses, whereby they prescribe after twenty years unless the pursuer proves by the defender's oath the verity

[1] Bell, *Prin.* §587–88.
[2] Prescription Act, 1579, c. 21; Stair II, 12, 30; Ersk. III, 7, 17; Bell, *Prin.* §628.
[3] Prescription Act, 1669, c. 14; Stair II, 12, 32; Ersk. III, 7, 20; Bell, *Prin.* §634.
[4] Bills of Exchange (Sc.) Act, 1772, S. 37; Bell, *Comm.* I, 393; *Prin.* §594.

of the said bond, letters and subscriptions, which is competent till the expiry of the long prescription formerly of forty years,[1] and now of twenty years.[2]

All these have been replaced with effect from 25 July 1976, by the Prescription and Limitation (Sc.) Act, 1973.[3]

Statutory limitations on time for bringing actions

Akin to the foregoing limitations are certain statutory limitations on the time for bringing certain actions. It is thought that they do not extinguish the obligation but merely render claims brought out of time unenforceable by action, so that a sum paid thereafter by way of compromise would be irrecoverable under a *conditio indebiti*. The protection may be waived.[4] The main provisions[5] are:

(1) carriage by air: action against the carrier must be brought within two years of arrival or scheduled arrival.[6]

(2) carriage by railway: action for injury to or death of a passenger must be brought within three years from the accident, or three years from the death or five years from the accident, whichever is earlier.[7]

(3) carriage by road: action for loss must be brought within one year or, in case of wilful misconduct or equivalent, three years.[8]

(4) carriage by sea: action must be brought within one year of delivery or the due date of delivery: the period may be extended.[9]

(5) international carriage of passengers by road: action must be brought within three years in case of death or injury, or one year in other cases.[10]

(6) civic amenities: a planning authority may within two years of discovering non-compliance, require a landowner to replant trees.[11]

(7) collisions at sea: a claim for damage or loss of life or for

---

[1] Prescription Act, 1669, c. 14; Stair II, 12, 35; Ersk. III, 7, 26; Bell, *Prin.* §590.
[2] Conveyancing (Sc.) Act, 1924, S. 17.
[3] As to transitional cases, see S. 16.
[4] *Burns* v. *Glasgow Corpn.*, 1917, 1 S.L.T. 301.
[5] Provisions applicable in public law or criminal law are not here listed.
[6] Carriage by Air Act, 1961, S. 5 and Sch. I, Art. 29.
[7] Carriage by Railway Act, 1972, Sch. Art. 17.
[8] Carriage of Goods by Road Act, 1965, Sch. Arts. 32, 39.
[9] Carriage of Goods by Sea Act, 1971, Sch. Art. III, para. 6.
[10] Carriage of Passengers by Road Act, 1974, Sch. Art. 22.
[11] Civic Amenities Act, 1967, S. 14.

salvage services must be brought within two years, unless the period is extended by the court.[1] A claim to enforce contribution in respect of an overpaid proportion of any damages for loss of life or personal injuries must be brought within one, unless the period is extended by the court.[2]

(8) compulsory powers of acquiring land: the powers of promoters must be exercised within three years from the passing of the special Act, or any other period prescribed,[3]

(9) contribution between wrongdoers: a claim to recover contribution in respect of damages or expenses must be brought within two years.[4]

(10) foreign jurisdiction: actions for any act done in pursuance or execution or intended execution of the Act must be brought within six months.[5]

(11) forestry: claims for compensation on refusal of a felling licence for trees must be brought within ten years of deterioration of the trees or one year from the date of their felling.[6]

(12) industrial disputes: complaints to the Industrial Court must be brought within six months, but the period may be modified.[7]

(13) merchant seamen: a creditor of a deceased seaman is not not entitled to payment unless the debt accrued less than three years before death and action is brought within two years thereafter.[8]

(14) mines and quarries: compensation for damage or disturbance to land resulting from operations must be brought within six years.[9]

(15) moneylenders: a claim for recovery of money lent, or interest, or the enforcement of an agreement or security must be commenced within twelve months of the accrual of the cause of action, or acknowledgment of the debt.[10]

---

[1] Maritime Conventions Act, 1911, S. 8. See *Birkdale S.S. Co.*, 1922 S.L.T. 575; *Reresby* v. *Cobetas*, 1923 S.L.T. 492, 719; *Dorie S.S. Co.*, 1923 S.C. 593; *Essien* v. *Clan Line* 1925 S.N. 75.

[2] Maritime Conventions Act, 1911, S. 8.

[3] Lands Clauses Consolidation (Sc.) Act, 1845, S. 116; see also Allotments (Sc.) Act, 1922, S. 13(1).

[4] Prescription and Limitation (Sc.) Act, 1973, S. 20.

[5] Foreign Jurisdiction Act, 1890, S. 13.   [6] Forestry Act, 1967, S. 11.

[7] Industrial Relations Act, 1971, Sch. 3, para. 25.

[8] Merchant Shipping Act, 1894, S. 178.

[9] Mines and Quarries (Tips) Act, 1969, S. 20.   [10] Moneylenders Act, 1927, S. 13.

(16) nuclear incidents: claims for injury or damage caused by an occurrence involving nuclear matter must be brought within twenty years.[1] Claims for compensation for breach of duty under the Act must be brought within thirty years.[1]

(17) oil pollution: claims for damage resulting from discharge or escape of oil from a ship must be brought within three years after claim arose and six years of occurrence resulting in discharge or escape.[2]

(18) personal injuries or death: action must be brought within three years from the date the injuries were sustained, or the date when the act, neglect or default giving rise to the injuries ceased, or the date of death, but in certain circumstances an extension of time is allowed.[3]

(19) Post Office: proceedings against the Post Office for loss of or damage to a registered inland packet must be begun within twelve months of posting.[4]

(20) protection of officials: action against anyone for anything done in execution of the Habitual Drunkards Act must be commenced within two years.[5] Proceedings against various officials for anything done in execution of the licensing acts must be commenced within two months.[6] Action for damages against officials for anything done under the Summary Jurisdiction Acts must be commenced within two months.[7] An action for anything done under the authority or in pursuance of any public local and personal, or local and personal, Act must be brought within two years, or one year after continuing damage has ceased.[8]

(21) recovery of property: a person presumed dead may recover property from one entitled under the Act only within thirteen years from the date when title was made up under the Act.[9] An action by a broker or dealer to recover possession of goods, stolen or fraudulently disposed of from a person to whom a magistrate has awarded them must be brought within three months.[10]

[1] Nuclear Installations Act, 1965, S. 15.
[2] Merchant Shipping (Oil Pollution) Act, 1971, S. 9.
[3] Prescription and Limitation (Sc.) Act, 1973, Ss. 17–19; see Walker, *Prescription*.
[4] Post Office Act, 1969, S. 30.
[5] Habitual Drunkards Act, 1879, S. 31.
[6] Licensing (Sc.) Act, 1959, S. 195, amd. Licensing (Sc.) Act, 1962, S. 26.
[7] Summary Jurisdiction (Sc.) Act, 1954, S. 75.
[8] Limitation of Actions and Costs Act, 1842, S. 5.
[9] Presumption of Life Limitation (Sc.) Act, 1891, S. 7.
[10] Burgh Police (Sc.) Act, 1892, S. 413.

(22) sewerage: claims for loss, injury or damage resulting from exercise of powers under the Act must be brought within twelve months.[1]

(23) social security: rights to benefits under the National Insurance Act, Industrial Injuries Act, Ministry of Social Security Act or Family Income Supplements Act must be claimed within twelve months.[2] The recovery of sums due to the National Insurance or Industrial Injuries Funds must be made within three years.[3]

(24) standard security: a notice calling up money is effective for five years only.[4] A notice of default authorises the exercise of certain powers within five years only.[5]

(25) trespass: actions for anything done in pursuance of the Act must be commenced within six months and subject to conditions.[6]

(26) wages: payments to, or deductions from wages by, an employer contrary to the Act may be recovered within six months.[7]

(27) wrongful imprisonment: an action of damages for wrongous imprisonment must be brought within three years of the end thereof.[8]

Periods of limitation under certain statutes may be extended in the case of a person within the Limitation (Enemies and War Prisoners) Act, 1945, as amended.

Statutory prescriptions—Negative prescriptions

The statutory prescriptions proper wholly extinguish the rights or obligations in question after the lapse of the stated time. The individual prescriptions within this class are:

(a) applicable till 25 July 1976, only:

(1) the triennial prescription of actions of spuilzie and ejection;[9]

[1] Sewerage (Sc.) Act, 1968, S. 20.

[2] National Insurance Act, 1965, S. 52, amd. 1969 Act, S. 2; National Insurance (Ind. Inj.) Act, 1965, S. 27, amd. 1969 Act, S. 2; Ministry of Social Security Act, 1966, S. 17, amd. 1969 Act, S. 2; Family Income Supplements Act, 1970, S. 10.

[3] National Insurance Act, 1965, S. 96; National Insurance (Industrial Injuries) Act, 1968, S. 68.

[4] Conveyancing and Feudal Reform (Sc.) Act, 1970, S. 19.

[5] Ibid., S. 21.

[6] Game (Sc.) Act, 1832, S. 17.

[7] Criminal Procedure Act, 1701 (c. 6).

[8] Truck Act, 1896, S. 5.

[9] Prescription (Ejections) Act, 1579, c. 19; Ersk. III, 7, 16.

(2) the septennial prescription of cautionary obligations, whereby a cautioner's liability is, subject to certain conditions, extinguished after seven years;[1]

(3) the decennial prescription of tutorial accounts, whereby the rights of actions of pupils and minors, against their tutors or curators for count and reckoning for intromissions with the ward's property is extinguished after ten years from the death or majority of the ward.[2] The contrary action against the ward's estate for reimbursement is also extinguished thereby.[3]

(4) the decennial prescription of actions proceeding on warnings, spuilzies, ejections, arrestments and for minister's stipends;[4]

(5) the vicennial prescription of retours which excludes challenge of retours or decrees of service of heirs after twenty years;[5]

(b) *applicable from* 25 *July* 1976, *only:*

(1) the quinquennial prescription of obligations to pay money (including interest, feuduty, ground annual and rent) and of obligations arising from, or by reason of breach of, contract or promise (unless constituted or evidenced by probative writ), from liability to make reparation (other than personal injuries or death), or from obligation of restitution, and of obligations of accounting.[6]

(c) *the long negative prescription*

The long negative prescription, created by the Prescription Acts, 1469, c. 28, and 1474, c. 54, and the second portion of the Prescription Act, 1617, c. 12, originally of forty years, and later[7] of twenty years, now replaced by the Prescription and Limitation (Sc.) Act, 1973, Ss. 7–8, extinguishes obligations of any kind and any right relating to property (unless a claim has been made in relation thereto, or its subsistence has been acknow-

[1] Cautioners Act, 1695, c. 7; Ersk. III, 7, 22; Bell, *Comm.* I, 396; *Prin.* §600.
[2] Prescription Act, 1696, c. 9; Ersk. III, 7, 25; Bell, *Prin.* §635, 2086, 2097.
[3] Prescription Act, 1669, c. 14; Ersk. III, 7, 27.
[4] Prescription Act, 1669, c. 14; Ersk. III, 7, 27.
[5] Reduction Act, 1617, c. 13; Bell, *Prin.* §2024.
[6] Prescription and Limitation (Sc.) Act, 1973, S. 6 and Sch. 1.
[7] Conveyancing (Sc.) Act, 1924, S. 17; Conveyancing Amdt. (Sc.) Act, 1938, S. 4.

ledged),[1] not being an imprescriptible obligation or right, after twenty years.[2]

(d) *other negative prescriptions*

Various other statutes extinguish various rights after the lapse of specified periods of time. The chief individual instances[3] are:

(1) arrestments prescribe in 3 years;[4]

(2) copyright in a published edition lapses after 25 years and an author's copyright after 50 years from his death, or 50 years from the year of first publication.[5]

(3) copyright in a registered design subsists for five years, which may be extended for two further periods of five years.[6]

(4) inhibitions registered in the Register of Inhibitions and Adjudications prescribe after five years but may be renewed for five years.[7]

(5) a marriage licence granted by a sheriff is void if marriage does not follow within ten days.[8]

(6) patents are valid for sixteen years but may be extended for five or ten years.[9]

(7) plant breeder's rights may be granted for fifteen (in certain cases eighteen) years and not exceeding twenty-five years.[10]

(8) registered trade marks subsist for seven years but may be renewed for fourteen years more.[11]

Statutory prescription—positive prescription

The Prescription Act, 1594, c. 218, provided that no one should be compelled to produce the warrants for his sasine of land after forty years' possession, and that the lack thereof should not be a ground of challenge of the infeftment. The Prescription Act, 1617, c. 12, created the rule that uninterrupted and peaceful

[1] As defined in 1973 Act, Ss. 9–10.

[2] 1973 Act, Ss. 7–8. Imprescriptible rights which cannot be extinguished by prescription are listed in Sch. 3.

[3] Certain extinctive provisions relevant only in public law, taxation or criminal law are not listed.

[4] Debtors (Sc.) Act, 1838, S. 22; it was formerly five years and is three months in the case of small debts: Small Debt (Sc.) Act, 1837, S. 6.

[5] Copyright Act, 1956, Ss. 2, 3, 12–15, 33, 39.

[6] Registered Designs Act, 1949, S. 8.

[7] Conveyancing (Sc.) Act, 1924, S. 44.

[8] Marriage (Sc.) Act, 1939, S. 2.

[9] Patents Act, 1949, Ss. 22–25.

[10] Plant Varieties and Seeds Act, 1964, S. 3.

[11] Trade Marks Act, 1938, S. 20.

possession of land for forty years by virtue of heritable infeftment for which charter and instrument of sasine was produced should not thereafter be challengeable.[1] The Conveyancing Act, 1874, S. 34, replaced by the Conveyancing Act, 1924, S. 16, enacted that any ex facie valid irredeemable title to an estate in land recorded in the appropriate register of sasines should be a sufficient foundation for prescription and that twenty years' possession should suffice except for servitudes, public rights of way or other rights. The Conveyancing and Feudal Reform (Sc.) Act, 1970, S. 8 reduced the period to ten years, with exceptions.

The Prescription and Limitation (Sc.) Act, 1973, Ss. 1–5, provides that if an interest in land has been possessed for a continuous period openly, peaceably and without judicial interruption,[2] and the possession was founded on a deed or decree[3] sufficient in its terms to constitute a title to that interest in the land, the validity of the title is thereafter exempt from challenge except on the ground that the deed is invalid *ex facie*[3] or is forged. The requisite periods are: interests in land generally: ten years;[4] an interest in the foreshore or salmon fishings as against the Crown,[4] an interest in land held on lease or allodially,[5] positive servitudes over land and public rights of way:[6] twenty years. The running of a prescriptive period may be interrupted judicially, by making a claim which challenges the possession.[7]

Decennalis et triennalis possessio

By a rule imported from canon law a churchman was deemed to have a title to any subject as part of his benefice from thirteen years possession, though he could produce no written title to it.[8]

Mora

Lapse of time short of the period of the long negative prescription, or a relevant shorter prescription, is not an absolute bar to a party's insistence on the right in question,[9] though delay enhances the onus of proof on the pursuer,[10] and may result in loss of

---

[1] Stair II, 12, 15; Ersk. III, 7, 8–15; Bell, *Prin.* §606, 2002.

[2] Defined, 1973 Act, S. 4.

[3] See also 1973 Act, S. 5.

[4] 1973 Act, S. 1.   [5] 1973 Act, S. 2.

[6] 1973 Act, S. 3.   [7] 1973 Act, S. 4.

[8] Ersk. III, 7, 33; *Cochrane* v. *Smith* (1859) 22 D. 252.

[9] *Cunninghame* v. *Boswell* (1868) 6 M. 890; *Halley* v. *Watt*, 1956 S.C. 370. But see *Russell* v. *McKnight's Tr.* (1900) 2 F. 520; *Smith* v. *Dixon*, 1910 S.C. 230.

[10] *C.B.* v. *A.B.* (1885) 12 R. (H.L.) 36; *Bain* v. *Assets Co.* (1905) 7 F. (H.L.) 104; *Bosville* v. *Lord Macdonald*, 1910 S.C. 597.

evidence.[1] To support a plea of mora[2] there must be such delay as raises an inference of acquiescence or waiver,[3] or cause prejudice to the other party.[4] Delay has frequently been held a ground for allowing inquiry by way of proof rather than jury trial.[5]

[1] *Jackson* v. *Swan* (1895) 3 S.L.T. 149; cf. *Eliott's Trs.* v. *E.* (1894) 21 R. 858; *McLellan* v. *Western S.M.T. Co.*, 1950 S.C. 112; *Moyes* v. *Burntisland Shipbuilding Co.*, 1952 S.C. 429; *Devine* v. *Beardmore*, 1955 S.C. 311.

[2] *Lees's Trs.* v. *Dun*, 1912 S.C. 50; 1913 S.C. (H.L.) 12.

[3] *Cook* v. *N.B. Ry.* (1872) 10 M. 513, 516; *Harrison* v. *N. of Scotland Bank* (1890) 28 S.L.R. 162; *Macdonald* v. *Newall* (1898) 1 F. 68; *Gamage* v. *Charlesworth's Tr.*, 1910 S.C. 257; cf. *Macfarlane* v. *M.*, 1956 S.C. 473.

[4] *Devine, supra*; *Clark* v. *Pryde*, 1959 S.L.T. (Notes) 16.

[5] *McLellan, supra*; *Milne* v. *Glasgow Corpn.*, 1951 S.C. 340; *Halley* v. *Watt*, 1956 S.C. 370; *Conetta* v. *Central S.M.T. Co.*, 1966 S.L.T. 302; *Graham* v. *A.E.I. Ltd.*, 1968 S.L.T. 81.

BOOK II

INTERNATIONAL PRIVATE LAW

CHAPTER 10

CASES INVOLVING FOREIGN ELEMENTS

THE principles of the international private law of Scotland or the Scottish principles as to conflict of laws are relevant where a legal problem arising in Scotland involves an element or factor which is non-Scottish, so that reference exclusively to Scots law might be unsatisfactory or unjust.[1] The non-Scottish factor may be such an element as that a party to a marriage is not Scottish, that a contract has been made furth of Scotland, or that a non-Scot dies possessed of property in Scotland and elsewhere. These principles are a branch of Scottish private law, and are not international in the sense of being common to many or all countries with distinct legal systems, though the principles accepted in Scots law show considerable similarity to those accepted in most Anglo-American legal systems, and extensive reliance is placed in Scotland on Anglo-American authorities. They constitute the Scottish principles relevant where a private law problem contains an international element, or one involving non-Scottish law as well as Scots law.[2]

The Scottish principles of international private law may be relevant in relation to any of the branches of domestic private law, persons, obligations, property, trusts, and so on. They do not themselves directly solve problems involving a foreign element, but guide the Scots lawyer on three preliminary problems: (1) jurisdiction, whether in the circumstances the Scottish courts can validly exercise jurisdiction to decide the dispute, or must decline;[3] (2) choice of law, whether, if the Scottish courts can validly exercise jurisdiction, the principles of Scots domestic or internal private law, or of some other system of domestic private law, fall to be applied to determine the rights, duties, and remedies

---

[1] England and Northern Ireland are non-Scottish or foreign for these purposes, as much as Canada or Germany. cf. *Orr Ewing's Trs.* v. *O.E.* (1885) 13 R. (H.L.) 1, 12.

[2] See generally Stair, More's Note A; Ersk. III, 2, 39–42; Bell, *Comm.* II, 375; *Prin.* §306, 1537, 1550; Duncan & Dykes, *Civil Jurisdiction*; Anton, *Private International Law*; Dicey and Morris, *Conflict of Laws*; Cheshire, *Private International Law*; Morris, *Conflict of Laws*; Graveson, *Conflict of Laws*.

[3] If the Scottish courts can validly exercise jurisdiction the subordinate question of jurisdiction may arise, whether the Court of Session, Sheriff Court, or some other Scottish court or tribunal, is the one competent to exercise that jurisdiction. This subordinate question is determined purely by Scots internal law.

of parties; and (3) what effect, if any, has to be given in Scotland
to any foreign judgment which may already have been issued in
relation to the dispute. It follows that, in some cases of problems
raising a foreign element, the Scottish courts, having considered
their own rules of international private law, must decline to
exercise jurisdiction, or, if they exercise it, must apply foreign
law, or must recognise an existing foreign judgment as decisive,
and give effect to it. It is only if the Scottish Courts feel entitled
to exercise jurisdiction and when they have selected the appropriate system of law, that they can proceed to ascertain the
relevant rules of law and apply them to decide the issue.

Preliminary issues

Before applying Scottish principles of international private
law to a situation involving a non-Scottish element the court or
legal adviser must be satisfied that the foreign element in the
situation is material to the question of jurisdiction or of choice of
law. It may be irrelevant; thus the foreign nationality of either or
both parties is generally irrelevant to a contract made, and to be
performed, or to a delict done, wholly in Scotland.[1] But such a
decision itself implies consideration of the possible effect of
international private law rules and rejection of them as irrelevant
in the circumstances.

Characterisation or classification

If, however, the foreign element is deemed material the court
must characterise or classify the facts raising the legal problem,
or assign the legal question raised thereby to the appropriate
legal category.[2] Thus if a young foreigner seeks to marry in
Scotland, and the law of the foreigner's country requires parental
consent, does the absence of such consent affect his capacity to
marry, or is it part of the formalities of marriage?[3] Is a claim for
breach of promise one for breach of contract or for a delict?[4]
Such characterisation may be differently done in different legal
systems. Characterisation of a legal question must probably be
effected in Scottish courts on the basis of legal concepts and categories recognized in internal Scots law, but sometimes recognizing wider and more general categories to take account of legal

---

[1] cf. *Branca* v. *Cobarro* [1947] K.B. 854.

[2] On this problem see Robertson, *Characterisation in the Conflict of Laws*, and chapters
in all the textbooks on international private law.

[3] *Bliersbach* v. *MacEwen*, 1959 S.C. 43.

[4] See further such cases as *De Nicols* v. *Curlier* [1900] A.C. 21; *Re Martin* [1900] P. 211.

concepts and relations unknown to Scots law but analogous thereto. Thus the distinction for purposes of characterisation is between immoveable and moveable property rather than between heritable and moveable or real and personal property.[1]

CONNECTING FACTORS

In relation both to jurisdiction and to choice of law there must be a connecting factor between the matter in controversy, and, so far as concerns jurisdiction, the Scottish courts or, so far as concerns choice of law, the principles of the system of law applied internally in Scotland or in the territory of another particular legal system, before the Scottish courts are justified in exercising jurisdiction, or in applying the principles of Scottish or another particular system of internal law, as the case may be.

Connecting factors—jurisdiction

In relation to jurisdiction, the main connecting factor in issues of personal status is the pursuer's having Scotland as his domicile or country of permanent home. In issues of obligations or property the general rule is *actor sequitur forum rei*, that the pursuer must seek his remedy in a court having jurisdiction over the defender, at the time when the summons is served,[2] so that the question is whether there is adequate connection between the court chosen and the defender. The principal connecting factor in such cases is the possibility, if the Scottish court exercises jurisdiction, of enforcing its decree against the defender by the appropriate diligence—the principle of effectiveness.[3]

The principal circumstances in which a decree can be made effective are where the defender is resident within the territorial area of the court's jurisdiction, or has property, heritable or moveable, situated therein, or has had moveables belonging to him arrested in the hands of a third party therein *jurisdictionis fundandae causa*. Jurisdiction founded by arrestment applies to all personal actions wherein a decree could be made effective by attachment of the property arrested.[4]

---

[1] *Re Fitzgerald* [1904] 1 Ch. 573, 588; *Re Hoyles* [1911] 1 Ch. 179, 185; on the distinctions in internal private law, see Ch. 71, *infra*.

[2] *Stewart* v. *North* (1889) 16 R. 927; 17 R. (H.L.) 60.

[3] Ersk. I, 2, 16; cf. *Henderson* v. *Patrick Thomson, Ltd.*, 1911 S.C. 246, 249.

[4] *L.N.W. Ry.* v. *Lindsay* (1858) 3 Macq. 99.

Prorogation of jurisdiction

The other main connecting factor in cases of obligations or property is that the defender has expressly or impliedly submitted himself to the jurisdiction of the Scottish courts. This may be done by prorogation of jurisdiction,[1] or voluntary submission to a court's jurisdiction, as by a foreigner.[2] It may be done expressly[3] or impliedly, as by lodging defences without objecting to the jurisdiction.[4] But prorogation is incompetent to confer a jurisdiction which the court could not otherwise exercise.[5]

Reconvention

Submission to the jurisdiction may also be made by reconvention, whereby it is held that one appealing to the courts of this country renders himself subject to the jurisdiction of these courts in a cross-action if arising *ex eodem negotio* or if *ejusdem generis*.[6] This principle also does not extend the court's jurisdiction to include subjects which it could not otherwise have disposed of. It does not amount to reconvention if the appeal to the Scottish courts was in self-defence.[7]

Connecting factors—choice of law

In relation to choice of law the main connecting factors between the parties' actings and one or more[8] particular legal systems are: the nationality of the parties; domicile of the parties; residence of the parties; presence of parties; the place of incorporation of a corporation; the intention of parties; the flag of a ship; the *locus* of an act or event, such as the celebration of a marriage, the making or performance of a contract, or the

---

[1] Ersk. I, 2, 27.

[2] *Thompson* v. *Whitehead* (1862) 24 D. 331; *Gill* v. *Cutler* (1895) 23 R. 371; cf. *Styring* v. *Mayor of Oporovec*, 1931 S.L.T. 493.

[3] *Longmuir* v. *L.* (1850) 12 D. 926; *Lord Macdonald* v. *His Next of Kin* (1864) 2 M. 1194; *Irvine* v. *Hart* (1869) 7 M. 723; *International Exhibition* v. *Bapty* (1891) 18 R. 843; *Elderslie S.S. Co.* v. *Burrell* (1895) 22 R. 389.

[4] *White* v. *Spottiswoode* (1846) 8 D. 952; *Dundee Investment Co.* v. *Macdonald* (1884) 11 R. 537; *Assets Co.* v. *Falla's Trs.* (1894) 22 R. 178; *D. Fife's Trs.* v. *Taylor*, 1934 S.L.T. 76; *Govt. of Spain* v. *National Bank of Scotland*, 1939 S.C. 413; *Grangemouth and Forth Towing Co.* v. *Netherlands E.I. Co.*, 1942 S.L.T. 228.

[5] Ersk. I, 2, 30; *Morton* v. *Gardiner* (1871) 9 M. 548; cf. *Ringer* v. *Churchill* (1840) 2 D. 307.

[6] *Thompson* v. *Whitehead* (1862) 24 D. 331; *Morison & Milne* v. *Massa* (1866) 5 M. 130; *Longworth* v. *Yelverton* (1868) 7 M. 70; *California Redwood Co. Liqdr.* v. *Walker* (1886) 13 R. 810; *Pacific Coast Mining Co. Liqdr.* v. *Walker* (1886) 13 R. 816; *Burrell* v. *Harding*, 1931 S.L.T. 76; *Kitson* v. *K.*, 1945 S.C. 434.

[7] *Davis* v. *Cadman* (1897) 24 R. 297; *Macaulay* v. *Hussain*, 1966 S.C. 204.

[8] Different parts of one controversy may have to be referred to different foreign legal systems.

commission of a delict; the *situs* or situation of property; and the *forum* in which proceedings are brought.

INDIVIDUAL CONNECTING FACTORS

Nationality

Nationality is a political relationship between a person and a state, and is only rarely a material connecting factor.[1] Apart from time of war[2] the fact that a party to a legal transaction connected with Scotland is a foreign national is usually irrelevant.[3]

Domicile

A person's domicile is the state, territory or country having a distinct legal system, which is regarded as the country of his permanent home.[4] No person can be without a domicile.[5] Law attributes to every person one domicile, and only one domicile at any given time.[6] What that domicile is is determined by the same rules in all branches of the law where domicile is relevant, and is a conclusion of law, determined by Scots law, on the basis of the facts of the particular case.[7]

Domicile of origin

Every person has initially a domicile of origin, which is, in the case of a legitimate child, the father's domicile,[8] of the child of a Scottish putative marriage, Scottish,[9] of an illegitimate or posthumous child, the mother's domicile,[10] and of a foundling the country where he is found. It is independent of the place of birth.[11] A domicile of origin may be transmitted through several generations though none of the later generations may have lived in the country of the domicile of origin.[12] On his father's death, a child

[1] European legal systems commonly rely on nationality rather than domicile as a connection between a person and a legal system.

[2] cf. *Van Uden* v. *Burrell*, 1916 S.C. 391; *Sovfracht* v. *Van Uden* [1943] A.C. 203.

[3] cf. *Powell* v. *Mackenzie* (1900) 8 S.L.T. 182; But only a British subject can own shares in a British ship (Merchant Shipping Act, 1894, S. 1) or a British aircraft.

[4] *Whicker* v. *Hume* (1858) 7 H.L.C. 124, 160.

[5] *Bell* v. *Kennedy* (1868) 6 M. (H.L.) 69; *Udny* v. *U.* (1869) 7 M. (H.L.) 89.

[6] *Winans* v. *A.G.* [1904] A.C. 287; *Marchioness of Huntly* v. *Gaskell* (1905) 8 F. (H.L.) 4; *Liverpool Royal Infirmary* v. *Ramsay*, 1930 S.C. (H.L.) 83.

[7] *L.A.* v. *Brown's Trs.*, 1907 S.C. 333; *Robinson* v. *R's Trs.*, 1930 S.C. (H.L.) 20.

[8] *Udny* v. *U.* (1869) 7 M. (H.L.) 89; *Fairbairn* v. *Neville* (1897) 25 R. 192; this is so even if the child is in the mother's custody after divorce: *Shanks* v. *S.*, 1965 S.L.T. 330.

[9] *Udny* v. *U.* (1869) 7 M. (H.L.) 89.   [10] *Smijth* v. *S.*, 1918, 1 S.L.T. 156.

[11] *Wylie* v. *Laye* (1834) 12 S. 927; *Corbidge* v. *Somerville*, 1913 S.C. 858.

[12] *Peal* v. *P.* (1930) 46 T.L.R. 645; *Grant* v. *G.*, 1931 S.C. 238.

takes the domicile of his mother, and it changes as her domicile changes.[1] In the absence of evidence of origin there is some presumption that a person is domiciled in a country of long residence.[2]

There is a presumption that a person's domicile of origin continues to be his domicile.[3] Domicile of origin continues to attach to a person despite absences abroad,[4] or involuntary residence, however long, in another state.[5] It is lost only by the acquisition of a domicile of choice,[6] which can only be done *animo et facto*, by settling in another state in circumstances evidencing intention to relinquish connection with the country of origin,[7] and it revives if a domicile of choice be abandoned.[8]

Domicile of choice

A person may acquire a domicile of choice *animo et facto* by residing in another state with the intention of remaining there indefinitely.[9] The court must have regard to the length of residence and any expressed intention,[10] or circumstances evidencing intention to make that his permanent home or otherwise.[11] Long residence abroad evidences acquisition of domicile but is not conclusive.[7] Short residence may suffice if there is clear intention.[8]

---

[1] *Crumpton's J.F.* v. *Fitch-Noyes*, 1918 S.C. 378.   [2] *Watts* v. *W.* (1885) 12 R. 894.

[3] *Fairbairn, supra*; *Winans* v. *A.G.* [1904] A.C. 287; *Marchioness of Huntly* v. *Gaskell* (1905) 8 F. (H.L.) 4; *Liverpool Royal Infirmary* v. *Ramsay*, 1930 S.C. (H.L.) 83.

[4] *Wilson* v. *W.* (1872) 10 M. 573; *In re Mitchell* (1884) 13 Q.B.D. 418; *Steel* v. *S.* (1888) 15 R. 896; *Hood* v. *H.* (1897) 24 R. 973; *Ross* v. *R.*, 1930 S.C. (H.L.) 1; *Sellars* v. *Sellars*, 1942 S.C. 206; see also *Brown* v. *B.*, 1928 S.C. 542.

[5] *Burton* v. *Fisher* (1828) Milw. 183; *In re Napoleon* (1853) 2 Rob. Eccl. 606 (prisoners); *Hoskins* v. *Matthews* (1856) 8 De G. M. & G. 13 (invalid); *Steel* v. *S.* (1888) 15 R. 896; *Crumpton's J.F., supra*.

[6] *Bell* v. *Kennedy* (1868) 6 M. (H.L.) 69; *Steel* v. *S.* (1888) 15 R. 896; *Liverpool R.I.*, *supra*.

[7] *Donaldson* v. *McClure* (1857) 20 D. 307; *Aikman* v. *A.* (1861) 3 Macq. 854; *Moorhouse* v. *Lord* (1863) 10 H.L.C. 272; *Steel, supra*; *Marchioness of Huntly, supra*.

[8] *Udny, supra*.

[9] *Aikman* v. *A.* (1861) 3 Macq. 854; *Bell, supra*; *Udny, supra*; *Liverpool R.I.* v. *Ramsay*, 1930 S.C. (H.L.) 83; *McLelland* v. *McL.*, 1942 S.C. 502.

[10] cf. *Robinson* v. *R's Trs.*, 1934 S.L.T. 183; *Rankin* v. *R.*, 1960 S.L.T. 308.

[11] *Low* v. *L.* (1891) 19 R. 115; *Marchioness of Huntly* v. *Gaskell* (1905) 8 F. (H.L.) 4; *Tasker* v. *Grieve* (1905) 8 F. 45; *Casdagli* v. *C.* [1919] A.C. 145; *Ross* v. *R.*, 1930 S.C. (H.L.) 1; *McLelland* v. *McL.*, 1942 S.C. 502; *Rankin* v. *R.*, 1960 S.L.T. 308; *Gould* v. *G.*, 1968 S.L.T. 98; *McEwan* v. *M.*, 1969 S.L.T. 342.

[12] *Jopp* v. *Wood* (1865) 4 De G. J. & S. 616; *Fairbairn* v. *Neville* (1897) 25 R. 192; *Ross* v. *R.* (1899) 1 F. 963; *Winans* v. *A.G.* [1904] A.C. 287; *Brown* v. *B.*, 1928 S.C. 542; *Liverpool R.I.* v. *Ramsay*, 1930 S.C. (H.L.) 83; *Gould* v. *G.*, 1968 S.L.T. 98.

[13] *Bell* v. *Kennedy* (1868) 6 M. (H.L.) 69; *Macphail* v. *M's Trs.* (1906) 14 S.L.T. 388; *Willar* v. *W.*, 1954 S.C. 144.

If there is doubt,[1] or until a domicile of choice has been acquired, the domicile of origin adheres.[2] A person residing in a country by reason of being stationed there may acquire a domicile of choice there, but only if the residence is continued voluntarily.[3] Voluntary residence abroad, even if motivated by health or fiscal reasons, may operate a change of domicile.[4] A move made to facilitate divorce may have the same effect.[5]

A domicile of choice may be abandoned *animo et facto*, and a new one acquired. Until then, or if none be acquired, the domicile of origin revives,[6] but mere absence or departure from the country of choice does not at once destroy domicile there.[7] Departure from the country of domicile of choice with ending of intention to return there is sufficient to end that domicile.[8]

The onus is on a person maintaining a change of domicile to prove intention to relinquish the domicile of origin and also the acquisition *animo et facto* of a new domicile.[9]

Domicile of dependants

A wife on contracting a valid or voidable marriage formerly acquired the domicile of her husband,[10] and retained it, even though actually or judicially separated,[11] and might have it changed by her husband's change of domicile,[12] until her husband's death, when she might by leaving the country revert to

---

[1] *Steel* v. *S.* (1888) 15 R. 896.

[2] *Moorhouse* v. *Lord* (1863) 10 H.L.C. 272; *Donaldson* v. *McClure* (1857) 20 D. 307; *Bell* v. *Kennedy* (1868) 6 M. (H.L.) 69; *Hood* v. *H.* (1897) 24 R. 973; *Marchioness of Huntly* v. *Gaskell* (1905) 8 F. (H.L.) 4; *Liverpool R.I.*, *supra*; *McLelland* v. *McL.*, 1942 S.C. 502.

[3] *Clarke* v. *Newmarsh* (1835) 14 S. 488; *Udny*, *supra*; *Grant* v. *G.*, 1931 S.C. 238; *Sellars* v. *S.*, 1942 S.C. 206; *Donaldson* v. *D.* [1949] P. 363; *Willar* v. *W.*, 1954 S.C. 144.

[4] *Hoskins* v. *Matthews* (1856) 8 De G. M. & G. 13.

[5] *Carswell* v. *C.* (1881) 8 R. 901; *Stavert* v. *S.* (1882) 9 R. 519; *Wood* v. *W.* [1957] P. 254.

[6] *Udny* v. *Udny* (1869) 7 M. (H.L.) 89; *Vincent* v. *Earl of Buchan* (1889) 16 R. 637; *Stewart* v. *S.* (1905) 13 S.L.T. 668; *Re Flynn* [1968] 1 All E.R. 49.

[7] *Hunter* v. *H.* (1893) 30 S.L.R. 915; *Pabst* v. *P.* (1898) 6 S.L.T. 117; *McNeill* v. *McN.*, 1919, 2 S.L.T. 127; *Labacianskas* v. *L.*, 1949 S.C. 280.

[8] *Re Flynn* [1968] 1 All E.R. 49.

[9] *Bell* v. *Kennedy* (1868) 6 M. (H.L.) 69; *Vincent* v. *Earl of Buchan* (1889) 16 R. 637; *McLelland* v. *McL.*, 1942 S.C. 502; *Holden* v. *H.* [1968] N.I. 7.

[10] Stair I, 4, 9; *Harvey* v. *Farnie* (1882) 8 App. Cas. 43; *Yelverton* v. *Y.* (1859) 1 Sw. & Tr. 574; *De Reneville* v. *De R.* [1948] P. 100.

[11] *Low* v. *L.* (1891) 19 R. 115; *Mackinnon's Trs.* v. *Inland Revenue*, 1920 S.C. (H.L.) 171; *A.G. for Alberta* v. *Cook* [1926] A.C. 444.

[12] *Mackinnon's Trs.* v. *Inland Revenue*, 1920 S.C. (H.L.) 171. Many proposals have been made for altering the rules set out in this sentence, e.g. Royal Commission on Marriage and Divorce, 1956.

her domicile of origin[1] or acquire a fresh domicile of choice.[2] A wife now has an independent domicile.[3] If the marriage is void, she does not thereby acquire her husband's domicile,[4] but may have acquired a domicile of choice in the country of her putative husband's domicile.[5]

A pupil cannot acquire a domicile of choice, but such may be acquired for him by his father,[6] failing whom, by his mother,[7] making a change of domicile, but a minor may acquire a domicile for himself.[8] After majority a person's domicile is not changed merely by his parent's change of domicile. A pupil child's domicile is, but a minor child's domicile is not, changed by his mother's remarriage.[9] If parents separate, the domicile of a pupil child is that of the mother if he lives with her.[10] After divorce of the parents a pupil child's domicile is determined by the father's domicile, even though the child is in the custody of the mother who has acquired a new domicile.[11]

An orphan child probably cannot have his domicile changed by his guardian. A legitimated child or an adopted child probably takes his father's domicile.

A person mentally incapax probably cannot have his domicile changed by himself or by his guardian.[12]

A husband cannot, by seeking to change his domicile after a cause of action has arisen in a matrimonial dispute, subject his wife to the exclusive jurisdiction of a foreign court.[13]

Presence of parties

The actual presence of a party in a country is frequently

---

[1] *In the goods of Raffenel* (1863) 32 L.J.P. & M. 203; *Crumpton's J.F. v. Finch-Noyes*, 1918 S.C. 378.

[2] *Re Wallach* [1950] 1 All E.R. 199.

[3] Domicile and Matrimonial Proceedings Act, 1973, S. 1.

[4] *De Reneville v. De R.* [1948] P. 100.

[5] *Administrator of Austrian Property v. von Lorang*, 1927 S.C. (H.L.) 80.

[6] *D'Etchegoyen v. D'E.* (1888) 13 P.D. 132; *Woodbury v. Sutherland's Trs.*, 1938 S.C. 689; *Henderson v. H.* [1965] 1 All E.R. 179.

[7] *Potinger v. Wightman* (1817) 3 Mer. 67; *Johnstone v. Beattie* (1843) 10 Cl. & F. 42, 138; *Arnott v. Groom* (1846) 9 D. 142; *Crumpton's J.F. v. Fitch-Noyes*, 1918 S.C. 378.

[8] *Harvey v. H.* (1860) 22 D. 1198; *Flannigan v. Bothwell Inspector* (1892) 19 R. 909; Clive, 1966 J.R. 1.

[9] *Crumpton's J.F.*, *supra*. See also *Re Beaumont* [1893] 3 Ch. 490. See also *Hope v. H.* [1968] N.I. 1.

[10] Domicile and Matrimonial Proceedings Act, 1973, S. 4, altering *Shanks v. S.*, 1965 S.L.T. 330.

[11] *Shanks v. S.*, 1965 S.L.T. 330. *Sed quaere*: see *Hope v. H.* [1968] N.I. 1.

[12] *Urquhart v. Butterfield* (1887) 37 Ch. D. 357; see also *Crumpton's J.F.*, *supra*.

[13] *Ramsay v. R.*, 1925 S.C. 216; *Hannah v. H.*, 1926 S.L.T. 370; *Lack v. L.*, 1926 S.L.T. 656; *Kelly v. K.*, 1927 S.N. 132; *Crabtree v. C.*, 1929 S.L.T. 675.

relevant to jurisdiction,[1] but rarely to choice of law as that presence may be explained by extraneous matters.

Residence

Habitual residence and ordinary residence are sometimes referred to[2] as connecting factors.

Residence is quite independent of domicile; it connotes physical presence, not necessarily permanent, but at least prolonged and not merely transitory presence. It is entirely a question of fact. A person may have a residence in more than one country, and it is immaterial to a question of residence in Scotland that he is not domiciled in Scotland.[3] By Scots law a person is 'resident' if he is physically present and has resided continuously in Scotland for 40 days.[4] Domicile even along with presence for less than 40 days does not confer jurisdiction on the ground of residence.[5] Residence must be actual; it requires physical presence and it is not sufficient merely to have one's home in Scotland.[6] Jurisdiction based on residence lapses when the person quits Scotland;[7] it does not continue for 40 days thereafter.[8]

Nationality, domicile, presence and residence of unincorporated associations

The domicile of an association is probably determined by the country in which it is established, its residence by having an office, and its presence established by its carrying on business. A friendly society registered in England, carrying on business in Scotland by a branch with rules registered in Scotland, has been held subject to Scottish jurisdiction.[9]

---

[1] e.g. *Dalziel* v. *Coulthurst's Exrs.*, 1934 S.C. 564; *Dallas* v. *McArdle*, 1949 S.C. 481 (need for personal citation in Scotland).

[2] e.g. Wills Act, 1963, S. 1; Adoption Act, 1968, S. 11.

[3] *Marchioness of Huntly* v. *Gaskell* (1905) 8 F. (H.L.) 4.

[4] *Tasker* v. *Grieve* (1905) 8 F. 45; *Carter* v. *Allison*, 1966 S.C. 257.

[5] *Tasker, supra*; *Hutchison* v. *H.*, 1912 1 S.L.T. 219.

[6] *Joel* v. *Gill* (1859) 21 D. 929; *Martin* v. *Szyszka*, 1943 S.C. 203; *Findlay* v. *Donachie*, 1944 S.C. 306; *McCord* v. *McC.*, 1946 S.C. 198; *Nicol* v. *Bruce*, 1965 S.C. 160.

[7] *Corstorphine* v. *Kasten* (1898) 1 F. 287; *Carter* v. *Allison*, 1966 S.C. 257.

[8] It continues for the purposes of the jurisdiction of a particular sheriff court, if the defender has ceased for less than 40 days to reside and has no known residence in Scotland; Sheriff Courts (Sc.) Acts, 1907, S. 6, and 1913, S. 3 and Sched. 1; *Martin, supra*; *Findlay, supra*; *McCord, supra*.

[9] *Sons of Temperance Friendly Socy.*, 1926 S.C. 418.

Nationality, domicile, presence, and residence of corporations

The nationality of a corporation depends on the country of its incorporation.[1] Its domicile is the country in which it is incorporated[2] and that legal system determines its creation and dissolution, attributes and powers.[3] The carrying on of business in Scotland by a corporation is equivalent to the physical presence of a natural person,[4] and its residence is determined by the place where the main controlling power of the corporation is situated.[5] The presence of an agent in Scotland does not make a company resident in Scotland.[6]

Intention of parties

Parties may, particularly in contracts and wills, indicate their intention as to which country's courts are to have jurisdiction and which system of law they desire to regulate their relations. This may be indicated expressly,[7] or impliedly, by the use of the forms or technical terminology of one legal system,[8] by reference to arbitration in a particular place,[9] by the place where the deed was executed[10] or the transaction took place.[11]

Flag of a ship

The law of a ship's flag, i.e. of the country in which is situated the port of registry, is a relevant connecting factor in some cases.[12] By the Merchant Shipping Act, 1894, Sec. 265, where in any

---

[1] *Janson* v. *Driefontein Consolidated Mines, Ltd.* [1902] A.C. 484.

[2] *Williams* v. *R.C.V.S.* (1897) 5 S.L.T. 208; *A.G.* v. *Jewish Colonisation Assocn.* [1900] 2 Q.B. 556; *Lazard Bros.* v. *Midland Bank* [1933] A.C. 289; *Gasque* v. *I.R.C.* [1940] 2 K.B. 80.

[3] *Risdon Iron Works* v. *Furness* [1906] 1 K.B. 49; *Banco de Bilbao* v. *Sancha* [1938] 2 K.B. 176; *Carse* v. *Coppen*, 1951 S.C. 233.

[4] *Thomson* v. *N.B. and Mercantile Ins. Co.* (1868) 6 M. 310; cf. *H.M.A.* v. *Hetherington*, 1915 S.C. (J.) 79; *O'Brien* v. *Davies*, 1961 S.L.T. 85.

[5] *San Paulo (Brazilian) Ry. Co.* v. *Carter* [1896] A.C. 31; *De Beers Mines Ltd.* v. *Howe* [1906] A.C. 455; *Unit Construction Co. Ltd.* v. *Bullock* [1960] A.C. 351.

[6] *Laidlaw* v. *Provident Plate Glass Ins. Co.* (1890) 17 R. 544.

[7] *Girvin, Roper & Co.* v. *Monteith* (1895) 23 R. 129; *Vita Food Products* v. *Unus Shipping Co.* [1939] A.C. 277.

[8] *Corbet* v. *Waddell* (1879) 7 R. 200; *Studd* v. *Cook* (1883) 10 R. (H.L.) 53; *Brown's Trs.* v. *Brown* (1890) 17 R. 1174; *Battye's Trs.* v. *B.*, 1917 S.C. 385; *Eadie's Trs.* v. *Henderson*, 1919 1 S.L.T. 253; see also *Mitchell & Baxter* v. *Davies* (1875) 3 R. 208; *Smith* v. *Smiths* (1891) 18 R. 1036; contrast *Mackintosh* v. *May* (1895) 22 R. 345.

[9] *Hamlyn* v. *Talisker Distillery* (1894) 21 R. (H.L.) 21; *Robertson* v. *Brandes Schonwald & Co.* (1906) 8 F. 815; *Kwik Ho Tong* v. *Finlay* [1927] A.C. 604.

[10] *Shedlock* v. *Hannay* (1891) 18 R. 663.

[11] *Scottish Provident Inst.* v. *Cohen* (1888) 16 R. 112.

[12] *R.* v. *Anderson* (1868) L.R. 1 C.C.R. 161; *R.* v. *Keyn* (1876) L.R. 2 Ex.D. 63, 94, 98.

matter relating to a ship or to a person belonging to a ship there appears to be a conflict of laws then, failing provision in Part II of that Act extending to that ship, the case has to be governed by the laws of the port of registry.[1]

Locus of fact or event

The place in which a cause of action arises may be a connecting factor with that country's courts or system of law. Thus the solemnizing of a marriage in Scotland,[2] the making or performing of a contract,[3] the commission of a wrong[4] may all be relevant connecting factors. The country in which some act or event happened may be a matter of dispute. It is probably the country where the last event necessary to make the act or event legally significant and, by Scots law, give a complete cause of action in respect thereof.[5]

Situs of property

The situation in Scotland of some property or right, such as land,[6] goods,[7] a debt,[8] or an estate[9] may also be relevant as a connection. Money in Scotland owed to, or property in Scotland pertaining to, a person furth of Scotland may be arrested *ad fundandam jurisdictionem*, thereby fixing the locality of the subjects in Scotland and rendering their foreign owner liable to be convened in a Scottish action.[10]

Forum of action

The initiation of legal proceedings in the courts of a particular legal system, if those courts accept jurisdiction, establishes a connection with that legal system, at least in matters of procedure.[11]

---

[1] Held inapplicable to the facts in *MacKinnon* v. *Iberia Shipping Co.*, 1955 S.C. 20.

[2] *Miller* v. *Deakin*, 1912, 1 S.L.T. 253.

[3] Personal citation of the defender in Scotland is also necessary: *Dallas* v. *McArdle*, 1949 S.C. 481.

[4] e.g. *Parnell* v. *Walter* (1889) 16 R. 917; *Toni Tyres Ltd.* v. *Palmer Tyre Ltd.* (1905) 7 F. 477. Personal citation in Scotland was also necessary: *Dalziel* v. *Coulthurst's Exor.*, 1934 S.C. 546, overruled by Law Reform (Jurisdiction in Delict) (Sc.) Act, 1971.

[5] See *Waygood* v. *Bennie* (1885) 12 R. 651; *Parnell, supra*; *Bata* v. *B.* [1948] W.N. 366.

[6] *Love* v. *L.*, 1907 S.C. 728.

[7] *Hay* v. *Jackson*, 1911 S.C. 876.

[8] *Bank of Scotland* v. *Gudin* (1886) 14 R. 213.

[9] *Kennedy* v. *K.* (1884) 12 R. 275; *Robertson's Tr.* v. *Nicholson* (1888) 15 R. 914; *McGennis* v. *Rooney* (1891) 18 R. 817; *Ashburton* v. *Escombe* (1892) 20 R. 187.

[10] *Cameron* v. *Chapman* (1837) 16 S. 907; *Trowsdale's Tr.* v. *Forcett Ry. Co.* (1870) 9 M. 88; *North* v. *Stewart* (1890) 17 R. (H.L.) 60; *Leggat Bros.* v. *Gray*, 1908 S.C. 67; *Sheaf S.S. Co.* v. *Compania Transmediterranea*, 1930 S.C. 660.

[11] e.g. *McElroy* v. *M'Allister*, 1949 S.C. 110.

CHAPTER 11

JURISDICTION OF THE SCOTTISH COURTS

JURISDICTION is the power of pronouncing a decree resolving the issue between the parties, which will be enforceable by the Scottish court and also be recognized as valid by foreign courts.[1] The question of jurisdiction must be considered by the court at the outset.[2] In general, the Scottish courts will exercise jurisdiction at the instance of any person over any other person, irrespective of the nationality or domicile of either, and without regard to where the cause of action arose or what it concerns, if the court can make the judgment effective within its own territory by its own processes, or if the defender has submitted himself to the jurisdiction of the court.[3]

Persons disabled from suing

The only person disabled from suing in the Scottish courts is an alien enemy, who is for this purpose any person, even a British subject or a neutral, voluntarily[4] residing or carrying on business in another country during the existence of a state of war between the United Kingdom and that country. His right of action is suspended during hostilities.[5] A person of enemy nationality resident in the United Kingdom in wartime by permission of the Crown, whether interned or not, is fully entitled to sue.[6] Actions may be brought against enemy aliens, who may in such a case defend, counter-claim, and appeal.[7]

---

[1] See generally Duncan and Dykes, *Civil Jurisdiction*; Anton, *Private International Law*, Ch. 5; Maclaren, *Court of Session Practice*.

[2] *McLeod v. Tancred Arrol & Co.* (1890) 17 R. 514; *Dallas v McArdle*, 1949 S.C. 481.

[3] A foreign pursuer will usually, and a foreign defender less usually, be ordained to sist a mandatary, but it is always a matter for the court's discretion: *Ondix v. Landay, Ltd.*, 1963 S. C. 270.

[4] *Vandyke v. Adams* [1942] Ch. 155.

[5] *Janson v. Driefontein Consolidated Mines* [1902] A.C. 484; *Porter v. Freudenberg* [1915] 1 K.B. 857; *Craig Line v. N. B. Storage Co.*, 1915 S.C. 113; *Van Uden v. Burrell*, 1916 S.C. 391; *Rodriguez v. Speyer* [1919] A.C. 59; *Soufracht v. Van Uden* [1943] A.C. 203.

[6] *Schulze, Gow & Co. v. Bank of Scotland*, 1914 2 S.L.T. 455; 1916 2 S.L.T. 207; *Princess Thurn and Taxis v. Moffitt* [1915] 1 Ch. 58; *Schaffenius v. Goldberg* [1916] 1 K.B. 284; *Schulze*, 1917 S.C. 400; *Johnstone v. Pedlar* [1921] 2 A.C. 262; *Weiss v. W.*, 1940 S.L.T. 467; *Crolla*, 1942 S.C. 21.

[7] *Robinson v. Continental Insurance Co. of Mannheim* [1915] 1 K.B. 155; *Porter, supra.*

Persons immune from being sued

The sovereigns of independent states outside the United Kingdom are personally immune from action,[1] as are sovereign foreign states which own,[2] or possess,[3] or have effective control of, the subject-matter in issue,[4] or are entitled to an immediate right of possession of the property in issue.[5] The status of a foreign sovereign as independent or otherwise, if in doubt, is determined conclusively[6] by a certificate from the Foreign and Commonwealth Relations Office.[7]

A foreign sovereign, or state, may waive the immunity,[8] or voluntarily submit to, or prorogate, the jurisdiction of the court, expressly, or by implication, as where he enters appearance to defend and takes no plea to the jurisdiction,[9] or himself makes a claim, in which case he lays himself open to a counter-claim,[10] and he may be called where the purpose of so doing is to give notice of a claim.[11] But to lodge a tender under reservation of all rights and pleas does not imply waiver of the claim to immunity.[12]

Persons immune—diplomatic and consular representatives

By the Diplomatic Privileges Act, 1964, members of a diplomatic mission enjoy certain immunity from jurisdiction. Members of the diplomatic staff of a mission and their families have full personal immunity, except in respect of (a) an action relating to private immoveable property; (b) an action relating to succession in which the diplomat is involved as a private person;

[1] *Mighell* v. *Sultan of Johore* [1894] 1 Q.B. 149; *Kahan* v. *Pakistan Federation* [1951] 2 K.B. 1003.

[2] *The Parlement Belge* (1880) 5 P.D. 197; *The Porto Alexandre* [1920] P. 30; *The Victoria* v. *The Quillwork*, 1932 S.L.T. 68.

[3] *The Gagara* [1919] P. 95; *The Christina* [1938] A.C. 485; *Govt. of Republic of Spain* v. *National Bank of Scotland*, 1939 S.C. 413.

[4] *The Broadmayne* [1916] P. 64; *The Arantzazu Mendi* [1939] A.C. 256.

[5] *U.S.A.* v. *Dollfus Mieg and Bank of England* [1952] A.C. 582; *Rahimtoola* v. *Nizam of Hyderabad* [1958] A.C. 379.

[6] *Foster* v. *Globe Venture Syndicate Ltd.* [1900] 1 Ch. 811; *Duff Development Co.* v. *Kelantan Government* [1924] A.C. 797.

[7] *Mighell, supra*; *Sayce* v. *Armeer* [1952] 2 Q.B. 390.

[8] *D. Brunswick* v. *King of Hanover* (1844) 6 Beav. 1, 37; *Sultan of Johore* v. *Abubaker Tunku Aris Bendahar* [1952] A.C. 318.

[9] *Rosses* v. *Bhagvat Sinhjee* (1891) 19 R. 31.

[10] *King of Spain* v. *Hullet* (1833) 1 Cl. & F. 333; *Rothschild* v. *Queen of Portugal* (1839) 3 Y. & C. Ex. 594; *Strousberg* v. *Republic of Costa Rica* (1881) 44 L.T. 199; *Govt. of Republic of Spain* v. *National Bank of Scotland*, 1939 S.C. 413; *Sultan of Johore* v. *Abubakar Tunku Aris Bendahar* [1952] A.C. 318.

[11] *Strousberg, supra*; *Mighell, supra*.

[12] *Grangemouth and Forth Towing Co.* v. *Netherlands E.I. Co.*, 1942 S.L.T. 228; cf. *S.S. Victoria* v. *S.S. Quillwork*, 1922 S.L.T. 68.

and (c) an action relating to any professional or commercial activity exercised by the diplomatic agent outside his official functions. A member of the administrative or technical staff of the mission and his family has full immunity for official acts, but is civilly liable for acts outside the course of his duties. A member of the service staff of the mission has immunity for official acts, but is liable civilly and criminally for acts outside the course of his duties.[1] Private servants of members of the mission may enjoy privileges and immunities only to the extent admitted by municipal law, so long as their functions are not unduly interfered with. Diplomatic staff who are British nationals or permanently resident in the U.K. have immunity only in respect of official acts.[2] Whether or not any person is entitled to any privilege or immunity is conclusively determined by a certificate of the Secretary of State.[3]

The head of the mission may expressly waive the immunity, and the initiation of proceedings by a diplomatic agent precludes him from invoking immunity in respect of any counter-claim. A separate waiver is necessary before a decree can be enforced against a person immune.[4]

The Crown may, by Order in Council, restrict the privileges of a mission whose country grants lesser privileges to the British mission in that country.[5]

Similar immunities are granted to representatives of Commonwealth countries and Ireland.[6]

Consular officers and employees are not amenable to the jurisdiction of the judicial or administrative authorities of the receiving state in respect of acts performed in the exercise of consular functions, but the sending state may expressly waive this immunity. Initiation of proceedings precludes invoking immunity in respect of any counter-claim.[7]

Persons immune—International Organizations and Conferences

The International Organizations Act, 1968,[8] provides that certain privileges and immunities, including immunity from suit,

---

[1] 1964 Act, Sched. I, Arts. 3, 37(2) and (3).
[2] Ibid., Art. 38.
[3] *Engelke* v. *Musmann* [1928] A.C. 433; 1964 Act, S. 4.
[4] Ibid., Art. 32.
[5] 1964 Act, S. 3.
[6] Diplomatic Immunities (Commonwealth Countries and Republic of Ireland) Act, 1952.
[7] Consular Relations Act, 1968, Sched. I, Arts. 43, 45, 53.
[8] Replacing International Organizations (Immunities and Privileges) Act, 1950, and European Coal and Steel Community Act, 1955.

may by Order in Council be conferred on certain international organizations and their officers, and on representatives at international conferences in the United Kingdom. The Diplomatic Immunities (Conferences with Commonwealth Countries and the Republic of Ireland) Act, 1961, later amended, confers immunities on the representatives of such countries attending conferences in the United Kingdom.

Matters exempted from jurisdiction

The Scottish courts will not entertain actions concerning title to, or possession of, land furth of Scotland,[1] save that these courts will entertain an action arising from a contract relative to foreign land.[2]

Nor will they entertain actions for penalties imposed by the law of other countries,[3] or to enforce foreign revenue laws.[4]

Concurrent jurisdiction—lis alibi pendens

A person may be liable to the jurisdiction of the courts of more than one country and be sued in both.[5] If the Scottish courts have jurisdiction they have no discretion whether to exercise that jurisdiction or not,[6] but may sist the action if the defender is being pursued oppressively and vexatiously by the concurrent actions[7] and they raise the same question.[8] The court is unlikely to sist an action if the defender in one action is pursuer in the other action.[9] The court will not sist an action to preserve the force of arrestments on the dependence until the pursuer raises an action elsewhere.[10] It will normally do so if the action is in

---

[1] Ersk. I, 2, 17; III, 2, 40. See also *British S.A. Co.* v. *Companhia de Moçambique* [1893] A.C. 602; *Cathcart* v. *C.* (1902) 12 S.L.T. 182.

[2] *Ruthven* v. *R.* (1905) 43 S.L.R. 11.

[3] *Huntington* v. *Attrill* [1893] A.C. 150; *A.G. for Canada* v. *Schulze & Co.* (1901) 9 S.L.T. 4; *Banco de Vizcaya* v. *Don Alfonso de Bourbon y Austria* [1935] 1 K.B. 140.

[4] *Govt. of India* v. *Taylor* [1955] A.C. 491; *Metal Industries (Salvage) Ltd.* v. *Owners of Harle*, 1962 S.L.T. 114; cf. *Buchanan and Macharg* v. *McVey* [1955] A.C. 516, n.

[5] e.g. *Hawkins* v. *Wedderburn* (1842) 4 D. 924, on which see *Atkinson & Wood* v. *Mackintosh* (1905) 7 F. 598. The plea of *lis alibi pendens* is a plea not strictly applicable where the other proceedings are in a foreign court; *Martin* v. *Stopford Blair's Exors.* (1879) 7 R. 329.

[6] *Clements* v. *Macaulay* (1866) 4 M. 583, 593, approved *Societe du Gaz* v. *Armateurs français*, 1926 S.C. (H.L.) 13, 19.

[7] *Cochrane* v. *Paul* (1857) 20 D. 178; *Rothfield* v. *Cohen*, 1919, 1 S.L.T. 138; see also *McHenry* v. *Lewis* (1882) 22 Ch. D. 397; *Cohen* v. *Rothfield* [1919] 1 K.B. 410; *Logan* v. *Bank of Scotland* [1906] 1 K.B. 141; *Devine* v. *Cementation Co. Ltd.* [1963] N.I. 65.

[8] *Wilson* v. *Dunlop, Bremner & Co.*, 1921, 1 S.L.T. 35.

[9] *Rothfield, supra.*

[10] *Atkinson & Wood, supra.*

breach of a contractual provision referring disputes to the jurisdiction of a foreign court.[1]

Concurrent jurisdiction—forum non conveniens

The Scottish court may in its discretion decline to exercise
jurisdiction where, though it has jurisdiction, a court in another
country also has jurisdiction, the parties are the same, and the
Scottish court considers that the other forum is more suitable and
appropriate having regard to the convenience of the parties and
the ends of justice.[2] The court may exercise jurisdiction even
though the defender is in Scotland only temporarily if the other
forum is less appropriate.[3] Factors weighing in favour of Scottish
jurisdiction are the express invocation of Scots law in a deed,[4]
the *de quo* being a purely Scottish right such as terce,[5] and
Scotland being the domicile of the parties,[6] and the parties to the
two actions, or the remedies sought, not being identical.[7] Contrary factors include the need to determine questions of the
validity and construction of a will by English law.[8] Priority of
initiation of process is important but not conclusive in relation to
appropriateness of forum.[9]

JURISDICTION IN PARTICULAR ACTIONS

(a) ACTIONS CONCERNING PERSONAL STATUS

In actions brought to declare or change personal status, such
as declarators of marriage, of nullity of marriage, of legitimacy
or of bastardy, and actions of divorce, the main ground of the
jurisdiction of the Scottish court is that the party or parties are

---

[1] cf. *The Cap Blanco* [1913] P. 130; *The Eleftheria* [1970] P. 94.
[2] *Longworth* v. *Hope* (1865) 3 M. 1049; *Clements* v. *Macaulay* (1866) 4 M. 583; *Martin* v. *Stopford-Blair's Exors.* (1879) 7 R. 329; *Orr-Ewing's Trs.* v. *O.E.* (1885) 13 R. (H.L.) 1; *Sim* v. *Robinow* (1892) 19 R. 665; *Hine* v. *McDowall* (1897) 5 S.L.T. 12; *Societe du Gaz* v. *Armateurs français*, 1926 S.C. (H.L.) 13; *Argyllshire Weavers* v. *Macaulay*, 1962 S.C. 388; *Balshaw* v. *B.*, 1967 S.C. 63; see also *Howden* v. *Powell Duffryn*, 1912 S.C. 920; *Foster* v. *F's Trs.*, 1923 S.C. 212; *Lawford* v. *L's Trs.*, 1927 S.C. 360; *Robinson* v. *R's Trs.*, 1930 S.C. (H.L.) 20.
[3] *Prescott* v. *Graham* (1883) 20 S.L.R. 573.
[4] *Bayley* v. *Johnstone*, 1928 S.N. 153; cf. *Drummond* v. *Bell-Irving*, 1930 S.C. 704.
[5] *Robinson, supra.*   [6] *McLean* v. *McL.*, 1947 S.C. 79.
[7] *Argyllshire Weavers, Ltd.* v. *Macaulay*, 1962 S.C. 388.
[8] *Jubert* v. *Church Commrs. for England*, 1952 S.C. 160.
[9] *Thomson* v. *N.B. and Mercantile Ins. Co.* (1868) 6 M. 310; *Robinson* v. *R's Trs.*, 1930 S.C. (H.L.) 20; *Woodbury* v. *Sutherland's Trs.*, 1938 S.C. 689; *Babington* v. *B.*, 1955 S.C. 115; *Argyllshire Weavers, Ltd.* v. *Macaulay*, 1962 S.C. 388.

domiciled in Scotland,[1] irrespective of where the parties may be actually resident,[2] and of whether the cause of action would be recognized in a former domicile,[3] but other grounds are recognized in certain cases.

Declarator of legitimacy or of bastardy

A declarator of legitimacy or of bastardy may be brought in the Scottish courts if the pursuer is domiciled in Scotland,[4] or seeks to establish rights, such as to property, over which the Scottish courts have jurisdiction.[5] If the child's father were domiciled in Scotland legitimation *per subsequens matrimonium* applies, wherever the birth took place and wherever the marriage took place.[6]

Declarator of freedom and putting to silence

The Scottish courts now have jurisdiction only where either party is domiciled in Scotland at the time of the action or has been habitually resident in Scotland for one year before the action was commenced,[7] but not merely because the husband was so domiciled at the time of the alleged marriage.[8]

Declarator of marriage or of nullity of marriage

The Scottish courts now have jurisdiction if either party is domiciled in Scotland, or habitually resident in Scotland for one year before the action was commenced, or had died and was previously thus qualified.[9]

Divorce

The Scottish court now has jurisdiction only if either party is domiciled in Scotland, or has been habitually resident in Scotland

---

[1] *Le Mesurier* v. *Le M.* [1895] A.C. 517; *Admin. of Austrian Property* v. *Von Lorang*, 1927 S.C. (H.L.) 80; *McLelland* v. *McL.*, 1942 S.C. 502; *Balshaw, supra.*

[2] cf. *Mangrulkar* v. *M.*, 1939 S.C. 239.

[3] *Carswell* v. *C.* (1881) 8 R. 901; see also *Stavert* v. *S.* (1882) 9 R. 519; *Steel* v. *S.* (1888) 15 R. 896;

[4] Hume, *Lect.* V, 244; *Balshaw* v. *B.*, 1967 S.C. 63, 82.

[5] See *Morley* v. *Jackson* (1888) 16 R. 78; *Smith* v. *S.*, 1918, 1 S.L.T. 156. See also *Shaw* v. *Gould* (1868) L.R. 3 H.L. 55.

[6] *Udny* v. *U.* (1869) 7 M. (H.L.) 89; *Blair* v. *Kay's Trs.*, 1940 S.L.T. 464.

[7] Domicile and Matrimonial Proceedings Act, 1973, S. 7(2).

[8] Fraser, *H. & W.*, II, 1271; *Yelverton* v. *Longworth* (1862) 2 M. (H.L.) 49; *A.B.* v. *C.D.* (1888) 25 S.L.R. 731; *McLelland* v. *McL.*, 1942 S.C. 502.

[9] Domicile and Matrimonial Proceedings Act, 1973, S. 7(3), superseding much conflicting older law.

for one year before the action was commenced.[1] Nationality does not give jurisdiction,[2] nor is the place of the marriage or of the matrimonial wrong relevant.[3]

The court's jurisdiction is not excluded by the existence of an order from an English magistrates' court made on a different ground from that in issue before the Scottish court,[4] nor by the existence of a decree of a Roman Catholic ecclesiastical tribunal that the marriage was null under canon law.[5] Divorce cannot be effected in the U.K. by any non-judicial process, religious or otherwise.[6]

Property rights arising on divorce

If the Scottish court has jurisdiction as to the marriage it also has jurisdiction as to ancillary and collateral orders[7] but enforcement of any award will be impossible unless the court granting divorce has effective jurisdiction over the defender's property.[8]

Reduction of decree of divorce

The court can reduce its own decree in consistorial proceedings whether or not it has jurisdiction otherwise.[9]

Dissolution on ground of presumed death

The Court of Session now has jurisdiction only if the petitioner is domiciled in Scotland or habitually has been resident there for one year immediately preceding the petition, or the person being presumed dead was so domiciled or resident.[10] Where the husband had acquired a domicile of choice in Scotland but had left Scotland and disappeared it was held that he must be presumed to have retained his Scottish domicile of choice in the absence of evident intention to change.[11]

---

[1] Domicile and Matrimonial Proceedings Act, 1973, S. 7(2). As regards domicile this repeats earlier law; as regards residence it extends a rule recognized only exceptionally.

[2] *Niboyet* v. *N.* (1878) 4 P.D. 1, 19.

[3] *Tulloh* v. *T.* (1861) 23 D. 639; *Mangrulkar* v. *M.*, 1939 S.C. 239.

[4] *Murray* v. *M.*, 1956 S.C. 376; *Richardson* v. *R.*, 1957 S.L.T. (Notes) 45.

[5] *Di Rollo* v. *Di R.*, 1959 S.C. 75.

[6] Domicile and Matrimonial Proceedings Act, 1973, S. 16.

[7] Domicile and Matrimonial Proceedings Act, 1973, S. 10.

[8] cf. *Fraser* v. *Fraser and Hibbert* (1870) 8 M. 400; *Thomson* v. *T.*, 1935 S.L.T. 24.

[9] Domicile and Matrimonial Proceedings Act, 1937, S. 9, overruling *Longworth* v. *Yelverton* (1868) 7 M. 70; *Acutt* v. *A.*, 1936 S.C. 386; *Jack* v. *J.*, 1940 S.L.T. 122.

[10] Domicile and Matrimonial Proceedings Act, 1973, S. 7(4).

[11] *Labacianskas* v. *L.*, 1949 S.C. 280.

Polygamous marriages

At common law the Scottish courts had no jurisdiction to grant matrimonial remedies to potentially or actually polygamous marriages.[1] But such marriages were not ignored in questions of bigamy,[2] legitimacy of children,[3] succession,[4] and claims for social security.[5] By the Matrimonial Proceedings (Polygamous Marriages) Act, 1972, a court in Scotland may (S. 2) grant decree of divorce, nullity, dissolution of marriage on the ground of presumed death, judicial separation, separation and aliment, adherence and aliment or interim aliment, declarator that the marriage is valid or invalid, or any other decree involving a determination as to the validity of a marriage, and make any ancillary order which it may make in such a case, and is not precluded by reason only that the marriage was entered into under a law which permits polygamy. This applies to both potentially and actually polygamous marriages.

Jurisdiction by virtue of other proceedings

If proceedings are pending in the Scottish courts, they may exercise jurisdiction in other proceedings in respect of the same marriage.[6]

(b) OTHER ACTIONS RELATING TO PERSONAL RELATIONS

Breach of promise, seduction, affiliation and aliment, etc.

In these actions the Scottish courts have jurisdiction only if they can exercise it in respect of a petitory claim.[7]

---

[1] *Hyde* v. *H.* (1866) L.R. 1 P. & M. 30; *Mohammed* v. *Suna*, 1956 S.C. 366. A marriage contracted in Britain is monogamous even though either or both parties might by their personal religious law contract polygamous marriage: *MacDougall* v. *Chitnavis*, 1937 S.C. 390; *Qureshi* v. *Q.* [1971] 1 All E.R. 325. A potentially polygamous marriage may become monogamous if the parties acquire an English or Scottish domicile: *Ali* v. *A.* [1968] P. 564.

[2] *Srini Vasan* v. *S.V.* [1946] P. 67; *Baindail* v. *B.* [1946] P. 122.

[3] *Sinha Peerage Case* [1946] 1 All E.R. 348 n.

[4] *Coleman* v. *Shang* [1961] A.C. 481. See also National Insurance Act, 1965, S. 113(2), and 1971 Act, S. 12.

[5] *Imam Din* v. *N.A.B.* [1967] 2 Q.B. 213.

[6] Domicile and Matrimonial Proceedings Act, 1973, S. 7(5).

[7] *Bald* v. *Dawson*, 1911 2 S.L.T. 459; *Martin* v. *Szyszka*, 1943 S.C. 203; *Findlay* v. *Donachie*, 1944 S.C. 306.

Judicial separation

An action for judicial separation does not fundamentally affect the status of the parties but only alters the obligations which otherwise flow from that status.[1] Jurisdiction accordingly depends on domicile[2] or habitual residence,[3] or exists if the action is begun when an original action is pending in respect of the marriage.[4] Once events giving a right to separation have happened, a husband cannot defeat his wife's right by changing his domicile.[5]

Aliment

A claim for aliment alone is a pecuniary one and the Scottish court can exercise jurisdiction only if it has jurisdiction in petitory actions against the defender,[6] or under the Maintenance Orders Act, 1950.

Jurisdiction under Maintenance Orders Act, 1950

Under this Act (S. 1) a court in England has jurisdiction in proceedings under the Summary Jurisdiction (Married Women) Act, 1895, against a man residing in Scotland if the applicant resides in England and the parties last ordinarily resided together as man and wife in England, or if the woman resides in Scotland against a man residing in England, and may revoke, revive or vary any such order. By S. 6 the sheriff has jurisdiction in an action by a married woman for aliment for herself and any child of the marriage[7] if the pursuer resides within the jurisdiction and the parties last ordinarily resided together as man and wife in Scotland, and the husband resides in England or Northern Ireland.[8]

A court having jurisdiction where the mother resides in England may grant custody of a child to the mother, with or without an order on the father to make payments for maintenance,

---

[1] cf. *Administrator of Austrian Property* v. *Von Lorang*, 1927 S.C. (H.L.) 80; *Jelfs* v. *J.*, 1939 S.L.T. 286; *McCord* v. *McC.*, 1946 S.C. 198.

[2] *Hood* v. *H.* (1897) 24 R. 973; *Eustace* v. *E.* [1924] P. 45; *Ramsay* v. *R.*, 1925 S.C. 216; *Jelfs* v. *J.*, 1939 S.L.T. 286; Domicile and Matrimonial Proceedings Act, 1973, S. 7(2), 8(2).

[3] *Armytage* v. *A.* [1898] P. 178; *Graham* v. *G.* [1923] P. 31; *Jelfs, supra*; *Sim* v. *S* [1944] P. 87; *McCord, supra*; *Matalon* v. *M.* [1952] P. 233; *Sinclair* v. *S.* [1967] 3 All E.R. 882; Domicile and Matrimonial Proceedings Act, 1973, S. 7(2), 8(2).

[4] Domicile and Matrimonial Proceedings Act, 1973, S. 7(2), 8(3).

[5] *Ramsay* v. *R.*, 1925 S.C. 216; *Crabtree* v. *C.*, 1929 S.L.T. 675.

[6] *Hutchison* v. *H.*, 1912, 1 S.L.T. 219; *McNeill* v. *McN.*, 1919, 2 S.L.T. 127.

[7] In *Wilson* v. *W.*, 1954 S.L.T. (Sh. Ct.) 68, 'child' was held to mean a child under 16.

[8] *Plant* v. *P.*, 1963 S.L.T. (Sh. Ct.) 58.

against a father residing in Scotland (S. 2). The sheriff court in Scotland has similar power in the converse case (S. 7).

An English court may grant an affiliation order against a man residing in Scotland if the intercourse took place in England, and the mother in Scotland may take proceedings for an affiliation order in a court in England having jurisdiction where the father resides (S. 3). Conversely (S. 8) the sheriff has jurisdiction in an action of affiliation and aliment if the mother resides within his jurisdiction, the intercourse took place in Scotland, and the father resides in England or Northern Ireland.

An English court has by S. 4 jurisdiction in proceedings against a person in Scotland for contribution under the Children and Young Persons Acts and the National Assistance Act; the Scottish courts have corresponding powers (S. 9).

Jurisdiction under Maintenance Orders (Reciprocal Enforcement) Act, 1972

Under the Maintenance Orders (Reciprocal Enforcement) Act, 1972, S. 4,[1] the sheriff has jurisdiction if the pursuer resides within the sheriff's jurisdiction, he is satisfied that the defender is residing in a reciprocating country under the Act, and he would not otherwise have jurisdiction, to make a provisional order for payment of aliment, including affiliation and aliment. In such a case the action may proceed without citation of the defender, but decree may be granted only after proof.

Custody of children

The Scottish courts have jurisdiction as to custody of pupils[2] and minors under sixteen.[3] They may determine custody and access if Scotland is the father's domicile,[4] and this is the pre-eminent forum,[5] or if Scotland is the child's domicile, or if there is reason to apprehend immediate danger to a child in Scotland, or to enforce the order for custody of a competent court.[6] It is immaterial that the child has been made a ward of court in

---

[1] Not yet brought into force.
[2] At common law.
[3] Custody of Children (Sc.) Act, 1939.
[4] *Barkworth* v. *B.*, 1913 S.C. 759; *Westergaard* v. *W.*, 1914 S.C. 977; *Ponder* v. *P.*, 1932 S.C. 233; *Kitson* v. *K.*, 1945 S.C. 434; *McLean* v. *McL.*, 1947 S.C. 79; *Babington* v. *B.*, 1955 S.C. 115; see also *Radoyevitch* v. *R.*, 1930 S.C. 619.
[5] *McLean, supra*; *Babington* v. *B.*, 1955 S.C. 115; *Oludimu* v. *O.*, 1967 S.L.T. 105.
[6] *McShane* v. *McS.*, 1962 S.L.T. 221; cf. *Oludimu* v. *O.*, 1967 S.L.T. 105.

England.[1] Under the Guardianship of Infants Acts, 1886 and 1925, the Court of Session has jurisdiction if the defender, either father or mother, is resident in Scotland.[2] The Court of Session also has jurisdiction at the instance of either party to an action in Scotland relating to the custody, maintenance or education of a child, or of the child's guardian, by interim interdict to prohibit the removal of the child furth of Scotland or out of the control of the person having custody.[3]

Under the Conjugal Rights (Sc.) Amendment Act, 1861, extended by the Matrimonial Proceedings (Children) Act, 1958, the court has power in actions for judicial separation, divorce and nullity of marriage to make orders as to the custody and maintenance of the children of the marriage. It may be that the court having jurisdiction in the principal action also has jurisdiction as to custody and maintenance,[4] or it may be that jurisdiction depends on the same considerations as in other custody cases.[5]

Jurisdiction to appoint guardians

The Scottish court has jurisdiction to appoint guardians to persons under legal or mental disability if the incapax is resident in Scotland, or if he has property situated in Scotland,[6] or probably if he is domiciled in Scotland.[7] A guardian appointed elsewhere will normally be recognized in Scotland, save as to the management of heritable property in Scotland,[8] and the Scottish court will normally assist a guardian lawfully entitled or appointed by other courts having jurisdiction.[9] A person residing outside Scotland will rarely be appointed.[10]

---

[1] McLean, supra; Babington, supra; Hoy v. H., 1968 S.C. 179. See also Johnstone v. Beattie (1843) 10 Cl. & F. 42; Stuart v. M. Bute (1861) 9 H.L.C. 440; Re X's Settlement [1945] Ch. 44.

[2] 1886 Act, S. 9.

[3] Low, 1920 S.C. 351; Matrimonial Proceedings (Children) Act, 1958, S. 13.

[4] Hamilton v. H., 1954 S.L.T. 16; Shanks v. S., 1965 S.L.T. 330; Battaglia v. B., 1966 S.L.T. (Notes) 85.

[5] McShane, supra; Robb v. R., 1953 S.L.T. 44, but on this see Hamilton, supra.

[6] Sawyer v. Sloan (1875) 3 R. 271; Reid v. R. (1887) 24 S.L.R. 281; Harper, 1932 S.L.T. 496; Waring, 1933 S.L.T. 190.

[7] Buchan v. Harvey (1839) 2 D. 275.

[8] Buchan v. Harvey (1839) 2 D. 275; Lamb (1858) 20 D. 1323; Sawyer v. Sloan (1875) 3 R. 271; Ogilvy v. O's Trs., 1927 S.L.T. 83; Forsyth, 1932 S.L.T. 462.

[9] Stuart v. Stuart (1861) 4 Macq. 1; Maquay v. Campbell (1888) 15 R. 606; Marchetti v. M. (1901) 3 F. 888.

[10] Fergusson v. Dormer (1870) 8 M. 426; Napier (1902) 9 S.L.T. 429; Forsyth, 1932 S.L.T. 462.

Adoption

The Scottish courts may make an adoption order if the applicant is domiciled in England or Scotland, and applicant and infant reside in Scotland, or exceptionally though the applicant is not ordinarily resident in Scotland.[1]

(c) IN RELATION TO CORPORATIONS

The Scottish courts have jurisdiction over corporate bodies registered in, having a place of business in, owning property in, or doing business in Scotland, but such jurisdiction is not necessarily exclusive.

They may wind up a company registered in Scotland[2] and, in certain circumstances, an unregistered company.[3]

(d) ACTIONS *IN PERSONAM*

Jurisdiction in actions *in personam*, such as actions arising *ex obligatione*, depends generally on the ability of the Scottish court to make its decree effective against the defender.[4] It follows that the maxim *actor sequitur forum rei* applies and the pursuer must bring his action in the country to which the defender is subject when action is commenced.[5] The date of citation in the action is the critical date.[6]

Presence

The main ground of this jurisdiction is the defender's personal presence in Scotland,[7] if substantially continuously[8] resident in one locality for forty days[9] and not merely itinerant.[9] A corporation is subject to jurisdiction if it has a place of business and

---

[1] Adoption Act, 1958, Ss. 1, 12. As to provisional adoption order, see S. 53. The Adoption Act, 1968 (not yet in force) will extend the jurisdiction to make adoption orders where the applicant is not domiciled in England or Scotland.

[2] Companies Act, 1948, S. 220.

[3] Ibid., Ss. 398–9.

[4] Ersk. I, 2, 16, and 20.

[5] *Joel* v. *Gill* (1859) 21 D. 929; *North* v. *Stewart* (1889) 17 R. (H.L.) 60; *McLeod* v. *Tancred Arrol & Co.* (1890) 17 R. 514.

[6] *North* v. *Stewart, supra*; *Smith* v. *Stuart* (1894) 22 R. 130.

[7] *Johnstone* v. *Strachan* (1861) 23 D. 758; *Buchan* v. *Grimaldi* (1905) 7 F. 917; *Kerr* v. *R. & W. Ferguson*, 1931 S.C. 736; *Findlay* v. *Donachie*, 1944 S.C. 306. See also *Young* v. *Harper*, 1970 S.C. 174.

[8] *Ritchie* v. *Fraser* (1852) 15 D. 205; *Prescott* v. *Graham* (1883) 20 S.L.R. 573.

[9] Ersk. I, 2, 16; Kames, *H.L.T.* 233; *Joel* v. *Gill* (1859) 21 D. 929. The forty days must be complete before citation: *Dallas* v. *McArdle*, 1949 S.C. 481; *McNeill* v. *McN.*, 1960 S.C. 30.

carries on business in Scotland.[1] This jurisdiction lapses immediately the defender quits Scotland.[2] An itinerant is subject to
the jurisdiction only if personally cited in Scotland.[3] A permanent home or address in Scotland does not amount to 'constructive residence'.[4] The defender's domicile is irrelevant.[5]

Ratione contractus vel delicti

Another ground of this jurisdiction is the occurrence of the
cause of action, such as the breach of a contract or the commission
of a wrong, within the jurisdiction, if coupled in the case of
contract with the personal citation of the defender therein.[6] The
defender's domicile in Scotland, even combined with the occurrence of the cause of action in Scotland, does not give jurisdiction,
in the absence of personal citation.[7]

Even where the Scottish courts do not have jurisdiction on
any other ground they may assume jurisdiction by interdict to
prevent the commission of a wrong in Scotland.[8] They may also,
if they have jurisdiction on another ground, interdict the commission of a wrong abroad.[9]

Ownership or tenancy of heritage

The ownership[10] or tenancy[11] of heritable property in Scotland
confers jurisdiction on the Scottish courts in all personal actions,

---

[1] *Laidlaw* v. *Provident Insce. Co. Ltd.* (1890) 17 R. 544; *Hughes* v. *Stewart*, 1907 S.C.
791; *L.A.* v. *Huron, etc. Co.*, 1911 S.C. 612.

[2] *Johnston, supra*; *Corstorphine* v. *Kasten* (1898) 1 F. 287; *Buchan, supra*; *Carter* v.
Allison, 1966 S.C. 257.

[3] Ersk. I, 2, 16; *Linn* v. *Casadinos* (1881) 8 R. 849; *Martin* v. *Szyska*, 1943 S.C. 203.

[4] *Nicol* v. *Bruce*, 1965 S.C. 160.

[5] *Tasker* v. *Grieve* (1905) 8 F. 45; *Bald* v. *Dawson*, 1911 2 S.L.T. 459; *Martin* v.
Szyszka, 1943 S.C. 203.

[6] *Sinclair* v. *Smith* (1860) 22 D. 1475; *Johnston, supra*; *Kermick* v. *Watson* (1871) 9 M.
984; *Maxwell* v. *Horwood's Trs.* (1902) 4 F. 489; *Kerr* v. *R. & W. Ferguson*, 1931 S.C.
736; *Dalziel* v. *Coulthurst's Exors.*, 1934 S.C. 564; *Dallas* v. *McArdle*, 1949 S.C. 481. The
need for personal citation in cases of delict was abrogated by the Law Reform (Jurisdiction
in Delict) (Sc.) Act, 1971.

[7] *Kerr, supra*, overruling *Glasgow Corpn.* v. *Johnston*, 1915 S.C. 555.

[8] *Campbell* v. *Arnott* (1893) 1 S.L.T. 159; *D. Hamilton* v. *McCracken* (1893) 1 S.L.T.
336; *Gill* v. *Cutler* (1895) 23 R. 371; *Toni Tyres Ltd.* v. *Palmer Tyre Co.* (1905) 7 F. 477.

[9] cf. *Liqdr. of California Redwood Co.* v. *Walker* (1886) 13 R. 810; *Liqdr. of Pacific
Mining Co.* v. *Walker* (1886) 13 R. 816; *Gill* v. *Cutler* (1895) 23 R. 371.

[10] Including having the radical right to heritage under a trust: *Smith* v. *Stuart* (1894)
22 R. 130; ownership as trustees: *Charles* v. *C's Trs.* (1868) 6 M. 772; possession of a
mid-superiority: *Kirkpatrick* v. *Irvine* (1841) 2 Rob. 475; and even though it has been
sold: *Caledonian Stores* v. *Hewson*, 1970 S.C. 168.

[11] *Fraser* v. *F. and Hibbert* (1870) 8 M. 400; *Weinschel*, 1916, 2 S.L.T. 91, 205.

and in causes relating to that property,[1] but not over an owner who is being sued in a representative capacity[2] nor over a claimant on a trust estate include Scottish heritage.[3] The radical right of a disponer in security probably gives jurisdiction,[4] as does a contract to purchase heritage.[5]

This ground of jurisdiction disappears when the owner is feudally divested of the heritage,[6] or even has delivered an absolute conveyance thereof,[7] and does not exist over trustees until they have completed title.[8]

The defender's interest is immaterial so long as it is capable of attachment.[9] Possession as trustee does not give jurisdiction against the trustee as an individual.[10]

Similarly executors or trustees may on this ground be sued as such executors or trustees, though not personally.[11]

The English courts assert jurisdiction in relation to implement of a contract to sell land in Scotland[12] but the Scottish courts would also have had jurisdiction.

Arrestment of moveables ad fundandam jurisdictionem

The last ground of personal jurisdiction is where moveable property of some commercial value[13] belonging or owed to the defender has been arrested in the hands of a third party within the jurisdiction.[14] Arrestments do not found jurisdiction if at the time they were laid on, the arrestee was under no liability to

---

[1] *McArthur* v. *McA.* (1842) 4 D. 354; *Ashburton* v. *Escombe* (1892) 20 R. 187; *Manderson* v. *Sutherland* (1899) 1 F. 621; *Thorburn* v. *Dempster* (1900) 2 F. 583; *Love* v. *L.*, 1907 S.C. 728; *Pagan & Osborne* v. *Haig*, 1910 S.C. 341; *Lawford* v. *L's Trs.*, 1927 S.C. 360. See also *Hastie* v. *Steel* (1886) 13 R. 843; *Buchan* v. *Grimaldi* (1905) 7 F. 917; *Wilson* (1895) 2 S.L.T. 567; *Jubert* v. *Church Commrs. for England*, 1952 S.C. 160.

[2] *Mackenzie* v. *Drummond's Exors.* (1868) 6 M. 932.

[3] *Gemmell* v. *Emery* (1905) 13 S.L.T. 490.

[4] *McBride* v. *Caledonian Ry.* (1894) 21 R. 620; *Low* v. *Scottish Amicable Socy.*, 1940 S.L.T. 295.

[5] *Thorburn* v. *Dempster* (1900) 2 F. 583; cf. *Caledonian Stores, supra.*

[6] *Shaw* v. *Dow & Dobie* (1869) 7 M. 449; *Buchan, supra; Caledonian Stores, supra.*

[7] *Bowman* v. *Wright* (1877) 4 R. 322; *Dowie* v. *Tennant* (1891) 18 R. 986; *Buchan* v. *Grimaldi* (1905) 7 F. 917; *Lindsay* v. *L's Trs., infra.*

[8] *Lindsay* v. *L's Trs.*, 1922 S.L.T. 363.

[9] *McArthur* v. *McA.* (1842) 4 D. 354; *Smith* v. *Stuart* (1894) 22 R. 130.

[10] *Hastie* v. *Steel* (1886) 13 R. 843.

[11] *Robertson's Tr.* v. *Nicholson* (1888) 15 R. 914; *Ashburton* v. *Escombe* (1892) 20 R. 187.

[12] *West and Partners* v. *Dick* [1969] 2 Ch. 424.

[13] *Shaw* v. *Dow & Dobie* (1869) 7 M. 449; *Trowsdale's Tr.* v. *Forcett Ry. Co.* (1870) 9 M. 88; *Ross* v. *R.* (1878) 5 R. 1013.

[14] *Cameron* v. *Chapman* (1838) 16 S. 907; *L.N.W. Ry.* v. *Lindsay* (1858) 3 Macq. 99; *North* v. *Stewart* (1890) 17 R. (H.L.) 60; *Leggat Bros.* v. *Gray*, 1908 S.C. 67; *O'Brien* v. *Davies*, 1961 S.L.T. 85.

account to the defender.[1] The property arrested need not be connected with the subject of the action.[2] A decree based on this ground of jurisdiction may well not be recognized furth of Scotland,[3] and it is probably a good ground of jurisdiction only in actions for debt or damages.[4] A ship may be arrested to found jurisdiction only so long as still in port.[5]

Prorogated jurisdiction

Personal jurisdiction may be conferred where parties prorogate the jurisdiction or submit themselves to it,[6] which may be done expressly,[7] or impliedly, as by lodging defences without objection to the jurisdiction,[8] but not in any case where the court could not competently exercise the jurisdiction.[9] It is questionable whether the courts can accept jurisdiction by prorogation where the case has no connection with Scotland or Scots law.[10]

Jurisdiction ex reconventione

It may also be conferred by reconvention, which doctrine holds that a person pursuing in the Scottish courts subjects himself to their jurisdiction in counter-actions[11] arising ex eodem negotio[12] or ejusdem generis,[13] unless the original action was one purely protective,[14] or he was involved in the actions in different capacities.[15]

Jurisdiction in personal actions cannot be founded on the defender's nationality, or domicile of origin being Scottish,

---

[1] *Kerr* v. *R. & W. Ferguson*, 1931 S.C. 736.

[2] *Sheaf S.S. Co.* v. *Compania Transmediterranea*, 1930 S.C. 660.

[3] *Schibsby* v. *Westenholz* (1870) L.R. 6 Q.B. 155; *Emanuel* v. *Symon* [1908] 1 K.B. 302.

[4] *Grant* v. *G.* (1867) 6 M. 155; *Shaw, supra*; *Union Electric Co.* v. *Holman*, 1913 S.C. 954.

[5] *Carlberg* v. *Borjesson* (1877) 5 R. (H.L.) 215.

[6] *Thompson* v. *Whitehead* (1862) 24 D. 331; *Gill* v. *Cutler* (1895) 23 R. 371.

[7] E.g. *International Exhibition* v. *Bapty* (1891) 18 R. 843; *Elderslie S.S. Co.* v. *Burrell* (1895) 22 R. 389.

[8] *Assets Co. Ltd.* v. *Falla's Tr.* (1894) 22 R. 178; *Gill, supra*.

[9] *Ringer* v. *Churchill* (1840) 2 D. 307.

[10] *Styring* v. *Mayor of Oporovec*, 1931 S.L.T. 493.

[11] *Thompson* v. *Whitehead* (1862) 24 D. 331; *Longworth* v. *Yelverton* (1868) 7 M. 70; *Davis* v. *Cadman* (1897) 24 R. 297.

[12] *Burrell* v. *Van Uden*, 1914 2 S.L.T. 394.

[13] *Morison & Milne* v. *Massa* (1866) 5 M. 130; *Hurst Nelson & Co.* v. *Whatley*, 1912 S.C. 1041; *Munro* v. *Anglo-American Nitrogen Co.*, 1917, 1 S.L.T. 24.

[14] *Davis* v. *Cadman* (1897) 24 R. 297; *Macaulay* v. *Hussain*, 1966 S.C. 204.

[15] *Ponton's Exors.* v. *P.*, 1913 S.C. 598.

though it may if domicile is combined with personal citation in Scotland.[1]

Jurisdiction in a personal action may be founded against executors, as such, if the executry estate is in Scotland, or both or all executors have been personally cited in Scotland, but not merely because the cause of action has arisen in Scotland.[2]

(e) ACTIONS *IN REM*

The only actions *in rem* are Admiralty actions to enable a person having a claim against a ship, its cargo or freight, or against an aircraft,[3] to have it satisfied out of the *res*. Such actions depend on effectiveness and the possibility of arresting the ship or aircraft within the jurisdiction.[4] Under the Administration of Justice Act, 1956, Ss. 45–50, the grounds of Admiralty jurisdiction are defined. The jurisdiction probably exists even though the claim involves land situated abroad.[5] By S. 47(1) arrest may be made of the ship concerned or of a sister ship wholly owned by the defender.[6]

(f) JURISDICTION IN TRUST QUESTIONS

No difficulty arises if all the trustees are in Scotland and the trust property in Scotland. The Scottish courts have also exercised jurisdiction where the trust is governed by Scots law, and may be said to be domiciled in Scotland, even though the trustees are not otherwise subject to the jurisdiction.[7] They also have jurisdiction over a foreign trust if all the trustees are personally subject to the Scottish jurisdiction,[8] or if it owns heritage in Scotland.[9] The truster's Scottish domicile does not necessarily make his trust a Scottish one so as to give jurisdiction.

---

[1] *Ritchie* v. *Fraser* (1852) 15 D. 205; *Tasker* v. *Grieve* (1905) 8 F. 45; *Kerr* v. *R. & W. Ferguson*, 1931 S.C. 736.

[2] *Dalziel* v. *Coulthurst's Exors.*, 1934 S.C. 564.

[3] e.g. *The Glider Standard Austria S.H.* 1964 [1965] P. 463.

[4] *Castrique* v. *Imrie* (1870) L.R. 4 H.L. 414; *Carlberg* v. *Borjesson* (1877) 5 R. (H.L.) 215.

[5] *The Tolten* [1946] P. 135 (ship damaging wharf at Lagos).

[6] cf. *The St. Elefterio* [1957] P. 179.

[7] *Cruikshanks* v. *C.* (1843) 5 D. 733; *Wick Mags.* v. *Forbes* (1849) 12 D. 299; *Kennedy* v. *K.* (1884) 12 R. 275; *Robertson's Tr.* v. *Nicholson* (1888) 15 R. 914; *Ashburton* v. *Escombe* (1892) 20 R. 187.

[8] *Peters* v. *Martin* (1825) 4 S. 107; *Hutchison* v. *H.*, 1912, 1 S.L.T. 219; cf. *Dalziel* v. *Coulthurst's Exors*, 1934 S.C. 564.

[9] *Charles* v. *C's Trs.* (1868) 6 M. 772; *Thomson* v. *Wilson's Trs.* (1895) 22 R. 866; *Mackay* v. *M.* (1897) 4 S.L.T. 337; *Jubert* v. *Church Commrs. for England*, 1952 S.C. 160.

Two or more courts may claim jurisdiction[1] and it must be decided which is *forum conveniens*, having regard to the truster's domicile, the residence of his trustees, the language of the trust deed, and the situation of the major part of the trust funds.[2] It is for the court of the domicile of the trust to determine the powers to be exercised by the trustees and to decide any questions with the beneficiaries.[3] The court cannot in the exercise of the *nobile officium* grant foreign trustees any indulgences not available to Scottish trustees.[4]

(g) JURISDICTION IN SUCCESSION

The *forum situs* has jurisdiction to determine whether property is immoveable or moveable in succession,[5] if indeed that distinction is relevant. The succession to immoveable property is governed by the *lex situs*[6] and the *forum situs* is alone competent to determine who is entitled on intestacy, or the validity of bequests, to administer the succession, and to grant the person entitled a legal title.[7] The succession to moveable property is determined by the *lex domicilii* and the *forum domicilii* has jurisdiction to determine who is entitled on intestacy, to adjudicate on the validity of, and interpret, a will[8] and to appoint and confirm executors,[9] but only to the extent of the estate situated within the jurisdiction. Estate situated elsewhere can be administered only under the authority of the courts there.[10]

The Scottish courts have jurisdiction to appoint or confirm an executor if there is property, heritable or moveable, in Scotland vested in the deceased, irrespective of his domicile.[11] The person selected as executor by the *forum domicilii* will normally be confirmed to the assets in Scotland by the Scottish courts.[12] As between Scotland and England or Northern Ireland, confirmation issued by a Scottish court may be resealed in those countries

---

[1] *Ewing* v. *Orr Ewing* (1883) 9 App. Cas. 34; *Orr Ewing's Trs.* v. *Orr Ewing* (1885) 13 R. (H.L.) 1.

[2] *Orr Ewing's Trs.*, *supra*; *Lawford* v. *L's Trs.*, 1927 S.C. 360.

[3] *Campbell, Petr.*, 1958 S.C. 275; *Campbell-Wyndham-Long's Trs.*, 1962 S.C. 132.

[4] *Horne's Trs.*, 1952 S.C. 70.

[5] *Downie* v. *D's Trs.* (1866) 4 M. 1067; *Monteith* v. *M's Trs.* (1882) 9 R. 982.

[6] Stair, More's Note A; Ersk. III, 8, 10.

[7] *Hewit's Trs.* v. *Lawson* (1891) 18 R. 793; *Foster* v. *F's Trs.*, 1923 S.C. 212.

[8] cf. *Elliot* v. *Joicey*, 1935 S.C. (H.L.) 57.

[9] Stair, More's Note A; Ersk. III, 9, 27.

[10] *Preston* v. *Melville* (1841) 2 Rob. App. 88.

[11] Executors (Sc.) Act, 1900, S. 6, amd. Succession (Sc.) Act, 1964, Sched. 2; *Hastings* v. *H's Exor.* (1852) 14 D. 489; *Goetze* v. *Aders* (1874) 2 R. 150.

[12] *Goetze, supra*.

and have the effect of a grant of probate by the competent courts there. The Scottish courts have jurisdiction in actions against executors if all of them are subject to its jurisdiction in personal actions,[1] or if the deceased's assets are within the jurisdiction[2] but not merely because an executor owns heritage in Scotland,[3] and if Scotland is not the place of the administration of the estate, there may be room for the plea of *forum non conveniens*.[4]

(h) JURISDICTION IN BANKRUPTCY

By statute[5] Scottish courts have jurisdiction to sequestrate the bankrupt estates of living debtors who are subject to the jurisdiction of the Supreme Courts of Scotland,[6] on their own petition, or on the petition of creditors if the debtor be notour bankrupt and had within a year before the petition resided or had a dwellinghouse or place of business in Scotland, and the bankrupt estates of deceased debtors who were then subject to the jurisdiction of the Supreme Courts of Scotland. Scottish domicile does not by itself confer jurisdiction,[7] nor does arrestment *ad fundandam*,[8] but possession of heritage in Scotland does even though the debtor resides elsewhere.[9] Where a bankrupt has been carrying on business in two or more jurisdictions, he may be subject to the bankruptcy jurisdiction of both or all. The jurisdiction in which proceedings are initiated first may be held to exclude that of the other jurisdictions.[10]

A Scottish court in awarding sequestration confers no title to heritable or real property outside Scotland, save in so far as the statute provides,[11] unless the Scottish title of the trustee is recognized by the *forum situs*. Creditors lodging claims thereby submit themselves to the jurisdiction of the Scottish courts in respect of the distribution of the estate.[12]

---

[1] *McTavish* v. *Saltoun*, 3 Feb. 1821, F.C.; *Peters* v. *Martin* (1825) 4 S. 107; *Dalziel* v. *Coulthurst's Exors.*, 1934 S.C. 564.

[2] *Grant's Trs.* v. *Douglas Heron & Co.* (1796) 3 Pat. 503.

[3] *Mackenzie* v. *Drummond's Exors.* (1868) 6 M. 932.

[4] *MacMaster* v. *MacM.* (1833) 11 S. 685.

[5] Bankruptcy (Scotland) Act, 1913, S. 11.

[6] *Joel* v. *Gill* (1859) 21 D. 929; *Wylie* v. *Bell & Jackson*, 1928 S.L.T. 665.

[7] *Obers* v. *Paton's Trs.* (1897) 24 R. 719.

[8] *Croil* (1863) 1 M. 509.

[9] *Joel, supra*; *Croil, supra*; *Weinschel*, 1916, 2 S.L.T. 91.

[10] *Goetze* v. *Aders* (1874) 2 R. 150; cf. *Young* v. *Buckle* (1864) 2 M. 1077; *Gibson* v. *Munro* (1894) 21 R. 840. See also 1913 Act, S. 43.

[11] 1913 Act, S. 97.

[12] *Barr* v. *Smith & Chamberlain* (1879) 7 R. 247.

A discharge in bankruptcy must be granted by the courts which had power to make bankrupt. The effect of such a discharge depends on the *lex fori* of the discharging court,[1] save that a discharge by a Scottish, English or Irish court operates as a discharge of all obligations, throughout the British Commonwealth.[2]

(i) JURISDICTION AS TO CIVIL REMEDIES

If the Scottish courts have jurisdiction to adjudicate on a controversy they have jurisdiction to grant only those remedies which they may grant in cases raising no foreign element. Remedies can be granted, moreover, only subject to the qualifications, limitations and restrictions applicable in purely Scottish cases. While the rights to awards of damages for particular kinds of losses arising from breach of contract or from delict are matters of substantive law,[3] the measure of the financial compensation, whether it is to be by a lump sum or by instalments, whether it carries interest or not, are matters for the *lex fori* exclusively.[4] Questions of remoteness of damage are matters of substantive law.[5] Similarly the Scottish courts can grant decrees for money only for money payable in sterling.[6]

(j) JURISDICTION UNDER INTERNATIONAL CONVENTION

Under the Carriage by Air Act, 1961, an action for damages under the Act, in the case of international carriage, may be brought in the territory of one of the High Contracting Parties to the convention made effective by the Act, before the court at the place of destination or before the court having jurisdiction where the carrier ordinarily resides or has his principal place of business or has an establishment by which the contract has been made.[7] The rules do not apply to non-international carriage.[8]

Under the Carriage by Air (Supplementary Provisions) Act, 1962, in the case of international carriage, a passenger or consignee may sue not only the airline which contracted with him,

---

[1] *Ellis* v. *McHenry* (1871) L.R. 6 C.P. 228.
[2] *Gill* v. *Barron* (1868) L.R. 2 P.C. 157; Bankruptcy (Sc.) Act, 1913, Ss. 137, 144.
[3] *Kendrick* v. *Burnett* (1897) 25 R. 82; *McElroy* v. *McAllister*, 1949 S.C. 110.
[4] *Kohnke* v. *Karger* [1951] 2 K.B. 670.
[5] *J. D'Almeida Araujo Lda.* v. *Becker* [1953] 2 Q.B. 329.
[6] *Hyslop* v. *Gordon* (1824) 2 Sh. App. 451; *Macfie's J.F.* v. *M.*, 1932 S.L.T. 460.
[7] 1961 Act, Sch. 1, Art. 28.
[8] Carriage by Air Acts (Application of Provisions) Order, 1967.

but the actual carrier to whom part or all of the carriage was subcontracted, before a court in which an action may be brought under the 1961 Act, or before the court having jurisdiction at the place where the actual carrier is ordinarily resident or has his principal place of business.[1] These rules apply to international carriage only.

The Carriage of Goods by Road Act, 1965, provides that legal proceedings arising out of carriage under the Geneva convention given effect to by the Act may be brought in any court or tribunal of a country which is party to the convention and designated by agreement between the parties, and also in the courts or tribunals of a country within whose territory (a) the defendant is ordinarily resident, or has his principal place of business, or the branch or agency through which the contract of carriage was made is situated, or (b) the place where the goods were taken over by the carrier, or the place designated for delivery is situated.[2]

The Carriage by Railway Act, 1972, provides that actions under the Act may only be instituted in the competent court of the State on whose territory the accident to the passenger occurred, unless otherwise provided in agreements between states, or in any licence or other document authorizing the operation of the railway concerned.[3]

The Carriage of Passengers by Road Act, 1974, applies to international carriage and provides that action may be brought in the court of the State on whose territory the accident occurred.[4]

[1] 1962 Act, Sch., Art. VIII.
[2] 1965 Act, Sched., Art. 31.
[3] 1972 Act, Sched., Art. 15.
[4] 1974 Act, Sched. Art. 21.

CHAPTER 12

CHOICE OF LAW

Where the Scottish court decides that it can exercise jurisdiction over the defender or in respect of the particular cause of action in issue, it must then determine whether to decide the rights and duties of the parties according to Scots law or the law of some other system involved. The Scottish courts do not necessarily or always apply Scots law to a case before them, nor are all matters in issue in one case necessarily decided by the rules of the same legal system. In many branches of the law the rules for choice of law are vague or uncertain, frequently the authorities are inadequate, ambiguous or hesitant, and frequently the authorities have been the subject of heavy criticism, so that it is difficult and dangerous to state the rules with any certainty.

The matters in dispute must first be classified or categorized to determine the juridical nature of the question for decision, as relating, e.g. to capacity to contract, or to the formalities of contract.[1] Secondly, the court must consider what legal system is indicated as appropriate by any connecting factors existing and relating the facts of that question and one or more particular systems of law. If the court decides that Scots law is applicable it must determine, if necessary after argument, what the content of the applicable rule is;[2] if it decides that a rule of foreign law is applicable it must ascertain, as a matter of fact, what the relevant rule prescribes.[3] Finally, the court must apply the rule thus revealed to the facts to reach a decision.

Exclusion of foreign law otherwise applicable

The court will not, however, give effect to a rule of a foreign system of law which would otherwise be applicable if it conflicts with the policy of Scots law.[4] In at least three sets of circumstances the foreign law will be rejected. These are where the foreign law is of a penal nature, such as confiscatory legislation,[5] where it is

---

[1] cf. Ch. 11, *supra*.   [2] Scots law in a Scottish court is a matter of law.
[3] Non-Scottish law in a Scottish court is a question of fact: see *infra*.
[4] *Connal* v. *Loder* (1868) 6 M. 1095, 1110; *Brodin* v. *A/R Seljan*, 1973 S.L.T. 198.
[5] *Banco de Vizcaya* v. *Don Alfonso de Borbon y Austria* [1935] 1 K.B. 140; cf. *Huntington* v. *Atrill* [1893] A.C. 150; *Luther* v. *Sagor* [1921] 3 K.B. 532.

part of the foreign revenue system, such as for the recovery of tax,[1] and where the rule of foreign law is contrary to the British concept of public policy,[2] such as a rule permitting what was to British eyes an illegal agreement,[3] or a contract contrary to good foreign relations,[4] or is contrary to British views of morality or the principles of justice.

THE LAW APPROPRIATE IN PARTICULAR QUESTIONS

Status—legitimacy or bastardy

The legitimacy or otherwise of a child must be determined by the *lex domicilii* of the father at the time of the child's birth,[5] or, if the father were unknown or the child posthumous, that of the mother. Hence the children of a man's several polygamous marriages may all be legitimate *lege paterni domicilii*,[6] and the child of a putative marriage is legitimate if the father's or mother's domicile is Scottish.[7]

Whether a child has been legitimated or not, *per subsequens matrimonium* or otherwise,[8] depends on whether the *lex domicilii* of the father at the time of the birth and of the subsequent marriage or other act or events alleged to effect legitimation recognizes that result.[9] The place of birth and of the later marriage are irrelevant.[10] If the father's domicile has changed the domicile at marriage probably rules.[11] Whether or not a child has been validly adopted may depend on the respective *leges domiciliorum* of adopter and adoptee.[12]

---

[1] *A.G. for Canada* v. *Schulze* (1901) 9 S.L.T. 4; *Raulin* v. *Fischer* [1911] 2 K.B. 93; *Govt. of India* v. *Taylor* [1955] A.C. 491; *Peter Buchanan Ltd. & McHarg* v. *McVey* [1955] A.C. 516 n.

[2] *Dynamit A/G* v. *Rio Tinto Co. Ltd.* [1918] A.C. 292.

[3] *Grell* v. *Levy* (1864) 16 C.B. (N.S.) 73; *Kaufman* v. *Gerson* [1904] 1 K.B. 591; *Addison* v. *Brown* [1954] 2 All E. R. 213.

[4] *Robson* v. *Premier Oil and Pipe Line Co.* [1915] 2 Ch. 124; *Foster* v. *Driscoll* [1929] 1 K.B. 470; *Regazzoni* v. *Sethia* [1958] A.C. 301.

[5] *Birtwhistle* v. *Vardill* (1835) 2 Cl. & F. 571; *Fenton* v. *Livingstone* (1859) 21 D. (H.L.) 10; *Beattie* v. *B.* (1866) 5 M. 181; *Re Goodman's Trusts* (1881) 17 Ch. D. 266; *Re Grove* (1888) 40 Ch. D. 216.

[6] *Bamgbose* v. *Daniel* [1955] A.C. 107.

[7] *Smijth* v. *S.*, 1918, 1 S.L.T. 156.

[8] As in *Re Luck* [1940] Ch. 864.

[9] *Shedden* v. *Patrick* (1808) 5 Pat. 194; *Munro* v. *M.* (1840) 1 Rob. 492; *Udny* v. *U.* (1869) 7 M. (H.L.) 89; *Re Grove* (1888) 40 Ch. D. 216; *Blair* v. *Kay's Trs.*, 1940 S.L.T. 464. See also Legitimation (Sc.) Act, 1968, S. 5.

[10] *Munro* v. *M.* (1840) 1 Rob. 492; *Shaw* v. *Gould* (1865) L.R. 3 H.L. 55; *Re Goodman's Trusts* (1881) 17 Ch. D. 266; *Re Andros* (1883) 24 Ch. D. 637; *Blair* v. *Kay's Trs.*, 1940 S.L.T. 464.

[11] *Munro, supra*; *McDouall* v. *Adair* (1852) 14 D. 525; *Aikman* v. *A.* (1859) 21 D. 757.

[12] See also Adoption Act, 1958, Ss. 1(1) and (5), 12.

Parent and child

Declarator of legitimacy or of bastardy determines whether a person has the status of legal parent vis-à-vis his child or merely that of natural parent, and conversely. The extent of the parent's rights and duties of maintenance, education, and correction, and over the child's property probably depend on the law of the place of residence, or in the case of a child's immoveable property, on the *lex situs* of the property. Hence the rights of all parents residing with their children in Scotland are determined by Scots law, and similarly with the rights of children against parents.

Guardian and ward

Whether a person has been duly constituted guardian of another, and the extent of his rights as such, depends on the law of the country where the ward was domiciled or resident when the guardian was appointed,[1] or where the ward has property requiring protection.[2] The Court of Session is the proper, and probably the only competent, court for deciding any question relating to Scottish heritage.

Engagement to marry

Whether a broken engagement to marry is actionable and, if so, what kinds of loss are relevant for consideration in assessing damages may be determined by the proper law of the contract or possibly by the law of the intended matrimonial domicile.[3]

Marriage

In an action of declarator of marriage or of nullity of marriage, whether as being null *ab initio* or as having been voidable and now being avoided, the existence or not of marriage depends on whether in respect of formalities, such as notice, banns, witnesses, ceremony, registration, need for parental consent,[4] need for personal presence,[5] and so on, the marriage satisfied the requirements of the *lex loci celebrationis*,[6] and in respect of

---

[1] *Sawyer* v. *Sloan* (1875) 3 R. 271; *Seddon* (1891) 19 R. 101; (1893) 20 R. 675; *Atherstone's Trs.* (1896) 24 R. 39; *Elder* (1903) 5 F. 307; *McFadzean*, 1917 S.C. 142.

[2] cf. *Stuart* v. *Moore* (1861) 23 D. 902; *Nugent* v. *Vetzera* (1866) L.R. 2 Eq. 704.

[3] cf. *Hamlyn* v. *Talisker Distillery* (1894) 21 R. (H.L.) 21; *Hansen* v. *Dixon* (1906) 23 T.L.R. 56; *Kremezi* v. *Ridgway* [1949] 1 All E.R. 662; Webb and Brown, 15 I.C.L.Q. 947.

[4] *Compton* v. *Bearcroft* (1767) 2 Hagg. Con. 444, note (Gretna Green runaways); *Simonin* v. *Mallac* (1860) 2 S. & T. 67; *Ogden* v. *O.* [1908] P. 46; *Bliersbach* v. *McEwen*, 1959 S.C. 43. See also *Pease* v. *P.*, 1967 S.C. 112; *Hoy* v. *H.*, 1968 S.C. 179. This element would be better classified as an element of essential validity.

[5] *Apt* v. *A.* [1948] P. 83; *Ponticelli* v. *P.* [1958] P. 204.

[6] *Di Rollo* v. *Di R.*, 1959 S.C. 75 (valid notwithstanding ecclesiastical ruling that void).

essentials of validity such as legal capacity or disability to marry,[1] consanguinity,[2] monogamous nature,[3] genuine consent,[4] sexual potency,[5] it satisfied the *lex domicilii* of each party,[6] or possibly the law of the matrimonial domicile,[7] unless one party only is subject to a domiciliary incapacity of a kind not recognized by Scots law.[8] Whether a particular element belongs to formalities or to essential validity is determined by Scots law as *lex fori*.[9] It is uncertain whether in respect of essential validity a marriage must also satisfy the *lex loci celebrationis*.[10] A marriage may be declared to exist, though Scots law would not declare it null nor dissolve it by divorce.[11]

Compliance in formalities with the *lex loci celebrationis* is not, however, demanded where there is no local form,[12] or it is inappropriate,[13] or the marriage satisfies the Foreign Marriages Acts, 1892 to 1947, the Foreign Marriage Order, 1964,[14] and the Foreign Marriages (Armed Forces) Order, 1904.

The court has held that an alleged rule of foreign law that a bigamous marriage was validated by the death of the first wife was not one which the Scottish courts were obliged to recognize.[15]

Judicial separation

The entitlement or not of the pursuer to a decree of judicial separation depends entirely on Scots law, as *lex fori*, because it is for the local system to give protection to a resident, whether or

---

[1] *Shaw v. Gould* (1868) L.R. 3 H.L. 55; *Chetti v. C.* [1909] P. 67; *Macdougall v. Chitnavis*, 1937 S.C. 390; *Pugh v. P.* [1951] P. 482; *R. v. Brentwood Registrar, ex p. Arias* [1968] 3 W.L.R. 531.

[2] *Mette v. M.* (1859) 1 S. & T. 416; *Brook v. B.* (1861) 9 H.L.C. 193; *Webster v. W's Tr.* (1866) 14 R. 90; *De Thoren v. Wall* (1876) 3 R. (H.L.) 28; *Sottomayor v. de Barros* (1877) 3 P.D. 1; (1879) 5 P.D. 94; *Martin v. Buret*, 1938 S.L.T. 479; *Cheni v. C.* [1965] P. 85.

[3] *Hyde v. H.* (1866) L.R. 1 P. & D. 130; *Ali v. A.* [1968] P. 564.

[4] *Kenward v. K.* [1951] P. 124; *H. v. H.* [1954] P. 258.

[5] *De Reneville v. De R.* [1948] P. 100.

[6] *Kenward v. K.* [1951] P. 124; *Pugh, supra.*

[7] *Warrender v. W.* (1835) 2 S. & MacL. 154; *Mackinnon's Trs. v. I.R.*, 1920 S.C. (H.L.) 171; cf. *Ramsay-Fairfax v. R.F.* [1956] P. 115.

[8] e.g. disability by religion: *Scott v. A.G.* (1886) L.R. 11 P.D. 128; *Chetti, supra*; *Macdougall v. Chitnavis*, 1937 S.C. 390. cf. *Sottomayor v. De Barros* (1879) 5 P.D. 94.

[9] *Bliersbach v. McEwen*, 1959 S.C. 43.

[10] cf. *Breen v. B.* [1964] P. 144.

[11] *Baindail v. B.* [1946] P. 122; *Muhammad v. Suna*, 1956 S.C. 366; *Risk v. R.* [1951] P. 50.

[12] *Wolfenden v. W.* [1946] P. 61; *Penhas v. Tan Soo Eng* [1953] A.C. 304.

[13] *Re Bethell* (1887) 38 Ch. D. 220; *Taczanowska v. T.* [1957] P. 301; *Kochanski v. K.* [1958] P. 147; *Merker v. M.* [1963] P. 283.

[14] cf. *Hay v. Northcote* [1900] 2 Ch. 262.

[15] *Prawdzic-Lazarska v. P.L.*, 1954 S.C. 98.

not the wrongs were committed within the jurisdiction, and because the decree does not fundamentally affect the status of the persons as married but only alters their mutual rights and duties.

Divorce

Where the court has jurisdiction, the right of the pursuer to the remedy sought depends on Scots law, as *lex domicilii*, or possibly as *lex fori*, irrespective of the place of marriage, of residence, of the place of the matrimonial offence, and of whether the marriage was dissoluble by the *lex loci celebrationis*.[1] Where the jurisdiction is statutory,[2] the issues fall to be determined as if both parties were domiciled in Scotland, i.e. by Scots law. Dissolution of marriage on the ground of presumed death is regulated by Scots law.

Guardianship

The rights and powers of a guardian are determined by the system of law under which he is appointed, save that a guardian appointed by the *lex domicilii* of a foreign infant has no authority to grant a discharge valid to exonerate trustees transferring Scottish heritage.[3]

Unincorporated associations

Whether an association has any existence or personality distinct from those of its members depends on the legal system of the country where the association has been formed.[4] In the absence of contrary evidence the character of a particular association will be presumed to be like its nearest Scottish counterpart.[5] An association's powers and legal capacities will be determined by the law of its country of creation, save that it probably could not in Scotland be conceded the ability or power to do anything for which no legal facilities exist by Scots law.

Corporations

The nationality of a corporation depends on the country where it is incorporated. The domicile of a corporation is the country by whose laws it is incorporated,[6] and its status, powers,

---

[1] *Warrender* v. *W.* (1835) 2 S. & MacL. 154.
[2] Law Reform (Miscellaneous Provisions) Act, 1949, S. 2(4).
[3] *Ogilvy* v. *O's Trs.*, 1927 S.L.T. 83.
[4] *Edinburgh and Glasgow Bank* v. *Ewan* (1852) 14 D. 547.
[5] *Reid and McCall* v. *Douglas*, 11 June 1814, F.C.; *Muir* v. *Collett* (1862) 24 D. 1119.
[6] *Leith and Flensburg Shipping Co. Ltd.*, 1925 S.N. 111; *Carse* v. *Coppen*, 1951 S.C. 233.

and characteristics are determined by that law,[1] as also are its internal affairs.[2] A corporation may be resident in as many countries as it carries on business in. But a corporation formed elsewhere cannot by Scots law do what is illegal by Scots law or anything for which no facilities exist by Scots law.[3] A company incorporated outside Great Britain which carried on business in Scotland but has ceased to do so may be wound up by the Scottish courts, even if it has been dissolved by the law of its place of incorporation.[4]

Contracts

In modern practice it is recognized that one legal system is not necessarily appropriate for application to all matters affecting a contract; the court must select the 'proper law' of the contract, namely that with which the contract has the most substantial connection,[5] or that which the parties intended to apply,[6] or would presumably have intended if they had considered the matter,[7] and this may vary where different parts of the contract are deemed to have been intended to be governed by different laws. Where the parties clearly express their intention, this is normally decisive.[8] Failing that, it has to be inferred from the terms of the contract and concomitant circumstances.[9] Some assistance may be got from presumptions in favour of the *lex loci contractus*,[10] or the *lex loci solutionis*,[11] or the *lex situs* of moveables,[12]

---

[1] *Carse, supra; Carl Zeiss Stiftung v. Rayner and Keeler* [1967] 1 A.C. 853.

[2] *Branley v. S.E. Ry.* (1862) 12 C.B. (N.S.) 63.

[3] *Carse, supra;* rule now altered by Companies (Floating Charges and Receivers) (Sc.) Act, 1972.

[4] Companies Act, 1948, S. 400; *Marshall* (1895) 22 R. 697.

[5] *Boissevain v. Weil* [1950] A.C. 327; *Bonython v. Australia* [1951] A.C. 201; *Miller & Partners v. Whitworth Street Estates, Ltd.* [1970] A.C. 583.

[6] *Lloyd v. Guibert* (1865) L.R. 1 Q.B. 115; *Mount Albert B.C. v. Australian Temperance Socy.* [1938] A.C. 224; *Vita Food Products v. Unus Shipping Co.* [1939] A.C. 277.

[7] *Lloyd, supra; Mount Albert B.C. v. Australian Life Assce. Socy. Ltd.* [1938] A.C. 224; *The Assunzione* [1954] P. 150.

[8] *Girvin, Roper & Co. v. Monteith* (1895) 23 R. 129; *Salt Mines Syndicate* (1895) 2 S.L.T. 489; *Montgomery v. Zarifi,* 1918 S.C. (H.L.) 128; *Bayley v. Johnstone,* 1928 S.N. 153; *Drummond v. Bell-Irving,* 1930 S.C. 704; *Vita Food Products v. Unus Shipping Co.* [1939] A.C. 277; *The Assunzione* [1954] P. 150, 175. For a case where it was held not decisive see *English v. Donnelly,* 1958 S.C. 494.

[9] *The Metamorphosis* [1953] 1 W.L.R. 543.

[10] The term *locus contractus* may mean the place of making the contract, but in general means the locality of the contract, as ascertained from its nature and what is to be done under it: *Parken v. Royal Exchange Assce. Co.* (1846) 8 D. 365, 374; *Valery v. Scott* (1876) 3 R. 965, 967.

[11] *Valery, supra.*

[12] *Connal v. Loder* (1868) 6 M. 1095; *Todd v. Armour* (1882) 9 R. 901; *Shedlock v. Hannay* (1891) 18 R. 663; *Inglis v. Robertson & Baxter* (1898) 25 R. (H.L.) 70; *Forbes v. Receiver in Bankruptcy,* 1924 S.L.T. 522.

or the *lex situs* of immoveables,[1] or the law of the flag of a ship.[2] The choice of arbitration in one country is normally deemed a choice of the arbiter's system of law.[3] The use of the legal terminology of one system may indicate that that system should apply.[4] Other factors, such as the nationality, domicile or residence of parties, may yield some indication of the proper law.

In relation to capacity to contract, the proper law is normally the *lex loci contractus*,[5] except, probably, in the case of contracts relating to immoveable property, where it is the *lex situs*, and marriage contracts, where it may be the law of the intended matrimonial domicile. What formalities of constitution need to be observed for validity, and whether they have been satisfied, generally falls to be regulated by the *lex loci contractus*[6] or by the proper law.[7]

The proper law also determines the essential validity of the contract,[8] whether there has been consensus or not, and the effect of alleged vitiating factors. Thus English courts have declined to enforce a contract illegal by the *lex loci contractus*,[9] or by the *lex loci solutionis*,[10] and Scottish courts have refused to enforce a contract legal by the *lex loci contractus* but illegal by Scots law,[11] and one to which English law was agreed to be applicable, when it contravened a Scottish Act.[12] In relation to contracts constituted by a bill of exchange, the choice of law to regulate the rights of parties is determined by statute.[13]

[1] *Mackintosh* v. *May* (1895) 22 R. 345; *Bank of Africa* v. *Cohen* [1909] 2 Ch. 129.

[2] *Lloyd* v. *Guibert* (1865) L.R. 1 Q.B. 115; *Immanuel* v. *Denholm* (1887) 15 R. 152; *R.* v. *International Trustee* [1937] A.C. 500, 529; *The Assunzione* [1954] P. 150.

[3] *Hamlyn* v. *Talisker Distillery* (1894) 21 R. (H.L.) 21; *Girvin, Roper & Co.*, *supra*; *Robertson* v. *Brandes, Schonwald & Co.* (1906) 8 F. 815; *Kwik Hoo Tong* v. *Finlay* [1927] A.C. 604; *Naamlooze Vennootschap* v. *A/S Ludwig Mowinckels Rederi* [1938] 2 All E.R. 152; *Tzortzis* v. *Monark Line* [1968] 1 All E.R. 949. But see *Compagnie d'Armement Maritime* v. *Compagnie Tunisienne de Navigation* [1970] 3 All E.R. 71.

[4] *Pender* v. *Commercial Bank*, 1940 S.L.T. 306.

[5] *Male* v. *Roberts* (1799) 3 Esp. 163; *De Virte* v. *Macleod* (1869) 7 M. 347; *Cooper* v. *C.* (1888) 15 R. (H.L.) 21; *McFeetridge* v. *Stewarts and Lloyds*, 1913 S.C. 773.

[6] *Guepratte* v. *Young* (1851) 4 De G. & Sm. 217.

[7] *Tayler* v. *Scott* (1847) 9 D. 1504; *Valery* v. *Scott* (1876) 3 R. 965.

[8] *Corbet* v. *Waddell* (1879) 7 R. 200; *Todd* v. *Armour* (1882) 9 R. 901; *Scottish Provident Instn.* v. *Cohen* (1888) 16 R. 112; *Shedlock* v. *Hannay* (1891) 18 R. 663; *Forbes* v. *Official Receiver in Bankruptcy*, 1924 S.L.T. 522; *Pender* v. *Commercial Bank*, 1940 S.L.T. 306; cf. *Hamlyn* v. *Talisker Distillery* (1894) 21 R. (H.L.) 21.

[9] *Vita Food Products Co.* v. *Unus Shipping Co.* [1939] A.C. 277.

[10] *Ralli Bros.* v. *Compania Naviera Sota y Aznar* [1920] 2 K.B. 287; *Boissevain* v. *Weil* [1950] A.C. 327; cf. *Regazzoni* v. *Sethia* [1958] A.C. 301.

[11] *Luszczewska* v. *L.*, 1953 S.L.T. (Notes) 73; cf. *O'Toole* v. *Whiterock Quarry Co.*, 1937 S.L.T. 521; *Duncan* v. *Motherwell Bridge Co.*, 1952 S.C. 131; contrast *Clayton* v. *C.*, 1937 S.C. 619.

[12] *English* v. *Donnelly*, 1958 S.C. 494.

[13] Bills of Exchange Act, 1882, S. 72; see also *Stewart* v. *Gelot* (1871) 9 M. 1057.

The interpretation of the parties' undertakings must probably be according to the proper law of the contract.[1]

Questions as to the due performance, or breach or discharge of the contract and of remoteness of damages fall to be determined by the proper law, normally *lex loci solutionis*.[2] Procedure, evidence, prescription[3] and measure of damages are, however, determined by the *lex fori*.[4] In assessing damages conversion must be made of foreign currency into sterling as at the date of the breach.[5]

Effect of Statutes

Certain statutes applicable to contracts make their own provisions. The Bills of Exchange Act, 1882, contains its own code of conflicts provisions as to bills. Others[6] contain provisions defining the scope of rules of English or Scottish domestic law and a statute may be held applicable to a contract, irrespective of its proper law, to give effect to its policy.[7]

Carriage by Air Act, 1961, and Carriage by Air (Supplementary Provisions) Act, 1962

These Acts give effect to international conventions, applicable to the carriage of goods, passengers and luggage, and substitute for the law which might be otherwise applicable the rules in the convention.[8]

Carriage of Goods by Road Act

The Carriage of Goods by Road Act, 1965, gives effect to a convention scheduled to the Act, signed at Geneva in 1956. The convention applies to every contract for the carriage of goods by road in vehicles for reward, when the place of taking over of the goods and the place designated for delivery are situated in two different countries, of which at least one is a contracting party.[9] It substitutes the rules of the convention for any rules otherwise applicable.[10]

[1] *Henderson's Trs.* v. *H.* (1868) 5 S.L.R. 394; *Hamlyn, supra*; *Robertson* v. *Brandes, Schonwald & Co.* (1906) 8 F. 815; see also *Mackintosh* v. *May* (1895) 22 R. 345.
[2] *Valery* v. *Scott* (1876) 3 R. 965; *Dallas* v. *McArdle*, 1949 S.C. 481; *J. D'Almeida Araujo* v. *Becker* [1953] 2 Q.B. 329.
[3] *Don* v. *Lippmann* (1837) 2 S. & Macl. 682; *Higgins* v. *Ewing's Trs.*, 1925 S.C. 440.
[4] *B.L. Co.* v. *Drummond* (1830) 10 B. & C. 903; *Westminster Bank* v. *McDonald*, 1955 S.L.T. (Notes) 73; *Stirling's Trs.* v. *Legal and General Assce. Soc. Ltd.*, 1957 S.L.T. 73.
[5] *Di Ferdinando* v. *Simon, Smits & Co.* [1920] 3 K.B. 409.
[6] e.g. Carriage of Goods by Sea Act, 1971; Contracts of Employment Act, 1972.
[7] *Duncan* v. *Motherwell Bridge Co.*, 1952 S.C. 131; *English* v. *Donnelly*, 1958 S.C. 494.
[8] See further Chap. 44, *infra*.
[9] Art. 1.   [10] See further Chap. 42, *infra*.

Carriage of Goods by Sea Act, 1971

This Act[1] applies to the carriage of goods by sea from ports in the United Kingdom under a contract providing for the issue of a bill of lading or similar document of title, and where it applies supersedes any rules which might otherwise apply to the contract.[2]

Carriage by Railway Act, 1972

The liability of a railway for damage caused to passengers by an accident on the territory of a state which is a party to the Convention scheduled to the Act is governed by the Convention.[3]

Uniform Laws on International Sales

The Uniform Laws on International Sales Act, 1967, S. 1, gives the force of law in the United Kingdom to the Uniform Law on the International Sale of Goods in Schedule 1 of the Act, being the convention on that topic done at the Hague in 1964. While an Order in Council is in force declaring that a declaration by the United Kingdom has been made[4] the Uniform Law applies to a contract of sale only if chosen by the parties to the contract as the law of the contract.

Section 2 of the same Act gives the force of law also to the Uniform Law on the Formation of Contracts for the International Sale of Goods in Schedule 2 of the Act, also being a convention done at the Hague in 1964, but not to negotiations before an Order in Council brings the convention into force.

Restitution

Whether a person can claim restitution, repayment, recompense, or reward for *negotiorum gestio* probably depends on whether Scots law is the proper law of the relationship giving rise to the claim.[5]

Delicts

A preliminary question, sometimes difficult, may arise of the place where a delict was committed. This is probably where the

---

[1] Not yet in force: until it comes into force the similar Act of 1924 applies.

[2] See further Chap. 43, *infra*.

[3] See further Chap. 42, *infra*.

[4] None has yet been made.

[5] *Rae* v. *Wright* (1717) Mor. 4506; *Batthyany* v. *Walford* (1887) 36 Ch. D. 269; *Cantiere San Rocco* v. *Clyde Shipbuilding Co.*, 1923 S.C. (H.L.) 105.

harm was suffered.[1] A question of a particular pursuer's title to sue depends on whether he could, in that capacity, claim both under Scots law and according to the law under which he claims a particular remedy.[2] The rights and liabilities of parties have to be determined by reference to both the *lex loci delicti* and Scots law as *lex fori*; the defender's conduct is actionable in Scotland as a delict only if, and in so far as, it is civilly actionable by both those systems,[3] and not if by either system it is innocent[4] or legalized[5] or subjects to no civil liability[6] or is no longer actionable by reason of lapse of time.[7] If it is so civilly actionable the pursuer's rights are those of the *lex loci delicti*.[8] Questions of remoteness of liability or of injury, of adequacy of causal connection between conduct and harm and of remoteness of damage all fall to be determined by the *lex loci delicti*.[9] Evidence, procedure, the effect of lapse of time, measure of damages, and enforcement are determined solely by the *lex fori*.[10] A claim by a spouse or other relative of a deceased for solatium in recognition of grief at the death is a distinct right of action, and not merely a head of damages.[11]

In the special case of collisions at sea the rules applicable are those of the general maritime law, particularly those of the Maritime Conventions Act, 1911.[12]

Property—classification

For the purpose of international private law property is divided into immoveable and moveable property, the former

[1] *Longworth* v. *Hope* (1865) 3 M. 1049; *Parnell* v. *Walter* (1889) 16 R. 917; *Evans* v. *Stein* (1904) 7 F. 65; *Thomson* v. *Kindell*, 1910, 2 S.L.T. 442. But see *Rosses* v. *Bhagvat Sinhjee* (1891) 19 R. 31; *Soutar* v. *Peters*, 1912, 1 S.L.T. 111; *Walker* v. *Ost* [1970] 2 All E.R. 106.

[2] *McElroy* v. *McAllister*, 1949 S.C. 110; cf. *Jones* v. *Somervell's Tr.*, 1907 S.C. 545.

[3] *Goodman* v. *L.N.W. Ry.* (1877) 14 S.L.R. 449; *Naftalin* v. *L.M.S. Ry.*, 1933 S.C. 259; *McElroy*, *supra*; *McKinnon* v. *Iberia Shipping Co.*, 1955 S.C. 20. *McLarty* v. *Steele* (1881) 8 R. 435, has been disapproved.

[4] *The M. Moxham* (1876) 1 P.D. 107; *Rosses* v. *Bhagvat Sinhjee* (1891) 19 R. 31; *McMillan* v. *C.N. Ry.* [1923] A.C. 120.   [5] *Phillips* v. *Eyre* (1870) L.R. 6 Q.B. 1.

[6] *Walpole* v. *C.N. Ry.* [1923] A.C. 113; *McMillan*, *supra*.

[7] *McElroy*, *supra*. See 1950 S.L.T. (News) 209; 63 J.R. 39; 65 L.Q.R. 313; 12 M.L.R. 248. For the view that liability depends on the 'proper law of the tort' see *Boys* v. *Chaplin* [1971] A.C. 356.

[8] *Naftalin*, *supra*; *McElroy*, *supra*.

[9] *Naftalin* v. *L.M.S. Ry.*, 1933 S.C. 259; *McElroy*, *supra*.

[10] *Goodman* v. *L.N.W. Ry.* (1877) 14 S.L.R. 449; *McElroy*, *supra*; *Kohnke* v. *Karger* [1951] 2 K.B. 670; cf. *J. D'Almeida Araujo* v. *Becker* [1953] 2 Q.B. 329.

[11] *McElroy*, *supra*.

[12] *Chartered Mercantile Bank of India* v. *Netherlands India S.N. Co.* [1883] 10 Q.B.D. 521; *Currie* v. *McKnight* (1896) 24 R. (H.L.) 1; *Reresby* v. *Cobetas*, 1923 S.L.T. 719; *Sheaf S.S. Co.* v. *Compania Transmediterranea*, 1930 S.C. 660.

including all things deemed immoveable, real or heritable by the *lex situs* and the latter all things deemed moveable or personal by the *lex situs*.[1] This division does not always coincide exactly with that drawn between heritable and moveable property by Scottish internal law. Thus a heritable bond, though deemed heritable only for certain purposes by Scots law, is immoveable property for purposes of international private law;[2] a mortgage of English land, being classified by English law as personalty, has been treated as moveable in succession.[3] A lease of land is an immoveable interest both by Scots[4] and English[5] law. But land is by nature immoveable and rights to land are always rights to an immoveable subject.[6]

Immoveable property

In general the *lex situs* regulates all questions regarding immoveable property, including capacity to hold land,[7] capacity to transfer it,[8] and the formalities and validity of transfer.[9] But the proper law of a contract to sell or mortgage land is not necessarily Scots law.[10] And English courts have long asserted jurisdiction *in personam* in relation to foreign land.[11] The mutual rights of spouses, as regards immoveables, are governed by the *lex situs*.[12] The proprietary and possessory rights attaching to particular interests in land depend on the *lex situs*.

Corporeal moveable property

The nature and extent of the rights which a person has in relation to corporeal moveable property are probably determined by the *lex situs* of the moveables. The capacity of a person to transfer corporeal moveables and matters of the contract are

---

[1] *Newlands v. Chalmers's Trs.* (1832) 11 S. 65; *Downie v. D's Trs.* (1866) 4 M. 1067; *Moss's Tr. v. M.*, 1916, 2 S.L.T. 31; *Macdonald v. M.*, 1932 S.C. (H.L.) 79.

[2] *Jerningham v. Herbert* (1828) 4 Russ. 388; *Allen v. Anderson* (1846) 5 Hare 163; *re Fitzgerald* [1904] 1 Ch. 573; but see *Train v. T's Exrx.* (1899) 2 F. 146, *sed quaere*.

[3] *Breadalbane's Trs. v. B.* (1843) 15 S. Jur. 389; *Monteith v. M's Trs.* (1882) 9 R. 982, both doubted in *Macdonald, supra*; see further *In re Hoyles* [1911] 1 Ch. 179.

[4] *Burns v. Martin* (1887) 14 R. (H.L.) 20.

[5] *Freke v. Carbery* (1873) L.R. 16 Eq. 461; *Duncan v. Lawson* (1889) 41 Ch. D. 394; *Macdonald, supra*.

[6] *Macdonald, supra*.   [7] *Duncan v. Lawson* (1889) 41 Ch. D. 394.

[8] *Bank of Africa, Ltd. v. Cohen* [1909] 2 Ch. 129; see also *Waring*, 1933 S.L.T. 190.

[9] Ersk. III, 2, 40; *Adams v. Clutterbuck* (1883) 10 Q.B.D. 403; *Hewitt's Trs. v. Lawson* (1891) 18 R. 793; cf. *Mackintosh v. May* (1895) 22 R. 345; *Re Grassi* [1905] 1 Ch. 584.

[10] *Miller and Partners v. Whitworth Street Estates, Ltd.* [1970] A.C. 583.

[11] *West & Partners, Ltd. v. Dick* [1969] 2 Ch. 424.

[12] *Welch v. Tennent* (1891) 18 R. (H.L.) 72; *Love v. L.*, 1907 S.C. 728.

probably governed by the proper law of the transaction, commonly the *lex loci contractus*, the formalities of the transfer by the *lex situs*,[1] and its essential validity and effect by the *lex situs*.[1] So too the validity and effect of a gift is *prima facie* determined by its *lex situs*.[2] The creation of rights in security over corporeal moveables is probably governed, as to formalities, validity, and effect by the *lex situs*.[3] Thus a purported transfer in security of a vehicle in Scotland by one foreigner to another in England would be void in the absence of *traditio*. The *lex situs* also regulates the kinds of diligence competent against moveables and their effect.

Incorporeal moveable property

Incorporeal moveable property includes a wide variety of rights and the same rules do not necessarily apply to all categories. The validity and enforceability of a claim of debt or a claim of damages probably normally depend on the legal system whereby the duty to pay was created, normally that of the debtor's residence, which is deemed the *lex situs* of the debt.[4] Thus share certificates issued by an English company have been held to be interpreted by English law.[5] The assignability of such a claim probably depends on the *lex situs*,[6] and its formal validity[7] probably on the *lex loci contractus* of the assignation[7] and whether it has been validly assigned probably on the *lex situs* of the claim.[8] The rule that intimation is required to complete an assignation seems to apply to Scottish debts wherever assigned.[9] Questions between assignor and assignee are probably determined by the rules relating to contracts.

The existence, validity, and extent of any such privileges as right of copyrights, patents, etc., depends on the system of law by which such right is alleged to be created, and whether it is recognized by bilateral or international convention as effective in Scotland also.

[1] *Cammell* v. *Sewell* (1860) 5 H. & N. 728; *Todd* v. *Armour* (1882) 9 R. 901.

[2] *Re Korvine's Trusts* [1921] 1 Ch. 343.

[3] *Connal* v. *Loder* (1868) 6 M. 1095; *N.W. Bank* v. *Poynter, Son & Macdonalds* (1894) 22 R. (H.L.) 1; *Inglis* v. *Robertson & Baxter* (1898) 25 R. (H.L.) 70.

[4] *Williamson* v. *Taylor* (1845) 8 D. 156; cf. *Thomson* v. *N.B. and Mercantile Ins. Co.* (1868) 6 M. 310; *Dinwoodie* v. *Carruthers' Exor.* (1895) 23 R. 234.

[5] *Connell's Trs.* v. *C's Trs.* (1886) 13 R. 1175.

[6] *Grant's Trs.* v. *Ritchie's Exors.* (1886) 13 R. 646; *Schumann* v. *Scottish Widow's Fund* (1886) 13 R. 678; *Pender* v. *Commercial Bank*, 1940 S.L.T. 306.

[7] *Erskine* v. *Ramsay* (1664) Mor. 4502; *Ross* v. *R.* (1806) Hume 187; *Tayler* v. *Scott* (1847) 9 D. 1504.

[8] *Scottish Provident Inst.* v. *Cohen* (1888) 16 R. 112.

[9] *Strachan* v. *McDougle* (1835) 13 S. 954; *Donaldson* v. *Ord* (1855) 17 D. 1053.

Universal assignations of property

Apart from death, universal assignation arises only, in some systems, on marriage, or on bankruptcy or the granting of a trust deed for creditors. Whether marriage does or does not operate any general assignation of a spouse's property depends, so far as concerns moveables, on the law of the matrimonial domicile at the time of the marriage,[1] and, *quoad* immoveables, on the *lex situs*.[2] A change of domicile probably does not subject the rights of the spouses in that property to the rule of the new domicile.[3]

Marriage contracts

A marriage contract or settlement is generally governed by the proper law of the transaction, which is *prima facie* the law of the matrimonial domicile,[4] capacity to enter into it by the domicile of each party at the time of the marriage[5] and, so far as concerns immoveables, the *lex situs*, formal validity by the proper law[6] or the *lex loci actus*,[7] and essential validity and revocability by the proper law[8] or, so far as concerns immoveables, the *lex situs*.[9] A subsequent change of domicile cannot affect the rights of parties under the settlement.[10]

Trusts

Capacity to create a trust probably depends, *quoad* moveables, on the truster's *lex domicilii* and, *quoad* immoveables, on their *lex situs*.[11] Formal validity, and essential validity[12] and interpretation,[13] probably depend on the proper law of the trust. Where a trust is Scottish in form, particularly if the truster is, or was at death, a domiciled Scotsman, and if the trust estate is situated in Scotland, Scots law must apply to the solution of any questions which arise

---

[1] *Corbet* v. *Waddell* (1879) 7 R. 200; *Welch, infra*; *Re Egerton's Will Trusts* [1956] Ch. 593.

[2] *Welch* v. *Tennent* (1891) 18 R. (H.L.) 72.

[3] *Lashley* v. *Hog* (1804) 4 Paton 581; *De Nicols* v. *Curlier* [1900] A.C. 21.

[4] *Corbet* v. *Waddell* (1879) 7 R. 200; *Re Fitzgerald* [1904] 1 Ch. 573; *Eadie's Trs.* v. *Henderson*, 1919, 1 S.L.T. 253; *D. Marlborough* v. *A.G.* [1945] Ch. 78. For cases of express choice of law see *Stair* v. *Head* (1844) 6 D. 904; *Montgomery* v. *Zarifi*, 1918 S.C. (H.L.) 128; *Drummond* v. *Bell-Irving*, 1930 S.C. 704.

[5] *Cooper* v. *C.* (1888) 15 R. (H.L.) 21; *Viditz* v. *O'Hagan* [1900] 2 Ch. 87.

[6] *Re Bankes* [1902] 2 Ch. 333.

[7] *Seafield* v. *S.*, 8 Feb. 1814, F.C.; *Van Grutten* v. *Digby* (1862) 31 Beav. 561.

[8] *Sawrey-Cookson* v. *S-C's Trs.* (1905) 8 F. 157.

[9] *Re de Nicols* [1900] 2 Ch. 410.

[10] *de Nicols* v. *Curlier* [1900] A.C. 21.

[11] *Black* v. *B's Trs.*, 1950 S.L.T. (Notes) 32.

[12] *Boe* v. *Anderson* (1862) 24 D. 732; *Irving* v. *Snow*, 1956 S.C. 257.

[13] *Ferguson* v. *Marjoribanks* (1853) 15 D. 637; *Eadie's Trs.* v. *Henderson*, 1919, 1 S.L.T. 253.

under the terms of the trust.[1] If the Scottish court exercises jurisdiction over trustees in the management of a trust estate, it must apply Scots law, whatever may be or have been the truster's domicile, or the *situs* of any part of the trust estate.[2] The rights, powers, duties, and liabilities of trustees are probably determined by the domicile of the trust.[3] The Scottish courts have frequently been appealed to to exercise an auxiliary jurisdiction to the effect of granting power in relation to property in Scotland to trustees of English trusts.[4] The capacity of a trust beneficiary to grant a valid discharge has been held determined by his *lex domicilii*.[5]

Intestate succession

Succession on death intestate to property classified by the *lex situs* as immoveable is regulated by the *lex situs* of that property.[6] Succession on death intestate to property classified by the *lex situs* as moveable is regulated by the *lex domicilii* of the deceased.[7] Hence the estate of a domiciled Scot is divided on intestacy by reference to the statutory rights, legal rights and rights of succession conferred by the Succession (Sc.) Act, 1964, in respect of heritage (immoveables) and moveables in Scotland, and property, wherever situated, which is deemed moveable by the *lex situs*.[8] Conversely heritable estate in Scotland belonging to a person dying domiciled elsewhere devolves by Scots law,[9] and moveable estate in Scotland devolves according to the *lex domicilii* of the deceased.[10]

In each case the designated legal system determines to whom, in what shares, and subject to what conditions, the property descends. But if by the *lex domicilii* property passes to some body

---

[1] *Orr Ewing's Trs. v. O.E.* (1885) 13 R. (H.L.) 1, 14; *Betts Brown Trust Fund Trs.*, 1968 S.C. 170.

[2] *Peters v. Martin* (1825) 4 S. 107.

[3] *Carruthers' Trs. and Allan's Trs.* (1896) 24 R. 238; *Campbell*, 1958 S.C. 275; cf. *Brower's Exor. v. Ramsay's Trs.*, 1912 S.C. 1374.

[4] *Allan's Trs.* (1897) 24 R. 718; *Pender's Trs.*, 1907 S.C. 207; *Harris's Trs.*, 1919 S.C. 432; *Lipton's Trs.*, 1943 S.C. 521; *Evans-Freke's Trs.*, 1945 S.C. 382; *Neech's Exors.*, 1947 S.C. 119; *Campbell-Wyndham-Long's Trs.*, 1951 S.C. 685; *Horne's Trs.*, 1952 S.C. 70; *Campbell*, 1958 S.C. 275; *Campbell-Wyndham-Long's Trs.*, 1962 S.C. 132; cf. *Rossmore's Trs. v. Brownlie* (1877) 5 R. 201.

[5] *Freeman v. Bruce's Exors.* (1905) 13 S.L.T. 97.

[6] *Duncan v. Lawson* (1889) 41 Ch. D. 394; *In re Rea* [1902] 1 Ir. R. 451; *Macdonald v. M.*, 1932 S.C. (H.L.) 79.

[7] Stair, More's Note A; *Hog v. Lashley* (1792) 3 Pat. 247; *Orr Ewing's Trs. v. O.E.* (1885) 13 R. (H.L.) 1; cf. *Monteith v. M's Trs.* (1882) 9 R. 982; *Macdonald, supra*; *In the Estate of Maldonado* [1954] P. 223.

[8] cf. *In the Estate of Musurus* [1936] 2 All E.R. 1666.

[9] *Ross v. R.*, 4 July 1809, F.C.; *Fenton v. Livingstone* (1859) 3 Macq. 497.

[10] *Macdonald, supra*.

as *res nullius*, this is not a rule of succession, and the Scottish courts may treat the property as *bona vacantia*.[1]

Testate succession—testamentary capacity

Capacity to test is determined, *quoad* immoveables, by the *lex situs*[2] and, *quoad* moveables, by the *lex domicilii*,[3] in both cases as the law stood at the time when the will was made.[4] The capacity of a legatee to take is determined by the *lex situs* of the immoveables,[5] or, in the case of moveables, his own *lex domicilii*,[6] as at the date when the bequest vests.

Formal validity of wills—execution

A will is to be treated as properly executed if its execution conforms to the internal law in force in the territory where it was executed, or in the territory where, at the time of its execution or of the testator's death, he was domiciled or had his habitual residence, or in a state of which at either of these times, he was a national.[7] There are also treated as properly executed (a) a will executed on board a vessel or aircraft conforming to the internal law with which the vessel or aircraft is most closely connected; (b) a will, so far as disposing of immoveable property, execution of which conformed to the *lex situs*; (c) a will, so far as revoking a will properly executed under the Act or revoking a provision which under the Act would be treated as comprised in a properly executed will, if the execution of the later will conformed to any law by reference to which the revoked will or provision would be so treated; (d) a will, so far as it exercises a power of appointment, if executed conform to the law governing the essential validity of the power. A will so far as exercising a power of appointment, is not to be treated as improperly executed by reason only that its execution was not in accordance with any formal requirements contained in the instrument creating the power.[8] A law in force

---

[1] cf. *Monteith* v. *M's Trs.* (1882) 9 R. 982; *Train* v. *T's Exrx.* (1899) 2 F. 146; *Moss's Trs.* v. *M.*, 1916, 2 S.L.T. 31.

[2] *Re Hernando* (1884) 27 Ch. D. 284; *Black* v. *B's Trs.*, 1950 S.L.T. (Notes) 33.

[3] *In the goods of Maraver* (1828) 1 Hagg. Ecc. 498; *In the Estate of Field* [1966] 2 W.L.R. 717.

[4] *Field, supra.*

[5] *Brown's Trs.* v. *Gregson*, 1920 S.C. (H.L.) 87.

[6] *Seddon* (1891) 19 R. 101; (1893) 20 R. 675; *Freeman* v. *Bruce's Exors.* (1905) 13 S.L.T. 97; see also *Re Hellman's Will* (1866) L.R. 2 Eq. 363; *Re Schnapper* [1928] Ch. 420.

[7] Wills Act, 1963, S. 1; cf. *Connel's Trs.* v. *C.* (1872) 10 M. 627; *Macdonald* v. *Cuthbertson* (1890) 18 R. 101; *Irving* v. *Snow*, 1956 S.C. 257; see also *Bradford* v. *Young* (1884) 11 R. 1135.

[8] Ibid., S. 2.

outside the U.K. requiring special formalities for particular testators or qualifications for witnesses are to be treated as formal requirements only.[1] A will executed in England by a testator domiciled there but formally invalid by English law has been said to be valid if by the time of his death he had acquired a domicile in Scotland and the will was formally valid by Scots law.[2]

Revocation

Capacity to revoke is normally determined by capacity to test. The validity and effect of a potentially revoking act, such as scoring-out, depends, *quoad* immoveables, on the *lex situs*[3] and, *quoad* moveables, on the *lex domicilii*. Revocation is not effected by a subsequent change of domicile,[4] but whether a subsequent marriage revokes a will depends on the testator's *lex domicilii* as affected by the marriage.[5]

Essential validity

This includes the non-contravention of restrictions on the creation of liferents, the validity of the extent of dispositions made, and the validity of the exercise of powers in the will. Essential validity is determined *quoad* immoveables by the *lex situs*,[6] and, *quoad* moveables, by the *lex domicilii* at the date of death.[7]

Construction of will

In interpreting a will the main consideration is the ascertainment of the testator's intention and the *lex situs* and *lex domicilii* may have to be subordinated to the proper law of the will, or that which the testator apparently intended to apply to his will.[8] This is particularly relevant where there is estate in several countries.[9] The use in the will of the technical terms of any particular system are strongly indicative of that as the proper law of the will.[10]

---

[1] Ibid., S. 3.
[2] *Chisholm* v. *C.*, 1949 S. C. 434.
[3] *In the estate of Alberti* [1955] 3 All E.R. 730.
[4] Wills Act, 1963, S. 1.
[5] *Westerman's Exor.* v. *Schwab* (1905) 8 F. 132; see also *Battye's Tr.* v. *B.*, 1917 S.C. 385.
[6] *Nelson* v. *Bridport* (1846) 8 Beav. 547; *Freke* v. *Carbery* (1873) L.R. 16 Eq. 461; *Studd* v. *Cook* (1883) 10 R. (H.L.) 53; *Hewit's Trs.* v. *Lawson* (1891) 18 R. 793; *Canterbury* v. *Wyburn* [1895] A.C. 89; *Brown's Trs.* v. *Gregson*, 1920 S.C. (H.L.) 87.
[7] *Keith's Trs.* v. *K.* (1857) 19 D. 1040; *Boe* v. *Anderson* (1862) 24 D. 732; *Canterbury, supra*; *Re Groos* [1915] 1 Ch. 572; *Black* v. *B's Trs.*, 1950 S.L.T. (Notes) 33; cf. *M. Bute* v. *Mss. Bute's Trs.* (1880) 8 R. 191.
[8] *Mitchell & Baxter* v. *Davies* (1875) 3 R. 208; *Smith* v. *S.* (1891) 18 R. 1036; *Re Gansloser's Will Trusts* [1952] Ch. 30; *McBride's Trs.*, 1952 S.L.T. (Notes) 59.
[9] *Iveagh* v. *I.R.C.* [1954] Ch. 364; *Philipson-Stow* v. *I.R.C.* [1961] A.C. 727.
[10] *Rainsford* v. *Maxwell* (1852) 14 D. 450; *Mitchell & Baxter* v. *Davies* (1875) 3 R. 208; *Studd* v. *Cook* (1883) 10 R. (H.L.) 53; *Robinson* v. *R's Trs.*, 1930 S.C. (H.L.) 20; *Re Allen's Estate* [1945] 2 All E.R. 264.

Failing that there is a presumption in favour of the *lex domicilii*
at the time the will was made, as being the system which the
testator probably knew best,[1] even though the will disposes of
interests in immoveables in another country[2] and particularly
in the case of moveables.[3] Whether a will executed abroad is
intended to carry Scottish heritage is usually treated as a question
of Scots law.[4] Where a will bequeathed a legacy to a legatee,
whom failing to his 'nearest heirs', it has been held that his
nearest heir fell to be ascertained by the law of the legatee's
domicile.[5] Special destinations of property fall to be construed
according to the *lex situs*.[6] The construction of a will is not
altered by reason of any change in the testator's domicile after
the execution of the will.[7] Similarly it has been held when
interpreting testamentary provisions of a marriage contract in
Scottish form that the ascertainment of the deceased's next of kin
fell to be made by Scots law, though he had subsequently
acquired a domicile of choice in Australia.[8]

Exercise of power of appointment by will

Whether a power of appointment conferred on the testator has
been validly exercised by his will is presumed to depend, *quoad*
immoveables, on the *lex situs* of the immoveables and, *quoad*
moveables, depends as regards capacity to appoint on the law
which determines capacity to test, as regards formal validity on
the law governing formal validity,[9] and as regards essential
validity and interpretation on the *lex domicilii*.[10]

Executors and the administration of estates

The *lex situs* of property must determine whether an executor
or administrator of the estate of a deceased need be appointed, if
so how and by whom, and what his powers are. In case of conflict,
the *forum* where the predominant part of the estate is situated is

---

[1] *Mitchell & Baxter* v. *Davies* (1875) 3 R. 208; *Smith, supra; Hewit's Trs.* v. *Lawson*
(1891) 18 R. 793; *McBride's Trs.*, 1952 S.L.T. (Notes) 59.

[2] *Philipson Stow* v. *I.R.C.* [1961] A.C. 727, but see *Nelson* v. *Bridport* (1846) 8 Beav.
547.

[3] *Re Price* [1900] 1 Ch. 442; *Re Connington* [1924] 1 Ch. 68.

[4] *Griffith's J.F.* v. *G's Exors.* (1905) 7 F. 470.

[5] *Smith's Trs.* v. *Macpherson*, 1926 S.C. 983; cf. *Mitchell's Tr.* v. *Rule* (1908) 16 S.L.T.
189.

[6] *Connell's Trs.* v. *C's Trs.* (1886) 13 R. 1175; *Cunningham's Trs.* v. *C.*, 1924 S.C. 581.

[7] Wills Act, 1963, S. 4.

[8] *Smart's Tr.* v. *Goold's Tr.*, 1947 S.L.T. 221.

[9] Wills Act, 1963, S. 2; *Kennion* v. *Buchan's Trs.* (1880) 7 R. 570.

[10] *Durie's Trs.* v. *Osborne*, 1960 S.C. 444. See also *Re Khan's Settlement* [1966] Ch. 567.

more appropriate for its main administration.[1] If the estate is heritable the *forum situs* is appropriate.[2] The mode of administration is determined in each country in which a grant of representation has been obtained by that country's rules.[3]

Bankruptcy

The sequestration by a Scottish court of a person subject to its jurisdiction vests in the trustee the bankrupt's moveables both in Scotland and elsewhere,[4] and possibly also his immoveables elsewhere as well as his Scottish heritage. If a person having assets in Scotland is sequestrated abroad, this has been held to render subsequent sequestration in Scotland incompetent,[5] but this is inaccurate. The Scottish courts are not precluded from appointing a trustee in Scotland,[6] but, unless this is done, will normally accept the title of a foreign administrator in bankruptcy to moveables in Scotland,[7] subject to all claims already constituted thereon by diligence under Scots law,[8] provided always that the debtor was only subject to the jurisdiction of the foreign court and was cognisant of the proceedings.[9] As regards immoveable property in Scotland a foreign administrator must petition the court, as *forum situs*, to vest such immoveable property in him and to authorize him to sell it.[10]

Within the United Kingdom the Act and Warrant of a trustee in bankruptcy appointed by a Scottish court vests in him, *inter alia*, moveable estate wherever situated and real estate in England or Ireland or any of Her Majesty's dominions, to the same effect as if the debtor had been adjudicated bankrupt there, subject to complying with certain formalities.[11] The converse applies in the

---

[1] *Orr Ewing's Trs.* v. *O.E.* (1885) 13 R. (H.L.) 1.

[2] *Hewit's Trs.* v. *Lawson* (1891) 18 R. 793; cf. Succession (Sc.) Act, 1964, S. 14.

[3] cf. *S.N.O. Society* v. *Thomson's Exor.*, 1969 S.L.T. 325.

[4] Bankruptcy (Sc.) Act, 1913, S. 97; see also *Lindsay* v. *Paterson* (1840) 2 D. 1373; *Galbraith* v. *Nicholson* (1888) 15 R. 914.

[5] *Goetze* v. *Aders* (1874) 2 R. 150; see also *Phosphate Sewage Co.* v. *Molleson* (1878) 5 R. 1125; affd. (1879) 6 R. (H.L.) 113; *Okell* v. *Foden* (1884) 11 R. 906.

[6] cf. *Queensland Mercantile and Agency Co.* v. *Australasian Investment Co.* (1888) 15 R. 935; *Gibson* v. *Munro* (1894) 21 R. 840; *Bank of Scotland* v. *Youde* (1908) 15 S.L.T. 847.

[7] *Obers* v. *Paton's Trs.* (1897) 24 R. 719; *Salaman* v. *Tod*, 1911 S.C. 1214; *Araya* v. *Coghill*, 1921 S.C. 462.

[8] *Connal* v. *Loder* (1868) 6 M. 1095; *Goetze, supra*; *Galbraith* v. *Grimshaw* [1910] A.C. 508.

[9] *Wilkie* v. *Cathcart* (1870) 9 M. 168; *Salaman* v. *Tod*, 1911 S.C. 1214; *Re Anderson* [1911] 1 K.B. 896.

[10] *Salaman* v. *Tod*, 1911 S.C. 1214; *Araya* v. *Coghill*, 1921 S.C. 462.

[11] Bankruptcy (Sc.) Act, 1913, S. 97(3).

cases of English and Irish bankruptcies.[1] The rights and powers of a Scottish trustee in bankruptcy to property situated outwith the United Kingdom depend on the recognition granted to such appointment by the *lex situs* of the property.

Any disabilities attaching to the status of bankrupt must be determined by the proper law of the bankruptcy.[2] Questions of competing rights of the trustee and creditors claiming preferences depend on the proper law of the sequestration.[3]

A discharge in bankruptcy granted in one part of the United Kingdom is effective in the others also. Outside that area, a discharge granted in a foreign country will probably be recognized if it is effective under the proper law of the bankruptcy.[4]

Remedies

An aggrieved person can claim only those remedies which the forum appealed to can grant according to its own law and practice.[5] The actionability of a claim depends on its proper law. The heads of damage for which damages may be claimed are fixed by the proper law of the contract, or the *lex loci delicti*.[6] Remoteness of damage, and other principles excluding certain losses from consideration in quantifying loss are regulated by the proper law of the contract or the *lex loci delicti*.[7] Whether an obligation has been extinguished by prescription depends on the proper law of the obligation.[8] Liability for interest on money depends on the same law.[9] The measure of damages and any liability for interest thereon is, however, a matter for the *lex fori*.[10] So also is the ranking of claimants on a fund.[11]

Evidence and procedure

The evidencing of disputed rights, and all matters of procedure for adjudicating them, fall to be determined solely by the *lex fori*.[12]

---

[1] Bankruptcy Act, 1914, Ss. 53, 121–2, 167; Bankruptcy and Insolvency (Ireland) Act, 1857, Ss. 267–8. See also *Scrivenor* v. *Home's Trs.*, 1926 S.L.T. 214.

[2] *Obers* v. *Paton's Trs.* (1897) 24 R. 719.

[3] *Sc. Provident Instn.* v. *Cohen* (1888) 16 R. 112.

[4] *Ellis* v. *McHenry* (1871) L.R. 6 C.P. 228; *Gibb* v. *Societe Industrielle* (1890) 25 Q.BD. 399.

[5] *McElroy* v. *McAllister*, 1949 S.C. 110; cf. *Phrantzes* v. *Argenti* [1960] 2 Q.B. 19.

[6] *McElroy, supra.* See also *Boys* v. *Chaplin* [1971] A.C. 356.

[7] *J. D'Almeida Araujo Lda.* v. *Becker* [1953] 2 Q.B. 329.

[8] *Stirling's Trs.* v. *Legal and General Assce. Socy.*, 1957 S.L.T. 73.

[9] *Cochrane* v. *Gilkison* (1857) 20 D 213; *Price and Logan* v. *Wise* (1862) 24 D. 491.

[10] *Kendrick* v. *Burnett* (1897) 25 R. 82; cf. *Boys* v. *Chaplin* [1971] A.C. 366.

[11] *Clark* v. *Bowring*, 1908 S.C. 1168.

[12] Ersk. III, 7, 48; *B.L. Co.* v. *Drummond* (1830) 10 B. & C. 903; *Don* v. *Lippmann* (1837) 2 Sh. & Macl. 682; *Jones* v. *Somervell's Tr.*, 1907 S.C. 545.

Procedure for this purpose includes selection of the court appropriate by the internal law, modes of initiation and conduct of proceedings, parties,[1] competency,[2] and relevancy of action, limitation of time for bringing the action, method, and burden of proof,[3] sufficiency of evidence,[4] appeal, diligence, and expenses.

Arbitration

The validity, interpretation and effect of an agreement to arbitrate are governed by the proper law of the parties' contract. There is a presumption that the proper law is the law of the country where the arbitration is to be held.[5] The law governing the arbitration proceedings may be stated expressly, but will be presumed to be that of the country where the arbitration is to take place.[6]

THE PROOF OF FOREIGN LAW

When the Scottish choice-of-law rules direct the Scottish court to apply rules of foreign law to determine the rights of parties, the Scottish court must not assume knowledge of the statutes, cases or rules of that foreign system nor itself look at the textbooks of the foreign legal system.[7] Rules of foreign law are, in a Scottish case, matters of fact which must be averred as such and proved to the satisfaction of the court.[8] The onus of averment and of proof is on the party founding on the foreign law as being different from Scots law.[9] It is uncertain whether the evidence must be corroborated; probably it must.[10] If he fails to make adequate averments of the foreign law, the case must be decided by Scots law.[11]

[1] *McElroy* v. *McAllister,* 1949 S.C. 110.   [2] *Hansen* v. *Dixon* (1906) 23 T.L.R. 56.

[3] *Mackenzie* v. *Hall* (1854) 17 D. 164; *Girvin, Roper & Co.* v. *Monteith* (1895) 23 R. 129.

[4] *Owners of Immanuel* v. *Denholm* (1887) 15 R. 152.

[5] *Hamlyn* v. *Talisker Distillery* (1894) 21 R. (H.L.) 21; *Tzortzis* v. *Monark Line* [1968] 1 All E.R. 949.

[6] *Miller and Partners, Ltd.* v. *Whitworth Street Estates Ltd.* [1970] A.C. 583.

[7] Save that by the Evidence (Colonial Statutes) Act 1907, copies of laws made by the legislature of any British possession can be received in evidence if purporting to be printed by the government printer, without proof that they were so printed: *Papadopoulos* v. *P.* [1930] P. 55.

[8] *Rosses* v. *Bhagvat Sinjhee* (1891) 19 R. 31; *Stuart* v. *Potter, Choate & Prentice,* 1911, 1 S.L.T. 377; *Higgins* v. *Ewing's Trs.,* 1925 S.C. 440; *Faulkner* v. *Hill,* 1942 J.C. 20; *McElroy* v. *McAllister,* 1949 S.C. 110.

[9] *Immanuel* v. *Denholm* (1887) 15 R. 152; *Dynamit A/G* v. *Rio Tinto Co.* [1918] A.C. 260, 295; *De Reneville* v. *De R.* [1948] P. 100; *Prawdzic-Lazarska* v. *P.L.,* 1954 S.C. 98.

[10] It was in *Parnell* (1889) 16 R. 917 and *Rosses, supra.*

[11] *Lloyd* v. *Guibert* (1865) L.R. 1 Q.B. 115; *Dynamit A/G, supra*; *Rodden* v. *Whatlings, Ltd.,* 1961 S.C. 132; *Pryde* v. *Proctor & Gamble,* 1971 S.L.T. (Notes) 18; *Bonnor* v. *Balfour Kilpatrick,* 1974 S.L.T. 187.

The House of Lords, however, has judicial knowledge of all the legal systems of the U.K. and the law of each part of the U.K. is a matter of law, not of fact, in an appeal to it from another part.[1]

Unless parties lodge an agreed statement of the foreign law, or of consent remit to a foreign lawyer for his opinion,[2] or consent to the judge investigating the issue for himself,[3] foreign law must be proved by expert witnesses, who must normally be practising members of the legal profession in the legal system in question,[4] or at least hold an office which requires practical acquaintance with that legal system,[5] giving oral expert opinion evidence, and not, in general, by persons who have only an academic knowledge of that legal system.[6] If the evidence as to foreign law is uncontradicted the court must accept it, unless the result is absurd.[7] If there is a conflict of evidence on the foreign law the court must interpret that law in the light of the evidence,[8] and once foreign law has been proved the court must interpret the evidence as law, not fact.[8] The court may, however, itself interpret an agreed statement of foreign law.[6]

Judicial ascertainment of foreign law

Statutory provisions permit Scottish courts to state and remit a case to a foreign court for a statement of its opinion on its own law applicable to the case. The British Law Ascertainment Act, 1859, authorizes a court[9] in one part of Her Majesty's dominions to prepare a case, setting out questions of law on which they desire to have the opinion of another court, and remit it[10] there

---

[1] *Stein's Assignee* v. *Gibson & Craig* (1831) 5 W. & S. 47; *Cooper* v. *C.* (1888) 15 R. (H.L.) 21; *Municipal Council of Johannesburg* v. *Stewart*, 1909 S.C. (H.L.) 53; *Elliot* v. *Joicey*, 1935 S.C. (H.L.) 57. See also *Inland Revenue* v. *Glasgow Police Athletic Assocn.*, 1953 S.C. (H.L.) 13.

[2] *Welsh* v. *Milne* (1845) 7 D. 213; *Higgins* v. *Ewing's Trs.*, 1925 S.C. 440.

[3] *Jabbour* v. *Custodian of Israeli Absentee Property* [1954] 1 W.L.R. 139, 147.

[4] *Parnell* v. *Walter* (1889) 16 R. 917; (1890) 17 R. 552; *Rosses* v. *Bhagvat Sinhjee* (1891) 19 R. 31; but see *Said Ajami* v. *Comptroller of Customs* [1954] 1 W.L.R. 1405.

[5] *Sussex Peerage Case* (1844) 11 Cl. & F. 85; *In bonis Dhost Aly Khan* (1880) 6 P.D. 6.

[6] *Bristow* v. *Sequeville* (1850) 19 L.J. Ex. 289; *In the goods of Bonelli* (1875) L.R. 1 P.D. 69; contrast *Brailey* v. *Rhodesia Consolidated Ltd.* [1910] 2 Ch. 95; *In the goods of Whitelegg* [1899] P. 267.

[7] *Buerger* v. *N.Y. Life Assce. Co.* (1926) 96 L.J.K.B. 930; *Koechlin* v. *Kestenbaum* [1927] 1 K.B. 616; *Sharif* v. *Azad* [1967] 1 Q.B. 605.

[8] *Kolbin* v. *Kinnear*, 1930 S.C. 724; *Lazard Bros.* v. *Midland Bank* [1933] A.C. 289; *Tallina Laevauhisus* v. *Estonian State S.S. Line* (1947) 80 Ll.L.R. 99.

[9] Including a Lord Ordinary: *Hewit's Trs.* v. *Lawson* (1891) 18 R. 793; *Macomish's Exors.* v. *Jones*, 1932 S.C. 108. The court may refuse to settle a case: *MacDougall* v. *Chitnavis*, 1937 S.C. 390.

[10] *Guthrie* (1880) 7 R. 1141.

for opinion.[1] A certified copy of the opinion being returned, the remitting court must apply the opinion on law to the facts. The Privy Council or House of Lords on appeal may reject the opinion if of a court whose judgments are reviewable by it.

The Foreign Law Ascertainment Act, 1861, authorizes superior courts within Her Majesty's dominions to remit a case, with questions of law, to a court of any foreign state with which a convention has been made for the purpose, and conversely.

RENVOI

Difficulties may arise where the Scottish rules for choice of law direct the courts to apply another legal system, and that system's rules for choice of law direct the application of Scots law.[2] There appears to be no Scottish authority. The most satisfactory principle is to treat the other legal system concerned as including only its substantive rules and excluding the other system's rules for choice of law, so that the reference by Scots law to the other system is treated as final.

[1] Cf. *Bradford* v. *Young* (1884) 11 R. 1135; *D. Wellington's Exor.*, 1946 S.C. 32.
[2] cf. *Collier* v. *Rivaz* (1841) 2 Curt. 855; *Bremer* v. *Freeman* (1857) 10 Moo. P.C. 306; *Hamilton* v. *Dallas* (1875) L.R. 1 Ch. D. 257.

CHAPTER 13

FOREIGN JUDGMENTS

THE problem may arise whether, where some legal issue has already been determined by the courts of another country, that judgment should be accepted by the Scottish courts as decisive, or as valid and enforceable in Scotland. Convenience and international comity require that foreign judgments only exceptionally be disregarded.

In general a foreign judgment will be recognized (a) if it were pronounced by a court apparently having jurisdiction under the principles of effectiveness or of submission, whether or not the court actually giving the judgment truly had competence, under its own internal law and procedure, to grant that judgment,[1] unless possibly it plainly appeared that the court had no competence by its internal law to do what it has purported to do; (b) if the judgment were final and conclusive, and not interlocutory, nor subject to variation, nor requiring a further order to complete it,[2] though it may be final even though still appealable;[3] and (c) if it is for a definite sum in money, in or convertible into sterling.[4]

A Scottish court will not enforce a decree of a foreign court in a penal or revenue claim.[5]

Foreign judgments affecting status

The judgment determining status is akin to a judgment *in rem*. The general principle is that if a foreign court exercises jurisdiction on grounds accepted by Scots law as adequate, its judgment will be treated as valid by the Scottish courts.[6] Thus a decree of nullity of marriage of the court of the foreign domicile is recognized in Scotland;[7] a decree from the court of the common

---

[1] *Pick* v. *Stewart, Galbraith & Co.* (1907) 15 S.L.T. 447; *Geiger* v. *Macdonald*, 1932 S.L.T. 70; *Scott* v. *S.*, 1937 S.L.T. 632.

[2] *Nouvion* v. *Freeman* (1889) 15 App. Cas. 1; *Harrop* v. *H.* [1920] 3 K.B. 386.

[3] *Scott* v. *Pilkington* (1862) 2 B. & S. 11; *Findlay* v. *Wickham*, 1920, 2 S.L.T. 325.

[4] *Sadler* v. *Robins* (1808) 1 Camp. 253; *Beatty* v. *B.* [1924] 1 K.B. 807.

[5] *Huntington* v. *Attrill* [1893] A.C. 150; *A.G. for Canada* v. *Schulze* (1901) 9 S.L.T. 4; *Metal Industries (Salvage) Ltd.* v. *Harle*, 1962 S.L.T. 114; *Govt. of India* v. *Taylor* [1955] A.C. 491; *Peter Buchanan Ltd.* v. *McVey* [1955] A.C. 516 n.

[6] Cf. Legitimation (Sc.) Act, 1968, S. 5.

[7] *Administrator of Austrian Property* v. *Von Lorang*, 1927 S.C. (H.L.) 80; cf. *Aldridge* v. *A.*, 1954 S.C. 58.

residence would similarly be recognized[1] but not a decree annulling a marriage by a court of the country where the marriage took place.[2] In divorce cases Scottish courts at common law treated as valid a decree of divorce pronounced by a foreign court if the parties were domiciled within the jurisdiction of that court,[3] or if the courts of the domicile recognize a decree pronounced elsewhere as valid within that domicile.[4]

Statutory recognition

By statute the validity of a decree of divorce or judicial separation granted after 1 January 1972 under the law of Scotland is recognized in England and Wales and conversely, and if granted under the law of Northern Ireland, the Channel Islands or the Isle of Man, it is recognized in Great Britain.[5] Divorces and legal separations obtained judicially outside the British Isles and effective under the law of the country of granting are recognized in Great Britain if at the date of the institution of the proceedings either spouse was habitually resident, or domiciled, in that country, or either spouse was a national of that country.[6] Divorce or separation obtained non-judicially,[7] if not required to be recognized by secs. 2–5, is not to be regarded as validly dissolving a marriage if both parties thereto have within the previous year been habitually resident in the U.K.[8] Where there are cross-actions the validity of an overseas divorce or separation obtained either in the original proceedings or in the cross proceedings is recognized if S. 3 is satisfied, and where a separation, the validity of which is entitled to recognition is converted in the country in which it was obtained into a divorce, the validity of the divorce is recognized.[9] In respect of recognition any

---

[1] *Ramsay-Fairfax* v. *R.F.* [1956] P. 115.

[2] *Casey* v. *C.* [1949] P. 420.

[3] *Shaw* v. *Gould* (1868) L.R. 3 H.L. 55; *Harvey* v. *Farnie* (1882) 8 App. Cas. 43; *Le Mesurier* v. *Le M.* [1895] A.C. 517; *Humphrey* v. *H's Trs.* (1895) 3 S.L.T. 151; *Makouipur* v. *M.*, 1967 S.C. 116. Declarator of the validity of a judicial divorce is unnecessary: *Arnott* v. *L.A.*, 1932 S.L.T. 46; *McKay* v. *Walls*, 1951 S.L.T. (Notes) 6. See also *Sim* v. *S.*, 1948 S.L.T. (Notes) 15.

[4] *Armitage* v. *A.G.* [1906] P. 135; *Perin* v. *P.*, 1950 S.L.T. 51; *McKay* v. *Walls*, 1951 S.L.T. (Notes) 6; cf. *Mather* v. *Mahoney* [1968] 3 All E.R. 223. See also *Galbraith* v. *G.*, 1971 S.L.T. 139; *Bain* v. *B.*, 1971 S.L.T. 141.

[5] Recognition of Divorces and Legal Separations Act, 1971, S. 1.

[6] Ss. 2–3; *Broit* v. *B.*, 1972 S.L.T. (Notes) 32; *Cruse* v. *Chittum* [1974] 2 All E.R. 940.

[7] This includes legislative, administrative, e.g. *Nachinson* v. *N.* [1930] P. 217, and religious divorces, e.g. *Qureshi* v. *Q.* [1971] 1 All E.R. 325; *Har-Shefi* v. *H.S.* [1953] P. 220.

[8] Domicile and Matrimonial Proceedings Act, 1973, S. 16.

[9] 1971 Act, S. 4.

finding of fact is conclusive evidence of the facts found if both spouses took part in the proceedings, and otherwise sufficient proof unless the contrary is shown.[1] The Act is without prejudice to the recognition of the validity of divorces and legal separations obtained outside the British Isles by virtue of any rule that the spouses had both been domiciled in that other country[2] or that it was recognized as valid under the law of that country,[3] and also if one spouse was domiciled in that country and the divorce or separation was recognized as valid under the law of the other spouse's domicile or, neither spouse being domiciled there, it was recognized as valid under the law of the domicile of each spouse respectively, or by virtue of any other enactment, but no other divorce or legal separation is to be recognized as valid.[4]

Neither spouse is precluded from remarrying in Great Britain if the validity of a divorce obtained elsewhere is entitled to recognition under the Act, even though it would not be recognized elsewhere.[5] Recognition is not granted if by Scots law there was no marriage between the parties, and may be refused only if it was granted outside the British Isles and proper notice of the proceedings were not given to the other party,[6] or the other party were not given such opportunity to take part in the proceedings as he should reasonably have been given, or recognition would manifestly be contrary to the public policy.[7] Nothing in the Act requires the recognition of findings of fault made in any proceedings or of any custody or maintenance order made therein.[8]

A decree, if valid under these principles, is a judgment *in rem* binding throughout the world, save that if it also imposes a restriction on remarriage, that might be disregarded in Scotland as being a penalty,[9] and that if it also prevents remarriage until after the lapse of a specified time, the decree may be held not to have finally determined the issue between the parties till that time has elapsed.[10] If such a foreign decree is invalid, it is ineffective to dissolve the marriage, so that a remarriage is adulterous

---

[1] Ibid., S. 5.
[2] e.g. *Le Mesurier* v. *Le M.* [1895] A.C. 517.
[3] e.g. *Armitage* v. *A.G.* [1903] P. 135.
[4] *Ibid.*, S. 6, replaced under Domicile and Matrimonial Proceedings Act, 1973, S. 2. This overrules *Travers* v. *Holley* [1953] P. 246; *Indyka* v. *I.* [1969] 3 A.C. 33.
[5] Ibid., S. 7.
[6] cf. *Crabtree* v. *C.*, 1929 S.L.T. 675.
[7] cf. *Macalpine* v. *M.* [1958] P. 35; *Meyer* v. *M.* [1971] 1 All E.R. 378.
[8] Ibid., S. 8.
[9] *Scott* v. *A.G.* (1886) 11 P.D. 128; see also *Martin* v. *Buret*, 1938 S.L.T. 479.
[10] *Warter* v. *W.* (1890) 17 P.D. 152.

and bigamous, and also ineffective in Scotland as to any consequential matters, such as aliment.[1]

The Scottish courts have refused to accept the decree of an
American court presuming the death of a person as valid in
Scotland,[2] and the decree of the Rota of the Roman Catholic
church as annulling a marriage contracted in Scotland.[3] Decrees
of English magistrates' courts for maintenance or permitting
non-cohabitation have been held not to bar proceedings in the
courts of the domicile determinative of status.[4]

Foreign decrees of judicial separation

Recognition of these is governed by the Recognition of
Divorces and Legal Separations Act, 1971.

Foreign judgments regulating custody

The Scottish courts recognize as valid the decree of a foreign
court, having jurisdiction in matrimonial affairs, settling the
custody of a child[5] or access to it,[6] but have taken account of
circumstances affecting the child's welfare before giving effect to
a petition by the entitled parent for actual custody.[7] Where the
child of a domiciled Scot had been made a ward of court in
England and access had been granted, the Scottish court declined
to make an order for access.[8]

Foreign judgments appointing guardians

A judgment of a court of that state in which a minor is domiciled and resident has been recognized, though the minor has been
held not entitled to grant an effective discharge for the transfer
to him of Scottish heritage, and his guardian unauthorized to
grant a discharge valid to exonerate Scottish trustees.[9] But the
court has refused to recognize an order by the High Court in
England making a girl, not then in Scotland, a ward of court as
being granted without jurisdiction.[10]

---

[1] *Papadopoulos* v. *P.* [1930] P. 55; *Simons* v. *S.* [1939] 1 K.B. 490.
[2] *Simpson's Trs.* v. *Fox*, 1951 S.L.T. 412. cf. *In the Goods of Wolf* [1948] P. 66.
[3] *Di Rollo* v. *D.R.*, 1959 S.C. 75.
[4] *Murray* v. *M.*, 1956 S.C. 376; *Richardson* v. *R.*, 1957 S.L.T. (Notes) 45.
[5] *Radoyevitch* v. *R.*, 1930 S.C. 619; see also *Battaglia* v. *B.*, 1966 S.L.T. (Notes) 85;
Kelly v. *Marks*, 1974 S.L.T. 118.
[6] *Westergaard* v. *W.*, 1914 S.C. 977.
[7] *Middleton* v. *M.* [1966] 1 All E.R. 168.
[8] *Calder* v. *C.*, 1960 S.L.T. (Notes) 52.
[9] *Ogilvy* v. *O's Trs.*, 1927 S.L.T. 83.   [10] *Hoy* v. *H.*, 1968 S.C. 179.

Foreign adoptions

As the Adoption Act 1958 applies to both Scotland and England English adoptions will be recognized in Scotland. The Adoption Act, 1964, provides for the recognition in Scotland of adoption orders made in Northern Ireland, the Channel Islands and the Isle of Man. An adoption elsewhere may be recognized if the adoptive parents are domiciled there and the child ordinarily resident there[1] or possibly if recognized by the courts of the adoptive parents' domicile. The Adoption Act, 1968,[2] will facilitate recognition of foreign adoptions.

Foreign judgments in personam

The common law principle is that a foreign judgment is not enforceable as such, but it has created an obligation which gives a good cause of action in an action for decree conform, which decree if granted by the Scottish court is enforceable as a Scottish decree. In the absence of statutory warrant for registering a foreign judgment the only method of enforcing it is to bring an action for decree conform in which the foreign decree, if prepared and authenticated according to the practice of the Court granting it,[3] is produced and proved. Such a judgment will be presumed to have been pronounced by a competent court and accordingly to be *res judicata*, but it may be challenged on the grounds that the foreign court did not have jurisdiction over the defender on a ground reasonably consistent with international law,[4] or the defender did not have due notice of the claim made against him,[5] or there was fraud on or by the foreign court,[6] or the decree was not final,[7] or was contrary to British ideas of natural justice,[8] or public policy.[9] A foreign judgment cannot be challenged on the merits either on fact or law.[10] Apart from direct enforcement a

---

[1] *Re Valentine's Settlement* [1965] Ch. 831. [2] Not yet in force.

[3] *Robertson* v. *Gordon*, 15 Nov. 1814, F.C.; cf. *Disbrow* v. *Mackintosh* (1852) 15 D. 123; *Whitehead* v. *Thompson* (1861) 23 D. 772; *Cooney* v. *Dunne*, 1925 S.L.T. 22.

[4] *Waygood* v. *Bennie* (1885) 12 R. 651; *Schibsby* v. *Westenholz* (1870) L.R. 6 Q.B. 155; *Sirdar Gurdyal Singh* v. *Rajah of Faridkote* [1894] A.C. 670; *Pemberton* v. *Hughes* [1899] 1 Ch. 781; *Carrick* v. *Hancock* (1895) 12 T.L.R. 59; *Geiger* v. *Macdonald*, 1932 S.L.T. 70.

[5] *Pemberton* v. *Hughes* [1899] 1 Ch. 781.

[6] *Vadala* v. *Lawes* (1890) 25 Q.B.D. 310; *Syal* v. *Heyward* [1948] 2 K.B. 443.

[7] *Pattison* v. *MacVicar* (1886) 13 R. 550; *Nouvion* v. *Freeman* (1889) 15 App. Cas. 1; *Delhi and London Bank* v. *Loch* (1895) 22 R. 849; *Administrator of Austrian Property* v. *Von Lorang*, 1927 S.C. (H.L.) 80.

[8] *Don* v. *Lippman* (1837) 2 Sh. & Macl. 682, 745; *Bethell* v. *Bethell* (1888) 38 Ch. D. 220; cf. *Cooney* v. *Dunne*, 1925 S.L.T. 22.

[9] *In re Macartney* [1921] 1 Ch. 522.

[10] *Gladstone* v. *Lindsay* (1868) 6 S.L.R. 71; *Castrique* v. *Imrie* (1870) L.R. 4 H.L. 414; *Nouvion* v. *Freeman* (1889) 15 App. Cas. 1; but see *Meyer* v. *Ralli* (1876) L.R. 1 C.P. 358.

foreign decree may sometimes be founded on as evidencing a debt sued for,[1] or be pleaded in defence as *res judicata*.[2]

Defences to actions on foreign judgments

While it is not open to challenge a foreign judgment on any ground of error in fact or law by the foreign court,[3] certain defences are competent, and render the foreign judgment unenforceable:

(1) Foreign judgment obtained by fraud: this includes collusion by the parties to give the foreign court jurisdiction,[4] or deception of that court and abuse of its procedure.[5]

(2) Judgment contrary to British public policy: such judgments include foreign judgments of a penal nature,[6] or foreign revenue claims.[7]

(3) Judgment contrary to natural justice: if reached in a manner contrary to natural justice the foreign judgment is unenforceable. This includes failure to hear one party,[8] or failure to give fair notice of the proceedings to a party,[9] but not merely apparent or obvious incorrectness of the judgment.[10]

Statutory enforcement of foreign judgments

By the Judgments Extension Act, 1868, judgments obtained in the superior courts of England[11] and Northern Ireland[12] for any debt, damages or costs[13] are enforceable in Scotland when a certificate of judgment from the adjudicating court is registered in the Register of English and Irish Judgments maintained by the Court of Session. A certificate so registered has the same effect as a Court of Session decree pronounced on the date of

---

[1] *Stiven* v. *Myer* (1868) 6 M. 885; *Phosphate Sewage Co.* v. *Molleson* (1879) 6 R. (H.L.) 113.

[2] *Phosphate Sewage Co.* v. *Lawson* (1878) 5 R. 1125; *Comber* v. *Maclean* (1881) 9 R. 215.

[3] *Castrique* v. *Imrie* (1870) L.R. 4 H.L. 414; *Godard* v. *Gray* (1870) L.R. 6 Q.B. 139.

[4] *Shaw* v. *Gould* (1868) L.R. 3 H.L. 55.

[5] *Boe* v. *Anderson* (1857) 20 D. 11; *Vadala* v. *Lawes* (1890) 25 Q.B.D. 310; *Macalpine* v. *M.* [1958] P. 35; see also *Perin* v. *P.*, 1950 S.L.T. 51.

[6] *Raulin* v. *Fischer* [1911] 2 K.B. 93; *Re Macartney* [1921] 1 Ch. 522.

[7] *Govt. of India* v. *Taylor* [1955] A.C. 491.

[8] *Don* v. *Lippmann* (1837) 2 S. & Macl. 682; *Det Norske Bjergnings og Dykkercompagni* v. *McLaren* (1885) 22 S.L.R. 861; *Pattison* v. *McVicar* (1886) 13 R. 550.

[9] *Rudd* v. *R.* [1924] P. 72; *Scott* v. *S.*, 1937 S.L.T. 632; *Igra* v. *I.* [1951] P. 404; *Maher* v. *M.* [1951] P. 342.

[10] *Castrique* v. *Imrie* (1870) L.R. 4 H.L. 414.

[11] See *English's Coasting Co.* v. *British Finance Co.* (1886) 14 R. 220, 225.

[12] As to judgments from the Republic of Ireland, see *Wakely* v. *Triumph Cycle Co.* [1924] 1 K.B. 214; *Cooney* v. *Dunne*, 1925 S.L.T. 22; *Doohan* v. *N.C.B.*, 1959 S.C. 310; *Harley* v. *Kinnear Moodie & Co.*, 1964 S.C. 99.

[13] *Wotherspoon* v. *Connelly* (1871) 9 M. 510.

registration.[1] The Scottish court cannot consider the merits of the English or Irish decision,[2] nor whether that court had jurisdiction, unless it is manifest that it exceeded its jurisdiction.[3] The debtor need not be subject to the jurisdiction of the Scottish courts.[4]

The Inferior Courts Judgments Extension Act, 1882, makes similar procedure applicable to English and Northern Irish County Courts judgments. A certificate is registered in the Sheriff Court Books and diligence may follow thereon as if it were a sheriff court decree.

The Administration of Justice Act, 1920, makes provision for the enforcement within the United Kingdom countries of judgments obtained in a superior court of any part of the British dominions, including any territory under Her Majesty's protection or mandate, with which reciprocal arrangements have been made. Registration is in the discretion of the Court of Session,[5] is competent only if for the payment of money,[6] and is not permitted in certain specified circumstances.[7]

The Foreign Judgments (Reciprocal Enforcement) Act, 1933, provides for the registration of judgments obtained in foreign countries for money, other than sums in respect of taxes, fines, or penalties, if reciprocal arrangements have been made.[8] In certain specified circumstances the judgment must, or may, be set aside.

The Act of Sederunt (Enforcement Abroad of Sheriff Court Judgments), 1962,[9] prescribes procedure whereby sheriff court judgments may be enforced abroad in countries with which the United Kingdom has a convention providing therefor.

Recognition of foreign adoptions

Certain adoptions authorized in countries outside the United Kingdom are entitled to recognition in Great Britain.[10]

---

[1] See e.g. *Cumming* v. *Parker, White & Co.*, 1923 S.L.T. 455; *Swaine* v. *Demetriades*, 1942 S.C. 1.

[2] *Wotherspoon, supra.*

[3] *Wotherspoon, supra*; *Gartland* v. *Sweeny*, 1920, 2 S.L.T. 152. See also *Laughland* v. *Wansborough Paper Co.*, 1921, 1 S.L.T. 341.

[4] *English's Coasting Co., supra.*

[5] Refused in *Ibbetson*, 1957 S.L.T. (Notes) 15.

[6] Inclusion of an order for costs does not make the judgment one for money: *Platt* v. *P.*, 1958 S.C. 95.

[7] *Bank of British W. Africa*, 1931 S.L.T. 83.

[8] See *Medinelli* v. *Malgras*, 1958 S.C. 489; *Jamieson* v. *Northern Electricity Sy. Corpn.* [1969] C.L.Y. 4189. See also *Black-Clawson* v. *Papierwerke A/G* [1974] 2 All E.R. 611.

[9] S.I. 1962, No. 1517.

[10] Adoption Act, 1968, Ss. 4–5. By Ss. 6–7 British courts may pronounce on the validity of adoptions and determinations made overseas.

Enforcement of Maintenance Orders

Under the Maintenance Orders Act, 1950, Ss. 16–18,[1] orders for payment of maintenance, i.e. aliment, to women and children made under specified statutes[2] by a court in any one part of the United Kingdom may be registered in a court in another part of the United Kingdom and enforced in that other part of the United Kingdom as if it had been made by the registering court. Such orders may similarly be discharged or varied,[3] and the registration may be cancelled.

Extensions of Act

Under the Family Law Reform Act, 1969, Ss. 4(5) and 6(7) orders made in England for maintenance of a person up to the age of 21, and orders for the maintenance of a ward of court are enforceable in Scotland under the 1950 Act, S. 16. Under the Matrimonial Proceedings and Property Act, 1970, S. 12, orders made in England for maintenance pending divorce, financial provision on divorce, nullity, or separation, financial provision for children in such cases, and in case of neglect by either party to a marriage to maintain the other or a child of the family, are enforceable in Scotland under the 1950 Act, S. 16. Under the Guardianship of Minors Act, 1971, S. 13, an English court may make an order relating to the custody of a minor, including an order on a father to make payments to the mother towards the minor's maintenance, and this also is enforceable under the 1950 Act, S. 16.

Reciprocal enforcement of maintenance orders

By the Maintenance Orders (Reciprocal Enforcement) Act, 1972,[4] maintenance orders made by courts in the United Kingdom may be transmitted to reciprocating countries for enforcement there, and orders made by courts in reciprocating countries may be sent to courts in this country and confirmed or not, or with alterations, registered, and enforced as if made by these courts, and varied or revoked.[5] Provision is made for applications by persons in the U.K. for recovery of maintenance in convention

---

[1] Extended by Maintenance Orders Act, 1958, S. 20 (3)(a).

[2] Listed in S. 16(2), extended by Succession (Sc.) Act, 1964, S. 26, and Social Work (Sc.) Act, 1967, Sch. 8.

[3] *Allum v. A.,* 1965 S.L.T. (Sh. Ct.) 26; see also *Thompson v. T.* (1953) 69 Sh. Ct. Rep. 193.

[4] Not yet brought into force.   [5] Ss. 1–24.

countries[1] and by persons in convention countries for recovery of maintenance in Scotland.[2] Extensive provision is made for transfer, enforcement, variation and revocation of registered orders.[3]

Foreign judgments in rem

A foreign judgment *in rem*, such as determining title to property, immoveable or moveable, falls to be recognized if proceeding from a court of the country where the property was situated at the date of the action.[4]

Enforcement of judgments under Carriage of Goods by Road Act, 1965

This Act gives effect to an international convention relating to carriage by road. Proceedings may be brought in the courts of a contracting country or of one where the defendant is ordinarily resident, or has his principal place of business, or the branch or agency through which the contract was made, or where the goods were taken over by the carrier or the place designated for delivery. Judgments from such courts are enforceable within the United Kingdom by registration under the Foreign Judgments (Reciprocal Enforcement) Act, 1933, Part I.

Enforcement of judgments under Carriage by Railway Act, 1972

This Act gives effect to an international convention relating to carriage of passengers and luggage by railway and governs the liability of railways for damage caused to passengers by an accident occurring on the territory of a party to the convention. Actions may only be instituted in the competent court of the state on whose territory the accident occurred, unless otherwise provided in agreements between States, or in any licence or other document authorizing the operation of the railway concerned.

Judgments of courts of contracting States other than the United Kingdom and enforceable under the law applied by that court are enforceable by registration under Part I of the Foreign Judgments (Reciprocal Enforcement) Act.

Enforcement of orders in company liquidation

An order made by a court in England for or in the course of winding up is enforceable in Scotland and Northern Ireland, if

---

[1] Ss. 25–6, i.e. countries which have acceded to the U.N. Convention on the Recovery Abroad of Maintenance, 1956.

[2] S. 31.   [3] Ss. 32–9.

[4] *Cammell* v. *Sewell* (1858) 3 H. & N. 728; *Castrique* v. *Imrie* (1870) L.R. 4 H.L. 414.

the courts there would have had jurisdiction if the company had been registered there, as if it had been made by them, and conversely.[1]

Enforcement of orders in bankruptcy

At common law the title of a trustee in bankruptcy or equivalent officer appointed by the court of the country where the bankrupt has been residing and carrying on business will be recognized by the Scottish courts.[2] The Scottish courts have held that they will accept the bankruptcy jurisdiction of English courts.[3] The Act and Warrant of confirmation of a trustee in bankruptcy vests in him moveable estate wherever situated, heritable estate in Scotland, real estate in England, Ireland or any of Her Majesty's dominions.[4] Orders made by a Scottish court are statutorily enforceable in England and Ireland as if made by the courts there. Similarly orders of a court of bankruptcy in England or Ireland are enforceable in Scotland as if made by the court required to enforce them. These courts are to be auxiliary to one another in all matters of bankruptcy.[5]

Foreign appointments of executors

If a deceased person left property in Scotland it can be dealt with only by an executor confirmed by the Scottish courts. By the Administration of Estates Act 1971, S. 3, a grant of probate or letters of administration from the High Court in England or Northern Ireland has, without being resealed, the same force, effect, and operation in relation to property in Scotland as a Scottish confirmation, and conversely. Under the Colonial Probates Act, 1892, a grant of representation made in a country to which the Act applies[6] may be resealed and have the same effect as confirmation. But representatives appointed by deceased persons elsewhere must obtain confirmation in the ordinary way.[7]

---

[1] Companies Act, 1948, S. 276; and see R.C. 216; it applies to orders for payment of money only: *Johnstone's Trs.* v. *Roose* (1884) 12 R. 1.

[2] *Obers* v. *Paton's Trs.* (1897) 24 R. 719.

[3] *Wilkie* v. *Cathcart* (1870) 9 M. 168; *Salaman* v. *Tod,* 1911 S.C. 1214.

[4] Bankruptcy (Sc.) Act, 1913, S. 97.

[5] Bankruptcy Act, 1914, Ss. 123–4; see also *Forbes* v. *Official Receiver in Bankruptcy,* 1924 S.L.T. 522; *Scrivenor* v. *Home's Trs.,* 1926 S.L.T. 214.

[6] This includes most Commonwealth countries.

[7] cf. *New York Breweries Co. Ltd.* v. *A.G.* [1899] A.C. 62.

Enforcement of European Community judgments

By the European Communities (Enforcement of Community Judgments) Order, 1972,[1] there may be registered in the Court of Session judgments and orders to which the Secretary of State has duly appended an order for enforcement, so that they are then, subject to the treaties, enforceable as if they were judgments or order of that court.

Enforcement of foreign arbitration awards

At common law the Scottish courts give effect to a final decree-arbitral valid by the proper law of the contract of submission to arbitration,[2] so long as not contrary to natural justice,[3] by decree-conform.

Foreign arbitral awards, as statutorily defined,[4] subject to certain conditions[5] and to being satisfactorily evidenced,[6] are enforceable in Scotland by action, or if the agreement for arbitration contains consent to the registration of the award in the Books of Council and Session for execution and it is so registered, by summary diligence.[7] Certain arbitration awards can be enforced by registration as if they were judgments?[8]

---

[1] S.I. 1972, No. 1590.

[2] *E. Hopetoun* v. *Scots Mines Co.* (1856) 18 D. 739; *Hope* v. *Crookston Bros.* (1890) 17 R. 868.

[3] *Hamlyn* v. *Talisker Distillery* (1894) 21 R. (H.L.) 21, 23.

[4] Arbitration Act, 1950, S. 35.

[5] Ibid., S. 37(1).

[6] Ibid., S. 38.

[7] Ibid., S. 41(3).

[8] i.e. those made in countries to which the Administration of Justice Act, 1920, Part II, or the Foreign Judgments (Reciprocal Enforcement) Act, 1933, Part I, has been extended, and certain awards made in pursuance of a contract for the international carriage of goods: Carriage of Goods by Road Act, 1965, Ss. 4, 7.

BOOK III

THE LAW OF PERSONS

CHAPTER 14

PERSONALITY

THE LAW of persons is properly studied first because the legal system operates by ascribing legal rights and duties to legal persons, and obligations exist between legal persons, property is possessed and owned by legal persons, and legal persons claim legal remedies from other legal persons. The concept of the legal person is accordingly fundamental.

Legal personality is the quality, attributed by the legal system, of being a legal person, an entity to which legal rights can attach and on which legal duties may be incumbent. A legal person is a right and duty bearing unit for legal purposes, having *persona standi in judicio*.

The category of legal persons is not confined to natural living persons. Scots law attributes legal personality to all living human beings (natural persons),[1] at least for some purposes to certain kinds of associations of living persons, particularly partnerships (sometimes called quasi-corporations),[2] though for other purposes these groups, and other kinds of groups for all purposes, are deemed merely groups or aggregates of natural persons,[3] and it attributes legal personality for all purposes to certain entities or groups or institutions held to be incorporated by law, and hence known as corporations, such as companies and local authorities.[4] Though in themselves inanimate and incorporeal, corporations (sometimes called artificial or juristic persons) are held in law to be single entities which have legal personality and existence in law quite independently of the legal personalities of all the members or officials thereof.[5] Whether the Crown, in the sense of the superior central government of the state, as distinct from the sovereign for the time being, is a corporation for any purpose is uncertain.[6]

---

[1] Ch. 15–19, *infra*.

[2] Ch. 23, *infra*.

[3] Chs. 20–3, *infra*.

[4] Chs. 24–8, *infra*; cf. Ersk. I, 7, 64; Bell, *Prin.* §2176–8.

[5] The Interpretation Act, 1889, S. 19, provides that in legislation generally, 'The expression "person" shall, unless the contrary intention appears, include any body of persons corporate or unincorporate'. But normally unincorporated groups or associations must be distinguished from incorporated bodies.

[6] Ch. 25, *infra*.

Animals do not have legal personality; though various rules of law exist for their benefit these confer no rights or duties on the beasts themselves.[1]

Whether legal personality, full or restricted, is attributed to particular categories of human beings is a matter of law, as is the question whether particular kinds of groups or entities can be, or have been, incorporated, and, in the latter event what powers, capacities, duties and liabilities attach to them thereby. So too the questions whether, and, if so, at what point of time, personality has come into being or terminated, are questions of law.

[1] cf. *Re Dean* (1889) 41 Ch. D. 552.

NATURAL PERSONS

CHAPTER 15

NATURAL PERSONS AND THEIR STATUS

NATURAL persons are living human beings and all are regarded by Scots law as endowed with legal personality. Though by Scots law all living human beings are natural persons, not all have the same legal attributes, powers, and capacities. These vary according to the status of the natural person.

Commencement of personality

Legal personality commences at least for certain purposes at conception, provided that the individual is subsequently born alive and has lived, for however short a time. Thus a claim may be open for ante-natal injuries[1] or loss,[2] and in the law of succession a child *in utero* is deemed already born if that will benefit it, under the maxim *nasciturus pro iam nato habetur quando agitur de ejus commodo*.[3] If the child is stillborn he is held never to have been a legal person.

Personality commences generally at birth, though by reason of a child's incapacity he has no legal powers to act on his own behalf so long as he remains a pupil. The precise time of birth is material as the periods of age are computed *de momento in momentum*.[4] Births must be registered under the Registration of Births, Deaths and Marriages (Scotland) Act, 1965, Ss. 13–21.

---

[1] Walker, *Delict*, 96; Atkinson (1904) 20 L.Q.R. 134; Winfield (1942) 8 Camb. L.J. 76; Veitch (1973) 24 N.I.L.Q. 40; see also *Walker* v. *G.N. Ry. of Ireland* (1890) 28 L.R. Ir. 69; *Montreal Tramways* v. *Leveille* [1933] 4 D.L.R. 337.

[2] *Connachan* v. *S.M.T. Co.*, 1946 S.C. 428; *Moorcraft* v. *Alexander*, 1946 S.C. 466; *Leadbetter* v. *N.C.B.*, 1952 S.L.T. 179 (damages to posthumous children for father's death).

[3] *Elliot* v. *Joicey*, 1935 S.C. (H.L.) 57, 70; *Allan's Trs.* v. *A.*, 1949 S.L.T. (Notes) 3; *Cox's Trs.* v. *C.*, 1950 S.C. 117.

[4] Craig II, 12, 14; Stair I, 6, 33; Ersk. I, 7, 36; Fraser, *P. & Ch.*, 200.

Presumption of life

A person once born is presumed to remain alive for a normal and substantial time[1] but at common law the Court may at any time presume his death at a stated date[2] if satisfied by evidence that his death by then is very probable.[3] It is a question of circumstances and it is relevant to consider what the absent person's age would have been, his health, and any circumstances which might shorten his normal expectation of life.[4] The issue may be tried in a multiplepoinding.[5]

Under the Presumption of Life Limitation (Scotland) Act, 1891, the Court may, where a person has disappeared and not been heard of for seven years or more, find the fact of disappearance, the date at which he was last known to be alive, and that he died at a specified date or that he is to be presumed to have died seven years after the date on which he was last known to be alive.[6] Petition is competent at the instance of anyone entitled to succeed to any estate on the death of the absentee,[7] or to any estate the transmission of which depends on the absentee's death, or by the fiar of any estate burdened by a liferent in favour of the absentee.[8] The absentee may, despite the decree, recover the estate from anyone who has obtained it under the decree[9] or from a gratuitous alienee from him, or, if it has been sold, recover the price thereof, within 13 years from the date when the title to the estate, if capable of registration in a public register, was so registered, or when possession was taken of other estate under the decree. Thereafter recovery of property is barred.[10] The Act does not exclude the rights of third parties having a right preferable to

---

[1] Stair IV, 45, 17, (19) mentions 80 or 100 years; Bankt. II, 6, 31; *Bruce* v. *Smith* (1871) 10 M. 130; *Barstow* v. *Cook* (1874) 11 S.L.R. 363; *Stewart's Trs.* v. *S.* (1875) 2 R. 488; *McLay* v. *Borland* (1876) 3 R. 1124; *Secy. of State for Scotland* v. *Sutherland*, 1944 S.C. 79, 84.

[2] *Rhind's Trs.* v. *Bell* (1878) 5 R. 527.

[3] *Greig* v. *Edinburgh Merchant Coy.*, 1921 S.C. 76; *Secy. of State for Scotland, supra*; contrast *Sharp* v. *S.* (1898) 25 R. 1132.

[4] e.g. *Garland* v. *Stewart* (1841) 4 D. 1; *Fairholme* v. *F's Trs.* (1858) 20 D. 813; *Bruce, supra*; *Rhind's Trs., supra*; *Williamson* v. *W.* (1886) 14 R. 226; *Greig, supra*.

[5] *Tait's Factor* v. *Meikle* (1890) 17 R. 1182.

[6] *X.* c. *S.S.C. Socy.*, 1937 S.L.T. 87; *Tait* v. *Sleigh*, 1969 S.L.T. 227. If the absentee is later found to have been alive at a date after he had been presumed dead, a second petition is competent: *Andrews* (1901) 9 S.L.T. 117.

[7] cf. *Shepherd's Trs.* v. *Brown* (1902) 9 S.L.T. 487; *Barr* v. *Campbell*, 1925 S.C. 317; including the case where the heir to a Scottish heritage, who had disappeared, was a domiciled Englishman: *Jones*, 1923 S.L.T. 31.

[8] On the effect of certificates of presumed death of persons on war service, see *Robson Scott's Trs.* v. *R.S.*, 1945 S.C. 52; *Hannay*, 1949 S.C. 304.

[9] See e.g. *Coull's Tr.*, 1934 S.C. 415.   [10] S. 6.

that of the absentee or his representatives,[1] and does not apply to claims under policies of insurance.[2] This Act may not be invoked where there is no patrimonial object, but merely for an ulterior motive, such as to reacquire the status of being unmarried.[3] It is incompetent to accept the decree of a foreign court on the matter of presumption of death.[4]

Under the Divorce (Scotland) Act, 1938, S. 5, the Court may decree the dissolution of a marriage on the ground of the presumed death of the other spouse, if satisfied that reasonable grounds exist for supposing that the other spouse is dead. The continuous absence of the other spouse for seven years is evidence of his death, if the petitioner has no reason to believe that the absent spouse had been living within that period and unless the contrary is proved.[5] This provision has no application for purposes other than dissolution of marriage.[6]

It is frequently important to determine whether one person survived another. At common law there is no presumption that one person survived another in any particular circumstances,[7] and survival has to be proved, but the Succession (Scotland) Act, 1964, S. 31 makes provision for a presumption in certain cases.[8]

Termination of personality

Legal personality terminates with natural death, though it may be said to continue to the extent that a deceased person's wishes for the disposal of his estate, if expressed in a document held to evidence testamentary intention, will be legally enforceable, and rights and liabilities vested in his estate will be exigible by or against his executor, who is accounted as *eadem persona cum defuncto*.[9] But all purely personal rights and liabilities perish with

---

[1] S. 7.

[2] S. 11; *Murray* v. *Chalmers*, 1913, 1 S.L.T. 223.

[3] *Brady* v. *Murray*, 1933 S.L.T. 534; *Fraser*, 1950 S.L.T. (Sh. Ct.) 51.

[4] *Simpson's Trs.* v. *Fox*, 1951 S.L.T. 412.

[5] *Labacianskas* v. *L.*, 1949 S.C. 280; see also *Lench* v. *L.*, 1945 S.C. 295; and, on evidence, *Gilchrist*, 1950 S.L.T. (Notes) 6.

[6] *Secy. of State for Scotland* v. *Sutherland*, 1944 S.C. 79.

[7] *Drummond's J. F.* v. *H.M. Advocate*, 1944 S.C. 298; *Mitchell's Exrx.* v. *Gordon*, 1953 S.C. 176; *Ross's J.F.* v. *Martin*, 1955 S.C. (H.L.) 56; see also *Tawse* (1882) 19 S.L.R. 829; *Dear* v. *Lumgair* (1905) 12 S.L.T. 862; (1906) 13 S.L.T. 850.

[8] Ch. 118, *infra*.

[9] e.g. right of action for patrimonial loss: *Smith* v. *Stewart*, 1961 S.C. 91; right to exact payment of money due to deceased, or to recover damages for breach of contract: *Riley* v. *Ellis*, 1910 S.C. 934; liability to pay: *Gardiner* v. *Stewart's Trs.*, 1908 S.C. 985; or to perform contract not involving *delectus personae*.

the deceased.[1] Deaths must be registered under the Registration of Births, Deaths, and Marriages (Scotland) Act, 1965, Ss. 22–28. Between the moment of death and the confirmation by the court of an executor, the deceased's property is *haereditas jacens*, vested in nobody, though the executor's confirmation vests it in him, retrospectively to the time of death.

STATUS

Natural persons are grouped for legal purposes according to their status.[2] Status is the legal standing or position of a person and consists in belonging to a particular class of persons to all of whom the law assigns particular legal powers, capacities, liabilities or incapacities. Membership of a particular status-group is in many cases attributed to persons entirely by force of law and independently of their volition; in other cases, such as that of being married, the individual may elect or decline to assume the status, but if he does elect, he cannot voluntarily divest himself of it. In all cases prescribed rights and duties, capacities and incapacities, attach by force of law to all persons having the particular status, and can be modified, if at all, by the parties only in details. Status is more than, and different from, a mere voluntary relationship between one person and another; it involves a general condition or standing in legal matters, which regulates generally the individual's capacities and incapacities.

A person's status is determined by the totality of various factors each of which has two or more mutually exclusive possibilities, and every person must fall into one or other of the possible classes of each. Each person's total status is determined by the aggregate of the various factors of status which apply in his case, and this totality accordingly determines the aggregate of his legal powers, capacities, immunities, disabilities, and so on. In particular contexts, e.g. as regards capacity to marry, or to contract, one factor of status may be more relevant than others;[3] in many contexts many of the factors are irrelevant. The factors are:

---

[1] e.g. right of action for solatium: *Smith* v. *Stewart*, 1960 S.C. 329; liability to perform contract involving *delectus personae*: *Hoey* v. *McEwan & Auld* (1867) 5 M. 814; *Mitchell* v. *Mackersy* (1905) 8 F. 198; *Cole* v. *Handasyde*, 1910 S.C. 68; *Tait's Exrx.* v. *Arden Coal Co.*, 1947 S.C. 100.

[2] On status see Graveson, *Status in the Common Law*; Allen, 'Status and Capacity' in *Legal Duties*, 28; *Admin. of Austrian Property* v. *Von Lorang*, 1927 S.C. (H.L.) 80, 85, 92.

[3] Some of the factors are important primarily in public law, and not in private law.

(a) (i) British subjects; (ii) aliens;
(b) (i) patrials; (ii) non-patrials;[1]
(c) (i) unborn child; (ii) pupil; (iii) minor; (iv) adult;
(d) (i) male; (ii) female;[2]
(e) (i) legitimate; (ii) illegitimate; (iii) legitimated; (iv) adopted;
(f) (i) bodily and mentally sound; (ii) bodily or mentally *incapax*;
(g) (i) single;[3] (ii) married;[4]
(h) (i) noble; (ii) commoner;
(j) (i) free; (ii) prisoner;
(k) (i) solvent; (ii) bankrupt;
(l) (i) lay; (ii) cleric;
(m) (i) civilian; (ii) member of one of the armed forces.

For legal purposes the norm or standard natural person is the adult male commoner of British nationality, of sound mind and body, legitimate, unmarried, free and solvent, lay and civilian and persons of different status have their status described as in some respect variations from that standard. In many respects the variations are insignificant.

Various factors relevant to status at other times or in other legal systems, but irrelevant in modern Scots law, are civil death, heresy, prodigality, serfdom or slavery,[5] outlawry,[6] race,[7] colour,[7] caste, position in the family (whether *sui juris* or *in potestate*) and others. Certain other factors, such as being facile, or under the influence of drink or a drug, may in particular circumstances be relevant to a person's capacity, but do not amount to a distinct element of status. Domicile is the connection between a person and a legal system attributed by law for certain purposes, not a status, and residence is a matter of fact.

Decrees of court altering the status of parties are reported by

---

[1] As defined by Immigration Act, 1971, S. 2.

[2] The hermaphrodite has been said to belong to the sex which he resembles more closely and *in dubio* deemed male: Forbes, p. 18. The transsexual belongs to the sex to which he or she belongs by virtue of chromosomal, gonadal, genital and psychological factors: *Corbett* v. *C.* [1970] 2 All E.R. 33. If a child's sex is wrongly described when its birth is registered a correction may be made in the Register of Corrected Entries: Registration of Births, Deaths, and Marriages (Sc.) Act, 1965, S. 42. This seems to be the only case of change of sex.

[3] Including, for all practical purposes, widowed and divorced.

[4] *Admin. of Austrian Property, supra,* 92.

[5] *Knight* v. *Wedderburn* (1778) Mor. 14545.

[6] Criminal Justice (Sc.) Act, 1949, S. 15.

[7] See Race Relations Act, 1968.

the court to the Registrar-General and entered by him in the Register of Corrections.[1]

The holding of an official position, or the membership of a particular profession, is sometimes spoken of as a status.[2] This is inaccurate, because any special rights or privileges attach to the individual only so long as he holds the office or is a member of the profession, and only in relation thereto, and does not affect his legal rights, powers, and capacities generally.

Status in general extra-domestic and in domestic relations

The rights, duties, capacities and incapacities of status-groups must be considered both generally, in relations with everyone, and in respect of domestic relations, with one another within the home and family.[3] The capacities and incapacities or disabilities implied in private law by membership of particular status groups are stated as deviations from the standard of the adult male.

(a) BRITISH SUBJECTS: ALIENS

British subjects include citizens of the United Kingdom and colonies, citizens of various Commonwealth countries, British protected persons and certain citizens of Ireland. Aliens are persons not British subjects, British protected persons or citizens of Ireland.[4] In the sphere of private law the differences are insubstantial in peace time.[5] Only a British subject by birth or naturalization may own any share in a British ship[6] or aircraft.[7] In most other respects an alien in Britain in peace time has ordinary civil or private rights though he must declare his nationality in prescribed business documents.[8] He may sue and be sued,[9] hold property, act as trustee, bequeath by will and take as legatee.

---

[1] Registration of Births, Deaths, and Marriages (Sc.) Act, 1965, S. 48. This deals with Scottish decrees only: *Smart* v. *Registrar General*, 1954 S.C. 81.

[2] cf. *Forbes* v. *Eden* (1865) 4 M. 143, 'a particular status, meaning the capacity to perform certain functions or hold certain offices'.

[3] Chs. 16–18, *infra*.

[4] See generally Bell, *Prin.* §2131–60; Status of Aliens Act, 1914, S. 17; Aliens Restrictions Act, 1919; British Nationality Acts, 1948, 1958 and 1965; Naturalization Act, 1870.

[5] As defined by British Nationality Acts, 1948, 1958, and 1965.

[6] Merchant Shipping Act, 1894, S. 1. As to pilotage certificates and employment on British Ships, see Aliens Restrictions Act, 1919, Ss. 4, 5.

[7] Air Navigation Order, 1960, arts. 21, 22, and 23.

[8] Registration of Business Names Act, 1916, S. 18; Companies Act, 1948, S. 201.

[9] *Porter* v. *Freudenberg* [1915] 1 K.B. 857; see also *Goldston* v. *Young* (1868) 7 M. 188.

In wartime, however, aliens of enemy nationality in this country may be interned but may still act in a representative capacity[1] and, if domiciled here, bring actions relative to status,[2] sue and be sued and appeal,[3] and contract.[4] Alien enemies outside the realm, including British nationals resident in enemy territory, cannot sue[5] and pending actions must be sisted till peace returns.[6] Save by royal licence a contract with an alien enemy is illegal, but executory contracts become illegal only if performance would involve dealings with or potential benefit to enemies.[7] Property rights are not affected[8] but are suspended and restored when peace returns.[9]

(b) PATRIALS: NON-PATRIALS

Only patrials have the right of abode in the United Kingdom. These are citizens of the United Kingdom and Colonies by birth, adoption, naturalization or, with exceptions, registration in the U.K., or certain other categories of such citizens, or in certain circumstances Commonwealth citizens. Save as provided by statute a non-patrial may not enter the U.K. unless given leave to do so, which leave may be limited or subject to conditions. They may live, work, and settle in the U.K. by permission only and subject to statutory regulation and control.[10] There appear to be no differences in private law between patrials and non-patrials while in the U.K.

(c) UNBORN CHILD: PUPIL: MINOR: ADULT

(i) *Unborn child*

The unborn child has legal personality before birth only to the limited extent that, if subsequently born alive, a claim of damages

---

[1] *Schulze,* 1917 S.C. 400; *Rodriguez* v. *Speyer* [1919] A.C. 59; *Crolla,* 1942 S.C. 21.

[2] *Weiss* v. *W.,* 1940 S.L.T. 467.

[3] *Porter* v. *Freudenberg* [1915] 1 K.B. 857.

[4] *Schulze, Gow & Co.* v. *Bank of Scotland,* 1914, 2 S.L.T. 455.

[5] *Johnson & Wight* v. *Goldsmid,* 15 Feb. 1809, F.C.; *Sovfracht* v. *van Uden,* [1943] A.C. 203.

[6] *Craig Line* v. *N.B. Storage Co.,* 1915 S.C. 113; *Van Uden* v. *Burrell,* 1916 S.C. 391.

[7] *Stevenson* v. *Cartonnagen Industrie* [1918] A.C. 239; *Ertel Bieber* v. *Rio Tinto* [1918] A.C. 260; *Rodriguez, supra.*

[8] *Halsey* v. *Lowenfeld* [1916] 2 K.B. 707; *Ertel Bieber, supra.*

[9] *Penney* v. *Clyde Shipbuilding Co.,* 1920 S.C. (H.L.) 68.

[10] Immigration Act, 1971, ss. 1–3.

may be brought on his behalf for loss suffered,[1] or ante-natal injuries,[2] and that, for the purposes of inheritance, he will be accounted already born if that would be to his advantage, on the basis of the maxim *nasciturus pro iam nato habetur quando de ejus commodo queritur*.[3] Only to this limited extent has he any legal status. If never born alive he is deemed in law never to have existed.[4]

(ii) *Pupils*

Pupils, that is boys aged under fourteen and girls aged under twelve, the traditional ages of presumed puberty, have, for reasons of their natural incapacity, strictly limited legal personality; indeed they are said to have no person in the legal sense of the word,[5] and to be in a state of absolute incapacity.[6] A pupil must, therefore, have a parent or other person to act as his tutor and administrator-in-law. At common law a pupil cannot marry but if parties continued to cohabit after the age of puberty a marriage was held validly constituted or ratified.[7] A pupil has by himself no contractual capacity, and an attempt to contract is a nullity, and a purported contract is challengeable within the twenty years of the long negative prescription.[8] Any contract must be entered into by his tutor on his behalf, but any such contracts are open to challenge by the child until four years after he has attained majority, on proof of lesion.[9] He is said to be able to enforce a contract made on his behalf which is beneficial to himself though it cannot be enforced against him.[10] Money lent to a pupil may be recovered from him if used beneficially by him,[11] and if neces-

---

[1] *Connachan* v. *S.M.T. Co.*, 1946 S.C. 428; *Moorcraft* v. *Alexander*, 1946 S.C. 466; *Leadbetter* v. *N.C.B.*, 1952 S.L.T. 179.

[2] Walker, *Delict*, 96; *Montreal Tramways* v. *Leveille* [1933] 4 D.L.R. 337; *Pinchin* v. *Santam Ins. Co.*, 1963 (2) S.A. 254.

[3] Dig. I, 6, 7, and 26; Fraser, *P. & Ch.*, 220; *Hardman* v. *Guthrie* (1828) 6 S. 920; *Elliot* v. *Joicey*, 1935 S.C. (H.L.) 57; *Cox's Trs.* v. *C.*, 1950 S.C. 117.

[4] Bankt. I, 2, 7–8.

[5] Ersk. I, 7, 14; cf. *Sinclair* v. *Stark* (1828) 6 S. 336.

[6] Bell. *Pr.* §2067. cf. *McAulay* v. *Renny* (1803) Bell, *Comm.* II, 514; *Calder* v. *Downie*, 11 Dec. 1811, F.C., affd. (1815) 18 F.C. 508; *Hill* v. *City of Glasgow Bank* (1879) 7 R. 68, 74. But a pupil is not a non-entity: see *Whitehall* v. *W.*, 1958 S.C. 252, 259.

[7] Ersk. I, 6, 2; Bell, *Pr.* §1523; Fraser, *H. & W.*, I., 53; *Johnston* v. *Ferrier* (1770) Mor. 8931.

[8] Ersk., *supra*; *Bruce* (1577) Mor. 8979.

[9] Ersk. I, 7, 34; Bell, *Prin.* §2098; *Falconer* v. *Thomson* (1792) Mor. 16380; cf. *Patrick* v. *Baird*, 1927 S.N. 32.

[10] Bankt. IV, 45, 13; Ersk. I, 7, 33; Fraser, *P. & Ch.*, 206.

[11] *E. Morton* v. *Muirhead* (1749) Mor. 8931; *Scott's Trs.* v. *S.* (1887) 14 R. 1043.

saries have been sold and delivered to him, he must pay a reasonable price therefor;[1] but these obligations are not contractual but arise *ex lege*, by quasi-contract.

He has no title by himself to sue for wrong done him, nor liability to be sued; the tutor must sue[2] or be called. A pupil can however commit wrong imposing liability on his tutor in reparation,[3] and may be guilty of contributory negligence, if old enough to appreciate the danger.[4] A pupil cannot grant a discharge for damages awarded him and this must be done by his tutor, or a judicial factor be appointed.[5]

Property can be held by a pupil, but must be administered by his tutor for behoof of the pupil.[6] A pupil has no capacity to make a will,[7] nor may he act as a trustee.

An action in name of a pupil without his tutor is incompetent, and a decree against one without his tutor is reducible as a decree in absence, though not wholly null.[8] If a pupil has no legal guardian, or the guardian has an adverse interest, or is incapax, action may be brought in his name and a *curator ad litem* appointed, with whose concurrence the case may proceed.[9] Both the pupil and his tutor should be called as defenders; if the latter is not known the action should be directed against the pupil and his tutors generally.[10] If necessary a *curator ad litem* must be appointed.[11]

(iii) *Minors*

Minors are young persons who have attained 14 (boys) or 12 (girls) but not adulthood. They attain the new status at the time

---

[1] Common law and Sale of Goods Act, 1893, S.2.

[2] e.g. *Davis's Tutor* v. *Glasgow Victoria Hospitals*, 1950 S.C. 382.

[3] *Somerville* v. *Hamilton* (1541) Mor. 8905; *Kerr* v. *Bremner* (1839) 1 D. 618; *Davie* v. *Wilson* (1854) 16 D. 956.

[4] *Cass* v. *Edinburgh Tramways*, 1909 S.C. 1068; *Holland* v. *Lanark C.C.*, 1909 S.C. 1142; *Plantza* v. *Glasgow Corpn.*, 1910 S.C. 786; *Allison* v. *Langloan Iron & Chemical Co.*, 1917, 2 S.L.T. 162.

[5] *Collins* v. *Eglinton Iron Co.* (1882) 9 R. 500; *Connolly* v. *Bent Colliery Co.* (1897) 24 R. 1172; *Boylan* v. *Hunter*, 1922 S.C. 80; *Fairley* v. *Allan*, 1948 S.L.T. (Notes) 81; *Falconer* v. *Robertson*, 1949 S.L.T. (Notes) 57.

[6] Title to heritage is commonly taken in name of a pupil himself without objection; see Titles to Land Consolidation (Sc.) Act, 1868, S. 24, as amended; Bell, *Prin.* §2084; Bell, *Convg.* I, 117; Fraser, *P. & Ch.*, 205; *Linton* v. *I.R.*, 1928 S.C. 209, 213. The tutor has no power to alienate or dispose of the heritage without court authority.

[7] Stair III, 8, 37.

[8] Bell, *Prin.* §2067; *Craven* v. *Elibank's Trs.* (1854) 16 D. 811; *Dingwall* v. *Burns* (1871) 9 M. 582.

[9] *M'Conochie* v. *Binnie* (1847) 9 D. 791; *Ward* v. *Walker*, 1920 S.C. 80; *Kirk* v. *Scottish Gas Board*, 1968 S.C. 328. The guardian would be better entitled a *tutor ad litem*.

[10] Fraser, *P. & Ch.*, 211; *Thomson's Trs.* v. *Livingston* (1863) 2 M. 114.

[11] *Drummond's Trs.* v. *Peel's Trs.*, 1929 S.C. 484.

of their birth on the fourteenth or twelfth anniversary thereof.[1]

A minor has legal personality and considerable though limited legal powers and capacities. He cannot be a trustee in sequestration[2] or a tutor, curator or judicial factor.[3] He is capable of entering into legal transactions, though requiring the protection of the law by reason of his inferior judgment or discretion.[4] He may, but need not, have a parent or other person to act as his curator.

A promise to marry is binding on a minor though his curators do not consent.[5] At common law any minor might marry without consent[6] but since 1929 a marriage is void if either party were under the age of 16.[7] Continuing cohabitation after attaining 16 may however create a marriage by cohabitation with habit and repute.[8]

Contractual powers

A minor's contractual powers vary according as he contracts with or without a curator's consent. A minor without a curator, or forisfamiliated,[9] has the full contractual powers of an adult.[10] But a party paying a capital sum to a minor may demand security for the investment or profitable employment of the money,[11] though he may safely pay a sum of the nature of income or interest, and the minor can grant a valid discharge.[12] A minor who has a curator may, with the consent and concurrence of the curator, enter into any contract,[13] though a contract between the minor and the curator himself is not validated by the latter's consent, and is voidable within the period of the long negative prescription.[14] A minor who has a curator but contracts without

---

[1] Ersk. I, 7, 36; Bell, *Prin.* §2091; Fraser, *P. & Ch.*, 201.

[2] Bankruptcy (S.C.) Act, 1913, S. 64.   [3] Ersk. I, 7, 12.

[4] Bell, *Prin.* §2088; *Harvey* v. *H.* (1860) 22 D. 1198; *Hill* v. *City of Glasgow Bank* (1879) 7 R. 68, 74.

[5] *Whitehead* v. *Phillips*, 1902, 10 S.L.T. 577.

[6] Ersk. I, 7, 33; *Bruce* v. *Hamilton* (1854) 17 D. 265.

[7] Age of Marriage Act, 1929; Ch. 16, *infra.*

[8] *A.B.* v. *C.D.*, 1957 S.C. 415.

[9] On forisfamiliation see Ersk. I, 6, 53; *Anderson* v. *A.* (1832) 11 S. 10; *McFeetridge, infra.*

[10] Ersk. I, 7, 33; Fraser, *P. & Ch.*, 436; *Thomson* v. *Stevenson* (1666) Mor. 8991; *Hill* v. *City of Glasgow Bank* (1879) 7 R. 68; *Brown's Tr.* v. *B.* (1897) 24 R. 962; *McFeetridge* v. *Stewarts & Lloyds*, 1913 S.C. 773.

[11] *Kirkman* v. *Pym* (1782) Mor. 8977.

[12] *Jack* v. *N.B. Ry. Co.* (1886) 14 R. 263.

[13] Ersk. I, 7, 33; Bell, *Prin.* §2096; Fraser, *P. & Ch.* 483; *Alexander* v. *Thomson* (1813) Hume 411; *Hill, supra.*

[14] *Mackenzie* v. *Fairholm* (1666) Mor. 8959; *Thomson* v. *Pagan* (1781) Mor. 8985; *Manuel* v. *M.* (1853) 15 D. 284.

the latter's consent may bind himself to contracts for necessaries[1] or for, or in the ordinary course of, employment;[2] but apart from those cases a contract without consent is void, and challengeable at any time within the period of the long negative prescription without need for proof of lesion,[3] though it is said to be enforceable by the minor if beneficial to him.[4] A minor contracting without his curator's consent is liable in so far as money obtained by him under the contract has been beneficially employed.[5] The curator by himself has no contractual power at all on behalf of the minor, his function being only to advise and consent, and any contract by him alone is a nullity.[6] Subject to these qualifications, a minor may bind himself to any personal obligation, engage in trade, or become a partner or a shareholder in a company.[7]

Avoidance of contract for minority and lesion

In all cases,[8] following the Roman law,[9] the minor's contracts are voidable at his instance until four years, the *quadriennium utile*, after he has attained majority,[10] on proof of his minority at the time, and of enorm lesion. The plea may also be taken by the minor's heirs, creditors, or assignees.[11] Enorm lesion is consideration for the contract immoderately disproportionate to what might have been got.[12] It must be positive loss, not merely loss of possible gain,[13] and be enorm, or substantial,[14] judged as at the date of the

---

[1] Sale of Goods Act, 1893, S. 2, repeating common law e.g. *Fontaine* v. *Foster* (1808) Hume 409. 'Necessaries' doubtless include food, clothing, and lodging; beyond that it is a question of fact in each case; see *Johnston* v. *Maitland* (1782) Mor. 9036; *Scoffier* v. *Read* (1783) Mor. 8936; cf. *Nash* v. *Inman* [1908] 3 K.B. 1.

[2] Ersk. I, 7, 38; Bell, *Comm.* I, 131; *Stevenson* v. *Adair* (1872) 10 M. 919; *McFeetridge, supra*; *O'Donnell* v. *Brownieside Coal Co.*, 1934 S.C. 534.

[3] Stair I, 6, 33; Bankt. I, 7, 56; Ersk. I, 7, 33; Fraser, *P. & Ch.* 493; *Manuel* v. *M.* (1853) 15 D. 284; see also *Stevenson* v. *Adair* (1872) 10 M. 919; *McFeetridge* v. *Stewarts & Lloyds*, 1913 S.C. 773; *Boyle* v. *Woodypoint Caravans*, 1970 S.L.T. (Sh. Ct.) 34.

[4] Ersk. I, 7, 33.

[5] Stair, *supra*.

[6] Bell, *Prin.* §2096; Fraser, *P. & Ch.* 471; *E. Bute* v. *Campbell* (1725) Mor. 16338.

[7] *Hill* v. *City of Glasgow Bank* (1879) 7 R. 68, 75.

[8] Even if the curator consented, though a higher degree of lesion must be shown in such a case: Ersk. I, 7, 33; or if the court had authorized the transaction: *Gillam's Curator* (1908) 15 S.L.T. 1043.

[9] D. 4, 4, 1, and see 49 J.R. 50.

[10] Stair I, 6, 44; Ersk. I, 7, 35; Bell, *Prin.* §2098; Fraser, *P. & Ch.*, 533. Lapse of the time renders the contract unchallengeable, even if the minor were unaware of the privilege: *Hill* v. *City of Glasgow Bank* (1879) 7 R. 68.

[11] Stair I, 6, 44; Ersk. I, 7, 42; *Hamilton* v. *Sharp* (1630) Mor. 8981, 10419.

[12] *Robertson* v. *Henderson* (1905) 7 F. 776, 785; *McGuire* v. *Addie's Collieries*, 1950 S.C. 537.

[13] *Cooper* v. *C.'s Trs.* (1885) 12 R. 473; *Patrick* v. *Baird*, 1927 S.N. 32.

[14] Ersk. I, 7, 36; Bell, *Prin.* §2100; *Robertson* v. *Henderson* (1904) 6 F. 770; 7 F. 776.

transaction.[1] The transaction will not be reduced if in the whole circumstances, it was, in the view of the court, reasonable.[2] A higher degree of lesion must be shown where the minor contracted with his curator's consent,[3] and no proof of lesion is required where a minor, having a curator, contracts without his consent.[4]

Enorm lesion is presumed in the cases of donations,[5] surrenders of rights,[6] cautionary obligations,[7] loans of money made to the minor,[7] or even capital payments to the minor,[8] unless it be shown that the lesion resulted subsequently from mismanagement, or that he had ratified the transaction after attaining majority, in the knowledge of his right to challenge.[10] A person lending money to a minor, or buying property from him, is entitled to demand evidence that the money is profitably employed, for otherwise he cannot recover the money or keep the property unless he can prove that the money was expended *in rem versum* of the minor.[11]

If the minor was engaged in trade or business and contracts in relation thereto,[12] or falsely represented himself to be major and was believed to be such on reasonable grounds,[13] he is not entitled to restitution at all. Reduction may also be barred if the minor has, after attaining full age, in the knowledge of his right of reduction,[14] freely[15] ratified or approbated a transaction inferring liability,[16] but is not barred merely because the minor has ratified a writ by his oath.[17]

[1] *Cooper, supra,* 486.   [2] *Robertson, supra.*

[3] Ersk. I, 7, 33; *Cooper, supra.*

[4] Stair I, 6, 33; Bankt. I, 7, 56; Ersk. I, 7, 33; Fraser, *P. & Ch.,* 493.

[5] Bell, *Prin.* §2100; *Heriot* v. *Blyth* (1681) Mor. 8935.

[6] *Cooper* v. *C's Trs.* (1885) 12 R. 473; revd. on another point (1887) 15 R. (H.L.) 21.

[7] Stair I, 6, 44; Bell, *Comm.* I, 135; Bell, *Prin.* §2100; *Wall* v. *Brownlee* (1724) Mor. 9035; *Macmichael* v. *Barbour* (1840) 3 D. 279.

[8] *Harkness* v. *Graham* (1833) 11 S. 760; *Ferguson* v. *Yuill* (1835) 13 S. 886; cf. Consumer Credit Act, 1974, S.50.

[9] Bell, *Prin.* §2100; *Jack* v. *N.B. Ry. Co.* (1886) 14 R. 263.

[10] *Dennistoun* v. *Mudie* (1850) 12 D. 613; *Henry* v. *Scott* (1892) 19 R. 545.

[11] *Harkness, supra; Stark* v. *Tennant* (1843) 5 D. 542; *Macara* v. *Wilson* (1848) 10 D. 707; *Gifford* v. *Rennie* (1853) 15 D. 451; *Scott's Trs.* v. *S.* (1887) 14 R. 1043.

[12] Ersk. I, 7, 38; Bell, *Prin.* §2100; obligations in trade do not include gambling on the Stock Exchange: *Dennistoun, supra.*

[13] Stair I, 6, 44; Ersk. I, 7, 36; Fraser, *P. & Ch.,* 527; *Wemyss* v. *His Creditors* (1637) Mor. 9025; *Kennedy* v. *Weir* (1665) Mor. 11658; see also *Sutherland* v. *Morson* (1825) 3 S. 449; *Harvie* v. *McIntyre* (1829) 7 S. 561.

[14] *McGibbon* v. *McG.* (1852) 14 D. 605.

[15] *Melvil* v. *Arnot* (1782) Mor. 8998; *Leiper* v. *Cochran* (1822) 1 S. 552.

[16] Stair I, 6, 44; Fraser, *P. & Ch.* 531; *Forrest* v. *Campbell* (1853) 16 D. 16; *Adam* v. *A.* (1861) 23 D. 859; *Henry* v. *Scott* (1892) 19 R. 545; *L.A.* v. *Wemyss* (1899) 2 F. (H.L.) 1.

[17] Oaths of Minors Act, 1681.

A minor seeking reduction on this ground must not only repudiate but bring his action of reduction before expiry of the *quadriennium utile*,[1] or plead minority and lesion as a defence *ope exceptionis* within that period. Reduction for minority and lesion does not apply to marriage, though it may to conventional provisions made in a marriage settlement.[2] In no case is the minor entitled to any advantage from the reduction, but only to be restored to his former position.[3] If he reduces the transaction he must restore what he received thereunder,[4] The lapse of the *quadriennium utile* does not preclude a challenge of the contract as being, not voidable, but wholly void, e.g. if the minor contracted without his curator's consent.[5]

Delict

A minor has a title to sue, with the consent of his curator, for wrong done him, and while he may be sued and held liable for delict, his curator, if he any have, must be called as defender with him. By wrongdoing a minor does not automatically render a parent or curator liable. A minor awarded damages can himself grant a valid discharge,[6] but in many cases the court has appointed a factor *loco tutoris* or *curator bonis* to receive and invest the money, and to discharge the defender.[7] Such a discharge is reducible on the ground of minority and lesion within the *quadriennium utile*.[8]

Property

A minor may hold property, heritable and moveable, in his own name and can validly deal with ordinary matters of administration; thus he can receive interest or rent and grant discharges therefor.[9] He may sell land and dispose of the price.[10] But he may not effectually grant a deed whereby he *inter vivos*

---

[1] Bell, *Prin.* §2099; *Stewart* v. *Snodgrass* (1860) 23 D. 187; *Hill* v. *City of Glasgow Bank* (1879) 7 R. 68, 75; see also *Patrick* v. *Baird*, 1927 S.N. 32.

[2] Bell, *Prin.* §2100; *Taylor's Trs.* v. *Dick* (1854) 16 D. 529; *Bruce* v. *Hamilton* (1854) 17 D. 265; *Cooper* v. *C's Trs.* (1885) 12 R. 473.

[3] Bell, *Prin.* §2100; Fraser, *P. & Ch.* 540.

[4] Ersk. I, 7, 41; Fraser, *P. & Ch.* 540; *Rose* v. *R.* (1821) 1 S. 154.

[5] *Kincaid* (1561) Mor. 8979; *Bell* v. *Sutherland* (1728) Mor. 8985.

[6] *Jack* v. *N.B. Ry.* (1886) 14 R. 263.

[7] *McAvoy* v. *Young's Paraffin Oil Co.* (1882) 19 S.L.R. 441; *Anderson* v. *Muirhead* (1884) 11 R. 870; *Sharp* v. *Pathhead Spinning Co.* (1885) 12 R. 574; *Fairley* v. *Allan*, 1948 S.L.T. (Notes) 81. A curator *ad litem* cannot grant a discharge: *Pratt* v. *Knox* (1855) 17 D. 1006.

[8] *Robertson* v. *Henderson* (1905) 7 F. 776.

[9] *Jack* v. *N.B. Ry. Co.* (1886) 14 R. 263. cf. Building Societies Act, 1962, S. 47.

[10] *Brown's Tr.* v. *B.* (1897) 24 R. 962.

gratuitously alters the succession to his heritable property,[1] and is deemed incapable of assenting to an arrangement varying trust purposes.[2] He may be made bankrupt.[3] He cannot be called on to defend the right he has to an ancestor's heritage.[4]

Trust

A minor may act as a trustee.[5]

Succession

A minor may validly make a will of moveables,[6] and a testamentary disposition or settlement of heritage, though null at common law,[7] is now competent by statute.[8] A minor may challenge the action of the trustees of an estate in which he may be interested as beneficiary *intra quadriennium utile*.[9]

Actions

A minor may sue and be sued alone, but if he has a curator he should himself sue with the consent and concurrence of his curator, and be sued himself and the curator called for his interest. If he has no curator either party may apply for a curator *ad litem* to be appointed.[10] Decree against a minor alone might be set aside as a decree in absence,[11] and, whether he has a curator or not, it is reducible on the ground of minority and lesion within the *quadriennium utile*.[12] A curator cannot sue alone with or without the minor's consent, nor if he disclaims.[13] A minor may himself grant a valid discharge for damages recovered,[14] but where a capital sum is involved the court may direct payment to a trustee to hold and invest the capital until majority.[15] A minor may not grant an effective discharge on receiving a transfer of

[1] Fraser, *P. & Ch.* 442; *Hunter* (1728) Mor. 8964; *McCulloch* v. *M.* (1731) Mor. 8965.
[2] Trusts (Sc.) Act, 1961, S. 1(2).
[3] *Gray* v. *Purves* (1816) Hume 411; *Miller* v. *Aitken* (1840) 2 D. 1112.
[4] *Minor non tenetur placitare super haereditate*: Stair I, 6, 45; Ersk. I, 7, 43; Bell, *Prin.* §2101. It is questionable if this principle is still extant.
[5] *Hill* v. *City of Glasgow Bank* (1879) 7 R. 68.
[6] *Brown's Tr.* v. *B.* (1897) 24 R. 962.
[7] Ersk. I, 7, 33; Bell, *Prin.* §2089; *Brand's Trs.* v. *B's Trs.* (1874) 2 R. 258.
[8] Succession (Sc.) Act, 1964, S. 28.
[9] *McLauchlan* v. *McL.'s Trs.*, 1941 S.L.T. 43.
[10] *Cunningham* v. *Smith* (1880) 7 R. 424; see also *Saunders* (1821) 1 S. 115; *Rankine* (1821) 1 S. 118; *McConochie* v. *Binnie* (1847) 9 D. 791.
[11] Ersk. I, 7, 33.
[12] Ersk. I, 7, 35, and 38; *Cunningham, supra*.
[13] *Allan* v. *Walker* (1812) Hume 586; Bell, *Prin.* §2096.
[14] *Jack* v. *N.B. Ry. Co.* (1886) 14 R. 263.
[15] *Anderson* v. *Muirhead* (1884) 11 R. 870; *Sharp* v. *Pathhead Spinning Co.* (1885) 12 R. 574. See also *Boylan* v. *Hunter*, 1922 S.C. 80.

heritage with which he cannot himself deal.[1] Some of the short statutory prescriptions do not run against a defender so long as he is in minority.[2]

Minors aged 16 or over

While minority continues to the age of eighteen various statutes confer particular powers on persons who have attained sixteen.

(iv) Adulthood

Adulthood or majority is the status of a person who has attained eighteen,[3] formerly twenty-one, years of age.[4] He attains this age on the eighteenth, formerly twenty-first, anniversary of his birth, at the hour of his birth.[5] He is then *sui juris* and has full legal rights and is subject to all legal liabilities without qualification, and this status is taken as the norm from which all other status are regarded as deviations. It is impossible to enumerate the legal attributes, powers and capacities, duties and liabilities of the adult status because the whole of the private law, so far as applicable to natural persons, is stated primarily with reference to the adult or person of full age.

(d) MALE:FEMALE

To which sex a person belongs is a question of fact.[6] An error in stating the sex of a child when registering the birth may be rectified by the Registrar General causing an appropriate entry to be made in the Register of Corrections.[7] If he refuses, a person claiming that an error has been made may appeal to the Sheriff.[8] A hermaphrodite has been said to belong to the sex which he more closely resembles, and *in dubio* to be presumed male.[9] A transsexual belongs to the sex to which he or she belongs having

[1] *Ogilvy* v. *O's Trs.*, 1927 S.L.T. 83.

[2] Ch. 32, *infra.*

[3] Age of Majority (Sc.) Act, 1969, S. 1. The change does not affect the meaning of such words as 'majority' in deeds executed before 1 January 1970, or in statutory provisions incorporated in any such deed.

[4] Bankt. I, 2, 11; I, 7, 61; Ersk. I, 7, 1; *Adam* v. *A.* (1861) 23 D. 859.

[5] Stair I, 6, 33; Ersk. I, 7, 36; Fraser, *P. & Ch.*, 201; *Drummond* v. *Cunningham-Head* (1624) Mor. 3465.

[6] See Bankt. I, 2, 2.

[7] This is the only true case of 'change of sex'.

[8] Registration of Births, Deaths, and Marriages (Sc.) Act, 1965, S. 42 (5). The birth might then be re-registered: S. 20.

[9] Dig. I, 5, 9; Forbes, *Inst.* I, 1, 1, 18; Bankt. I, 2, 8.

regard to chromosomal, gonadal, genital, and psychological factors.[1] A person may belong to one sex biologically but be advised to belong socially to the other sex.[1] Where a person has elected for psychological reasons to pass as one of the other sex the only formal means of having the fact recognized would probably be a petition to the *nobile officium* of the Court of Session for declarator of change of apparent sex, and possibly of dissolution of marriage by reason thereof, the decree being notified by the court to the Registrar General.[2]

For the purposes of private law the distinction between the sexes is relevant as to the age at which a pupil child becomes minor,[3] to capacity to marry,[1] to certain regulations affecting employment, and to certain rules of national insurance legislation.

At common law no distinction existed between the rights and capacities of adult males and females so long as unmarried. But when a female married she passed into the curatory of her husband[4] so that she could not sue without his consent, even in actions relating to injuries to her, or to her own property or rights.[5] This now happens only if, and so long as, she is in minority.[6] She long had her domicile determined by her husband.[7] In modern law a woman, married or not, has full liberty of contract.[8]

A married woman may be liable for delict, independently of her husband; she does not make him liable unless they were acting jointly or she was acting as his agent or servant.[9] She may sue alone for delict done to her, or in the same action, if her husband had also been injured by the same wrong.[10] Husband and wife may sue each other.[11]

At common law by the *jus mariti* a woman's moveable property passed outright to her husband on marriage and by the *jus administrationis* he acquired the right to administer her heritable property. These rights have been abolished,[12] and a married

[1] *Corbett v. C.* [1970] 2 All E.R. 33.
[2] 1965 Act, S. 48; see also *X, Petr.*, 1957 S.L.T. (Sh. Ct.) 61.
[3] Ch. 18, *supra*.
[4] cf. Roman *perpetua tutela mulierum*: Gaius I, 190; Inst. I, 13.
[5] Stair I, 4, 22; Ersk. I, 6, 21; Bell, *Prin.* §1548.
[6] Married Women's Property (Sc.) Act, 1920, S. 20.   [7] Ch. 10, *supra*.
[8] Married Women's Property (Sc.) Act, 1920, S. 3; *Millar v. M.*, 1940 S.C. 56; *Horsburgh v. H.*, 1949 S.C. 227.
[9] *Barr v. Neilsons* (1868) 6 M. 651; *Milne v. Smith* (1892) 20 R. 95; *Hook v. McCallum* (1905) 7 F. 528.
[10] cf. *Finburgh v. Moss' Empires, Ltd.*, 1908 S.C. 928.
[11] Law Reform (Husband and Wife) Act, 1962, S. 2.
[12] Conjugal Rights (Sc.) Act, 1861; Married Women's Property (Sc.) Acts, 1877, 1881, and 1920.

woman has the same rights to own and dispose of property as if she were unmarried. A survival of the former rules is the rule that only a woman may, by ante-nuptial marriage contract, create an alimentary liferent in her own favour.[1]

A married woman has always had freedom to dispose of property by will,[2] as had an unmarried woman. If judicially separated, or divorced, or carrying on a separate business, a woman has always been entitled to sue and be sued as if unmarried.[3] Since 1920 all women can sue and be sued as if they were unmarried, unless still subject to curatory.[4]

Since the Sex Disqualification (Removal) Act, 1919, no person is disqualified by sex or marriage from holding any appointment or entering any profession, but women may still not be ordained priests or ministers in certain religious denominations.

(e) LEGITIMATE: ILLEGITIMATE: LEGITIMATED: ADOPTED

In relation to third parties no distinction exists in the capacities and incapacities of these categories of status.[5] A gift by will to the 'children' of a person formerly *prima facie* included his legitimate children only, but might in particular circumstances have to be construed more widely.[6] In deeds executed after 25 November 1968, words of relationship include illegitimate relations unless the contrary intention appears, and subject to certain exceptions.[6]

(f) BODILY AND MENTAL CAPACITY OR INCAPACITY

The whole private law is stated by reference to the individual who is bodily and mentally *capax*, and every person is presumed *capax*.[7] Bodily incapacity does not in general entail any legal incapacities, though a blind person cannot witness a deed[8] and may have a deed executed on his behalf by a notary public.[9] But serious bodily incapacity, such as paralysis, would justify the court, on petition supported by medical evidence, appointing a *curator bonis* to manage the affairs of the incapax and to supersede

[1] *Burn Murdoch's Trs. v. Tinney*, 1937 S.C. 743; *Pearson*, 1968 S.C. 8.

[2] Ersk. I, 6, 28.

[3] Conjugal Rights (Sc.) Amdt. Act, 1861, S. 6; *Cullen* v. *Ewing* (1833) 6 W. & S. 566; *Ritchie* v. *Barclay* (1845) 7 D. 819.

[4] Married Women's Property (Sc.) Act, 1920, S. 3.

[5] cf. *Clarke* v. *Carfin Coal Co.* [1891] 18 R. (H.L.) 63. As regards parents see Chap. 17.

[6] *Purdie's Trs.* v. *Doolan*, 1929 S.L.T. 273.

[6] Law Reform (Misc. Prov.) (Sc.) Act, 1968, S. 5, and see also S. 6.

[7] *Lindsay* v. *Watson* (1843) 5 D. 1194.

[8] Burn's *Conveyancing Practice*, 5.

[9] Conveyancing (Sc.) Act, 1924, S. 18.

him therein.[1] Mental incapacity[2] entails total legal incapacity when the court, acting on certificates by two independent medical men that the person is incapable of attending to his affairs or of giving instructions for their management, appoints a *curator bonis* to manage the affairs of the incapax.[3] In this event the capacity to transact legally and to sue is vested in the *curator bonis* alone.[4] Similarly the *curator bonis* alone should be sued.[5] If not under curatory an incapax may sue and be sued himself, his capacity and responsibility in relation to the matter in issue being a question of fact. It is always a question of fact whether the alleged incapax did or did not, at the material time, have the mental capacity to appreciate the legal force of the transaction he was entering into. Thus a will made during a lucid interval may be sustained.[6] Conversely deeds executed while subject to alienation of mind may be reduced on proof of derangement at the time.[7] A contract made by an insane person though not judicially found so, is void.[8] It is questionable whether an incapax, not under curatory, can be held liable for wrongdoing.[9]

Drunkenness may be so disabling as to render a person temporarily incapax,[10] and if a person was thereby rendered incapable at the time of transacting the kind of business which is in question the transaction is voidable.[11] The plea that a transaction was reducible because the granter was facile by reason of intoxication has been admitted.[12]

---

[1] *Duncan*, 1915, 2 S.L.T. 50.

[2] Ersk. I, 7, 48; Bell, *Prin.* §2103–22. In *Mears* v. *M.*, 1969 S.L.T. (Sh. Ct.) 21, it was held that a declarator that a person was of sound mind did not come within 'the personal status of individuals' under the Sheriff Courts (Sc.) Act, 1907, S. 5. *Sed quaere.*

[3] *Loudon* v. *Elder's C.B.*, 1923 S.L.T. 226.

[4] Bankt. I, 7, 10; Ersk. I, 7, 50; Fraser, *P. & Ch.*, 685; *Mitchell & Baxter* v. *Cheyne* (1891) 19 R. 324; cf. *Cole-Hamilton* v. *Boyd*, 1963 S.C. (H.L.) 1.

[5] *Anderson's Trs.* v. *Skinner* (1871) 8 S.L.R. 325.

[6] *Nisbet's Trs.* v. *N.* (1871) 9 M. 937; *Ballantyne* v. *Evans* (1886) 13 R. 652; *Hope* v. *H's Trs.* (1898) 1 F. (H.L.) 1; *Sivewright* v. *S's Trs.*, 1920 S.C. (H.L.) 63; see also *Maitland's Trs.* v. *M.* (1871) 10 M. 79.

[7] Bankt. I, 7, 10; Ersk. I, 7, 51; Bell, *Comm.* I, 133; *Lindsay* v. *Trent* (1683) Mor. 6280; *Currie* v. *Jardine* (1827) 5 S. 838.

[8] Stair I, 10, 13; Ersk. III, 1, 16; *Moncrieff* v. *Maxwell* (1710) Mor. 6286; cf. *Gall* v. *Bird* (1855) 17 D. 1027; *Loudon, supra.* But if necessaries are sold to a person, unable to contract by mental incapacity, he must pay a reasonable price therefor: *Ballantyne* v. *Evans* (1886) 13 R. 652; Sale of Goods Act, 1893, S. 2. If money is lent to a lunatic it may be recovered if profitably expended by him.

[9] cf. Divorce (Sc.) Act, 1964, S. 5(2).

[10] Stair I, 10, 13; Ersk. III, 1, 18.

[11] *Johnston* v. *Clark* (1854) 17 D. 228; *Taylor* v. *Provan* (1864) 2 M. 1226; *Pollok* v. *Burns* (1875) 2 R. 497; see also *Harvey* v. *Smith* (1904) 6 F. 511; *sed quaere.*

[12] *Jardine* v. *Elliot* (1803) Hume 684; *Hunter* v. *Stevenson* (1804) Hume 686; *Jackson* v. *Pollok* (1900) 8 S.L.T. 267; cf. *Taylor, supra.*

(g) SINGLE AND MARRIED

A single person is one who has not been married, or whose marriage has been annulled, or dissolved by death or divorce, whereas a married person is a party to a subsisting valid marriage, even though voidable. A party to a null marriage is single even before the nullity has been declared judicially. As regards third parties a married person cannot validly promise marriage,[1] or enter into a valid marriage,[2] sexual relations constitute adultery,[3] and a child born of such relations is normally illegitimate and until 1968 could not be legitimated.[4] His freedom of testation is limited by the doctrine of the legal rights of his spouse and children,[5] and the division of his estate on intestacy is different.[6] But in other respects this aspect of status makes no difference.

(h) NOBLE AND COMMONER

In private law the only differences of status are that a peer of the realm is exempt from arrest and imprisonment for a civil cause, even though Parliament is not sitting.[7]

(j) FREE AND PRISONER

As regards private law the person lawfully imprisoned now suffers no legal disabilities or incapacities, save the loss of liberty and liability to discipline and training, but may otherwise exercise his civil rights in the same way as a free man. His domestic relations are unaffected, though if in desertion when imprisoned he is presumed to continue to have *animus deserendi*.[8] His property rights are unaffected. He may sue[9] and be sued.[10]

---

[1] *Spiers v. Hunt* [1908] 1 K.B. 720; *Wilson v. Carnley* [1908] 1 K.B. 729.

[2] *Ballantyne v. B.* (1866) 4 M. 494; *Petrie v. Ross* (1894) 4 S.L.T. 63; *Bairner v. Fels*, 1931 S.C. 674.

[3] Ch. 16, *infra*.

[4] Ch. 17, *infra*.

[5] Ch. 119, *infra*.

[6] Ch. 120, *infra*.

[7] Bell, *Prin.* §2138–48; *Digby v. Lord Stirling* (1831) 8 Bing. 55; *D. Newcastle v. Morris* (1870) L.R. 4 H.L. 661.

[8] *Parker v. P.*, 1926 S.C. 574; *Anderson v. A.*, 1955 S.C. 428.

[9] Including suing the prison authorities for injuries while in prison: *Keatings v. Secy. of State for Scotland*, 1961 S.L.T. (Sh. Ct.) 63; cf. *Ellis v. Home Office* [1953] 2 All E.R. 149; *Pullen v. Prison Commrs.* [1957] 3 All E.R. 470.

[10] *Young v. Y.* (1882) 10 R. 184.

(k) SOLVENT AND BANKRUPT

The insolvent suffers no legal disabilities or incapacities until adjudicated bankrupt. Even then his domestic relations are not affected, nor his capacity to hold private offices such as tutor or factor, though he may be superseded in such offices if their interests conflict with those of the creditors in the sequestration.[1] His holding of public offices is restricted.[2] He may carry on his business or commence a new business but may not obtain credit beyond £10 without disclosing that he is an undischarged bankrupt.[3] A mandate to an agent falls, however.[4] No act or deed is effectual without the consent of his trustee, save in certain cases as regards bona fide third parties.[5] Though divested of all his property by the award of sequestration, the radical right remains in him,[6] and he can demand an accounting for the trustee's intromissions with the estate.[7]

He may sue alone for personal injuries but may be required to find caution for expenses,[8] and any damages fall to the trustee for behoof of the creditors;[9] he may be sued, and may, exceptionally, be required to find caution as a condition of defending.[10] The trustee may sue for patrimonial loss to the estate[11] but not for solatium to the bankrupt.[12] Once discharged, whether on composition or on payment of dividend, a bankrupt is restored to the position of a solvent person.

(l) LAY AND CLERIC

Persons ordained to the ministry of a branch of the Christian church or the Jewish faith[13] are subject to the jurisdiction of their

---

[1] Bell, *Comm.* I, 121; *Horn* v. *Sanderson* (1872) 10 M. 295; *Sawers* v. *Penney* (1881) 19 S.L.R. 258; *Whittle* v. *Carruthers* (1896) 23 R. 775.

[2] Bankruptcy (Sc.) Act, 1913, Ss. 183–4; Local Govt. (Sc.) Act, 1947, S. 52(1)(b).

[3] 1913 Act, S. 182; *Maclean* v. *McCord*, 1965 S.L.T. (Sh. Ct.) 69, *sed quaere*.

[4] *McKenzie* v. *Campbell* (1894) 21 R. 904.

[5] 1913 Act, S. 107.

[6] *Air* v. *Royal Bank of Scotland* (1886) 13 R. 734; *Whyte* v. *Northern, etc. Investment Co.* (1891) 18 R. (H.L.) 37; *Cooper* v. *Frame* (1893) 20 R. 920.

[7] 1913 Act, Ss. 82, 139; *Burt* v. *Bell* (1863) 1 M. 382.

[8] Bell, *Comm.* II, 324; *Clarke* v. *Muller* (1884) 11 R. 418; *Scott* v. *Roy* (1886) 13 R. 1173.

[9] *Thom* v. *Bridges* (1857) 19 D. 721; *Jackson* v. *McKechnie* (1875) 3 R. 130.

[10] *Taylor* v. *Fairlie* (1833) 6 W. & Sh. 301; *Buchanan* v. *Stevenson* (1880) 8 R. 220; *Lawrie* v. *Pearson* (1888) 16 R. 62.

[11] *Thom, supra*; *Howden* v. *Rocheid* (1868) 6 M. 300; Bankruptcy (Sc.) Act, 1913, S. 70.

[12] *Muir's Tr.* v. *Braidwood*, 1958 S.C. 169.

[13] It is questionable whether, e.g. a Mohammedan imam, is entitled to be treated as a cleric in Scots law. See also *Walsh* v. *Lord Advocate*, 1956 S.C. (H.L.) 126.

respective church courts and codes of discipline as well as to the ordinary law, and, as well as superior status in religious matters, have certain legal privileges, such as to perform marriages and, in certain cases, to act in notarial execution of a will.[1]

(m) CITIZEN AND MEMBER OF THE ARMED FORCES

Persons who join one or other of the armed forces of the Crown become subject to the code of discipline of that service and to courts-martial as well as to the ordinary law,[2] but have some legal privileges, in relation to death duties.[3]

Other status-distinctions

Older authorities refer to other status-distinctions not now of relevance for private law, such as prodigals.[4] Interdiction of lavish and prodigal persons is now abolished.[5]

Representative capacity

Apart from the capacities and powers which a person enjoys by virtue of his status, he may enjoy further powers by virtue of being appointed to act in a representative capacity, such as agent or trustee for another, or executor of or judicial factor on the estates of another. Such powers and duties are temporary only and affect the person only in so far as he represents the other person. They do not amount to a distinct status.

NAMES[6]

By custom a child when born, if legitimate, is normally given the surname of its father, or, if illegitimate, of its mother, but any name can be given. The surname is that by which the person is designated and identified,[7] and registration of birth by that name initiates a repute normally lifelong. But if the Crown has conferred a name of dignity, descending to heirs, this name is necessarily attached to all within the destination. The designation of a landowner as 'of' his lands was recognized by statute in 1672[8] as

---

[1] Ersk. I, 5, 1–31; Bell, *Prin.* §2160; Conveyancing (Sc.) Act, 1924, S. 18.

[2] cf. *O'Brien* v. *Strathern*, 1922 J.C. 55.

[3] cf. *Lord Advocate* v. *Mirrielees' Trs.*, 1945 S.C. (H.L.) 1.

[4] Bankt. I, 2; Ersk. I, 7, 54; II, 11, 45; Bell, *Prin.* §2123–8.

[5] Conveyancing (Sc.) Act, 1924, S. 44 (3)(6).

[6] See generally Seton, *Law and Practice of Heraldry*; Stevenson, *Heraldry in Scotland*.

[7] Bell, *Convg.*, I, 213.

[8] Lyon King of Arms Act, 1672, c. 47.

part of his name,[1] and a title of dignity is also part of a person's name. Children are also given at baptism one or more Christian names or forenames. Peers subscribe by their titles alone and bishops by their Christian name followed by the name of the see. Scottish judges subscribe their personal names, their titles being honorary only. The officers of arms subscribe by their titles only.[2] Commoners subscribe by their forenames, in full or abbreviated, and surname, adding any property or title, or profession. By custom a married woman normally takes her husband's surname, but she is designated for formal legal purposes by her Christian name, maiden surname or married surname or successive married surnames.[3] A husband may adopt, or be required to adopt, his wife's surname.[4] The misnaming of a party to an action or petition may invalidate the proceedings.[5]

Change of name

A person may assume a new forename or Christian name or a new surname,[6] or add to or alter it, without the authority of the court.[7] But it is necessary in the case of persons holding public offices or enrolled members or professions to mark the change and establish the identity of the bearer of the former and of the new names by obtaining a private Act of Parliament, or obtaining the authority of the Court of Session on petition to the *nobile officium*,[8] or obtaining a decree or certificate of change of name from the Lord Lyon King of Arms,[9] or by executing and recording in the Books of Council and Session or Lyon Court or Sheriff Books a deed stating the change, and by making advertisement in the press. Where a person is required, as a condition of succeeding to particular lands, to assume a stated surname, it must be assumed exactly as prescribed.[10]

[1] cf. *Moir of Leckie* (1794) Mor. 15537; *Eliot of Stobs* (1803) Mor. 15542.

[2] Lyon King of Arms Act, 1672, c.47.

[3] e.g. Mrs. Mary McAlister or Donoghue; see (1933) 49 L.Q.R. 1; (1965) 61 L.Q.R. 109.

[4] *Eliot of Stobs* (1803) Mor. 15542.

[5] *Brown* v. *Rodger* (1884) 12 R. 340; *Overseas League* v. *Taylor*, 1951 S.C. 105. Contrast *Spalding* v. *Valentine* (1883) 10 R. 1092; *Cruickshank* v. *Gow* (1888) 15 R. 326; *Anderson* v. *Stoddart*, 1923 S.C. 755.

[6] *Kinloch* v. *Lourie* (1853) 16 D. 197.

[7] *Young* (1835) 13 S. 262; *Finlayson* (1844) 2 Broun 17; *Kinloch, supra*; *Johnston* (1899) 2 F. 75; *Robertson* (1899) 2 F. 127; *Clark* v. *Chalmers*, 1961 J.C. 60.

[8] *Forlong* (1880) 7 R. 910; *Robertson, supra*; *Silverstone*, 1935 S.C. 223.

[9] *M'Donell* v. *M'Donald* (1826) 4 S. 371.

[10] *Sir Hugh Munro-Lucas-Tooth*, 1965 S.L.T. (Lyon Ct.) 2; see also *Munro's Trs.* v. *Monson*, 1965 S.C. 84.

To give as one's name an untrue name or the name of another determinate person and thereby seek to pass oneself off as that other person is personation and may involve criminal sanctions if done fraudulently, and have civil consequences also.[1] To give a false name may also infer criminal penalties.[2] But a person may legitimately practise a profession or business under a name different from his usual name.[3]

Registration of change of name

The Registrar-General records in the Register of Corrections a change in a child's registered name made within 12 months of the birth, or a name given to it after registration, if a certificate is given him within two years of the birth.[4] Provision is also made for the recording of changes of name or surname of a child under 16,[5] a person between 16 and 21 or over 21,[6] or of an alternative name, being the English equivalent of a non-English name.[7] Registration in the Register of Corrections may also be made of a decree or certificate of change of name or surname granted by the Lord Lyon, or a copy of a deed containing a condition that a person shall adopt another name with evidence that it has been so changed, or a decree or certificate of the change of name or surname of a male person following his marriage.[8]

Registration of Business Names

By the Registration of Business Names Act, 1916, a person or persons who carry on a business or profession must, unless the business name consists of the name of the individual or corporation which is solely concerned, or of all the partners, individual or corporate, or with an addition indicating merely that the business is carried on in succession to a former owner, register specified particulars, and any alterations therein, with the Registrar of Companies. The Registrar may refuse to register any name which in his opinion is undesirable.[9] Failure to register imports liability to penalties and a disability to enforce any contract whether in the business name or otherwise,[10] unless the

---

[1] *Wilson* v. *Horn* (1904) 11 S.L.T. 702 (nullity of marriage); *Morrisson* v. *Robertson*, 1908 S.C. 332; *MacLeod* v. *Kerr*, 1965 S.C. 253; *Clark* v. *Chalmers*, 1961 J.C. 60.

[2] *Clark, supra.*

[3] e.g. authors, actors, bookmakers. cf. *Galbraith* v. *Provident Bank, Ltd.* (1900) 2 F. 1148.

[4] Registration of Births, Deaths, and Marriages (Sc.) Act, 1965, S. 43(3).

[5] 1965 Act, S. 43(4).   [6] 1965 Act, S. 43(5).

[7] 1965 Act, S. 43(7).   [8] 1965 Act, S. 43(6).

[9] S. 14, amd. Companies Act, 1947, S. 116.

[10] cf. *Kinnear* v. *Paper Shavings Co.*, 1967 S.L.T. (Sh. Ct.) 75.

Court on application by the defaulting persons, grants relief on the ground that the failure was accidental or inadvertent, or that, on other grounds,[1] it is just and equitable to grant relief.[2] The fact that a person's name is or is not registered as a partner of a firm is not, unless the registration was effected by himself, evidence in any question of his liability for the firm debts. The register may be amended on application to the Court of Session by any person who conceives that his name should or should not be registered. The Act also requires publication of the name or names of the person carrying on the business or the partners, and stated particulars relative thereto, in all trade catalogues, circulars, show cards and business letters sent to any person within the British Empire, subject to penalties. Failure probably, however, does not invalidate any contract entered into.

KINSHIP

Kinsmen are persons related to each other by having a common ancestor. Their relationship is measured in degrees, each representing the step between a parent and his child. Two methods of reckoning degrees of kinship have been recognized. In the Roman law method the degree between one kinsman and another is reckoned by counting the steps from one up to the common ancestor and then the steps down to the other; thus cousins are related in the fourth degree and uncle and niece in the third degree.[3] In the canon law method the degree is ascertained by counting up each line to the common ancestor and taking the longer line. Thus cousins are related in the second degree and uncle and niece in the second degree.[4] The canon law computation was followed in Scotland prior to the Reformation and sometimes thereafter[5] but subsequently the Roman law method has been generally followed.

Agnates and cognates

Agnates are those of a person's kindred who are related to

---

[1] Including ignorance of the Act; *Clydesdale Motor Transport Co.*, 1922 S.C. 18; *McLachlan, Petr.*, 1929 S.C. 357.

[2] This may be by allowing amendment of the instance of a summons: *J. and F. Anderson* v. *Balnagown Estates Co.*, 1939 S.N. 1.

[3] Inst. III, 6; Dig. 38, 1; Bankt. I, 5, 37–8; Ersk. I, 6, 9; Fraser, *H. & W.* I, 105.

[4] Decretals, IV, 4; Fraser, *H. & W.* I, 107.

[5] e.g. Marriage Act, 1567.

him through his father;[1] cognates are those who are related to him through his mother.[2]

Full and half blood

Persons are german or related by full blood who are descended, however remotely, from the same father and mother,[3] whereas half-blood relatives share the same father or mother but not both. Kinsmen of the half blood consanguinean share the same father, of the half blood uterine the same mother.[4]

Consanguinity and affinity

Persons are related by consanguinity if related by blood, by affinity if related through marriage only.

[1] Stair, III, 4, 8; Bell, *Prin.* §2078, 2111. In Roman law agnates were persons related to him through males only.

[2] Ersk. I, 7, 4. In Roman law cognates were persons related to him through one or more females.

[3] Craig II, 17, 11; Stair, III, 3, 47; Ersk. III, 10, 2; Bell, *Prin.* §1651-2.

[4] Bell, *Prin.* §1653-4.

CHAPTER 16

THE DOMESTIC RELATIONS
(1) HUSBAND AND WIFE

THE relationship of husband and wife[1] and the status of married persons is constituted by marriage, which is the voluntary union of one man and one woman for the duration of their joint lives, unless judicially terminated earlier.[2] Marriage[3] is based upon a contract by the parties, but is productive of a new status for each, and the contract differs from commercial contracts in respect of personal capacity, formalities, grounds for avoidance or dissolution, and the legal consequences of the contract are fixed by law and unalterable, save in detail, by the will of the parties. Unlike a commercial contract, marriage cannot be discharged by agreement, breach, or frustration. Furthermore the rights and duties of each of the spouses vis-à-vis third parties are modified by their marriage.[4]

While Scots law is concerned for the most part with monogamous unions, and provides for the creation of monogamous unions only, a polygamous or potentially polygamous union contracted elsewhere, in a country where such unions are recognized,[5] if deemed valid by the law of the husband's domicile, will be recognized for some purposes,[6] including the grant of divorce, nullity, dissolution on the ground of presumed death, judicial separation, separation and aliment, adherence and aliment and

---

[1] The Scots law of marriage is based on the canon law as administered in ecclesiastical courts prior to the Reformation. At the Reformation jurisdiction was transferred to the Commissary Court of Edinburgh with appeal to the Court of Session, and in 1830 to the Court of Session. The canon law principles have in certain respects been altered by statutes and decisions. See generally Stair I, 4, 1; Mack. I, 6, 1; Bankt. I, 5, 1; Ersk. I, 6, 1; Hume, *Lect.* I, 19; Bell, *Prin.* §1506–1623; More, *Lect.* I, 17; Fraser, *H. & W., passim.*

[2] *Hyde* v. *H.* (1866) 1 P. & D. 130; *Lang* v. *L.*, 1921 S.C. 44; *Nachimson* v. *N.* [1930] P. 217.

[3] The word 'marriage' is used both for the ceremony and for the relationship, or state of being married, to which it gives rise.

[4] Fraser, *H. & W.*, I, 155.

[5] Whether a marriage is polygamous or not depends on the *lex loci celebrationis*, whether it recognizes such unions or not; *R.* v. *Hammersmith Registrar, ex p. Mir-Anwaruddin* [1917] 1 K.B. 634. It is questionably open to parties to give evidence that their intention was to contract a monogamous union: *Warrender* v. *W.* (1835) 2 Sh. & Macl. 154. See also *Mehta* v. *M.* [1945] 2 All E.R. 690.

[6] cf. *Srini Vasan* v. *S.V.* [1946] P. 67; *Baindail* v. *B.* [1946] P. 122. (legitimacy of children—social welfare legislation).

aliment and decrees involving determination of the validity of the marriage.[1] It is not essential that either or both parties to a marriage by Scots law should profess Christianity.[2]

ENGAGEMENT

Engagement

Parties contemplating marriage customarily enter first into an engagement or betrothal, *sponsalia per verba de futuro*, an exchange of mutual promises subsequently to contract marriage.[3] This is a bare contract similar to a commercial contract and by itself does not effect change of status. Capacity to promise is regulated by principles of capacity to contract, not capacity to marry. No particular formalities are required. It may be proved by parole evidence[4] and the parties are competent witnesses. An inference of engagement to marry may be drawn from the conduct of parties though no express promise be proved.[5]

Either or both parties to the engagement may be too young to marry, but this will not invalidate their engagement. The contract may be avoided if induced by misrepresentation[6] or undue influence, or, probably, essential error.

The contract may be to marry at a certain time, or on the occurrence of a certain event,[7] or be conditional on some uncertain event. If no time or certain event be stated, the contract will be construed as a promise to marry within a reasonable time of the engagement.[8]

The contract may be conditional, but if the condition is contrary to public policy[9] or conducive to immorality[10] the whole contract is probably null. If the condition is illegal but can be severed from the rest of the contract, it may be enforced except for the objectionable condition. The contract is not always null

---

[1] Matrimonial Proceedings (Polygamous Marriages) Act, 1972, S. 2, overruling *Muhammad* v. *Suna*, 1956 S.C. 366.

[2] cf. *MacDougall* v. *Chitnavis*, 1937 S.C. 390.

[3] Ersk. I, 6, 3.

[4] *Murray* v. *Napier* (1861) 23 D. 1243; *Sinclair* v. *Rowan* (1861) 23 D. 1365.

[5] *Hogg* v. *Gow*, 27 May 1812, F.C.; *Scott* v. *Stewart* (1870) 8 S.L.R. 44. Contrast *Morrison* v. *Dobson* (1869) 8 M. 347.

[6] *Wharton* v. *Lewis* (1824) 1 C. & P. 529.

[7] *Frost* v. *Knight* (1872) L.R. 7 Ex. 111.

[8] *Potter* v. *Deboos* (1815) 1 Stark. 82.

[9] e.g. promise to marry if man can get rid of present wife: cf. *Spiers* v. *Hunt* [1908] 1 K.B. 720; *Wilson* v. *Carnley* [1908] 1 K.B. 729.

[10] e.g. promise to marry if the girl will allow intercourse and should become pregnant.

merely because one party is already married; if the other party is ignorant of this the married party cannot rely on his own fraud in defence to an action for breach of promise;[1] and a person a party to an English divorce may, after decree nisi but before decree absolute of divorce, validly promise to marry.[2]

Cancellation of engagement

The parties may by agreement rescind their engagement,[3] or be held to have let it lapse.[4] In such a case gifts made to each other in contemplation of marriage should be returned, though gifts made outright may be retained. An engagement will also be held cancelled by the death or supervening incapacity of either party.

Inducing breach of engagement

It is an actionable wrong for any person to persuade or induce a party to break off an engagement, but, at least in the case of a parent and a child under age, the parent may advise the child and will not be liable if he induces the child to break off an unsuitable engagement, unless he can be shown to have acted maliciously.[5]

Breach of promise

Either party may be in breach of the contract of engagement, by expressly refusing beforehand to have the marriage solemnized,[6] by delaying unjustifiably for longer than a reasonable time to implement the contract,[7] by failing to appear at the wedding, by conduct which justifies the pursuer in refusing to proceed with the marriage,[8] or by conduct inconsistent with the contract, such as by marrying another.[9] In case of delay a request to the defender to fix a date for the wedding and refusal or prevarication may be necessary to evidence the unwillingness to perform.[10]

---

[1] *Millward* v. *Littlewood* (1850) 5 Ex. 775; *Shaw* v. *S.* [1954] 2 Q.B. 429.
[2] *Fender* v. *Mildmay* [1938] A.C. 1.
[3] *Davis* v. *Bomford* (1860) 6 H. & N. 245.
[4] *Macgillivray* v. *Mackintosh* (1891) 28 S.L.R. 488; cf. *Colvin* v. *Johnstone* (1890) 18 R. 115.
[5] *Findlay* v. *Blaylock*, 1937 S.C. 21.
[6] *Frost* v. *Knight* (1872) L.R. 7 Exch. 111.
[7] *Cattanach* v. *Robertson* (1864) 2 M. 839; *Currie* v. *Guthrie* (1874) 12 S.L.R. 75.
[8] *Turnbull* v. *Dodds* (1869) 6 S.L.R. 353; contrast *Stoole* v. *McLeish* (1870) 8 M. 613.
[9] *Short* v. *Stone* (1846) 8 Q.B. 358; *Colvin* v. *Johnstone* (1890) 18 R. 115; cf. *Cattanach* v. *Robertson* (1864) 2 M. 839.
[10] cf. *Gough* v. *Farr* (1827) 2 C. & P. 631; *Colvin, supra*.

Such breach of promise, if without legal justification, gives the other party an action for damages for solatium for hurt to feelings and for patrimonial loss sustained in consequence of the breach.[1] A disappointed party of either sex may bring the action.[2] The claim must be insisted on within a reasonable time, and will not be kept alive indefinitely even by intimation that it is not departed from.[3] It probably cannot be pursued after the pursuer's death by his executor,[4] but may be insisted on against the defender's executor.[5] An action for breach of promise may in appropriate cases be combined with a claim for seduction,[6] and, if necessary, also with claims for inlying expenses and aliment for an illegitimate child.[7]

There is said[3] to be no prescription of marriage promises, so that lapse of time does not preclude a claim, but lapse of time without pressing a claim may imply acquiescence in the cancellation of the engagement or abandonment of the claim for breach.

Justifications for breach

A party has legal justification for non-implement if the promise was procured by fraud, or misrepresentation or concealment of material facts,[8] or if the man has proceeded under a mistaken belief in the woman's chastity, whether before[9] or after[10] the engagement, or if either party were mistaken about the other's moral character in any material respect,[11] or if a legal impediment

---

[1] *Hogg* v. *Gow*, 27 May 1812, F.C.; *Rose* v. *Golkan* (1816) 1 Mur. 82; *Tucker* v. *Aitchison* (1846) 9 D. 21; *Scott* v. *Stewart* (1870) 8 S:L.R. 44; *Colvin, supra.*

[2] cf. *Thomson* v. *Wright* (1767) Mor. 13915; *Longmore* v. *Massie* (1883) 2 Guthrie 450; *MacGillivray* v. *Mackintosh* (1891) 28 S.L.R. 488.

[3] *Colvin* v. *Johnstone* (1890) 18 R. 115. *Quaere*, does the long negative prescription not apply?

[4] cf. *Smith* v. *Stewart*, 1960 S.C. 329.

[5] *Liddell* v. *Easton's Trs.*, 1907 S.C. 154.

[6] *McCandy* v. *Turpy* (1826) 4 S. 520; *Walker* v. *McIsaac* (1857) 19 D. 340; *Paton* v. *Brodie* (1858) 20 D. 258; *Forbes* v. *Wilson* (1868) 6 M. 770; *Cathcart* v. *Brown* (1905) 7 F. 951; *Murray* v. *Fraser*, 1916 S.C. 623, 625. See also *Linning* v. *Hamilton* (1748) Mor. 13909; *Kay* v. *Wilson's Trs.* (1850) 12 D. 845; *Gray* v. *Brown* (1878) 5 R. 971; *Borthwick* v. *B.* (1896) 24 R. 211 (breach of promise and seduction, failing declarator of marriage).

[7] *Trotter* v. *Happer* (1888) 16 R. 141.

[8] *Wharton* v. *Lewis* (1824) 1 C. & P. 529; *Foote* v. *Hayne* (1824) 1 C. & P. 545; cf. *Lang* v. *L.*, 1921 S.C. 44.

[9] *Bench* v. *Merrick* (1844) 1 C. & K. 463; *Fletcher* v. *Grant* (1878) 6 R. 59.

[10] *Irving* v. *Greenwood* (1824) 1 C. & P. 350; *Hall* v. *Wright* (1859) E.B. & E. 765. Post-engagement unchastity with the promisor himself does not give him any ground for breach.

[11] *Baddeley* v. *Mortlock* (1816) Holt N.P. 151.

to the marriage has been discovered,[1] or if either party has been rendered impotent or otherwise unfit, physically or mentally, by supervening event,[2] to marry, or in general if there has been discovered after the engagement some radical defect rendering either party unfit for marriage. The defender can rely on supervening defect in himself only in the case of serious physical or mental defect,[2] not on his own subsequent immorality. Change in financial situation does not justify breach, nor any defect known at the time of the engagement, nor mere suspicion or mistaken belief as to defect in the pursuer.[3]

Damages

Damages fall to be awarded as *solatium* for hurt to feelings, as compensation for loss of the particular marriage[4] and for possibly diminished chance of marriage altogether, for loss of the financial advantages of that marriage,[5] and for outlays and expenses fruitlessly incurred on the faith of and financial loss consequent on the cancellation of the promised marriage.[6]

Return of gifts on breaking off of engagement

Gifts given outright by either party to the other are not recoverable,[7] but gifts such as a ring made in contemplation of marriage may be recoverable.[8] The principle probably is that if the man breaks off the engagement without legal justification, the woman may keep the engagement ring, but if he has legal justification he may recover the ring.[9] If the woman breaks off without justification, she must return the ring, but if she has justification she may keep the ring.[10] If the engagement is broken off by mutual consent or by reason of death or disability, all gifts must be re-

---

[1] cf. *Beachey* v. *Brown* (1860) E.B. & E. 796.

[2] *Atchinson* v. *Baker* (1797) Peake Add. Cas. 103; *Hall* v. *Wright* (1859) E.B. & E. 765; *Liddell* v. *Easton's Trs.*, 1907 S.C. 154; *Gamble* v. *Sales* (1920) 36 T.L.R. 427.

[3] *Jefferson* v. *Paskell* [1916] 1 K.B. 57.

[4] *Hogg* v. *Gow*, 27 May 1812, F.C.; *Tucker* v. *Aitchison* (1846) 9 D. 21; *Smith* v. *Woodfine* (1857) 1 C.B. (N.S.) 660; *Berry* v. *Da Costa* (1866) L.R. 1 C.P. 331; *Somerville* v. *Thomson* (1896) 23 R. 576; *Brodie* v. *McGregor* (1900) 8 S.L.T. 200; *Stroyan* v. *McWhirter* (1901) 9 S.L.T. 242.

[5] *Berry, supra*; *Brodie, supra*; *Stroyan, supra*; *Robertson* v. *Hamilton*, 1915, 2 S.L.T. 195; *Quirk* v. *Thomas* [1916] 1 K.B. 516; cf. *Shaw* v. *S.* [1954] 2 Q.B. 429.

[6] *Finlay* v. *Chirney* (1888) 20 Q.B.D. 494. See also *Liddell, supra*.

[7] *Gold* v. *Hume* (1950) 66 Sh. Ct. Rep. 85.

[8] *Savage* v. *McAllister* (1952) 68 Sh. Ct. Rep. 11.

[9] *Cohen* v. *Sellar* [1926] 1 K.B. 536.

[10] *Jacobs* v. *Davis* [1917] 2 K.B. 532.

turned. Gifts made by third parties should be returned if the marriage does not take place.[1]

Discharge by performance

The contract of engagement is discharged when the parties perform their mutual undertakings, by solemnizing a valid marriage between themselves. If the marriage should be invalid, the engagement subsists as a cause of action and could be sued on.[2]

CONSTITUTION OF MARRIAGE

For the constitution of a legally valid marriage the parties must each have legal capacity to marry, in that they must be of opposite sexes, of single status, of age to marry, there must be no legal impediments, they must truly consent to contract matrimony, and the requisite formalities must be complied with. A seeming marriage which by reason of some defect is not legally valid may be either void or voidable. A marriage which is void is a legal nullity and never takes effect in law as a marriage; no declarator of nullity is necessary to set it aside, though such a decree is commonly sought to establish the fact and regularize the position.[3] A marriage which is merely voidable is good and valid but is subject to a resolutive condition in that it contains a flaw entitling either party to have it set aside; if not challenged it continues valid; until declared void by declarator of nullity, it is valid, but once declared null it is deemed void from the start.[4]

The differences between void and voidable marriages are that (i) a void marriage is always a nullity, whereas a voidable marriage is valid until and unless declared null, but when this happens, the decree has retrospective effect: (ii) any person having an interest may challenge a void marriage,[5] but only the parties may challenge a voidable marriage:[6] (iii) a void marriage may be challenged even after the death of one spouse;[5] a voidable marriage becomes unchallengeable if continued till one spouse dies;[6] and (iv) the issue of a void marriage are illegitimate; the

---

[1] Stair I, 7, 7.
[2] *Shaw* v. *S.* [1954] 2 Q.B. 429.
[3] e.g. *Ballantyne, infra; Aldridge, infra.*
[4] *S.G.* v. *W.G.*, 1933 S.C. 728. See also Clive, 1968 J.R. 209.
[5] *Fenton* v. *Livingstone* (1861) 23 D. 366.
[6] *L.* v. *L.*, 1931 S.C. 477; *F.* v. *F.*, 1945 S.C. 202.

issue of a voidable marriage legitimate.[1] But the issue of a putative marriage[2] are also deemed legitimate though the marriage
is void.

Capacity to marry

Scots law has adopted from the canon law the distinction
between *impedimenta dirimentia* (irritant impediments) and
impedimenta impeditiva (prohibitive impediments).[3] The former
are fundamental and a marriage conflicting with one of them is
void. They are sex, prior marriage, nonage, insanity, and relationship.[4] These are disabilities which affect a domiciled Scot,
wherever he may wish to marry.[5] The latter include clandestine
marriages,[6] and cases where one party lacks parental consent
required by the law of his domicile.[7] Impediments of this kind
are concerned with the conditions under which marriage may be
solemnized and are regulated by Scots law as *lex loci celebrationis*.

Sex

The parties must be biologically male and female respectively.
It will not suffice that one appears to be, and dresses and passes
as, of one sex if he or she is biologically of the other.[8]

Single status

Both parties must be of single status (whether single, widowed,
or divorced) and a marriage is void if either party were already
validly married to another,[9] even though that party honestly
believed, on reasonable grounds, that he was free to marry.[10] But

---

[1] Law Reform (Misc. Prov.) Act, 1949, S. 4.   [2] See *infra*.

[3] Fraser, *H. & W.*, I, 49; *Administrator of Austrian Property* v. *Von Lorang*, 1927 S.C.
(H.L.) 80, 96; *Bliersbach* v. *McEwen*, 1959 S.C. 43, 49.

[4] Fraser, *supra*, adds impotency, which is now treated as a resolutive condition, not a
condition precedent, and adultery and, in irregular marriages, non-residence, which have
been repealed.

[5] *Bliersbach*, *supra*, citing *Sussex Peerage Case* (1844) 11 Cl. & F. 85; *Sottomayor* v.
de Barros (1877) 3 P.D. 1.

[6] Fraser, *supra*.

[7] *Bliersbach*, *supra*.

[8] *Corbett* v. *C.* [1970] 2 All E.R. 33.

[9] Ersk. I, 6, 7; *Ballantyne* v. *B.* (1866) 4 M. 494; *Petrie* v. *Ross* (1894) 4 S.L.T. 63; cf.
Jack v. *J.*, 1940 S.L.T. 122; *Aldridge* v. *A.*, 1954 S.C. 58. Decree under the Presumption
of Life Limitation (Scotland) Act, 1891, does not permit a subsequent marriage: *Brady*
v. *Murray*, 1933 S.L.T. 534; *Fraser*, 1950 S.L.T. (Sh. Ct.) 51; nor does an invalid
divorce: *Van Mehren* v. *V.M.*, 1948 S.L.T. (Notes) 62.

[10] Bell, *Prin.* §1525; *Dalrymple* v. *D.* (1811) 2 Hagg. C.R. 54; *Jolly* v. *McGregor* (1828)
3 W. & S. 85, 202; *Wright* v. *W's Trs.* (1837) 15 S. 767. cf. *Prawdzic-Lazarska* v. *P.L.*,
1954 S.C. 98.

in the latter event, by the doctrine of putative marriage, the children are accounted legitimate. If the earlier 'marriage' were legally void the later marriage is not invalid by reason thereof.

Age

While by canon law and at common law persons could marry if they had attained the respective ages of puberty (or minority),[1] now by statute a marriage is void if either party has not attained sixteen.[2] But though a regular marriage be void by reason of the non-age of one party a valid irregular marriage may be constituted by their subsequent cohabitation and acquisition of the habit and repute of being married.[3]

Persons marrying in Scotland do not require any parental or other consent to their marriage when under 18.[4]

Mental incapacity

A marriage is null if either party was at the time of unsound mind so as to be incapable of understanding the nature of the relation being entered into or of truly consenting to marry.[5] The onus of proof is on the party seeking to establish the incapacity; the onus is lightened if it be established that the incapax had been of unsound mind shortly before the marriage, and this may cast on the defender the onus of establishing that it took place during a lucid interval.[6] The matter may be raised by either spouse, by the tutor-dative, but not the *curator bonis*, of the insane spouse if placed under guardianship,[7] and by any interested party after the death of either spouse,[8] and even if there has been issue of the marriage.[9] A marriage challengeable on this ground

---

[1] Bell, *Prin.* §1523.

[2] Age of Marriage Act, 1929, S. 1; cf. *Pugh* v. *P.* [1951] P. 482.

[3] *A.B.* v. *C.D.*, 1957 S.C. 415.

[4] Ersk. I, 6, 6; Bell, *Prin.* §1523; *Bliersbach* v. *McEwen*, 1959 S.C. 43; *Pease* v. *P.*, 1967 S.C. 112; *Hoy* v. *H.*, 1968 S.C. 179.

[5] Stair I, 4, 6; Ersk. I, 6, 2; Bell, *Prin.* §1523; Fraser, *H. & W.* I, 55; *Hunter* v. *Edney* (1881) 10 P.D. 93; *Durham* v. *D.* (1885) 10 P.D. 80; *Graham* v. *G.* (1907) 15 S.L.T. 33; *Park* v. *P.*, 1914, 1 S.L.T. 88; *Calder* v. *C.*, 1942 S.N. 40; *In the Estate of Park* [1954] P. 112; cf. *Johnston* v. *Brown* (1823) 2 S. 495. As to mental deficiency see *Long* v. *L.*, 1950 S.L.T. (Notes) 32.

[6] *Turner* v. *Meyers* (1808) 1 Hagg. C.R. 414, 417.

[7] cf. *Thomson* v. *T.* (1887) 14 R. 634.

[8] Fraser, *H. & W.* I, 74; *Loch* v. *Dick* (1638) Mor. 6278; *Christie* v. *Gib* (1700) Mor. 6283.

[9] *Jackson* v. *J.* [1908] P. 308.

may be approbated if the insane spouse recovers sanity.[1] Intoxication or drugs probably have the same effect in that a marriage is void if either spouse was at that time incapable on that account of understanding the contract being entered into, or of consenting.[2]

Prohibited degrees of relationship

Among the irritant impediments are the existence between the prospective spouses of a degree of relationship deemed to be too close to be permissible, and any such relationship is deemed incestuous.[3] If parties are related within the prohibited degrees of consanguinity or affinity, the marriage will be void, even though they were ignorant of the relationship. The Marriage Act, 1567, c. 16, legalized all marriages not forbidden by the Book of Leviticus, c. 18, verses 6–18, by providing that seconds in degree of consanguinity and affinity,[4] and all more remote degrees not repugnant to the said Biblical prescription, may lawfully marry, but the courts have extended the express prohibitions by implication to others of the same degree of relationship.[5] Under these principles marriage is forbidden between any two persons related to each other in the direct line of descent, however remotely, and to collateral relations within the second degree, even though the relationship be illegitimate.[6] Marriage is also prohibited between collaterals where one party stands *in loco parentis* to the other, as being a sibling of a direct ascendant,[7] unless the relationship is illegitimate.[8] Prohibitions extend equally to relatives of the whole and of the half-blood.

Marriage with relatives by affinity, i.e. blood relatives of one's late spouse, are subject to analogous prohibitions,[9] but the Marriage (Enabling) Act, 1960[10] provides that no marriage

---

[1] *Johnston* v. *Brown* (1823) 2 S. 495.

[2] *Johnston, supra*; cf. *Gall* v. *G.* (1870) 9 M. 177.

[3] For the reasons for this prohibition see *Philp's Tr.* v. *Beaton*, 1938 S.C. 733, 745. Incest as a crime is governed by the Incest Act, 1567 (c. 15), and refers to the same passage in scripture.

[4] Computed by the canon law method. See Ch. 15. Relations by consanguinity are those related by blood; relationship by affinity is that between a married person and his spouse's blood-relations.

[5] *Fenton* v. *Livingstone* (1861) 23 D. 366; *Purves' Trs.* v. *P.* (1895) 22 R. 513.

[6] *Robertson* v. *Channing*, 1928 S.L.T. 376; (man and late wife's sister's bastard daughter).

[7] Craig II, 18, 18; Stair I, 4, 4; Ersk. I, 6, 9; Bankt. I, 5, 39, and 47; Bell, *Prin.* §1527.

[8] *Philp's Trs.* v. *Beaton*, 1938 S.C. 733 (man and brother's daughter's bastard daughter).

[9] *Purves' Trs.* v. *P.* (1895) 22 R. 513.

[10] Replacing Deceased Wife's Sister's Marriage Act, 1907; Deceased Brother's Widow's Marriage Act, 1921; and Marriage (Prohibited Degrees of Relationship) Act, 1931.

between a man and a woman who is the sister, aunt or niece of a former wife of his (whether living or not), or was formerly the wife of his brother, uncle or nephew (whether living or not), shall be void or voidable on the ground of affinity; the provisions apply equally to kin of the whole and of the half blood.

Relatives of spouses are not *affines* to each other, so that a husband's brother may marry the wife's sister. A person may possibly marry the illegitimate child of one of his or her parents,[1] person adopted by his or her parents, but an adopter and his adoptive child are deemed within the prohibited degrees, even if the adoptive child is later again adopted.[2]

Marriage of divorced person with paramour

By statute[3] a marriage between a divorced person and the paramour with whom he committed adultery was null, and the children of such a union could not inherit from their parents. The statute was said to be applicable only if the paramour was expressly named in the decree, which was only done if specially requested.[4] It was long questionable whether the statute was in observance,[5] and it is now repealed.[6]

Royal Marriages Act, 1772

This Act provides that no descendant of King George II (other than the issue of princesses who have married into foreign families) may marry without the previous consent of the Sovereign granted under the great seal and declared in Council on pain of nullity, unless the descendant is over 25 and has given twelve months notice of the marriage to the Privy Council in which case the marriage is good unless both Houses of Parliament have expressly disapproved of it.[7]

Consent to marriage

It is essential, however the marriage be contracted, that the parties consent: *consensus non concubitus facit matrimonium*. The parties must give voluntary, real, and genuine consent to marriage,

---

[1] cf. *Philp's Trs., supra*, 746.

[2] Adoption Act, 1958, S. 13.

[3] Act 1600, c. 20; Stair, I, 4, 7; Ersk. I, 6, 43; III, 10, 9: Bell, *Prin.* §1526; Ferguson, *Consistorial Law*, 172; Fraser, *H. & W.* I, 140; *Lyle* v. *Douglas* (1670) Mor. 329.

[4] More, Notes, xvi; Riddell, *Peerage Law*, 391, 410.

[5] Bell, *Prin.* §1526; Fraser, *H. & W.* I, 144, 150; *Campbell* v. *C.* (1866) 4 M. 867, 5 M. (H.L.) 115; *Beattie* v. *B.* (1866) 5 M. 181.

[6] Statute Law Revision (Sc.) Act, 1964, Sched. I.

[7] See Farran, 14 M.L.R. 53.

or at least facts must be established from which the exchange of such consent may be inferred. Absence of genuine consent renders the alleged marriage a nullity *ab initio*.[1]

The consent must be to marriage, not to mere betrothal,[2] nor to any other relationship, e.g. concubinage. A marriage for an ulterior motive is void.[3] Consent is not valid if given under essential error as to the identity of the other party,[4] nor if induced by fraud or deception,[5] (though it is valid if the error relates merely to the chastity or other qualities or attributes of the other[6]), nor if there is error as to the nature and effect of the ceremony,[7] nor if induced by fear or coercion,[8] nor if not deliberate,[9] nor if parties have a mental reservation and do not regard themselves as truly married.[10] If consent is obtained by fraud the marriage may still be ratified by the innocent party.[11]

If parties have truly consented, the validity of the marriage is not affected by one party's subsequent erroneous belief that the marriage was invalid for lack of a formality,[12] nor by the fact that one party was disabled by his religion from marrying outside that religion.[13] Consent may be held not to have been given, when, even though statutory formalities had been fulfilled, the marriage was a sham, contracted purely for some ulterior purpose,[14] though it is more difficult to establish absence of true consent in a case of

---

[1] Stair I, 4, 6; More's Notes, xiii; Ersk. I, 6, 2, and 5; Hume, *Lect.* I, 26; Bell, *Prin.* §1517; Fergusson, *Consist. Law*; Fraser *H. & W.* I, 435. Cases of no serious or genuine consent include *Gall v. G.* (1870) 9 M. 177; *Steuart v. Robertson* (1875) 2 R. (H.L.) 80; *Davidson v. D.*, 1921 S.C. 341.

[2] *Ford v. Stier* [1896] P. 1; *Hall v. H.* (1908) 24 T.L.R. 756; *Kelly v. K.* (1932) 49 T.L.R. 99; *Mehta v. M.* [1945] 2 All E.R. 690; cf. *S.G. v. W.G.*, 1933 S.C. 728.

[3] More, Notes, 14; *Browne v. B.* (1843) 5 D. 1288, 1295; *Orlandi v. Castelli*, 1961 S.C. 113. See also *H. v. H.* [1953] 2 All E.R. 1229; *Buckland v. B.* [1967] 2 All E.R. 300; *Szechter v. S.* [1970] 3 All E.R. 905.

[4] e.g. where there has been personation: *Lang, infra*, 49; cf. *Wilson v. Horn* (1904) 11 S.L.T. 702; *McLeod v. Adams*, 1920, 1 S.L.T. 229.

[5] Fraser, *H. & W.* I, 457, 461; *Lang, infra*, 50.

[6] *Lang v. L.*, 1921 S.C. 44 (wife concealing that she was pregnant by another), overruling *Stein v. S.*, 1914 S.C. 903; cf. *Moss v. M.* [1897] P. 263.

[7] *Valier v. V.* (1925) 133 L.T. 830; *Lendrum v. Chakravarti*, 1929 S.L.T. 96; *Kelly, supra*; *Mehta, supra*.

[8] *Cameron v. Malcolm* (1756) Mor. 12680; *Jolly v. McGregor* (1828) 3 W. & S. 85; *Scott v. Sebright* (1886) 12 P.D. 21; *Griffith v. G.* [1944] Ir. R. 35.

[9] *Blair v. Fairie* (1766) 5 B.S. 921.

[10] *Brady v. Murray*, 1933 S.L.T. 534.

[11] *Alexander v. A.*, 1920 S.C. 327.

[12] *Courtin v. Elder*, 1930 S.C. 68.

[13] *MacDougall v. Chitnavis*, 1937 S.C. 390.

[14] *H. v. H.* [1954] P. 258; *Silver v. S.* [1955] 2 All E.R. 614; *Orlandi v. Castelli*, 1961 S.C. 113.

regular marriage,[1] and the court is reluctant to recognize the misuse of marriage for ulterior purposes by allowing parties to controvert the consent exchanged.

Formalities of marriage

The formalities of marriage are determined by the *lex loci celebrationis*. The Scots law was shaped by the canon law as it stood before the Council of Trent (1563) and the pre-Tridentine law was continued in Scotland after and notwithstanding the Reformation. Under this no religious ceremony was necessary, but only acceptance by the parties of each other as husband and wife *per verba de praesenti*, in which case marriage was at once constituted, or *per verba de futuro*, in which case marriage became binding as soon as consummated, or parties might be deemed married if they cohabited openly and continuously so as to acquire the reputation of being married, but it became common to celebrate marriage *in facie ecclesiae* after publication of banns and with a religious service. Hence until recent times marriage might be constituted in Scotland irregularly or regularly. There were three modes of irregular marriage: (1) by declaration *de praesenti*; (2) by promise *subsequente copula*; and (3) by cohabitation with habit and repute. Since 1 July 1940 contracting marriage in either of the first two modes is incompetent.[2] There are now two modes of regular marriage: (1) before a minister of religion after due notice; and (2) before an authorized registrar after due notice.[3]

Irregular marriage

Though marriage may no longer be contracted by either of the first two modes of irregular marriage, marriages previously constituted in those modes remain valid and questions of their constitution may still arise. Circumstances may justify the plea of more than one mode of constitution of marriage alternatively, and one may succeed and another fail.[4]

---

[1] See cases of *McInnes* v. *More* (1782) 2 Pat. 598; *Taylor* v. *Kello* (1787) 3 Pat. 56; *Sassen* v. *Campbell* (1826) 2 W. & S. 309; *Stewart* v. *Menzies* (1841) 2 Rob. App. 547; *Lockyer* v. *Sinclair* (1846) 8 D. 582; *Robertson* v. *Steuart* (1874) 1 R. 532, 667; *Imrie* v. *I.* (1891) 19 R. 185; *Lang* v. *L.* 1921 S.C. 44, 54.

[2] Marriage (Sc.) Act, 1939, S. 5.

[3] Ibid., S. 1.

[4] e.g. *Petrie* v. *P.*, 1911 S.C. 360.

Prerequisite residence

Originally parties could marry irregularly in Scotland without any need for prior residence; hence 'Gretna Green' and other 'runaway' marriages were valid by Scots law.[1] After 1856 no irregular marriage contracted by declaration, acknowledgement or ceremony[2] is valid unless one of the parties had his or her usual place of residence[3] in Scotland, or had lived in Scotland for twenty-one days[4] next preceding the marriage.[5] This Act was repealed when irregular marriages by declaration after 1 July 1940 were invalidated, but it applies to such marriages prior thereto.

Marriage by declaration de praesenti

This mode of marriage, recognized in canon law, consisted in a mutual declaration of consent there and then[6] to take each other as spouses.[7] If the mutual consent were proved, matrimony was at once thereby constituted, whether concubitus followed or not.[8] The consent might be proved by witnesses,[9] or by the testimony of one of the parties, if corroborated by facts and circumstances,[10] or by the giving and acceptance of a written declaration or acknowledgment of marriage,[11] if proved to be written, or adopted and signed, by the giver.[12] If written declarations were exchanged, the pursuer had to prove the circumstances in which they were exchanged, and that these were consistent with the matrimonial intention expressed therein.[13] The question was always whether there was a genuine exchange of consent to marriage there and

---

[1] On history see *Mackie* v. *Dumfriesshire Assessor*, 1932 S.C. 397, 404; Anton and Francescaskis, 1958 J.R. 253.

[2] This seems to refer to clandestine, not regular, marriages. The Act does not appear to cover marriages by cohabitation.

[3] Interpreted: *Gray* v. *G.*, 1941 S.C. 461; *Cooke* v. *Taylor*, 1941 S.C. 461.

[4] *Lawford* v. *Davies* (1878) 4 P.D. 61.

[5] Marriage (Scotland) Act, 1856 (Lord Brougham's Act); *Miller* v. *Deakin*, 1912, 1 S.L.T. 253; *Bach* v. *B.* (1927) 43 T.L.R. 493; and see Adamson, 1958 J.R. 148.

[6] *Brady* v. *Murray*, 1933 S.L.T. 534.

[7] Generally, Stair I, 4, 6; Ersk. I, 6, 5; Bell, *Prin.* §1508, 1514.

[8] *Dalrymple* v. *D.* (1811) 2 Hagg. C.R. 54; *Walker* v. *Macadam* (1813) 1 Dow 148; *Aitchison* v. *Incorpn. of Solicitors* (1838) 1 D. 42; *Leslie* v. *L.* (1860) 22 D. 993.

[9] *Craigie* v. *Hoggan* (1839) Macl. & R. 942.

[10] *Dysart Peerage Case* (1881) 6 App. Cas. 489, 538; *Glass* v. *G's Trs.* (1907) 15 S.L.T. 716; *Petrie* v. *P.*, 1911 S.C. 360; *Polack* v. *Shiels*, 1912, 2 S.L.T. 329.

[11] *Richardson* v. *Irving* (1785) Hume 361; *Dunn* v. *D's Trs.*, 1930 S.C. 131; cf. *Strathern* v. *Stuart*, 1926 J.C. 114; *Reid* v. *H.M.A.*, 1934 J.C. 7.

[12] *Mackenzie* v. *Stewart* (1848) 10 D. 611; *Forster* v. *F.* (1872) 10 M. (H.L.) 68; *Imrie* v. *I.* (1891) 19 R. 185.

[13] *Imrie, supra*; *Duran* v. *D.* (1904) 7 F. 87.

then,[1] and a writing might be proved to have some other purpose than marriage.[2] The court had to have regard to the whole conduct of parties before and after, and the concomitant circumstances, as evidencing their intention.[3] Subsequent conduct might indicate absence of genuine consent to marriage.[4] Evidence of subsequent acknowledgment before witnesses,[5] of *concubitus*, and of children being registered as legitimate or illegitimate was relevant.[6] If the facts indicated an exchange of matrimonial consent, it was not necessary to prove the exact time or place of marriage, or the exact words used.[7] The exchange of consent as constituting marriage was not vitiated by an agreement to keep the marriage secret,[8] nor even by the fact that a declaration that a woman was the writer's wife was not delivered to her but to an agent, though she knew of its existence,[9] nor by the fact that one party subsequently reached an erroneous conclusion that the marriage was invalid for lack of a formality.[10] If the natural interpretation of a writing was that it inferred present marriage, and the woman understood it in that way, the man was barred from contending that he intended another meaning.[11] But an acknowledgment of marriage found in a man's repositories after his death and not to be opened till then was held not to be a consent to present marriage but an invalid attempt to bequeath a mistress the status of widow.[12] Marriage in this mode could be established after the other spouse's death.[13] Such a marriage was

---

[1] *Taylor v. Kello* (1787) 3 Pat. 56; *Aitchison v. Incorpn. of Solicitors* (1838) 1 D. 42; *Courtin v. Elder*, 1930 S.C. 68; *Brady v. Murray*, 1933 S.L.T. 534.

[2] *More v. McInnes* (1782) 2 Pat. 598; *Sassen v. Campbell* (1826) 2 W. & S. 309; *Stewart v. Menzies* (1841) 2 Robin. 547; *Lockyer v. Sinclair* (1846) 8 D. 582, 616; *Fleming v. Corbet* (1859) 21 D. 1034; *Duran v. D.* (1904) 7 F. 87.

[3] *Jolly v. McGregor* (1828) 3 W. & Sh. 85, 179; *Lockyer, supra*; *Fleming, supra*; *Beattie v. Baird* (1863) 1 M. 273; *Steuart v. Robertson* (1875) 2 R. (H.L.) 80; *Maloy v. Macadam* (1885) 12 R. 431; *Imrie, supra*; *Davidson v. D.*, 1921 S.C. 341; *Dunn v. D's Trs.*, 1930 S.C. 131.

[4] *Davidson, supra*.

[5] *Walker v. Macadam* (1813) 1 Dow 148; *Macdouall v. Lady Dalhousie* (1840) 1 Robin. 475.

[6] *Reid v. Laing* (1823) 1 Sh. App. 440; *Forster v. F.* (1872) 10 M. (H.L.) 68; *Beattie v. Nish* (1878) 5 R. 775; *Mackenzie v. M's Trs.*, 1916, 1 S.L.T. 349.

[7] *Leslie v. L.* (1860) 22 D. 993, 1017.

[8] *Hamilton v. H.* (1842) 1 Bell 736; *Leslie v. L.* (1860) 22 D. 993; *Brebner v. Bell* (1904) 12 S.L.T. 2; *Mackenzie v. M's Trs.*, 1916, 1 S.L.T. 349.

[9] *Hamilton v. H.* (1842) 1 Bell's App. 736.

[10] *Courtin v. Elder*, 1930 S.C. 68.

[11] *Fleming v. Corbet* (1859) 21 D. 1034, 1045; *Duran v. D.* (1904) 7 F. 87.

[12] *Anderson v. Fullarton* (1795) Hume 365.

[13] *Glass v. G's Trs.* (1907) 15 S.L.T. 716; *Davidson v. D.*, 1921 S.C. 341; *Dunn v. D's Trs.*, 1930 S.C. 131; *Gray v. G.*, 1941 S.C. 461.

frequently followed by petitioning the sheriff to certify that marriage had taken place and to grant warrant to the appropriate registrar to register the marriage.[1]

Marriage by promise subsequente copula

In the mediaeval canon law parties were held married if they uttered words denoting a future intention to become man and wife and subsequently had intercourse in reliance thereon; promise to marry became marriage by consummation. This mode of marriage was accepted in Scots law also,[2] prior to 1 July 1940.[3] Probably both promise and *copula* had to take place in Scotland.[4] If both were proved marriage was held constituted at the time of the *copula*.[5] The *copula* was held to imply consent to marriage in implement of the prior promise.[6] There had to be promise to marry, not merely courtship.[7] The promise of subsequent marriage had to be admitted by, or proved by the writ of, the defender, or by reference to his oath.[8] It would not necessarily be inferred from the fact that the parties were engaged,[9] but might be from the tenor of a correspondence.[10] The writing relied on had to be holograph of the defender, or signed and be proved to be signed by him.[11] The precise time and place of the promise need not be proved.[12] The requisite *copula* must have taken place after the promise and in reliance thereon. It might be proved *prout de jure*. If the promise were established it was usually presumed that subsequent *copula* was in reliance thereon, but this could be rebutted.[13] Though promise and subsequent *copula* be proved, other facts might disprove any consent

---

[1] Marriage (Sc.) Act, 1856, S. 2; *Courtin, supra*.

[2] Stair I, 4, 6; Ersk. I, 6, 4; Bell, *Prin.* §1515; *Dalrymple* v. *D.* (1811) 2 Hagg. C.R. 54.

[3] Marriage (Sc.) Act, 1939, S. 5.

[4] *Yelverton* v. *Longworth* (1864) 4 Macq. 745, 834, 879, 902.

[5] *Mackie* v. *M.*, 1917 S.C. 276.

[6] *Stewart* v. *Menzies* (1841) 2 Rob. 547, 591; *Yelverton, supra*; *N.* v. *C.*, 1933 S.C. 492.

[7] *Monteith* v. *Robb* (1844) 6 D. 934.

[8] Competency of reference to oath doubted in *Longworth* v. *Yelverton* (1867) 5 M. (H.L.) 144. Subsequent cases do not share this doubt: see *Morrison, infra*, 353; *Mackie, supra*, 282, 283; *Lindsay* v. *L.*, 1927 S.C. 395.

[9] *Cameron* v. *C.* (1814) Ferg. Con. Cas. 139; *Monteith* v. *Robb* (1844) 6 D. 934; *Ross* v. *McLeod* (1861) 23 D. 972, 981.

[10] *Campbell* v. *Honeyman* (1831) 5 W. & Sh. 92; *Yelverton* v. *Longworth* (1864) 4 Macq. 856; *Morrison* v. *Dobson* (1869) 8 M. 347, 353; *Mackie, supra; X.* v. *Y.*, 1921, 1 S.L.T. 79; *Lindsay* v. *L.*, 1927 S.C. 395.

[11] *Mackenzie* v. *Stewart* (1848) 10 D. 611, 638.

[12] *Campbell, supra*.

[13] *Morrison* v. *Dobson* (1869) 8 M. 347; *N.* v. *C.*, 1933 S.C. 492.

to marriage.[1] The court had to consider the whole circumstances and conduct of the parties, before and after the alleged marriage, to discover the parties' intention.[2] It was irrelevant, if the woman consented to *copula* in reliance on the promise, that she was ignorant that this would constitute marriage.[3] If there had been *copula* prior to the promise, there was no presumption that subsequent *copula* was in reliance on the promise, but this might be proved.[4] Marriage would not be constituted by conditional promise, to marry if the girl became pregnant, followed by *copula*, because there the marriage was to be, if at all, after the *copula*, and not constituted thereby.[5] But marriage might be constituted by promise to marry when a condition was purified, if *copula* subsequently took place, it being held that the condition had been waived, but this inference could be disproved.[6] Declarator of marriage constituted by this mode is competent at the instance of either party,[7] and after the death of one spouse, proof of the promise being then necessarily restricted to writ,[8] and might be brought by a child of the marriage after the death of one spouse.[9]

Marriage by Cohabitation with Habit and Repute

By an old Act[10] it was provided that a woman who had been reputed to be a man's wife during his lifetime should be entitled to terce from his estate unless it were proved that she was not married to him. From this arose the doctrine that if a couple cohabit openly and constantly as husband and wife so as to produce a general belief that they are married, they will be presumed to have exchanged matrimonial consent.[11] This mode of irregular marriage remains competent. The question in every case is one of fact, whether the proper inference from the evidence is that the parties must have exchanged matrimonial consent.[12] There must

[1] *Morrison, supra.*   [2] *Maloy* v. *Macadam* (1885) 12 R. 431.

[3] *Reid* v. *Laing* (1823) 1 Sh. App. 440, 451; *Yelverton, supra,* 854.

[4] *Sim* v. *Miles* (1829) 85, 89; *Ross* v. *McLeod* (1861) 23 D. 972, 994; *Surtees* v. *Wotherspoon* (1873) 11 M. 384, 389; *M.* v. *Y.,* 1934 S.L.T. 187.

[5] *Kennedy* v. *Macdouall* (1800) Ferg. Con. Cas. 163; *Stewart* v. *Menzies* (1841) 2 Rob. App. 547. See also *Surtees* v. *Wotherspoon* (1873) 11 M. 384.

[6] Walton, 30.

[7] *Hardie* v. *H.,* 1931 S.L.T. 198.

[8] *Mackie* v. *M.,* 1917 S.C. 276; *X.* v. *Y.,* 1921, 1 S.L.T. 79.

[9] *X.* v. *Y.,* 1921, 1 S.L.T. 79.

[10] 1503, c. 77 (repealed).

[11] Stair, I, 46, III, 3, 42; Ersk. I, 6, 6; Bell, *Prin.* §1516; *Elder* v. *McLean* (1829) 8 S. 56; *Lapsley* v. *Grierson* (1845) 8 D. 34; *Campbell* v. *C.* (1867) 5 M. (H.L.) 115. See also Ashton-Cross, 1961 J.R. 21.

[12] *Low* v. *Gorman,* 1970 S.L.T. 356.

be cohabitation at bed and board[1] in Scotland[2] by parties free to marry, or cohabitation continued after they have become free to marry,[3] unless the circumstances of continuance do not imply consent to marry.[4] If the parties knew that their relationship was initially illicit, concubinage or adultery, no presumption of marriage arises from its continuance after the impediment has been removed,[5] unless there is clear evidence of matrimonial intent.[6] If at the commencement of the relationship, one of the parties is proved to have intended to remain single, the onus of proof of marriage is increased.[7] No particular period of cohabitation is requisite, so long as it is sufficient reasonably to support the presumption of exchange of matrimonial consent.[8] The relationship must also have given rise to substantially consistent and unvarying reputation of being married,[9] as evidenced preferably by the opinions of friends and relatives, rather than by the views of servants, shopkeepers, and casual acquaintances.[10] Acknowledgment of marriage to friends is favourable,[11] but concealment of the marriage from friends and connections is unfavourable.[12] Disparity of social position between the parties is also relevant.[13] The registration of children as legitimate suggests marriage.[14] Uncertain or divided repute will not suffice.[15] Marriage may be held not constituted if one party has delayed to have it declared,[16]

---

[1] *Lowrie* v. *Mercer* (1840) 2 D. 953, 963; *Hamilton* v. H. (1842) 1 Bell 736.

[2] *Macdouall* v. *Lady Dalhousie* (1840) 1 Robin. 475; *Dysart Peerage Case* (1881) 6 App. Cas. 489.

[3] *Campbell, supra*; *De Thoren* v. *Wall* (1876) 3 R. (H.L.) 28; *A.B.* v. *C.D.*, 1957 S.C. 415; see also *Secretary of State for Scotland* v. *Sutherland*, 1944 S.C. 79, 84.

[4] *Bairner* v. *Fels*, 1931 S.C. 674.

[5] *Cuninghame* v. *C.* (1814) 2 Dow. 482; *Lapsley* v. *Grierson* (1845) 8 D. 34; (1848) 1 H.L.C. 498; *Campbell* v. *C.* (1867) 5 M. (H.L.) 115; *Dysart Peerage Case, supra*.

[6] *Elder* v. *Maclean* (1829) 8 S. 56; *Wood's Trs.* v. *Findlay*, 1909, 1 S.L.T. 156; *Cossar* v. *C.* (1901) 9 S.L.T. 44; *A.B., supra*; *Low* v. *Gorman*, 1970 S.L.T. 356.

[7] *Nicol* v. *Bell*, 1954 S.L.T. 314.

[8] Insufficient: *Wallace* v. *Fife Coal Co.*, 1909 S.C. 682 (10½ mos.); sufficient: *A.B.* v. *C.D.*, 1957 S.C. 415 (6 years); *Petrie* v. *P.*, 1911 S.C. 360 (8 years); *Hendry* v. *L.A.*, 1930 S.C. 1027 (20 years); *Nicol* v. *Bell*, 1954 S.L.T. 314 (22 years); *Wood's Trs.* v. *Findlay*, 1909, 1 S.L.T. 156 (38 years). cf. *Low, supra* (10 mos.).

[9] *Petrie* v. *P.*, 1911 S.C. 360.

[10] *Thomas* v. *Gordon* (1829) 7 S. 872; *Hamilton* v. H. (1839) 2 D. 89; *Lapsley* v. *Grierson, supra*; *Cossar, supra*; *Lynch* v. *L.*, 1926 S.N. 172; *Hendry* v. *L.A.*, 1930 S.C. 1027; see also *Longworth* v. *Yelverton* (1862) 24 D. 696 and 28 J.R. 38 thereon.

[11] *Inglis* v. *Robertson* (1787) 3 Pat. 53; *MacGregor* v. *Campbell*, 28 Nov. 1801, F.C.; *Aitchison* v. *Incorporation of Solicitors* (1838) 1 D. 42; *Lang* v. *L.* (1841) 3 D. 980.

[12] *Thomas, supra*; *Lowrie* v. *Mercer* (1840) 2 D. 953, 961.

[13] *Hamilton, supra*; cf. *MacGregor* v. *Campbell*, 29 Nov. 1801, F.C.

[14] *A.B., supra*.

[15] *Hamilton, supra*.

[16] *Darsie* v. *Sceales* (1867) 39 Sc. Jur. 191.

or has acquiesced in inconsistent conduct, such as the other taking up cohabitation with a third party.[1] If the evidence points to marriage by cohabitation with habit and repute, no regard will be paid to a subsequent writing acknowledging that the parties did not cohabit as man and wife.[2] If the facts justify an inference of an exchange of matrimonial consent, this may be deemed to have taken place at the outset of the cohabitation, or when some event indicative of marriage took place, such as registering a child as legitimate,[3] or when the parties became free to marry.[4]

Regular marriage-preliminaries

As a preliminary to a regular marriage parties must, in the case of a marriage *in facie ecclesiae*, have banns called in church, or give notice to the local registrar of births, deaths, and marriages,[5] or obtain a sheriff's licence, or, in the case of marriage before an authorized registrar, give notice in respect of both parties, or obtain a sheriff's licence. Failing compliance with the preliminaries, the marriage is null and void.[6]

Banns

The calling of banns is regulated by Acts of Assembly of the Church of Scotland.[7] The names and designations of the parties and their purpose of marriage are proclaimed at public worship in a designated church of the registration district where the parties reside, or in the churches of each, if they reside in different districts, on two consecutive Sundays, or on one if the parties are known to the minister. At least one party must have resided in the district for at least fifteen days previously. If the session clerk is not aware of the residence qualification and that the parties are free to marry, he must be furnished with a certificate of these facts signed by an elder or by two householders. When due proclamation has been made, a certificate of proclamation is

---

[1] *Napier* v. *N.* (1801) Hume 367; *Wright* v. *W.'s Trs.* (1837) 15 S. 767. Contrast *Reid* v. *Robb* (1813) Hume 378.

[2] *Mackenzie* v. *M.*, 8 Mar. 1810, F.C.

[3] *Nicol* v. *Bell*, 1954 S.L.T. 314.

[4] *Campbell* v. *C.* (1867) 5 M. (H.L.) 115; *A.B.* v. *C.D.*, 1957 S.C. 415.

[5] Banns may be called in respect of one party and notice given in respect of the other, or banns may be called or notice given in respect of both.

[6] *Bradley* v. *Mochrie*, 1947 S.L.T. (Notes) 27.

[7] Marriage Notice (Sc.) Act, 1878, S. 18; Marriage (Sc.) Act, 1956, S. 3. For history see *Hutton* v. *Harper* (1875) 2 R. 893; 3 R. (H.L.) 9. Banns may be published in Scotland by a clergyman of the Church of England, if either party resides in Scotland, for marriage in England: Marriage Act, 1949, S. 13.

issued by the session clerk valid for three months only. A statutory schedule is issued and partly completed by the registrar and has to be completed at the marriage ceremony by the officiating minister, the spouses, and two witnesses, and transmitted to the registrar of the district within three days. Banns should probably be called in the name by which the party is generally known, whether or not that is the baptismal name,[1] but publication is invalid if a false name has been assumed.[2] Although other churches have adopted the custom of giving notice in the form of proclamation of banns only banns proclaimed in a church of the Church of Scotland are valid as a legal prerequisite to marriage.

Notice to registrar

Alternatively, parties may give notice of intended marriage to the registrars of the districts in which each had his usual residence or has resided for at least fifteen days; one notice suffices when both reside in the same district. The registrar enters the particulars in a book and exhibits a public notice of the intended marriage on the door or outer wall of his office for seven days. If no objection appears *ex facie* of the notice, or is stated to him, the registrar may then grant a certificate of publication of notice, which is equivalent to a proclamation of banns.[3] The certificate is valid for three months only.[4] Objections may be made in writing, lodged personally and supported by a statutory declaration, before the certificate is issued. If the objection relates to stated formal defects the sheriff may direct amendment or cancellation of the notice; if to fundamental impediments, the registrar must suspend the issue of his certificate until a competent court has decided that the parties are not disqualified from marrying.[5]

Where one party lives in Scotland and the other in England, the party residing in Scotland may, subject to the 1878 Act, give notice of the intended marriage as if the parties were residing in

---

[1] cf. *Dancer* v. *D.* [1949] P. 147.

[2] cf. *Tooth* v. *Barrow* (1854) 1 Ecc. & Ad. 371; *Gompertz* v. *Kensit* (1872) L.R. 13 Eq. 369; *Chipchase* v. *C.* [1939] P. 391; *Chipchase* v. *C.* [1942] P. 37.

[3] Marriage Notice (Sc.) Act, 1878, Ss. 6–9. A marriage has been held valid though false information as to residence had been given to the registrar: *Gall* v. *G.*, 1968 S.C. 332.

[4] Ibid., S. 11.

[5] Ibid., S. 10; *Bliersbach* v. *McEwen*, 1959 S.C. 43. As to risks of objector see *Henderson* v. *H.* (1855) 17 D. 348. It is incompetent to interdict the Registrar General from issuing forms of intention to marry or performing the ceremony: *Butler* v. *Registrar General*, 1962 S.L.T. (Notes) 12.

different parishes or districts in Scotland, and the party residing in England similarly. The registrar of the Scottish parish may accept notice given by the party residing in his district, subject to the 1878 Act, as if both parties resided in different districts in Scotland.[1]

A party residing in England intending marriage in Scotland and having a parent whose usual residence is in Scotland, may give notice to the registrar of the parish of the parent's usual residence, as if he had resided in that parish for fifteen days.[2] Where both parties contemplating marriage in Scotland reside in England and one has a parent whose usual residence is in Scotland, the other may give notice to the superintendent registrar of the district in which he has resided for seven days. If the parties reside in different registration districts notice need not be given in the other district. Section 28(1) of the (English) Marriage Act, 1949, applies, with modifications, to the declaration which accompanies the notice of marriage.[3] A notice given under the latter subsection, if in other respects complying with the Marriage Act, 1949, is to be treated as a notice in accordance with that Act, and the provisions of that Act relative to certificates for marriage apply as if the marriage were to be in England. Such a certificate is equivalent to a certificate issued by a Scottish registrar.[4]

Sheriff's licence

Where one party to a marriage intended in Scotland has a Scottish residential qualification, there is no legal impediment to the marriage,[5] the parties are unable to obtain a certificate of proclamation of banns or of publication of notice until after the date of the intended marriage, and, in respect of the illness of one of the parties or other unforeseen and exceptional circumstance,[6] there is reasonable excuse for the failure of the parties to secure such proclamation or publication, the sheriff may on joint application grant a licence in lieu, which has the same effect as a registrar's certificate.[7] The licence is void if the marriage does not take place within ten days after the grant thereof.

---

[1] Marriage Act, 1939, Ss. 1 and 2.
[2] Marriage (Scotland) Act, 1956, S. 1(1).
[3] Ibid., S. 1(2).
[4] Ibid., S. 1(3) and (4).
[5] *Rojas*, 1967 S.L.T. (Sh. Ct.) 24.
[6] *Doherty and Thomson*, 1949 S.L.T. (Sh. Ct.) 73.
[7] Marriage (Sc.) Act, 1939, S. 2(1).

Marriage in facie ecclesiae

This is a marriage celebrated by a minister of religion[1] before two witnesses. No particular formalities are required by law[2] though it is probably essential that the officiating clergyman obtain the oral consent of each party to take the other as spouse, and that he then declare them to be married. Beyond that, the order of service is a matter of religious form only. It need not take place in a consecrated building, but may be in a house or hotel.

Marriages of Episcopalians, Roman Catholics, Quakers, Jews, Etc.

Episcopal ministers may marry only persons whose banns have been published on three Sundays in the episcopal congregations which the parties frequent and in the churches to which they belong as parishioners.[3] After proclamation of banns or notice to the registrar, persons may be married by priests or ministers not of the Established Church.[4] Quakers and Jews may contract regular marriage according to their own usages provided both are Jews and that notice to the registrar has been given and his certificate obtained,[5] or provided both are, or one is a Quaker or an attender associated therewith, and notice has been given.[6]

Civil marriage

Marriages may be celebrated by authorized registrars. Parties produce certificates that notice of the intended marriage has been published, or a sheriff's licence, complete the prescribed form, declare in the presence of the registrar and two witnesses that they know of no legal impediment to their marriage, and accept each other as husband and wife. The form is subscribed, or signed by mark, by parties, registrar, and witnesses, and the marriage registered.[7]

---

[1] This term includes, as well as Church of Scotland ministers, priests or ministers not of the Established Church, (Marriage (Sc.) Act, 1834, S. 2), a 'minister, clergyman, pastor or priest of any Christian denomination' (Registration of Births, etc., (Sc.) Act, 1965, S. 29), a Jewish rabbi, or a person performing such ceremonies among Quakers (Marriage (Sc.) Act, 1939, S. 3). In practice registrars issue marriage schedules to pastors of many denominations, officers of the Salvation Army, and others approved by the Registrar-General.

[2] Bell, *Pr.* §1511–13.

[3] Scottish Episcopalians Act, 1711, S. 7.

[4] Marriage (Sc.) Act, 1834, S. 2. It is uncertain what 'priests or ministers' covers. Query as to e.g. Mohammedans.

[5] Marriage Notice (Scotland) Act, 1878, S. 5.

[6] Ibid., amd. Marriage (Sc.) Act, 1939, S. 3.

[7] Marriage (Sc.) Act, 1939, S. 1; Marriage (Sc.) Act, 1942, S. 4.

Registration of marriages

Irregular marriages might be registered on the warrant of a sheriff, granted on joint application of parties within three months of the marriage.[1] If the marriage is established by declarator, the decree is intimated to the Registrar-General for registration.[2]

Regular marriages must be registered with the registrar of the parish in which it was solemnized. A Marriage Schedule, issued by the registrar to the parties on production of evidence of proclamation of banns or certificate of publication of notice, must be signed by the officiating person, the parties, and two witnesses and delivered to the district registrar within three days, under penalties.[3] The registrar registers civil marriages performed by him.[4] Registration does not settle the essential validity or otherwise of a marriage, but the validity of a registered regular marriage may not be questioned in any legal proceedings on the grounds that the celebrant was not competent or qualified to do so.[5]

Clandestine marriage

A clandestine marriage is one celebrated by a person falsely assuming the character of a clergyman,[6] or by a clergyman, without banns having been called or notice of marriage given.[7] It is an offence to celebrate marriage with religious ceremony but without publication of banns or certificate,[8] or to personate a clergyman, or without authority to perform a marriage ceremony.[9] Such a marriage is now void; formerly it could have had effect as a marriage by *de praesenti* consent,[10] and it might yet be the basis for marriage by cohabitation with habit and repute.

---

[1] Bell, *Prin.* §1514A; Marriage (Sc.) Act, 1916, S. 3, replacing Marriage (Sc.) Act, 1856, S. 2, and repealed by 1939 Act, S. 8. See practice described in *Courtin* v. *Elder*, 1930 S.C. 68, 76.

[2] Marriage (Sc.) Act, 1939, S. 6.

[3] Registration of Births, etc. (Sc.) Act, 1965, S. 30.

[4] Marriage (Sc.) Act, 1939, S. 1(2).

[5] Marriage (Sc.) Act, 1939, S. 4. Under this provision registrars allow pastors of various sects to celebrate marriages which are recognized as regular, and registered, but the legality of this is doubtful.

[6] cf. *H.M.A.* v. *Ballantyne* (1859) 3 Irv. 352. *Quaere* as to one of the sect of Jehovah's Witnesses? See *Walsh* v. *L.A.*, 1956 S.C. (H.L.) 126.

[7] Scottish Episcopalians Act, 1711, S. 7; Ersk. I, 6, 11; Bell, *Prin.* §1514.

[8] Marriage Notice (Sc.) Act, 1878, S. 12; cf. *Strathern* v. *Stuart*, 1926 J.C. 114.

[9] *H.M.A.* v. *Ballantyne, supra.*

[10] Stair I, 4, 6.

Marriages in England

The formalities of marriage in England are prescribed by the Marriage Act, 1949, as amended.

Marriages in Naval, Military, and Air Force Chapels

Under the Marriage Act, 1949, Part V, persons at least one of whom is or was a regular member of the forces, or of the women's services, or the daughter of any such person, may marry in a garrison church, subject to certain qualifications of the rules applicable to marriages in England.

Declarator of marriage

Declarator of marriage is the process for seeking to have a doubtful marriage judicially recognized as valid and binding, or to have established a marriage which is denied by the other party.[1] It may be a necessary preliminary to an action of divorce, may be brought by a child of the marriage after the death of one spouse,[2] and may be continued by the pursuer's executor after her death *pendente lite*.[3] An alternative conclusion may be for damages for breach of promise and seduction.[4] The existence of marriage may also be decided incidentally in other actions.[5]

Declarator of freedom and putting to silence

Declarator of freedom and putting to silence is the process whereby a person, troubled by another falsely calling himself or herself that person's spouse, may have himself declared free of the alleged marriage and the other enjoined to preserve silence as to the false claim.[6] It is a competent defence that marriage was truly constituted.[7]

Declarator of nullity

Declarator of nullity is the process to have declared that an apparent marriage was truly void on any ground on which it is

---

[1] e.g. *Steuart* v. *Robertson* (1875) 2 R. (H.L.) 80; *Nicol* v. *Bell*, 1954 S.L.T. 314.

[2] *X.* v. *Y.*, 1921, 1 S.L.T. 79.

[3] *Borthwick* v. *B.* (1896) 24 R. 211; cf. *Mackie* v. *M.*, 1917 S.C. 276.

[4] *Borthwick, supra.*

[5] *Wright* v. *Sharp* (1880) 7 R. 460. But contrast *Lenaghan* v. *Monkland Iron Co.* (1857) 19 D. 975; *Wallace* v. *Fife Coal Co.*, 1909 S.C. 682.

[6] *Williams* v. *Forsythe*, 1909, 2 S.L.T. 252; cf. *A.B.* v. *C.D.* (1901) 8 S.L.T. 406.

[7] *H.* v. *R.* (1844) 16 Sc. Jur. 576; *Longworth* v. *Yelverton* (1862) 1 M. 161; (1864) 2 M. (H.L.) 49.

void *ab initio*,[1] or that, being voidable, it should now be declared void.[2] In a declarator of nullity on the ground of prior subsisting marriage which was not registered, it is competent to include a conclusion for declarator that the defender was previously married to another named person.[3]

RELATIONS *STANTE MATRIMONIO*

The constitution of marriages effects substantial changes in the rights and duties of the spouses *inter se*.

Change of name

By modern custom a married woman usually takes the title Mrs. and substitutes her husband's surname for her own but there is no obligation to do this.[4] For legal purposes she is designated Mrs. [Christian names] [maiden surname] or [married surname]. Her husband's designation, if any, may be assumed with the rest of his name.

Husband's curatory

At common law a married woman fell under her husband's curatory and could sue or be sued only with his concurrence. But now this curatory exists only if, and so long as, she is in minority.[5] Neither spouse may represent the other in litigation.[6]

Litigation

Either spouse can sue or be sued alone, and the other incurs no liability merely by reason of marriage, but either may incur liability by taking control of the action.[7]

Obligations inter se

Spouses may contract with one another and sue each other for breach of contract.[8] Either may stand to the other in the relation of landlord to tenant and may eject the other from the house,[9] or

---

[1] See *infra*.
[2] See *infra*.
[3] *Courtin* v. *Elder*, 1930 S.C. 68.
[4] This is a modern practice under English influence: Seton, *Law and Practice of Heraldry*, 392.
[5] Married Women's Property (Sc.) Act, 1920, S. 2; cf. *Mullen* v. *March's Trs.*, 1920, 2 S.L.T. 372.
[6] *Gordon* v. *Nakeski-Cumming*, 1924 S.C. 939.
[7] *Swirles* v. *Isles*, 1930 S.C. 696.
[8] *Horsburgh* v. *H.*, 1949 S.C. 227.
[9] *MacLure* v. *M.*, 1911 S.C. 200; *Millar* v. *M.*, 1940 S.C. 56.

the relation of creditor to debtor and sue for repayment.[1] Each owes duties of care to the other and may now sue for injury or damage caused by breach thereof.[2] Neither is vicariously liable to a third party for the other's wrong,[3] unless the wrongdoing one were at the time acting as agent or servant of the other. One spouse may steal from the other,[4] or commit any other kind of crime against the other.

Property

At common law, by the *jus mariti*, a wife's whole moveable property passed automatically to her husband on marriage as his absolute property, including all moveables which she might acquire during the marriage, but excluding all items from which the *jus mariti* was excluded by the destination thereof.[5] The husband also acquired the *jus administrationis*, a right of management of the wife's heritable estate springing from his curatorial power over her.[6] Statute intervened in the nineteenth century; by the Conjugal Rights (Scotland) Amendment Act, 1861, Ss. 1–5, a wife deserted by her husband might obtain from the court a protection order which had the effect of a decree of separation, and thereafter she held, exclusive of the husband's rights, property acquired by her own industry or to which she succeeded or acquired right after desertion. Her property belongs to her as if unmarried. By S. 6, after decree of separation her property belonged to her as if unmarried. By S. 16 if a wife succeeded to property, the husband could not claim it except on condition of making therefrom a reasonable provision for the wife's maintenance and support, if claimed before the husband had obtained possession of the property.[7] By the Married Women's Property (Sc.) Act, 1877, S. 3 the husband's right was excluded from the wife's earnings in any employment or trade, or in business carried on under her own name, and from money or property acquired by the exercise of literary, artistic, or scientific skill.[8] The Married Women's Property (Scotland) Act, 1881, abolished the

[1] *Aitken* v. *A.*, 1954 S.L.T. (Sh. Ct.) 60.
[2] Law Reform (Husband and Wife) Act, 1962, overruling *Young* v. *Y.* (1903) 5 F. 330; *Harper* v. *H.*, 1929 S.C. 220; *Cameron* v. *Glasgow Corpn.*, 1936 S.C. (H.L.) 26.
[3] *Barr* v. *Neilson* (1868) 6 M. 651; *Milne* v. *Smiths* (1892) 20 R. 95.
[4] *Harper* v. *Adair*, 1945 J.C. 21.
[5] Stair I, 4, 17; Ersk. I, 6, 12; Bell, *Prin.* §1547, 1561; Fraser, *H. & W.*, I, 679.
[6] Bell, *Prin.* §1563.
[7] Bell, *Prin.* §1560A; Fraser, *H. & W.*, I, 831.
[8] Bell, *Prin.* §1560C.

jus mariti, vested the wife's whole moveable property in her as her separate estate, and excepted the income of such estate from the *jus administrationis*. The income of her heritage was also to belong to her alone.[1] The Married Women's Property (Scotland) Act, 1920, abolished the *jus administrationis*, and gave a married woman full power of disposal of her estate as if unmarried.

Wife's separate estate

Where a wife possessed funds exclusive of her husband's *jus mariti* and *jus administrationis* she could incur obligations personally in respect thereof, which were ineffectual against her husband.[2]

Paraphernalia

At common law a wife's paraphernalia were always her own property.[3] These were her clothing, jewellery, and personal trinkets.[4] The concept is now obsolete.

Liability for each other's debts

Under the *jus mariti* the husband acquired liability for his wife's ante-nuptial debts, whether or not he benefited from the marriage. Such debts included her liability to aliment her indigent parents,[5] or an illegitimate child.[6] By the 1877 Act, S. 4, this was limited to the value of property received through her,[7] and he is now no longer liable for her ante-nuptial debts at all.[8] By the 1881 Act, S. 1, a wife's moveable property, if placed in her name, was not liable for the husband's debts, but if lent or entrusted to the husband or inmixed with his funds, had to be treated as assets in the husband's bankruptcy, the wife having a claim to a dividend for her property.

Marriage-contracts

While the *jus mariti* and *jus administrationis* subsisted, it was common where the wife had, or might inherit, substantial

---

[1] Bell, *Prin.* §1560D.

[2] *Biggart* v. *City of Glasgow Bank* (1879) 6 R. 470.

[3] Ersk. I, 6, 15; Bell, *Prin.* §1554–9; *Craig* v. *Monteith* (1684) Mor. 5819; *Cameron* v. *McLean* (1876) 13 S.L.R. 278; *Young* v. *Johnson* (1880) 7 R. 760; *Sleigh* v. *S's J.F.* (1901) 9 S.L.T. 35.

[4] *Dicks* v. *Massie* (1655) Mor. 5821; *Cameron* v. *McLean* (1870) 13 S.L.R. 278.

[5] *Reid* v. *Moir* (1866) 4 M. 1060; *Foulis* v. *Fairbairn* (1887) 14 R. 1088.

[6] *Aitken* v. *Anderson* (1815) Hume 217.

[7] Bell, *Prin.* §1570–3; *McAllan* v. *Alexander* (1888) 15 R. 863; *Dear* v. *Duncan* (1896) 3 S.L.T. 241.

[8] Married Women's Property (Sc.) Act, 1920, S. 3(1).

property, for the spouses and their parents to enter into ante-nuptial or post-nuptial marriage contracts whereby property was assigned to trustees to be held for the wife or the survivor of the spouses and the children of the marriage on such terms as might be arranged, exclusive of the husband's rights. The necessity for such arrangements has largely disappeared and they are now much less common. Such contracts commonly provide provisions to a surviving spouse and children in lieu of legal rights.[1]

Wife as husband's agent

A wife may act as her husband's agent and render him liable on contracts concluded by her, either where she had actual or express authority to act as such, either generally or in regard to particular kinds of transactions only, or where such authority is held implied by a past course of dealings which has led persons to believe that the wife had authority.[2]

Agency of necessity

A wife also has an implied agency in case of necessity. This confers on her an implied power to pledge his credit and render him liable for necessary goods and services supplied to her.[3] It is founded on the husband's obligation to maintain his wife and children and arises if she is living apart, with her husband's consent or with reasonable cause, and is without means.[4] It does not arise if she was in receipt of an adequate allowance,[5] is in desertion of her husband, nor if she has separate estate. 'Necessaries' include food, clothing, lodging, medical care, and legal advice, even for proceedings against the husband,[6] unless the solicitor acted negligently, or knew, or could by ordinary reasonable inquiries, have ascertained that proceedings were unfounded.[7] The husband's liability arises only if the creditor intended to give credit to the husband, and not if he relied on the wife's credit exclusively or she incurred the obligation on her own behalf.[8]

---

[1] On legal rights, see Ch. 119, *infra*.

[2] *Slowey* v. *Robertson and Moir* (1865) 4 M. 1.

[3] Fraser, *H. & W.*, I, 638.

[4] M.W.P. (Sc.) Act, 1920, S. 3(2).

[5] *Star Stores Ltd.* v. *Joss* [1955] C.L.Y. 3288.

[6] *McAlister* v. *McA.* (1762) Mor. 4036; *Macgregor* v. *Martin* (1867) 5 M. 583; *Clark* v. *Henderson* (1875) 2 R. 428; *Milne* v. *M.* (1885) 13 R. 304; *A.B.* v. *C.B.* (1906) 8 F. 973; *Warden* v. *W.*, 1962 S.C. 127; *Lawrie* v. *L.*, 1965 S.C. 49.

[7] *Robertson* v. *R.* (1881) 6 P.D. 119.

[8] Married Women's Property (Sc.) Act, 1920, S. 3(1).

Praepositura

More important is the agency presumed from cohabitation, that the wife, as *praeposita rebus domesticis*, has her husband's presumed authority to act as agent in all matters of household administration normally entrusted to a wife.[1] The wife's presumed authority to bind her husband extends only to contracts for necessaries, such goods and services as are necessary to maintain the home in the manner permitted by the husband, but not necessarily such as the wife deems desirable or appropriate to her station in life. The presumption arises notwithstanding that the wife has separate estate, and though the wife was given money for household purposes, but it does not extend to transactions unconnected with management of the household, in which the husband's credit is not relied on.[2] It does not extend to receiving notice to quit premises leased.[3] The onus is on the creditor to prove that the articles or services supplied were necessaries, suitable to the style of living adopted by the husband.[4] A similar presumption arises where the household management is in the hands of a sister, daughter, or housekeeper.[5] The husband may rebut the presumption by showing that he had made a sufficient allowance and had not in fact authorized the contract in question[6] but it is strengthened if in fact the husband had paid previous accounts and not intimated to the supplier that he was not to give the wife credit in future.[7]

The husband may terminate his wife's presumed authority by express intimation to suppliers,[8] but not by general advertisement that he will not be responsible for debts unless personally contracted, unless he proves that this had come to the supplier's knowledge.[9] He may terminate it formally by executing Letters of Inhibition against her, which are deemed published to the world when recorded in the Register of Inhibitions and Adjudications and are effective though not known to the supplier.[10] But such

[1] Stair, More's Notes xxii; Ersk. I, 6, 20; Bell, *Prin.* §1565; *Debenham* v. *Mellon* (1880) 6 App. Cas. 24.
[2] *Arnot* v. *Stevenson* (1698) Mor. 6017.   [3] *Lambert* v. *Smith* (1864) 3 M. 43.
[4] *Phillipson* v. *Hayter* (1870) L.R. 6 C.P. 38.
[5] Ersk. I, 6, 26; Bell, *Comm.* I, 479; *Prin.* §1565; *Hamilton* v. *Forrester* (1825) 3 S. 572.
[6] *Morel* v. *Westmorland* [1904] A.C. 11.
[7] *Jolly* v. *Rees* (1864) 15 C.B. (N.S.) 628.
[8] *Buie* v. *Gordon* (1831) 9 S. 923; *Jolly, supra*; *Debenham* v. *Mellon* (1880) 6 App. Cas. 24.
[9] *Hodge* v. *Cooper* (1841) 10 L.J.C.P. 218. He is not entitled to advertise unless he had *bona fide* ground for believing that the wife intended to pledge his credit; *Vickers* v. *V.*, 1966 S.L.T. (Notes) 69.
[10] *Topham* v. *Marshall* (1808) Mor. Appx. Inhibition, 2.

action cannot relieve the husband of his duty to aliment his wife, so that she may, notwithstanding the inhibition, pledge his credit for necessaries.[1] The husband may, notwithstanding the inhibition, ratify or acquiesce in her contracts and thereby bar himself from pleading the inhibition.[2]

Housekeeping allowance

Where a husband allows his wife a periodical lump sum for housekeeping and similar expenses, she administers the money as his agent and has no right, unless authorized, to keep any periodical balance for herself. Any balance, savings made therefrom, or property purchased with such savings, in the absence of contrary agreement, belong to the husband.[3] Contributions made by adult children must be deemed to have been made in consideration of maintenance and similarly fall to the husband.[4] If the wife makes money from keeping boarders in the husband's house, the profits belong to him.[5] Money remitted to the wife for her maintenance belongs, so far as unspent, to the husband.[6] If the wife maintains herself or the household out of funds of her own, she does not acquire any right to the unspent allowance.[7] The Married Women's Property Act, 1964, provides that money derived from any allowance made by the husband[8] for the expenses of the matrimonial home or for similar purposes,[9] or property acquired out of such money, shall, in the absence of contrary agreement, be treated as belonging to the husband and wife in equal shares.[10]

Moveable property in matrimonial home

Moveable property in the matrimonial home belongs to the spouse who brought it into the home, whose funds paid for it, or

---

[1] Stair I, 4, 17; Ersk. I, 6, 26; *Gordon* v. *Sempill* (1776) Mor. Appx. Husband and Wife, 4.

[2] *Ker* v. *Gibson* (1709) Mor. 6023.

[3] *Henry* v. *Fraser* (1906) 14 S.L.T. 164; *Dryden* v. *McGibbon*, 1907 S.C. 1131; *Smith* v. *S.*, 1933 S.C. 701; *Blackwell* v. *B.* [1943] 2 All E.R. 579; *Hoddinott* v. *H.* [1949] 2 K.B. 406; *Preston* v. *P.*, 1950 S.C. 253; *Ireland* v. *I.*, 1954 S.L.T. (Notes) 14; cf. *McGinty* v. *McAlpine* (1892) 19 R. 935; *Dryden* v. *McGibbon*, 1907 S.C. 1131.

[4] *Smith, supra*; *Johnson* v. *J's Trs.*, 1949 S.L.T. (Notes) 36, 40.

[5] *Horsburgh* v. *H.*, 1949 S.L.T. 357.

[6] *Logan* v. *L.*, 1920 S.C. 537; *Preston, supra*.

[7] *Preston, supra*, 257.

[8] The provision is inapplicable where the wife provides the money and the husband does the housekeeping.

[9] Held not to include money out of which mortgage repayments were made: *Tymoszczuk* v. *T.* (1964) 108 Sol. Jo. 676.

[10] On the death of one spouse that spouse's share will fall into his estate, not go to the surviving spouse. See also *Pyatt* v. *P.*, 1966 S.L.T. (Notes) 73.

by whom the property is exclusively used. There is no presumption that furniture must be presumed joint property, if bought by one.[1] But some articles, e.g. wedding presents, may be deemed to belong to the spouses jointly.

Heritable property

Where title to heritable property is taken in the joint names of husband and wife they are deemed joint proprietors; if survivorship be expressed, the survivor has the benefit of accretion.[2] The spouse paying the price in such a case has been held entitled by will to evacuate the destination *quoad* his own *pro indiviso* share only.[3] Though title is taken in the name of one spouse only, if the price was borrowed on the security of the obligations of both, each has an equal half-share in the profits on sale.[4] It may be proved, but only by writ or oath, that heritable property in the name of one was held in trust for the other.[5]

Donations between spouses

At common law donations between spouses during the marriage were revocable by the donor; but they are now irrevocable, though any donation made within a year and a day before sequestration of the donor's estate is revocable at the instance of his creditors.[6] In case of dispute the donee has to establish delivery sufficient to evidence gift and circumstances showing *animus donandi*.[7]

Personal allowance

A husband normally provides for his wife, while living with him, by the *praepositura*, but may also make a personal allowance to her for her own use, independently thereof. Such falls to be regarded as periodical donations, and become her absolute property.

Wife's earnings

A wife's earnings are her own absolute property. Though she is now obliged to aliment her indigent husband,[8] there seems to

---

[1] *Harper* v. *Adair*, 1945 J.C. 21.

[2] *Walker* v. *Galbraith* (1895) 23 R. 347. For more complicated destinations see Fraser, *H. & W.*, II, 1428; Craigie, *Heritable*, 567.

[3] *Hay's Tr.* v. *Hay's Trs.*, 1951 S.C. 329.   [4] *McDougall* v. *M.*, 1947 S.N. 102.

[5] *Adam* v. *A.*, 1962 S.L.T. 332; cf. *Galloway* v. *G.*, 1929 S.C. 160; *Weissenbruch* v. *W.*, 1961 S.C. 340.

[6] Married Women's Property (Sc.) Act, 1920, S. 5.

[7] *Donald* v. *D.*, 1953 S.L.T. (Sh. Ct.) 69.

[8] Married Women's Property (Sc.) Act, 1920, S. 4.

be no legal duty in other circumstances on her to maintain the common home or even to contribute to its cost.[1] Nor is she apparently bound to support the children if the husband is alive but is unable himself to do so, and if she does she probably has a claim against the husband's estate for relief when he can repay her.[2] If, however, the husband dies, she is bound to aliment the children.[3]

Where income pooled

Prima facie the income of each spouse, however earned, remains his or her private property. But if spouses pool the whole or part of their incomes they probably acquire a joint right of property in the fund, irrespective of the amounts contributed by each thereto,[4] the whole accrescing to the survivor on the death of either. Joint property is not, however, necessarily constituted by a bank account in joint names and on which either may draw, as such may be merely a convenient arrangement.[5] Property purchased from a joint fund will belong to the purchaser, unless it appears to be a joint investment, in which case it will be joint property. Thus a house bought by contributions from both spouses may be deemed joint property, each being entitled to half the proceeds on sale.[6]

Life insurance policies

Each spouse has an insurable interest in the life of the other, and may insure the other's life and recover on the other's death without proof of actual loss.[7] Under the Married Women's Policies of Assurance (Sc.) Act, 1880, a policy of assurance effected by a married man[8] on his own life and expressed to be for the benefit of his wife or children[9] or wife and children[9] shall be deemed a trust for her or them, and vest in him or any trustee appointed, and shall not otherwise be subject to his control, or

[1] *Preston* v. *P.*, 1950 S.C. 253, 257; cf. *Fingzies* v. *F.* (1890) 28 S.L.R. 6.

[2] See Stair I, 5, 7; More's Notes, xxix; Bankt. I, 6, 15; Ersk. I, 6, 56; Fraser, *P. & Ch.*, 100.

[3] Fraser, *supra.*

[4] cf. *Jones* v. *Maynard* [1951] Ch. 572.

[5] *Marshal* v. *Crutwell* (1875) L.R. 20 Eq. 328.

[6] cf. *Rimmer* v. *R.* [1953] 1 Q.B. 63; *Cobb* v. *C.* [1955] 2 All E.R. 696. See also *Fribance* v. *F.* [1957] 1 All E.R. 357.

[7] *Griffiths* v. *Fleming* [1909] 1 K.B. 805.

[8] Including a widower: *Kennedy's Trs.* v. *Sharpe* (1895) 23 R. 146. As to man about to be married see *Coulson's Trs.* v. *C.* (1901) 3 F. 1041.

[9] Including illegitimate children: Family Law Reform Act, 1969, S. 19.

form part of his estate,[1] or be liable to the diligence of his creditors,[2] or be revocable as a donation, or reducible on any ground of excess or insolvency, though if it is proved that the policy was effected and the premiums paid with intent to defraud creditors, or the husband be made bankrupt within two years from the date of the policy, the creditors may claim repayment of the premiums from the trustee of the policy out of the proceeds thereof. Such a policy may be surrendered at any time by the trustee with the wife's concurrence.[3]

DUTIES TO EACH OTHER

Duties to each other—aliment

The husband is bound to aliment his wife, and furnish her with necessary food, clothing, and lodging, so long as the marriage endures.[4] This obligation is normally satisfied by maintaining her in family with him, or by providing a home and money during his necessary absence. It subsists even if she has been guilty of cruelty for which he has obtained decree of separation,[5] or she has committed adultery[6] or has been put out of the house,[7] or is with just cause living in separation from the husband by reason of the desertion or other conduct of the husband,[8] so long as she is willing to adhere[8] but not if she has left him without legal justification and refuses to adhere.[9] She is entitled to an award of aliment if she has obtained decree of adherence and aliment, so long as her husband refuses to adhere, or decree of separation and aliment, so long as the separation stands unrevoked,[10] or if the spouses have separated by consent, or if she has justification for divorce and has withdrawn from cohabita-

---

[1] cf. *Walker's Trs.* v. *L.A.*, 1955 S.C. (H.L.) 74. But see *Sharp's Trs.* v. *L.A.*, 1951 S.C. 442, where husband retained contingent interest, and Finance Act, 1968, Ss. 37–38, limiting amounts.

[2] *Chrystal's Trs.* v. *C.*, 1912 S.C. 1003.

[3] *Schumann* v. *Scottish Widows Fund* (1886) 13 R. 678.

[4] *Donnelly* v. *D.*, 1959 S.C. 97.

[5] *Nisbet* v. *N.* (1896) 4 S.L.T. 142.

[6] Fraser, *H. & W.*, 644; *Milne* v. *M.* (1901) 8 S.L.T. 375; *Donnelly* v. *D.*, 1959 S.C. 97; *Harkness* v. *H.* (1961) 77 Sh. Ct. Rep. 165.

[7] *Croall* v. *C.* (1832) 11 S. 185; *McMillan* v. *M.* (1870) 9 M. 1067; *MacLure* v. *M.*, 1911 S.C. 200; *Donnelly, supra.*

[8] Divorce (Sc.) Act, 1964, S. 6, altering *Jack* v. *J.*, 1962 S.C. 24; *Barbour* v. *B.*, 1965 S.C. 158; *Barr* v. *B.*, 1968 S.L.T. (Sh. Ct.) 37.

[9] *Bell* v. *B.*, 22 Feb. 1812, F.C.; *Coutts* v. *C.* (1866) 4 M. 802; *Cameron* v. *C.*, 1956 S.L.T. (Notes) 7; *Beveridge* v. *B.*, 1963 S.C. 572.

[10] cf. *Lawson* v. *Bain* (1830) 8 S. 923.

tion,[1] even if no longer willing to adhere.[2] A sufficient answer to her claim is an offer to entertain her at bed and board, if *bona fide* and reasonable in the circumstances.[3]

A wife is bound to aliment her husband only if he be indigent[4] Persons do not by marriage assume liability to aliment the spouse's relatives,[5] nor acquire rights to aliment against the spouse's relatives.[6] The sanction for wilful failure to pay aliment due under a decree is civil imprisonment at the instance of the pursuer holding the decree.[7]

Interim awards of aliment may be made to a wife *pendente lite*,[8] but this is inexpedient, if not incompetent, in a declarator of marriage where the marriage is denied.[9]

Interim aliment alone may be claimed by a wife, justifiably expelled from the house by her husband, so long as he refuses to receive her back,[10] but is normally conjoined with a claim for adherence, being due failing adherence and so long as non-adherence continues, or a claim for separation, being due so long as the separation stands unrevoked.[11] Decrees for aliment consequential on the decision of an issue of adherence or separation are permanent, though subject to review at the instance of either party if financial circumstances change.[12] There is no rule that a wife earning money must expend the whole of it on her maintenance to the relief of her husband's obligation under a decree for aliment.[13] Aliment should be calculated by reference to the husband's gross

---

[1] *Scott* v. *Selbie* (1835) 13 S. 278; *McFarlane* v. *McF.* (1844) 6 D. 1220; *Fyffe* v. *F.*, 1954 S.C. 1; Divorce (Sc.) Act, 1964, S. 6; *Barr* v. *B.*, 1968 S.L.T. (Sh. Ct.) 37.

[2] *Stirling* v. *S.*, 1971 S.L.T. 322.

[3] *Paterson* v. *P.* (1861) 24 D. 215. For inadequate offers see *Arthur* v. *Gourley* (1769) 2 Pat. 184; *Reid* v. *R.* (1823) 2 S. 468.

[4] *Fingzies* v. *F.* (1890) 28 S.L.R. 6; Married Women's Property (Sc.) Act, 1920, S. 4; *Adair* v. *A.*, 1924 S.C. 798.

[5] *McAllan* v. *Alexander* (1888) 15 R. 863 (wife's mother); *Dear* v. *Duncan* (1896) 3 S.L.T. 241 (wife's father).

[6] *Hoseason* v. *H.* (1870) 9 M. 37; *Reid* v. *R.* (1897) in 6 F. 935; *Mackay* v. *M.'s Trs.* (1904) 6 F. 936 (against father-in-law).

[7] *Macdonald* v. *Denoon*, 1929 S.C. 172; *Brunt* v. *B.*, 1954 S.L.T. (Sh. Ct.) 74; *Cassells* v. *C.*, 1955 S.L.T. (Sh. Ct.) 41; *McWilliams* v. *McW.*, 1963 S.C. 259.

[8] *Macfarlane* v. *M.* (1844) 6 D. 1220; *Borthwick* v. *B.* (1848) 10 D. 1312; *Hoey* v. *H.* (1883) 11 R. 25; *A.D.* v. *W.D.*, 1909, 1 S.L.T. 342; *Pirrie* v. *P.* (1903) 10 S.L.T. 598; *Robertson* v. *R.* (1905) 13 S.L.T. 114; *Barbour* v. *B.*, 1965 S.C. 158.

[9] *Murison* v. *M.*, 1923 S.C. 40.

[10] *Pearce* v. *P.* (1898) 5 S.L.T. 338; *Gatchell* v. *G.* (1898) 6 S.L.T. 224; *Hicks* v. *H.* (1899) 6 S.L.T. 261; *Milne* v. *M.* (1901) 8 S.L.T. 375; *Donnelly* v. *D.*, 1959 S.C. 97.

[11] *Williamson* v. *W.* (1860) 22 D. 599; see also *Adair* v. *A.*, 1924 S.C. 798.

[12] *Donald* v. *D.* (1862) 24 D. 499; *Christie* v. *C.*, 1919 S.C. 576; *Adair* v. *A.*, 1932 S.N. 47, 69; *Donnelly, supra.*

[13] *Dowswell* v. *D.*, 1943 S.C. 23.

income and be made 'less tax'.[1] It is incompetent to seek, or for the court to grant, decree for aliment to be paid in all time coming.[2] The Maintenance Orders Act, 1950, S. 6, confers jurisdiction on the sheriff if (a) the husband resides in England or Northern Ireland; and (b) the parties last ordinarily resided as spouses in Scotland; and (c) the pursuer resides within the sheriff's jurisdiction.[3] Orders made under this Act are registrable and enforceable in England or Northern Ireland under Part II thereof.

Statutory duty to aliment

By statute, for the purposes of the Act,[4] each spouse is liable to maintain the other spouse and his or her children, and a man to maintain children his paternity of whom has been admitted or established, and a woman to maintain her illegitimate children. It is a criminal offence persistently to refuse or neglect to do so.[5] Where assistance is given by the Supplementary Benefits Commission or a local authority the court may order the person liable to maintain the person assisted to pay such sum as the court considers appropriate.[6]

Duties to each other—adherence

The spouses should adhere to each other, and cohabit at bed and board. The husband has the prior right to determine the place of the matrimonial home, and the prior duty to provide it. The wife must accompany him there, provided it is reasonably suitable in the circumstances.[7] He may insist on her living in a house provided for her separate use,[8] and, if he offers aliment, have her ejected from his house and interdicted from returning.[9] A wife may now act similarly towards her husband if the house is hers.[10] But refusal to receive her into his house, if persisted in without reasonable cause for three years, would be desertion justifying divorce.[11]

[1] *Thomson* v. *T.*, 1943 S.C. 154.

[2] *Duncan* v. *Forbes* (1878) 15 S.L.R. 371; *Brunt* v. *B.*, 1958 S.L.T. (Notes) 41.

[3] cf. *Plant* v. *P.*, 1963 S.L.T. (Sh. Ct.) 58.

[4] National Assistance Act, 1948, Ss. 42–43, amd. Min. of Social Security Act, 1966, S. 39.

[5] *Corcoran* v. *Muir*, 1954 J.C. 46.

[6] *Supplementary Benefits Commission* v. *Black*, 1968 S.L.T. (Sh. Ct.) 90.

[7] Stair I, 4, 8; *Muir* v. *M.* (1879) 6 R. 1353; *Young* v. *Y.*, 1947 S.L.T. 5. But see *Martin* v. *M.*, 1956 S.L.T. (Notes) 41.

[8] *Colquhoun* v. *C.* (1804) Mor. Appx. Husband and Wife, 5.

[9] *MacLure* v. *M.*, 1911 S.C. 200.

[10] *MacLure, supra*; *Millar* v. *M.*, 1940 S.C. 56. [11] See *infra*.

If either spouse ceases to adhere without adequate legal justification the other may seek to enforce the obligation by an action of adherence, calling on the other to adhere. Such an action requires that the pursuer be willing to adhere,[1] and it is accordingly inconsistent with an action of divorce.[2] The only relevant defences to such an action are averments of such conduct as would justify separation or divorce at the defender's instance,[3] or of certain lesser matrimonial wrongs.[4] The duty to adhere is not specifically enforceable and the action of adherence is now, if brought by the wife, always combined with an alternative crave, until or failing adherence, for aliment. The amount of aliment depends on the circumstances of the case, but should be enough to enable the wife reasonably to support herself.[5] In determining the amount of aliment regard should be had to gross income, and the award made 'less tax'.[6] Only the husband's legal obligation of support should be considered and not payments to another woman.[7] If the defender in defence offers to adhere, an opportunity should be given to test the genuineness of the offer[8] before decree is granted. If bona fide it is a good defence.[9] If the pursuer refuses the defender's offer to adhere and the offer was genuine and included an adequate offer of accommodation, the pursuer is in desertion from that date.[10] A pursuer is not entitled to aliment if not willing to adhere,[11] and is not entitled to qualify his or her willingness to adhere by a condition, such as that the defender give up a friendship with another person which is not proved to be illicit.[12]

---

[1] Beveridge v. B., 1963 S.C. 572.

[2] Farquharson v. F., 1968 S.L.T. (Sh. Ct.) 45.

[3] Mackenzie v. M. (1895) 22 R. (H.L.) 32. See also A.B. v. C.B., 1937 S.C. 408, 696.

[4] Hastings v. H., 1941 S.L.T. 323; Hamilton v. H., 1953 S.C. 383; Richardson v. R., 1956 S.C. 394.

[5] Thomson v. T., 1951 S.L.T. (Sh. Ct.) 56.

[6] Thomson v. T., 1943 S.C. 154; but see Alexander v. A., 1957 S.L.T. 298. On the sanction for wilful non-payment of aliment see McWilliams v. McW., 1963 S.C. 259.

[7] McCarroll v. McC., 1966 S.L.T. (Sh. Ct.) 45; Hawthorne v. H., 1966 S.L.T. (Sh. Ct.) 47. The husband's duty to illegitimate children by another woman must be considered: McAuley v. McA., 1968 S.L.T. (Sh. Ct.) 81.

[8] Macdonald v. M. (1903) 10 S.L.T. 578; Samson v. S. (1925) 41 Sh. Ct. Rep. 251; Bisset v. B., 1933 S.C. 764; Coyle v. C., 1950 S.L.T. (Notes) 22; Martin v. M., 1956 S.L.T. (Notes) 41.

[9] Paterson v. P. (1861) 24 D. 215; Hood v. H. (1871) 9 M. 449; Brown v. B., 1970 S.L.T. (Notes) 79.

[10] Darroch v. D., 1947 S.C. 110.

[11] Cameron v. C., 1956 S.L.T. (Notes) 7; Beveridge v. B., 1963 S.C. 572.

[12] Burnett v. B., 1958 S.C. 1.

Either party is relieved of the duty to adhere if the other has been guilty of such conduct as would justify an action of divorce against him or her,[1] or of certain lesser matrimonial wrongs,[2] or if either has obtained a decree of separation. There is no duty to adhere if the marriage were void *ab initio*,[3] and it is ended if a voidable marriage is declared void.[4]

Deserted spouse's title to matrimonial home

If one spouse has been deserted and left in occupation of the former matrimonial home, the other spouse, if owner of the home,[5] may eject the deserted spouse[6] so long as the permission to occupy does not amount to a tenancy.[7] If the deserting spouse was tenant of a house subject to the Rent Acts he cannot on desertion confer on his spouse any right to remain in occupation.[8]

Voluntary separation

Parties may by agreement separate and live apart, but the courts will not enforce any contract providing for this,[9] though an agreement to make financial provision for an already agreed separation is enforceable.[10] Any such agreement is at any time revocable by agreement, or by either party calling on the other to adhere,[11] if accompanied by *bona fide* intention to adhere and, if made by the husband, by a genuine offer of a home.[12] Despite separation the husband is still liable to aliment his wife, and this is frequently provided for in a separation agreement.[13] The wife may sue for arrears of aliment due thereunder,[14] and for interim aliment for the future, but the court will not grant decree for the future if the husband *bona fide* offers to take her back,[15] and in

---

[1] *Mackenzie v. M.* (1895) 22 R. (H.L.) 33.

[2] *Hastings v. H.*, 1941 S.L.T. 323; *Hamilton v. H.*, 1953 S.C. 383; *Richardson v. R.*, 1956 S.C. 394; *McMillan v. McM.*, 1962 S.C. 115.

[3] *Jack v. J.*, 1940 S.L.T. 122.

[4] *Allardyce v. A.*, 1954 S.C. 419.

[5] As to spouses' joint title, see *Cairns v. Halifax Bldg. Soc.*, 1951 S.L.T. (Sh. Ct.) 67.

[6] *Millar v. M.*, 1940 S.C. 56; *Scott v. S.* (1948) 64 Sh. Ct. Rep. 119; *Macpherson v. M.*, 1950 S.L.T. (Sh. Ct.) 24; *McLeod v. McL.*, 1958 S.L.T. (Sh. Ct.) 31.

[7] *Donachie v. D.* (1948) 64 Sh. Ct. Rep. 120; cf. *Labno v. L.*, 1949 S.L.T. (Notes) 18.

[8] *Temple v. Mitchell*, 1956 S.C. 267.

[9] *Macdonald v. M's Trs.* (1863) 1 M. 1065.

[10] *Webster v. W's Trs.* (1886) 14 R. 90; *Scott v. S.* (1894) 21 R. 853.

[11] Ersk. I, 6, 30, Fraser *H. & W.* II, 911; *A.B. v. C.D.* (1853) 16 D. 111; *Macdonald, supra.* cf. *Barr v. B.*, 1939 S.C. 696.

[12] *Adair v. A.*, 1932 S.N. 47, 69.

[13] *Davidson v. D.* (1867) 5 M. 710; *Jameson v. J.* (1886) 23 S.L.R. 402; *Thomson v. T.* (1890) 17 R. 1091; *Scott v. S.* (1894) 21 R. 853; *Campbell v. C.*, 1923 S.L.T. 670.

[14] *Malcolm v. Mack* (1805) Hume 2.

[15] *Hood v. H.* (1871) 9 M. 449; *Bonnar v. B.*, 1911 S.C. 854; *Douglas v. D.*, 1932 S.C. 680.

such an action may try the issue whether or not a decree of separation would have been warranted, if the husband pleads that the contract was not binding.[1] The amount of aliment fixed by agreement may be revised by the court as if it had been fixed by decree.[2] If aliment exceeds what is necessary for maintenance the wife may keep the excess.[3]

Judicial separation[4]

The court may on the application of one spouse permit them to cease cohabitation and order the defender to separate himself from the pursuer. The effect of such a decree is to leave the marriage standing,[5] but relieve parties of the obligation of adherence, and the main justification has been the protection of the pursuer from the defender's conduct.[6] An action by an insane wife is incompetent.[7] A conclusion for interdict against the defender molesting the pursuer may be added.[8]

It may be granted only on the grounds of adultery, or of cruelty. The requisites of adultery are the same as must be proved to justify divorce,[9] and the same defences are competent as in an action for divorce.[10] The requisites of cruelty are the same as were required to justify divorce prior to the Divorce (Sc.) Act, 1964.[11] Cruelty includes habitual drunkenness[12] and causing harm to health by excessive drinking even if not amounting to statutory habitual drunkenness.[13] Cruelty established by a wife in defence to an action for divorce for her desertion is not res judicata entitling her to separation and aliment.[14] The pursuer's own adultery

---

[1] Campbell, supra.

[2] Scott, supra; McKeddie v. McK. (1902) 9 S.L.T. 381.

[3] Davidson, supra; Henry v. Fraser (1907) 14 S.L.T. 164; Preston v. P., 1950 S.C. 253.

[4] This is the old divortium a mensa et thoro or separatio quoad thorum of the canon law which did not admit of divorce a vinculo matrimonii. It was continued after and notwithstanding the Reformation by the Scottish courts.

[5] cf. Shirrefs v. S. (1896) 23 R. 807.

[6] Adair v. A., 1924 S.L.T. 749.

[7] Thomson v. T. (1887) 14 R. 634.

[8] Gunn v. G., 1955 S.L.T. (Notes) 69.

[9] See infra; cf. Hall v. H., 1958 S.C. 206.

[10] Watson v. W. (1874) 12 S.L.R. 78; Graham v. G. (1878) 5 R. 1093; Smeaton v. S. (1900) 2 F. 837; Smith v. S. (1904) 12 S.L.T. 341; Paterson v. P., 1938 S.C. 251; Richards v. R., 1939 S.C. 554.

[11] McLachlan v. McL., 1945 S.C. 382; Jack v. J., 1962 S.C. 24; Boyd v. B., 1968 S.L.T. (Sh. Ct.) 17. S. 4 of the 1964 Act does not apply to actions for separation for cruelty: hence the need for future protection of the pursuer is still relevant in separation cases.

[12] Habitual Drunkards Act, 1879, S. 3; Licensing (Sc.) Act, 1903, S. 73; Cox v. C., 1942 S.C. 352; Hutchison v. H., 1945 S.C. 427.

[13] Hutchison, supra.

[14] Stevens v. S. (1882) 9 R. 730.

does not bar an action,[1] nor does the existence of a voluntary separation agreement.[2] The grant of judicial separation does not prejudice a subsequent action for divorce on the same ground and alleging the same facts,[3] and a separation may be brought while divorce is pending.[4] It has been held incompetent to refuse separation merely because the defender had given an undertaking to refrain from further cruelty.[5] A husband may obtain decree of separation but remains liable to aliment his wife.[6] A decree lapses if parties resume cohabitation but the pursuer may later again seek decree of separation if there are fresh grounds.[7]

A claim for separation, if brought by the wife, is normally conjoined with one for aliment for the pursuer and her children.[8] Any such award is *ad interim* and either party may apply for it to be increased or restricted in view of changed circumstances.[9] If the wife has separate income it must be taken into account,[10] and where it was as great as that of the husband aliment has been refused.[11] There is no rule that a wife earning money must spend it all on her maintenance to the relief of her husband's obligation to aliment her.[12] It is incompetent to award aliment for a past period even though the pursuer had had to rely on charity because the wife could have pledged her husband's credit in case of need.[13]

If the wife is maintaining a child or children of the marriage she is entitled to aliment for them also.[14] The decree will not be recalled by the court on averments by the defender that the pursuer no longer needs the protection it affords,[15] but the decree

---

[1] *Taylor* v. *T.* (1903) 11 S.L.T. 487.

[2] *Martin* v. *M.* (1895) 3 S.L.T. 150.

[3] *Stewart* v. *S.* (1906) 8 F. 769; *Summers* v. *S.*, 1935 S.C. 537; Divorce (Sc.) Act, 1938, S. 4; *Wilson* v. *W.*, 1939 S.C. 102; *McFarlane* v. *McF.*, 1951 S.C. 530.

[4] *Stewart*, *supra*.

[5] *Dawson* v. *D.*, 1925 S.C. 221.

[6] *Nisbet* v. *N.* (1896) 4 S.L.T. 142; see also *Hastings* v. *H.*, 1941 S.L.T. 323.

[7] *Donachie* v. *D.*, 1965 S.L.T. (Sh. Ct.) 18.

[8] On amount of aliment see *Lang* v. *L.* (1868) 7 M. 24; *Wotherspoon* v. *W.* (1869) 8 M. 81; *Maitland* v. *M.*, 1912, 1. S.L.T. 350.

[9] *Hay* v. *H.* (1882) 9 R. 667; *Stewart* v. *S.* (1886) 13 R. 1052; (1887) 15 R. 113; *Purdom* v. *P.*, 1934 S.L.T. 315; *Dowswell* v. *D.*, 1943 S.C. 23. On interim aliment pending appeal see *Cunningham* v. *C.*, 1965 S.C. 78.

[10] *Overbeck-Wright* v. *O.W.*, 1929 S.L.T. 653.

[11] *Thacker* v. *T.*, 1928 S.L.T. 248.

[12] *Dowswell* v. *D.*, 1943 S.C. 23.

[13] *McMillan* v. *M.* (1871) 9 M. 1067; *Smith* v. *S's Trs.* (1882) 19 S.L.R. 552; *Bruce* v. *B.*, 1945 S.C. 353.

[14] cf. *Hay* v. *H.* (1882) 9 R. 667; *Scott* v. *S.* (1894) 21 R. 853.

[15] *Strain* v. *S.* (1890) 17 R. 297.

lapses if cohabitation is resumed by common consent. If one spouse offers to adhere, the other must at least test the genuineness of the offer.[1]

A wife who holds a decree of separation may hold and dispose of all property which she may acquire, as if unmarried, and on her death intestate her property passes to her heirs on intestacy as if her husband were dead.[2]

Rights on death

Each spouse, by marriage, acquires rights to certain proportions of the other spouse's estate on the latter's predecease, testate or intestate, and to provisions from the latter's estate, if dying intestate.[3]

NULLITY OF MARRIAGE

A petition for declarator of nullity of marriage may be brought either on the ground that the marriage is void, or that it is voidable.[4] In either case the decree declares that a seeming marriage has never had legal existence and that the parties have never had the status of married persons; but a void marriage is, and has been *ab initio*, a nullity and the declarator is necessary only to determine and record that fact, whereas a voidable marriage, despite its inherent flaw, is good until or unless set aside by declarator, which, when granted, has retrospective effect.[5] Decree of nullity of a void marriage makes no change in status, but merely declares authoritatively that the parties have never been married, whereas decree of nullity of a voidable marriage causes the status of married parties to revert to that of single persons. A void marriage cannot be ratified or approbated; a voidable marriage can. A decree of nullity is a judgment *in rem*.[6]

Grounds on which marriage is void ab initio

A marriage may be declared void on any of the following grounds:[7] (a) legal incapacity of either party to marry by reason of

---

[1] *Fletcher* v. *Young*, 1936 S.L.T. 572.
[2] Conjugal Rights Amdt. (Sc.) Act, 1861, S. 6.
[3] Chs. 119–20, *infra*.
[4] *S.G.* v. *W.G.*, 1933 S.C. 728; see also *F.* v. *F.*, 1945 S.C. 202.
[5] Stair I, 4, 6; Bankt. I, 5, 27; Ersk. I, 6, 7; *F.* v. *F.*, *supra*, 211.
[6] *Administrator of Austrian Property* v. *Von Lorang*, 1927 S.C. (H.L.) 80.
[7] cf. Fraser, *H. & W.*, I, 51–79, 105–39.

non-age;[1] (b) unsoundness of mind;[2] (c) existing marriage;[3] (d) impediment of consanguinity or affinity;[4] (e) failure to comply with formalities of marriage;[5] or (f) absence of true consent to marriage by reason of e.g. intoxication, intimidation, or error as to the other party or the nature of the ceremony.[6] It does not follow that any or every failure in the formalities of marriage will result in nullity. In some cases, such as non-registration, the only sanction will be a penalty for non-compliance.

Ground on which marriage is voidable

The sole ground on which a marriage is voidable is the sexual impotence of either spouse,[7] which consists in total physical incapacity for sexual intercourse, or in invincible repugnance to and revulsion from intercourse with that partner,[8] existing at, and continuously since, the date of the 'marriage', and wholly preventing consummation. Till consummation, by intercourse after the marriage, the 'marriage' is voidable. The defect of impotence is not a flaw making the marriage void *ab initio* but rather a resolutive condition invalidating the marriage retrospectively.[9] Hence the spouses may waive the objection. Either spouse may petition, and on the ground of his or her own,[10] or the other spouse's,[11] impotence, or the impotence of either alternatively,[12] but the plea is personal to the spouses and cannot be raised by a third party having a patrimonial interest.[13] A person

---

[1] *Johnston* v. *Ferrier* (1770) Mor. 8931; *A.B.* v. *C.D.*, 1957 S.C. 415.

[2] *Graham* v. *G.* (1907) 15 S.L.T. 33; *A.B.* v. *C.D.* (1908) 15 S.L.T. 911; *Park* v. *P.*, 1914, 1 S.L.T. 88; *Calder* v. *C.*, 1942 S.N. 40.

[3] *Ballantyne* v. *B.* (1866) 4 M. 494; *Mackenzie* v. *Macfarlane* (1891) 5 S.L.T. 292; *Macdonald* v. *Parkinson* (1905) 12 S.L.T. 710; *Courtin* v. *Elder*, 1930 S.C. 68; *Bairner* v. *Fels*, 1931 S.C. 674; *Martin* v. *Buret*, 1938 S.L.T. 479; *Aldridge* v. *A.*, 1954 S.C. 58; *Balshaw* v. *B.*, 1967 S.C. 63.

[4] *Purves' Trs.* v. *P.* (1895) 22 R. 513.

[5] *Miller* v. *Deakin*, 1912, 1 S.L.T. 253; *Admin. of Austrian Property* v. *Von Lorang*, 1927 S.C. (H.L.) 80; *Bradley* v. *Mochrie*, 1947 S.L.T. (Notes) 27.

[6] *Brebner* v. *Bell* (1904) 12 S.L.T. 2; *McLeod* v. *Adams*, 1920, 1 S.L.T. 229; *Brady* v. *Murray*, 1933 S.L.T. 534; *Orlandi* v. *Castelli*, 1961 S.C. 113; *Balshaw* v. *B.*, 1967 S.C. 63.

[7] Stair I, 4, 6; Bankt. I, 5, 27, 56; Ersk. I, 6, 7; Bell, *Prin.* §1524; Fraser, *H. & W.* I, 80; *C.B.* v. *A.B.* (1885) 12 R. (H.L.) 36; *L.* v. *L.*, 1931 S.C. 477; *S.G.* v. *W.G.*, 1933 S.C. 728.

[8] *A.B.* v. *C.D.* (1903) 10 S.L.T. 266; *C.* v. *C.* [1921] P. 399; *G.* v. *G.*, 1924 S.C. (H.L.) 42.

[9] Fraser, *H. & W.*, I, 83; *Admin. of Austrian Property* v. *Von Lorang*, 1926 S.C. 598, 616.

[10] *F.* v. *F.*, 1945 S.C. 202; *H.* v. *H.*, 1949 S.C. 587. Such a pursuer must prove his or her defect to be irremediable.

[11] Stair I, 4, 6; Ersk. I, 6, 7; *A.B.* v. *C.B.* (1906) 8 F. 603; *G.* v. *G.*, 1924 S.C. (H.L.) 42.

[12] *M.* v. *M.*, 1967 S.L.T. 157.

[13] Bell, *Prin.* §1524; Fraser, *H. & W.*, I, 98.

may be impotent, either physically[1] or psychologically,[2] and *quoad* the present partner only, and not *quoad omnes*. If the ground is physical incapacity, the court must be satisfied that the defect is incurable,[3] and has been so for the whole duration of the 'marriage',[4] or not curable without danger to life or the infliction of unreasonable pain,[5] or that the impotent spouse is unlikely ever to submit to treatment.[6] If the evidence shows that an impotent defender may be cured, the defender, if willing, is entitled to an opportunity to undergo treatment.[7] Absence of evidence of structural defect does not preclude nullity, if the other circumstances indicate incapacity.[8] The petition is barred if the marriage has been consummated at any time since the marriage. Once consummated it is valid, though intercourse be never repeated. There is no matrimonial relief for cases of supervening impotence, whatever its cause. Refusal of sexual relations is not a ground for relief, but may amount to cruelty and justify divorce.[9]

Consummation requires normal penetration of the female vagina by the male organ, but not necessarily any emission of semen. There is no consummation if there is only partial or imperfect penetration[10] or if one party has an artificial organ.[11] A marriage may be held consummated though the husband practised *coitus interruptus*,[12] though a contraceptive was used,[13] or though ejaculation was impossible.[14] Nullity has been granted in England even though the wife had become pregnant by *fecundatio ab extra*,[15] or by artificial insemination by the husband;[16] the birth of a child accordingly does not necessarily establish consummation. Nullity is not competent if there is merely wilful delay or refusal to consummate,[17] though evidence of such conduct, if

---

[1] *G.* v. *G.* (1909) 25 T.L.R. 328.

[2] *A.B.* v. *C.D.* (1903) 10 S.L.T. 266.

[3] *C.* v. *M.* (1876) 3 R. 693; cf. *L.* v. *L.* (1882) 7 P.D. 16; *H.* v. *H.*, 1949 S.C. 587.

[4] *M.* v. *M.*, 1966 S.L.T. 25.

[5] *C.* v. *M.* (1876) 3 R. 693.

[6] *W.Y.* v. *A.Y.*, 1946 S.C. 27; cf. *G.* v. *B.*, 1934 S.L.T. 421.

[7] *W.Y.*, *supra*.

[8] *A.B.* v. *C.D.* (1900) 38 S.L.R. 559; *M.* v. *G.* (1902) 10 S.L.T. 264; *A.B.* v. *C.B.* (1906) 8 F. 603; *G.* v. *G.*, 1924 S.C. (H.L.) 42.

[9] *H.* v. *H.*, 1968 S.L.T. 40.

[10] *D.E.* v. *A.G.* (1845) 1 Rob. Eccl. 279.

[11] *D.* v. *D.* [1955] P. 42; *Corbett* v. *C.* [1970] 2 All E.R. 33.

[12] *White* v. *W.* [1948] P. 330; *Cackett* v. *C.* [1950] 1 All E.R. 677.

[13] *Baxter* v. *B.* [1948] A.C. 274.   [14] *R.* v. *R.* [1952] 1 All E.R. 1194.

[15] *Snowman* v. *S.* [1934] P. 186; *Clarke* v. *C.* [1943] 2 All E.R. 540; *L.* v. *L.* [1949] P. 211.

[16] *L.* v. *L.* [1949] P. 211.

[17] *Paterson* v. *P.*, 1958 S.C. 141.

prolonged, may suggest an inference of impotence.[1] So too absence of desire or attempt to consummate may be evidence, but is not conclusive. If there is *potentia copulandi* it matters not that there is *impotentia procreandi*: sterility is irrelevant.[2] Parties may each aver that the other is impotent, and one may adopt the other's allegations as alternative to his allegations against the other.[3]

Psychological impotence

Where the ground of action is psychological the pursuer must establish that non-consummation resulted not from indifference or lack of attempt on his part, nor from wilful refusal, nor mere temporary objection to intercourse on the defender's part, but from permanent invincible repugnance to or revulsion from intercourse.[4] The onus is on the pursuer to prove the case on balance of probabilities.[4] The court may infer incapacity if after a reasonable period of cohabitation there has been no intercourse and reasonable attempts have met with resistance or produced mental upsets.[5]

Nullity barred by insincerity

Decree may be held barred where the pursuer's case lacks substantial justification,[6] as where a woman married solely to obtain a settlement for herself and her child.[7] Knowledge at the time of the marriage of the defender's impotence is not *per se* a bar to decree, but may amount to approbation.[8] Decree is not barred, if otherwise admissible, merely because the pursuer wishes to rid himself of liability to aliment the defender,[9] or has another collateral reason for wishing the marriage avoided.[10]

Nullity barred by approbation

Nullity will not be granted where, despite non-consummation, the parties have by their conduct approbated and ratified the

---

[1] *A.B.* v. *Y.Z.* (1900) 8 S.L.T. 253; *A.B.* v. *C.B.* (1906) 8 F. 603; *G.* v. *G.*, 1924 S.C. (H.L.) 42.

[2] Stair I, 4, 6; Ersk. I, 6, 7; *A.B.* v. *C.B.*, *supra*, 607; *G.* v. *G.*, *supra*; cf. *Baxter* v. *B.* [1948] A.C. 274.

[3] *M.* v. *M.*, 1967 S.L.T. 157.

[4] *M.* v. *M.*, 1966 S.L.T. 153.

[5] *A.B.* v. *C.B.* (1906) 8 F. 603; *G.* v. *G.*, 1924 S.C. (H.L.) 42.

[6] *C.B.* v. *A.B.* (1885) 12 R. (H.L.) 36, 45.

[7] *L.* v. *L.*, 1931 S.C. 477.

[8] *L.* v. *L.*, *supra*; *Nash* v. *N.* [1940] P. 60; *J.* v. *J.* [1947] P. 158.

[9] *Allardyce* v. *A.*, 1954 S.C. 419.   [10] *C.B.*, *supra*.

marriage, as where the wife has had a child by artificial insemination with the husband's semen,[1] or by *fecundatio ab extra*,[2] or the
parties have adopted a child.[3] Nullity may be held barred by the
petitioner's knowledge of his own impotence, certainly if the
defender does not concur.[4] There can, however, be no approbation where the petitioner is ignorant of the facts or the law,[5] the
onus of proof of which is on him.[6] To bring an action for divorce
does not imply approbation of the marriage sufficient to bar a
subsequent petition for nullity.[7] If the defender is relying on
personal bar she must prove facts from which it can be inferred
that she has been prejudiced and that justice requires that nullity
be refused.[8]

Bar by delay

Delay in seeking nullity is a factor to be considered though no
particular lapse of time will automatically bar an action.[9] Delay
is ineffective if the pursuer did not have the knowledge of facts
and law essential to the decision whether to avoid or approbate
the marriage.[10] If delay extends to the death of either spouse, it
is too late thereafter to have the marriage avoided.

Consequences of nullity

On decree of nullity being pronounced parties must effect a
separation of their property interests, so far as in joint names, and
make restitution *hinc inde* of all transfers of property made in
contemplation of, or during, the supposed marriage.[11] They are
after the decree as if they had never been in the apparent relationship of marriage, and neither has, on the other's death, any claim
as a surviving spouse.

DISSOLUTION OF MARRIAGE

Dissolution of marriage is effected only by the death of either
spouse or by the decree of a competent court. It differs from

---

[1] *A.B.* v. *C.B.*, 1961 S.C. 347; cf. *L.* v. *L.* [1949] P. 211; *Slater* v. *S.* [1953] P. 235.
[2] *Pettit* v. *P.* [1963] P. 177.
[3] *W.* v. *W.*, 1933 S.N. 73; *W.* v. *W.* [1952] P. 152.
[4] *Harthan* v. *H.* [1949] P. 115.   [5] *G.* v. *M.* (1885) 10 App. Cas. 171.
[6] *Allardyce* v. *A.*, 1954 S.C. 419.   [7] *M.* v. *M.*, 1966 S.L.T. 25.
[8] *M.* v. *M.*, 1966 S.L.T. 153.
[9] *C.B.* v. *A.B.* (1885) 12 R. (H.L.) 36; *W.* v. *W.*, 1933 S.N. 73.
[10] *Allardyce* v. *A.*, 1954 S.C. 419; *M.* v. *M.*, 1966 S.L.T. 153.
[11] Stair I, 4, 20; Ersk. I, 6, 43; Fraser, *H. & W.*, I, 149; see also *Wright* v. *Sharp* (1880)
7 R. 460, 464; *Henderson* v. *Wilkie* (1908) 15 S.L.T. 895.

nullity in that the marriage is for all purposes good and valid so long as it lasted, and parties acquired married status.

Dissolution by death

On the death of either spouse, the marriage is dissolved and the surviving spouse restored to the status of single person and entitled to remarry. The surviving spouse is entitled to certain rights from the estate of the deceased[1] and may be entitled to payments under the deceased's will or the provision of a marriage-contract. Bona fide belief in the other spouse's death does not entitle a spouse to remarry.[2]

Dissolution by decree of court

The Court of Session may dissolve a marriage by divorcing one spouse from the other *a vinculo matrimonii* on the grounds of adultery,[3] desertion,[4] incurable insanity,[5] cruelty,[5] sodomy or bestiality,[5] or dissolve the marriage on the ground of the presumed death of the other party.[6] The principle underlying all the grounds of divorce, except insanity, is that divorce is a remedy granted for the commission of a matrimonial offence, or wrong done to the innocent spouse by conduct contradictory of the fundamental obligations of the matrimonial relationship.[7] Even if the action is undefended, the court may not grant decree unless satisfied by evidence of the factual justification for the action.[8] Adultery and sodomy or bestiality must also be proved beyond reasonable doubt, which is a higher standard of proof than usually required in civil actions.[9] More than one ground of dissolution may arise in particular circumstances; which is founded on depends on the evidence available.[10] Failure on one ground does not preclude action on another ground.[11] A party detained in hospital as

---

[1] Ch. 119, *infra*.

[2] *Hunter* v. *H.* (1900) 2 F. 771.

[3] At common law, since the Reformation.

[4] Act 1573, c. 55, superseded by Divorce (Scotland) Act, 1938, S. 1(1)(a).

[5] Divorce (Scotland) Act, 1938, S. 1(1)(b), (c), and (d).

[6] Divorce (Scotland) Act, 1938, S. 5.

[7] See *Report of Royal Commission on Marriage and Divorce*, 1956 (Cmnd. 9678). The introduction of a basis of 'the breakdown of the marriage' is now increasingly favoured.

[8] Court of Session Act, 1830, S. 36; *Smith* v. *S.*, 1929 S.C. 75; *Macfarlane* v. *M.*, 1956 S.C. 472.

[9] *Currie* v. *C.*, 1950 S.C. 10; *Burnett* v. *B.*, 1955 S.C. 183.

[10] Decree may be granted on more than one ground or in more than one action: *Mansfield* v. *M.*, 1970 S.L.T. (Notes) 14.

[11] cf. *Lench* v. *L.*, 1945 S.C. 295.

mentally defective has been held capable of understanding divorce and entitled to bring an action.[1]

Oath of calumny

In all actions of divorce the Lord Ordinary administers to the pursuer the oath of calumny,[2] to the effect that there has been no collusion or agreement between the parties for the purpose of substantiating a false case or withholding a just defence.[3]

Proof of marriage

The parties must be proved to be married, normally by production of an extract from the Register of Births, Deaths, and Marriages.[4] If the marriage was irregular it may be necessary to preface the divorce by a declarator of marriage.[5] In defence it may be contended that the 'marriage' was null.[6]

Cross actions

It is competent for spouses to bring cross-actions, each charging the other with a matrimonial offence justifying divorce,[7] and for the court to grant decree in either action, or in both.[8] Decree in one suffices to dissolve the marriage.

Jurisdiction

The pursuer must specifically aver and prove facts sufficient to entitle the court to assume jurisdiction.[9]

Divorce for adultery

Adultery consists in voluntary[10] sexual relations[11] between a married person and a person of the opposite sex, other than his or

---

[1] *Gibson* v. *G.*, 1970 S.L.T. (Notes) 60.

[2] For its history see *Paul* v. *Laing* (1855) 17 D. 604; *Riddell* v. *R.*, 1952 S.C. 475, 482. See also Divorce (Sc.) Act, 1938, S. 4(2).

[3] The present form of oath is founded on *Walker* v. *W.*, 1911 S.C. 163 and *Fairgrieve* v. *Chalmers*, 1912 S.C. 745.

[4] cf. *McDonald* v. *McD.*, 1924 S.L.T. 200.   [5] *Nicol* v. *Bell*, 1954 S.L.T. 314.

[6] *C.B.* v. *A.B.* (1885) 12 R. (H.L.) 36; *Sharp* v. *S.* (1898) 25 R. 1132.

[7] Cross actions each alleging desertion cannot both result in decree. Apart from that both actions may be on the same, or on different grounds.

[8] *Brodie* v. *B.* (1870) 8 M. 854; *Connell* v. *C.*, 1950 S.C. 505. Either spouse may reclaim to obtain a finding that he or she was not in fault: *Connell, supra.*

[9] *Horn* v. *H.*, 1935 S.L.T. 589.

[10] *Long* v. *L.* (1890) 15 P.D. 218; *Hanbury* v. *H.* [1892] P. 222; *Yarrow* v. *Y.* [1892] P. 92; *Stewart* v. *S.*, 1914, 2 S.L.T. 310; *Clarkson* v. *C.* (1930) 46 T.L.R. 623; *S.* v. *S.* [1962] P. 133; Insanity is a defence: Fraser, *H. & W.*, II, 1143.

[11] *MacLennan* v. *M.*, 1958 S.C. 105; *sed quaere*; see *Russell* v. *R.* [1924] A.C. 687, 721.

her spouse, during the subsistence of the marriage.[1] A woman raped is not guilty of adultery.[2] It is adultery to have intercourse with one other than one's spouse, notwithstanding separation, voluntary or judicial, desertion by, or reasonable belief in the death of, the other spouse.[3] If *coitus* be admitted, the onus of proving that it was involuntary lies on the party admitting.[4] It has been held that only physical *coitus* amounts to adultery, and not even the birth to a wife of a child conceived by artificial insemination by a donor amounts to adultery.[5] Sexual gratification without penetration of the female is, however, not adultery.[6] Emission need not be proved, still less impregnation. Only the injured spouse has a title to sue and the right of action falls on his death.[7]

The other spouse has title and interest to defend, but not his creditors, nor a child of the marriage. Where the defender cannot be found the summons must be intimated to the children of the marriage, if any, above the age of puberty, and on one or more of the defender's next of kin, any one of whom may appear and lodge defences.[8]

The Lord Advocate may state defences.[9] The paramour with whom adultery is alleged must, if known,[10] have intimation of the action, and he may apply to be sisted as a party to the action, and is then entitled to a decision as to his guilt or innocence.[11] He may be called as co-defender,[12] and found liable in damages and or

---

[1] Mack, *Crim. L.* 86; Fraser, *H. & W.*, II, 1142; Hume, *Lect.* I, 83. See also *Sands v. S.*, 1964 S.L.T. 80.

[2] *Clarkson, supra*; cf. *Black v. Duncan*, 1924 S.C. 738.

[3] Ersk. I, 6, 44; *Donald v. D.* (1863) 1 M. 741, 749; *Hunter v. H.* (1900) 2 F. 771, 774, 775.

[4] *Stewart v. S.*, 1914, 2 S.L.T. 310; cf. *Redpath v. R.* [1950] 1 All E.R. 600.

[5] *McLennan, supra.* But the essence of adultery is infidelity, granting the use of the sexual organs to another than one's spouse, whether for gratification or reproduction, and whether or not pregnancy results, though carnal connection is the normal form of this infidelity. cf. Bartholomew, 21 M.L.R. 236; Tallin, 34 Can. B.R. 1, 166.

[6] *Sapsford v. S.* [1954] P. 394; *Dennis v. D.* [1955] P. 153; cf. *Clarke v. C.* [1943] 2 All E.R. 540; *L. v. L.* [1949] P. 211.

[7] *Clement v. Sinclair* (1762) Mor. 337; *Ritchie v. R.* (1874) 1 R. 826; but personal representatives have an interest to prosecute a reclaiming motion; *Fenton v. Livingstone* (1859) 3 Macq. 497; *Ritchie, supra.*

[8] R.C. 160.

[9] Conjugal Rights (Sc.) Amdt. Act, 1861, S. 8; see *Ralston v. R.* (1881) 8 R. 371; *Riddell v. R.*, 1952 S.C. 475.

[10] It is competent to charge adultery with a person whose name is unknown: *Smith v. S.* (1838) 16 S. 499; *Gray v. G.* (1865) 37 S. Jur. 566.

[11] *Raeside v. R.*, 1913 S.C. 60.

[12] 1861 Act, S. 7.

expenses,[1] provided he is shown to have known that the defender was married.[2] His liability does not transmit on his death against his estate.[3]

A pursuer is not barred from suing by his own adultery. It is competent for spouses to bring cross-actions of divorce for adultery.[4]

The averments of time and place, or circumstances giving rise to the inference of adultery, must be as specific as possible, and vague allegations will not be admitted to probation.[5]

Proof of adultery

Only one act of illicit coitus need be proved, not necessarily a course of adultery or adulterous cohabitation.[6] The onus is on the pursuer and he cannot found on the fact that the defender has abstained from giving evidence.[7] Adultery must be proved beyond reasonable doubt,[8] or facts and circumstances be proved from which the court is prepared to infer adultery. There may be direct evidence of persons being seen or found *in flagrante delicto*. Failing that, the facts must be inconsistent with innocence before an inference will be drawn,[9] but adultery may be inferred from facts and circumstances without direct proof of any specific act of adultery.[10] An inference of adultery may be drawn if one spouse is proved to have shared a bedroom for the night with a third party.[11] It will not necessarily be drawn, in the absence of other evidence of mutual passion, merely from propinquity, opportunity, or evidence of familiarities.[12] The defender's conviction of rape,[13] or his frequenting a brothel,[14] are

---

[1] *Fraser* v. *F. and Hibbert* (1870) 8 M. 400; *Duncan* v. *D.*, 1948 S.C. 666; *Reynolds* v. *R.*, 1965 S.C. 150; *Morrison* v. *M.*, 1970 S.L.T. 116.

[2] *Miller* v. *Simpson* (1863) 2 M. 225; *Kydd* v. *K.* (1864) 2 M. 1074; *Laurie* v. *L.*, 1913, 1 S.L.T. 117; *Heggie* v. *H.*, 1917, 2 S.L.T. 246; *Forrester* v. *F.*, 1963 S.C. 662.

[3] *Kelly* v. *K.*, 1953 S.L.T. 284.   [4] e.g. *Connell* v. *C.*, 1950 S.C. 505.

[5] *Walker* v. *W.* (1869) 41 S. Jur. 502; *Soeder* v. *S.* (1897) 24 R. 278; *Blakely* v. *B.*, 1947 S.N. 10; *Smith* v. *S.*, 1947 S.N. 80.

[6] e.g. *Smith* v. *S.*, 1930 S.C. 75.

[7] *Bird* v. *B.*, 1931 S.C. 731.

[8] *Currie* v. *C.*, 1950 S.C. 10.

[9] *Wilson* v. *W.* (1898) 25 R. 788; *Bennet Clark* v. *B.C.*, 1909 S.C. 591, 609.

[10] *Walker* v. *W.* (1871) 9 M. 1091; *Fullerton* v. *F.* (1873) 11 M. 720; *McInnes* v. *McI.*, 1954 S.C. 396.

[11] *Hannah* v. *H.*, 1931 S.C. 275; cf. *Smith* v. *S.*, 1929 S.C. 75.

[12] *McIver* v. *M.* (1859) 21 D. 655; *Bennet Clark, supra*; *Ross* v. *R.*, 1930 S.C. (H.L.) 1; *Burnett* v. *B.*, 1955 S.C. 183; *Hall* v. *H.*, 1958 S.C. 206.

[13] *Galbraith* v. *G.* (1902) 9 S.L.T. 346. On evidence see Law Reform (Misc. Prov.) (Sc.) Act, 1968, S. 10.

[14] *Marshall* v. *M.* (1881) 8 R. 702; contrast *Edward* v. *E.* (1879) 6 R. 1255; see also *Tennant* v. *T.* (1883) 10 R. 1187.

factors justifying an inference of adultery. Condoned acts of adultery may not be founded on, but may be proved to cast light on the defender's conduct thereafter.[1]

Adultery may be inferred from proof of the birth of a child to the wife at a time so long after the latest possible opportunity for intercourse with her husband, or so soon after the first possible opportunity following long absence, that the child must have been begotten by another.[2] While the normal duration of pregnancy is 280 days, no set periods give rise to presumptions and courts have, on the strength of medical evidence, held that unusually long,[3] or short,[4] periods of gestation have not been impossible, so as inevitably to give rise to the inference of adultery, but exceptional periods of gestation go someway to yield an inference of adultery.[5] It is in each case a question of fact and evidence, and the presumption *pater est quem nuptiae demonstrant* has to be overcome.[6] Even where parties lived in the same town, but apart, the presumption *pater est* may be rebutted and adultery inferred.[7] Similarly acknowledgment by a wife that a child is illegitimate is evidence of adultery.[8] It has also been held proved where the alleged paramour had given birth to a child of which the defender acknowledged paternity,[9] or had obtained decree of affiliation and aliment against the defender.[10] The fact that a person has been found guilty of adultery in any matrimonial proceedings or has been found to be the father of a child in affiliation proceedings in any court in the United Kingdom, is admissible evidence to prove that he committed that adultery, or is the father of that child, and in a subsequent case that fact will be held established unless the contrary is proved.[11]

[1] *Collins* v. *C.* (1884) 11 R. (H.L.) 19; *Robertson* v. *R.* (1888) 15 R. 1001; *Nicol* v. *N.*, 1938 S.L.T. 98.

[2] *Pegg* v. *P.* (1859) 21 D. 820; *Tulloh* v. *T.* (1861) 23 D. 639.

[3] *Whyte* v. *W.* (1884) 11 R. 710 (297 days); *Marshall* v. *M.*, 1934 S.N. 39 (308 days); *McIntosh* v. *M.*, 1947 S.N. 23 (316 days); *Gaskill* v. *G.* [1921] P. 425 (331 days); *Gray* v. *G.*, 1919, 1 S.L.T. 163 (331 days); *Currie* v. *C.*, 1950 S.C. 10 (336 days); *M.T.* v. *M.T.* [1949] P. 331 (340 days); *Wood* v. *W.* [1947] P. 103 (346 days); *Doherty* v. *D.*, 1922 S.L.T. 245 (348 days); *Hadlum* v. *H.* [1949] P. 197 (349 days); *Preston-Jones* v. *P.J.* [1951] A.C. 391 (360 days).

[4] *Clark* v. *C.* [1939] P. 228 (174 days); contrast *Re S.B.* [1949] Ch. 108 (188 days: no evidence that child premature).

[5] *Currie* v. *C.*, *supra.*

[6] cf. *Marshall* v. *M.*, 1934 S.N. 39.

[7] *Steedman* v. *S.* (1887) 14 R. 1066.

[8] *Fullerton* v. *F.* (1873) 11 M. 720; *Duncan* v. *D.* (1893) 30 S.L.R. 435.

[9] *Campbell* v. *C.* (1860) 23 D. 99; *McDougall* v. *M.*, 1927 S.C. 666; see also *Stewart* v. *S.*, 1930 S.L.T. 363.

[10] *Mathieson* v. *M.*, 1914, 1 S.L.T. 511.

[11] Law Reform (Misc. Prov.) (Sc.) Act, 1968, s. 11.

Evidence that the defender had contracted venereal disease is relevant.[1] The court will not ordain a defender and her child, allegedly illegitimate, to submit to blood tests.[2] It is relevant to prove that the defender had had an immoral relationship with the co-defender before the marriage, but not to prove that the co-defender had previously had immoral relations with other women,[3] though it is to prove that the defender was guilty of indecent conduct with another woman at the same period as the alleged adultery.[4]

A judicial admission by the defender is admissible but not conclusive evidence, unless corroborated to eliminate the risk of collusion.[5] A written confession by the defender, even of adultery with the co-defender, is admissible but is not evidence against the co-defender.[6] Judicial admissions by paramours are admissible, but not conclusive.[7] The pursuer cannot found on the fact that the defender, though denying adultery on record, has neither given nor led evidence.[8]

An extra-judicial confession by the defender, made *ante litem motam*, is admissible but requires corroboration.[9] Letters from, or the diaries of, the defender may be interpreted as admissions of adultery.[10] Extrajudicial confessions by the co-defender are not evidence against the defender.[11] No witness in any proceedings instituted in consequence of adultery is liable to be asked or bound to answer any question tending to show that he or she has been guilty of adultery.[12]

A subsisting decree of separation on the ground of adultery may be treated as sufficient proof of the adultery founded on, but

---

[1] *Kelly* v. *K.*, 1946 S.L.T. 208; *McRae* v. *M.*, 1947 S.C. 173.

[2] *Whitehall* v. *W.*, 1958 S.C. 252; contrast *Borthwick* v. *B.*, 1929 S.L.T. 596.

[3] *Johnston* v. *J.* (1903) 5 F. 659.

[4] *Whyte* v. *W.* (1884) 11 R. 710.

[5] *Muirhead* v. *M.* (1846) 8 D. 786; *Laidlaw* v. *L.* (1894) 2 S.L.T. 168; *Macfarlane* v. *M.*, 1956 S.C. 472; cf. *Ramsay* v. *R.* (1880) 17 S.L.R. 793; *Whyte* v. *W.* (1884) 11 R. 710; *Barnes* v. *B.*, 1935 S.C. 646. See also *Chatman* v. *C.*, 1944 S.C. 494.

[6] *Laidlaw* v. *L.* (1894) 2 S.L.T. 168; *Ramsay* v. *R.* (1880) 17 S.L.R. 793; *Smith* v. *S.*, 1929 S.C. 75.

[7] *Sim* v. *Miles* (1834) 12 S. 633; *Barnes, supra*; *Michlek* v. *M.*, 1971 S.L.T. (Notes) 50.

[8] *Bird* v. *B.*, 1931 S.C. 731.

[9] *Smith* v. *S.* (1866) 2 S.L.R. 243; *Fullerton* v. *F.* (1873) 11 M. 720; *Duncan* v. *D.* (1893) 30 S.L.R. 435; *Stewart* v. *S.*, 1930 S.L.T. 363; *Mackay* v. *M.*, 1946 S.C. 78; *MacColl* v. *MacC.*, 1948 S.C. 500; *Hamilton* v. *H.*, 1953 S.C. 383.

[10] *McNeill* v. *M.*, 1929 S.L.T. 251; *Creasey* v. *C.*, 1931 S.C. 9; *Watson* v. *W.*, 1934 S.C. 374; *Barnes, supra*; *Argyll* v. *A.*, 1962 S.C. (H.L.) 88; see also *Turner* v. *T.*, 1930 S.L.T. 393; *Smith* v. *S.*, 1929 S.C. 75.

[11] *Swapp* v. *S.*, 1931 S.L.T. 199; contrast *Reid* v. *R.*, 1926 S.L.T. 102.

[12] Evidence (Further Amdt.) (Sc.) Act, 1874, S. 2; *Bannatyne* v. *B.* (1886) 13 R. 619; *McDougall* v. *McD.*, 1927 S.C. 666.

the pursuer must still take the oath of calumny and give evidence.[1] An extract conviction of the husband for rape, together with a letter containing vague expressions of regret, has been held sufficient.[2]

Divorce for desertion[3]

The court may grant divorce where one spouse has wilfully and without reasonable cause deserted the other and persisted in such desertion for not less than three years.[4] Action cannot be brought until the three years have elapsed.[5] The pursuer has then a vested right to divorce,[6] so that the defender's subsequent insanity does not affect the issue.[7] It is constituted by cessation of adherence at bed and board by one spouse *animo deserendi*, the other spouse being willing to adhere, and normally by the departure of one spouse from the matrimonial home. This separation constitutes actual desertion where the deserting spouse leaves the matrimonial home and remains apart, despite the willingness of the other to adhere,[8] or constructive desertion where the deserting spouse, though remaining in the matrimonial home, has put the other out, or made life so intolerable for the other as to have driven that other to leave, though willing to adhere.[9]

There may be desertion though the spouses continue both to occupy the same house, if there are truly separate establishments and no cohabitation, social contact, mutual assistance or services.[10] The refusal of sexual relations not acquiesced in, by itself does

[1] Law Reform (Misc. Prov.) (Sc.) Act, 1968, S. 11, replacing Divorce (Scotland) Act, 1938, S. 4(2); cf. *Macpherson* v. *M.*, 1911, 2 S.L.T. 99.

[2] *Galbraith* v. *G.* (1902) 9 S.L.T. 346. On admissibility of conviction see Law Reform (Misc. Prov.) (Sc.) Act, 1968, S. 10.

[3] Introduced by Act 1573, c. 55, and requiring four years' malicious non-adherence. Until the Conjugal Rights Act, 1861, an action of adherence, non-implement of that decree and an application to the presbytery, were necessary preliminaries to an action for divorce for desertion: see Stair I, 4, 8; Ersk. I, 6, 44; Bell, *Prin.* §1535; Fraser, *H. & W.* II, 1207; *Watson* v. *W.* (1890) 17 R. 736; *Mackenzie* v. *M.* (1895) 22 R. (H.L.) 32.

[4] Divorce (Sc.) Act, 1938, S. 1(1)(a).

[5] *Ross* v. *R.* (1899) 1 F. 963; *Martin* v. *M.*, 1968 S.C. 205.

[6] *Bell* v. *B.*, 1941 S.C. (H.L.) 5; *Graham* v. *G.*, 1942 S.L.T. 142.

[7] *Scott* v. *S.*, 1908 S.C. 1124.   [8] e.g. *Bell* v. *B.*, 1941 S.C. (H.L.) 5.

[9] *Winchcombe* v. *W.* (1881) 8 R. 726; *Gow* v. *G.* (1887) 14 R. 443; *Murray* v. *M.* (1894) 21 R. 723; *Mackenzie, supra*; *Munro* v. *M.* (1895) 2 S.L.T. 598; cf. *Bowman* v. *B.* (1866) 4 M. 384; *Forbes* v. *F.* (1881) 19 S.L.R. 118; contrast *Gibson* v. *G.* (1894) 21 R. 470.

[10] *Forbes* v. *F.* (1881) 19 S.L.R. 118; *Goold* v. *G.*, 1927 S.C. 177, 183; *Lennie* v. *L.*, 1950 S.C. (H.L.) 1, 5, 16; *Cooke* v. *C.*, 1946 S.L.T. (Notes) 28; cf. *Smith* v. *S.* [1940] P. 49; *Littlewood* v. *L.* [1943] P. 11; *Wilkes* v. *W.* [1943] P. 41; *Hopes* v. *H.* [1949] P. 227; *Bartram* v. *B.* [1950] P. 1; *Naylor* v. *N.* [1962] P. 253.

not now amount to desertion.[1] Divorce for desertion is not precluded by the pursuer having previously obtained decree of separation and aliment, after which the defender had disappeared,[2] or refused the pursuer's offer to resume cohabitation.[3]

Wilful desertion

The desertion must be wilful or intentional, not mere disappearance,[4] or separation enforced by business, duty, illness, imprisonment, or other overriding compulsion,[5] nor consensual separation.[6] Separation initially consensual becomes wilful desertion when one spouse refuses the other's *bona fide* call to resume co-habitation,[7] or breaks off communication.[8] Similarly a spouse holding a decree of separation may offer to resume cohabitation; the other spouse, if refusing unjustifiably, is thereafter in desertion.[9] If, however, the defender was in desertion when imprisoned and continues to be so on release the triennium is deemed not thereby interrupted.[10] This conclusion will not necessarily be drawn if the triennium has expired while the imprisonment continues.[11] If one spouse is in desertion and offers *bona fide* to resume cohabitation but the other refuses, the latter is in desertion,[12] but an offer which is not *bona fide* may be ignored.[13] Wilful desertion may be inferred from conduct inconsistent with willingness to adhere, such as forming an association with another while justifiably abroad. An insane person cannot form *animus deserendi* so that insanity is a defence.[14]

---

[1] *Lennie* v. *L.*, 1950 S.C. (H.L.) 1, overruling *Stair* v. *S.* (1905) 12 S.L.T. 788; *A.* v. *B.* (1905) 13 S.L.T. 532; *Goold, supra*; *Pinder* v. *P.*, 1932 S.L.T. 292; *Burrell* v. *B.*, 1947 S.C. 569; *Macdonald* v. *M.*, 1948 S.L.T. 380; cf. *A.* v. *B.* (1905) 13 S.L.T. 532; *X.* v. *Y.*, 1914, 1 S.L.T. 366; *C.* v. *D.*, 1921, 2 S.L.T. 82; *G.* v. *G.*, 1923 S.C. 175; *Robertson* v. *R.*, 1939 S.L.T. 432.

[2] *Whalley* v. *W.*, 1921 2 S.L.T. 135; *Summers* v. *S.*, 1935 S.C. 537.

[3] *Macdonald* v. *M.*, 1912, 2 S.L.T. 14; cf. *Horsley* v. *H.*, 1914, 1 S.L.T. 92; *Smellie* v. *S.*, 1914, 2 S.L.T. 240.

[4] *Lench* v. *L.*, 1945 S.C. 295; contrast *Lough* v. *L.*, 1930 S.C. 1016.

[5] *Irvine* v. *I.* (1884) 21 S.L.R. 493; *Ross* v. *R.* (1899) 1 F. 963.

[6] *Barrie* v. *B.* (1882) 10 R. 208; *Gibson* v. *G.* (1894) 21 R. 470.

[7] cf. *Barr* v. *B.*, 1939 S.C. 696.

[8] *Mason* v. *M.* (1877) 14 S.L.R. 592; *Muir* v. *M.* (1879) 6 R. 1353; *Jeffrey* v. *J.* (1901) 9 S.L.T. 54; *Smellie* v. *S.*, 1914, 2 S.L.T. 240; *Mitchell* v. *M.*, 1931 S.L.T. 484; cf. *Stair* v. *S.* (1905) 12 S.L.T. 788.

[9] *Irvine* v. *I.* (1884) 21 S.L.R. 493; *Horsley* v. *H.*, 1914, 1 S.L.T. 92;

[10] *Hunter* v. *H.* (1898) 5 S.L.T. 384; *Parker* v. *P.*, 1926 S.C. 574; *Trondsen* v. *T.*, 1948 S.L.T. (Notes) 85; *Anderson* v. *A.*, 1955 S.C. 428; contrast *Young* v. *Y.* (1882) 10 R. 184, where defender still in prison.

[11] *Parker, supra*, 578.

[12] *Forbes* v. *F.* (1881) 19 S.L.R. 118.   [13] *Chalmers* v. *C.* (1868) 6 M. 547.

[14] *Gilfillan* v. *G.* (1902) 10 S.L.T. 295; *Mudie* v. *M.*, 1956 S.C. 318.

Desertion without reasonable cause

Separation amounts to desertion only if the non-adhering spouse had no reasonable cause for leaving the other spouse or staying apart. That spouse has a good defence if he or she can establish reasonable cause for non-adherence. The defences of being willing to adhere, and of having reasonable cause for non-adherence, are not mutually exclusive.[1] Reasonable cause includes conduct by the pursuer such as would entitle the defender to defend an action for adherence, or himself to bring an action of divorce,[2] such as adultery,[3] cruelty,[4] or sodomy,[5] but not insanity, which is not an offence but an involuntary misfortune.[6] But reasonable cause as a defence also includes circumstances which do not by themselves give any positive remedy, as where the wife was willing to live with the husband only on condition that no marital intercourse took place,[6] or the husband was alleged to have attempted connection with the wife's niece,[7] or where the wife had tricked the husband into marriage by falsely representing that he was the cause of her pregnancy,[8] where the only home the pursuer had offered was with his relatives,[9] or where the pursuer had confessed to adultery,[10] or had committed crime so long as associated with the matrimonial relationship,[11] or conduct such that it would shock the conscience of reasonable men to ordain the spouses to cohabit again,[12] or was guilty of ill-treatment not amounting to legal cruelty justifying separation or divorce.[13] It is no longer a defence that the pursuer has committed adultery, unless that was a cause of the defender's desertion.[14]

Proceedings taken in good faith, though unjustifiably, for the defender's detention as a person of unsound mind have been

---

[1] *Sinclair v. S.*, 1950 S.L.T. (Notes) 65.

[2] *Mackenzie v. M.* (1895) 22 R. (H.L.) 32.

[3] *Auld v. A.* (1884) 12 R. 36; *Hunter v. H.* (1900) 2 F. 771; *Wilkinson v. W.*, 1943 S.C. (H.L.) 61.

[4] *Stevens v. S.* (1882) 9 R. 730; *Mackenzie v. M.* (1895) 22 R. (H.L.) 32; *Anderson v. A.*, 1958 S.L.T. (Notes) 31.

[5] *Borland v. B.*, 1947 S.C. 432, 444; *Jack v. J.*, 1962 S.C. 24, 31.

[6] *Stair v. S.* (1905) 12 S.L.T. 788.

[7] *A. v. B.* (1896) 23 R. 588.

[8] *Hastings v. H.*, 1941 S.L.T. 323; cf. *Lang v. L.*, 1921 S.C. 44.

[9] *Young v. Y.*, 1947 S.L.T. 5.

[10] *Wilkinson v. W.*, 1943 S.C. (H.L.) 61; *Hamilton v. H.*, 1953 S.C. 383. But see now Divorce (Sc.) Act, 1964, S. 5.

[11] *Brown v. B.*, 1955 S.L.T. 48; *A.B. v. C.B.*, 1959 S.C. 27.

[12] *Richardson v. R.*, 1956 S.C. 394; cf. *McMillan v. McM.*, 1962 S.C. 115.

[13] *Jack v. J.*, 1962 S.C. 24.

[14] Divorce (Sc.) Act, 1964, S. 5; *Muir v. M.*, 1967 S.L.T. 264.

held not to be reasonable ground for non-adherence,[1] as has been a wife's refusal to cohabit unless she could bring her grown-up children with her,[2] and a wife's refusal, after a brief cohabitation, to have her husband's sister continue to stay with them.[3] Nor does a wife have reasonable cause because she is employed and her husband (pursuer) is unemployed,[4] nor because she holds a non-cohabitation order granted by magistrates in England,[5] nor because he had formed an association, not adulterous, with another woman.[6] Unhappiness or matrimonial disharmony is not reasonable cause for non-adherence.

Pursuer's willingness to adhere

Desertion is bilateral in involving a spouse who deserts and a spouse who is willing to adhere.[7] This distinguishes it from consensual separation. Offers to adhere, ignored or rejected by the defender, or requests to resume cohabitation, are material evidence in a pursuer's case.[8] The sincerity of the offers must be judged by the court.[9] To raise an action for adherence and aliment during the triennium constitutes an offer to adhere.[10] To allow a spouse to live apart without serious effort to induce her to return suggests consensual separation.[11] The pursuer had formerly to be able to aver, and satisfy the court, in all cases, that he remained willing to adhere to the deserting spouse for at least three years after the date of desertion;[12] this is no longer so, so long as he has not refused any genuine offer to resume cohabitation.[13] Once desertion is proved, the pursuer's willingness to adhere is presumed, unless the defender rebuts that presumption, as by showing the pursuer's refusal of a genuine offer to adhere.[14] On

---

[1] *Cathcart* v. *C.* (1900) 2 F. 404; cf. *Gould* v. *G.* (1887) 15 R. 229.

[2] *Inglis* v. *I.*, 1919, 1 S.L.T. 184.   [3] *Anderson* v. *A.*, 1928 S.L.T. 199.

[4] *Knox* v. *K.*, 1934 S.C. 240.

[5] *Murray* v. *M.*, 1956 S.C. 376; cf. *Richardson* v. *R.*, 1957 S.L.T. (Notes) 45.

[6] *Richardson*, 1956 S.C. 394.   [7] *Burrell* v. *B.*, 1947 S.C. 569, 578.

[8] *Willey* v. *W.* (1884) 11 R. 815; *Watson* v. *W.* (1890) 17 R. 736; *Gibson* v. *G.* (1894) 21 R. 470; *Murray* v. *M.* (1894) 21 R. 723; *Munro* v. *M.* (1895) 2 S.L.T. 598; *Shaw* v. *S.* (1908) 16 S.L.T. 371; *McEwan* v. *McE.*, 1908 S.C. 1263; *Robertson* v. *R.* (1908) 16 S.L.T. 641; *Farrow* v. *F.*, 1920 S.C. 707; *Woodhouse* v. *W.*, 1936 S.C. 523.

[9] *Lilley* v. *L.* (1884) 12 R. 145; *Mackenzie* v. *M.* (1893) 20 R. 636, 657; *Hutchison* v. *H.*, 1909 S.C. 148; *Mulherron* v. *M.*, 1923 S.C. 461; *Summers* v. *S.*, 1935 S.C. 537.

[10] *Deans* v. *D.*, 1965 S.L.T. (Notes) 9.   [11] *Barrie* v. *B.* (1882) 10 R. 208.

[12] *Macaskill* v. *M.*, 1939 S.C. 187; *Bell* v. *B.*, 1941 S.C. (H.L.) 5; *Borland* v. *B.*, 1947 S.C. 432.

[13] Divorce (Sc.) Act, 1964, S. 3; *Thomson* v. *T.*, 1965 S.L.T. 343; *Donnelly* v. *D.*, 1969 S.L.T. 52; *Burgess* v. *B.*, 1969 S.L.T. (Notes) 22; *McLean* v. *McL.*, 1969 S.L.T. (Notes) 67; but see *Greenwald* v. *G.*, 1967 S.L.T. (Notes) 97; *Thomson* v. *T.*, 1969 S.L.T. 364.

[14] *Thomson* v. *T.*, 1965 S.L.T. 343.

the expiry of this *triennium* he acquires a vested right to divorce,[1] though the right is barred if during the triennium the pursuer refused a genuine and reasonable offer by the defender to adhere.[2] After the expiry of the triennium an offer by the defender to adhere comes too late,[3] and a pursuer is not bound to accept an offer by the defender to adhere after twenty years' desertion when she refused to give information about her life in the interval.[4] A spouse is not unwilling to adhere merely because she declines to join her husband in inadequate or unsatisfactory accommodation.[5] It is a valid defence that during the triennium the pursuer has refused a genuine and reasonable offer by the defender to adhere.[6]

The pursuer's adultery during the triennium formerly excluded his action, since it was inconsistent with willingness to adhere, and absolved the defender from the duty of adherence,[7] but this is no longer a defence, unless it appears to the court that the adultery was a cause of the defender's desertion or persistence in desertion;[8] after the triennium it has no effect.[9]

Three years' desertion

The three year period runs from the date when the parties finally separated, the pursuer unwillingly, the defender *animo deserendi*,[10] or from the date when, the parties being already separated, one declares an intention not to resume cohabitation,[11] or unjustifiably refuses an offer of a home,[12] or forms a connection with another,[13] or has disappeared and ceased to communicate

---

[1] *Muir v. M.* (1879) 6 R. 1353; *Auld v. A.* (1884) 12 R. 36; *Forbes v. F.* (1900) 8 S.L.T. 51; *Scott v. S.*, 1908 S.C. 1124; *Bell, supra*; *Graham v. G.*, 1942 S.L.T. 142; *Wilson v. W.*, 1944 S.L.T. 223; *Wright v. W.*, 1966 S.L.T. (Notes) 86, superseding *Bisset v. B.*, 1933 S.C. 764.

[2] Divorce (Sc.) Act, 1964, S. 3; *Thomson v. T.*, 1965 S.L.T. 343.

[3] *Muir, supra*; *Pirie v. P.*, 1927 S.N. 124; cf. *Bisset v. B.*, 1933 S.C. 764; *Gilfillan v. G.*, 1931 S.L.T. 454.

[4] *Forbes v. F.* (1900) 8 S.L.T. 51.

[5] *Fletcher v. F.* [1945] 1 All E.R. 582; *Young v. Y.*, 1947 S.L.T. 5; contrast *St. Wart v. S.*, 1959 S.L.T. (Notes) 70.

[6] Divorce (Sc.) Act, 1964, S. 3.

[7] *Wilkinson v. W.*, 1943 S.C. (H.L.) 61.

[8] Divorce (Sc.) Act, 1964, S. 5. This is retrospective: *Muir v. M.*, 1967 S.L.T. 264.

[9] *Bell, supra*, modifying principles stated in *Auld v. A.* (1884) 12 R. 36; *Hunter v. H.* (1900) 2 F. 771; and *Wooler v. W.*, 1940 S.L.T. 66; *Graham v. G.*, 1942 S.C. 575.

[10] *Trondsen v. T.*, 1948 S.L.T. (Notes) 85.

[11] *Belken v. B.* [1948] P. 302.

[12] *Darroch v. D.*, 1947 S.C. 110.

[13] *Stickland v. S.* (1876) 35 L.T. 767.

with the pursuer.[1] The proved period of desertion must be three full years,[2] and continuous. If interrupted, the *triennium* commences afresh. Interruption is constituted by the resumption of matrimonial cohabitation, but not necessarily by living in the same house, though separately,[3] nor by unsuccessfully suing for separation during the triennium,[4] nor by sharing a bed for one night when there was no intention to resume cohabitation,[5] nor by a brief return with the intention of interrupting the triennium,[6] though the court will not in general inquire into the alleged purpose of resumed cohabitation.[7] A brief resumption of cohabitation after the expiry of the triennium, and in ignorance of facts as to the defender's conduct during the triennium does not cancel that desertion.[8] Since 1964 no account falls to be taken of any one period not exceeding three months during which the parties resumed cohabitation with a view to reconciliation.[9]

If *currente triennio* the defender became insane, he or she could not be held to be in wilful desertion.[10] If not certified insane, it was a question of fact whether the defender was capable of *animus deserendi*.[11] The Divorce (Insanity and Desertion) Act, 1958, S. 2,[12] allows the court to treat desertion as having continued at a time when the deserting party was incapable of continuing the necessary intention if the evidence is that otherwise the court would have inferred that the intention continued. If during the triennium a period of imprisonment has interposed that does not interrupt the period unless there is evidence of no *animus deserendi* during that period.[13] It is no bar to divorce that, the triennium having expired, the defender has become insane, because the pursuer's right has vested.[14]

---

[1] *Lough* v. *L.*, 1930 S.C. 1076.

[2] cf. *Darroch, supra.* Action cannot be brought until the three years have expired: *Martin* v. *M.*, 1968 S.C. 205.

[3] *McEwan* v. *McE.*, 1908 S.C. 1263.

[4] *Forbes* v. *F.* (1881) 19 S.L.R. 118.

[5] *Crawford* v. *C.*, 1946 S.L.T. 138; cf. *Calder* v. *C.*, 1962 S.L.T. (Notes) 78; contrast *Meiklem* v. *M.*, 1949 S.L.T. 370, where one night's resumption of full cohabitation.

[6] *Wallace* v. *W.*, 1952 S.C. 197.

[7] *Beggs* v. *B.*, 1947 S.N. 182; *Wallace, supra.*

[8] *Wilson* v. *W.*, 1944 S.L.T. 223; contrast *Grant* v. *G.*, 1961 S.L.T. 322.

[9] Divorce (Sc.) Act, 1964, S. 2(2); *Leishman* v. *L.*, 1969 S.L.T. (Notes) 16.

[10] *Williams* v. *W.* [1939] P. 365; *Rushbrook* v. *R.* [1940] P. 24; *Mudie* v. *M.*, 1956 S.C. 318.

[11] *Monckton* v. *M.* [1942] P. 28.

[12] Repealed, at least *quoad* England, by Matrimonial Causes Act, 1965.

[13] *Hunter* v. *H.* (1898) 5 S.L.T. 384; *Parker* v. *P.*, 1926 S.C. 574; *Trondsen* v. *T.*, 1948 S.L.T. (Notes) 85; contrast *Young* v. *Y.* (1882) 10 R. 184.

[14] *Scott* v. *S.*, 1908 S.C. 1124; cf. *Bell* v. *B.*, 1941 S.C. (H.L.) 5.

Termination of desertion

Desertion is terminated if, before the triennium has expired, the spouses resume cohabitation, or the deserted spouse consents to their living apart, as by coming to an agreement for aliment, or commits some act which justifies the other in living apart, or if the spouse in desertion *bona fide* offers to resume cohabitation; if such an offer is unjustifiably refused the spouse refusing becomes in desertion and a new triennium commences. If the spouse in desertion has also been guilty of adultery, cruelty or sodomy, the innocent spouse is not bound to take the other back as this would effect condonation of the additional offence and bar the innocent spouse's remedy on that ground.[1] If the spouse in desertion has also been guilty of conduct giving the innocent spouse reasonable ground for non-adherence it is probably a question of circumstances whether the innocent spouse should take the guilty spouse back if the latter, apparently *bona fide*, offers to resume cohabitation.

Divorce for incurable insanity

Divorce may be granted on the ground that the defender is incurably insane;[2] a presumption of incurable insanity, sufficient, unless rebutted, to justify decree,[3] is raised if it is proved that the defender is, and has been for a period of five years continuously immediately preceding the raising of the action, under care and treatment as an insane person.[4] This includes detention as a State mental patient,[5] or as a voluntary patient,[6] and probably also detention during Her Majesty's pleasure after acquittal on the ground of insanity,[5] but not detention on grounds of mental deficiency.[7] 'Care and treatment' probably excludes persons received into guardianship for mental disorder.[8] A patient absent

---

[1] *Everitt* v. *E.* [1949] P. 374.   [2] Divorce (Sc.) Act, 1938, S. 1(1)(b).

[3] Ibid., S. 6(2); *Ramsay* v. *R.*, 1964 S.C. 289.

[4] Defined, S. 6(3), as amd. Mental Health (Sc.) Act, 1960, Sched. 4, as 'while liable to be detained by reason of mental illness in a hospital or place of safety under the Mental Health (Sc.) Act, 1960, or in a hospital, mental nursing home, or place of safety under the [English] Mental Health Act, 1959; and not otherwise'. Procedure for admission and detention in mental hospital is regulated by the Mental Health (Sc.) Act, 1960, Part IV. The Divorce (Insanity and Desertion) Act, 1958, S. 1(1), provides that a person shall be deemed to be under care and treatment as an insane person at any time when he is receiving care and treatment for mental illness as a resident in a hospital of certain classes in the U.K. or abroad.

[5] *Lang* v. *L.*, 1945 S.C. 471.

[6] Divorce (Insanity and Desertion) Act, 1958, S. 4, amending 1938 Act, S. 6(3), overruling *W.* v. *W.*, 1945 S.L.T. 9.

[7] *Murray* v. *M.*, 1942 S.C. 579.

[8] Mental Health (Sc.) Act, 1960, S. 25.

without leave from hospital for certain periods[1] ceases to be liable
to be detained, and this accordingly interrupts the quinquennium
required for divorce.[2]

A *curator ad litem* must be appointed to the defender by the
Court,[3] and he may lodge defences,[4] and the summons must be
intimated to minor children of the marriage and to one or more
of the next-of-kin. A report on the defender's condition and
prospects of recovery must be furnished by the Mental Welfare
Commission for Scotland.[5] The warrant under which the defender
is detained should be exhibited at the proof.[6]

As divorce on this ground is a relief from hardship, not a
matrimonial offence, a pursuer is not barred by his own adultery,[7]
nor by intercourse with the defender within the quinquennium,[8]
but the court is not bound to grant divorce if the pursuer's
wilful neglect or misconduct conduced to the insanity.[9] The
court may order payment by the pursuer of a capital sum or
periodical allowance to or for behalf of the defender and their
children.[10] A statement of the financial position of the parties
should be lodged with any proposals the pursuer has for making
provision for the defender.[11]

Divorce for cruelty

Divorce may be granted where the defender 'has been guilty
of such cruelty towards the pursuer as would justify, according
to the law existing at the passing of [the Divorce (Scotland) Act,
1938] the granting of a decree of separation *a mensa et thoro*'.[12]
Cases discussing cruelty for the purposes of separation prior
to the 1938 Act are accordingly relevant to both separation and

---

[1] 1960 Act, S. 36(3): mental deficiency—3 months; patients admitted in emergency—7
days; other cases—28 days.

[2] cf. *Ironside* v. *I.*, 1955 S.C. 471; *Peden* v. *P.*, 1957 S.C. 409; contrast *Ramsay* v. *R.*,
1960 S.L.T. (Notes) 17.

[3] 1938 Act, S. 3.

[4] e.g. *McFarlane* v. *M.*, 1951 S.C. 530.

[5] Established by Mental Health (Sc.) Act, 1960, S. 2, replacing General Board of
Control. As to the evidential value of the report see *Ramsay* v. *R.*, 1964 S.C. 289.

[6] *Adamson* v. *A.*, 1939 S.L.T. 272.

[7] *Brown* v. *B.*, 1940 S.C. 474.

[8] *M.* v. *M.*, 1944 S.C. 491.

[9] 1938 Act, S. 1(1)(b); *Aitchison* v. *A.*, 1958 S.L.T. 47.

[10] 1938 Act, S. 2(2) and (3).

[11] *Adamson* v. *A.*, 1939 S.L.T. 272; see also *Docherty* v. *Greenock Corpn.*, 1946 S.L.T. 90.

[12] Divorce (Sc.) Act 1938, S. 1(1)(c). Prior to the 1938 Act cruelty justified only
judicial separation; separation and divorce are now alternatives, and separation does not
preclude a subsequent divorce on the same facts. Prior to the Divorce (Sc.) Act, 1964, the
concept of cruelty was the same for separation and for divorce, but the changes made by
S. 4 of that Act apply to cruelty for divorce only.

divorce thereafter. A pursuer holding a decree of separation on the ground of cruelty may subsequently seek divorce for the same cruelty. The decree of separation may be treated as sufficient proof of the cruelty but the pursuer must still take the oath of calumny and give evidence.[1] A previous unsuccessful action for separation and aliment in the Sheriff court is not *res judicata* so as to bar a later action for divorce on the ground of the same alleged cruelty.[2] A person may seek divorce for cruelty despite having failed to establish a defence of justifiable non-adherence in a previous action of adherence and aliment against him.[3] Cruelty may be committed by either spouse,[4] and where a wife is guilty it may be relevant to consider the danger of provoking retaliation.[5]

Nature of cruelty

Cruelty is conduct of such a character as causes danger to life, limb or health (whether of body or mind) or as to give rise to a reasonable apprehension of such danger.[6] The grounds of action must be grave and weighty and regard must be had to the nature and quality of the conduct, and its effect on the other spouse, realized or apprehended.[7] At common law the question was whether the pursuer could with safety to life and health live with the defender at the date of the action.[8] Formerly a main consideration was the need for the present and future protection of the pursuer by relieving him or her of the duty to adhere, if he or she were called on to adhere or continue adherence,[9] so that divorce had to be refused where there seemed no reason to apprehend further or future harm.[10] In separation cases future protection is still relevant, but in divorce cases[11] the court need

---

[1] 1938 Act, S. 4; *Wilson* v. *W.*, 1939 S.C. 102; *McFarlane* v. *McF.*, 1951 S.C. 530.

[2] *Hynds* v. *H.*, 1966 S.C. 201.

[3] *Rorie* v. *R.*, 1967 S.L.T. 75.

[4] *Nisbet* v. *N.* (1896) 4 S.L.T. 142; *Main* v. *M.*, 1945 S.C. 469; *Thomas* v. *T.*, 1947 S.C. (H.L.) 45; *Walker* v. *W.*, 1953 S.C. 297; *Tullis* v. *T.*, 1953 S.C. 312.

[5] *Main, supra*; *Thomas, supra*; cf. *Mackay* v. *M.*, 1958 S.L.T. (Notes) 35.

[6] Fraser, *H. & W.* II, 878–9.

[7] *Paterson* v. *Russell* (1850) 7 Bell 337; *Russell* v. *R.* [1897] A.C. 395; *Graham* v. *G.* (1878) 5 R. 1093; *Thomas, supra*.

[8] *Paterson* v. *Russell* (1850) 7 Bell 337, 363; *McDonald* v. *McD.*, 1939 S.C. 173, 177, 181.

[9] *Paterson, supra*; *Graham* v. *G.* (1878) 5 R. 1093, 1095; *Russell* v. *R.* [1897] A.C. 395; *McDonald, supra*; *Dobbie* v. *D.*, 1955 S.C. 371; cf. *Adair* v. *A.*, 1924 S.L.T. 749; *Bennett* v. *B.*, 1949 S.L.T. (Notes) 40.

[10] *Duffy* v. *D.*, 1947 S.C. 54; *Dunlop* v. *D.*, 1950 S.C. 227; cf. *Dawson* v. *D.*, 1925 S.C. 221; *McFarlane* v. *McF.*, 1951 S.C. 530; *Dobbie* v. *D.*, 1955 S.C. 371.

[11] Divorce (Sc.) Act, 1964, S. 4.

no longer have regard to the need for present or future protection, so that proven cruelty now gives a vested right to divorce. Opinions have been expressed that there is no difference in principle between Scots law and English as to the kind or degree of cruelty necessary for divorce.[1] The question of cruelty must be considered on the whole facts and not by considering the conduct of one party in isolation.[2]

Physical cruelty

Cruelty may be constituted by assaults, blows, personal violence, or threats thereof, or any conduct which leads to physical injury or creates danger to life or health.[3] Normally there is a sustained course of incidents,[4] but a single act may be sufficient, if serious and if there appears reason to apprehend repetition.[5] It is cruelty to communicate venereal disease to the pursuer, if the defender's conduct showed reckless indifference to the pursuer's health.[6]

Mental cruelty

Though there be no physical maltreatment, selfish, thoughtless, or indifferent conduct, neglect, persecution or disregard, may amount to cruelty if grave and weighty in character, striking at the matrimonial relationship and causing material deterioration of physical or mental health.[7] This may take the form of false accusations of adultery,[8] persistent unfounded accusations of immorality,[9] possibly of unnatural sexual relations between the defender and a third party,[10] persistent deliberate refusal of sexual relations,[11] or excessive sexual demands,[12] or abnormal sexual

---

[1] *Jamieson v. J.*, 1952 S.C. (H.L.) 44; *White v. W.*, 1966 S.C. 187.

[2] *Paterson v. P.*, 1965 S.L.T. (Notes) 51. On various incidents see *Walker, supra; Tullis, supra.*

[3] *Paterson, supra; Graham, supra; McGaan v. McG.* (1880) 8 R. 279; *Russell, supra.*

[4] *Steuart v. S.* (1870) 8 M. 821; *Mackenzie v. M.* (1895) 22 R. (H.L.) 32, 36; cf. *Bennett v. B.*, 1949 S.L.T. (Notes) 40.

[5] *Stewart, supra; Forbes v. F.*, 1965 S.L.T. 109.   [6] *Strain v. S.* (1885) 13 R. 132.

[7] *Mackenzie v. M.* (1895) 22 R. (H.L.) 32; *Russell v. R.* [1897] A.C. 395; *Aitchison v. A.* (1903) 10 S.L.T. 331; *Jamieson v. J.*, 1952 S.C. (H.L.) 44.

[8] *Jackson v. J.* (1906) 14 S.L.T. 331.

[9] *Russell, supra; Aitchison, supra; Duffy v. D.*, 1947 S.C. 54.

[10] *Gardner v. G.* [1947] 1 All E.R. 630; cf. *Hutchison v. H.*, 1945 S.C. 427, 431; *M. v. M.*, 1967 S.L.T. (Notes) 116.

[11] *Scott v. S.*, 1960 S.C. 36; *P. v. P.* [1965] 2 All E.R. 456; *Evans v. E.* [1965] 2 All E.R. 789; contrast *P. v. P.* [1964] 3 All E.R. 919; *B. v. B.* [1965] 3 All E.R. 263; *H. v. H.*, 1968 S.L.T. 40.

[12] *Holborn v. H.* [1947] 1 All E.R. 32.

practices,[1] improper practices towards the parties' child,[2] insults and neglect,[3] fraudulent conduct towards business associates,[4] dishonesty and criminality resulting in frequent imprisonment,[5] repeatedly leaving home without warning, failing to maintain the pursuer, and removing a child without notice,[6] drunkenness and neglect of the family,[7] murdering and attempting to murder certain of the pursuer's close relatives,[8] committing gross indecency with another male in a public lavatory,[9] spending money on his own pursuits and keeping the pursuer short of money,[10] insistence on the use of contraceptives,[11] sexual indifference and refusal of sexual intercourse,[12] unreasonable conduct to the pursuer,[13] outbreaks of temper and violence.[14]

It has been held not to extend to lewd practices by a husband towards young girls, but not involving the wife.[15]

Cruelty to the parties' child, or possibly to another relative, or possibly to an animal, or false accusations of conduct on the pursuers' part, may be constructive mental cruelty to the pursuer, if it causes the pursuer actual or apprehended injury to health, but it probably must be in the presence or within the actual knowledge of the pursuer.[16]

Mental factors in cruelty

Formerly it was held that the defender's conduct, alleged to be cruel, had to be intentional[17] or show unwarrantable indifference to the pursuer's feelings, or, if it did not strike directly at the matrimonial relationship, such as dishonesty or criminality causing deterioration to the pursuer's health, the guilty spouse had to have aimed it at, and intended thereby to implicate or hurt,

[1] *White* v. *W.* [1948] P. 330; *Cackett* v. *C.* [1950] 1 All E.R. 677.
[2] *Duffy, supra.*
[3] *Jamieson* v. *J.*, 1951 S.C. 286; 1952 S.C. (H.L.) 44.
[4] *Waite* v. *W.*, 1961 S.C. 266.
[5] *Hutton* v. *H.*, 1962 S.C. 10.
[6] *Rose* v. *R.*, 1964 S.L.T. (Notes) 15.
[7] *Campbell* v. *C.*, 1973 S.L.T. (Notes) 82.
[8] *Christie* v. *C.*, 1964 S.L.T. 72; cf. *A.B.* v. *C.D.*, 1959 S.C. 27.
[9] *White* v. *W.*, 1966 S.C. 187; cf. *Coffer* v. *C.* (1964) 108 Sol. Jo. 465 (lesbianism); *M.* v. *M.*, 1967 S.L.T. 119.
[10] *Kerr* v. *K.*, 1967 S.L.T. (Notes) 77.
[11] *Jamieson, supra.*
[12] *H.* v. *H.*, 1968 S.L.T. 40.
[13] *Craig* v. *C.*, 1970 S.L.T. (Notes) 43.
[14] *Purdie* v. *P.*, 1970 S.L.T. (Notes) 58.
[15] *Rintoul* v. *R.*, 1964 S.L.T. 183.
[16] *Duffy, supra.*
[17] *Inglis* v. *I.*, 1911 S.C. 547; *Jamieson* v. *J.*, 1951 S.C. 286; altered 1952 S.C. (H.L.) 44.

the pursuer.[1] But the House of Lords[2] and statute[3] have now laid down that it is not a defence that the defender had no malicious intent towards the pursuer.

Formerly it was also held that the defender must have been in control of his conduct. He was not guilty of cruelty if he suffered from insanity or unsoundness of mind related to the acts complained of and rendering him irresponsible for his conduct.[4] The House of Lords[5] and statute[6] have now laid down that the insanity of the defender at the time of the conduct complained of as cruel is not a defence.[7] An action is not barred because the defender is then detained as a patient in a mental hospital if he had been guilty of cruelty before being certified.[8]

Habitual drunkenness as cruelty

At common law habitual drunkenness was not cruelty *per se*,[9] but was relevant if it endangered the health or safety of the other spouse.[10] By statute,[11] where either spouse is a habitual drunkard,[12] proof of this fact in a consistorial action has the same legal consequences as cruelty and bodily violence, if it has brought about one of the stated consequences,[13] and therefore justifies

---

[1] *Tullis* v. *T.*, 1953 S.C. 312; *Waite* v. *W.*, 1961 S.C. 266; *Hutton* v. *H.*, 1962 S.C. 10; *Mathieson* v. *M.*, 1962 S.L.T. 229; *Rintoul* v. *R.*, 1964 S.L.T. 183; disapproving *Scott* v. *S.*, 1960 S.C. 36.

[2] *Gollins* v. *G.* [1964] A.C. 644.

[3] Divorce (Sc.) Act, 1964, S. 5(2)(b); *Anderson* v. *A.*, 1971 S.L.T. 303. But where the misconduct did not affect health seriously, intention to injure has been held requisite: *Anderson* v. *A.*, 1970 S.L.T. (Notes) 64.

[4] Fraser, *H. & W.* II, 891; *Steuart* v. *S.* (1870) 8 M. 821; *Inglis* v. *I.*, 1931 S.C. 547; *Breen* v. *B.*, 1961 S.C. 158, disapproving *McKenzie* v. *McK.*, 1960 S.C. 322; *Brennan* v. *B.*, 1963 S.L.T. (Notes) 79. *McLachlan* v. *McL.*, 1945 S.C. 382, is a doubtful case.

[5] *Williams* v. *W.* [1964] A.C. 698, not following *Breen, supra.*

[6] Divorce (Sc.) Act, 1964, S. 5(2)(a).

[7] cf. *Crump* v. *C.* [1965] 2 All E.R. 980 (compulsive psycho-neurosis).

[8] *Dobbie* v. *D.*, 1955 S.C. 371, applying *McDonald* v. *McD.*, 1939 S.C. 173, not following *McFarlane* v. *McF.*, 1951 S.C. 530.

[9] *Fulton* v. *F.* (1850) 12 D. 1104.

[10] *McGaan* v. *McG.* (1880) 8 R. 279; *Dunlop* v. *D.*, 1950 S.C. 227.

[11] Licensing (Scotland) Act, 1903, S. 73.

[12] Defined (Habitual Drunkards Act, 1879, S. 3, amended Mental Health (Sc.) Act, 1960, Sched. 4) as a person who, not being a person suffering from mental disorder within the meaning of the Mental Health (Scotland) Act, 1960, is notwithstanding, by reason of habitual intemperate drinking of intoxicating liquor, at times dangerous to himself or herself or others, or incapable of managing himself or herself, or his or her affairs: see also *Hutchison* v. *H.*, 1945 S.C. 427, 433.

[13] viz.: danger to himself or herself or others, or incapacity to manage himself or herself, or his or her affairs.

separation[1] or divorce.[2] It is sufficient, unless there is delay in raising the action, to prove that the defender was an habitual drunkard when the pursuer left him, the presumption being that the habit persists.[3] An action may be founded on cruelty or on cruelty by habitual drunkenness.[4]

Divorce for Sodomy or Bestiality

Divorce may be granted on the ground that the defender has committed either of these offences.[5] Either may be proved by an extract of a conviction of the defender for the offence in any part of the United Kingdom,[6] but the wrong may be proved otherwise even if there has been no conviction.[7] It has been held in England that a wife cannot found a petition for divorce on sodomy committed on herself if she was a consenting party.[8] In the case of sodomy intimation must be made to the defender's coparticipant in the offence. There is no remedy for lesbianism, but such conduct might justify a husband in non-adherence.

Dissolution of marriage on the ground of presumed death

The Court may declare a marriage dissolved on the ground of the presumed death of the other spouse, if satisfied that reasonable grounds[9] exist for supposing that the other spouse is dead.[10] If the defender has been continuously absent from the petitioner for a period of seven years or upwards and the petitioner has no reason to believe that the other party has been living within that time, that is evidence of death unless the contrary be proved.[10] The onus is on the petitioner to make enquiries so as reasonably to satisfy the court that the defender has disappeared rather than merely deserted,[11] and search should be made in the national Registers.[12] The reappearance of the spouse judicially presumed dead has no effect by itself, but would justify reduction of the decree at the instance of either party. This would restore the dissolved marriage and nullify any second marriage contracted

---

[1] *Isles* v. *I.* (1906) 14 S.L.T. 118; *A.B.* v. *C.D.*, 1911, 1 S.L.T. 407; *X.T.* v. *Z.Y.*, 1911, 1 S.L.T. 459; *Low* v. *L.*, 1931 S.L.T. (Sh. Ct.) 14.

[2] *Rooney* v. *R.*, 1962 S.L.T. 294.   [3] *Cox* v. *C.*, 1942 S.C. 352.

[4] *Stephen* v. *S.*, 1967 S.L.T. (Notes) 51.   [5] Divorce (Sc.) Act, 1938, S. 1(1)(d).

[6] Ibid., S. 1(2).

[7] *Coffey* v. *C.* [1898] P. 169.

[8] *Statham* v. *S.* [1929] P. 131; *Davidson* v. *D.* [1953] 1 All E.R. 611; *T.* v. *T.* [1964] P. 85.

[9] cf. *Cumming* (1944) 60 Sh. Ct. Rep. 142; *Hannay* ; *Holmes*, 1949 S.C. 304.

[10] Divorce (Sc.) Act, 1938, S. 5.

[11] *Labacianskas* v. *L.*, 1949 S.C. 280; cf. *Lench* v. *L.*, 1945 S.C. 295.

[12] *Gilchrist*, 1950 S.L.T. (Notes) 6.

while the decree stood. Alternatively the court could at common law hold that evidence had overcome the presumption that life continues for a substantial period,[1] and this also would permit remarriage. But a finding of death under the Presumption of Life Limitation (Scotland) Act, 1891, has no effect on marriage and does not permit remarriage.[2]

Cross-actions of divorce

It is competent for each spouse simultaneously to seek divorce from the other; the grounds may be the same, or different. Normally such actions will be heard together.[3] Where decree in one action had become final, it has been held that the pursuer in the other no longer had a title to reclaim in the other action, the marriage having been dissolved.[4] If decree is granted in both actions simultaneously either party may reclaim to avoid the finding that he or she was guilty of adultery, and to alter the consequences of the actions so far as concerning property.[5] Similarly there may be cross actions of divorce and of nullity of marriage, in which case the divorce will be sisted to await the decision of the action for nullity.[6]

Absolute bars to action for divorce

There are three pleas, the establishment of any one of which wholly bars the pursuer from obtaining judicial separation or divorce.

Condonation

Condonation or forgiveness of the offence bars an action of divorce on the ground of adultery or desertion or cruelty, and may well do so also where the ground is sodomy or bestiality. Adultery[7] cannot be condoned by mere expressions of forgiveness,[8] nor will it inferred from anything less than a continuance or resumption of full matrimonial relations in the full knowledge of the other spouse's adultery,[9] or at least genuine belief in its having taken place,[10] but not if there is merely suspicion of

---

[1] See chap. 15, *supra.*
[2] *Brady* v. *Murray,* 1933 S.L.T. 534; *Fraser,* 1950 S.L.T. (Sh. Ct.) 51.
[3] *Gray* v. *G.,* 1968 S.C. 185.
[4] *Bridges* v. *B.,* 1911 S.C. 250.   [5] *Connell* v. *C.,* 1950 S.C. 505.
[6] *A.B.* v. *C.B.,* 1911, 2 S.L.T. 99.   [7] Bell, *Prin.* §1531.
[8] *Ralston* v. *R.* (1881) 8 R. 371; *Annan* v. *A.,* 1948 S.C. 532; *Dick* v. *D.,* 1949 S.C. 66.
[9] *Hunt* v. *H.* (1893) 31 S.L.R. 244; *Edgar* v. *E.* (1902) 4 F. 632; *Steven* v. *S.,* 1919, 2 S.L.T. 239.
[10] *Wemyss* v. *W.* (1866) 4 M. 660; *Paterson* v. *P.,* 1938 S.C. 251.

infidelity.[1] It may be inferred even though the condoner did not have full knowledge of the extent of the other's guilt, if no further inquiry is made.[2] If sexual relations are resumed in the full knowledge of adultery condonation will be held established[3] and this result cannot be escaped by a denial of real forgiveness,[4] or by the imposition of any condition.[2] Even the resumption of cohabitation without sexual relations may amount to condonation[5] and if the parties resume or continue residence in the same house condonation will be presumed unless disproved.[6] Any presumption of condonation arising from the continuance or resumption of marital intercourse may be rebutted by a pursuer of either sex.[7] Condonation of adultery is not now to be inferred by reason only of a continuation or resumption of cohabitation between the parties for any one period not exceeding three months, or of anything done during such cohabitation, if it were done with a view to a reconciliation.[8] If condonation is held proved, the effect is to wipe out all known incidents of adultery prior to the condonation, but not any acts of adultery then unknown to the pursuer.[9] It matters not that there might not have been condonation had they been known.[10] But even condoned adultery may subsequently be referred to, not as a ground of action, but as casting light on subsequent suspicious conduct by the defender.[11] It does not prejudice an action for subsequent adultery, even with the same paramour. Condonation does not bar an action of damages against the paramour for the wrong of interfering with the pursuer's domestic relations.[12] The onus of proof is on the defender pleading condonation.[13]

Condonation of desertion may be inferred from a resumption of matrimonial relations after the triennium for divorce has run, in the full knowledge of all material circumstances, or by a substantial period of resumed cohabitation, but apart from these cases,

---

[1] *Collins* v. *C.* (1884) 11 R. (H.L.) 19.
[2] *A.* v. *B.* (1870) 8 S.L.R. 258; *Smith* v. *S.* (1904) 12 S.L.T. 341.
[3] *Edgar* v. *E.* (1902) 4 F. 632.
[4] *Wemyss* v. *W.* (1866) 4 M. 660; *Collins* v. *C.* (1884) 11 R. (H.L.) 19.
[5] *Edgar, supra; Dick* v. *D.,* 1949 S.C. 66, 68; but see *Mitchell* v. *M.,* 1947 S.L.T. (Notes) 9.
[6] *Edgar, supra.*
[7] Divorce (Sc.) Act, 1964, S. 1.
[8] Ibid., S. 2(1).
[9] *Ralston* v. *R.* (1881) 8 R. 371; *Steven* v. *S.,* 1919, 2 S.L.T. 239.
[10] *Ralston, supra.*
[11] *Robertson* v. *R.* (1888) 15 R. 1001; *Nicol* v. *N.,* 1938 S.L.T. 98.
[12] *Macdonald* v. *M.* (1885) 12 R. 1327.
[13] *Andrews* v. *A.,* 1961 S.L.T. (Notes) 48.

the vested right to divorce is not lost by a brief temporary resumption of cohabitation.[1]

Condonation of cruelty is not to be inferred from refusal or failure to seek a judicial remedy on the occurrence of one or two acts of cruelty.[2] Even where cohabitation has been continued or resumed after cruelty those incidents are not excluded from consideration if there is a subsequent incident, because the inquiry must consider the whole married life and determine whether the pursuer can with safety continue to live with the defender.[3] But if there are no subsequent incidents the continuance of cohabitation may yield an inference of forgiveness and suggests an absence of danger to life or health.[4] Condonation of cruelty is not to be inferred by reason only of a continuation or resumption of cohabitation for any one period not exceeding three months, or of anything done during such cohabitation, if it were done with a view to a reconciliation.[5]

Connivance or lenocinium

This is a bar to divorce on the ground of adultery and might be relevant also in a case founded on sodomy or bestiality. Lenocinium is whoremongering, and in Scotland[6] the substance of the plea is that the husband was actively accessory to, or participant in, or the direct occasion of, or otherwise promoted or positively encouraged, his wife's adultery.[7] It is not inferred from mere lack of care[8] or indifference[9] or imprudence[10] or acquiescence,[11] or even permission to act when there were grounds of suspicion.[12] The wife's misconduct must be causally connected with her husband's encouragement to adultery, and not too

---

[1] *Wilson* v. *W.*, 1944 S.L.T. 223; Divorce (Sc.) Act, 1964, S. 2 (2).

[2] *Richards* v. *R.*, 1939 S.C. 554.

[3] *Macfarlane* v. *M.* (1848) 10 D. 962; *Graham* v. *G.* (1878) 5 R. 1093; *Martin* v. *M.* (1895) 3 S.L.T. 150; *Smeaton* v. *S.* (1900) 2 F. 837; *Richards, supra; Adams* v. *A.*, 1964 S.L.T. (Notes) 101. See also *Watson* v. *W.* (1874) 12 S.L.R. 78.

[4] By virtue of the Divorce (Sc.) Act, 1964, S. 4, future safety is relevant only in separation cases.

[5] Divorce (Sc.) Act, 1964, S. 2(1); cf. *Herridge* v. *H.* [1966] 1 All E.R. 93.

[6] The English concept of connivance is different; see *Wemyss* v. *W.* (1866) 4 M. 660; *Riddell* v. *R.*, 1952 S.C. 475.

[7] Bell, *Prin.* §1532; Fraser, *H. & W.*, II, 1184; *Wemyss* v. *W.* (1866) 4 M. 660, 662; (1877) 4 R. 332; *Marshall* v. *M.* (1881) 8 R. 702; *Hunter* v. *H.* (1884) 11 R. 359; *Thomson* v. *T.*, 1908 S.C. 179; *Gallacher* v. *G.*, 1928 S.C. 586; *Hannah* v. *H.*, 1931 S.C. 275; *Riddell* v. *R.*, 1952 S.C. 475. A wife also can probably be guilty of lenocinium.

[8] *Fletcher* v. *F.* (1902) 10 S.L.T. 296.

[9] *Erskine* v. *E.* (1907) 15 S.L.T. 144.

[10] *Hunter* v. *H.* (1883) 11 R. 359.

[11] *McMahon* v. *McM.*, 1928 S.N. 37, 158 (bigamous marriage).

[12] *Thomson* v. *T.*, 1908 S.C. 179.

remotely connected in time.[1] It is not lenocinium to have suspicions but conceal them and have the defender watched,[2] nor to say that divorce will be considered if evidence is furnished,[3] nor even to take a wife to a brothel, unless to tempt her to adultery.[4]

Collusion

Collusion is a bar to divorce on the ground of adultery only.[5] It also differs from collusion in English law. It consists not in a common desire to have the marriage ended, nor in allowing an action to pass undefended, nor even in co-operation to secure divorce, as by communicating evidence, but only in permitting a false case to be substantiated or withholding a just defence.[6] It will not be held established unless facts are proved which show that the oath of calumny has been falsely sworn.[7] It does not strike at an agreement to withdraw defences,[8] or even acting in fulfilment of a promise to divorce if the parties quarrelled.[9]

Pursuer's conduct as bar to divorce

The pursuer's own misconduct is in some cases a bar to divorce. In adultery the pursuer's own adultery or other misconduct is no bar, though it grounds a cross-action.[10] In desertion the pursuer's conduct giving reasonable cause for non-adherence is a bar. In insanity the pursuer's neglect or misconduct conducing to the defender's insanity is a discretionary bar.[11] In cruelty the pursuer's misconduct of any kind is probably irrelevant.

Discretionary bars to action for divorce

In certain circumstances the court may hold that a pursuer is barred by his own conduct from obtaining divorce, but the court is not obliged in such a case to refuse decree. The grant or refusal of decree is discretionary in the circumstances. The main conditional bar is mora. Lapse of time after adultery before bringing action is not a bar if the pursuer was ignorant of the wrong,[12] and

[1] *Marshall, supra; Hunter, supra; Gallacher v. G.*, 1928 S.C. 586; 1934 S.C. 339.
[2] *Fraser, H. & W.* II, 1186; *McIntosh v. M.* (1882) 20 S.L.R. 117; *Thomson, supra.*
[3] *Hannah, supra.*
[4] *Donald v. D.* (1863) 1 M. 741; *Wemyss, supra.*
[5] Bell, *Prin.* §1530; cf. *Shaw v. Gould* (1868) L.R. 3 H.L. 55.
[6] *Walker v. W.*, 1911 S.C. 163, 169; see also *McKenzie v. McK.*, 1935 S.L.T. 198.
[7] *Fairgrieve v. Chalmers*, 1912 S.C. 745; *Riddell v. R.*, 1952 S.C. 475.
[8] *Williamson v. W.*, 1932 S.N. 65; cf. *Graham v. G.* (1881) 9 R. 327.
[9] *McKenzie v. M.*, 1935 S.L.T. 198.
[10] *Marchant v. M.*, 1948 S.L.T. 143; cf. *Connell v. C.*, 1950 S.C. 505.
[11] 1938 Act, S. 1(1) (c); see *Aitchison v. A.*, 1958 S.L.T. 47.
[12] *Gatchell v. G.* (1898) 6 S.L.T. 218; *Robertson v. R.* (1901) 9 S.L.T. 332.

if the wrong were known delay bars only if circumstances suggest condonation or acquiescence.[1] Mora and acquiescence may bar an action though they fall short of condonation.[2] An action of divorce for desertion is not necessarily prejudiced by even long delay after the triennium has expired,[3] but it may be held barred.[4]

EFFECT OF DIVORCE ON PROPERTY RIGHTS

At common law

Decree of divorce on any ground, except incurable insanity,[5] formerly entitled the innocent spouse at once[6] to claim from the estate of the guilty party the legal rights which could have been claimed on death,[7] i.e. a capital payment once and for all, but not any periodical payments of aliment. The innocent wife might accordingly exact terce and *jus relictae*,[8] the innocent husband courtesy (if the requisites for that claim had been satisfied)[9] but not *jus relicti*.[10] The fiction that the guilty spouse was treated as dead was not rigidly applied, and the innocent spouse was held entitled to legal rights out of the capital value of liferent interests enjoyed by the guilty,[11] though not out of capital in which the guilty spouse had only a contingent interest.[12] The innocent spouse might also exact provisions conventionally payable, as under a marriage contract, by the guilty spouse, or any third party on his behalf, on the termination of the marriage, to the survivor, not only funds actually contributed by the other and forfeited by him.[13] But the innocent spouse could not exact pay-

[1] *A.B.* v. *C.D.* (1853) 15 D. 976; *Hellon* v. *H.* (1873) 11 M. 290; *Holmes* v. *H.*, 1927 S.L.T. 20; *Johnstone* v. *J.*, 1931 S.C. 60; see also *Cocozza* v. *C.*, 1955 S.L.T. (Notes) 29; *Macfarlane* v. *M.*, 1956 S.C. 472.

[2] *Macfarlane, supra.*

[3] *Mackenzie* v. *M.* (1883) 11 R. 105; *Monahan* v. *M.*, 1930 S.C. 221; see also *Goold* v. *G.*, 1927 S.C. 177.

[4] *Grant* v. *G.*, 1961 S.L.T. 322.

[5] Divorce (Scotland) Act, 1938, S. 1(1)(b); see also *infra*.

[6] *Smith* v. *McLean*, 1940 S.L.T. (Sh. Ct.) 22.

[7] For further discussion see Ch. 119, *infra*.

[8] Stair I, 4, 20; Ersk. I, 6, 46, and 48; Fraser, *H. & W.* II, 1216; *Harvey* v. *Farquhar* (1871) 10 M. (H.L.) 26; *Montgomery* v. *Zarifi*, 1918 S.C. (H.L.) 128, 137; *Manderson* v. *Sutherland* (1899) 1 F. 621.

[9] Fraser, *supra*.

[10] Married Women's Property (Sc.) Act, 1881, S. 6; *Eddington* v. *Robertson* (1895) 22 R. 430.

[11] *Scott* v. *S.*, 1930 S.C. 903; *Selsdon* v. *S.*, 1934 S.C. (H.L.) 24.

[12] *Wright* v. *Bryson*, 1935 S.C. (H.L.) 49.

[13] *Thom* v. *T.* (1852) 14 D. 861; *Harvey* v. *Farquhar* (1872) 10 M. (H.L.) 26; *Johnstone-Beattie* v. *J.* (1867) 5 M. 340; *Somervell's Tr.* v. *Dawes* (1903) 5 F. 1065; *Fortington* v. *Kinnaird*, 1942 S.C. 239; *Coat's Trs.* v. *Lord Advocate*, 1965 S.C. (H.L.) 45.

ment of testamentary bequests by his or her own relatives conditional on his or her survivance, unless this intention was apparent,[1] and divorce is not equivalent to death in relation to the rights of children.[2]

Conversely the guilty spouse on being divorced forfeited all claims to conventional provisions under marriage contracts.[3] In the case of cross actions of divorce, if decree were granted in both actions, neither party had any claim on the other's property.[4]

Under statute

The Succession (Scotland) Act, 1964, Part V, applicable to divorces brought after the commencement of that Act, provides (Ss. 25–26) that in an action on any ground other than incurable insanity the pursuer may, at any time prior to decree, apply to the court for an order for the payment to him by the defender,[5] or the defender's executor, of a capital sum,[6] or a periodical allowance,[7] or both;[8] and either party may apply to the court for an order varying the terms of any settlement made in contemplation of or during marriage, so far as taking effect on or after the termination of the marriage.[9] The court may on granting divorce make such order, if any, as it thinks fit having regard to the means of the parties and the circumstances of the case.[10]

---

[1] *Mason* v. *Beattie's Trs.* (1878) 6 R. 37.

[2] *Harvey's J.F.* v. *Spittal's Curator* (1893) 20 R. 1016; *Dawson* v. *Smart* (1903) 5 F. (H.L.) 24; *Montgomery* v. *Zarifi,* 1918 S.C. (H.L.) 128; *Coats's Trs., supra.*

[3] *Johnstone-Beattie* v. *Dalzell* (1868) 6 M. 333; *Ritchie* v. *R's Trs.* (1874) 1 R. 987; *Hedderwick* v. *Morison* (1901) 4 F. 163.

[4] *Thomson* v. *Donald's Exor.* (1871) 9 M. 1069; *Fraser* v. *Walker* (1872) 10 M. 837.

[5] Arrestment on the dependence of the action is warranted only exceptionally: see *Gillanders* v. *G.,* 1966 S.C. 54; *Brash* v. *B.,* 1966 S.C. 56; *Tweedie* v. *T.,* 1966 S.L.T. (Notes) 89.

[6] *Galloway* v. *G.,* 1965 S.L.T. (Notes) 92; *Hogg* v. *H.,* 1967 S.L.T. (Notes) 91; *Murray* v. *M.,* 1967 S.L.T. (Notes) 103; *Gould* v. *G.,* 1969 S.L.T. (Notes) 89; *Sharpe* v. *S.,* 1970 S.L.T. (Notes) 26.

[7] e.g. *Cartwright* v. *C.,* 1965 S.L.T. (Notes) 59. The basis of calculation is the payer's gross income. The amount is in the court's discretion and the court is not bound to make a deduction because of the wife's (pursuer's) own adultery: *Gray* v. *G.,* 1968 S.C. 185.

[8] e.g. *Patterson* v. *P.,* 1966 S.L.T. (Notes) 20; *Robertson* v. *R.,* 1967 S.L.T. (Notes) 78; *Nicol* v. *N.,* 1969 S.L.T. (Notes) 67.

[9] In *Holmpatrick* v. *Ainsworth,* 1943 S.C. 75, the divorced husband surrendered his liferent interest in a marriage-contract trust.

[10] A wife has been granted a periodical allowance though the husband was successful in his cross-action: *Thomson* v. *T.,* 1966 S.L.T. (Notes) 49. In undefended cases detailed evidence of means will generally not be required: *Gould* v. *G.,* 1966 S.C. 88. As to appeal against award on the ground of manifest inequity see *Nicol* v. *N.,* 1970 S.L.T. 302. An award is discretionary, and may be refused if there is no basis in evidence for an award: *Seed* v. *S.,* 1971 S.L.T. 305.

Application may be made after divorce if there has been a change in circumstances. An order for a periodical allowance may be varied or recalled by a subsequent order. Except as to arrears, an order for a periodical payment lapses on the pursuer's death or remarriage. Such an order is enforceable throughout the United Kingdom under the Maintenance Orders Act, 1950. The pursuer may (S. 27) until a year after the disposal of such an application apply to the court for an order to prevent the defender defeating any claim the pursuer has or might make under s. 26.[1]

Exception—Divorce for incurable insanity

In the case of divorce for incurable insanity, the decree never had automatic effect on property rights, and the court may make such order, if any, as having regard to the respective means of the parties it shall think fit, for the payment by either party, or out of any estate belonging to him or held for his behoof, or in the event of his predecease, by his executors, of a capital sum or an annual or periodical allowance to or for behoof of the other party or of any children of the marriage. Such an order may be varied or recalled.[2] Such a divorce may result in the total failure of a marriage-contract trust.[3]

Other provisions

Provisions for children in a marriage-contract, to become operative on their parents' death, are not rendered payable by divorce,[4] and powers granted thereunder are still exercisable.[5] The Act 1592, c. 11, enacted that a wife divorced for adultery who married or openly cohabited with her paramour could not alienate her heritage to any person to the prejudice of the issue of the dissolved marriage or of her lawful heirs at law,[6] but this has been repealed.[7]

Reduction of decree of divorce

A decree of divorce may be reduced, as having been granted without jurisdiction, or by perjured evidence or concealment of

---

[1] e.g. *Johnstone* v. *J.*, 1967 S.C. 143.

[2] Divorce (Sc.) Act, 1964, S. 7, replacing Divorce (Sc.) Act, 1938, S. 2.

[3] *Adamson's Trs.* v. *A's C.B.*, 1940 S.C. 596.

[4] *Harvey's J.F.* v. *Spittal's Curator* (1893) 20 R. 1016; *Dawson* v. *Smart* (1903) 5 F. (H.L.) 24.

[5] *McGrady's Trs.* v. *McG.*, 1932 S.C. 191; *Peel's Trs.* v. *Drummond*, 1936 S.C. 786.

[6] Ersk. II, 3, 16; Fraser, *H. & W.* II, 1224; *Irvine* v. *Skeen* (1707) Mor. 6350.

[7] Succession (Sc.) Act, 1964, Sched. 3.

known facts. This necessarily restores the marriage and rein-
states the parties in married status. Hence intercourse by one
spouse with a third party, even between the raising of the action
of reduction and decree therein is adultery,[1] and *a fortiori* after
decree of reduction.

Registration

When a decree altering the status of a person has been granted
the court notifies the Registrar-General who causes an appropriate entry to be made in the Register of Corrections.[2]

[1] *Sands* v. *S.*, 1964 S.L.T. 80.
[2] Registration of Births, etc. (Sc.) Act, 1965, S. 48. This is concerned only with
Scottish decrees: *Smart* v. *Registrar-General*, 1954 S.C. 81.

CHAPTER 17

THE DOMESTIC RELATIONS
(2) PARENT AND CHILD

THE mutual obligations and legal relations between parent and child are obediential, not voluntary, and are defined by law itself.[1] They vary according as, in the first place, the child is of legitimate, illegitimate, legitimated or adopted status, and in the second place according to the age of the child. Scots law, following Roman law, distinguishes the status of the pupil (from birth to puberty, fixed as 14 in the case of boys, 12 in the case of girls), from that of the minor (from these ages till the attainment of majority at 18) and of the adult or person of full age.[2] Statute has intervened in many circumstances to modify the common law principles.

Legitimacy or illegitimacy

The issue of legitimacy or illegitimacy if in doubt is determined by an action of declarator of legitimacy or of bastardy. With either may be combined a conclusion for decree of putting to silence, ordaining the defender to desist from asserting falsely that the pursuer was illegitimate, or as the case may be.[3] The competency of combining a declarator of bastardy with a divorce has been doubted.[4] Where a decree altering the status of any person has been granted, its import must be notified to the Registrar General who will have it entered in the Register of Corrections.[5]

LEGITIMATE CHILDREN

Legitimate children

A legitimate child is one either conceived or born in lawful marriage, or to parties to a putative marriage, i.e. one which, though null, at least one party honestly though erroneously

---

[1] Stair I, 5, 1; Mack. I, 7, 1; Bankt. I, 6, 1; Ersk. I, 6, 49; Hume, *Lect.* I, 191; Bell, *Prin.* §1624–36; More, *Lect.* I, 78; Fraser, *P. & Ch., passim.*

[2] Stair I, 5, 2; Ersk. I, 7, 1; Bell, *Prin.* §2066.

[3] cf. *Imre* v. *Mitchell*, 1958 S.C. 439.

[4] *Jamieson* v. *J.*, 1969 S.L.T. (Notes) 11. See also *Curran* v. *C.*, 1957 S.L.T. (Notes) 47.

[5] Registration of Births, Deaths, and Marriages (Sc.) Act, 1965, S. 48.

believed to be valid.[1] In accordance with the maxim *pater est quem nuptiae demonstrant* a child born to a married woman, if born sufficiently long after her marriage, or sufficiently shortly after its termination, that it could have been conceived in wedlock,[2] is presumed begotten by her husband and therefore legitimate.[3] The presumption is strong and is not redargued merely by evidence of her adultery, but only by clear and conclusive facts.[4] The presumption is inapplicable if the birth is so shortly after the marriage, or so long after its dissolution, that the child could not have been conceived in wedlock,[5] though if a man has arranged to marry a woman already, to his knowledge, pregnant, and there were opportunities for pre-marital intercourse, a similar presumption arises that he is the father.[6] If he did not know of her pregnancy a presumption will arise if he take no action to repudiate the wife and child when he has ground for suspicion.[7] The presumption does not arise when a man marries a woman who has had an illegitimate child, even shortly before the marriage.[8] The presumption is probably inapplicable if the marriage was irregular,[9] and does not arise if the legal issue in doubt is of the existence of the marriage or otherwise.[10] The fact that parties have registered their child as legitimate is evidence, but by no means conclusive, of that fact, or at least of their belief at the time.[11] The presumption still applies though parties live apart or have separated voluntarily, but may be rebutted by proof of non-access by the husband.[12]

The presumption does not, however, apply if the parties have been judicially separated before the probable date of conception, since after judicial separation a husband is not entitled to access to his wife. The presumption, though strong, may be rebutted by clear evidence of the husband's impotence, or of his not

[1] Ersk. I, 6, 49, 52; Bell, *Prin.* §1624–5.

[2] *Gardner* v. *G.* (1876) 3 R. 695; 4 R. (H.L.) 56.

[3] Stair III, 3, 42; Ersk. I, 6, 49; Bell, *Prin.* §1626.

[4] *Routledge* v. *Carruthers* (1816) 4 Dow 392; *Imre* v. *Mitchell*, 1958 S.C. 439.

[5] Stair, *supra*; *Lepper* v. *Watson* (1802) Hume 488; *Aitken* v. *Mitchell* (1806) Hume 489; see also *Jobson* v. *Reid* (1827) 5 S. 715; (1830) 8 S. 343; (1832) 10 S. 594.

[6] *Gardner*, *supra*; *Reid* v. *Mill* (1879) 6 R. 659; *Kerr* v. *Lindsay* (1890) 18 R. 365; *Imre* v. *Mitchell*, 1958 S.C. 439.

[7] cf. *Lang* v. *L.*, 1921 S.C. 44; *Hastings* v. *H.*, 1941 S.L.T. 323, where in such circumstances the husband left the wife.

[8] *Imre*, *supra*; *Brooks's Exrx.* v. *James*, 1970 S.C. 147.

[9] *Baptie* v. *Barclay* (1665) Mor. 8431; *Swinton* v. *S.* (1862) 24 D. 833.

[10] *Deans's J.F.* v. *D.*, 1912 S.C. 441.

[11] *Imre*, *supra*.

[12] *Montgomery* v. *M.* (1881) 8 R. 403; *Colquhoun* v. *C.* (1891) 28 S.L.R. 689; *Marshall* v. *M.*, 1934 S.N. 39; *Ballantyne* v. *Douglas*, 1953 S.L.T. (Notes) 10.

possibly having had access to his wife at or about the date of conception.[1] It is not sufficient by itself to show that the wife was guilty of adultery at or about that time.[2] Blood tests alone are insufficient to rebut the presumption.[3] The presumption may also be rebutted by inference, based on evidence of unreasonably short pregnancy after the first cohabitation following the husband's absence, or of unreasonably long pregnancy after the last cohabitation before his absence.[4]

A married woman may bring an action of affiliation and aliment against a man not her husband and thereby rebut the presumption, even though there had been a possibility of access by him.[5] Evidence by the parents themselves tending to bastardize their child is competent[6] but possibly not sufficient by itself to rebut the presumption.[7]

When a man marries the mother of an illegitimate child there is no presumption that he is the father.[8]

The status of legitimacy also attaches, as in canon law, to the children of a putative marriage, i.e. one where one or both parties honestly believed themselves free to marry, though their marriage was in fact null by reason of the existence of an impediment.[9] The marriage may have been irregular[10] but the parties' error must have been one of fact and not of law.[11] If a person has by common reputation enjoyed the status of legitimacy throughout his life this is presumed justified.[12]

---

[1] Craig II, 18, 13, and 20; Stair III, 3, 42; IV, 45, 20; Bankt. I, 2, 3; Ersk. I, 6, 50; *Mackay* v. *M.* (1855) 17 D. 494; *Brodie* v. *Dyce* (1872) 11 M. 142; *Steedman* v. *S.* (1887) 14 R. 1066; *Tennent* v. *T.* (1890) 17 R. 1205; *Coles* v. *Homer & Tulloh* (1895) 22 R. 716. Many such cases raise questions of the maximum and minimum possible durations of pregnancy, on which see Ch. 16, *supra*, and *infra*.

[2] *Routledge* v. *Carruthers*, 19 May 1812, F.C.; *Ballantyne, supra.*

[3] *Imre* v. *Mitchell*, 1958 S.C. 439. *Sed quaere.*

[4] Stair III, 3, 42; IV, 45, 20; Ersk. I, 6, 49, and 50; *Gray* v. *G.*, 1919, 1 S.L.T. 163; *McIntosh* v. *M.*, 1947 S.N. 23; *Currie* v. *C.*, 1950 S.C. 10.

[5] *Mackay, supra*; *Brodie, supra*; *Ballantyne, supra*; cf. *Reid* v. *Mill* (1879) 6 R. 659.

[6] *Burman* v. *B.*, 1930 S.C. 262.

[7] *Tennent* v. *T.* (1890) 17 R. 1205, 1223; *Burman* v. *B.*, 1930 S.C. 262; *Imre, supra.*

[8] *Brooks's Exrx.* v. *James*, 1970 S.C. 147.

[9] Craig II, 18, 18; Stair III, 3, 42; Ersk. I, 6, 51; Bell, *Prin.* §1625; *Jolly* v. *McGregor* (1828) 3 W. & S. 85; *Petrie* v. *Ross* (1896) 4 S.L.T. 63; *Smijth* v. *S.*, 1918, 1 S.L.T. 156. See also *Purves's Trs.* v. *P.* (1895) 22 R. 513; *Kirkcaldy Parish Council* v. *Traquair Parish Council*, 1915 S.C. 1124.

[10] *Smijth* v. *S.*, 1918, 1 S.L.T. 156.

[11] Fraser, *P. & Ch.* 33; *Purves's Trs.* v. *P.* (1896) 22 R. 513; *Philp's Trs.* v. *Beaton*, 1938 S.C. 733.

[12] *Brook's Exrx., supra.*

Statute[1] has also provided that where a decree of nullity of a voidable marriage is granted, any child who would have been legitimate had the marriage been dissolved and not annulled is to be deemed legitimate.

The child of adultery, of concubinage or casual cohabitation, or of a void marriage is not legitimate. Though the artificial insemination of a married woman with the semen of a donor is not adultery,[2] a child by A.I.D., not being begotten by the husband, is presumably illegitimate.

Registration of birth

A parent or the parents or any relative of either having knowledge of the birth, or the occupier of the premises in which the birth takes place, or any person present at the birth or having charge of the child must within 21 days attend personally at the local registrar's office to give information of statutory particulars regarding the birth.[3] An abbreviated extract of the entry is given to the informant and further copies may be obtained.[4]

Name

A legitimate child is normally given a christian or baptismal name and the surname of the parents, or of the father. The right to change a child's surname before majority probably resides primarily in the father, as the natural guardian, and a widowed or divorced mother, having custody of the child and having re-married, is probably not entitled to change the child's name without at least the father's consent, if still alive, and, probably, if the child is a minor, the child's consent.[5]

Parental rights over child

Parental rights and powers are of two kinds, that of guiding and directing the persons of children under full age, and that of legal administration, of managing their property and legal business or advising thereon.

---

[1] Law Reform (Misc. Prov.) Act, 1949, S. 4. This can in Scotland cover only the case of a child conceived by fecundation *ab extra*, and possibly also the case of the child conceived by A.I.H., where the marriage has not been consummated naturally; cf. *MacLennan* v. *McL.*, 1958 S.C. 105.

[2] As held in *MacLennan* v. *McL.*, 1958 S.C. 105. *Sed quaere.*

[3] Registration of Births, Deaths, and Marriages (Sc.) Act, 1965, S. 14. As to registrar's powers to require information, see Ss. 16, 21, 56(1). As to events in institutions, see S. 50.

[4] Ss. 19, 40.

[5] Note, 1949 S.L.T. (News) 95; cf. *Re T.* [1962] 3 W.L.R. 1477; Registration of Births, Deaths, and Marriages (Sc.) Act, 1965, S. 43.

In relation to a pupil or minor and to the administration of any property belonging to or held in trust for a pupil or minor or the application of income of any such property, a mother now[1] has the same rights and authority as a father; the parents' rights and authority are equal and exercisable by either without the other. An agreement by either to surrender any such rights is unenforceable, save during the parents' separation and even then not if the court is of opinion that it will not be for the benefit of the child to give effect to it. If the parents disagree either may apply to the Court of Session or any sheriff court for the court's direction, except in relation to custody or access.

Patria potestas

So long as a child is a pupil, the father had at common law, and now each parent has, the right of custody, and the power and authority to regulate the child's upbringing and discipline and govern its person;[2] this power is diminished but not ended when the pupil child becomes minor,[3] and terminates when the minor child becomes major.[4] During minority the father's authority may be lost by apparent intention to abandon it or by inability or unwillingness to discharge rightly the parental duty towards his child,[5] and in determining such a question the wishes and feelings of the child are entitled to weight.[6] The authority is also lost if the father dies or the child, while minor, is forisfamilated, i.e. has, with the father's consent, set out on its own by leaving home or taking employment, or, being a daughter, has married.[7]

Older authorities[8] state that the father is entitled to all the profits accruing from children's labour and industry, while they are living in family or maintained by him, but it is questionable if this right would be enforceable today, beyond what is a fair contribution to the expenses of the family home. Donations to children from the father or third parties have always been their own property.[9]

---

[1] Guardianship Act, 1973, S. 10.

[2] Stair I, 5, 13; Ersk. I, 6, 53; Bell, *Prin.* §1636; *Harvey* v. *H.* (1860) 22 D. 1198; but see *Young* v. *Rankin*, 1934 S.C. 499, 507.

[3] *Fisher* v. *Edgar* (1894) 21 R. 1076; *Greenock* v. *Kilmarnock and Stirling*, 1911 S.C. 570.

[4] The child then becomes *sui juris.*

[5] Stair, *supra*; Ersk. I, 6, 53.

[6] *Harvey, supra*; *Craig* v. *Greig* (1863) 1 M. 1172.   [7] Ersk., *supra.*

[8] Stair I, 5, 8; Ersk. I, 6, 53.

[9] Ersk., *supra.*

Custody and access

Custody is concerned with control of the physical person of the child only. By virtue of the *nobile officium* the Court of Session has power to deal with all questions of custody,[1] but it and the Sheriff Court also have power under statute.[2] At common law the father was alone entitled to the custody of a pupil child; the court would in the exercise of its *nobile officium* interfere only if the child's health or morals were in danger.[3] As custodier the father could fix the residence and regulate the upbringing of the child.[4] The court sometimes conferred custody on a factor *loco tutoris* after the father's death rather than leave the child with the mother.[5]

The Guardianship of Children (Scotland) Acts, 1886 to 1973,[6] provide that on all questions of custody or upbringing or administration of any property or application of income thereof the court must regard the welfare of the child as the first and paramount consideration.[7] The claim of the father from any other point of view, is not to be considered.[8] The court may exercise its powers though the parents are living together.[9] Interim custody may be granted pending a consistorial action between the parents.[10]

The Custody of Children (Scotland) Act, 1939, extends the powers of the court to make orders as to the custody, maintenance, or education of, or access to, pupil children, and minor children under 16.[11] After the father's death a minor child can

---

1 *McCallum* v. *McC.* (1893) 20 R. 293; *S.* v. *S.*, 1967 S.C. (H.L.) 46, 51.

2 Conjugal Rights (Sc.) Amdt. Act, 1861, S. 9; Sheriff Courts (Sc.) Acts, 1907, S. 5; 1913, S. 3; *Brown* v. *B.*, 1948 S.C. 5; *Campbell* v. *C.*, 1956 S.C. 285, 289; cf. *Curran* v. *C.*, 1957 S.L.T. (Notes) 47.

3 *A.B.* v. *C.D.* (1847) 10 D. 229; *McIver* v. *M.* (1859) 21 D. 1103; *Harvey* v. *H.* (1859) 22 D. 1198; *Lang* v. *L.* (1869) 7 M. 445; *Nicolson* v. *N.* (1869) 7 M. 1118; *Steuart* v. *S.* (1870) 8 M. 821; *Ketchen* v. *K.* (1870) 8 M. 952; *Symington* v. *S.* (1875) 2 R. (H.L.) 41; 2 R. 974; *Lilley* v. *L.* (1877) 4 R. 397.

4 Even if he were resident abroad: *Pagan* v. *P.* (1883) 10 R. 1072.

5 *Gulland* v. *Henderson* (1878) 5 R. 768.

6 Viz.: Guardianship of Infants Acts, 1886 and 1925; Guardianship Act, 1973, Part II. Applicable to legitimate pupil children only: 1886 Act, S. 8; *Brand* v. *Shaw* (1888) 16 R. 315. Extended to children under 16: 1973 Act, Ss. 10, 13.

7 1925 Act, S. 1; *Maquay* v. *Campbell* (1888) 15 R. 606; *Rintoul* v. *R.* (1898) 1 F. 22; *Marchetti* v. *M.* (1901) 3 F. 888; *M.* v. *M.*, 1926 S.C. 778; *Hume* v. *H.*, 1926 S.C. 1008; *Christison* v. *C.*, 1936 S.C. 381; *McLean* v. *McL.*, 1947 S.C. 79; *Brown* v. *B.*, 1948 S.C. 5.

8 *Sleigh* v. *S.* (1893) 30 S.L.R. 272; *Mackellar* v. *M.* (1898) 25 R. 883; *A.C.* v. *B.C.* (1902) 5 F. 108; *Fairley* v. *F.* (1904) 12 S.L.T. 140; *Campbell* v. *C.*, 1920 S.C. 31.

9 1925 Act, S. 3, amd. 1973, Sch. 4.

10 *Beattie* v. *B.* (1883) 11 R. 85; *McCallum* v. *M.* (1893) 20 R. 293; *Stevenson* v. *S.* (1894) 21 R. (H.L.) 96; *Reid* v. *R.* (1901) 3 F. 330.

11 In such a case the minor has a right to be heard: *Morrison*, 1943 S.C. 481.

choose his own residence and is not, unless by court order made under statute, subject to regulation as to its person by curators.[1]

Under all these acts the paramount consideration is the welfare of the child in the whole circumstances of the case.[2] Custody may be regulated pending consistorial proceedings.[3] Factors held to tip the balance in favour of one parent include the provision of a religious upbringing for the child.[4] If considerations of welfare are equally balanced, the father is still preferred.[5] Where both parents had died the nearest male agnate has been preferred.[6]

In an application under the 1886, 1925, 1928, and 1939 Acts relative to custody, if it appears to the court that there are exceptional circumstances making it impracticable or undesirable for the child to be entrusted to either parent or to anyone else, the court may commit the child to a specified local authority, or award custody to a person but order that the child be under the supervision of a specified local authority, subject to any directions from the court. Any such order lapses when the child attains 16. The parents may be ordered to pay for the child's maintenance.[7] Such an order may be varied or discharged.[8]

At common law a widowed mother has a legal title to custody, which will usually be enforced against any other custodier.[9] The court has several times refused to give custody of an orphan to a grandparent in preference to leaving him in an institution.[10] The power of the Scottish courts to grant custody is not limited by the fact that the parties are furth of Scotland.[11]

Custody of children in separation, nullity and divorce cases

The Court has jurisdiction in separation, nullity, and divorce cases to regulate the custody, maintenance, and education of any

---

[1] Ersk. I, 7, 14; Bell, *Prin.* §2090; *Harvey* v. *H.* (1860) 22 D. 1198, 1207; *Flannigan* v. *Bothwell Inspector* (1892) 19 R. 909.

[2] 1925 Act, S. 1. cf. *Zagrodnik* v. *Z.*, 1925 S.C. 258; *Macallister* v. *M.*, 1962 S.C. 406.

[3] *Beattie* v. *B.* (1883) 11 R. 85; *Sleigh* v. *S.* (1893) 30 S.L.R. 272; *Stevenson* v. *S.* (1894) 21 R. (H.L.) 96; *Reid* v. *R.* (1901) 3 F. 330; *B.* v. *B.*, 1907 S.C. 1186.

[4] *Mackay* v. *M.*, 1957 S.L.T. (Notes) 17; *McClements* v. *M.*, 1958 S.C. 286.

[5] *Douglas* v. *D.*, 1950 S.C. 453; *Hannah* v. *H.*, 1971 S.L.T. (Note) 42.

[6] *Alexander* v. *McGarrity* (1903) 5 F. 654.

[7] Guardianship Act, 1973, S. 11.

[8] Ibid., S. 12.

[9] *Macallister, supra.*

[10] *Smith* v. *S's Trs.* (1890) 18 R. 241; *Flannigan* v. *Bothwell Inspector* (1892) 19 R. 909; *Morrison* v. *Quarrier* (1894) 21 R. 889. Contrast *Low*, 1920 S.C. 351.

[11] *Ponder* v. *P.*, 1932 S.C. 233.

child of the marriage under the age of sixteen[1] and to decree aliment for such child, liberty being reserved to either party to reapply to the Court on these matters until the date when the child last to attain 16 will do so.[2] The paramount consideration is the welfare of the child or children,[3] and the court will consider the child's wishes, and a child in minority is entitled to be heard on the matter.[4] Accordingly though custody is commonly granted to the innocent party to such proceedings[5] it may be granted to a parent guilty of adultery[6] or of desertion.[7] The tender age of a child is a relevant factor, but not conclusive.[8] Where the welfare would be equally regarded, the father still has the superior claim.[9] The court may, in granting decree, declare the culpable spouse unfit to have the custody of the children, and in that event that parent is not entitled to the custody or guardianship of the children as of right on the death of the other.[10] The court may refuse to remove children from the custody of grandparents who have been caring for them.[11]

By the Matrimonial Proceedings (Children) Act, 1958,[12] the power of the court to deal with custody, maintenance, and education applies also[13] in relation to an illegitimate child of both parties,[14] or to the child of one party (including an illegitimate or adopted child) who has been accepted as one of the family by the other party.[15] The court is not to grant divorce, nullity, or

[1] Conjugal Rights (Sc.) Amdt. Act, 1861, S. 9; Guardianship of Infants Acts, 1886 and 1925; Custody of Children (Sc.) Act, 1939; Matrimonial Proceedings (Children) Act, 1958. As to jurisdiction see *McShane* v. *M.*, 1962 S.L.T. 221. Under the 1861 Act at least, no order could be made if the court refused separation or divorce: *McArthur* v. *M.*, 1955 S.C. 414; and any order made ceased to apply to each child as it emerged from pupillarity: *Watson* v. *W.* (1895) 23 R. 219.

[2] Where custody was awarded to the mother and she died, it was held incompetent for her parents to apply by minute in the process for custody: *McKenzie*, 1963 S.C. 266; contrast *Smith* v. *S.*, 1964 S.C. 218.

[3] *Symington* v. *S.* (1875) 2 R. (H.L.) 41; 1964 S.C. 218; *Huddart* v. *H.*, 1961 S.C. 393.

[4] *Morrison* v. *M.*, 1943 S.C. 481.

[5] *Ketchen* v. *K.* (1870) 8 M. 952; *Minto* v. *M.*, 1914, 2 S.L.T. 381; *Hume* v. *H.*, 1926 S.C. 1008; *Christison* v. *C.*, 1936 S.C. 381.

[6] *McCurdie* v. *McC.*, 1918, 2 S.L.T. 250; *Allan* v. *A.*, 1919, S.L.T. 88; *Stewart* v. *S.*, 1914, 2 S.L.T. 310; *McCarroll* v. *McC.*, 1937 S.N. 62; *Christie* v. *C.* 1945 S.L.T. 300; *Johnston* v. *J.*, 1947 S.L.T. (Notes) 26; *Wallace* v. *W.*, 1947 S.L.T. (Notes) 47.

[7] *Gibson* v. *G.* (1894) 2 S.L.T. 71; *Maclean* v. *M.*, 1947 S.C. 79.

[8] *Christison* v. *C.*, 1936 S.C. 381; *McLean, supra*; *Brown* v. *B.*, 1948 S.C. 5.

[9] *Mackellar* v. *M.* (1898) 25 R. 883.

[10] 1886 Act, S. 7.

[11] *Pow* v. *P.*, 1931 S.L.T. 485; contrast *Klein* v. *K.*, 1969 S.L.T. (Notes) 53.

[12] Ss. 7–15.   [13] S. 7.

[14] e.g. a child of a void marriage, not being a putative marriage.

[15] e.g. child by one spouse's previous marriage. Despite denial of such acceptance, the court has awarded a wife interim aliment under this section: *Hart* v. *H.*, 1960 S.L.T. (Notes) 33; 1961 S.L.T. (Notes) 14.

separation unless and until satisfied that arrangements have been
made for care and upbringing of each child which are satisfactory
or are the best which can be devised in the circumstances, or that
it is impracticable for the parties appearing to make any such
arrangements. Exceptionally the court may grant decree on an
undertaking by the parties to bring the arrangements for the
children before the court within a specified time.[1] The court may
also make provision for custody and maintenance where an
action is dismissed or the defender assoilzied,[2] or where one
spouse has not obtempered a decree of adherence[3] and may
commit the care of a child to a local authority or another person.[4]
Probation officers or other persons may be appointed to report
on the child's circumstances and the proposed arrangements for
its care and upbringing,[5] and a probation officer or local authority
may be appointed to supervise a child which is in the care of any
person.[6] The court may prohibit removal of a child furth of
Scotland or out of the control of a person having custody of it.[7]
There is power to entrust custody to a person other than a parent.[8]
Access may be regulated though custody is not in issue.[9] All
orders may subsequently be varied or revoked. The court may
in its discretion allow a third party to lodge a minute in the
divorce process relating to the custody of the children.[10]

Access

The parent not having or refused custody is normally entitled
to reasonable access to the child, by agreement or by order of
the court.[11] But the court may decline to allow access if the

---

[1] S. 8.
[2] Overruling *Pringle* v. *P.*, 1953 S.L.T. (Notes) 49; *McArthur* v. *McA.*, 1955 S.C. 414.
The court has no jurisdiction where a nullity petition is dismissed before proof on the
merits: *Gall* v. *G.*, 1968 S.C. 333.
[3] S. 9; *Driffel* v. *D.*, 1971 S.L.T. (Notes) 60.   [4] S. 10.
[5] S. 11; *MacIntyre* v. *M.*, 1962 S.L.T. (Notes) 70; only the court may invoke S. 11:
Wallace v. *W.*, 1963 S.C. 256.
[6] S. 12.   [7] S. 13.
[8] S. 14 (2); *S.* v. *S.*, 1967 S.C. (H.I.) 46.
[9] S. 14(2); *Huddart* v. *H.*, 1960 S.C. 300 (sequel 1961 S.C. 393).
[10] *Smith* v. *S.*, 1964 S.L.T. 309. Such a minute was incompetent where divorce has been
granted, and the party granted custody has died: *Sutherland* v. *S.*, 1959 S.L.T. (Notes)
61; *McKenzie* v. *McK.*, 1963 S.C. 266; see now R.C. 166(b); *Copeland* v. *C.*, 1969 S.L.T.
(Notes) 70.
[11] *A.* v. *B.* (1870) 7 S.L.R. 276; *Symington* v. *S.* (1875) 2 R. (H.L.) 41; 2 R. 976; *Lilley* v.
L. (1877) 4 R. 397; *Mackenzie* v. *M.* (1881) 8 R. 574; *Bloe* v. *B.* (1882) 9 R. 894; *Bowman*
v. *Graham* (1883) 10 R. 1234; *Mackenzie* v. *M.* (1887) 25 S.L.R. 183; *Mackellar* v. *M.*
(1898) 25 R. 883; *C.D.* v. *A.B.* (*Kiegler* v. *Hamilton*) 1908 S.C. 737; *McLean* v. *McL.*,
1947 S.C. 79; *Murray* v. *M.*, 1947 S.N. 102.

parent's circumstances, character, or conduct render this un-desirable in the child's interests.[1] Access may be granted to a person other than the parent refused custody,[2] and an applica-tion for access can be dealt with whether custody is raised or not.[3]

Children in the custody of third parties

A parent or parents may entrust custody to a third party and at common law the father, having the preferable right, could reclaim custody unless he were manifestly unsuitable.[4] By the Custody of Children Act, 1891, the Court of Session[5] may (S. 1) refuse to make an order for the production of a child by a third-party[6] custodier if of opinion that the parent applying has abandoned or deserted the child or so conducted himself that the court should refuse to enforce his right to custody.[7] If it makes a delivery order under the 1891 Act the court may (S. 2) require the petitioner to repay to the custodier money spent on rearing the child.[8] The Court is not (S. 3) to make an order for delivery of a child to a parent if the parent has abandoned or deserted his child or allowed it to be brought up by another at the latter's expense for so long and under such circumstances as to satisfy the Court that the parent was unmindful of his parental duties.[9] If it refuses to order delivery the court may make an order to ensure that the child is brought up in the religion which the parent wishes (S. 4). The welfare of the child, in the whole circumstances of the case, is the paramount consideration of the court.[10]

[1] *McAllister* v. *McA.*, 1947 S.N. 41; *Urquhart* v. *U.*, 1961 S.L.T. (Notes) 56; *Gray* v. *G.*, 1961 S.L.T. (Notes) 83; *Gover* v. *G.*, 1969 S.L.T. (Notes) 78.

[2] *McCallum* v. *McDonald* (1853) 15 D. 535; *S.* v. *S.*, 1967 S.C. (H.L.) 46.

[3] *Huddart* v. *H.*, 1960 S.C. 300; *S.* v. *S.*, *supra*, 52.

[4] *Russell* (1873) 10 S.L.R. 314; *Leys* v. *L.* (1886) 13 R. 1223; *Markey* v. *Colston* (1888) 15 R. 921; *Smith* v. *S's Trs.* (1840) 18 R. 241; *Moncrieff* (1891) 18 R. 1029; *Edgar* v. *Fisher's Trs.* (1893) 21 R. 59; *Fisher* v. *Edgar* (1894) 21 R. 1076. Similarly tutors-nomi-nate under the father's will may claim custody of children from other relatives: *Hogan* v. *McCrossan* (1899) 7 S.L.T. 22. A widowed mother has a primary right to custody in a question with the child's half-sister, subject to the best interests of the child: *Macallister* v. *M.*, 1962 S.C. 406.

[5] *Campbell* v. *C.*, 1956 S.C. 285; cf. *Mackenzie* v. *Keillor* (1892) 19 R. 963; *Murray* v. *Forsyth*, 1917 S.C. 721; *McLean* v. *Hardie*, 1927 S.C. 344.

[6] *Murray, supra*; *Campbell, supra*; *Macallister* v. *M.* 1962 S.C. 406.

[7] *Campbell* v. *Croall* (1895) 22 R. 869; *Mitchell* v. *Wright* (1905) 7 F. 568; *McLean* v. *Hardie*, 1927 S.C. 344; *Begbie* v. *Nichol*, 1949 S.C. 158.

[8] *Soutar* v. *Carrie* (1894) 21 R. 1050; *Begbie* v. *Nichol*, 1949 S.C. 158.

[9] cf. *Gillan* v. *Barony Parish* (1898) 1 F. 183; *Gibson* v. *Hagen*, 1960 S.L.T. (Notes) 24; *Macallister, supra*.

[10] *Fenwick* v. *Hannah's Trs.* (1893) 20 R. 848; *Campbell* v. *Croall* (1895) 22 R. 869; *Alexander* v. *McGarrity* (1903) 5 F. 654; *Pow* v. *P.*, 1931 S.L.T. 485; *Nicol* v. *N.*, 1953 S.L.T. (Notes) 68; *Macallister, supra*.

Enforcement

Orders for the delivery of custody of a child must be obeyed under pain of being in contempt of court. The court may grant warrant to messengers-at-arms to take the child,[1] or to search for and recover the child,[2] and impose imprisonment,[3] or sequestration of estates[4] on the contumacious party. Interdict may be granted against an attempt to remove the child from Scotland.[5]

Divestiture of custody

Where on the trial of an offence under the Criminal Law Amendment Act, 1885, it is proved that the seduction or prostitution of a girl under 16 has been caused, encouraged or favoured by her parent, guardian, master or mistress, the court may divest such person of all authority over her and appoint any person or persons willing to take charge of such girl to be her guardian till she is 21, or less as the court may direct.[6]

Management of legitimate children's legal affairs

At common law the father was by natural right the tutor and administrator in law of his pupil child and as such managed the pupil's property and acts for him in all legal transactions.[7] When the child became a minor the father became curator, and the child then managed his own property and transacted legally, but with the father's consent and concurrence, unless forisfamiliated, when he might act alone.[8] The curatory terminated when the child became adult, unless the child was bodily or mentally incapax; if a daughter marries while a minor the curatory devolves on her husband so long as she remains a minor.[9]

Failing the father, the mother was, by statute,[10] guardian, alone, or jointly with any guardian appointed by the father or by the

[1] *Hutchison* v. *H.* (1890) 18 R. 237; *Low*, 1920 S.C. 351.
[2] *Guthrie* v. *G.* (1906) 8 F. 545.
[3] *Muir* v. *Milligan* (1868) 6 M. 1125; *Leys* v. *L.* (1886) 13 R. 1223.
[4] *Ross* v. *R.* (1885) 12 R. 1351; *Edgar* v. *Fisher's Trs.* (1893) 21 R. 59, 325; *Fisher* v. *Edgar* (1894) 21 R. 1076.
[5] *Robertson*, 1911 S.C. 1319; cf. *Lumsden* (1882) 20 S.L.R. 240.
[6] 1885 Act, S. 12.
[7] cf. *Dumbreck* v. *Stevenson* (1861) 4 Macq. 86; *Murray's Trs.* v. *Bloxsom's Trs.* (1887) 15 R. 233.
[8] Ersk. I, 6, 54; Bell, *Prin.* §2068.
[9] Ersk., *supra*; Married Women's Property (Sc.) Act, 1920, S. 2.
[10] Guardianship of Infants Act, 1925, S. 4. ('Infant' is defined as pupil.) *Willison* (1890) 18 R. 228. She is not disqualified by remarriage: *Campbell* v. *Maquay* (1888) 15 R. 784.

Court,[1] but her power of administration terminated when the child became a minor; she did not, as mother, automatically become curatrix, nor might she nominate a curator. She might be appointed curatrix by the father's will, and a minor might by petition have his mother appointed as curatrix, in which case she was not subject to the Account of Court, nor obliged to find caution.[2]

By the Guardianship Act, 1973, S. 10, a mother now has the same rights and authority as the father and can hold the offices of tutor or curator, and the rights of each parent are equal and exercisable by either alone. In case of disagreement the court may give directions.

A mother may, by deed or will, appoint guardians of her pupil child after the death of the father and herself, or to act jointly with the father after her death.[3]

Where a conflict of interest arises the court may appoint a factor *loco tutoris* to supersede the parent as a pupil's guardian.[4]

A third party making a gift or bequest to a minor may make it exclusive of the father's administration, nominating a curator for the purpose; if no curator is named, the court may appoint a curator other than the father.[5] Where the child has a claim against the father, the court will appoint a curator *ad litem* to advise in the suit.[6]

Powers of parent as tutor

A parent acting as tutor of a pupil at common law or under the Guardianship of Children (Scotland) Acts, 1886 to 1973, is deemed a trustee within the meaning of the Trusts (Scotland) Acts, 1921 and 1961.[7] In the ordinary case he need not find caution,[8] but exceptionally the court may require him to do so, or appoint a factor *loco tutoris*.[9] The pupil may hold property but has no capacity to transact legally and all legal powers are vested in the parent as tutor for behoof of the child. A parent as tutor has

---

[1] *Martin* v. *Stewart* (1888) 16 R. 185; such an appointment falls on the mother's death, but the tutor has a right and interest to see that a suitable successor is appointed: *Fraser* (1893) 1 S.L.T. 126.

[2] *Maclean, Petr.*, 1956 S.L.T. (Sh. Ct.) 90.

[3] Guardianship of Infants Act, 1925, S. 5.

[4] *Mann* (1851) 14 D. 12; *Cochrane* (1891) 18 R. 456; *Balfour Melville* (1903) 5 F. 347.

[5] *Robertson* (1865) 3 M. 1077.

[6] Ersk. I, 6, 54.

[7] 1925 Act, S. 10.

[8] Ersk. I, 6, 54; Bell, *Prin.* §2068.

[9] Bell, *Prin.*, *supra*; *Stevenson's Trs.* v. *Dumbreck* (1859) 19 D. 462; 4 Macq. 86; *Cochrane* (1891) 18 R. 456.

power to sue[1] and be sued, to grant a valid discharge of damages paid for the pupil's behoof,[2] and to compromise an action without the court's authority.[3] He may sell the pupil's heritage,[4] or feu it.[5] The court may, on application, grant special powers deemed necessary.[6]

Powers of parent as curator

As curator a parent has no power to deal with the minor's estate, but only the power of consenting to the minor's own transactions therewith. Even if the parent withholds consent that does not nullify or invalidate the minor's actings.[7] The curator is guardian of the estate, not of the minor's person.[8] As curator, the parent cannot compel the minor to take any step, nor to refrain; if the minor be obstinate he may act alone,[9] but deeds by the curator alone are null.[10] The minor's powers of administration, with or without his curator's consent, are unlimited, but all actings are voidable at any time within four years of majority, on proof of minority and lesion.[11] If the parent declines to concur or has an adverse interest a curator *ad litem* may be appointed. A father as curator is entitled to advise his child against risking a contemplated marriage, and is not liable in damages for preventing it, unless he acted maliciously.[12] A father as curator who takes an active part in litigation on behalf of the minor may render himself licote for expenses.[13]

Aliment

A father is under a natural obligation to aliment his child,[14] and maintain it from want,[15] a standard which is relative to the

---

[1] e.g. *Davis's Tutor* v. *Glasgow Victoria Hospitals*, 1950 S.C. 382. As to expenses see *White* v. *Steel* (1894) 21 R. 649. If the parent is dead: *Ward* v. *Walker*, 1920 S.C. 80; or refuses to sue, the court may appoint a curator *ad litem*: *McConochie* v. *Dinnie* (1847) 9 D. 791; *Kirk* v. *Scottish Gas Board*, 1969 8 S.C. 328.

[2] *Jack* v. *N.B. Ry. Co.* (1886) 14 R. 263.

[3] *Gow* v. *Henry* (1899) 2 F. 48; *Murphy* v. *Smith*, 1920 S.C. 104.

[4] *Logan* (1897) 25 R. 51. Authority of the court is not now requisite in cases within the Trusts Acts: see *Ferrier's Tutrix*, 1925 S.C. 571; *Dempster*, 1926 S.L.T. 157; *Cunningham's Tutrix*, 1949 S.C. 275, explaining *Linton* v. *I.R.*, 1928 S.C. 209.

[5] *Lord Clinton* (1875) 3 R. 62; *Campbell* (1880) 7 R. 1032; *Shearer*, 1924 S.C. 445.

[6] *Hamilton's Tutors*, 1924 S.C. 364; *Brunton*, 1928 S.N. 112.

[7] See further, *infra*.   [8] Bell, *Prin.* §2090, 2096.

[9] *Stevenson* v. *Adair* (1872) 10 M. 919.   [10] Bell, *Prin.* §2096.

[11] See further, *infra*.   [12] *Findlay* v. *Blaylock*, 1937 S.C. 21.

[13] *Rodger* v. *Weir*, 1917 S.C. 300.

[14] Stair I, 3, 3; I, 9, 1; Ersk. I, 6, 56; III, 1, 9; Bell, *Prin.* §1629–31; *Fairgrieves* v. *Hendersons* (1885) 13 R. 98. The obligation covers posthumous children: *Spalding* v. *S's Trs.* (1874) 2 R. 237. See also National Assistance Act, 1948, S. 42.

[15] *Maule* v. *M.* (1825) 1 W. & S. 266.

social and financial position of the parent.[1] The obligation
subsists until the child can, legally and in fact, maintain himself
by his own exertions,[2] and for life if the child, by reason of
physical or mental incapacity, or inability to obtain employment,
cannot support himself.[3] The obligation is normally discharged
by maintaining the child in a family home, but may be discharged by making an allowance for the child's support.[4] If not
done in either way, the father will be liable to persons who supply
the child with necessaries.[5]

The father may discharge his obligation in the way least
burdensome to himself, and meet a claim for aliment by an offer
to maintain the child in family, unless his conduct to the child
has been such as to forfeit this alternative.[6] The court is much less
willing to award aliment to a child who has completed education
and training than to one who has not, unless the child's need is
due to physical or mental incapacity or inability to obtain suitable employment.[7]

On the father's death a child in need of aliment has a claim
against the father's representatives, postponed to ordinary
creditors but preferred to special and general legatees.[8]

If the father is dead, missing, or indigent, the child may claim
aliment from his relatives in this order:[9] (1) his mother;[10] (2) his
paternal grandfather;[11] (3) his paternal grandmother;[12] (4) higher
ascendants in the paternal line; (5) his maternal grandfather;[13]
(6) his maternal grandmother;[14] (7) higher ascendants in the
maternal line. If, however, the child himself has children his

---

[1] *Thom v. MacKenzie* (1864) 3 M. 177; *Smith v. S* (1885) 13 R. 126.

[2] *Smith, supra*; *Whyte v. W.* (1901) 3 F. 937.

[3] *Bain v. B.* (1860) 22 D. 1021; *Smith v. S.* (1885) 13 R. 126; *Watson v. W.* (1896) 4
S.L.T. 39; *Fife C.C. v. Rodger*, 1937 S.L.T. 638; cf. *Beaton v. B.*, 1935 S.C. 187 (son aged
62).

[4] *Ketchen v. K.* (1871) 9 M. 690; *Whyte v. W.* (1901) 3 F. 937.

[5] Stair I, 5, 7; Ersk. I. 6, 57.

[6] Ersk. I, 6, 56; Bell. *Prin.* §1630; *Smith, supra*; *Westlands v. Pirie* (1887) 14 R. 763;
Bell v. B. (1890) 17 R. 549.

[7] Ersk., *supra*; *Reid v. Moir* (1866) 4 M. 1060; *Smith, supra*; *Watson v. W.* (1896) 33
S.L.R. 771; *Whyte v. W.* (1901) 3 F. 937.

[8] *Ker's Trs. v. K.*, 1927 S.C. 52; see also *Hutcheson v. Hoggan's Trs.* (1904) 6 F. 594.

[9] Bell, *Prin.* §1632–3; Fraser, *P. & Ch.* 100.

[10] *Macdonald v. M.* (1846) 8 D. 830; *Fairgrieves v. Henderson* (1886) 13 R. 98; *Ewart
v. R. & W. Ferguson*, 1932 S.C. 277.

[11] *Bell v. B.* (1895) 2 S.L.T. 598; *Leslie Parish Council v. Gibson's Trs.* (1899) 1 F. 601;
Hanlin v. Melrose & Thomson (1899) 1 F. 1012; *Mackenzie's Tutrix v. M.*, 1928 S.L.T.
649; *Ewart, supra*; *Gay's Tutrix v. G's Tr.*, 1953 S.L.T. 278.

[12] cf. *Muirhead v. M.* (1849) 12 D. 356.

[13] *Cooper v. Fife Coal Co.*, 1907 S.C. 564.

[14] Fraser, *P. & Ch.* 102.

claim lies first against them, if they are able to aliment him.[1] No
natural claim for aliment lies against brothers or sisters or other
collaterals.[2] If the father has left legacies to the children their
aliment must be paid in the first instance from their own income
therefrom.[3] But if the father's estate has passed chiefly to one
child, the inheritance carries with it the father's liability to
aliment the other children, so far as *lucratus* by the succession,
and in such a case one child may claim aliment from another, *jure
representationis* as representing the father.[4] There is no such claim
where all children have succeeded equally.[5] This liability by
representation may extend to the representatives of grandparents,[6] certainly where the more distant relative has acknowledged the obligation during his lifetime.[7] A posthumous child
has been held entitled to aliment out of the father's trust estate.[8]

Where a child is infirm or incapax, the father's executors or
trustees are not bound to set aside funds for that child's maintenance beyond the legal share due to him on the father's death, but
may distribute the estate, the other children being bound to
give their undertakings to provide for the maintenance of the
incapax child.[9] If the child has independent estate the mother
certainly,[10] and now even the father, despite the greater duty
incumbent on him,[11] may claim reimbursement from the income
or capital of that estate. No repayment could formerly be claimed
from capital without a contract with the child or his tutor,[12] but

---

[1] Fraser, *P. & Ch.* 100; *Beaton* v. *B.*, 1935 S.C. 187.

[2] Fraser, *P. & Ch.* 102; *Greenhorn* v. *Addie* (1855) 17 D. 860; *Eisten* v. *N.B. Ry. Co.*
(1870) 8 M. 980.

[3] *Ker's Trs.*, *supra*.

[4] Fraser, *P. & Ch.* 128; *Mackintosh* v. *Taylor* (1868) 7 M. 67; *Davidson's Trs.* v. *D.*,
1907 S.C. 16; *Beaton* v. *B's Trs.*, 1935 S.C. 187; *Hutchison* v. *H's Trs.*, 1951 S.C. 108;
cf. *Stevenson* v. *McDonald's Trs.*, 1923 S.L.T. 451.

[5] Fraser, *P. & Ch.* 129; *Beaton*, *supra*.

[6] Ersk. I, 6, 58; *Spalding* v. *S's Trs.* (1874) 2 R. 237; *Anderson* v. *Grant* (1899) 1 F. 484;
Gay's Tutrix v. *G's Tr.*, 1953 S.L.T. 278.

[7] *Leslie Parish Council* v. *Gibson's Trs.* (1899) 1 F. 601.

[8] *Spalding* v. *S's Trs.* (1874) 2 R. 237.

[9] *Mackintosh* v. *Taylor* (1868) 7 M. 67; *Howard's Exor.* v. *H's C.B.* (1894) 21 R. 787;
McKenna v. *Ferguson* (1894) 1 S.L.T. 599; *Davidson's Trs.* v. *D.*, 1907 S.C. 16; *Edinburgh
Parish Council* v. *Couper*, 1924 S.C. 139; cf. *Hutchison* v. *H's Trs.*, 1951 S.C. 108.
supra.

[10] *Baird* v. *B's Trs.* (1872) 10 M. 482; *Douglas* v. *D's Trs.* (1872) 10 M. 943; *Christie* v.
C's Trs. (1877) 4 R. 620; *Fairgrieves* v. *Henderson* (1885) 13 R. 98; *Ker's Trs.* v. *K.*,
1927 S.C. 52; see also *Ross* v. *R.* (1896) 23 R. (H.L.) 67.

[11] *Edmiston* v. *Miller's Trs.* (1871) 9 M. 987; *Stewart's Trs.* v. *S.* (1871) 8 S.L.R. 367;
Duke of Sutherland (1901) 3 F. 761; *Hutcheson* v. *Hoggan's Trs.* (1904) 6 F. 594; *Ker's Trs.*,
supra; *Polland* v. *Sturrock's Exors.*, 1952 S.C. 535.

[12] *Galt* v. *Boyd* (1830) 8 S. 332; *Milne* (1888) 15 R. 437;

there is now no absolute rule forbidding this,[1] though the acquisition of property by the child does not justify a claim for reimbursement of past outlays.[2] A father who has been alimenting his son has no right of recovery against the son's wife.[3]

A father is not obliged to aliment his daughter-in-law,[4] nor a stepmother her step-son,[5] nor a son-in-law his father-in-law,[6] or mother-in-law.[7]

Under the National Assistance Act[8] and the Ministry of Social Security Act, 1966,[9] each parent is liable to maintain his or her spouse and children; the Supplementary Benefits Commission may recover from persons liable to maintain the cost of assistance given to an indigent child.[10] It is an offence wilfully to neglect a child of which one has custody.[11]

Where spouses are judicially separated or divorced the wife, if awarded custody, is normally also awarded aliment for the children in her charge, for whose aliment the husband remains primarily liable.[12] The amount of aliment may be altered on change of circumstances.[13]

Parents' claim against children

The parents and other ascendants who are obliged to aliment a child have a corresponding claim against all their children who are capable of contributing, jointly and severally, to be supported and alimented by them in case of need![14] This ranks prior to any

---

[1] *Polland* v. *Sturrock's Exors.*, 1952 S.C. 535.

[2] Fraser, *P. & Ch.*, 119.

[3] *Fingzies* v. *F.* (1890) 28 S.L.R. 6; see now Married Women's Property (Sc.) Act, 1920, S. 4.

[4] *Hoseason* v. *H.* (1870) 9 M. 37; *Reid* v. *R.* (1904) 6 F. 935; *Mackay* v. *M.'s Trs.* (1904) 6 F. 936. But if living with her husband she may benefit from any aliment he gets from his father.

[5] *Macdonald* v. *M.* (1846) 8 D. 830; *Barty's Trs.* v. *B.* (1888) 15 R. 496.

[6] *Dear* v. *Duncan* (1896) 3 S.L.T. 241.

[7] *McAllan* v. *Alexander* (1888) 15 R. 863.

[8] 1948 Act, S. 42–3, amd. Ministry of Social Security Act, 1966, S. 39; *Corcoran* v. *Muir*, 1954 J.C. 46.

[9] S. 22; cf. *Duncan* v. *Forbes* (1878) 15 S.L.R. 371.

[10] Parents' liability is joint and several: *N. A. Board* v. *Casey*, 1967 S.L.T. (Sh. Ct.) 11.

[11] Children and Young Persons (Sc.) Act, 1937, Ss. 12, 27; *Henderson* v. *Stewart*, 1954 J.C. 94.

[12] *Foxwell* v. *Robertson* (1900) 2 F. 932; *Matthew* v. *M.*, 1926 S.L.T. 723; *Dickinson* v. *D.*, 1952 S.C. 27.

[13] *Hay* v. *H.* (1882) 9 R. 667; *Rowat* v. *R.* (1904) 12 S.L.T. 449; *Maitland* v. *M.*, 1912, 1 S.L.T. 350; *Melvin* v. *M.*, 1918, 2 S.L.T. 209; *Dickinson, supra.*

[14] Stair I, 5, 8; Ersk. I, 6, 57; Bell, *Prin.* §1634; Fraser, *P. & Ch.*, 136; *Muirhead* v. *M.* (1849) 12 D. 356; *Landers* v. *L.* (1859) 21 D. 706; *Buie* v. *Stiven* (1863) 2 M. 208; *Thom* v. *Mackenzie* (1864) 3 M. 177; *Hamilton* v. *H.* (1877) 4 R. 688; *Duncan* v. *D.* (1882) 19 S.L.R. 696; *Foulis* v. *Fairbairn* (1887) 14 R. 1088; *Dear* v. *Duncan* (1896) 3 S.L.T. 241; *Sagar* v. *N.C.B.*, 1955 S.C. 424; *Dickson* v. *N.C.B.*, 1957 S.C. 157.

claim on their own ascendants.[1] A child is not now bound to support his parents-in-law, except so far as *lucratus* by his marriage.[2]

Education

Parents are obliged to provide education for their children, normally by ensuring attendance at a local authority or other school till at least the minimum school-leaving age.[3] At common law the father has the main right to regulate the children's education.[4] A parent is guilty of an offence if the child fails to attend regularly at public school.[5] There is no legal obligation to provide better or further education than that required by statute.[6]

Religious upbringing

Formerly the father had the prior right to dictate in what religion the child was to be brought up.[7] Since the Guardianship of Infants Act, 1925, the parents have equal rights in the matter,[8] and the court has refused to disturb a widow's arrangements for upbringing at the request of the nearest male agnates.[9] The parents' views, though weighty, are not conclusive on the matter.[10] Where the father was an atheist, the court has awarded custody to a mother, though guilty of adultery, on the ground that a child should during its formative years have the opportunity of a religious upbringing.[11] Under the Custody of Children Act, 1891, S. 4, if the court refuses a parent custody, it may make an order to secure that the child be brought up in the religion in which the parent has a legal right that the child be brought up. The child's wishes may be consulted and if old enough to do so, it may exercise its own free choice.

Other relations between parent and child

There is no bar to contractual relations between parent and child, though such a transaction may be reduced if it be shown

---

[1] Bell, *Prin., supra.*

[2] Fraser, *P. & Ch.*, 102; Married Women's Property (Sc.) Act, 1877, S. 4; *McAllan v. Alexander* (1888) 15 R. 863; *Dear v. Duncan* (1896) 3 S.L.T. 241.

[3] Education (Sc.) Act, 1962, S. 31.

[4] *Pagan v. P.* (1883) 10 R. 1072.

[5] Ibid., S. 35–6; 1949 Act, S. 5; 1956 Act, Ss. 3, 13(1).

[6] Bell, *Prin.* §1635, 2083.   [7] *O'Donnell v. O'D.*, 1919 S.C. 14.

[8] cf. *Re Collins* [1950] Ch. 498; *Barr v. B.*, 1950 S.L.T. (Notes) 15; *Zamorski v. Z.*, 1960 S.L.T. (Notes) 26.

[9] *Kincaid v. Quarrier* (1896) 23 R. 676; *Murray v. Maclay* (1903) 6 F. 160.

[10] *Morrison v. Quarrier* (1894) 21 R. 1071; *Reilly v. Quarrier* (1895) 22 R. 879.

[11] *McClements v. M.*, 1958 S.C. 286; see also *Mackay v. M.*, 1957 S.L.T. (Notes) 17.

that the parent had exercised undue influence on the child.[1] Parent may sue child[2] and conversely[3] for damages for delict. The parent is not automatically liable for the child's delicts, but may be if he authorized or ratified them, or if the child were acting at the time as his agent or servant in the course of his employment.

Children's obligations inter se

Children have no legal liability to look after or aliment each other,[4] except in the case where, *jure repraesentationis*, one or more children have inherited the whole or the major part of the father's estate and another child is unable to earn, in which case those who inherit take the estate under burden of alimenting those whom the deceased was under a natural obligation to aliment.[5] This liability subsists until the child not provided for attains majority or, if a girl, marries under that age, or becomes able to earn his own livelihood.

Children have full liberty of transacting legally one with another as if with third parties.

ILLEGITIMATE CHILDREN

Illegitimate children

A natural, illegitimate, or bastard child is one born to a woman who was not at the time of its conception or of its birth or at any time between validly married to the father of the child, or was joined to him in a union deemed legally null.[6] If a man marries a woman who is, to his knowledge pregnant, and there had been opportunities for pre-marital intercourse, the child is deemed his and legitimate.[7] The relationship between a father and his bastard child is not in any proper civil sense that of parent and child. A bastard is in law *filius nullius*.[8] A bastard child was en-

---

[1] *Smith Cunninghame* v. *Anstruther's Trs.* (1872) 10 M. (H.L.) 39; *Gray* v. *Binny* (1879) 7 R. 332; *Menzies* v. *M.* (1893) 20 R. (H.L.) 108; *Allan* v. *A.*, 1961 S.C. 200.

[2] *Wood* v. *W.*, 1935 S.L.T. 431.   [3] *Young* v. *Rankin*, 1934 S.C. 499.

[4] Stair I, 5, 10; *Greenhorn* v. *Addie* (1855) 17 D. 860; *Eisten* v. *N.B. Ry.* (1870) 8 M. 980.

[5] Stair, *supra*; Ersk. I, 6, 58; Bell, *Prin.* §1632; Fraser, *P. & Ch.*, 128; *Marshall* v. *Gourley* (1836) 15 S. 313; *Stuart* v. *Court* (1848) 10 D. 1275; *Mackintosh* v. *Taylor* (1868) 7 M. 67; *Beaton* v. *B's Trs.*, 1935 S.C. 187; *Hutchison* v. *H's Trs.*, 1951 S.C. 108 (adopted child).

[6] Stair III, 3, 43–6; Ersk. I, 6, 51; Bell, *Prin.* §2058–63.

[7] *Gardner* v. *G.* (1877) 4 R. (H.L.) 56; *Reid* v. *Mill* (1879) 6 R. 659; *Kerrs* v. *Lindsay* (1890) 18 R. 365.

[8] *Corrie* v. *Adair* (1860) 22 D. 897; *Silver* v. *Walker*, 1938 S.C. 595.

titled at common law to none of the civil rights conferred on legitimate children, but this position has been alleviated by statute. In case of doubt or dispute the child's status must be determined by a declarator of legitimacy,[1] or of bastardy.[2] With the latter may be combined a conclusion putting the defender to silence as to the child's legitimacy.[3]

Foundlings

A living child found exposed, in default of discovery of its parentage, must be deemed illegitimate.[4]

Child of rape

A child conceived by an unmarried woman in consequence of rape is illegitimate,[5] proof thereof being relevant to rebut the presumption *pater est* in the case of a married woman.[6]

Name

An illegitimate child is normally given a christian name and the mother's surname. Where the mother of a bastard proposed to adopt it and give it the name of her late husband who was not the child's father, it was held permissible with the consent of the late husband's relatives.[7]

Registration

An illegitimate child's birth must be registered in the same way as a legitimate one, but the registrar may not register on information supplied by the father alone, nor enter the name of any person as the father unless at the joint request of both parents, in which case the father must attend personally and sign as informant along with the mother. The mother must produce a declaration stating that a particular person is the father and a statutory declaration by him acknowledging himself to be the father. Where the name of the father has not been registered, it may be recorded in the Register of Corrections if decree of paternity has been granted, or declarations are produced by both parents, or,

[1] e.g. *Tennent* v. *T.* (1890) 17 R. 1205.
[2] e.g. *Smith* v. *Dick* (1869) 8 M. 31; *Steedman* v. *S.* (1887) 14 R. 1066; *Whitehall* v. *W.*, 1958 S.C. 252; *Imre* v. *Mitchell*, 1958 S.C. 439.
[3] *Imre, supra.*
[4] As to registration of its birth see Registration of Births, etc. (Sc.) Act, 1965, Ss. 15 and 20(1)(b).
[5] cf. *H.M.* v. *W.M.* (1953) 69 Sh. Ct. Rep. 271.
[6] cf. *Black* v. *Duncan*, 1924 S.C. 738.
[7] *Mrs. C. Cn. or Cl.*, 1951 S.L.T. (Sh. Ct.) 83.

where the mother is dead, he is ordered to do so by the sheriff on application by the father. Where paternity has been established by decree, notice of the import of the decree is sent to the Registrar general.[1] An abbreviated birth certificate may be obtained containing no mention of parentage.[2]

Determination of paternity

Where paternity is doubtful or disputed,[3] and in order to obtain a contribution to its aliment, and to her inlying expenses, the mother may bring an action of affiliation and aliment against the alleged father.[4] Decree in such an action does not affect the status of the child as illegitimate.[5] A married woman may bring such an action against a man other than her husband, but must discharge the heavy onus of rebutting the presumption *pater est quem nuptiae demonstrant*.[6] A pregnant unmarried woman may bring an action of affiliation and aliment against the alleged father not more than 3 months before the child's birth if she produces a sworn declaration that the defender is the father and a medical certificate of pregnancy certifying the expected date of delivery, but no declarator of paternity may be pronounced for payment until after the birth, save that if the action is undefended or paternity admitted, the court may before birth grant decree for a payment to account of inlying expenses, and for periodical payments of aliment from the date of birth, and may subsequently grant decree for a further payment for inlying expenses, and review or alter the sums decerned for as aliment.[7]

If the mother has died an action of affiliation and aliment may be brought by the bastard child through its tutor.[8]

In establishing paternity there is frequently *penuria testium*;[9]

---

[1] Registration of Births, Deaths, and Marriages (Sc.) Act, 1965, S. 18.

[2] 1965 Act, S. 19.

[3] As to blood test evidence see *Sproat* v. *McGibney*, 1968 S.L.T. 33.

[4] Such an action is one for debt and not a declarator of status: *Silver* v. *Walker*, 1938 S.C. 595. The rate of aliment is in the court's discretion and is not limited by the Affiliation Orders Act, 1952, which does not apply to Scotland: *Halkett* v. *McSkeane*, 1962 S.L.T. (Sh. Ct.) 59.

[5] cf. *McDonald* v. *Ross*, 1929 S.C. 240, 249.

[6] cf. *Lepper* v. *Brown* (1802) Hume 488; *Aitken* v. *Mitchell* (1806) Hume 489; *Routledge* v. *Carruthers* (1816) 4 Dow 392; *Jobson* v. *Reid* (1827) 5 S. 715; (1830) 8 S. 343; *Mackay* v. *M.* (1855) 17 D. 494; *Brodie* v. *Dyce* (1872) 11 M. 142; *McLachlan* v. *Lewis*, 1925 S.C. 886; *Imre* v. *Mitchell*, 1958 S.C. 439.

[7] Illegitimate Children (Sc.) Act, 1930, S. 3. As to right of appeal, see *McDonald* v. *Ross*, 1929 S.C. 240.

[8] *Robertson* v. *Hutchison*, 1935 S.C. 708.

[9] On evidence generally see *Young* v. *Nicol* (1893) 20 R. 768.

inferences may be drawn from evidence of courtship about the time of conception,[1] opportunities,[2] familiarities[3] and suspicious circumstances.[4] If the defender admits intercourse prior to that alleged to have started the child little corroboration of the pursuer's evidence is necessary,[5] but intercourse subsequent thereto requires substantial corroboration.[6] Subsequent marriage raises no presumption that the husband was father of the child.[7]

Evidence by the defender which is disbelieved or proved false may justify an unfavourable inference, particularly if the pursuer's contrary evidence is corroborated.[8] The practice of calling the defender as the pursuer's first witness has been disapproved.[9] If the defender is not called by the pursuer, his failure to give or lead evidence is not an admission, nor corroboration of the pursuer's evidence.[10] Where a woman has been promiscuous she cannot sue both or all her paramours, nor can she elect which one to sue. She must sue the one whom she believes was the father and establish his paternity of her child.[11] Hence proof of intercourse also with another man may throw doubt on a pursuer's case.[12] But if she fails against one man, she may subsequently sue another.

[1] *Lawson* v. *Eddie* (1861) 23 D. 876; *Harper* v. *Paterson* (1896) 33 S.L.R. 657.

[2] *Ruddiman* v. *Bruce* (1863) 2 M. 70; *Costley* v. *Little* (1892) 30 S.L.R. 87; *Dawson* v. *McKenzie*, 1908 S.C. 648; but see *Morrison* v. *Monaghan*, 1969 S.L.T. (Notes) 25.

[3] *Muir* v. *Tweedie* (1883) 21 S.L.R. 241; *Scott* v. *Dawson* (1884) 11 R. 518; *Buchanan* v. *Finlayson* (1900) 3 F. 245.

[4] *Dunn* v. *Chalmers* (1875) 3 R. 236; *Macfarlane* v. *Raeburn*, 1946 S.C. 67; cf. *Gray* v. *Marshall* (1875) 2 R. 907.

[5] *McDonald* v. *Glass* (1883) 11 R. 57; *Havery* v. *Brownlee*, 1908 S.C. 424. As to medical evidence see *Sproat* v. *McGibney*, 1968 S.L.T. 33.

[6] *Muir* v. *Tweedie* (1883) 21 S.L.R. 241; *Havery*, *supra*; *Buchanan* v. *Finlayson* (1900) 3 F. 245.

[7] *Imre* v. *Mitchell*, 1958 S.C. 439.

[8] The so-called doctrine of corroboration by contradiction: see *McBayne* v. *Davidson* (1860) 22 D. 738; *Dunn* v. *Chalmers* (1875) 3 R. 236; *Harper* v. *Paterson* (1896) 33 S.L.R. 657; *Macpherson* v. *Largue* (1896) 23 R. 785; *Dawson* v. *McKenzie*, 1908 S.C. 648; *McWhirter* v. *Lynch*, 1909 S.C. 112; *Florence* v. *Smith*, 1913 S.C. 978; *Lowdon* v. *McConnachie*, 1933 S.C. 574; *Macfarlane* v. *Raeburn*, 1946 S.C. 67; *Macpherson* v. *Beaton*, 1955 S.C. 100; *Roy* v. *Pairman*, 1958 S.C. 334; see also *McWhirter* v. *Lynch*, 1909 S.C. 122 where false denial was of immaterial circumstances, and *Rathmill* v. *McInnes*, 1946 S.L.T. (Notes) 3. On procedure see *Pirie* v. *Leask*, 1964 S.C. 103.

[9] *McArthur* v. *McQueen* (1901) 3 F. 1010; *Darroch* v. *Kerr* (1901) 4 F. 396; *McWhirter* v. *Lynch*, 1909 S.C. 112; *Fraser* v. *Smith*, 1937 S.N. 67; *Finnegan* v. *Maan*, 1966 S.L.T. (Notes) 47.

[10] *Faddes* v. *McNeish*, 1923 S.C. 443.

[11] See *Lawson* v. *Eddie* (1861) 23 D. 876; *Barr* v. *Bain* (1896) 23 R. 1090; *Butter* v. *McLaren*, 1909 S.C. 786; *Sinclair* v. *Rankin*, 1921 S.C. 933; *Robertson* v. *Hutchison*, 1935 S.C. 708.

[12] *Butter*, *supra*; *Sinclair*, *supra*; *Robertson*, *supra*. See also *Scrimgeour* v. *Stewart* (1864) 2 M. 667.

In all cases there must be specific averment of the date and place of the intercourse alleged, and proof at least of circumstances yielding an inference of very probably intercourse then. The courts have frequently been faced by the problem of whether certain periods of gestation were too short or too long since any proven intercourse to make paternity probable and have frequently held unusually long or short periods not to be impossible, and therefore not to rebut any normal inference.[1] The defence of total physical capacity or sterility is relevant.[2]

Obligation to aliment

If paternity is not established the mother must bear the whole expense of alimenting her child. If paternity is admitted or proved both parents are liable jointly and severally to aliment their child until he is old enough to earn his own living[3] and, if need be, throughout his life.[4] Without prejudice to the common law,[5] statute has provided that this obligation continues until the child attains sixteen,[6] with possible extension for two years, or further but not beyond 21, if the child is undertaking full-time education.[7] The mother is entitled to constitute her claim for aliment against the father by decree even if he has admitted paternity, if he will not make arrangements for future aliment, but at her own expense.[8] The claim transmits against the parents' representatives.[9] If either parent is unable to contribute, the whole liability falls on the other. If the mother supports the child she has a claim of relief against the father for a share, formerly a half, but now a

---

[1] See e.g. *Ritchie* v. *Cunningham* (1857) 20 D. 35 (228 days inadequate); *Pitcairn* v. *Smith* (1872) 9 S.L.R. 608 (237 days); *McDonald* v. *Main* (1897) 4 S.L.T. 252 (244 days); *Whyte* v. *W.* (1884) 11 R. 710 (297 days); *Cook* v. *Rattray* (1880) 8 R. 217 (305 days); *Boyd* v. *Kerr* (1843) 5 D. 1213 (306 days); *Williamson* v. *McClelland*, 1913 S.C. 678 (306 days); *Jamieson* v. *Dobie*, 1935 S.C. 415 (306 days); *Henderson* v. *Somers* (1876) 3 R. 997 (311 days impossible); *Gibson* v. *McFagan* (1874) 1 R. 853 (312 days impossible); *Gray* v. *G.*, 1919, 1 S.L.T. 163 (331 days impossible); *Doherty* v. *D.*, 1922, S.L.T. 245 (348 days impossible). See also *Grassie* v. *Couper* (1829) 8 S. 259; Ch. 16, *supra*.

[2] *McDonald* v. *Gilruth* (1874) 12 S.L.R. 43.

[3] *Hardie* v. *Leith* (1878) 6 R. 115; *Dunnet* v. *Campbell* (1883) 11 R. 280. Aliment was discontinued in *Purves's Trs.* v. *P.* (1900) 8 S.L.T. 179, where the child had succeeded to funds sufficient for its support.

[4] Ersk. I, 6, 56; Bell, *Prin.* §2062; *Oncken's J.F.* v. *Reimers* (1892) 19 R. 519; *A.B.* v. *C.D.'s Exor.* (1900) 2 F. 610. But see *Stewart's J.F.* v. *Law*, 1918, 2 S.L.T. 319. An action for aliment need not contain a conclusion declaratory of paternity but the crave of the writ must include an assertion of the fact: *Silver* v. *Walker*, 1938 S.C. 595.

[5] *S.* v. *P's Trs.*, 1941 S.L.T. 35.

[6] Illegitimate Children (Sc.) Act, 1930, S. 4.

[7] Affiliation Orders Act, 1952, S. 3.

[8] *Oncken's J.F.*, *supra*.

[9] *Robbie* v. *Dawes*, 1924 S.C. 749.

greater or lesser share depending on the means of the parties and the whole circumstances of the case,[1] of the cost of upbringing. She can recover unpaid arrears.[2] If the mother deserts the child and the father supports it he may sue her, if she has means, for a share of the cost. A third party having custody of the child may claim aliment.[3] The amount which may be awarded as aliment depends on the means of the parties,[4] the minimum being the amount of support beyond want which must be accorded to an illegitimate child.[5]

The child's claim for aliment was exigible as a debt against the father's executors in preference to the rights in succession of his widow and legitimate children,[6] or against the trustee in the father's sequestration in priority to the bankrupt's family.[7] By the Law Reform (Miscellaneous Provisions) (Sc.) Act, 1968, S. 4, a bastard is to have the same right to aliment from a deceased parent's estate, or from any person who had received property from that estate, *quantum lucratus*, as he would if legitimate. Any agreement for the bastard's aliment after the parent's death may be varied by the court.

When the bastard had reached seven or, if a girl, ten, the father could formerly, unless in exceptional circumstances, discharge any further claim for aliment by the mother by offering *bona fide* to take the maintenance and upbringing into his own hands,[8] even if he intended to put the child in the custody of a stranger.[9] This is not now competent.[10]

---

[1] 1930 Act, S. 1; *Shearer* v. *Robertson* (1877) 5 R. 263; *Mottram* v. *Butchart*, 1939 S.C. 89; *Terry* v. *Murray*, 1947 S.C. 10. She may claim on the father's bankrupt estate for future aliment as a contingent debt: *Downs* v. *Wilson's Tr.* (1886) 13 R. 1101.

[2] *Shearer* v. *Robertson* (1877) 5 R. 263; *Dunnet* v. *Campbell* (1883) 11 R. 280.

[3] 1930 Act, S. 1(3).

[4] 1930 Act, S. 1(2); *Terry, supra*; but a maximum of £1.50 per week was fixed by the Affiliation Orders Act, 1952, S. 1 (now Affiliation Proceedings Act, 1957, S. 4) and raised to £2.50 by the Matrimonial Proceedings (Magistrates Courts) Act, 1960, S. 15. Query, whether S. 1 applied to Scotland: held it did not, in *Halkett* v. *McSkeane*, 1962 S.L.T. (Sh. Ct.) 59, 80.

[5] *Fraser* v. *Campbell*, 1927 S.C. 589.

[6] *Oncken's J.F.* v. *Reimers* (1892) 19 R. 519; *Hare* v. *Logan's Trs.*, 1957 S.L.T. (Notes) 49.

[7] *Gairdner* v. *Monro* (1848) 10 D. 650.

[8] *Ballantine* v. *Malcolm* (1803) Hume 424; *Corrie* v. *Adair* (1860) 22 D. 897; *Grant* v. *Yuill* (1872) 10 M. 511; *Shearer, supra*; *Brown* v. *Halbert* (1896) 23 R. 733; *Millar* v. *Melville* (1898) 1 F. 367; *Moncrieff* v. *Langlands* (1900) 2 F. 1111; *Macdonald* v. *Denoon*, 1929 S.C. 172; cf. *Brown* v. *Ferguson*, 1912 S.C. 22, where mother died.

[9] *Corrie* v. *Adair* (1860) 22 D. 897; *Grant* v. *Yuill* (1872) 10 M. 511; *Shearer* v. *Robertson* (1877) 5 R. 263; *Westland* v. *Pirie* (1887) 14 R. 763; *Wilson* v. *Lindsay* (1893) 1 S.L.T. 272; *Oliver* v. *Bayne* (1894) 2 S.L.T. 106; *Moncrieff* v. *Langlands* (1900) 2 F. 1111.

[10] 1930 Act, S. 2(2).

The parents are liable, jointly or in such proportions as the sheriff may determine, for the funeral expenses of a bastard who dies while under sixteen.[1]

Where assistance is given from social security funds[2] a local authority[3] and the Supplementary Benefits Commission[4] have the same right as the mother to bring an action for affiliation and aliment concluding for aliment for a bastard, and the court may order that the sums due under the decree, or part thereof, shall be paid to the Commission or the local authority or such other person as the court may direct, and such payee may enforce the decree. Such payments are to recompense the authority or Commission for assistance given under the Acts.[5, 6] The Supplementary Benefits Commission may also seek to recover from the parents of a bastard sums expended on the child's maintenance and the parents are jointly and severally liable therefor.[5]

Where a child maintainable by the local authority is illegitimate, the authority has the same right as the mother to bring an action of affiliation and aliment. If a decree for aliment is in force the local authority may have a court order the payments to be made to the local authority entitled thereto.[6]

Custody and Guardianship—illegitimate children

The father of a bastard has no common law right of *patria potestas*, or of custody.[7] Nor has a grandparent.[8] The mother is the natural custodier of her own bastard child and has the primary right to custody.[9] The court may on the application of either parent, or in an action for aliment, make an order regarding custody and the right of access thereto of either parent, having regard to the welfare of the child, to the conduct of the parents and the wishes of each of them, and may on the application of either recall or vary such order.[10] The paramount consideration

---

[1] 1930 Act, S. 5.

[2] Under Ministry of Social Security Act, 1966, Part II.

[3] National Assistance Act, 1948, S. 44(7).

[4] Ministry of Social Security Act, 1966, S. 24(10).

[5] *N.A.B.* v. *Casey*, 1967 S.L.T. (Sh. Ct.) 11. See also *Supplementary Benefits Commn.* v. *Black*, 1968 S.L.T. (Sh. Ct.) 90.

[6] Social Work (Sc.) Act, 1968, S. 81.

[7] *Corrie* v. *Adair* (1860) 22 D. 897; *Macpherson* v. *Leishman* (1887) 14 R. 780; *Greenock Parish Council* v. *Kilmarnock and Stirling*, 1911 S.C. 570; *A.* v. *B.*, 1955 S.C. 378; *A.* v. *N.*, 1973 S.L.T. (Sh. Ct.) 34.

[8] *Brown* v. *Ferguson*, 1912 S.C. 22.

[9] *Macpherson, supra*; *Brand* v. *Shaws* (1888) 15 R. 449; *Kerrigan* v. *Hall* (1901) 4 F. 10; *Walter* v. *Culbertson*, 1921 S.C. 490; *Duguid* v. *McBrinn*, 1954 S.C. 105.

[10] 1930 Act, S. 2(1); *Duguid, supra*; *A.* v. *B., supra*. Custody awarded to father in *Sutherland* v. *Taylor* (1888) 15 R. 224; *A.B.* v. *C.D.*, 1962 S.L.T. (Sh. Ct.) 16.

is the welfare of the child.[1] The court may commit the care of the child to a local authority.[2] The court may make an order for payment to the person entitled to custody, whether father, mother or a third party, by the father or mother or both, of such aliment as the court thinks reasonable, having regard to the means and position of the parents and the whole circumstances of the case, and may recall or vary any such order.[3] The court's power on divorce to regulate custody, maintenance and education[4] applies to an illegitimate child of the parties, or of one party who has been accepted as one of the family by the other party.

Tutory and curatory—illegitimate children

The father has no common law right to the administration of his bastard child's legal affairs.[5] Nor has the mother such a right.[6] Where a bastard pupil sues he may do so in his own name, and the court will appoint a tutor ad litem, with whose concurrence the action proceeds.[7]

Relations between parents and natural child

The legal relations between the parents of a bastard and it are limited.[8] A bastard was at common law filius nullius and, save under statute, has no reciprocal rights and duties with his parents. Neither parent is deemed a blood relative of the child, and neither has any right to aliment from the bastard in case of need.[9] Nor are different bastards by the same parent or parents deemed in any way connected. Natural parent and natural child may transact with one another as if they were strangers.

At common law no right of succession was recognized in favour of, or through, illegitimate children. By the Succession (Scotland) Act, 1964, S. 4, illegitimate children were entitled on intestacy, failing legitimate issue, to the whole of their mother's estate, and, failing legitimate issue and other relatives of a bastard who died intestate, his mother is entitled to the whole of his

---

[1] *Duguid, supra.*

[2] Guardianship Act, 1973, S. 11.

[3] 1930 Act, S. 1(3). See also Affiliation Orders Act, 1952, S. 1.

[4] Matrimonial Proceedings (Children) Act, 1958, Ss. 7–15.

[5] *Corrie* v. *Adair* (1860) 22 D. 897.

[6] *Jones* v. *Somervell's Tr.*, 1907 S.C. 545.

[7] Mackay, *Manual of Practice*, 148; in *Ward* v. *Walker*, 1920 S.C. 80, the court appointed a curator *ad litem.*

[8] Bell, *Prin.* §2058.

[9] *Weir* v. *Coltness Iron Co.* (1889) 16 R. 614; *Clarke* v. *Carfin Coal Co.* (1891) 18 R. (H.L.) 63; *Clement* v. *Bell* (1899) 1 F. 924. *Samson* v. *Davie* (1886) 14 R. 113 is overruled by *Clarke, supra.*

intestate estate. By the Law Reform (Miscellaneous Provisions) (Scotland) Act, 1968, S. 1, S. 4 of the 1964 Act is replaced by a new S. 4, which gives legitimate and illegitimate children of an intestate equal rights to his whole estate, and the parents of an illegitimate person, if dying intestate and without issue, have right to his whole estate, it being presumed that the illegitimate was not survived by his father unless the contrary be shown. Apart from these provisions nothing in Part I of the 1964 Act is to be held to import any rule of succession through illegitimate relationship. The 1968 Act, S. 2, enacts a new S. 10A of the 1964 Act giving an illegitimate child a right to legitim.

LEGITIMATED CHILDREN

Legitimated children

In accordance with the civil and canon law doctrine of *legitimatio per subsequens matrimonium*,[1] a child born out of wedlock was at common law held legitimated if the natural parents were under no legal impediment to marry at the time the child was conceived, and subsequently did marry, and the husband admitted paternity, expressly or impliedly, or if it was proved against him.[2] The place of birth was immaterial.[3] But if there were a legal impediment to marriage, such as a subsisting marriage of either parent to another, legitimation could not take place; hence an adulterine bastard could never be legitimated, nor could the offspring of incest. Declarator of legitimation may be granted long after the death of the person involved at the instance of his descendants.[4] Where the doctrine of legitimation operates it does so independently of the consent of the child.[5] If the mother of a bastard marries it is still competent to prove, even after the deaths of the spouses and of the child, that the child was illegitimate.[6] The marriage by itself does not prove, nor even raise a presumption of, paternity by the husband.[7] A child cannot be legitimated by the marriage of its parents after it has

---

[1] Stair III, 3, 42; Bankt. I, 5, 54; Ersk. I, 6, 52; III, 10, 7; Bell, *Prin.* §1627, 2064; Fraser, *P. & Ch.* 37. See also history and authorities cited in *Kerr* v. *Martin* (1840) 2 D. 752.

[2] *Innes* v. *I.* (1837) 2 S. & Macl. 417; *Udny* v. *U.* (1869) 7 M. (H.L.) 89; *Imre* v. *Mitchell*, 1958 S.C. 439, 469.

[3] *Blair* v. *Kay's Trs.*, 1940 S.N. 82.   [4] *Bosville* v. *Lord Macdonald*, 1910 S.C. 597.

[5] *Hume* v. *Macfarlane* (1908) 16 S.L.T. 123.

[6] *Smith* v. *Dick* (1869) 8 M. 31.

[7] *Imre, supra; Brooks's Exrx.* v. *James*, 1970 S.C. 147; cf. *Gaffney* v. *Connerton*, 1909 S.C. 1009.

died,[1] but it may be legitimated, though one parent had married a third party and been widowed between the birth of the child and her marriage to the child's other parent.[2] Where the doctrine applies the bastard is retrospectively deemed legitimate from birth and has the same status as a fully legitimate child.[3] It is probable that such a child takes priority over later children born legitimate.[4] A bastard may also be legitimated by royal letters of legitimation.[5] By the Legitimation (Sc.) Act, 1968, S. 1, where the parents of a bastard marry after the commencement of the Act,[6] if the father is then domiciled in Scotland and the bastard is alive, the marriage legitimates the bastard from the date of the marriage. By S. 4, where the parents of a bastard had married each other before the Act, the father was domiciled in Scotland at the date of the marriage, the bastard was alive at the date of the marriage, and by reason of the existence at any time previous to the marriage of an impediment thereto, the marriage did not, at common law, effect legitimation, the marriage does so with effect from the commencement of the Act, or if he had died the Act applies to determine the rights and obligations of persons living thereafter as if the bastard had been legitimated as from that date.

Where a child has been registered as illegitimate entry may be made in the Register of Corrections respecting its legitimation *per subsequens matrimonium* only where such legitimation has been found by decree of court.[7] The Registrar-General may, in case of legitimation, authorize re-registration of the birth, but not where paternity of the bastard had not been registered, unless with the sanction of the sheriff on the application of both parents, or the survivor or of or on behalf of the legitimated bastard, after intimation and inquiry.[8]

Effect of legitimation

Under the Legitimation (Sc.) Act, 1968, S. 2, legitimation under the Act confers no status or right, and imposes no obliga-

---

[1] *McNeill* v. *McGregor* (1901) 4 F. 123; contrast *McLean* v. *Glasgow Corpn.*, 1933 S.L.T. 396.

[2] *Kerr* v. *Martin* (1840) 2 D. 752.

[3] *Crawford's Trs.* v. *Hart* (1802) Mor. 12698; *Kerr, supra*; see also *Munro* v. *Ross* (1827) 5 S. 605.

[4] Ersk. I, 6, 52; Bell, *Prin.* §1627; *Kerr, supra*.

[5] Ersk. III, 10, 7; Fraser, *P. & Ch.*, 51. cf. legitimation *per rescriptum principis*: Nov. 74, 89.

[6] 8th June 1968.

[7] Registration of Births, Deaths, and Marriages (Sc.) Act, 1965, Ss. 44, 48.

[8] 1965 Act, S. 20(1)(c). Re-registration was held incompetent where there was no evidence of legitimation by English law, the father's *lex domicilii*: *Mr. and Mrs. X.*, 1966 S.L.T. (Sh. Ct.) 86.

tion in respect of any time prior to the legitimation.[1] A person is not entitled, by virtue of the legitimation of anyone, to any right in the intestate estate of a person dying after the Act and before the legitimation, nor to legitim from the estate of any such person.[2] A person's legitimation does not affect any right under a deed coming into operation after the Act if the right has become indefeasibly vested in any other person before the legitimation, but,[3] subject to that, a legitimated person is entitled to any right under a deed coming into operation after the Act if his entitlement depends on his legitimacy and another person is entitled if his entitlement depends on the legitimacy of the legitimated person.[4] A reference in a deed coming into operation after the Act to a child or issue of a marriage is to be construed as including a reference to any child legitimated by the marriage.[5] Where a right is conferred or an obligation imposed by law or under a deed operative after the Act by reference to the relative seniority of the members of a class in terms which indicate that the class consists of legitimate persons only, any member of the class who is legitimated ranks as if born on the date of legitimation, and, if two or more, according to the respective times of birth.[6] Subject to these provisions, legitimation enures to the benefit of any other person claiming any right arising after the Act if entitlement depends on the legitimacy of the legitimated person.[7]

Where an illegitimate has died or dies, and would otherwise have been legitimated by the 1968 Act, the rights and obligations of any person living at or after the relevant date are determined by the Act as if legitimation had occurred.[8]

Where the parents of a bastard married before the Act, the father was domiciled in Scotland, the bastard was living, but the marriage did not effect legitimation at common law, marriage legitimates from the date of the Act; if the bastard were not living the Act determines the rights and obligations of any person living after the Act as if legitimation had operated.[9]

Legitimation includes recognition by Scots law of legitimation *per subsequens matrimonium* under the law of another country.[10]

Where the parents of a bastard married and adopted their bastard the adoption may be revoked without prejudice to succession rights acquired before the revocation.[11]

---

[1] 1968 Act, S. 2(1) and (8).   [2] S. 2(2).   [3] S. 2(3).   [4] S. 2(4).
[5] S. 2(5).   [6] S. 2(6).   [7] S. 2(7).   [8] S. 3.   [9] S. 4.
[10] S. 5.   [11] S. 6.

ADOPTIVE CHILDREN

Adoptive children

At common law an arrangement for the adoption of a child so as to make him legally the child of another parent or other parents was not recognized though such arrangements as fostering were permissible contractually.[1] By statute adoption has been introduced,[2] having definite legal consequences and creating the status of adoptive child. Only local authorities and registered adoption societies may make arrangements for the adoption of children.[3] Advertisement relating to adoption and certain payments in relation thereto are forbidden.[4]

On application by the mother or father of the child, alone or jointly with his or her spouse,[5] or by spouses,[6] domiciled and, normally, also resident in Scotland,[7] the Court of Session or Sheriff Court may make an order authorizing the adoption of a person aged under 21,[8] but not one who is or has been married,[9] who is resident in Scotland.[10] A person must be appointed to act as curator *ad litem* to the child to safeguard his interests.[11] The applicant must be mother or father of the child, or a relative of the child and aged 21, or be aged 25; if spouses are

---

[1] cf. *Kerrigan* v. *Hall* (1901) 4 F. 10; *Briggs* v. *Mitchell*, 1911 S.C. 765.

[2] Adoption of Children (Sc.) Act, 1930, now replaced by Adoption Act, 1958.

[3] 1958 Act, Ss. 28–33. The court will normally refuse an adoption of a child obtained from an unregistered person: *Mr. and Mrs. S.S.*, 1953 S.L.T. (Sh. Ct.) 29.

[4] Ss. 50–1.

[5] S. 1(3): A mother may adopt her own illegitimate child: *D.*, 1938 S.C. 223; *Re D.* [1958] 3 All E.R. 716.

[6] S. 1(2). Grandparents have been permitted to adopt their daughter's illegitimate child: *T.F. and H.F.*, 1949 S.L.T. (Sh. Ct.) 48; *Re. D.X.* [1949] Ch. 320; contrast *Mr. and Mrs. A.B.*, (1962) 78 Sh. Ct. Rep. 148; *C.D.*, 1963 S.L.T. (Sh. Ct.) 7. Spouses may adopt the wife's legitimate children by a previous marriage: *B. and B.*, 1936 S.C. 256; *I. and I.*, 1947 S.C. 485; or the legitimate but unwanted child of another couple: *Mr. and Mrs. L.*, 1965 S.L.T. (Sh. Ct.) 66. But parents may not adopt their own child legitimated *per subsequens matrimonium*: *M. and M.*, 1950 S.L.T. (Sh. Ct.) 3. A grandparent may adopt her own grandchild whose parents were dead: *Mrs. D.*, 1951 S.L.T. (Sh. Ct.) 19; contrast *Mr. and Mrs. A.B.*, (1962) 78 Sh. Ct. Rep. 148. A divorced mother and her second husband may adopt the children of her previous marriage: *Z.* v. *Z.*, 1954 S.L.T. (Sh. Ct.) 47. A childless couple may adopt their nephew or niece, unwanted by its parents: *Mr. and Mrs. L.*, 1965 S.L.T. (Sh. Ct.) 66.

[7] S. 12; *H.* (1949) 65 Sh. Ct. Rep. 7; *B.* (1949) 65 Sh. Ct. Rep. 45; *M.* (1949) 65 Sh. Ct. Rep. 91; *C.* (1949) 65 Sh. Ct. Rep. 93; as to adoption by persons domiciled outside Great Britain, see S. 52.

[8] *G. Petr.*, 1939 S.C. 782; *K. Petr.*, 1949 S.C. 140; *T.B.*, 1950 S.L.T. (Sh. Ct.) 74; *R.B.*, 1950 S.L.T. (Sh. Ct.) 73; *M. Petr.*, 1953 S.C. 227.

[9] Overruling *L.*, 1951 S.C. 605.

[10] 1958 Act, S. 1.

[11] Ibid., S. 11(4).

joint applicants, one must be mother or father of the child,[1] or one spouse must be a relative of the child and aged 21, or be aged 25, and the other spouse must be 21. Only in special circumstances will a single male be permitted to adopt a female child.[2] The child must have been continuously in the care and possession of the applicant[3] for at least three consecutive months before the order and after attaining the age of six weeks. Except where one applicant is a parent of the child three months' notice of intention to apply for an adoption order must be given to the local authority.[4]

The consent is required of every parent[5] or guardian[6] of the child and of an applicant's own spouse, and of the child itself, if a minor,[7] but the court may dispense with consent if the consenter has neglected the child or cannot be found[8] or is incapable of giving consent or is withholding it unreasonably,[9] or has persistently failed to discharge the obligations of a parent or guardian.[10] If a minor is incapable of giving consent, the court may dispense with it.[11] A person who has consented may not, while an adoption application is pending, without leave of the court, remove the child from the applicant's possession.[12] An adopted child may be re-adopted by other persons.[13]

Before making an order the court must be satisfied that all the requisite consents have been given and the consenters understand the effect of an adoption order, that the order will be for the

---

[1] *B. and B.*, 1936 S.C. 256.

[2] Ibid., S. 2; for special circumstances see *H.*, 1960 S.L.T. (Sh. Ct.) 3.

[3] See *E.O., Petr.*, 1951 S.L.T. (Sh. Ct.) 11; *M., Petr.*, 1953 S.C. 227; *A. Petr.*, 1953 S.L.T. (Sh. Ct.) 45; *X.Y., Petr.*, 1954 S.L.T. (Sh. Ct.) 86; *F.*, 1955 S.L.T. (Sh. Ct.) 12; *G., Petr.*, 1955 S.L.T. (Sh. Ct.) 27; *A., Petrs.*, 1958 S.L.T. (Sh. Ct.) 61.

[4] S. 3.

[5] The father of a bastard is not a 'parent': *A.* v. *B.*, 1955 S.C. 378. It will rarely be necessary to appoint a curator *ad litem* to a mother who is a minor: *A.B. and C.B.* v. *X's Curator*, 1963 S.C. 124.

[6] Defined: S. 4(3); *C. and C.*, 1936 S.C. 257. Disclosure to the natural parent of the identity of the proposed adopters is not essential: *H. and H.*, 1944 S.C. 347. See also *K.*, 1949 S.C. 140.

[7] S. 4; *A., Petr.*, 1936 S.C. 255; *McD. and McD.* (1949) 65 Sh. Ct. Rep. 42; *Mr. and Mrs. A.*, 1953 S.L.T. (Sh. Ct.) 45; *Y.Z., Petr.*, 1954 S.L.T. (Sh. Ct.) 98.

[8] *Mr. and Mrs. O.*, 1950 S.L.T. (Sh. Ct.) 64.

[9] *Mr. and Mrs. A.B.*, 1959 S.L.T. (Sh. Ct.) 49. The whole circumstances, including the child's welfare, have to be considered in determining whether consent has been unreasonably withheld: *A.B. and C.B.* v. *X's Curator*, 1963 S.C. 124; *C.* v. *D.*, 1964 S.L.T. (Sh. Ct.) 39; *X.* v. *Y.*, 1967 S.L.T. (Sh. Ct.) 87; *C.* v. *D.*, 1968 S.L.T. (Sh. Ct.) 39; *A.B.* v. *C.D.*, 1970 S.C. 268.

[10] S. 5; see also *X.* v. *Y.*, 1967 S.L.T. (Sh. Ct.) 87; as to evidence of consent, see S. 6.

[11] S. 5(5) added by Law Reform (Misc. Prov.) (Sc.) Act, 1966, S. 4, curing defect revealed by *B. and B.*, 1965 S.C. 44, *sub. nom. P.Q. and R.Q.*, 1965 S.L.T. 93.

[12] S. 34.

[13] Ss. 23–4; *E. and E.*, 1939 S.C. 165; *F., Petr.*, 1939 S.C. 166.

welfare of the infant,[1] and that no unauthorized payments have been made in respect of the adoption; the order may be made subject to terms and conditions.[2] The court may make an interim order for a two-year probationary period.[3] An adoption order once made cannot be set aside on the ground of essential error.[4]

While an application for an adoption order is pending a parent or guardian who has consented thereto may not, save by leave of the court, remove the child from the care and possession of the applicant.[5] A prospective adopter may decide not to retain the child, and an adoption society recall the child before an adoption order has been made.[6] Where notice of intention to adopt a child has been given, the child is deemed a protected child, and the local authority must satisfy itself as to its well-being.[7] The court may order a protected child to be removed from unsuitable surroundings.[8]

When an adoption order has been made all rights, duties, obligations, and liabilities of natural parents or guardians in relation to custody, maintenance, and education and the appointment of guardians are extinguished, and they vest in and are enforceable against the adopter(s) as if the child were one born in lawful wedlock.[9] It becomes liable to aliment its adoptive parent(s) and is within the prohibited degrees of relationship to him or them.[10] Unless made in favour of the child's mother who is single an adoption order supersedes a decree of affiliation and aliment and any agreement whereby the father has undertaken to make payments for the child's benefit, without prejudice to recovery of arrears, and no such decree shall be subsequently granted.[11] An adoption order also supersedes a committal order under the Children and Young Persons (Scotland) Act, 1937, or the assumption of parental functions by a local authority under the Children Act, 1948.[12] An adoption order may be revoked

---

[1] The factors the court must consider (S. 7(2)) include the health and wishes of the child: see also *H., Petrs.*, 1951 S.L.T. (Sh. Ct.) 17. Petitions have been refused as being *contra bonos mores*: *E.* (1949) 65 Sh. Ct. Rep. 8; *J.S.*, 1950 S.L.T. (Sh. Ct.) 3; for reasons of health: *G. and G.*, 1949 S.L.T. (Sh. Ct.) 60; contrast *K. and K.*, 1950 S.L.T. (Sh. Ct.) 1; as ratifying a separation of spouses: *H.*, 1951 S.L.T. (Sh. Ct.) 17; contrast *L.H.*, 1951 S.L.T. (Sh. Ct.) 46.

[2] S. 7, e.g. undertaking by natural father to aliment child in case of need: *G.D.*, 1950 S.L.T. (Sh. Ct.) 34.

[3] S. 8. [4] *J. & J.* v. *C's Tutor*, 1948 S.C. 636.

[5] 1958 Act, S. 34. [6] S. 35.

[7] Ss. 37–40. [8] S. 43.

[10] cf. *Hutchison* v. *H's Trs.*, 1951 S.C. 108.

[11] Ss. 13–14. But it is not incest to have intercourse with an adopted daughter who is the accused's wife's illegitimate child: *H.M.A.* v. *McKenzie*, 1970 S.L.T. 81.

[12] S. 15.

where a person adopted by one parent has been legitimated *per subsequens matrimonium*.[1]

Adoptions are recorded in an Adopted Children Register kept by the Registrar General for Scotland, and provision is made for relating entries in the Register of Births to entries in the Adopted Children Register.[2] The entry in the Register of Births relating to the child is to be marked 'adopted'.

The name or surname of a child adopted may be changed and the change registered.[3]

On the death of one of two jointly adopting parents the adoptive child stands in the same relation to the survivor as a legitimate child would.[4]

Formerly[5] an adopted child retained rights of succession to his natural parents and did not acquire such rights to his adoptive parents. By the Succession (Scotland) Act, 1964, Ss. 23–4, an adopted child is now deemed the legitimate child of his adoptive parents for purposes of succession and has no claim on his natural parents. But where the adoptive parent had died, or both adoptive parents had died, before 10 September 1964, the adoptee is treated, for the purposes of succession as the child of the natural parent, if dying after 3 August 1966.[6]

Custody and guardianship of adoptive child

A child once adopted is subject to the custody of the adoptive parent or parents as if that relationship were legitimate.[7] The adoptive parent is tutor to the adoptive child in legal business in the same way as if the relationship were legitimate.[8]

---

[1] Ss. 26–7; Legitimation (Sc.) Act, 1968, S. 6.
[2] Ss. 22–3.
[3] 1958 Act, Ss. 22(6) and 24(1).
[4] *Hutchison* v. *H's Trs.*, 1951 S.C. 108.
[5] 1930 Act, S. 5; 1958 Act, S. 18.
[6] Law Reform (Misc. Prov.) (Sc.) Act, 1966, S. 5.
[7] Adoption Act, 1958, S. 13.
[8] *Hutchison, supra.*

CHAPTER 18

THE DOMESTIC RELATIONS— (3) GUARDIAN AND WARD

PUPILS, minors, and persons physically or mentally incapax require for their own protection and good to be under the guardianship of persons of greater maturity both for physical care, custody, and upbringing, and for advice in business transactions and legal relations.[1] In the case of pupils and minors both custody and guidance are normally provided by the natural parents, or persons nominated by them or designated by law as guardians, failing the parents.[2] Extensive statutory provision is now made for the custody and guidance of children in other cases, and of incapaces.

PUPILS AND MINORS

In its doctrines of guardianship of children Scots law closely resembles Roman law. Corresponding to the two stages of life short of majority, there are two kinds of guardianship, tutory and curatory.

Tutory is a power and faculty to govern the person, and to manage the estate of a pupil; curatory is the power of managing the estate of a minor, or of a major who is incapable of acting for himself through defect of judgment.[3] *Tutor datur personae, curator rei.* Failing a parent, a tutor is essential for a pupil, but a curator is not essential to a minor, since he has capacity to act on his own. The rules as to guardianship vary according as the child is legitimate, legitimated, or adopted on the one hand, or illegitimate on the other.

Guardianship of legitimate pupils—Tutors testamentary or nominate

At common law, on the father's death, the office of tutor to his pupil children devolves on one or more tutors nominate or testamentary named in his will, to control the pupil's person and manage his estate.[4] The father's testamentary trustees are

---

[1] See generally Stair I, 6, 1; Ersk. I, 7, 1; Bell, *Prin.* §2065–2128; Fraser, *P. & Ch.,* passim.

[2] Chap. 17, *supra.*

[3] Stair I, 6, 1; Ersk. I, 7, 1; Bell, *Prin.* §2065–6, 2088–90.

[4] Ersk. I, 7, 2–3; Bell, *Prin.* §2071; Fraser, *P. & Ch.,* 239.

frequently so named.[1] They need neither take the oath *de fideli administratione*, nor find caution for their intromissions, unless the court had reason to suspect their honesty or their circumstances,[2] but must make up an inventory as a check on administration.

A person devising any property to a pupil may nominate a person to manage it during the pupillarity, but such a person is not tutor for any other purpose.

Tutor of law or tutor-legitim

Failing any tutors-nominate, the office, as in Roman law, devolves by law on the nearest of the male agnates, i.e. kinsmen on the father's side, the one who would by common law be the pupil's heir at law, if aged 25, as tutor-legitim or tutor of law.[3] Even after accepting office a tutor-legitim must relinquish the office if a tutor-testamentary offers to accept.[4] The tutor of law obtains appointment by petition to the Sheriff for service as tutor-legitim, after such inquiry as may be necessary. He must take the oath *de fideli*, find caution for his intromissions,[5] and is subject to the supervision of the Accountant of Court.[6] But a tutor-legitim might not be sufficiently careful to preserve the pupil's life so that, while he has the direction of the pupil's education and of the expenses attaching to him, the mother, if still a widow, has the custody, at least till the pupil is seven. If she remarries or her mode of life be bad, the custody is given to the next of the cognates, i.e. all relations by the mother.[7]

Tutor-dative

In default of tutor-legitim, a tutor-dative may be appointed by the court. To enable a tutor-legitim to decide whether to serve or not, no appointment as tutor-dative can be made till a year from the time when the first tutor of law might have served.[8] A tutor-dative must find caution, and is subject to the supervision of the Accountant of Court.[9]

[1] e.g. *McCrossan's Trs.* v. *McC.* (1899) 7 S.L.T. 22; see, however, *Walker* v. *Stronach* (1874) 2 R. 120.

[2] Ersk. I, 7, 1–3; Bell, *Prin.* §2081; Guardianship of Infants Act, 1886, S. 12.

[3] Ersk. I, 7, 4–5; Bell, *Prin.* §2078–9; Fraser, *P. & Ch.*, 249; *McLay* v. *Thornton* (1868) 41 S. Jur. 68; *Alexander* v. *McGarrity* (1903) 5 F. 654.

[4] Ersk. I, 7, 4–5.

[5] Ersk. I, 7, 6.

[6] Judicial Factors (Sc.) Act, 1849, Ss. 3, 25, 30.

[7] Ersk. I, 7, 7; Bell, *Prin.* §2078.

[8] Ersk. I, 7, 8; Bell, *Prin.* §2080; Fraser, *P. & Ch.*, 258; *Martin* (1859) 22 D. 45; *Urquhart* (1860) 22 D. 932; *Simpson* (1861) 23 D. 1292.

[9] Bell, *Prin.* §2081–81A; Judicial Factors (Sc.) Act, 1849, S. 26.

The usual practice is, however, on the petition of any kinsman of the pupil, to appoint a judicial factor *loco tutoris* to the pupil, for the management of his affairs.[1] He should be a neutral person.[2] The court may, on cause shown, remove or accept the resignation of any tutor of law or tutor dative and appoint a factor *loco tutoris* in his place.[3] A father's poverty alone is not a sufficient ground for depriving him of the administration of his pupil child's property,[4] nor the mere possibility of conflict of interest between him and his child.[5] On a father's death a mother cannot be appointed factor *loco tutoris* since she is now, by the Guardianship of Children (Sc.) Acts, 1886 to 1973, guardian.[6] A temporary appointment may be made while the Court is dissatisfied with the administration of a tutor-nominate.[7]

A factor *loco tutoris* who continues to act after the pupil becomes minor becomes a *curator bonis*.[8]

Statutory provisions

In most cases the common law provisions are now superseded by statutory ones. By the Guardianship of Children (Scotland) Acts, 1886 to 1973[9] both parents have equal rights. On the death of either the survivor is to be tutor,[10] alone or jointly with any tutor appointed by the deceased parent. Failing any such appointment the court may appoint a tutor to act jointly with the survivor.[11] If a pupil has no parent or tutor the court may appoint any applicant to be tutor.[12] Either parent may by deed or will appoint any person to be tutor after his death; such a tutor will act jointly with the surviving parent, unless the latter objects. If so, or if the tutor considers the parent unfit to have custody, the tutor may apply to the court, which may make either parent or tutor

---

[1] Ersk. I, 7, 10; Bell, *Prin.* §2068.

[2] *Hutcheon* v. *Alexander*, 1909, 1 S.L.T. 71.

[3] Judicial Factors (Scotland) Act, 1849, S. 31.

[4] *Wardrop* v. *Gossling* (1869) 7 M. 532.

[5] *Cochrane* (1891) 18 R. 456; contrast *Allan* (1895) 3 S.L.T. 87.

[6] *Willison* (1890) 18 R. 228.

[7] *Edgar* v. *Fisher's Trs.* (1893) 21 R. 59, 325, 1076.

[8] Judicial Factors (Sc.) Act, 1889, S. 11; *Stiven* v. *Masterton* (1892) 30 S.L.R. 50.

[9] 'Guardian' is defined as 'tutor' and 'infant' as 'pupil': 1886 Act, S. 8. The Acts apply only to legitimate children: *Brand* v. *Shaws* (1888) 16 R. 315; 1973 Act, S. 10(6).

[10] A mother's tutory is not affected by remarriage: *Campbell* v. *Maquay* (1888) 15 R. 784. In view of the Acts a mother cannot now be appointed factor *loco tutoris*: *Willison* (1890) 18 R. 228.

[11] *Martin* v. *Stewart* (1888) 16 R. 185; *Sim* v. *Robertson* (1901) 3 F. 1027. It is incompetent to seek to have a factor *loco tutoris* appointed to act with the mother: *Speirs*, 1946 S.L.T. 203.

[12] 1925 Act, S. 4.

sole tutor, or make them joint tutors, and may, if making the tutor sole tutor, regulate custody and access to the child by the parent and order the parent to make payments towards maintenance. Where both parents appoint tutors, they act jointly after the death of the surviving parent. A tutor appointed by the court continues to act after the death of the surviving parent and jointly with any tutor appointed by the survivor.[1] Disputes between joint tutors may be settled by the court on application.[2]

Powers of tutors—custody

A tutor, except a tutor of law who is heir-at-law, has custody of the person of the pupil. If the mother be not tutor, she will have the custody of the pupil till seven, unless she is unfit therefor. The tutor may direct the residence and education of the pupil, subject to the control of the Court of Session.[3] A factor *loco tutoris* may be granted custody in preference to the father.[4]

Powers of tutors—estate and actions

A tutor of law, tutor dative or factor *loco tutoris* is subject to the Judicial Factors (Scotland) Acts, 1849 to 1889,[5] and a tutor who is administrator-in-law, tutor nominate or guardian under the 1886 Act is deemed a tutor within the meaning of the Judicial Factors (Scotland) Act, 1849 and subject to the provisions thereof.[6] A parent acting as tutor at common law or under the 1886 to 1973 Acts is a trustee within the meaning of the Trusts (Scotland) Acts, 1921 and 1961,[7] and any tutor or judicial factor is deemed, and has the powers of, a trustee under those Acts.[8] All such tutors have ordinary powers of administration of the pupil's property.[9] They bring and defend legal proceedings alone, for behoof of the pupil.[10] A tutor *ad litem* may be appointed to a pupil, called as defender, for whom appearance has not been entered.[11] A mother, as tutor under the 1886 Act, has been held

[1] 1925 Act, S. 5, overruling *Fraser* (1893) 1 S.L.T. 126.

[2] 1925 Act, S. 6.

[3] Bell, *Prin.* §2083.

[4] *Moncreiff* (1891) 18 R. 1029.

[5] 1849 Act, S. 1.

[6] 1886 Act, S. 12.

[7] Guardianship of Infants Act, 1925, S. 10.

[8] Trusts (Sc.) Act, 1921, S. 2.

[9] Bell, *Prin.* §2082, 2084.

[10] Fraser, *P. & Ch.*, 208; cf. *Craven* v. *Elibank's Trs.* (1854) 16 D. 811; *Davis's Tutor* v. *Glasgow Victoria Hospitals*, 1950 S.C. 382.

[11] *Macdonald's Trs.* v. *Medhurst*, 1915 S.C. 879; *Ward* v. *Walker*, 1920 S.C. 80; *Aitken's Trs.* v. *Milne*, 1921 S.C. 454; *Drummond's Trs.* v. *Peel's Trs.*, 1929 S.C. 484; the court in the last case speaks of a curator *ad litem*, which seems a misnomer.

entitled to grant a good discharge for damages awarded to her pupil children.[1] In other cases the Court has sometimes *de plano* appointed a factor *loco tutoris*[2] and sometimes required a formal petition for such a factor to administer awards of damages.[3]

Expiry of office

The office expires on the death of tutor or pupil, or the pupil's attainment of minority.[4] A tutor may be removed by the Court of Session.[5] Mutual actions lie for an accounting for intromissions with the pupil's estate, and for loss or damage from any transaction against which the pupil cannot be restored,[6] and on the other hand for reimbursement of outlays, relief of engagements undertaken and discharge. These actions prescribe in five years.[7] A discharge under the 1849 Act is generally conclusive against all parties.[8]

Guardianship of minors—estate and actions

The minor manages his property and transacts legally himself, but with the consent and concurrence of his curator, as his adviser.[9] Transactions by the curator himself are null, and he cannot compel the minor to any course of action; if the minor is obstinate, the curator should apply to be discharged.[10] The minor's powers of administration, with his curator's concurrence, are unlimited. If a minor is a defender in litigation and has no curator, the court may appoint a curator *ad litem* to him.[11]

Powers of curators

A curator is deemed to be, and has the powers of, a trustee under the Trusts (Scotland) Acts, 1921 and 1961.[12] But the function of

---

[1] *Jack v. N.B. Ry. Co.* (1886) 14 R. 263.

[2] *Collins v. Eglinton Iron Co.* (1882) 9 R. 500; *McAvoy v. Young's Paraffin Oil Co.* (1882) 19 S.L.R. 441; *Boylan v. Hunter*, 1922 S.C. 80.

[3] *Connolly v. Bent Colliery Co.* (1897) 24 R. 1172; cf. *Anderson v. Muirhead* (1884) 11 R. 870.

[4] Bell, *Prin.* §2086.

[5] *Butchart v. B.* (1851) 13 D. 1258; *Dewar* (1853) 16 D. 163, 489; *Fleming v. Craig* (1863) 1 M. 850; *Mitchell* (1864) 2 M. 1378; see also Judicial Factors (Sc.) Act, 1849, Ss. 25, 31; Guardianship of Infants Act, 1886, S. 6.

[6] *A.B.* (1854) 16 D. 1004; *Guthrie* (1853) 16 D. 214; *Cochrane v. Black* (1855) 17 D. 321; 19 D. 1019; *Laird v. L.* (1855) 17 D. 984; *Acct. of Court v. Geddes* (1858) 20 D. 1174.

[7] Prescription and Limitation (Sc.) Act, 1973, S. 6.

[8] 1849 Act, S. 34.

[9] Ersk. I, 7, 16; Bell, *Prin.* §2096.

[10] *Mackenzie's Tr. v. M.*, 1908 S.C. 995, 999.

[11] cf. *Drummond's Trs. v. Peel's Trs.*, 1929 S.C. 484 (pupil).

[12] 1921 Act, S. 2.

a curator is not to administer, but to interpose consent and concurrence to the minor's actings. Thus minors can themselves
grant a valid discharge for damages,[1] though if the sum is
substantial the court may direct it to be paid to a person in trust
for the minor.[2]

Guardianship of minors

At common law the father is the natural curator of his minor
child,[3] but the minor may by forisfamiliation, i.e. by setting out,
with the father's consent, on an independent career,[4] or, if a
girl, by marriage, release himself from the father's curatory.
With the father's consent, however, or if he has acted in violation
of paternal duty, or if there is conflict of interest between father
and child, another person may be appointed curator to guide the
child in managing his affairs.[5] By the Tutors and Curators Act,
1696, c. 8, fathers while still in health, in *liege poustie*,[6] may
nominate curators to their children.[7] Failing the father the mother
was not automatically curator, but might be appointed to the
office by the father's will. Under the Guardianship Act, 1973,
a mother is now curator. A person appointed factor *loco tutoris*
automatically becomes curator when the child attains puberty
unless the child chooses curators for himself.[8] A minor might,
under the Act 1555, c. 35, bring an action for choosing curators
for himself.[9] Now, if a minor desires a curator he may have one
appointed by petitioning the Court of Session.[10]

A curator may be named to a minor for a special purpose, as
where a third party has devised property to the minor, but such is
more properly a *curator bonis* than a guardian,[11] and such an
appointment does not prejudice a petition for choosing curators.[12]

---

[1] *Jack* v. *N.B. Ry. Co.* (1886) 14 R. 263; cf. *Macdonald* (1896) 4 S.L.T. 4.

[2] *Sharp* v. *Pathhead Spinning Co.* (1885) 12 R. 574; *Spring* v. *Blackhall* (1901) 9 S.L.T.
162; See also *Anderson* v. *Muirhead* (1884) 11 R. 870; *McIntosh* v. *Wood*, 1970 S.C. 179.

[3] Ersk. I, 6, 54; Bell, *Prin.* §2092.

[4] Fraser, *P. & Ch.*, 499; *Thomson* v. *Gibson & Borthwick* (1851) 13 D. 683; *McFeetridge*
v. *Stewarts & Lloyds*, 1913 S.C. 773.

[5] Ersk. I, 6, 54; *McNab* v. *McN.* (1871) 10 M. 248.

[6] i.e. *in legitima potestate*.

[7] Ersk. I, 7, 11; Bell, *Prin.* §2093; Fraser, *P. & Ch.*, 455; see e.g. *Greig* v. *G.* (1872)
11 M. 20.

[8] Judicial Factors (Sc.) Act, 1889, S. 11; *Ferguson* v. *Blair* (1908) 16 S.L.T. 284.

[9] Ersk. I, 7, 11; Bell, *Prin.* §2095; Fraser, *P. & Ch.*, 459; *Fergusson* v. *Dormer* (1870)
8 M. 426.

[10] Administration of Justice (Sc.) Act, 1933, S. 12; cf. *Thomson* (1881) 19 S.L.R. 105;
Hutchison (1881) 18 S.L.R. 725.

[11] *Macdonald* (1896) 4 S.L.T. 4; *Perry* (1903) 10 S.L.T. 536.

[12] Ersk. I, 7, 13; Bell, *Prin.* §2094.

Also, where a minor is involved in litigation with his curator, or having no curator, with a stranger, a curator *ad litem* must be appointed by the court.[1]

While tutory was at common law *officium virile* which could not be exercised by women, all persons may be appointed curators to minors who are fit to manage an estate. Hence a father may nominate his widow, or any unmarried woman, and doubtless now,[2] any woman at all, to be curatrix.[3]

A minor need not have a curator at all and may manage his affairs himself without any curatorial guidance.

Guardianship of minors—control of the person

A minor without parents is not subject to custody or control of his person or residence, and may choose his or her own residence.[4] Even where a minor has a curator, the latter has no control of the minor's person or residence. A curator may advise as to education and training for a career, but cannot compel.[5]

Termination of curatory

Curatory terminates by the death of curator or minor, or by the minor's attaining majority[6] or, if a girl, marrying, when she passes into the curatory of her husband.[7] The office falls by supervening incapacity, natural or legal. Curators may be removed by the court.[8] If the minor refuses to accept advice, or to sign necessary deeds, the curator should apply to the court to be discharged.[8]

Accounting

On the termination of tutory or curatory, a minor or adult has an *actio directa tutelae vel curatelae* against the guardian for an accounting for intromissions in the management of the ward's affairs, payment of any balance due and restoration of papers in the guardian's possession.[9] Guardians may bring an *actio tutelae*

---

[1] Fraser, *P. & Ch.*, 466; *Cunningham* v. *Smith* (1880) 7 R. 424; *Young* v. *Rankin*, 1934 S.C. 499. If such a minor later becomes insane the office of *curator ad litem* falls and a *curator bonis* must be appointed: *Moodie* v. *Dempster*, 1931 S.C. 553.

[2] *Chalmers' Trs.* v. *Sinclair* (1897) 24 R. 1047 is probably superseded, at least *quoad* married women over 18, who are not now themselves subject to curatory.

[3] Ersk. I, 7, 12.

[4] *Flannigan* v. *Inspector of Bothwell* (1892) 19 R. 909; *Morrison* v. *Quarrier* (1894) 21 R. 889, 1071; *Fisher* v. *Edgar* (1894) 21 R. 1076.

[5] Bell, *Prin.* §2090; Fraser, *P. & Ch.*, 470.

[6] cf. *McIntosh* v. *Wood*, 1970 S.C. 179.

[7] Ersk. I, 7, 29; Married Women's Property (Sc.) Act, 1920, S. 2.

[8] Ersk., *supra*.

[9] Ersk. I, 7, 31; Bell, *Prin.* §2097.

vel curatelae contraria against the minor or adult to obtain discharge from their office and administration, to obtain relief from all engagements undertaken, for reimbursement of outlays and charges, but not for any remuneration or reward for their services.[1]

Administration by tutors, factors loco tutoris and curators

The main distinction between the offices of tutor and curator is expressed in the maxim *tutor datur personae, curator rei*. The tutor has the governance of the pupil's person and the sole management of his estate; the curator has no power of governance of the minor's person, and cannot prescribe where he may reside, and no power of management, but only of advising, and consenting and concurring with, the minor in the latter's management of his own estate.[2] In most other respects the powers privileges, duties, and obligations of the offices of tutory and curatory coincide. The offices are gratuitous, though a father may allow a tutor-testamentary and a minor allow his curator an allowance, presumed to be in full of all charges and outlays.[3] Tutors, and factors *loco tutoris* are subject to the Judicial Factors (Scotland) Acts, 1849,[4] 1880, and 1889, and are subject to the supervision of the Accountant of Court. A factor appointed to a pupil automatically becomes a curator bonis when the pupil becomes a minor.[5]

No person can be compelled to accept either office and acceptance is not to be inferred by implication.[6] Having accepted, however, tutors and curators are accountable for their intromissions from the time of acceptance.[7] They must first make an inventory of the pupil or minor's whole estate.[8]

Tutors and curators must not be *auctores in rem suam* or act contrary to their trust, as by entering into obligations in which they have an interest, or which favours or benefits them.[9] Thus a curator cannot lend money to the minor, nor purchase anything from the minor, nor employ a firm in which he was a partner to conduct a lawsuit.[10]

---

[1] Ersk. I, 7, 32; Bell, *Prin., supra.*

[2] Ersk. I, 7, 14; Bell, *Prin.* §2090. See also *Browning's Factor* (1905) 7 F. 1037.

[3] Ersk. I, 7, 15.

[4] Sometimes called the Pupils' Protection Act, 1849.

[5] 1889 Act, S. 11.

[6] As to modes of express acceptance, see Ersk. I, 7, 20.

[7] Ersk. I, 7, 20.

[8] Ersk. I, 7, 21; Act 1672, c. 2.

[9] Ersk. I, 7, 19; cf. *Dunn* v. *Chambers* (1897) 25 R. 247.

[10] *Mitchell* v. *Burness* (1878) 5 R. 1124.

The court will not sanction the expenditure of the ward's funds to support a person whom the ward is under no legal obligation to support[1] but expenditure of this kind may be allowed in special circumstances, if the funds are ample,[2] the beneficiary is of kin[3] and the beneficiary be destitute, particularly if the ward would probably have made the expenditure.[4] The court may even sanction it retrospectively.[5]

Pro-tutors and pro-curators

Persons who act as tutors or curators without having a legal title to the office, whether they believe themselves guardians or know that they are not, are deemed pro-tutors or pro-curators. They are on the same footing as tutors or curators as to the obligations incumbent on them but have none of the powers competent to those duly appointed, such as to sue third parties for payment or to grant valid discharges.[6]

Guardianship of illegitimate children

The father of a bastard pupil has no common law right of *patria potestas*, of custody or administration, and cannot appoint tutors to the child.[7] The mother is the natural custodier and tutor of her own bastard child, the only person with a legal title to its custody,[8] and probably cannot by agreement deprive herself of the right to its custody.[9] She cannot nominate a guardian to her bastard, either at common law or under the Guardianship of Infants Acts.[10] But in a question between the mother and a person to whom the mother has given the child to be brought up the court must consider the child's welfare and may refuse the mother custody.[11] After the mother's death her expressed wishes may be

---

[1] *Court* (1848) 10 D. 822; *Primerose* (1852) 15 D. 37; *Dunbar* (1876) 3 R. 554; *Balfour* (1889) 26 S.L.R. 268.

[2] *Primerose, supra; Robertson* (1853) 25 Sc. Jur. 554.

[3] But see *Boyle* (1854) 17 D. 790.

[4] *Gardner* (1882) 20 S.L.R. 165; *Blackwood* (1890) 17 R. 1093; *Bowers* v. *Pringle-Pattison's C.B.* (1892) 19 R. 941.

[5] *Hamilton's Tutors,* 1924 S.C. 363.

[6] Stair I, 6, 12; Bankt. I, 7, 19; Ersk. I, 7, 28; Bell, *Prin.* §2098; Fraser, *P. & Ch.,* 561; *Fultons* v. *F.* (1864) 2 M. 893.

[7] Bell, *Prin.* §2071.

[8] *Sutherland* v. *Taylor* (1887) 15 R. 224.

[9] *Macpherson* v. *Leishman* (1887) 14 R. 780; *Kerrigan* v. *Hall* (1901) 4 F. 10.

[10] *Brand* v. *Shaws* (1888) 16 R. 315.

[11] Custody of Children (Sc.) Act, 1891; *Mackenzie* v. *Keillor* (1892) 19 R. 963; *Campbell* v. *Croall* (1895) 22 R. 869; *Kerrigan, supra; Mitchell* v. *Wright* (1905) 7 F. 568; *Walter* v. *Culbertson,* 1921 S.C. 490.

given effect to,[1] but apart from that the bastard has no tutor but if he litigates a *tutor ad litem* will be appointed.[2] A bastard minor is not subject to his mother's control as to his person, nor is she his curator for business matters. He has no curator, unless he chooses one for himself, but if he litigates a curator *ad litem* may be appointed.[3]

Guardianship of legitimated children

Till legitimation the child is under the mother's guardianship as a bastard. After legitimation it passes into the tutory or curatory of its father and is thereafter regarded as if legitimate from birth.

Guardianship of adopted children

On adoption a child passes into the guardianship of its adoptive parents and falls to be treated as if legitimate from birth.

Factors loco tutoris *and* curators bonis

Failing tutors or curators appointed under other principles the Court of Session[4] and Sheriff Court[5] may appoint a judicial factor *loco tutoris*[6] or a *curator bonis*[7] to supply the need. Such factors are officers of the court and subject to the supervision of the Accountant of Court, and must conform to the relevant statutes.[8] A factor *loco tutoris* becomes a *curator bonis* on the ward becoming a minor.[9] He has no control of the person of the pupil.[10]

Appointments have been made where the tutor was acting improperly,[11] to administer sums of damages awarded to pupils[12]

---

[1] *Brand, supra.*

[2] *Ward* v. *Walker,* 1920 S.C. 80.

[3] *Young* (1828) 7 S. 220.

[4] At common law and under Judicial Factors Acts, 1849 and 1889.

[5] By Judicial Factors (Sc.) Act, 1880, where the yearly value of the estate is not above £100: see e.g. *Penny* v. *Scott* (1894) 22 R. 5 (curator bonis to minor).

[6] Ersk. I, 7, 10; Bell, *Prin.* §2114.

[7] Bell, *Prin.* §2121.

[8] Judicial Factors (Sc.) Acts, 1849 (Pupils' Protection Act), 1880 and 1889.

[9] 1889 Act, S. 11; *Stiven* v. *Masterton* (1892) 30 S.L.R. 50.

[10] *Bryce* v. *Graham* (1828) 3 W. & S. 323.

[11] *Edgar* v. *Fisher's Trs.* (1893) 21 R. 59, 325; *Fisher* v. *Edgar* (1894) 21 R. 1076.

[12] *Collins* v. *Eglinton Iron Co.* (1882) 9 R. 500; *McAvoy* v. *Young's Paraffin Oil Co.* (1882) 19 S.L.R. 441; *Anderson* v. *Muirhead* (1884) 11 R. 870; *Connolly* v. *Bent Colliery Co.* (1897) 24 R. 1172; *Boylan* v. *Hunter,* 1922 S.C. 80; *Fairley* v. *Allan,* 1948 S.L.T. (Notes) 81; *Falconer* v. *Robertson,* 1949 S.L.T. (Notes) 57; *McIntosh* v. *Wood,* 1970 S.C. 179.

or minors,[1] to supersede the father as curator,[2] to enable a
minor to sell heritage,[3] to complete title to land in a minor's
name and complete sale thereof,[4] to advise in managing inherited estate.[5] A factor *loco tutoris* cannot be appointed to act
jointly with a surviving widow.[6]

Protected children

A child placed in the care and possession of a person not a
parent, guardian, or relative of his, or of an applicant for an
adoption order, is a protected child till he attains 18 or is adopted.[7]
Notice must be given to the local authority which may inspect
premises and ensure the well-being of protected children.[8] The
sheriff may order his removal to a place of safety and he may be
taken into the care of a local authority.[9]

Care of children by local authorities

A local authority must take into their care a child apparently
under 17 who has neither parent nor guardian, or has been
abandoned or lost, or whose parent or guardian is prevented
by illness, infirmity or incapacity from providing for his proper
accommodation, maintenance and upbringing, if it appears that
the local authority's intervention is necessary in the interests of the
welfare of the child. If assumed, this care lasts so long as the
child's welfare appears to require it and the child has not attained
18. The local authority must try to have the care of the child
assumed by a parent or guardian, or a relative or friend, if
possible of the same religious persuasion.[10] The local authority
may, in the case of a child in care whose parents are dead and
who has no guardian, or whose parent or guardian has abandoned him or is incapable of caring for the child or is unfit
to have the care of the child, resolve that all the rights and
powers of the parents or guardian shall vest in the local authority.[11]
The local authority may nevertheless allow the child to be under

---

[1] *Sharp* v. *Pathhead Spinning Co.* (1885) 12 R. 574; cf. *Jack* v. *N.B. Ry.* (1886) 14 R.
263.

[2] *McNab* v. *McN.* (1871) 10 M. 248.   [3] *Perry* (1903) 10 S.L.T. 536.

[4] *Waring*, 1933 S.L.T. 190.   [5] *Penny, supra.*

[6] *Speirs*, 1946 S.L.T. 203.   [7] Adoption Act, 1958, S. 37.

[8] Ss. 38–40.   [9] S. 43.

[10] Social Work (Sc.) Act, 1968, S. 15 replacing Children Act, 1948, S. 1.

[11] 1968 Act, S. 16. Once a child has been committed parental rights and powers, including access, vest in the local authority to the exclusion of the parent: *Gilmour* v. *Ayr C.C.*,
1968 S.L.T. (Sh. Ct.) 41. In such a case it is incompetent to grant an order for access:
McGuire v. *M.*, 1969 S.L.T. (Notes) 36.

the control of a parent, guardian, relative, or friend. Its assumption of parental rights does not relieve anyone from the liability to maintain or contribute to maintenance of the child.[1] The authority's parental rights continue, unless rescinded, till the child is eighteen.[2] The general duty of the local authority is to further the best interests of the child and afford him opportunity for the proper development of his character and abilities.[3] Accommodation and maintenance is provided by boarding the child out, or maintaining him in a home provided by a local authority or a home maintained by a voluntary body or any other person.[4] The local authority may arrange for the emigration of children,[5] assist in the training of persons over school age and advise children formerly in care and still under 18.[6] The parents of such a child are liable to make contributions towards maintenance till the child is 16; once the child is 16, if engaged in remunerative full-time work, he is liable to make contributions in respect of himself.[7] Local authorities must also ensure the well-being of foster-children, i.e. children maintained for reward by persons other than relatives or guardian, and may inspect premises and impose conditions.[8] The sheriff may order the removal of a foster-child kept in unsuitable surroundings.[9]

Children in need of compulsory care

A child who has not attained 16, or one between 16 and 18 in respect of whom a children's hearing has made a supervision requirement, or a child whose case has been referred to a children's hearing, may be in need of compulsory measures of care if he is beyond the control of his parent, is falling into bad associations or is exposed to moral danger, or lack of care is likely to cause him unnecessary suffering or to impair his health or development, or an offence has been committed against him, or is a female member of a household and another female has been subjected to incest, or he has failed to attend school regularly or has committed an offence or his case has been referred to a

[1] 1968 Act, S. 17.
[2] 1968 Act, S. 18.
[3] 1968 Act, S. 20.
[4] 1968 Act, Ss. 21–4.
[5] 1968 Act, S. 23.
[6] 1968 Act, Ss. 24–6.
[7] 1968 Act, Ss. 78–83.
[8] Children Act, 1958, Ss. 2–6, amd. Social Work (Sc.) Act, 1968, Sched. 1.
[9] 1958 Act, S. 7.

children's hearing.[1] Such a child may be brought before a children's hearing and may be required to submit to supervision in accordance with conditions, or to reside in a residential establishment.[2] A supervision requirement may be terminated[3] and ends when the child attains 18.[4] Contributions in respect of a child subject to a supervision requirement are payable by his parents while he is under 16 and by the child himself if over 16 and engaged in remunerative employment.[5]

Right of local authority to aliment

Where a maintainable child is illegitimate the local authority has the same right as the mother to bring an action for affiliation and aliment for aliment in respect of the child. Where a decree for aliment of an illegitimate child is in force the local authority may have the court order payments under the decree to be paid to it.[6]

INCAPACES

Persons physically incapacitated

A person physically incapacitated is not thereby deprived of any legal capacity or power for managing his affairs, but if his incapacity is of such a nature or gravity that he cannot execute necessary deeds or attend to affairs, the court may appoint a *curator bonis* on the petition of any relative or interested person, supported by two medical certificates of incapacity to manage his affairs.[7]

Persons mentally incapacitated: care of person

At common law the court may appoint the nearest male agnate as tutor-at-law, or appoint a suitable person as guardian (tutor-dative) of the person of an incapax, without prejudice to administration of his property by a *curator bonis*.[8] If the nearest male agnate were served tutor-at-law he was formerly debarred from custody of the ward's person, because suspicion attached to him as the ward's heir,[9] but little force now attaches to this.[8]

---

[1] Social Work (Sc.) Act, 1968, Ss. 30, 32.

[2] Ibid., S. 44. On children's hearings see Ss. 33–58. On residential establishments see Ss. 59–68.

[3] Ibid., Ss. 47, 52. [4] Ibid., S. 47.

[5] Ibid., Ss. 78–83. [6] Ibid., S. 81.

[7] *Kirkpatrick* (1853) 15 D. 734; *Duncan*, 1915, 2 S.L.T. 50.

[8] *Dick* v. *Douglas*, 1924 S.C. 787. Such a person may seek delivery of the person of the ward into his custody.

[9] Ersk. I, 7, 7.

A person over 21 suffering from mental disorder may be detained in hospital or received into guardianship only if suffering from mental deficiency such that he is incapable of living an independent life or of guarding himself against serious exploitation, or from mental illness other than a persistent disorder which is manifested only by abnormally aggressive or seriously irresponsible conduct. Detention or guardianship lasts only till 25 unless he is still suffering from mental deficiency or mental illness or would be likely to act in a manner dangerous to himself or others. Alternatively such a person may receive treatment as a voluntary patient.[1] Admission and detention requires an application to the hospital management board by the patient's nearest relative[2] or a mental health officer, accompanied by two medical recommendations, and approved by the sheriff. Guardianship requires a similar application to the local health authority, accompanied by two medical recommendations, and approved by the sheriff, and naming as guardian the local health authority, a person chosen by that authority, or any other person including the applicant, accepted as a suitable person to act in that behalf by that authority.[3] Guardianship may be transferred in case of death or incapacity of the guardian.[4]

Approval of an application for admission is authority for the patient's removal and admission within seven days;[5] approval of a guardianship application confers on the local health authority or the guardian named, to the exclusion of anyone else, the powers of a father in relation to a pupil child, but not as to property nor does it confer any power of corporal punishment.[6] A patient may be transferred from detention to another hospital or to the guardianship of a local health authority or of a person approved by such authority.[7] If a guardian dies or wishes to relinquish the post, guardianship vests in the local health authority.[8]

In a case of urgent necessity an emergency recommendation may be made justifying detention for seven days.[9]

A patient who absents himself may be taken into custody but not after three months, in the case of a patient liable to be de-

[1] Mental Health (Sc.) Act, 1960, S. 23.
[2] Defined, Ss. 45–9.
[3] 1960 Act, Ss. 24–8.
[4] 1960 Act, S. 38.
[5] 1960 Act, S. 29(1)–(3).
[6] 1960 Act, S. 29(4)–(6).
[7] 1960 Act, S. 37.
[8] 1960 Act, S. 38.
[9] 1960 Act, S. 31–2.

tained or subject to guardianship by reason of mental deficiency, or seven days, in the case of a patient liable to be detained under an emergency recommendation, or twenty-eight days in other cases.[1]

Detention or guardianship lasts only for a year but may be renewed for a further year and thereafter for periods of two years.[2] A patient aged at least 16 may appeal to the sheriff to order his discharge.[2]

The Mental Welfare Commission for Scotland (replacing the General Board of Control for Scotland) has the duty of exercising protective functions in respect of persons who by reason of mental disorder are incapable of adequately protecting their persons or their interests.[3]

Persons mentally incapacitated: care of property

At common law a person found incapax by the process of cognition of the insane was superseded in the management of his property by the nearest male agnate of full age or a near male relative as tutor-at-law,[4] and this is still competent.[5] Alternatively, a person might be appointed tutor-dative to an incapax.[6] Subsequently it became normal for the court on the petition of a relative[7] supported by two medical certificates[8] to appoint a suitable person, frequently the petitioner, to be *curator bonis* to the incapax.[9] The alleged incapax may oppose the petition.[10] Such a *curator bonis* is subject to the Judicial Factors Acts and subject to the supervision of the Accountant of Court.[11] Hence the court will rarely appoint as curator a person residing outwith the jurisdiction.[12] A married

---

[1] 1960 Act, S. 36.

[2] 1960 Act, S. 39; *W.* v. *Carstairs State Hospital*, 1967 S.L.T. (Sh. Ct.) 18.

[3] 1960 Act, Ss. 1–4.

[4] Stair I, 6, 25; Bankt. III, 47; Ersk. I, 7, 50; Bell, *Prin.* §2103–12; Fraser, *P. & Ch.*, 651; *Irving* v. *Swan* (1868) 7 M. 86; *Larkin* v. *McGrady* (1874) 2 R. 170; see also *C.B.* v. *A.B.* (1891) 18 R. (H.L.) 40 (incapax not entitled to insist on cognition); *Simpson* v. *S.* (1891) 18 R. 1207; *A.B.* v. *C.B.*, 1937 S.C. 408.

[5] Court of Session Act, 1868, S. 101, replacing Act, 1585, c. 18.

[6] *Urquhart* (1860) 22 D. 932; *Simpson* (1861) 23 D. 1292; *Graham* (1881) 8 R. 996.

[7] Or of the incapax himself: *A.B.* (1908) 16 S.L.T. 557.

[8] On these see *McKechnie* (1890) 27 S.L.R. 261; *Knox* (1894) 2 S.L.T. 388; *Leslie* (1895) 3 S.L.T. 128; *Calderwood* v. *Duncan* (1907) 14 S.L.T. 777. For remit to neutral medical man see *Davies* v. *D.*, 1928 S.L.T. 142; *Shand* v. *S.*, 1950 S.L.T. (Notes) 32; *Brown* v. *Hackston*, 1960 S.C. 27.

[9] *Johnstone* v. *Barbe*, 1928 S.N. 86.

[10] e.g. *Dowie* v. *Hagart* (1894) 21 R. 1052; *Greig*, 1923 S.L.T. 434; *Davies, supra*; *Shand, supra*.

[11] Judicial Factors Acts, 1880, S. 4; 1889, S. 14.

[12] *Napier* (1902) 9 S.L.T. 439; *Duff*, 1910 2 S.L.T. 202; *Forsyth*, 1932 S.L.T. 462.

woman may be curator.[1] Such an appointment supersedes a factory and commission granted by the ward while capax.[2] Service of a relative as tutor-at-law supersedes the appointment of a tutor-dative or *curator bonis*.[3]

Under the Mental Health (Scotland) Act, 1960, S. 91, a local health authority must, in case of need, petition for such an appointment. Hospital boards of management have limited powers to receive and hold money and valuables.

A *curator bonis* to an incapax supersedes the *incapax* in the management of his estates, but the ward is not divested of those estates;[4] the curator has the powers of a trustee under the Trusts (Scotland) Acts, 1921 and 1961. He has no power over the person of the incapax[5] but may if necessary apply to the court for the ward's protection.[6] He may sue for damages for a delict which caused the ward's incapacity,[7] take legal advice and make inquiries relative to a contemplated action of divorce against the ward's wife.[8] It is incompetent for an incapax to bring an action and have a curator *ad litem* appointed when the action comes into court.[9] When a person becomes insane during the dependence of an action the process should probably be sisted until a *curator bonis* is appointed.[10] The curator may be authorized to elect on the ward's behalf between legal and testamentary provisions accruing to the ward on another person's death,[11] to sell heritage,[12] or to compromise an action.[13]

The *curator bonis* may petition for discharge when the ward recovers,[14] on having his accounts audited by the Accountant of

---

[1] *Smith Sligo*, 1914 1 S.L.T. 287.

[2] *Dick* (1901) 9 S.L.T. 177.

[3] Ersk. I, 7, 51; *Young* v. *Rose* (1839) 1 D. 1242; *Dick* v. *Douglas*, 1924 S.C. 787.

[4] Bell, *Prin.* §2121; Irons, 310; *Yule* v. *Alexander* (1891) R. 167; *Mitchell & Baxter* v. *Cheyne* (1891) 19 R. 324; *I.R.* v. *McMillan's C.B.*, 1956 S.C. 142.

[5] *Robertson* v. *Elphinstone*, 28 June 1814, F.C.; *Bryce* v. *Graham* (1832) 3 W. & S. 323.

[6] *Robertson, supra*; *Gardiner* (1869) 7 M. 1130.

[7] *Cole-Hamilton* v. *Boyd*, 1963 S.C. (H.L.) 1; see also *Calver* v. *Howard Baker & Co.* (1894) 22 R. 1.

[8] *Thyne's C.B.* (1882) 19 S.L.R. 724.

[9] *Reid* v. *R.* (1839) 1 D. 400; *Mackenzie* (1845) 7 D. 283; *Moodie* v. *Dempster*, 1931 S.C. 553.

[10] *Anderson's Trs.* v. *Skinner* (1871) 8 S.L.R. 325; *Moodie, supra*.

[11] *McCall's Tr.* v. *McCall's C.B.* (1901) 3 F. 1065; *Neave's J.F.* v. *Neave's Trs.*, 1928 S.L.T. 411; *Burns' C.B.* v. *Burns' Trs.*, 1961 S.L.T. 166; see also *Skinner's C.B.* (1903) 5 F. 914.

[12] *Lothian's C.B.*, 1927 S.C. 579; *Cameron's C.B.*, 1961 S.L.T. (Notes) 21; *Barclay, Petr.*, 1962 S.C. 594.

[13] *Tennent's J.F.* v. *T.*, 1954 S.C. 215.

[14] *Inglis* v. *I.*, 1927 S.N. 181; *A.B.* v. *C.B.*, 1929 S.L.T. 517.

Court and being discharged by the ward, or when the ward dies, on confirmation of the ward's executor and discharge by the latter.

There was formerly a process of interdiction[1] whereby persons liable to be imposed on were restrained from executing any deed, not being rational or onerous, affecting heritage to their prejudice without the consent of the interdictors. It was established in 1924.[2]

[1] Ersk. II, 7, 53.
[2] Conveyancing (Sc.) Act, 1924, S. 44 (3).

CHAPTER 19

SOCIAL SECURITY

A T C O M M O N law persons had to support themselves and
those having claims against them, and to provide by saving
or insurance against diminution in earnings caused by ill-
health, unemployment or old age. In case of poverty the poor law
system provided for the diseased and impotent poor, so far as
necessary to supply deficiencies in church-door and other contributions, able-bodied poor being left to the resources of private
charity.[1] Since the beginning of the twentieth century an extensive system of social security has developed, but without prejudice
to private provision by savings or insurance.

NATIONAL INSURANCE

The national insurance scheme[2] tries to make provision by
compulsory insurance against the main contingencies which
interfere with the normal earning of a livelihood and the support
of relatives, such as unemployment, sickness and old age. Under
the National Insurance Acts, 1965 to 1974,[3] all persons resident
in Great Britain, except some married women, students and persons of small incomes,[4] between school-leaving age and pensionable age, are classified into employed,[5] self-employed,[6] and non-
employed persons, and all are insured under the Acts and required to pay contributions at varying rates into the National
Insurance Fund. Married women who are not employed may
elect not to become or remain insured. Even if employed a married woman may rely on her husband's contributions, though she

---

[1] Ersk. I, 7, 63; Bell, *Prin.* §2190–2204.

[2] See generally Potter & Stansfield, *National Insurance*.

[3] Replacing National Insurance Act, 1946 to 1964. The National Insurance scheme,
introduced in 1948 under the 1946 Act, in partial implement of the (Beveridge) Report
on Social Insurance and Allied Services (1942) (Cmd. 6404), superseded more limited
provisions for unemployment and health insurance dating from 1911 and for contributory
pensions from 1925. The Acts are supplemented by numerous sets of regulations.

[4] See *Longsdon* v. *Minister of Pensions and National Insurance* [1956] 1 Q.B. 587.

[5] See *Gould* v. *Minister of National Insurance* [1951] 1 K.B. 731; *Stagecraft Ltd.* v.
Minister of National Insurance, 1952 S.C. 288; *Vandyck* v. *Minister of Pensions and National
Insurance* [1955] 1 Q.B. 29; *Benjamin* v. *M.P.N.I.* [1960] 2 All E.R. 851; *Market In-
vestigations Ltd.* v. *Minister of Social Security* [1968] 3 All E.R. 732.

[6] See *Ready Mixed Concrete Ltd.* v. *M.P.N.I.* [1968] 2 Q.B. 497; *Argent* v. *M.O.S.S.*
[1968] 3 All E.R. 208.

must pay the industrial injuries portion. An Exchequer supplement is added and employers must also pay contributions in respect of each person employed by them. Graduated contributions are also payable in respect of persons earning above £9 per week.[1] In the case of employed persons they are payable by the employer, who may recover the employee's portion from his pay. Persons may not pay contributions other than those they are liable to pay. Contributions are normally paid by affixing stamps each week to cards for each contributor.[2] Certain employments may be non-participating employments.[3]

Benefits

The benefits which may be claimed[4] are:

(a) unemployment benefit,[5] payable, subject to satisfying contribution conditions,[6] for any day of unemployment,[7] except the first three days. After 312 working days a person is not entitled to unemployment benefit until he has requalified for benefit. A person is disqualified for receiving unemployment benefit if he lost employment by reason of a stoppage of work due to a trade dispute, unless he was not participating in the dispute, and disqualified for limited periods, if he lost employment through misconduct, voluntarily left employment without just cause, or in certain other circumstances.[8]

(b) sickness benefit,[9] payable, subject to satisfying contribution conditions,[10] in respect of any day of incapacity for work[11] which forms part of a period of interruption of employment, except for the first three days of any period of interruption of employment, up to 168 days. A person is not entitled to benefit after 312 working days unless he has requalified for benefit. A person may be disqualified for receiving sickness benefit if he became incapable of work through his own misconduct, or failed without good

---

[1] National Insurance Act, 1965, Ss. 1–7.

[2] The stamp includes the contribution for the national health service under the National Health Service Contributions Acts 1965 and 1970.

[3] National Insurance Act, 1965, Ss. 56–63.

[4] National Insurance Act, 1965, S. 17, as amended.

[5] 1965 Act, Ss. 19–22, amd. Social Security Act, 1971, S. 7.

[6] 1965 Act, Sched. 2, para. 1.

[7] Defined, 1965 Act, S. 20.

[8] Ibid., S. 22(1), (2), (4)–(6), amd. Social Security Act, 1971, S. 7.

[9] Ibid., Ss. 18–22, amd. Social Security Act, 1971, S. 7.

[10] Ibid., Sched. 2, para. 1.

[11] Defined, S. 20.

cause to attend for medical or other examination or treatment.[1]

(bb) invalidity benefit,[2] consisting of (i) invalidity pension payable after 168 days sickness benefit, subject to contribution conditions, and (ii) invalidity allowance, payable in addition if a person entitled to invalidity pension is more than five years below pensionable age.

(c) maternity benefit, including (i) maternity grant,[3] subject to contribution conditions; and (ii) maternity allowance,[4] for 18 weeks, subject to contribution conditions. Maternity benefit is not taken into account by a court awarding inlying expenses in connection with the birth of an illegitimate child.[5]

(d) widow's benefit, including (i) widow's allowance for 26 weeks after her husband's death, subject to contribution conditions and to not then remarrying or cohabiting with a man;[6] (ii) widowed mother's allowance, if she has a family, as defined, or has residing with her a person under 19 who is a child of the family, subject to contribution conditions and only until the widow remarries or cohabits with a man;[7] and (iii) widow's pension, subject to conditions as to contributions and age, payable till she is 65 if not entitled to a widow's or widowed mother's allowance, and only until the widow remarries or cohabits with a man.[8]

(e) guardian's allowance, payable in respect of any child who is for the time being a child of the claimant's family if the child's parents are dead and one of them was an insured person. Special provisions may apply where the child has been adopted, is illegitimate, or the child's parents' marriage was terminated by divorce, or one of them has died and the claimant was unaware of the death and has failed to discover the whereabouts of the other parent.[9]

(f) retirement pension, if the claimant is over pensionable age, has retired from regular employment, and satisfies the

[1] Ibid., S. 22(3)–(6).
[2] National Insurance Act, 1971, S. 3 and Sched. 5.
[3] 1965 Act, S. 23.
[4] Ibid., S. 24, amd. National Insurance Act, 1966, S. 4.
[5] Ibid., S. 25(2).
[6] Ibid., S. 26.
[7] Ibid., S. 27.
[8] Ibid., S. 28, amended National Insurance (Old persons, etc.) Act, 1970, S. 2.
[9] Ibid., S. 29.

contribution conditions.[1] This is subject to reductions in respect of earnings, or to increase in respect of contributions made after pensionable age.[2] A woman may be entitled to a retirement pension by virtue of her husband's insurance.[3]

(ff) age addition[4] payable to persons over eighty entitled to a retirement pension, or not so entitled but fulfilling other conditions to be prescribed.

(g) graduated retirement benefit, payable to retired persons in respect of graduated contributions paid by them.[5]

(h) child's special allowance, payable to a woman whose marriage has been terminated by divorce if her husband is dead and satisfied certain contribution conditions and she has a family, including a child of her family or of her husband's family, and her husband had been contributing to the cost of providing for that child, but only until she remarries or cohabits with a man as his wife.[6]

(i) death grant, payable in respect of the death of any person if he satisfied certain contribution conditions, or was one of specified relatives of a person satisfying those conditions, and in certain other cases.[7]

(j) attendance allowance, payable if a person satisfies prescribed conditions and is so severely disabled as to require frequent attention or continual supervision.[8]

The weekly rates of benefit under heads (a), (b), (c(ii)), (d(i)), and (f) are increased in respect of each child for any period for which the beneficiary has a family which includes children, and in certain other cases.[9] Weekly rates of benefit under heads (a), (b) or (f) are increased if the beneficiary is residing with his wife, or contributing to her support and she is not engaged in gainful employment with earnings exceeding the amount of the increase,

---

[1] Ibid., S. 30.

[2] Ibid., S. 31. The earnings rules may be altered by regulations: S. 44.

[3] Ibid., Ss. 32–35. Persons over pensionable age in 1948 were granted pensions under the National Insurance (Old Persons' and Widows' Pensions and Attendance Allowance) Act, 1970, S. 1.

[4] National Insurance Act, 1971, S. 5 and Sched. 5.

[5] 1965 Act, Ss. 36–37.

[6] Ibid., S. 38.

[7] Ibid., S. 39, amd. National Insurance Act, 1969, S. 4.

[8] National Insurance (Old Persons' and Widows' Pensions and Attendance Allowance) Act, 1970, Ss. 4, 6. The operation of this provision is under the oversight of an Attendance Allowance Board.

[9] 1965 Act, Ss. 40–2.

and in certain other cases of adult dependants.[1] Increased benefit is payable under heads (a), (b), and (d) by way of earnings-related supplement.[2] Reduced benefits may be paid if contribution conditions have been only partially satisfied.[3]

In certain cases a person may be disqualified from benefit, or benefit suspended.[4] Benefits under the Act may not be assigned, not used as scrutiny, and do not pass to a trustee in sequestration.[5]

Certain questions arising under the Act must be determined by the Minister of Social Security and any question of law may be referred for decision to the Court of Session,[6] but questions as to rights to benefit and disqualification are determined by an insurance officer, with appeal to a local tribunal and to the National Insurance Commissioner.[7]

NATIONAL INSURANCE (INDUSTRIAL INJURIES)

The industrial injuries scheme[8] replaces the former workmen's compensation scheme[9] and provides a system of compulsory insurance of persons employed in insurable employment against 'personal injury caused after 4 July 1948 by accident arising out

---

[1] Ibid., S. 43. See also S. 43A added by National Insurance Act, 1971, S. 4.

[2] National Insurance Act, 1966, Ss. 2, 4.

[3] 1965 Act, S. 45.

[4] Ibid., S. 49.

[5] Ibid., S. 53.

[6] Ibid., Ss. 64–6; see *Dept. of Health & Social Security* v. *Walker* [1970] 1 All E.R. 757.

[7] Ibid., Ss. 67–80.

[8] National Insurance (Industrial Injuries) Acts, 1965 to 1971, replacing National Insurance (Industrial Injuries) Acts, 1946 to 1964, implementing other parts of the (Beveridge) Report on Social Insurance and Allied Services (1942) (Cmd. 6404). The Acts are supplemented by numerous sets of Regulations. See generally Potter & Stansfield, *National Insurance (Industrial Injuries) Act.*

[9] Under the Workmen's Compensation Acts, 1925 to 1945, superseding the Workmen's Compensation Act, 1897, as later amended, employers were required to compensate workmen who sustained 'personal injury by accident arising out of and in the course of the employment', without proof of fault or negligence on the part of the employer or of anyone for whom he was responsible. The phrase quoted gave rise to much litigation and was interpreted by the courts in numerous cases. Claims were disposed of by arbitration under statutory conditions, usually by a sheriff, who might be required to state a case on a question of law to the Court of Session, with appeal to the House of Lords. A right to compensation did not exclude a claim for damages at common law or under the (now repealed) Employers' Liability Act, 1880, but there could be no double compensation. An election to accept compensation, or the final rejection of a claim for compensation, barred an action for damages; a successful claim for damages barred a claim for compensation but an unsuccessful claim left it open to the workman to claim compensation. The Workmen's Compensation Acts continue to apply where the right to compensation arose before 5 July 1948, but the payments are supplemented under the Industrial Injuries and Diseases (Old Cases) Acts, 1967 to 1971.

of and in the course of the employment',[1] and against prescribed diseases and prescribed personal injuries due to the nature of a person's employment.[2] Employers and employees contribute to the industrial injuries fund by affixing stamps to cards at rates fixed from time to time, and the Exchequer makes further contributions. The contribution is incorporated with the contributions to the national insurance fund and those due in respect of national health service contributions.

Industrial injuries contributions are due and benefits are payable only in respect of persons employed under a contract of service, and certain categories of persons are deemed to be so employed.

'Personal injury' means physical or mental hurt, not *injuria*.[3] 'Accident' has its ordinary meaning[4] of unlooked-for mishap or untoward event not expected or designed, and includes unexpected occurrences but not self-inflicted injury; it may include nervous shock, strain, and exposure, but is distinct from any continuing process producing injury or incapacity.[5] An accident 'arising out of' the employment is one to the risk of which the person is exposed by being in that employment, as distinct from those common to the general public.[6]

An accident arising in the course of an insured person's employment is deemed, in the absence of evidence to the contrary, also to have arisen out of that employment,[7] and is deemed to arise out of and in the course of the employment even though the injured person was then acting in contravention of any statutory or other regulations applicable to his employment, or of orders given by or on behalf of his employer or without instructions from his employer if it would have been deemed so to have arisen without such contravention, and it was done for the purposes of and in connection with the employer's trade or business,[8] or while travelling in the employer's transport,[9] or

---

[1] 1965 Act, S. 1; see *M.O.S.S.* v. *A.E.U.* [1967] 1 A.C. 725; *Jones* v. *Secretary of State for Social Services* [1972] A.C. 944.

[2] 1965 Act, S. 56.

[3] cf. *Yates* v. *S. Kirkby Collieries, Ltd.* [1910] 2 K.B. 538; *Woodcock* v. *L.N.W. Ry.* [1913] 3 K.B. 139; *Ex p. Haines* [1945] K.B. 183.

[4] cf. *Fenton* v. *Thorley* [1903] A.C. 443.

[5] cf. *Roberts* v. *Dorothea Slate Quarries Co. Ltd.* [1948] 2 All E.R. 201.

[6] cf. *Dennis* v. *White* [1917] A.C. 479.

[7] 1965 Act, S. 6, and see *R.* v. *National Ins. (Ind. Inj.) Commr., ex parte Richardson* [1958] 2 All E.R. 689.

[8] Ibid., S. 7.

[9] Ibid., S. 8.

while acting in emergency,[1] or if caused by another person's misconduct.[2]

An accident takes place 'in the course of' the employment only while the person was doing something which he was required to do as part of his job, or something reasonably incidental thereto.[3]

Benefits

The benefits which may be claimed are:[4]

(a) industrial injury benefit, for any day during the benefit period of 156 working days beginning with the day of the accident, on which as a result of the relevant injury the claimant was incapable of work, except for the first three days;[5] injury benefit is increased in certain circumstances in respect of children or adult dependants.[6]

(b) industrial disablement benefit, if the claimant suffers as a result of the accident from loss of physical or mental faculty to an extent assessed as at least one per cent. It is not available until after the third day of the period of 156 days beginning with the day of the accident nor until after the last day of that period on which he is incapable of work. If assessed at less than 20 per cent disablement benefit is paid as a lump sum disablement gratuity. If assessed at 20 per cent or more disablement benefit is paid as disablement pension.[7] The weekly rate of disablement pension may be increased on account of unemployability,[8] in cases of special hardship,[9] where constant attendance is necessary,[10] or during hospital treatment.[11] Disablement pension is increased in certain circumstances in respect of children or adult dependants.[12]

(c) industrial death benefit, payable to a widow, in the form of a pension for life or until she remarries or cohabits with

---

[1] Ibid., S. 9.

[2] Ibid., S. 10.

[3] cf. R. v. *Industrial Injuries Commr., ex parte A.E.U.* [1966] 2 Q.B. 21.

[4] National Insurance (Ind. Inj.) Act, 1965, S. 5, amd. National Insurance Act, 1971, S. 8.

[5] Ibid., S. 11, amd. National Insurance Act, 1966, S. 5, and Social Security Act, 1971, S. 7.

[6] Ibid., Ss. 17–18, amd. National Insurance Act, 1971, S. 8 and Sched. 5.

[7] Ibid., S. 12; see also 1966 Act, S. 6.

[8] Ibid., S. 13; see also 1971 Act, S. 9.

[9] Ibid., S. 14.

[10] Ibid., S. 15, amd. National Insurance Act, 1966, S. 6.

[11] Ibid., S. 16.

[12] Ibid., Ss. 17–18, amd. National Insurance Act, 1971, S. 8 and Sched. 5.

a man as his wife and a gratuity on remarriage,[1] or to a widower, if maintained by the deceased and permanently incapable of self-support, a pension for life.[2] Death benefit is also payable in respect of children,[3] to parents maintained by the deceased,[4] any such relative maintained by the deceased as may be prescribed,[5] and a female residing with the deceased and having the care of his children.[6]

Claimants may be required to submit to medical examination, to medical treatment, or to attend a vocational training course or industrial rehabilitation course,[7] and claimants may be disqualified for, *inter alia*, failure to do so or acting in a manner calculated to retard recovery.[8] Adjustment may be made in case of successive accidents.[9]

Benefits may not be assigned nor used as security and do not pass to a trustee in sequestration.[10] Certain questions are determined by the Secretary of State for Social Security, disablement questions by medical boards or medical appeal tribunals, and claims for benefit by insurance officers, local appeal tribunals and the National Insurance Commissioner.[11]

Industrial diseases

Insured persons are also insured against any prescribed disease and any prescribed injury not caused by accident, if the disease or injury were due to the nature of the employment.[12] A disease or injury may be prescribed if it should be treated as a risk of the occupation and not one common to all persons. The benefits payable in respect of a prescribed disease or injury are generally the same as in the case of personal injury by accident.

FAMILY ALLOWANCES

Under the Family Allowances Act, 1965,[13] weekly allowances are paid, without contribution, at rates fixed from time to time, for every family which includes two or more children, in respect of

---

[1] Ibid., S. 19.   [2] Ibid., S. 20.   [3] Ibid., S. 21.
[4] Ibid., S. 22.   [5] Ibid., S. 23.   [6] Ibid., S. 24.
[7] Ibid., S. 25.   [8] Ibid., S. 31.   [9] Ibid., S. 29.
[10] Ibid., S. 28.

[11] Ibid., Ss. 35–49, amd. National Insurance Act, 1966, S. 9. See also *R.* v. *Deputy Industrial Injuries Commissioner, ex p. Moore* [1965] 1 Q.B. 456; *M.O.S.S.* v. *A.E.U.* [1967] 1 A.C. 725; *R.* v. *National Ins. Commr., ex parte Hudson and Jones* [1970] 1 All E.R. 97.

[12] Ibid., Ss. 56–58.

[13] Replacing Family Allowances Act, 1945 to 1964. The Act is supplemented by various Regulations.

each child other than the eldest, for the benefit of the family as a whole.[1] The payments are made so long as there are at least two children in the family under school-leaving age, or receiving full-time education and under nineteen, or under sixteen and incapacitated by illness or disability of mind or body for regular employment.[2] A child is not counted in certain circumstances.[3]

A 'family' means a man and his wife living together,[4] any child or children being issue of theirs, his or her, and any child or children being maintained by them; a man not having a wife or not living with her, any child or children being issue of his, and any child or children being maintained by[5] him; and a woman not having a husband or not living with him, any child or children being issue of hers, and any child or children being maintained by her; or in any of these cases that the cost of providing for[6] the child elsewhere is contributed to by them, him or her at a stated rate.[7] Allowances belong to the woman in the first and third cases and to the man in the second case, but in the first case are payable to either, save in exceptional cases.[8] Questions as to rights to allowances are determined by the Minister of Social Security.[9] Allowances are not assignable, nor can they be used as security.[10] Questions as to the right to an allowance fall to be determined by the same authorities as questions as to the right to national insurance benefits.[11]

SUPPLEMENTARY BENEFITS

The National Assistance Act, 1948, replaced the provisions made by the old poor law, and established the National Assistance Board which in turn was replaced by the Supplementary Benefits Commission in 1966.[12] Under this every person in Great Britain of or over 16 whose resources are insufficient to meet his requirements is entitled to a supplementary allowance or, if he has

[1] 1965 Act, S. 1.
[2] Ibid., S. 2; *Fraser* v. *Min. of National Insurance*, 1947 S.C. 594.
[3] Ibid., S. 11.
[4] Ibid., S. 3. For additional conditions see Ss. 17, 20.
[5] Ibid., Sched.
[6] Ibid., S. 18.
[7] Ibid., S. 3; see also S. 17.
[8] Ibid., S. 4.
[9] Ibid., S. 5.
[10] Ibid., S. 10.
[11] Family Allowances (Determination of Claims and Questions) Regs. 1967 (S.I. 1967 No. 1572).
[12] Ministry of Social Security Act, 1966, S. 3. The 1948 Act is still in force so far as concerns duties imposed on local authorities by Parts III and IV thereof.

attained pensionable age, to a supplementary pension.[1] The only qualifying condition is the need for assistance, and the question whether a person is entitled to benefit and the amount of any benefit is determined by the Commission,[2] subject to an appeal tribunal.[3] A person is not generally entitled to benefit while engaged in remunerative full-time work,[4] nor while attending school or receiving full-time instruction,[5] nor, in general, if unemployed by reason of a stoppage due to a trade dispute.[6] Persons refusing or neglecting to maintain themselves or their dependants may be made subject to special provisions.[7] Exceptions may be made in urgent cases.[8] Benefit is normally in cash but may be given in kind,[9] and provision is made to prevent duplication with other social security payments.[10] Benefit paid during a stoppage of work is recoverable after the stoppage has ended in certain cases.[11] Benefits are not assignable, cannot be used as security, and do not pass to a trustee in sequestration.[12]

Where benefit is paid to meet requirements for spouse or child which some person is liable to discharge the Commission may recover the cost of benefit from the person liable,[13] and the Commission has the same right as the mother to bring an action for affiliation and aliment of an illegitimate child.[14]

The Commission is also responsible for re-establishment centres and reception centres.[15]

FAMILY INCOME SUPPLEMENT

Under the Family Income Supplement Act, 1970, family income supplement may be claimed for any family[16] in Great Britain if the weekly amount of its resources, so far as taken into

[1] Ibid., S. 4.
[2] Ibid., S. 5 and Sched. 2, amd. Social Security Act, 1971, S. 1.
[3] Ibid., S. 18.
[4] Ibid., S. 8.
[5] Ibid., S. 9.
[6] Ibid., S. 10.
[7] Ibid., S. 12.
[8] Ibid., S. 13.
[9] Ibid., S. 14.
[10] Ibid., S. 16, amd. Social Security Act, 1971, S. 3.
[11] Social Security Act, 1971, S. 2.
[12] Ibid., S. 20.
[13] Ibid., Ss. 22–3; as to polygamous marriage see *Din* v. *National Assistance Board* [1967] 2 Q.B. 213.
[14] Ibid., S. 24; and see *Clapham* v. *N.A.B.* [1961] 2 Q.B. 77; *Payne* v. *Critchley* [1962] 2 Q.B. 83.
[15] Ibid., S. 34 and Sched. 4.
[16] Defined, 1970 Act, S. 1.

account for the purposes of the Act,[1] falls short of the prescribed amount.[2] The amount of the supplement is half of the difference between the prescribed amount and the weekly resources.[3] Questions of right to, and amount of, family income supplement are determined by the Supplementary Benefit Commission, subject to appeal to the Appeal Tribunal.[4] There is provision to avoid overlapping with supplementary benefits.[5] The assignation, or using as security of a family income supplement is void, and supplement does not pass to a trustee in sequestration.[6]

NATIONAL HEALTH SERVICE

The national health service came into operation in 1948[7] and provides hospital and specialist services, general medical services, general dental services, pharmaceutical services, and supplementary ophthalmic services. Through local authorities it provides midwifery services, health visitors, home nursing and domestic help. The services are available to all without charge, save where expressly imposed by regulations, but persons insured under the National Insurance Act pay, as an element in their weekly contribution, a contribution to the National Health Service.[8]

Where no suitable arrangements are made otherwise it is the duty of the local authority to arrange for the burial or cremation of the body of any person who has died or is found dead in their area.[9]

SOCIAL WELFARE

Under the Social Work (Scotland) Act, 1968, a local authority may give assistance in cash or kind to a person,[10] assist persons to

---

[1] Defined, S. 4.

[2] Ibid., Ss. 1–2.

[3] Ibid., S. 3.

[4] Ibid., Ss. 6–7, amd. Pensioners and Family Income Supplement Payments Act, 1972, S. 3.

[5] Ibid., S. 8.

[6] Ibid., S. 9.

[7] National Health Service (Sc.) Act, 1947, replacing provisions under the National Health Insurance Acts, 1936 to 1941, and hospitals managed by local authorities, by voluntary bodies, and under the poor law.

[8] National Health Service Contributions Acts, 1965 and 1970.

[9] National Assistance Act, 1948, S. 50; *Secretary of State for Scotland* v. *Fife C.C.*, 1953 S.C. 257.

[10] 1968 Act, S. 12.

dispose of their work,[1] provide home helps, where necessary, and may provide or arrange for the provision of laundry facilities,[2] take into its care children orphaned, abandoned or lost, or lacking proper accommodation, maintenance, and upbringing[3] and in such cases assume parental rights over the children,[4] in which case it becomes the local authority's duty to further the best interests of the children and afford opportunity for their proper development.[5] It may maintain such children by boarding-out, or in a residential establishment,[6] arrange for the emigration of children[7] and give financial assistance towards the cost of the accommodation and maintenance of persons over school age but under 21 or till he completes a course of education or training.[8] It must offer guidance and assistance to children formerly in the care of local authorities or voluntary organizations until they are 18.[9]

[1] Ibid., S. 13.
[2] Ibid., S. 14.
[3] Ibid., S. 15.
[4] Ibid., Ss. 16–19.
[5] Ibid., S. 20.
[6] Ibid., Ss. 21–2.
[7] Ibid., S. 23.
[8] Ibid., Ss. 24–5.
[9] Ibid., S. 26.

PART 2

UNINCORPORATED ASSOCIATIONS

Natural persons frequently associate themselves in groups for particular purposes. In some cases these groups are deemed by law to be unincorporated associations in which case the group is not incorporated or treated as a legal entity distinct from the members of the group. In other cases the group is incorporated and forms a legal entity quite distinct from the natural persons who are its officials or members.[1]

The main unincorporated associations are voluntary associations, which include clubs and societies, churches other than the Church of Scotland, and organizations of workers or of employers.[2]

CHAPTER 20

VOLUNTARY ASSOCIATIONS

VOLUNTARY associations are groups of natural persons who have voluntarily associated themselves for some common lawful purpose.[3] But the group they form is not recognized by the law as a corporation or legal entity endowed with legal personality, and it has no existence in law distinct from the aggregate of the members, unless it can be, and has been, incorporated as a company.[4] Hence such a body must be represented in legal transactions by its authorized office-bearers,[5] or the office-bearers and authorized representative members may sue jointly,[6] or mandatories specially authorized may sue.[7] It is necessary when suing such an association only to call the society

---

[1] Chaps 24–28, *infra*.
[2] For these see Chap. 22, *infra*.
[3] See generally More, *Lect.* I, 210.
[4] e.g. *St. Johnstone F.C.* v. *S.F.A., Ltd.*, 1965 S.L.T. 171.
[5] *Edinburgh Veterinary Medical Society* v. *Dick's Trs.* (1874) 1 R. 1072.
[6] *Renton F.C.* v. *McDowall* (1891) 18 R. 670; *Bridge* v. *South Portland St. Synagogue*, 1907 S.C. 1351.
[7] *Chapter-General of the Temple* v. *Mackersey* (1903) 11 S.L.T. 516; *Pagan & Osborne* v. *Haig*, 1910 S.C. 341.

and its office-bearers.[1] A member has no title to sue for a wrong
to the association.[2] An unincorporated association carrying on
business under a descriptive name may sue and be sued in that
name.[3] An association is liable for wrong done by an employee
while acting in the course of his employment.[4]

The relations between members of an association are contractual and the courts will intervene to secure a member's contractual
rights only if some civil right or patrimonial interest under contract is involved,[5] and not if merely social claims are in issue.[6]

Types of voluntary associations

The main types are members' clubs, associations, and societies,[7]
churches, other than the Church of Scotland, and societies
formed for religious or charitable purposes or the promotion of
some other serious purpose, trade associations, and organizations
of workers or of employers not being trade unions or employers'
associations.

Clubs, associations, and societies

The relations of members of an unincorporated[8] members'
club[9] with one another are determined by principles of contract
and the joint ownership of property. Persons who join contract
with the other members on the terms set out in the constitution
and rules of the club.[10] The constitution and rules fall to be
interpreted in the last resort by the court as a matter of law, and
the committee or other managing body cannot validly be made
the final arbiter on their interpretation.[11] The constitution and rules

[1] *Somerville* v. *Rowbotham* (1862) 24 D. 1187; *Skerret* v. *Oliver* (1896) 23 R. 468; *Bridge, supra.*
[2] *Campbell* v. *Wilson*, 1934 S.L.T. 249.
[3] Sheriff Courts (Sc.) Act, 1913, Sched. 2, R. 11.
[4] *Ellis* v. *National Free Labour Assocn.* (1904) 7 F. 629.
[5] *McMillan* v. *Free Church* (1862) 24 D. 1282; *Forbes* v. *Eden* (1867) 5 M. (H.L.) 36; *Cocker* v. *Crombie* (1893) 20 R. 954; *Brook* v. *Kelly* (1893) 20 (H.L.) 104; *Murdison* v. *S. Football Union* (1896) 23 R. 449; *Mulcahy* v. *Herbert* (1898) 25 R. 1136; *Anderson* v. *Manson*, 1909 S.C. 838.
[6] *Forbes* v. *Eden* (1867) 5 M. (H.L.) 36; *Skerret* v. *Oliver* (1896) 23 R. 468; *Drennan* v. *Associated Ironmoulders*, 1921 S.C. 151.
[7] Including an unregistered friendly society: *Young* v. *Waterson*, 1918 S.C. 9; or an unregistered trade union: *Wilson* v. *Scottish Typographical Assocn.*, 1912 S.C. 534.
[8] A members' club may be incorporated, by registration as a company limited by shares or by guarantee under the Companies Act, in which case the membership rules are contained in, or appended to, the articles of association of the company.
[9] It is otherwise with a proprietary club, owned by a person, where members by joining obtain only the privileges of using the premises for the purposes allowed by their member-ship. Such a club may be conducted as a limited company.
[10] *Lyttleton* v. *Blackburne* (1875) L.J. Ch. 219.
[11] *Baker* v. *Jones* [1954] 2 All E.R. 553.

can be altered only with the consent of all the members,[1] unless they contain provisions for alteration by other means, in which case any alteration *bona fide* and validly made is binding on all the members unless it is at variance with the fundamental purposes of the association.[2] Unless the constitution provides for dissolution, it is *ultra vires* for a majority to dissolve it against the wishes of a dissentient minority.[3]

A member is liable to contribute to the club only the agreed subscription;[4] by membership he incurs no liability to creditors of the club, unless he has acted so as to make himself liable as an agent[5] or has otherwise undertaken personal liability.

In the ordinary administration of the club, the views of the majority normally rule. Elected officers do not incur personal liability to outside creditors unless they have represented themselves as acting in a personal capacity.[6] They act normally as agents for the whole body of members. How far they may bind the members depends on the constitution and rules of the club.[7] Similarly an elected officer may incur liability as an agent for injuries sustained by a member on club property.[8] The whole club may be liable for carrying on a nuisance or causing harm to a third party.[9]

All members have a right of joint or common property in the club property, heritable and moveable.[10] But a member cannot insist on a sale thereof and division of the price, and on his death or resignation his right lapses and does not transmit to anyone.[11] Nor may a majority gratuitously alienate club property against the wishes of a minority.[12] If the club is wound up any surplus after meeting liabilities may be distributed among the

---

[1] *Dawkins* v. *Antrobus* (1881) 17 Ch.D. 615; *Harington* v. *Sendall* [1903] 1 Ch. 921. But see *Wilson* v. *Scottish Typographical Assocn.*, 1912 S.C. 534; *Abbatt* v. *Treasury Solicitor* [1969] 3 All E.R. 1175.

[2] *Thellusson* v. *Valentia* [1907] 2 Ch. 1; *Morgan* v. *Driscoll* (1922) 38 T.L.R. 251.

[3] *Peake* v. *Assoc. of English Episcopalians in Scotland* (1884) 22 S.L.R. 3; *Gardner* v. *McLintock* (1904) 11 S.L.T. 654.

[4] *Wise* v. *Perpetual Trustee Co.* [1903] A.C. 139.

[5] *Flemyng* v. *Hector* (1836) 2 M. & W. 172; *Todd* v. *Emly* (1841) 7 M. & W. 427; *Thomson* v. *Victoria Eighty Club* (1905) 13 S.L.T. 399.

[6] *Overton* v. *Hewett* (1886) 3 T.L.R. 246; *McMeekin* v. *Easton* (1889) 16 R. 363; *Thomson, supra.*

[7] *Flemyng, supra; Draper* v. *Manners* (1892) 9 T.L.R. 73.

[8] *Prole* v. *Allen* [1950] 1 All E.R. 476.

[9] *Castle* v. *St. Augustine's Links* (1922) 38 T.L.R. 615; cf. *Bolton* v. *Stone* [1951] A.C. 850.

[10] *Edinburgh Y.W.C.A.* (1893) 20 R. 894; *Murray* v. *Johnstone* (1896) 23 R. 981.

[11] *Graff* v. *Evans* (1881) 8 Q.B.D. 373; *Murray, supra.*

[12] *Murray, supra.*

members at the time.[1] A club cannot be made notour bankrupt or sequestrated.[2]

A member aggrieved by expulsion may appeal to the courts which will entertain his complaint only if the effect of the expulsion has been to deprive him of his enjoyment of club property or of other patrimonial rights and if the expulsion is not authorized by the rules,[3] or was not arrived at in good faith,[4] or if the proceedings were contrary to natural justice, as where the member was not given notice or permitted to state his case.[5] If the rules make no provision for it, expulsion must be done by the whole membership.[6] If the expulsion were wrongful a claim lies for damages. If the expulsion were authorized and fairly carried through, the courts will not investigate the merits of the decision of the committee or club members.[7] Subject to the rules, a member may resign at any time on communicating his desire to do so to the secretary.[8]

Religious, charitable, and other similar associations

Such associations are formed for the furtherance of particular objects set out in their constitution or other fundamental documents. The relations of members are contractual, and the courts will intervene only if pecuniary or proprietary issues are involved, such as deprivation of quasi-status,[9] injury to character,[10] or alleged misapplication of property.[11] Their funds and property are held in trust by the members, or persons nominated as trustees,

---

[1] *Baird* v. *Wells* (1890) 44 Ch. D. 661; *Re St Andrews Allotment Assocn.* [1969] 1 All E.R. 147.

[2] *Pitreavie Golf Club* v. *Penman*, 1934 S.L.T. 247.

[3] *Labouchere* v. *Earl Wharncliffe* (1879) 13 Ch.D. 346; *Young* v. *Ladies Imperial Club* [1920] 2 K.B. 523.

[4] *Tantussi* v. *Molli* (1886) 2 T.L.R. 731.

[5] *Fisher* v. *Keane* (1878) 11 Ch.D. 353; *Labouchere, supra*; *Dawkins* v. *Antrobus* (1881) 17 Ch.D. 615; *Anderson* v. *Manson*, 1909 S.C. 838; *Young* v. *Ladies Imperial Club* [1920] 2 K.B. 523; *Burn* v. *National Amalgamated Labourers' Union* [1920] 2 Ch. 364; *Maclean* v. *Workers' Union* [1929] 1 Ch. 602. The exercise of the power of expulsion of a member from an association, incorporated as a company limited by guarantee, need not conform to the principles of natural justice: *Gaiman* v. *National Association for Mental Health* [1970] 2 All E.R. 362.

[6] *Innes* v. *Wylie* (1844) 1 C. & K. 257.

[7] *Dawkins, supra*; *Weinberger* v. *Inglis* [1919] A.C. 606; *Thompson* v. *B.M.A.* [1924] A.C. 764.

[8] *Finch* v. *Oake* [1896] 1 Ch. 409.

[9] *McMillan* v. *Free Church of Scotland* (1861) 23 D. 1314; *Forbes* v. *Eden* (1867) 5 M. (H.L.) 36.

[10] *Dunbar* v. *Skinner* (1841) 11 D. 945.

[11] *Craigdallie* v. *Aikman* (1813) 1 Dow 1; *Smith* v. *Galbraith*, 6 June 1839, F.C.

for the objects of the society, and in case of dispute, the funds and property belong, in trust, to those who adhere to the principles of the body,[1] unless the society has the power to modify its principles or objects or has made provision in its constitutional documents for disposal of the property in the kind of event which has happened.[2]

Donations, contributions, or subscriptions are held in trust by the society for the furtherance of its objects[3] and are not revocable so long as those purposes are capable of fulfilment.[4] A subscription does not, unless the constitution provides therefor, make the subscriber a member.[5] If the purposes cease to be capable of fulfilment but there is an overriding general charitable intent the court will settle a scheme for the administration of the funds *cy près*,[6] but if there is no such intent the funds will be repayable to the subscribers.[7] If a subscriber cannot be traced his share probably falls to the Crown as *bona vacantia*.[8] But subscriptions may have been paid in return for benefits and hence not be returnable.[9]

The relations of a clergyman or member with such an association are contractual and if either be expelled he may recover damages if he has suffered patrimonial loss thereby.[10] The court will not require the church or association to readmit the expelled person.[11]

---

[1] *Free Church of Scotland* v. *Lord Overtoun* (1904) 7 F. (H.L.) 1; cf. *Ferguson Bequest Fund* (1879) 6 R. 486.

[2] *Kennedy* v. *Morrison* (1879) 6 R. 879.

[3] *Ewing* v. *McGavin* (1831) 9 S. 622; *Connell* v. *Ferguson* (1857) 19 D. 482.

[4] *Ewing, supra; Peake* v. *Assocn. of English Episcopalians* (1884) 22 S.L.R. 3; *Stuart's Exors.* v. *Colclough* (1900) 8 S.L.T. 236.

[5] *Goodall* v. *Bilsland*, 1909 S.C. 1152.

[6] *Clephane* v. *Edinburgh Mags.* (1869) 7 M. (H.L.) 7; *Prestonpans Kirk Session* v. *Prestonpans School Board* (1891) 19 R. 193; *Gibson* (1900) 2 F. 1195; *Anderson's Trs.* v. *Scott*, 1914 S.C. 942; *Clyde Industrial Training Ship Assocn.*, 1925 S.C. 676.

[7] *Bain* v. *Black* (1849) 11 D. 1287; 6 Bell 317; *Connell* v. *Ferguson* (1857) 19 D. 482; *Mitchell* v. *Burness* (1878) 5 R. 954; *Simpson* v. *Moffat Working Men's Institute Trs.* (1892) 19 R. 389; *Re British Red Cross Balkan Fund* [1914] 2 Ch. 419. *Emslie's Trs.* v. *Aberdeen Female Society*, 1949 S.L.T. (Notes) 61; *E. Kilbride District Nursing Assocn.*, 1951 S.C. 64. See also *Leven Penny Savings Bank*, 1948 S.C. 147.

[8] *Incorporated Maltmen of Stirling*, 1912 S.C. 887; *Anderson's Trs.* v. *Scott*, 1914 S.C. 942; *Caledonian Employees' Benevolent Socy.* 1928 S.C. 633.

[9] *Smith* v. *Lord Advocate* (1899) 1 F. 741.

[10] *Forbes* v. *Eden* (1867) 5 M. (H.L.) 36; *Brook* v. *Kelly* (1893) 20 R. (H.L.) 104; *Skerret* v. *Oliver* (1896) 23 R. 468; *McDonald* v. *Burns*, 1940 S.C. 376. Such loss includes loss of quasi-status, the capacity to hold certain offices and to perform certain functions.

[11] *Skerret, supra; Gall* v. *Loyal Glenbogie Lodge* (1900) 2 F. 1187.

Trade associations

A trade association is a body of persons formed for the purposes of furthering the trade interests of its members, or persons represented by them.[1] It may be an unincorporated association,[2] or a trade union within the definition of the Trade Union Acts, or formed as a company under the Companies Acts.[3] Its functions are normally to put the views of its members before government departments and other bodies, to collect and exchange information, to carry out research, to negotiate on behalf of its members with trade unions and generally to promote the interests of the trade in question.[4]

Organizations of workers and employers' organizations

Organizations of workers[5] and organizations of employers,[6] not registered as trade unions or employers' associations under statute,[7] are voluntary associations having none of the privileges of registered bodies.[8] Such organisations were commonly illegal at common law because their objects were in restraint of trade but were legalized by the Trade Union Act, 1871, S. 3.[9] They are not now illegal merely because their purposes are in restraint of trade.[10]

Relations between the organization and the member and between members, are contractual, regulated by the rules of the organization.[11] The 1974 Act formulates guiding principles for such organizations[12] and the courts have long sought to protect members from oppression by their organizations of their fellow members, as by expulsion unauthorised by the rules or in manner conflicting with natural justice or by unfair disciplinary action.[13]

[1] Restrictive Trade Practices Act, 1956, S. 6(8). Cf. *Johnston* v. *Aberdeen Master Plumbers Assocn.,* 1921 S.C. 62.

[2] But membership is limited to 20: Companies Act, 1948, S. 434.

[3] See Ch. 25, *infra.*   [4] See list in P.E.P., *Industrial Trade Associations* (1957).

[5] Defined: Trade Union and Labour Relations Act, 1974, s. 9.

[6] Defined: ibid., S. 62.   [7] 1974 Act, SS. 2, 3, 8.

[8] On these see Ch. 28, *infra.* The earlier trade union Acts, having been repealed, do not apply to non-registered unions, i.e. "organisations'.

[9] cf. *Bernard* v. *N.U.M.,* 1971 S.L.T. 177.

[10] 1974 Act, SS. 2, 3.

[11] cf. *Martin* v. *Scottish T. & G.W.U.,* 1952 S.C. (H.L.) 1.

[12] S 5.

[13] *Gardner* v. *McLintock* (1904) 11 S.L.T. 654; *McDowall* v. *McGhee,* 1913, 2 S.L.T. 238; *Kelly* v. *Natsopa* (1915) 31 T.L.R. 632; *Blackall* v. *N.U. Foundry Workers* (1923) 39 T.L.R. 431; *Abbott* v. *Sullivan* [1952] 1 K.B. 189; *Lee* v. *Showmen's Guild* [1952] 2 Q.B. 329; *Huntly* v. *Thornton* [1957] 1 All E.R. 234; *Lawlor* v. *U.P.O.W.* [1965] 1 All E.R. 353; *Walker* v. *A.U.E.W.* 1969 S.L.T. 150; *Leary* v. *N.U.V.B.* [1970] 2 All E.R. 713; *Edwards* v. *S.O.G.A.T.* [1970] 3 All E.R. 689.

The property of such organizations must be held by trustees[1] but they may sue and be sued in the name of the organization and decrees are enforceable against the property belonging to or held in trust for the organization.[2]

[1] cf. *Re N.U.R.'s Rules* [1968] 1 All E.R. 5.
[2] 1974 Act, SS. 2, 3. cf. *Hodgson* v. *N.A.L.G.O.* [1972] 1 All E.R. 15.

CHAPTER 21

FRIENDLY AND OTHER SIMILAR SOCIETIES

F RIENDLY societies are unincorporated societies formed for the provision by voluntary subscriptions of members for the relief or maintenance of members and their relatives, during sickness, old age, widowhood, or minority, for insuring money to be paid on a birth or death, for funeral expenses, for relief when seeking employment, and for other kindred purposes.[1] There are various types; some accumulate their funds, others divide their surpluses periodically, and some societies operate more than one system of benefit. Akin to these are cattle insurance societies, benevolent societies for any benevolent or charitable purpose, working men's clubs, old people's home societies, and specially authorized societies for any purpose which the Treasury may authorize under the Acts.[1]

Creation

The Friendly Societies Acts, now of 1974, provide for a central office of the registry of friendly societies, with a chief registrar, and an assistant registrar for Scotland.[2] Societies registrable under the Acts are societies formed for the purpose of providing, by voluntary subscriptions of the members, for one or more of the statutory purposes,[3] viz.: relief or maintenance of members or relatives in sickness or old age, insuring money to be paid on a birth or death, relief or maintenance during unemployment, endowment on marriage, and other specified purposes. There are financial limits on permissible assurances.

A society need not register under the Acts but, if it does not, it may not have more than twenty members.[4] If a society con-

---

[1] cf. Friendly Societies Act, 1974, S.7. For origins and development of Friendly Societies see Clapham, *Economic History of Modern Britain*; Cole, *Short History of British Working Class Movement*; Gregg, *Social and Economic History of Britain*; Beveridge, *Voluntary Action*. Statutory authority and regulation dates from 1793.

[2] 1974 Act, SS. 1–6.

[3] S. 7(1).

[4] Companies Act, 1948, S. 434; *Jennings* v. *Hammond* (1881) 9 Q.B.D. 225; *Shaw* v. *Benson* (1883) 11 Q.B.D. 563; *Shaw* v. *Simmons* (1883) 12 Q.B.D. 117. There is no legal definition of an unregistered friendly society, but its purposes must be generally similar to those of a registered society. It is an unincorporated association and its property is normally vested in trustees. The Acts, in general, apply only to registered societies.

sists of at least seven members it may be registered, on submitting an application with copies of its rules containing specified particulars.[1] Amendments of the rules must be registered.[2] The rules must contain all the matters mentioned in Schedule I of the 1896 Act. They may permit a minor to be a member.[3] The registrar has discretion to reject an unsuitable name.[4] Societies may have branches, which may have separate trustees and rules, be separately registered and administered, and may secede from the parent society.[5] Every society and branch must have a registered office, specified in the rules and notified to the assistant registrar.[6]

A registered society or branch is excepted from the Unlawful Societies Act, 1799 and the Seditious Meetings Act, 1817, so long as it confines itself to society business.[7] It also has certain priorities on the death or bankruptcy of an officer of the society having money or property of the society in his possession.[8]

Management

The affairs of a society or branch are managed by its officers; the rules must provide for trustees, a secretary, a treasurer, and a committee of management,[9] and two auditors or an approved auditor. There may be other officers. The rules must provide for the removal of officers.[10] Every officer having the receipt or charge of money must, if required by the rules, find security for the rendering of his accounts.[11] All property of a society vests in the trustees thereof for the time being for the benefit of the society, the members thereof, and persons claiming through them.[12] The trustees are liable only for sums of money actually received on account of the society or branch.[13]

[1] 1974 Act, Ss. 8–16; see also *Finlay* v. *Royal Liver Friendly Socy.* (1901) 4 F. 34; *Batty* v. *Scottish Legal Life Assce. Socy.* (1902) 4 F. 954; cf. *Mackendrick* v. *Union of Dock Labourers*, 1911 S.C. 83.

[2] 1974 Act, S. 18. See also *Davie* v. *Colinton Friendly Socy.* (1870) 9 M. 96 (registration not conclusive of legality of rules).

[3] S. 60.

[4] S. 8; *R.* v. *Registrar of Friendly Societies* (1872) L.R. 7 Q.B. 741; cf. Companies Act, 1948, S. 17.

[5] Ss. 11–14.

[6] S. 7 and Sch. 2.

[7] S. 24.

[8] S. 59.

[9] S. 7 and Sched. 2.

[10] See *Glasgow District of Ancient Order of Forresters* v. *Stevenson* (1899) 2 F. 14; *Liverpool Victoria Loyal Friendly Socy.* v. *Honston* (1900) 3 F. 42.

[11] S. 27.

[12] S. 54.

[13] S. 54; *Re Cardiff Savings Bank* [1892] 2 Ch. 100, 108.

A member's subscriptions are not recoverable at law,[1] save that sums payable to a registered cattle insurance society or branch or to such specially authorized societies or branch thereof as the Treasury may allow are recoverable in the Sheriff court.[2]

Every registered society and branch must have its accounts audited annually,[3] make an annual return to the registrar,[4] and have its assets and liabilities valued at least quinquennially.[5]

A registered society or branch enjoys certain privileges including exemption from income tax and stamp duty[6] and a priority over diligence and bankruptcy in recovering property from officers having it in their possession.[7]

The trustees may invest the society's funds in specified ways, make advances or loans to members, and hold land and transact with it.[8] All property vests in the trustees,[9] who are liable for their own defaults only.[10] Officers having charge of money must give in accounts to be examined and pay over money on demand by the society.[11]

The trustees of a society or branch may bring or defend legal proceedings concerning any property, right or claim of the society or branch in their proper names, with the title of their office.[12] In proceedings by a member a society may also be sued in the name of an officer who receives contributions on behalf of the society.[13]

Members

There is no limit on the number of members. The rules may permit minors to be members.[14] The terms and manner of admission must be provided in the rules, and also the rights and liabilities of members. Members also have numerous statutory rights, such as to obtain a copy of the last annual return of the society[15] and to inspect the books.[16] Specified proportions or numbers of members have further statutory rights, such as to apply for appointment of an inspector to investigate the affairs

[1] S. 61   [2] S. 22.   [3] S. 31.   [4] S. 43.
[5] S. 41.
[6] See *Incorporation of Tailors in Glasgow* v. *I.R.C.* (1887) 14 R. 729.
[7] SS. 59.
[8] SS. 46–53; *United Deposit Friendly Relief Socy.* (1903) 11 S.L.T. 85.
[9] Ss. 54.
[10] S. 54.
[11] S. 28; cf. *First Edinburgh & Leith, etc. Socy.* v. *Munro* (1883) 11 R. 5.
[12] S. 56; *Simpson* v. *Ramsay* (1874) 2 R. 129; *Kelly* v. *Peacock* (1917) 55 S.L.R. 65.
[13] S. 56; *Blue* v. *Pollock* (1866) 4 M. 1042; *General Railways Workers' Union* v. *Macdonald* (1900) 37 S.L.R. 721.
[14] S. 60.   [15] S. 44.   [16] S. 62.

of a society.[1] The amount which a member, or a person claiming through a member, may recover from societies is limited.[2] A member may recover damages from the funds of the society for a wrong done to him through violation of the society's rules by one of the society's officers.[3] A member may terminate his membership as provided by the rules, or at any time. It is usually provided that membership shall cease if contributions are in arrears for a specified period. A member cannot be expelled unless the rules give power to do so.[4] Any power must be exercised in good faith, in accordance with the rules, and for the benefit of the society.[5]

Meetings

The rules must provide for holding general meetings. The assistant registrar may call a special meeting on the requisition of a number of members.[6] Certain changes require a special resolution.[7]

Accounts

Every society must keep proper books of accounts and comply with statutory requirements as to accounts, balance sheets, and auditors.[8]

Functioning

Members pay their contributions periodically to the society, or collectors call at their homes to collect contributions. Friendly societies which receive contributions for death benefit or other assurances on life by collectors at the homes of members or persons assured at intervals of less than two months are known as collecting societies and subject to the Industrial Assurance Acts, 1923 to 1958. A member's subscriptions are not recoverable at law,[9] save in certain cases.[10]

---

[1] S. 90.
[2] S. 64.
[3] Blue v. Pollock (1866) 4 M. 1042.
[4] Dawkins v. Antrobus (1881) 17 Ch. D. 615; cf. Bonsor v. Musicians' Union [1956] A.C. 104.
[5] cf. Wood v. Woad (1874) L.R. 9 Ex. 190; Fisher v. Keane (1878) 11 Ch. D. 353; Burn v. Nat. Amalgamated Labourers [1902] 2 Ch. 364.
[6] S. 90.
[7] S. 86.
[8] Ss. 29–40.
[9] S. 61.
[10] S. 22.

Property and Funds

The rules must provide for the investment of the society's funds, and the trustees may invest in stated ways, including land and trustee securities.[1] Societies have power, if the rules permit, to borrow on the security of land or buildings and to accept deposits made by members to a separate loan fund.[2] There are close restrictions on lending the society's money.[3]

Payments on death

The moneys payable on death may include sums insured on on his life, moneys in a loan account and money accumulated for the member. Save in exceptional cases a death certificate must be produced.[4]

Nominations

A member may, by writing under his hand[5] delivered to the society's registered office or made in a book kept there, nominate a person to whom any money payable by the society on his death, not exceeding £500, shall be paid.[6] He may revoke and vary the nomination.[7] Marriage revokes a nomination.[8] On receiving satisfactory proof of the nominator's death the society pays the nominee.[9] Nomination does not imply that the nominee is to have the sole beneficial interest in the money affected.[10] On the member's death, not having made a nomination, the society may pay to those whom it considers entitled without need for confirmation. If an illegitimate member dies, not having made a nomination, the trustees may pay to the person who, in the committee's opinion, would have been entitled if the member had been legitimate.[11] A society may insure the life of a child only to a limited extent, except where the person insuring has an insurable interest in the child's life.[12]

---

[1] S. 46.
[2] S. 49.
[3] S. 48.
[4] S. 70.
[5] *Morton* v. *French*, 1908 S.C. 171.
[6] S. 66.
[7] cf. *Young* v. *Waterson*, 1918 S.C. 9.
[8] S. 66(7).
[9] S. 67.
[10] *Young, supra*, where nominee had to account to executor under subsequent will for money due.
[11] SS. 68–71; cf. *Symington* v. *Galashiels Co-operative Store Co.* (1894) 21 R. 371.
[12] SS. 71; cf. *Carmichael* v. *C's Exrx.*, 1919 S.C. 636.

Disputes

Disputes within the society[1] are to be decided as the society rules provide,[2] which may be by arbitration,[3] and are not removable into any court; they may be referred to the assistant registrar or to the sheriff court.[4] A case may be stated on a question of law for the opinion of the Inner House.[5] But the jurisdiction of the Court is not excluded where it is alleged that the society has acted in contravention of its rules.[6] The court cannot enforce a decree ordering a branch to reinstate a member, as ordered by a superior court of the society, and a petition for such a decree is therefore incompetent,[7] but declarator of membership is competent.[8]

Change of status

A society may change its name, amalgamate with or transfer its engagements to another society, or convert itself into a company under the Companies Acts, or transfer its engagement to such a company. It may become a branch of another society.[9]

The assistant registrar may, on application by members, appoint an inspector to examine into and report on the affairs of the society or call a special meeting of the society, or may suspend or cancel the society's registration.[10]

Dissolution

A society may dissolve itself on the happening of an event having this effect under the rules, or, with certain consents, by

---

[1] *Melrose* v. *Adam* (1897) 34 S.L.R. 346; *Glasgow District A.O.F.* v. *Stevenson* (1899) 2 F. 14; *Lewis* v. *Paulton* (1907) 14 S.L.T. 818; *Catt* v. *Wood* [1910] A.C. 404; see also *Blue* v. *Pollock* (1866) 4 M. 1042; *Davie* v. *Colinton Friendly Socy.* (1870) 9 M. 96; *Symington, supra*; *Gall* v. *Loyal Glenbogie Lodge* (1900) 2 F. 1187; *McGowan* v. *City of Glasgow Friendly Socy.*, 1913 S.C. 991.

[2] S. 76(1); *Somerville* v. *Meters of Leith* (1868) 6. M. 796; *McKernan* v. *Operative Masons* (1873) 11 M. 548; *Finlay* v. *Royal Liver Friendly Socy.* (1901) 4 F. 34; *Batty* v. *Scottish Legal Life Assce. Socy* (1902) 4 F. 954; *Collins* v. *Barrowfield Lodge*, 1915 S.C. 190.

[3] *Galashiels Provident Bldg. Socy.* v. *Newlands* (1893) 20 R. 821; *Rombach* v. *McCormack* (1896) 4 S.L.T. 174.

[4] *Leitch* v. *Scottish Legal Burial Socy.* (1870) 9 M. 40; *Davie* v. *Colinton Friendly Socy.* (1870) 9 M. 96.

[5] S. 78; *Manners* v. *Fairholme* (1872) 10 M. 520; *Smith* v. *Scottish Legal Life Assce. Socy.*, 1912 S.C. 611.

[6] *McGowan* v. *City of Glasgow Friendly Socy.*, 1913 S.C. 991; Contrast *Crichton* v. *Free Gardeners* (1904) 6 F. 398.

[7] *Gall* v. *Loyal Glenbogie Lodge* (1900) 2 F. 1187.

[8] *Collins* v. *Barrowfield United Oddfellows*, 1915 S.C. 190.

[9] Ss. 81–86; *Blythe* v. *Birtley* [1910] 1 Ch. 226, *Wilkinson* v. *City of Glasgow Friendly Socy.*, 1911 S.C. 476.

[10] Ss. 87–92; *Professional, etc., Supply Assocn.* v. *Dougal* (1898) 5 S.L.T. 359.

an instrument of dissolution,[1] or by the award of the assistant registrar, following on an application by members and investigation.[2] If a society fails for lack of members surviving annuitants are not entitled to appropriate the funds.[3]

[1] S. 93; *Second Edinburgh, etc., Building Socy.* v. *Aitken* (1892) 19 R. 603; *Kelly* v. *Peacock* (1917) 55 S.L.R. 65. As to winding-up unregistered societies see *Smith* v. *Irvine and Fullarton Bldg. Socy.* (1903) 6 F. 99; *Sharp* v. *Dunbar Sailors Socy.* (1903) 10 S.L.T. 572.

[2] Ss. 95–97.

[3] *Mitchell* v. *Burness* (1878) 5 R. 954; cf. *Smith* v. *Lord Advocate* (1899) 1 F. 741; *Sharp* v. *Sailors of Dunbar* (1903) 10 S.L.T. 572.

CHAPTER 22

TRADE UNIONS AND EMPLOYERS'
ASSOCIATIONS

THE law of trade unions is understandable only in the light of the history of the trade union movement and related social and economic conflicts.[1] At common law a trade union was an association of employers, or workmen, or employers and workmen, formed normally to impose restrictions on the conduct of trade or business and normally, therefore, existing for purposes contrary to public policy, and consequently an unlawful association.[2]

The Trade Union Act, 1871, was the first Act which fully recognized and legalized unions even though their objects were in restraint of trade, and for a century it was the basis of the law, materially amended, however, by Acts of 1876, 1906, 1913, 1945 and 1965. Most of this legislation was superseded by the Industrial Relations Act, 1971, itself replaced by the Trade Union and Labour Relations Act, 1974.

For the purpose of the Trade Union Acts, 1871 and 1876 (now repealed), a trade union was any combination, whether temporary or permanent, for regulating the relations between workmen[3] and masters, or between workmen and workmen, or between masters and masters, or for imposing restrictive conditions on the conduct of any trade or business,[4] whether such combination would or would not, if the 1871 Act had not been been passed, have been deemed an unlawful combination by reason of some one or more of its purposes being in restraint of trade.[5] The Trade Union Act, 1913, defined a trade union as any

[1] See Webb, *History of Trade Unionism*; Hedges and Winterbottom, *Legal History of Trade Unionism*; Cole, *Short History of the British Working Class Movement*; Pelling, *History of British Trade Unionism*; Clegg, Fox and Thompson, *History of British Trade Unions*. For modern law see Citrine, *Trade Union Law*; Vester and Gardner, *Trade Union Law and Practice*; Grunfeld, *Modern Trade Union Law*.

[2] Bell, *Prin.* §. 40, 193; *Osborne v. A.S.R.S.* [1911] 1 Ch. 540, 565, 572; *Bernard v. N.U.M.*, 1971 S.L.T. 177.

[3] Probably including employed persons of all kinds.

[4] See e.g. *Glasgow Potted Meat Mfrs. Socy. v. Geddes* (1902) 10 S.L.T. 481; *Edinburgh Aerated Water Mfrs. Defence Assocn. v. Jenkinson* (1902) 5 F. 1159; *Rae v. Plate Glass Merchants' Assocn.*, 1919 S.C. 426; *Johnston v. Aberdeen Plumbers*, 1921 S.C. 62.

[5] Trade Union Act Amdt. Act, 1876, S. 16, replacing Trade Union Act, 1871. S. 23, except proviso.

combination, temporary or permanent, the principal objects of which were one or more of the statutory objects,[1] i.e. regulating relations or imposing restrictive conditions, and also the provision of benefits to members.[2]

Under these Acts unions might be temporary or permanent, registered or unregistered, but were not incorporated bodies, though in some respects they were treated as semi-corporations. Registration was of very limited importance.

Lawful and unlawful organizations at common law

Organizations which have purposes and objects lawful at common law are lawful voluntary associations.[3] A trade combination is, however, unlawful at common law if its objects or rules or practices are in unreasonable restraint of trade,[4] and such combinations are lawful only under statute.[5] A trade combination whose purposes are criminal, or actionable as a conspiracy to injure, is not lawful either at common law or under statute.[6]

Definition of trade union

A trade union is an organization, permanent or temporary, which consists wholly or mainly of workers and is an organization whose principal purposes include the regulation of relations between workers and employers or employers' associations or consists wholly or mainly of constituent or affiliated organizations or representatives thereof with such a principal purpose.[7]

Definition of employers' associations

An employers' association is an organization, permanent or temporary, which consists wholly or mainly of employers or proprietors and its principal purposes include the regulation of relations between employers and workers or trade unions, or con-

---

[1] 1913 Act, S. 2(1) and 1(2), later amended by Industrial Relations Act, 1971, Sched. 8.
[2] 1913 Act S. 1(2). The provision of benefits alone would not make an organisation a trade union.
[3] *Gozney* v. *Bristol Trade Society* [1909] 1 K.B. 901; *Russell* v. *Amalgamated Carpenters* [1912] A.C. 421.
[4] *Osborne* v. *A.S.R.S.* [1911] 1 Ch. 540, 565, 572.
[5] cf. *Rigby* v. *Connol* (1880) 14 Ch.D. 482; *Yorkshire Miners Assoc.* v. *Howden* [1905] A.C. 256; *Russell, supra; Briggs* v. *N.U.M.*, 1968 S.L.T. (Notes) 59. See also Kahn-Freund (1944) 7 M.L.R. 202.
[6] cf. *Crofter Co.* v. *Veitch*, 1942 S.C. (H.L.) 1.
[7] Trade Union and Labour Relations Act, 1974, S. 28(1). 'Workers' are defined in S. 30.

sists wholly or mainly of constituent or affiliated organizations or representatives thereof with such a principal purpose.[1]

Status of trade union

A trade union which is not a special register body is not to be treated as a body corporate but it is capable of making contracts, all property belonging to it is vested in trustees in trust for the union, it is capable of suing and being sued in its own name and may be prosecuted in its own name, but any judgment or order is enforceable against property held in trust for it as if it were a body corporate. Such a union may not be registered as a company, friendly society or industrial and provident society.

The purposes of such a trade union and, so far as relating to the regulation of relations between employers and workers, the purposes of any trade union are not, by reason only that they are in restraint of trade, unlawful so as to make any member liable to criminal proceedings for conspiracy or otherwise or to make any agreement or trust void or voidable, nor is any rule of such a trade union or, so far as it so relates, any rule of any trade union unlawful or unenforceable by reason only that it is in restraint of trade.[2]

Status of employers' association

An employers' association may be a body corporate or an unincorporated institution. In the latter case it is capable of making contracts, all property is vested in trustees in trust for the association, it is capable of suing and being sued in its own name and may be prosecuted in its own name, but any judgment or order is enforceable as if it were a body corporate.

The purposes of an unincorporated employers' association and, so far as relating to the regulation of relations between employers and workers or unions, of an incorporated association are not, by reason only that they are in restraint of trade, unlawful so as to make any member criminally liable for conspiracy or otherwise or to make any agreement or trust void or voidable, nor is any rule unlawful or unenforceable by reason only that it is in restraint of trade.[3]

---

[1] Trade Union and Labour Relations Act, 1974, S. 28(2). Employers are defined in S. 30

[2] Trade Union and Labour Relations Act, 1974, S. 2. As to trustees of property see also S. 4.

[3] Trade Union and Labour Relations Act, 1974, S. 3. As to trustees of property see also S. 4.

Lists of trade unions

The Registrar of Friendly Societies must maintain a list of trade unions, and any organization of workers may apply to be registered on submitting specified particulars.[1] An appeal against refusal to register lies to the Court of Sessions.[2] Organizations must keep accounting records and make annual returns.[3]

Lists of employers' associations

The Registrar of Friendly Societies must maintain a list of employers' organizations and any organization of employers may apply to be registered on submitting specified particulars.[4] An appeal against refusal to register lies to the Court of Sessions.[5] Organizations must keep accounting records and make annual returns.[6]

Relations between unions and members: rule books

Membership of a union is constituted by contract, and the rules of the union are the terms of the contract between the members and between the union and each member.[7] Qualifications for membership may be imposed,[8] but contribution to an organization's political fund may not be a condition of membership.[9] An appropriately specified person may not, by arbitrary or unreasonable discrimination, be excluded from membership.[10] The rules of a trade union or employers' association must comply with statutory requirements.[11] Unless there is provision to the contrary a member may resign but may not be expelled.[12] The qualifications, powers, rights and duties of all officials should be defined by the union rules, and they are its agents and bind the union if acting within the scope of their authority.[13] Acts outwith the rules by union, committees or officials are *ultra vires* and void.[14]

---

[1] 1974 Act, S. 8.   [2] S. 8(7).   [3] Ss. 10–11.

[4] 1974 Act, S. 8.   [5] S. 8(7).   [6] Ss. 10–11.

[7] *Martin* v. *Scottish T. & G.W.U.*, 1952 S.C. (H.L.) 1; *Haggarty* v. *Scottish T. & G.W.U.*, 1955 S.C. 109; *Bonsor* v. *Musicians' Union* [1956] A.C. 104; *Faramus* v. *Film Artistes Assocn.* [1964] A.C. 925 contrast *Nisbet* v. *Percy*, 1951 S.C. 350.

[8] cf. *Russell* v. *D. Norfolk* [1949] 1 All E.R. 109; *Nagle* v. *Fielden* [1966] 2 Q.B. 633.

[9] Trade Union Act, 1913, S. 3(1).

[10] 1974 Act, S. 5.   [11] 1974 Act, S. 6.

[12] *Luby* v. *Warwickshire Miners* [1912] 2 Ch. 371.

[13] Cf. *N.U. Bank Employees* v. *Murray*, 1948 S.L.T. (Notes) 51; *Bonsor* v. *Musicians' Union* [1956] A.C. 104.

[14] *Yorkshire Miners* v. *Howden* [1905] A.C. 256; *Martin* v. *Scottish T. & G.W.U.*, 1952 S.C. (H.L.) 1.

The terms of employment of paid union officials, and their dismissal or removal are regulated by the rules and by the ordinary law of employment.[1]

Meetings and elections

The occasions for which meetings are required, their calling, composition, procedure, and powers are determined mainly by the rules. Interdict may be granted against an irregularly convened or conducted meeting[2] or against the implement of *ultra vires* resolutions. The conduct of elections, eligibility, candidature, and campaign, are also determined by the rules,[3] supplemented by the general law as to elections.

Disciplinary powers over members

A union can suspend, expel, fine, impose forfeitures, exclude from union office, or otherwise discipline a member only by virtue of powers contained in its rules and accepted in the contract between union and member.[4] There are statutory restrictions on unfair or unreasonable disciplinary action.[5] Such powers may be exercised only by the committee or other body specified in the rules, acting as a domestic tribunal. Rules establishing a domestic tribunal and requiring resort to it before going to law,[6] and even making it final on questions of fact,[7] are valid. A member would not be held bound by rules deemed by the court unreasonable[8] or wholly withdrawing disputes from the jurisdiction of the courts[9] or excluding the application of the principles of natural justice from a domestic inquiry.[10] Any appeals procedure within the union rules should be utilized but failure to utilise it does not prevent, if appropriate, an appeal to the ordinary courts.[11]

---

[1] See *Byrne* v. *K.R.A.* [1958] 2 All E.R. 579; *Lawlor* v. *U.P.O.W.* [1965] 1 All E.R. 353. Cf. *Ridge* v. *Baldwin* [1964] A.C. 40.

[2] The court may ignore an unimportant irregularity: *Cotter* v. *N.U.S.* [1929] 2 Ch. 58.

[3] *Watson* v. *Smith* [1941] 2 All E.R. 725.

[4] *Parr* v. *Lancashire Miners* [1913] 1 Ch. 366; *Spowart* v. *T & G.W.U.*, 1926 S.L.T. 245; *Wolstenholme* v. *Amalg. Musicians' Union* [1920] 2 Ch. 388; *Lee* v. *Showmen's Guild* [1952] 2 Q.B. 329; *Martin* v. *Scottish T. & W.G.U.*, 1952 S.C. (H.L.) 1.

[5] Trade Union and Labour Relations Act, 1974, S. 5.

[6] *Scott* v. *Avery* (1856) 5 H.L.C. 811; *White* v. *Kuzych* [1951] A.C. 585.

[7] *Lee, supra.*

[8] *Baker* v. *Jones* [1954] 2 All E.R. 553; *Edwards* v. *S.O.G.A.T.* [1971] Ch. 354.

[9] *Scott* v. *Avery* (1856) 5 H.L.C. 811; *Lee, supra.*

[10] *Russell* v. *D. Norfolk* [1949] 1 All E.R. 109; *Lee, supra; Lawlor* v. *Post Office Workers* [1965] 1 All E.R. 353.

[11] *Annamunthodo* v. *Oilfield Workers* [1961] A.C. 945. See also 1971 Act, S. 65(8).

Either party may appeal to the ordinary courts only if it is alleged that the union had no such disciplinary powers as it claimed, or that, if it had, they were not validly exercised[1] or not exercised in conformity with the principles of natural justice. Disciplinary powers must be exercised in good faith,[2] in accordance with the rules of the union,[3] and the proceedings of the domestic tribunal must be conducted in accordance with the requirements of natural justice,[4] and the facts must be reasonably capable of supporting the tribunal's decision.[5] The courts will not inquire whether the decision of the domestic tribunal of the union is correct, or fair,[6] or reasonable;[7] they will not act as court of appeal.[8] In appropriate cases the courts may grant declarator that the discipline was *ultra vires*, or interdict against expulsion, or damages for breach by the union of the contract of membership.[9] Exceptionally, union pressure on a member or former member may justify damages for conspiracy to injure.[10]

Welfare activities

Benevolent objects, including legal aid,[11] may be provided by a union.[12] The rules must provide for any contributions payable in respect thereof and for the payment of benefits. A member may seek interdict against expenditure on unauthorized objects.[13]

---

[1] e.g. *Blackall* v. *N.U. of Foundry Workers* (1923) 39 T.L.R. 431; *Huntley* v. *Thornton* [1957] 1 All E.R. 234.

[2] Cf. *McDowall* v. *McGhee*, 1913, 2 S.L.T. 238; *Kelly* v. *Natsopa* (1915) 31 T.L.R. 632; *Wolstenholme* v. *Amalg. Musicians' Union* [1920] 2 Ch. 388; *Evans* v. *N.U. of Printing Workers* [1938] 4 All E.R. 51.

[3] *Spowart* v. *T. & G.W.U.*, 1926 S.L.T. 245. In this respect the rules must be construed strictly: *Blackall* v. *N.U. Foundry Workers* (1923) 39 T.L.R. 431; *Huntley* v. *Thornton* [1957] 1 All E.R. 234.

[4] These are: The member must be informed of the charge and given time to prepare his defence; both sides must be given a fair and equal hearing; and the decision must be reached honestly and without bias: see *Maclean* v. *Workers' Union* [1929] 1 Ch. 602; *White* v. *Kuzych* [1951] A.C. 58; *Walker* v. *A.U. Engineers* 1969 S.L.T. 150; *Leary* v. *N.U.V.B.* [1970] 2 All E.R. 713; *Breen* v. *A.E.U.* [1971] 1 All E.R. 1148; 1974 Act, S. 5.

[5] *Allison* v. *G.M.C.* [1894] 1 Q.B. 750; *Lee, supra.*

[6] *Maclean* v. *Workers' Union* [1929] 1 Ch. 602.

[7] *Weinberger* v. *Inglis* [1919] A.C. 606; *Thompson* v. *B.M.A.* [1924] A.C. 764.

[8] cf. *Leeson* v. *G.M.C.* (1889) 43 Ch.D. 615; *Young* v. *Ladies Imperial Club* [1920] 2 K.B. 523.

[9] *Bonsor* v. *Musicians' Union* [1956] A.C. 104.

[10] *Huntley* v. *Thornton* [1957] 1 All E.R. 234.

[11] cf. *Mackendrick* v. *N.U. Dock Labourers*, 1911 S.C. 83; *McGahie* v. *U.S.D.A.W.*, 1966 S.L.T. 74; on the extent of the union's duty, see *Buckley* v. *N.U.G.M.W.* [1967] 3 All E.R. 767; *Cross* v. *B.I.S.K.T.A.* [1968] 1 All E.R. 250.

[12] Trade Union Act, 1913, S. 1(2); *P.R.S.* v. *London Theatre of Varieties Ltd.* [1922] 2 K.B. 433.

[13] *Oram* v. *Hutt* [1914] 1 Ch. 98; *Re National Union of Seamen* [1929] 1 Ch. 216.

Political activities

Trade unions may apply funds to specified political objects, national or local,[1] provided they have obtained the approval of the specified political objects as objects of the union at a ballot vote of members held under special rules approved by the Registrar,[2] have adopted rules providing for the setting up of a separate 'political fund'[3] and make payments only out of the political fund. A member need not contribute to his union's political fund, but may not be excluded from any union benefits nor placed under any disability for that reason.[4] A member not wishing to contribute may 'contract out' by giving notice in a statutory form.[5] A member aggrieved by breach of any of the political fund rules may complain to the Registrar who may make an order for remedying the breach, which is conclusive and not appealable.[6]

Nominations by members of trade unions

The Secretary of State may make provision by regulations (a) for enabling members of trade unions not under 16 to nominate a person or persons to become entitled, at the death of the nominator, to the whole or part of the moneys payable on his death out of any funds of the union, and (b) for enabling such moneys to an amount not exceeding £500 (which sum may be increased) to be paid or distributed on his death without confirmation, probate or letters of administration. Nominations made under superseded enactments continue to be valid.[7]

Termination of membership

A member is entitled to terminate his membership of a union.[8]

---

[1] Trade Union Act, 1913, S. 3(3), overruling *A.S.R.S.* v. *Osborne* [1910] A.C. 87 and *Wilson* v. *Scottish Typographical Assocn.*, 1912 S.C. 534. The definition of trade union is modified by 1974 Act, S. 8.

[2] 1913 Act, S. 4(1).

[3] Ibid., S. 3(1).

[4] Ibid., S. 3(1); *Birch* v. *N.U.R.* [1950] Ch. 602.

[5] Ibid., Ss. 5, 6. From 1927 to 1946, under the Trade Union and Trade Disputes Act, 1927 (repealed 1946), a member had to 'contract-in'.

[6] 1913 Act, S. 3(2); *Forster* v. *National Shop Assistants* [1927] 1 Ch. 539.

[7] Trade Unions and Labour Relations Act, 1974, Sch. 1, para. 31. cf. *Symington* v. *Galashiels Co-op Socy.* (1894) 21 R. 371; *Morton* v. *French*, 1908 S.C. 171.

[8] 1974 Act, S. 7.

Contracts

A union's contracts, including those with its own members, so long as not objectionable on any other ground, are valid and legally enforceable.[1]

Delicts

A trade union can recover damages for any kind of wrong done to it as an entity.[2]

A union is not now wholly protected, as it formerly was,[3] from being sued for delict but is given protection in particular circumstances.

Immunity from actions for delict

No action for delict lies in respect of any act alleged to have been done by or on behalf of a trade union which is not a special register body[4] or an unincorporated employers' association, or alleged to have been done in connection with the regulation of relations between employers or employers' associations and workers or trade unions by or on behalf of a trade union which is a special register body[4] or by or on behalf of an employers' association which is a body corporate, or alleged to be threatened or intended to be done as above, against the union or association in its own name, or the trustees of either, or any members or officials on behalf of themselves and all other members. But this does not affect liability, not arising from trade dispute, for negligence, nuisance or breach of duty resulting in personal injury, or breach of duty in connection with ownership, possession, control or use of property.[5]

Collective bargaining

The main functions of a trade union are to bargain collectively on behalf of its members with employers or employers' associations about the terms and conditions of employment of the members or groups of them. At common law such collective bargains are not enforceable as terms of the contracts of individual em-

---

[1] *Swaine* v. *Wilson* (1890) 24 Q.B.D. 252; *Gozney* v. *Bristol Trade Society* [1909] 1 K.B. 901; *Osborne* v. *A.S.R.S.* [1911] 1 Ch. 540. Restrictions on the direct enforceability of certain contracts with members under the 1871 Act were repealed by the 1971 Act.

[2] *N.U.G.M.W.* v. *Gillian* [1946] K.B. 81; *Willis* v. *London Compositors* [1947] 1 All E.R. 191.

[3] Trade Disputes Act, 1906, S. 3.

[4] Defined, 1974 Act, S. 30.

[5] 1974 Act, S. 14.

ployees,[1] unless imported into such contracts by reference, or by custom of trade.[2]

Collective agreements

Any collective agreement made after 31st July 1974 is conclusively presumed not to have been intended to be legally enforceable unless it is in writing and contains a provision stating that the parties intend it to be a legally enforceable contract. It may be in part not enforceable and in part enforceable.

Terms of a collective agreement which restrict the right of workers to strike or take industrial action do not form part of a contract between worker and employer unless it is in writing, contains a provision expressly stating that those terms may be incorporated in such a contract, is reasonably accessible to the worker, is one where each trade union a party to it is an independent one, and unless the contract with that worker expressly or impliedly incorporates these terms in the contract.[3]

Code of Labour Relations Practice

It is the duty of the Secretary of State to maintain a Code of Labour Relations Practice, containing such practical guidance as would be helpful for promoting good industrial relations.[4] Failure on the part of any person to observe any provision of a code of practice then in force shall not of itself render him liable to any proceedings, but in any proceedings before an industrial tribunal under the 1974 Act, any such code is admissible in evidence, and any provision of such a code which appears to the tribunal to be relevant to any question arising in the proceedings shall be taken into account by the Court or tribunal in determining that question.[5]

Trade disputes

A trade dispute[6] is a dispute between employers and workers or workers and workers connected with one or more of (a) terms and conditions of employment, (b) engagement, non-engagement, termination or suspension of employment or duties thereof, (c) allocation of work, (d) matters of discipline, (e) membership

---

[1] *Hulland* v. *Saunders* [1945] K.B. 78; *Ford Motor Co. A.U. Engineers* [1969] 2 Q.B. 393.

[2] *Devonald* v. *Rosser* [1906] 2 K.B. 728.

[3] 1974 Act, S. 18.

[4] 1971 Act, S. 2–4. The Code is re-enacted in the 1974 Act, Sch. 1, Part I, paras. 1–3.

[5] Ibid., S. 4; cf. The Highway Code under Road Traffic Act, 1972, S.37.

[6] 1974 Act, S. 29. 'Employment' and 'worker' are widely defined in the section. The definition extends also to the Conspiracy and Protection of Property Act 1875.

or non-membership of a trade union, (f) facilities for trade union officials, and (g) machinery for negotiation or consultation, including recognition. It includes disputes between a minister of the Crown and any workers though he is not their employer, in certain cases, and disputes to which a trade union or employers' association is a party.

Strikes and lockouts

In industrial relations pressure by one side on the other may take the form of a threat of, or an actual, strike or lockout. A strike is a concerted stoppage of work by a group of workers, in contemplation or furtherance of a trade dispute, whether they are parties to the dispute or not, whether (in the case of all or any of those workers) the stoppage is or is not in breach of their terms and conditions of employment, and whether it is carried out during, or on the termination of, their employment. A lockout is action which, in contemplation or furtherance of an industrial dispute, is taken by one or more employers, whether parties to the dispute or not, and which consists in the exclusion of workers from one or more factories, offices or other places of employment or of the suspension of work in one or more such places or of the collective, simultaneous or otherwise connected termination or suspension of employment of a group of workers.

A strike is at common law a breach of each employee's contract of employment, unless all employees concerned have given due notice of termination of employment.[1] A strike not called by a union or without such due notice is commonly termed an 'unofficial strike'; a strike called by a union and with due notice given is an official strike. A strike of either kind is not illegal, nor criminal.[2]

No legal compulsion to work

No court may by order of specific implement or interdict compel an employee to do any work or attend at any place for the doing of any work.[3]

---

[1] *Rookes* v. *Barnard* [1964] A.C. 1129. In *Morgan* v. *Fry* [1968] 2 Q.B. 710 it was suggested that a strike after notice merely suspended the contract; but there is no unilateral right of suspension.

[2] Criminality attaches to breach of the Conspiracy and Protection of Property Act, 1875, S. 5.

[3] 1974 Act, S. 16.

Liability of unions for harm done while pursuing objectives

A union which calls a strike may be liable at common law for the delict of inducing breach of contract, either directly by procuring parties to the contract not to implement it, or indirectly by inducing others to act so that a party to the contract is driven into the position of breaking his contract.[1] The latter arises only where actionably wrongful means are employed. It may even be wrongful to interfere with performance of a contract without causing actual breach.[2] Or a union may be liable for the delict of intimidation of the employer, or of an employee, or of other persons (such as the employer) to the harm of the pursuer (such) as the employee).[3] What is threatened must be actionable. Or a union may be liable for the delict of conspiracy to injure, if the predominant purpose of a combination is to do unjustifiable harm rather than to promote the interests of members, or if unlawful means are used.[4]

Restrictions on legal liability

An act done by a person in contemplation or furtherance of a trade dispute is not actionable as a delict in the ground only (a) that it induces another person to break a contract of employment, or (b) that it consists in his threatening that a contract of employment (whether he is a party to it or not) will be broken or that he will induce another person to break a contract of employment to which that other person is a party.[5] An act done by a person in contemplation or furtherance of a trade dispute is not actionable as delict on the ground only that it is an interference with the trade, business or employment of another person or with the right of another person to dispose of his capital or his labour as he wills.[6] An act which by reason of these provisions is not actionable, and a breach of contract in contemplation or furtherance of a trade dispute are not to be regarded as the doing of an unlawful act or as the use of unlawful means for the purpose of establishing delictual liability.[7] An agreement or combination by two or more persons to do or procure the doing of any act in contemplation or furtherance of a trade dispute is not actionable

---

[1] *D. C. Thomson* v. *Deakin* [1952] Ch. 646; *Stratford* v. *Lindley* [1965] A.C. 269.
[2] *Torquay Hotels* v. *Cousins* [1969] 2 Ch. 106.
[3] *Rookes* v. *Barnard* [1964] A.C. 1129.
[4] *Crofter Co.* v. *Veitch*, 1942 S.C. (H.L.) 1.
[5] 1974 Act, S. 13(1). cf. Trade Disputes Act, 1906, S. 3.
[6] 1974 Act, S. 13(2).
[7] 1974 Act, S. 13(3).

as delict if the act, done without any such agreement or combination, would not be actionable as delict.[1]

Criminal actings in relation to industrial disputes

Under the Conspiracy and Protection of Property Act, 1875, S. 4 it is an offence wilfully and maliciously to break a contract of service or hiring, knowing and having reasonable cause to believe that the consequence will be to endanger human life or cause serious bodily injury or expose valuable property to destruction or serious injury. By the same Act, S. 7, it is illegal to use violence to or intimidate[2] a person to compel him to do or abstain from doing what he is entitled to do, persistently follow him[3] about, hide his tools, clothes or other property,[4] watch or beset his house or follow him in a disorderly manner[5] in any street.

Peaceful picketing

It is lawful for one or more persons in contemplation or furtherance of a trade dispute to attend at or near a place where another person works or carries on business, or any other place where another person happens to be, not being a place where he resides, for the purpose only of peacefully obtaining or communicating information, or peacefully persuading any person to work or abstain from working.[6]

Amalgamation and Dissolution

Organizations, if the proposal to do so on the basis of an agreed Instrument of Amalgamation, approved by the registrar, is carried by a simple majority of the votes recorded by the members of each organization concerned, may amalgamate.[7] The organizations must apply to the assistant registrar for registration of the Instrument; after a period for challenge it becomes effective. Alternatively an organization may by special resolution passed by specified majorities transfer its engagements to another which undertakes to fulfil those engagements. Notice of the

---

[1] 1974 Act, S. 13(4).

[2] See *Gibson* v. *Lawson* [1891] 2 Q.B. 545; *Curran* v. *Treleaven, ibid.*

[3] *Smith* v. *Thomasson* (1899) 62 L.T. 68.

[4] *Fowler* v. *Kibble* [1922] 1 Cr. 487.

[5] *R.* v. *McKenzie* (1892) 2 Q.B. 519.

[6] 1974 Act, S. 15. cf. *Lyons* v. *Wilkins* [1899] 1 Ch. 255; *Ward Lock & Co.* v. *Operative Printers* (1906) 22 T.L.R. 327; *Agnew* v. *Monro* (1891) 2 White 611; *Stuart* v. *Clarkson* (1894) 22 R. 5; *Piddington* v. *Bates* [1960] 3 All E.R. 660; *Tynan* v. *Balmer* [1966] 2 All E.R. 133; *Broome* v. *D.P.P.* [1974] 1 All E.R. 314.

[7] Trade Union (Amalgamations) Act, 1964, S. 1, amd. 1971 Act, Sched. 8.

transfer must be registered.[1] An organization may dissolve itself only in accordance with its own rules, by the unanimous consent of its members, or by the court finding that the interests of those to whom the funds belong can no longer be carried into effect under the rules.[2] In such a case the court will order surplus assets to be distributed to the members at the date of dissolution in proportion to their contributions. If there are no surviving members any surplus falls to the Crown as *bona vacantia*.[3]

---

[1] 1964 Act, S. 1, as amended.
[2] *Re Lead Co.'s Workmen's Fund* [1904] 2 Ch. 196.
[3] *Braithwaite* v. *A.G.* [1909] 1 Ch. 510.

CHAPTER 23

PARTNERSHIPS

THE Scottish law of partnerships is based on the Roman *societas* and while the law has been substantially codified by the Partnership Act, 1890, that Act preserves the common law rules except so far as inconsistent with the Act,[1] and makes little change on the common law.

Partnership is the relation which subsists between persons[2] carrying on a business (including every trade, occupation, or profession)[3] in common with a view of profit.[4] Members of a company or other incorporated body are excluded from the definition.[4] Each person must have the legal capacity to enter into the contract of copartnery.[5] The trade or occupation in question must be legal and not contrary to public policy and no rights arise between the parties to partnership for an illegal purpose.[6] In certain cases a partnership with an unqualified person is illegal.[7] By custom the profession of advocate may not be carried on in partnership. Association for purposes other than profit is not partnership but merely voluntary association.[8] Partnership is distinguished from joint adventure, which is a partnership confined to a particular adventure, speculation, course of trade or

---

[1] 1890 Act, S. 46. See generally Stair I, 10, 12; I, 16, 1; Bankt. I, 22, 1; Ersk. III, 3, 18; Hume, *Lect.* II, 171; Bell, *Comm.* II, 499; *Prin.* §350–91; More *Lect.* I, 198; Clark, Bennett Miller, Lindley, and Pollock on *Partnership*.

[2] Including natural and also juristic persons; hence a 'consortium' of engineering companies, each of which is a limited company, may be a partnership; cf. *Stevenson* v. *Cartonnagen-Industrie* [1918] A.C. 239. A body of trustees may be a partner: *Beveridge* v. *B.* (1872) 10 M. (H.L.) 1; *Alexander's Trs.* v. *Thomson* (1885) 22 S.L.R. 828.

[3] 1890 Act, S. 45.

[4] S. 1; cf. Stair, I, 16, 3; *Keith Spicer* v. *Mansell* [1970] 1 All E.R. 462.

[5] cf. *Blackwood* v. *Thorburn* (1868) 7 M. 318.

[6] *Everet* v. *Williams* (1725) Lindley, 130; (1893) 9 L.Q.R. 197 (highwaymen); *Gibson* v. *Stewart* (1840) 1 Robin. 260; *Foster* v. *Driscoll* [1929] 1 K.B. 470; cf. *Gordon* v. *Howden* (1845) 4 Bell 254; *Fraser* v. *Hair* (1848) 10 D. 1402; *Fraser* v. *Hill* (1853) 1 Macq. 392; *Fraser* v. *Bell* (1854) 16 D. 789; *Lindsay* v. *Inland Revenue*, 1933 S.C. 33. By S. 34 a partnership, initially legal, is dissolved by the happening of any event which makes it unlawful for the business of the firm to be carried on, or for the members of the firm to carry it on in partnership. See e.g. *Esposito* v. *Bowden* (1857) 7 E. & B. 763; *Stevenson, supra.*

[7] e.g. Solicitors (Sc.) Act, 1933, Ss. 36–8; Moneylenders Act, 1927, S. 1; Dentists Act, 1957, Ss. 34, 36, 37; *A.B.* v. *C.D.*, 1912, 1 S.L.T. 44.

[8] cf. *Pitreavie Golf Club* v. *Penman*, 1934 S.L.T. 247.

voyage,[1] but the incidents of the relation are similar, and in some
respect indistinguishable.[2]

Size of Partnership

There must be at least two partners,[3] though a single person
trading under a firm name may be a 'firm' for certain provisions
of the Act,[4] and not more than twenty,[5] save for partnerships of
solicitors, accountants, or stockbrokers, or other kinds of partnerships permitted by Department of Trade and Industry regulations.[6] A partnership exceeding, or by the admission of fresh
partners coming to exceed, the permitted size is an illegal association which is debarred from suing, and each member, as a partner,
is responsible for all the firm's debts.[7]

Constitution of partnership

Partnership may be constituted by express contract,[8] oral or
written, or its existence may be inferred from the conduct and
relations of parties.[9] The relationship being contractual questions
may arise of capacity to contract, or of error or fraud affecting
the contract. Its existence is a question of the intention of
the parties as disclosed by the whole circumstances of the case.[10]
Not every agreement involving the sharing of the profits of a
business amounts to partnership,[11] but partnership may be held
to exist in face of the terms of the agreement between the parties,[12]
and a person may be held liable as a partner if he be held to have
assumed that position, despite his contrary view or even dis-

[1] See *infra*.

[2] *Mair* v. *Wood*, 1948 S.C. 83, 86, 90.

[3] The phrase 'sole partner' is meaningless: *Wallace* v. *W's Tr.* (1906) 8 F. 558.

[4] e.g. Ss. 14, 17, 18.

[5] Companies Act, 1948, Ss. 429, 434, amd. Companies Act, 1967, Ss. 119–20; Limited
Partnerships Act, 1907, S. 4 amd. 1967 Act, S. 121.

[6] 1967 Act, S. 120, 121. Regulations have been made in relation to various professions.

[7] *Shaw* v. *Benson* (1883) 11 Q.B.D. 563; *Shaw* v. *Simmons* (1883) 12 Q.B.D. 117;
Greenberg v. *Cooperstein* [1926] 1 Ch. 657.

[8] On which see Chap. 38, *infra*. The alleged contract must be capable of indicating the
partnership terms: *McArthur* v. *Lawson* (1877) 4 R. 1134; *Traill* v. *Dewar* (1881) 8 R.
583.

[9] cf. *Warner* v. *Cuninghame* (1815) 3 Dow 76; *Dundee Ry. Co.* v. *Miller* (1832) 10 S.
269; *Gunn* v. *Ballantyne* (1870) 7 S.L.R. 289; *Aitchison* v. *A.* (1877) 4 R. 899; *Kinnell* v.
Peebles (1890) 17 R. 416.

[10] *Morrison* v. *Service* (1879) 6 R. 1158; cf. *Lawrie* v. *L's Trs.* (1892) 19 R. 675;
Thomson v. *Bell* (1894) 1 S.L.T. 433; *Menzies' Trs.* v. *Black's Trs.*, 1909 S.C. 239; *Scott* v.
Dick, 1909, 2 S.L.T. 118. See also *Clippens Oil Co.* v. *Scott* (1876) 3 R. 651..

[11] *Cox* v. *Hickman* (1860) 8 H.L.C. 268.

[12] *Stewart* v. *Buchanan* (1903) 6 F. 15.

claimer.[1] He may be held to have acted as a partner towards third parties though he might not be so held as regards the other partners.[2] Distinguishable from partnership are cases of service,[3] security for repayment of debt,[4] sale,[5] and carrying on a testator's business.[6] The partners may participate in different ways, some contributing services, others only capital. The same principles apply to all partners, whether active or dormant, known or latent.[7]

Rules for determining existence of partnership

In determining whether partnership does or does not exist regard must be had to the rules laid down in the Act:[8] viz.:

(1) Joint tenancy, tenancy in common, joint property, common property or part ownership does not of itself create a partnership as to anything so held or owned, whether the tenants or owners do or do not share any profits made by the use thereof.

(2) The sharing of gross returns does not of itself create a partnership, whether the persons sharing such returns have or have not a joint or common right or interest in any property from which or from the use of which the returns are derived.[9]

(3) The receipt by a person of a share of the profits of a business is *prima facie* evidence that he is a partner in the business, but the receipt of such a share, or of a payment contingent on or varying with the profits of a business does not of itself make him a partner in the business;[10] and in particular—

[1] *Adam* v. *Newbigging* (1888) 13 App. Cas. 308; *McCosh* v. *Brown's Tr.* (1899) 1 F. (H.L.) 86; *Charlton* v. *Highet*, 1923 S.L.T. 493.

[2] Bell, *Comm.* II, 511; *Clippens Oil Co.* v. *Scott* (1876) 3 R. 651; *Walker* v. *Hirsch* (1884) 27 Ch. D. 460.

[3] *Geddes* v. *Wallace* (1820) 6 Pat. 643; *Kinnell* v. *Peebles* (1890) 17 R. 416; *Walker* v. *Reith* (1906) 8 F. 381. See also *Gunn* v. *Ballantyne* (1870) 7 S.L.R. 289; *Allison* v. *A's Trs.* (1904) 6 F. 496.

[4] *Eaglesham & Co.* v. *Grant* (1875) 2 R. 960; *Stott* v. *Fender* (1878) 5 R. 1104; cf. *Miller* v. *Downie* (1876) 3 R. 548.

[5] *Moore* v. *Dempster* (1879) 6 R. 930.

[6] *Paterson's Trs.* v. *Learmont & Co.* (1870) 8 M. 500; *Lawrie* v. *L's Trs.* (1892) 19 R. 675.

[7] *Cameron* v. *Young* (1871) 9 M. 786.

[8] 1890 Act, S. 2, substantially re-enacting Law of Partnership Act, 1865 (Bovill's Act), and stated to make no change in the law: *Davis* v. *D.* [1894] 1 Ch. 393.

[9] The sharing of both profits and losses is indicative of partnership.

[10] *Laing Bros. & Co.'s Tr.* v. *Low* (1896) 23 R. 1105; *Allison* v. *A's Trs.* (1904) 6 F. 496; *Eadie* v. *Crawford*, 1912, 2 S.L.T. 360. But a right to a share in profits and also a right to receive or dispose of partnership assets implies partnership: *McCosh* v. *Brown's Tr.* (1899) 1 F. (H.L.) 86; *Charlton* v. *Highet*, 1923 S.L.T. 493. A share in profits and also a power to control the business may imply partnership: *Stewart* v. *Buchanan* (1903) 6 F. 15. See also *Bolton* v. *Mansfield* (1787) 3 Pat. 70.

(a) the receipt by a person of a debt or other liquidated amount by instalments or otherwise out of the accruing profits of a business does not of itself make him a partner in the business or liable as such:[1]

(b) a contract for the remuneration of a servant or agent of a person engaged in a business by a share of the profits of the business does not of itself make the servant or agent a partner in the business or liable as such:[2]

(c) a person being the widow or child of a deceased partner, and receiving by way of annuity a portion of the profits made in the business in which the deceased person was a partner, is not by reason only of such receipt a partner in the business or liable as such:[3]

(d) the advance of money by way of loan to a person engaged or about to engage in any business on a contract with that person that the lender shall receive a rate of interest varying with the profits, or shall receive a share of the profits arising from carrying on the business, does not of itself make the lender a partner with the person or persons carrying on the business or liable as such.[4] Provided that the contract is in writing, and signed by or on behalf of all the parties thereto:

(e) a person receiving by way of annuity or otherwise a portion of the profits of a business in consideration of the sale by him of the goodwill of the business is not by reason only of such receipt a partner in the business or liable as such.[5]

If a debtor who has borrowed money on such a contract as is mentioned in S. 2, or a buyer of goodwill on the terms of paying a share of profits in the business, is adjudicated bankrupt, enters into an agreement to pay his creditors less than the full sum due, or dies insolvent, the lender or seller is entitled to recover nothing in

---

[1] cf. *McKinlay* v. *Gillon* (1831) 5 W. & Sh. 468; *Cox* v. *Hickman* (1860) 8 H.L.C. 268; *Stott* v. *Fender* (1878) 5 R. 1104; *Gosling* v. *Gaskell* [1897] A.C. 575.

[2] *Kinnell* v. *Peebles* (1890) 7 R. 416; *Lawrie* v. *L's Trs.* (1892) 19 R. 675; *Gatherer* (1893) 1 S.L.T. 401; *Walker* v. *Reith* (1906) 8 F. 381; *Clark* v. *Jamieson*, 1909 S.C. 132; *Sharpe* v. *Carswell*, 1910 S.C. 391; *A.B.* v. *C.D.*, 1912, 1 S.L.T. 44.

[3] cf. *Paterson's Tr.* v. *Learmont* (1870) 8 M. 500; *Thomson* v. *T.*, 1962 S.C. (H.L.) 28.

[4] cf. *Pooley* v. *Driver* (1876) 5 Ch. D. 458; *Re Howard* (1877) 6 Ch.D. 303; *Re Megevand* (1878) 7 Ch.D. 511; *Thomson* v. *Bell* (1894) 1 S.L.T. 433; *Laing Bros. & Co.'s Tr.* v. *Low* (1896) 23 R. 1105; *McCosh* v. *Brown & Co.'s Tr.* (1899) 1 F. (H.L.) 86; *Stewart* v. *Buchanan* (1903) 6 F. 15.

[5] cf. *Alexander* v. *Clark* (1862) 24 D. 323.

respect of his loan or share of profits respectively, until the claims of the other creditors have been satisfied.[1]

The firm and its quasi-personality

Persons who have entered into partnership form collectively a firm or company,[2] which in Scotland is a legal person distinct from the partners of whom it is composed.[3] The firm is in Scotland not merely a collective name for the individual partners. From this certain consequences follow. It may sue and be sued, and partners may sue the firm and conversely.[4] It may be debtor or creditor to any partner. It may commit actionable wrong, even a wrong requiring proof of malice,[5] or suffer wrong and sue therefor.[6] A partner cannot sue alone for the enforcement of the firm's obligations, but may be sued, but only if the debt has first been constituted against the firm.[7] In relation to third parties, the firm is the primary debtor, the partners being deemed cautioners for the firm. A firm can be sequestrated without individual partners being sequestrated, and conversely. On the sequestration of a firm and the partners, the creditors rank in the first place on the firms estate and, if not paid in full, for the balance on the estates of the partners. Creditors of a partner can arrest his share in the hands of the firm.

Though the firm is a legal person it is not a full corporation or legal entity in itself.[8] The fact that it is not a corporation is shown by the facts that it is created by contract, not by charter, statute, or registration, that it can be dissolved by consent, that the firm cannot in the firm name hold heritable property, the title to which must be taken in the name of partners as trustees for the firm,[9]

[1] S. 3. See *ex p. Mills* (1873) L.R. 8 Ch. 569; *Re Hildesheim* [1893] 2 Q.B. 357; *Re Mason* [1899] 1 Q.B. 810 cf. Married Women's Property (Sc.) Act, 1881, S. 1(4), postponing claim of one spouse on another in bankruptcy where loan made for business.

[2] 'Company' as a term equivalent to firm or partnership must be distinguished from 'company' signifying an incorporated company, usually with limited liability, on which see Ch. 26, *infra*.

[3] 1890 Act, S. 4(2); Bell, *Comm.* II, 507; *Prin.* §357; *Mair* v. *Wood*, 1948 S.C. 83, 86.

[4] e.g. *Malcolm* v. *West Lothian Ry. Co.* (1835) 13 S. 887; *Glebe Sugar Co.* v. *Lusk* (1866) 2 S.L.R. 9.

[5] *Gordon* v. *British and Foreign Metaline Co.* (1886) 14 R. 75.

[6] *May* v. *Matthews* (1833) 11 S. 305.

[7] *Johnston* v. *Duncan* (1823) 2 S. 532; *Geddes* v. *Hopkirk* (1828) 5 S. 697; *Munnoch* v. *Dewar* (1831) 9 S. 487; *Muir* v. *Collett* (1862) 24 D. 1119; *Neilson* v. *Wilson* (1890) 17 R. 608, 612.

[8] 'It is a quasi corporation possessing many, but not all the privileges which law confers upon a duly constituted corporation': *Forsyth* v. *Hare* (1834) 13 S. 42, 47.

[9] Bell, *Prin.* §357; *Kelly's Tr.* v. *Moncreiff's Tr.*, 1920 S.C. 461; but a firm is capable of holding a lease: *Dennistoun, Macnayr & Co.* v. *McFarlane*, 16 Feb. 1808, F.C.; *Cooke's Circus Co.* v. *Welding* (1894) 21 R. 339.

that the firm comes to an end by the death or bankruptcy of any partner of the firm,[1] and that an individual partner may be charged on a decree or diligence directed against the firm, being entitled on payment to relief *pro rata* from the firm and its other members.[2] It is an open question whether a firm can employ one of its partners under a contract of service.[3] The firm has no claim if it loses profits by reason of injuries caused to a partner by a third party.[4]

The firm name

The name under which parties carry on business is the firm name.[5] The firm name may be a social name comprising the names of individual partners, in which case the firm may sue and be sued in that name even though the names are not those of the existing partners,[6] or a descriptive name, in which case the firm name is not enough without the addition of the names of the partners, or at least three of them.[7] A firm may use any name it pleases, but may not take such a name, or use partners' names, in such a way as to deceive the public.[8] Where one partner purchased the firm's business and goodwill and subsequently his former partner began to trade in the same business in the same town in partnership with a third party of the same name as the first partner, he was held entitled to interdict against their trading under that name.[9] A firm name must normally be registered under the Registration of Business Names Act, 1916,[10] and the true names of the partners disclosed in all trade catalogues, trade

[1] 1890 Act, S. 33.

[2] 1890 Act, S. 4(2); *Thomson* v. *Liddell*, 24 July 1812, F.C.; *Wallace* v. *Plock & Logan* (1841) 3 D. 1047; *Ewing* v. *McClelland* (1860) 22 D. 1347.

[3] *Fife C.C.* v. *Minister of Nat. Insurance*, 1947 S.C. 629; but see *Allison* v. *A's Trs.* (1904) 6 F. 496; *Ellis* v. *E.* [1905] 1 K.B. 324.

[4] *Gibson* v. *Glasgow Corpn.*, 1963 S.L.T. (Notes) 16.   [5] 1890 Act, S. 4(1).

[6] *Forsyth* v. *Hare* (1834) 13 S. 42; *Wallace* v. *Plock & Logan* (1841) 3 D. 1047; *Paton* v. *Neill, Edgar & Co.* (1873) 10 S.L.R. 461; *Brims & Mackay* v. *Pattullo*, 1907 S.C. 1106.

[7] *Culcreugh Cotton Co.* v. *Mathie* (1822) 2 S. 47; *Commercial Bank* v. *Pollock* (1828) 3 W. & Sh. 365; *Kerr* v. *Clyde Shipping Co.* (1839) 1 D. 901; *London Shipping Co.* v. *McCorkle* (1841) 3 D. 1045; *McMillan* v. *McCulloch* (1842) 4 D. 492; *Nat. Exchange Co.* v. *Drew* (1848) 11 D. 179; *Antermony Coal Co.* v. *Wingate* (1866) 4 M. 1017. In the Sheriff Court a firm may sue by its descriptive name alone: Sheriff Courts (Sc.) Act, 1907 (amd. 1913) R. 11. See also *Gordon* v. *British and Foreign Metaline Co.* (1886) 14 R. 75; *City and Suburban Dairies* v. *Mackenna*, 1918 J.C. 105.

[8] *Croft* v. *Day* (1843) 7 Beav. 84; *Levy* v. *Walker* (1879) 10 Ch.D. 436; *Massam* v. *Thorley's Cattle Food Co.* (1880) 14 Ch. D. 748; *Tussaud* v. *T.* (1890) 44 Ch. D. 678; *North Cheshire and Manchester Brewery Co.* v. *Manchester Brewery Co.* [1899] A.C. 83; *Cowan* v. *Millar* (1895) 22 R. 833 (name attached to premises).

[9] *Smith* v. *McBride and Smith* (1888) 16 R. 36.

[10] For exceptions see 1916 Act, S. 1; Ch. 14, *supra.*

circulars, showcards and business letters on or in which the business name appears.[1] The Registrar of Business Names may refuse to register any name which in his opinion is undesirable.[2]

Actions by and against firm

As the firm has a separate legal personality it alone has a title to sue for the enforcement of obligations to it.[3] A firm in default in registering its name under the Registration of Business Names Act, 1916 cannot enforce rights under contract by action or otherwise.[4] An individual partner cannot sue, though all the partners can, if it clearly appears that they are suing for a debt to the firm.[5] Similarly an action against the firm should be directed against it, not against any individual partner, and even though the firm has been dissolved.[6] A partner can be sued only if the debt has first been constituted against the firm, unless the firm has previously been dissolved.[7]

Diligence against firm

Diligence following on a decree against the firm may proceed against the firm,[8] but also against any individual partner,[9] whether or not he is named in the decree, he being entitled on payment to *pro rata* relief against his partners.[10] But a person not a partner cannot be charged to pay under a decree against the firm, even though it be alleged that he is truly liable, having held himself out to be a partner.[11] A person wrongly charged may bring a suspension of the diligence. Poinding of the ground is competent to attach the property of one partner in buildings owned by the firm when the partners had the sole control of and interest in

---

[1] 1916 Act, S. 18.

[2] 1916 Act, S. 14, amd. Companies Act, 1947, S. 116.

[3] e.g. *Brims & Mackay* v. *Pattullo*, 1907 S.C. 1106 (social name); *Antermony Coal Co.* v. *Wingate* (1866) 4 M. 1017 (descriptive name).

[4] *Anderson* v. *Livingstone*, 1932 S.N. 82; see also *J. J. & P. McLachlan*, 1929 S.C. 357; *J. & F. Anderson* v. *Balnagown Estates Co.*, 1939 S.C. 168; *Kinnear* v. *Paper Shavings Co.*, 1967 S.L.T. (Sh. Ct.) 75.

[5] *Plotzker* v. *Lucas*, 1907 S.C. 315.

[6] *McNaught* v. *Milligan* (1885) 13 R. 366; *Brims* v. *Mackay, supra.*

[7] *Johnston* v. *Duncan* (1823) 2 S. 532; *Geddes* v. *Hopkirk* (1828) 5 S. 697; *Munnoch* v. *Dewar*, 23 Feb. 1831, F.C.; *Muir* v. *Collett* (1862) 24 D. 1119; *Neilson* v. *Wilson* (1890) 17 R. 608.

[8] *Rosslund Cycle Co.* v. *McCreadie*, 1907 S.C. 1208.

[9] *Brember* v. *Rutherford* (1901) 4 F. 62.

[10] *Ewing* v. *McClelland* (1860) 22 D. 1347; 1890 Act, S. 4(2).

[11] *Brember* v. *Rutherford* (1901) 4 F. 62.

the firm for which, as trustees, they held the title to the buildings.[1] A creditor of one partner cannot attach the partner's share in the firm by poinding to the prejudice of a creditor of the firm,[2] nor arrest it in the hands of the firm, it not being an ascertained debt,[3] nor arrest a firm debt for a debt of one of the partners.[4]

RELATION OF PARTNERS TO THIRD PARTIES

Contracts with third parties

A firm may bind itself contractually by the act of a partner as agent for the firm, or of a servant or agent as such agent.[5] The authority of any partner, acting as agent for the firm, to bind the firm contractually may, as between the partners themselves, be regulated by the contract of copartnery. As regards third parties his mandate is implied by law.

Implied mandate

Every partner is held to be *praepositus negotiis societatis*, and is an agent of the firm and his other partners for the purpose of the partnership business, and the acts of every partner who does any act for carrying on in the usual way business of the kind carried on by the firm bind the firm and his partners, unless that partner has in fact no authority to act for the firm in the particular matter, and the person with whom he is dealing either knows that he has no authority, or does not know or believe him to be a partner.[6] As regards third parties every partner is an unlimited agent of every other in every matter relating to their business, or which he represents as firm business and which is not, in its nature, beyond the scope of the partnership.[7] Hence he normally has implied authority to buy and sell goods, engage staff, receive payment and grant discharges

---

[1] *Kelly's Tr.* v. *Moncreiff's Tr.*, 1920 S.C. 461.

[2] *Dawson* v. *Cullen* (1825) 4 S. 39; *Fleming* v. *Twaddle* (1828) 7 S. 92.

[3] *Parnell* v. *Walter* (1889) 16 R. 917, 925.

[4] *Corrie* v. *Calder's Crs.* (1741) Mor. 14596.

[5] e.g. a salaried manager: the authority of such a person depends on the principles of agency.

[6] 1890 Act, S. 5; Stair I, 16, 4; Ersk. III, 3, 20; Bell, *Prin.* §354; *Nisbet's Trs.* v. *Morrison's Trs.* (1829) 7 S. 307; *Cooke's Circus Buildings Co.* v. *Welding* (1894) 21 R. 339; *Fortune* v. *Young*, 1918 S.C. 1; *Mercantile Credit Co.* v. *Garrod* [1962] 3 All E.R. 1103; *Mann* v. *D'Arcy* [1968] 2 All E.R. 172.

[7] *Baird's Case* (1870) L.R. 5 Ch. 725, 733.

therefor,[1] borrow money[2] and undertake financial transactions,[3] and possibly to litigate for recovery of debts due to the firm even if a copartner disclaims.[4] A partner in a firm of solicitors has implied authority to grant an obligation to clear a title and exhibit clear searches.[5] A document written and signed by a partner in the firm's name is holograph of the firm.[6] When all the partners of a firm grant a bill, the presumption is that it is for firm purposes, but the contrary may be proved.[7] The extent of a partner's implied authority to act as an agent for the firm depends on the nature of the firm business.[8] If the obligation undertaken is in exceptional terms, or the circumstances unusual or suspicious, there may be an onus on the other party to ascertain if the partner undertaking truly had authority to grant the obligation in question.[9] An obligation undertaken in the firm name which is beyond the real or ostensible authority of the partner undertaking and is therefore not binding on the firm is still binding on that partner as an individual.[10] The firm is not bound by an undertaking granted, even in the firm name, by a partner if it is known to be granted in his private interest,[11] or granted outwith the ordinary course of the firm's business,[12] or known to be granted without authority.[13]

Partners bound by acts on behalf of firm

A firm and its partners are bound by an act or instrument relating to the business of the firm and done or executed in the firm name, or in any other manner showing an intention to bind the firm, by any person thereto authorized, whether a partner or

---

[1] *Nicoll* v. *Reid* (1878) 6 R. 216; *Powell* v. *Brodhurst* [1901] 2 Ch. 160.

[2] *Bank of Australasia* v. *Breillat* (1847) 6 Moo. P.C. 152, 194; *Cumming* v. *Hay & Stephen* (1879) 17 S.L.R. 207; *Bryan* v. *Butters Bros.* (1892) 19 R. 490.

[3] *Williamson* v. *Johnson* (1823) 1 B. & C. 146; *Garland* v. *Jacomb* (1873) L.R. 8 Ex. 216: including power to agree to a composition arrangement with a debtor to the firm: *Mains & McGlashan* v. *Black* (1895) 22 R. 329; as to cautionary obligation see *Fortune* v. *Young*, 1918 S.C. 1, 6.

[4] *Kinnes* v. *Adam* (1882) 9 R. 698, 700.   [5] *Walker* v. *Smith* (1906) 8 F. 619, 624.

[6] *Nisbet* v. *Neil's Trs.* (1869) 7 M. 1097.

[7] *Rosslund Cycle Co.* v. *McCreadie*, 1907 S.C. 1208; see also *Paterson Bros.* v. *Gladstone* (1891) 18 R. 403.

[8] See *Bryan* v. *Butters* (1892) 19 R. 490; *Cooke's Circus Buildings Co.* v. *Welding* (1894) 21 R. 339; *Mains & McGlashan* v. *Black* (1895) 22 R. 329; *Ciceri* v. *Hunter* (1904) 12 S.L.T. 293.

[9] *Paterson Bros.* v. *Gladstone* (1891) 18 R. 403.

[10] *Fortune* v. *Young*, 1918 S.C. 1.

[11] *Crum* v. *McLean* (1858) 20 D. 751; *Walker* v. *Smith* (1906) 8 F. 619.

[12] Ersk. III, 3, 20; *Paterson Bros.*, *supra*; *Gilmour* v. *Nunn's Trs.* (1899) 7 S.L.T. 292.

[13] *Paterson Bros.*, *supra*.

not,[1] without prejudice to the general rules relating to the execution of deeds or negotiable instruments.[2] If in fact the person was so acting, the firm is bound, though its existence was not disclosed and the other party was unaware that he was dealing with a firm.[3] But the firm is not bound by an act by a partner not in the way of the firm's business.[4]

Partner using firm credit for private purposes

Where a partner pledges the credit of the firm for a purpose apparently not connected with the firm's ordinary course of business, the firm is not bound, unless the partner is in fact specially authorized by the other partners; but this does not affect any personal liability of an individual partner.[5] Where a partner not authorized to sign the firm name adhibited the firm name to bills which he discounted with a moneylender and applied the proceeds to his own use, it was held that the partners were not liable as they were ignorant of the transaction and it was not in the course of the firm's business or for its behoof.[6]

Restriction on power of one to bind firm

If partners have agreed that any restriction be placed on the power of one or more to bind the firm no act in contravention of this binds the firm with respect to persons having notice of the agreement.[7] But such an agreement is ineffective against third parties ignorant of it.[8]

Liability of firm and partners

The liability of a firm on its obligations, contractual and delictual, is unlimited and in no respect limited to the capital

---

[1] cf. *Beveridge* v. *B's Trs.* (1872) 10 M. (H.L.) 1.

[2] 1890 Act, S. 6; *Turnbull* v. *McKie* (1822) 1 S. 353; *Edmond* v. *Robertson* (1867) 5 S.L.R. 30; *Bryan* v. *Butters Bros. & Co.* (1892) 19 R. 490. As to execution see *Mellis* v. *Royal Bank*, 22 June 1815, F.C.; *Blair Iron Co.* v. *Alison* (1855) 18 D. (H.L.) 49; *Nisbet* v. *Neil's Tr.* (1869) 7 M. 1097.

[3] *Beckham* v. *Drake* (1843) 11 M. & W. 315; cf. *Watson* v. *Smith* (1806) Hume 756.

[4] *McNair* v. *Gray, Hunter & Speirs* (1803) Hume 753; *Miller* v. *Douglas*, 22 Jan. 1811, F.C.; *Kennedy*, 22 Dec. 1814, F.C.; *Jardine* v. *McFarlane* (1828) 6 S. 564; *McLeod* v. *Tosh* (1836) 14 S. 1058; *Finlayson* v. *Braidbar Quarry Co.* (1864) 2 M. 1297; *Paterson Bros.* v. *Gladstone* (1891) 18 R. 403.

[5] 1890 Act, S. 7; cf. *McNair* v. *Gray, Hunter & Speirs* (1803) Hume 753; *Kennedy*, 22 Dec. 1814, F.C.

[6] *Paterson Bros.* v. *Gladstone* (1891) 18 R. 403.

[7] 1890 Act, S. 8.

[8] *Cox* v. *Hickman* (1860) 8 H.L. Cas. 268, 304; cf. *Paterson Bros.* v. *Gladstone* (1891) 18 R. 403, 404-5.

employed in the firm business. The liability of the partners is also unlimited,[1] though secondary to the liability of the firm.

Liability of partners

Every partner is jointly and severally liable for all debts and obligations of the firm, incurred while he is a partner, and after his death his estate remains severally liable.[2] But partners are liable only subsidiarily to the liability of the firm, and are in substance guarantors or cautioners for the firm's obligations, each being entitled on payment to *pro rata* relief from the others.[3] The firm's liability must be constituted first.[4] A latent partner is liable, even though the third party did not know of his existence.[5] A retired partner is still liable for all debts incurred while he was a partner. Any arrangement between him and his partners is ineffectual against a creditor, unless the creditor is a party to the arrangement.[6] This may be implied by a subsequent course of trading but the court is unwilling to infer it, and will not do so merely from the creditor's acceptance of interest or part-payment from the new firm, or from his ranking in their bankruptcy.[7] A retired partner who has not given adequate notice of retiral may be liable on obligations undertaken after his retiral.[8] Once a firm has been dissolved an action for a firm debt cannot be brought against one partner without being constituted against the firm,[9] unless where the firm and the other partners are outwith the jurisdiction.[10]

Liability of firm for wrongs

A partner who, while acting as such in the ordinary course of the firm's business, or with the authority of his co-partners, by any wrongful act or omission causes loss or injury to a third party, is personally liable, and the firm is also liable to the same

---

[1] All partners except one may have limited liability if the partnership is formed under the Limited Partnership Act, 1907.

[2] 1890 Act, S. 9.

[3] Bell, *Comm.* II, 508; *Prin.* §356; 1890 Act, S. 4(2).

[4] But if one partner admits the firm's liability, decree may pass against him, reserving his rights of relief, without constituting the debt against the firm: *Elliot* v. *Aiken* (1869) 7 M. 894; *sed quaere.*

[5] *Cameron* v. *Young* (1871) 9 M. 786.

[6] 1890 Act, S. 17(3).

[7] *Morton's Trs.* v. *Robertson's J.F.* (1892) 20 R. 72; *Smith* v. *Patrick* (1901) 3 F. (H.L.) 14. Contrast *Goldfarb* v. *Bartlett* [1920] 1 K.B. 639; *Rouse* v. *Bradford Banking Co.* [1894] A.C. 586.

[8] 1890 Act, S. 36; cf. *Scarf* v. *Jardine* (1882) 7 App. Cas. 345.

[9] *McNaught* v. *Milligan* (1885) 13 R. 366.

[10] *Muir* v. *Collett* (1862) 24 D. 1119.

extent.[1] If there are no averments of individual fault by partners the action is against the firm only.[2] The liability of the partners is joint and several.[3] The firm is vicariously liable also for its agents and servants acting within the scope of their authority or course of their employment respectively.[4] But the firm is not vicariously liable for the wrong of one partner, while acting as such and within the scope of his implied mandate, done to another partner; only the wrongdoing partner is liable.[5] Nor, in general, is the firm liable for the fraud of one partner committed outside the ordinary course of the firm's business.[6] One partner who is innocent is entitled to relief against others who have without his knowledge engaged in wrongdoing.[7] It is incompetent to sue a firm for damages for fraud, unless the names of the partners alleged to have committed the fraud are specified, fraud being personal to the individual.[8] A firm may be sued for wrong, even though in the circumstances malice has to be proved.[9]

Misapplication of money or property

The firm is liable to make good the loss where one partner, acting within the scope of his apparent authority, receives the money or property of a third person and misapplies it, and also where a firm in the course of its business receives money or property of a third person, and it is misapplied by one or more of the partners while in the firm's custody.[10] The liability of the partners is joint and several.[11] Thus where a partner had, with the

[1] 1890 Act, S. 10; *National Exchange Co.* v. *Drew* (1855) 2 Macq. 103; *Jardine's Trs.* v. *Drew* (1864) 2 M. 1101; *Trail* v. *Smith's Trs.* (1875) 3 R. 770; *Blyth* v. *Fladgate* [1891] 1 Ch. 337; *Rhodes* v. *Moules* [1895] 1 Ch. 236; *Hamlyn* v. *Houston* [1903] 1 K.B. 81; *New Mining Syndicate* v. *Chalmers,* 1912 S.C. 126; *Meekins* v. *Henson* [1962] 1 All E.R. 899; see also *Tully* v. *Ingram* (1891) 19 R. 65; *Kirkintilloch Co-operative Socy.* v. *Livingstone,* 1972 S.L.T. 154.

[2] *Gordon* v. *British and Foreign Metaline Co.* (1886) 14 R. 75.

[3] 1890 Act, S. 12; cf. *McGee* v. *Anderson* (1895) 22 R. 274.

[4] *Barwick* v. *English Joint Stock Bank* (1867) L.R. 2 Ex. 259; *British Legal Life Assce. Co.* v. *Pearl Life Assce. Co. Ltd.* (1887) 14 R. 818; *Lloyd* v. *Grace Smith & Co.* [1912] A.C. 716.

[5] *Mair* v. *Wood,* 1948 S.C. 83; *Parker* v. *Walker,* 1961 S.L.T. 252.

[6] *Cleather* v. *Twisden* (1884) 28 Ch. D. 340; *Hughes* v. *Twisden* (1886) 34 W.R. 498; *Mara* v. *Browne* [1896] 1 Ch. 199.

[7] *Campbell* v. *C.* (1839) Macl. & R. 387; cf. Law Reform (Misc. Prov.) (Sc.) Act, 1940, S. 3.

[8] *Scott* v. *Napier* (1827) 5 S. 414; *Thomson* v. *Pattison Elder & Co.* (1895) 22 R. 432.

[9] *Gordon* v. *British and Foreign Metaline Co.* (1886) 14 R. 75.

[10] 1890 Act, S. 11; *Dundonald* v. *Masterman* (1869) L.R. 7 Eq. 504; *New Mining and Exploring Syndicate* v. *Chalmers & Hunter,* 1912 S.C. 126.

[11] 1890 Act, S. 12; see e.g. *Devaynes* v. *Noble (Clayton's Case)* (1816) 1 Mer. 529, 572; *Blyth* v. *Fladgate* [1891] 1 Ch. 337.

knowledge of his firm, occupied a fiduciary position towards a company and received promotion money from it, the firm was bound to repay the money.[1]

Improper use of trust property

If a partner who is a trustee improperly employs trust property in the business or on the account of the partnership, no other partner is liable for the trust property to the persons beneficially interested therein; but this rule does not affect any liability incurred by any partner by reason of his having notice of a breach of trust; nor does it prevent trust money being followed and recovered[2] from the firm if still in its possession or under its control.[3]

Liability by holding-out

A person who by words or conduct represents himself, or knowingly suffers himself to be represented, as a partner in a particular firm,[4] is liable as a partner to anyone who has given credit to the firm on the faith of such representation, whether made to him by or with the knowledge of the apparent partner or not.[5] But the continued use of the old firm name after a partner's death, or of the deceased partner's name as part thereof, does not by itself make his estate liable for any partnership debts contracted after his death.[6] The rule of holding out is an application of the principle of personal bar. It applies also to a partner who has retired but not given notice.[7] It does not apply if a man's name is mentioned as a partner without his knowledge, nor even if he misrepresents himself not knowingly but carelessly,[8] nor if the creditor knows the true facts.[9] The representation need not have been made to the creditor directly. A man whose name is mentioned as a partner without his consent may interdict the misuse thereof.[10] Conversely it has been held that payment of a debt due

---

[1] *Scottish Pacific Coast Mining Co.* v. *Falkner, Bell & Co.* (1888) 15 R. 290.

[2] As to following trust property, see Ch. 114, *infra*.

[3] 1890 Act, S. 13; *New Mining Syndicate* v. *Chalmers,* 1912 S.C. 126, 133; as to case where other partners implicated see *Blyth* v. *Fladgate* [1891] 1 Ch. 337.

[4] *Brember* v. *Rutherford* (1901) 4 F. 62.

[5] 1890 Act, S. 14(1); cf. *McNair* v. *Fleming* (1812) 5 Pat. 639; *Moyes* v. *Cook* (1829) 7 S. 793; *Gardner* v. *Anderson* (1862) 24 D. 315; *Stocks* v. *Simpson* (1905) 13 S.L.T. 422.

[6] 1890 Act, S. 14(2); *Morrison* v. *Leamont* (1869) 8 M. 500.

[7] 1890 Act, S. 36.

[8] *Tower Cabinet Co.* v. *Ingram* [1949] 2 K.B. 397.

[9] *Mann* v. *Sinclair* (1879) 6 R. 1078.

[10] *Walker* v. *Ashton* [1902] 2 Ch. 282.

to a firm to a person who has been held out as a partner therein, and in the *bona fide* belief that he is one, is a good payment.[1]

Evidence

An admission or representation made by any partner concerning the partnership affairs, and in the ordinary course of its business, is evidence against the firm.[2] Similarly a letter written and signed by one partner in the firm name is holograph of the firm.[3]

Notice

Notice, i.e. the coming of facts to knowledge, to any partner who habitually acts in the partnership business, of any matter relating to partnership affairs, operates as notice to the firm, except in the case of a fraud on the firm committed by or with the consent of that partner.[4] Hence notice to a sleeping partner is not notice, nor, probably is notice to a man who subsequently becomes a partner notice to the firm.[5]

Liabilities of incoming and outgoing partners

A person admitted as a partner into an existing firm does not thereby become liable to the creditors of the firm for anything done before he became a partner,[6] but a retiring partner does not thereby cease to be liable for partnership debts or obligations incurred before his retirement.[7] A retiring partner may be discharged from any existing liabilities by an agreement to that effect between himself and the members of the firm as newly constituted and the creditors, which may be express or inferred from the course of dealing between the creditors and the firm as newly constituted.[8] A person may be held by his course of dealing with the new firm to have accepted it as his debtor and to

[1] *Hosie* v. *Waddell* (1866) 3 S.L.R. 16.

[2] 1890 Act, S. 15.

[3] *Nisbet* v. *Neil's Tr.* (1869) 7 M. 1097.

[4] 1890 Act, S. 16; Stair III, 1, 10.

[5] cf. *Williamson* v. *Barbour* (1877) 9 Ch. D. 529.

[6] 1890 Act, S. 17(1); *Mercer* v. *Peddie* (1832) 10 S. 405; *Nelmes* v. *Montgomery* (1883) 10 R. 974; cf. *New Mining Syndicate* v. *Chalmers*, 1912 S.C. 126, 135. But see *Miller* v. *Thorburn* (1861) 23 D. 359.

[7] 1890 Act, S. 17(2); *Blacks* v. *Girdwood* (1885) 13 R. 243; *Beveridge* v. *Forbes, Bryson & Carrick* (1897) 5 S.L.T. 115.

[8] 1890 Act, S. 17(3); cf. *Pollock* v. *Murray and Spence* (1863) 2 M. 14; *Smith* v. *Patrick* (1901) 3 F. (H.L.) 14; *Roughead* v. *White*, 1913 S.C. 162.

have discharged the retired partner.[1] Where the business of an existing partnership is transferred to a new one and the business continues on the same basis as before, the presumption is that the new firm assumes liability for all the liabilities which are taken over with the business,[2] but this may be rebutted, as where the new partner contributes substantial fresh capital,[3] or the new firm is carried on on the basis that there shall be no liability for prior debts and no right to collect sums due to the old firm or its partners.[4]

Change in firm revokes continuing cautionary obligation

A continuing guarantee or cautionary obligation given to a firm or to a third party in respect of the transactions of a firm is, in the absence of agreement to the contrary, revoked as to future transactions by any change in the constitution of the firm to which, or of the firm in respect of the transactions of which, the guarantee or obligation was given.[5] A similar principle may apply in respect of any contract which involves an element of *delectus personae*.[6]

Ordinary contracts, as of employment, are not revoked by a change in the constitution of the firm,[7] but contracts involving personal service may be terminated thereby.[8] The conversion of a partnership into a limited company dissolves the firm utterly and releases all employees from their contracts,[9] and terminates contracts involving *delectus personae*.[10]

---

[1] *Ker* v. *McKechnie* (1845) 7 D. 494; *Pearston* v. *Wilson* (1856) 19 D. 197; contrast *Campbell* v. *Cruickshank* (1845) 7 D. 548; *Muir* v. *Dickson* (1860) 22 D. 1070. cf. *Price & Logan* v. *Wise* (1862) 24 D. 491.

[2] *Miller* v. *Thorburn* (1861) 23 D. 359; *McKeand* v. *Laird* (1861) 23 D. 846; *Heddle's Exrx.* v. *Marwick & Hourston's Tr.* (1888) 15 R. 698; *Thomson & Balfour* v. *Boag*, 1936 S.C. 2; *Miller* v. *Mcleod & Parker*, 1974 S.L.T. 99.

[3] *Thomson & Balfour* v. *Boag*, 1936 S.C. 2.

[4] *Stephen's Tr.* v. *Macdougall & Co.'s Tr.* (1889) 16 R. 779; *Tully* v. *Ingram* (1891) 19 R. 65; *Thomson & Balfour*, supra, 10.

[5] 1890 Act, S. 18, replacing Mercantile Law Amdt. (Sc) Act, 1856, S. 7; cf. *Speirs* v. *Royal Bank* (1822) 1 S. 516; *Aytoun* v. *Dundee Bank* (1844) 6 D. 1409; *Alexander* v. *Lowson's Trs.* (1890) 17 R. 571.

[6] cf. *Hoey* v. *McEwan & Auld* (1867) 5 M. 814; *Smith* v. *Patrick* (1901) 3 F. (H.L.) 14.

[7] *Campbell* v. *Baird* (1827) 5 S. 335.

[8] *Hoey*, supra.

[9] *Berlitz School* v. *Duchene* (1903) 6 F. 181; *Garden, Haig-Scott & Wallace* v. *Prudential Assce. Socy.*, 1927 S.L.T. 393.

[10] *Grierson, Oldham & Co.* v. *Forbes, Maxwell & Co.* (1895) 22 R. 812; *Brown* v. *Carron Co.* (1898) 6 S.L.T. 90.

RELATIONS OF PARTNERS *INTER SE*

Relations fixed by contract or Act, but variable

The relations and mutual rights and duties of partners may be defined by their contract of copartnery,[1] but, whether ascertained by agreement or defined by the Act, these may be varied by the consent of all the partners, express or inferred from a course of dealing.[2] Variations assented to bind a partner's assignees or representatives. Partners are not related as debtor and creditor unless and until an accounting after dissolution has shown that one is indebted to another or others; nor are they trustees for each other or for the firm,[3] unless expressly so designated, as when taking title to land, or after dissolution of the partnership.[4] Partners owe each other the duty to take the care and show the diligence in firm business which they habitually take and show in their own affairs,[5] and must act honestly and honourably towards each other.[6]

Partnership property

Partnership property, i.e. property and rights and interests in property brought into the partnership stock or acquired on account of the firm, or for the purposes and in the course of the partnership business, must be held and applied by the partners exclusively for the purpose of the partnership and in accordance with the partnership agreement.[7] The title to and interest in any heritable estate belonging to the partnership devolves according to the general rules of law but in trust for the persons beneficially interested therein in the partnership.[8] If co-owners of heritable estate, not itself partnership property, who are partners as to profits made by the use of that land, purchase other land, it belongs to them, failing contrary agreement, not as partners, but as co-owners as in the case of the first land.[9] Disputes have frequently arisen as to whether certain property is firm property

---

[1] See Ch. 38, *infra*.

[2] 1890 Act, S. 19; see also *Const* v. *Harris* (1824) T. & R. 496; *Coventry* v. *Barclay* (1864) 3 De G. J. & S. 320; *Ex p. Barber* (1870) L.R. 5 Ch. 687.

[3] *Piddocke* v. *Burt* [1894] 1 Ch. 343.

[4] *Gordon* v. *Gonda* [1955] 2 All E.R. 762.

[5] Ersk. III, 3, 21; if one does not the remedy is the dissolution of the partnership: *MacCredie's Trs.* v. *Lamond* (1886) 24 S.L.R. 114.

[6] *Cassels* v. *Stewart* (1881) 8 R. (H.L.) 1.

[7] 1890 Act, S. 20(1); cf. *Pillans Bros.* v. *P.* (1908) 16 S.L.T. 611.

[8] 1890 Act, S. 20(2); *Morrison* v. *Miller* (1818) Hume 720; as to completion of title see *Scott's Trs.*, 1957 S.L.T. (Notes) 45; as to proof see *Adam* v. *A.*, 1962 S.L.T. 332.

[9] 1890 Act, S. 20(3); *Davis* v. *D.* [1894] 1 Ch. 393.

or personal property of a partner.[1] A partner may insist on having firm property entered in the balance sheet at a real value, and not one stated in the copartnery.[2] It is competent to prove by parole evidence that certain heritage is partnership property.[3] Property bought with firm money is deemed to have been bought on account of the firm.[4] Land held as partnership property is to be treated, as between partners, their heirs and representatives, as moveable, not heritable property.[5] A lease may be granted to be held in the firm name,[6] but heritage held feudally is vested in the partners as trustees.[7] Each partner has a *pro indiviso* right in the firm's assets,[8] which is wholly moveable, and may be attached by arrestment in the hands of the firm,[9] but a creditor may not arrest money due to the firm for a partner's debt because the partner has no separate share in the firm assets.[10]

Rights of partners inter se

The interest of partners in the partnership property and their rights and duties in relation to the partnership are regulated by their contract of copartnery or any agreement implied by their conduct, failing which by the rules of the 1890 Act.[11] These are:

(1) All the partners are entitled to share equally in the capital and profits of the business[12] and must contribute equally towards the losses whether of capital or otherwise sustained by the firm.[13]

---

[1] e.g. *Wilson* v. *Laidlaw* (1816) 6 Pat. 222; *Wilson* v. *Threshie* (1825) 4 S. 361; *Cox* v. *Stead* (1834) 7 W. & S. 497; *Mabon* v. *Christie* (1844) 6 D. 619; *McArthurs* v. *McBrair & Johnstone's Tr.* (1844) 6 D. 1174; *Ord.* v. *Barton* (1846) 8 D. 1011; *Miles* v. *Clarke* [1953] 1 All E.R. 779.

[2] *Noble* v. *N.*, 1965 S.L.T. 415.

[3] *Munro* v. *Stein*, 1961 S.C. 362.

[4] 1890 Act, S. 21.

[5] 1890 Act, S. 22; Bell, *Comm.* II, 501; *Murray* v. *M.*, 5 Feb. 1805, F.C.; *Sime* v. *Balfour* (1811) 5 Pat. 525; *Minto* v. *Kirkpatrick* (1833) 11 S. 632; *Irvine* v. *I.* (1851) 13 D. 1367; *Wray* v. *W.* [1905] 2 Ch. 349.

[6] *Denniston, McNayr & Co.* v. *McFarlane*, 16 Feb. 1808, F.C.

[7] Bell, *Prin.* §357. Proof of the trust is limited to writ or oath of the partners: *Laird* v. *Laird & Rutherford* (1884) 12 R. 294. But see *Munro* v. *Stein*, 1961 S.C. 362.

[8] As to the difference between the interest of a partner in a firm and that of a shareholder in a company see *Dove* v. *Young* (1868) 7 M. 304; see also *Arthur* v. *Baird* (1868) 7 M. 308.

[9] Ersk. III, 3, 24.

[10] *Parnell* v. *Walter* (1889) 16 R. 917, 925.

[11] 1890 Act, S. 24; Stair I, 16, 4.

[12] Stair I, 16, 3; Ersk. III, 3, 19; *McWhirter* v. *Guthrie* (1823) 1 S. 319; *Fergusson* v. *Graham's Trs.* (1836) 14 S. 871; *Campbell's Trs.* v. *Thomson* (1831) 5 W. & Sh. 16; *Aberdeen Town & County Bank* v. *Clark* (1859) 22 D. 44; *Aitchison* v. *A.* (1877) 4 R. 899.

[13] *Binney* v. *Mutrie* (1886) 12 App. Cas. 160; *Garner* v. *Murray* [1904] 1 Ch. 57.

(2) The firm must indemnify every partner in respect of payments and personal liabilities incurred by him—

(a) in the ordinary and proper conduct of the business of the firm; or

(b) in or about anything necessarily done for the preservation of the business or property of the firm.[1]

(3) A partner making, for the purpose of the partnership, any normal payment or advance beyond the amount of capital which he has agreed to subscribe, is entitled to interest at 5% p.a. from the date thereof.[2]

(4) A partner is not entitled, before the ascertainment of profits, to interest on the capital subscribed by him.[3]

(5) Every partner may take part in the management of the partnership business.[4]

(6) No partner shall be entitled to remuneration for acting in the partnership business.[5]

(7) No person may be introduced as a partner without the consent of all existing partners.[6]

(8) Any difference arising as to ordinary matters connected with the partnership business may be decided by a majority of the partners,[7] but no change may be made in the nature of the partnership business without the consent of all existing partners.[8]

(9) The partnership books are to be kept at the place of business of the partnership (or the principal place, if there is more than one) and every partner may, when he thinks fit, have access to and inspect and copy any of them.[9]

It is incompetent for one partner of a dissolved company to use summary diligence against a co-partner on a decree acquired from a creditor of the firm.[10]

---

[1] *Stroyan* v. *Milroy*, 1910 S.C. 174.

[2] *Bate* v. *Robbins* (1863) 32 Beav. 73;

[3] *Kerr, Duff & Co.* v. *Cossar* (1902) 10 S.L.T. 27. If there is provision in the copartnery for interest it ceases to be payable when the partnership is dissolved: *Barfield* v. *Loughborough* (1872) 8 Ch. App. 1.

[4] *Dickson* v. *D.* (1823) 2 S. 462; *Fleming* v. *Campbell* (1845) 7 D. 935; contrast *Duff* v. *Corsar* (1902) 10 S.L.T. 27.

[5] *Geddes* v. *Hamilton* (1801) 4 Pat. 657; *McWhirter* v. *Guthrie* (1821) Hume 760; *Pender* v. *Henderson* (1864) 2 M. 1428; *Faulds* v. *Roxburgh* (1867) 5 M. 373; *Lawrie* v. *L's Trs.* (1892) 19 R. 675.

[6] cf. *Hill* v. *Wylie* (1865) 3 M. 541; cf. *Thomson* v. *T.*, 1962 S.C. (H.L.) 28.

[7] Mere questions of disputed management and general disagreement do not justify an action of damages between partners: *Ferguson* v. *Mackenzie* (1870) 8 S.L.R. 273.

[8] *Maxton* v. *Brown* (1839) 1 D. 367.

[9] He may call on an accountant or solicitor for assistance: *Fife Bank* v. *Halliday* (1831) 9 S. 693; *Cameron* v. *McMurray* (1858) 17 D. 1142; *Bevan* v. *Webb* [1901] 1 Ch. 724.

[10] *Pearson* v. *Lockhart* (1867) 5 M. 301; *Hamilton* v. *Steele* (1871) 9 M. 805.

Expulsion of partner

No majority of partners can expel any partner unless a power
to do so has been conferred by express agreement between the
partners.[1] Such a power is very narrowly interpreted.[2] Even
then the court may decline to give effect to such a provision
if convinced that the expulsion is not in the interests of the
firm but for a private reason.[3] But a partner may be prevailed
on to agree to leave the partnership; such an agreement may
be attacked as impetrated by undue influence,[4] but is not necessarily objectionable.[5]

Retirement from partnership at will

Where no fixed term has been agreed upon for the duration
of the partnership, any partner may determine it at any time on
giving notice of his intention to all the other partners. If the
partnership was entered into by deed, written notice, signed, is
sufficient.[6]

Continuance of partnership—tacit relocation

If a partnership is entered into for a fixed period[7] it determines
without notice on the expiry of that period. But if after the expiry
of the period, without express new agreement, or agreement to
prolong the term, the business is continued for a substantial
period[8] by the partners who habitually acted in the firm affairs
without any settlement or liquidation of the partnership affairs,
the court will infer an intention to continue the partnership as a
partnership at will, on the terms and conditions, so far as still
applicable, obtaining at the end of the former partnership.[9]
Continuance by tacit relocation requires that at least two partners
survive the term; it will not suffice that only one survives and
carries on the business.[8]

---

[1] 1890 Act, S. 25; cf. Stair I, 16, 4; *Carmichael* v. *Evans* [1904] 1 Ch. 486.

[2] *Clarke* v. *Hart* (1858) 6 H.L.C. 633, 650.

[3] *Blisset* v. *Daniel* (1853) 10 Hare 493; *Wood* v. *Woad* (1874) L.R. 9 Ex. 190; *Green* v.
Howell [1910] 1 Ch. 495. See also *Montgomery* v. *Forrester* (1791) Hume 748; *Cunninghame*
v. *Warner* (1824) 2 Sh. App. 225.

[4] *Tennent* v. *T's Trs.* (1870) 8 M. (H.L.) 10.

[5] *McKirdy* v. *Paterson* (1854) 16 D. 1013.

[6] 1890 Act, S. 26.

[7] cf. *Gracie* v. *Prentice* (1904) 12 S.L.T. 15.

[8] *Wallace* v. *Wallace's Trs.* (1906) 8 F. 558.

[9] 1890 Act, Ss. 27, 32; *Marshall* v. *M.*, 23 Feb. 1816, F.C.; *Neilson* v. *Mossend Iron Co.*
(1886) 13 R. (H.L.) 50; *Browns* v. *Kilsyth Police Commrs.* (1886) 13 R. 515; *McGown* v.
Henderson, 1914 S.C. 839.

A partnership at will may be terminated by any partner giving reasonable notice to the others,[1] or in any event by the death of the second last surviving partner.

Duty to account

Partners are bound to render true accounts and full information of all things affecting the partnership to any partner or his legal representatives.[2] A partner must also account to the firm for any benefit derived by him without the consent of the other partners from any transaction concerning the partnership,[3] or from any use by him of the partnership property, name or business connection, including transactions undertaken after a partnership has been dissolved by the death of a partner and before the affairs thereof have been completely wound up, either by a surviving partner or by the deceased partner's representatives.[4] A partner may accordingly not make any private profit or benefit from the firm business, but may make private profit outside the scope of, and not competing with the firm business.[5] The same principle applies where a partner dissolves the partnership to obtain for his private benefit a contract which the firm might have obtained.[6]

Profits of competing business

If a partner without the consent of the other partners carries on a business of the same nature as and competing with that of the firm, he must account for and pay over to the firm all profits made by him in that business.[7] If there is no competition there is no obligation to account, even though the position of profit would not have been achieved without connection with the partnership.[8]

---

[1] 1890 Act, S. 26(1).

[2] 1890 Act, S. 28; *Law* v. *L.* [1905] 1 Ch. 140; *Smith* v. *Barclay*, 1962 S.C. 1. See also *McIntyre* v. *Maxwell* (1831) 9 S. 284; *Pollock, Gilmour & Co.* v. *Ritchie* (1850) 13 D. 640; *McLaren* v. *Liddell's Trs.* (1862) 24 D. 577; *Lawson* v. *L's Trs.* (1872) 11 M. 168.

[3] Not including the purchase by one partner of a second's share in the firm without the knowledge of the third partner: *Cassels* v. *Stewart* (1881) 8 R. (H.L.) 1; see also *Lister* v. *Marshall's Tr.*, 1927 S.N. 55.

[4] 1890 Act, S. 29; cf. Ersk. III, 3, 20; Bell, *Comm.* II, 522; *Marshall* v. *M.*, 23 Feb. 1816, F.C.; *Bayne* v. *Fergusson & Kyd* (1817) 5 Dow 151; *Wallace, Hamilton & Co.* v. *Campbell* (1824) 2 Sh. App.; *Pender* v. *Henderson* (1864) 2 M. 1428; *McNiven* v. *Peffers* (1868) 7 M. 181; *Manners* v. *Raeburn & Verel* (1884) 11 R. 899; *Sc. Pacific Coast Mining Co.* v. *Falkner, Bell & Co.* (1888) 15 R. 290.

[5] *Aas* v. *Benham* [1891] 2 Ch. 244; *Trimble* v. *Goldberg* [1906] A.C. 494.

[6] Bell, *Comm.* II, 522; *McNiven, supra*.

[7] 1890 Act, S. 30; *Stewart* v. *North* (1893) 20 R. 260; *Pillans Bros.* v. *P.* (1908) 16 S.L.T. 611.

[8] *Aas* v. *Benham* [1891] 2 Ch. 244.

Assignation of interests

The partnership relation demands full mutual confidence, so that no partner can, without the consent of all the others, assign his interest to the effect of making the assignee a partner in the firm,[1] except under the provisions of the Limited Partnership Act, 1907.[2] But a partner may assign his interest, either absolutely or in security.[3] The assignee acquires thereby no right to interfere in the management of the firm, to require accounts, or inspect the partnership books, but only the right, so long as the firm continues, to receive the share of profits to which his cedent was entitled, and he must accept the account of profits to which the partners have agreed.[4] He has no power to dissolve the firm, but if it is dissolved, he is entitled to receive the share of the partnership assets which the cedent would have been entitled to receive, and for this purpose, he is entitled to an account as from the date of the dissolution.[5] Similarly a partner may, if the copartnery permits, nominate a relative to his share in the partnership, but this confers only an interest in the partnership assets and does not make the relative a partner.[6]

DISSOLUTION OF PARTNERSHIP

Subject to any agreement between the partners, a partnership is dissolved (a) by the expiry of any fixed term for which it was entered into,[7] or (b) by the termination of any single adventure or undertaking for which it was entered into,[8] or (c) if entered into for an undefined time, by any partner giving notice to the other or others of his intention to dissolve the partnership,[9] in which case the partnership is dissolved as from any date fixed in the notice as the date of dissolution or, if no date is mentioned, from the date of the communication of the notice.[10] It is also dissolved

---

[1] 1890 Act, S. 31; cf. Ersk. III, 3, 22.

[2] See further, *infra.*

[3] See *Lonsdale Hematite Iron Co.* v. *Barclay* (1874) 1 R. 417; *Cassels* v. *Stewart* (1881) 8 R. (H.L.) 1.

[4] S. 31(1).   [5] S. 31(2).

[6] *Thomson* v. *T.*, 1962 S.C. (H.L.) 28.

[7] *Wallace's Trs.* v. *W.* (1906) 8 F. 558. If continued after the expiry of the fixed term it subsists as a partnership at will: S. 27(1). Bell, *Comm.* II S. 21; *Neilson* v. *Mossend Iron Co.* (1886) 13 R. (H.L.) 50.

[8] *Gracie* v. *Prentice* (1904) 12 S.L.T. 15.

[9] Ersk. III, 3, 26; cf. *Marshall* v. *M.*, 26 Jan. 1815, F.C.; notice given cannot, save by consent, be withdrawn: *Jones* v. *Lloyd* (1874) L.R. 18 Eq. 265.

[10] 1890 Act, S. 32.

in the absence of agreement to the contrary,[1] by the death or bankruptcy of any partner,[2] or by the happening of any event which makes it unlawful for the business to be carried on or for the members of the firm to carry it on in partnership,[3] and may, at the option of the other partners, be dissolved if any partner suffers his share of the partnership property to be charged under the Act for his separate debt.[4] The executor of a predeceasing partner has been said to be absolutely entitled to insist on a public sale of the business, to ascertain the deceased's share.[5]

Dissolution by the Court

The Court may dissolve a partnership on the application of a partner on the following grounds:[6]

(a) When a partner is found a lunatic by cognition, or is shown to the satisfaction of the Court to be of permanently unsound mind,[7] application being competent by the incapax partner's *curator bonis* or by another partner:

(b) When a partner, other than the partner suing, becomes in any other way permanently incapable of performing his part of the partnership contract:

(c) When a partner, other than the partner suing, has been guilty of such conduct as, in the opinion of the Court, having regard to the nature of the business, is calculated prejudicially to affect the carrying on of the business:[8]

(d) When a partner, other than the partner suing, wilfully or

---

[1] e.g. *Hill* v. *Wylie* (1865) 3 M. 541; cf. *Sclater* v. *Clyne* (1831) 5 W. & S. 625; *Beveridge* v. *B's Trs.* (1872) 10 M. (H.L.) 1; *Alexander* v. *Lowson's Trs.* (1890) 17 R. 571.

[2] S. 33(1); Stair I, 16, 5; Ersk. III, 3, 25; *Aitken's Trs.* v. *Shanks* (1830) 8 S. 753; *Christie* v. *Royal Bank* (1840) 2 Robin. 118; *Aytoun* v. *Dundee Bank* (1844) 6 D. 1409; *Hoey* v. *McEwan & Auld* (1867) 5 M. 814; *Oswald's Trs.* v. *City of Glasgow Bank* (1879) 6 R. 461; *Hannan* v. *Henderson* (1879) 7 R. 380; see also *Fleming's Trs.* v. *Henderson*, 1962 S.L.T. 401; *Inland Revenue* v. *Graham's Trs.*, 1871 S.L.T. 46; *Thomson* v. *T.*, 1962 S.C. (H.L.) 28.

[3] S. 34; *Esposito* v. *Bowden* (1857) 7 E. & B. 763; *Stevenson* v. *Cartonnagen Industrie* [1918] A.C. 239.

[4] S. 33(2); this is ineffective in Scotland by reason of S. 23.

[5] *McKersies* v. *Mitchell* (1872) 10 M. 861.

[6] 1890 Act, S. 35; application may be made by petition or action of declarator: *McNab Petr.*, 1912 S.C. 421; *Thomson, Petr.*, 1923, 1 S.L.T. 73; cf. *Gordon* v. *Howden* (1854) 4 Bell 254; *Russell* v. *R.* (1874) 2 R. 93; a summary application under this section is not always convenient or competent: *Wallace* v. *Whitelaw* (1900) 2 F. 675; this statutory power does not exclude a provision in the copartnery for arbitration as to dissolution: *Hackston* v. *H.*, 1956 S.L.T. (Notes) 38.

[7] cf. *Eadie* v. *McBean's C.B.* (1885) 12 R. 660; *Cleghorn* (1901) 8 S.L.T. 409.

[8] e.g. conviction for dishonesty though not affecting the firm: *Carmichael* v. *Evans* [1904] 1 Ch. 486; see also *McCredies' Trs.* v. *Lamond* (1886) 24 S.L.R. 114; *Macnab* v. *M.*, 1912 S.C. 421; *Tomkins* v. *Cohen*, 1951 S.C. 22.

persistently commits a breach of the partnership agreement, or otherwise so conducts himself in matters relating to the partnership business that it is not reasonably practicable for the other partner or partners to carry on the business in partnership with him:[1]

(e) When the business of the partnership can only be carried on at a loss:[2]

(f) Whenever in any case circumstances have arisen which, in the opinion of the Court, render it just and equitable that the partnership be dissolved.[3]

Rights against apparent partners

A person who deals with a firm after a change in its constitution is entitled to treat all apparent members of the old firm as still being members of the firm until he has notice of the change.[4] Hence express notice of change to parties dealing with the firm is prudent. An advertisement in the *Edinburgh Gazette* in respect of a firm whose principal place of business is in Scotland, is notice to all persons who had no prior dealings with the firm.[5] Direct intimation, by circular or obvious change in the firm name, is necessary in the case of persons who have had dealings with the firm;[6] advertisement or notice in the *Gazette* is insufficient unless the third party can be shown to have had actual knowledge of the change.[6] The estate of a partner who dies, or becomes bankrupt, or who retires, not having been known to third parties to be a partner, is not liable for partnership debts contracted after his death, bankruptcy or retirement respectively.[7]

Right to notify dissolution

On the dissolution of a firm or retirement of a partner any partner may publicly notify the fact and may require the other

---

[1] cf. *A.B.* (1884) 22 S.L.R. 294; *Thomson* (1893) 1 S.L.T. 59. See observations on this in *Elder* v. *Elder & Watson*, 1952 S.C. 49.

[2] *Miller* v. *Walker* (1875) 3 R. 242.

[3] *Olver* v. *Hillier* [1959] 2 All E.R. 220. cf. Companies Act, 1948, S. 222(f), and cases thereon.

[4] 1890 Act, S. 36(1); *Campbell, Thomson & Co.* v. *McLintock* (1803) Hume 755; *Kay* v. *Pollock*, 27 Jan. 1809, F.C.; contrast *Dunbar* v. *Remmington Wilson & Co.*, 10 Mar. 1810, F.C.; *Blacks* v. *Girdwood* (1885) 13 R. 243.

[5] S. 36(2); *McMillan* v. *Walker* (1814) Hume 755; *Mann* v. *Sinclair* (1879) 6 R. 1078.

[6] Bell, *Comm.* II, 530; *Prin.* §384; cf. *Dunbar* v. *Remmington, Wilson & Co.*, 10 Mar. 1810, F.C.; *Sawers* v. *Tradestown Victualling Socy.*, 24 Feb. 1815, F.C.; *McMillan* v. *Walker* (1814) Hume 755.

[7] S. 36(3). cf. Bell, *Comm.* II, 529.

partner or partners to concur for the purpose in all necessary or proper acts which cannot be done without their concurrence.[1]

Effect of dissolution

The authority of each partner to bind the firm, and the other rights and obligations of the partners, continue notwithstanding dissolution so far as necessary to complete business in progress at the date of dissolution and to wind up the partnership affairs.[2] But the firm is in no case bound by the acts of a partner who has become bankrupt, without prejudice to the liability of any one who after the bankruptcy represented himself or knowingly suffered himself to be represented as a partner of the bankrupt.[3]

Dissolution by the death of one partner terminates contracts of personal service with employees, but is not breach of contract with them,[4] but probably does not terminate other contracts. It may terminate a partnership obligation to pay an annuity to a former partner's widow.[5] On dissolution followed by the creation of a new firm obligations with the old firm may be held novated into obligations with the new one, as by a course of dealing with the new firm and acceptance of it as the debtor.[6] But, in the absence of express or implied agreement to the contrary, a new firm incurs no liability for prior trade debts.[7]

Assets and liabilities of firm

What the assets and liabilities of the firm at the time of dissolution are, are questions of fact, frequently involving interpretation of any relevant provisions in the contract of copartnery.[8]

---

[1] 1890 Act, S. 37.

[2] 1890 Act, S. 38; *Gordon* v. *Douglas Heron & Co.* (1795) 3 Pat. 428; *Paul* v. *Taylor* (1826) 4 S. 572; *Wotherspoon* v. *Henderson's Trs.* (1868) 6 M. 1052; *Dickson* v. *National Bank*, 1917 S.C. (H.L.) 50; *Goldfarb* v. *Bartlett* [1920] 1 K.B. 639; *Public Trustee* v. *Elder* [1926] Ch. 776; cf. *Muir* v. *Dickson* (1860) 22 D. 1070; *Goodwin* v. *Industrial and General Trust* (1890) 18 R. 193; *Welsh* v. *Knarston*, 1972 S.L.T. 96.

[3] S. 38, proviso.

[4] *Hoey* v. *McEwan & Auld* (1867) 5 M. 814.

[5] *Menzies' Trs.* v. *Black's Trs.*, 1909 S.C. 239.

[6] *Ker* v. *McKechnie* (1845) 7 D. 494; *Price & Logan* v. *Wise* (1862) 24 D. 491; contrast *Campbell* v. *Cruickshank* (1845) 7 D. 548; *Pollock* v. *Murray & Spence* (1863) 2 M. 14; *Heritable Securities Investment Assocn.* v. *Wingates* (1891) 29 S.L.R. 904; *Morton's Trs.* v. *Robertson's J. F.* (1892) 20 R. 72; cf. *Mackintosh* v. *Gibb & Co's Trs.* (1828) 6 S. 992.

[7] *Nelmes* v. *Montgomery* (1883) 10 R. 974.

[8] See *Forrester* v. *Robson's Trs.* (1875) 2 R. 755; *Glass* v. *Haig* (1877) 4 R. 875; *Charlton* v. *C.* (1894) 2 S.L.T. 61; *Eadie* v. *Crawford*, 1912, 2 S.L.T. 360 (assets); *MacCredie's Trs.* v. *Lamond* (1886) 24 S.L.R. 114; *Menzies' Trs.* v. *Black's Trs.*, 1909 S.C. 239 (liabilities).

It is a question of fact whether a firm has any goodwill accountable as an asset.[1]

Application of property

Every partner is entitled to have the partnership property
applied in payment of the debts and liabilities of the firm, and
the surplus assets applied in payment of what may be due to
the partners respectively after deducting what may be due from
them as partners to the firm; for this purpose any partner or
his representative may apply to the Court to wind up the business
and affairs of the firm.[2] In dividing firm property among the
partners any one can insist on public sale.[3]

Appointment of judicial factor

The court may at common law sequestrate the estate of a
partnership and appoint a judicial factor thereon,[4] not to carry on
the business but normally only to protect the assets pending
dissolution, or where the partners are at loggerheads.[5] An
interim appointment may be made.[6] The court may appoint a
judicial factor to wind up the estate if a partner has been guilty
of misconduct,[7] all the partners have died,[8] or any surviving
partners are unfit to, or incapable of winding up the affairs,[9] or
there is danger of a partner not obtaining his due rights on
dissolution,[10] but not if there are surviving partners not prevented
by fault or incapacity from winding up their affairs,[11] or if the
differences between the partners relate to accounting only,[12] or it is

[1] *Mackenzie* v. *Macfarlane*, 1934 S.N. 16; *Reid* v. *R.*, 1938 S.L.T. 415; cf. *Ventisei* v.
V.'s Exors., 1966 S.C. 21. Under the National Health Service the goodwill of a medical
practice cannot be sold.

[2] 1890 Act, S. 39; Ersk. III, 3, 27; *Thomson* (1893) 1 S.L.T. 59; *Robertson* (1902) 10
S.L.T. 417; *Elliott* v. *Cassils* (1907) 15 S.L.T. 190.

[3] *Stewart* v. *Simpson* (1835) 14 S. 72; *Mackersies* v. *Mitchell* (1872) 10 M. 861. See also
Marshall v. *M.*, 23 Feb. 1816, F.C.; *Aitken's Trs.* v. *Shanks* (1830) 8 S. 753; *McWhannell* v.
Dobbie (1830) 8 S. 914.

[4] A petition for appointment of a judicial factor must contain a crave for sequestration
of the estate: *Booth* v. *MacKinnon* (1908) 15 S.L.T. 848.

[5] *Carabine* v. *C.*, 1949 S.C. 521; *McCulloch* v. *McC.*, 1953 S.C. 189.

[6] *McCulloch, supra.*

[7] *Macpherson* v. *Richmond* (1869) 6 S.L.R. 348.

[8] *Dixon* v. *D.* (1832) 6 W. & S. 229.

[9] *Dickie* v. *Mitchell* (1874) 1 R. 1030; *Russell* v. *R.* (1874) 2 R. 93; *Miller* v. *Walker*
(1875) 3 R. 242; *Gow* v. *Schulze* (1877) 4 R. 928; *Gatherer* (1893) 1 S.L.T. 401; *Paterson*
(1894) 1 S.L.T. 564; *Robertson* (1902) 10 S.L.T. 417.

[10] *Allan* v. *Gronmeyer* (1891) 18 R. 784; *Carabine, supra.*

[11] *Young* v. *Collins and Feely* (1853) 15 D. (H.L.) 35; 1 Macq. 385; *Russell, supra*;
Thomson (1893) 1 S.L.T. 59.

[12] *Gow* v. *Schulze* (1877) 4 R. 928; *Elliott* v. *Cassils* (1907) 15 S.L.T. 190.

otherwise unnecessary.[1] Minor differences between partners do not justify the appointment of a factor.[2] A petition for appointment of a factor is not a suitable process for determining substantive issues such as whether a partnership existed,[2] the construction of the partnership units,[3] or whether there was goodwill to be sold.[4]

Where a partnership is prematurely dissolved, the Court may order repayment in whole or in part of any premium paid by one partner to another on entering into partnership, unless the dissolution is wholly or chiefly due to the misconduct of the partner who paid the premium, or the partnership has been dissolved by an agreement containing no provision for return of any part of the premium.[5]

Where a partnership contract is rescinded on the ground of the fraud or misrepresentation of one of the parties,[6] the party rescinding is, apart from any other right, entitled—

(a) to a lien on the surplus of partnership assets after satisfying liabilities, for any money paid by him for a share in the partnership and for any capital contributed by him; and

(b) to stand in the place of the firm creditors for any payments made by him in respect of partnership liabilities; and

(c) to be indemnified by the person guilty of the fraud or making the representation against all the debts and liabilities of the firm.[7]

Where a member of a firm has died or otherwise ceased to be a partner[8] and the surviving or continuing partners carry on business without any final settlement of accounts, failing contrary agreement, the outgoing partner or his estate is entitled in his option to such share of the profits made since dissolution as the Court may find attributable to the use of his share of the partnership assets, or to interest on the amount of his share at five per cent.[9] But where the survivors have an option to purchase his

---

[1] *Eadie* v. *MacBean's C.B.* (1885) 12 R. 660.

[2] *Anderson* v. *Blair*, 1935 S.L.T. 377.

[3] *Blake's Trs.* v. *Jolly*, 1920, 1 S.L.T. 304.

[4] *Mackenzie* v. *M.*, 1934 S.N. 16.

[5] 1890 Act, S. 40.

[6] *Adam* v. *Newbigging* (1888) 13 App. Cas. 308; *Manners* v. *Whitehead* (1898) 1 F. 171; *Ferguson* v. *Wilson* (1904) 6 F. 779.

[7] 1890 Act, S. 41; and see further *infra*.

[8] Including ceasing by reason of becoming an alien enemy on the outbreak of war: *Stevenson* v. *Cartonnagen Industrie* [1918] A.C. 239.

[9] 1890 Act, S. 42(1); *Vyse* v. *Foster* (1874) L.R. 7 H.L. 318; *Yates* v. *Finn* (1880) 13 Ch. D. 839.

share and exercise it, he is not entitled to any further or other share of the profits unless there is material non-compliance with the terms of the option.[1] The amount due to an outgoing partner in respect of his share is a debt accruing at the date of dissolution or death.[2]

Priority of payments in final settlement

In the absence of contrary agreement the following rules apply in settling the accounts of a partnership after dissolution:

(a) losses, including losses and deficiencies of capital, are paid first out of profits, next out of capital, and lastly, if necessary, by the partners individually in the proportion in which they were entitled to share profits:

(b) assets, including such contributions, fall to be applied (1) in paying debts and liabilities of the firm to non-partners;[3] (2) in paying each partner rateably which is due him for advances,[4] and (3) for capital;[5] (4) the residue is divided among the partners in the proportion in which profits are divisible.[6]

The doqueted accounts of a mercantile firm must be taken as conclusive in the absence of anything casting doubt on their accuracy, but are open to correction at the instance of a representative of one of the partners.[7] They may be challenged on the ground of *error calculi*.[8]

Liability of partners after dissolution

When a firm has been dissolved the partners remain jointly and severally liable for the firm's debts, but no one partner can be sued without calling all the others, so far as that is possible, unless the firm obligation has been previously constituted by writing or decree.[9]

---

[1] 1890 Act, S. 42(2).

[2] 1890 Act, S. 43.

[3] Liabilities include the legal and accountancy fees incurred in winding up the firm's affairs, but these are postponed to business creditors.

[4] *Potter v. Jackson* (1880) 13 Ch. D. 845.

[5] 1890 Act, S. 44.

[6] *Garner v. Murray* [1904] 1 Ch. 57.

[7] *Findlay, Bannatyne & Co.'s Assignee v. Donaldson* (1865) 2 M. (H.L.) 86; cf. *Russel v. Glen* (1827) 5 S. 221; *Blair v. Russell* (1828) 6 S. 836.

[8] *McLaren v. Liddell's Tr.* (1862) 24 D. 577.

[9] *Johnston v. Duncan* (1823) 2 S. 625; *Geddes v. Hopkirk* (1828) 5 S. 747; *Dewar v. Munnoch* (1831) 9 S. 487; *Muir v. Collett* (1862) 24 D. 1119; *Neilson v. Wilson* (1890) 17 R. 608, 612, 614.

Bankruptcy

The law relating to the bankruptcy of a firm or of the individual partners thereof in Scotland is unaffected by the 1890 Act.[1]

JOINT ADVENTURE

Joint adventure is a co-operative enterprise confined to a particular adventure, speculation, course of trade or voyage in which the partners use no firm or social name and incur no responsibility beyond the limits of the adventure.[2] It may be of some duration, such as the lease of a farm[3] but is differentiated from partnership by its limited purpose and duration.[4] It is established by contract, express or implied, and evidenced by the same kind of evidence as partnership, but is not necessarily to be inferred from the joint ownership of a ship, unless there has been participation in the mercantile employment of the ship in which the joint adventure is said to have consisted,[5] nor necessarily from taking shares in a company to which one sells property.[6]

It is doubtful whether a joint adventure creates any body having a quasi-persona as does a firm.[7] There can be no contract by the joint adventure as such,[8] and one joint adventurer can sue another or an agent of the adventure for an accounting.[9] A company can be party to a joint adventure.[10]

Each adventurer is *praepositus negotiis societatis* and has an implied mandate in dealing within the limits of the adventure,

---

[1] S. 47. See Ch. 124, *infra*.

[2] Ersk. III, 3, 29; Hume *Lect.* II, 194; Bell, *Comm.* II, 538; *Prin.* §392; More, *Lect.* I, 199; *Wilkie* v. *Johnstone, Bannatyne & Co.* (1808) 5 Pat. 191; *Logan* v. *Brown* (1824) 3 S. 15; *Ferguson* v. *Graham's Trs.* (1836) 14 S. 871; *Venables* v. *Wood* (1839) 1 D. 659; *Orr* v. *Pollock* (1840) 2 D. 1902; *White* v. *McIntyre* (1841) 3 D. 334; *Baxter* v. *Aitchison* (1841) 3 D. 391; *B.L. Co.* v. *Alexander* (1853) 15 D. 277; *Clements* v. *Macaulay* (1866) 4 M. 583; *Aitchison* v. *A.* (1877) 4 R. 899; *Pyper* v. *Christie* (1878) 6 R. 143; *Young* v. *Dougans* (1887) 14 R. 490; *Cooke's Circus Building Co.* v. *Welding* (1894) 21 R. 338; *Livingstone* v. *Allans* (1900) 3 F. 233; *Clayton* v. *C.*, 1937 S.C. 619; *Parker* v. *Walker*, 1961 S.L.T. 252; *Adam* v. *A.*, 1962 S.L.T. 332.

[3] *Cameron* v. *Young* (1871) 9 M. 786.

[4] *Mair* v. *Wood*, 1948 S.C. 83, 86.

[5] Bell, *Prin.* §392; *Logan, supra; Fergusson, supra*.

[6] *Moore* v. *Dempster* (1879) 6 R. 930; see also *Beresford's Tr.* v. *Argyll Assessor* (1884) 11 R. 818; *Clark* v. *Jamieson*, 1909 S.C. 132; *Sc. Ins. Commrs.* v. *McNaughton*, 1914 S.C. 826.

[7] Bell, *Comm.* II, 539, says there is no firm; cf. *Livingstone* v. *Allans* (1900) 3 F. 233, 237; but see *Mair* v. *Wood*, 1948 S.C. 83, 89.

[8] Ersk. III, 3, 29.

[9] *Manners* v. *Raeburn & Verel* (1884) 11 R. 899.

[10] Bell, *Prin.* §394.

but not to bind the partners generally.[1] When goods are purchased or money borrowed for the joint adventure, the adventurers are jointly and severally liable therefor.[2] There is no such liability for goods purchased previously by any one and subsequently brought into the stock of the adventure.[3] Each adventurer's liability is limited to that adventure.[4]

Each joint adventurer is jointly and severally liable for wrongs done to third parties in pursuance of the joint adventure.[5] The shares of the adventurers are presumed equal. Their stock is common property and held in trust for the creditors.[6]

The duration of a joint adventure may be evident from the circumstances. Any one adventurer may end it if it comes to be attended with greater risk than when the contract was entered into, or if there be no reasonable belief that profit will be made for either party.[7] It is also terminable at will on reasonable notice.[8] In partnership proper the firm is a separate persona and subsists in that capacity for winding-up, while a joint adventure, when completed, is resolved into its elements and each person may maintain his own interests in the common funds by direct action in his own name without the co-operation of the rest. Each joint adventurer is proprietor of his share of the funds, and may vindicate them from anyone in whose hands they are and who holds them on his account.[9]

LIMITED PARTNERSHIPS

By the Limited Partnerships Act, 1907 it is permissible to create a partnership of one or more general partners, liable for all the debts and obligations of the firm, and one or more limited partners, who contribute to the firm capital or property valued at a stated amount and are not liable for the debts or obligations of

---

[1] Bell, *Prin.* §396; *Cameron* v. *Young* (1871) 9 M. 786.

[2] Bell, *Prin.* §395; *Cameron, supra*; *Lockhart* v. *Moodie* (1877) 4 R. 859; *Lockhart* v. *Brown* (1888) 15 R. 742; *Mollison* v. *Noltie* (1889) 16 R. 350; *Fowler* v. *Paterson's Trs.* (1896) 3 S.L.T. 305; *Hay* v. *Douglas*, 1922 S.L.T. 365. As to bills given for the price see Ersk. III, 3, 29.

[3] *Venables* v. *Wood* (1839) 1 D. 659; *White* v. *McIntyre* (1841) 3 D. 334; *Lockhart* v. *Brown* (1888) 15 R. 742.

[4] *Jardine* v. *Macfarlan* (1828) 6 S. 564.

[5] *McGee* v. *Anderson* (1895) 22 R. 274; *Mair* v. *Wood*, 1948 S.C. 83.

[6] Bell, *Prin.* §396; *McCaul* v. *Ramsay & Ritchie* (1740) Mor. 14608; *Fergusson* v. *Graham* (1836) 14 S. 871; *Buchanan* v. *Lennox* (1838) 16 S. 824; *Keith* v. *Penn* (1840) 2 D. 633; *Livingstone* v. *Allans* (1900) 3 F. 233.

[7] *Miller* v. *Walker* (1875) 3 R. 242, 249.

[8] *Young* v. *Dougans* (1887) 14 R. 490.   [9] *Pyper* v. *Christie* (1878) 6 R. 143.

the firm beyond that amount.[1] A corporate body may be a limited partner. The general law and the 1890 Act apply, save in so far as the 1907 Act makes special provisions.[2] During the continuance of the partnership a limited partner may not, directly or indirectly, withdraw any part of his contribution, on pain of liability for firm debts up to the amount so drawn out.[3] Limited partnerships must be registered as such[4] in the manner provided,[4] failing which it shall be deemed a general partnership and every limited partner deemed a general partner.[5]

A limited partner may not take part in the management of the partnership business and has no power to bind the firm, but he may inspect the firm books and examine the state and prospects of the partnership business and advise with the partners thereon. If he takes part in the management he is liable for all debts and obligations of the firm incurred while doing so as if he were a general partner.[6] A limited partnership is not dissolved by the death or bankruptcy of a limited partner, and his lunacy is not a ground for dissolution by the Court unless his share cannot otherwise be ascertained and realized.[7] In the event of dissolution the affairs of a limited partnership are wound up by the general partners unless the court otherwise orders.[8] A petition by a partner for dissolution may be brought under the Companies Act, 1948, S. 398, but it is competent for the Court to appoint a judicial factor to wind up.[9]

Subject to any agreement expressed or implied between the partners (a) any difference arising as to ordinary matters connected with the partnership business may be decided by a majority of the general partners; (b) a limited partner may, with the consent of the general partners, assign his share in the partnership;[10] (c) the other partners are not entitled to dissolve the partnership by reason of any limited partner suffering his share to be charged for his separate debt; (d) a person may be introduced as a partner without the consent of the existing limited partners; and (e) a

[1] As to number of partners see 1907 Act, S. 4(2), amd. Companies Act, 1967, S. 121.

[2] 1907 Act, S. 7; see also *Re Barnard* [1932] 1 Ch. 269.

[3] 1907 Act, S. 4.

[4] 1907 Act, Ss. 5, 14–16. Duty must be paid on the amount contributed by the limited partners: S. 5, 11.

[5] 1907 Act, Ss. 8–9. Changes must be notified: S. 9. Notice of a general partner becoming a limited partner or of assigning a share must be given: S. 10.

[6] 1907 Act S. 6(1).

[7] 1907 Act, S. 6(2).

[8] 1907 Act, S. 6(3).

[9] *Muirhead* v. *Borland*, 1925 S.C. 474.

[10] This must be advertised in the *Gazette*: S. 10.

limited partner is not entitled to dissolve the partnership by notice.[1]

The winding-up of an insolvent limited partnership may be conducted under the Companies Act, 1948, S. 398, or by a judicial factor.[2]

UNINCORPORATED COMPANIES

It was formerly common and is still competent, to form a joint stock company with transferable shares, not incorporated[3] in any of the ways by which corporate status can be obtained.[4] Such a company was in effect a large partnership, and the members were personally liable to an unlimited extent to the company's creditors. The maximum number of members of such an association is now restricted to twenty,[5] otherwise the association is illegal. This form of association is accordingly now unimportant.

[1] 1907 Act, S. 6(5).

[2] *Muirhead, supra.*

[3] An example was The Western Bank of Scotland, on which see *Western Bank* v. *Addie* (1867) 5 M. (H.L.) 80. See history set out in *Muir* v. *City of Glasgow Bank* (1878) 6 R. 392, 399. On the different interests of a partner in an unincorporated company and in one incorporated, see *Dove* v. *Young* (1868) 7 M. 304. See also Bell, *Prin.* §398.

[4] On these see Ch. 26, *infra.*

[5] Companies Act, 1948, Ss. 429, 434, amd. Companies Act, 1967, S. 119.

PART 3

JURISTIC PERSONS:
INCORPORATED BODIES

CHAPTER 24

CORPORATIONS

A CORPORATION or corporate body is a juristic person or legal entity capable of existing, of sustaining legal rights and duties, and of suing and being sued, by itself, wholly independently of the natural persons who are for the time being officers or members of the group incorporated.[1] It is not a collective name for the members, nor any aggregate of them, but a separate legal entity. The word 'person' in a public general statute generally includes a corporation as well as a natural person. In every Act of Parliament since 1890 the expression 'person', unless a contrary intention appears, includes any body of persons corporate or unincorporate.[2] But a corporation cannot be a person practising certain professions.[3]

A corporation is an incorporated aggregate or group of co-existing persons; English law knows also the corporation sole, where a person as the holder of his office is deemed incorporated.[4] Bell[5] states that a parish minister is a corporation sole but this is unwarranted and the concept of the corporation sole seems unknown in Scots law.

The characteristics of a corporation are: it is incorporated, or created a corporation under a corporate name,[6] by, or in accordance with, some State authority, and not wholly by the acts of

[1] Stair II, 3, 39; II, 4, 20; Bankt. I, 2, 18–27; Ersk. I, 7, 64; Bell, *Comm.* II, 157; *Prin.* §2176. See also history in *University of Glasgow* v. *Faculty of Physicians and Surgeons* (1834) 13 S. 9; (1835) 2 S. & McL. 275; (1837) 15 S. 736; (1840) 1 Rob. 397.

[2] Interpretation Act, 1889, Ss. 19, 42.

[3] e.g. solicitors: Solicitors Act, 1934, S. 1.

[4] In English law the sovereign is a corporation sole; *quaere* as to Scots law. Some Ministers of the Crown have been created corporations sole, e.g. Minister of Transport (Ministry of Transport Act, 1919, S. 26(3), and Ministers of the Crown (Transfer of Functions) Act, 1946, S. 6). As to the position of such a Minister in Scots law, *quaere*.

[5] *Prin.* §2176.

[6] As to protection of names see Chartered Associations (Protection of Names and Uniforms) Act, 1926.

private individuals;[1] once created it has perpetual succession[2] and continues in being indefinitely until dissolved by or under State authority; it exists wholly independently of the natural persons who are at any time its officers or members[3] and exists though they change or even though all the officers and members die; all rights and property are vested in the corporation itself, and no member has a claim on any identifiable part thereof,[4] nor is any member liable for the liabilities of the corporation but only for any obligation he has undertaken to contribute to its funds;[5] the members have implied power to elect their own officers, and to make by-laws and regulations for the management of the internal affairs of the corporation; and it possesses a common seal the use of which is necessary to authenticate deeds binding the corporation and expressing its will.

Kinds of corporations

Corporations are established for numerous purposes; public corporations exist to manage public utilities and social services;[6] local authorities to administer local government functions;[7] companies to conduct businesses;[8] building societies to lend money for house purchase;[9] industrial and provident societies to improve the conditions of members of the community;[10]

---

[1] Ersk. I, 7, 64; *Crawford* v. *Mitchell* (1761) Mor. 1958, 14553.

[2] Stair II, 3, 41; exceptionally a corporation may be created for a limited time; e.g. the B.B.C., the charter of which (1927) was for ten years, but has been subsequently renewed for further periods.

[3] cf. *G. E. Ry.* v. *Turner* (1872) L.R. 8 Ch. 152; *Flitcroft's Case* (1882) 21 Ch. D. 519, 536; *Salomon* v. *S. & Co.* [1897] A.C. 22, 51.

[4] *Short* v. *Treasury Comms.* [1948] 1 K.B. 116, 122.

[5] *Muir* v. *City of Glasgow Bank* (1878) 6 R. 392, 401, 405; 6 R. (H.L.) 21, 39. This obligation might, and may, be unlimited; but a creditor's claim is against the corporation, not against all or any members. In the case of public and municipal corporations, and, possibly, chartered and statutory companies, the members are under no liability to the corporation at all, unless and so far as the charter or statute so provides: cf. *Elve* v. *Boyton* [1891] 1 Ch. 501, 507.

[6] e.g. The National Coal Board; the Scottish Gas Board; the Clyde Port Authority; on such bodies see *London T.A.F.A.* v. *Nichols* [1949] 1 K.B. 35; *Tamlin* v. *Hannaford* [1950] 1 K.B. 18; *Glasgow Corpn.* v. *Central Land Board*, 1956 S.C. (H.L.) 1; and generally Robson, *Nationalized Industry and Public Ownership*; Friedmann, *Law and Social Change*, Ch. 9; Chester, *The Nationalized Industries*. Many of the principles of law applicable to corporations generally cannot be easily applied to these public corporations.

[7] See Bennett Miller, *Outline of Administrative and Local Government Law in Scotland*, Ch. 4. As to burghs in private law see *Banff Mags.* v. *Ruthin Castle*, 1944 S.C. 36; *McDougal's Trs.* v. *L.A.*, 1952 S.C. 260.

[8] Ch. 26, *infra*.

[9] Ch. 27, *infra*.

[10] Ch. 28, *infra*.

and corporations of many kinds and titles to further academic, professional, charitable, and other purposes. The last class include universities, royal colleges of practitioners of particular professions, and similar institutions. Whether a particular kind of association is, or can be, incorporated or not may be as much a matter of legal history as of the wish of the persons composing it.[1] The powers and functions of public corporations and local authorities are determined mainly by public law, but these and all other corporations transact in spheres of private law, when they contract, commit wrongs, hold property, sue and are sued, in much the same way as private persons of full age and capacity.

Modes of creation

A corporation may be created only by public authority,[2] the modes recognized being: by Royal Charter,[3] by letters patent,[4] by special public Act of Parliament,[5] by public general Act of Parliament,[6] by private Act,[7] by registration under and in terms of a public general Act,[8] by the grant by a common law chartered corporation of subordinate corporate powers by grant of a seal of cause,[9] and by long recognition at common law as a corporate

---

[1] Thus friendly societies may be registered but are not and cannot be incorporated. Many societies and bodies remain unincorporated, their property vested in trustees.

[2] Hence a body of trustees is not a corporation: *Martin* v. *Wight* (1841) 3 D. 485; *Muir* v. *City of Glasgow Bank* (1879) 6 R. (H.L.) 21, 33, 38, 39; nor is a kirk-session; *Kirk Session of North Berwick* v. *Sime* (1839) 2 D. 23.

[3] e.g. The Royal Bank of Scotland; Carron Company (see *I.R.C.* v. *Carron Co.*, 1968 S.C. (H.L.) 47); The National Trust for Scotland; The University of Strathclyde. In the case of Royal Charter the grant of privileges may imply incorporation, though there be no express grant thereof nor bestowal of a corporate name: *University of Glasgow* v. *Faculty of Physicians and Surgeons* (1840) 1 Rob. 397. As to the term 'chartered banks' see *Sanders* v. *S's Trs.* (1879) 7 R. 157.

[4] e.g. S.S.P.C.K.; *Bonar* v. *S.S.P.C.K.* (1846) 8 D. 660.

[5] e.g. The Bank of Scotland (Act 1695; see Bell, *Comm.* I, 102 and *Sanders* v. *S's Trs.* (1879) 7 R. 157, 165); The National Coal Board (Coal Industry Nationalization Act, 1946, S. 1).

[6] e.g. Regional councils and district councils: Local Government (Sc.) Act, 1973, S. 2.

[7] e.g. Clyde Navigation Trust (Clyde Navigation Acts, 1858–1899: see 1927 S.C. 626) and railway companies in the nineteenth century; see e.g. *Clouston* v. *Edinburgh & Glasgow Ry.* (1865) 4 M. 207; such statutes latterly incorporated provisions of the Companies Clauses Consolidation (Sc.) Act, 1845, or other Clauses Acts.

[8] e.g. Companies registered under Companies Act, 1948 and 1967: see Ch. 26, *infra*.

[9] See Kames, *Elucidations*, 53; *Ritchie* v. *Cordiners of Edinburgh* (1823) 2 S. 565; *Mowat* v. *Tailors of Aberdeen* (1825) 4 S. 52; *Fleshers* of Canongate v. *Wight* (1835) 14 S. 135; *Anderson* v. *Wrights of Glasgow* (1865) 3 M. (H.L.) 1; *Morris* v. *Guildry of Dunfermline* (1866) 4 M. 457; *Tailors of Edinburgh* v. *Muir's Tr.* 1912 S.C. 603. The exclusive privileges of trading in burghs were abolished by the Burgh Trading Act, 1846.

body.[1] The three oldest Scottish universities were founded, and probably impliedly incorporated, by Papal bulls, though subsequently regulated also by statute.[2] Some corporations may act under powers conferred by more than one of these creative acts. Registration of a body under the appropriate legislation does not automatically incorporate it.[3]

Officers

The constitutive charter or Act normally provides for the existence of certain officers to administer and manage the corporation's affairs and for their appointment or election, tenure of office, powers and duties.[4]

Though a corporation has full legal personality by itself it can act only through the agency of natural persons appointed as its officers, usually by the natural persons who are the members for the time being of the incorporated body. The members are not necessarily the only persons beneficially interested in the corporation; thus a council performing local government functions must do so for the general benefit of the community in its area of responsibility.

Meetings

A corporation may act as such, unless the constitutive document directs otherwise, only by corporate meeting duly convened at which the head of the corporation and a majority, or other specified quorum, of members is present, and a majority approves a resolution to do the act in question. But the execution of policy and routine administration of the corporation's affairs may be delegated to committees and officers. These may act only within the scope of the remit or authority given them, and any act beyond such limits is *ultra vires* and void, though it may be adopted and ratified by the corporation,[5] unless it is of a kind

---

[1] See Bell, *Prin*, §2177; *Skirving* v. *Smellie*, 19 Jan. 1803, F.C.; *Dempster* v. *Masters and Seamen of Dundee* (1831) 9 S. 313; e.g. The Dean and Faculty of Advocates. As to whether the W.S. Society is a corporation see *Writers to the Signet* v. *Grahame* (1823) 2 S. 214, 456, 765; (1824) 3 S. 237; (1825) 1 W. & Sh. 538; *Solicitors* v. *Clerks to the Signet*, 25 Feb. 1800, F.C. and observations in 15 S. 744; *Writers to the Signet* v. *Inland Revenue* (1886) 14 R. 34. Bankton I, 2, 25, states that the Established Church is a great corporation.

[2] cf. *University of Glasgow* v. *Faculty of Physicians* (1840) 1 Rob. 397; Universities (Sc.) Acts, 1858 (esp. S. 25), 1889 (esp. S. 5(3)) and 1966.

[3] *Muir* v. *City of Glasgow Bank* (1878) 6 R. 392, 401; cf. registration of friendly societies.

[4] e.g. Local Government (Sc.) Act, 1947, Ss. 28–37 (provosts and magistrates of burghs).

[5] *Irvine* v. *Union Bank of Australia* (1877) 2 App. Cas. 366.

ultra vires not merely of the officer but of the corporation itself, in which case it cannot be adopted or ratified at all.[1]

Powers of corporations

All kinds of corporations have power to sue, and liability to be sued, as entities, by the corporate name,[2] power to elect or admit new members and to appoint officers for the administration of the corporate affairs,[3] to have and use a common seal, to hold property, heritable and moveable,[4] to act in accordance with the views of a majority of the managers or members in any matter within the scope of the purposes of the corporation as fixed by Charter or Act,[5] and to make by-laws, ordinances or regulations for the administration of its affairs within the limits of the constitution and purposes of the corporation.[6] A corporation incorporated by royal charter cannot, by its own rules, confer on itself powers wider than those given by the charter and the general law.[7]

Contractual powers

The contractual powers of a corporation depend in the first place on its constitutive deed. Corporations created by Royal Charter have power to do any act or enter into any contract not expressly forbidden by their charter, as interpreted by usage, though certain kinds of conduct may be challengeable as a breach of trust on its members or contrary to public policy.[8] Corporations

[1] *Ashbury Ry. Carriage Co. v. Riche* (1875) L.R. 7 H.L. 653; *Mann v. Edinburgh Northern Tramways Co.* (1892) 20 R. (H.L.) 7.

[2] Bell, *Prin.* §2178; *Eadie v. Glasgow Corpn.*, 1908 S.C. 207; but they must be represented in litigation by counsel and agents, not by directors: *Equity, etc. Life Assce. Socy. v. Tritonia, Ltd.*, 1943 S.C. (H.L.) 88; nor employees; *Scottish Gas Board v. Alexander*, 1963 S.L.T. (Sh. Ct.) 27.

[3] Ersk. I, 7, 64; see also *Loudon v. Tailors of Ayr* (1891) 18 R. 549.

[4] *Thomson v. Incorpn. of Candlemakers* (1855) 17 D. 765; *Webster v. Tailors of Ayr* (1893) 21 R. 107.

[5] *Gray v. Smith* (1836) 14 S. 1062; *Howden v. Goldsmiths* (1840) 2 D. 996; *Rodgers v. Tailors of Edinburgh* (1842) 5 D. 295; *Balfour's Trs. v. Edin. & Northern Ry.* (1848) 10 D. 1240; *Wedderburn v. Sc. Central Ry.* (1848) 10 D. 1317; *Galloway v. Ranken* (1864) 2 M. 1199; *Clouston v. Edin. & Glasgow Ry.* (1865) 4 M. 207; but see *Baird v. Dundee Mags* (1865) 4 M. 69; *Morrison v. Fleshers of Edinburgh* (1853) 16 D. 86.

[6] Ersk. I, 7, 64; *Gray v. Smith* (1836) 14 S. 1062; *University of Glasgow v. Faculty of Physicians and Surgeons* (1840) 1 Rob. 397; *Tailors of Glasgow v. Trades' House of Glasgow* (1901) 4 F. 156. See also *Dinning v. Procurators of Glasgow* (1817) Hume 166; *Hill v. Fairweather* (1823) 2 S. 569.

[7] *S.S.A.F.A. v. A.G.* [1968] 1 All E.R. 448.

[8] *Sanderson v. Lees* (1859) 22 D. 24; *Baroness Wenlock v. River Dee Co.* (1885) 10 App. Cas. 354; *Kesson v. Aberdeen Wrights Incorpn.* (1898) 1 F. 36; *A.G. v. Manchester Corpn.* [1906] 1 Ch. 643; *Conn v. Renfrew Corpn.* (1906) 8 F. 905; *Kemp v. Glasgow Corpn.*, 1920 S.C. (H.L.) 73; *Graham v. Glasgow Corpn.*, 1936 S.C. 108.

created by statute have only those powers expressly or impliedly conferred by the statute and powers implied as necessarily incidental thereto, and any act exceeding those powers is *ultra vires* and void.[1] Corporations incorporated under the Companies Acts have only those powers which they have expressly taken in their Memorandum and Articles of Association and powers reasonably incidental thereto, and any act or contract outwith those powers is *ultra vires* and void.[2] Where an act or contract is *ultra vires* of the corporation even the unanimous ratification of all the members thereof cannot validate it,[3] and a corporation cannot be barred from pleading that its own acts were *ultra vires*.[4] All corporations have by legal implication contractual powers essential to their existence and operation, such as to open a bank account and operate thereon, to employ staff, to lease premises and to purchase necessaries.[5] No particular form is essential for a contract by a corporation,[6] unless the relevant charter or Act provides otherwise.

Liabilities of corporation and members

If a corporation is created at common law, it has its own estate and liabilities and the members are not liable for its debts, but only to it within the limit of the obligation they have undertaken to subscribe to its funds, unless the charter of incorporation expressly makes the corporators liable without limitation for its debts.[7] The liability of corporations established by statute and of their members are determined by the relevant Act. Companies may be incorporated under the Companies Acts with unlimited or limited liability of members. A corporation may be rendered notour bankrupt and sequestrated [8] though special provision is made for companies.

---

[1] *Ashbury Ry. Carriage Co.* v. *Riche* (1875) L.R. 7 H.L. 653; *Caledonian & Dumbarton Ry.* v. *Helensburgh Mags.* (1856) 2 Macq. 391; *Scottish N.E. Ry.* v. *Stewart* (1859) 3 Macq. 382; *Mann* v. *Edinburgh Northern Tramways* (1892) 20 R. (H.L.) 7; *Nicol* v. *Dundee Harbour Trs.*, 1915 S.C. (H.L.) 7; *Newburgh & N. Fife Ry.* v. *N.B. Ry.*, 1913 S.C. 1166; *Grieve* v. *Edinburgh Water Trs.*, 1918 S.C. 700.

[2] *Ashbury, supra*; *Shiell's Trs.* v. *Scottish Property Investment Co.* (1884) 12 R. (H.L.) 14. See further Ch. 26, *infra*.

[3] *Ashbury, supra*; *Mann, supra*.

[4] *General Property Inv. Co.* v. *Matheson's Trs.* (1888) 16 R. 282.

[5] Ersk. I, 7, 64; Bell, *Prin.* §2178.

[6] *Park* v. *Glasgow University* (1675) Mor. 2535; cf. *Cook* v. *N.B. Ry.* (1872) 10 M. 513.

[7] *Muir* v. *City of Glasgow Bank* (1878) 6 R. 392, 401, 405; *Sanders* v. *S's Trs.* (1879) 7 R. 157, 162, 168.

[8] *Wotherspoon* v. *Linlithgow Mags.* (1863) 2 M. 348.

Title to sue for delict

A corporation may sue for harm done to it or its rights or property in its corporate capacity.[1]

Delictual liability

A corporation is liable for unjustifiable harm done by an agent acting within the scope of his authority, or by an employee acting in the course of his employment,[2] both where intention or malice is a necessary element of the wrong[3] and where the agent or employee has been merely negligent.[4]

Criminal liability

A corporation may be incapable of incurring liability for common law crimes,[5] but it may be held liable for statutory offences[6] and be responsible for the misdeeds of its executives.[7]

Dissolution of corporations

A corporation can be dissolved only by public authority, by expiry, surrender or forfeiture of its charter, by Act of Parliament, by dissolution in accordance with the provisions of an Act of Parliament,[8] or by lapse of time, in the case of a creation for a limited time.[9]

[1] *North of Scotland Bank* v. *Duncan* (1857) 19 D. 881; *Glebe Sugar Refining Co.* v. *Lusk* (1866) 3 S.L.R. 33; *Thorley's Cattle Food Co.* v. *Massam* (1880) 14 Ch. D. 763; *South Hetton Coal Co.* v. *N.E. News Assocn.* [1894] 1 Q.B. 133. Some delicts, from their nature, e.g. assault, cannot be committed against a corporation.

[2] e.g. *Beaton* v. *Glasgow Corpn.*, 1908 S.C. 1010; *Riddell* v. *Glasgow Corpn.*, 1911 S.C. (H.L.) 35; *Percy* v. *Glasgow Corpn.*, 1922 S.C. (H.L.) 144; contrast *Aiken* v. *Caledonian Ry.*, 1913 S.C. 66.

[3] *Gordon* v. *British and Foreign Metaline Co.* (1886) 14 R. 75; *Citizens Life Assce. Co. Ltd.* v. *Brown* [1904] A.C. 423; *Finburgh* v. *Moss's Empires, Ltd.*, 1908 S.C. 928.

[4] e.g. *O'Hanlon* v. *Stein*, 1963 S.C. 357.

[5] But see *R.* v. *I.C.R. Haulage Ltd.* [1944] K.B. 551.

[6] *Galbraith's Stores* v. *McIntyre* (1912) 6 Adam 641; *Clydebank Cooperative Socy.* v. *Binnie*, 1937 J.C. 17; *D.P.P.* v. *Kent and Sussex Contractors Ltd.* [1944] K.B. 146.

[7] *Lennard's Carrying Co.* v. *Asiatic Petroleum Co.* [1915] A.C. 705; *Clydebank, supra*, cf. *Sarna* v. *Adair*, 1945 J.C. 141.

[8] Including, in the case of a company, dissolution by liquidation, which may follow on insolvency.

[9] Ersk. I, 7, 64; Bell, *Prin.* §2179; *Thomson* v. *Candlemakers of Edinburgh* (1855) 17 D. 765; *Wrights of Leith* (1856) 18 D. 981.

CHAPTER 25

THE CROWN

THE term, the Crown, is applied both to the sovereign for the time being[1] and used as the title for Her Majesty's government, including departments of state and crown servants. It may be that the Crown, in the sense of the State, the community as legally organized, can be treated as a corporation aggregate.[2] It is not always clear which aspect of the Crown has certain rights. Specialties, moreover, arise from the fiction that Ministers and their departments and crown servants are still the personal servants of the sovereign, and entitled to the privileges which attached to the sovereign personally at common law.

It may be a matter of doubt whether a particular person or body is a department of state, or crown servant, or acting on behalf of the Crown, in such a way as to be entitled to the privileged position of the Crown. Thus Crown privileges attach to the (former) Central Land Board,[3] and custodians of enemy property,[4] and to the Lord Advocate as head of the criminal administration,[5] but not to the British Transport Commission,[6] the B.B.C.,[7] nationalized industries generally, local authorities, health boards,[8] the police,[9] or other public bodies,[10] still less to private bodies, though acting for the public benefit.[11] In all civil litigation and other private law contexts the Crown and public departments are represented by the Lord Advocate.[12]

---

[1] Whether, as in English law, the sovereign is a corporation sole, is a difficult question. It is submitted that she is not.

[2] Walker, 65 J.R. 255.

[3] Glasgow Corpn. v. Central Land Board, 1956 S.C. (H.L.) 1.

[4] Bank Voor Handel v. Admin. of Hungarian Property [1954] A.C. 584.

[5] McKie v. Western S.M.T., 1952 S.C. 206.

[6] Tamlin v. Hannaford [1950] 1 K.B. 18.

[7] B.B.C. v. Johns [1964] 1 All E.R. 923.

[8] National Health Service (Sc.) Act, 1972, S. 13(10).

[9] The chief constable is liable: Police (Sc.) Act, 1967, S. 39.

[10] London T. & A.F.A. v. Nicholls [1948] 2 All E.R. 432.

[11] Whitehall v. W., 1957 S.C. 30.

[12] Crown Suits (Sc.) Act, 1857, S. 1; Law Officers Act, 1944, S. 2. For development see King's Advocate v. Lord Dunglas (1836) 15 S. 314; see also Lord Advocate v. Meiklam (1860) 22 D. 1427; Macgregor v. Lord Advocate, 1921 S.C. 847; Cameron v. L.A., 1952 S.C. 165.

Subjection to jurisdiction

At common law the Crown could be impleaded only in the Court of Session,[1] but by the Crown Proceedings Act, 1947, S. 44, subject to that Act and to any Act limiting the jurisdiction of the sheriff court, civil proceedings against the Crown may be instituted in the sheriff court as if against a subject, but may be remitted to the Court of Session at the Lord Advocate's instance.

The Crown is not subject to the jurisdiction of the Dean of Guild Court of a burgh, unless by voluntary submission thereto.[2]

Contractual powers and capacity

The Crown, acting through the agency of departments of state or Crown officials, may contract in the same way as any other corporation and be liable for breach of contract.[3] But any undertaking to pay money, or damages, is impliedly subject to the condition that Parliament provides funds for that particular purpose.[4] A department or official, in contracting, is presumed to act in his official capacity and subject to the constitutional limits of his authority, but may so contract as to incur personal liability.[5] Certain exceptions and qualifications arise from the Crown's unique position. Save under statute[6] all Crown employees hold office at the Crown's pleasure only, and have no civilly enforceable contract of employment.[7] Nor does a Crown servant engaging a lower employee warrant his authority to do so, or bind the Crown, though he may bind himself.[8] It is also established that the Crown or its agents cannot by contract restrict the future freedom of action of the executive.[9]

---

[1] *Somerville* v. *L.A.* (1893) 20 R. 1050, 1067, 1073.

[2] *Somerville* v. *L.A.* (1893) 20 R. 1050.

[3] *Windsor & Annapolis Ry.* v. *The Queen* (1886) 11 App. Cas. 607; *Parkinson* v. *Commrs. of Works* [1949] 2 K.B. 632 (building contract); *Cameron* v. *L.A.*, 1952 S.C. 165 (civilian employment).

[4] *Churchward* v. *The Queen* (1865) L.R. 1 Q.B. 173; *Auckland Harbour Bd.* v. *The King* [1924] A.C. 318; *A.G.* v. *Great Southern Ry.* [1925] A.C. 754.

[5] *Dunn* v. *Macdonald* [1897] 1 Q.B. 555; *Commercial Cable Co.* v. *Govt. of Newfoundland* [1916] 2 A.C. 610.

[6] e.g. *Gould* v. *Stuart* [1896] A.C. 575; *Leaman* v. *The King* [1920] 3 K.B. 663.

[7] *Shenton* v. *Smith* [1895] A.C. 229; *Dunn* v. *The Queen* [1896] 1 Q.B. 116; *Smith* v. *L.A.* (1897) 25 R. 112 (pay); *Mackie* v. *L.A.* (1898) 25 R. 769 (pension); *Mulvenna* v. *The Admiralty*, 1926 S.C. 842 (pay); *Griffin* v. *L.A.*, 1950 S.C. 448 (pension); see also Crown Proceedings Act, 1947, S. 46.

[8] *Dunn* v. *Macdonald* [1897] 1 Q.B. 555; *Kenny* v. *Cosgrove* [1926] I.R. 517.

[9] *The Amphitrite* v. *The King* [1921] 3 K.B. 500.

Title to sue for delict

The Crown can sue for delict done to it as a corporation, as by damage done to one of H.M. ships.[1]

Delictual liability

It is probable that the Crown in Scotland has never enjoyed any exemption from delictual liability[2] though certain cases, on English analogy, held the Crown exempt from liability.[3] The actual wrongdoer seems never to have been protected.[4] The Crown Proceedings Act, 1947, provides (S. 2(1)) that, subject to the Act, the Crown shall be subject to all those liabilities in reparation for delict to which, if it were a private person of full age and capacity, it would be subject: (a) in respect of delicts committed by its servants or agents;[5] (b) in respect of any breach of those duties which a person owes to his servants or agents[5] at common law by reason of being their employer; and (c) in respect of any breach of the duties attaching at common law to the ownership, occupation, possession or control of property:[6] Provided that no proceedings shall lie against the Crown by virtue of para. (a) unless the servant's act or omission would have given rise to an action of delict against the servant or agent or his estate apart from the Act. Statutory duties incumbent on the Crown and also on private persons give rise to delictual liability.[7] The Crown is liable for delict committed by an officer while performing functions conferred or imposed on him by common law or statute as if the functions had been imposed by Crown instructions.[8] The Crown can rely on enactments negativing or limiting the liability of any government department or officer of the Crown in respect of delict committed by it or him as if the proceedings had been against it or him.[9] No proceedings lie against the Crown

---

[1] *Admiralty Commrs.,* v. *S.S. Chekiang* [1926] A.C. 637; *Admiralty Commrs.* v. *S.S. Susquehanna* [1926] A.C. 655; *Admiralty* v. *S.S. Divina* [1952] P. 1.

See also *Officers of State* v. *Smith* (1849) 6 Bell 847; *Cameron & Gunn* v. *Ainslie* (1848) 10 D. 446; *Alexander* v. *Officers of State* (1868) 6 M. (H.L.) 54, 67; *Agnew* v. *L.A.* (1873) 11 M. 309; *Young* v. *N.B. Ry.* (1887) 14 R. (H.L.) 53; *Boy Andrew* v. *St. Rognvald,* 1947 S.C. (H.L.) 70.

[2] *Hay* v. *Officers of State* (1832) 11 S. 196; *Macgregor* v. *L.A.,* 1921 S.C. 847, 850, argument; Philip, 40 J.R. 238.

[3] *Smith* v. *L.A.* (1897) 25 R. 112; *Wilson* v. *Edinburgh City R.G.A. Volunteers* (1904) 7 F. 168; *Macgregor, supra,* 852, 853, which goes too far.

[4] *Wilson, supra*; *Macgregor, supra*.

[5] Including, by S. 38(2), an independent contractor employed by the Crown; but see S. 40(2)(d).

[6] The Occupiers Liability (Sc.) Act, 1960, binds the Crown: S. 4 thereof.

[7] S. 2(2) e.g. Factories Act, 1961, which by S. 173, binds the Crown.

[8] S. 2(3).   [9] S. 2(4).

under S. 2 in respect of anything done or omitted by any person in the discharge of duties of a judicial nature or responsibilities in connection with the execution of judicial process.[1] No proceedings lie against the Crown under S. 2 in respect of any act, neglect or default of any officer of the Crown unless he has been directly or indirectly appointed by the Crown and was at the material time paid wholly out of the Consolidated Fund, moneys provided by Parliament, the Road Fund, or any other Fund certified by the Treasury for the purposes of the subsection, or was at the material time holding an office in respect of which the Treasury certify that the holder thereof would normally be so paid.[2] Civil proceedings lie against the Crown for infringement of patent, registered trade mark, copyright or registered design, by a servant or agent with the authority of the Crown.[3] The rules as to indemnity,[4] contribution,[4] joint and several wrongdoers,[5] and contributory negligence[6] are enforceable by or against the Crown as if it were a private person.[7] The limitation of liability of shipowners[8] limits the liability of the Crown in respect of H.M. ships,[9] as do the rules as to division of loss.[10] The limitation of the liability of the owners of docks and canals limits the liability of the Crown as such owner.[11] The law relating to civil salvage[12] applies, with certain exceptions, to salvage services to H.M. ships and to Crown claims to salvage.[13] No act or omission by a member of the armed forces of the Crown while on duty as such subjects him or the Crown to delictual liability for causing the death of another person, or for causing personal injury to another person, in so far as the death or personal injury is due to anything suffered by that person while he is a member of the armed forces of the Crown if he was either on duty or was on premises used for armed forces purposes and the death or

[1] S. 2(5), cf. *Smith* v. *L.A.* (1897) 25 R. 112 where said that no action lay against the War Department for wrongful acts of a court-martial; cf. *Hester* v. *Macdonald*, 1961 S.C. 370.

[2] S. 2(6).

[3] S. 3.

[4] Law Reform (Misc. Prov.) (Sc.) Act, 1940, S. 3; Ch. 55, *infra*.

[5] At common law: see Ch. 55, *infra*.

[6] Law Reform (Contributory Negligence) Act, 1945; Ch. 56, infra.

[7] S. 4.

[8] Merchant Shipping Act, 1894, S. 503, amd. M.S. (Liability of Shipowners and Others) Act, 1958.

[9] S. 5; *The Admiralty* v. *S.S. Divina* (*H.M.S. Truculent*) [1952] P. 1.

[10] S. 6; Maritime Conventions Act, 1911, Ss. 1–3; see also S. 30.

[11] S. 7.

[12] Ch. 53, *infra*.

[13] S. 8.

injury falls to be treated as attributable to service for pension purposes.[1]

The Crown is not vicariously liable for public services provided by corporations and persons who are not Crown departments or servants.[2] Nothing in the 1947 Act authorises or applies to proceedings against the Queen in her private capacity.[3]

The Lord Advocate as head of the public system of criminal prosecution is immune from delictual liability, and this extends also to his deputies, procurators-fiscal and their deputies acting in trials on indictment.[4]

Crown property

The sovereign personally owns certain property in Scotland. The Crown originally personally, holds the ultimate radical right to all land in Scotland held on feudal tenure,[5] and has a reserved right to certain minerals, salmon-fishings, forests and other subjects.[6] Treasure, and property not inherited by anyone on the owner's death, fall to the Crown.[7]

Remedies against the Crown

Under the 1947 Act[8] the court may make all such orders as it may in proceedings between subjects, save that it may not grant interdict or specific implement[9] but may in lieu thereof make an order declaratory of the rights of the parties,[10] and may not make an order for the recovery of land or the delivery of property, but may in lieu declare the pursuer's entitlement thereto: nor may it grant interdict or make an order against an officer of the Crown if the effect would be to give any relief against the Crown not directly obtainable. Proceedings *in rem* against the Crown are excluded.[11] Proceedings by or against the Crown are not affected by the demise of the Crown.[12]

---

[1] S. 10; *Adams* v. *War Office* [1955] 3 All E.R. 245.

[2] Its former limited liability for the Post Office (1947 Act, S. 9; *Triefus* v. *Post Office* [1957] 2 Q.B. 352) disappeared with the Post Office Act, 1969.

[3] S. 40.

[4] *Hester* v. *Macdonald*, 1961 S.C. 370.

[5] cf. *Burmah Oil Co.* v. *Lord Advocate*, 1964 S.C. (H.L.) 117, 127.

[6] Chaps. 72–3, *infra*.

[7] *Lord Advocate* v. *Aberdeen University*, 1963 S.C. 533.

[8] S. 21, as applied by S. 43.

[9] This restricts the remedies, in that interdict against the Crown was formerly competent: *Bell* v. *Secretary of State*, 1933 S.L.T. 519; cf. *Carlton Hotel Co.* v. *L.A.*, 1921 S.C. 237.

[10] A final declaration only: There is no jurisdiction to make an interim declaration: *Underhill* v. *Ministry of Food* [1950] 1 All E.R. 591; *Griffin* v. *L.A.*, 1950 S.C. 448; *Ayr Mags.* v. *Secretary of State for Scotland*, 1965 S.C. 394.

[11] S. 29. [12] S. 32.

Special pleas

By the Crown Proceedings Act, 1600, c. 14, the Crown cannot be prejudiced by the negligence of its servants in litigation to which it is a party and may accordingly state a plea formerly omitted by its servants by exception or reply.[1] A plea of bar founded on the error of Crown servants does not lie against the Crown.[2] Both positive[3] and negative[4] prescription run against the Crown, but an action of warrandice will not lie against the Crown.[5] The Crown is not bound by statute unless the intention that it is to be so bound is expressed[6] but may take advantage of provisions of a statute though not named therein.[7]

[1] Mack. *Observations*, 311; Stair IV, 35, 1; Ersk. I, 2, 27; *Crawford* v. *Kennedy* (1694) Mor. 7866.

[2] *L.A.* v. *Meiklam* (1860) 22 D. 1427; *L.A.* v. *Miller's Trs.* (1884) 11 R. 1046; *L.A.* v. *D. Hamilton* (1891) 29 S.L.R. 213; *Alston's Trs.* v. *L.A.* (1896) 33 S.L.R. 278.

[3] Prescription and Limitation (Sc.) Act, 1973, S. 1; Stair II. 3, 33; Ersk. III, 7, 31; Bell, *Prin.* §2025; *H.M.A.* v. *Graham* (1844) 7 D. 183; *L.A.* v. *Hunt* (1867) 5 M. (H.L.) 1.

[4] *E. Fife's Trs.* v. *Commrs. of Woods and Forests* (1849) 11 D. 889; *Deans of Chapel Royal* v. *Johnstone* (1869) 7 M. (H.L.) 19.

[5] Ersk. II, 3, 27.

[6] *Edinburgh Mags.* v. *L.A.*, 1912 S.C. 1085. See, however, *Somerville* v. *L.A.* (1893) 20 R. 1050.

[7] Crown Proceedings Act, 1947, S. 31.

CHAPTER 26

COMPANIES

COMPANIES[1] are the principal form of corporation where the purpose of the association is business and economic gain.[2] The modern incorporated company has developed out of the partnership and the common law joint stock company, incorporation being appropriate when the need for greater capital required a larger membership than could conveniently be managed in the form of partnership.[3] Since 1856 incorporation may include provision for limiting the liability of members of the company to the amount, if any, still unpaid on the nominal value of their shares, or to the amount they guarantee to pay in the event of the company being wound up.

The principal forms now recognized are companies established by special Act,[4] by Royal Charter[5] or letters patent,[6] statutory companies,[7] and, most commonly, companies incorporated by registration under the Companies Act, 1948 to 1967.[8] The constitutions, government, powers and functions of all kinds depend on their individual incorporating documents, the statutes relevant in the case and the general principles of law, particularly of contract, agency and trust.

The 1948 Act makes general provision for the incorporation

[1] The word 'company' is not exclusively appropriated to companies registered under the Acts. It is commonly used in older cases of partnerships. See also Evans, 'What is a Company?' (1910) 26 L.Q.R. 259.

[2] See generally Palmer, *Company Law*; Gower, *Modern Company Law*; Buckley on *The Companies Acts*; Halsbury, *Laws of England*, Vol. 6.

[3] On the development see Bell, *Comm.* II, 516; Gower, *Modern Company Law*, Chs. 2 and 3; Palmer, *Company Law*, Ch. 2. The first Act permitting incorporation by registration at a public office was in 1844, and the ffrst Act applicable to Scotland was in 1856.

[4] e.g. The Bank of Scotland (Act, 1695; see Bell *Comm.* I, 102).

[5] e.g. Hudson's Bay Company; The Royal Bank of Scotland; London Assurance Corpn.; Carron Company.

[6] Under Chartered Companies Acts, 1837 and 1884. Such letters patent do not incorporate the company but confer corporation privileges.

[7] Incorporated by private Act, normally incorporating the provisions of the Companies Clauses Consolidation (Sc.) Acts, 1845, 1863, and 1869, or the Companies Clauses Acts, 1845, 1863, 1869, and 1888, or other appropriate Clauses Act. See e.g. *Campbell* v. *Edinburgh & Glasgow Ry.* (1855) 17 D. 613; *Newburgh & North Fife Ry.* v. *N.B. Ry.*, 1913 S.C. 1166; as to interpretation see *Scottish Drainage and Improvement Co.* v. *Campbell* (1889) 16 R. (H.L.) 16.

[8] These Acts are the Companies Act, 1948 (the principal Act), Part I of the Companies Act, 1967, and the Companies (Floating Charges and Receivers) (Scotland) Act, 1972.

of companies by registration at a public office of a Memorandum and Articles of Association, containing respectively the constitution and objects, and the regulations for management, of the company, and on payment of the requisite fees and stamp duties.

Companies registered under former Companies Acts[1] repealed by the 1948 Act are governed by the 1948 Act and need not re-register thereunder,[2] though they may do so,[3] but if they have adopted Schedule I, Table A, of the Act as their Articles of Association, it is the Table A of the Act in force at the time of original registration, not that of the 1948 Act. The repeal of earlier Acts does not affect the incorporation of any company registered under a repealed Act.[4] Unincorporated joint-stock companies formed at common law prior to any of the Companies Acts[5] may still exist but cannot now be formed if having more than twenty partners or members, and formed to carry on any business for the purpose of gain.[6]

Forms of companies registrable under 1948 Act

The Act authorizes two forms of companies, public and private. Either form may be registered as (a) a company the liability of whose members is limited by shares, or (b) as a company the liability of whose members is limited by guarantee, or (c) as a company the liability of whose members is unlimited. Public companies of the latter two types may have, or not have, a share capital, but private companies of all three types must have a share capital.[7] Certain exceptional types may also be registered.[8] All these types of companies are incorporated bodies and have independent legal personality. But it is still competent to form, outwith the Act, an unincorporated company, but, if formed for business or gain, not of more than twenty members.[9] The provisions of the 1948 to 1967 Acts and the general law apply equally

---

[1] Joint Stock Companies Act, 1856 and 1857; Companies Acts, 1862, 1908, and 1929.

[2] S. 377, 455.

[3] Ss. 16, 382.

[4] S. 459(14).

[5] e.g. The Western Bank of Scotland: see *Lumsden* v. *Buchanan* (1864) 2 M. 695, 729–30; affd. (1865) 3 M. (H.L.) 89.

[6] S. 429, 434; cf. *Anderson* v. *Lauder Mags.*, 1930 S.L.T. 725; see also *Caledonian Employees' Benevolent Socy.*, 1928 S.C. 633.

[7] A private company limited by guarantee and not having a share capital cannot be formed because it could not satisfy the rule (S. 28) that it must restrict the right to transfer its shares.

[8] See Ss. 406–15, 416, 382.

[9] Ss. 429, 434. On 'for gain' see *Re Padstow Total Loss Assocn.* (1882) 20 Ch. D. 137; *Re Siddall* (1885) 29 Ch. D. 1; *Greenberg* v. *Cooperstein* [1926] Ch. 657.

to public and private companies unless otherwise stated. A company is presumed to be public unless it is clear from its constitution that it is a private company.[1]

Public companies

A public company has no restriction on the number of members so long as there are at least <u>seven</u>, nor on the offer or transfer of its shares or debentures to the public, though it may restrict the issue or transfer of shares of one or more of its classes of shares, particularly those carrying effective control of the company. Only the shares of public companies are dealt in on the stock exchanges, and then only if the Stock Exchange on application permits dealing and quotation, not automatically.

Private companies

Private companies must by their Articles (a) restrict the right of members to transfer their shares, (b) limit the number of members to fifty (excluding present employees and past employees continuing to hold shares after the termination of their employment, and counting joint shareholders as one) and (c) prohibit any invitation to the public to subscribe to the shares or debentures of the company.[2] Shares or debentures of a private company cannot be dealt in on the stock exchange. A private company which in fact fails to comply with these three restrictions is treated as if the minimum number of members required were seven and not two, but in other respects does not cease to be a private company. If the failure was accidental or inadvertent the court may relieve from these consequences.[3] A private company requires a minimum of two members only, not seven,[4] need not, before allotting shares or debentures, deliver a statement in lieu of prospectus for registration,[5] may commence business as soon as incorporated,[6] need not hold a statutory meeting nor make a statutory report,[7] need have only one director,[8] and its directors may be voted into office as a group[9] and need not retire at an age limit.[10] It must, however, along with its annual return file a certificate that it has not issued any invitation to the public to subscribe for shares or debentures and, if the membership exceeds 50, a certificate that the excess consists of persons authorized by S. 28.[11]

[1] About 97% of all companies registered under the Companies Acts are private.
[2] S. 28. As to whether an 'invitation to the public' has been issued see *Booth* v. *New Afrikander Gold Mining Co., Ltd.* [1903] 1 Ch. 295; *Nash* v. *Lynde* [1929] A.C. 158.
[3] S. 29.   [4] S. 1.   [5] S. 48.   [6] S. 109.   [7] S. 130.
[8] S. 176.   [9] S. 183.   [10] S. 185.   [11] S. 128.

Exempt private company

Between 1948 and 1967 a category of exempt private companies was recognized. An exempt private company enjoyed all the privileges of a private company and, in addition, did not need to attach its balance sheet and profit and loss account to the annual return filed with the Registrar of Companies nor to comply with certain other statutory requirements.

Companies limited by shares

A company limited by shares has the liability of its members limited by its Memorandum of Association to the amount, if any, unpaid on the shares respectively held by them.[1] The company obtains its capital by the issue of shares to the signatories of the memorandum or to applicants, in return for money or money's worth, such as the transfer of a business. The shareholder may not be required to pay the full nominal value of his shares to the company when acquiring the shares, but the unpaid portion may be called up at any time by the directors.

Companies limited by guarantee

Such a company has the liability of its members limited by the Memorandum to such amount as the members may respectively thereby undertake to contribute to the assets in the event of its being wound up.[2] A guarantee company does not obtain its capital from its members, and this form of company is therefore suitable only if no capital is necessary or it is obtained from, e.g., subscriptions. The guarantee company is suited therefore to clubs, trade organizations or professional bodies rather than to business enterprises. The guarantee materializes only in the event of winding-up to pay the debts and liabilities of the company, the expenses of winding-up, and the adjustment of the rights of members *inter se*, and affects members at the commencement of the winding-up and, if need be, past members who ceased to be members within a year prior to that date. In its pure form the guarantee company has no share capital,[3] but it may have a share capital[4] in which case the guarantee reinforces the company's assets comprised by the share capital.

---

[1] S. 1(2)(a). For exception, where liability is unlimited see S. 31.
[2] S. 1(2)(b).
[3] S. 11(b).
[4] S. 11(c).

Unlimited companies

Partnerships and unincorporated business associations of more than 20 persons, with certain exceptions, are prohibited,[1] but may exist if registered as incorporated companies the liability of whose members is unlimited. Such a company differs from a partnership only in that the entity enjoys full separate legal personality, and is unlimited as to numbers.[2] The liability of members, though unlimited, is to the company and not directly to the company's creditors. The memorandum and articles have to be in the form of Table E or as near thereto as circumstances permit.[3] An unlimited company may be converted into a company limited by shares or by guarantee,[4] but such a change does not affect the rights or liabilities of the company acquired or incurred prior to such registration.

Conversion of companies

A private company may be converted into a public company by removing from its Articles the three restrictions of S.28, and filing a statement in lieu of prospectus or issuing a prospectus.[5] A public company may convert itself into a private company by adopting the restrictions of S. 28 in its Articles and removing any provisions which conflict with the requisites for a private company. A company limited by shares may convert itself into one limited by guarantee, and vice versa, and one limited by guarantee having a share capital into one without a share capital, and vice versa, by re-registration under S. 16. An unlimited company may convert itself into one limited by shares or guarantee by registration under S. 16.[6]

Oversea companies

An oversea company is one incorporated outside Great Britain but having a place of business in Britain.[7] It must deliver certain documents to the Registrar of Companies,[8] and state the country of incorporation in every prospectus and in official publications[9] and give notice of the limited liability of its members in publications and at places of business.[9] The Crown's

---

[1] Ss. 429, 434 amd. 1967 Act, Ss. 119–21. If not formed for gain the association, though of more than 20, does not require to be registered: *Campbell* v. *C.*, 1917, 1 S.L.T. 339.

[2] It falls to be distinguished from an unincorporated company.

[3] S. 11 (d).

[4] e.g. *Proprs. of Royal Exchange Buildings, Glasgow*, 1911 S.C. 1337.

[5] S. 30.

[6] e.g. *Proprs. of Royal Exchange Buildings, Glasgow*, 1911 S.C. 1337.

[7] S. 406.   [8] S. 407, 410.   [9] S. 411.

right to its property as *bona vacantia* is modified in relation to the winding up of a dissolved oversea company.[1]

Insurance companies

Insurance companies are governed by the Companies Acts, 1948 to 1967 and also by the Insurance Companies Act, 1974. The 1974 Act imposes restrictions on the commencement or carrying on of insurance business and provides special rules as to accounts and balance sheets, the amalgamation of insurance companies and transfer of business from one to another, and as to insolvency and liquidation.

Official notification by the registrar

The registrar of companies must publish in the Edinburgh Gazette official notification of the issue or receipt by him of documents of stated descriptions, stating the name of the company, the description of document and the date of issue or receipt of the document. The descriptions of documents are (a) certificates of incorporation; (b) changes in memorandum or articles; (c) returns relating to the register of directors; (d) the annual return; (e) notice of situation of registered office; (f) winding-up orders; (g) orders for dissolution on winding up; (h) returns by liquidators of final meetings of companies on winding up.[2] A company is not entitled to rely against other persons on the happening of a winding up order, the appointment of a liquidator, an alteration in the memorandum or articles, a change in the directors or a change in the registered office if the event had not been officially notified and is not shown to have been known to the person concerned, or fifteen days had elapsed after notification, unless the third party was prevented from knowing of the event.[3]

FORMATION OF COMPANY

A company is formed by preparing a Memorandum of Association and, usually, Articles of Association, and registering these with and paying certain fees to the Registrar of Companies, who, if satisfied, issues a Certificate of Registration and thereby brings the company into existence as a legal person.[4] The Registrar must register the company if the documents are *ex*

---

[1] See *Re Banque Industrielle de Moscou* [1952] Ch. 919.

[2] European Communities Act, 1972, S. 9(3).

[3] Ibid., S. 9(4).

[4] Ss. 12–13. The Registrar will refuse if e.g. the company is being formed for an illegal purpose.

facie regular and in proper form.[1] A statutory declaration by a solicitor engaged in the formation of the company, or by a person named in the Articles as director or secretary, of compliance with the Act is necessary, and may be accepted as sufficient evidence of compliance.[2] A list of the persons who have consented to be directors is also necessary in certain cases,[3] and a statement of the nominal share capital.[4] The Certificate of Incorporation is conclusive that the requirements of the Act have been complied with and that the association is a company authorized to be registered, and registered under the Act.[2]

The Memorandum

The Memorandum is the essential and fundamental constitutional document of the company and alterable only to the extent permitted by the Act.[5] It must be, according to the kind of company, in the form set out in Tables B, C, D, or E of Schedule I of the Act, or as near thereto as circumstances permit.[6] It must contain clauses stating (1) the name of the company; (2) the country of the United Kingdom in which the registered office is to be situated; (3) the objects of the company; (4) (except in the case of unlimited companies) the statement that the liability of the members is limited; (5) (except in the case of unlimited companies and companies not having a share capital) a statement of the authorized capital of the company, or an undertaking to contribute a stated sum in the event of winding up; and a statement that the subscribers desire to be formed into a company. The Memorandum must be subscribed by at least seven persons (public company) or at least two (private company), each in the presence of one witness who attests his signature. Each subscriber must state the number of shares he will take, not less than one each.[7] One witness may attest all the subscriptions.[8] A subscriber may be an alien, a minor,[9] a trustee for another subscriber,[10] a corporation, limited company,[11] or a partnership.[12] The Memorandum is the fundamental document and the

---

[1] *Peel's Case* (1867) L.R. 2 Ch. 674; *Re Nassau Phosphate Co.* (1876) 2 Ch. D. 610.
[2] S. 15. See also *Jubilee Cotton Mills Ltd.* v. *Lewis* [1924] A.C. 958.
[3] S. 181.
[4] To comply with the Stamp Act, 1891, S. 112, as amended.
[5] S. 4.   [6] S. 11.
[7] cf. *Molleson & Grigor* v. *Fraser's Trs.* (1881) 8 R. 630.
[8] S. 3.
[9] cf. *Hill* v. *City of Glasgow Bank* (1880) 7 R. 68.
[10] *Salomon* v. *S.* [1897] A.C. 22.
[11] S. 139; Interpretation Act, 1889, S. 19.
[12] *Weikersheim's Case* (1873) 8 Ch. App. 831.

Articles are subordinate thereto; any Articles which go beyond the company's sphere of activity are inoperative and anything done under their authority is void.[1] The Articles may, however, be used to explain an ambiguity in the Memorandum.[2] Both documents are public documents in that they are registered in a public register and are open for public inspection,[3] and everyone who transacts with a registered company is held to have notice of the Memorandum and Articles of the company. The Memorandum may include further clauses, such as one enabling the company to invest its reserve funds in stocks and securities.[4]

Name clause

The Memorandum states the Company's name with 'Limited' as the last word (unless the company is unlimited). The word 'company' is not essential. The Dept. of Trade may license a non-profit-making association to omit the word Limited.[5] The use of the word 'Limited' by a person or body not so incorporated is punishable.[6] The Dept. of Trade may in its discretion refuse to register an undesirable name, e.g. if it is misleading or suggests royal or governmental connection or is too like the name of an existing company,[7] and may require a change of name within six weeks.[8] The name may not include the words 'Building Society' and may include such words as 'Bank' or 'Trust' only if justified. The unauthorized use of certain names is prohibited.[9] An existing firm or company may interdict a new company from registering a name which is so similar as to be likely to confuse or mislead.[10] The company may subsequently, with the approval of the Dept. of Trade, change its name.[8] The name must be painted up or fixed to the outside of every office or place where the company's business is carried on, mentioned in all business letters, notices, and official publications, and all bills, cheques, invoices, receipts and similar documents.[11]

[1] *Ashbury Ry. Carriage Co.* v. *Riche* (1875) L.R. 7 H.L. 653.
[2] *Guinness* v. *Land Corpn. of Ireland* (1882) 22 Ch. D. 349, 381.
[3] S. 426.   [4] *J. & P. Coats* (1900) 2 F. 829.
[5] S. 19. See *Incorporated Glasgow Dental Hospital* v. *L.A.*, 1927 S.C. 400; *Re Scientific Poultry Breeder's Assocn.* [1933] 1 Ch. 227.
[6] S. 439.   [7] S. 17.   [8] S. 18; 1967 Act, S. 46.
[9] Geneva Convention Act, 1911, S. 1; Anzac (Restriction on Trade Use of Word) Act, 1916; Chartered Associations (Protection of Names and Uniforms) Act, 1926, S. 1.
[10] *Reddaway* v. *Banham* [1896] A.C. 199; *North Cheshire and Manchester Brewery Co.* v. *Manchester Brewery Co.* [1899] A.C. 83; *Dunlop Pneumatic Tyre Co.* v. *Dunlop Motor Co.*, 1907 S.C. (H.L.) 15; *Scottish Union and National Ins. Co.* v. *Scottish National Ins. Co.*, 1909 S.C. 318; *Standard Bank of S. Africa* v. *Standard Bank* (1909) 25 T.L.R. 420; *Ewing* v. *Buttercup Margarine Co.* [1917] 2 Ch. 1.
[11] S. 108; *Stacey* v. *Wallis* (1912) 28 T.L.R. 209.

A company must state in all business letters and order forms
(a) the place of registration and the number with which it is
registered; (b) the address of its registered office; and (c) if it
is exempted from the obligation to use the word 'limited', the
fact that it is a limited company. If there is reference to the
amount of share capital, it is to paid-up share capital.[1] A company may carry on business under a name other than its corporate name but must register that other name under the
Registration of Business Names Act, 1916.[2] If a company
contracts without using the word 'limited' the contract will bind
the signatory personally.[3]

Registered Office Clause

This clause states in which country of the United Kingdom
the registered office is to be located. This determines the nationality and domicile of the company,[4] and the jurisdiction of the
courts. But within the country chosen the place of the registered
office may be anywhere, and may be changed periodically; notice
of change must be sent to the Registrar.[5] Every company must
have a registered office to which all communications and notices
may be sent; notice of the address must be given to the Registrar.[5]
At the registered office must be kept the register of members;[6]
the register of debenture holders;[7] the register of charges;[8]
copies of instruments creating charges requiring registration;[9]
the minute books of general meetings;[10] the register of directors'
shareholdings;[11] the register of directors and secretaries;[12] copies
of each director's contract of service;[13] a register of interests in
one-tenth or more of the shares[14] and, in certain cases, financial
statements.[15]

The Objects Clause

The statement in the Memorandum of the objects of the
company defines the purposes of the company. The objects may

---

[1] European Communities Act, 1972, S. 9(7).

[2] 1948 Act, Sched. 16, para. 4.

[3] *Atkins* v. *Wardle* (1889) 58 L.J.Q.B. 377.

[4] *Janson* v. *Driefontein Consolidated Mines Ltd.* [1902] A.C. 484; *Gasque* v. *I.R.C.* [1940]
2 K.B. 80.

[5] S. 107; change is ineffective till intimated: *Ross* v. *Invergordon Distillers, Ltd.*, 1961
S.C. 286; but service of a writ at an unregistered office is valid: *Re Fortune Copper
Mining Co. Ltd.* (1870) L.R. 10 Eq. 390.

[6] S. 110.

[7] S. 86.

[8] Ss. 104, 106 I.

[9] Ss. 95, 97, 103, 104, 106 H.

[10] S. 146.

[11] S. 195.

[12] S. 200.

[13] 1967 Act, S. 26.

[14] 1967 Act, Ss. 33–4.

[15] S. 433.

be any lawful purposes, but may not include anything in contravention of any rule of the general law[1] or of the Act.[2] By being stated in the Memorandum the objects are made plain to the share-holders, and to persons dealing with the company.[3] The objects clause is important because the company exists only for the purposes of incorporation stated in the objects, and enjoys only the powers necessary for the attainment of these objects, or reasonably incidental thereto, or given by statute.[4] Actings outwith those powers are *ultra vires* of the company, wholly void, and incapable of ratification by even all the shareholders.[4] Consequently the objects clause frequently lists a large number of objects, some of which the law would probably imply as incidental to the main objects. Unless all are stated as main objects, one or two will be interpreted as main objects and the rest as subsidiary.[5] Whether a particular transaction is within the company's powers is a question of interpretation of the objects clause.

The Limited Liability Clause

Companies limited by shares or by guarantee must state that the liability of the members is limited, i.e. to the amount, if any, unpaid on their shares, or to the amount of their guarantee, or both.[6] No alteration in the Memorandum or Articles can increase the member's liability to pay money.[7] The limitation on liability ceases if, to the member's knowledge, the number of shareholders has fallen below the legal minimum and so remained for six months, in which case each member is severally liable to the creditors for all debts contracted thereafter,[8] or if he agrees in writing to be bound by an alteration requiring him to take more shares or increasing his liability.[9]

The Capital Clause

In a company limited by shares the capital clause states the amount of nominal capital, the classes of shares, and the number and the nominal value of each. There is no fixed minimum or

---

[1] *Evans* v. *Heathcote* [1918] 1 K.B. 418.

[2] *Victor Battery Co.* v. *Curry's Ltd.* [1946] Ch. 242.

[3] *Cotman* v. *Brougham* [1918] A.C. 514.

[4] *Ashbury Ry. Carriage Co.* v. *Riche* (1875) L.R. 7 H.L. 653; *A.G.* v. *G.E. Ry.* (1880) 5 App. Cas. 473; see further, *infra*.

[5] *Re German Date Coffee Co.* (1882) 20 Ch. D. 169; *Anglo Overseas Agencies, Ltd.* v. *Green* [1961] 1 Q.B. 1.

[6] S. 2.   [7] S. 22; *McKewan's Case* (1877) 6 Ch. D. 447.

[8] S. 31.

[9] S. 22, proviso.

maximum capital. There may be various classes of shares, such as preference, ordinary, and deferred shares, and the rights of the different classes of shares are usually defined in the Articles.

Association Clause

The association clause states the desire of the subscribers to be incorporated as a company. There must be at least seven subscribers (public company) or two (private company) who must each sign, and undertake each to take at least one share.[1] Each signature, or all if all subscribe before the one witness, must be attested by at least one witness.[2] Any person having legal personality, including a minor,[3] a company, and a firm, may be a subscriber. A subscriber cannot subsequently repudiate his undertaking on the ground of misrepresentation.[4]

Alteration of Memorandum

Alteration of the Memorandum is prohibited[5] save in the modes and to the extent expressly permitted. The name clause may be altered by special resolution with the approval of the Dept. of Trade.[6] The registered office clause can be altered only by re-registering the company as incorporated in another country of the United Kingdom. The objects may be altered by special resolution so far as required to enable the company to do one or more of seven specified things.[7] Confirmation of the change by the court is no longer necessary (since 1948), though a specified minority of shareholders or of certain debenture holders may apply to the court to cancel the alteration.[8] The limited liability

---

[1] Ss. 1–2. [2] S. 3. [3] *Re Laxon and Co.* [1892] 3 Ch. 555.

[4] *Metal Constituents Ltd., Lord Lurgan's Case* [1902] 1 Ch. 707. [5] S. 4.

[6] S. 18; *Scottish Accident Ins. Co.* (1896) 23 R. 586; *Scottish Employers Liability etc. Ins. Co.* (1896) 23 R. 1016; *Kirkcaldy Steam Laundry Co.* (1904) 6 F. 778.

[7] These are (a) to carry on the business more economically or efficiently; (b) to attain the main purpose by new or improved means; (c) to enlarge or change the local area of operations; (d) to carry on some business which may conveniently or advantageously be combined with the business of the company; (e) to restrict or abandon any of the objects specified in the Memorandum; (f) to sell or dispose of the whole or any part of the undertaking of the company; (g) to amalgamate with any other company or body of persons.

[8] S. 5. See e.g. *Glasgow Tramways Co.* v. *Glasgow Mags.* (1891) 18 R. 675; *Scottish American Investment Co.* (1891) 28 S.L.R. 421; *Northern Accident Ins. Co.* (1893) 30 S.L.R. 834; *Young's Paraffin Light Co.* (1894) 21 R. 384; *King Line* (1902) 4 F. 504; *John Walker & Sons*, 1914 S.C. 280; *Macfarlane Strang & Co.*, 1915 S.C. 196; *Kirkcaldy Cafe Co.*, 1921 S.C. 681; *Hugh Baird & Sons*, 1932 S.C. 455; *Dundee Aerated Water Mfg. Co.*, 1932 S.C. 473; *Strathspey Hall Co.* v. *Anderson's Trs.*, 1934 S.C. 385; *Mutual Property Ins. Co.*, 1934 S.C. 61; *Scottish Veterans' Garden City Assocn.*, 1946 S.C. 416; *Sc. Special Housing Assocn.*, 1947 S.C. 17. Since 1948 see *Re Hampstead Garden Suburb Trust, Ltd.* [1962] Ch. 806. A printed copy of the memorandum as altered must be delivered to the registrar (S. 5(7)).

clause may be altered only by re-registering the company as unlimited.[1] The capital clause may be altered when, if authorized by the Articles, capital is increased or diminished, or shares consolidated or subdivided, by ordinary resolution;[2] a reduction of capital requires a special resolution and confirmation by the court.[3]

If additional provisions are included in the Memorandum they can be altered only in the same manner as the objects clause, and subject to the rights of minorities to object, unless the Memorandum itself prohibits alteration or provides for means of alteration. But this does not apply to a variation or abrogation of class rights of any class of members.[4] Alterations must be embodied in all copies of the Memorandum.[5]

Where an alteration is made in a memorandum or articles by any statutory provision, in Act of Parliament or instrument made thereunder, a printed copy of the Act or instrument must, under penalty, be forwarded to the registrar and recorded by him, along with a printed copy of the memorandum or articles as altered.[6] This provision is retrospective,[7] and the same applies to previous alterations made in any manner.[7]

The Articles of Association

The Articles of Association contain the regulations for managing the internal affairs of the company.[8] Articles must be registered by guarantee and unlimited companies,[9] and may be registered by companies limited by shares. If in the last case none are registered, those set out in Schedule I, Table A, of the Act apply, except in so far as modified or excluded.[10] Articles must be printed, subscribed in the same way as the Memorandum, and stamped.[11] They should not contain anything *ultra vires* the company or illegal. Articles substantially to the same effect as Table A cannot be illegal.[12] An article is not invalid by reason of not being in Table A or other appropriate Table.[13]

---

[1] 1967 Act, Ss. 43–44. Cf. *Proprietors of Royal Exchange Bldgs., Glasgow,* 1911 S.C. 1337.
[2] S. 61; cf. *Ramsbotham v. Scottish American Investment Co.* (1891) 18 R. 558.
[3] S. 66.
[4] S. 23. This does not prevent a company varying the rights of a class of members by a scheme of arrangement under S. 206: *City Property Investment Trust Corpn.,* 1951 S.C. 570.
[5] Ss. 24–5.
[6] European Communities Act, 1972, S. 9(5).
[7] Ibid., S. 9(6).
[8] *Lawrence's case* (1866) L.R. 2 Ch. 412.
[9] S. 6.   [10] S. 8.   [11] S. 9.
[12] *Lock v. Queensland Investment Co.* [1896] A.C. 461.
[13] *Gaiman v. National Assocn. for Mental Health* [1970] 2 All E.R. 362.

Alteration of Articles

Subject to the Act and any conditions contained in the Memorandum the Articles are freely alterable by special resolution,[1] even retrospectively[2] or so as to effect existing rights,[3] or in breach of contract,[4] but bona fide for the benefit of the company as a whole and not so as to defraud or oppress a minority of shareholders.[5] Without his consent in writing no member is bound by an alteration binding him to take or subscribe for more shares than held by him, or increasing his liability to pay money to the company.[6] An alteration not properly made may bind third parties though invalid within the company.[7] Copies of special resolutions in force are to be annexed to copies of the Articles issued thereafter.[8] Alterations to the Articles by statutory provisions require a printed copy to be forwarded to the registrar and recorded.[9]

Relation of Articles to Memorandum

The Memorandum contains fundamental provisions and the Articles are subordinate thereto[10] and cannot authorize anything inconsistent with the Memorandum, still less anything contrary to the Act or the general law. But they may be utilized to explain an ambiguity in the Memorandum.[11]

Effect of Memorandum and Articles

Both Memorandum and Articles when registered bind the company and the members as if signed by each member and containing covenants by each to observe all the provisions thereof.[12] In effect they constitute a contract between each

---

[1] S. 10; cf. *Andrews* v. *Gas Meter Co.* [1897] 1 Ch. 361; *Punt* v. *Symons & Co.* [1903] 2 Ch. 506; *Shirlaw* v. *Southern Foundries* [1940] A.C. 701.

[2] *Allen* v. *Gold Reefs of W. Africa* [1900] 1 Ch. 656; but see *McArthur* v. *Gulf Line, Ltd.*, 1909 S.C. 732; *Moir* v. *Duff & Co.* (1900) 2 F. 1265.

[3] *Sidebottom* v. *Kershaw, Leese & Co.* [1920] 1 Ch. 154; see also *Moir* v. *Duff* (1900) 2 F. 1265; *McArthur* v. *Gulf Line*, 1909 S.C. 732; *Crookston* v. *Lindsay Crookston & Co.*, 1922 S.L.T. 62; *Caledonian Ins. Co.* v. *Scottish American Investment Co.*, 1951 S.L.T. 23.

[4] *Shirlaw, supra.*

[5] *Burland* v. *Earle* [1902] A.C. 83; *Brown* v. *British Abrasive Wheel Co.* [1919] 1 Ch. 290; *Shuttleworth* v. *Cox* [1927] 2 K.B. 9; *Greenhalgh* v. *Arderne Cinemas* [1951] Ch. 286; *Rights and Issues Investment Trust Ltd.* v. *Stylo Shoes, Ltd.* [1965] Ch. 250.

[6] S. 22.

[7] *Muirhead* v. *Forth and North Sea Ins. Assocn.* (1894) 21 R. (H.L.) 1.

[8] S. 143.

[9] European Communities Act, 1972, S. 9(5) and (6).

[10] *Ashbury Ry. Carriage Co.* v. *Riche* (1875) L.R. 7 H.L. 653, 671; *Scottish National Trust Co.*, 1928 S.C. 499; *Re Duncan Gilmour & Co.* [1952] 2 All E.R. 871.

[11] *Re Wedgewood Coal & Iron Co.* (1877) 7 Ch. D. 75; *Guinness* v. *Land Corpn. of Ireland* (1882) 22 Ch. D. 349, 381.   [12] S. 20.

member and the company,[1] but not between members and each other, save through the intervention of the company,[2] nor between company and members, if not acting in the capacity of members.[3] They are binding on the directors, who must observe any restrictions imposed on them by the Articles. Being public documents, anyone who has dealings with a registered company is deemed to have notice thereof and to have understood them.[4]

Incorporation

The Memorandum and Articles and certain other documents (Ss. 15, 181, and Stamp Act, 1891, S. 112) are registered by the Registrar of Companies and fees paid, and a certificate of incorporation issued, whereupon the company comes into existence as a legal person.[5] The certificate is conclusive that all formalities have been complied with and that the company is registered under the Act,[6] but not as to the legality of all the objects.[7]

Legal personality

The company once incorporated is a full corporation or juristic person entirely independent of all its members. It matters not that one person owns nearly all the shares and entirely controls the company.[8] In consequence the company owns its assets and title to property is taken in its name. It may subscribe the Memorandum and Articles of, or take shares in, another company, or be a partner in a partnership, contract, commit wrongs, sue and be sued,[9] and continue in being indefinitely until dissolved on winding-up. In consequence of the company having full legal personality third parties have rights only against the company, and none against the members.[10] Members can contract with or sue the company and conversely. The company's

---

[1] *Oakbank Oil Co.* v. *Crum* (1882) 10 R. (H.L.) 11; *Bradford Banking Co.* v. *Briggs* (1886) 12 App. Cas. 29; *Welton* v. *Saffery* [1897] A.C. 299; see also *Hickman* v. *Kent, etc., Sheep Breeders' Assoc.* [1915] 1 Ch. 881; *St. Johnstone F.C.* v. *S.F.A., Ltd.*, 1965 S.L.T. 171.

[2] *Welton, supra*; *Borland's Trs.* v. *Steel Bros. & Co.* [1901] 1 Ch. 279.

[3] *Eley* v. *Positive Life Assocn. Co.* (1876) 1 Ex. D. 20, 88; *Beattie* v. *B.* [1938] Ch. 708.

[4] *Mahony* v. *East Holyford Mining Co.* (1875) L.R. 7 H.L. 869; *Griffith* v. *Paget* (1877) 6 Ch. D. 517; *Oakbank Oil Co.* v. *Crum* (1882) 10 R. (H.L.) 11.

[5] S. 13.

[6] S. 15; *Re Peel's Case* (1867) L.R. 2 Ch. App. 674; *Oakes* v. *Turquand* (1867) L.R. 2 H.L. 325; *Cotman* v. *Brougham* [1918] A.C. 514.

[7] *Bowman* v. *Secular Society* [1917] A.C. 406.

[8] *Salomon* v. *Salomon & Co.* [1897] A.C. 22.

[9] But it must appear in court by counsel: *Equity and Law Life Assce. Socy.* v. *Tritonia*, 1943 S.C. (H.L.) 88.

[10] Except under S. 31.

personality is such that it has a commercial reputation which may be impugned by defamation (though it cannot claim solatium for hurt feelings).[1]

Lifting the Veil

Only exceptionally does the law look behind the screen of corporate personality at those who actually compose or control the company.[2] This happens when the number of members falls below the minimum,[3] where there has been fraudulent trading,[4] where the Dept. of Trade is making an investigation of related companies, where the company is acting as agent of the share-holders,[5] when it is necessary to determine whether persons controlling a company are alien enemies or not,[6] when companies stand in the relationship of holding and subsidiary companies to one another,[7] and in various matters relating to stamps, taxation, and death duties.[8]

Statutory and common law powers

A company established by Royal charter has all the powers of a natural person, unless these are expressly or impliedly excluded or abridged by the Charter.[9] A company established by statute has its powers limited by the purposes of incorporation defined by the statute.[10] A company incorporated under the Companies Act has only those powers expressly or impliedly conferred as neces-sary to attain its declared objects, and powers necessarily inci-dental thereto.[11] Formerly Memoranda tended to state a main object or objects, other powers being deemed merely incidental thereto, but today Memoranda usually state a large number of independent main objects.[12] A company incorporated under the

---

[1] South Hetton Coal Co. v. N.E. News Assocn. [1894] 1 Q.B. 133; D. & L. Caterers Ltd. v. D'Ajou [1945] K.B. 364.
[2] See generally Gower, 183 et seq.
[3] S. 31.   [4] S. 332.
[5] Smith, Stone & Knight, Ltd. v. Birmingham Corpn. [1939] 4 All E.R. 116.
[6] Daimler Co. v. Continental Tyre & Rubber Co. [1916] 2 A.C. 307.
[7] S. 150.
[8] Unit Construction Co., Ltd. v. Bullock [1960] A.C. 351.
[9] Ellis v. Henderson (1844) 1 Bell 1; Sanderson v. Lees (1859) 22 D. 24; Kesson v. Aberdeen Wrights Incorpn. (1898) 1 F. 36.
[10] Ashbury Ry. Carriage Co. v. Riche (1875) L.R. 7 H.L. 628, 653; Baroness Wenlock v. River Dee Commrs. (1885) 10 App. Cas. 354; Mann v. Edinburgh Northern Tramways Co. (1892) 20 R. (H.L.) 7.
[11] Ashbury, supra; Shiell's Trs. v. Scottish Property Investment Socy. (1884) 12 R. (H.L.) 14; Life Assocn. v. Caledonian Heritable Security Co. (1886) 13 R. 750.
[12] e.g. Cotman v. Brougham [1918] A.C. 514; Anglo Overseas Agencies, Ltd. v. Green [1961] 1 Q.B. 1.

Companies Act has also numerous powers conferred on it by the Act, independently of those taken in the Memorandum of Association, some of which can be exercised only if the company's Articles so permit, other powers conferred, exercisable subject to confirmation by the court, and other powers again expressly withheld entirely or unless conditions are satisfied. It has also, at common law, though these are frequently also expressly taken in the Memorandum, power to enter into the ordinary kinds of contracts and to do the kinds of things naturally and normally incidental to its kinds of business, such as to employ staff, open bank accounts, and bring legal proceedings.

The ultra vires *rule*

The deduction from the rule that a company's objects define and limit its powers is that any transaction outwith those powers is wholly void and expenditure thereon is unwarranted, and neither can be ratified by the shareholders.[1] The company cannot lawfully do anything outside the powers given it in its Memorandum or fairly incidental thereto,[2] or by the Act. An alteration of the Memorandum cannot retrospectively validate earlier *ultra vires* actings. Moreover, since the Memorandum and Articles are registered and public documents, third parties dealing with the company were at common law deemed to have notice of the company's objects and powers, and had no remedy if they transacted innocently with the company in what is held to be an *ultra vires* transaction.[3] But now, in favour of a person dealing with the company in good faith any transaction decided on by the directors shall be deemed to be one which it is within the capacity of the company to enter into, and the power of the directors to bind the company shall be deemed to be free of any limitation under the memorandum or articles of association, and a party to a transaction so decided on shall not be bound to enquire as to the capacity of the company to enter into it or as to any such limitation on the powers of the directors, and shall be presumed to have acted in good faith unless the contrary is proved.[4] The *ultra vires* rule does not, however, prevent a company being held liable for

---

[1] *Ashbury Ry. Carriage Co.* v. *Riche* (1875) L.R. 7 H.L. 653; *General Property Co.* v. *Matheson's Trs.* (1888) 16 R. 282.

[2] *Foster* v. *L.C. & D. Ry. Co.* [1895] 1 Q.B. 711; *L.C.C.* v. *A.G.* [1902] A.C. 165.

[3] *Re Jon Beauforte (London) Ltd.* [1953] Ch. 131.

[4] European Communities Act, 1972, S. 9(1).

delicts[1] or crimes.[2] The plea that a transaction is *ultra vires* is personal to the contracting parties.[3]

Contractual powers

Prior to incorporation the company has no contractual powers,[4] and is not bound by a contract,[5] nor can anyone contract as agent for it,[6] but an agreement may be made by a person as trustee for the company, and adopted by it once it is incorporated.[7] Where a contract purports to be made by a company, or by a person as agent for a company, at a time when the company has not been formed, then subject to any agreement to the contrary the contract has effect as one entered into by the person purporting to act for the company or as agent for it, and he is personally liable on the contract accordingly.[8] Once incorporated, a company has, within the limits of the *ultra vires* rule, full contractual powers, though contracts must be in fact negotiated and signed by persons acting within the scope of their express or implied authority as agents for the company. Authority is normally conferred in the Articles on directors, managers and others, and this power may be delegated to others. An act by a manager in excess of authority may be ratified by the person entitled to authorize him. A third party dealing with a company cannot assume that an officer has authority to contract unless the company has held him out as having such authority or, possibly, unless the act would be within the ordinary scope of the officer's duties. Contracts which are *intra vires* the company but *ultra vires* the directors may be ratified by the company.[9] Contracts are made in the same form as those by a private person, orally on behalf of the company by any person acting under its authority, express or implied, or in writing signed on behalf of the company by such

---

[1] *Mersey Dock and Harbour Board* v. *Gibbs* (1866) L.R. 1 H.L. 93; *Barwick* v. *English Joint Stock Bank* (1867) L.R. 2 Ex. 259; *Houldsworth* v. *City of Glasgow Bank* (1880) 7 R. (H.L.) 53.

[2] *R.* v. *I.C.R. Haulage Ltd.* [1944] K.B. 551; *Lott* v. *Macdonald*, 1963 J.C. 57.

[3] *Clyde Steam Packet Co.* v. *G.S.W. Ry.* (1897) 4 S.L.T. 327.

[4] *Newborne* v. *Sensolid (G.B.) Ltd.* [1954] 1 Q.B. 45.

[5] *Re English and Colonial Produce Co., Ltd.* [1906] 2 Ch. 435.

[6] *Kelner* v. *Baxter* (1866) L.R. 2 C.P. 174; *Tinnevelly Sugar Refining Co.* v. *Mirrlees Watson & Yaryan Co.* (1894) 21 R. 1009. See also *Struthers Patent Co.* v. *Clydesdale Bank* (1886) 13 R. 434.

[7] *James Young & Sons Ltd.* v. *James Young & Sons' Trs.* (1902) 10 S.L.T. 85.

[8] European Communities Act, 1972, S. 9(2).

[9] *Gillies* v. *Craigton Garage Co., Ltd.*, 1935 S.C. 423; *Bamford* v. *B.* [1968] 2 All E.R. 655.

a person.[1] Where formal writing is required a contract is validly executed if executed in accordance with the provisions of the Act or sealed with the common seal and subscribed by two directors or by a director and the secretary, witnesses being unnecessary.[2]

The doctrine of notice

Persons dealing with the company must satisfy themselves that the company has power to enter into the proposed transaction, and that the agent for the company is authorized to act in that respect on its behalf. The Memorandum and Articles and special resolutions of the company, being registered, are public documents and everyone dealing with the company is deemed to have notice of their contents, including the extent of the company's powers and any limitations imposed by the Articles on the directors' powers.[2] This rule operates only in the company's favour, not against it.[3] Hence even an innocent person who in ignorance transacts with a company to do something *ultra vires* the company has no remedy against it. Fraud is, however, an exception.[4] If the transaction is *intra vires* the company but *ultra vires* the directors and the latter fact is not disclosed by the public documents, a person who innocently transacts in ignorance of that limitation may assume that all matters of procedure internal to the company, such as conferring the requisite authority on the directors with whom he deals, have been duly complied with, and he need not inquire into the company's internal management,[5] on the basis that *omnia praesumuntur rite ac solemniter esse acta*. The other person has no protection if the agent purporting to act on behalf of the company purports to make a contract not within the powers ordinarily or ostensibly possessed by such an agent,[6] nor, probably, if he did not have actual knowledge of the

---

[1] S. 32; the Articles may prescribe the manner of affixing the common seal: *Clydesdale Bank (Moore Place) Nominees, Ltd.* v. *Snodgrass*, 1939 S.C. 805.

[2] *Mahony* v. *East Holyford Co.* (1875) L.R. 7 H.L. 869; *Oakbank Oil Co.* v. *Crum* (1882) 10 R. (H.L.) 11.

[3] *Rama Corpn. Ltd.* v. *Proved Investments Ltd.* [1952] 2 K.B. 147.

[4] *Venezuela Central Ry.* v. *Kisch* (1867) 2 H.L.C. 99; cf. *Heiton* v. *Waverley Hydropathic Co.* (1877) 4 R. 830.

[5] This is 'the rule in *Royal British Bank* v. *Turquand* (1856) 6 E. & B. 327'. See *Mahony, supra*; *Re County Life Assce. Co.* (1870) L.R. 5 Ch. App. 288; *Duck* v. *Tower Galvanizing Co., Ltd.* [1901] 2 K.B. 314; *Gillies* v. *Craigton Garage Co.*, 1935 S.C. 423. Contrast *Irvine* v. *Union Bank of Australia* (1877) 2 App. Cas. 366. See also *National Bank Glasgow Nominees Ltd.* v. *Adamson*, 1932 S.L.T. 492.

[6] *Houghton* v. *Nothard, Lowe & Wills, Ltd.* [1927] 1 K.B. 246; *Rama Corpn., supra*.

public documents.[1] Reliance on the rule in *Turquand's case*[2] is not possible where the person transacting with the company was ignorant of the contents of the Articles,[3] or knew of the irregularity in internal matters,[4] or had been put on his inquiry and should have investigated further,[5] or if the transaction is based on a forged document.[6]

Delictual liability

As a juristic person a company cannot by itself commit wrongs, but it can be held vicariously liable[7] for wrongs committed by its agents acting within the scope of their authority, or by its servants acting in the course of their employment,[8] even where intention, malice or other mental element is of the essence of the wrong.[9] It is questionable whether the company is liable if the agent or servant, when doing wrong, was acting *ultra vires*.[10] An act is not, however, automatically *ultra vires* merely because the agent, in doing it, is committing delict.

Power to hold property

If authorized by its Memorandum and Articles a company may hold any kind of property in its corporate name.

Title to sue and to defend

A company may sue and defend all kinds of legal proceedings in its corporate name, but can appear in court only by counsel.[11]

Criminal liability

A company may similarly be held liable for criminal wrongdoing, though the actual wrong must have been that of an agent

[1] *Rama Corpn. Ltd.* v. *Proved Investments Ltd.* [1952] 2 K.B. 147.

[2] (1856) 6 E. & B. 327.

[3] *Rama Corpn. Ltd.*, *supra*; *Hely Hutchinson* v. *Brayhead, Ltd.* [1967] 3 All E.R. 98.

[4] *Houghton* v. *Nothard, Lowe & Wills* [1928] A.C. 1; *Morris* v. *Kanssen* [1946] A.C. 459.

[5] *Underwood* v. *Bank of Liverpool* [1924] 1 K.B. 775; *Houghton*, *supra*; *E.B.M. Co.* v. *Dominion Bank* [1937] 3 All E.R. 555.

[6] *Ruben* v. *Great Fingall Consolidated* [1906] A.C. 439; *Kreditbank Cassel* v. *Schenkers, Ltd.* [1927] 1 K.B. 826; *South London Greyhound Racecourses* v. *Wake* [1931] 1 Ch. 496.

[7] On vicarious liability see Ch. 55, *infra*.

[8] *Barwick* v. *English Joint Stock Bank* (1867) L.R. 2 Ex. 259; *Houldsworth* v. *City of Glasgow Bank* (1880) 7 R. (H.L.) 53; *Wright* v. *Dunlop & Co.* (1893) 20 R. 363; *Citizens Life Assce. Co.* v. *Brown* [1904] A.C. 423; *Finburgh* v. *Moss's Empires*, 1908 S.C. 928; *Power* v. *Central S.M.T. Co.*, 1949 S.C. 376.

[9] *Gordon* v. *British and Foreign Metaline Co.* (1886) 14 R. 75.

[10] *Poulton* v. *L.S.W. Ry.* (1867) L.R. 2 Q.B. 534; *Campbell* v. *Paddington Corpn.* [1911] 1 K.B. 869.

[11] *Equity and Law Life Assce. Socy.* v. *Tritonia Ltd.*, 1943 S.C. (H.L.) 88.

or servant of the company,[1] except, probably, for such kinds of crimes as only a natural person can commit, the requisite criminal intent of the agent being ascribed to the company.

FLOTATION

The promoters of a company are those who participate, in other than a professional capacity,[2] in bringing a company into being, as by raising capital, placing shares, or negotiating with a seller of a business or other interest.[3] The promoters stand in a fiduciary relation to the nascent company and consequently may not make any direct or indirect profit from the promotion without the knowledge of the company.[4] They may not sell their own property to the company without disclosing their interest.[5] Any transaction not adequately disclosed may be reduced by the company[6] and any secret profit may be recovered by the company.[7] Promoters may be legitimately remunerated by receiving certain shares allotted as fully paid, or obtaining an option to take unissued shares, or selling a business or asset to the new company at a profit.[8] But if a promoter is selling his own property to the company he must furnish it with an independent board of directors and disclose his interest in the sale.[9] Payments to a firm of which the promoter is a partner must equally be disclosed.[10] A promoter may recover preliminary expenses only where he established a contract by the company to pay.[11] The

---

[1] *D.P.P.* v. *Kent & Sussex Contractors Ltd.* [1944] K.B. 146; *R.* v. *I.C.R. Haulage, Ltd.* [1944] K.B. 551. As to summary offences see *Henderson* v. *Forster*, 1944 J.C. 91.

[2] *Re Great Wheal Polgooth Co.* (1883) 53 L.J. Ch. 42 (solicitors); *Mann* v. *Edinburgh Northern Tramways Co.* (1896) 23 R. 1056.

[3] *Lindsay Petroleum Co.* v. *Hurd* (1874) L.R. 5 P.C. 221; *Twycross* v. *Grant* (1877) 2 C.P.D. 469; *Emma Silver Mining Co.* v. *Lewis* (1879) 4 C.P.D. 396; *Whaley Bridge Printing Co.* v. *Green* (1879) 5 Q.B.D. 109; *Gluckstein* v. *Barnes* [1900] A.C. 240.

[4] *Henderson* v. *Huntington Copper & Sulphur Co.* (1877) 5 R. (H.L.) 1; *Erlanger* v. *New Sombrero Phosphate Co.* (1887) 3 App. Cas. 1218; *Mann* v. *Edinburgh Northern Tramways* (1892) 20 R. (H.L.) 7; (1896) 23 R. 1056.

[5] *Henderson* v. *Huntington Copper Co.* (1877) 5 R. (H.L.) 1.

[6] *Erlanger* v. *New Sombrero Phosphate Co.* (1878) 3 App. Cas. 1218; *Jubilee Cotton Mills, Ltd.* v. *Lewis* [1924] A.C. 958.

[7] *Lagunas Nitrate Co.* v. *Lagunas Syndicate* [1899] 2 Ch. 392; *Re Leeds and Hanley Theatre of Varieties* [1902] 2 Ch. 809; *Jubilee Cotton Mills* v. *Lewis* [1924] A.C. 958.

[8] cf. *Mason's Trs.* v. *Poole & Robinson* (1903) 5 F. 789.

[9] *Erlanger*, *supra*.

[10] *Scottish Pacific Coast Mining Co.* v. *Falkner, Bell & Co.* (1888) 15 R. 290.

[11] *Mason's Trs.*, *supra*; *English and Colonial Produce Co.* [1906] 2 Ch. 435; *National Motor Mail Coach Co.* [1908] 2 Ch. 515. See also *Scott* v. *Money Order Co. of G.B.* (1870) 42 S. Jur. 212.

remuneration or benefit, whatever its nature, must be disclosed in the prospectus if paid within the past two years or intended to be paid at any time.[1]

The raising of capital

A public company may raise money required for capital by issuing a prospectus and inviting applications from the public for shares, or by an offer for sale, by allotting shares in bulk to an issuing house which invites the public to take shares in smaller quantities and also for a commission underwrites the issue, thus taking the risk that the public will not subscribe for all the shares,[2] or by the issuing house 'placing' shares with clients and business associates without issuing invitations to the general public to take shares.[3] An issue of invitations to make application for shares must be accompanied by a prospectus (defined, S. 455) which must be dated,[4] and a copy delivered to the Registrar for registration.[5] It must contain the information required by the Act (S. 38 and Sched. 4), including certain reports. To obtain a quotation of the shares on a Stock Exchange the prospectus must contain the information required by the rules of the stock exchange in question. The prospectus must give a full, fair, and accurate picture of the state and prospects of the company, make full disclosure, and not contain any misrepresentations, ambiguities or misleading statements.[6] The company putting it forward is responsible for the truth of statements in a report contained therein.[7]

A prospectus is addressed only to those who subscribe on the faith of it, and only they can sue for misrepresentation.[8] In many cases individuals who subscribed for shares, induced by material mis-statements in the prospectus, have had their contracts set

---

[1] S. 38; *Henderson v. Huntington Copper and Sulphur Co.* (1877) 5 R. (H.L.) 1.

[2] On underwriting see *Premier Briquette Co. v. Gray*, 1922 S.C. 329; *Australian Inv. Tr. v. Strand Properties* [1932] A.C. 735. Underwriting commission is a legitimate expense, subject to S. 53. See also *Andreae v. Zinc Mines of G.B.* [1918] 2 K.B. 454.

[3] cf. *Sleigh v. Glasgow and Transvaal Options* (1904) 6 F. 420.

[4] S. 37.

[5] S. 41.

[6] Ss. 30, 46; *New Brunswick Ry. Co. v. Muggeridge* (1860) 1 Dr. & Sm. 383; *Henderson v. Lacon* (1867) L.R. 5 Eq. 249; *Central Ry. of Venezuela v. Kisch* (1867) L.R. 2 H.L. 123; *Reese River Co. v. Smith* (1869) L.R. 4 H.L. 64; *Arnison v. Smith* (1889) 41 Ch. D. 348; *Aaron's Reefs v. Twiss* [1896] A.C. 273.

[7] *Mair v. Rio Grande Rubber Estates*, 1913 S.C. (H.L.) 74.

[8] *Peek v. Gurney* (1873) L.R. 6 H.L. 337; *McMorland's Trs. v. Fraser* (1896) 24 R. 65.

aside and their money returned,[1] or recovered damages from the company or the directors for loss caused if they can prove fraud.[2] They must prove that they were induced by the prospectus and applied for shares on the faith of the prospectus.[3] The right to rescind the contract to take shares will be lost if the contract has been ratified expressly or impliedly, as by trying to sell the shares, receiving dividends,[4] or otherwise acting as a member.[5] It is lost when winding-up commences, as the interests of creditors then intervene,[6] or if restitutio *in integrum* cannot be made.[7]

Damages may also be recovered at common law from the promoters or directors or experts for fraud, if the misleading statements were made by them knowingly, or without belief in their truth, or recklessly, careless whether they were true or false, but not merely because they were made negligently or without reasonable grounds for belief in their truth.[8] By S. 43, however, an allottee is entitled to sue directors and promoters who authorized the issue of the prospectus[9] for compensation without need to prove fraud, but the directors have possible defences open to them.[10] An expert who has consented to a statement in the prospectus may also be liable, but only in respect of an untrue statement purporting to be made by him as an expert. Damages may also be claimed for non-compliance with S. 38 by omission of something which should have been included in a prospectus.[11]

A person induced by misrepresentation to take shares may apply to have the register of members rectified by removal of his

[1] *Western Bank of Scotland* v. *Addie* (1867) 5 M. (H.L.) 80; *Central Ry. of Venezuela* v. *Kisch* (1867) L.R. 2 H.L. 99; *Reese River Co.* v. *Smith* (1869) L.R. 4 H.L. 64.

[2] e.g. *National Exchange Co. of Glasgow* v. *Drew* (1855) 2 Macq. 124; *Houldsworth* v. *City of Glasgow Bank* (1880) 7 R. (H.L.) 53; *Arnison* v. *Smith* (1889) 41 Ch. D. 348; *Lagunas Nitrate Co.* v. *Lagunas Syndicate* [1899] 2 Ch. 392.

[3] *McMorland's Trs.* v. *Fraser* (1896) 24 R. 65.

[4] *Scholey* v. *Venezuela & Central Ry.* (1868) L.R. 9 Eq. 266n.

[5] *Ex p. Briggs* (1866) L.R. 1 Eq. 483; *Scholey, supra*; *Sharpley* v. *Louth Co.* (1876) 2 Ch. D. 663; *Caledonian Debenture Co.* v. *Bernard* (1898) 5 S.L.T. 392.

[6] *Oakes* v. *Turquand* (1867) L.R. 2 H.L. 325; *Tennant* v. *City of Glasgow Bank* (1879) 6 R. (H.L.) 69.

[7] *Houldsworth* v. *City of Glasgow Bank* (1880) 7 R. (H.L.) 53.

[8] *Derry* v. *Peek* (1889) 14 App. Cas. 337; cf. *Tulloch* v. *Davidson* (1858) 3 Macq. 783; *Cullen* v. *Thomson's Trs.* (1862) 4 Macq. 424; *Western Bank, supra*; *New Brunswick Ry.* v. *Conybeare* (1862) 9 H.L. Cas. 724; *City of Edinburgh Brewery Co.* v. *Gibson's Tr.* (1869) 7 M. 886; *Smith* v. *Chadwick* (1883) 9 App. Cas. 187; *Chambers* v. *Edinburgh & Glasgow Aerated Bread Co.* (1891) 18 R. 1039; *Blakiston* v. *London, etc. Discount Corpn.* (1894) 21 R. 417; contrast *Honeyman* v. *Dickson* (1896) 4 S.L.T. 150.

[9] cf. *Sleigh* v. *Glasgow and Transvaal Options* (1904) 6 F. 420.

[10] *Macleay* v. *Tait* [1906] A.C. 24; *Clarke* v. *Urquhart* [1930] A.C. 28; cf. *Smith* v. *Moncrieff* (1894) 2 S.L.T. 140; *Davidson* v. *Hamilton* (1904) 12 S.L.T. 353.

[11] *Nash* v. *Lynde* [1929] A.C. 158.

name therefrom, and the return of his money with interest,[1] but must not have acted as a shareholder after discovering the misrepresentation.[2] Rectification may also be ordered in an action of reduction.[3]

Criminal liability may also be incurred.[4]

A statement in lieu of prospectus conforming to Schedule 3 is required when a private company is converted into a public one, unless it in fact issues a prospectus,[5] or when a public company is formed which has not obtained its initial working capital on the basis of a prospectus, in which case it must conform to Schedule 5.[6]

A private company may not issue a prospectus but obtains its initial capital from the promoters and persons whom they induce to contribute capital such as banks.

The practice of 'share-pushing' is limited by the Prevention of Fraud (Investments) Act, 1958, and the Protection of Depositors Act, 1963. The latter Act also prohibits fraudulent inducements to invest money on deposit.

Allotment of shares

An applicant's offer to take shares is accepted in whole or in part when shares are allotted to him and he is notified of the fact by letter of allotment[7] or otherwise. The court may order specific implement of the contract to allot, or to take, shares.[8] The allotment must not contain conditions not in the application for shares.[9] When a public company for the first time invites the public to subscribe for shares, no allotment of shares may take place until the minimum subscription fixed by the directors as giving essential initial capital has been taken up and the sums in respect thereof paid.[10] If the minimum subscrip-

---

[1] S. 116; *Anderson's Case* (1881) 17 Ch. D. 373; *Re London and Staffordshire Fire Ins. Co.* (1883) 24 Ch. D. 149. See also *Blaikie* v. *Coats* (1893) 21 R. 150; *Colquhoun's Tr.* v. *B.L. Co.* (1900) 2 F. 945; *Sleigh* v. *Glasgow and Transvaal Options, Ltd.* (1904) 6 F. 420; *Gowans* v. *Dundee S.N. Co.* (1904) 6 F. 613.

[2] *First National Reinsurance Co. Ltd.* v. *Greenfield* [1921] 2 K.B. 260.

[3] *Kinghorn* v. *Glenyards Fireclay Co.* (1907) 14 S.L.T. 683.

[4] Ss. 44, 438; cf. *R.* v. *Kylsant* [1932] 1 K.B. 442.

[5] S. 30.   [6] S. 48

[7] *Pellatt's Case* (1867) L.R. 2 Ch. App. 527; *Re Scottish Petroleum Co.* (1883) 23 Ch. D. 413; *Chapman* v. *Sulphite Pulp Co.* (1892) 19 R. 837; *Nelson* v. *Fraser* (1906) 14 S.L.T. 513; cf. *Molleson & Grigor* v. *Fraser's Trs.* (1881) 8 R. 630. As to letter not arriving see *Household Fire Ins. Co.* v. *Grant* (1879) 4 Ex. D. 216.

[8] S. 92; *Beardmore* v. *Barry*, 1928 S.C. 101; affd. 1928 S.C. (H.L.) 47.

[9] *Consolidated Copper Co. of Canada* v. *Peddie* (1877) 5 R. 393; *Swedish Match Co.* v. *Seivwright* (1889) 16 R. 989; *National House Property Investment Co.* v. *Watson*, 1908 S.C. 888.   [10] S. 47.

tion has not been received within 40 days of the first issue of the prospectus money received must be repaid.[1] Shares may be issued at a premium,[2] but the premium must be credited to a special account and may be used only for specified purposes.[3] They may not be issued at a discount, save under statutory conditions.[4] Full payment for shares is frequently not required on allotment, and shares may remain partly-paid shares for some time, the directors making calls from time to time. Payment for shares allotted may be in money or money's worth, such as services or property.[5] An allotment which is irregular may in certain circumstances be voidable[6] or void.[7] Within one month of allotment the company must make a return giving prescribed particulars thereof.[8] Shares are held to be issued to an allotee only when he has been placed on the register or a share certificate issued to him.[9]

Commencement of business

Private companies and companies having no share capital may commence business as soon as incorporated. Other companies may not do so until the Registrar has issued a trading certificate which requires the prior fulfilment of the conditions that, if the company has issued a prospectus, shares to the amount of the minimum subscription (determined by S. 47) have been allotted, and that no money is or may become liable to be repaid to applicants by reason of any failure to apply for or to obtain permission for shares or debentures to be dealt in on any stock exchange, and, if the company has not issued a prospectus, that a statement in lieu of prospectus has been delivered to the registrar for registration; and, further, in both cases, that every director has paid, on each of the shares taken or contracted to be taken and for which he is liable to pay, a proportion equal to the proportion payable on application and allotment on the shares payable in cash, and that there has been delivered for registration

[1] *Glasgow Pavilion Ltd.* v. *Motherwell* (1903) 6 F. 116.
[2] *Cameron* v. *Glenmorangie Distillery Co.* (1896) 23 R. 1092.
[3] S. 56; *Head & Co.* v. *Ropner Holdings Ltd.* [1951] 2 All E.R. 994.
[4] Ss. 53, 57; *Ooregum Gold Mining Co. of India* v. *Roper* [1892] A.C. 125; *Mosely* v. *Koffyfontein Mines, Ltd.* [1904] 2 Ch. 108; cf. *Klenck* v. *East India Co.* (1888) 16 R. 271; *Newburgh, etc. Ry. Co.* v. *N.B. Ry. Co.*, 1913 S.C. 1166.
[5] *Larocque* v. *Beauchemin* [1897] A.C. 358; *Pelican, etc. Insce. Co.* v. *Bruce* (1904) 11 S.L.T. 658. But shares may not be allotted in return for future services: *Gardner* v. *Iredale* [1912] 1 Ch. 700.
[6] S. 49.
[7] S. 51.
[8] S. 52.
[9] *Blyth's Case* (1876) 4 Ch. D. 140; *Clarke's Case* (1878) 8 Ch. D. 635.

a statutory declaration by the secretary or a director that the conditions have been complied with.[1] Such other companies must also within one to three months from the date when the company is entitled to commence business hold a statutory general meeting at which the members consider a statutory report circulated by the directors, a copy of which is sent to the registrar for registration.[2] The trading certificate is conclusive evidence that the company is entitled to commence business.[3]

MANAGEMENT OF THE COMPANY

Directors

The members of a company are usually too numerous all to participate in managing its affairs and to act as agents for the company. The Articles normally therefore name the first directors[4] and provide thereafter for the election by the members of directors to manage the affairs of the company. The Articles may prescribe qualifications for appointment, such as holding a certain number of shares. Every public company must now[5] have at least two directors, and every private company at least one director. There must also be a secretary and a sole director cannot also be secretary.[6] A register of directors and secretaries must be maintained at the registered office showing specified particulars of all directors.[7] Similar particulars must be sent to the Registrar of Companies.[7] A register must also be maintained of directors' service contracts[8] and their holdings of shares or debentures in it or associated companies.[9] The names, former names, and nationality of directors must be published in trade catalogues, trade circulars, showcards and business letters in which the company's name appears.[10]

Directors are agents of the company and the principles of agency apply to their relationship.[11] They are not by election as directors employees of the company, but an employee may be a director.

[1] S. 109.

[2] S. 130.   [3] S. 109.

[4] Nomination is valid only if the conditions of S. 181 are satisfied. Failing nomination the first directors are appointed by the subscribers to the Memorandum: *John Morley Building Co.* v. *Barras* [1891] 2 Ch. 386.

[5] S. 176; a limited company may be sole director: *Re Bulawayo Market Co.* [1907] 2 Ch. 458.

[6] Ss. 177–8.   [7] S. 200.

[8] 1967 Act, S. 26.   [9] 1967 Act, Ss. 27–29.

[10] S. 201.

[11] *Ferguson* v. *Wilson* (1866) L.R. 2 Ch. App. 77. They may be personally liable under S. 108.

Directors are also trustees for the company, in that they must act for the benefit of the general body of members,[1] though not for individual shareholders,[2] may not, as directors, transact with themselves as individuals,[3] must account to the company for any profit made,[4] must show diligence and care in the execution of their duties and not abuse their powers.[5] They may not delegate their powers or duties save in so far as power to do so is expressed or implied in the Articles.[6] A director may incur liability for breach of trust, either personally or by concurring in conduct by fellow-directors of that nature.[7]

Directors must act honestly towards the company,[8] not contract with the seller of a business to the company for their own benefit,[9] not accept bribes or private benefits or otherwise make secret profits,[10] exercise diligence and care in the company's affairs,[11] and in appropriate circumstances take and act on independent skilled advice.[12] They are not liable for errors of judgment[13] but are for gross negligence. But a director of a parent company may contract with a subsidiary which has an independent board of directors.[14]

A director who is in breach of duty is liable to an action by the company to recover the profit made by him or the loss sustained

[1] *G. E. Ry.* v. *Turner* (1872) L.R. 8 Ch. App. 149; *Smith* v. *Anderson* (1880) 15 Ch. D. 247; *Re Faure Electric Accumulator Co.* (1888) 40 Ch. D. 141; *Re City Equitable Fire Ins. Co.* [1925] Ch. 407; *Harris* v. *H.*, 1936 S.C. 183; *Selangor Rubber Estates* v. *Cradock* [1968] 2 All E.R. 1073.

[2] *Percival* v. *Wright* [1902] 2 Ch. 421; *Wilson* v. *Dunlop, Bremner & Co.*, 1921, 1 S.L.T. 354.

[3] *Jacobus Marler Estates* v. *Marler* (1916) 85 L.J.P.C. 167; *Hely-Hutchinson* v. *Brayhead* [1968] 1 Q.B. 549.

[4] *Allen* v. *Hyatt* (1914) 30 T.L.R. 444; *Regal (Hastings) Ltd.* v. *Gulliver* [1942] 1 All E.R. 378.

[5] *Punt* v. *Symons & Co.* [1903] 2 Ch. 506; *Brenes & Co.* v. *Downie*, 1914 S.C. 97; *Piercy* v. *Mills & Co.* [1920] 1 Ch. 77.

[6] *Cobb* v. *Becke* (1845) 6 Q.B. 930; *Leeds Estate Co.* v. *Shepherd* (1887) 36 Ch. D. 787; *Mahony* v. *East Holyford Mining Co.* (1875) L.R. 7 H.L. 869; *Allison* v. *Scotia Motor and Engineering Co.* (1906) 14 S.L.T. 9.

[7] *Caledonian Heritable Security Co.* v. *Curror's Tr.* (1882) 9 R. 1115.

[8] *Industrial Development Consultants, Ltd.* v. *Cooley* [1972] 2 All E.R. 162.

[9] *Henderson* v. *Huntington Copper Co.* (1877) 5 R. (H.L.) 1; cf. *G.N.S. Ry.* v. *Urquhart* (1884) 21 S.L.R. 377.

[10] *Re George Newman & Co.* [1895] 1 Ch. 674; *Laughland* v. *Millar Laughland & Co.* (1904) 6 F. 413; *Industrial Development Consultants, supra.*

[11] *Rance's Case* (1870) L.R. 6 Ch. App. 104; *Re City Equitable Fire Ins. Co.* [1925] 1 Ch. 407.

[12] *Re Faure Electric Accumulator Co.* (1888) 40 Ch. D. 141.

[13] *Overend & Gurney Co.* v. *Gibb* (1872) L.R. 5 H.L. 480; *Liqrs. of City of Glasgow Bank* v. *Mackinnon* (1882) 9 R. 535.

[14] *Lindgren* v. *L. & P. Estates Co.* [1968] 1 All E.R. 917.

by the company.[1] On winding-up the liquidator or a creditor may apply to the court[2] to examine the conduct of a director or past director and require repayment by him.[3] The court has a discretion, whether to grant relief and how much.[4] The Articles may contain provisions for indemnifying directors from liability,[5] but only so far as permitted by S. 205, but S. 448 empowers the court, in proceedings against a director for negligence, default, breach of duty or breach of trust to relieve him from liability, wholly or partly, if in the opinion of the court he acted honestly and reasonably and in the circumstances ought fairly to be relieved.[6]

Appointment of directors

First directors are usually named in the Articles, failing which all or a majority of the subscribers may by writing appoint them. Thereafter directors are elected at a general meeting. Casual vacancies may be filled by co-option, subject to ratification at the next general meeting. No qualification is required save that an undischarged bankrupt may not act unless authorized by the court[7] and a person guilty of fraud or breach of duty may be disqualified by the court.[8] A director need not be a shareholder but the Articles may provide that he hold a specified number of shares, in which case he must acquire the qualifying holding within two months.[9] Subject to certain exceptions a person cannot be elected a director of a public company, or a private company which is a subsidiary of a public company, when over the age of 70, unless he is appointed in general meeting in terms of an ordinary resolution of which special notice has been given, stating the director's age.[10] The Articles may provide for permanent directors[11] but frequently provide for directors retiring in rotation, and frequently for re-election unless the general meeting resolves not to fill the vacancy or a resolution for his re-election

---

[1] *Joint Stock Discount Co.* v. *Brown* (1869) L.R. 8 Eq. 381; *Industrial Development Consultants, supra.*

[2] S. 338; *Re Forest of Dean Mining Co.* (1878) 10 Ch. D. 450; *Cavendish-Bentinck* v. *Fenn* (1887) 12 App. Cas. 652; *Re City Equitable Fire Insce. Co.* [1925] Ch. 407.

[3] *Liqr. of Caledonian Heritable Security Co.* v. *Curror's Tr.* (1882) 9 R. 1115.

[4] *Sunlight Incandescent Gas Lamp Co.* (1900) 16 T.L.R. 535.

[5] *Tomlinson* v. *Liqrs. of Scottish Amalgamated Silks, Ltd.,* 1935 S.C. (H.L.) 1.

[6] cf. *National Trustee Co. of Australasia* v. *General Finance Co.* [1905] A.C. 373; *Re Claridges Patent Asphalte Co.* [1921] 1 Ch. 543; *Re City Equitable Co., supra.*

[7] S. 187.

[8] S. 188.

[9] S. 182; cf. *Brown's case* (1874) L.R. 9 Ch. 102; *Kingsburgh Motor Construction Co.* v. *Scott* (1902) 10 S.L.T. 424.

[10] S. 185.

[11] e.g. *Bersel* v. *Berry* [1968] 2 All E.R. 552.

has been lost. A director may resign at any time or sell his qualification shares and vacate office in consequence.[1]

Disqualification of directors

A director becomes disqualified if he loses any qualification required by the Articles or does anything which is thereby stated to be a disqualification.[2] A director who becomes bankrupt cannot act as a director without leave of the court.[3] A director must retire after he has attained 70, unless his continuance in office is approved by a general meeting, special notice having been given.[4] The Articles may modify the rule, which does not apply to private companies unless they are subsidiaries of public companies.[4]

Benefits to directors

Loans by a company to a director or director of its holding company are prohibited, nor may a company guarantee or provide security for a loan to a director by anyone, subject to limited exceptions.[5] A director may not, unless permitted by the Articles, contract with the company as this might result in conflict between his interest and his duty of trust, not even if the contract were perfectly fair.[6] Any interest in a contract or proposed contract with the company must be disclosed.[7] It is an offence for a director to deal in options on the company's shares.[8] A director who obtains any secret benefit by virtue of his position must account to the company for it,[9] and the company may rescind the contract[10] or recover from a third party any benefit it has obtained by bribing a director.[11] Directors have, as such, no claim to remuneration[12] but the Articles normally authorize such remuneration as shall be voted in general meeting.[13] Expenses are frequently also authorized.[14] To take unauthorized remuneration is

---

[1] *Gilbert's Case* (1870) L.R. 5 Ch. App. 559.

[2] See e.g. Table A, Art. 88.

[3] S. 187.

[4] S. 185.

[5] S. 190. See also *Baird* v. *J. Baird & Co.*, 1949 S.L.T. 368.

[6] *Aberdeen Ry.* v. *Blaikie Bros.* (1854) 1 Macq. 461; *Bray* v. *Ford* [1896] A.C. 44.

[7] S. 199.   [8] 1967 Act, S. 25.

[9] *Boston Co.* v. *Ansell* (1888) 39 Ch. D. 339; *Eden* v. *Ridsdale Co.* (1889) 23 Q.B.D. 368.

[10] *Shipway* v. *Broadwood* [1889] 1 Q.B. 369.

[11] *Mayor of Salford* v. *Lever* [1891] 1 Q.B. 168; *Grant* v. *Gold Exploration Syndicate* [1900] 1 Q.B. 233.

[12] *McNaughtan* v. *Brunton* (1882) 10 R. 111; *Hutton* v. *West York Ry. Co.* (1883) 23 Ch. D. 654. See also *Fife Linoleum Co.* v. *Lornie* (1905) 13 S.L.T. 670.

[13] *Woolf* v. *East Nigel Co.* (1905) 21 T.L.R. 660.

[14] *Marmor* v. *Alexander*, 1908 S.C. 78.

breach of trust and directors are liable to refund the amount paid.[1] Unless authorised by the Articles directors cannot vote themselves remuneration or appoint one of themselves to a salaried office.[2] All sums paid must be shown in the accounts.[3] They are also entitled to be indemnified for all liabilities properly incurred in managing the company's affairs, including legal expenses,[4] but not for wrongful or *ultra vires* actings.[5] A company must keep at an appropriate place a copy of every written contract of service with a director or, if it is not in writing, a memorandum setting out its terms, and these must be open to public inspection.[6]

Removal of directors

The general meeting may by ordinary resolution requiring special notice remove a director, notwithstanding any agreement with him or anything in the Articles.[7] Special notice must be given of the resolution and the director may have circulated to the members written representations, or may make them at the meeting. A director removed from office is not thereby deprived of any claim for compensation or damages which he might have.[7] Compensation for loss of office or in connection with retirement must be disclosed to the shareholders and approved by the company.[8]

Directors' powers

The directors' powers are limited to those acts which the company, their principal, is empowered to do, so that they cannot do anything *ultra vires* of the company, and further limited to those powers which the company has by the Articles delegated to them and anything fairly incidental thereto. Acts *intra vires* of the company but *ultra vires* of the directors may be ratified by the members in general meeting,[9] failing which the directors will be personally liable to the parties with whom they have dealt for

---

[1] *Leeds Estate Co.* v. *Shepherd* (1887) 36 Ch. D. 787.

[2] *Kerr* v. *Marine Products, Ltd.* (1928) 44 T.L.R. 292.

[3] S. 196; 1967 Act, S. 6.

[4] *James* v. *May* (1873) L.R. 6 H.L. 328; *Re Famatina Development Corpn.* [1914] 2 Ch. 271; but see *Tomlinson* v. *Scottish Amalgamated Silks, Ltd.*, 1935 S.C. (H.L.) 1.

[5] *Moxham* v. *Grant* [1900] 1 Q.B. 88; *Re Claridge's Patent Asphalte Co., Ltd.* [1921] 1 Ch. 543.

[6] 1967 Act, S. 26.

[7] S. 184; *Read* v. *Astoria Garage (Streatham) Ltd.* [1952] Ch. 637; *Yetton* v. *Eastwoods Froy, Ltd.* [1966] 3 All E.R. 353. But see *Bushell* v. *Faith* [1970] 1 All E.R. 53.

[8] Ss. 191–2.

[9] *Grant* v. *U.K. Switchback Ry.* (1888) 40 Ch. D. 135; *Re Oxted Motor Co.* [1921] 3 K.B. 32.

breach of warranty of authority.[1] Persons transacting with the company are entitled to assume that the directors have the authority they claim to have and that the internal rules of management of the company have been complied with.[2] A general conferment of powers by the Articles is valid.[3] Unless they have express or implied powers to do so, they may not delegate their powers,[4] but power of delegation is common. Directors must, in exercising their powers, have regard to the benefit of the company and may not abuse a power or use it unfairly.[5] Directors, as agents, are not personally liable on contracts made professedly on behalf of the company,[6] but may render themselves personally liable, deliberately, or by contracting without disclosing that they are acting as agents for the company, or without purporting to bind the company.[7] They are not personally liable for wrongs committed by the company, unless personally parties to the wrong; they may be liable along with the company.[8] The acts of a director or manager are valid despite any defect later discovered in his appointment.[9]

Board meetings

The directors in general act as a body at board meetings, but the Articles may authorize the appointment of one or more as managing directors who take day-to-day decisions,[10] or the delegation of powers to committees. The Articles fix, or authorize the directors to fix, the quorum who may act for the whole board. If

[1] *Firbank's Exors.* v. *Humphreys* (1886) 18 Q.B.D. 54; *Starkey* v. *Bank of England* [1903] A.C. 114.

[2] *Royal British Bank* v. *Turquand* (1856) 6 E. & B. 327; *Gillies* v. *Craigton Garage Co.*, 1935 S.C. 423; *Freeman & Lockyer* v. *Buckhurst Park Properties* [1964] 2 Q.B. 480; *Hely-Hutchinson* v. *Brayhew* [1968] 1 Q.B. 549.

[3] *Re Patent File Co.* (1870) L.R. 6 Ch. App. 83; *Re Anglo-Danubian Co.* (1875) L.R. 20 Eq. 339.

[4] *Leeds Estate Co.* v. *Shepherd* (1887) 36 Ch. D. 787; *Dunn* v. *Banknock Coal Co.* (1901) 9 S.L.T. 51.

[5] *Alexander* v. *Automatic Telephone Co.* [1900] 2 Ch. 56; *Punt* v. *Symons* [1903] 2 Ch. 506; *Cook* v. *Barry, Henry & Cook*, 1923 S.L.T. 692.

[6] *Ferguson* v. *Wilson* (1866) L.R. 2 Ch. App. 77.

[7] *McCollin* v. *Gilpin* (1880) 5 Q.B.D. 390; *Dermatine Co.* v. *Ashworth* (1905) 21 T.L.R. 510.

[8] *Cullen* v. *Thomson's Trs.* (1862) 4 Macq. 424.

[9] S. 180; *Dawson* v. *African Consolidated Co.* [1898] 1 Ch. 6; contrast *Morris* v. *Kanssen* [1946] A.C. 459.

[10] On their position see *Allison* v. *Scotia Motor Co.* (1906) 14 S.L.T. 9; *Hindle* v. *John Cotton, Ltd.* (1919) 56 S.L.R. 625; *Kerr* v. *Walker*, 1933 S.C. 458; *Anderson* v. *James Sutherland (Peterhead) Ltd.*, 1941 S.C. 203; *Caddies* v. *Harold Holdsworth & Co. (Wakefield) Ltd.*, 1955 S.C. (H.L.) 27; *Shindler* v. *Northern Raincoat Co.* [1960] 1 W.L.R. 1038. See also *Nelson* v. *James Nelson & Sons, Ltd.* [1914] 2 K.B. 770; *Southern Foundries Ltd.* v. *Shirlaw* [1940] A.C. 701; *Read* v. *Astoria Garage (Streatham) Ltd.* [1952] 1 Ch. 637.

no quorum is fixed a majority can act.[1] Unless meetings are held at fixed times due notice must be given calling a meeting a reasonable time beforehand.[2] Decisions are reached in the form of resolutions, and minutes of all directors' proceedings must be recorded in a book kept for the purpose.[3] A managing director is usually an employee of the company as well as a director and his dismissal may be a breach of his contract of employment.[4] A director is entitled to a court order for inspection of the minutes of board meetings.[5]

Secretary

Every company must have a secretary and a sole director cannot also be secretary.[6] No qualifications are specified and the office may be held by a person, a firm, or, subject to qualifications, another company.[71] He is appointed and removed by the directors and is a servant of the company. His functions are administrative, not managerial; he has no power to bind the company contractually nor to make representations on behalf of the company unless express or implied authority is given him.[8] His duties include notices, correspondence, board and company meetings, the register of members, share transfer procedure, and numerous statutory duties, but not advice on law.[9] Apart from showing due care, skill and diligence in the performance of his duties he is, like a director, in a fiduciary position to the company and must not let his interest conflict with his duty, or make a secret profit.[10] Particulars of the secretary must be given in the register of directors and secretaries.[11]

Auditors

A company must at every annual general meeting appoint an auditor or auditors[12] who must possess stated professional qualifications or be authorized by the Dept. of Trade.[13] Retiring

---

[1] *York Tramways Co.* v. *Willows* (1882) 8 Q.B.D. 685.

[2] *Browne* v. *La Trinidad* (1887) 37 Ch. D. 1; see also *Re Homer Gold Mines* (1888) 39 Ch. D. 546.

[3] S. 145; *City of Glasgow Bank Liqrs.* (1880) 7 R. 1196.

[4] See p. 463, note 10.

[5] *McCusker* v. *McRae*, 1966 S.C. 253.

[6] S. 177.   [7] S. 178.

[8] *Barnet, Hoares & Co.* v. *South London Tramways Co.* (1887) 18 Q.B.D. 815; *Houghton* v. *Nothard Lowe & Wills Ltd.* [1928] A.C. 1.

[9] *Niven* v. *Collins Patent Lever Gear Co.* (1900) 7 S.L.T. 476.

[10] cf. *Regal (Hastings) Ltd.* v. *Gulliver* [1942] 1 All E.R. 378.

[11] S. 200.

[12] S. 159.   [13] S. 161.

auditors are to be reappointed unless there is a contrary resolution, of which special notice must be given, or they are not qualified or unwilling to act. If none are appointed or reappointed the Dept. of Trade may appoint.[1] Their remuneration is fixed by the company in general meeting. They are agents of the members, whose duty is to examine the company's accounts and report on them, and their report must contain statements as to the matters contained in Sched. 9.[2] An auditor is a 'watchdog, not a bloodhound'.[3] Auditors must exercise reasonable skill, care, and caution in carrying out their duties; they must have access to the books and obtain such information as they may think necessary for the performance of their duties.[4] If there is anything to excite suspicion it must be investigated.[5] The auditors' report must be attached to the balance-sheet and laid before the company in general meeting.[6] Auditors may be liable for loss caused by their negligence and failure to exercise due care,[7] or for misfeasance in an investigation under S. 333,[8] or criminally.[9]

Accounts

Every company must keep books of account sufficient to give a true and fair view of the company's affairs and to explain its transactions, and prepare a balance sheet, profit and loss account, group accounts (in certain cases), a directors' report, and an auditor's report.[10] The balance sheet must comply with the 1948 Act, Sched. 8, amended by the 1967 Act, Sched. 1.[11] The profit and loss account must comply with the same requirements.[12] In the case of a holding company, group accounts are necessary.[13] A directors' report must be attached to the balance sheet, stating specified matters.[14] An auditors' report must be made, stating specified particulars, and read to the company in general meeting.[15] A director is entitled to a court order for inspection of accounts.[16]

---

[1] S. 159.

[2] S. 162; 1967 Act, S. 14; *Re Republic of Bolivia Exploration Syndicate, Ltd.* [1914] 1 Ch. 139.

[3] *Re Kingston Cotton Mill Co. (No. 2)* [1896] 2 Ch. 279, 288.

[4] *Leeds Estate Building and Investment Co. v. Shepherd* (1887) 36 Ch. D. 787; *Re London and General Bank* [1895] 2 Ch. 673.

[5] *Re Thomas Gerrard & Son* [1968] Ch. 455.   [6] S. 156.

[7] *Leeds Estate Bldg. Co. v. Shepherd* (1887) 36 Ch. D. 787; *Re City Equitable Fire Ins. Co.* [1925] Ch. 407.

[8] *Re London and General Bank (No. 2)* [1895] 2 Ch. 673; *Re Kingston Cotton Mill Co. (No. 2)* [1896] 2 Ch. 279; *Re Thomas Gerrard, supra.*

[9] S. 438; *R. v. Kylsant* [1932] 1 K.B. 442.

[10] S. 147.   [11] Ss. 148–9.   [12] Ss. 149, 156.   [13] Ss. 152–4.

[14] S. 157 amd. 1967 Act, Ss. 16–22.   [15] 1967 Act, S. 14.

[16] *McCusker v. McRae,* 1966 S.C. 253.

The Annual Return

Every year a company having a share capital must, within 42 days after the annual general meeting, make a return to the Registrar[1] containing the particulars set out in Sched. 6 to the 1948 Act, having annexed thereto a certified copy of every balance sheet laid before the company during the period covered and copies of the auditors' and directors' reports.[2]

Investigations

In certain circumstances the Dept. of Trade must, or may, appoint inspectors to investigate a company's affairs[3] or the ownership of shares in a company.[4] Such an inspector is an investigator, not a judge or prosecutor; he has wide powers.[5] The Dept. of Trade may inspect a company's books and papers,[6] investigate a director's dealings in options[7] or interest in shares.[8]

MEMBERSHIP

Members of the company

The members collectively do not compose the company, which is a separate entity, but they own it by virtue of owning shares therein.[9] A person becomes a member by subscribing the Memorandum,[10] by signing and delivering to the Registrar an undertaking to take and pay for qualification shares as a director[11] by agreeing to take shares on allotment and being registered,[12] by taking a transfer of shares and being registered, by taking the estate of a deceased or bankrupt member and being registered,[13] or by otherwise allowing his name to be on the register or holding himself out to be a member.[14] A company can be a member of another company, but may not, without statutory

---

[1] Ss. 124–6.

[2] S. 127.

[3] Ss. 164–5. As to conduct see *Re Pergamon Press* [1970] 3 All E.R. 535.

[4] Ss. 172–5.

[5] Ss. 167–8.　　[6] S. 109.　　[7] 1967 Act, S. 32.　　[8] 1967 Act, S. 32.

[9] As to the difference between a member and a partner, see *Dove* v. *Young* (1868) 7 M. 304.

[10] S. 26; *Migotti's Case* (1867) L.R. 4 Eq. 238; *Re London and Provincial Coal Co.* (1877) 5 Ch. D. 525; *Nicol's Case* (1885) 29 Ch. D. 444; *Alexander* v. *Automatic Telephone Co.* [1900] 2 Ch. 63.

[11] S. 181.

[12] *Miln* v. *N.B. Fresh Fish Supply Co.* (1887) 15 R. 21.

[13] *McEwen* v. *City of Glasgow Bank* (1879) 6 R. 1315; *Gordon* v. *City of Glasgow Bank* (1879) 7 R. 55; *Galloway Saloon S.P. Co.* v. *Wallace* (1891) 19 R. 330.

[14] *Sewell's case* (1868) L.R. 3 Ch. 138.

authority,[1] holds its own shares,[2] nor shares in its own holding company,[3] nor may it assist a person financially to acquire its shares.[4] A person ceases to be a member if he has the contract of membership rescinded for error or misrepresentation, or has the register rectified to the effect of removing his name, or by transferring his shares to another and the other person being registered, or by death, when another person receives a transfer from his executor and is registered, or if he is adjudicated bankrupt and his trustee disclaims the shares, or if his shares are forfeited, or sold by the company under a provision in the articles and the purchaser is registered in his place, or surrendered.

The Register of Members

Every company must keep a register of members at its registered office containing stated particulars of each member,[5] and changes in particulars must be registered. Companies registered in Scotland may, but those registered in England may not, record notice of any trust.[6] The register must be open for public inspection[7] but may be closed for not more than 30 days each year on notice given in the press.[8] A dominion register may be maintained [9] The register is *prima facie* evidence of any matter directed or authorized to be inserted therein.[10] A person must notify the company if he becomes interested in or acquires the shares of a company carrying unrestricted voting rights and quoted on a stock exchange if his holding thereby amounts to a tenth or more of the nominal value of the issued share capital of that class, and also if his holding ceases to amount to one-tenth.[11] The company must keep a register of such information.[12]

---

[1] S. 210(2).

[2] *Trevor* v. *Whitworth* (1887) 12 App. Cas. 409.

[3] S. 27.

[4] S. 54.

[5] Ss. 110, 436.

[6] S. 117. See *Muir* v. *City of Glasgow Bank* (1879) 6 R. (H.L.) 21; *Cree* v. *Somervail* (1879) 6 R. (H.L.) 90; *Cuninghame* v. *City of Glasgow Bank* (1879) 6 R. (H.L.) 98; contrast *Simpson* v. *Molson's Bank* [1895] A.C. 270.

[7] S. 113; 1967 Act, S. 52.

[8] S. 115. See *Oakes* v. *Turquand* (1867) L.R. 2 H.L. 325, 366.

[9] S. 119.

[10] S. 118; *Reese River Silver Mining Co.* v. *Smith* (1869) L.R. 4 H.L. 80. It is not conclusive in questions between husband and wife: *Thomas* v. *City of Glasgow Bank* (1879) 6 R. 607; *Steedman* v. *Same* (1879) 7 R. 111; *Carmichael* v. *Same* (1879) 7 R. 118.

[11] 1967 Act, S. 33.

[12] 1967 Act, S. 34.

The court may, on application by the person aggrieved or any member of the company or the company, rectify the register where the name of any person is without sufficient cause[1] entered in or omitted from the register of members, or where default is made or unnecessary delay takes place in entering on the register the fact that any person has ceased to be a member.[2] A person claiming to have his name removed should claim without delay after discovering that fact, or otherwise he may be held to have approbated his registration.[3] Application may be made on such grounds as that the applicant had been induced to take shares by misrepresentation,[4] that the company has neglected to register a transfer,[5] that shares had been improperly forfeited,[6] that the company, acting on a forged transfer, had removed the applicant's name.[7] An action of declarator is also competent.[8] It is questionable whether rectification by way of reduction *ope exceptionis* is competent.[9]

The rights of members

Members are entitled to numerous rights under statute, the Articles, and the general law, including the rights to annual reports from the directors on the affairs of the company and annual accounts, to payment of dividends as provided by the Articles and resolved on by the company and to repayment on winding-up and possibly to participate in surplus assets then. They may sue the company to restrain deviations from the company's purpose, without needing to show that the thing done is hurtful to the company's interests.[10]

Liabilities of members

A member is liable, if the company is limited by shares, to pay

[1] *Elliot* v. *Mackie*, 1935 S.C. 81.

[2] S. 116; *Re Sussex Brick Co.* [1904] 1 Ch. 598.

[3] *Re Scottish Petroleum Co.* (1883) 23 Ch. D. 434; *Property Investment Co. of Scotland* v. *Duncan* (1887) 14 R. 299; *Linz* v. *Electric Wire Co. of Palestine* [1948] A.C. 371.

[4] *Stewart's Case* (1866) L.R. 1 Ch. App. 574; *City of Edinburgh Brewery Co.* v. *Gibson's Tr.* (1869) 7 M. 886; *Anderson's Case* (1881) 17 Ch. D. 373; *Chambers* v. *Edinburgh and Glasgow Aerated Bread Co.* (1891) 18 R. 1039; *Blakiston* v. *London, etc., Discount Corpn.* (1894) 21 R. 417; *Mair* v. *Rio Grande Rubber Estates,* 1913 S.C. (H.L.) 74. Contrast *Blaikie* v. *Coats* (1893) 21 R. 150; see also *Scottish Amalgamated Silks Ltd.* v. *Macalister,* 1930 S.L.T. 593.

[5] *Re Stranton Iron & Steel Co.* (1873) L.R. 16 Eq. 559.

[6] *Re Ystalyfera Gas Co.* [1887] W.N. 30.

[7] *Re Bahia etc. Ry. Co.* (1868) L.R. 3 Q.B. 584.

[8] *Kinghorn* v. *Glenyards Fireclay Co.* (1907) 14 S.L.T. 683.

[9] *National Bank of Scotland Glasgow Nominees Ltd* v. *Adamson,* 1932 S.L.T. 492.

[10] *Smith* v. *G.S.W. Ry.* (1897) 4 S.L.T. 327; *Dunn* v. *Banknock Coal Co.* (1901) 9 S.L.T. 51.

if called on, the amount, if any, remaining unpaid of the nominal value of his shares.[1] If the company is limited by guarantee he is liable to have to pay the amount which he has undertaken by the Memorandum to contribute to the company's assets in the event of it being wound up.[1] If the company is unlimited, he is liable, jointly and severally with the other solvent members, for the whole debts of the company.[1] If at any time the number of members is reduced below the legal minimum and the company carries on business for more than six months while so reduced, every member thereafter cognisant of the fact is severally liable for the whole debts of the company.[2] A shareholder who transfers his shares within one year before the company is wound up is liable to be put on the 'B' list of contributories, and liable to the amount unpaid on his shares if debts exist incurred while he was a member, and members on the 'A' list cannot satisfy the contributions required from them.[3]

Meetings

A public company limited by shares and any company limited by guarantee and having a share capital must hold a statutory meeting between one and three months of the date when it is entitled to commence business, at which a statutory report is considered.[4] The members of any company must be summoned to a general meeting within 18 months of incorporation, and thereafter every year and not more than 15 months from the previous one.[5] The usual business is to hear an address on the state of the company's business, to consider and approve the accounts, authorize a dividend, elect or re-elect directors, and vote the auditors' remuneration. On default the Board of Trade may call a meeting.[5] A quorum must be present throughout.[6] Extraordinary general meetings may be called at any time, and must be called when a proportion of the members request one.[7] Meetings of classes of shareholders have to be held when the Act or Articles or the terms of issue of shares require, particularly when it is proposed to vary the rights of some class of shareholders.

---

[1] S. 212.   [2] S. 31.   [3] S. 212.
[4] S. 130.   [5] S. 131.

[6] *Henderson* v. *Louttit & Co.* (1894) 21 R. 674; as to quorum see S. 134 and *M. Harris, Ltd.*, 1956 S.C. 207; *Neil McLeod & Sons Ltd.* 1967 S.C. 16. One person does not make a 'meeting': *Prain & Sons*, 1947 S.C. 325. See also *Edinburgh Workmen's Houses Improvement Co.*, 1935 S.C. 56.

[7] S. 132. The requisition for such a meeting must state the objects of calling it but other competent business can be dealt with: *Ball* v. *Metal Industries, Ltd.*, 1957 S.C. 315.

Meetings require 14 days' notice (21 days for A.G.M.), and notice must be given of resolutions proposed.[1] Voting at general meetings is by show of hands,[2] without regard to number of shares held or proxies held. Any member may demand a poll[3] and the Articles frequently provide that in such a case each member has a vote for each share held.[4] Articles usually recognize voting by proxy; i.e. by a member appointing another person, not necessarily a member, to vote for him.[5]

Resolutions

Decisions are expressed by resolutions; for most purposes an ordinary resolution[6] passed by a simple majority of those present and voting is enough. An extraordinary resolution is one passed by a three-fourths majority of those voting in person or by proxy at a general meeting of which notice specifying the intention to propose the resolution as an extraordinary resolution has been duly given.[6] Such resolutions are frequently required to sanction winding-up or voluntary liquidation or to obtain the sanction of a class of shareholders. A special resolution requires the same majority and at least 21 days' notice must have been given of intention to propose it as a special resolution.[7] Special resolutions are required for important business such as altering the Memorandum or Articles or reducing capital.[8] Unless a poll is demanded, a declaration by the chairman that the resolution is carried is conclusive.[9] A resolution requiring special notice requires that prior notice must be given to the company, and by the company to the shareholders when calling the meeting.[10] A resolution cannot receive effect if the Minute of Meeting shows that it had not been passed by the requisite majority.[11] Printed copies of extraordinary and special resolutions and those binding on classes of shareholders must be registered with

---

[1] S. 133; see *Aberdeen Comb Works Co.* (1902) 10 S.L.T. 210; *Neil McLeod & Sons, Ltd.*, 1967 S.C. 16.

[2] Even if there is no opposition failure to call for a show of hands may be fatal: *Citizens Theatre*, 1946 S.C. 14; see also *Fraserburgh Commercial Co.*, 1946 S.C. 444.

[3] S. 137.   [4] S. 134.   [5] Ss. 136–7.

[6] See *Bushell* v. *Faith* [1970] 1 All E.R. 53.

[7] S. 141; see *N. of Scotland, etc. S.N. Co.*, 1920 S.C. 94; *Rennie* v. *Crichton's, Ltd.*, 1927 S.L.T. 459; *Neil McLeod & Sons, Ltd., supra.* Extraordinary resolutions are required by Ss. 278, 303, 306.

[8] Special resolutions are required by Ss. 5, 10, 18, 66, 278, 287.

[9] S. 141.

[10] S. 142. Special notice resolutions are required by Ss. 160, 184, and 185.

[11] *Cowan* v. *Scottish Publishing Co.* (1892) 19 R. 437; *J. T. Clark & Co.*, 1911 S.C. 243; *Graham's Morocco Co., Ltd.*, 1932 S.C. 269; *Citizen's Theatre, Ltd.*, 1946 S.C. 14; *Fraserburgh Commercial Co.*, 1946 S.C. 444.

the Registrar.[1] A shareholder is entitled to a court order for inspection of the minutes of general meetings.[2]

Majority and minority rights

Members are deemed to agree to accept the will of the majority if expressed in accordance with law and the Articles, in respect of corporate membership rights.[3] But a majority cannot ratify an act illegal or *ultra vires* of the company,[4] or an act in fraud of the minority and not for the benefit of the company as a whole when the wrongdoers are in control of the company,[5] or a resolution requiring a qualified majority but passed only by a simple majority.[6] A minority of a specified size may requisition an extraordinary general meeting,[7] requisition the circulation of resolutions and notices,[8] demand a poll at a meeting,[9] object to the alteration of the company's objects,[10] or of non-obligatory clauses in the Memorandum,[11] or of the rights of a class of shares,[12] or apply for an investigation into the company's affairs,[13] or into the membership of the company.[14] But a minority is not obliged to accept the will of the majority in matters affecting individual membership rights, such as to have the requirements of law and the Articles observed in relation to them, to receive notices, to attend meetings and vote. An aggrieved minority may petition the court to have the company wound up on the ground that it is just and equitable to do so,[15] or petition the court, if the affairs of the company are conducted in a manner oppressive to some part of the members[16] and the court would be prepared to make a winding-up order but such would unfairly prejudice the members,[17] in which case the court may make such order as it thinks fit for resolving the conflict,[18] or apply to the Dept. of Trade to have the affairs of the company investigated.

[1] S. 143 amd. 1967 Act, S. 51.

[2] *McCusker* v. *McRae*, 1966 S.C. 253.

[3] *Foss* v. *Harbottle* (1843) 2 Hare 461; *N.W. Transportation Co.* v. *Beatty* (1887) L.R. 12 App. Cas. 589; *Burland* v. *Earle* [1902] A.C. 83.

[4] *Edwards* v. *Halliwell* [1950] 2 All E.R. 1064; *Pavlides* v. *Jensen* [1956] Ch. 565.

[5] *Orr* v. *Glasgow, etc. Ry. Co.* (1860) 3 Macq. 799; *Brown* v. *Stewart* (1898) 1 F. 316; *Cook* v. *Deeks* [1916] 1 A.C. 554; *Harris* v. *A. Harris, Ltd.*, 1936 S.C. 183; *Oliver's Trs.* v. *Walker*, 1948 S.L.T. 140.

[6] *Edwards, supra,* 1067.

[7] S. 132. [8] S. 140. [9] S. 137.

[10] S. 5. [11] S. 23. [12] S. 72.

[13] S. 164. [14] S. 172. [15] S. 222(f).

[16] *Elder* v. *Elder & Watson*, 1952 S.C. 49.

[17] S. 210.

[18] S. 210; *Meyer* v. *S.C.W.S.*, 1958 S.C. (H.L.) 40; *Re Jermyn Street Public Baths* [1970] 3 All E.R. 57.

SHARE CAPITAL, SHARES AND DIVIDENDS

Every company having a share capital, whether limited by shares or by guarantee, must have a nominal or authorized capital with which it is incorporated.[1] It need not, however, issue shares to this full extent; the issued capital is the amount of shares actually issued to shareholders, the remainder being unissued capital. The full nominal value of the shares issued is not always fully paid-up and there may be a liability on the shareholders for the amount uncalled on each share; hence there may be paid-up and uncalled capital. Reserve capital is any part of the uncalled capital which the company has determined may be called up only if the company is being wound up.[2] Shares are designated as of stated nominal values but their true economic and exchange values may be more or less than the nominal values, depending on the company's record, earnings and prospects.

Shares

A share is an incorporeal right of ownership of a determinate fraction of the company.[3] It carries the rights to receive reports and accounts from the directors, to attend and vote at meetings, to receive a dividend in accordance with the company's prosperity and the conditions attaching under the Articles to the class of shares, and, on winding up, to a proportionate share of the capital and other realized assets of the company. It carries the liability on call to pay to the company any proportion of the nominal value of the share as yet uncalled and on winding-up to be put on the B list of contributories.[4] It is arrestable in security or in execution,[5] save that stock of the Royal Bank of Scotland is, by the bank's charter, adjudgeable only.

The company may, if authorized by its Articles,[6] create differ-

---

[1] S. 2(4).   [2] *Re Mayfair Property Co.* [1898] 2 Ch. 28.

[3] Not of the company's assets; the shareholders own the company; the company owns its property and assets. See also *Borland's Tr.* v. *Steel Bros.* [1901] 1 Ch. 279; *I.R.C.* v. *Crossman* [1937] A.C. 26.

[4] S. 212.

[5] *Sinclair* v. *Staples* (1860) 22 D. 600; *Valentine* v. *Grangemouth Coal Co.* (1897) 35 S.L.R. 12; *Harvey's Yoker Distillery, Ltd.* v. *Sinclair* (1901) 8 S.L.T. 369; *American Mortgage Co. of Scotland* v. *Sidway*, 1908 S.C. 500.

[6] If the Memorandum expressly provides for equality or specifies the classes of shares, this cannot be altered by the Articles: *Campbell* v. *Rofe* [1933] A.C. 91; *Marshall, Fleming & Co. Ltd.*, 1938 S.C. 873, 878. If the Memorandum does not provide for equality preferential rights may be conferred by the Articles, there being no implication in the Memorandum that all shares shall be equal: *Humboldt Redwood Co. Ltd.* v. *Coats*, 1908 S.C. 751.

ent classes of shares having different rights, particularly in relation to voting, dividends, and winding-up. The Articles may contain provisions for the variation of the rights of the classes of shares. Preference shares may have a preference as to capital or dividend, or both, or carry other preferential rights. Preference shares may be redeemable on conditions.[1] If preference shares carry a preferential right to dividend, the dividend is prima facie cumulative,[2] but may be non-cumulative.[3] Prima facie a preferential dividend[4] of specified percentage excludes further participation in profits. Non-privileged shares are usually designated ordinary shares. There may also be deferred shares, or shares of other categories with particular rights and conditions attached to them. Shares may carry no, or only restricted, voting rights. The right of preference shareholders to vote at meetings is usually restricted to occasions when their rights are being varied or their dividend in arrears.

Variation of rights of shareholders

If the Articles permit, the rights of any class of shareholders may be varied or abrogated by the consent of a specified proportion of the holders of shares of that class or by a resolution passed at a separate meeting of the holders of those shares, but the holders of at least fifteen per cent of the issued shares of that class may apply to the court to have the variation cancelled, and the variation is then ineffective until confirmed by the court.[5] The company may validly pay money to the shareholders to secure their acquiescence.[6]

Partly-paid shares: calls

When shares are issued the full nominal value thereof is normally paid-up at once or by instalments over a short period, but it is competent to have the shares only partly paid and the balance liable to be called up when the company so decides. The power to make a call must be exercised for the general benefit of the company[7] and is exercised by resolution of the directors in

[1] S. 58.

[2] *Webb* v. *Earle* (1875) L.R. 20 Eq. 556; *Partick, etc. Gas Co.* v. *Taylor* (1888) 15 R. 711; *Miln* v. *Arizona Copper Co.* (1899) 1 F. 935; *Ferguson & Forrester, Ltd.* v. *Buchanan,* 1920 S.C. 154.

[3] *Staples* v. *Eastman Photographic Co.* [1896] 2 Ch. 303; *Thornycroft & Co. Ltd.* v. *T.* (1927) 44 T.L.R. 9.

[4] *Will* v. *United Lankat Plantations Co. Ltd.* [1914] A.C. 11.

[5] S. 72; *White* v. *Bristol Aeroplane Co. Ltd.* [1953] Ch. 65.

[6] *Caledonian Ins. Co.* v. *Scottish American Investment Co. Ltd.,* 1951 S.L.T. 23.

[7] *Alexander* v. *Automatic Telephone Co.* [1900] 2 Ch. 56.

accordance with the Articles.[1] Payment may be enforced. Shares may be issued at a premium, the excess receipts over nominal value being carried to a special share premium account,[2] or with the sanction of the court and on conditions, at a discount,[3] and either for cash or for consideration other than cash, such as fully paid-up shares in another company, or the goodwill of a business.

Acquisition of shares

Shares are acquired by application and allotment when an issue of shares is made, or subsequently by purchase, gift or bequest from an existing holder. If an application for an allotment of shares is accepted, the applicant may be entered on the register of members.[4] Allotment letters may be subject to conditions.[5] In the case of a public company, on first allotment of shares offered to the public for subscription, no allotment may be made unless the minimum subscription has been subscribed and the sum payable on application therefor has been received by the company.[6]

Share certificates and share warrants

Share certificates issued under the seal of the company, specifying the shares held by the member, are the shareholder's *prima facie* evidence of title to his shares in the company.[7] Certificates must be completed by the company and ready for delivery within two months after allotment.[8] A share certificate is not negotiable and confers no right by being handed to another. The company is barred from maintaining that a share certificate, accepted in good faith, untruly represents what it states, e.g. that the shares are fully paid,[9] but a company is not liable on a

---

[1] *Odessa Tramways* v. *Mendel* (1878) 8 Ch. D. 235; *Universal Corpn. Ltd.* v. *Hughes,* 1909 S.C. 1434.

[2] S. 56; prior to 1948 premiums could be distributed as dividends; cf. *Cameron* v. *Glenmorangie Distillery Co.* (1896) 23 R. 1092.

[3] S. 57; prior to 1929 this was generally incompetent: see *Klenck* v. *E.I. Co. for Exploration and Mining* (1888) 16 R. 271; *Newburgh and N. Fife Ry.* v. *N.B. Ry.,* 1913 S.C. 1166; *Penang Foundry Co.* v. *Gardiner,* 1913 S.C. 1203.

[4] See *Mason* v. *Benhar Coal Co.* (1882) 9 R. 883; *Goldie* v. *Torrance* (1882) 10 R. 174; *Chapman* v. *Sulphite Pulp Co.* (1892) 19 R. 837; *Nelson* v. *Fraser* (1906) 14 S.L.T. 513.

[5] *Liqr. of Consolidated Copper Co. of Canada* v. *Peddie* (1877) 5 R. 393; *National House Property Investment Co.* v. *Watson,* 1908 S.C. 888.

[6] S. 47.

[7] S. 81; see also *Woodhouse & Rawson* v. *Hosack* (1894) 2 S.L.T. 279.

[8] S. 80.

[9] *Re Bahia and San Francisco Ry.* (1868) L.R. 3 Q.B. 584; *Penang Foundry Co.* v. *Gardiner,* 1913 S.C. 1203; cf. *Balkis Consolidated Co.* v. *Tomlinson* [1893] A.C. 396; *Bloomenthal* v. *Ford* [1897] A.C. 156.

forged certificate.[1] Share warrants to bearer can be issued only if the shares are fully paid up and the Articles so authorize, and only by public companies.[2] Where issued, they are customarily treated as negotiable instruments,[3] and are transferred by the delivery of the warrant. Subject to the Articles, the bearer of a warrant is entitled to surrender it and be registered as a member.

Transfer and transmission of shares

Shares are incorporeal moveable property and may be transferred voluntarily, unless restricted by the Articles, mortgaged or transferred in security of debt, and are transmitted on death or bankruptcy. Shares are freely transferable in pursuance of a contract of sale entered into privately or through the intervention of stockbrokers, or by way of gift. The sale or gift is effected by completion of a share transfer form in the form authorized by the Articles, or a stock transfer form in the form introduced by the Stock Transfer Act, 1963, and the lodging of it with the share certificate at the company's transfer office. The directors of private companies normally have under the Articles a discretion to refuse to register transfers, which will not be interfered with by the court unless the directors have acted corruptly or capriciously.[4] The power will be presumed to have been properly exercised, for the company's benefit.[5] So, too, the Articles may require a shareholder first to offer his shares to the company or other shareholders therein.[6] The directors must refuse to register a transfer when the company has stopped payment or ceased to be a going concern, although liquidation has not commenced.[7] A forged transfer is a nullity and a company which has removed the holder's name in reliance on a forged transfer must replace it.[8]

---

[1] *Clavering, Son & Co.* v. *Goodwins, Jardine & Co.* (1891) 18 R. 652; *Ruben* v. *Great Fingall Consolidated* [1906] A.C. 439; *South London Greyhound Racecourses, Ltd.* v. *Wake* [1931] 1 Ch. 496.

[2] S. 83.

[3] *Webb, Hale & Co.* v. *Alexandria Water Co.* (1905) 21 T.L.R. 572.

[4] *Re Coalport China Co.* [1895] 2 Ch. 404; *Stewart* v. *James Keiller & Sons* (1902) 4 F. 657; *Stevenson* v. *Wilson*, 1907 S.C. 445; *Kennedy* v. *N.B. Wireless Schools*, 1916, 1 S.L.T. 407; *Re Bede S.S. Co.* [1917] 1 Ch. 123. The refusal must be exercised by resolution: *Shepherd's Trs.* v. *S.*, 1950 S.C. (H.L.) 60.

[5] *Berry* v. *Tottenham Hotspur F.C.* [1936] 3 All E.R. 554; *Re Smith and Fawcett, Ltd.* [1942] Ch. 304.

[6] *Smith, Ltd.* v. *Colquhoun's Tr.* (1901) 3 F. 981; see also *Shepherd's Trs.* v. *S.*, 1950 S.C. (H.L.) 60; *Lyle & Scott* v. *Scott's Trs.*, 1959 S.C. (H.L.) 64.

[7] *Nelson Mitchell* v. *City of Glasgow Bank* (1879) 6 R. (H.L.) 66; *Dodds* v. *Cosmopolitan Ins. Corpn., Ltd.*, 1915 S.C. 992.

[8] *Sheffield Corpn.* v. *Barclay* [1905] A.C. 392.

The Forged Transfers Acts, 1891 and 1892, empower a company to make pecuniary compensation for any loss arising from a transfer of shares or stock in pursuance of a forged transfer, or of a transfer under a forged power of attorney.

On death shares pass as moveable property to the member's executor, who may be registered[1] but may[2] transfer the deceased's shares without himself being registered. If the executor becomes registered, he becomes a shareholder for all purposes.[3] So long as the deceased's name remains on the register his estate is liable in connection with the shares.[4] On bankruptcy shares are vested in the trustee in bankruptcy by the Act and Warrant,[5] and he may thereby become registered,[6] but may transfer them without so doing.

Mortgage of shares

Shares may be transferred in security of a loan or other obligation. The shares may be transferred outright to the lender who becomes registered, but is under an obligation to retransfer the shares when his debt is repaid.[7] Or the shares may be transferred to a nominee who holds them in trust for the lender till the debt is repaid, and then for the borrower and, it may be, for the lender again for another advance. A deposit of the share certificate by itself creates no right of security whatever in Scotland,[8] but it may be accompanied by a transfer signed by the borrower, enabling the lender at any time to have himself registered, or to hand back the certificate and destroy the transfer when his loan is repaid. Such a transfer may be void under the Blank Bonds and Trusts Act, 1696, c. 25,[9] and an uncompleted transfer could be defeated by another creditor's diligence or by the debtor's obtaining a duplicate certificate from the company and selling the shares to an innocent purchaser who has himself registered.

---

[1] *Trotter* v. *B.L. Bank* (1898) 6 S.L.T. 213; *Craig* v. *Caledonian Ry.* (1905) 13 S.L.T. 643.

[2] S. 76.

[3] *Buchan* v. *City of Glasgow Bank* (1879) 6 R. (H.L.) 44; *Bell* v. *Same* (1879) 6 R. (H.L.) 55; *McEwen* v. *Same* (1879) 6 R. 1315; *Gordon* v. *Same* (1879) 7 R. 55.

[4] cf. *Stewart's Trs.* v. *Evans* (1871) 9 M. 810; *Heritable Securities Investment Assocn. Ltd.* v. *Miller's Trs.* (1893) 20 R. 675.

[5] Bankruptcy (Sc.) Act, 1913, Ss. 70, 97; *Lindsay* v. *City of Glasgow Bank* (1879) 6 R. 671; *Myles* v. *City of Glasgow Bank* (1879) 6 R. 718.

[6] *Lumsden* v. *Peddie* (1866) 5 M. 34.

[7] *Morrison* v. *Harrison* (1876) 3 R. 406; *Siemens Bros.* v. *Burns* [1918] 2 Ch. 324.

[8] *Christie* v. *Ruxton* (1862) 24 D. 1182; *Scottish Provident Inst.* v. *Cohen* (1888) 16 R. 112; *Robertson* v. *B.L. Co.* (1891) 18 R. 1225.

[9] cf. *Shaw* v. *Caledonian Ry.* (1890) 17 R. 466, 478; see also *Guild* v. *Young* (1884) 22 S.L.R. 520; *Gourlay* v. *Mackie* (1887) 14 R. 403.

If valid, the borrower must do nothing to prevent the lender having himself registered.[1]

Calls on shares

Where shares have not been fully paid up the directors may call up part or all of the amount still unpaid on each share. The power to make calls must be exercised for the benefit of the company[2] and normally on all the shareholders *pari passu*.[3] Any limitations on calls,[4] and the procedure therefor, provided in the Articles must be adhered to. A member is entitled to notice stating when, where and to whom the call is payable.[5] The sum called up may be enforced by action[6] or, if authorized, by forfeiture of the shares.[7] The member may be able, in defence, to plead that he was induced by misrepresentation to become a member,[8] or that the call was not validly made.[9] A call may be made to equalize the values of shares prior to liquidation.[10] In a liquidation the court may make and enforce payment of calls.[11]

Lien on shares

A company has at common law,[12] and commonly by its Articles also reserves for itself,[13] a lien on a member's shares for his debts and liabilities to the company,[14] for such debts as money due under a call or other claims. The lien is enforceable according to the Articles, usually by power to sell the shares on default. It is doubtful if a lien can be enforced by forfeiture of shares.[15]

[1] *Hooper* v. *Herts* [1906] 1 Ch. 549.

[2] *Alexander* v. *Automatic Telephone Co.* [1900] 2 Ch. 56.

[3] *Galloway* v. *Hallé Concerts Society* [1915] 2 Ch. 233.

[4] *Universal Corpn.* v. *Hughes*, 1909 S.C. 1434.

[5] *Ferguson* v. *Central Halls Co.* (1887) 8 R. 997; *Re Cawley and Co.* (1889) 42 Ch. D. 209.

[6] *Galloway Saloon S.P. Co.* v. *Wallace* (1891) 19 R. 330.

[7] *Ferguson* v. *Central Halls Co.* (1887) 8 R. 997; *Re Cawley and Co.* (1889) 42 Ch. D. 209.

[8] *City of Edinburgh Brewery Co.* v. *Gibson's Tr.* (1867) 7 M. 886; *Scottish Amalgamated Silks* v. *Macalister*, 1930 S.N. 121.

[9] *Ferguson, supra.*

[10] *Paterson* v. *McFarlane* (1875) 2 R. 490; *Stewart* v. *Liqr. of Scoto-American Sugar Syndicate, Ltd.* (1901) 3 F. 585.

[11] Ss. 260, 275. [12] *Bell's Tr.* v. *Coatbridge Tinplate Co.* (1886) 14 R. 246.

[13] As to changing the Articles to create a lien, see *Liqr. of McArthur, Ltd.* v. *Gulf Line, Ltd.*, 1909 S.C. 732.

[14] *Re General Exchange Bank* (1871) L.R. 6 Ch. App. 818; *Bradford Banking Co.* v. *Briggs* (1887) 12 App. Cas. 29; *Stark* v. *Fife and Kinross Coal Co.* (1899) 1 F. 1173; *Paul's Tr.* v. *Thomas Justice & Sons*, 1912 S.C. 1303.

[15] *General Property and Investment Co.* v. *Matheson's Trs.* (1888) 16 R. 282; *Salt* v. *Marquis of Northampton* [1892] A.C. 1.

Forfeiture and surrender of shares

The Articles commonly provide for the forfeiture of shares for non-payment of calls.[1] The power must be exercised *bona fide* and for the benefit of the company,[2] and in strict accordance with the Articles.[3] If exercised the shareholder ceases to be a member[4] and the shares may be sold by the company. Forfeiture prima facie prevents a claim for unpaid calls, but the Articles may provide that such liability continues, and such an obligation is enforceable.[5] The court may set aside a forfeiture as invalid[6] and give damages for an irregular forfeiture,[6] but will not relieve a shareholder from a forfeiture if duly incurred and properly effected.[7] The company may have power to, and in fact, annul a forfeiture but only with the consent of the former member.[8] A forfeited share may normally, under the Articles, be sold to a third party, who acquires a good title thereto from the company, free from liability for past calls. If the Articles empower the company to accept surrender, shares may be surrendered to it in lieu of forfeiture,[9] but surrender is incompetent as a means of avoiding liability for uncalled capital, as this would amount to an unauthorized reduction of capital.[10] If surrender is valid, the shares can be re-issued.

Rights issues and bonus issues

When an existing company wishes to raise further capital it may make a fresh issue of shares by the same means as an initial issue, but frequently makes a 'rights' issue, giving existing shareholders the right to acquire new shares in a fixed proportion to their existing holdings, e.g. one for every five held, or it may make a bonus issue, in which shares are paid for out of profits and distributed free to the existing shareholders in proportion to their holdings, in lieu of or in addition to dividend. Issues to existing

---

[1] *Ferguson v. Central Halls Co.* (1881) 8 R. 997; *Allen v. Gold Reefs of W. Africa* [1900] 1 Ch. 656; *Hopkinson v. Mortimer, Harley & Co.* [1917] 1 Ch. 646.

[2] *Clarke v. Hart* (1858) 6 H.L.C. 633; *Garden Gully Mining Co. v. McLister* (1875) 1 App. Cas. 39; *In re Esparto Trading Co.* (1879) 12 Ch. D. 191.

[3] *Clarke, supra; Ferguson, supra.*

[4] *Liqrs. of Mount Morgan (West) Gold Mine v. McMahon* (1891) 18 R. 772;

[5] *Mount Morgan, supra; Ladies Dress Assocn. v. Pulbrook* [1900] 2 Q.B. 376.

[6] *Re New Chile Co.* (1890) 45 Ch. D. 598.

[7] *Sparks v. Liverpool Waterworks Co.* (1807) 13 Ves. 428.

[8] *Taylor v. Union Heritable Securities Co.* (1889) 16 R. 711; *Lackworthy's Case* [1903] 1 Ch. 711.

[9] *General Property Investment Co. and Liqr. v. Craig* (1891) 18 R. 389; *Trevor v. Whitworth* (1887) 12 App. Cas. 409; *Gill v. Arizona Copper Co.* (1900) 2 F. 843.

[10] *Bellerby v. Rowland and Marwood's SS. Co.* [1902] 2 Ch. 14.

members, including rights issues and bonus issues, have to satisfy the requirements of a prospectus, though it may be abridged.[1]

Profits and dividends

Unless restricted by its Memorandum or Articles a company has implied power to distribute some of its profits to its members as dividend.[2] It is in the discretion of the directors to recommend how much of any year's divisible profits shall be resolved by the members to be distributed as dividend. No dividend may be paid out of capital save as permitted by S. 65; this is completely *ultra vires*[3] and directors who are parties thereto are jointly and severally liable to repay the sum.[4] Dividends may be paid only out of divisible profits, which includes reserves of past trading profits and realized capital profits but requires provision out of profits for the depreciation or loss of circulating capital.[5] In the absence of provision in the Articles dividend falls to be distributed in proportion to amounts of nominal rather than paid-up capital.[6] On declaration a dividend becomes a debt by the company to the shareholders.[7] Where shares are entitled by the Articles to a preferential rate of dividend, prima facie this is cumulative.[8] Profits not distributed as dividend may, subject to the Memorandum and Articles, be put in reserve, or capitalized for redemption of redeemable preference shares, or otherwise applied as permitted by the Act.[9]

Alteration of capital

A company may alter its capital by increase, consolidation of

[1] S. 38.

[2] See *Paterson* v. *R. Paterson & Sons*, 1917 S.C. (H.L.) 13.

[3] *Beaumont* v. *G.N.S. Ry.* (1868) 6 M. 1027; *Flitcroft's Case* (1882) 21 Ch. D. 519; *Trevor* v. *Whitworth* (1887) 12 App. Cas. 409.

[4] *Flitcroft's case, supra; Liqrs. of City of Glasgow Bank* v. *Mackinnon* (1882) 9 R. 535.

[5] *Lee* v. *Neuchatel Asphalte Co. Ltd.* (1889) 41 Ch. D. 1; *Lubbock* v. *British Bank of S. America* [1892] 2 Ch. 198; *Verner* v. *General and Commercial Investment Trust Ltd.* [1894] 2 Ch. 239; *Wilmer* v. *McNamara & Co. Ltd.* [1895] 2 Ch. 245; *Cadell* v. *Scottish Investment Trust Co.* (1901) 8 S.L.T. 480; 9 S.L.T. 299; *Foster* v. *New Trinidad Lake Asphalt Co. Ltd.* [1901] 1 Ch. 208; *Bond* v. *Barrow Haematite Steel Co.* [1902] 1 Ch. 353; *Ammonia Soda Co. Ltd.* v. *Chamberlain* [1918] 1 Ch. 266.

[6] *Oakbank Oil Co.* v. *Crum* (1882) 10 R. (H.L.) 11; *Birch* v. *Cropper* (1889) 14 App. Cas. 525; contrast *Hoggan* v. *Tharsis Sulphur & Copper Co.* (1882) 9 R. 1191.

[7] *Carron Co.* v. *Hunter* (1868) 6 M. (H.L.) 106; *Re Severn and Wye and Severn Bridge Co.* [1896] 1 Ch. 559.

[8] *Webb* v. *Earle* (1875) L.R. 20 Eq. 556.

[9] S. 58; see *Arizona Copper Co.* v. *London Scottish American Trust* (1897) 24 R. 658; *Scottish Investment Trust* (1901) 9 S.L.T. 299; *Wemyss Collieries Trust, Ltd.* v. *Melville* (1905) 8 F. 143.

shares, conversion of shares into stock and vice versa, subdivision of shares, and diminution of capital, by cancellation of shares not taken up,[1] and by reduction of share capital.[2] Any of the alterations permitted by S. 61 requires the authority of the Articles and a resolution of the members in general meeting. The alterations under S. 61 and S. 66 are mutually exclusive. Increase of nominal capital involves alteration of the Memorandum but does not automatically require a further issue of shares.[3] Notice must be given to the Registrar. Consolidation involves combining shares into a lesser number of shares of equivalent nominal value, e.g. shares of £1 instead of 4 shares of 25p. Subdivision is the converse process. Notice of either must be given to the Registrar. Shares, if fully paid-up, may be converted into stock; stock is not numbered like shares, and is divisible into and transferable as so much money's worth of stock instead of so many shares of a stated nominal value. Since the 1948 Act fully paid-up shares ranking *pari passu* need not be numbered.[4] Diminution of nominal capital is the cancellation of shares authorized but unissued. Reduction of capital may be necessary where the company has too much capital,[5] or has suffered serious capital losses;[6] it requires authority in the Articles,[7] a special resolution, and confirmation by the court. It may be done in any way, including the ways mentioned in S. 66.[8] This may involve reduction in the nominal capital, and of either or both of the issued and unissued capital, and of the paid-up capital.[9] A reduction of capital should generally be an all round one, the same percentage being reduced in respect of each share and each class of share.[10] If preference shares have priority as to capital in winding up, the loss should fall first on the ordinary shares.[11] But reduction affecting only some of the shares is

---

[1] S. 61.

[2] S. 66.

[3] cf. *Metropolitan Cemetery Co.*, 1934 S.C. 65.

[4] S. 74. [5] e.g. *Alloa Coal Co.*, 1947 S.C. 651.

[6] *West End Cafe Co.* (1894) 21 R. 381; *City Property Investment Trust Corpn.* (1896) 23 R. 400; *Caldwell & Co. v. Caldwell*, 1916 S.C. (H.L.) 120; *Gardiner & Sons*, 1948 S.C. 34; *Halley & Sons*, 1948 S.C. 612.

[7] *Avery & Co.* (1890) 17 R. 1101; *Oregon Mortgage Co.*, 1910 S.C. 964.

[8] *British and American Tr. Co. v. Couper* [1894] A.C. 399; *Poole v. National Bank of China* [1907] A.C. 229.

[9] *Peebles Hotel-Hydropathic*, 1920 S.C. 303; *Ormiston Coal Co.*, 1949 S.C. 516.

[10] *Walker Steam Trawl Fishing Co.*, 1908 S.C. 123; *Wilsons and Clyde Coal Co. v. Scottish Insurance Corpn.*, 1949 S.C. (H.L.) 90.

[11] *Re Thomas de la Rue & Co.* [1911] 2 Ch. 361.

competent.[1] Where the rights of creditors may be affected the court may settle a list of them, and permit them to object.[2] The court may sanction reduction even if one class of shareholders thereby loses a potential future benefit, as where preference shareholders were paid out in full and thereby lost the possibility of sharing in capital compensation payments,[3] if arrears of dividend on preference shares are cancelled,[4] or if the preference shareholders' rights are diminished.[5] Capital may be reduced on the footing that the money returned may be called up again.[6] The fairness of a proposed reduction is a matter for the court, having regard to the evidence and the circumstances.[7] The fact that a reduction has some ulterior motive is irrelevant,[8] unless it is simply a device to avoid taxation.[9] The court may confirm the reduction on such terms and conditions as it thinks fit, and may direct the company to add to its name 'and reduced' for a period.[10]

BORROWING AND DEBENTURES

Borrowing

A company may borrow money only if it has power to do so; such a power is incidental to the company's objects in the case of a trading company.[11] A non-trading company must have the power in its constitution.[12] A company with power to borrow has power to charge its property and give security for repayment;[13] power

---

[1] *Re Gatling Gun, Ltd.* (1890) 43 Ch. D. 628; *British and American Tr. Corpn.* v. *Couper* [1894] A.C. 399; *Donaldson Line, Ltd.*, 1945 S.C. 162; *D. M. Stevenson & Co.*, 1947 S.C. 646; *Fife Coal Co.*, 1948 S.C. 505; *William Dixon, Ltd.*, 1948 S.C. 511; *Frazer Bros., Ltd.* 1963 S.C. 139.

[2] S. 67; see *Cranston's Tea Rooms, Ltd.*, 1919, 1 S.L.T. 107; *Unifruitco S.S. Co.*, 1930 S.C. 1104; *Cadzow Coal Co.*, 1931 S.C. 272; *Lawrie & Symington Ltd.*, 1969 S.L.T. 221. The court may dispense with the list: *Anderson, Brown & Co.*, 1965 S.C. 81.

[3] *Wilson & Clyde Coal Co., supra.*

[4] *Oban and Aultmore-Glenlivet Distilleries* (1903) 5 F. 1140.

[5] *Balmenach-Glenlivet Distillery* v. *Croall* (1906) 8 F. 1135.

[6] *Scottish Vulcanite Co.* (1894) 21 R. 752; *Stevenson, Anderson & Co.*, 1951 S.C. 346 settling doubt expressed in *William Brown, Son & Co. Ltd.*, 1931 S.C. 701.

[7] *Carruth* v. *I.C.I. Ltd.* [1937] A.C. 707.

[8] *Westburn Sugar Refineries, Ltd.*, 1951 S.C. (H.L.) 57; *David Bell, Ltd.*, 1954 S.C. 33.

[9] *A. & D. Fraser, Ltd.*, 1951 S.C. 394.

[10] S. 68.

[11] *General Auction Co.* v. *Smith* [1891] 3 Ch. 432; *Re Badger, Mansell* v. *Cobham* [1905] 1 Ch. 568.

[12] *Wenlock* v. *River Dee Co.* (1885) 10 App. Cas. 354.

[13] *Paterson's Trs.* v. *Caledonian Heritable Security Co.* (1886) 13 R. 369; *General Auction Co.* v. *Smith* [1891] 3 Ch. 432.

to borrow may include power to assign in security uncalled capital.[1] The Articles usually authorize the directors to exercise the borrowing powers, sometime subject to the sanction of a general meeting, and may impose a limit on amount, any borrowing beyond which is *ultra vires*. If borrowing is *ultra vires* of the directors it may be ratified by the company.[2] If borrowing is *ultra vires* of the company, securities given are void, and the lender may recover damages for the directors' breach of warranty that they had power to borrow.[3]

A company having power may borrow in any way competent to a natural person, by bank overdraft, unsecured loan, or by granting bills or promissory notes. In security for repayment a company may grant any security over its heritage or moveables which a natural person could. Uncalled share capital may, if the Articles permit, be assigned to creditors in security, but this must be intimated to each shareholder.[4] It may also issue debentures or grant a floating charge over its undertaking.

Debentures

Debentures are bonds or instruments acknowledging the company's indebtedness for a fixed sum and providing for payment of interest.[5] Debentures may be redeemable,[6] or perpetual, i.e. repayable only on notice or winding-up, or convertible, containing an option to the holder to convert his claim against the company into shares at stated times and rates of exchange. They may be made payable to bearer,[7] or to registered holder, or be a

---

[1] *Newton* v. *Anglo-Australian Co's Debenture Holders* [1895] A.C. 244; *Liqr. of Ballachulish Slate Quarries Co.* v. *Malcom* (1908) 15 S.L.T. 963; *Liqr. of Union Club* v. *Edinburgh Life Assce. Co.* (1906) 8 F. 1143; contrast *Bank of South Australia* v. *Abrahams* (1875) L.R. 6 P.C. 265. A company limited by guarantee cannot hypothecate the guarantee obligation of its members, prestable only on winding-up: *Robertson* v. *B.L. Co.* (1891) 18 R. 1225, but can assign a guarantee from a third party, not enforceable only on winding-up: *Lloyds Bank* v. *Morrison*, 1927 S.C. 571.

[2] *Irvine* v. *Union Bank of Australia* (1877) 2 App. Cas. 366.

[3] *Weeks* v. *Propert* (1873) L.R. 8 C.P. 427; *Firbank's Exors.* v. *Humphreys* (1886) 18 Q.B.D. 54; see also *Neath Building Socy.* v. *Luce* (1889) 43 Ch. D. 158; *Re Wrexham, Mold and Connah's Quay Ry. Co.* [1899] 1 Ch. 440; *Re Introductions* [1969] 1 All E.R. 887.

[4] *Union Club* v. *Edinburgh Life Assce Co.* (1906) 8 F. 1143; *Ballachulish Slate Quarries Co.* v. *Malcolm* (1908) 15 S.L.T. 963.

[5] S. 455; see also *British India S.N. Co.* v. *I.R.C.* (1881) 7 Q.B.D. 165; *Knightsbridge Estates Trust* v. *Byrne* [1940] A.C. 613.

[6] e.g. *United Collieries* v. *L.A.*, 1950 S.C. 458.

[7] Expressly legalized for Scotland, notwithstanding the Blank Bonds and Trusts Act, 1696, c. 25, by S. 93. Such debentures are negotiable instruments; *Goodwin* v. *Robarts* (1876) 1 App Cas. 476; *Bechuanaland Exploration Co.* v. *London Trading Bank* [1898] 2 Q.B. 658.

combination of these forms. Debentures redeemed may be re-issued.[1] They are often issued as a series,[2] all of the same date and ranking *pari passu*, and may create a charge or security over company assets, frequently by way of floating charge. Debenture stock or loan stock is generally constituted by a trust deed trans-ferring assets to, or granting a floating charge over property in favour of, named persons as trustees for the debenture holders, providing for payment of interest, and issuing, for cash,[3] stock which gives the holder a claim against the trust fund, or the debenture or loan stock may be unsecured and contain only a personal obligation to repay. A sinking fund may be established to enable debentures to be paid off after a time.[4] Debentures are transferable only as units, whereas debenture stock is evidenced by certificates and transferable in units of convenient amounts such as £1, a register of holders of debenture stock being main-tained by the company.

Issue of debentures

Statutory provisions as to prospectuses apply also to the offering for sale of debentures,[5] but they may be issued at a discount,[6] though not if convertible into paid-up shares of the same amount as the face value of the debentures.[7]

Transfer of debentures

A debenture payable to bearer is transferable by mere delivery and conveys a good title to a holder who has taken in good faith, for value and without notice of any defect or limitation thereon.[8] A debenture to registered holder is transferable as specified therein, but there must be an instrument of transfer.[9] Normally a register of debenture-holders is maintained, transfers are regis-tered, and a note of the registration endorsed on the debenture. The rules applicable to transfer of shares in security apply equally to transfer of debentures.

---

[1] S. 90.

[2] An example of a single debenture is *Tennant's Trs.* v. *T.*, 1946 S.C. 420.

[3] The contract to take and pay for debentures may be enforced by decree for specific implement: S. 92.

[4] *Arizona Copper Co.* v. *London Scottish American Trust* (1897) 24 R. 658.

[5] Ss. 38–40; see also *Dunnett* v. *Mitchell* (1885) 12 R. 400.

[6] *Campbell's Case* (1876) 4 Ch. D. 470.

[7] *Mosely* v. *Koffyfontein Mines, Ltd.* [1904] 2 Ch. 108.

[8] *Bechuanaland Exploration Co.* v. *London Trading Bank* [1898] 2 Q.B. 658.

[9] S. 75; *Re Rhodesia Goldfields, Ltd.* (1880) 14 Ch. D. 859.

Remedies of debenture-holders

Where the debenture is not secured the holder may, as an unsecured creditor, sue thereon and do diligence on the decree, or petition for winding-up, or claim in the winding-up. If the debenture is secured it is usually provided that the debenture holders, or the trustee for them, may on default by the company take possession of the security subjects and sell them for the benefit of the debenture holders. Debentures of a company registered in Scotland can now contain power to appoint a receiver or manager on the company's property in specified events, as can debentures of a company registered in England, and the trustees may be authorized to take possession of and carry on a company's business. A debenture-holder, or the trustee, may petition for winding-up.

Floating Charges

By statute[1] a company may, to secure any debt or other obligation (including a cautionary obligation) incurred or to be incurred by or binding upon the company or any other person, create in favour of the creditor in the debt or obligation a floating charge,[2] by executing, under seal or by attorney, an instrument of charge[3] over all or any part of the property, heritable and moveable (including uncalled capital), which is, or may be from time to time, while the instrument is in force, comprised in the company's property and undertaking, save any property expressly excepted therefrom, or executing a bond or other written acknowledgment which purports to create such a charge. It is effectual in relation to heritage though not recorded in the Register of Sasines.[4] An instrument of charge may be altered by an instrument of alteration.[5] It does not affect any property so long as the company is a going concern, but attaches to the property comprised in the company's undertaking on the commencement of winding up, but is subject to the rights of any person who has effectually executed diligence on the property, or holds a fixed security[6] over the property or part of it ranking

[1] Companies (Floating Charges and Receivers) (Sc.) Act, 1972, Ss. 1–2, replacing Companies (Floating Charges) (Sc.) Act, 1961. This was incompetent at common law: *Ballachulish Slate Quarries Co.* v. *Menzies* (1908) 16 S.L.T. 48; *Carse* v. *Coppen*, 1951 S.C. 233.

[2] On its nature see *Governments Stock Inv. Co.* v. *Manila Ry.* [1897] A.C. 81; *Re Yorkshire Woolcombers Assocn.* [1903] 2 Ch. 284.

[3] Form in 1961 Act, Sched. 1; no form in 1972 Act.

[4] 1972 Act, S. 3.

[5] 1972 Act, S. 7.

[6] Defined, 1972 Act, S. 31(1).

in priority to the floating charge, or holds over the property or part of it another floating charge ranking in priority.[1] In winding-up a fixed security has priority over a floating charge unless the latter was registered before the creditor in the fixed security constituted his right as a real right.[2] Among floating charges themselves, priority is determined by time of registration unless the instruments provide that they are to rank *pari passu*.[3] Where the holder of a registered floating charge has received written intimation of the subsequent registration of another floating charge over the same property the preference of the earlier floating charge is restricted to security for present advances, further advances required to be made under the floating charge, interest due or to become due on all such advances, and expenses or outlays.[4] All charges, including floating charges, must be registered with the Registrar within 21 days, and copies of every such instrument must be kept at the registered office.[5] A creditor who holds a floating charge may seek to obtain payment of the debt secured thereby either by petitioning to wind up the company or he may appoint a receiver.

Registration of charges

A charge on land, wherever situated,[6] or any interest therein, over the uncalled share capital of the company, over incorporeal moveable property of stated kinds,[7] a security over a ship or any share therein or an aircraft, or a floating charge, if created after the 1961 Act, is void against the liquidator and any creditor of the company unless prescribed particulars and a certified copy of the instrument of charge are lodged with the Registrar for registration within 21 days.[8] Where a debenture contains a charge over the company's assets, a copy of the deed containing the charge or of one of the debentures must be registered, with stated particulars.[9] If property is acquired subject to a charge,

---

[1] 1972 Act S. 1. A floating charge granted to a bank in respect of advances under a cash-credit bond covers interest to the date of payment: S. 1(4); *National Commercial Bank* v. *Liqdrs of Telford Grier Mackay & Co.*, 1969 S.C. 181.

[2] 1972 Act, S. 5(2) and (3).   [3] 1972 Act, S. 5(4).

[4] 1972 Act, Sched. 2; cf. *M. Milne, Ltd.* (1963) 79 Sh. Ct. Rep. 105; *Archd. Campbell, Hope & King, Ltd.*, 1967 S.C. 21; *Amalgamated Securities Ltd.*, 1967 S.C. 56.

[5] 1972 Act, S. 5(5).

[6] Including land in England: *Amalgamated Securities, Ltd.*, 1967 S.C. 56.

[7] For an exception see *Scottish Homes Investment Co.*, 1968 S.C. 244.

[8] Ss. 106A–106B, added by Companies (Floating Charges and Receivers) (Sc.) Act, 1972; *M. Milne, Ltd.* (1963) 79 Sh. Ct. Rep. 105; *Archibald Campbell, Hope & King, Ltd.*, 1967 S.C. 21; *Scottish and Newcastle Breweries* v. *Rathburne Hotel Liqdr.*, 1970 S.L.T. 313.

[9] S. 106A(7).

particulars of the charge must be intimated.[1] The Registrar maintains a register of charges for each company and gives a certificate of registration of a charge; he also records the satisfaction of debts and the release of property from charge in security therefor.[2] The court may rectify the register.[3] The company must keep copies of every instrument creating a charge, and a register of charges, both open to inspection.[4] These provisions apply also to charges on property in Scotland created or acquired by a company not registered in Scotland if it has a place of business in Scotland.[5] Charges on property in England created or acquired by a company incorporated in Scotland with a place of business in England must similarly be registered with the Registrar in England.[6]

Receivers

The holder of a floating charge, or the court on the application of the holder of a floating charge, may appoint a receiver of the part of the company's property subject to the charge[7] on the occurrence of any event provided for by the instrument of charge or on the occurrence of any of stated events.[8] Business letters and documents must state that a receiver has been appointed,[9] and he must intimate his appointment to the company.[10] He must report his transactions annually to the registrar, the company and others.[11] He has the powers given him by the instrument of charge and extensive statutory powers.[12] He is deemed to be the agent of the company and, unless the contract provides otherwise, personally liable on contracts.[13] He must pay out of assets coming into his hands certain preferential claims,[14] then pay the holder of the floating charge in satisfaction of the debt secured thereby,[15] and distribute any balance among other claimants according to their respective interests.[16] He may resign or be removed by the court, and may apply to the court for directions in any matter arising in connection with the performance of his functions.

[1] S. 106C.
[2] S. 106D–106F.
[3] S. 106G.
[4] Ss. 106H–106J.
[5] S. 106K.
[6] Companies Act, 1948, S. 106; cf. *Amalgamated Securities, Ltd.*, 1967 S.C. 56.
[7] Companies (Floating Charges and Receivers) (Sc). Act, 1972, S. 11. As to modes of appointment see Ss. 13–14. As to suspension see S. 16. As to remuneration see S. 18.
[8] 1972 Act, S. 12.
[9] 1972 Act, S. 24.
[10] 1972 Act, S. 25.
[11] 1972 Act, S. 25.
[12] 1972 Act, Ss. 15, 21.
[13] 1972 Act, S. 17.
[14] 1972 Act, Ss. 19, 20(1).
[15] 1972 Act, S. 20(2) and (3).
[16] 1972 Act, Ss. 22–23.

REORGANIZATION

Reorganization is necessary where a company's capital structure is unsatisfactory or it has pressing claims by members or creditors or both. A company may make a compromise or arrangement with its creditors, or members, or any class or classes of either or both of these, under Ss. 206–8.[1] The procedure is for the company to formulate a scheme and petition the court requesting authority to summon separate meetings of each class of person affected by the proposed scheme;[2] notices calling the meetings are accompanied by a circular explaining the proposals,[3] and proxy forms. The results of the meetings are reported to the court which may, if satisfied of its fairness, sanction the scheme, in which event it is binding on the company and all classes of persons parties to the arrangement.[4] The court may require the rights of dissentient shareholders to be protected.[5]

Under S. 287 a company may be reconstructed by a voluntary liquidation wherein the liquidator transfers the company's assets to a new company for shares in the new company which are allotted to shareholders of the old company. Provided the section is complied with, any such arrangement is binding on all members of the company. A dissentient member may require the liquidator to abstain from carrying into effect the resolution to wind up and sell to the other company, or to purchase his interest at a price to be determined by agreement or by arbitration.[6] Any provision in the Articles depriving members of their rights under S. 287 is void.[7]

Amalgamation

If a company has power under its Memorandum to sell its business, it may sell its whole undertaking to another company for shares in the other company, which are distributed among the members in proportion to their rights. The selling company may

---

[1] See e.g. *Oban and Aultmore-Glenlivet Distilleries* (1903) 5 F. 1140; *Balmenach-Glenlivet Distillery Co.*, 1916 S.C. 639; *Clydesdale Bank*, 1950 S.C. 30.

[2] See *Cayzer Irvine & Co., Ltd.*, 1963 S.C. 25.

[3] *Scott & Co.*, 1950 S.C. 507; In particular the circular must state any material interests of the directors in the scheme: see *Rankin & Blackmore, Ltd.*, 1950 S.C. 218; *Coltness Iron Co.*, 1951 S.C. 476; *City Property Investment Trust Corpn.*, 1951 S.C. 570; *Second Scottish Investment Trust Co., Ltd.*, 1962 S.L.T. 392.

[4] e.g. *R. A. Munro & Co.*, 1913 S.C. 456; *British Assets Trust*, 1913 S.C. 661; *Scottish India Rubber Co.*, 1920 S.C. 1. See also *Re National Bank, Ltd.* [1966] 1 All E.R. 1006.

[5] *Re Sandwell Park Colliery Co., Ltd.* [1914] 1 Ch. 589.

[6] S. 287(3); *Re Union Bank of Kingston-upon-Hull* (1880) 13 Ch. D. 808; *Re Demerara Rubber Co., Ltd.* [1913] 1 Ch. 331; *Brailey v. Rhodesia Consolidated, Ltd.* [1910] 2 Ch. 95.

[7] *Payne v. Cork Co., Ltd.* [1900] 1 Ch. 308.

then be wound up, or continue in being as a wholly owned subsidiary of the other company. Any agreement to sell must make proper provision for the rights of dissentient shareholders.[1]

Take-overs

Where one company wishes to acquire all the shares of another company, or the whole of any class of shares, it makes an offer to the shareholders to acquire their shares, normally conditional on acceptance by the holders of a stated percentage of shares, sufficient to give the acquiring company full control. If this is achieved the offer becomes unconditional. If acceptances are received from holders of 90 per cent of the shares concerned within four months of the offer, the acquiring company may within two months of the expiry of the period for acceptance of the offer intimate to any dissenting shareholder that it desires to acquire his shares.[2] Such a shareholder may apply to the court to declare that the terms are not fair, the onus of proof of unfairness being on him.[3] Unless there is dissent, the fairness of the scheme need never come before the court.[4] The directors of an offeree company must be honest and not mislead their shareholders in advising them whether to accept the offer to buy their shares or not.[5]

Remedy for oppression

Where a member of a company complains that the affairs of the company are being conducted in a manner oppressive to some part of the members, including himself, the court may make an order for the purchase of any members' shares by other members, if winding-up would unfairly prejudice the other members but otherwise the facts would justify the making of a winding-up order as being just and equitable.[6] Thus a majority shareholder who oppresses minority shareholders by driving

---

[1] *Bisgood* v. *Henderson's Transvaal Estates, Ltd.* [1908] 1 Ch. 743.

[2] S. 209; *Musson* v. *Howard Glasgow Associates, Ltd.*, 1960 S.C. 371; *Nidditch* v. *C.P.A., Ltd.*, 1961 S.L.T. 282.

[3] *Re Press Caps* [1949] Ch. 434; *Re Sussex Brick Co. Ltd.* [1961] Ch. 289; *Re Grierson, Oldham and Adams, Ltd.* [1967] 1 All E.R. 192.

[4] The requirements of disclosure and fairness in take-over bids are controlled not so much by law as by 'The City Code on Takeovers and Mergers' formulated by the London Stock Exchange, issuing houses, bankers and others in 1968 and operating through a Panel on Takeovers and Mergers. A company contravening the code would find it practically impossible to get professional guidance or assistance, and quotation on the Stock Exchange might be suspended. Certain mergers might be referred to the Monopolies Commission under the Monopolies and Mergers Act, 1965.

[5] *Gething* v. *Kilner* [1972] 1 All E.R. 1166.

[6] S. 210.

down the company's business and the value of their shares may be required to buy out the minority shareholders.[1] To amount to oppression the conduct of the company's affairs must be burdensome, harsh and wrongful to the other members of the company and force them to submit to something unfair.[2]

WINDING-UP OR LIQUIDATION

Winding-up or liquidation is the process whereby a company is brought to an end. A winding-up may be (a) by the court; (b) voluntary; or (c) under the supervision of the court. The company need not be insolvent.[3] A company can be made notour bankrupt to the effect of equalizing diligences and entitling creditors to reduce preferences struck at by the Bankruptcy Act, 1696,[4] but cannot be sequestrated.[5]

(a) WINDING-UP BY THE COURT

The Court of Session may wind up any company registered in Scotland and the Sheriff court of the Sheriffdom where the registered office is situated may do so where the paid-up capital does not exceed £10,000.[6] An unregistered company[7] may be wound up as if registered in Scotland, but only by the court and in stated circumstances.[8] A company may be wound up by the court if[9]

(a) the company has by special resolution resolved that it be wound up by the court;

(b) default is made in delivery of the statutory report to the registrar or in holding the statutory meeting;[10]

(c) the company does not commence its business within a year from its incorporation or suspends its business for a whole year;[11]

---

[1] *Meyer* v. *S.C.W.S.*, 1954 S.C. 381; 1958 S.C. (H.L.) 40; see also *Elder* v. *Elder & Watson*, 1952 S.C. 49.

[2] *Meyer, supra*; *Re H. R. Harmer* [1958] 3 All E.R. 689; *Re Five Minute Car Wash Service, Ltd.* [1966] 1 All E.R. 242; *Re Jermyn Street Turkish Baths, Ltd.* [1971] 3 All E.R. 184.

[3] *Queensland Mercantile and Agency Co.* v. *Australasian Investment Co.* (1888) 15 R. 935.

[4] *Clark* v. *Hinde, Milne & Co.* (1884) 12 R. 347; *Athole Hydropathic Co.* v. *Scottish Provincial Assce. Co.* (1886) 13 R. 818.

[5] *Standard Property Investment Co.* v. *Dunblane Hydropathic Co.* (1884) 12 R. 328.

[6] Ss. 220-1; *Chaney & Bull Ltd., Petrs.*, 1930 S.C. 759; *Steel Scaffolding Co.* v. *Buckleys*, 1935 S.C. 617.

[7] Defined, S. 398; see *Smith's Trs.* v. *Irvine and Fullarton Property Socy.* (1903) 6 F. 99; *Re Caledonian Employees' Benevolent Socy.*, 1928 S.C. 633; *Canavan*, 1929 S.L.T. 636.

[8] S. 399.

[9] S. 222.

[10] Under S. 130 (public companies only); see also S. 225(3).

[11] *Re Middlesborough Assembly Rooms* (1880) 14 Ch. D. 104.

(d) the number of members is reduced, in the case of a private company, below two, or, in the case of any other company, below seven;

(e) the company is unable to pay its debts;[1]

(f) the court is of opinion that it is just and equitable that the company should be wound up;[2] and also if there is subsisting a floating charge over property comprised in the company's property and undertaking and the court is satisfied that the security of the creditor entitled to the benefit of the floating charge is in jeopardy.[3]

An application to the court for winding-up is made by petition, by the company or any creditor or creditors, contributory or contributories, or any or all of these parties,[4] or by the Dept. of Trade under S. 169(3). The court may dismiss the petition,[5] adjourn it conditionally or unconditionally, or make any interim order or other order it thinks fit, as for advertisement of the petition.[6] Answers may be lodged and parties heard.[7] The court may stay or restrain proceedings against the company.[8]

Winding-up is generally deemed to commence at the time of the presentation of the petition.[9] A copy of the order must be forwarded to the Registrar and minuted by him.[10] Thereafter no action or proceeding shall be commenced or proceeded with except by leave of the court.[11] The order operates in favour of all the creditors and contributories.[12] Any disposition of the property of the company, or transfer of shares, or alteration in the status of

---

[1] S. 223 states cases in which a company is 'deemed unable to pay its debts.' See also *Cuninghame* v. *Walkinshaw Coal Co.* (1886) 14 R. 87; *Pollok* v. *Gaeta Mining Co.*, 1907 S.C. 182. If the debt is disputed the petition may be sisted till the creditor constitutes his debt: *Landauer* v. *Alexander*, 1919 S.C. 492.

[2] See e.g. *Re T. E. Brinsmead & Sons* [1897] 1 Ch. 45, 406; *Pirie* v. *Stewart* (1904) 6 F. 847; *Black* v. *United Collieries* (1904) 7 F. 18; *Symington* v. *S's Quarries* (1906) 8 F. 121; *Loch* v. *John Blackwood Ltd.* [1924] A.C. 783; *Baird* v. *Lees*, 1924 S.C. 83; *Thomson* v. *Drysdale*, 1925 S.C. 311; *Zolkwer* v. *Reid Carr & Co.*, 1946 S.N. 141; *Galbraith* v. *Merito Shipping Co.*, 1947 S.C. 446; *Elder* v. *Elder & Watson*, 1952 S.C. 49; *Levy* v. *Napier*, 1962 S.C. 468; *Lewis* v. *Haas*, 1970 S.L.T. (Notes) 67. See also S. 225(2).

[3] Added by Companies (Floating Charges and Receivers) (Sc.) Act, 1972, S. 4.

[4] S. 224.

[5] e.g. *Macdonell's Trs.* v. *Oregonian Ry.* (1884) 11 R. 912; *Black* v. *United Collieries* (1904) 7 F. 18.

[6] S. 225.   [7] e.g. *Galbraith* v. *Merito Shipping Co.*, 1947 S.C. 446.

[8] S. 226; cf. *Martin* v. *Port of Manchester Ins. Co.*, 1934 S.C. 143.

[9] S. 229; *Liqdr. of Property Investment Co. of Scotland* v. *National Bank of Scotland* (1891) 28 S.L.R. 884.

[10] S. 230.

[11] S. 231; cf. *Martin, supra*; see also *Radford & Bright* v. *Stevenson* (1902) 10 S.L.T. 82; *Coclas* v. *Bruce Peebles & Co.* (1908) 16 S.L.T. 7.

[12] S. 232.

the members of the company after the commencement of winding up is void unless the court otherwise orders.[1] Winding up does not terminate current contracts and the liquidator may perform them,[2] or repudiate them, being then liable in damages for non-performance.[3]

Effect of winding up on antecedent transactions

Any transaction which, if done by or against an individual within six months before petition for his sequestration would be deemed in his bankruptcy a fraudulent preference,[4] if done by or against the company, is deemed a fraudulent preference and invalid accordingly.[5] Any conveyance or assignation by a company of all its property to trustees for the benefit of all its creditors is void to all intents.[4] A floating charge created within twelve months before winding-up is invalid, unless the company immediately thereafter was solvent, except to the amount of any cash then paid to the company in consideration for the charge, and interest thereon.[6] The winding-up is equivalent to an arrestment in execution and decree of furthcoming, and to an executed poinding, and no arrestment or poinding of the company's funds or effects within 60 days before the winding-up is effectual.[7] It is also equivalent to an adjudication of the company's heritable estates for debt, subject to such preferable heritable rights and securities as then existed and are valid and un-challengeable, and the right to poind the ground.[8] No poinding of the ground not carried into execution by sale sixty days before the commencement of winding-up is available in any question with the liquidator, save that no creditor holding a security over heritage prior to the liquidator is prevented from executing a poinding thereafter, but it is available only for the current half-year's interest on the debt, and for one year's arrears.[9]

---

[1] S. 227.

[2] *British Waggon Co.* v. *Lea* (1880) 5 Q.B.D. 149; *Tolhurst* v. *Assoc. Portland Cement Manufacturers* [1903] A.C. 414.

[3] *Asphaltic Limestone Co.* v. *Glasgow Corpn.*, 1907 S.C. 463.

[4] This includes any alienation or preference voidable by statute or at common law on the ground of insolvency or notour bankruptcy. See Ch. 124, *infra.*

[5] S. 320; *T.* v. *L.*, 1970 S.L.T. 243.

[6] S. 322.

[7] S. 327(1)(a); *Property Investment Co. of Scotland* (1891) 28 S.L.R. 884; *Campbell* v. *Edinburgh Parish Council*, 1911 S.C. 280; *Johnston* v. *Cluny Trs.*, 1957 S.C. 184.

[8] S. 327(1)(b); *Turnbull* v. *Scottish County Investment Co.*, 1939 S.C. 5; the Bankruptcy (Sc.) Act, 1913, Ss. 108 to 113 apply to the realization of heritable estates, affected by such heritable rights and securities: S. 327(1)(c).

[9] S. 327(1)(d); *Campbell, supra.*

The liquidator

The court appoints one or more liquidators,[1] who thereby become officers of the court and subject to its jurisdiction.[2] A provisional liquidator may be appointed at any time after the petition has been presented.[3] The court may determine what caution, if any, is required of the liquidator. He receives such remuneration as the court may direct.[4] He may resign, or on cause shown be removed by the court.[5] He must take into his custody or under his control all the company's property: so long as there is no liquidator, the company's property is deemed in the custody of the court.[6] There are statutory disqualifications for appointment[7] and penalties for corrupt inducement affecting appointment.[8]

The function of the liquidator is to ingather assets, adjust the rights of creditors and contributories *inter se*, apply the assets in discharge of liabilities and distribute any surplus among the persons entitled thereto. He is not a trustee,[9] nor vested with the property of the company; but an administrator who must have regard to the interests of the creditors.[10] The right of property remains in the company for which he administers it,[11] but the court may direct that property shall vest in him by his official name.[12]

The liquidator has wide statutory powers,[13] some of which require the sanction of the court or of the committee of inspection,

[1] Ss. 237–8, 242; *Gilmour's Trs.* v. *Kilmarnock Heritable Investment Co.* (1883) 10 R. 1221; *Broad* v. *Edinburgh Northern Tramways Co.* (1888) 15 R. 641; *Barberton Development Syndicate* (1898) 25 R. 654; *Argylls, Ltd.* v. *Ritchie & Whiteman*, 1914 S.C. 915.

[2] *Robertson* (1875) 3 R. 17; *Liqrs. of Bruce Peebles & Co.* v. *Shiells*, 1908 S.C. 692.

[3] S. 238; *Levy* v. *Napier*, 1962 S.C. 468; *Levy*, 1963 S.C. 46. If his appointment is recalled he may retain funds for his fees and expenses: *Booth* v. *Thomson*, 1972 S.L.T. 141.

[4] Ss. 241–2; *Jamieson* v. *Gaepel Haematite Co.* (1877) 14 S.L.R. 667; *Glasgow Commercial Co.*, 1913, 1 S.L.T. 117.

[5] S. 242; see *Lysons* v. *Liqr. of Miraflores Gold Syndicate* (1895) 22 R. 605; see also *Highland and Northern Dairy Farms, Ltd.*, 1964 S.C. 1.

[6] S. 243.

[7] S. 335.

[8] S. 336.

[9] *Gray's Trs.* v. *Benhar Coal Co.* (1881) 9 R. 225; *Clark* v. *West Calder Oil Co.* (1882) 9 R. 1017; *Liqr. of Style & Mantle, Ltd.* v. *Price's Tailors Ltd.*, 1934 S.C. 548.

[10] *Waterhouse* v. *Jamieson* (1870) 8 M. (H.L.) 88; *Bank of Scotland* v. *Liqrs. of Hutchison, Main & Co.*, 1914 S.C. (H.L.) 1.

[11] *Gray's Trs.*, *supra*; *Bank of Scotland*, *supra*; *Liqr. of Style & Mantle, Ltd.*, *supra*.

[12] S. 244.

[13] S. 245; court sanction to sell heritage is unnecessary: *Galbraith*, 1964 S.L.T. (Sh. Ct.) 75; as to powers and obligations when selling heritage see *Liqr. of Style & Mantle, Ltd.* v. *Price's Tailors Ltd.*, 1934 S.C. 548.

but others may be exercised at his own hand. The exercise of his powers is subject to the control of the court, which may permit him, where there is no committee of inspection, to exercise certain powers without the court's sanction. He may carry on the company's business[1] or litigate[2] if necessary for the beneficial winding-up. Hence contracts in progress may be completed,[3] unless involving an element of *delectus personae*. The company is liable in damages if the liquidator repudiates an uncompleted contract or if it is defectively performed. Subject to general rules, he has the same powers as a trustee on a bankrupt estate.[4] He may challenge payments made by the company as amounting to illegal preferences under the Bankruptcy Act, 1696, as amended by the Companies Act, 1947, S. 115(3).[5]

Committee of inspection

The liquidator must summon separate meetings of creditors and contributories to determine whether or not application should be made to the court for appointment of a committee of inspection,[6] which, if appointed, has statutory functions, and such powers and duties of commissioners on a bankrupt estate as may be conferred by general rules.[7] Its members are in a position of trust.[8]

The court may stay a winding-up, altogether or for a limited time, on such conditions as it thinks fit.[9] The court must as soon as possible settle a list of contributories, or persons liable to contribute to the company's assets on winding-up.[10] Settling the lists may involve rectifying the register of members. Usually there are the A list, of members of the company at the date of winding-up, and the B list, of past members still liable under the Act. The court must also cause the company's assets to be collected

---

[1] S. 245(1)(b); *Re Wreck Recovery & Salvage Co.* (1880) 15 Ch. D. 353; *Liqr. of Burntisland Oil Co.* v. *Dawson* (1892) 20 R. 180; *Liqr. of Victoria Public Buildings Co.* (1893) 30 S.L.R. 386; as to obligations binding in honour only see *Clyde Marine Ins. Co.* v. *Renwick*, 1924 S.C. 113.

[2] S. 245(1)(a); *Millar* (1890) 18 R. 179; *S.S. Camelot* (1893) 1 S.L.T. 358; *Kilmarnock Theatre Co.* v. *Buchanan*, 1907 S.C. 607. The liquidator is personally liable for the expenses of litigation: *Liqr. of Consolidated Copper Co. of Canada* (1877) 5 R. 393; *Kilmarnock, supra.*

[3] *Asphaltic Limestone Co.* v. *Glasgow Corpn.*, 1907 S.C. 463.

[4] S. 245(5).

[5] *Walkcraft Paint Co.* v. *Lovelock*, 1964 S.L.T. 103; *Walkcraft Paint Co.* v. *Kinsay*, 1964 S.L.T. 104.

[6] S. 252. For the constitution of the committee see S. 253.

[7] S. 255.

[8] *N.B. Locomotive Co. Liqdrs.* v. *L.A.*, 1963 S.C. 272.

[9] S. 256.

[10] Who are contributories is determined by Ss. 212–17.

and applied in discharge of its liabilities.[1] It may require contributories and other persons to hand over to the liquidator money, property, or papers to which the company is *prima facie* entitled,[2] and make an order on a contributory to pay money due to the company.[3] The court may make calls on all or any contributories to the extent of their liability for money needed to pay the company's debts and the expenses of winding-up.[4] It may exclude creditors not proving their claims in time[5] and adjust the rights of contributories among themselves and distribute any surplus among the persons entitled thereto.[6] It may summon and examine persons suspected of having company property[7] and may require the attendance of officers of the company to give information about the company.[8]

Proof and ranking of claims

Debts payable on a contingency, and claims present or future, certain or contingent, ascertained or sounding only in damages may be proved in liquidation, a just estimate being made of those not ascertained.[9] The provision of Ss. 45–62, 96 and 105 of the Bankruptcy (Sc.) Act, 1913, apply as they do in a sequestration,[10] provided that the holder of a debenture is not required to value and deduct the security for the purpose of voting at meetings of creditors.[11] Funds held by the company belonging to third parties and distinguishable from the company's own funds are payable to the third parties.[12]

Distribution of assets

The expenses of the liquidation and the liquidator's remuneration are the first charge.[13] There must be paid in priority to all

---

[1] S. 257. [2] S. 258.

[3] S. 259; see also S. 262. On enforcement of such orders see Ss. 275–6; on appeals see S. 277; *Levy*, 1963 S.C. 46.

[4] S. 260.

[5] S. 264; late claimants may participate in later distributions: *Dickey* v. *Ballantine*, 1939 S.C. 783.

[6] S. 265.

[7] S. 268.

[8] S. 269.

[9] S. 316. As to ranking for annuity, see *Kerr* v. *Walker*, 1933 S.C. 458.

[10] S. 318; see also *Clydesdale Bank* v. *Allan*, 1926 S.C. 235.

[11] Proviso added by 1961 Act, S. 7(a).

[12] *Smith* v. *Liqdr. of James Birrell, Ltd.*, 1968 S.L.T. 174.

[13] S. 309; as to insufficient assets, see S. 267; *Edinburgh Pavilion Co.* v. *Walker* (1906) 14 S.L.T. 61; *Falconer* v. *Drummond* (1908) 15 S.L.T. 1067.

other debts certain statutorily preferred debts.[1] These rank
equally *inter se* and must be paid in full, unless the assets are
insufficient to meet them in which case they abate in equal
proportions and, so far as the assets of the company available for
payment of the general creditors are insufficient to meet them,
have priority over the claims of holders of debentures under any
floating charge and must be paid out of any property comprised
in or subject to that charge.[2] Thereafter must be paid debts for
which security was held, unsecured debts, and any surplus is
divided among the persons entitled thereto, in proportion to the
nominal capital held by them.[3]

Dissolution of the company

When the company's affairs have been completely wound up,
the court will, on application by the liquidator, order that the
company be dissolved from that date. A copy of the order is sent
to the Registrar.[4] Within two years the dissolution may be
declared void.[5]

Discharge of liquidator

The liquidator seeks discharge by petition to the court. It may
be refused if he has failed in his duties.[6]

(b) VOLUNTARY WINDING-UP

Voluntary winding-up may be at the instance of members or
creditors; it may take place when the period fixed for the company's duration has expired or the event has happened on which
the company is to be dissolved and the company has resolved to
wind up voluntarily, or on a special resolution of the members, or
on an extraordinary resolution that the company cannot, by
reason of its liabilities, continue in business and that it is advisable
to wind it up.[7] Due notice of the resolution must be given, and

---

[1] S. 319(1)–(4); see also *L.A. v. Purvis Industries, Ltd.*, 1958 S.C. 338.

[2] S. 319(5) amd. 1961 Act, S. 7(b).

[3] S. 265; *Birch v. Cropper* (1889) 14 App. Cas. 525; cf. *Wilsons & Clyde Coal Co. v. Scottish Ins. Corpn.*, 1949 S.C. (H.L.) 90.

[4] S. 274.

[5] S. 352; *Charles Dale, Ltd.*, 1927 S.C. 130. The court may extend the period: *Collins Bros. & Co.*, 1916 S.C. 620. Avoidance was refused in *Lord Macdonald's C.B.*, 1924 S.C. 163; *Forth Shipbreaking Co.*, 1924 S.C. 489 but granted in *Champdany Jute Co.*, 1924 S.C. 209; see also *Dowling*, 1960 S.L.T. (Notes) 76.

[6] *Lovat Mantle Mfrs. Ltd.*, 1960 S.L.T. (Sh. Ct.) 52.

[7] S. 278; as to the need for stating the character of the resolution, see *Rennie v. Crichton's, Ltd.*, 1927 S.L.T. 459. As to overriding creditors' wishes and making winding-up compulsory, see *Bouboulis v. Mann, Macneal & Co.*, 1926 S.C. 637.

when passed, it must be advertised in the Edinburgh Gazette.[1]
The winding-up dates from the passing of the resolution and the
company must cease to carry on business except so far as necessary
for the winding-up, though the company continues in being.[2]
Any transfer of shares or alteration in the status of members of
the company thereafter is void.[3] If the directors can, and do,
within 5 weeks before the resolution to wind up, make a statutory
declaration of the company's solvency[2] it is a members' voluntary
winding-up.[2]

Member's voluntary winding-up

If it is a members' voluntary winding-up the company in general
meeting must appoint one or more liquidators, on whose appointment all the powers of the directors cease, unless their continuance
be sanctioned.[4] The liquidator may sell the company's property
for shares in another company.[5] If of opinion that the company
will not be able to pay its debts in full the liquidator must
summon a meeting of creditors forthwith and state the company's
assets and liabilities.[6] He must call a general meeting at the end
of each year and report on the progress of the winding-up.[7]
When the company's affairs are fully wound up the liquidator
must summon a final meeting, present an account of the winding-
up and transmit a copy to the Registrar. Three months later the
company is deemed dissolved,[8] but the dissolution may be
declared void within two years.[9] In case of insolvency alternative
provisions apply.[10]

Creditors' voluntary winding-up

If it is a creditors' voluntary winding-up[11] a meeting of
creditors must be called on the same day as the members' meeting
to pass the winding-up resolution, or on the following day; the
directors must put before the meeting a statement of the company's position with a list of creditors.[12] The company or its

---

[1] S. 279; see *Liqdr. of Nairn Public Hall Co.*, 1946 S.C. 395.
[2] Ss. 280–1.   [3] S. 282.
[4] S. 285; the company may fill a vacancy in the office: s. 286.
[5] S. 287.
[6] S. 288.
[7] S. 289.
[8] S. 290.
[9] S. 352.
[10] S. 291.
[11] This covers all cases other than where the declaration of solvency has been made
and whether or not the company is in fact solvent.
[12] S. 293.

creditors appoints a liquidator.[1] The creditors may appoint a committee of inspection of not more than five, to whom the members may add not more than five, subject to the creditors' objections.[2] The committee of inspection or the creditors may fix the liquidator's remuneration.[3] The liquidator may sell the company's property for shares in another company.[4] The directors' powers cease.[2] The liquidator must call meetings of the company and of the creditors at the end of each year and report on the conduct of the winding-up during the year.[5] When the company's affairs are fully wound up the liquidator lays an account before a general meeting of the company and a meeting of creditors. The Registrar registers the account and the company is deemed dissolved three months later, unless the court defers the date.[6]

Provisions applicable to both kinds of voluntary winding-up

The provisions as to proof and ranking of claims (Ss. 316–18), preferential debts (S. 319), fraudulent preferences (S. 320), floating charges (S. 322), and the effect of diligence within 60 days of winding-up (S. 327) apply. Subject to S. 319, the company's property is to be applied in satisfaction of its liabilities *pari passu* and, subject thereto, shall be distributed among the members according to their rights and interests in the company.[7] The court may appoint a liquidator, or remove him and appoint another.[8] The liquidator has statutory powers, including the power to settle the list of contributories[9] and he or any contributory or creditor may apply to the court to determine any question arising in the winding-up, or to exercise any power which it might in a winding-up by the court.[10] Any arrangement between a company being wound up and its creditors is binding on the company if sanctioned by an extraordinary resolution and on the creditors if acceded to by three-fourths in number and value of the creditors, but any creditor or contributory may appeal to the court against it.[11] The court may stay

---

[1] S. 294; the creditors may fill a vacancy in office: S. 297.

[2] S. 295; *Liqr. of Clyde Marine Insce. Co.*, 1921 S.C. 472; *Webb*, 1922 S.C. 226. A member of the committee of inspection is in a quasi-fiduciary position: *N.B. Locomotive Co. Liqdrs. v. L.A.*, 1963 S.C. 272.

[3] S. 296.   [4] S. 298.

[5] S. 299.   [6] S. 300.

[7] S. 302.

[8] S. 304: he must intimate his appointment to the Registrar: S. 305.

[9] S. 303.

[10] S. 307: but see *Crawford v. McCulloch*, 1909 S.C. 1063.

[11] S. 306.

actions against the company.[1] The costs of a voluntary winding-up, including the liquidator's remuneration, are payable in priority to all other claims.[2]

(c) WINDING-UP SUBJECT TO SUPERVISION BY THE COURT

Where a company has resolved to wind up voluntarily the Court may make an order that the winding-up shall continue but subject to such supervision by the court, and with such liberty to creditors, contributories or others to apply to the court as the court thinks just.[3] The court may appoint an additional liquidator to act with the existing liquidator.[4] The effect of a supervision order is that the liquidator may exercise all his powers, with certain exceptions, without the sanction of the court as if the company were being wound up voluntarily.[5] The rules as to proof and ranking of claims (Ss. 316 to 318), preferential payments (S. 319), fraudulent preferences (S. 320), floating charges (S. 322), and the effect of diligence within 60 days before winding up (S. 327) apply in this case also. When the winding-up has been completed the company may be dissolved under S. 274.

Removal of company from register

Apart from dissolution following on liquidation, a company may be removed from the register when the Registrar has reasonable cause to believe that it is not carrying on business or in operation.[6] A company may be restored to the register if the court is satisfied that it is just so to order.[7] The property of dissolved company is *bona vacantia* and belongs to the Crown, though the Queen's and Lord Treasurer's Remembrancer may disclaim title thereto.[8]

---

[1] S. 308.

[2] S. 309.

[3] S. 311; see *Re Varieties Ltd.* [1893] 2 Ch. 235; *Re Medical Battery Co.* [1894] 1 Ch. 444.

[4] S. 314.

[5] S. 315.

[6] S. 353; cf. *Alliance Heritable Security Co.* (1886) 14 R. 34.

[7] S. 353(6); *Charles Dale, Ltd.*, 1927 S.C. 130; *Beith Unionist Assocn. Trs.*, 1950 S.C. 1; *Re Harvest Lane Motor Bodies* [1968] 2 All E.R. 1012; *Re Test Holdings Ltd.* [1969] 3 All E.R. 517.

[8] Ss. 354-5.

CHAPTER 27

BUILDING SOCIETIES

BUILDING societies are societies established for the purpose of raising by the subscriptions of the members, a fund for making advances to members out of the funds of the society on the security of land and buildings.[1] Societies lend not only the subscriptions of investing members but money deposited at interest by the public and money lent by banks and other sources. The purpose of the advances is to finance the building or purchase of houses. Societies may be either permanent or terminating,[2] and either of these may be incorporated or unincorporated; today practically all are incorporated permanent societies.[3] A company may carry on the business of a building society, but cannot contain those words in its name,[4] and the rights of such a company and its members is determined by the law of companies.

Formation

Any ten or more persons may establish a building society by agreeing on rules and making application to the Assistant Registrar of Friendly Societies for Scotland with copies of the rules agreed upon for the society.[5] The assistant registrar may reject an undesirable name; the last words of the name must be 'Building Society.'[6] There are penalties for persons representing themselves to be a society and commencing business without a certificate of incorporation.[7] If the registrar is satisfied he registers the rules and issues a certificate of incorporation, whereby the society becomes a corporate body by its registered name.[6]

---

[1] Building Societies Act, 1962, S. 1(1). See *Fleming* v. *Self* (1854) 3 De G.M. & G. 997, and generally Wurtzburg and Mills, *Building Society Law*. They originated in the 18th century and were originally temporary and terminating and only later formed as permanent organizations. They are another facet of the Victorian drive for thrift and self-help. The first statutory regulation was in 1836, superseded in 1874, and now replaced by the 1962 Act, except as to unincorporated societies.

[2] These include the Bowkett and Starr-Bowkett Societies.

[3] Unincorporated societies were all formed under the Building Societies Act, 1836, and are regulated by the pre-1962 legislation, which by S. 133(2) is saved.

[4] Companies Act, 1948 Ss. 1(4), 17.

[5] 1962 Act, S. 1.

[6] 1962 Act, Ss. 2, 3; cf. *Glover* v. *Giles* (1881) 18 Ch. D. 173.

[7] 1962 Act, S. 12.

The court cannot declare the incorporation void as having been obtained by fraud or irregularity.[1] A society may not use any name or title other than its registered name.[2] It may subsequently change its name by special resolution, notice of which must be sent to the assistant registrar.[3] The use of even a registered name may be interdicted if the court considers that there is danger of deception or confusion.[4] The corporate name is a sufficient description without further designation or address.[5] The assistant registrar retains powers of control over a society once it is incorporated, and may suspend borrowing and subscription for shares,[6] regulate advertising,[7] require documents and information,[8] and generally control advertisements and other communications.[9] He has special powers in relation to small societies.[10] He may also suspend or cancel registration on specified grounds.[11]

Commencing business

A new society cannot commence business or borrow money until the registrar has certified that each of the ten founding members has subscribed £500 and undertaken to leave it for five years. On failure the registration may be cancelled.[12] A new society may not issue advertisements until the registrar has on written application given permission in writing, which he may do if the society has satisfied the requirement of Schedule 2.[13]

Officers and administration

The society's affairs are normally managed by directors, managers, and a secretary.[14] Appointments have to be intimated to the registrar.[15] An auditor is an officer only for certain purposes.[16] All officers are bound by the rules of the society which must set out their duties and powers.[17] The position of directors vis-a-vis the society is similar to that of directors of a company. Officers having the receipt or charge of any money must find

---

[1] *Glover, supra.*
[2] 1962 Act, S. 15.
[3] 1962 Act, S. 16.
[4] *Accident Insce. Co.* v. *Accident Disease and General Insce. Corpn.* (1884) 54 L.J. Ch. 104.
[5] *Improved Edinburgh, etc. Bldg. Socy.* v. *White* (1906) 8 F. 903.
[6] 1962 Act, Ss. 48–50.   [7] 1962 Act, Ss. 51–2.
[8] 1962 Act, Ss. 53–4.   [9] 1962 Act, S. 57.
[10] 1962 Act, Ss. 55–6.   [11] 1962 Act, Ss. 13, 113–15.
[12] 1962 Act, S. 13.   [13] 1962 Act, S. 14.
[14] S. 129.   [15] S. 75.
[16] S. 84.   [17] S. 4.

caution for faithful performance of their duties.[1] They must account on demand for money, securities, books and other society property in their custody.[2] Directors must disclose any interest in a proposed contract with the society, and no officer may accept any commission for or in connection with any loan by the Society.[3] Officers may not be exempted by the rules from liability for negligence, default, breach of duty or breach of trust, nor provision made for indemnifying officers for such conduct, but the court may in its discretion relieve officers from liability.[4] Under many provisions of the 1962 Act officers are liable criminally for the society's failure to comply with the Act's requirements.

Societies must maintain proper books, a system of supervision of books and money, and a system for the safe custody of title deeds of property.[5] A revenue and appropriation account and a balance sheet with auditors' report must be laid before the society at the annual general meeting.[6] The directors must also submit a report on the state of affairs of the society,[7] and copies must be sent to the assistant registrar and to members.[8]

An annual return with auditors' report thereon must be made to the assistant registrar containing prescribed information.[9] He may in certain circumstances forbid the society to receive money[10] or to issue advertisements.[11]

Rules

The rules form the contract between the society and its members and, when registered, are binding on the society, and the members and officers of the society, and on all persons claiming under the rules.[12] All such persons are deemed to have full notice of the rules.[12] The rules must contain the matters required by the Act,[13] but may contain other matters,[14] so long as consistent with the general law and the 1962 Act.[15]

---

[1] S. 71.   [2] S. 72.   [3] Ss. 73–4.
[4] S. 92, incorporating Companies Act, 1948, S. 448.   [5] 1962 Act, S. 76.
[6] 1962 Act, Ss. 77–81, 84–7.
[7] 1962 Act, S. 82.
[8] 1962 Act, S. 83.
[9] 1962 Act, Ss. 88–91.
[10] 1962 Act, S. 48.
[11] 1962 Act, Ss. 51, 57.
[12] 1962 Act, S. 5; *Walton* v. *Edge* (1884) 10 App. Cas. 33; *Auld* v. *Glasgow Working Men's Building Socy.* (1887) 14 R. (H.L.) 27; *Galashiels Provident Bldg. Socy.* v. *Newlands* (1893) 20 R. 821.   [13] 1962 Act, S. 4.
[14] The Building Societies Association has produced a set of Model Rules.
[15] *Murray* v. *Scott* (1884) 9 App. Cas. 519, 538; *Cullerne* v. *London etc. Bldg. Socy.* (1890) 25 Q.B.D. 485.

A society may alter or add to its rules only by special resolution, the change being registered with the assistant registrar.[1] The alteration must always be consistent with the constitution of the society.[2] A member may be barred by acquiescence from challenging a rule as *ultra vires*.[3] Certain transactions, if not authorized by the rules, may be *ultra vires* of the directors.[4] A society admittedly insolvent cannot alter its rules so as to vary the rights of members in its liquidation, though it may merely so as to facilitate ingathering of assets.[5]

Members

The members of a society are usually investing (or unadvanced) members who subscribe for shares, receiving interest thereon, and borrowing (or advanced) members who borrow money on the security of heritage. A person may be permitted by the rules to become a member without holding a share in the society, and a person need not become a member to obtain an advance.[6] A society must maintain a register of members.[7] The rights and liabilities of investing members depend on the society's rules; and those of borrowing members on the rules and the bond by which they undertake to repay advances. The liability of members of an incorporated society is limited, investing members with shares to the amount paid or in arrear on their shares, borrowing members with an advanced share to the amount payable on their shares, under their bonds or the society's rules, and borrowing members without a share to the amount payable under their bonds.[8] Members are entitled to copies of the annual accounts and annual returns.[9] A member may retire from the society or withdraw and require the return of money paid on his shares. The rules must state the terms on which he may withdraw,[10] and may provide for repayment in rotation. Death operates as with-

---

[1] 1962 Act, S. 17; *Auld, supra*; *Alliance Perpetual Bldg. Socy. v. Clifton* [1962] 3 All E.R. 828.

[2] *Bradbury v. Wild* [1893] 1 Ch. 377; *Strohmenger v. Finsbury Bldg. Socy.* [1897] 2 Ch. 469.

[3] *Sinclair v. Mercantile Bldg. Investment Socy.* (1885) 12 R. 1243; *Biddulph, etc., Socy. v. Agricultural Wholesale Socy., Ltd.* [1927] A.C. 76.

[4] *Shiell's Trs. v. Scottish Property Investment Co.* (1884) 12 R. (H.L.) 14.

[5] *Sixth West Kent Mutual Bldg. Socy. v. Hills; Same v. Shore* [1899] 2 Ch. 60, 64.

[6] 1962 Act, S. 8.　　　　　　　　[7] 1962 Act, S. 62.

[8] 1962 Act, S. 11; *Re Sheffield, etc. Bldg. Socy.* (1889) 22 Q.B.D. 470 (investing member); *Brownlie v. Russell* (1883) 10 R. (H.L.) 19 (advanced member).

[9] 1902 Act, Ss. 83, 88.

[10] 1962 Act, S. 4; cf. *Auld v. Glasgow, etc. Bldg. Socy.* (1887) 14 R. (H.L.) 27; *Glasgow etc. Bldg. Socy. v. Galbraith* (1884) 21 S.L.R. 782; *Scottish Property etc. Socy. v. Stewart* (1885) 12 R. 925.

drawal.[1] Once repaid, the member ceases to be a member and is free of all liability, even on winding-up.[2] Till repaid, a withdrawing member remains a member and remains bound by the rules.[3] If during a member's period of notice of withdrawal the society is ordered to be wound up[4] or dissolved, or orders a stoppage of business,[5] the notice becomes ineffective and confers no priority in the distribution of assets. Membership may be terminated by reason of a shareholder's default.[6]

Shares

Whereas a company share is a fractional part of the capital and ownership of the company, a building society has no fixed capital,[7] but may raise funds by shares issued as persons wish to take them up, limited only by the number the public is prepared to subscribe for and the amount of money the society can usefully lend. The rules must set out the terms on which shares are to be issued.[8] A member may withdraw and obtain repayment of his shares, whereas a shareholder in a company can only sell his shares (except in a winding-up). Investment shares may be preferential shares, if authorized, may have preference under the rules as to interest, withdrawal, in relation to losses and to payment on dissolution.[9] Paid-up shares have a nominal value which is paid up in full at the time of issue. Subscription shares have a nominal value, payable by monthly subscriptions of so many shillings per share. Failing contrary provision in the rules, shares are freely transferable, and may be gifted or bequeathed.[10] If a member dies having less than £500 in the society's funds the directors may pay the person who appears to be entitled, subject to certain conditions, without requiring production of confirmation.[11]

Meetings

The society's rules must provide for the calling and holding of meetings.[12] There must be an annual general meeting.[13] Meetings

[1] *Re Counties, etc. Bldg. Socy., Davis v. Norton* [1900] 2 Ch. 819.
[2] cf. *Meiklejohn v. Glasgow, etc. Bldg. Socy.* (1885) 13 R. 144.
[3] *Mitchells v. Caledonian Bldg. Socy.* (1886) 13 R. 918.
[4] *N.B. Bldg. Socy. v. McLellan* (1887) 14 R. 827.
[5] *Re Sunderland Bldg. Socy.* (1890) 24 Q.B.D. 394; *Re Ambition Investment Socy.* [1896] 1 Ch. 89.
[6] *Liqr. of Irvine and Fullarton etc. Bldg. Socy. v. Cuthbertson* (1905) 8 F. 1.
[7] *Irvine and Fullarton, etc., Bldg. Socy. v. Cuthbertson* (1905) 8 F. 1.
[8] 1962 Act, S. 4.   [9] *Alliance Perpetual Bldg. Socy. v. Clifton* [1962] 3 All E.R. 828.
[10] *Collins v. C.* (1871) 40 L.J. Ch. 541; *Allan v. Urquhart* (1887) 25 S.L.R. 47.
[11] 1962 Act, S. 46, amd. Administration of Estates (Small Payments) Act, 1965, S. 1.
[12] 1962 Act, S. 4.   [13] 1962 Act, S. 64.

must be called on written notice of at least 21 and not more than 56 days, sent to all members holding shares valued at at least £25. Proxies may attend but may vote only on a poll, which may be demanded by 10 members.[1]

Borrowing powers

A society may within limits, and if authorized by its rules, borrow and receive deposits or loans at interest to be applied for the purposes of the society.[2] It may give security for loans made to it.[3] Directors are personally liable for any excess.[4] A common form of borrowing is by receiving deposits from members and non-members on which interest is paid.[5] The minimum permitted notice of withdrawal is one month.[6] One society, if in difficulties, may be authorized to borrow from another.[7] Share investments in designated building societies are 'wider-range' trustee investments and deposits are 'narrower-range investments requiring advice' under the Trustee Investments Act, 1961.[8] The designation is entrusted to the Chief Registrar. The onus of discovering whether a society has borrowing power or has exceeded its powers is on the lender.[9]

Investment and banking

A society may invest surplus funds only in a manner authorized by the Act, or keep them on current account with an authorized bank.[10]

Advances on heritable security

This is the main purpose and business of a society. Applicants for advances are not to be required or permitted to ballot for precedence or otherwise have their chances determined by lot.[11] The applicant is made a member of the society, if not already one, for the purpose of receiving an advance, but the actual issue of

---

[1] 1962 Act, Ss. 64–70.

[2] 1962 Act, S. 39; cf. *Sinclair* v. *Brougham* [1914] A.C. 398; *Sun Permanent Bldg. Socy.* v. *Western Suburban etc. Bldg. Socy.* [1921] 2 Ch. 438.

[3] 1962 Act, Ss. 4, 41; cf. *Murray* v. *Scott* (1884) 9 App. Cas. 519.

[4] 1962 Act, S. 40; *Looker* v. *Wrigby* (1882) 9 Q.B.D. 397; *Cross* v. *Fisher* [1892] 1 Q.B. 467.

[5] 1962 Act, S. 45.

[6] 1962 Act, S. 42.

[7] 1962 Act, S. 44.

[8] Sched. 1, Parts 2 and 3.

[9] *Sun Permanent Socy.*, *supra*.

[10] 1962 Act, Ss. 58–61.

[11] 1962 Act, S. 35.

borrowers' shares is unnecessary[1] and now unusual. The society must be satisfied that the borrower has legal capacity to borrow and give security and is a satisfactory person, lending to whom does not involve unreasonable risk. When a society makes an advance for the purchase of heritage, it is deemed, unless it gives contrary notice, to warrant that the purchase price is reasonable.[2] A 'special advance' is an advance made on heritable security (a) to a body corporate; (b) of more than £5000 to a person other than a body corporate; (c) of any amount to a person other than a body corporate who, after the advance is made to him, is indebted to the society in an amount exceeding the limit in force for the purposes of the paragraph.[3] Special advances may be made only as authorized by Ss. 22–4.

Security for advances

Advances made by a society to a borrowing member are determined in large part by the ordinary law of dispositions of heritage in security,[4] but also by his contract of membership of the society.[5] The security must be primarily heritable subjects, but additional security of the kinds specified in the Act is competent.[6] A person having a financial interest who misrepresents that a property is sufficient security for an advance is subject to penalties.[7] In view of fluctuations of the general rate of interest on money lent, the bond normally reserves power to modify, within limits, the rate of interest. It is also commonly provided that all future instalments become immediately payable on default in regular repayment.[8]

Society directors must satisfy themselves that the adequacy of security will be assessed by them or a competent person, and that an appropriate signed report by a competent and prudent independent person is made available to the person assessing. Certain persons are disqualified from reporting.[9] Additional security, but only of specified kinds, may be taken into account.[10]

---

[1] 1962 Act, S. 8.

[2] 1962 Act, S. 30.

[3] 1962 Act, S. 21; the limit is stated in S. 21(2) and (3).

[4] Ch. 82, *infra*; cf. *Provident Bldg. Socy.* v. *Greenhill* (1878) 9 Ch. D. 122.

[5] *Galashiels Provident Bldg. Socy.* v. *Newlands* (1893) 20 R. 821.

[6] 1962 Act, S. 26 and Sched. 3. This may include a postponed security: *Hayes Bridge Estate* v. *Portman Bldg. Socy.* [1936] 2 All E.R. 1400.

[7] 1962 Act, S. 31.

[8] cf. *Leeds and Hanley Theatre* v. *Broadbent* [1898] 1 Ch. 343; *Gatty* v. *Maclaine*, 1921 S.C. (H.L.) 1.

[9] 1962 Act, S. 25.

[10] 1962 Act, S. 26 and Scheds. 3 and 4.

Records of advances must be kept, showing the value of the security.[1] Where security is taken from a third party, the society must, before seeking to recover any sums in respect of an advance, give the borrower a written notice stating prescribed particulars.[2] A society may not advance money on land subject to a prior security, with certain exceptions, unless it is in favour of the society. Directors are jointly and severally liable for loss occasioned by contravention of this restriction.[3]

Repayment of advances

The main systems in use for the repayment of advances made by a society are the flat rate system, whereby instalments covering both interest and principal are paid over an agreed term of years, the capital element increasing as time passes, or the fixed principal instalment system, whereby fixed instalments of principal are repaid periodically with interest on the outstanding balance, the total instalment diminishing as time passes, and the endowment assurance system, whereby the borrower pays interest only but maintains for the benefit of the society an endowment policy on his own life for the period of the advance, which when it matures, is applied to repaying the principal advanced.[4] More than one system may apply to one advance. The rules may permit suspension of repayments. When all moneys secured by a disposition in security to a building society have been fully paid or discharged the society should discharge the security in the usual way.[5] On default under a security a society has all the ordinary powers of a security-holder, as may be stated in the deed, to enter into possession, sell or foreclose. Where a society, having exercised its power of sale, acquires an irredeemable title to land, it must as soon as conveniently practicable sell or convert the land into money.[6]

Disputes

Disputes between a society and a member as such[7] or a person claiming through him, except the construction or effect of a security deed or any other contract contained in a document other

---

[1] 1963 Act, S. 27.

[2] 1962 Act, S. 28.

[3] 1962 Act, S. 32.

[4] The society may advance the premium for a single premium life policy for this purpose: 1962 Act, S. 33.

[5] 1962 Act, S. 37 does not apply to Scotland.

[6] 1962 Act, S. 109.

[7] *Municipal, etc., Bldg. Socy.* v. *Richards* (1888) 39 Ch. D. 372.

than the rules, and any other disputes specified in the rules, must be determined by arbitration, reference to the assistant registrar or application to the sheriff court, whichever the rules provide.[1] The arbiter, assistant registrar, or sheriff court may, at the request of either party, state a case for the opinion of the Court of Session on any question of law. Subject thereto, the determination of the dispute is final, not appealable nor removeable into any court.[2] This does not cover a dispute whether a person is a member.[3] If an application for settlement of a dispute by arbitration is not complied with within 40 days, the sheriff may determine the dispute.[4] But it was held under former legislation that the courts have jurisdiction to give a remedy to a person complaining of *ultra vires* actings by a society.[5]

Inspections

The assistant registrar may, on the application of a specified number of members or *ex proprio moto*, appoint an inspector to inquire into and report on the affairs of a society, and/or call a special meeting.[6]

Unions and transfers of engagements

Two or more societies may unite, if the terms of union are approved by special resolution of each society and either have the consent in writing of the holders of at least $\frac{2}{3}$ of the whole number of shares in each society, or the registrar, on application, after notice and hearing objections, confirms the union. A statement, approved by the registrar, must be sent to each member before-hand, and notice of the union given to the registrar. Registration of the notice conveys all funds, property and assets of the uniting societies to the combined society.[7] A society may by special resolution transfer its engagements to a society which under-takes to fulfil them. This requires also the same approved state-ment and members' consents as for a union, and registration of notice of the transfer and of a copy of the Instrument of Transfer of Engagements by the registrar, which registration makes the

---

[1] 1962 Act, Ss. 4, 93–6, 129; these provisions probably supersede *Dundee Provident Co.* v. *Macdonald* (1884) 11 R. 537. See also *First Edinburgh, etc. Socy.* v. *Munro* (1883) 11 R. 5.

[2] 1962 Act, Ss. 97–8.

[3] *Prentice* v. *London* (1875) L.R. 10 C.P. 679.

[4] cf. *Sinclair* v. *Mercantile Bldg. Investment Socy.* (1885) 12 R. 1243; *Galashiels Provident Bldg. Socy.* v. *Newlands* (1893) 20 R. 821.

[5] *Hastie* v. *First Edinburgh, etc. Socy.* (1884) 21 S.L.R. 284.

[6] 1962 Act, S. 110.

[7] 1962 Act, Ss. 18–20.

transfer effective and conveys the assets as provided by the Instrument to the transferee society.[1]

Dissolution

A society may terminate or be dissolved on the happening of any event declared to be the termination of the society,[2] or by dissolution in the manner prescribed by its rules,[3] or by an Instrument of Dissolution setting out prescribed particulars,[4] or by dissolution by award of the registrar,[5] or by winding-up, voluntarily under the supervision of the court, or by the court.[6] Notice of dissolution or winding-up must be sent to the registrar.[3] On dissolution or winding-up a society may, if the bond permits it, call up the bond to facilitate the winding-up;[7] apart from that an advanced member cannot be made to pay off his advance other than as provided in the bond or the rules of the society.[8] Investing members are liable to contribute to the assets only to the extent to which payments due on their shares are in arrears.[9] Borrowing members may pay off sums due by them and are not bound to remain members so as to share losses.[10]

[1] 1962 Act, Ss. 19–20.
[2] 1962 Act, S. 106.
[3] 1962 Act, S. 99.
[4] 1962 Act, S. 100; *Second Edinburgh, etc. Socy.* v. *Aitken* (1892) 19 R. 603.
[5] 1962 Act, S. 101.
[6] 1962 Act, S. 103; Building Societies Acts, 1874, S. 22 and 1891, S. 8.
[7] *N.B. Bldg. Socy.* (1885) 12 R. 1271.
[8] 1962 Act, S. 104; *Scottish Property, etc. Socy.* v. *Boyd* (1884) 12 R. 127.
[9] 1962 Act, S. 11; *Brownlie* v. *Russell* (1883) 10 R. (H.L.) 19; *Tosh* v. *N.B. Bldg. Socy.* (1886) 14 R. (H.L.) 6; *Auld* v. *Glasgow, etc. Bldg. Socy.* (1887) 14 R. (H.L.) 27.
[10] *Re Middlesbrough, etc., Bldg. Socy.* (1889) 58 L.J. Ch. 771; cf. *N.B. Bldg. Socy.* v. *McLellan* (1887) 14 R. 827.

CHAPTER 28

INDUSTRIAL AND PROVIDENT SOCIETIES

A SOCIETY for carrying on any industry, business or trade (including dealings with land) wholesale or retail, specified in its rules, may be registered under the Industrial and Provident Societies Act, 1965 to 1968,[1] if it is a bona fide co-operative society or, being conducted for the benefit of the community, there are special reasons why the society should be registered under the Act rather than as a company, and the rules contain provisions as to the matters contained in Schedule 1 and the registered office is to be in Great Britain or the Channel Islands.[2]

Registration

Registration is effected by application to the Assistant Registrar of Friendly Societies by seven members and the secretary of the society with two printed copies of the society's rules. A society may be formed by two or more registered societies. An acknowledgment of registration is conclusive evidence that the society is duly registered.[3] By virtue of registration a society is a body corporate with limited liability and may sue and be sued by its registered name.[4] The assistant registrar may reject an undesirable name; the name must contain 'Limited' as its last word unless the assistant registrar dispenses with this, where the objects are wholly charitable or benevolent; the name may be changed, and must be used on all premises, publications, and documents.[5] Change in the situation of the registered office must be notified to the assistant registrar.[6] Registration may be cancelled or suspended;[7] an appeal lies from refusal to register, cancellation or suspension, to the chief registrar and to the Court

---

[1] The first legislation dealing with such societies was in 1852; but such societies had been established under a Friendly Societies Act of 1834.

[2] 1965 Act, S. 1. A society for constructing or improving housing accommodation may be registered under this head.

[3] S. 2. Societies registered under previous Acts are deemed registered under the 1965 Act, S. 4.

[4] S. 3. As to carrying on business also in England, see S. 8.

[5] S. 5.   [6] S. 10.

[7] Ss. 16–17.

of Session.[1] A registered society may by special resolution convert itself into a company registered under the Companies Acts,[2] and conversely.[3]

Rules

Every society must have rules,[4] and acknowledgment of registration of the society is conclusive evidence of the registration of its rules.[5] Amendments thereof must be registered.[6] The registered rules bind the society and all members and all persons claiming through them as if each member had subscribed them and undertaken to conform thereto.[7] Any person may on demand and on payment receive a copy of the rules.[8] The rules must provide for entrusting the management of the society's affairs to a committee.[9] They may be challenged as being in unreasonable restraint of trade,[10] or illegal, though some illegal rules does not make the society an illegal association.[11] A society carrying on the business of banking cannot provide in its rules for its shares being withdrawable.[12]

Management

The rules must make provision for the appointment of a committee of management and of managers and other officers. Where under the rules the control of the society's affairs is vested in the committee the members cannot exercise that control.[13] It has statutory functions in connection with transfers of property[14] and the general function of carrying on the business in accordance with the Act.

Members

Individuals or other registered societies or corporate bodies may be members. The rules must set out the terms of admission

---

[1] S. 18.   [2] S. 52.

[3] S. 53; Companies Act, 1948, S. 141.

[4] Schedule 1 lists matters to be provided for in a society's rules.   [5] S. 9.

[6] S. 10. Further provisions as to rules are in Ss. 11–13. As to amendment see *Auld* v. *Glasgow, etc., Bldg. Soc.* (1887) 14 R. (H.L.) 27; *Strohmenger* v. *Finsbury Bldg. Soc.* [1897] 2 Ch. 469.

[7] S. 14. The section provides certain exceptions: see also *Hole* v. *Garnsey* [1930] A.C. 472.

[8] S. 15.

[9] As to the powers of a committee see *Alexander* v. *Duddy*, 1956 S.C. 24.

[10] *McEllistrim* v. *Ballmacelligott Co-operative Socy.* [1919] A.C. 548; *Bellshill and Mossend Co-operative Socy., Ltd.* v. *Dalziel Co-operative Socy. Ltd.*, 1958 S.C. 400; affd. on other points, 1960 S.C. (H.L.) 64.

[11] *Swaine* v. *Wilson* (1889) 24 Q.B.D. 252.   [12] S. 7.

[13] *Alexander* v. *Duddy*, 1956 S.C. 24.   [14] Ss. 23–7.

of members; members become shareholders, and a register of members must be maintained. Members have various statutory rights and limited liability for the society's debts.[1]

Meetings

The rules must provide for the mode of holding meetings and for voting thereat and the mode of making, altering, or rescinding rules.[2]

Capital

The share capital is not usually fixed; it consists normally of withdrawable or transferable shares, and possibly of other classes as provided by the rules. No member, with certain exceptions, may have an interest in the shares of the society exceeding £1000.[3] A society with withdrawable share capital may not carry on the business of banking.[4] The rules may provide for shares being paid up in full when issued, or paid by instalments or on call. Subject to the rules a corporate body may hold shares, as may a minor over 16.[5] There is no requirement of issuing share certificates and provision therefor is unusual. The rules must provide whether and, if so, by what authority and in what manner any of the society's funds may be invested.[6] A society's borrowing powers depends on its rules. It may grant security for money borrowed in any way competent to a natural person and also, like an incorporated company, grant a floating charge over its property, heritable and moveable, in accordance with the Industrial and Provident Societies Act, 1967, Part II and Schedule, amended by the Companies (Floating Charges and Receivers) (Sc.) Act, 1972, S. 10, and subject to compliance with the requirements of the 1967 Act, Part II.

Accounts

Every society must keep proper books of accounts and comply with statutory requirements as to accounts, balance sheets, and auditors.[7]

---

[1] Ss. 44, 57.
[2] Sched. 1, para. 5.
[3] S. 6.
[4] S. 7.
[5] Ss. 19–20.
[6] Sched. 1, para. 14.
[7] Ss. 37–40, partly replaced by Friendly and Industrial Provident Societies Act, 1968.

Application of profits

The rules must provide for the mode of application of the society's profits including, if authorised, the furtherance of political objects.[1]

Loans

The society's rules may provide for advances of money to members on the security of heritable or moveable estate or, if registered to carry on banking, in any manner customary in such business.[2] Debts due by members are recoverable in the sheriff court where the registered office is situated or the member resides. The society has a lien on the member's share for any debt due by the member to the society and may set off any sum credited to the member thereon towards the debt.[3]

Nominations

A member may[4] by signed writing,[5] delivered at or sent to the society's registered office or made in a book kept at that office, nominate a person[6] or persons to become entitled on his death to the whole or part of the property in the society (shares, loans, deposits etc.) which he may have at the time of his death, to the extent of £500.[7] A nomination may be varied or revoked by a subsequent nomination but not by the nominator's will or codicil. Marriage revokes a nomination.[8] The committee of the society may, on receiving satisfactory proof of the death of the member, transfer or pay the value of the property to which the nominee is entitled.[9] On a member's death with property in the society not exceeding £500 and not the subject of any nomination, the committee may, without confirmation being expede,[10] distribute that property among such persons as appear to the committee on such evidence as they deem satisfactory to be entitled by law to

---

[1] *Cahill* v. *London Cooperative Socy. Ltd.* [1937] Ch. 265. See also *Lafferty* v. *Barrhead Cooperative Soc.*, 1919, 1 S.L.T. 257; *Warburton* v. *Huddersfield Industrial Soc.* [1892] 1 Q.B. 817 (strike fund).

[2] S. 21.

[3] S. 22; see also *Lloyd* v. *Francis* [1937] 4 All E.R. 489.

[4] S. 23.

[5] See *Morton* v. *French*, 1908 S.C. 171 (authentication by mark only).

[6] Not an officer or servant of the society save in special cases: S. 23 (2).

[7] S. 23(3)(c) amd. Administration of Estates (Small Payments) Act, 1965, S. 2; (£100 if nomination made between 1.1.1914 and 5.8.1954: S. 23(3)(b); £200 if before 5.9.1965).

[8] S. 23 (4)–(6).

[9] S. 24.

[10] The society can demand production of confirmation: *Escritt* v. *Todmorden Coop. Soc.* [1896] 1 Q.B. 461.

receive it.[1] In so deciding the committee may dispense with evidence of title and relationship, but may not alter the title or select one of the next of kin as payee even with the consent of the majority.[2] If the deceased member were illegitimate and left no widow, widower, or issue and was not survived by his mother, the committee must deal with his property as the Treasury shall direct.[3] If a claiming member is mentally incapable the society may pay to any person whom they judge proper to receive the property on his behalf.[4] Such payments are valid and effectual against demands by other persons.[5]

Powers and duties

A registered society may contract, grant bills, purchase, lease, and transact with land, and invest its funds in any security authorized by its rules.[6] It must have its accounts audited and make an annual return to the assistant registrar.[7] Officers may be required to find caution for intromissions, and must account for monies handled.[8] It must maintain a register of members showing shares and property held; a member may inspect his own account and the assistant registrar may on the requisition of 10 members have the books inspected, or require the production of books, accounts, and documents.[9] The assistant registrar may on application appoint an inspector to examine into and report on the affairs of the society, or call a special meeting of the society.[10]

Amalgamation and dissolution

Societies may amalgamate or one may transfer its engagements to another, or a society may convert itself into or amalgamate with or transfer its engagements to a company under the Companies Acts. A company may convert itself into a registered society.[11] A society may be dissolved on being wound up by order or resolution as under the Companies Act, 1948,[12] or by instrument of dissolution signed by three-fourths of the members.[13]

---

[1] S. 25(1).
[2] *Symington's Exor.* v. *Galashiels Coop. Store Co. Ltd.* (1894) 21 R. 371.
[3] S. 25(2).
[4] S. 26.
[5] S. 27.
[6] Ss. 28–35. As to execution of deeds see S. 36.
[7] Ss. 37–40.　　　　　　　　　　　[8] Ss. 41–3.
[9] Ss. 44–8.　　　　　　　　　　　[10] S. 49.
[11] Ss. 50–4.　　　　　　　　　　　[12] Ss. 55–7, 59.
[13] S. 58.

Disputes

Disputes between a society or an officer and a member,[1] an aggrieved ex-member or person claiming through him, or any person claiming under the rules of the society, are to be decided in the manner provided by the rules, which may be by arbitration[2] or referred to the assistant registrar, whose decision is enforceable on application to the sheriff court, or referred to the sheriff. At the request of either party the assistant registrar or sheriff may state a case for the opinion of the Court of Session.[3] The courts' jurisdiction is not ousted if the dispute has not been decided according to the rules,[4] or if the dispute relates to a matter *ultra vires* of the society.[5] The Court of Session may overrule the sheriff if he has erred in determining whether or not a dispute is one to be decided in accordance with the rules of the society.[6]

[1] *Municipal, etc. Soc.* v. *Richards* (1888) 39 Ch. D. 372.
[2] As to dispute between two cooperative societies see *Bellshill and Mossend Co-op. Socy.* v. *Dalziel Co-op. Socy.*, 1960 S.C. (H.L.) 64.
[3] S. 60.
[4] *Andrews* v. *Mitchell* [1905] A.C. 78.
[5] *McEllistrim* v. *Ballymacelligott Coop. Soc. Ltd.* [1919] A.C. 548; *Todd* v. *Kelso Coop. Soc. Ltd.*, 1953 S.L.T. (Sh. Ct.) 2.
[6] cf. *Gall* v. *Loyal Glenbogie Lodge* (1900) 2 F. 1187; *Collins* v. *Barrowfield United Oddfellows*, 1915 S.C. 190.

BOOK IV

THE LAW OF OBLIGATIONS

CHAPTER 29

OBLIGATIONS IN GENERAL

A N obligation is *juris vinculum*, a legal bond or tie between two legal persons by which one is bound to pay or perform something to or for the benefit of the other.[1] When such a bond exists it creates rights to performance in the one party, and imposes correlative duties, liabilities or burdens of performance on the other.

The rights created by obligation are personal rights enforceable, in general, against the other party to the obligation only, *jura in personam*, as distinct from real rights, *jura in rem*, existing in respect of some claim or thing of a proprietary nature, and enforceable against all other persons in general.[2] The duties to which personal rights correspond are particular duties owed only by the other party in the obligation, whereas the duties to which real rights correspond are owed by everyone, by persons generally, to the person entitled thereto in respect of his claim or proprietary right. The term 'rights' is also used in the senses of legal advantages, such as liberties or privileges, powers, and immunities, and the corresponding term 'duties' in the senses of inabilities, subjections or liability and disabilities.[3] The term obligation is also used for the duties, which are the counterparts of rights derived through personal engagement,[4] for the duties arising from a unilateral agreement,[5] and for an enforceable document of debt.[6] With merely social or moral obligation or duties the law has no concern.

Classification of obligations

Obligations were said in the Roman law[7] to be all grounded on either express contract, *ex contractu*, or on something resembling a

---

[1] *Inst.* 3, 13, 2; *Dig.* 44, 7, 3, pr.; Stair I, 3, 1; Ersk. III, 1, 2; a person cannot create an obligation to himself: *Church of Scotland Endowment Cttee.* v. *Provident Assoc. of London*, 1914 S.C. 165.

[2] Stair I, 1, 22; Ersk. III, 1, 2. The main real right is the ownership of property. See also Holland, *Jurisprudence*, Ch. 12; Salmond, *Jurisprudence*, Ch. 11; Paton, *Jurisprudence*, Chs. 17–18.

[3] Hohfeld 'Fundamental Legal Conceptions' (1913) 23 Yale L.J. 16; (1917) 26 Yale L.J. 710; Pound 'Fifty Years of Jurisprudence' (1937) 50 H.L.R. 557.

[4] Stair I, 1, 22; Bell, *Prin.* §5.   [5] Bell, *Prin.* §5.

[6] Subscription of Deeds Act, 1579, c. 80; Balf., *Prac.* 149.

[7] *Inst.*, 3, 13, 2; cf. Stair I, 3, 2.

contract, *quasi ex contractu*, or in delinquency, *ex delicto*, or in some
fact resembling delinquency, *quasi ex delicto*.[1] But this classification, though followed by later jurists,[2] is unsatisfactory. Stair[3]
distinguished obediential or natural obligations and obligations
conventional or by engagement, the former including the duty on
parents to maintain their children,[4] the duty to make restitution,[5]
to make recompense,[6] and to make reparation for delinquency,[7]
the latter including obligations by contract,[8] including trust.[9] But
obligation may also spring from statute, or from decree of court.
The fundamental division is that of Stair, according to the cause
or ground of the obligation, into obligations springing *ex
voluntate vel ex conventione*, deliberately undertaken, and those
arising *ex lege*, imposed by law, independently of the will of the
parties.[10] The former group includes obligations voluntarily
undertaken by one party to another, or by mutual agreement
between the parties.[11] The latter includes the obligations arising
from family and domestic relations,[12] those of making restitution
and recompense,[13] of making reparation for harm done in breach
of a general duty not to do so,[14] of implementing a statutory
duty,[15] or of obtempering a decree of court.[16]

In some cases duties may arise on both grounds; the carrier of
passengers or of goods assumes duties by his contract to carry and
owes them also under the law, and if he causes injury or harm his
liability may be founded alternatively on breach of contract or on
breach of his legal duty of care. In other cases a person may
simultaneously owe a contractual duty to one and a legal duty to
another, both arising from one set of circumstances.

The obligations imposed by such relationships as landlord and
tenant or master and servant and those imposed by the relation-

---

[1] Ersk. III, 1, 9.
[2] e.g. Mack. III, 1; cf. IV, 4; Bankt. I, 4, 25–7; Ersk. III, 1, 19; Hume, *Lect.* II, 3;
see also *Campbell* v. *Kennedy* (1864) 3 M. 121, 125.
[3] I, 3, 2.
[4] Stair I, 5, 1; Ersk. III, 1, 9.
[5] Stair I, 7, 1; Ersk. III, 1, 10.
[6] Stair I, 8, 1; Ersk. III, 1, 11.
[7] Stair I, 9, 1; Ersk. III, 1, 12–15.
[8] Stair I, 10, 1 to I, 12, 16; I, 13, 1 to I, 18, 9; Ersk. III, I, 16 to III, 4, 27.
[9] Stair I, 12, 17; Ersk. III, 1, 32.
[10] Stair I, 3, 2; Bell, *Comm.* I, 312.
[11] Book IV, Parts 1 and 2, *infra*.
[12] Book III, Part I, *supra*.
[13] Book IV, Parts 3 and 4, *infra*.
[14] Book IV, Parts 5 and 6, *infra*.
[15] Book IV, Part 7, *infra*.
[16] Book IV, Part 8, *infra*.

ships of trust and other fiduciary relations are of a mixed character in that the individual enters into the relationship voluntarily but the duties which thereby become incumbent on him are principally determined by law.[10] Again if persons by agreement or contract create a conventional obligation but one fails to implement his duties thereunder a fresh obligation arises *ex lege*, to make reparation in damages for his breach of contract. Unless expressly excluded law implies this consequential remedial obligation into every contract in the event of it being breached.

A distinction has also been drawn between natural obligations, which are incumbent by the law of nature only and may be morally binding but are not sanctioned by any legal remedy,[2] or are ineffectual without the requisite mode of proof thereof, and civil obligations, which are legally enforceable.[3] The court may occasionally have regard to whether or not there was a natural or moral obligation, irrespective of there being a legal obligation.[4] The term natural obligation is also sometimes used for those assumed to be created by nature, such as the reciprocal obligation of aliment between parent and child.

The effect of obligation on persons

Obligation, once attached to persons voluntarily or by law, confers on them antecedent or primary rights to claim to have performed the duties required by the agreement or by law under the obligation in question. If the primary duties of obligation incumbent on one party are not implemented, there arise secondary, consequential or remedial rights in the other party to legal remedies for securing implement of the obligation, or reparation for its non-implement.[5] Thus an agreement between A and B confers on each mutual primary duties of implement, and mutual rights to expect performance; if any duty on either part is not implemented, the other thereby acquires a remedial right to have due performance exacted by law, or to have damages paid him in compensation. Similarly A owes a primary duty to persons who might be injured by his failure to do so a duty to take care not to cause them unjustifiable harm in person or property; if by such failure he causes harm to one such person, B,

---

[1] cf. *Allen* v. *McCombie's Trs.*, 1909 S.C. 710.
[2] cf. *Clyde Marine Ins. Co.* v. *Renwick*, 1924 S.C. 113.
[3] Stair I, 3, 5.
[4] Mack. III, 1, 5; Ersk. III, 3, 54; *Clark* v. *C.* (1869) 7 M. 335.
[5] Holland, *Jurisprudence*, Ch. 13; Paton, *Jurisprudence*, Ch. 19; Chap. 125, *infra*.

he comes under a secondary or consequential duty to make reparation to B for the loss caused by his breach of primary duty, and B acquires a secondary or remedial right to obtain such reparation for the loss he has suffered by the breach of his primary right, not to be harmed in person or property.

PART 1

VOLUNTARY AND CONVENTIONAL OBLIGATIONS—GENERAL PRINCIPLES

CHAPTER 30

VOLUNTARY OBLIGATIONS

VOLUNTARY and conventional obligations are both undertaken by parties of their own volition, though the incidents of such an obligation may be determined in part by rules of law. An important distinction is that drawn in Scots law between unilateral voluntary undertakings or promises, and conventional or consensual mutual agreements or contracts. The latter group is divided into bilateral gratuitous contracts, where one party alone is bound to do something and the other is bound merely to accept but not to do or pay anything in return, and bilateral onerous contracts, where each party is bound to do or pay something to or for the other. All three categories equally may produce legally enforceable obligations.[1] Of these bilateral onerous contracts are more numerous and more important than voluntary undertakings or bilateral gratuitous contracts, and the distinction between a unilateral voluntary undertaking and a bilateral gratuitous contract may be very narrow.[2] In doubtful cases a proposal will more readily be construed as an offer to contract than as a unilateral promise, obligatory by itself.[3]

Such obligations, particularly consensual contracts, are of many kinds, most of which have particular names, such as sale, hiring, or lease, and which, increasingly in modern law, have statutory peculiarities and incidents applicable to contracts of that kind only.[4] Yet there remain many principles, discussed in this Part, common to all or at least most of the particular and

[1] Stair I, 10, 3; Mack. III, 1, 5; Bankt. I, 11, 6; Ersk. III, 1, 16; III, 2, 1; Bell, *Comm.* I, 312, 332, 351; *Prin.* §7, 70; cf. Dig. 50, 12, 3; Smith, *Studies*, 168.

[2] The distinction is not settled conclusively by the use of such words as 'promise', 'offer' or 'agree': see *Macfarlane v. Johnston* (1864) 2 M. 1210, 1213.

[3] *Macfarlane, supra*; *Malcolm v. Campbell* (1891) 19 R. 278; *Forbes v. Knox*, 1957 S.L.T. 102, 103.

[4] *Infra*, Chaps. 38–51, 82–86, 91–2, 97–104, 109–110.

specific kinds of obligations, derived inductively from the study of, and illustrated by, contracts of many different kinds, and which fall to be invoked and applied in cases to which no peculiarity, special to the kind of specific contract in question, is applicable. These general principles are in fact the most general issues, of capacity to contract, of the formalities and proof of contract, of breach, and remedies, and so on.

UNILATERAL VOLUNTARY OBLIGATIONS

An enforceable obligation arises from the expression of a definite promise or undertaking by one party,[1] as distinct from an offer,[2] or merely an expressed desire or intention,[3] or a proposal[4] or a warning[5] or merely an honourable understanding,[6] to give or do something to or for another, without any need for the promisee's assent or acceptance,[7] still less for any undertaking or payment in return. The promisor, having capacity to bind himself legally and intent to assume a legal obligation, must undertake a certain and definite liability to, or for the benefit of, a determinate person or object. Thus a promise to give a present,[8] or a donation,[9] or a reward,[10] or pay an annuity,[11] or to leave a legacy,[12] or make an *ex gratia* payment,[13] or keep an offer open,[14] or subscribe for shares,[15] creates an obligation and performance is enforceable.

Such a promise may bind the promisor's representatives after his death.[16] It may be conditional.[16] The promise, to be enforce-

[1] *Cambuslang West Church* v. *Bryce* (1897) 25 R. 322; *Smith* v. *Oliver*, 1911 S.C. 103; cf. *Mackersy* v. *Davis* (1895) 22 R. 368; *Ritchie* v. *Cowan & Kinghorn* (1901) 3 F. 1071; *Paterson* v. *Highland Ry.*, 1927 S.C. (H.L.) 32; *Denny's Trs.* v. *Dumbarton Mags.*, 1945 S.C. 147.

[2] *Macfarlane* v. *Johnston* (1864) 2 M. 1210; *Malcolm* v. *Campbell* (1891) 19 R. 278; *Morton's Trs.* v. *Aged Christian Friend Socy.* (1899) 2 F. 82. See also *Anderson* v. *A.*, 1961 S.C. 59.

[3] *Scott* v. *Dawson* (1862) 24 D. 440; *Gray* v. *Johnston*, 1928 S.C. 659.

[4] *Forbes* v. *Knox*, 1957 S.L.T. 102.

[5] *Mackersy* v. *Davis* (1895) 22 R. 368.

[6] *Ritchie, supra.*

[7] Stair I, 10, 4; Bankt. I, 4, 5; *Cambuslang West Church, supra*; Ashton-Cross, 1957 J.R. 147. Acceptance would make the obligation bilateral.

[8] cf. *Shadwell* v. *S.* (1860) 9 C.B. (N.S.) 159; *Malcolm* v. *Campbell* (1891) 19 R. 278.

[9] *Cambuslang West Church* v. *Bryce* (1897) 25 R. 322; cf. *Morton's Trs., supra.*

[10] *Petrie* v. *E. Airlie* (1834) 13 S. 68.

[11] *Macqueen* v. *McTavish*, 3 March, 1812, F.C.

[12] *Edmondston* v. *E.* (1861) 23 D. 995; *Mackenzie's Trs.* v. *Kilmarnock's Trs.*, 1909 S.C. 472; *Smith* v. *Oliver*, 1911 S.C. 103.

[13] *Shaw* v. *Muir's Exrx.* (1892) 19 R. 997; *Campbell* v. *Glasgow Police Commrs.* (1895) 22 R. 621; *Wick Harbour Trs.* v. *Admiralty*, 1921, 2 S.L.T. 109.

[14] *Littlejohn* v. *Hadwen* (1882) 20 S.L.R. 5.

[15] *Beardmore* v. *Barry*, 1928 S.C. 101; affd. 1928 S.C. (H.L.) 47.

[16] *Petrie, supra*; cf. *Morton's Trs., supra*; *Denny's Trs., supra.*

able, must be communicated to the promisee[1] or have come to his notice before he claims performance. The promisee need not consent to or accept the promise,[2] but if he declines, the promisor is no longer bound and the promise falls. Such a promise can be proved only by the writ (not necessarily probative), or admission on reference to oath, of the promisor.[3]

It is enforceable only against the promisor and his representatives, and only by a, or the, promisee; it is unenforceable against the promisee. A unilateral promise cannot be converted into a bilateral contract by alleging that things were done by the other party in reliance on the promise.[4] It is questionable whether such an obligation can be undertaken in favour of persons generally, or of anyone who cares to claim performance of, or to exercise, the right created, though a guarantee by Y of X's financial standing, not addressed to anyone, has been held to ground an action by a party whose reliance thereon was contemplated and who in fact relied thereon.[5] An obligation can, however, certainly be undertaken to the bearer or holder of a particular document, such as a bill of exchange,[6] and to anyone who satisfies a condition attached to the promise, such as to anyone who returns lost property.[7]

---

[1] *Smeaton* v. *St. Andrews Police Commrs.* (1871) 9 M. (H.L.) 24; *Shaw, supra*; *Denny's Trs., supra*; contrast *Burr* v. *Bo'ness Police Commrs.* (1896) 24 R. 148.

[2] *Smeaton* v. *St. Andrews Police Commrs.* (1871) 9 M. (H.L.) 24; *Campbell* v. *Glasgow Police Commrs.* (1895) 22 R. 621; *Beardmore* v. *Barry*, 1928 S.C. 101.

[3] *Shaw* v. *Muir's Exrx.* (1892) 19 R. 997; *Hallet* v. *Ryrie* (1907) 15 S.L.T. 367; *Smith, supra*, and 1911, 1 S.L.T. 451.

[4] *Millar* v. *Tremamondo* (1771) Mor. 12395; *Smith, supra*; *Forbes* v. *F's Trs.*, 1957 S.C. 325; 1957 S.L.T. 102, 103.

[5] *Fortune* v. *Young*, 1918 S.C. 1.

[6] Bills of Exchange Act, 1882, Ss. 3, 20, 73, 83.

[7] cf. *Petrie* v. *E. Airlie* (1834) 13 S. 68.

CHAPTER 31

CONVENTIONAL OBLIGATIONS—
CONSENSUAL AGREEMENTS OR CONTRACTS

OBLIGATION arises from mutual agreement or contract more commonly than from unilateral promise. A contract is an agreement which produces an obligation,[1] or an agreement normally intended to be legally enforceable whereby one or both parties agree to do or give or abstain from something for the other's benefit.[2]

Agreement between the parties or *consensus in idem* is the basis of contractual obligation, but increasingly in modern practice one party has little or no freedom to negotiate the terms of the agreement but must accept whatever terms the other party offers, or do without the contract.[3] In many cases also statute imports terms into contracts of particular kinds, independently of the wills of the parties.[4] It is only subject to these important qualifications that the principle survives that persons have freedom of contract and their agreements, freely entered into, will be upheld and enforced. Where the contract is in a standard form prepared by one party, or the parties differ materially in bargaining power, the courts interpret the contract strictly and *contra proferentem*. It is sometimes difficult to determine whether parties' relations were intended to be contractual and legally obligatory, or gratuitous and on the basis of friendship, or regulated by non-legal rules.[5]

PREREQUISITES OF CONTRACT

For an arrangement to be valid and enforceable in law as a contract

(a) both parties must have had, at the time of contracting,

---

[1] *Jackson* v. *Broatch* (1900) 37 S.L.R. 707, 714. The term 'contract' is also used for purported agreements intended to produce an obligation, but which fail for some legal reason, i.e. the so-called unenforceable and void contracts.

[2] cf. Stair I, 10, 6; Ersk. III, 1, 16; Bell, *Comm.* I, 454.

[3] e.g. *McKay* v. *Scottish Airways*, 1948 S.C. 254; *McCutcheon* v. *MacBrayne*, 1964 S.C. (H.L.) 28.

[4] e.g. Sale of Goods Act, 1893, Ss. 12–15; Supply of Goods (ImpliedTerms) Act, 1973, Ss. 7–12.

[5] e.g. *Brook* v. *Kelly* (1893) 20 R. (H.L.) 104; *Cappon* v. *L.A.*, 1920, 1 S.L.T. 261.

general contractual capacity,[1] and also legal power or authority to make the kind of contract in question;

(b) they must reach agreement on reasonably definite terms;

(c) they must intend to effect a legal relationship;[2]

(d) the object contemplated by their agreement must be possible of attainment in fact, legally possible, and not illegal or otherwise objectionable in law.[3] There is no need for consideration or *quid pro quo* and a consensual agreement is actionable as a contract though one party has merely agreed to accept or receive benefit, and is doing or giving nothing in return.

Valid, voidable, void and unenforceable contracts

An agreement which satisfies the prerequisites and is not defective on any other ground[4] is a valid contract and the obligation created is enforceable by either party. A voidable contract is one which is valid and creative of obligation but contains a defect entitling one party to rescind it, or have it reduced by a court, in which case it is treated as if it had never been constituted.[5] A void contract is a merely apparent contract, which *ab initio* has no existence or legal effect, produces no obligation, and can be repudiated or ignored by either party with impunity.[6] An unenforceable contract is one which is valid and creative of obligation but by reason of defective evidence or of statutory provision cannot be enforced by law.[7]

(a) CAPACITY AND POWER TO CONTRACT

Capacity to contract is a function of a person's legal status, or of the powers of a body, unincorporated or incorporated, and discussed thereunder.[8] If either party did not at the time of contracting have contractual capacity, the purported contract is void and no rights arise from it enforceable by either party. The classes of natural persons having restricted contractual capacity are pupils, minors, persons of unsound mind, persons incapacitated by drink, alien enemies and bankrupts.

---

[1] cf. Stair I, 10, 13.

[2] cf. Stair I, 10, 13(2).

[3] cf. Stair I, 10, 13(3).

[4] e.g. defective formal constitution (Ch. 32), or brought about by error or fraud (Ch. 33).

[5] e.g. some cases of contracts induced by fraud.

[6] In some statutes provisions purporting to render certain transactions void have been interpreted as making them voidable only.

[7] e.g. contracts requiring to be constituted in a particular form, and lacking that form.

[8] See Chs. 15–28, *supra*.

Power to contract

A party must not only have contractual capacity but, particularly if acting as agent, trustee or otherwise in a representative capacity, also have power to make a contract of the kind he seeks to make. Thus the actual or ostensible authority of an agent may be limited, and trustees have various powers by statute only if their exercise is not at variance with the purposes of the trust.[1] Absence of the power to make that kind of contract in the circumstances does not, in at least certain kinds of transactions, invalidate the transaction so far as concerns the other party thereto, though as regards the beneficiaries it is a breach of trust.[2]

In the case of contracts by unincorporated bodies the powers of the agent for the body are relevant, and in the case of contracts by corporate bodies the contractual powers of the body conferred by its constitutive deed are relevant.[3]

(b) AGREEMENT

The parties must reach agreement on all the material terms of their contract. Whether they have done so or not is a question of fact.[4] This falls to be judged objectively,[5] independently of whether they think or say that they had reached agreement; failing agreement, the contract is a nullity.[6] There is no contract if parties have not agreed on all the material terms of their bargain,[7] nor if any material term is neither settled, nor implied by law, and the agreement has made no provision for determining it,[8] nor if it subsequently emerges that parties had been fundamentally mistaken about some matter of the contract,[9] nor can a party be heard to say that he meant other than what would be reasonably understood by the other party.[10] But agreement does not require that the parties state all the terms of their agreement, as some at

---

[1] Trusts (Sc.) Act, 1921, S. 4. The court may grant power (ibid., S. 5) if satisfied that the act is expedient for the execution of the trust.

[2] Trusts (Sc.) Act, 1961, S. 2, covering exercise of powers in 1921 Act, S. 4(a) to (ee).

[3] Thus the *ultra vires* rule denies validity to contracts beyond the powers of a company, e.g. *Ashbury Ry. Carriage Co.* v. *Riche* (1875) L.R. 7 H.L. 653; *Re Jon Beauforte (London) Ltd.* [1953] Ch. 131.

[4] *Harvey* v. *Smith* (1904) 6 F. 511; *Gray* v. *Edinburgh Univ.*, 1962 S.C. 157.

[5] *Muirhead and Turnbull* v. *Dickson* (1905) 7 F. 686, 694; *Brownlee* v. *Robb*, 1907 S.C. 1302, 1312; *Norwich Union Ins. Socy.* v. *Price* [1934] A.C. 455, 463; *Chappell* v. *Nestlé* [1960] A.C. 87, 108.

[6] *Came* v. *Glasgow Friendly Socy.*, 1933 S.C. 69; *Mathieson Gee, Ltd.* v. *Quigley*, 1952 S.C. (H.L.) 38; *Gray, supra;* cf. *Houldsworth* v. *Gordon Cumming*, 1910 S.C. (H.L.) 49, 52.

[7] *Heiton* v. *Waverley Hydropathic Co.* (1877) 4 R. 830; cf. *Harvey, supra.*

[8] *Foley* v. *Classique Coaches, Ltd.* [1934] 2 K.B. 1, 13.   [9] Ch. 33, *infra.*

[10] *Muirhead and Turnbull, supra;* *Brownlee* v. *Robb*, 1907 S.C. 1302, 1312.

least of these may be supplied by implication of law or imported by statute or the custom of business or previous dealings between the parties. Thus agreement may be reached though the price has later to be agreed.[1] A statement of willingness or intention by one party is not an agreement.[2]

In seeking to ascertain whether negotiations between parties have resulted in agreement on all material terms, the courts normally consider whether the communications and negotiations between the parties amount to an exchange of offer by one party and acceptance by the other justifying an inference of agreement. The parties are held to have contracted when an unqualified offer has been met by an unqualified acceptance of the terms proposed, indicating that the parties have reached *consensus in idem*.

Offer and acceptance

There are no formalities nor *voces signatae* requisite for offer or acceptance, and the court may have to infer either or both from speech, writings, or conduct, or some of these taken together.[3] In substance there is most commonly an undertaking to act in return for a counter-undertaking,[4] but there may be a promise for an act,[5] an act for a promise,[6] or an act for an act,[7] and the question is always whether the conduct of parties yields the inference of offer and acceptance. Thus an inference of acceptance of an offer to buy property may be drawn from allowing the offeror to take possession.[8] If either party founds on the other's signed writing he must, if necessary, prove the other's signature.[9]

Offers to contract

A distinction must be taken between unilateral promises,[10] or enquiries, or advertisements, or expressions of intention to do something,[11] or expressions of willingness to do business, or

[1] *Dempster* v. *Motherwell Bridge Co.*, 1964 S.C. 308. cf. *Freeman* v. *Maxwell*, 1928 S.C. 682.

[2] *Todd* v. *Millen*, 1910 S.C. 868.

[3] cf. *Clarke* v. *Dunraven* [1897] A.C. 59.

[4] e.g. to hand over an article in return for payment.

[5] e.g. to give a reward for returning lost property.

[6] e.g. a taxi lifting a passenger who hails it and thereby impliedly promises to pay the fare.

[7] e.g. holding out coins to a newsvendor who holds out a newspaper.

[8] *Errol* v. *Walker*, 1966 S.C. 93.

[9] *S. Scotland Electricity Board* v. *Robertson*, 1968 S.L.T. (Sh. Ct.) 3.

[10] Ch. 30, *supra*.

[11] *Shaw* v. *Muir's Exrx.* (1892) 19 R. 997; *Burr* v. *Bo'ness Police Commrs.* (1896) 24 R. 148; contrast *Smeaton* v. *St. Andrews Police Commrs.* (1871) 9 M. (H.L.) 24; *Campbell* v. *Glasgow Police Commrs* (1895) 22 R. 621.

requests for tenders,[1] and offers to contract. Thus a reply to an enquiry is not necessarily an offer,[2] and an advertisement of goods for sale,[3] or a priced catalogue,[4] or the exhibition of goods in a shop, with or without price tags,[5] are only indications of willingness to trade, not offers to sell, capable of acceptance, though a quotation of prices for a commodity may be held an offer to sell,[6] and a circular may be an offer to all the addressees, capable of and requiring acceptance by them.[7] Exposing goods for sale by auction is not an offer to sell to the highest bidder.[8] An apparent unilateral undertaking to sell property may be held to be an offer requiring acceptance.[9] Innkeepers and common carriers, who exercise a common calling, are held, however, by being in business, to make a continuing offer to provide their services to any person who chooses to accept, so long as they have accommodation and the person is unobjectionable and willing to pay.[10] An intimation of intention to trade on particular terms for a period may be neither a unilateral promise, nor a continuing offer capable of conversion into a contract by acceptance, but merely a revocable disclosed intention.[11]

Communication of offer

The offer must be communicated to the offeree or offerees.[12] It is effective, failing express provision, from the time it comes to the notice of the offeree and any period limited for acceptances runs from that time. Nothing done prior to, or done in ignorance of, the offer can be construed as acceptance thereof.[13] Only an offeree, or one with his authority, can accept an offer,[14] and not a person

[1] *G.N. Ry.* v. *Witham* (1873) L.R. 9 C.P. 16.

[2] *Milne* v. *Anderson* (1836) 14 S. 533; *Harvey* v. *Facey* [1893] A.C. 552; *Clifton* v. *Palumbo* [1944] 2 All E.R. 497; contrast *Bigg* v. *Boyd Gibbins* [1971] 2 All E.R. 183.

[3] *Harris* v. *Nickerson* (1873) L.R. 8 Q.B. 286; *Fenwick* v. *Macdonald, Fraser & Co.* (1904) 6 F. 850; contrast *Warlow* v. *Harrison* (1859) 1 E. & E. 295.

[4] *Grainger* v. *Gough* [1896] A.C. 325.

[5] *Pharmaceutical Socy.* v. *Boots* [1953] 1 Q.B. 401; *Fisher* v. *Bell* [1961] 1 Q.B. 394.

[6] *Philp* v. *Knoblauch*, 1907 S.C. 994, distinguishing *Harvey, supra*; *Bigg, supra*.

[7] *Liqr. of Edinburgh Employers Co.* v. *Griffiths* (1892) 19 R. 550.

[8] *Fenwick* v. *Macdonald, Fraser & Co.* (1904) 6 F. 850; contrast *Warlow* v. *Harrison* (1859) 1 E. & E. 295, 309.

[9] *Malcolm* v. *Campbell* (1891) 19 R. 278.

[10] Bell, *Prin.* §159; *Campbell* v. *Ker*, 24 Feb. 1810, F.C.; *Ewing* v. *Campbells* (1878) 5 R. 230; *Strathearn Hydro Co.* v. *I.R.* (1881) 8 R. 798; *Clark* v. *West Ham Corpn.* [1909] 2 K.B. 858; *Rothfield* v. *N.B. Ry.*, 1920 S.C. 805.

[11] *Paterson* v. *Highland Ry.*, 1927 S.C. (H.L.) 32.

[12] *Wiles* v. *Maddison* [1943] 1 All E.R. 315.

[13] *R.* v. *Clarke* (1927) 40 C.L.R. 227.

[14] *Powell* v. *Lee* (1908) 99 L.T. 835; cf. *Henkel* v. *Pape* (1870) L.R. 6 Ex. 7; *Verdin* v. *Robertson* (1871) 10 M. 35.

who did not reasonably believe that the offer was made to him. There may be several offers in different terms, as at an auction or where a house is advertised for sale.

To whom offer made

An offer may be made to a particular person, or to a class of persons,[1] or to any member of the public who cares to accept by doing what is required.[2] A general offer may permit many acceptances,[3] or it may be expressed or implied that only the first or certain acceptors can claim to have contracted. Acceptance may be implied by doing the required thing rather than communicating an acceptance.[4]

Standing offer

Where tenders are sought for the supply of indefinite quantities as and when required, or in similar terms, the offerors make a standing offer to supply as required, capable of acceptance by particular orders,[5] or possibly acceptance concludes a contract to implement subsequent particular contracts by supplying quantities ordered. Similarly the terms of an insurance policy have been held to amount to a standing offer to pay the surrender value.[6]

Offer to be held open

If an offerer undertakes to keep his offer open for a stated time, the undertaking is a separate voluntary obligation, and withdrawal of the offer before the stated time is an actionable breach of contract.[7]

---

[1] cf. *Paterson* v. *P.* (1849) 11 D. 441.

[2] e.g. offer of reward to person giving information: *Williams* v. *Carwardine* (1833) 4 B. & Ald. 621; *Petrie* v. *E. of Airlie* (1834) 13 S. 68; *Taylor* v. *Commercial Bank* (1838) MacF. 62: offer of reward to any unsuccessful user of patent medicine: *Carlill* v. *Carbolic Smoke Ball Co.* [1893] 1 Q.B. 256; offer of insurance to any purchaser of diary who completed form therein: *Law* v. *Newnes* (1894) 21 R. 1027; *Hunter* v. *H.* (1904) 7 F. 136; *Hunter* v. *General Accident Co.*, 1909 S.C. (H.L.) 30.

[3] e.g. *Hunter, supra.*

[4] e.g. *Petrie, supra.*

[5] e.g. *G.N. Ry.* v. *Witham* (1873) L.R. 9 C.P. 16; *Percival* v. *L.C.C. Asylum Cttee.* (1918) 87 L.J.K.B. 677.

[6] *Ingram-Johnson* v. *Century Insce. Co.*, 1909 S.C. 1032.

[7] *Littlejohn* v. *Hadwen* (1882) 20 S.L.R. 5, approved *Paterson* v. *Highland Ry.*, 1927 S.C. (H.L.) 32, 38. In England such an undertaking is revocable; *Routledge* v. *Grant* (1828) 4 Bing. 653; unless the undertaking is supported by consideration or made under seal: *Dickinson* v. *Dodds* (1876) 2 Ch. D. 463.

Irrevocable offer

An offer may be stated to be irrevocable in which case it may be accepted at any time,[1] until or unless rejected.

Withdrawal of offer

If not declared irrevocable an offer may be withdrawn at any time before acceptance, by intimation to the offeree.[2] At an auction a bidder may withdraw his bid at any time before the hammer falls,[3] and the exposer may withdraw the goods exposed.[4]

Lapse of offer

An offer lapses on the death, bankruptcy, or insanity of the offeror, even though not determined publicly, and though the offer has been accepted in ignorance of that fact,[5] and possibly on the death of the offeree.[6] It lapses also on any important change of circumstances,[7] on the expiry of any time stated for which it was open, or after the lapse of a time reasonable in the circumstances, if not accepted by then.[8] It also lapses if refused, and therefore cannot be accepted subsequently on a change of mind,[9] but does not lapse merely because the offeree had made an inquiry about different terms.[10] It lapses if made on the basis of a state of affairs which has ceased to exist,[11] and may lapse on the death, bankruptcy or insanity of the offeree.[12]

Cross-offers

If offers cross in the post, there can be no contract if they differ in terms; even if the parties agree, there may well be no contract until one accepts the other's offer.[13]

---

[1] *Premier Briquette Co.* v. *Gray*, 1922 S.C. 329.

[2] *Byrne* v. *Van Tienhoven* (1880) 5 C.P.D. 344; *Stevenson* v. *McLean* (1880) 5 Q.B.D. 346; *Henthorn* v. *Fraser* [1892] 2 Ch. 27.

[3] Sale of Goods Act, 1893, S. 58; *Fenwick, infra*.

[4] *Fenwick* v. *Macdonald, Fraser & Co.* (1904) 6 F. 850.

[5] *Thomson* v. *James* (1855) 18 D. 1, 10; *Dickinson* v. *Dodds* (1876) 2 Ch. D. 463, 475; *Loudon* v. *Elder's C.B.*, 1923 S.L.T. 226.

[6] *Sommerville* v. *N.C.B.*, 1963 S.C. 666.

[7] *Macrae* v. *Edinburgh Street Tramways* (1885) 13 R. 265, 269; *Bright* v. *Low*, 1940 S.C. 280.

[8] *Ramsgate Victoria Hotel Co.* v. *Montefiore* (1866) L.R. 1 Exch. 109.

[9] *Hyde* v. *Wrench* (1840) 3 Beav. 334.

[10] *Stevenson, Jacques & Co.* v. *McLean* (1880) 5 Q.B.D. 346; *Brown & Gracie* v. *Green* [1960] 1 Lloyd's Rep. 289.

[11] *Financings, Ltd.* v. *Stimson* [1962] 3 All E.R. 386; *Sommerville, supra*.

[12] Bell, *Prin.* § 79; Gloog, 37; but see *Sommerville, supra*.

[13] *Tinn* v. *Hoffman* (1873) 29 L.T. 271; *Harvey* v. *Smith* (1904) 6 F. 511.

Acceptance

A party may bind himself to accept the highest or lowest offer,[1] but apart from that he is not obliged to accept any offer. Only the, or an, offeree can validly accept an offer.[2] Mental acceptance, or acquiescence, does not amount to acceptance.[3] The offer must be accepted in the way prescribed by the offeror,[4] if any, failing which in any manner appropriate to the offer,[5] as by express communication,[6] even unauthorized,[7] or by conduct yielding an inference of acceptance, such as sending goods ordered,[8] taking possession of property bought,[9] complying with the terms of the offer,[10] or returning lost property for which a reward is offered.[11] Conduct which in fact meets the offer is not an acceptance if the offer were unknown,[12] though if it were known the motive for actings amounting to acceptance is irrelevant,[13] but it may be held an acceptance despite denial that it was so intended.[14]

The acceptance must be made within any time fixed by the offeror,[15] failing which, within a reasonable time,[16] the period of which depends on the custom of the particular trade,[17] or on the circumstances of the case. If so made it is valid, even though in the interval the offeror had sold the goods to another.[18] The onus is on a party accepting out of time and alleging that the time had been extended to establish that fact.[19] Acceptance need not re-

---

[1] *Paton* v. *Macpherson* (1889) 17 R. 52.

[2] *Greer* v. *Downs Supply Co.* [1927] 2 K.B. 28.

[3] *Brogden* v. *Metropolitan Ry.* (1877) 2 App. Cas. 666.

[4] cf. *Jaeger Bros., Ltd.* v. *McMorland* (1902) 10 S.L.T. 63.

[5] *Household Fire Ins. Co.* v. *Grant* (1879) 4 Ex. D. 216; *Henthorn* v. *Fraser* [1892] 2 Ch. 27.

[6] *Chapman* v. *Sulphite Pulp Co.* (1892) 19 R. 837.

[7] *Smeaton* v. *St. Andrews Police Commrs.* (1871) 9 M. (H.L.) 24.

[8] Bell, *Comm.* I, 343; *Brogden, supra;* cf. *Wallace* v. *Gibson* (1859) 22 R. (H.L.) 56; *Clarke* v. *Dunraven* [1897] A.C. 59.

[9] *Errol* v. *Walker,* 1966 S.C. 93.

[10] *Carlill* v. *Carbolic Smokeball Co.* [1893] 1 Q.B. 256.

[11] cf. *Petrie* v. *E. Airlie* (1834) 13 S. 68.

[12] *Neville* v. *Kelly* (1862) 12 C.B. (N.S.) 740; *Wylie and Lochhead* v. *McElroy* (1873) 1 R. 41; *Gibbons* v. *Proctor* (1891) 64 L.T. 594; *Hall Maxwell* v. *Gill* (1901) 9 S.L.T. 222.

[13] *Williams* v. *Carwardine* (1833) 5 C. & P. 566.

[14] *Robertson* v. *Royal Exchange Assce.,* 1925 S.C. 1.

[15] *Jacobsen* v. *Underwood* (1894) 21 R. 654. Within that period it may be that the offeror cannot withdraw: *Littlejohn* v. *Hadwen* (1882) 20 S.L.R. 5.

[16] Bell, *supra; Heron* v. *Caledonian Ry.* (1867) 5 M. 935; *Wylie & Lochhead* v. *McElroy* (1873) 1 R. 41; *Glasgow S.S. Co.* v. *Watson* (1873) 1 R. 189.

[17] *Murray* v. *Rennie* (1897) 24 R. 965; *Hall-Maxwell* v. *Gill* (1901) 9 S.L.T. 222.

[18] *Adams* v. *Lindsell* (1818) 1 B. & Ald. 681.

[19] *Glasgow S.S. Co.* v. *Watson* (1873) 1 R. 189.

iterate all the terms of the offer,[1] but should mention all material elements of the contract.[2] If goods are ordered after discussion of the terms of sale, no acceptance is necessary and the order must be implemented.[3]

Acceptance cannot be thrust on an offeree by a term in an offer that silence will be taken as assent.[4] Goods sent unasked may be rejected;[5] if kept, liability at common law is for recompense for their value, not under any contract.[6]

By the Unsolicited Goods and Services Act, 1971, S. 1, a person who receives unsolicited goods may use, deal with or dispose of them as if they were an unconditional gift to him and any right of the sender to the goods is extinguished, if they were sent to him with a view to his acquiring them, if he has no reasonable cause to believe that they were sent with a view to their being acquired for the purposes of a trade or business and has neither agreed to acquire nor agreed to return them, and either (a) during the six months after he received the goods the sender did not take possession of them and he did not unreasonably refuse to permit the sender to do so, or (b) at least 30 days before the end of the six months he gave the sender written notice and during the next 30 days the sender did not take possession of the goods and he did not unreasonably refuse to permit the sender to do so. Demands for and threats regarding payment for unsolicited goods are an offence (S. 2)[7] and it is an offence to include an entry as to a person or his trade in a directory with his written order (S. 3) or to send unsolicited any book or publication describing human sexual techniques (S. 4).

An acceptance made too late is ineffective; it may, however, be treated as a counter-offer. An acceptance in error of an offer which has been confused in transmission is not binding and may be repudiated when the mistake is discovered.[8] It may be a question of interpretation whether an acceptance is of the whole offer, or of part only, such as a specification.[9] Where the offer was held to be

---

[1] *Erskine* v. *Glendinning* (1871) 9 M. 656; *Philp* v. *Knoblauch*, 1907 S.C. 994.

[2] *Harvey* v. *Smith* (1904) 6 F. 511.

[3] *Barry, Ostlere & Shepherd* v. *Edinburgh Cork Importing Co.*, 1909 S.C. 1113.

[4] *Jaffray, infra*; *Felthouse* v. *Bindley* (1862) 11 C.B. (N.S.) 869.

[5] *Jaffray* v. *Boag* (1824) 3 S. 375; *Watson* v. *O'Reilly* (1826) 4 S. 475.

[6] *Webster* v. *Thomson* (1830) 8 S. 528.

[7] cf. *Readers Digest Assocn.* v. *Pirie*, 1973 S.L.T. 170.

[8] *Henkel* v. *Pape* (1870) L.R. 6 Ex. 7 (order for 'the' articles transmitted as for 'three'); *Verdin* v. *Robertson* (1871) 10 M. 35 (order received different from that sent).

[9] *Pollock* v. *Macrae*, 1922 S.C. (H.L.) 192; cf. *Star Insce. Co.* v. *Davidson* (1902) 5 F. 83.

one to several defenders jointly, an acceptance by one was held not to conclude any contract, not even with the one acceptor.[1]

Qualified acceptance

An acceptance which does not meet the offer but introduces or is subject to conditions or qualifications falls to be treated as a rejection of the offer, which cannot subsequently be accepted,[2] and also as a counter-offer which itself can be accepted.[3] Till itself accepted there is no contract.[3] But the offeree may seek clarification of the offer, and such would not be a rejection of the offer so as to preclude later acceptance,[4] and an addition to the acceptance not amounting to a new condition does not prevent the conclusion of agreement.[5]

Communication of acceptance

Acceptance must be communicated to the offeror by some overt act. The offeror may require acceptance to be notified by a stated date or time,[6] or by particular means. Failing compliance, no contract exists, possibly even if the alternative means of communication was, or should have been, as prompt.[7] In contracts made orally or by telephone acceptance is effective when and if the message reaches the offeror's consciousness.[8] In contracts made by post or telegram, the Post Office is deemed the agent of the offeror, or possibly of both parties, and, in the absence of contrary provision, the acceptance is effective from the time it is posted, even though it does not reach the offeror till later,[9] but possibly not if it never arrives,[10] in which event there would be no contract. A possibly invalid or inadequate acceptance may be

---

[1] *Anderson* v. *Sillars* (1894) 22 R. 105.

[2] *Hyde* v. *Wrench* (1840) 3 Beav. 334; *Johnston* v. *Clark* (1855) 18 D. 70; *Wylie & Lochhead* v. *McElroy* (1873) 1 R. 41; *Ocean Coal Co.* v. *Powell Duffryn* [1932] 1 Ch. 654.

[3] *Hart* v. *Mills* (1846) 15 M. & W. 85; *Johnston* v. *Clark* (1855) 18 D. 70; *Canning* v. *Farquhar* (1886) 16 Q.B.D. 727; *Jones* v. *Daniel* [1894] 2 Ch. 332; *Star Fire Ins. Co.* v. *Davidson* (1902) 5 F. 83; *Roberts and Cooper, Ltd.* v. *Salvesen*, 1918 S.C. 794; *Mathieson Gee, Ltd.* v. *Quigley*, 1952 S.C. (H.L.) 38; cf. *Nelson* v. *Assets Co.* (1889) 16 R. 898.

[4] *Stevenson* v. *McLean* (1880) 5 Q.B.D. 346.

[5] *Tait & Crichton* v. *Mitchell* (1889) 26 S.L.R. 573.

[6] e.g. *Jacobsen* v. *Underwood* (1894) 21 R. 654.

[7] e.g. if acceptance by post is requested and acceptance is telephoned. cf. *Manchester Diocesan Fund* v. *Commercial Investments* [1969] 3 All E.R. 1593.

[8] *Entores* v. *Miles Far East Corpn.* [1955] 2 Q.B. 327.

[9] Bell, *Comm.* I, 344; *Adams* v. *Lindsell* (1818) 1 B. & Ald. 681; *Dunlop* v. *Higgins* (1848) 6 Bell. 195; *Household Fire Insce. Co.* v. *Grant* (1879) 4 Ex. D. 216; *Cowan* v. *O'Connor* (1888) 20 Q.B.D. 640 (telegram); *Henthorn* v. *Fraser* [1892] 2 Ch. 27; *Jacobsen* v. *Underwood* (1894) 21 R. 654.

[10] *Mason* v. *Benhar Coal Co.* (1882) 9 R. 883, doubting *Household Co., supra.*

ratified if the contract be acted on by the offeror for a substantial period.[1]

Revocation of offer or acceptance

An offer unless declared irrevocable, or to be open for a period, may be withdrawn at any time before acceptance,[2] but the withdrawal becomes effective only when notice of it reaches the offeree,[3] or, possibly, when it would in the normal course have reached the offeree,[4] and it is too late if an acceptance has already been sent.[5] *Prima facie*, an acceptance once posted is irrevocable. It has been held, however, that an acceptance may be withdrawn by any cancellation thereof arriving with or before the acceptance.[6]

Modification of contract after acceptance

After an offer has been accepted any qualification of offer or acceptance is too late,[7] and can be taken account of only in an agreement to modify the concluded contract. Similarly if a deed containing an agreement is not in accordance with the offer as accepted there is no contract.[8] But exceptionally, it has been held that an alteration made on execution by one party in a written agreement embodying a prior agreement did not entitle the other to resile.[9] An oral agreement has been held not capable of being qualified by the terms of invoices sent with the goods,[10] and if a contract has been embodied in a formal deed it is incompetent by parole evidence to seek to establish that the intention of parties was other than set out in the deed.[11] Exceptionally one party has been held to have waived objections to a clause added by the other party after the first party had signed a contract and to be barred from maintaining that there was no concluded contract.[12]

Certainty of terms

The terms agreed on by the parties must be reasonably certain; the court will not fix matters left vague and cannot enforce an

[1] *National Benefit Socy.* v. *Coulter,* 1911 S.C. 545.

[2] *J. M. Smith, Ltd.* v. *Colquhoun's Tr.* (1901) 3 F. 981.

[3] *Byrne* v. *Van Tienhoven* (1880) 5 C.P.D. 344.

[4] *Burnley* v. *Alford,* 1919, 2 S.L.T. 123.

[5] *Thomson* v. *James* (1855) 18 D. 1; *Byrne, supra; Henthorn* v. *Fraser* [1892] 2 Ch. 27.

[6] *Dunmore* v. *Alexander* (1830) 9 S. 190 (inconsistent with rule that acceptance effective from time of posting); explained in *Thomson, supra.*

[7] *Jaeger Bros., Ltd.* v. *McMorland* (1902) 10 S.L.T. 63.

[8] *Star Fire Ins. Co.* v. *Davidson* (1902) 5 F. 83.

[9] *Bernards, Ltd.* v. *N.B. Ry.* (1899) 36 S.L.R. 683.

[10] *Buchanan* v. *Macdonald* (1895) 23 R. 264.

[11] *Steuart's Trs.* v. *Hart* (1875) 3 R. 192; *Burrell* v. *Russell* (1900) 2 F. (H.L.) 81.

[12] *Roberts & Cooper* v. *Salvesen,* 1918 S.C. 794.

indefinite agreement,[1] nor one where terms can be determined only by a further agreement.[2] The question is whether the court could grant a decree of implement giving the pursuer what he bargained for;[3] if not the contract is void for uncertainty.[4] But terms not expressly mentioned may be deemed implied by law,[5] by the custom of the trade or profession,[6] or from a previous course of dealing between the parties;[7] the courts will seek to interpret an agreement so as to uphold it as valid,[7] and an uncertain or meaningless subsidiary term may be disregarded if severable from the rest of the agreement without prejudice thereto.[8] Parties may be held to have reached agreement though no price has been fixed,[9] though in sale agreement on the price is essential.[10] Even after agreement had apparently been reached it may appear that there is no concluded contract.[11]

Whether agreement immediately obligatory

It is a question of interpretation[12] whether an apparent agreement concludes an obligation immediately[13] or one still subject to suspensive condition, i.e. suspended or otherwise conditional,[14] or

[1] *Cook* v. *N.B. Ry.* (1872) 10 M. 513; *Montreal Gas Co.* v. *Vasey* [1900] A.C. 595; *Murray's Trs.* v. *St. Margaret's Convent,* 1907 S.C. (H.L.) 8; *British Homophone Co.* v. *Kunz* (1935) 152 L.T. 589; *Scammell* v. *Ouston* [1941] A.C. 251; *Bishop & Baxter* v. *Anglo-Eastern Trading Co.* [1944] K.B. 12; *British Electrical Industries* v. *Patley Pressings* [1953] 1 All E.R. 94.

[2] *May & Butcher* v. *The King* [1934] 2 K.B. 17.

[3] *Macarthur* v. *Lawson* (1877) 4 R. 1134; *Traill* v. *Dewar* (1881) 8 R. 583.

[4] e.g. *Lord Clinton* v. *Brown* (1874) 1 R. 1137; *Macarthur, supra; Traill, supra; British Workmen's Ins. Co.* v. *Wilkinson* (1900) 8 S.L.T. 67.

[5] e.g. *Wilson* v. *Mann* (1876) 3 R. 527; *Dunlop* v. *Steel Co. of Scotland* (1879) 7 R. 283; *Christie* v. *Fife Coal Co.* (1899) 2 F. 192; *Lawrie* v. *Brown,* 1908 S.C. 705.

[6] Bell, *Comm.* I, 465; *Buchanan* v. *Riddell* (1900) 2 F. 544.

[7] *Hillas* v. *Arcos* (1932) 147 L.T. 503 (H.L.); *McCutcheon* v. *MacBrayne,* 1964 S.C. (H.L.) 28.

[8] *Nicolene* v. *Simmonds* [1953] 1 Q.B. 543.

[9] *Dempster* v. *Motherwell Bridge Co.,* 1964 S.C. 308.

[10] *Foley* v. *Classique Coaches, Ltd* [1934] 2 K.B. 1; *May and Butcher* v. *The King* [1934] 2 K.B. 17; *Hillas, supra.*

[11] *Heiton* v. *Waverley Hydropathic Co.* (1877) 4 R. 830; *E. Kilbride Dev. Corpn.* v. *Pollok,* 1953 S.C. 370.

[12] *Chinnock* v. *Marchioness of Ely* (1865) 4 De G. J. & S. 638; *Rossiter* v. *Miller* (1878) 3 App. Cas. 1124, 1137; *Tait & Crichton* v. *Mitchell* (1889) 26 S.L.R. 573; *Gordon's Exor.* v. *G.,* 1918, 1 S.L.T. 407; *Stobo* v. *Morrisons (Gowns) Ltd.,* 1949 S.C. 184.

[13] *Erskine* v. *Glendinning* (1871) 9 M. 656 ('subject to lease drawn out'); *Branca* v. *Cobarro* [1947] K.B. 854 ('provisional agreement'); cf. *Dewar* v. *Ainslie* (1892) 20 R. 203; *Gow* v. *Henry* (1899) 2 F. 48.

[14] *Winn* v. *Bull* (1877) 7 Ch. D. 29; *Johnston* v. *Clark* (1855) 18 D. 70; *Van Laun* v. *Neilson, Reid & Co.* (1904) 6 F. 644; *Gordon's Exor.* v. *G.,* 1918, 1 S.L.T. 407; *Eccles* v. *Bryant & Pollock* [1948] Ch. 93; *Stobo* v. *Morrisons (Gowns) Ltd.,* 1949 S.C. 184 ('subject to contract').

one subject to resolutive condition, i.e. liable to be rescinded if stated conditions are not met.[1]

Effect of concluded agreement

If parties have reached *consensus in idem* both are bound from that time to perform their undertakings under the contract and there is, in general, no *locus poenitentiae* and neither party can, without incurring liability for breach of contract, thereafter repudiate the contract.[2] So long as there is no concluded agreement either party may resile.[3] But exceptions to this exist (a) where formalities requisite for the constitution of the contract have not been complied with;[4] and (b) where the agreement is future or conditional, i.e. to be performed at a later time, or if some prior condition is satisfied.

(c) INTENTION TO AFFECT LEGAL RELATIONS

The agreement must have been intended to produce a legally binding and enforceable contract and affect the parties' legal relations, not merely to create a social or private arrangement,[5] morally binding only. Thus an arrangement between spouses[6] or between members of the family[7] has been held presumably not intended to be a legal bargain, though a legal contract between spouses is competent.[8] An advertisement of a bursary followed by a competitive examination therefor has been held not to constitute a contract between the bursary trustees and a competitor,[9] a nun's relations with her convent are not necessarily contractual,[10] and the relations between a college and its students are not necessarily contractual.[11] A person discharging a *munus publicum* is not employed contractually.[12] A collective bargain

---

[1] *Head* v. *Tattersall* (1871) L.R. 7 Ex. 7.

[2] *Dewar* v. *Ainslie* (1892) 20 R. 203; cf. *Gow* v. *Henry* (1899) 2 F. 48; *White & Carter* v. *McGregor*, 1962 S.C. (H.L.) 1.

[3] *Van Laun* v. *Neilson Reid & Co.* (1904) 6 F. 644; *Reid & Laidlaw* v. *Reid* (1905) 7 F. 457; *Murphy* v. *Smith*, 1920 S.C. 104.

[4] Ch. 32, *infra.*

[5] cf. *Parker* v. *Clark* [1960] 1 All E.R. 93.

[6] *Balfour* v. *B.* [1919] 2 K.B. 571; cf. *Coward* v. *Motor Insurers Bureau* [1963] 1 Q.B. 259; *Buckpitt* v. *Oates* [1968] 1 All E.R. 1145; *Gould* v. *G.* [1970] 1 Q.B. 275.

[7] *Jones* v. *Padavatton* [1969] 2 All E.R. 616.

[8] *Horsburgh* v. *H.*, 1949 S.C. 227; *Hoddinott* v. *H.* [1949] 2 K.B. 406; *Simpkins* v. *Pays* [1955] 3 All E.R. 10; cf. *Parker* v. *Clark* [1960] 1 All E.R. 93; *Merritt* v. *M.* [1970] 2 All E.R. 760.

[9] *Martins* v. *MacDougall's Trs.* (1885) 13 R. 274; *McDonald* v. *McColl* (1890) 17 R. 951; cf. *McQuaker* v. *Ballantrae Trust* (1891) 18 R. 521; *Rooke* v. *Dawson* [1895] 1 Ch. 480.

[10] *Mulcahy* v. *Herbert* (1898) 25 R. 1136.

[11] *Cadells* v. *Balfour* (1890) 17 R. 1138; see also *Caird* v. *Sime* (1887) 14 R. (H.L.) 37.

[12] *Hastie* v. *McMurtrie* (1889) 16 R. 715.

between employers and trade unions may or may not be a contract.[1]

Parties may, moreover, expressly declare their agreement not to be legally enforceable but only an honourable understanding or gentlemen's agreement.[2] Where the subject of agreement relates to business affairs the onus of establishing that it was not intended to create legal relations is on the party setting up that defence and is a heavy onus.[3] In certain cases, whatever the parties' intentions, their agreement is deemed by law unenforceable, though not illegal nor a nullity.[4]

Absence of patrimonial interest

In some cases the courts treat an agreement as not creating a legal relationship because it involves no element of patrimonial right or interest. Thus a person expelled from a club or church cannot claim for breach of contract unless he has thereby lost some patrimonial right such as to property or to the use of property. Thus patrimonial interest has been held involved in a clergyman's loss of benefice[5] but not in an alteration of his church's doctrinal standards,[6] in a member's loss of the use of club property[7] but not in the loss of association with others,[8] in a person's loss of a professional status[9] but not in the mere chance of being employed or winning a prize.[10]

(d) FACTUAL AND LEGAL POSSIBILITY, AND LEGALITY OF OBJECT

Factual possibility of object

The agreed object of the parties' contract must be possible of attainment in fact,[11] such an object as reasonable men, versed in the

---

[1] *Ford Motor Co.* v. *A.U.E.W.* [1969] 2 All E.R. 481. Trade Unions and Labour Relations Act, 1974, S. 18.

[2] e.g. *Woods* v. *Cooperative Ins. Socy.*, 1924 S.C. 692; *Rose and Frank* v. *Crompton* [1925] A.C. 445; *Jones* v. *Vernons* [1938] 2 All E.R. 626; *Appleson* v. *Littlewood* [1939] 1 All E.R. 464; cf. *Clyde Marine Ins. Co.* v. *Renwick*, 1924 S.C. 113.

[3] *Edwards* v. *Skyways, Ltd.* [1964] 1 All E.R. 494.

[4] See *infra*.

[5] *McMillan* v. *Free Church of Scotland* (1861) 23 D. 1314.

[6] *Forbes* v. *Eden* (1867) 5 M. (H.L.) 36.

[7] *Labouchere* v. *Wharncliffe* (1879) 13 Ch. D. 346; *Renton F.C.* v. *McDowall* (1891) 18 R. 670; *Murray* v. *Johnstone* (1896) 23 R. 981; *Gardner* v. *McLintock* (1904) 11 S.L.T. 654; *Yonge* v. *Ladies Imperial Club* [1920] 2 K.B. 523.

[8] *Forbes, supra*; *Aitken* v. *Assoc. Carpenters* (1885) 12 R. 1206; *Skerret* v. *Oliver* (1896) 23 R. 468; *Anderson* v. *Manson*, 1909 S.C. 838.

[9] *McMillan, supra*; *Forbes, supra*; *Skerret, supra*.

[10] *Cocker* v. *Crombie* (1893) 20 R. 954; *Anderson, supra*.

[11] Inst. 3, 19, 1; Dig. 44, 7, 31; 45, 1, 35.

subject concerned, reasonably believe to be, at the time of the contract,[1] possible of attainment or of performance. If generally deemed impossible at that time, the contract is a nullity, even though the parties believe it possible.[2] Extreme difficulty of performance, uncertainty of success, the need for inordinate expense, or the party's eventual failure or inability to perform do not, however, nullify a contract if attainment is at all possible. Parties may, however, competently contract on the basis of taking a chance on the possibility of attainment of the object intended.

Legal possibility of object

The agreed object of the parties' contract must also be legally possible of attainment, in that legal means must exist for performing the contract, and the subject matter must be susceptible of being dealt with legally in the way contemplated. A contract attempting to bring about a legal impossibility is a nullity.[3] Thus to contract to create a right in security over moveable property without delivery of possession thereof is, in general, legally impossible and quite incompetent.[4] A contract to assign a permit to withdraw liquor from bond has been held incompetent and illegal.[5]

Legality of object—pacta illicita

The object of the parties' contract must also be legal and not deemed criminal, civilly wrongful or otherwise objectionable and contrary to public policy under any rule of common law or statute. Many such rules do stigmatize certain kinds of conduct and contracts connected therewith as void, as being illegal or contrary to public policy.[6] In this context 'illegal' covers not only conduct contrary to the criminal law and punishable, but conduct possibly civilly actionable as harmful, or contrary to public morality or to public policy.

(i) CONTRACTS DEEMED ILLEGAL AT COMMON LAW

The illegality which at common law vitiates a contract may be in the purpose of the contract,[7] the manner of performance, or in

[1] Contrast *Gillespie* v. *Howden* (1885) 12 R. 800, and cases of supervening impossibility.
[2] Stair I, 10, 13; II, 3, 56; Ersk. III, 3, 84; Bell, *Comm.* I, 313.
[3] Ersk. III, 3, 84; e.g. to create a strict entail of land has been impossible since 1914.
[4] *Orr's Tr.* v. *Tullis* (1870) 8 M. 936; *Stiven* v. *Cowan* (1878) 15 S.L.R. 422; *Heritable Securities Inv. Assocn.* v. *Wingate's Tr.* (1880) 7 R. 1094.
[5] *Trevalion* v. *Blanche*, 1919 S.C. 617.
[6] Bell, *Comm.* I, 317; *Prin.* §35.
[7] e.g. *Pearce* v. *Brooks* (1866) L.R. 1 Ex. 213 (carriage hired to facilitate prostitution).

the consideration given or to be given for the promisor's undertaking.[1] Such contracts are nullities.[2] It is *pars judicis* to notice that a contract is *pactum illicitum* and the court may *ex proprio motu* decline to enforce a transaction thus vitiated, if the party invoking the court's aid was implicated in and cognisant of the illegality of purpose, manner or consideration.[3] But a contract is not illegal if it may be performed legally and only possibly involve illegality.[4]

Contracts productive of crime or delict

Illegality affects contracts to bring about any kind of crime or delict,[5] such as to print a libel,[6] to deliver blasphemous lectures,[7] to defraud shareholders,[8] or a third party,[9] or the public,[10] to obtain goods by false pretences,[11] artificially to inflate the values of shares,[12] to pay a secret commission,[13] or to assign a permit to withdraw spirits from bond.[14]

Contracts interfering with due process of law

Similarly contracts involving interference with the course of justice, such as a *pactum de quota litis*, by which counsel or agent agrees to take a share of the sum in issue as remuneration for his services,[15] a collusive agreement for divorce,[16] or a contract (other than one providing for arbitration), purporting wholly to exclude resort to the courts of law,[17] or an agreement to share fees

[1] *Hamilton* v. *Main* (1823) 2 S. 356 (bill granted for cost of drunken orgy with prostitute).

[2] Stair I, 10, 8; Ersk. III, 1, 10; Bell, *Prin.* §37.

[3] *Scott* v. *Brown, Doering, McNab & Co.* [1892] 2 Q.B. 724; *Hamilton* v. *McLauchlan* (1908) 16 S.L.T. 341; *N.W. Salt Co.* v. *Electrolytic Alkali Co.* [1914] A.C. 461; *Alexander* v. *Rayson* [1936] 1 K.B. 169.

[4] *Fegan* v. *Dept. of Health for Sc.*, 1935 S.C. 823.

[5] *Macdougall* v. *Bremner* (1907) 15 S.L.T. 193.

[6] *Clay* v. *Yates* (1856) 1 H. & N. 73; *Apthorp* v. *Neville* (1907) 23 T.L.R. 575.

[7] *Cowan* v. *Milbourn* (1867) L.R. 2 Ex. 230.

[8] *Begbie* v. *Phosphate Sewage Co.* (1875) L.R. 10 Q.B. 491; *Laughland* v. *Millar* (1904) 6 F. 413.

[9] *Henderson* v. *Caldwell* (1890) 28 S.L.R. 16.

[10] *Arrol* v. *Montgomery* (1826) 4 S. 499.

[11] *Berg* v. *Sadler & Moore* [1937] 2 K.B. 158.

[12] *Scott* v. *Brown, Doering, McNab & Co.* [1892] 2 Q.B. 724.

[13] *Macdougall, supra.*

[14] *Trevalion* v. *Blanche*, 1919 S.C. 617.

[15] Stair I, 10, 8; Bell, *Prin.* §36(2); *Glasford* v. *Morrison* (1823) 2 S. 417; *Rucker* v. *Fischer* (1826) 4 S. 438; *Johnston* v. *Rome* (1831) 9 S. 364; *Gilfillan* v. *Henderson* (1833) 6 M. & S. 489; but it has been held permissible to act for ordinary remuneration recoverable only in case of success: *Taylor* v. *Forbes* (1853) 24 D. 19; *Bell* v. *Ogilvie* (1863) 2 M. 336; *Scotland* v. *Henry* (1865) 3 M. 1125; *Moscrip* v. *O'Hara* (1880) 8 R. 36.

[16] *Emanuel* v. *E.* [1946] P. 115.

[17] *Wylie* v. *Heritable Securities Investment Assocn.* (1871) 10 M. 253; *Lee* v. *Showmen's Guild* [1952] 2 Q.B. 329; *Baker* v. *Jones* [1954] 2 All E.R. 553.

in violation of the bankruptcy laws,[1] though not, as against participating creditors, to give certain creditors in bankruptcy an illegal preference,[2] or an agreement between a friend of the bankrupt and a creditor to pay the latter to withdraw a claim,[3] or any contract interfering with the administration of justice, are void.[4]

An agreement to refrain from giving information for a criminal prosecution may be *pactum illicitum*.[5] So is a bribe to procure a pardon or stifle a prosecution.[6]

Contracts promoting corruption

Contracts likely to promote corruption in public life are similarly void, including a bond to secure the grantee's vote,[7] an undertaking to vote in Parliament as directed by an outside body,[8] a promise to procure a knighthood in return for a donation,[9] a contract for the sale of a public office or appointment,[10] one which entails a public officer in neglect of his duties,[11] or one for a secret commission.[12] This includes the avoidance of contracts for the assignation of the salaries of public officials paid from national funds. But a contract which involves refusal to take the oath of allegiance to the Crown is not, at least for some purposes, *pactum illicitum*.[13]

---

[1] *Farmers' Mart.* v. *Milne*, 1914 S.C. (H.L.) 84; see also *Robertson* v. *Ainslie's Trs.* (1837) 15 S. 1299; *Macfarlane* v. *Nicoll* (1864) 3 M. 237; *Pendreigh's Tr.* v. *McLaren* (1871) 9 M. (H.L.) 49; *Thomas* v. *Sandeman* (1872) 11 M. 81.

[2] *Munro* v. *Rothfield*, 1920 S.C. (H.L.) 165.

[3] *Thomas* v. *Waddell* (1869) 7 M. 558.

[4] *Stewart* v. *E. Galloway* (1752) Mor. 9465; *Henderson* v. *Mackay* (1832) 11 S. 225; *Ord* v. *Hill & Paul* (1847) 9 D. 1118.

[5] *Stewart* v. *E. Galloway* (1752) Mor. 9465; *Grant* v. *Davidson* (1786) Mor. 9571; *McLeod* v. *Fraser* (1758) Mor. 9563; *Lee* v. *Watson's Exors.* (1795) Bell's Cas. 176; *Kennedy* v. *Cameron* (1823) 2 S. 192; *Ferrier* v. *Mackenzie* (1899) 1 F. 597; *Smith* v. *Buchanan*, 1910, 2 S.L.T. 387; *Lamson Paragon Supply Co.* v. *MacPhail*, 1914 S.C. 73.

[6] Bell, *Prin.* §37; *Stewart* v. *E. Galloway* (1752) Mor. 9465.

[7] *Glen* v. *Dundas* (1822) 1 S. 234.

[8] *A.S.R.S.* v. *Osborne* [1910] A.C. 87; cf. *Hoggan* v. *Wardlaw* (1735) 1 Pat. 148; *Paterson* v. *Stirling Mags.* (1775) Mor. 9527.

[9] *Parkinson* v. *College of Ambulance Ltd.* [1925] 2 K.B. 1; see now Honours (Prevention of Abuses) Act, 1925.

[10] Bell, *Prin.* §36(5); *Richardson* v. *Mellish* (1824) 2 Bing. 229; *Gardiner* v. *Grant* (1835) 13 S. 664; *Bruce* v. *Grant* (1839) 1 D. 583; *Hill* v. *Paul* (1841) 2 Rob. 524; *Ord* v. *Hill and Paul* (1847) 9 D. 1118; *Eyre* v. *Forbes* (1862) 12 C.B. (N.S.) 191. See also *E. Lauderdale* v. *Scrymgeour Wedderburn*, 1910 S.C. (H.L.) 35; Sale of Offices Act, 1809.

[11] *Hughes* v. *Statham* (1825) 4 B. & C. 187; *Mason* v. *Wilson* (1844) 7 D. 160.

[12] *Macdougall* v. *Bremner* (1907) 15 S.L.T. 193.

[13] *Ferguson Bequest Fund* (1879) 6 R. 486.

Contracts to defraud the revenue

Contracts involving fraud on the public revenue, whether national[1] or local,[2] are similarly void.[3]

Contracts with the enemy

The same result attaches to contracts with enemy aliens[4] during wartime.[5]

Contracts prejudicial to foreign relations

The same attaches also to contracts likely to be prejudicial to good relations with another state in peacetime.[6]

Contracts deemed contrary to public policy

Various classes of contracts are held void if their effect is deemed detrimental to public morality or public policy.[7] Public policy has been said[8] to be the principle of law which holds that no subject can lawfully do that which has a tendency to be injurious to the public or against the public good. But this has been criticized as a vague standard[9] and the view expressed that, unless in clear cases, it is no longer legitimate for the courts to invent new heads of public policy,[10] though the precedents may be developed by analogy.[11] The main recognized classes are:

[1] Ersk. III, 3, 3; Bell, *Prin.*, §42(4); *Brown* v. *Limond* (1791) Hume 672; *Isaacson* v. *Wiseman* (1806) Hume 714; *Russel* v. *Liston's Trs.* (1844) 6 D. 1138; *Greig* v. *Conacher* (1876) 4 R. 187; *Cairns* v. *Walker*, 1914 S.C. 51; *Miller* v. *Karlinski* (1945) 62 T.L.R. 85; *Napier* v. *National Agency, Ltd.* [1951] 2 All E.R. 264.

[2] *Alexander* v. *Rayson* [1936] 1 K.B. 169; *Berg* v. *Sadler and Moore* [1937] 2 K.B. 158; *Chettiar* v. *C.* [1962] A.C. 294.

[3] *Secus,* if one party is innocent: *Mason* v. *Clarke* [1955] 1 All E.R. 914.

[4] Including British subjects or neutrals carrying on business in enemy territory: *Sovfracht* v. *Van Uden* [1943] A.C. 203.

[5] Stair II, 2, 10; Bell, *Comm.* I, 303; *Prin.* §43(5); *Halsey* v. *Lowenfeld* [1916] 2 K.B. 707; *Ertel Bieber* v. *Rio Tinto* [1918] A.C. 260; *Fibrosa* v. *Fairbairn* [1943] A.C. 32.

[6] *Foster* v. *Driscoll* [1929] 1 K.B. 470; *O'Toole* v. *Whiterock Quarry Co.,* 1937 S.L.T. 521; *Regazzoni* v. *Sethia* [1956] 2 All E.R. 487.

[7] Bell, *Prin.* §38–43.

[8] *Egerton* v. *Earl Brownlow* (1853) 4 H.L. Cas. 1, 196.

[9] *Richardson* v. *Mellish* (1824) 2 Bing. 229 ('a very unruly horse'); *Re Mirams* [1891] 1 Q.B. 594; *Janson* v. *Driefontein Mines* [1902] A.C. 484.

[10] *Janson, supra; Fender* v. *St. John Mildmay* [1938] A.C. 1.

[11] *E. Caithness* v. *Sinclair,* 1912 S.C. 79.

Contracts in contravention of marriage

Contracts in total restraint of marriage[1] or unreasonably limiting the choice of marriage partner,[2] or interfering with matrimonial obligations, such as providing for future separation,[3] or promising to marry while still married to another,[4] are void on this ground. A marriage brokage agreement, to pay for an introduction with a view to, or influence to bring about, a marriage, is likewise void.[5] But this principle does not strike at a contract regulating the terms of a separation which has taken place or is about to take place,[6] nor at a provision for forfeiture if the beneficiary married without the obligor's consent.[7]

Contracts interfering with parental relations

A contract whereby a parent surrenders the right to custody of a child is not illegal[8] though ineffective against a demand for return of the child.[9] But a contract that a child should not live with either parent, without provision for maintenance by a third party, might be void.[10]

Contracts relative to immorality

Contracts for the furtherance of,[11] or known to be incidental to[12] sexual immorality, or for future illicit cohabitation,[13] are void, but this does not strike at a contract in consideration of past immorality.[14]

---

[1] *Lowe* v. *Peers* (1768) 4 Burr. 2225; *Re Lanyon* [1927] 2 Ch. 264.

[2] *Perrin* v. *Lyon* (1807) 9 East 170; *Hermann* v. *Charlesworth* [1905] 2 K.B. 123; cf. *Ommaney* v. *Bingham* (1796) 3 Pat. 448; *Forbes* v. *F's Trs.* (1882) 9 R. 675; *Aird's Exors.* v. *A.*, 1949 S.C. 154.

[3] *Brodie* v. *B.* [1917] P. 271.

[4] *Prevost* v. *Wood* (1905) 21 T.L.R. 684; *Speirs* v. *Hunt* [1908] 1 K.B. 720; *Wilson* v. *Carnley* [1908] 1 K.B. 729; *Skipp* v. *Kelly* (1926) 42 T.L.R. 258; *Siveyer* v. *Allison* [1935] 2 K.B. 403; cf. *Fender* v. *Mildmay* [1938] A.C. 1; *Shaw* v. *S.* [1954] 2 Q.B. 429.

[5] *Campbell* v. *Burns & Stewart* (1678) Mor. 9505; *Buchan* v. *Cochran* (1698) Mor. 9507; *Thomson* v. *McKail* (1770) Mor. 9519; *Hermann, supra.*

[6] *Clark* v. *C.* (1885) 10 P.D. 188.

[7] *Hay* v. *Wood* (1781) Mor. 2982.

[8] *Macpherson* v. *Leishman* (1887) 14 R. 780.

[9] *Kerrigan* v. *Hall* (1901) 4 F. 10.

[10] cf. *Fraser* v. *Rose* (1849) 11 D. 1466; *Grant's Trs.* v. *G.* (1898) 25 R. 929.

[11] Bell, *Prin.* §37; *Hamilton* v. *de Gares* (1765) Mor. 9471; *Johnstone* v. *McKenzie's Exor.* (1835) 14 S. 106; *Graham* v. *Kennedy* (1860) 22 D. 560; *Smith* v. *White* (1866) L.R. 1 Eq. 626; *Pearce* v. *Brooks* (1866) L.R. 1 Ex. 213; *Upfill* v. *Wright* [1911] 1 K.B. 506.

[12] *Hamilton* v. *Main* (1823) 2 S. 356.

[13] *Walker* v. *Perkins* (1764) 1 W. Bl. 517; *Ayerst* v. *Jenkins* (1873) L.R. 16 Eq. 275.

[14] Bell, *Prin.* §37; *Vallance* v. *Blagden* (1884) 26 Ch. D. 353; *Webster* v. *W's. Trs.* (1886) 14 R. 90; cf. *Young* v. *Johnson and Wright* (1880) 7 R. 760.

Contracts in restraint of personal liberty

Contracts in complete restraint of personal liberty are void.[1] Contracts, or terms of contracts, which are considered by the courts unreasonably to restrict the liberty of a person freely to carry on a profession, trade or business are held *prima facie* void as being contrary to public policy, but may be valid if the restriction is in the circumstances reasonable, in the interests of the public and of the person bound himself.[2]

A restraint deemed reasonable between the parties has rarely been held void as unreasonable in the public interest.[3] The onus of proof of reasonableness lies on the party imposing the restriction and benefited thereby;[4] the onus of proof of public injury is on the party bound.[5] Whether a restraint is reasonable or not is a question of law, not of fact.[6] In judging of reasonableness the court considers particularly the extent of restriction imposed in point of area and the time or duration for which it is to apply. In particular circumstances restrictions wholly unlimited in area,[7] or in duration,[8] have been upheld, though none unlimited in both respects. In case of doubt the interpretation will be adopted which renders the contract valid rather than invalid.[9]

The cases fall into four main groups: (a) where an employee undertakes not to compete with his employer after leaving the employment; (b) where the seller of a business undertakes not to compete with the buyer; (c) where manufacturers regulate the output or disposal or price of their products; and (d) where manufacturers restrict the trading of a distributor. Greater liberty of contractual restraint is permissible in cases of the second and third, than of the first, class.[10]

The courts will not cut down, or enforce within a restricted sphere, unduly wide restrictions imposed by parties; if deemed too wide, the restriction is unreasonable and falls.[11] But severable

[1] Bell, *Prin.* §40(2); *Allan & Mearns* v. *Skene* (1728) Mor. 9454; see also *Knight* v. *Wedderburn* (1778) Mor. 14545. But see Ersk. I, 7, 61–2; *Stewart* v. *S.* (1899) 1 F. 1158.

[2] *Nordenfelt* v. *Maxim Nordenfelt, Ltd.* [1894] A.C. 535; *Mason* v. *Provident Clothing Co.* [1913] A.C. 724; *Morris* v. *Saxelby* [1916] 1 A.C. 688; *Attwood* v. *Lamont* [1920] 3 K.B. 571.

[3] *A.G. for Australia* v. *Adelaide S.S. Co.* [1913] A.C. 781, 797.

[4] *Mason, supra,* 733; *Morris, supra,* 700; *Attwood, supra,* 587.

[5] *A.G. for Australia, supra,* 796.

[6] *Mason, supra,* 732.

[7] *Nordenfelt, supra* (world-wide).

[8] *Fitch* v. *Dewes* [1921] 2 A.C. 158 (lifelong).

[9] Sc. *Farmers Dairy Co.* v. *McGhee,* 1933 S.C. 148.

[10] *Leather Cloth Co.* v. *Lorsont* (1869) L.R. 9 Eq. 345; *Mason, supra; Morris, supra.*

[11] *Dumbarton Steamboat Co.* v. *MacFarlane* (1899) 1 F. 993.

restrictions may be distinguished and the reasonable part enforced, the rest being ignored as void.[1] This may be competent only if there are in substance two or more restrictions.[2]

A restrictive covenant is enforceable only if, and so long as, the party in right has an interest to enforce it,[3] and it falls if that party is in material breach of contract, as by dismissing unjustifiably a servant contractually restricted.[4]

The benefit of a covenant is not generally assignable in the case of a contract of service,[5] but, in the case of sale of a business, it is assignable on the resale of the business, unless it was undertaken in favour of the buyer alone.[6]

(a) Contracts restricting competition with former employer

An employer is not entitled to obtain by contract complete protection from competition by his former employee, but only to protection of his own business custom or trade secrets, and only within such limits of space and time as are deemed reasonably necessary.[7] If deemed excessive in space or time the restriction is void.[8] If reasonable between the parties it is unlikely to be unreasonable in respect of the public interest.[9]

(b) Contracts restricting competition by seller of business

A condition imposed on the seller of a business, restrictive of his *prima facie* right[10] to set up a rival business, is *prima facie* void, but may be valid if not wider in space and time than deemed reasonably necessary to protect the goodwill and connection of the business bought.[11] A world-wide restriction, limited in time, has

---

[1] *Mulvein v. Murray*, 1908 S.C. 528; *Attwood, supra.*

[2] *Mason v. Provident Clothing Co.* [1913] A.C. 724; *Attwood, supra.*

[3] *Berlitz School v. Duchene* (1903) 6 F. 181; *Rodger v. Herbertson*, 1909 S.C. 256; cf. *Ballachulish Slate Quarries v. Grant* (1903) 5 F. 1105.

[4] *General Billposting Co. v. Atkinson* [1909] A.C. 118; cf. *Measures Bros. v. Measures* [1910] 2 Ch. 248.

[5] *Berlitz, supra; Methven, Simpson & Co. v. Jones*, 1910, 2 S.L.T. 14.

[6] *Rodger v. Herbertson*, 1909 S.C. 256.

[7] *Watson v. Neuffert* (1863) 1 M. 1110; *Macintyre v. MacRaild* (1866) 4 M. 571; *Meikle v. M.* (1895) 3 S.L.T. 204; *Williams v. Fairbairn* (1899) 1 F. 944; *Dumbarton Steamboat Co. v. MacFarlane* (1899) 1 F. 993; *Stewart v. S.* (1899) 1 F. 1158; *Lyddon v. Thomas* (1901) 17 T.L.R. 450; *Ballachulish Slate Quarries v. Grant* (1903) 5 F. 1105; *Berlitz School v. Duchene* (1903) 6 F. 181; *Mulvein v. Murray*, 1908 S.C. 528; *Mason v. Provident Clothing Co.* [1913] A.C. 724; *Morris v. Saxelby* [1916] 1 A.C. 688; *Forster v. Suggett* (1918) 35 T.L.R. 87; *Fitch v. Dewes* [1921] 2 A.C. 158; *Taylor v. Campbell*, 1926 S.L.T. 260; *Scottish Farmers Dairy Co. v. McGhee*, 1933 S.C. 148.

[8] e.g. *Mason v. Provident Clothing Co.* [1913] A.C. 724; *Remington Typewriter Co. v. Sim*, 1915, 1 S.L.T. 168; *Fitch, supra; Pratt v. Maclean*, 1927 S.N. 161.

[9] The main instance is *Wyatt v. Kreglinger and Fernau* [1933] 1 K.B. 793.

[10] *Trego v. Hunt* [1896] A.C. 7.

[11] *Brodie v. Aitken*, 1927 S.N. 101; *Barr v. Lions*, 1956 S.C. 59.

been upheld[1] but in other cases restrictions over much smaller areas have been held invalid as too wide.[2] A restriction for the rest of the covenantor's life has been upheld[3] but normally only a restriction for a much shorter period will be held reasonable and enforceable.[4] The restriction must be reasonable as between the parties and the interests of the public, but the latter factor is rarely material. The same considerations apply to restrictions on a partner after quitting the partnership.[5]

(c) Contract restricting freedom of trade

At common law manufacturers or traders might enter into joint agreements to regulate production, quotas, marketing, standards and prices of their products. Such agreements also were at common law *prima facie* void,[6] but might be upheld if deemed reasonable as between the parties and in the public interest.[7] If freely entered into such a restraint was rarely deemed unreasonable as between the parties.[8]

The Restrictive Trade Practices Act, 1956, provides for the compulsory registration of most such agreements and their consideration by the Restrictive Practices Court, which may prohibit those deemed contrary to the public interest (there being a statutory presumption to that effect),[9] though parties may satisfiy the Court on specified grounds that their agreement is in the circumstances not contrary to the public interest.[9] Any agreements not covered by this Act remain subject to the common law principles.[10]

The Resale Prices Act, 1964, invalidates any term in a contract between a supplier and a dealer providing for the maintenance of

---

[1] *Nordenfelt, supra*; cf. *Leather Cloth Co.* v. *Lorsont* (1869) L.R. 9 Eq. 345; *Connors Bros. Ltd.* v. *Connors* [1940] 4 All E.R. 179.

[2] *Dumbarton Steamboat Co.* v. *MacFarlane* (1899) 1 F. 993; *British Workman's Assce. Co.* v. *Wilkinson* (1900) 8 S.L.T. 67.

[3] *Elves* v. *Crofts* (1850) 10 C.B. 241.

[4] e.g. *Stalker* v. *Carmichael* (1735) Mor. 9455; *Meikle* v. *M.* (1895) 33 S.L.R. 362; *Rodger* v. *Herbertson*, 1909 S.C. 256.

[5] *Whitehill* v. *Bradford* [1952] Ch. 236.

[6] *McEllistrim* v. *Ballymacelligot Co operative Socy.* [1919] A.C. 548; *Evans* v. *Heathcote* [1918] 1 K.B. 418.

[7] *N.W. Salt & Co.* v. *Electrolytic Alkali Co.* [1914] A.C. 461; *English Hop Growers, Ltd.* v. *Dering* [1928] 2 K.B. 174.

[8] *English Hop Growers, Ltd., supra.*

[9] 1956 Act, S. 21.

[10] *Kores Mfg. Co.* v. *Kolok Mfg. Co. Ltd.* [1959] Ch. 108.

minimum resale prices for the goods. In all other respects the contract is unaffected.[1]

(d) Restraint by manufacturer on distributor

The same principle applies to restrictions imposed by a manufacturer or importer on a distributor, binding him, in return for favourable terms of trade, to sell only that manufacturer's products.[2] Similar considerations may apply where such a restriction is a part of a contract of sale of or security over the subjects in which the distributor carries on his business.[3]

(e) Other cases

Restrictive conditions may arise in cases other than the four main groups, such as a restriction on a borrower from competing in business with the lender,[4] or on a proprietor letting a shop to compete with an existing tenant,[5] or on a professional football player's transfer,[6] or on the regulation of the trading activities of members of a profession.[7] At common law the activities of trade unions were void as in restraint of trade, but they have been legalized by statute.[8] The categories of restraint of trade are not closed, but must expand to take account of new methods of trade.[9]

Interpretation and enforcement of contracts in restraint of liberty

The validity of such contracts is normally challenged and determined in proceedings for interdict against conduct infringing the restriction. If the validity of the restriction is doubtful the court will prefer the interpretation which makes the contract valid and enforceable,[10] but will not permit evasion of the restriction by

---

[1] S. 1. Certain classes of goods may be exempted: Ss. 5–8.

[2] *Petrofina (G.B.) Ltd.* v. *Martin* [1966] Ch. 146; *Regent Oil Co.* v. *Leavesley* [1966] 2 All E.R. 454; *Esso* v. *Harper's Garage* [1967] 1 All E.R. 699.

[3] *Macintyre* v. *Cleveland Petroleum Co.*, 1967 S.L.T. (Notes) 14.

[4] *Stewart* v. *S.* (1899) 1 F. 1158. See also *Brown* v. *Muir* (1737) Mor. 9464.

[5] *Randall* v. *Summers*, 1919 S.C. 396.

[6] *Eastham* v. *Newcastle United F.C.* [1964] Ch. 413.

[7] *Pharmaceutical Socy.* v. *Dickson* [1970] A.C. 403.

[8] Trade Union Act, 1871, S. 3 (now Trade Union and Labour Relations Act, 1974, S. 2(5); *Russell* v. *Amalgamated Carpenters* [1912] A.C. 421.

[9] *Petrofina, supra*, 131, instancing cases where a tradesman agrees to limit his mode of trade, such as to execute orders for one person only: *Collins* v. *Locke* (1879) 4 App. Cas. 674; or to make one particular kind of machine only: *Jones* v. *Lees* (1856) 1 H. & N. 189. In *B.M.T.A.* v. *Gray*, 1951 S.C. 586, an agreement between an association of motor dealers and a dealer restricting dealings in motor vehicles during a shortage was held not to be in restraint of trade.

[10] *Watson* v. *Neuffert* (1863) 1 M. 1110; but see *Mulvein* v. *Murray*, 1908 S.C. 528.

a narrow reading of its terms.[1] If the restrictive undertaking is too vague it is unenforceable.[2]

(ii) CONTRACTS DECLARED ILLEGAL OR VOID BY STATUTE

Statute may, expressly or impliedly, declare any kind of contract to be illegal, null, void, prohibited, or subject to penalty. The terminology varies. Thus statutes have declared a contract which contravenes the Act in question to be illegal, null and void,[3] or wholly null and void,[4] or, if not satisfying the section of the Act, to have no effect,[5] or to be illegal in part only,[6] or void in part only,[7] or made it unlawful, and participation an offence,[8] or made contracting a criminal offence, save under conditions, such as obtaining a licence,[9] or made contracting a criminal offence without affecting the validity of the contract,[10] or prohibited certain practices, without directly saying anything as to the validity of the transaction itself.[11] The effect of the particular statute on a contract is always a question of interpretation. A contract declared null, or void, or null and void, is wholly ineffective legally. A contract declared illegal is normally also wholly ineffective. A contract declared criminal, or prohibited, or subject to penalty, is normally deemed thereby impliedly made illegal and void,[12] but it may be that the penalty is imposed merely to deter or to protect the revenue,[13] and does not avoid the contract, and a contract may subject to criminal penalties, but expressly without effect on its civil validity.[14] If the contract is merely declared unenforceable it is valid and effective but cannot be enforced by any legal process.[15]

---

[1] *Williams* v. *Fairbairn* (1899) 1 F. 944.

[2] *British Workman's and General Assce. Co.* v. *Wilkinson* (1900) 8 S.L.T. 67.

[3] e.g. Truck Act, 1831, S. 2; *Duncan* v. *Motherwell Bridge Co.*, 1952 S.C. 131.

[4] e.g. Life Assurance Act, 1774, S. 1; cf. *Hadden* v. *Bryden* (1899) 1 F. 710; Banking Companies (Shares) Act, 1867, S. 1 (Leeman's Act) (repealed); *Mitchell* v. *City of Glasgow Bank* (1878) 6 R. 420; 6 R. (H.L.) 66.

[5] Mercantile Law Amdt. (Sc.) Act, 1856, S. 6.

[6] e.g. Moneylenders Act, 1927, S. 7 (illegal so far as providing for compound interest); *Malcolm Muir, Ltd.* v. *Jamieson*, 1947 S.C. 314.

[7] e.g. Resale Prices Act, 1964, S. 1 (void so far as contract purports to establish minimum prices).

[8] Betting and Lotteries Act, 1934, Ss. 21, 22; *Clayton* v. *C.*, 1937 S.C. 619.

[9] e.g. *Eisen* v. *McCabe*, 1930 S.C. (H.L.) 146; *Jamieson* v. *Watt's Tr.*, 1950 S.C. 265; c.f. *Designers & Decorators (Sc.)* v. *Ellis*, 1957 S.C. (H.L.) 69.

[10] e.g. Road Traffic Act, 1972, S. 60; cf. *Mair* v. *Chalmers* (1948) 64 Sh. Ct. Rep. 221. *Smith* v. *Nugent*, 1955 S.L.T. (Sh. Ct.) 60 is overruled by the 1972 Act.

[11] Mock Auctions Act, 1961, S. 1; see also S. 3(6).

[12] Bell, *Prin.* §36; *Re Mahmoud and Ispahani* [1921] 2 K.B. 716; *Anderson* v. *Daniel* [1924] 1 K.B. 138; *Bostel Bros. Ltd.* v. *Hurlock* [1949] 1 K.B. 74.

[13] *Learoyd* v. *Bracken* [1894] 1 Q.B. 114.

[14] Road Traffic Act, 1972, S. 60, overruling *Smith* v. *Nugent*, 1955 S.L.T. (Sh. Ct.) 60; cf. *Mair* v. *Chalmers* (1948) 64 Sh. Ct. Rep. 221.   [15] See *infra*.

A contract is not, however, necessarily affected merely because one party, in the course of performing a lawful contract, infringes the criminal law, as by overloading a ship.[1] But the statute may prohibit the contract as performed, rendering the whole transaction illegal.[2]

Contracts declared wholly or partly void by statute include those providing for restrictions on the spending of, or for prohibited deductions from, earnings;[3] provisions in contracts for the sale of articles outright, or by instalment payments, or on hire-purchase, whereby any party to the contract prorogates the jurisdiction of a particular sheriff court;[4] agreements by an incoming tenant to pay compensation due to the outgoing tenant of an agricultural holding;[5] assignments of, charges on, and agreements to assign or charge military or air force pay, pensions or allowances;[6] contracts by crofters relinquishing statutory rights;[7] contracts restricting liability for death or injury to persons in public service vehicles;[8] contracts so far as purporting to fix minimum prices for resale;[9] statutes also frequently declare void any contract, or provision in a contract, excluding or limiting the effect of the statute.[10]

Contracts expressly or impliedly declared illegal by statute include insuring the life of a person while having no insurable interest in the life;[11] corruptly inducing or procuring any person to withdraw from being a candidate at an election;[12] those for the import into or export from the United Kingdom, or sale or distribution of certain dangerous drugs;[13] the sale of goods not complying with regulations imposing safety requirements;[14] the sale of goods so far as subject to a condition purporting to fix a minimum resale price therefor.[15]

By the Land Purchase Act, 1594,[16] no member of the College of

---

[1] St. John Shipping Corpn. v. Rank [1957] 1 Q.B. 267; Archbolds (Freightage) Ltd. v. Spanglett Ltd., [1961] 1 Q.B. 374.

[2] Anderson v. Daniel [1924] 1 K.B. 138; B. & B. Viennese Fashions v. Losane [1952] 1 All E.R. 909.

[3] Truck Acts, 1831, 1887, 1896 and 1940.

[4] Law Reform (Misc. Prov.) (Sc.) Act, 1940, S. 4.

[5] Agricultural Holdings (Sc.) Act, 1949, S. 11.

[6] Army Act, 1955, S. 203; Air Force Act, 1955, S. 203.

[7] Crofters (Scotland) Act, 1955, S. 3(4).

[8] Road Traffic Act, 1960, S. 151.   [9] Resale Prices Act, 1964, S. 1.

[10] e.g. Trading Stamps Act, 1964, S. 3.

[11] Life Assurance Act, 1774; Hadden v. Bryden (1899) 1 F. 710; Harse v. Pearl Life Assce. Co. [1904] 1 K.B. 558.

[12] Representation of the People Act, 1949, S. 92.

[13] Dangerous Drugs Act, 1951.   [14] Consumer Protection Act, 1961, S. 2.

[15] Resale Prices Act, 1964, S. 1.   [16] 1594, c. 26.

Justice or inferior court may purchase heritage while it is subject of a pending case. The contract is not null, but the purchaser is deprived of the lands. This has been extended by construction to all matters in pending cases.[1] But security for expenses may be taken over the subject of the cause.[2]

It is an offence to use for trade any unit of measurement other than those authorized by statute,[3] and contracts doing so are null,[4] but contracts utilizing other measures have been held not wholly to preclude claims for the value of goods sold.[5]

The fact that statute renders a contract void or unenforceable does not necessarily avoid all claims between the parties. Thus where goods were supplied under a contract null and void as contravening a statute providing for measurement by imperial standards, a claim for recompense for the value of the goods was competent,[6] and where a contract was illegal, null and void a counter-claim for recompense was competent.[7]

Consequences of illegal transactions

Where individuals have entered into what the law deems to be *pactum illicitum*, it is void and no action will lie for enforcement or breach of a party's obligation:[8] *ex turpi causa non oritur actio*. The taint of illegality extends to avoiding a subsequent security for the payment of money due under an illegal contract,[9] and to avoiding a claim alternative to the claim vitiated by illegality.[10]

In general also money paid or property transferred under an illegal agreement is irrecoverable: *in turpi causa melior est conditio possidentis*.[11] Thus a loan by an unregistered moneylender is irrecoverable.[12] But where the parties are not *in pari delicto* the less

[1] Ersk. II, 3, 16; Bell, *Prin.* §36(1); *Purves* v. *Keith* (1683) Mor. 9500; *Home* v. *E. Home* (1713) Mor. 9502. The Act does not strike at third parties.

[2] *Forbes* v. *Blair* (1774) 5 B.S. 530.

[3] Weights and Measures Act, 1963, S. 10.

[4] *McDade* v. *Henshilwood* (1868) 5 S.L.R. 539; contrast *Henderson* v. *Davidson* (1871) 8 S.L.R. 633; *Lang* v. *Cameron* (1894) 21 R. 337.

[5] *Cuthbertson* v. *Lowes* (1870) 8 M. 1073.

[6] *Cuthbertson, supra.*

[7] *Duncan* v. *Motherwell Bridge Co.*, 1952 S.C. 31.

[8] *Bruce* v. *Grant* (1839) 1 D. 583; *Stewart* v. *Gibson* (1840) 1 Rob. 260; *Alexander* v. *McGregor* (1845) 7 D. 915; *Handyside* v. *Pringle and McDougal* (1863) 1 M. 1154; *Duncan* v. *Motherwell Bridge Co.*, 1952 S.C. 131.

[9] Bell, *Prin.* §35; *Strachan* v. *Graham* (1823) 2 S. 391; *Russell* v. *Liston's Trs.* (1844) 6 D. 1138.

[10] *Bolden* v. *Fogo* (1850) 12 D. 798.

[11] Bell, *Prin.* §35; *Fraser* v. *Hill* (1852) 14 D. 335; *A.B.* v. *C.D.*, 1912, 1 S.L.T. 44; cf. *Cuthbertson* v. *Lowes* (1870) 8 M. 1073.

[12] *Shaw* v. *Duffy*, 1943 S.C. 350; *Premor* v. *Shaw* [1964] 2 All E.R. 583.

culpable may be permitted to recover property transferred;[1] so too where the transaction is statutorily prohibited for the protection of a particular class of persons.[2] So too if one party is innocently a party to an unlawful contract he may probably obtain restitution or repetition on equitable grounds though the contract has been performed.[3] But if unperformed he must not perform and if he does can neither recover payment or restitution.[4] Where, however, an unlawful part can be severed from a lawful part of a contract, the lawful can be enforced without taint from the unlawful.[5] The fact that a contract of employment was illegal has been held not to exclude a claim founded on delict for injuries arising therefrom.[6] Though a contract is avoided by statute, or rendered unenforceable, a claim founded on recompense in respect of a collateral transaction may be competent.[7] An innocent party to such a contract cannot be held barred from objecting to the contract by acquiescence or ratification, the contract being incapable of ratification.[8]

UNENFORCEABLE CONTRACTS

Some contracts, though not *pacta illicita*, are by common law or statute unenforceable, in which case no action will lie for specific implement, nor for damages for non-implement. But if performance or payment is made under such a contract, it cannot be sought back as paid unjustifiably, as it was due in equity.

Contracts unenforceable (though not void) by common law

This category includes some contracts with persons not having full contractual capacity, such as minors;[9] contracts validly constituted but of which the evidence requisite for enforcement is lacking;[10] and contracts imperfectly constituted, such as those requiring but lacking constitution by probative writing.[11]

---

[1] *Arrol* v. *Montgomery* (1826) 4 S. 499; *MacFarlane* v. *Nicoll* (1864) 3 M. 237; *Harse* v. *Pearl Life Assce. Co.* [1904] 1 K.B. 558; *McCarroll* v. *Maguire*, 1920, 2 S.L.T. 220; *Bigos* v. *Boustead* [1951] 1 All E.R. 92.
[2] *Phillips* v. *Blackhurst*, 1912, 2 S.L.T. 254.
[3] Bell, *Prin.* §35; *McCarroll* v. *Maguire*, 1920, 2 S.L.T. 220.
[4] *Hamilton* v. *De Gares* (1756) Mor. 947; *Hamilton* v. *Main* (1823) 2 S. 356.
[5] cf. *Farmers' Mart.* v. *Milne*, 1914 S.C. (H.L.) 84, 87.
[6] *Richardson* v. *Beattie*, 1923 S.L.T. 440.
[7] *Duncan* v. *Motherwell Bridge Co.*, 1952 S.C. 131.
[8] *Penman* v. *Fife Coal Co.*, 1935 S.C. (H.L.) 39.
[9] Ch. 15, *supra*.
[10] e.g. contracts requiring proof by writ or oath: Ch. 32, *infra*.
[11] Ch. 32, *infra*.

Contracts declared unenforceable by statute

Contracts declared unenforceable by statute include contracts by firms which have failed to comply with the Registration of Business Names Act, 1916;[1] and contracts by unregistered medical practitioners.[2]

SPONSIONES LUDICRAE : BETTING AND GAMING TRANSACTIONS

Sponsiones ludicrae are transactions deemed unworthy to occupy judicial time and therefore legally unenforceable, though not necessarily illegal or void.[3] The most important category are betting and gaming transactions, including football pools,[4] where money becomes payable according to the outcome of an uncertain event. Bets and wagers are probably also illegal at common law and therefore unenforceable,[5] irrespective of whether the contest on which the bet is placed is lawful or not.[6]

The courts will accordingly not entertain questions of the result of a race,[7] enforce payment of a bet,[8] nor assist recovery of money lost even if it be alleged the play was unfair,[9] and may take judicial notice of the fact that a claim is based on a wager or competition.[10] Even if betting debts are admitted, payment is legally unenforceable,[11] and a supervening contract to pay winnings is equally unenforceable.[11]

But collateral transactions connected with gaming are not rendered unenforceable. Thus the winner of a bet may recover from a stakeholder the prize in a contest of skill, prowess or merit

---

[1] S. 8; *Daniel* v. *Rogers* [1918] 2 K.B. 228; *Watson* v. *Park Royal (Caterers) Ltd.* [1961] 2 All E.R. 346.

[2] Medical Act, 1956, S. 27.

[3] See Kames, *Equity*, 22; Bell, *Comm.* I, 320; *Prin.* §37; *Wordsworth* v. *Pettigrew* (1709) Mor. 9524; *Stewart* v. *E. Dundonald* (1753) Mor. 9514; *Calder* v. *Stevens* (1871) 9 M. 1074, 1077; *Kelly* v. *Murphy*, 1940 S.C. 96.

[4] *Wilson* v. *Murphy*, 1936 S.L.T. 564; *Kelly, supra*.

[5] Bell, *Comm.* I, 319; *Prin.* §37; *Bruce* v. *Ross* (1788) 3 Pat. 107; *Wordsworth* v. *Pettigrew* (1709) Mor. 9524; *Cumming Gordon* v. *Campbell* (1804) Mor. App. *Pactum Illicitum*, 3; *Graham* v. *Pollok* (1848) 10 D. 646; *O'Connell* v. *Russell* (1864) 3 M. 89, 94; *Calder* v. *Stevens* (1871) 9 M. 1076; *Robertson* v. *Balfour.* 1938 S.C. 207.

[6] The courts have repeatedly recognized the legality of horse-racing and other sports. If the contest on which the bets are placed is illegal, e.g. cock-fighting, the gambling is all the more illegal.

[7] *Graham, supra*; *O'Connell, supra*; *Calder* v. *Stevens* (1871) 9 M. 1074. cf. *Wilson* v. *Murphy*, 1936 S.L.T. 564.

[8] *Wordsworth, supra*; *Gordon* v. *Campbell* (1804) Mor. App. *Pactum Illicitum*, 3.

[9] *Paterson* v. *Macqueen* (1866) 4 M. 602.

[10] *Paterson, supra*; *Hamilton* v. *McLauchlan* (1908) 16 S.L.T. 341.

[11] *Robertson* v. *Balfour*, 1938 S.C. 207.

if the result of the event is undisputed;[1] an agent for a gambler may recover money paid on the latter's behalf;[2] money lent to pay gambling losses is recoverable;[3] the purchase of gaming chips is enforceable[4] and a joint adventure for gaming purposes may be investigated.[5] But a supervening contract to accept partial payment of a gambling debt and not press for full payment till later is subsidiary to the original wagering contract, still tainted by it, and unenforceable.[6]

It is a question of fact whether a contract for the sale or purchase of shares or goods is a genuine transaction, in which parties are bound to give and take delivery, or a mere speculation on the movement of the market price. If the latter, it is unenforceable as a wager.[7]

Lotteries are not illegal at common law.[8] The Betting, Gaming and Lotteries Act, 1963, declares all lotteries unlawful except small lotteries incidental to certain entertainments, subject to conditions, private lotteries, where the sale of tickets is confined to members of one society, persons all working or residing on the same premises, subject to conditions, and lotteries of Art Unions.[9] No action lies to recover a subject won in an unlawful lottery.[10] Participation by persons in Scotland in a lottery abroad is not unlawful, and the courts may give effect to collateral and consequential transactions, such as a contract to share equally the proceeds of a lottery ticket bought by one for others.[11]

Statutes relative to gaming

By the Gaming Act, 1710, S. 1, all notes, bills, bonds, judgments, mortgages or other securities or conveyances whatsoever

[1] *Graham* v. *Pollok* (1848) 10 D. 646; *O'Connell* v. *Russell* (1864) 3 M. 89; *Calder* v. *Stevens* (1871) 9 M. 1074; *Knight* v. *Stott* (1892) 19 R. 959; *Kelly* v. *Murphy*, 1940 S.C. 96.
[2] *Foulds* v. *Thomson* (1857) 19 D. 803; *Risk* v. *Auld & Guild* (1881) 8 R. 729; *Gillies* v. *McLean* (1885) 13 R. 12; *Maffett* v. *Stewart* (1887) 14 R. 506; *Knight* v. *Stott* (1892) 19 R. 959; *Levy* v. *Jackson* (1903) 5 F. 1170.
[3] *Hopkins* v. *Baird*, 1920, 2 S.L.T. 94.
[4] *Cumming* v. *Mackie*, 1973 S.L.T. 242.
[5] *Mollison* v. *Noltie* (1889) 16 R. 350.
[6] *Robertson* v. *Balfour*, 1938 S.C. 207.
[7] Bell, *Prin.* §37; *Foulds* v. *Thomson* (1857) 19 D. 803; *Risk* v. *Auld & Guild* (1887) 8 R. 729; *Newton* v. *Cribbes* (1884) 11 R. 554; *Gillies* v. *McLean* (1885) 13 R. 12; *Heimann* v. *Hardie & Co.* (1885) 12 R. 406; *Maffett* v. *Stewart* (1887) 14 R. 506; *Mollison* v. *Noltie* (1889) 16 R. 350; *Shaw* v. *Caledonian Ry.* (1890) 17 R. 466; *Universal Stock Exchange Co.* v. *Howat* (1891) 19 R. 128; *Mole* v. *Turner, Lupton & Co.* (1894) 2 S.L.T. 352; *Symonds* v. *Davis* (1899) 7 S.L.T. 291; *Johnston* v. *Gordon* (1899) 7 S.L.T. 294.
[8] *Clayton* v. *C.*, 1937 S.C. 619.
[9] Ss. 41–5, amd. Gaming Act, 1968, S. 53.
[10] *Christison* v. *McBride* (1881) 9 R. 34.
[11] *Clayton, supra.*

granted as consideration for money won by gaming or playing at cards, dice, tables, tennis, bowls or other game or games whatsoever or by betting on the hands of those who game or for the reimbursement of money knowingly lent or advanced for such gaming or betting, shall be utterly void and of no effect for any purpose. Hence a bond for money lost could not be enforced even against a *bona fide* assignee, though he might recover from the assignor on the basis of implied warrandice *debitum subesse*.[1] The Gaming Act, 1835, S. 1, however, provides that securities within the 1710 Act given for considerations arising from illegal transactions are not to be void, but be taken to have been given for an illegal consideration. Hence a security originally given for a gaming debt is enforceable by a subsequent *bona fide* assignee for value.[2] An I.O.U. can be founded on though the money was lent to make or pay bets.[3] It has been held in England, however, that the combined effect of the 1710 and 1835 Acts was to avoid all loans where the money lent is to be used, to the lender's knowledge, in playing or betting on games.[4] It has been held that the Gaming Acts 1845 and 1892 do not apply to Scotland.[5]

The Betting, Gaming and Lotteries Act, 1963, regulates licensed betting shops, legalizes gambling subject to statutory conditions, and makes all lotteries illegal, with certain exceptions. But though betting and gaming are in many cases no longer criminal, a contract connected therewith is still *sponsio ludicra*.[6]

CONSIDERATION—GRATUITOUS CONTRACTS

Scots law does not require, as a prerequisite of the validity or enforceability of an agreement or contract, that the promisee should have given any consideration for the promise, or *quid pro quo* for what is being done or given or promised to him under the agreement. Hence a consensural agreement is enforceable though gratuitous; if the promisee or offeree has accepted the promise or offer there is a contract just as much as if he had agreed to do or

---

[1] *Ferrier* v. *Graham's Trs.* (1828) 6 S. 818. See also *Cumming* v. *Mackie*, 1973.

[2] *Woolf* v. *Hamilton* [1898] 2 Q.B. 337.

[3] *Hopkins* v. *Baird*, 1920, 2 S.L.T. 94.

[4] *Carlton Hotel Club* v. *Lawrence* (1929) 2 K.B. 153.

[5] *Russell* v. *Grey* (1894) 1 S.L.T. 529; *Levy* v. *Jackson* (1903) 5 F. 1170; *Robertson* v. *Balfour*, 1938 S.C. 207; *Kelly* v. *Murphy*, 1940 S.C. 96.

[6] *MacAffer* v. *Scott*, 1963 S.L.T. (Sh. Ct.) 39; *Johnston* v. *Archibald*, 1966 S.L.T. (Sh. Ct.) 8.

pay something in return.[1] Such an agreement may be difficult to distinguish from a unilateral voluntary undertaking;[2] but while such a unilateral undertaking cannot be enforced against the beneficiary, a bilateral agreement is so enforceable, as the other party has accepted, and must accept performance, even though he is not bound to do anything else.[3] Also a unilateral promise can be revoked, but an accepted offer cannot be, even though gratuitous.

A contract may still be gratuitous though one party can only accept by undertaking to implement the conditions of the offer, the quality of the contract as onerous or gratuitous being fixed while matters are entire.[4]

A gratuitous bilateral contract must, like a unilateral voluntary undertaking, be proved by the writ or admission on oath of the person sought to be made liable.[5]

In cases of error, the courts have been more ready to set aside a contract if gratuitous than if onerous[6] and serious inadequacy of consideration may be an element in determining whether or not a contract was affected by fraud, undue influence, facility or other vitiating factor.[7]

IMPLIED CONTRACTS

Apart from contracts created by express offer and acceptance or by actings yielding an inference of such agreement, a contract may be held implied from the actings of parties.[8] It is only in the clearest cases, however, that a court will hold that parties neither of whom has contracted expressly must be held to have bound themselves to a similar effect by mere conduct.[9] Thus a person working for a relative is not entitled to wages in the absence of express contract.[10] An agent who contracts as such with a third party is held impliedly to undertake or warrant that he had

---

[1] Stair I, 10, 12; Bell, *Prin.* §63–4. *Morton's Trs.* v. *Aged Christian Friend Socy.* (1899) 2 F. 82.

[2] cf. *Paterson* v. *Highland Ry.*, 1927 S.C. (H.L.) 32.

[3] Contrary dictum in *Douglas Hamilton* v. *Hamilton's Trs.*, 1961 S.C. 205, is unsound.

[4] *Hawick Heritable Inv. Bank* v. *Huggan* (1902) 5 F. 75.

[5] *Edmondston* v. *E.* (1861) 23 D. 995; *Hawick Heritable Inv. Bank* v. *Huggan* (1902) 5 F. 75, 78.

[6] *McConechy* v. *McIndoe* (1853) 16 D. 315; *Purdon* v. *Rowat's Trs.* (1856) 19 D. 206; *McLaurin* v. *Stafford* (1875) 3 R. 265; *McCaig* v. *Glasgow University* (1904) 6 F. 918; *Macandrew* v. *Gilhooley*, 1911 S.C. 448; *Sinclair* v. *S.*, 1964 S.L.T. (Notes) 16.

[7] Ch. 33, *infra.*

[8] *Clarke* v. *Dunraven* [1897] A.C. 59.

[9] *Houldsworth* v. *Wishaw* (1887) 14 R. 920, 927; *Mackison* v. *Dundee*, 1910 S.C. (H.L.) 27.

[10] *Miller* v. *M.* (1898) 25 R. 995; *Urquhart* v. *U's Tr.* (1906) 8 F. 42; *Russel* v. *McClymont* (1906) 8 F. 821.

authority to do so and, if the contract fails by reason of his lack of authority, he is liable to the other contracting party, as being in breach of his implied undertaking, for loss caused by his breach of contract.[1] Again a person who consults a practitioner of any profession on a matter within the scope of his professional practice impliedly employs him professionally, unless the circumstances indicate that it was merely obtaining information on the basis of friendship.[2] An agent of a friendly society may not, after leaving the post, give lists of members to a rival society.[3] Where an employer used a process patented by an employee, there was held to be an implied contract to pay for the use of the process.[4] A notice on a receipt for goods delivered for processing that goods were covered by insurance was held to constitute a contract so to insure.[5] Implied contracts also arise where parties continue in contractual relations after notice to terminate their express contract though required, has not been given, or where notice is not requisite, as in a contract for a fixed term. This implied contract may, in cases of tacit relocation,[6] be a renewal of the old contract,[7] or a renewal subject to modification[8] but in other cases it is a contract on the terms·which the law would imply in a contract of that kind, independent of what may have been the terms of the former contract.[9] It may be a narrow question whether a claim to be reimbursed lies on implied contract, or for recompense on the basis of quasi-contract.[10] In the former case the duty to pay is imposed by facts implying a contract; in the latter it is imposed by law, implying an obligation to reward for the avoidance of unjust benefit.

CANCELLATION

Once a contract has been validly constituted and any necessary formalities[11] compiled with, both parties are bound and

[1] *Collen* v. *Wright* (1857) 8 E. & B. 647; *Re National Coffee Palace Co.* (1883) 24 Ch. D. 367; *Firbank's Exors.* v. *Humphreys* (1886) 18 Q.B.D. 54; *Anderson* v. *Croall* (1903) 6 F. 153; *Salvesen* v. *Rederi A/B Nordsjernan* (1905) 7 F. (H.L.) 101; *Yonge* v. *Toynbee* [1910] 1 K.B. 215.

[2] cf. *Cappon* v. *L.A.*, 1920, 1 S.L.T. 261.

[3] *Liverpool Victoria Friendly Socy.* v. *Houston* (1900) 3 F. 42.

[4] *Mellor* v. *Beardmore*, 1927 S.C. 597.

[5] *Cochran* v. *Leckie's Tr.* (1906) 8 F. 975.

[6] Chs. 37, 85, *infra.*

[7] *Neilson* v. *Mossend Iron Co.* (1886) 13 R. (H.L.) 50; *Wallace* v. *W's Trs.* (1906) 8 F. 558; *McGown* v. *Henderson*, 1914 S.C. 839; Partnership Act, 1890, S. 27.

[8] *McFarlane* v. *Mitchell* (1900) 2 F. 901.

[9] *Lennox* v. *Allen* (1880) 8 R. 38, 40; *Stanley* v. *Hanway*, 1911, 2 S.L.T. 2.

[10] Chap. 53, *infra.*   [11] Chap. 32, *infra.*

neither party may resile or withdraw from, nor cancel, the contract, save by agreement with the other party on such terms as may be agreed. But in certain cases[1] statute confers a right of cancellation within a prescribed period.

[1] e.g. hire-purchase contracts.

CHAPTER 32

FORMAL VALIDITY—
FORMALITIES AND PROOF OF CONTRACT

General principle

IN considering formalities it is essential to distinguish between any formalities required to create or constitute a contract, without which it is a nullity, formalities required to evidence a contract, without which it exists but is legally unenforceable,[1] and formalities required to execute or give effect to the contract. The first two kinds are intimately connected whereas the third is concerned with proprietary consequences of contract. In general a contract may be constituted by any means whereby agreement can be reached, orally, by writing, or by conduct implying agreement, and, if disputed, the fact of agreement, and the nature and terms thereof, may be proved by any kind of evidence.[2] To this general principle there are several classes of exceptions.

Contract in fact reduced to writing

If the parties, though not obliged by law in the circumstances to do so, in fact reduce their agreement to writing to have a record of its terms and to prevent disputes,[3] that writing probably does not require to be in any particular form or in any way authenticated. It is then part of the evidence as to the contract.[4] If on the other hand the parties, though not obliged in the circumstances by law to constitute their agreement in writing, have elected to do so with the intention of superseding thereby their prior oral agreement, this writing must be holograph or authenticated.[5] Into which class a case falls depends upon the intention of the parties, not solely upon the terms of the writing.

Transactions in re mercatoria

Moreover, if the transaction falls within the category of contracts *in re mercatoria*, any writing made, whether necessary or not, agreed to be made or not, may be informal both as to form,

---

[1] *Paterson v. P.* (1897) 25 R. 144, 150, 164, 173, 183, 191.
[2] Stair III, 2, 7; IV, 43, 4; Ersk. III, 2, 1; *Taylor v. Nisbet* (1901) 4 F. 79; *McConnachie v. Geddes*, 1918 S.C. 391, 398.
[3] e.g. *Ireland v. Rosewell Coal Co.* (1900) 7 S.L.T. 445.
[4] *Stuart v. Potter, Choate & Prentice*, 1911, S.L.T. 377.
[5] Ersk. III, 2, 6; Bell, *Prin.* §18; *Paterson, supra,* 168, 183.

contents, and execution, and the rules as to authentication have no application. Common law has settled that, for the convenience of business, contracts *in re mercatoria* are binding though not solemnly authenticated unless the signature be challenged.[1] They may be merely signed, initialled, signed by agent or facsimile signature, and may be proved *prout de jure*. They also prove their own dates.[2] Documents *in re mercatoria* include[2] all the variety of engagements or mandates or acknowledgements which the infinite occasions of trade may require, including bills of exchange, promissory notes and cheques, orders for goods, mandates and procurations, guarantees, offers and acceptances to sell or buy merchandise, or transport it from place to place, and in general all the variety of engagements or mandates or acknowledgements which the infinite occasions of trade may require.[3] The privileges of such writings are that, though not holograph, witnesses are not necessary to prove their authenticity, nor to prove the date, and even subscription by initials or a mere mark, if it be proved or admitted to be genuine, and to be the accustomed mode of the person transacting business, is sufficient.[4]

Exception I: contracts requiring expression in writing

In certain cases statute, while not requiring the contracts in question to be constituted in any form, requires them to be expressed in writing, and usually also to be signed by the granter, though not necessarily solemnly authenticated. The main instances are:

(a) All guarantees, securities or cautionary obligations made or granted by any person for any other person, and all representations and assurances as to the character, conduct, credit, ability, trade or dealings of any person, made or granted to the effect or for the purpose of enabling such person to obtain credit, money, goods or postponement of payment of debt, or of any other obligation demandable from him, shall be in writing and subscribed by the person undertaking or representing, or by some person duly authorized by him or them, otherwise the same shall have no

---

[1] Stair IV, 43, 3; Ersk. III, 2, 10 and 24–5; Bell, *Comm.* I, 342.

[2] Bell, *Comm.*, I, 342.

[3] The category includes also the hiring of advertising space: *U.K. Advertising Co.* v. *Glasgow BagWash Laundry*, 1926 S.C. 303; an obligation to take shares: *Beardmore* v. *Barry*, 1928 S.C. 101; agreement to buy fittings in premises: *Kinninmont* v. *Paxton* (1893) 20 R. 128; award in a trade arbitration: *Dykes* v. *Roy* (1869) 7 M. 357; and business arbitrations: *Hope* v. *Crookston Bros.* (1890) 17 R. 868; *McLaren* v. *Aikman*, 1939 S.C. 222.

[4] Bell, *Comm.* I, 343.

effect.[1] No action accordingly lies on an oral representation, even though allegedly made fraudulently,[2] nor can an oral statement be founded on in defence to an action on an obligation induced by it.[3]

(b) Contracts with a pawnbroker in respect of pledges must be signed by or on behalf of the pawnbroker and signed by the pawner.[4]

(c) Agreements between employer and employee for certain permitted deductions from wages must be in writing and signed by the workman.[5]

(d) Bills of exchange, cheques and promissory notes must be expressed in writing;[6] an order or promise to pay money, not in writing, is valid, but cannot have any of the legal characteristics of a bill or note, such as negotiability.

(e) A contract of marine insurance is inadmissible in evidence unless embodied in a marine policy in accordance with the Marine Insurance Act, 1906,[7] and such a contract must, to be valid, be in writing,[8] and signed by or on behalf of each insurer.[9]

(f) Agreements between masters and seamen must be entered into in writing and signed.[10]

(g) Contracts with moneylenders for repayment or for interest are unenforceable unless a note or memorandum of the contract is made and signed personally by the borrower before the money is lent or security given.[11]

(h) Loans to persons in business when the rate of interest is to vary with profits or the lender is to receive a share of profits but does not wish to incur the liabilities of a partner must be in writing and signed by or on behalf of all the parties thereto.[12]

(j) The Memorandum and Articles of Association of a company must be in writing and signed by all the subscribers before one witness.[13]

---

[1] Mercantile Law Amendment (Sc.) Act, 1856, S. 6.

[2] *Clydesdale Bank* v. *Paton* (1896) 23 R. (H.L.) 22; *Irving* v. *Burns,* 1915 S.C. 260.

[3] *Union Bank* v. *Taylor,* 1925 S.C. 835.

[4] Consumer Credit Act, 1974, S. 61.

[5] Truck Acts, 1831, S. 23; 1896, Ss. 1–3; and 1940; *Pratt* v. *Cook, Son & Co. (St. Paul's) Ltd.* [1940] A.C. 437.

[6] Bills of Exchange Act, 1882, Ss. 3, 73, 83.

[7] S. 22. By S. 21 the contract is concluded when the proposal is accepted by the insurer, whether the policy be then issued or not.

[8] Stamp Act, 1891, S. 93(1).

[9] 1906 Act, S. 24.

[10] M.S.A., 1970, S. 1; *Moore* v. *City of Malines* (1947) 81 Ll.L. Rep. 96; an oral agreement is enforceable subject to penalties.

[11] Consumer Credit Act, 1974, S. 61.

[12] Partnership Act, 1890, S. 2(3)(d); *Pooley* v. *Driver* (1876) 5 Ch. D. 458.

[13] Companies Act, 1948, Ss. 1–3.

(k) A contract of hire-purchase, credit sale or conditional sale within the Consumer Credit Act, 1974, must be in writing and signed by the hirer or buyer and by or on behalf of all other parties to the agreement, otherwise it is unenforceable.[1] A contract of guarantee relating to such an agreement is unenforceable unless signed before two witnesses by the guarantor.[2]

Exception 2: Contracts requiring proof by writ or oath

Certain kinds of contracts may be entered into orally but must, if challenged, be proved only by the writ of the other party, or alternatively by the admission of the other party obtained on referring the case to his oath. Parole evidence is inadequate, and incompetent. The writ need not be in any set form, nor need it be holograph or attested,[3] and may be proved to be holograph of him by parole evidence.[4] It may be entries in the defender's business books,[5] unsigned jottings if admitted or proved to be holograph,[6] or the writ of an authorized agent,[7] or the writ of the pursuer received and retained by the defender and held constructively to have become his writ.[8] But any such holograph writing does not prove its own date.[9] An entry by a party's solicitor in his business books has been held not to be the writ of that party.[10]

Reference to oath[11] is initiated by minute referring to the opponent's oath the whole or part of a claim. The deponent is put on oath, or affirms, and is examined by counsel for the party referring; his own counsel may not cross-examine him but may suggest questions which the judge may put;[12] an admission by the

[1] Consumer Credit Act, 1974, S. 61.

[2] This does not require execution according to solemnities; it is not stated that the witnesses must sign. It might be competent to lead parole evidence that two witnesses did see the guarantor sign.

[3] *Paterson* v. *P.* (1897) 25 R. 144.

[4] *Christie's Trs.* v. *Muirhead* (1870) 8 M. 461; *Dunn's Tr.* v. *Hardy* (1890) 23 R. 621; *Borland* v. *Macdonald*, 1940 S.C. 124.

[5] *Thomson* v. *Lindsay* (1873) 1 R. 65; *McRae* v. *Williamson Bros.* (1877) 14 S.L.R. 562; *Muir* v. *Goldie's Trs.* (1898) 6 S.L.T. 188; *Hope* v. *Derwent Rolling Mills Co.* (1905) 7 F. 837; *Jackson* v. *Ogilvie's Exor.*, 1935 S.C. 154, 163.

[6] *Storeys* v. *Paxton* (1878) 6 R. 293; see also *Wink* v. *Speirs* (1868) 6 M. 657.

[7] *Bryan* v. *Butters Bros.* (1892) 19 R. 490; *Clark's Exrx.* v. *Brown*, 1935 S.C. 110; *Dryburgh* v. *Macpherson*, 1944 S.L.T. 116; *Fisher* v. *Fisher's Trs.*, 1952 S.C. 347.

[8] *Wood* v. *Howden* (1843) 5 D. 507; *Thomson* v. *Lindsay* (1873) 1 R. 65; *Rennie* v. *Urquhart* (1880) 7 R. 1030; *Campbell's Trs.* v. *Hudson's Exor.* (1895) 22 R. 943; *MacBain* v. *MacBain*, 1930 S.C. (H.L.) 72.

[9] *Purvis* v. *Dowie* (1869) 7 M. 764.   [10] *Fisher* v. *F.*, 1952 S.C. 347.

[11] See generally Bell, *Prin.* §2263-9; Walkers, *Evidence*, Ch. 25; *Pollok* v. *Whiteford* 1936 S.C. 402; *Hamilton* v. *H's Exrx.*, 1950 S.C. 39.

[12] *Heslop* v. *Runcie* (1894) 22 R. 83.

deponent is conclusive of the matter referred. If his answers are qualified they must be interpreted by the court to determine whether they are affirmative or negative of the reference.[1]

The requisite of proof by writ or oath applies to the following cases:

(a) averments of loan,[2] advance[3] or payment[4] of money exceeding £100 Scots (£8.33 stg.), but not of loan of corporeal moveables.[5] An unqualified receipt for money implies loan, and the granter must discharge the onus of proving that there was some other cause of granting.[6] An I.O.U. is competent evidence of loan.[7] A cheque does not prove loan to the payee.[8] If the proof is by writ, the interpretation is a matter for the court; letters not repudiating do not imply admission.[9] Loan may also be evidenced by a formal bond to repay, with or without a disposition or assignation of property in security for repayment. Donation, whether *inter vivos* or *mortis causa*, may, however, be proved by parole

---

[1] *Thomson* v. *Duncan* (1855) 17 D. 1081; *Gow's Exors.* v. *Sim* (1866) 4 M. 578; *Wilson* v. *W.* (1871) 9 M. 920; *Fenning* v. *Meldrum* (1876) 4 R. 148; *Cooper* v. *Marshall* (1877) 5 R. 258; *Newlands* v. *McKinlay* (1885) 13 R. 353; *Broatch* v. *Dodds* (1892) 19 R. 855; *Penney* v. *Aitken*, 1927 S.C. 673.

[2] Stair IV, 43, 4; Ersk. IV, 2, 20; Bell, *Prin.*, §§2257; *Martin* v. *Crawford* (1850) 12 D. 960; *Robertson* v. *R.* (1858) 20 D. 371; *Annand* v. *A.* (1869) 7 M. 526; *Haldane* v. *Speirs* (1872) 10 M. 537; *Bryan* v. *Butters Bros. & Co.* (1892) 19 R. 490; *Paterson* v. *P.* (1897) 25 R. 144; *Field* v. *Thomson* (1902) 10 S.L.T. 261; *Morison's Trs.* v. *Mitchell*, 1925 S.L.T. 231; *Penney* v. *Aitken*, 1927 S.C. 673; *McMenemy* v. *Forster's Tr.*, 1938 S.L.T. 555; *Kennedy* v. *Macrae*, 1946 S.C. 118. But a writ dated after the borrower's sequestration will not suffice: *Carmichael's Tr.* v. *C.*, 1929 S.L.T. 230. In *Clark's Exor.* v. *Brown*, 1935 S.C. 110, in special circumstances a wider proof was allowed. See also *Boyd* v. *Millar*, 1934 S.N. 7.

[3] *Macfarquhar* v. *McKay* (1869) 7 M. 766; *Murray* v. *Wright* (1870) 8 M. 722; *McAdie* v. *McA's Exrx.* (1883) 10 R. 741; cf. *Stuart* v. *S.* (1869) 7 M. 366; *Govan New Bowling Club* v. *Geddes* (1898) 25 R. 485.

[4] *Mackenzie* v. *Brodie* (1859) 21 D. 1048; *White* v. *Arthur* (1864) 2 M. 1154; *McLaren* v. *Howie* (1869) 8 M. 106; *Thiem's Trs.* v. *Collie* (1899) 1 F. 764; *Campbell* v. *C's Exors.*, 1910 2 S.L.T. 240. But not payment of a cash sale: *Shaw* v. *Wright* (1877) 5 R. 245; nor payment coupled with mandate to deal with the money: *Burt* v. *Laing*, 1925 S.C. 181.

[5] Such may be proved by any evidence: *Scot* v. *Fletcher* (1665) Mor. 11616; *Geddes* v. *G.* (1678) Mor. 12730.

[6] *Martin* v. *Crawford* (1850) 12 D. 960; *Fraser* v. *Bruce* (1857) 20 D. 115; *Robertson* v. *R.* (1858) 20 D. 371; *Thomson* v. *Geekie* (1861) 23 D. 693; *Christie's Trs.* v. *Muirhead* (1870) 8 M. 461; *Duncan's Trs.* v. *Shand* (1873) 11 M. 254; *Gill* v. *G.*, 1907 S.C. 532.

[7] *Nicholson* v. *Stuart's Exor.* (1896) 3 S.L.T. 233. See also *Bowe & Christie* v. *Hutchison* (1868) 6 M. 642; *Christie's Trs.* v. *Muirhead* (1870) 8 M. 461; *Neilson's Trs.* v. *N's Trs.* (1883) 11 R. 119; *Paterson* v. *Wilson* (1883) 21 S.L.R. 272; *Thiem's Trs.* v. *Collie* (1899) 1 F. 764; *Bishop* v. *Bryce*, 1910 S.C. 426; *Black* v. *Gibb*, 1940 S.C. 24.

[8] *Haldane* v. *Speirs* (1872) 10 M. 537; *Scotland* v. *S.*, 1909 S.C. 505.

[9] *MacBain* v. *MacBain*, 1930 S.C. (H.L.) 72.

evidence.[1] Payment or discharge may also be proved by facts and circumstances giving rise to the inevitable inference that the debt has been satisfied or discharged in some way.[2] If repayment is alleged, both constitution and resting-owing of the loan must be proved by writ or oath.[3]

(b) allegations that property, *ex facie* held absolutely under a ꭎeed or document of title, is truly held in trust may be proved only, at least as between truster and trustee,[4] and not where the case is mandate rather than trust,[5] by the writ or oath of the alleged trustee.[6] If the existence of the trust is judicially admitted or proved by writ or oath, the terms thereof may be proved *prout de jure*.[7] Discharge of trust may similarly in general be proved by writ or oath only.[8]

(c) obligations of relief, as by one co-acceptor of a bill against another,[9] or one guarantor against another,[10] though this rule has no application where the right of relief is implied by law, and as between cautioners and co-obligants one party may prove that he is truly a cautioner and thus entitled to relief.[11]

(d) the discharge or performance of an obligation constituted by writing, or vouched by a document of debt.[12] Thus if an action is brought on a bill or I.O.U. and the defence is payment, payment must be established by the pursuer's writ or oath,[13] or by

---

[1] *Morris* v. *Riddick* (1867) 5 M. 1036; *Wright's Exors.* v. *City of Glasgow Bank* (1880) 7 R. 527, 535; *Sharp* v. *Paton* (1883) 10 R. 1000; *Milne* v. *Grant's Exors.* (1884) 11 R. 887; *Penny* v. *Aitken*, 1927 S.C. 673. Older cases required proof by writ or oath, e.g. *Robertson* v. *R.* (1858) 20 D. 371.

[2] *Campbell* v. *C's Exors.*, 1910, 2 S.L.T. 240; *Bishop* v. *Bryce*, 1910 S.C. 426; cf. *Stenhouse* v. *S's Trs.* (1899) 6 S.L.T. 368; *Kilpatrick* v. *Dunlop*, 1909, 2 S.L.T. 307; *Semple's Exors.* v. *S.*, 1912, 1 S.L.T. 382.

[3] *Walker* v. *Garlick*, 1940 S.L.T. 208.

[4] *Wink* v. *Speirs* (1867) 6 M. 77; *Forrester* v. *Robson's Trs.* (1875) 2 R. 755; *Hastie* v. *Steel* (1886) 13 R. 843; *Galloway* v. *G.*, 1929 S.C. 160.

[5] *Horne* v. *Morrison* (1877) 4 R. 977; *Pant-Mawr Quarry Co.* v. *Fleming* (1883) 10 R. 457; *McConnachie* v. *Geddes*, 1918 S.C. 391; cf. *McNair's Exrx.* v. *Litster*, 1939 S.C. 72.

[6] Blank Bonds and Trusts Act, 1696 (c. 25); Bell, *Prin.* §1995; *Thomson* v. *Lindsay* (1873) 1 R. 65; *Laird* v. *Laird and Rutherford* (1884) 12 R. 294; *Purnell* v. *Shannon* (1894) 22 R. 74; *Dunn* v. *Pratt* (1898) 25 R. 461; *Govan Bowling Club* v. *Geddes* (1898) 25 R. 485; *Anderson* v. *Yorston* (1906) 14 S.L.T. 54; *Robertson* v. *R.*, 1929 S.L.T. 510; *Pickard* v. *P.*, 1963 S.C. 604.

[7] *Livingstone* v. *Allan* (1900) 3 F. 233; *National Bank* v. *Mackie's Trs.* (1905) 13 S.L.T. 383; *Cairns* v. *Davidson*, 1913 S.C. 1054.

[8] *Keanie* v. *K.*, 1940 S.C. 549.

[9] *Thoms* v. *Thoms* (1867) 6 M. 174; *Crosbie* v. *Brown* (1900) 3 F. 83.

[10] *Devlin* v. *McKelvie*, 1915 S.C. 180; contrast *Hamilton* v. *Freeth* (1889) 16 R. 1022.

[11] Bell, *Prin.* §267; cf. *Hamilton*, *supra*; *Thow's Tr.* v. *Young*, 1910 S.C. 588.

[12] *Woddrop* v. *Speirs* (1906) 14 S.L.T. 319.

[13] *Robertson* v. *Thomson* (1900) 3 F. 5; *Nicol's Trs.* v. *Sutherland*, 1951 S.C. (H.L.) 21; cf. *Young* v. *Thomson*, 1909 S.C. 529; *Keanie* v. *Keanie*, 1940 S.C. 549.

proof of facts and circumstances which give rise to the inevitable inference that the debt has been discharged in some way.[1] But performance of obligations by supplying goods or otherwise performing actual services may be proved *prout de jure*.[2]

(e) the payment of money in implement of an antecedent obligation, even if not expressed in writing, unless the sum does not exceed £100 Scots:[3] instances are repayment of a loan,[4] and payment of sums which should earlier have been paid weekly.[5]

(f) renunciation, without payment or performance, of rights constituted in writing,[6] such as of a stipulation in a feu-charter,[7] or of an acknowledgment of trust.[8] If the rights were constituted orally, the same rule may apply,[9] or parole proof of renunciation may be competent.[10] The renunciation or discharge of a claim of damages, or an agreement not to proceed with diligence can similarly be proved only by writ or oath.[11]

(g) the modification of an agreement constituted in writing,[12] such as an agreement to give an abatement from the rent stated in the lease,[13] or to make up any deficiency in the value of firm assets if a new valuation were required,[14] or to vary the terms on which an action had been compromised,[15] unless the written contract contemplated subsidiary or explanatory oral agreements,[16] or there has been oral agreement to modify followed by actings inconsistent with or contradictory of the original obligation.[17]

(h) promises or gratuitous obligations, whether unilateral or bilateral, where there is no *quid pro quo* for the undertaking or

---

[1] *Campbell* v. *C's Exors.*, 1910, 2 S.L.T. 240; *Bishop* v. *Bryce*, 1910 S.C. 426.

[2] Stair IV, 43, 4; Ersk. IV, 2, 21; Gloag, 720.

[3] Ersk. IV, 2, 21; *Shaw* v. *Wright* (1877) 5 R. 245; *Young* v. *Thomson*, 1909 S.C. 529; *Burt* v. *Laing*, 1925 S.C. 181.

[4] *Thiem's Trs.* v. *Collie* (1899) 1 F. 764; *Jackson* v. *Ogilvie's Exor.*, 1935 S.C. 154.

[5] *Hope Bros.* v. *Morrison*, 1960 S.C. 1.

[6] Ersk. III, 4, 8; Gloag, 722.

[7] *Scot* v. *Cairns* (1830) 9 S. 246.

[8] *Keanie* v. *K.*, 1940 S.C. 549.

[9] *Kilpatrick* v. *Dunlop*, 1909, 2 S.L.T. 307; cf. *Cochrane* v. *Traill* (1900) 2 F. 794; *McFadzean's Exor.* v. *McAlpine*, 1907 S.C. 1269.

[10] Ersk. III, 4, 8; Gloag, 722.

[11] *Cochrane* v. *Trail* (1900) 2 F. 794; *Reid* v. *Gow* (1903) 10 S.L.T. 606; *McFadzean's Exor.* v. *McAlpine*, 1907 S.C. 1269; contrast *Downie* v. *Black* (1885) 13 R. 271.

[12] *Steuart's Trs.* v. *Hart* (1875) 3 R. 192; *Ireland* v. *Rosewall Coal Co.* (1900) 7 S.L.T. 445. cf. *Tharsis Sulphur Co.* v. *McElroy* (1878) 5 R. (H.L.) 171.

[13] *Turnbull* v. *Oliver* (1891) 19 R. 154.

[14] *Barr's Trs.* v. *Barr & Shearer* (1886) 13 R. 1055.

[15] *Hamilton & Baird* v. *Lewis* (1893) 21 R. 120.

[16] *Merrow & Fell* v. *Hutchison & Brown* (1873) 10 S.L.R. 338; *Davidson* v. *Bisset* (1878) 5 R. 706.

[17] *Kirkpatrick* v. *Allanshaw Coal Co.* (1881) 8 R. 327; *Lavan* v. *Aird*, 1919 S.C. 345.

promise,[1] such as a promise to give a benefit[2] or to renounce a right to share in an estate,[3] or the gratuitous discharge of a debt,[4] though it is competent to prove by any evidence facts and circumstances giving rise to an inference that a debt has been discharged,[5] or tending to rebut the presumptions of payment.[6]

(j) innominate and unusual obligations, i.e. such agreements as are not within one of the recognized classes of named contracts, and are also anomalous or extraordinary or peculiar in their terms,[7] such as an alleged agreement to grant a deed regulating succession,[8] or to share the expenses of a shooting,[9] or by a landlord to repay a tenant's losses if the latter would remain in occupancy and pay the rent,[10] or that one would leave all his property to the other if the latter would settle as a doctor in Shetland,[11] or that the pursuer had been appointed to a post on highly exceptional terms,[12] or that parties had agreed to a capital payment instead of weekly payments of workmen's compensation,[13] or an agreement not to proceed with diligence,[14] or an agreement by a bank to grant an overdraft,[15] or an agreement by a cautioner not to plead the septennial prescription,[16] or an agreement between husband and wife that he would, for certain considerations, make a will irrevocably bequeathing a house to her,[17] or a compromise whereby an injured man was allegedly re-employed permanently,[18] or a peculiar arrangement between

[1] Stair I, 10, 4; *Deuchar* v. *Brown* (1672) Mor. 12387; *Harvie* v. *Crawford* (1732) Mor. 12388.

[2] e.g. *Morton's Trs.* v. *Aged Christian Friend. Socy.* (1899) 2 F. 82; *Smith* v. *Oliver*, 1911 S.C. 103.

[3] *Jackson* v. *Ogilvie*, 1933 S.L.T. 533.

[4] *Anderson's Trs.* v. *Webster* (1883) 11 R. 35; *Cameron* v. *Panton's Trs.* (1891) 18 R. 728.

[5] *Chrystal* v. *C.* (1900) 2 F. 373; *Kirkpatrick* v. *Dunlop*, 1909, 2 S.L.T. 307; *Campbell* v. *C's Exors.*, 1910, 2 S.L.T. 240; *Bishop* v. *Bryce*, 1910 S.C. 426.

[6] *Stenhouse* v. *S's Trs.* (1899) 6 S.L.T. 368 (*apocha trium annorum*); *Semple's Exors.* v. *S.*, 1912 1 S.L.T. 382 (*chirographum apud debitorem repertum praesumitur solutum*). On these presumptions see Ch. 37, *infra*.

[7] Ersk. IV, 2, 20; Bell, *Prin.* §2257; *Forbes* v. *Caird* (1877) 4 R. 1141; *Allison* v. *A's Trs.* (1904) 6 F. 496; *Hendry* v. *Cowie* (1904) 12 S.L.T. 261.

[8] *Johnston* v. *Goodlet* (1868) 6 M. 1067.

[9] *Stewart & Craig* v. *Phillips* (1882) 9 R. 501.

[10] *Garden* v. *Earl of Aberdeen* (1893) 20 R. 896.

[11] *Edmondston* v. *E.* (1861) 23 D. 995.

[12] *Copeland* v. *Lord Wimborne*, 1912 S.C. 355.

[13] *McFadzean's Exors.* v. *McAlpine*, 1907 S.C. 1269, doubted in *Smith* v. *Reekie*, 1920 S.C. 188; see also *Cochrane* v. *Traill* (1900) 2 F. 794.

[14] *Reid* v. *Gow* (1903) 10 S.L.T. 606.

[15] *Ritchie* v. *Clydesdale Bank* (1886) 13 R. 866.

[16] *McGregor's Exors.* v. *Anderson's Trs.* (1893) 21 R. 7.

[17] *Fisher* v. *F.*, 1952 S.C. 347.

[18] *Cook* v. *Grubb*, 1963 S.C. 1.

merchants,[1] or an agreement to divide funds destined by statute to the survivor of them,[2] or an agreement between two managing directors to share an increase in salary for the one if the other voted for it,[3] or to leave a person money by will,[4] or an agreement as to sharing the expenses of a feu,[5] or to give an abatement from the agreed rent,[6] or to relieve a cautioner if financial circumstances permitted.[7] But the rule has not been applied to such cases as an agreement not to purchase heritage without giving the other a chance to join in the purchase,[8] nor an agreement to pay a bonus to fishermen engaging on Admiralty service in wartime.[9] The rule does not apply to agreements which are innominate but not also unusual in their terms.

Exception 3: contracts requiring proof by writ or oath after lapse of time

By certain old prescription statutes the lapse of time did not extinguish or render unenforceable the obligations affected but after the lapse of the prescribed periods the obligation could be proved to be still subsisting only by the defender's writ (not necessarily probative) or his admission on oath. These were obligations falling under the triennial prescription,[10] the quinquennial prescription,[11] the sexennial prescription[12] or the vicennial prescription.[13] By the Prescription and Limitation (Sc.) Act, 1973, all these statutes were repealed with effect from 25 July 1976, and the obligations within the categories formerly affected are now free from restrictions as to proof, but most now fall within the provisions of the 1973 Act extinguishing them completely after five years.[14]

---

[1] *Muller* v. *Weber & Schaer* (1901) 3 F. 401.

[2] *McMurrich's Trs.* v. *McM's Trs.* (1903) 6 F. 121.

[3] *Jackson* v. *Elphick* (1902) 10 S.L.T. 146.

[4] *Hallet* v. *Ryrie* (1907) 15 S.L.T. 367.

[5] *Woddrop* v. *Speirs* (1906) 14 S.L.T. 319.

[6] *Turnbull* v. *Oliver* (1891) 19 R. 154.   [7] *Williamson* v. *Foulds*, 1927 S.N. 164.

[8] *Mungall* v. *Bowhill Coal Co.* (1904) 12 S.L.T. 80, 262.

[9] *Smith* v. *Reekie*, 1920 S.C. 188; see also *Thomson* v. *Fraser* (1868) 7 M. 39; *Dobie* v. *Lauder's Trs.* (1873) 11 M. 749; *Forbes* v. *Caird* (1877) 4 R. 1141; *Downie* v. *Black* (1885) 13 R. 271; *Reid* v. *Reid Bros.* (1887) 14 R. 789; *Moncrieff* v. *Sievwright* (1896) 3 S.L.T. 314; *Lightbody* v. *Reid* (1894) 1 S.L.T. 581; *Jack* v. *McGrouther* (1901) 38 S.L.R. 701; *Allison* v. *A's Trs.* (1904) 6 F. 496; *Henderson, Tucker & Co.* v. *United Collieries* (1904) 11 S.L.T. 653; *Smith* v. *Reekie*, 1920 S.C. 188; *Denvir* v. *D.*, 1969 S.L.T. 301.

[10] Prescription Act, 1579, c. 21; see Stair II, 12, 30; Ersk. III, 7, 17–18; Bell, *Comm.* I, 348; *Prin.* §628.

[11] Prescription Act, 1669, c. 14; Ersk. III, 7, 20; Bell, *Prin.* §634.

[12] Bills of Exchange (Sc.) Act, 1772, S. 37; Ersk. III, 7, 29; Bell, *Comm.* I, 418; *Prin.* §594–9.

[13] Prescription Act, 1669, c. 14; Ersk. III, 7, 26; Bell, *Comm.* I., 346; *Prin.* §590–2.

[14] See further Chap. 37, *infra*.

Exception 4: Obligationes literis

Obligationes literis are those categories of obligations of great importance which must be constituted in writing executed by the granter in accordance with the statutory solemnities,[1] and also may be proved only by the terms of these writings.[2] A writ so authenticated is held probative, i.e. proves itself, and no further evidence of its authenticity is necessary.

By custom writs which are holograph of the granter[3] or adopted as holograph[4] by him are deemed equivalent to writ solemnly executed. Such writs are not probative, but if proved to be holograph, are equivalent to solemnly executed writing.[5]

Where probative writing is demanded by law, informal or improbative writing is by itself insufficient,[6] judicial admission is inadequate,[7] and reference to oath incompetent.[8] Despite agreement there is *locus poenitentiae* open to either party until or unless the agreement be constituted in writing authenticated by the party bound, and in mutual obligations, by both parties.[9]

What are obligationes literis

The category of *obligatio literis* includes all 'obligations of great importance'.[10] As explained by decisions this includes:

(a) contracts relating to heritage, including writings constituting offers and acceptances for the purchase or sale of heritage,[11]

---

[1] The statutory solemnities of execution are those prescribed by the Subscription of Deeds Acts, 1540 (c. 37), 1579 (c. 18) and 1681 (c. 5), the Deeds Act, 1696 (c. 15). See Ch. 6, *supra*.

[2] See generally Stair I, 10, 9; Bell, *Comm.* I, 340.

[3] The onus of proving that a writing is holograph is on the party proponing it: *Anderson* v. *Gill* (1858) 3 Macq. 180.

[4] A writing printed, typewritten or otherwise reproduced, or handwritten by another, may be 'adopted as holograph' by the granter himself writing those words, or words to the same effect, at the end and signing it. Witnesses and their signatures are then unnecessary. See *Bryson* v. *Crawford* (1833) 12 S. 39; *McIntyre* v. *McFarlane*, 1 Mar. 1821, F.C.; *Christie's Trs.* v. *Muirhead* (1870) 8 M. 461; *Maitland's Trs.* v. *M.* (1871) 10 M. 29; *Weir* v. *Robertson* (1872) 10 M. 438; *Gavine's Trs.* v. *Lee* (1883) 10 R. 448. See also *McGinn* v. *Shearer*, 1947 S.C. 334. If the docquet and signature are proved holograph, the deed, though not probative, is also equivalent to a solemnly executed writing. The docquet and signature may, very exceptionally, be also typewritten: *McBeath's Trs.* v. *McBeath*, 1935 S.C. 471.

[5] *Harper* v. *Green*, 1938 S.C. 198.

[6] *Goldston* v. *Young* (1868) 7 M. 188; as to its sufficiency when supplemented by evidence of conduct in reliance thereon, see *infra*.

[7] *Jamieson* v. *Edinburgh Mutual Investment Bldg. Socy.*, 1913, 2 S.L.T. 52.

[8] *Paterson* v. *P.* (1897) 25 R. 144, 174; *Perdikou* v. *Pattison*, 1958 S.L.T. 153.

[9] Bell, *Comm.* I, 345.

[10] Subscription of Deeds Act, 1579; see also *Paterson* v. *P.* (1897) 25 R. 144, 173.

[11] Ersk. III, 2, 2 and 10; *Goldston* v. *Young* (1868) 7 M. 188; *Allan* v. *Gilchrist* (1875) 2 R. 587; *Shiell* v. *Guthrie's Trs.* (1874) 1 R. 1083; *McGinn* v. *Shearer*, 1947 S.C. 334.

deeds conveying title to heritage, and agreements for, and deeds actually constituting, servitudes,[1] heritable securities,[2] and leases for longer than one year.[3] Exceptions have been recognized in cases involving heritage only incidentally,[4] such as the compromise of an action providing *inter alia* for the purchase of heritage.[5]

(b) bonds or obligations for the payment of money,[6] but not mere receipts for money lent[7] or paid, and instruments of intimation of assignations, translations or retrocessions to bonds, contracts or other writs.[8]

(c) contracts of service for more than one year, which must be solemnly authenticated, holograph, or adopted as holograph by both parties.[9] The requirement does not apply to an agency engagement at a salary plus commission on sales,[10] nor to a contract of indefinite duration to do a particular piece of work,[11] and when services have in fact been rendered for a period of years without remuneration, the facts from which the right to remuneration may be inferred may be proved *prout de jure*.[12]

(d) cautionary obligations: a cautionary obligation or guarantee had at common law to be constituted by writing solemnly authenticated, unless in a proper *res mercatoria*.[13] But in view of the Mercantile Law Amendment (Sc.) Act, 1856, S. 6,[14] signed writing (not formally authenticated) appears now sufficient.[15] An

[1] *Dundas* v. *Blair* (1886) 13 R. 759; *Inglis* v. *Clark* (1901) 4 F. 288; *Metcalfe* v. *Purdon* (1902) 4 F. 507.

[2] *Gilchrist* v. *Whyte*, 1907 S.C. 984.

[3] *Sproul* v. *Wilson* (1809) Hume 920; *Fowlie* v. *McLean* (1868) 6 M. 254; *Sinclair* v. *Weddell* (1868) 41 S. Jur. 121; *Gibson* v. *Adams* (1875) 3 R. 144.

[4] *Kinninmont* v. *Paxton* (1892) 20 R. 128 *Moncrieff* v. *Seivwright* (1896) 33 S.L.R. 456; *Hamilton* v. *Lochrane* (1899) 1 F. 478; *Mungall* v. *Bowhill Coal Co.* (1904) 12 S.L.T. 262; *Woddrop* v. *Speirs* (1906) 44 S.L.R. 22; *Mackay* v. *Rodger* (1907) 15 S.L.T. 42; *Anderson* v. *Dick* (1901) 4 F. 68; *Paterson* v. *Brown*, 1913 S.C. 292; *Allan* v. *Millar*, 1932 S.C. 620.

[5] *Torbat* v. *T's Trs.* (1906) 14 S.L.T. 830; cf. *Love* v. *Marshall* (1872) 10 M. 795; *Anderson* v. *Dick* (1901) 4 F. 68.

[6] Subscription of Deeds Act, 1540.   [7] *Paterson* v. *P.* (1897) 25 R. 144, 177, 181.

[8] Subscription of Deeds Act, 1681.

[9] Bell, *Prin.* §173; Fraser, *M. & S.*, 30; *Stewart* v. *McCall* (1869) 7 M. 544; *Reuter* v. *Douglas* (1902) 10 S.L.T. 294; *Nisbet* v. *Percy*, 1951 S.C. 350; *Cook* v. *Grubb*, 1963 S.C. 1; *Walker* v. *Greenock Hospital Board*, 1951 S.C. 464, 469. But see *Brown* v. *Scottish Antarctic Expedition* (1902) 10 S.L.T. 433.

[10] *Pickin* v. *Hawkes* (1878) 5 R. 676.

[11] Gloag, 180.

[12] *Thomson* v. *Thomson's Tr.* (1889) 16 R. 333.

[13] *Walker's Trs.* v. *McKinlay* (1880) 7 R. (H.L.) 85.

[14] *Church of England, etc., Co.* v. *Hodges* (1857) 19 D. 414, 421.

[15] See opinion of L.O. Wellwood in *Wallace* v. *Gibson* (1895) 22 R. (H.L.) 56, 58–59; *Snaddon* v. *London, etc. Assce. Co.* (1902) 5 F. 182; *Fortune* v. *Young*, 1918 S.C. 1; cf. *Gibson* v. *Alston's Trs.* (1893) 1 S.L.T. 62.

informal writing is certainly sufficient where an advance has been made on the faith thereof.[1] This Act covers also a written undertaking to give a guarantee when required.[2]

(e) submissions to arbitration and decrees-arbitral: submissions and decrees-arbitral in arbitrations relating to heritage must be authenticated, holograph or adopted as holograph,[3] excepting arbitrations relating to incidents of agricultural leases, which need only be in writing and signed;[4] arbitrations *in re mercatoria* may similarly be informal.[5]

(f) where a term in a compromise agreement is one of the *obligationes literis*, the agreement must be constituted in writing.[6]

Where necessary formalities absent or defective

Where solemnly authenticated writing is necessary for the constitution of an obligation but there is no writing, or any writing is not properly authenticated, holograph or adopted as holograph, but merely informal, the obligation is held merely inchoate, and *locus poenitentiae* is open to both parties equally, so that either may resile without being in breach of contract.[7] In such a case, however, the right to resile may be held personally barred if material actings amounting to partial performance have followed on the faith of the contract, on the equitable basis that a party cannot be heard to deny an obligation which he has impliedly approbated by his actings. The essence of the plea is the occurrence, subsequent to the informally constituted agreement, of acts on the part of either party which would render it inequitable to hold that there was still a *locus poenitentiae*.[8] These acts may be held to amount to *rei interventus* or to homologation.

Rei interventus *and homologation*

The right to resile is accordingly held barred if the antecedent agreement of parties is proved by judicial admission, or by writ or

---

[1] *Johnston* v. *Grant* (1844) 6 D. 875; *Church of England, etc., Co.* v. *Wink* (1857) 19 D. 1079; *National Bank* v. *Campbell* (1892) 19 R. 885.

[2] *Wallace* v. *Gibson* (1895) 22 R. (H.L.) 56.

[3] Bell, *Arbitration*, S. 93–4; *Robertson* v. *Boyd and Winans* (1885) 12 R. 419; *McLaren* v. *Aikman*, 1939 S.C. 222.

[4] *Davidson* v. *Logan*, 1908 S.C. 350; *Gibson* v. *Fotheringham*, 1914 S.C. 987; *Cameron* v. *Nicol*, 1930 S.C. 1; *McLaren* v. *Aikman*, 1939 S.C. 222. But see Agricultural Holdings (Sc.) Act, 1949, and Connell thereon, p. 75.

[5] *Dykes* v. *Roy* (1869) 7 M. 357; *Hope* v. *Crookston Bros.* (1890) 17 R. 868; *McLaren, supra.*

[6] *Cook* v. *Grubb*, 1963 S.C. 1.

[7] Bell, *Comm.* I, 345; *Goldston* v. *Young* (1868) 7 M. 188; *Sinclair* v. *Weddell* (1868) 5 S.L.R. 664; *Gavine's Trs.* v. *Lee* (1883) 10 R. 448; *Paterson* v. *P.* (1897) 25 R. 144, 173.

[8] *Mitchell* v. *Stornoway Trs.*, 1936 S.C. (H.L.) 56, 64.

oath, and was followed by proven actings on one or the other part, held by the court to amount to partial implement or performance of the contract, and done in reliance thereon.[1] If the actings are those of the party seeking to establish the obligation, permitted by the party denying the obligation, to take place on the faith of the contract as if it were perfect, they are held to amount to *rei interventus*.[2] If they are those of the party seeking to deny the obligation, they are held to be homologation.[3] Thus the party who seeks to enforce an informal contract against the party who seeks to disown it may found upon his own actings on the faith of the contract, if these actings have been known to and were permitted by the other party, in which case he invokes the doctrine of *rei interventus*; or he may found upon the actings of the party seeking to disown the contract as being actings which imply the latter's approbation or confirmation of the contract, in which case he invokes the doctrine of homologation.[4] Both pleas may arise on the facts of one case.[5]

Proof of the concluded agreement

Rei interventus or homologation will not cure absence of agreement of parties, but only defect in formalities.[6] A concluded agreement of parties must first be proved, by judicial admission,[7] or by writ or oath,[8] or partly by each of these.[8] The writ or writs need

---

[1] Bell, *Prin.* §25.

[2] cf. Bell, *Prin.* §26: '*Rei interventus* is inferred from any proceedings not unimportant on the part of the obligee, known to and permitted by the obligor to take place on the faith of the contract as if it were perfect; provided they are unequivocally referable to the agreement and productive of alteration of circumstances, loss or inconvenience, though not irretrievable.' See also Bell, *Comm.* I, 346.

[3] cf. Ersk. III, 3, 47; Bell, *Prin.* §27: 'Homologation (in principle similar to *rei interventus*) is an act approbatory of a preceding engagement, which in itself is defective or informal, either confirming or adopting it as binding. It may be express or inferred from circumstances. It must be absolute, and not compulsory, nor proceeding on error or fraud, and unequivocally referable to the engagement; and must imply assent to it, with fully knowledge of its extent, and of all the relative interests of the homologator.' See also Bell, *Comm.* I, 139.

[4] *Mitchell* v. *Stornoway Trs.*, 1936 S.C. (H.L.) 56, 63.

[5] *Station Hotel, Nairn* v. *Macpherson* (1905) 13 S.L.T. 456; *Mitchell, supra.*

[6] *Mowat* v. *Caledonian Banking Co.* (1897) 23 R. 270; *Ker* v. *Forrest's Trs.* (1902) 10 S.L.T. 67; *Mitchell* v. *Stornoway Trs.*, 1936 S.C. (H.L.) 56, 66, explaining *Colquhoun* v. *Wilson's Trs.* (1860) 22 D. 1035 (but on this see also *Errol* v. *Walker*, 1966 S.C. 93); *E. Kilbride Development Corpn.* v. *Pollok*, 1953 S.C. 370. A unilateral promise cannot be converted into a bilateral contract by *rei interventus*: *Smith* v. *Oliver*, 1911 S.C. 103.   [7] *Church of England Assce. Co.* v. *Wink* (1857) 19 D. 1079; *Mitchell, infra.*

[8] *Gowans' Trs.* v. *Carstairs* (1862) 24 D. 1382; *Walker* v. *Flint* (1863) 1 M. 417; *Paterson* v. *Earl of Fife* (1865) 3 M. 423; *Fowlie* v. *McLean* (1868) 6 M. 254; *Philip* v. *Gordon Cumming's Exors.* (1869) 7 M. 859; *Sellar* v. *Aiton* (1875) 2 R. 381; *Allan* v. *Gilchrist* (1875) 2 R. 587; *Gibson* v. *Adams* (1875) 3 R. 144; *Errol* v. *Walker*, 1966 S.C. 93 seems very questionable.

not be authenticated and may be informal, such as a docquet on a plan,[1] entries in the landlord's books,[2] an offer from a tenant,[3] and a receipt for feu duty.[4] But if there was no *consensus* of parties,[5] or if the contract was not sufficiently certain in terms to be enforceable, there is no basis which the subsequent actings can complete.[6] While to form a basis for *rei interventus* or homologation, the agreement must be concluded in all substantials, not every detail need have been settled; if any matters are not settled it depends on their importance whether the agreement can be held concluded or not.[7] Actings earlier than the conclusion of the underlying agreement of parties cannot be relied on as amounting to *rei interventus* or homologation.[8]

In a few cases actings similar to those evidencing *rei interventus* have been held to evidence the fact that agreement has been reached, and in these cases proof of agreement constituted, at least on one part, by mere actings, may be by parole.[9]

Actings constituting rei interventus

Actings, or abstentions,[10] if not judicially admitted,[11] may be proved by parole evidence.[12] To be effective as *rei interventus*, they must be on the part of the pursuer himself and be 'not unimportant', not so much in extent as in nature or significance in showing reliance on the prior agreement.[13] They must have been known to, and permitted by, the defender as if there was a binding contract,[14] or at least be such as would naturally be expected to

---

[1] *Mitchell* v. *Stornoway Trs.*, 1936 S.C. (H.L.) 56.

[2] *Wares* v. *Duff Dunbar's Trs.*, 1920 S.C. 5.

[3] *Forbes* v. *Wilson* (1873) 11 M. 454.

[4] *Stodart* v. *Dalzell* (1876) 4 R. 236.

[5] *Buchanan* v. *Duke of Hamilton* (1878) 5 R. (H.L.) 69; *Kay* v. *Forrest's Trs.* (1902) 10 S.L.T. 67.

[6] *Van Laun & Co.* v. *Neilson, Reid & Co.* (1904) 6 F. 644, 652.

[7] *Erskine* v. *Glendinning* (1871) 9 M. 656; *Westren* v. *Millar* (1879) 7 R. 173; *Wight* v. *Newton*, 1911 S.C. 762; *Stobo* v. *Morrisons Gowns*, 1949 S.C. 184; *Heiton* v. *Waverley Hydropathic Co.* (1877) 4 R. 830; *Mitchell, supra*, 59, 66.

[8] *Mowat* v. *Caledonian Banking Co.* (1895) 23 R. 270; *Rigg* v. *Mather* (1902) 10 S.L.T. 426; *Van Laun & Co.* v. *Neilson, Reid & Co.* (1904) 6 F. 644, 653; *Mitchell, supra*, 61, 64.

[9] *Stewart* v. *Moray* (1773) 2 Pat. 317; *Keir* v. *D. Atholl* (1815) 6 Pat. 130; *Colquhoun* v. *Wilson's Trs.* (1860) 22 D. 1035; *Ballantine* v. *Stevenson* (1881) 8 R. 959; *Errol* v. *Walker*, 1966 S.C. 93; Gloag, 46.

[10] *Danish Dairy Co.* v. *Gillespie*, 1922 S.C. 656.

[11] *Beardmore* v. *Barry*, 1928 S.C. 107.

[12] *Walker* v. *Flint* (1863) 1 M. 417; *Mitchell* v. *Stornoway Trs.*, 1936 S.C. (H.L.) 56.

[13] *McLean* v. *Scott* (1902) 10 S.L.T. 447; *Mitchell, supra*.

[14] *Stewart* v. *Burns* (1877) 4 R. 427; *Bell* v. *Goodall* (1883) 10 R. 905; *Simpson* v. *Mason & McRae* (1884) 21 S.L.R. 413; *Danish Dairy Co., supra*.

follow on the agreement.[1] Knowledge and permission by an agent suffices, if he had authority to make the agreement and allow the acts.[2] They must have taken place on the faith of the contract as if it were perfect and be unequivocally referable thereto. Hence they must be later than the agreement,[3] and be fairly explicable only on the hypothesis of the agreement alleged, rather than a similar agreement.[4] Lastly, the actings must have been productive of change of circumstances and loss or inconvenience.[5]

Examples of conduct amounting to rei interventus

In cases of feu or sale of heritage *rei interventus* has included being allowed to take possession of land feued orally, to build thereon, and being granted receipts for 'feuduty', the first of which contained a note of the area feued and the feu-duty,[6] a purchaser of premises letting them to a tenant and seeking to obtain a licence for the premises,[7] a purchaser getting possession of the keys, allowing the 'For Sale' notice to be taken down, and superintending the layout of the garden,[8] and a vassal, while an agreement for the alteration of a building restriction in the title was in draft, erecting a building inconsistent with the former restrictions but consistent with the new ones.[9] Payment of £5 to account of a price of £6000 and the incurring of certain expenses have been held insufficient.[10]

In the case of leases the principle has extended to entry into possession, and erection of buildings for the purposes of the lease,[11] entry and possession on terms advertised,[12] entry into possession and expenditure on the land leased,[13] a draft lease followed by demolition of ruinous buildings and improvements

[1] *Gardner* v. *Lucas* (1878) 5 R. 638; *National Bank* v. *Campbell* (1892) 19 R. 885; *Danish Dairy Co., supra; Boyd* v. *Shaw,* 1927 S.C. 414.

[2] *Heiton* v. *Waverley Hydropathic Co.* (1877) 4 R. 830.

[3] *Mowat* v. *Caledonian Banking Co.* (1895) 23 R. 270; *Van Laun* v. *Neilson, Reid & Co.* (1904) 6 F. 644; *Pollok* v. *Whiteford,* 1936 S.C. 402.

[4] *Philip* v. *Gordon Cumming's Exor.* (1869) 7 M. 859; *Bathie* v. *Lord Wharncliffe* (1873) 11 M. 489; *Sutherland's Tr.* v. *Miller's Tr.* (1888) 16 R. 10; *Mowat, supra; Gow* v. *McEwan* (1901) 8 S.L.T. 484; *Pollok, supra; Rigg* v. *Mather* (1902) 10 S.L.T. 426; cf *Lavan* v. *Gavin Aird & Co.,* 1919 S.C. 345.

[5] *Simpson* v. *Mason & McRae* (1884) 21 S.L.R. 413.

[6] *Stodart* v. *Dalzell* (1876) 4 R. 236.

[7] *Stewart* v. *Burns* (1877) 4 R. 427.

[8] *Westren* v. *Millar* (1879) 7 R. 173.

[9] *Simpson* v. *Mason & McRae* (1884) 21 S.L.R. 413.

[10] *McLean* v. *Scott* (1902) 10 S.L.T. 447; *Rigg* v. *Mather* (1902) 10 S.L.T. 426.

[11] *Walker* v. *Flint* (1863) 1 M. 417.

[12] *Campbell* v. *McLean* (1870) 8 M. (H.L.) 40.

[13] *Forbes* v. *Wilson* (1873) 11 M. 454.

of the lands,[1] oral agreements followed by four years' possession,[2] improbative writings followed by possession,[3] remaining in possession after signing a new lease and paying rent on the basis thereof,[4] being allowed to possess, and grant a sub-lease of part of, lands, in reliance on an invalid lease,[5] remaining in possession on improbative missives for a new lease,[6] making an informal application for the renewal of a lease and staying on in reliance thereon,[7] taking possession in reliance on a draft lease,[8] possessing land in accordance with the stipulations of a copy lease engrossed in a book of estate leases and subscribed only by the tenant's mark.[9] It has been questioned whether a tenant's absention from giving notice of intention to terminate a lease is sufficient *rei interventus* to validate an informal agreement for a new lease.[10]

In the case of contracts of service *rei interventus* applies equally,[11] and could be constituted by entry on the service and actual service for more than a year.[12]

In the case of cautionary obligations the principle covers receiving money advanced on the faith of an improbative bond,[13] and making advances on the faith of an improbative guarantee.[14]

In other cases the principle has also applied: thus marriage has been held to validate an invalidly executed antenuptial marriage-contract;[15] divorce has been held to complete an improbative agreement to make provision for the wife by gift of heritage.[16]

Homologation

Homologation may be inferred from some act by the party against whom the informal contract is sought to be enforced, subsequent thereto, which unequivocally implies approbation of

---

[1] *Bathie* v. *Lord Wharncliffe* (1873) 11 M. 490.
[2] *Sellar* v. *Aiton* (1875) 2 R. 381.
[3] *Grieve* v. *Barr*, 1954 S.C. 414.
[4] *Ballantine* v. *Stevenson* (1881) 8 R. 959.
[5] *Bell* v. *Goodall* (1883) 10 R. 905.
[6] *Buchanan* v. *Harris & Sheldon* (1900) 2 F. 935.
[7] *Station Hotel, Nairn* v. *Macpherson* (1905) 13 S.L.T. 456.
[8] *Wight* v. *Newton*, 1911 S.C. 762.
[9] *Wares* v. *Duff Dunbar's Trs.*, 1920 S.C. 5.
[10] *Sutherland's Tr.* v. *Miller's Tr.* (1888) 16 R. 10; cf. *Gardner* v. *Beresford's Trs.* (1878) 5 R. 638.
[11] *Stewart* v. *McCall* (1869) 7 M. 544; *Nisbet* v. *Percy*, 1951 S.C. 350.
[12] *Gow* v. *McEwan* (1901) 8 S.L.T. 484.
[13] *Church of England Life Assce. Co.* v. *Wink* (1857) 19 D. 415, 1079.
[14] *National Bank* v. *Campbell* (1892) 19 R. 885; cf. *Baird's Tr.* v. *Murray* (1883) 11 R. 153; *MacLeish* v. *B.L. Bank*, 1911, 2 S.L.T. 168.
[15] *Lang* v. *L's Trs.* (1889) 16 R. 590.
[16] *Stewart* v. *S.*, 1953 S.L.T. 267.

the informal contract.[1] He must have had full legal capacity, and had full knowledge of the circumstances and the contract he is alleged to have homologated.[2] It need not be important, not amount to alteration of circumstances or to loss.[1] Instances of homologation include circumstances implying acceptance by a landlord of a tenant's offer and allowing possession thereon,[3] retaining a lease signed by the tenant,[4] continuing to make arrangements to take over a licensed business and applying for transfer of the licence,[5] applying for the renewal of a hotel licence, following acceptance of an improbative application for renewal of the lease,[6] and assisting a feuar to have his plans approved by the Dean of Guild Court.[7]

Adoption of null deeds

Rei interventus and homologation apply only to transactions unenforceable by reason of the imperfections of the necessary deeds, not to transactions which are wholly null in law. Such cannot be approbated. But a party, in full knowledge of the nullity, may adopt a null transaction and assume liability thereunder,[8] as by accepting liability on a bill to which the person's signature had been forged,[9] though adoption will not be inferred from mere silence in face of a demand for payment of the bill.[10]

Formalities required to give effect to contracts

In certain cases at common law or under statute further formalities by way of writing or registration or both are required to give effect to the parties' contract, particularly to pass title to property. Thus at common law a contract to feu, or sell, or lease, or otherwise create or transfer any real right in or to heritable property, must be given effect to by a feu-contract or feu-charter, or disposition, or lease, or other appropriate probative deed, and

---

[1] Ersk. III, 3, 47–50; Bell, *Prin.* §27; *Mitchell* v. *Stornoway Trs.*, 1936 S.C. (H.L.) 56, 62.

[2] *Paterson* v. *Moncrieff* (1866) 4 M. 706; *Logan* v. *L.* (1869) 7 S.L.R. 40; *Gillespie* v. *City of Glasgow Bank* (1879) 6 R. 813; *Donaldson* v. *Tainsh's Trs.* (1886) 13 R. 967; *Inglis's Tr.* v. *I.* (1890) 17 R. (H.L.) 76.

[3] *Forbes* v. *Wilson* (1873) 11 M. 454.

[4] *Ballantine* v. *Stevenson* (1881) 8 R. 959.

[5] *Charles* v. *Shearer* (1900) 8 S.L.T. 273.

[6] *Station Hotel, Nairn* v. *Macpherson* (1905) 13 S.L.T. 456.

[7] *Mitchell* v. *Stornoway Trs.*, 1936 S.C. (H.L.) 56.

[8] Ersk. III, 3, 47; Bell, *Prin.* §27.

[9] *Greenwood* v. *Martin's Bank* [1933] A.C. 51.

[10] *McKenzie* v. *B.L. Co.* (1881) 8 R (H.L.) 8; *B.L. Co.* v. *Cowan* (1906) 8 F. 704; *Muir's Exrx.* v. *Craig's Trs.*, 1913 S.C. 349.

in most cases this must also be registered in the appropriate division of the General Register of Sasines.[1]

Among cases required by statute to be effectuated by writing are the following:

(a) an agreement to assign, outright or in security, translate, or retrocess any personal bond or conveyance of moveable property must be effected by assignation in statutory form, written on the bond or conveyance or in a separate deed, and intimated to the debtor.[2]

(b) the sale or transfer of registered ships or shares therein must be effected by bill of sale executed by the transferor before one witness and registered.[3]

(c) the mortgage of a registered ship or a share therein must be effected by mortgage executed by the mortgagor before one witness and registered.[4]

(d) the transfer of shares or debentures in a company cannot be registered unless a proper instrument of transfer signed by the transferor has been delivered to the company;[5] various categories of registered securities may be transferred by a stock transfer executed by the transferor, not attested, registered by the company or issuing authority.[6]

(e) copyright can be assigned only in writing signed by or on behalf of the assignor.[7]

(f) an assignation of a patent,[8] registered trade mark,[9] or registered design[10] must be made by deed and registered at the Patent Office.

(g) an assignation of plant breeder's rights must be made by deed registered at the Plant Variety Rights Office.[11]

(h) the mortgage of an aircraft must be effected by an aircraft mortgage in statutory form entered in the register of aircraft mortgages kept by the Civil Aviation Authority.[12]

---

[1] See generally Chaps. 76, 85, 86, *infra*.

[2] Transmission of Moveable Property (Sc.) Act, 1862; see Chaps. 109–110, *infra*.

[3] Merchant Shipping Act, 1894, S. 24. But writing is not necessary for the sale of a ship or shares therein: *McConnachie* v. *Geddes*, 1918 S.C. 391.

[4] M.S.A., 1894, S. 31. As to transfer of mortgage see S. 37.

[5] Companies Act, 1948, S. 75; writing is not necessary for the contract.

[6] Stock Transfer Act, 1963, S. 1.

[7] Copyright Act, 1956, S. 36(3).

[8] Patents Act, 1949, Ss. 73–4.

[9] Trade Marks Act, 1938, Ss. 22–5.

[10] Registered Designs Act, 1949, Ss. 17–19.

[11] Plant Varieties and Seeds Act, 1964, Ss. 4(4), 9(5), 11.

[12] Mortgaging of Aircraft Order, 1972 (S.I. 1972, 1268) Reg. 4 and Sched. 2.

Stamping

The Stamp Act, 1891, as amended, imposes in many circumstances the requirement that a document constituting or evidencing or discharging a contract be stamped. Stamp duties are applicable to documents, not to transactions, so that they never apply where an oral transaction is competent, and is in fact entered into. The liability of a document to duty is to be judged not according to its title or language but according to its substance, or true nature and effect. Where several instruments are contained in one deed, each one falls to be separately stamped.[1] Once a document has been executed the commissioners of Inland Revenue may be required to give an opinion as to whether it is liable to duty and, if so, to how much;[2] it can then be stamped with an adjudication stamp, which is conclusive that the deed is properly stamped or is not liable to duty. In certain cases duty must be adjudicated. The duties are in some cases fixed, in others varying with the value of the transaction.[3] An instrument required to be, but not, duly stamped may not, except in criminal proceedings, be received in evidence or be available for any purpose whatever unless or until stamped. Deeds should in theory be stamped before execution, and after-stamping is permissible only under penalty, and not in all cases.[4]

Delivery

Mutual obligations or contracts require no delivery.[5] But unilateral deeds are not obligatory on the granter without delivery to the grantee, or a third party on his behalf,[6] and remain revocable by the granter,[7] except for deeds containing a clause dispensing with delivery, testamentary deeds, bonds by a parent in favour of his children, deeds in which the granter has a reserved interest, deeds which the granter was under an antecedent obligation to execute, and deeds recorded in a public register for publication.[5] Where delivery is necessary to bind the granter, the grantee is not bound until he accepts the deed with all its limitations and burdens.[8]

[1] For table of duties see [1964] C.L.Y. §3483.

[2] e.g. *Paul* v. *I.R.*, 1936 S.C. 443.

[3] Stamp Act, 1891, S. 14; see *Don Francesco* v. *De Meo*, 1908 S.C. 7; *Watson* v. *W.*, 1934 S.C. 374.

[4] *Simpson's Trs.* v. *S.*, 1933 S.C. 128; *Thomson* v. *Black*, 1936 S.N. 78.

[5] Ersk. III, 2, 44; Bell, *Prin.* §24.

[6] *McAslan* v. *Glen* (1859) 21 D. 511; *Martini* v. *Steel and Craig* (1878) 6 R. 342.

[7] Bell, *Prin.* §23; *Shaw* v. *Muir's Exrx.* (1892) 19 R. 997.

[8] Ersk. III, 2, 45.

CHAPTER 33

ESSENTIAL VALIDITY— AGREEMENTS WITH INHERENT DEFECTS

A N agreement apparently validly concluded may subsequently be challenged by one party as being invalid by reason of inherent defect. The categories of invalidity are (1) where the agreement was affected by the error of one or both parties; (2) where the contract was extorted, or (3) assent was obtained under force or fear, or (4) where one contracting party suffered from facility and was circumvented; and (5) where undue influence was exercised. The party alleging that he has been mistaken or over-reached may refuse to perform, alleging the error or other defect as a defence, or bring an action of reduction of the contract as vitiated by error or other defect in its constitution.

ERROR

Error[1] is a mistaken belief or understanding in the mind of one or of both parties to a contract as to some material element of their agreement. It may be as to some collateral matter or as to some matter which is an essential of the contract; it may affect the expression of the parties' intentions, or the substance of their contract, and be in a matter of law or of fact; it may affect the minds of both parties or that of one only, and in the latter case be unknown or known to the other, be the result of pure ignorance or mistake or be induced by the representations of the other. The cases must be finely distinguished and the effect of error on a contract differs in different circumstances.

Collateral error and essential error

Error is collateral or concomitant when it existed in the mind of at least one party but related to some collateral fact and did not affect any fundamental element of the agreement. Thus a man's motive or reason for contracting may turn out unfounded,[2] but if he obtained what he contracted for, that error does not affect the

---

[1] The corresponding concept in English law is mistake. But many English cases of mistake have been decided on different principles which are an unsafe guide to Scottish cases involving problems of error. See also Gow, 65 J.R. 221; 66 J.R. 253.
[2] *Cloup* v. *Alexander* (1831) 9 S. 448; *Hogg* v. *Campbell* (1864) 2 M. 848.

validity of the contract. Similarly a mistaken belief in the suitability or utility of the subject of agreement leaves the contract unaffected.[1] It is thought that collateral or concomitant error never justifies rescission of the contract or its reduction by the court.

Essential error

Error can be effective, if at all, as a ground for a contract being reduced by the court, only if it was essential, or in respect of some substantial or fundamental element of the agreement.[2] Error is essential if it is such that 'but for it one of the parties would have declined to contract,'[3] or which affected the substance of the contract,[4] or was in one of the respects fundamental to the agreement such as parties, subject or price,[5] or as to some qualities expressly or tacitly essential to the bargain,[6] or was an error material to the entering into the contract, and the consequent acceptance of its rights and obligations.[7] Small discrepancies between contract and reality, in extent, quality or value, do not amount to essential error.[8] In cases of error as to fact such error in substantials may arise in relation to any one or more of (1) the subject of the contract or obligation, (2) the other party to the obligation, wherever personal identity is essential, (3) the price or consideration for the undertaking, (4) the quality, quantity or extent of the thing, if expressly or tacitly essential to the bargain, and (5) the nature of the contract itself supposed to be entered into.[9] In nominate contracts the essentials of the contract are usually well settled; thus in sale the essentials are identification of the parties, the subjects sold, and the price. Nothing can be an essential of a contract which does not concern both parties.[10]

Error common, mutual, unilateral and unilateral induced

A distinction also falls to be drawn between cases of (1) error common to both contracting parties, (2) error in the mind of each

---

[1] cf. Ersk. III, 1, 16.

[2] *Stewart* v. *Kennedy* (1890) 17 R. (H.L.) 25; cf. *Edinburgh Brewery Co.* v. *Gibson's Tr.* (1869) 7 M. 886; *Morton* v. *Smith* (1877) 5 R. 83; *Wood* v. *Edinburgh Mags.* (1886) 13 R. 1006; *Woods* v. *Tulloch* (1893) 20 R. 477; *Pender-Small* v. *Kinloch's Trs.*, 1917 S.C. 307.

[3] *Menzies* v. *M.* (1893) 20 R. (H.L.) 108, 142. ct. Ersk. III, 1, 16.

[4] *Stewart*, *supra*, 26.

[5] *Stewart* v. *Kennedy* (1889) 16 R. 857, 864.

[6] *Woods*, *supra*, 479. cf. *Munro* v. *Strain* (1874) 1 R. 522, 525.

[7] *Westville S.S. Co.* v. *Abram S.S. Co.*, 1922 S.C. 571, 579.

[8] *Wood*, *supra*; *Woods*, *supra*.

[9] Bell, *Prin.* §11, approved in *Stewart*, *supra*, 28. See also Ersk. III, 1, 16; Bell, *Comm.* I, 313–14.

[10] *Stewart* v. *Kennedy* (1889) 16 R. 857, 864, per L. P. Inglis.

party as to the other's intention (mutual error), (3) error in the
mind of one party only but realized by the other to exist, though
not induced by him (unilateral error uninduced), and (4) error in
the mind of one party only but known by the other to exist because induced by a representation made by the other contracting
party. Cases of error in the mind of one party only induced by
mis-statements by the other party made in the course of negotiations are referable to misrepresentation rather than pure error.

The groups of cases

The cases where essential error has arisen may be divided into
firstly cases where the error was in the expression, transmission
or effectuation of the parties' intentions, and secondly cases where
the error affected their actual intentions, comprising cases where
error in law is alleged and also cases where error in fact is alleged,
though it is frequently difficult to draw a line between errors in
law and errors in fact.

Error in expression or transmission or effectuation of parties' intention

Where an error is made by one party in the expression of an
offer, as where he mistakenly quotes too low a price, the other
party, if he realizes the mistake, is possibly not entitled to accept,[1]
and if he does the contract is reducible. Even if the other party
does not realize the mistake and accepts in good faith, he possibly
may not, on discovering the mistake, hold the offeror to his
bargain if he could reasonably have discovered it previously.[2]

If an error is made in the transmission of an offer so that it
reaches the offeree in terms materially different from those
intended, an acceptance does not conclude a contract.[3] There is
no true *consensus* between parties.

Where agreement has been reached but the contract or deed
embodying or giving effect to the agreement contains an error,
so that it does not correctly state or give effect to what the parties
agreed on, the court will not permit one party to take advantage
of what is admitted, or held proved, to be an incorrect expression

---

[1] *Steuart's Tr.* v. *Hart* (1875) 3 R. 192 (inconsistent with *Stewart* v. *Kennedy* (1890) 17 R.
(H.L.) 25, 27, 29 and *Menzies* v. *M.* (1893) 20 R. (H.L.) 108, 142).

[2] *Sword* v. *Sinclair* (1771) Mor. 14241; *Jamieson* v. *McInnes* (1887) 15 R. 17; *Wilkie* v.
Hamilton Lodging House Co. (1902) 4 F. 951 (contracts by schedule rates, not lump sum);
Mitchell v. *Dalkeith Mags.*, 1930 S.L.T. 80; *Contra, Seaton Brick Co.* v. *Mitchell* (1900) 2 F.
550, where contract for lump sum and mistake not discoverable by offeree.

[3] *Henkel* v. *Pape* (1870) L.R. 6 Ex. 7 (order for 'the' transmitted as 'three'); *Verdin
Bros.* v. *Robertson* (1871) 10 M. 35; see also *Falck* v. *Williams* [1900] A.C. 176.

of their underlying agreement.[1] Even where a deed giving incorrect effect to a sale of heritage has been recorded in the Register of Sasines it may be reduced for an accurate deed to be substituted.[2]

Error in intention—Error in law

Error in law covers both mistaken understanding of some matter of general law, such as of the rights of a buyer or a seller of goods, or of the beneficiaries under a trust, and mistaken interpretation of the legal effect of some deed affecting the rights of the parties only. Despite the generality of the proposition 'Error in substantials, whether in fact or in law, invalidates consent where reliance is placed on the thing stated',[3] it is thought that a person cannot reduce a contract on the ground that he was mistaken as to some matter of general law affecting it.[4] A man must be taken to know the general law; if he does not he should find out, or take the consequences. A contract deliberately executed in the terms which the parties agreed cannot, save by agreement, be set aside on the ground that one or both of them was under essential error as to its construction and legal effect.[5] They are bound according to the true interpretation of the contract as decided by the court. It may, however, be otherwise where the party can satisfy the court that he was mistaken as to the category of contract being entered into. Similarly a party may contract on the basis of taking the risk that the other's representations as to a matter of law were incorrect, and cannot then complain if the legal position is found to be otherwise.[6] So also the modern view is that money paid under a mistaken understanding of the general law,[7] though not of an agreement between parties,[8] is not recoverable.

---

[1] Ersk. III, 3, 87; *Waddell* v. *W.* (1863) 1 M. 635; *N.B. Insce. Co.* v. *Tunnock* (1864) 3 M. 1; *Johnston* v. *Pettigrew* (1865) 3 M. 954; *Dundee Mags.* v. *Duncan* (1883) 11 R. 145; *Glasgow Feuing Co.* v. *Watson's Trs.* (1887) 14 R. 610; *Glen's Trs.* v. *Lancashire Insurance Co.* (1906) 8 F. 915; *Krupp* v. *Menzies,* 1907 S.C. 903; cf. *Aitken's Exors.* v. *Brown* (1862) 24 D. 506.

[2] *Anderson* v. *Lambie,* 1954 S.C. (H.L.) 43.

[3] Bell, *Prin.* §11; cf. Stair I, 10, 13; Ersk. III, 1, 16.

[4] *Cloup* v. *Alexander* (1831) 9 S. 448; *Manclark* v. *Thomson's Trs.,* 1958 S.C. 147, 161.

[5] *Stewart* v. *Kennedy* (1889) 16 R. 857, 862; (1890) 17 R. (H.L.) 25; see also *Cloup* v. *Alexander* (1831) 9 S. 448; *MacLagan* v. *Dickson* (1832) 11 S. 165; *Johnston* v. *Goodlet* (1868) 6 M. 1067; *Stewart* v. *Kennedy* (1890) 17 R. (H.L.) 25; *Muirhead & Turnbull* v. *Dickson* (1905) 7 F. 686; *Laing* v. *Provincial Homes Investment Co.,* 1909 S.C. 812; *Britannia Insce. Co.* v. *Duff,* 1909 S.C. 1261; *Manclark* v. *Thomson's Trs.,* 1958 S.C. 147.

[6] *Brownlie* v. *Miller* (1880) 7 R. (H.L.) 66.

[7] *Young* v. *Campbell* (1851) 14 D. 63; *Dickson* v. *Halbert* (1854) 16 D. 586; *Baird's Trs.* v. *B.* (1877) 4 R. 1005; *Glasgow Corpn.* v. *Lord Advocate,* 1959 S.C. 203.

[8] *British Hydro Carbon Chemicals* v. *B.T.C.,* 1961 S.L.T. 280.

Error in interpretation

The proper interpretation of a contract is a matter of law for the court and, save by agreement, parties cannot resile from or rescind the contract because it is held to mean other than they thought.[1] Where a contract has been concluded in terms agreed by the parties but the court attaches to those words a meaning other than that which the parties or one of them intended, the parties are held to their words and neither party can attack the contract on the ground of error.[2] If the court finds the contract unintelligible or meaningless the contract is void.[3]

Error in law affecting parties' rights only

But it is otherwise where there has been essential error on a point of law affecting the parties only, such as on the interpretation of a marriage contract. In such a case common error justifies reduction of the contract entered into subject to the error.[4]

While a discharge for onerous consideration or compromise is not reducible on the ground of alleged unilateral error in law[5] in cases of unilateral grants, renunciations and discharges, and gratuitious undertakings the court has, moreover, sometimes permitted reduction on the ground that the grant had been made under mistaken belief as to its legal consequences.[6] So too a widow's election whether to accept legal rights or a testamentary provision is alterable if she was in error as to the consequences of her election.[7]

If one party's erroneous belief as to his rights was induced by misrepresentations by the other party the contract is probably reducible.[8]

Error in intention—Error in fact

Error in fact exists where one or both of the contracting parties find that he or they have been under a misapprehension in some

---

[1] *Stewart v. Kennedy* (1890) 17 R. (H.L.) 25; *Laing, supra.*

[2] *Anderson v. Lambie*, 1954 S.C. (H.L.) 43, 57–8.   [3] *Laing, supra.*

[4] *Mercer v. Anstruther's Trs.* (1871) 9 M. 618, 628, 649, 652; affd. (1872) 10 M. (H.L.) 39.

[5] *Kippen v. K's Tr.* (1874) 1 R. 1171, 1179; *Manclark v. Thomson's Trs.*, 1958 S.C. 147, 162. cf. *Forbes v. F's Trs.*, 1957 S.C. 325.

[6] *Ross v. Mackenzie* (1842) 5 D. 151; *Dickson v. Halbert* (1854) 16 D. 586; *Purdon v. Rowat's Trs.* (1856) 19 D. 206; *Johnston v. J.* (1857) 19 D. 706; 3 Macq. 619; *McLaurin v. Stafford* (1875) 3 R. 265; *McCaig's Tr. v. Glasgow University* (1904) 6 F. 918; *Hunter v. Bradford Property Trust*, 1970 S.L.T. 173. cf. *Macandrew v. Gilhooley*, 1911 S.C. 448. See also *Kippen v. K's Tr.* (1874) 1 R. 1171, 1179.

[7] *Dawson's Trs. v. D.* (1896) 23 R. 1006; *Stewart v. Bruce's Trs.* (1898) 25 R. 965.

[8] cf. *Laing v. Provincial Homes*, 1909 S.C. 812; *McCulloch v. McC.*, 1950 S.L.T. (Notes) 29.

substantial or essential respect as to some matter of fact relevant to their contract, such as the subject-matter or the price. The cases may be grouped according as the error alleged was common to both parties, mutual, unilateral or unilateral but induced by the other party to the contract.

(1) COMMON ERROR

Common error[1] arises where both parties have made the same mistake about some fact underlying and material to their contract. They agree that they had reached agreement, but it appears that both were then under the same misapprehension. Where the mistaken belief relates to the existence of a certain state of facts essential to the contract, the contract is void. Thus if goods are sold and without the seller's knowledge had perished at the time the contract was made, it is void.[2] So too where an annuity was bought on the life of a person already dead,[3] or the life assurance policy of a dead man assigned,[4] or a thing was sold which, unknown to the parties, already belonged to the purchaser,[5] or a house was let in ignorance that it had been burned down,[6] or a ship chartered when it had in fact been lost,[7] or a sale was negotiated of land, part of which was found to belong to a third party,[8] or a person paid premiums on a life assurance policy in which she had no insurable interest and for which she had made no proposal,[9] or a company made an *ultra vires* issue of shares.[10]

The contract will, however, be valid if one party warranted the existence of the thing, or if both parties took a chance on the existence of a thing, the existence of which was known by both to be doubtful.[11] The contract is valid if the common error was as to

[1] Not infrequently mis-called 'mutual error'. 'Common' means 'pertaining to both'; 'Mutual' means 'in respect of each other'. For mutual error see (2), *infra*.

[2] Sale of Goods Act, 1893, S. 6; *Couturier* v. *Hastie* (1856) 5 H.L. Cas. 673; cf. *Bell* v. *Lever Bros.* [1932] A.C. 161.

[3] *Strickland* v. *Turner* (1852) 7 Ex. 208.

[4] *Scott* v. *Coulson* [1903] 2 Ch. 249.

[5] *Morton* v. *Smith* (1877) 5 R. 83.

[6] Dig. 18, 1, 57.

[7] *Sibson & Kerr* v. *Barcraig Co.* (1896) 24 R. 91; cf. *Couturier* v. *Hastie* (1856) 5 H.L.C. 673; *Paine* v. *Hutchinson* (1868) L.R. 3 Ch. 388.

[8] *Hamilton* v. *Western Bank* (1861) 23 D. 1033; cf. *Dowell's Ltd.* v. *Heriot's Trust*, 1941 S.C. 13, 19.

[9] *Came* v. *City of Glasgow Friendly Socy.*, 1933 S.C. 69.

[10] *Waverley Hydropathic Co.* v. *Barrowman* (1895) 23 R. 136.

[11] *Pender-Small* v. *Kinloch's Trs.*, 1917 S.C. 307.

a matter of opinion[1] or of future prospects,[2] or if a thing sold turns out to have unexpected value or qualities,[3] or to lack a particular quality,[4] or involved an element of transaction or compromise.[5]

(2) MUTUAL ERROR

Mutual[6] error arises where the parties have misunderstood each other and are at cross-purposes, or where one has, unknown to the other, misunderstood the other's intention, and in consequence denies the existence of true agreement.[7] In such circumstances the court must ascertain the terms of the offer and acceptance and enforce the contract in favour of the party whose understanding is deemed correct and consistent with what a reasonable person would have understood from the negotiations. The contract is therefore valid, unless the court holds that the difference of view has disclosed a concealed failure ever to reach agreement, in which case the contract is void. Examples are where one party thought the transaction was hire-purchase, the other that it was sale with instalment payments,[8] or one thought the price agreed was 'per (lineal) foot' and the other 'per (superficial) foot',[9] or that the sale of entailed lands was subject to certain Entail Acts procedure, and the other to different procedure,[10] or one thought the price of cattle was £15 per head, the other £13 per head,[11] or one thought he was buying goods of one shipment, the other that he was selling goods of a different shipment,[12] or one bid at an auction for a bale containing one commodity and the auctioneer knew the bale contained a different

---

[1] *Leaf* v. *International Galleries* [1950] 2 K.B. 86.

[2] *Wood* v. *N.B. Ry.* (1891) 18 R. (H.L.) 27; *Dornan* v. *Allan* (1900) 3 F. 112; *McGuire* v. *Paterson*, 1913 S.C. 400.

[3] *Dawson* v. *Muir* (1851) 13 D. 843; *Leaf, supra.*

[4] *Harrison and Jones Ltd.* v. *Bunten and Lancaster Ltd.* [1953] 1 Q.B. 646; cf. *Rose* v. *Pim* [1953] 2 Q.B. 450.

[5] *Manclark* v. *Thomson's Trs.*, 1958 S.C. 147.

[6] 'Mutual' is frequently used meaning 'common'; it is properly used as meaning 'by each towards the other'.

[7] Common instances are the so-called 'ticket cases', where one party thinks the contract is conditional, the other that it is unconditional: see Chap. 34.

[8] *Muirhead & Turnbull* v. *Dickson* (1905) 7 F. 686 (contract valid).

[9] *Stuart* v. *Kennedy* (1885) 13 R. 221 (contract void).

[10] *Kennedy* v. *Stewart* (1889) 16 R. 421; (1890) 17 R. (H.L.) 1 (contract valid: see also sequel: *Stewart* v. *Kennedy* (1889) 16 R. 857; (1890) 17 R. (H.L.) 25).

[11] *Wilson* v. *Marquis of Breadalbane* (1859) 21 D. 957 (contract void).

[12] *Raffles* v. *Wichelhaus* (1864) 2 H. & C. 906 (two ships of same name sailing in successive months) (contract void).

commodity but thought the bid was intended for the latter,[1] or one thought that the contract was *locatio rei* and the other that it was *locatio operis faciendi*,[2] or one party to an agreement to sell was not owner of the property,[3] or one thought that the contract was insurance and the other thought it insurance and copartnery,[4] or one made an offer ignorant of the fact that the other had made a better cross-offer.[5] Very common cases of mutual error are the so-called 'ticket cases',[6] where one party thinks that the contract is unconditional, the other that it is subject to conditions he has sought to attach to the contract. If the contract is in writing the court must interpret the written contract and may find that there was no true consensus and the contract is void[7] or that one party's understanding was correct and that the contract can be enforced as he understood it.[8]

(3) UNILATERAL ERROR UNINDUCED

In cases of unilateral error one party only has made a mistake and the other knows, or must be held to know, that, though he had not induced the error.[9] The party in error may consequently deny that there was true agreement. But in normal cases each contracting party must be on his guard and satisfy himself as to the nature, qualities and value of the subject of contract, and the other party is under no duty to prevent him making a bad bargain, beyond not misrepresenting to, or concealing from, him.[10] If a man buys too dear, or sells too cheap, he is not by reason of his mistake protected from loss.[11] It is no ground for interfering with the contract that one party agreed to it under a mistake, even in an essential respect.[12] The contract is therefore valid, notwithstanding the error of one realized by the other,[13] unless possibly the party in error reasonably believed that the subject of contract was

---

[1] *Scriven* v. *Hindley* [1913] 3 K.B. 564 (contract void).

[2] *Mathieson Gee* v. *Quigley*, 1952 S.C. (H.L.) 38 (contract void).

[3] *Dowell's Ltd.* v. *Heriot's Trust*, 1941 S.C. 13 (contract void).

[4] *Star Fire Ins. Co.* v. *Davidson* (1902) 5 F. 83 (contract void).

[5] *Welsh* v. *Cousin* (1900) 2 F. 277 (contract void).

[6] Chap. 34, *infra*.

[7] *Mathieson Gee* v. *Quigley*, 1952 S.C. (H.L.) 38 (contract void).

[8] *Houldsworth* v. *Gordon Cumming*, 1910 S.C. (H.L.) 49 (contract valid). cf. *Tamplin* v. *James* (1880) 15 Ch. D. 215.

[9] If the other party does not realize that the first party is in error, it is a case of mutual error.

[10] cf. *Patterson* v. *Landsberg* (1905) 7 F. 675, 678.

[11] Bell, *Prin.* §11.

[12] *Hunter* v. *Bradford Property Trust*, 1970 S.L.T. 173; *Steel* v. *Bradley Homes*, 1974 S.L.T. 133.

[13] Stair I, 9, 9; Bankt. I, 11; Ersk. III, 1, 16; Bell, *Comm.* I, 314; Gloag, 449.

so different from what it really was as to amount to a complete difference in kind, so that he had never truly consented to the contract he in fact made.[1] Unilateral essential error does not justify rescission or reduction of an onerous contract unless that error was induced by the other party's misrepresentation.[2] If, however, the deed or transaction were gratuitous it may be reduced if the error is essential, even though not induced by the other party.[3]

Instances of unilateral error uninduced include:

(i) (*subject-matter of contract*) undertaking an obligation in respect of one property thinking it was in respect of another property;[4] taking a lease of land as a deer-forest when it was not such;[5]

(ii) (*other party to the contract, where personal identity essential*) selling goods to a person who presented himself as buyer but whose identity was unknown;[6]

(iii) (*price or consideration*) selling goods at lower than the market price by reason of ignorance of what was known to the buyer, that legislation would raise the price;[7] settling an action for £20 in ignorance of a tender of £50 lodged in defence to the pursuer's action.[8]

(iv) (*quantity, quality or extent of the subject of contract*) undertaking to guarantee a person's overdraft at the bank in ignorance of the extent thereof;[9] buying fake antiques, thinking they were genuine;[10] but if the difference in quantity, quality or extent were so great that the thing given in fulfilment were of a different category from that contracted for, it might be that the contract would be void.[11]

(v) (*nature of the bargain itself*) signing a deed thinking it was a deed of another kind altogether, such as a conveyance thinking it

---

[1] Dig. 18, 1, 11; Stair I, 10, 13; Gloag, 441.

[2] *Stewart* v. *Kennedy* (1890) 17 R. (H.L.) 25, 27, 29; *Menzies* v. *M.* (1893) 20 R. (H.L.) 108, 142; *Stein* v. *S.*, 1914 S.C. 903, 908; cf. *Murray* v. *Marr* (1892) 20 R. 119, 125; and see further *infra*. *Steuart's Trs.* v. *Hart* (1875) 3 R. 192, so far as to the contrary effect, seems doubtful.

[3] *McLaurin* v. *Stafford* (1875) 3 R. 265; *McCaig* v. *Glasgow Univ.* (1904) 6 F. 918; *Sinclair* v. *S.*, 1949 S.L.T. (Notes) 16.

[4] *Bennie's Trs.* v. *Couper* (1890) 17 R. 782.

[5] *Wemyss* v. *Campbell* (1858) 20 D. 1090 (where court allowed an issue: *sed quaere*).

[6] *Macleod* v. *Kerr*, 1965 S.C. 253 (where contract challengeable as induced by fraud); cf. *Phillips* v. *Brooks* [1919] 2 K.B. 243; *Lake* v. *Simmons* [1927] A.C. 487.

[7] *Morison* v. *Boswell* (1801) Hume 679; *Paterson* v. *Allan* (1801) Hume 681.

[8] *Welsh* v. *Cousin* (1899) 2 F. 277; cf. *Steel* v. *Bradley Homes*, 1974 S.L.T. 133.

[9] *Royal Bank* v. *Greenshields*, 1914 S.C. 259.

[10] *Edgar* v. *Hector*, 1912 S.C. 348 (where held that error induced and contract consequently rescinded).

[11] cf. Dig. 18, 1, 9, 2.

was a will;[1] or granting a discharge of compensation claims thinking it was only a receipt for payments;[2] or a discharge of damages claims for an inadequate sum.[3]

Unilateral error wholly excluding consent

Unilateral error may, however, render the contract void if it existed in such fundamental respects as truly to have excluded consent, where the party in error cannot be said to have agreed at all to the contract which he apparently assented to.[4] Thus an issue was allowed where a tenant believed he was taking a lease of a deer-forest but found that the lands were not a deer-forest, as that term was truly understood,[5] and where a person signed a deed in ignorance that a material clause had been omitted from the copy signed.[6] In the case, moreover, of unilateral and gratuitous undertakings, grants or renunciations, essential error alone justifies reduction, even without averments of inducement by misrepresentation.[7]

MISREPRESENTATION

(4) UNILATERAL ERROR INDUCED BY MISREPRESENTATION

Where, however, a party contracts under essential error induced by a misrepresentation made to him[8] by the other party,[9] in the course of the negotiations leading up to the contract, the contract is at least voidable and reducible at the instance of the

---

[1] Bell, *Prin.* §11; cf. *Selkirk* v. *Ferguson*, 1908 S.C. 26, where held no error as to nature of contract.

[2] *Mathieson* v. *Hawthorn* (1899) 1 F. 468; *Ellis* v. *Lochgelly Iron Co.*, 1909 S.C. 1278; *Macandrew* v. *Gilhooley*, 1911 S.C. 448.

[3] *N.B. Ry.* v. *Wood* (1891) 18 R. (H.L.) 27; *Mackie* v. *Strachan, Kinmond & Co.* (1896) 23 R. 1030; cf. *Welsh* v. *Cousin* (1899) 2 F. 277.

[4] Stair I, 10, 13.

[5] *Wemyss* v. *Campbell* (1858) 20 D. 1090, explained in *Steel* v. *Bradley Homes*, 1974 S.L.T. 133.

[6] cf. *Hogg* v. *Campbell* (1864) 2 M. 848, where fraud was alleged.

[7] *Ross* v. *Mackenzie* (1842) 5 D. 151; *Hutchison* v. *Anderson's Trs.* (1853) 15 D. 570; *Dickson* v. *Halbert* (1854) 16 D. 586; *Purdon* v. *Rowatt's Trs.* (1856) 19 D. 206; *Priestnell* v. *Hutcheson* (1857) 19 D. 495; *Mercer* v. *Anstruther's Trs.* (1871) 9 M. 618; 10 M. (H.L.) 39; *McLaurin* v. *Stafford* (1875) 3 R. 265; *Baird's Trs.* v. *B.* (1877) 4 R. 1005; *Scottish Life Assce. Co.* v. *Donald* (1901) 9 S.L.T. 200; *McCaig* v. *Glasgow University Court* (1904) 6 F. 918; *Macandrew* v. *Gilhooley*, 1911 S.C. 448; *McAdam* v. *Scott*, 1913, 1 S.L.T. 12.

[8] *Woods* v. *Tulloch* (1893) 20 R. 477; *Ferguson* v. *Wilson* (1904) 6 F. 779, 782.

[9] Not by a third party: *Young* v. *Clydesdale Bank* (1889) 17 R. 231; *Thin & Sinclair* v. *Arrol* (1896) 24 R. 198; *Aitken* v. *Pyper* (1900) 8 S.L.T. 258; *Ellis* v. *Lochgelly Iron Co.*, 1909 S.C. 1278. They may, however, be made indirectly: *Gillies* v. *Campbell, Shearer & Co.* (1902) 10 S.L.T. 289.

party induced,[1] and may be wholly void, if the error has been essential and so fundamental as wholly to preclude *consensus*.[2] Claims for repetition of money and damages may sometimes also be available. It is unsettled whether reduction of a contract induced by misrepresentation is competent where it is not averred that it produced essential error, but merely that the contract was induced by misrepresentation.[3] The better view seems to be that 'as a ground of rescinding the contract, error and misrepresentation must be *in essentialibus*'.[4]

What are misrepresentations

A misrepresentation is an inaccurate[5] statement of past or present fact[6] made, expressly or impliedly, by assertion or concealment, or a failure to disclose in circumstances where there is a positive duty to disclose, made prior to or at the time of contracting, by one party to the other, which is a material factor in inducing the other party to contract on the terms on which he did. Such misrepresentation may be made in any of the respects regarded as essentials of a contract.[7] A mis-statement of law[8] is not in general a misrepresentation but may in particular circumstances imply a misrepresentation of fact, and conversely.

Not everything stated to the other party in the course of negotiations amounts to representation, or misrepresentation. Misrepresentations of fact must be distinguished from (a) exaggerated or unduly laudatory or optimistic advertisements, *verba jactanctia*; for such are common, not usually thought of as obligatory, and some latitude is permitted to persons seeking to do business:[9] *simplex commendatio non obligat*; (b) expressions of opinion, which, so long as honestly held, may with impunity be

---

[1] *Tulloch* v. *Davidson* (1860) 22 D. (H.L.) 7; *Graham* v. *Western Bank* (1864) 2 M. 559; *Western Bank* v. *Addie* (1867) 5 M. (H.L.) 80; *Stewart* v. *Kennedy* (1890) 17 R. (H.L.) 25; *Price & Pierce* v. *Bank of Scotland*, 1910 S.C. 1095; affd. 1912 S.C. (H.L.) 19.

[2] e.g. *Morrisson* v. *Robertson*, 1908 S.C. 332.

[3] See e.g. *Hart* v. *Fraser*, 1907 S.C. 50.

[4] *Boyd & Forrest* v. *G.S.W. Ry.*, 1915 S.C. (H.L.) 20, 35, per Lord Shaw; cf. *Woods* v. *Tulloch* (1893) 20 R. 477, where error held not essential. *Bell, Prin.* §13A, suggests that an obligation induced by fraud is voidable, one induced by fraud resulting in essential error wholly void. The modern practice is to desiderate averment of essential error in all cases.

[5] cf. *MacDonald* v. *Fyfe, Ireland & Dangerfield* (1895) 3 S.L.T. 124.

[6] cf. *Zurich Ins. Co.* v. *Leven*, 1940 S.C. 406.

[7] cf. Bell, *Prin.* §14.

[8] *Brownlie* v. *Miller* (1880) 7 R. (H.L.) 66 (erroneous statement that lands were held of the Crown).

[9] Stair I, 9, 10; *Dimmock* v. *Hallett* (1866) L.R. 2 Ch. 21; *City of Edinburgh Brewery Co.* v. *Gibson's Tr.* (1869) 7 M. 886; *Dunnett* v. *Mitchell* (1887) 15 R. 131. cf. *Paul* v. *Glasgow Corpn.* (1900) 3 F. 119.

unfounded;[1] though it is otherwise if an opinion is stated as a fact;[2] (c) expressions of intention or expectation, which may with impunity be changed,[3] though it is misrepresentation to state as entertained an intention not truly or in fact held;[4] and (d) promises or undertakings,[5] unless the promisor was misrepresenting the state of his own mind and his willingness to perform. For none of these, even if unfounded, does the law give a remedy, as the other party is not entitled to rely on them. Moreover the Trade Descriptions Act, 1968, which creates the offences of applying a false trade description to goods, of supplying or offering to supply goods to which a false trade description is applied, of offering to supply goods with a false indication that the price is equal to or less than a recommended price at which goods were previously offered, and of making false or misleading statments as to services, provides (S. 35) that a contract for the supply of any goods shall not be void or unenforceable by reason only of a contravention of any provision of the 1968 Act.[6]

Representations of fact in negotiations and inducing contract must also be distinguished from statements agreed to be, or held to have been intended as, contractual warranties, or undertakings intended to be guarantees and to enter as terms into the contract,[7] and from statements outside of but collateral to the contract.[8]

Express misrepresentation

Misrepresentation may be made expressly, as by a positive statement which is inaccurate in fact, such as erroneous statements as to the profits of a business,[9] or mis-statements of the strata through which contractors had to dig,[10] or by conduct designed to conceal and prevent discovery of the truth.[11]

---

[1] *Gowans* v. *Christie* (1873) 11 M. (H.L.) 1; *Brownlie* v. *Miller* (1880) 7 R. (H.L.) 66; *Smith* v. *Land and House Property Corpn.* (1884) 28 Ch. D. 7; *Woods* v. *Tulloch* (1893) 20 R. 477; *Sutherland* v. *Bremner's Trs.* (1903) 10 S.L.T. 565; *Hamilton* v. *Duke of Montrose* (1906) 8 F. 1026; *Gilchrist* v. *Whyte*, 1907 S.C. 984; *Bisset* v. *Wilkinson* [1927] A.C. 177; *Flynn* v. *Scott*, 1949 S.C. 442.

[2] *Reese River Co.* v. *Smith* (1869) L.R. 4 H.L. 64.

[3] *Harvey* v. *Seligmann* (1883) 10 R. 680; *Ferguson* v. *Wilson* (1904) 6 F. 779.

[4] *Edgington* v. *Fitzmaurice* (1885) 29 Ch. D. 459.

[5] *Bell Bros. (H.P.) Ltd.* v. *Reynolds*, 1945 S.C. 213.

[6] But ordinary remedies may be available on other grounds.

[7] *Buist* v. *Scottish Equitable Life Assce. Socy.* (1878) 5 R. (H.L.) 64; *Standard Life Assce. Co.* v. *Weems* (1884) 11 R. (H.L.) 48; *Reid* v. *Employers', etc., Insce. Co.* (1899) 1 F. 1031; *Hyslop* v. *Shirlaw* (1905) 7 F. 875; see also *Craig* v. *Palatine Insce. Co.* (1894) 1 S.L.T. 646.

[8] *Robey* v. *Stein* (1900) 3 F. 278.   [9] *Ferguson* v. *Wilson* (1904) 6 F. 779.

[10] *Boyd & Forrest* v. *G.S.W. Ry.*, 1912 S.C. (H.L.) 93.

[11] *Schneider* v. *Heath* (1813) 3 Camp. 506; cf. *White* v. *Dougherty* (1891) 18 R. 972.

Implied misrepresentation

A misrepresentation may also be made by implication,[1] as where a person buys goods knowing that he cannot pay for them or not intending to pay for them[2] or indifferent to his ability or inability to pay, as the buying implies a representation of ability to pay, but it is very difficult to prove that such was the buyer's state of mind. Such an implied misrepresentation may render the contract voidable,[3] but it is questionable if such would ever render it wholly void. It is otherwise if he merely has doubts about his ability to pay when payment is due.[4] To offer for sale goods apparently other than they truly are may similarly be an implied misrepresentation.[5]

Concealment

Concealment may have the same effect as actual representation to the contrary.[6] If the pursuer establishes a prima facie case of concealment there may be some onus on the defender to prove fair disclosure.[7]

No general duty of disclosure

In normal cases each party to a contract must ascertain facts for himself and rely on his own information and judgment; the other party is not obliged to volunteer information nor to prevent the first party making a bad bargain.[8] There is no legal objection to selling defective goods,[9] nor to buying goods having a value unsuspected by the seller.[10] If, however, questions are asked they

[1] Is it an express or an implied misrepresentation for a non-member to wear a club tie and thereby induce a contract?
[2] *Schuurmans* v. *Tweedie's Tr.* (1828) 6 S. 1110; *Watt* v. *Findlay* (1846) 8 D. 529; *Ex parte Whittaker* (1875) L.R. 10 Ch. 446; *Edgington* v. *Fitzmaurice* (1885) 29 Ch. D. 459; *Gamage* v. *Charlesworth's Tr.*, 1910 S.C. 257.
[3] *Gamage* v. *Charlesworth's Tr.*, *supra*.
[4] *Ehrenbacher* v. *Kennedy* (1874) 1 R. 1131; *Clarke* v. *Miller & Co.'s Tr.* (1885) 12 R. 1035.
[5] cf. *Patterson* v. *Landsberg* (1905) 7 F. 675; *Edgar* v. *Hector*, 1912 S.C. 348; *Gibson* v. *National Cash Register Co.*, 1925 S.C. 500; cf. *Gordon* v. *Watson & Montgomery* (1899) 6 S.L.T. 274.
[6] *Shankland* v. *Robinson*, 1920 S.C. (H.L.) 103; *The Spathari*, 1925 S.C. (H.L.) 6.
[7] *Gibson* v. *National Cash Register Co.*, 1925 S.C. 500.
[8] *Morison* v. *Boswell* (1801) Hume 679; *Paterson* v. *Allan* (1801) Hume 681; *Young* v. *Clydesdale Bank* (1889) 17 R. 231; *Welsh* v. *Cousin* (1899) 2 F. 277; *Russell* v. *Farrell* (1900) 2 F. 892; *Aitken* v. *Pyper* (1900) 8 S.L.T. 258; *Royal Bank* v. *Greenshields*, 1914 S.C. 259; *Park* v. *Anderson Bros.*, 1924 S.C. 1017; cf. *N. of S. Bank* v. *Mackenzie*, 1925 S.L.T. 236.
[9] *Smith* v. *Hughes* (1871) L.R. 6 Q.B. 597; *Patterson* v. *Landsberg* (1905) 7 F. 675.
[10] *Gillespie* v. *Russell* (1856) 18 D. 677; 19 D. 897; 3 Macq. 757.

must be answered honestly, and there is authority for the view that disclosure of known defects should be made in the sale of specific articles where the circumstances preclude effective examination by the buyer.[1] But, in general, there is no duty of disclosure, and accordingly, in general, mere silence or non-disclosure does not amount to a representation or misrepresentation.[2] In particular, in contracts of sale or employment there is no duty to disclose defects. If concealment or non-disclosure is to be the ground of action, there must have been a duty to disclose.[3] But it is otherwise if silence in the circumstances implies a positive statement, if there is active or deliberate concealment of defects,[4] or there is non-disclosure where the goods appear to be what they are not.[5]

The Trade Descriptions Act, 1968 (extended 1972), makes it an offence to supply or offer to supply any goods to which a false trade description is applied (S. 1), or to give any false indication as to price (S. 11), or to make a statement known to be false or recklessly to make a false statement as to the provision of services (S. 14), but (S. 35) a contract for the supply of any goods shall not be void or unenforceable by reason only a contravention of the Act. The Trading Representations (Disabled Persons) Amendment Act, 1972, S. 1, makes it an offence to sell goods advertised as made by or sold for the benefit of blind or disabled persons.

Where duty of disclosure exists

Exceptionally, a party is legally obliged, though unasked, to make full and frank disclosure of every fact which might influence the mind of the other contracting parties.[6] This duty arises:

(a) in cases of contracts *uberrimae fidei*, which category includes contracts of insurance, where there is a duty to disclose all known facts, whether or not the proposer considered the information

---

[1] Gloag, 458.

[2] *Young* v. *Clydesdale Bank* (1889) 17 R. 231; *Welsh* v. *Cousin* (1899) 2 F. 277; *Russell* v. *Farrell* (1900) 2 F. 892; *Aitken* v. *Pyper* (1900) 8 S.L.T. 258; *Walker* v. *Greenock Hospitals Board*, 1951 S.C. 464, 470; *Zurich Ins. Co.* v. *Leven*, 1940 S.C. 406, 415.

[3] *Kirkpatrick* v. *Irvine* (1850) 7 Bell 186; *Broatch* v. *Jenkins* (1866) 4 M. 1030; cf. *Assets Co.* v. *Tosh's Trs.* (1898) 6 S.L.T. 96; *Bain* v. *Assets Co.* (1905) 7 F. (H.L.) 104.

[4] *Schneider* v. *Heath* (1813) 3 Camp. 506; *Duthie* v. *Carnegie*, 21 Jan., 1815, F.C.; *Paul* v. *Old Shipping Co.* (1816) 1 Mur. 64, 70.

[5] *Patterson, supra* (fake antiques); *Edgar* v. *Hector*, 1912 S.C. 348; *Gibson* v. *National Cash Register Co.*, 1925 S.C. 500 (reconditioned machine).

[6] Bell, *Prin.* §14.

relevant or material,[1] contracts of caution for the intromissions of an employee,[2] though not necessarily all cautionary obligations,[3] and possibly contracts to enter into partnership[4] or to take shares in a company;[5]

(b) in any case where silence or non-disclosure renders incomplete or inaccurate another statement,[6] or where circumstances have changed requiring a correction to a prior statement.[7] In such cases any statement made must be complete and not leave a misleading impression.[8] This principle may extend to imposing a duty to disclose unexpected restrictions in the titles of land sold;[9]

(c) where there is a fiduciary or similar relationship between the parties, as between trustee and beneficiary,[10] or parent and child,[11] or different beneficiaries under a settlement.[12] A solicitor contracting with a client must not only disclose all material facts but show that the contract is one which an independent adviser would have advised.[13]

Duty of care not to misrepresent

Similarly, though there is always a duty not deliberately or knowingly to misrepresent, there is in general no duty to take care not to represent incorrectly, carelessly or inaccurately, unless such a duty is created by contract, or arises from such circumstances as

---

[1] *Life Assocn. of Scotland* v. *Foster* (1873) 11 M. 351; *Hutchison* v. *Aberdeen Sea Insce. Co.* (1876) 3 R. 682; *London Assce.* v. *Mansel* (1879) 11 Ch. D. 363; *Blackburn* v. *Vigors* (1886) 12 App. Cas. 531; *Craig* v. *Imperial Union Assce. Co.* (1894) 1 S.L.T. 646; *Equitable Life Assce. Socy.* v. *General Accident Assce. Corpn.* (1904) 12 S.L.T. 348; *The Spathari*, 1925 S.C. (H.L.) 6; *Locker and Woolf, Ltd.* v. *Western Australian Insce. Co.* [1936] 1 K.B. 408; *N.F.U. Mutual Insce. Socy.* v. *Tully*, 1935 S.L.T. 574; *Zurich General Accident Co.* v. *Leven*, 1938 S.C. 582; 1940 S.C. 406; cf. Marine Insurance Act, 1906, S. 18. See also *Harvey* v. *Seligmann* (1883) 10 R. 680; *Joel* v. *Law Union Insce. Co.* [1908] 2 K.B. 863.

[2] *French* v. *Cameron* (1893) 20 R. 966; *L.G.O.C.* v. *Holloway* [1912] 2 K.B. 72.

[3] *Royal Bank* v. *Greenshields*, 1914 S.C. 259; cf. *Cooper* v. *Nat. Prov. Bank* [1946] K.B. 1.

[4] *Ferguson* v. *Wilson* (1904) 6 F. 779; cf. *Manners* v. *Whitehead* (1898) 1 F. 171.

[5] *New Brunswick Ry.* v. *Muggeridge* (1860) 1 Dr. & Sm. 363; *Central Ry. of Venezuela* v. *Kisch* (1867) L.R. 2 H.L. 99; cf. Companies Act, 1948, Ss. 38, 43 and Sched. IV.

[6] *Dimmock* v. *Hallett* (1866) L.R. 2 Ch. App. 21; *Oakes* v. *Turquand* (1867) L.R. 2 H.L. 325; *Peek* v. *Gurney* (1873) L.R. 6 H.L. 377; *Curtis* v. *Chemical Cleaning Co.* [1951] 1 K.B. 805; cf. *Brownlie* v. *Miller* (1880) 7 R. (H.L.) 66, 79.

[7] *Davies* v. *London Marine Insce. Co.* (1878) 8 Ch. D. 469; *Shankland* v. *Robinson*, 1920 S.C. (H.L.) 103; *With* v. *O'Flanagan* [1936] Ch. 575.

[8] *Falconer* v. *N. of S. Bank* (1863) 1 M. 704; *Royal Bank* v. *Greenshields*, 1914 S.C. 259.

[9] *Smith* v. *Soeder* (1895) 23 R. 60; sed quaere.

[10] *Dougan* v. *Macpherson* (1902) 4 F. (H.L.) 7.

[11] *Smith Cuninghame* v. *Anstruther's Trs.* (1872) 10 M. (H.L.) 39; cf. *Woodward* v. *W.*, 1910, 2 S.L.T. 163.

[12] *Dempster* v. *Raes* (1873) 11 M. 843.

[13] *Aitken* v. *Campbell's Trs.*, 1909 S.C. 1217; *Gillespie* v. *Gardner*, 1909 S.C. 1053.

that information is given in reply to a question and in the knowledge that the inquirer or a known third party intends to act in reliance thereon.[1] In such circumstances there is a duty to take reasonable care for the accuracy of the statement.

Materiality of misrepresentation

To be effective the misrepresentation must have been material and not have been negligible in extent nor have related to some unimportant element of the contract; *de minimis non curat lex*.[2] Thus a discrepancy between reality and statement was held immaterial when not referred to in the subsequent contract.[3]

Inducement

A misrepresentation has no effect on a contract unless it was intended to induce, and did in fact induce, the other party to contract on the terms on which he did contract.[4] To be actionable it must have been addressed to the party who contracted and not come to the latter's notice indirectly.[5] To be a ground of relief, it must have been relied on and induced the contract; it must have been *dolus dans causam contractui*.[6] Misrepresentation is accordingly not a ground for relief if the complainer was unaware of the misrepresentation, and was not deceived, as where he did not inspect the thing,[7] or was aware that the representation was incorrect,[8] or does not allege that it was untrue,[9] or was not influenced by the misrepresentation.[10] If it is alleged that the complainer knew of the misrepresentation, it must be shown that

[1] *Robinson* v. *National Bank*, 1916 S.C. (H.L.) 154; *Hedley Byrne & Co.* v. *Heller & Partners* [1964] A.C. 465.

[2] *Burnett* v. *B.* (1859) 21 D. 813; *City of Edinburgh Brewery Co.* v. *Gibson's Tr.* (1869) 7 M. 886, 891; *Lees* v. *Tod* (1882) 9 R. 807, 846, 848; *Harvey* v. *Seligmann* (1883) 10 R. 680; *Wood* v. *Edinburgh Mags.* (1886) 13 R. 1006; *Woods* v. *Tulloch* (1893) 20 R. 477; *Zurich Ins. Co.* v. *Leven*, 1940 S.C. 406.

[3] *Ritchie* v. *Glass*, 1936 S.L.T. 591

[4] *McLellan* v. *Gibson* (1843) 5 D. 1032; *Burnett* v. *B.* (1859) 21 D. 813.

[5] *Peek* v. *Gurney* (1873) L.R. 6 H.L. 377; see also *Andrews* v. *Mockford* [1896] 1 Q.B. 372; *McMorland's Trs.* v. *Fraser* (1896) 24 R. 65.

[6] *City of Edinburgh Brewery Co.* v. *Gibson's Tr.* (1869) 7 M. 886, 891; *Ehrenbacher* v. *Kennedy* (1874) 1 R. 1131; *Lees* v. *Tod* (1882) 9 R. 807, 846, 853; *Gamage* v. *Charlesworth's Tr.*, 1910 S.C. 257; *Boyd & Forrest* v. *G.S.W. Ry.*, 1915 S.C. (H.L.) 20.

[7] *Horsfall* v. *Thomas* (1862) 1 H. & C. 90; *Arkwright* v. *Newbold* (1881) 17 Ch. D. 301; *Smith* v. *Chadwick* (1884) 9 App. Cas. 187.

[8] *Irving* v. *Burns*, 1915 S.C. 260.

[9] *Irvine* v. *Kirkpatrick* (1850) 7 Bell 186; *Hannah* v. *H.* (1869) 6 S.L.R. 329; *Edinburgh United Breweries* v. *Molleson* (1893) 20 R. 581; cf. *Patterson* v. *Landsberg* (1905) 7 F. 675.

[10] *Attwood* v. *Small* (1838) 6 Cl. & Fin. 232 (reliance on independent investigation); *Redgrave* v. *Hurd* (1881) 20 Ch. D. 1; *Smith* v. *Chadwick* (1884) 9 App. Cas. 187.

he had actual knowledge, not merely the means of knowledge; it is no defence that he might have discovered the misrepresentation by investigating or checking the representations.[1] The complainer need not, however, prove that the misrepresentation was the sole inducing factor, so long as it was one of the factors, and was in the circumstances material.[2]

Innocent, Negligent and Fraudulent Misrepresentation

A misrepresentation is innocent if the representer honestly but mistakenly believed what he asserted and had no intention to deceive.[3] It is negligent if he believed what he asserted and did not intend to deceive, but should in the circumstances have taken, and failed to take, care reasonable in the circumstances to ascertain the correctness of his representation.[4] It is fraudulent if he intended to deceive, or had no honest belief in the accuracy of his representation, if he made a false statement 'knowingly, or without belief in its truth, or recklessly, careless whether it be true or false'.[5] Only intentional, or reckless,[6] dishonesty amounts to fraudulent misrepresentation, and not only erroneous though honest,[7] but ignorant, foolish, credulous, and careless misrepresentation is innocent[8] misrepresentation. A person having *bona fide* belief in the truth of his representation is not fraudulent, even though he had inadequate grounds for the belief, unless indeed the inadequacy were such as to destroy the idea of good faith.[9] Older cases treated negligent misrepresentation as innocent,[10] but it now appears that if misrepresentation were made negligently, i.e. without taking due care in circumstances where the law imposes a duty to take care, the effect is the same as fraudulent misrepresentation.[11]

---

[1] *Redgrave v. Hurd* (1881) 20 Ch. D. 1; *Nocton v. Ashburton* [1914] A.C. 932; see also *Central Ry. of Venezuela v. Kisch* (1867) L.R. 2 H.L. 99, 120.

[2] *Western Bank v. Addie* (1867) 5 M. (H.L.) 80; *Smith v. Chadwick* (1882) 20 Ch. D. 27; *Edgington v. Fitzmaurice* (1885) 29 Ch. D. 459; *Gamage v. Charlesworth's Tr.*, 1910 S.C. 257.

[3] e.g. *Duncan, Galloway & Co. v. Duncan Falconer & Co.*, 1913 S.C. 265. This category includes cases where fraud is alleged but not proved, as in *Lees v. Tod* (1882) 9 R. 807; *Boyd & Forrest v. G.S.W. Ry.*, 1912 S.C. (H.L.) 93.

[4] *Hedley Byrne & Co. v. Heller & Partners* [1964] A.C. 465.

[5] *Derry v. Peek* (1889) 14 App. Cas. 337, 374, per Lord Herschell. Fraud is a machination or contrivance to deceive: Ersk. III, 1, 16; Bell, *Prin.* §13.

[6] *Culpa lata aequiparatur dolo*; see also Bell, *Comm.* I, 316.

[7] *Lees v. Tod* (1882) 9 R. 807, 853; *Boyd & Forrest v. G.S.W. Ry.*, 1912 S.C. (H.L.) 93.

[8] *Robinson v. National Bank of Scotland*, 1916 S.C. (H.L.) 154.

[9] *Lees, supra*, 854.

[10] *Derry, supra*; but see *Lees, supra*, 833.

[11] *Hedley Byrne & Co. v. Heller & Partners* [1964] A.C. 465; see also *Robinson, supra*.

Unilateral error induced by misrepresentation

Many cases illustrate the effect of unilateral error induced by misrepresentation, whether innocent, negligent or fraudulent.

(i) *(subject of the contract)*: An action for reduction of a lease was held relevant on averments of misrepresentation of the quantity of stock on, and the quality of, the land.[1]

(ii) *(person)*: where a party is induced to contract and the identity of the other contracting party is material and is misrepresented the contract is void,[2] but is only voidable where the misrepresentation was as to some fact less fundamental than his identity, such as his giving a false name,[3] or as to his solvency[4] or ability to pay[5] or his capacity to contract.[6]

(iii) *(price or consideration)*: where a party entered into partnership induced by misrepresentation as to the profits of the business;[7] where a buyer of land was misled as to the feuduty;[8] or a buyer of a business as to its profitability;[9] or a person settled a claim for an inadequate sum;[10] or a person sold shares, induced by misrepresentations as to the company's condition;[11] or a person disponed a house gratuitously;[12] or a person bought timber by fraudulent misrepresentations of the seller's solvency.[13]

(iv) *(quantity, quality or extent of the subject-matter)*: where goods were totally different from what they were represented to be;[14] where a hotel was sold as being reputable whereas there had been complaints as to its conduct;[15] where sellers represented that buildings belonged to them whereas they belonged to the landlord;[16] where a railway represented to contractors that a proposed

[1] *McPherson v. Campbell's Trs.* (1869) 41 S. Jur. 634.

[2] *Hardman v. Booth* (1857) 27 L.J. Ex. 117; *Cundy v. Lindsay* (1878) 3 App. Cas. 459; *Morrisson v. Robertson*, 1908 S.C. 332; *Lake v. Simmons* [1927] A.C. 487; *Ingram v. Little* [1961] 1 Q.B. 31.

[3] *King's Norton Metal Co. v. Edridge, Merrett & Co.* (1897) 14 T.L.R. 98; *Phillips v. Brooks* [1919] 2 K.B. 243; *Macleod v. Kerr*, 1965 S.C. 253; *Lewis v. Averay* [1971] 3 All E.R. 907.

[4] *Price & Pierce v. Bank of Scotland*, 1912 S.C. (H.L.) 19.

[5] *Gamage v. Charlesworth's Tr.*, 1910 S.C. 257.

[6] *Laing v. Provincial Homes Ins. Co.*, 1909 S.C. 812.

[7] *Ferguson v. Wilson* (1904) 6 F. 779; cf. *Adam v. Newbigging* (1888) 13 App. Cas. 308.

[8] *Clason v. Steuart* (1844) 6 D. 1201.

[9] *Straker v. Campbell*, 1926 S.L.T. 262.

[10] *Docherty v. McAlpine* (1899) 2 F. 128.

[11] *Spence v. Crawford*, 1939 S.C. (H.L.) 52.

[12] *Woodward v. W.*, 1910, 2 S.L.T. 163.

[13] *Price & Pierce, Ltd. v. Bank of Scotland*, 1912 S.C. (H.L.) 19.

[14] *Patterson v. Landsberg* (1905) 7 F. 675; *Edgar v. Hector*, 1912 S.C. 348; contrast *Woods v. Tulloch* (1893) 20 R. 477.

[15] *Hart v. Fraser*, 1907 S.C. 50.

[16] *Duncan Galloway & Co. v. Duncan Falconer & Co.*, 1913 S.C. 265.

line had to be constructed through soft ground not rock;[1] where a prospectus misstated the company's prospects;[2] and where one party misrepresented the benefits from an arrangement.[3]

(v) (*nature of the contract itself*): Again where signature is obtained by misrepresentation to a document wholly different in nature and category from that contemplated by the signatory, such as a conveyance believing it to be a will,[4] a bill of exchange instead of a guarantee,[5] a promissory note instead of witnessing a deed,[6] a guarantee instead of a paper concerning insurance,[7] an acceptance of an agreement instead of a reference to arbitration,[8] or a discharge of future claims instead of a receipt for part payments,[9] the signatory is not bound, and can repudiate liability. But he is bound if his mistake related only to the contents, effect, terms or interpretation of the document signed.[10] He cannot be released from a signed undertaking on·a plea of ignorance or misunderstanding. But if he was negligent in signing and he has sustained loss or a third party has lost in consequence, as by advancing money in reliance on the signature, the signatory is personally barred from denying his signature.[11] It has been indicated that error as to some essential stipulation even if not as to the legal category of the contract may amount to error regarding the nature of the contract.[12]

Effect on contract of its having been induced by misrepresentation

If the requisites are satisfied, misrepresentation renders the contract induced thereby voidable,[13] whether it was innocent,[14]

---

[1] *Boyd and Forrest v. G.S.W. Ry.*, 1912 S.C. (H.L.) 93.

[2] *Mair v. Rio Grande Rubber Estates, Ltd.*, 1913 S.C. (H.L.) 74; cf. *Chambers v. Edinburgh & Glasgow Aerated Bread Co.* (1891) 18 R. 1039; *Blakiston v. London & Scottish Banking Co.* (1894) 21 R. 417; *Romanes v. Garman*, 1912, 2 S.L.T. 104.

[3] *Laing v. Provincial Homes Ins. Co.*, 1909 S.C. 812.

[4] Bell, *Prin.*, §11.

[5] *Foster v. Mackinnon* (1869) L.R. 4 C.P. 704; cf. *Selkirk v. Ferguson*, 1908 S.C. 26.

[6] *Lewis v. Clay* (1897) 67 L.J. Q.B. 224.

[7] *Carlisle and Cumberland Bank v. Bragg* [1911] 1 K.B. 489 (but see *Saunders, infra*).

[8] *Fletcher v. Lord Advocate*, 1923 S.C. 27.

[9] cf. *Ellis v. Lochgelly Iron Co.*, 1909 S.C. 1278; *Macandrew v. Gilhooley*, 1911 S.C. 448.

[10] *McLeish v. B.L. Bank*, 1911, 2 S.L.T. 168; *Boyd v. Shaw*, 1927 S.C. 414; *Saunders v. Anglia Building Socy.* [1971] A.C. 1004.

[11] *Foster, supra*; *Young v. Clydesdale Bank* (1889) 17 R. 231; *Saunders, supra*.

[12] *Stewart v. Kennedy* (1890) 17 R. (H.L.) 25; *Laing, supra*; *Westville S.S. Co. v. Abram*, 1922 S.C. 573, 580.

[13] cf. *Smyth v. Muir* (1891) 19 R. 81, 89; *Tennent v. City of Glasgow Bank* (1879) 6 R. 554; 6 R. (H.L.) 69; *Price & Pierce, Ltd. v. Bank of Scotland*, 1910 S.C. 1095, 1106–07, 1117; 1912 S.C. (H.L.) 19.

[14] e.g. *Adamson v. Glasgow Waterworks Commrs.* (1859) 21 D. 1012; *Wilson v. Caledonian Ry.* (1860) 22 D. 1408; *Fletcher v. L.A.*, 1923 S.C. 27.

negligent or fraudulent.[1] It is not necessary to prove that the misrepresentation produced such error as wholly to exclude true consent to the contract, but if it has done so, the contract is wholly void.[1] 'Error becomes essential whenever it is shown that but for it one of the parties would have declined to contract. He cannot rescind unless his error was induced by the representations of the other party, or of his agent, made in the course of negotiation, and with reference to the subject matter of the contract. If his error is proved to have been so induced, the fact that the misleading representations were made in good faith affords no defence against the remedy of rescission.'[2] A party induced to contract by misrepresentation may accordingly rescind the contract, by an action of reduction, if need be, and recover anything paid or transferred under the contract, himself making restitution of anything received under the contract. But rescission is an equitable remedy and may be precluded where the representations were such that the party defrauded was disregarding ordinary business precautions in relying on them.[3] Alternatively he may plead the invalidity of the contract in defence to an action for specific implement or claiming damages for non-performance.[4] Or he may elect to approbate, affirm or acquiesce in the contract and choose not to rescind it.[5]

Remedies

The remedy in such cases is to rescind or repudiate liability under the contract and, if this is not accepted, to bring an action of reduction thereof. It is a condition of reduction that *restitution in integrum* is still possible, and is in fact made. Thus reduction is impossible after engineering works have been completed,[6] or after the company, shares in which had been agreed to be taken, had gone into liquidation,[7] or after an article bought has been re-sold,[8] or used up. But if the resale or other subsequent dealing with the subject is cancelled the title to rescind the original contract revives.[9] It is not competent for the court to revise the

---

[1] e.g. *Morrisson* v. *Robertson*, 1908 S.C. 332.

[2] *Menzies* v. *M.* (1893) 20 R. (H.L.) 108, 142; cf. *Stein* v. *S.*, 1914 S.C. 903, 908.

[3] *Gamage* v. *Charlesworth's Tr.*, 1910 S.C. 257.

[4] *Ritchie* v. *Glass*, 1936 S.L.T. 591; *Bell Bros. (H.P.) Ltd.* v. *Aitken*, 1939 S.C. 577.

[5] *Panmure* v. *Crokat* (1854) 17 D. 85, 92; *Westville S.S. Co.*, *supra*.

[6] *Boyd and Forrest* v. *G.S.W. Ry.*, 1915 S.C. (H.L.) 20.

[7] *Addie* v. *Western Bank* (1867) 5 M. (H.L.) 80, 89; *Houldsworth* v. *City of Glasgow Bank* (1880) 7 R. (H.L.) 53.

[8] *Edinburgh United Breweries* v. *Molleson* (1894) 21 R. (H.L.) 10; *Westville Shipping Co.* v. *Abram*, 1923 S.C. (H.L.) 68.

[9] *Westville*, *supra*.

contract to make it conform to what is believed to have been the true intention of the parties.[1]

Conditions of rescission of contract

The contract cannot be rescinded if the misrepresentation were by a third party and not by the other contracting party,[2] nor if the party imposed on, in the full knowledge of his rights, has affirmed the contract expressly, or impliedly,[3] or has failed within a reasonable time to seek to rescind,[4] or if mutual restitution *in integrum*, i.e. restoration of parties to their pre-contract position, is no longer possible,[5] though this rule is not to be applied too literally,[6] or if an innocent third party has for value acquired rights in the subject matter of contract,[7] as where goods bought have been resold to the third party,[8] or if nothing is alleged against some of the defenders, who desire the contract to stand.[9]

The fact that the contract has been executed does not by itself preclude rescission.[10]

Claims for damages or indemnity

Where the misrepresentation is innocent, the pursuer cannot recover damages or any compensation for loss instead of or in addition to reducing the contract,[11] but may recover payments made without consideration under the influence of the mis-

---

[1] *Steuart's Trs.* v. *Hart* (1875) 2 R. 192; *Krupp* v. *Menzies*, 1907 S.C. 903; *Pender-Small, supra.*

[2] *Young* v. *Clydesdale Bank* (1889) 17 R. 231; *Thin & Sinclair* v. *Arrol* (1896) 24 R. 198; *Aitken* v. *Pyper* (1900) 8 S.L.T. 258. The only remedy in such a case, if the misrepresentation is negligent or fraudulent, is damages against the maker thereof.

[3] *Re Hop and Malt Exchange and Warehouse Co.* (1866) L.R. 1 Eq. 483; *Clough* v. *L.N.W. Ry.* (1871) L.R. 7 Exch. 26; *Scholey* v. *Central Ry. of Venezuela* (1868) L.R. 9 Eq. 266.

[4] *Clough, supra; Re Scottish Petroleum Co.* (1883) 23 Ch. D. 413.

[5] *Western Bank of Scotland* v. *Addie* (1867) 5 M. (H.L.) 80; *Hay* v. *Rafferty* (1899) 2 F. 302; *Boyd & Forrest* v. *G.S.W. Ry.*, 1915 S.C. (H.L.) 20; *Spence* v. *Crawford*, 1939 S.C. (H.L.).

[6] *Erlanger* v. *New Sombrero Phosphate Co.* (1878) 3 App. Cas. 1218; *Adam* v. *Newbigging* (1888) 13 App. Cas. 308; *Lagunas Nitrate Co.* v. *Lagunas Syndicate* [1899] 2 Ch. 392; *Armstrong* v. *Jackson* [1917] 2 K.B. 822; *Spence, supra.*

[7] *White* v. *Garden* (1851) 10 C.B. 919; cf. *Oakes* v. *Turquand* (1867) L.R. 2 H.L. 325. If the misrepresentation induced fundamental error, the contract is void, and even an innocent third party acquires no title at all: see e.g. *Morrisson* v. *Robertson*, 1908 S.C. 332.

[8] Sale of Goods Act, 1893, S. 23; *Peirce* v. *London Horse and Carriage Repository* [1922] W.N. 170.

[9] *Rose* v. *McDonald* (1899) 7 S.L.T. 288.

[10] *Straker* v. *Campbell*, 1926 S.L.T. 262; contrast *Boyd & Forrest, supra,* where contract executed but restitution *in integrum* impossible.

[11] *Manners* v. *Whitehead* (1898) 1 F. 171; *Boyd & Forrest* v. *G.S.W. Ry.*, 1915 S.C. (H.L.) 20.

representation.[1] Where the misrepresentation is negligent or fraudulent the aggrieved party may recover damages for the loss caused him by the fraud, negligent harm and fraud being both actionable civil wrongs independently of contract,[2] instead of[3] or in addition to[4] obtaining reduction of the contract.

Consequences of contract being avoided

As between the parties to the contract it matters not whether a contract induced by misrepresentation is held voidable and reduced, or declared void *ab initio*. But if the contract is merely voidable the party obtaining goods under the contract acquires a good title thereto, and if he resells to an innocent third party before the contract is avoided, the latter obtains a good title to the property.[4] If the contract is void the party obtaining goods acquires no title thereto and if he resells, the sub-purchaser, however innocent, obtains no title and must restore the goods to the true owner (the party defrauded).[5]

Similarly a purchaser who has induced the purchase by fraudulent misrepresentation has a title to the goods, prior to the sale being reduced, sufficient to entitle him to pledge delivery-orders for the goods in security of money borrowed and confer a good title to the goods valid against the unpaid seller.[6]

EXTORTION

Extortion, the imposition of extremely onerous terms, or the inadequacy of consideration, is not always or automatically a ground of reduction,[7] though it may be in very extreme circumstances,[8] particularly if the person imposed upon was ignorant or without advice.[9] In contracts with moneylenders the court has statutory power,[10] if satisfied that the interest charged in respect of

---

[1] *Adam* v. *Newbigging* (1888) 13 App. Cas. 308; *Heilbut Symons* v. *Buckleton* [1913] A.C. 30; *Duncan Galloway & Co.* v. *Duncan Falconer & Co.*, 1913 S.C. 265.

[2] *Hedley Byrne & Co.* v. *Heller & Partners Ltd.* [1904] A.C. 465 (negligence); *Thin & Sinclair* v. *Arrol* (1896) 24 R. 198 (fraud).

[3] *Graham* v. *Western Bank* (1865) 3 M. 617; *Campbell* v. *Blair* (1897) 5 S.L.T. 28; *Manners* v. *Whitehead* (1898) 1 F. 171; *Bryson & Co.* v. *B.*, 1916, 1 S.L.T. 361; *Smith* v. *Sim*, 1954 S.C. 357.

[4] *Macleod* v. *Kerr*, 1965 S.C. 253.

[5] *Morrisson* v. *Robertson*, 1908 S.C. 332.

[6] *Price & Pierce, Ltd.* v. *Bank of Scotland*, 1912 S.C. (H.L.) 19.

[7] *McLachlan* v. *Watson* (1874) 11 S.L.R. 549.

[8] *Young* v. *Gordon* (1896) 23 R. 419; *Gordon's Admin.* v. *Stephen* (1902) 9 S.L.T. 397.

[9] cf. *Fry* v. *Lane* (1888) 40 Ch. D. 312.

[10] Consumer Credit Act, 1974, Ss. 137–140.

the sum actually lent is excessive,[1] or that the amounts charged for expenses, inquiries, fines, bonus, premium renewals or any other charges are excessive, and, in either case, that the transaction is harsh and unconscionable,[2] to reopen the transaction and relieve the borrower from any sum in excess of that which the Court, having regard to the risk and all the circumstances adjudges to be reasonable.[3]

FORCE AND FEAR

An agreement[4] is void and reducible if one party's consent was given under the influence of such force or fear, imposed by the other contracting party,[5] as would have overcome the resistance of a reasonable man,[6] or such, applied to a weaker person, as have an overpowering influence. Such duress includes intimidation,[7] actual or threatened physical violence, threats of death, infamy and disgrace, violence to one's spouse, parent or child,[8] or even loss of property,[9] warnings of financial ruin,[10] and obtaining an undertaking from a person while incarcerated at the other party's instance.[11] The threats must be illegal or unjustifiable.[12]

But the threat to exert legitimate pressure or take legitimate action, such as to prosecute for a crime,[13] or to take legal action for recovery of a sum due,[14] or to do diligence on a decree, or to petition for sequestration, is unobjectionable.[15] So too is threat to put a trader on a stop-list.[16] And a deed granted to avoid harmful consequences to another person is not necessarily voidable.[17]

---

[1] *Samuel v. Newbold* [1906] A.C. 461.

[2] *Midland Discount Co. v. Macdonald,* 1909 S.C. 477.

[3] 1974 Act, Ss. 137–140.

[4] Similar considerations apply to wills: cf. *Love v. Marshall* (1870) 9 M. 291.

[5] *Stewart Bros. v. Kiddie* (1899) 7 S.L.T. 92.

[6] Stair I, 9, 8; Ersk. III, 1, 16; IV, 1, 26; Bell, *Comm.* I, 314; *Prin.* §12; *Gelot v. Stewart* (1870) 8 M. 649; (1871) 9 M. 957, 1057; cf. *Young v. Healy,* 1909 S.C. 687.

[7] *E. Orkney v. Vinfra* (1606) Mor. 16481; *Cairns v. Marianski* (1850) 12 D. 919, 1286.

[8] Dig. 4, 2, 8; Stair, *supra*; *McIntosh v. Farquharson & Spalding* (1671) M. 16485; *Priestnell v. Hutcheson* (1857) 19 D. 495.

[9] *Wiseman v. Logie* (1700) M. 16505; *Dundas v. Hardie* (1700) M. 16506; *Foreman v. Sheriff* (1791) M. 16515.

[10] *Murray v. M.* (1826) 4 S. 374; *Ewen v. E's Trs.* (1830) 4 W. & S. 346.

[11] *McIntosh v. Chalmers* (1883) 11 R. 8. See also *Arratt v. Wilson* (1718) Robert. 234; *Gordon v. Crawford* (1730) 1 Pat. 47; *Craig v. Paton* (1865) 4 M. 192.

[12] *Dumfriesshire Education Authy. v. Wright,* 1926 S.L.T. 217.

[13] *Fisher v. Apollinaris Co.* (1875) 10 Ch. App. 297; cf. *Williams v. Bayley* (1866) L.R. 1 H.L. 200.

[14] *Craig v. Paton* (1865) 4 M. 192.   [15] *Bell, supra; McIntosh, supra.*

[16] *Thorne v. M.T.A.* [1937] A.C. 797; but see Restrictive Trade Practices Act, 1956, S.24.

[17] *Priestnell, supra.*

FACILITY AND CIRCUMVENTION

A contract is reducible if it is established both that the pursuer was facile, or weak in mind or body so as to be easily imposed on, and that the defender influenced, persuaded and got round him, and by fraud and circumvention secured his assent to the contract.[1] Facility falls short of insanity or incapacity, but may be constituted by senility[2] or simple-mindedness.[3] The absence of independent legal advice is a material point.[2] The facility need not be general; it suffices to prove facility in relation to the persuasion used.[4] Circumvention need not be more than persuasion which the granter was in no state to resist,[5] but specific facts and circumstances must be averred from which circumvention may be inferred.[6]

The resulting contract must have been detrimental to the pursuer, as by inadequate price. But, despite facility, a transaction will be upheld if there has been no circumvention.[7]

UNDUE INFLUENCE

A contract is voidable and reducible if one party establishes that the other party stood in a position of confidence, influence or trust in relation to him, and abused that position by letting his own interest conflict with the pursuer's, and thereby induced or permitted him to make a detrimental bargain.[8] ' The essence of undue influence is that a person who has assumed or undertaken a position of quasi-fiduciary responsibility in relation to the affairs of

---

[1] Stair I, 9, 9; Bell, Prin. §141A; *McNeill* v. *Moir* (1824) 2 Sh. App. 206 (age); *McDiarmid* v. *McD.* (1828) 3 W. & S. 37; *Jackson* v. *Pollok* (1900) 8 S.L.T. 267 (weakness through intoxication); *Sutherland* v. *Low* (1901) 3 F. 972 (age and frailty); *Bremner* v. *B.*, 1939 S.L.T. 448; *Mackay* v. *Campbell*, 1966 S.C. 237; cf. *McCulloch* v. *McCracken* (1857) 20 D. 206; *Mathieson* v. *Hawthorns* (1899) 1 F. 468. There are also many cases relating to reduction of wills on this ground. See Ch. 121, *infra*.

[2] *Sutherland, supra; Bremner* v. *B.*, 1939 S.L.T. 448.

[3] If the pursuer was incapable of understanding the agreement at all, the case is one of absence of consent, or error as to the nature of the contract itself.

[4] *Morrison* v. *Maclean's Trs.* (1862) 24 D. 625; *Munro* v. *Strain* (1874) 1 R. 1039.

[5] *Clunie* v. *Stirling* (1854) 17 D. 15.

[6] *Mackay* v. *Campbell*, 1967 S.C. (H.L.) 53.

[7] *Scott* v. *Wilson* (1825) 3 Mur. 526; *Morrison* v. *M.* (1841) 4 D. 337; *Home* v. *Hardy* (1842) 4 D. 1184. See also *Liston* v. *Cowan* (1865) 3 M. 1041.

[8] Bell, *Prin.* §14B; Undue influence may also be a ground for reducing a will, but the meaning and effect of the objection may not be the same in both classes of cases: *Forrest* v. *Low's Trs.*, 1907 S.C. 1240, 1255; affd. 1909 S.C. (H.L.) 16; *Forbes* v. *F's Trs.*, 1957 S.C. 325, 331.

another, allows his own self-interest to deflect the advice or guidance he gives, in his own favour.'[1]

In English cases a rebuttable presumption of undue influence arises in transactions between persons, where one stands in a fiduciary or quasi-fiduciary position to the other,[2] such as trustee and beneficiary,[3] parent and child,[4] guardian and ward,[5] religious,[6] legal[7] or medical[8] adviser and parishioner or client, and similar relationships, and it may be proved to have existed in any other case.[9] In Scotland there is no such presumption,[10] but in any case undue influence may be proved to have existed in fact. It is most easily proved where one of the parties stood in a fiduciary or quasi-fiduciary relationship to the other, such as clergyman to parishioner,[11] parent to child,[12] trustee to beneficiary,[13] and solicitor to client,[14] but even in such cases it may be shown that the person in whom confidence was reposed had no adverse personal interest and was acting in the interest of the person claiming reduction.[15] In the case of transactions between solicitor and client the test is whether an independent legal adviser would have advised the agreement.[16] Examples include a mother obtaining from her son consent to disentail for a grossly inadequate con-

---

[1] Ross v. Gosselin's Exors., 1926 S.C. 325, 334, approved in Forbes v. F's Trs., 1957 S.C. 325, 332; cf. Gray v. Binny (1879) 7 R. 332, 342.

[2] Nottidge v. Prince (1860) 2 Giff. 246; Tate v. Williamson (1866) L.R. 2 Ch. App. 55; Allcard v. Skinner (1887) 36 Ch. D. 145.

[3] Ellis v. Barker (1871) 7 Ch. App. 104; Beningfield v. Baxter (1886) 12 App. Cas. 167.

[4] Bainbrigge v. Brown (1881) 18 Ch. D. 188; Powell v. P. [1900] 1 Ch. 243; Lancashire Loans v. Black [1934] 1 K.B. 380; Bullock v. Lloyds Bank [1955] Ch. 317.

[5] Taylor v. Johnston (1882) 19 Ch. D. 603.

[6] Huguenin v. Baseley (1807) 14 Ves. 273; Allcard, supra; Morley v. Loughnan [1893] 1 Ch. 736.

[7] Wright v. Carter [1903] 1 Ch. 27.

[8] Mitchell v. Homfray (1881) 8 Q.B.D. 587; Radcliffe v. Price (1902) 18 T.L.R. 466.

[9] Williams v. Bayley (1866) L.R. 1 H.L. 200.

[10] But some Scottish cases, by incautious following of English authority, suggest that there is: see Grieve v. Cunningham (1869) 8 M. 317; Gray, supra; Winder, 56 L.Q.R. 97.

[11] Munro v. Strain (1874) 1 R. 522.

[12] Woodward v. W., 1910, 2 S.L.T. 163; Forbes v. F's Trs., 1957 S.C. 325; cf. Tennent v. T's Trs. (1870) 8 M. (H.L.) 10; Menzies v. M. (1893) 20 R. (H.L.) 108; Carmichael v. Baird (1899) 6 S.L.T. 369; Allan v. A., 1961 S.C. 200.

[13] Dougan v. Macpherson (1902) 4 F. (H.L.) 7.

[14] McPherson's Trs. v. Watt (1877) 5 R. (H.L.) 9; Cleland v. Morrison (1878) 6 R. 156; Logan's Trs. v. Reid (1885) 12 R. 1094; Love v. Kelly (1902) 10 S.L.T. 268; Rigg's Exrx. v. Urquhart (1902) 10 S.L.T. 503; Gillespie v. Gardner, 1909 S.C. 1053. See also Noble v. Campbell (1876) 4 R. 77; Rutherford v. MacGregor (1891) 18 R. 1061 and cases of testamentary bequests to solicitors: Grieve v. Cunningham (1869) 8 M. 317; Rooney v. Cormack (1895) 22 R. 761; Weir v. Grace (1899) 2 F. (H.L.) 30; Forrest v. Low's Trs., 1909 S.C. (H.L.) 16; Stewart v. MacLaren, 1920 S.C. (H.L.) 148.

[15] Gillespie, supra; Forbes, supra.

[16] Aitken v. Campbell's Trs., 1909 S.C. 1217.

sideration,[1] a father purchasing from his daughter her share in expectancy in his marriage contract trust fund,[2] a mother and stepfather obtaining from her son a gratuitous surrender to her of trust income,[3] a son agreeing to disentail estates for an inadequate consideration at his father's instigation,[4] a person under pressure of debts renouncing his interest in a partnership with his father and brother.[5] In rebutting a charge of undue influence a material factor is whether the pursuer had adequate independent legal or other advice.[6]

[1] *Gray* v. *Binny* (1879) 7 R. 332.

[2] *Smith Cuninghame* v. *Anstruther's Trs.* (1872) 10 M. (H.L.) 29.

[3] *Carmichael* v. *Baird* (1899) 6 S.L.T. 369.

[4] *Menzies* v. *M.* (1893) 20 R. (H.L.) 108.

[5] *Tennent* v. *T's Trs.* (1870) 8 M. (H.L.) 10 (action failed). See also *Johnston* v. *Goodlet* (1868) 6 M. 1067.

[6] *Cleland, supra*; *Gray, supra*; *Menzies, supra*; cf. *Stewart* v. *Bruce's Trs.* (1898) 25 R. 965; *Younger* v. *Y's Trs.* (1900) 7 S.L.T. 543; *Rigg's Exrx.* v. *Urquhart* (1902) 10 S.L.T. 503.

CHAPTER 34

THE CONTENTS OF THE CONTRACT

THE contents of the contract are the whole body of terms, stipulations and undertakings prescribing the rights and duties of the parties to the contract. The terms of a contract may be (1) express terms, stated by the parties when they contracted; or (2) terms imported by the parties by reference to a document outwith the contract; or (3) terms implied into the contract by force of law, independently of the will of the parties. If the court holds that parties have validly contracted it must then, before it can decide issues of enforcement or breach, discover what each party stipulated or undertook, which involves (a) ascertaining what were the terms agreed upon; and (b) interpreting the contract, or deciding the meaning to be attributed in the circumstances to the terms used. Only then can the court decide whether a party is in breach or whether a party should be ordained to perform, and what he is to perform.

EXPRESS TERMS

(a) ASCERTAINMENT

(i) *Contracts which are proved by parole evidence*

The court must determine from the oral evidence of parties and witnesses what was said and done relative to the proposed contract before and at the time of contracting, and what was agreed upon.[1]

(ii) *Contracts which are proved by writing*

Where the terms of a contract have to be, or are in fact, evidenced by writings of the parties, the general rule is that the court will look only at the writings and not investigate prior oral communings or negotiations between the parties,[2] nor even at words in the contract deleted before execution,[3] though prior communications may be looked at to determine the meaning of a

---

[1] *Muirhead & Turnbull* v. *Dickson* (1905) 7 F. 686.

[2] *McGregor* v. *Strathallan* (1862) 24 D. 1006; *Inglis* v. *Buttery* (1878) 5 R. (H.L.) 87; *Largue* v. *Urquhart* (1881) 18 S.L.R. 491; *Tininver Lime Co.* v. *Coghill* (1881) 19 S.L.R. 7; *Muller* v. *Weber & Schaer* (1901) 3 F. 401; *Paterson* v. *Inglis* (1902) 10 S.L.T. 449; *McAllister* v. *McGallagley*, 1911 S.C. 112.

[3] *Inglis, supra.*

term in the contract,[1] or the factual background to the parties' contract,[2] or to supplement the contract on a point on which it is silent,[3] or ambiguous.[4] Furthermore where a formal deed, such as a disposition or lease, is executed in implement of a previous contract, it supersedes it and becomes the sole measure of the rights and liabilities of the contracting parties,[5] so far as it implements the contract, but not as to any subjects of contract not covered therein,[6] nor if parties have agreed that this rule should not apply.[7]

Standard form contracts

Increasingly in modern practice the terms of a contract, particularly with a dominant or monopoly undertaker, are not truly negotiated but are presented to the party in the form of a standard printed contract devised by the undertaker which the other party must accept, or do without the contract. Any alternative supplier will have the same or very similar standard conditions of contract, and rarely if at all will the dominant undertaker vary the terms at the request of the other contracting party. Thus insurance policies, contracts for carriage, the supply of electricity, telephone and other services, are settled by the supplier of the service in question rather than by negotiation.

Qualification of terms of contract

Where a contract is evidenced in writing the general rule is that it is not competent to vary, modify, qualify, contradict or explain the terms thereof by parole evidence,[8] such as that parties' intention was different from that set forth in the deed,[9] or of alleged contrary custom of trade,[10] or of the subjects intended to

---

[1] *Temperance Halls Co-operative Bldg. Soc.* v. *Glasgow Pavilion Co.* (1908) 16 S.L.T. 112; *Crondace* v. *Annandale S.S. Co.*, 1925 S.L.T. 449.

[2] *Prenn* v. *Simonds* [1971] 1 W.L.R. 1381 (H.L.).

[3] *Riemann* v. *John Young & Co.* (1895) 2 S.L.T. 426.

[4] *Houldsworth* v. *Gordon Cumming*, 1910 S.C. (H.L.) 49.

[5] *Robertson's Trs.* v. *Lindsay* (1873) 1 R. 323; *Lee* v. *Alexander* (1883) 10 R. (H.L.) 91; *Orr* v. *Mitchell* (1893) 20 R. (H.L.) 27; *Edinburgh United Breweries* v. *Molleson* (1894) 21 R. (H.L.) 10; *Baird* v. *Alexander* (1898) 25 R. (H.L.) 35; *Butter* v. *Foster*, 1912 S.C. 1218. See also *Houldsworth* v. *Gordon Cumming*, 1910 S.C. (H.L.) 49. Contrast *Morrison* v. *Gray*, 1932 S.C. 712, where disposition not delivered and earlier contract still ruled.

[6] *Jamieson* v. *Welsh* (1900) 3 F. 176; *Masson* v. *Scottish Brewers, Ltd.*, 1966 S.C. 9.

[7] *Fraser* v. *Cox*, 1938 S.C. 506.

[8] *Inglis* v. *Buttery* (1878) 5 R. (H.L.) 87; *Burrell* v. *Russell* (1900) 2 F. (H.L.) 80; *Lindsay* v. *Craig*, 1919 S.C. 139; *Pickard* v. *P.*, 1963 S.C. 604.

[9] *Steuart's Trs.* v. *Hart* (1875) 3 R. 192; *Largue* v. *Urquhart* (1881) 18 S.L.R. 491; *Ayr District Board of Control* v. *L.A.*, 1926 S.L.T. 233; *Lloyds Bank* v. *Walker*, 1928 S.N. 7.

[10] *Tancred Arrol & Co.* v. *Steel Co. of Scotland* (1890) 17 R. (H.L.) 31; *P. & W. MacLellan* v. *Peattie's Trs.* (1903) 5 F. 1031; *Forth Collieries* v. *Hume* (1904) 11 S.L.T. 576.

be included,[1] or that a party was acting as agent only,[2] or that conditions implied by law were not to hold in that case,[3] or that there was an agreement to grant an abatement from the rent specified,[4] or that an *ex facie* permanent appointment was revocable,[5] or that a time limit would not be enforced,[6] or that payment was to be postponed,[7] or that certain additional terms of a lease existed,[8] or that a verbal agreement qualified the terms of a formal contract of copartnery,[9] or, probably, that a term not implied by law was intended to be a term of the contract.[10]

The terms of the written contract can be varied only by subsequent writ[11] or admission on oath[12] or by oral agreement followed by acts amounting to *rei interventus*.[13] Acquiescence in conduct contravening the original contract may bar a claim of damages therefor, but cannot ratify an alleged oral agreement to vary the original contract.[14] Where a mercantile document contained interlined manuscript words inconsistent with printed words, which had not been deleted, it was held that the intention disclosed by the written portion must prevail over that in the printed words.[15]

Challenge of validity or completeness of contract

Parole evidence is, however, admissible if the validity of the contract is challenged on such a ground as illegality, error or misrepresentation,[16] or if both parties admit that the contract is incomplete[17] or is merely a memorandum in writing of an oral

[1] *Gregson* v. *Alsop* (1897) 24 R. 1081.
[2] *Lindsay* v. *Craig*, 1919 S.C. 139.
[3] *Johnston* v. *Edinburgh, etc. Canal Co.* (1835) 1 S. & McL. 117; *Henderson* v. *Arthur* [1907] 1 K.B. 10.
[4] *Turnbull* v. *Oliver* (1891) 19 R. 154.
[5] *Hilson* v. *Otto* (1870) 9 M. 18.
[6] *Paterson* v. *Inglis* (1902) 10 S.L.T. 449.
[7] *McAllister* v. *McGallagley*, 1911 S.C. 112.
[8] *Norval* v. *Abbey*, 1939 S.C. 724.
[9] *Starrett* v. *Pia*, 1968 S.L.T. (Notes) 28.
[10] *Renison* v. *Bryce* (1898) 25 R. 521.
[11] *Stewart* v. *Clark* (1871) 9 M. 616; cf. *Dickson* v. *Bell* (1899) 36 S.L.R. 343.
[12] *Sinclair* v. *McBeath* (1869) 7 M. 934; *Muller* v. *Weber & Schaer* (1901) 3 F. 401.
[13] *Bargaddie Coal Co.* v. *Wark* (1859) 3 Macq. 467; *Kirkpatrick* v. *Allanshaw Coal Co.* (1880) 8 R. 327, 332.
[14] *Carron Co.* v. *Henderson's Trs.* (1896) 23 R. 1042; *Lavan* v. *Gavin Aird & Co.*, 1919 S.C. 345.
[15] *Rowtor Steamship Co.* v. *Love & Stewart*, 1916 S.C. (H.L.) 199.
[16] *Kirkwood* v. *Bryce* (1871) 8 S.L.R. 435; *Steuart's Trs.* v. *Hart* (1875) 3 R. 192; *Ross* v. *Cowie's Exrx.* (1888) 16 R. 224; *Krupp* v. *Menzies*, 1907 S.C. 903; *Bell Bros. (H.P.) Ltd.* v. *Aitken*, 1939 S.C. 577.
[17] *Riemann* v. *Young* (1895) 2 S.L.T. 426; *Masson* v. *Scottish Brewers Ltd.*, 1966 S.C. 9.

agreement,[1] or does not truly express the agreement between them,[2] or if it is averred that a document has been delivered subject to a suspensive condition,[3] or if there is latent ambiguity as to the subject of contract,[4] or as to the lands actually possessed under an unclear description,[5] or, if the contract has been partially performed before the formal contract was executed, to establish the relations of parties before that date.[6]

Collateral agreements

Parole evidence is also admissible as to any agreement collateral to the main agreement contained in the writings, though an agreement is not collateral if its effect would be to alter an express stipulation in the writing embodying the main agreement.[7]

(b) INTERPRETATION

Once it has been established what the terms of the parties' undertakings are, it is for the court to interpret the contract. The court must proceed on the basis that parties must be taken to have intended what they said and wrote, or what is the natural meaning of the words they used. They cannot be heard to say that they meant other than that.[8] The function of the court is generally to ascertain the common intention of the parties, as evidenced by their contract, and give effect to it. *Prima facie* words are understood in their ordinary plain and literal meaning,[9] unless circumstances disclose that a word is to be understood in an unusual or technical sense. Technical terms must be interpreted according to their usage in the trade in question, and extrinsic evidence of the meaning of such terms is admissible.[10] In doubt, the court will

---

[1] *Ireland* v. *Rosewall Coal Co.* (1900) 37 S.L.R. 521; *Lindsay* v. *Craig*, 1919 S.C. 139.

[2] *Grant's Trs.* v. *Morison* (1875) 2 R. 377; *Grant* v. *Mackenzie* (1899) 1 F. 889; *Miller* v. *M.* (1905) 12 S.L.T. 743; *Cairns* v. *Davidson*, 1913 S.C. 1054; *McMenemy* v. *Forster's Tr.*, 1938 S.L.T. 555.

[3] *Semple* v. *Kyle* (1902) 4 F. 421; *Abrahams* v. *Miller (Denny) Ltd.*, 1933 S.C. 171.

[4] *Macdonald* v. *Newall* (1898) 1 F. 68; *Houldsworth* v. *Gordon Cumming*, 1910 S.C. (H.L.) 49.

[5] *Girdwood* v. *Paterson* (1873) 11 M. 647; *Dalhousie's Tutors* v. *Minister of Lochlee* (1890) 17 R. 1060; *Mackay* v. *Maclachlan* (1899) 7 S.L.T. 48.

[6] *Korner* v. *Shennan*, 1950 S.C. 285.

[7] *Perdikou* v. *Pattison*, 1958 S.L.T. 153; *Masson* v. *Scottish Brewers, Ltd.*, 1966 S.C. 9, 16.

[8] *Muirhead & Turnbull* v. *Dickson* (1905) 7 F. 686; cf. *Steuart's Trs.* v. *Hart* (1875) 3 R. 192.

[9] *Tancred Arrol & Co.* v. *Steel Co. of Scotland* (1890) 17 R. (H.L.) 31.

[10] *Sutton* v. *Ciceri* (1890) 17 R. (H.L.) 40; *Von Mehren* v. *Edinburgh Roperie* (1901) 4 F. 232.

prefer a meaning which renders the contract valid rather than ineffective, and will seek to give effect to the contract as a whole; it may ignore or read as corrected apparent omissions or mistakes.[1] Many words and phrases occurring in common kinds of contracts have previously been construed by courts and these interpretations may be valuable in a subsequent similar case. Usage of trade may be put in evidence to show the meaning words may bear in a particular context,[2] but may not contradict the plain meaning of words used.[3]

General canons of interpretation, such as the *ejusdem generis* principle, may be invoked,[4] and ambiguous words are generally construed against the party using them (*contra proferentem*). Where an obligation can be performed in alternative ways the debtor in the obligation may choose in which way to perform.[5] A contract is to be interpreted by reference to the law applicable when it was constituted, not when the question of interpretation arose.[6] A patent ambiguity in a contract must be resolved by interpretation, though the actings of parties may assist. A latent ambiguity may be resolved by evidence of surrounding circumstances.[7] The court may be assisted by the actings of parties, as where parties have long acted on the basis of a particular interpretation,[8] or one party has not denied the other's interpretation.[9] Parole evidence is competent to establish the state of the parties' knowledge at the time of contracting where this is relevant,[10] and to establish the relations inter se of parties, such as joint obligants.[11]

Materiality of terms

The court must distinguish between on the one hand words of advertisement, opinion, intention or promise, which are not

[1] *Glen's Trs. v. Lancashire, etc. Ins. Co.* (1906) 8 F. 915.
[2] *Fleming v. Airdrie Iron Co.* (1882) 9 R. 473.
[3] *Tancred Arrol & Co. v. Steel Co. of Scotland* (1890) 17 R. (H.L.) 31; *McLellan v. Peattie's Trs.* (1903) 5 F. 1031.
[4] *Lilly v. Stevenson* (1895) 22 R. 278; *Admiralty v. Burns*, 1910 S.C. 531; *Abchurch S.S. Co. v. Stinnes*, 1911 S.C. 1010.
[5] *Christie v. Wilson*, 1915 S.C. 645.
[6] *Gregory's Trs. v. Alison* (1889) 16 R. (H.L.) 10.
[7] *McAdam v. Scott*, 1913, 1 S.L.T. 12.
[8] *Ainslie v. Edinburgh Mags.* (1842) 4 D. 639; *Hewats v. Roberton* (1881) 9 R. 175; *Hunter v. Barron's Trs.* (1886) 13 R. 883; *Jopp's Trs. v. Edmond* (1888) 15 R. 271; *Bank of Scotland v. Stewart* (1891) 18 R. 957; *Macgill v. Park* (1899) 2 F. 272; *N.B. Ry. v. Edinburgh Mags.*, 1920 S.C. 409.
[9] *Dowling v. Henderson* (1890) 17 R. 921.
[10] *Jacobs v. Scott* (1899) 2 F. (H.L.) 70; *Claddagh S.S. Co. v. Steven*, 1919 S.C. (H.L.) 132.
[11] *Crosbie v. Brown* (1900) 3 F. 83; *Gordon's Trs. v. Young*, 1909, 1 S.L.T. 202; *Thow's Tr. v. Young*, 1910 S.C. 588.

generally held obligatory, words of representation, which may have induced the contract, and which, if inaccurate, may give rise to a claim to rescind the contract as having been induced by misrepresentation, and on the other hand those other stipulations, known variously as essential or fundamental terms or warranties, the satisfaction of which the contracting party guarantees and for failure to satisfy which the other party may rescind the contract and claim damages,[1] and inessential terms or conditions, nonperformance of which is not so serious and for failure to perform which the other party may recover damages only, but may not rescind the contract.[2]

The parties may specify that any term or terms, however apparently unimportant, are to be deemed fundamental terms, but failing such specification it is a question of interpretation whether a particular term is fundamental or not.[3] Thus payment of the price of heritage[4] or moveables[5] on the date stipulated is not normally of the essence of the contract, but the supply of goods on or by the stipulated date may well be of the essence, and the quality of goods is normally of the essence of the contract.[5]

Modification of terms

If one party continues to act on a contract after intimation by the other that a term is to be altered, e.g. the rate of charge, he is held to have accepted the modification and is liable thereunder.[6]

Obligations present or future

A contract may be present or future, according as the obligations undertaken are immediately exigible, or are expressed to be

---

[1] e.g. *Robey* v. *Stein* (1900) 3 F. 278; *Hyslop* v. *Shirlaw* (1905) 7 F. 875; *Kyle* v. *Sim*, 1925 S.C. 425; *Kelly* v. *Clark*, 1967 S.L.T. (Notes) 115.

[2] Terms of the contract called 'conditions' must be distinguished from conditions, suspensive or resolutive, on which the validity of the contract depends. In Scots law a 'warranty' is a fundamental term of the contract, or guarantee; a 'condition' is a less material term. In English law a 'condition' is a fundamental stipulation, breach of which justifies rescission of the contract, but 'warranty' is a less important stipulation, breach of which justifies damages but not total rescission of the contract: see Sale of Goods Act, 1893, Ss. 11 and 62; *Wallis* v. *Pratt & Haynes* [1910] 2 K.B. 1003, 1012; *Dawsons Ltd.* v. *Bonnin*, 1922 S.C. (H.L.) 156, 161, 170.

[3] *Wade* v. *Waldon*, 1909 S.C. 571; *Dawsons, Ltd.* v. *Bonnin*, 1922 S.C. (H.L.) 156.

[4] *Burns* v. *Garscadden* (1900) 8 S.L.T. 321; *Rodger* v. *Fawdry*, 1950 S.C. 483.

[5] Sale of Goods Act, 1893, S. 10(1).

[6] *McFarlane* v. *Mitchell* (1900) 2 F. 901; *G.S.W. Ry.* v. *Polquhairn Coal Co.*, 1916 S.C. 36; *Caledonian Ry.* v. *Stein*, 1919 S.C. 324.

exigible only at a stated future time or on the occurrence of some future event which is certain to happen.[1]

COMMON EXPRESS TERMS OF CONTRACT

(1) CONDITIONS

Obligations pure or conditional

A contract may also be pure or unconditional, or conditional, i.e. contingent on the satisfaction of some condition.[2] A condition in this context[3] is an uncertain future event, external to the contract, on which its existence or the enforceability of some stipulation thereof depends.[4] An unlawful condition, or one wholly impossible of satisfaction, falls to be ignored.[5]

Suspensive and resolutive conditions

Conditions are distinguished as suspensive,[6] which withholds the operation of the obligation until the event predicated happens, when it becomes perfect: there is no liability until the event happens;[7] and resolutive,[8] which terminates or dissolves the obligation if or when the event predicated happens, such as a provision for terminating a lease on the tenant's bankruptcy.[9]

Potestative, casual and mixed conditions

Conditions may also be distinguished[10] as potestative, when it is in the power of one or both parties to implement the condition;[11] casual, when the purification depends on chance, or the act of a

---

[1] Stair I, 3, 7; Ersk. III, 1, 6; Bell, *Prin.* §§45–46.

[2] Bell, *Prin.* §47.

[3] Contrast 'condition' as meaning a less important stipulation of the contract.

[4] Bell, *Prin.* §47.

[5] *Shearer* v. *Alexander* (1875) 12 S.L.R. 333.

[6] In English terminology a 'condition precedent', which phrase also sometimes connotes a prerequisite, not in time but in efficiency; see further *infra*.

[7] Bell, *Prin.* §47; e.g. 'if X happens' or 'when Y happens'; see e.g. *Murdoch* v. *Greig* (1889) 16 R. 396; *McArthur's Exors.* v. *Guild*, 1908 S.C. 743; *Donaldson's Exor.* v. *Sharp*, 1922 S.C. 566; *Abrahams* v. *Miller*, 1933 S.C. 171; *Stobo* v. *Morrison's (Gowns) Ltd.*, 1949 S.C. 184.

[8] In English terminology a 'condition subsequent'; e.g. 'until X happens' or 'in the event of Y'; see *National & House Property Co.* v. *Watson*, 1908 S.C. 888; *Eisen* v. *McCabe*, 1920 S.C. (H.L.) 146; *Hardy* v. *Sime*, 1938 S.L.T. 18.

[9] *Bidoulac* v. *Sinclair's Tr.* (1889) 17 R. 144; *Noble* v. *Hart* (1890) 24 R. 174.

[10] Stair I, 3, 8; Ersk. III, 1, 6; III, 3, 85; Bell, *Prin.* §50.

[11] e.g. *Pirie* v. *P* (1873) 11 M. 941; *Paterson* v. *McEwan's Trs.* (1881) 8 R. 646; *Mackay* v. *Dick & Stevenson* (1881) 8 R. (H.L.); see also *Kedie's Trs.* v. *Stewart & McDonald*, 1926 S.C. 1019; *Simpson* v. *Roberts*, 1931 S.C. 259.

third party;[1] or mixed, when it depends on both potestative and casual events.[2] A potestative condition is held satisfied if the party bound has done all in his power to satisfy it.[3]

Condition precedent

A condition precedent is commonly a condition the satisfaction or performance of which is a prerequisite of some claim or action.[4] Unless the contract specifies so, it is a matter of interpretation whether performance of some step is a condition precedent to enforcing the contract.[5]

A party bound conditionally is not impliedly bound to perform the condition and complete the contract, but has an option to do it or not.[6] He is held to have implemented the condition if he does all in his power to implement it and his failure is attributable only to something beyond his control.[7] The other party is held bound to do nothing to prevent or impede the satisfaction of the condition by the party bound, and it is held satisfied if he has done so.[8] If a condition is conceived entirely in favour of one party that party may waive the condition and insist on the contract being implemented, and the other party is not released by the non-fulfilment of the condition.[9]

(2) CONDITIONS AND WARRANTIES

These words are used indifferently for the stipulations in the contract of what parties undertake to do. Properly speaking a condition is a stipulation not fundamental to the contract, for the

---

[1] e.g. *Maxwell's Trs.* v. *Warnock* (1900) 8 S.L.T. 144 (consent of landlord); *Halcroft* v. *West End Playhouse*, 1916 S.C. 182.

[2] e.g. *Waddell's Trs.* v. *Monkland Iron Co.* (1885) 13 R. 237 (lease terminable if minerals exhausted and engineer's report to that effect obtained).

[3] *Mackay* v. *Dick & Stevenson* (1881) 8 R. (H.L.) 37; *Munro's Trs.* v. *Monson*, 1965 S.C. 84.

[4] e.g. *Waddell's Trs.* v. *Monkland Iron Co.* (1885) 13 R. 237; *Shiells* v. *Scottish Assce. Corpn.* (1889) 16 R. 1014; *Caledonian Ins. Co.* v. *Gilmour* (1892) 20 R. (H.L.) 13; *Law* v. *Newnes* (1894) 21 R. 1927; *Howden* v. *Powell Duffryn*, 1912 S.C. 920; *Clydebank Water Trs.* v. *Fidlitty Co. of Maryland*, 1916 S.C. (H.L.) 69; *Dawson's Ltd.* v. *Bonnin*, 1922 S.C. (H.L.) 156.

[5] e.g. *National House Property Investment Co.* v. *Watson*, 1908 S.C. 888.

[6] *Philp* v. *Edinburgh Ry.* (1857) 2 Macq. 514; *Paterson* v. *McEwan's Trs.* (1881) 8 R. 646; *Maconochie Welwood* v. *Midlothian C.C.* (1894) 22 R. 56.

[7] cf. *Duncanson* v. *Scottish County Inv. Co. Ltd.*, 1915 S.C. 1106; *Halcroft* v. *West End Playhouse*, 1916 S.C. 182; *Dowling* v. *Methven*, 1921 S.C. 948.

[8] Bell, *Prin.* §50; *Hunter* v. *E. Hopetoun* (1865) 3 M. (H.L.) 50; *Pirie* v. *P.* (1873) 11 M. 941; *Mackay* v. *Dick & Stevenson* (1881) 8 R. (H.L.) 37; *Paterson, supra*; cf. *Kilmarnock District Cttee.* v. *Somervell* (1906) 14 S.L.T. 567.

[9] *Dewar & Finlay, Ltd.* v. *Blackwood*, 1968 S.L.T. 196.

breach of which damages are recoverable but which would not justify rescission of the contract, whereas a warranty is a fundamental stipulation, something guaranteed, for non-implement of which the contract can be rescinded and damages claimed.[1] Whether a stipulation is a condition or a warranty does not depend on the words used, but on whether one party's undertaking is substantially a guarantee or not that the subject-matter of contract has certain qualities.[2]

(3) IRRITANCY CLAUSE

In contracts of feu, ground annual and of lease and in deeds constituting entails an irritancy clause is common. An irritancy is a provision giving power to terminate the contractual relationship on the occurrence of certain specified breaches. An irritancy may be legal, imposed by law, or conventional, agreed upon in a particular contract.

Legal irritancies are incurred in the case of feu-rights, for failure to pay feu-duty for five years[3] (formerly known as tinsel of the feu-right), and in the case of leases, when the rent is two full years in arrears.[4]

A conventional irritancy may be included in any contract in such terms as the parties may agree, but it is common to provide for irritancy in the event of a tenant's assignation,[5] sequestration[6] or incapacity, and possibly for such as the vassal's failure to build,[7] or the tenant's failure to reside on a farm[8] or his misconducting himself.[9] A contract of ground annual, by analogy with a feu, may contain an irritancy in the event of the ground annual

---

[1] The usage of the words in English law is precisely the opposite, and the English usage appears in the Sale of Goods Act, 1893.

[2] See e.g. *Paul* v. *Glasgow Corpn.* (1900) 3 F. 119; *Hyslop* v. *Shirlaw* (1905) 7 F. 875, 881.

[3] Feu-Duty Act, 1597 (c. 17) amd. Land Tenure Reform (Sc.) Act, 1974, S. 15; Ersk. II, 5, 26. The Act refers to the irritancy of the right of an *emphyteuta* under the Roman law, and by analogy therewith this is called the irritancy *ob non solutum canonem*. See also *Hope* v. *Aitken* (1872) 10 M. 347; *Cassels* v. *Lamb* (1885) 12 R. 722; *Sandeman* v. *Scottish Property Investment Co.* (1885) 12 R. (H.L.) 67.

[4] A.S., 14 Dec. 1756.

[5] *Lyon* v. *Irvine* (1874) 1 R. 512.

[6] *Waugh* v. *More Nisbett* (1882) 19 S.L.R. 427; *Walker's Trs.* v. *Manson* (1886) 13 R. 1198; *Bidoulac* v. *Sinclair's Tr.* (1889) 17 R. 144; *Buttercase & Geddie's Tr.* v. *Geddie* (1897) 24 R. 1128.

[7] *Borland & Co's Tr.* v. *Paterson* (1881) 19 S.L.R. 261; *Glasgow Mags.* v. *Hay* (1883) 10 R. 635; cf. *Welsh* v. *Jack* (1882) 10 R. 113.

[8] *Stuart* v. *Warnocks* (1883) 20 S.L.R. 863.

[9] *Guild* v. *McLean* (1897) 25 R. 106; cf. *Noble* v. *Hart* (1896) 24 R. 174.

falling two years in arrear.[1] A party can enforce an irritancy despite having previously waived his power to enforce.[2]

Enforcement

An irritancy, whether legal or conventional, if incurred, renders the contract voidable only, not automatically void,[3] and it must generally be declared by the court to have been incurred before it can be enforced, though in a case of conventional irritancy the need for declarator was held to be a matter for the discretion of the court.[4] It is settled that a legal irritancy is purgeable by the tender of payment at any time before decree of declarator is granted,[5] but that a conventional irritancy, unless it is one merely expressing what the law implies,[6] is not purgeable once incurred, notwithstanding questions of hardship, and a tender of payment after it has been incurred but before declarator comes too late.[7] The court however may, unless the parties have stipulated that purgation was prohibited[8] always allow an irritancy to be purged if it is being used oppressively or misused.[9] It is no defence, however, that there is a subsisting question between superior and vassal, such as in regard to the latter's right to build.[10]

An irritancy is enforceable only by the party aggrieved by the breach; it cannot be used by the party in breach as a means of having the contract terminated.[11] If enforced, failing contrary stipulation,[12] it bars any action for the arrears of feuduties or rent,[13] and also precludes any claim for damages,[14] unless such a claim has been expressly reserved.[15] If incurred it annuls the right of the feudal vassal or tenant and all that has flowed therefrom, such as sub-feus.[16]

[1] *Wingate's Trs.* v. *W.* (1892) 29 S.L.R. 406.
[2] *Lurie* v. *Demarco*, 1967 S.L.T. (Notes) 110.
[3] *Bidoulac* v. *Sinclair's Tr.* (1889) 17 R. 144.
[4] *Duke of Argyll* v. *Campbeltown Coal Co.*, 1924 S.C. 844.
[5] *Maxwell's Trs.* v. *Bothwell School Board* (1893) 20 R. 953.
[6] *Duncanson* v. *Giffen* (1878) 15 S.L.R. 356.
[7] *Lyon* v. *Irvine* (1874) 1 R. 512; *Chalmer's Tr.* v. *Dick's Tr.*, 1909 S.C. 761; *McDouall's Trs.* v. *MacLeod*, 1949 S.C. 593.
[8] *E. Elgin* v. *Whittaker & Street* (1901) 9 S.L.T. 375.
[9] *Stewart* v. *Watson* (1864) 2 M. 1414; *McDouall's Trs.*, *supra*.
[10] *Thom* v. *Chalmers* (1886) 13 R. 1026.
[11] *Bidoulac* v. *Sinclair's Trs.* (1889) 17 R. 144; *N.Z. Shipping Co.* v. *Société des Ateliers* [1919] A.C. 1.
[12] *Marquis of Breadalbane* v. *Stewart* (1904) 7 F. (H.L.) 23.
[13] *Edinburgh Mags.* v. *Horsburgh* (1834) 12 S. 593.
[14] *Buttercase and Geddie's Tr.* v. *Geddie* (1897) 24 R. 1128.
[15] *Walker's Trs.* v. *Manson* (1886) 13 R. 1198.
[16] *Sandeman* v. *Scottish Property Investment Co.* (1885) 12 R. (H.L.) 67; *Cassels* v. *Lamb* (1885) 12 R. 722.

(4) FORFEITURE CLAUSES

Contracts, particularly relating to building and engineering works, frequently contain a provision empowering one party to forfeit certain property or rights of the other on the happening of specified events.[1] The right must be exercised unequivocally[2] and any prerequisites or formalities complied with.[3] Wrongful forfeiture is a fundamental breach of contract.[4] Any contract may provide for the payment of a deposit, to be forfeited if one party fails to complete the contract. At least where there is no justification for failure to complete, the deposit falls to the other party without proof of loss.[5]

(5) CLAUSES CONFERRING POWER TO DETERMINE

At common law either party has power to rescind or determine a contract if the other party has repudiated the obligations incumbent on him thereunder or has acted in material breach of contract, and a continuing contract may be terminated by either party on reasonable notice to the other. But a contract may contain express power to either party to determine the contract though there be no breach, in such circumstances and on such terms and conditions as may be provided.[6] Such determination may be provided to be exercisable wholly independently of fault or breach of contract by the other party. Thus charter-parties frequently contain a cancelling clause in the event of the non-arrival of the ship at the named port.[7]

(6) INDEMNITY CLAUSE

A contract may contain a provision whereby, if one party incurs specified legal liability to a third party, the second party will indemnify the first party. Whether a claim arises depends on the interpretation of the contract in the light of the circumstances

---

[1] cf. *Commercial Bank* v. *Beal* (1890) 18 R. 80; *British Glanzstoff Mfg. Co.* v. *General Accident, etc. Assce. Corpn.*, 1913 S.C. (H.L.) 1.

[2] *Roberts* v. *Davey* (1833) 4 B. & Ad. 664; *Re Tout and Finch, Ltd.* [1954] 1 All E.R. 127.

[3] *Drew* v. *Josolyne* (1887) 18 Q.B.D. 590.

[4] *Lodder* v. *Slowey* [1904] A.C. 442; *Roberts* v. *Bury Improvement Commrs.* (1870) L.R. 5 C.P. 310.

[5] *Commercial Bank* v. *Beal* (1890) 18 R. 80; *Roberts & Cooper* v. *Salvesen*, 1918 S.C. 794.

[6] e.g. power to architect to determine building contract if dissatisfied with progress of work: *Scott* v. *Gerrard*, 1916 S.C. 793.

[7] *Bank Line* v. *Capel* [1919] A.C. 435.

which have happened.[1] An undertaking to indemnify against claims for damages incurred 'at common law' includes claims for common law damages though founded on breach of a duty of care imposed by statute.[2] A party is not entitled to be indemnified against loss for which he would be legally responsible by reason of his own fault unless that is clearly covered by the indemnity clause.[3] In case of doubt such a clause must be construed *contra proferentem*.[4]

(7) CLAUSE OF RELIEF

A party may by a provision in a contract undertake to free and relieve the other party of certain liabilities which would otherwise fall on that other. Thus a granter of lands may undertake to free and relieve the grantee for the future from certain financial burdens exigible from the lands;[5] similarly a lessee may undertake to relieve the lessor of certain burdens.[6] Prima facie such a clause does not extend to burdens or taxes imposed by future or supervening laws,[5] but it may.[7] The usage of parties may assist in the interpretation of such a clause.[8] Essentially similar clauses have arisen in other kinds of contracts.[9]

(8) LIQUIDATE DAMAGES AND PENALTY CLAUSES

To encourage satisfactory performance and to minimize disputes as to damages for breach of contract parties frequently include in their contract provision for payment by the party in breach of a sum or sums of money to the other. Such a provision may be held to be a provision for liquidate damages, or for a penalty. Which it is is a question of the intention of parties as

---

[1] cf. *McGill* v. *Pirie & Co. (Paisley) Ltd.*, 1967 S.L.T. 152; *Mackay* v. *Balfour, Beatty & Co.*, 1967 S.L.T. (Notes) 15; *Wright* v. *Tyne Improvement Commrs.* [1968] 1 All E.R. 807.

[2] *Hamilton* v. *Anderson*, 1953 S.C. 129.

[3] *N. of S. Hydro-Electric Board* v. *Taylor*, 1956 S.C. 1.

[4] *N. of S. Hydro-Electric Board*, *supra*.

[5] *Scott* v. *Edmond* (1860) 12 D. 1077; *Wilson* v. *Musselburgh Mags.* (1868) 6 M. 483; *Dunbar's Trs.* v. *British Fisheries Socy.* (1878) 5 R. (H.L.) 221; *Welwood's Trs.* v. *Mungall*, 1921 S.C. 911.

[6] *Jopp's Trs.* v. *Edmond* (1888) 15 R. 271.

[7] *Stenhouse's Trs.* v. *St. Andrew's Mags.*, 1933 S.C. 373; cf. *Dunbar Mags.* v. *Mackersy*, 1931 S.C. 180.

[8] *Welwood's Trs.*, *supra*; *Dunbar Mags.*, *supra*.

[9] e.g. *Edinburgh Corpn.* v. *L.A.*, 1923 S.C. 112; *Secretary of State for Scotland* v. *Portkil Estates*, 1957 S.C. 1.

ascertained by the court from the terms of the contract.[1] The words used, though *prima facie* indicative, are not conclusive.[2] 'The essence of a penalty is a payment stipulated as *in terrorem* of the offending party; the essence of liquidated damages is a genuine covenanted pre-estimate of damages.'[3] 'The question whether a sum stipulated is penalty or liquidated damages is a question of construction to be decided upon the terms and inherent circumstances of each particular contract, judged of as at the time of making the contract, not as at the time of the breach.[4] To assist in this task of construction various tests have been suggested which if applicable to the case under consideration may prove helpful, or even conclusive. Such are: (a) it will be held to be penalty if the sum stipulated for is extravagant and unconscionable in amount in comparison with the greatest loss that could conceivably be proved to have followed from the breach.[5] (b) It will be a penalty if the breach consists only in not paying a sum of money and the sum stipulated is a sum greater than the sum which ought to have been paid.[6] (c) There is a presumption (but no more) that it is a penalty when a single lump sum is made payable by way of compensation, on the occurrence of one or more or all of several events, some of which may occasion serious and others but trifling damage.[7] On the other hand (d) It is no obstacle to the sum stipulated being a genuine pre-estimate of damage, that the consequences of the breach are such as to make precise pre-estimation almost an impossibility. On the contrary that is just the situation when it is probable that pre-estimated damage was the true bargain between the parties.[8,9]

---

[1] *Robertson* v. *Driver's Trs.* (1881) 8 R. 555; *Elphinstone* v. *Monkland Iron Co.* (1886) 13 R. (H.L.) 98; *Dunlop Tyre Co.* v. *New Garage Co.* [1915] A.C. 79; *Cellulose Acetate Silk Co.* v. *Widnes Foundry Co.* [1933] A.C. 20; *Bell Bros.* (*H.P.*) *Ltd.* v. *Aitken*, 1939 S.C. 577; *Paterson* v. *S.W.S.E.B.*, 1950 S.C. 582.

[2] 'Liquidate damages' held to be penalty: *Re Newman, ex p. Capper* (1876) 4 Ch. D. 724; 'Penalty' held to be penalty: *Craig* v. *McBeath* (1863) 1 M. 1020; *Dingwall* v. *Burnett*, 1912 S.C. 1097; 'Penalty' held to be liquidate damages: *Galsworthy* v. *Strutt* (1848) 1 Exch. 659; *Johnston* v. *Robertson* (1861) 23 D. 646; *Re White & Arthur* (1901) 84 L.T. 594; *Beattie* v. *Ritchie* (1801) 9 S.L.T. 2; *Cape of Good Hope* v. *Hills* (1906) 22 T.L.R. 589; *Steel* v. *Bell* (1900) 3 F. 319; *Clydebank, infra*; *Cameron-Head* v. *Cameron*, 1919 S.C. 627; cf. *Page* v. *Sherratt* (1907) 15 S.L.T. 731.

[3] *Clydebank Engineering Co.* v. *Castaneda* (1904) 7 F. (H.L.) 77.

[4] *Public Works Commr.* v. *Hills* [1906] A.C. 368; *Webster* v. *Bosanquet* [1912] A.C. 394.

[5] *Clydebank, supra*, 78, per Lord Halsbury; cf. *Cameron-Head, supra*.

[6] *Kemble* v. *Farran* (1829) 6 Bing. 141.

[7] *Elphinstone, supra*, 106, per Lord Watson; contrast *Dingwall, supra*.

[8] *Clydebank, supra*, 79, per Lord Halsbury; *Webster, supra*, per Lord Mersey.

[9] *Dunlop, supra*, 86, per Lord Dunedin.

It is important that the date from which liquidated damages are to run be specified, or at least be ascertainable, by the contract.[1] The party claiming must also satisfy the court that the circumstances in which the liquidated damages provision is applicable have arisen.[2]

If the sum stated is liquidated damages, the party aggrieved may recover that sum on proof of breach but without proof of loss, and even if he has not suffered so much loss, though the court may modify the sum if it is exorbitant,[3] but he may not claim more nor seek to prove greater loss.[4] If the sum is a penalty, he may exact the penalty, though the defender may set forth grounds for modification of it,[5] or he may ignore the penalty clause and claim damages, recovering for loss actually proved, even if greater than the stated penalty,[6] but cannot claim more than one penalty.[7]

The party aggrieved may lose his right to liquidated damages if he does not deduct them from sums payable to the party in breach, unless the latter has undertaken independently to pay them if due.[8] But he retains the right to claim unliquidated damages.[9] He may also lose the right if he invokes another conventional remedy, such as to take possession of the works and have them completed by another contractor,[10] or if the event giving rise to the claim, e.g. delay, has been caused partly by the claimant.[11]

Other similar conventional provisions are competent, such as an abatement of the price by way of damages.[12]

Penalty provisions in leases and feu-contracts are deemed compulsitors for performance, 'by and attour performance' and do not give a party an option to infringe on paying the penalty.[13]

---

[1] *Dodd* v. *Churton* [1897] 1 Q.B. 562.

[2] *British Glanzstoff Mfg. Co.* v. *General Accident, etc., Assce. Corpn.*, 1913 S.C. (H.L.) 1.

[3] *Forrest & Barr* v. *Henderson* (1869) 8 M. 187.

[4] *Hyndman's Trs.* v. *Miller* (1895) 3 S.L.T. 170.

[5] *Craig* v. *McBeath* (1863) 1 M. 1020.

[6] *Dingwall* v. *Burnett*, 1912 S.C. 1097; *Wall* v. *Rederi A/B Luggude* [1915] 3 K.B. 66.

[7] *Hyndman's Trs.* v. *Miller* (1895) 3 S.L.T. 170.

[8] *Mackintosh* v. *G.W. Ry.* (1865) 11 Jur. (N.S.) 681; contrast *Fletcher* v. *Dyche* (1787) 2 T.R. 32; *Davis* v. *Hedges* (1871) L.R. 6 Q.B. 687.

[9] *Ford* v. *Cotesworth* (1870) L.R. 5 Q.B. 544; *Tyers* v. *Rosedale Iron Co.* (1875) L.R. 10 Ex. 195.

[10] *British Glanzstoff Mfg. Co.* v. *General Accident Assce. Corpn.*, 1913 S.C. (H.L.) 1.

[11] *McElroy* v. *Tharsis Sulphur Co.* (1877) 5 R. 161 (revd. on another point (1878) 5 R. (H.L.) 171); cf. *Steel* v. *Bell* (1900) 3 F. 319, where held that onus of proving this defence was on the party pleading it.

[12] *McCormick* v. *Rittmeyer* (1869) 7 M. 854.

[13] *Gold* v. *Houldsworth* (1870) 8 M. 1006; *Dalrymple* v. *Herdman* (1878) 5 R. 847.

A clause referring disputes to arbitration may be limited to disputes arising in the execution of the contract, or may refer to arbitration every claim and obligation at any time arising out of the contract.[1] It is a question of interpretation what is the scope of the reference clause and whether a particular dispute falls within it.[2]

TERMS IMPORTED BY REFERENCE

Parties may competently, by appropriate reference in a contract, import into it some or all of the terms, provisions, conditions and stipulations set out in full in some other document. This may be a standard or model form of contract conditions settled by the parties or one of them, or a standard form settled by an outside person or body, such as the R.I.B.A. or an Institute of professional engineers.[3] Contracts with government departments normally incorporate standard conditions settled by the government. Or the parties' contract may incorporate some or all of the rules of a trading association,[3] or of the Stock Exchange. Particular details may also be determined in the contract by reference to specifications, plans, drawings, or schedules relative thereto,[4] or to external standards such as those of the British Standards Institution. Or an order form or letter of acceptance may contain or refer to some terms of sale.[5] In such cases the questions arise (a) whether the alleged term has been validly imported into the parties' contract; (b) what it is; and (c) what its effect is in the circumstances.

(a) ASCERTAINMENT

(a) *Whether term imported into contract or not*

It is not necessary that the term alleged have been copied *ad longum* into the parties' contract; an adequate reference suffices.

---

[1] *Wright* v. *Greenock & Port-Glasgow Tramways Co.* (1891) 29 S.L.R. 53.

[2] *Gerry* v. *Caithness Flagstone Quarrying Co.* (1885) 12 R. 543; cf. *Kilmarnock Dist. Cttee.* v. *Somervell* (1906) 14 S.L.T. 567. See also *Hagarty & Kelly* v. *Cosmopolitan Insce. Corpn.*, 1913 S.C. 377; *Sanderson* v. *Armour*, 1922 S.C. (H.L.) 117; *Scott* v. *Del Sel*, 1923 S.C. (H.L.) 37. See generally Chap. 3, *supra.*

[3] cf. *Stewart Brown & Co.* v. *Grime* (1897) 24 R. 414; *Morrison* v. *Rome*, 1964 S.C. 160.

[4] *Goodwins, Jardine & Co.* v. *Brand* (1905) 7 F. 995.

[5] *Smith* v. *Waite, Nash & Co.* (1888) 15 R. 533; *Oakbank Oil Co.* v. *Love & Stewart*, 1918 S.C. (H.L.) 54; *Rutherford* v. *Miln*, 1941 S.C. 125; cf. *Stewart, Brown & Co.* v. *Grime* (1897) 24 R. 414; *McConnell & Reid* v. *Smith*, 1911 S.C. 635; *Mechans Ltd.* v. *Highland Marine Charters*, 1964 S.C. 49.

No question arises where parties both admit that a particular term was imported, or where one party knows that the other has imported some provision and does not demur to contracting on these terms.[1] The onus is on the party relying on the imported term to show that it has been adequately brought to the other's attention.[2]

Conditions imported by one party unknown to other

Difficult issues may arise where one party intends that a term shall be imported into a contract but the other does not appreciate this. The attempt is frequently made by handing over a ticket or similar document or exhibiting a notice, usually with the purpose of excluding or limiting liability for default on the contract.

The court will hold such a document to be evidence of the contract and habile to import terms into it only if it was, and should reasonably have been understood in the circumstances to be, a contractual document[3] rather than merely a receipt or identification check.[4] It must moreover have been imported into the contract before or when it was made and not intimated subsequently,[5] unless there is evidence of agreement to subsequent modification of contract, or, possibly, evidence that the party had previously contracted on the same terms.[6]

If the document is contractual and has been signed by the acceptor he will normally, unless he can prove fraud or misrepresentation,[7] be held to have assented to and be bound thereby, whether he read it or understood it or not.[8]

If the document is contractual but has not been signed the acceptor is not held to have assented and to be bound if he did not see or know that there were contractual terms stated thereon; if he knew that there was something printed, and knew or believed that it contained conditions, he is bound thereby even though he did not, or could not,[9] read them or know what they were. Failing

---

[1] cf. *Rutherford* v. *Miln*, 1941 S.C. 125.

[2] *F.M.C. (Meat)* v. *Fairfield Cold Stores* [1971] 2 Lloyd's Rep. 221.

[3] *Hood* v. *Anchor Line*, 1918 S.C. (H.L.) 143.

[4] *Parker* v. *S.E. Ry.* (1877) 2 C.P.D. 416, 422; *Skrine* v. *Gould* (1912) 29 T.L.R. 19; *Chapelton* v. *Barry U.D.C.* [1940] 1 K.B. 532; *Taylor* v. *Glasgow Corpn.*, 1952 S.C. 440; *McCutcheon* v. *MacBrayne*, 1964 S.C. (H.L.) 28.

[5] *Olley* v. *Marlborough Court, Ltd.* [1949] 1 K.B. 532; *McCutcheon* v. *MacBrayne*, 1964 S.C. (H.L.) 28.

[6] *Grieve* v. *Turbine Steamers, Ltd.* (1903) 11 S.L.T. 379; cf. *Caird* v. *Adam* (1907) 15 S.L.T. 543.

[7] *Curtis* v. *Chemical Cleaning Co.* [1951] 1 K.B. 805.

[8] *Parker* v. *S.E. Ry.* (1877) 2 C.P.D. 416, 421; *Hood, supra*; *Aberdeen Grit Co.* v. *Ellerman's Wilson Line*, 1933 S.C. 9; *L'Estrange* v. *Graucob* [1934] 2 K.B. 394.

[9] *Thompson* v. *L.M.S. Ry.* [1930] 1 K.B. 41; *Gray* v. *L.N.E. Ry.*, 1930 S.C. 989.

such knowledge he is bound only if the offering party took reasonable steps to give notice of the terms to the acceptor. Reasonableness is a question of fact,[1] in which the position of the writing on the document, the size of print, and the presence or absence of anything specially drawing attention to the terms have been held relevant.[2]

If terms are validly incorporated into a contract, it is sufficient that they be merely a reference to the full conditions.[3] Such clauses, even if validly incorporated in the contract, can protect only the contracting party, and not third parties, such as the latter's employees.[4] Where it is apparent from the contract that one party would have to avail himself of a sub-contractor to enable him to perform part of the contract, the contract may import limitations of liability contained in the sub-contract.[5]

Importation by note on or with contract

A note or notice on or sent with a contractural document, such as a sale note,[6] letter of acceptance,[7] or covering letter[8] or receipt[9] may be held to give the other party reasonably adequate notice of the conditions of contract and hence to bind him.

Importation by notice

Importation of a condition by notice publicly exhibited at the place of contracting is possible,[10] but it must be established that the notice was intended to be part of each contract, and was known to and accepted by the other party as such.[11]

[1] *Parker* v. *S.E. Ry.* (1877) 2 C.P.D. 416; *Richardson* v. *Rowntree* [1894] A.C. 217; *Hood, supra.*

[2] *Henderson* v. *Stevenson* (1875) 2 R. (H.L.) 71; *Parker, supra; Burke* v. *S.E. Ry.* (1879) 5 C.P.D. 1; *Richardson, supra; Stephen* v. *International Sleeping Car Co.* (1903) 19 T.L.R. 621; *Hooper* v. *Furness Ry.* (1907) 23 T.L.R. 451; *Lyons* v. *Caledonian Ry.,* 1909 S.C. 1185; *Grand Trunk Ry.* v. *Robinson* [1915] A.C. 740; *Cooke* v. *Wilson* (1915) 85 L.J. K.B. 888; *Williamson* v. *N. of S.S.N. Co.,* 1916 S.C. 554; *C.P. Ry.* v. *Parent* [1917] A.C. 195; *Hood, supra; Lewis* v. *Laird Line,* 1925 S.L.T. 316; *Morris* v. *Laird Line,* 1925 S.L.T. 321; *Thompson* v. *L.M.S. Ry.* [1930] 1 K.B. 41; *Gray* v. *L.N.E. Ry.,* 1930 S.C. 989; *Coyle* v. *L.M.S. Ry.,* 1930 S.L.T. 349; *Penton* v. *S. Ry.* [1931] 2 K.B. 103; *Sugar* v. *L.M.S. Ry.* [1941] 1 All E.R. 172; *Thornton* v. *Shoe Lane Parking* [1971] 1 All E.R. 686.

[3] *Thompson, supra; Gray* v. *L.N.E. Ry.,* 1930 S.C. 989.

[4] *Adler* v. *Dickson* [1955] 1 Q.B. 158; *Scruttons* v. *Midland Silicones, Ltd.* [1962] A.C. 446.

[5] *Aberdeen Grit Co.* v. *Ellerman's Wilson Line,* 1933 S.C. 9.

[6] *McConnell & Reid* v. *Smith,* 1911 S.C. 635.

[7] *Smith* v. *Waite, Nash & Co.* (1888) 15 R. 533.

[8] *Oakbank Oil Co.* v. *Love & Stewart,* 1918 S.C. (H.L.) 54.

[9] *Ballingall* v. *Dundee Ice Co.,* 1924 S.C. 238.

[10] *Wood* v. *Burns* (1893) 20 R. 602; cf. *Lightbody's Tr.* v. *Hutchison* (1886) 14 R. 4.

[11] *Watkins* v. *Rymill* (1883) 10 Q.B.D. 178; *White* v. *Dougherty* (1891) 18 R. 972; *Wright* v. *Howard, Baker & Co.* (1893) 21 R. 25; *Harling* v. *Eddy* [1951] 2 K.B. 739; cf. *McCutcheon* v. *MacBrayne,* 1964 S.C. (H.L.) 28.

Course of dealing

A term expressed in one contract is not automatically held imported into subsequent contracts between the same parties, even though *in pari materia*,[1] particularly if earlier transactions were written and the present one oral,[2] but a contract may be on the usual terms of business and thereby have imported a condition.[3]

(b) *What the imported term is*

This is a question of evidence.

(b) INTERPRETATION

(c) *The effect of the imported term*

This is a question of interpretation, but the courts, recognizing that exemption clauses are commonly incorporated by dominant parties and imposed on individuals who have no option but to accept them, generally construe them strictly and *contra proferentem*, against the dominant party.[4] Any ambiguity in the contract will be decided against the dominant party who framed the contract and the imported exemption.[5] An exemption clause will not be held to exclude liability for fault or negligence unless this is expressed, or there is no other liability to which it can refer.[6] An exemption from liability for all damage, howsoever caused, will normally exempt from liability for negligence.[7] If words used clearly exclude all liability they must receive effect,[8] as they must if they can only fairly be read as covering the default alleged.[9]

The four corners rule

A party can normally rely on an exemption clause only if the loss or damage comes within the four corners of the contract and does not arise outside the contract altogether, as in unauthorized

---

[1] *Straiton Oil Co.* v. *Sanderson* (1882) 9 R. 929.

[2] *McCutcheon* v. *MacBrayne*, 1964 S.C. (H.L.) 28.

[3] *Rutherford* v. *Miln*, 1941 S.C. 125.

[4] *Baldry* v. *Marshall* [1925] 1 K.B. 260; *Andrews* v. *Singer* [1934] 1 K.B. 17.

[5] *L.N.W. Ry.* v. *Neilson* [1922] 2 A.C. 263; *McKay* v. *Scottish Airways*, 1948 S.C. 254, 256; *Lee* v. *Railway Executive* [1949] 2 All E.R. 581; *White* v. *Warwick* [1953] 1 W.L.R. 1285; *Houghton* v. *Trafalgar Insce. Co.* [1954] 1 Q.B. 247; *Morris* v. *Martin* [1966] 1 Q.B. 716; *Kendall* v. *Lillico* [1968] 2 All E.R. 444; *Hutchinson* v. *B.R. Board*, 1970 S.L.T. 72.

[6] *Alderslade* v. *Hendon Laundry* [1945] K.B. 189; *Canada S.S. Lines, Ltd.* v. *R.* [1952] A.C. 192.

[7] *Rutter* v. *Palmer* [1922] 2 K.B. 87; *Akerib* v. *Booth* [1960] 1 All E.R. 481.

[8] e.g. *Gibaud* v. *G.E. Ry.* [1921] 2 K.B. 426; *Rutter* v. *Palmer* [1922] 2 K.B. 87; *Ashby* v. *Tolhurst* [1937] 2 K.B. 242; *McKay, supra.*

[9] *Ballingall* v. *Dundee Ice Co.*, 1924 S.C. 238; *Alderslade* v. *Hendon Laundry, Ltd.* [1945] K.B. 189.

delegation of performance,[1] or conduct inconsistent with the main purpose of the contract.[2]

The principle of fundamental breach

When faced by increasingly compendious exemptions from liability for breach the courts have developed the doctrine of the fundamental term or fundamental breach, to the effect that an exception clause will not protect a party who has been in breach of the basic duties of the contract unless the provision is clear and unambiguous. He cannot easily escape the duty to perform his contract in its essential respects, and is *prima facie* in breach if performance is different from what the contract contemplates.[3] But the only kind of breach disentitling a party from relying on an exemption clause is performance wholly different from that contemplated by the contract.[4] Thus a shipowner who deviated from the agreed course has been held disentitled to claim the benefit of stipulations in his favour in the bill of lading.[5] A depositary who misdelivers goods deposited may be unprotected even if a term in the contract appears to cover him.[6] A seller of peas who delivers beans is not protected by a term merely excluding liability for all defects: he has fundamentally not performed his contract.[7] A seller who has not title to sell is not protected if the subject is recovered by the true owner.[8] A supplier has been held not protected if the goods have so many defects that they are practically unserviceable.[9] There is, however, no rule of law that an exceptions clause is nullified by a fundamental breach of contract or breach of a fundamental term; in each case the ques-

---

[1] *Davies* v. *Collins* [1945] 1 All E.R. 247; cf. *Woolmer* v. *Delmer Price, Ltd.* [1955] 1 Q.B. 291.

[2] *Glynn* v. *Margetson & Co.* [1893] A.C. 351; see also *Lilley* v. *Doubleday* (1881) 7 Q.B.D. 510; *Gibaud* v. *G.E. Ry.* [1921] 2 K.B. 426; *Suisse Atlantique Société d'Armement Maritime S.A.* v. *N.V. Rotterdamsche Kolen Centrale* [1967] A.C. 361.

[3] *Smeaton Hanscomb* v. *Sassoon Setty & Co.* [1953] 1 W.L.R. 1468.

[4] *Kenyon* v. *Baxter, Hoare & Co.* [1971] 2 All E.R. 708.

[5] *Thorley* v. *Orchis S.S. Co. Ltd.* [1907] 1 K.B. 660; cf. *Bontex Knitting Works* v. *St. John's Garage* [1944] 1 All E.R. 381.

[6] *Alexander* v. *Railway Executive* [1951] 2 K.B. 882; cf. *Spurling* v. *Bradshaw* [1956] 2 All E.R. 121.

[7] *Chanter* v. *Hopkins* (1838) 4 M. & W. 399; cf. *Pinnock Bros.* v. *Lewis & Peat* [1923] 1 K.B. 690.

[8] *Rowland* v. *Divall* [1923] 2 K.B. 500.

[9] *Pollock* v. *Macrae*, 1922 S.C. (H.L.) 192; *Mechans, Ltd.* v. *Highland Marine Charters, Ltd.*, 1964 S.C. 48; cf. *Karsales (Harrow) Ltd.* v. *Wallis* [1956] 2 All E.R. 866; *Yeoman Credit Ltd.* v. *Apps* [1962] 2 Q.B. 508.

tion is whether the exceptions clause was intended to exempt from the consequences of fundamental breach.[1]

Limits on conditions excluding liability

Conditions limiting or excluding liability, if wholly unreasonable, may be held not binding on a party even if steps reasonable in the circumstances have been taken to give him notice of them.[2] It is, however, competent for the railway authority to carry passengers at their own risk entirely.[3]

Statutory avoidance of exemption clauses

Statutes have in certain cases provided that clauses exempting from liability are void.[4]

IMPLIED TERMS

In some circumstances the law holds implied in a contract terms not expressed therein nor imported by reference, and in others the courts will hold that some term must be held implied to give efficacy to the parties' agreement. Terms may be implied by statute, by common law, by the custom of a particular trade, or by the court. It is for the court to say in each case whether a term should be held implied, in what terms, and what the effect of the implication is on the contract.[5]

(a) ASCERTAINMENT

Terms implied by statute

Statute frequently provides that in contracts of particular kinds terms to certain effects shall be implied. Sometimes the implication arises only in the absence of express contrary provision; sometimes it overrides any inconsistent express stipulation.

---

[1] *Suisse Atlantique Société d'Armement Maritime S.A.* v. *N.V. Rotterdamsche Kolen Centrale* [1967] A.C. 361. But see *Harbutt's Plasticene Ltd.* v. *Wayne Tank Co.* [1970] 1 Q.B. 447.

[2] *Parker* v. *S.E. Ry.* (1877) 2 C.P.D. 416, 428; *Thompson* v. *L.M.S. Ry.* [1930] 1 K.B. 41; but see *McKay* v. *Scottish Airways*, 1948 S.C. 254, 263; *Lee* v. *Railway Executive* [1949] 2 All E.R. 581, 584.

[3] *Gallin* v. *L.N.W. Ry.* (1875) L.R. 10 Q.B. 212; *Hall* v. *N.E. Ry.* (1875) L.R. 10 Q.B. 437; *Rogers* v. *L.M.S. Ry.* (1930) 46 T.L.R. 238.

[4] Carriers Act, 1830 (carriage of goods by carriers); Railway and Canal Traffic Act, 1854, S. 7 (carriage of goods by rail); Road Traffic Act, 1960, S. 151 (carriage of passengers by road); Transport Act, 1962, S. 43(7) (carriage of passengers by rail).

[5] *O'Brien* v. *Assoc. Fire Alarms* (1968) 3 K.I.R. 223.

The terms implied in particular cases are dealt with in relation to the particular contracts.[1]

Terms implied by common law

Whether a particular term falls to be implied into a particular contract by common law is determined by precedent or by the court's view of whether such implication is reasonable as supplying the presumed common intention of parties.[2] In the main kinds of contracts many terms are held implied by well-settled precedents.[3] Terms implied may confer authority,[4] impose a duty of reasonable skill and care,[5] confer a right to remuneration,[6] impose a duty of care for the safety of the other party,[7] and the like. But in other cases the court has held that a term must be implied, such as that money paid under protest and subsequently held illegally demanded should be repaid with interest.[8]

Terms implied by custom or usage of trade

Parties transacting in particular trades may have their contracts held supplemented by terms implied by the proved custom of the particular trade or of the community in relation to the particular relationship.[9] The alleged term must be proved to be well-known in the trade, certain, reasonable, not contrary to any general rule of law, and such that parties must be presumed to have accepted it as part of their contract.[10] Some statutes[11] have in substance enacted general usages of the business community in

---

[1] See e.g. Sale of Goods Act, 1893, Ss. 10–15; Marine Insurance Act, 1906, Ss. 33–41; Trading Stamps Act, 1964, S. 4; Consumer Credit Act, 1974, Sch. 4.

[2] See e.g. *Convery* v. *Summerlee Iron Co.* (1884) 12 R. 191; *Craig* v. *Millar* (1888) 15 R. 1005; *Patmore* v. *Cannon* (1892) 19 R. 1004; *S.S. State of California Co.* v. *Moore* (1895) 22 R. 562; *L.A.* v. *Anderson* (1895) 3 S.L.T. 115; *Moore's Carving Machine Co.* v. *Austin* (1896) 4 S.L.T. 38; *Murray* v. *Rennie & Angus* (1897) 24 R. 965; *Teacher* v. *Calder* (1899) 1 F. (H.L.) 39; *Hong Kong, etc., Dock Co.* v. *Netherton Shipping Co.*, 1909 S.C. 34; *Sturrock* v. *Murray*, 1952 S.C. 454.

[3] See further chapters on Specific Contracts.

[4] *Black* v. *Cornelius* (1879) 6 R. 581; *Steel* v. *Young*, 1907 S.C. 360; *Knox & Robb* v. *Scottish Garden Suburb Co.*, 1913 S.C. 872; *Forrest* v. *Scottish County Investment Co.*, 1915 S.C. 115.

[5] Bell, *Prin.* §153; *Dickson* v. *Hygienic Institute*, 1910 S.C. 352.

[6] *Thomson* v. *McBain* (1889) 16 R. 333.

[7] *English* v. *Wilsons & Clyde Coal Co.*, 1937 S.C. (H.L.) 46.

[8] *Haddon's Exrx.* v. *Scottish Milk Marketing Board*, 1938 S.C. 168.

[9] *Moss* v. *Cunliffe & Dunlop* (1875) 2 R. 657; *Livesey* v. *Purdom* (1894) 21 R. 911; *Duthie* v. *Merson & Gerry*, 1947 S.C. 43.

[10] *Brown* v. *McConnell* (1876) 3 R. 788; *Clacevich* v. *Hutcheson* (1887) 15 R. 11; *Bruce* v. *Smith* (1890) 17 R. 1000; *Cazalet* v. *Morris*, 1916 S.C. 952; *Wilkie* v. *Scottish Aviation*, 1956 S.C. 198.

[11] e.g. Bills of Exchange Act, 1882; Sale of Goods Act, 1893.

particular kinds of transactions. Thus it has been held implied that in the lace trade goods would not be manufactured from pattern cards except for the original owner of the designs.[1] Similarly an architect has been held to have by custom an implied authority to employ a surveyor[2] or to sanction deviations from the plans.[3]

It is in every case a question of fact whether an alleged custom has been adequately averred and proved so as to justify the court in holding that there existed an accepted custom to the effect of implying a term into the contract in question.[4] Such an implied term can always be excluded or negatived by express contrary provision in the contract, and alleged, or even proved, custom of trade can never override a clear contrary or inconsistent statement in the contract.[5] It has been held also that a contract made with a firm after a change therein was impliedly subject to the conditions previously applying.[6]

Terms implied judicially

The courts may also sometimes imply a term to complete the presumed intention of both parties, or to give 'business efficacy' to the contract.[7] The term implied must be some stipulation which is not expressed but which the court is confident that both parties took for granted and would certainly have expressed had they foreseen the contingency,[8] and particularly if the contract would fail completely if such a term were not implied.[9]

Exclusion or variation of implied terms

An implied term, unless implied by a statute which expressly forbids the exclusion of implied terms,[10] can always be excluded or

---

[1] *Morton* v. *Muir Bros.*, 1907 S.C. 1211; cf. *Eldon* v. *Hedley* [1935] 2 K.B. 1.

[2] *Black* v. *Cornelius* (1879) 6 R. 581; contrast *Knox & Robb* v. *Scottish Garden Suburb Co.*, 1913 S.C. 872.

[3] *Forrest* v. *Scottish County Investment Co.*, 1916 S.C. (H.L.) 28.

[4] *Hong Kong Dock Co.* v. *Netherton Shipping Co.*, 1909 S.C. 34.

[5] *Tancred Arrol & Co.* v. *Steel Co. of Scotland* (1890) 17 R. (H.L.) 31; *P. & W. MacLellan* v. *Peattie's Trs.* (1903) 5 F. 1031; *Forth Collieries* v. *Hume* (1904) 11 S.L.T. 576; *Affreteurs Reunis* v. *Walford* [1919] A.C. 801; *London Export Corpn.* v. *Jubilee Coffee Roasting Co.* [1958] 2 All E.R. 411.

[6] *Garden, Haig-Scott & Wallace* v. *Prudential Approved Socy.*, 1927 S.L.T. 393.

[7] *The Moorcock* (1889) 14 P.D. 64; *McWhirter* v. *Longmuir*, 1948 S.C. 577; see also *Morton* v. *Muir Bros.*, 1907 S.C. 1211, 1224.

[8] *Reigate* v. *Union Mfg. Co.* [1918] 1 K.B. 592; *Shirlaw* v. *Southern Foundries Ltd.* [1939] 2 K.B. 206; *McClelland* v. *Northern Ireland General Health Services Board* [1957] 2 All E.R. 129; *Narbeth* v. *James* [1968] 1 Lloyd's Rep. 168; *Cummings* v. *Connell*, 1968 S.C. 305.

[9] *Miller* v. *Cannon Hill Estates, Ltd.* [1931] 2 K.B. 113; *Lynch* v. *Thorne* [1956] 1 W.L.R. 31.

[10] e.g. Housing (Sc.) Act, 1966, S. 10.

varied by an inconsistent or contrary express term of the contract.[1] Such exclusion provisions, if incorporated in the contract at all,[2] are strictly construed;[3] thus in sale an express exclusion of 'warranties', does not exclude an implied 'condition';[4] nor does an exclusion of 'implied terms' exclude express terms;[5] but if the exclusion clearly covers the kind of term founded on, it is valid.[6] Moreover even a wide exclusion of implied terms and conditions cannot receive effect where the party sued is in fundamental breach of contract.[7]

(b) INTERPRETATION

Once it has been determined that a term to a particular effect is to be implied into a contract the court must interpret the contract, including the term, in the usual way, and determine the rights of parties accordingly,[8]

STATUTORY POWERS OF COURTS TO MODIFY TERMS OF CONTRACTS

Certain statutes confer powers on courts to modify or determine contracts in particular circumstances. Thus the court may modify contracts relating to land subjected to war damage.[9] The sheriff may set aside or modify an agreement between an owner and an occupier of a factory which prevents necessary structural alterations.[10] The sheriff has wide powers to terminate or vary the lease of premises consisting of or comprising a house subject to a control order made by the local authority,[11] to vary the conditions or restrictions of a feu charter or feu contract or lease to enable a house to be converted into two or more dwellings,[12] and to modify agreements and leases to permit alterations required for fire precautions.[13]

[1] *Duthie* v. *Merson & Gerry*, 1947 S.C. 43.

[2] On this see *supra*.

[3] *Pollock* v. *Macrae*, 1922 S.C. (H.L.) 192, 199; *Van Til-Hartman* v. *Thomson*, 1931 S.N. 30.

[4] *Wallis* v. *Pratt & Haynes* [1911] A.C. 394; *Baldry* v. *Marshall* [1925] 1 K.B. 260.

[5] *Andrews* v. *Singer* [1934] 1 K.B. 17.

[6] *L'Estrange* v. *Graucob* [1934] 2 K.B. 394.

[7] *Pollock, supra*; *Pinnock Bros.* v. *Lewis and Peat, Ltd.* [1923] 1 K.B. 690; *Rowland* v. *Divall* [1923] 2 K.B. 500; *Smeaton Handscomb* v. *Sassoon I. Setty* [1953] 2 All E.R. 1471; *Mechans, Ltd.* v. *Highland Marine Charters*, 1964 S.C. 48.

[8] For cases interpreting implied terms of the Sale of Goods Act, 1893, see Chap. 103, *infra*.

[9] War Damage to Land (Sc.) Act, 1939, S. 4.

[10] Factories Act, 1961, S. 169.

[11] Housing (Sc.) Act, 1966, S. 128; see also S. 187.

[12] Ibid., S. 189.

[13] Fire Precautions Act, 1971, S. 28.

CHAPTER 35

THE SCOPE OF THE CONTRACT

JOINT OBLIGATIONS

WHERE two or more persons bind themselves on one part to a contract, whether as creditors or debtors, the general rule and presumption is that each co-obligant is *prima facie* bound for his own share only, not for the whole.[1] Joint creditors have each right to a *pro rata* share only of the debt, and each may sue for, assign or discharge his own share,[2] unless the obligation is undertaken to them *in solidum*, when any one may sue for or discharge the debt. Joint debtors are similarly presumed liable *pro rata* only,[3] but exceptions[4] are recognized: (1) if they are expressly taken bound jointly and severally, or as co-principals and full debtors;[5] (2) if the obligation be *ad factum praestandum*, or indivisible,[6] though a pecuniary penalty stipulated for, failing the promised act, is divisible;[7] (3) if they are partners or joint adventurers or joint mandants;[8] (4) if they purchase, order or instruct together;[9] and (5) if they are jointly drawers or acceptors of a bill.[10] In such cases the creditor may recover the whole debt from any one or more of the debtors.[11]

Joint and several liability also arises where breaches of their respective contracts with the pursuer by two or more defenders cause a single and indivisible loss.[12]

---

[1] Stair I, 17, 20; Ersk. III, 3, 74; Bell, *Comm.* I, 361; Bell, *Prin.* §51; *Coats v. Union Bank,* 1929 S.C. (H.L.) 114.

[2] Bell, *Prin.* §52; *Lawson v. Leith & Newcastle S.P. Co.* (1850) 13 D. 175; *Pyper v. Christie* (1878) 6 R. 143; *Detrick & Webster v. Laing's Sewing Machine Co.* (1885) 12 R. 416; *Shaw v. Gibb's Trs.* (1893) 20 R. 718.

[3] Stair III, 5, 14; Bell, *Prin.* §53; *Coats, supra.* In some cases debtors have bound themselves severally for stated sums each: *Milne v. Souter* (1868) 6 M. 977; *Milne v. Kidd* (1869) 8 M. 250.   [4] cf. *Coats v. Union Bank,* 1928 S.C. 711, 722.

[5] Ersk. III, 3, 74; Bell, *Prin.* §54, 56; *Richmond v. Grahame* (1847) 9 D. 633; *Dundee Police Commrs. v. Straton* (1884) 11 R. 586; *Burns v. Martin* (1887) 14 R. (H.L.) 20.

[6] Bell, *Prin.* §58; *Darlington v. Gray* (1836) 15 S. 197; *Rankine v. Logie Den Land Co.* (1902) 4 F. 1074.

[7] Bell, *Prin.* §58.

[8] Bell, *Prin.* §59, 60; *Walker v. Brown* (1803) Mor. *Solidum et Pro Rata,* Appx. 1; *Wilson v. Dunfermline Mags.* (1822) 1 S. 417; *Commercial Bank v. Sprot* (1841) 3 D. 939; *Webster v. McLellan* (1852) 14 D. 932; *Smith v. Harding* (1877) 5 R. 147.

[9] *Walker v. Brown* (1803) Mor. *Solidum et Pro Rata,* Appx. 1.

[10] Ersk. III, 3, 74; Bell, *Prin.* §61; *Milne's Trs. v. Ormiston's Trs.* (1893) 20 R. 523.

[11] *Gibson v. Irvine* (1900) 7 S.L.T. 391; *Fleming v. Gemmill,* 1908 S.C. 340.

[12] *Grunwald v. Hughes,* 1965 S.L.T. 209.

Relief

No question of relief arises where joint debtors each pay their *pro rata* share, but if less than the full sum due is exacted one who has paid his full *pro rata* share is entitled to relief from the co-debtors.[1]

Though they may be liable *in solidum* to the creditor, debtors bound jointly and severally are liable *inter se* to relieve any one who has paid more than his proportionate share.[2] In fixing the shares any debtor who is bankrupt is excluded from account.[3] No express assignation of the creditor's right is essential,[4] but it may be taken.[5] A debtor paying more than his share is also entitled to an assignation from the creditor of any securities held by him for the debt, to assist in working out his relief. Assignation may be refused if such would conflict with any legitimate interest of the creditor,[6] as where he holds another security over the same subjects for a separate debt. He cannot, however, refuse assignation merely because he had made subsequent advances on the same security.[7]

If the obligation be indivisible, or expressly several, the party satisfying it has no claim for relief. Nor has he if he was under only a moral obligation to pay.[8]

A co-obligant who has paid and claims relief must communicate to his co-debtors the proportionate share of any benefit he may receive at settlement, or which may accrue from the estates of insolvent co-debtors.[9] Where an obligation is joint, no one signatory thereto is held bound until and unless all are, as otherwise his implied right of relief would be prejudiced.[10] Hence the forgery of one signature releases all those who have already signed.[11]

Prejudicing right of relief

If the creditor does anything which prejudices the rights of relief *inter se* of co-debtors bound jointly and severally, as by discharging one co-debtor, the others are relieved so far as their

---

[1] Bell, *Comm.* I, 367; cf. *Ellesmere Brewery Co.* v. *Cooper* [1896] 1 Q.B. 75.

[2] Bell, *Prin.* §62; *Marshall* v. *Pennycook*, 1908 S.C. 276.

[3] *Buchanan* v. *Main* (1900) 3 F. 215.

[4] Stair I, 8, 9; Ersk. III, 3, 74; Bell, *Prin.* §§62, 255.

[5] *Mackay* v. *M.* (1896) 4 S.L.T. 200.   [6] *Bruce* v. *Scottish Amicable*, 1907 S.C. 637.

[7] *Sligo* v. *Menzies* (1840) 2 D. 1478.   [8] *Henderson* v. *Paul* (1867) 5 M. 628.

[9] Stair I, 8, 9; II, 17, 13; Ersk. *Prin.* III, 3, 29; Bell, *Prin.* §62; *Ledingham* v. *McKenzie* (1824) 3 S. 113.

[10] *Paterson* v. *Bonar* (1844) 6 D. 987 (caution); contrast *Simpson* v. *Fleming* (1860) 22 D. 679, *sed quaere*; cf. *York Building Co.* v. *Baillie* (1724) M. 8435; *Gordon's Exors.* v. *G.* (1918) 55 S.L.R. 497.

[11] *Sc. Provincial Assce. Co.* v. *Pringle* (1858) 20 D. 465.

right of relief has been prejudiced, but remain liable for the proportions of the debt originally applicable to them.[1] If they are co-cautioners, they are completely discharged.[2] But this consequence does not follow if the creditor, without discharging a co-debtor, merely undertakes not to sue him (*pactum de non petendo*),[3] nor if the creditor expressly reserves his rights against the remaining co-debtors.[4] Probably also if a creditor relinquishes a security granted by one co-debtor he relieves the others in so far as their rights of relief have been prejudiced thereby.[5]

RIGHTS OF THIRD PARTIES UNDER CONTRACT

In the ordinary case, where a contract is made between two parties, they alone acquire rights and come under liabilities thereunder, and no third party acquires either rights or liabilities under the contract. The fact that a third party has an interest in, or will benefit from, a contract, or lose by its non-performance, gives him no title to sue for its enforcement, nor for damages for its breach.[6] Thus a creditor cannot sue his debtor's debtor,[7] nor a beneficiary of a trust sue a debtor to the trust estate,[8] nor a contracting party sue the debtor in a sub-contract with the other contracting party,[9] nor a dismissed employee sue the company which had taken over his employer's business.[10] Nor can an outsider reduce a contract between two partners.[11]

But to this general principle there are important exceptions:

(1) CONTRACT CONFERRING *JUS QUAESITUM TERTIO*

A contract between two parties may be held to confer a *jus quaesitum tertio* on a third party where it appears that an object of the contract was to benefit the third party's interests; this appears only if he is named or referred to, or is one of a distinct identifiable

---

[1] *Smith* v. *Harding* (1877) 5 R. 147.

[2] Mercantile Law Amdt. (Sc.) Act, 1856, S. 9.

[3] *Muir* v. *Crawford* (1875) 2 R. (H.L.) 148.

[4] *Morton's Trs.* v. *Robertson's J.F.* (1892) 20 R. 72; cf. Bankruptcy (Sc.) Act, 1913, S. 52.

[5] *Marshall* v. *Pennycook*, 1908 S.C. 276.

[6] *Peddie* v. *Brown* (1857) 3 Macq. 65; *Finnie* v. *G.S.W. Ry.* (1857) 3 Macq. 75; *Blumer* v. *Scott* (1874) 1 R. 379; *Henderson* v. *Robb* (1889) 16 R. 341; *Henderson* v. *Stubbs* (1894) 22 R. 51.

[7] *Henderson* v. *Robb, supra.*

[8] *Hinton* v. *Connell's Trs.* (1883) 10 R. 110; *Rae* v. *Meek* (1888) 15 R. 1033.

[9] *Blumer, supra.*

[10] *Taylor* v. *Thomson* (1901) 9 S.L.T. 373.

[11] *Edinburgh United Breweries* v. *Molleson* (1894) 21 R. (H.L.) 10.

class referred to, in the contract.[1] Whether a *jus quaesitum* will be held conferred on a *tertius* depends on the intention of both contracting parties as shown in their contract. It may be conferred expressly, as where money is banked on deposit receipt, made payable to a *tertius*, who may then uplift the money.[2] It may be conferred impliedly, where some *tertius* is the only person having any substantial interest in having the contract implemented, as where A promises B to benefit C.[3]

A *jus quaesitum* may be held conferred on a *tertius* notwithstanding that the creditor in the contract himself also retains a title and interest to enforce it.[4] But for the court to reach this conclusion there must be more than an interest in the *tertius*, but also a clear indication of intention to have the contract enforceable also by the *tertius*.[5] Thus where a heritable superior imposed building restrictions on various co-feuars, no one feuar has a title to sue another merely by reason of his interest, since the superior has the main interest and a clear contractual title to enforce the restrictions.[6] But where in similar circumstances there has been reference in the titles of each feuar to a common building plan or similar restrictions, or a stipulation in each title that the same restrictions were to be imposed on all co-feuars, and the restrictions are such that each feuar has an interest to enforce them, the court has inferred the intention that any one feuar, as well as the superior, might sue to enforce the restrictions on any one in breach.[7]

Jus quaesitum *and irrevocability*

It is said to be a condition of an enforceable *jus quaesitum* that it be irrevocable,[8] which is established by delivery of the contractual

---

[1] *Greenlees* v. *Manchester Ins. Co.*, 1933 S.C. 383, 403.

[2] *Crosbie's Trs.* v. *Wright* (1880) 7 R. 823; *Jamieson* v. *McLeod* (1880) 7 R. 1131; *Dickson* v. *National Bank*, 1917 S.C. (H.L.) 50; cf. *Jarvie's Tr.* v. *Jarvie's Trs.* (1887) 14 R. 411; *Henderson* v. *Stubbs* (1894) 22 R. 51; *Hadden* v. *Bryden* (1899) 1 F. 710; *Lawrence* v. *Scott*, 1965 S.C. 403.

[3] *Morton's Trs.* v. *Aged Christian Friend Socy.* (1899) 2 F. 82; *Rose, Murison & Thomson* v. *Wingate, Birrell & Co.'s Tr.* (1889) 16 R. 1132; *Cambuslang West Church* v. *Bryce* (1897) 25 R. 322; *Lamont* v. *Burnett* (1901) 3 F. 797; *Love* v. *Amalgamated Printers*, 1912 S.C. 1078.

[4] *Lamont* v. *Burnett* (1901) 3 F. 797.

[5] *Finnie* v. *G.S.W. Ry.* (1857) 3 Macq. 75; *Lamont, supra.*

[6] *Hislop* v. *Macritchie's Trs.* (1881) 8 R. (H.L.) 95; *Braid Hills Hotel Co.* v. *Manuel*, 1909 S.C. 120; *Nicholson* v. *Glasgow Blind Asylum*, 1911 S.C. 391.

[7] *Heriot's Hospital* v. *Cockburn* (1826) 2 W. & S. 302; *Edinburgh Mags.* v. *Macfarlane* (1858) 20 D. 156; *McGibbon* v. *Rankin* (1871) 9 M. 423; *Robertson* v. *N.B. Ry.* (1874) 1 R. 1218; *Johnston* v. *Walker's Trs.* (1897) 24 R. 1061; *Botanic Gardens Picture House* v. *Adamson*, 1924 S.C. 549; *Girls School Co.* v. *Buchanan*, 1958 S.L.T. (Notes) 2.

[8] *Carmichael* v. *C's Exrx.*, 1920 S.C. (H.L.) 195, explaining Stair I, 10, 5.

document to the *tertius*,[1] by registration for publication in the Books of Council and Session,[2] by intimation to the tertius,[3] by the tertius coming under onerous undertakings on the faith of having a *jus quaesitum*,[4] or by evidence that the tertius knew of the provision intended for his benefit.[5] But it is more consistent with Stair[6] to hold that irrevocability, even by both parties, is a consequence of the creation of a *jus quaesitum tertio*. Parties may doubtless reserve power to revoke, or evidence intent not to bind themselves irrevocably, as by not informing the *tertius* of the contract. It is presumed irrevocable, unless with the consent of the *tertius*. There seem to be two groups of cases: in the first the *tertius* acquires a right on the constitution of the contract in his favour and its intimation to him, which then becomes irrevocable. In the other the right of the *tertius* depends on donation, and delivery or registration is necessary to give him an irrevocable right.

Remedies of tertius

A person having a *jus quaesitum tertio* under a contract can enforce performance of the contract according to its terms,[7] or recover damages for non-performance. Some cases[8] have, however, been interpreted[9] as laying down that a *tertius* cannot sue for damages for defective performance, but such cases are all instances of defective performance of contracts collateral to the contract or gift giving rise to the *jus quaesitum*, and not truly affecting that principle at all. There is no good reason why conferment of a *jus quaesitum* implies conferment of title to enforce performance[10] but not, as is said, title to recover damages for defective performance,[11] though this does not exclude possible claims of damages founded on delict.[12]

[1] e.g. *Crosbie's Trs., supra*; *Middleton's Trs.* v. *M.*, 1909 S.C. 67; delivery is not essential: *B.L. Bank* v. *Martin* (1849) 11 D. 1004; *Gibson* v. *Hutchison* (1872) 10 M. 923.

[2] *Carmichael, supra*, 201.   [3] e.g. *Burr* v. *Bo'ness Police Commrs.* (1896) 24 R. 148.

[4] *Carmichael, supra*, 203.   [5] *Carmichael, supra*, 204, 207.

[6] I, 10, 5: see Smith, *Studies*, 183; Cameron, 1961 J.R. 103; Rodger, 1969 J.R. 41; McCormick, 1970 J.R. 228, cf. *Middleton's Trs.* v. *M.*, 1909 S.C. 67; *Allan's Trs.* v. *I.R.C.*, 1970 S.L.T. 73.

[7] e.g. *Carmichael, supra*.

[8] *Robertson* v. *Fleming* (1861) 4 Macq. 167; *Tully* v. *Ingram* (1891) 19 R. 65. See also *Goldie* v. *G.* (1842) 4 D. 1489; *Raes* v. *Meek* (1889) 16 R. (H.L.) 31.

[9] Gloag, 239.

[10] e.g. if A buys a car for B from C and C refuses to deliver it to B. This seems settled: e.g. *Crosbie's Trs.* v. *Wright* (1880) 7 R. 823; *Johnston, supra*.

[11] e.g. if A buys a car for B from C and C delays to deliver it to B.

[12] e.g. if A buys a car for B from C and it causes B injuries by a defect attributable to C's fault; cf. *Edgar* v. *Lamont*, 1914 S.C. 277.

Statutory right of third party

Statute may confer on a third party a similar right. By the Third Parties (Rights against Insurers) Act, 1930, if a person insured against liabilities to third parties becomes bankrupt or goes into liquidation, his rights against the insurer are transferred to any third party to whom he had incurred liability and who has obtained decree against him. By the Merchant Shipping Act, 1970, S. 14, a person to whom any part of a seaman's wages has been allotted may recover in his own name and has the same remedies as the seaman has for the recovery of his wages.

(2) ASSIGNATION

With the consent of the other party to the contract the benefits or the burdens of a contract may be assigned to a third party by the party primarily entitled or bound by the contract. This is essentially a novation of the former agreement, and the new party comes to stand in all respects in place of the original party.

Benefit of executed contract

Without the other's consent, however, the benefit under an executed contract, such as the right to receive payment, or take delivery or accept other performance, is, in the absence of express contrary stipulations, assignable.[1] The assignee may sue as such, or sist himself in an action commenced by the cedent.[2] The burden under an executed contract having been *ex hypothesi* performed, it is not assignable.

Benefit of executory contract

Without the other party's consent, the benefit of an executory contract is not assignable if there is any inherent element of *delectus personae*, so that it matters to or for whom performance has to be made by the other party. Assignation of contracts is excluded wherever the contract involves personal confidence or where personal considerations are of the essence of the agreement, or its terms or nature show that it was to be fulfilled on one or both

---

[1] Stair III, 1, 3; Ersk. III, 5, 2; Bell, *Prin.* §1459; *Aurdal* v. *Estrella*, 1916 S.C. 882. Payments due to a person under an alimentary liferent, national insurance and industrial injuries insurance benefits, family allowances, old age pensions, local government superannuation, services, police and fire brigade pensions, and post-war credits are not assignable by him.

[2] *Fraser* v. *Duguid* (1838) 16 S. 1130.

sides only by the parties themselves.[1] Thus a contract of service cannot be assigned to another employer.[2] An agricultural lease cannot be assigned by the tenant.[3] A landlord may on the other hand sell his interest in the lands, or a superior his superiority, without the consent of the tenant or vassal. A shipowner may assign the contract for a ship being built for him.[4] A life assurance policy may be assigned in security or outright without the consent of the insurers. An annuity or liferent may be declared alimentary in which case it is not assignable by the beneficiary,[5] except in so far as it exceeds the sum necessary for the latter's reasonable maintenance.[6]

Burden of executory contract

Without the creditor's consent the burden of performing an executory contract is similarly not assignable if it is provided in, or can reasonably be inferred from, the contract that it contained an element of *delectus personae*, i.e. that the person bound to perform had been chosen for his particular skill, qualities or abilities. This applies to all cases of personal services and cases where personal attention to the contract is requisite.[7] If, however, the contract involves no such reliance on personal skill, experience or performance, the debtor in the obligation may delegate or sub-contract the duty of performance to a third party and assign to the latter the right to sue for the price.[8] Where, however, an obligant is entitled to, and does, delegate the duty of performance to a third party, the obligant normally remains personally liable under his contract and must answer for the default or defective performance of the delegate.[9] He may still himself tender performance of the contract assigned, and the creditor cannot object to such performance.[10]

---

[1] Bell, *Prin.* §1459.

[2] *Nokes* v. *Doncaster Amalgamated Collieries* [1940] A.C. 1014; cf. *Griffith* v. *Tower Publishing Co.* [1897] 1 Ch. 21.

[3] Bell, *Prin.* §1214; *Mackintosh* v. *May* (1895) 22 R. 345.

[4] *Westville S.S. Co.* v. *Abram*, 1923 S.C. (H.L.) 68.

[5] *Lord Ruthven* v. *Drummond*, 1908 S.C. 1154.

[6] *Cuthbert* v. *C's Trs.*, 1908 S.C. 967.

[7] *Hoey* v. *McEwan & Auld* (1867) 5 M. 814; *Grierson, Oldham & Co.* v. *Forbes, Maxwell & Co.* (1895) 22 R. 812; *Berlitz Schools* v. *Duchene* (1903) 6 F. 181; *Cole* v. *Handasyde*, 1910 S.C. 68; *Thomas* v. *I.R.C.*, 1941 S.C. 356, 361.

[8] *British Waggon Co.* v. *Lea* (1880) 5 Q.B.D. 149; *Asphaltic Co.* v. *Glasgow Corpn.*, 1907 S.C. 463; *Cole, supra*; *Stevenson* v. *Maule*, 1920 S.C. 335; see also *Moore* v. *Gledden* (1869) 7 M. 1016.

[9] *Asphaltic Limestone Co.* v. *Glasgow Corpn.*, 1907 S.C. 463; *Stevenson* v. *Maule*, 1920 S.C. 335.

[10] *Fratelli Sorrentino* v. *Buerger* [1915] 3 K.B. 367.

An exception arises where the contract is of such duration that parties must be taken to have intended that it should be completely assignable,[1] and in any case where the parties are held to have intended that the debtor, on assigning the burden of performance, shall cease to be liable under the contract. In some cases it has been held that an obligant might delegate performance only of the main obligation undertaken, though he might not assign his obligations as a whole and remained liable for the whole obligations undertaken by him.[2]

Where assignation is competent it may be effected informally, intimation to the other contracting party being necessary, but rights of the nature of moveable property, including rights of action, must be assigned formally and intimated to the other party concerned. The assignee may sue to enforce performance in his own name, or may sist himself a party to an action brought by the cedent.[3]

Contractual stipulations transmitting with heritable property

In the case of feu-contracts between superior and vassal some of the obligations undertaken are personal to the parties[4] but some may be created real burdens affecting the lands themselves,[5] in which case they are assigned automatically with the lands to each successive holder of the position of superior or vassal. The same principle applies to contracts of ground annual. Similarly servitudes over land continue to affect the land notwithstanding transfer to other parties,[6] and an obligation to relieve an owner of land from public taxation for ever was held to transmit with the lands.[7] Conditions of a lease may transmit with the lands to successors of landlord or tenant.[8]

The principle that contractual rights and duties undertaken in respect of land transmit with it does not apply to similar rights and duties undertaken in respect of moveables. On the sale or other

---

[1] *Arbroath Mags.* v. *Strachan's Trs.* (1842) 4 D. 538; cf. *Tolhurst* v. *Assoc. Portland Cement Co.* [1903] A.C. 414; *Crawford* v. *Livingstone's Trs.*, 1938 S.C. 609 (lease for 354 years).

[2] *International Fibre Syndicate* v. *Dawson* (1901) 3 F. (H.L.) 32.

[3] *Fraser* v. *Duguid* (1838) 16 S. 1130.

[4] *Croall* v. *Edinburgh Mags.* (1870) 9 M. 323; *Edinburgh Mags.* v. *Begg* (1883) 11 R. 352; *Liddall* v. *Duncan* (1898) 25 R. 1119; cf. *Rankine* v. *Logie Den Land Co.* (1902) 4 F. 1074.

[5] *Bell, Prin.* §700; *Tailors of Aberdeen* v. *Coutts* (1840) 1 Rob. 296; *E. Zetland* v. *Hislop* (1882) 9 R. (H.L.) 40; *Macrae* v. *Mackenzie's Tr.* (1891) 19 R. 138; *Marshall* v. *Callander Hydro* (1896) 23 R. (H.L.) 55.

[6] *Cooper & McLeod* v. *Edinburgh Improvement Trs.* (1876) 3 R. 1106; *Tennant* v. *Napier Smith's Trs.* (1888) 15 R. 671.

[7] *Dunbar Mags.* v. *Mackersy*, 1931 S.C. 180.

[8] *Huber* v. *Ross*, 1912 S.C. 898; contrast *Turner* v. *Nicolson* (1835) 13 S. 633.

transfer of moveables contractual claims relative thereto, unless expressly assigned therewith, do not transmit with the goods, not even if the purchaser has notice of the condition or contract affecting it.[1] Thus if a thing let on hire is sold by the owner the purchaser takes it free of the letting, though the seller is liable to the hirer for breach of contract.[2]

Negotiable instruments

Where the contract is constituted by a negotiable instrument the benefit of the contract is assignable by mere negotiation of the document of debt.[3] The negotiability of a particular instrument may be curtailed by the terms in which it is drawn or indorsed.

Bills of lading

A bill of lading granted for goods shipped is not a negotiable instrument but may be used as a document of title to and a symbol of the goods and, if indorsed in favour of and delivered to a third party, gives him a title to the goods described therein. The Bills of Lading Act, 1855, S. 1, confers also on the assignee of a bill all rights of suit and the same liabilities in respect of the goods, as if the contract contained in the bill of lading had been made with himself. The transfer of a bill of lading, however, does not give any better title to the indorsee than to the cedent, and is expressly subject to equities.[4]

(3) TRANSMISSION ON DEATH

Death of a party to a contract is not a breach of contract.[2] Where there is no element of *delectus personae* the right to exact payment or performance under a contract transmits to the executors of a deceased creditor, and the liability to pay or perform transmits against the executors of a deceased debtor.[5] Thus a

---

[1] *Blumer* v. *Scott* (1874) 1 R. 379.

[2] *Morton* v. *Muir Bros.*, 1907 S.C. 1211, conflicts with this statement but is, on this point, unsound, and the reasons given are unconvincing. *Lord Strathcona S.S. Co.* v. *Dominion Coal Co.* [1926] A.C. 108 seemed to recognize an exception for ships sold while subject to charter-party, but the decision is insupportable and has been disapproved: *Clore* v. *Theatrical Properties, Ltd.* [1936] 3 All E.R. 483; *Port Line* v. *Ben Line Steamers* [1958] 2 Q.B. 146.

[3] See further Ch. 49, *infra*.

[4] 1855 Act, S. 2.

[5] *Hoey* v. *MacEwan and Auld* (1867) 5 M. 814; cf. *Re General Rolling Stock Co.* (1866) L.R. 1 Eq. 346; *Brace* v. *Calder* [1895] 2 Q.B. 253; *Beardmore* v. *Barry*, 1928 S.C. (H.L.) 47. cf. *Gardiner* v. *Stewart's Trs.*, 1908 S.C. 985, 989.

tenant's interest in a lease passes to his executors[1] in the absence of contrary provision. But if there is *delectus personae*, as in the case of personal service, or the undertaking be personal only, the contract is terminated by the death of either party.[2]

The involuntary dissolution of partnership, as by a death, does not necessarily terminate a contract,[3] but does in the case of personal services.[4] But the voluntary dissolution of partnership, or the creation of a new one by the assumption of a new partner, or the conversion of a firm into a limited company, is a breach of contract as regards employees or parties to other contracts with the firm involving *delectus personae*,[5] but not of contracts not involving that element.[6] Where a new firm is created and the business continued as before the presumption is that assets and liabilities are taken over by the new firm.[7]

(4) TRANSMISSION ON BANKRUPTCY OR LIQUIDATION

Bankruptcy or liquidation may be contractually deemed a breach of contract or a ground for the other party rescinding the contract.[8] Apart from that neither is a breach of contract, unless there is *delectus personae*.[9] On the bankruptcy of the creditor under a contract the trustee in bankruptcy is entitled to enforce any contract beneficial to the estate, though a contract of service under the bankrupt is terminated, the bankruptcy being then accounted a breach of contract.[10] On the bankruptcy of the debtor under a contract the trustee is not bound to implement the bankrupt's executory contracts and may disclaim them, subject to rendering the trust estate liable in damages to the creditor for breach of contract.[11] He may, however, adopt and perform a contract, even though the bankrupt could not have assigned it voluntarily,[12] unless it is one involving *delectus personae* which can

---

[1] Bell, *Prin.* §1219; Rankine, *Leases*, 157.
[2] *Hoey, supra.*
[3] *Alexander* v. *Lawson's Tr.* (1890) 17 R. 571.
[4] *Hoey* v. *MacEwan and Auld* (1867) 5 M. 814.
[5] *Grierson Oldham & Co.* v. *Forbes Maxwell & Co.* (1895) 22 R. 812.
[6] *Brown* v. *Carron Co.* (1898) 6 S.L.T. 90.
[7] *Miller* v. *Thorburn* (1861) 23 D. 359; *McKeand* v. *Laird* (1861) 23 D. 846; *Heddle's Exrx.* v. *Marwick & Hourston's Tr.* (1886) 13 R. 698; *Thomson & Balfour* v. *Boag*, 1936 S.C. 2.
[8] *Bidoulac* v. *Sinclair's Tr.* (1890) 17 R. 144.
[9] *Agra Bank, ex p. Tondeur* (1867) L.R. 5 Eq. 165 (liquidation); *Asphaltic Co.* v. *Glasgow Corpn.*, 1907 S.C. 463.
[10] *Hoey* v. *MacEwan and Auld* (1867) 5 M. 814, 817.
[11] *Kirkland* v. *Cadell* (1838) 16 S. 860; *Asphaltic Limestone Co., supra.*
[12] *Asphaltic Co., supra.*

be performed only by the personal services of the bankrupt.[1] The bankrupt's interest in a lease, even though not assignable, will pass to the trustee, unless that is expressly precluded.[2] Where the trustee can adopt the contract he must elect whether to do so or not within a reasonable time, and if he delays unduly the other party may treat the contract as repudiated and claim damages.[3] If the trustee can, and does, adopt a contract he can demand implement of the contract so far as beneficial to him only when he is prepared to implement the correlative conditions incumbent on him.[4] He may adopt one or some of the contracts between the bankrupt and a particular creditor and disclaim others.[5] Where he does adopt a contract he renders himself personally liable for the debts incurred thereby, such as, in the case of a lease, rent and arrears thereof.[6]

(5) CONTRACTS MADE BY AGENTS AND MANDATARIES

Where contracts are made by or with persons acting as agents or mandataries for other parties, who are their principals,[7] the question arises whether it is the agent or the principal who acquires contractual rights or comes under contractual liabilities. The answer depends in every case on the interpretation of the contract in the circumstances, but rebuttable presumptions arise if no clear indication of the parties' intention appears from the contract.[8] Whether an agent has authority to make a particular contract or not is a question of fact, the onus of proof being on the party who asserts that he has authority.[9]

(a) *Where agent acting for named principal*

Where an agent, having authority to contract, discloses when contracting the existence and the name of his principal, the general rule is that only the principal can sue and be sued on the contract,[10]

---

[1] *Anderson v. Hamilton* (1875) 2 R. 355; *Caldwell v. Hamilton*, 1919 S.C. (H.L.) 100.

[2] Stair II, 9, 26; Bell, *Prin.* §1216.

[3] *Anderson v. Hamilton* (1875) 2 R. 355.

[4] *Mitchell's Tr. v. Galloway's Trs.* (1903) 5 F. 612.

[5] *Gray's Ts. v. Benhar Coal Co.* (1881) 9 R. 225; *Asphaltic Co., supra.*

[6] *Gibson v. Kirkland* (1833) 6 W. & S. 340; Rankine, *L.,* 698.

[7] The relationship of principal and agent is itself a contract, discussed in Ch. 40, *infra.*

[8] Bell, *Comm.* I, 541; *Prin.* §224A; *Millar v. Mitchell* (1860) 22 D. 833.

[9] *Wylie & Lochhead v. Hornsby* (1889) 16 R. 907; *Laing v. Provincial Homes Investment Co.,* 1909 S.C. 813.

[10] *Levy v. Thomsons* (1883) 10 R. 1134, 1137; *Montgomerie v. U.K. Steamship Assocn.* [1891] 1 Q.B. 370; *Royal Bank v. Skinner*, 1931 S.L.T. 382.

and that the agent acquires neither rights nor liabilities there-from.[1] This is particularly clear where the terms of the contract negative the agent's personal liability.[2] But an agent may contract on terms of personal liability, particularly where the contract is in writing and the obligations are *ex facie* undertaken by the agent,[3] even though the other party knew of the agency and even the identity of the principal,[4] though in such cases the principal may also sue and be sued.[5] The agent is also personally liable if the principal for whom he acts is an unincorporated body which can-not be sued, such as a congregation,[6] or a club,[7] or a company not yet incorporated.[8] But no action lies against an agent acting for a government department[9] or a foreign government[10] merely because such a principal cannot be sued. There may also be a proven custom in a particular trade for agents to be liable as principals.[11] Where an agent is a party to a negotiable instrument he can escape personal liability only by clear indication of his capacity.[12] The view was formerly held that an agent contracting for a principal not subject to the jurisdiction of the British courts was presumed to have incurred personal liability,[13] but more modern authority suggests that it is a question of fact and no liability is incurred on this ground alone.[14] Where foreign prin-cipals hold out certain parties as their agents they are liable on the contracts made by those agents, notwithstanding a private arrangement that the agents should transact with the public as

---

[1] Bell, *Comm.* I, 540, note; *Fairlie v. Fenton* (1870) L.R. 5 Exch. 169; *Paquin v. Beau-clerk* [1906] A.C. 148; *Craig v. Blackater*, 1923 S.C. 472, 486.

[2] *Universal S.N. Co. v. McKelvie* [1923] A.C. 492; *Stone & Rolfe v. Kimber Coal Co.*, 1926 S.C. (H.L.) 45.

[3] *Woodside v. Cuthbertson* (1848) 10 D. 604; *Webster v. McCalman* (1848) 10 D. 1133; *Millar v. Mitchell* (1860) 22 D. 833; cf. *Gadd v. Houghton* (1876) 1 Ex. D. 357.

[4] *Stewart v. Shannessey* (1900) 2 F. 1288; *Lindsay v. Craig*, 1919 S.C. 139.

[5] *Fisher v. Marsh* (1865) 6 B. & S. 411, 415.

[6] *McMeekin v. Easton* (1889) 16 R. 363.

[7] *Thomson v. Victoria Eighty Club* (1905) 43 S.L.R. 628.

[8] *Kelner v. Baxter* (1866) L.R. 2 C.P. 174; *Tinnevelly Sugar Refining Co. v. Mirrlees Watson* (1894) 21 R. 1009.

[9] *Dunn v. Macdonald* [1897] 1 Q.B. 555.

[10] *Twycross v. Dreyfus* (1877) 5 Ch. D. 605.

[11] *Fleet v. Murton* (1871) L.R. 7 Q.B. 126.

[12] Bills of Exchange Act, 1882, S. 26; *Elliott v. Bax-Ironside* [1925] 2 K.B. 301.

[13] *Millar v. Mitchell* (1860) 22 D. 833; *Athya v. Buchanan* (1872) 10 S.L.R. 18; *Bennett v. Inveresk Paper Co.* (1891) 18 R. 975; *Girvin, Roper & Co. v. Monteith* (1895) 23 R. 129.

[14] *Miller Gibb & Co. v. Smith, Tyrer & Co.* [1917] 2 K.B. 141; *Brandt v. Morris* [1917] 2 K.B. 784; *Holt and Moseley v. Cunningham* (1949) 83 Ll.L.R. 141; *Teheran-Europe Co. v. Belton* [1968] 2 All E.R. 886.

principals.[1] An auctioneer or other mercantile agent has a right of action even though his principal is disclosed.[2]

(b) *Where agent acting for disclosed but unnamed principal*

Where an agent, having authority to contract, discloses when contracting the existence but not the name of his principal, the presumption is again that the principal is bound and not the agent,[3] but parties may more readily in this case be held to have contracted on the basis that the agent acquired the rights and liabilities under the contract.[4] A principal may be held disclosed where their existence could have been discovered by reference to the Register of Shipping.[5] In such a case the other party cannot plead compensation between a debt due to the agent and a claim by the principal.[6] Where a person contracts, purporting to be an agent, but in fact on his own behalf, he is personally bound[7] and can sue, so long as the alleged principal was not named and the identity of the principal was not material.[8]

(c) *Where agent acting for undisclosed principal*

Where an agent, having authority to contract, does not disclose when contracting the fact that he is truly acting for a principal, he can himself sue or be sued on the contract, being *ex facie* the contracting party.[9] But if the principal is subsequently disclosed to the other party the principal may sue on the contract,[10] but is subject to all pleas which could have been maintained against the agent, and the other party must elect whether to sue agent or principal.[11] They are liable alternatively, not jointly, nor jointly and severally.[12] The contract, may, however, indicate expressly or

---

[1] *Hayman* v. *American Cotton Co.* (1907) 15 S.L.T. 606.

[2] *Mackenzie* v. *Cormack*, 1950 S.C. 183.

[3] *Fenwick* v. *Macdonald, Fraser & Co.* (1904) 6 F. 850; *Armour* v. *Duff*, 1912 S.C. 120; *Craig* v. *Blackater*, 1923 S.C. 472, 486.

[4] Bell, *Comm.* I, 536; *Prin.* §224A; *Ferrier* v. *Dods* (1865) 3 M. 561; *Brydon* v. *Muir* (1869) 7 M. 536; *Levy* v. *Thomsons* (1883) 10 R. 1134.

[5] *Armour* v. *Duff*, 1912 S.C. 120.

[6] *Lavaggi* v. *Pirie* (1872) 10 M. 312; *Matthews* v. *Auld & Guild* (1874) 1 R. 1224.

[7] *Jenkins* v. *Hutchinson* (1849) 13 Q.B. 744.

[8] *Schmaltz* v. *Avery* (1851) 16 Q.B. 655; *Harper* v. *Vigers* [1909] 2 K.B. 549.

[9] *Sims* v. *Bond* (1833) 5 B. & Ad. 369; *Saxon* v. *Blake* (1861) 29 Beav. 438; *Athya* v. *Buchanan* (1872) 10 S.L.R. 18; *Macphail* v. *Maclean's Tr.* (1887) 15 R. 47; *Craig* v. *Blackater*, 1923 S.C. 472, 486; cf. *Shiells* (1902) 10 S.L.T. 123.

[10] *Skinner* v. *Stocks* (1821) 4 B. & Ald. 437; *Bennett* v. *Inveresk Paper Co.* (1891) 18 R. 975; *Craig, supra.*

[11] *Bennett, supra; Craig, supra.*

[12] *Thomson* v. *Davenport* (1829) 9 B. & C. 78; *Keighley Maxsted* v. *Durant* [1901] A.C. 240; *Craig, supra.*

impliedly an intention to be limited to the contracting parties.[1]
It is not competent to qualify a contract in which an agent contracts *ex facie* as principal by parole evidence that he was truly
acting as agent only.[2] An undisclosed foreign principal may sue
just as may a British principal.[3] Election to sue principal or agent
may be made expressly or inferred from conduct,[4] but nothing
prior to the disclosure of the principal's existence can be held to
amount to election. It does not necessarily amount to election to
debit the agent,[5] nor even to sue him,[6] but to take decree against
either amounts to election, even though it prove valueless,[7] as does
ranking in the bankruptcy of either,[8] unless a claim against the
other party be expressly reserved.[9]

(d) *Where agent not authorized*

Where an agent, not authorized to act as such, or acting in
excess of any authority actually or ostensibly conferred, contracts
on behalf of a named principal, the agent acquires no rights.[10] The
principal may ratify the contract or may repudiate it.[11] If the agent
contracts on behalf of a disclosed but unnamed principal, or on
behalf of an undisclosed principal, he may himself sue.[12] If the
agent knew that he had no authority to contract and causes the
other party loss by his misrepresentation of authority and the
consequent failure of the contract he is liable in damages therefor[13]
on the ground of fraud. If, however, he believed honestly but
mistakenly that he had authority, he is liable for loss caused by
reliance thereon, as being in breach of his implied warranty or

---

[1] *Humble* v. *Hunter* (1848) 12 Q.B. 310; *Formby Bros.* v. *F.* (1910) 102 L.T. 116;
contrast *Drughorn* v. *Rederi A/B Transatlantic* [1919] A.C. 203; *Danziger* v. *Thompson*
[1944] K.B. 654; *Epps* v. *Rothnie* [1948] K.B. 562.

[2] *Gibb* v. *Cunningham & Robertson*, 1925 S.L.T. 608.

[3] *Teheran-Europe* v. *Belton* [1968] 2 All E.R. 886.

[4] e.g. *Ferrier* v. *Dods* (1865) 3 M. 561; *Lamont, Nisbett & Co.* v. *Hamilton*, 1907 S.C. 628;
cf. *McIntosh* v. *Ainslie* (1872) 10 M. 304.

[5] *Stevenson* v. *Campbell* (1836) 14 S. 562; *Cory Bros.* v. *McLean* (1898) 6 S.L.T. 103.

[6] *Meier* v. *Kuchenmeister* (1881) 8 R. 642; *Green, Holland & Co.* v. *A/S City of Richmond*
(1894) 1 S.L.T. 483.

[7] *Kendall* v. *Hamilton* (1879) 4 App. Cas. 504; *Morel* v. *E. Westmoreland* [1904] A.C. 11;
Moore v. *Flanagan* [1920] 1 K.B. 919; *Craig, supra*.

[8] *Scarf* v. *Jardine* (1882) 7 App. Cas. 345; *Logan and Son* v. *Schuldt* (1903) 10 S.L.T.
598.

[9] *Blacks* v. *Girdwood* (1885) 13 R. 243.

[10] *Bickerton* v. *Burrell* (1816) 5 M. & S. 383; *Fairlie* v. *Fenton* (1870) L.R. 5 Ex. 169.

[11] *Strickland* v. *Neilson and MacIntosh* (1869) 7 M. 400; *Sinclair, Moorhead & Co.* v.
Wallace (1880) 7 R. 874; *Morrison* v. *Statter* (1885) 12 R. 1152.

[12] *Schmaltz* v. *Avery* (1851) 20 L.J. Q.B. 228; *Harper* v. *Vigers* [1909] 2 K.B. 549.

[13] *Polhill* v. *Walter* (1832) 3 B. & Ad. 114.

collateral representation of authority.[1] The latter principle would apply also where his actual authority had, unknown to the agent, been terminated by the death or insanity of his principal.[2]

The principal may, however, incur liability if, even though the contract was outwith the agent's actual authority, it was within the scope of his ostensible or apparent authority. Ostensible authority arises only if there was some previous, or existing, relationship between principal and agent, or circumstances which indicate that the agent was held out as having the principal's authority. Thus an agent employed to do certain business is deemed to have authority to do everything usually incidental to that kind of business.[3] Alternatively the principal may, if capable of doing so,[4] ratify the agent's unauthorized act and by adoption become a party to the contract. A person cannot, purporting and professing to act on his own behalf, make a contract with the undisclosed intention to give the benefit of the contract to a third party, so as to give the third party any rights thereunder, nor can the third party ratify or adopt the contract to that effect.[5]

[1] *Collen* v. *Wright* (1857) 8 E. & B. 647; *Firbank's Exors.* v. *Humphreys* (1886) 18 Q.B.D. 54; *Anderson* v. *Croall* (1903) 6 F. 153; *Starkey* v. *Bank of England* [1903] A.C. 114; *Rederi A/B Nordstjernan* v. *Salvesen* (1905) 7 F. (H.L.) 101; *Irving* v. *Burns*, 1915 S.C. 260.

[2] *Yonge* v. *Toynbee* [1910] 1 K.B. 215.

[3] *Edmunds* v. *Bushell and Jones* (1865) L.R. 1 Q.B. 97; *Watteau* v. *Fenwick* [1893] 1 Q.B. 346; *Ryan* v. *Pilkington* [1959] 1 All E.R. 689.

[4] *Tinnevelley Sugar Refining Co.* v. *Mirrlees, Watson & Yaryan Co.* (1894) 21 R. 1009.

[5] *Keighley, Maxsted & Co.* v. *Durant* [1901] A.C. 240.

CHAPTER 36

BREACH OF CONTRACT

BREACH of contract consists in the refusal or failure by either party to implement any of the terms or stipulations of the contract thereby incumbent on that party. There must be a concluded, and legally valid and unobjectionable contract,[1] and the party alleging breach must prove in what respects the contract was not properly performed, and fails if he cannot prove the respects alleged to be defective.[2] Breach always gives the innocent party a right of action for damages in compensation for loss caused by the breach; it may also in some circumstances entitle him to withhold performance of the obligations incumbent on him, or to rescind the contract and claim damages on the basis of a total failure to perform. Breach may take place by anticipation, as where one party, before the due date for performance, intimates his inability to or his intention not to perform,[3] or disables himself from performing,[4] or take place at the due date of performance, by one party then refusing to perform, or delaying to do so, or performing defectively, or wholly failing to perform. In both cases the contract is binding from its constitution till the due performance and repudiation before is as much a breach as repudiation or failure at the due date of performance.

Anticipatory breach

Anticipatory breach may be made expressly, as by repudiation or request for cancellation or intimation that performance will not be tendered when the due date arrives,[5] or impliedly, by the party now putting it outwith his power then to tender performance.[6] If

---

[1] *Van Laun* v. *Neilson Reid & Co.* (1904) 6 F. 644.

[2] *Morrison* v. *Rome,* 1964 S.C. 160.

[3] e.g. *Hochster, infra; Frost* v. *Knight* (1872) L.R. 7 Ex. 111.

[4] e.g. *Linton* v. *Sutherland* (1889) 17 R. 213; *Omnium D'Enterprises* v. *Sutherland* [1919] 1 K.B. 618.

[5] e.g. *Hochster* v. *De la Tour* (1853) 2 E. & B. 678; *Frost* v. *Knight* (1872) L.R. 7 Ex. 111; *Dingwall* v. *Burnett,* 1912 S.C. 1097; *White & Carter (Councils)* v. *McGregor,* 1962 S.C. (H.L.) 1.

[6] e.g. by selling the subject-matter of sale to another, or destroying it: *Short* v. *Stone* (1846) 8 Q.B. 358; *Lovelock* v. *Franklyn* (1846) 8 Q.B. 371; *Synge* v. *S.* [1894] 1 Q.B. 466; *Leith School Board* v. *Rattray's Trs.,* 1918 S.C. 94; *Omnium D'Enterprises* v. *Sutherland* [1919] 1 K.B. 618; *Universal Cargo Carriers Corpn.* v. *Citati* [1957] 2 Q.B. 401; or by closing the business, or ceasing to produce goods required to implement the contract.

performance is due on demand, or on the occurrence of an uncertain event, inability to perform at any time is a breach because the other party is entitled to a continuous expectation of due performance.[1] If performance is due only at a fixed future date, inability to perform prior to that date is a breach only if irremediable.[2] Breach is not constituted by mere warnings, or expressions of doubt, as to ability to perform when the time comes,[3] or by a request for greater time in which to perform, but may be by conduct such as to lead a reasonable person to the conclusion that the other person does not intend to fulfil his part of the obligation, whatever that party's actual intention may have been.[4] Anticipatory breach does not by itself or unilaterally terminate the contract, but it is a repudiation by the one party of his obligations which entitles the other party to sue for damages for loss due to the breach, and also to rescind or cancel the contract if the breach is in a material stipulation,[5] or evidences an intention no longer to be bound by the contract,[6] or is a total repudiation of the contract.[7] Such an intention may be expressed, or inferred from the repudiating party's conduct and the circumstances.[8] It should not lightly be inferred.

Courses open to innocent party

The innocent party may at once elect to treat the repudiation as a total breach of contract, rescind the contract, and at once claim damages for total non-performance.[9] In such an event the party repudiating may not subsequently tender performance, and it does not avail to argue that he might be,[10] nor if he is in fact, able to perform when the due date for performance arrives.[11] Alternatively the innocent party may decline to accept the repudiation, allow the contract to stand, await the due date of performance, and if performance is not then made, rescind the contract and claim

[1] *Sanderson* v. *Armour*, 1921 S.C. 18; affd. 1922 S.C. (H.L.) 117.

[2] *Smith* v. *Butler* [1900] 1 Q.B. 694; *Harvey* v. *Smith* (1904) 6 F. 511.

[3] *Johnstone* v. *Milling* (1886) 16 Q.B.D. 460; *Thornloe* v. *Macdonald* (1892) 29 S.L.R. 409.

[4] *Forslind* v. *Bechely-Crundall*, 1922 S.C. (H.L.) 173; cf. *Carswell* v. *Collard* (1893) 20 R. (H.L.) 47.

[5] *Mersey Steel & Iron Co.* v. *Naylor* (1884) 9 App. Cas. 434, 443.

[6] *Freeth* v. *Burr* (1874) L.R. 9 C.P. 208; *Mersey Steel, supra*.

[7] *White & Carter (Councils) Ltd., supra*.

[8] *Mersey Steel, supra*; *Shaffer* v. *Finlay, Durham & Brodie* [1953] 1 W.L.R. 106; *Dumenil* v. *Ruddin* [1953] 2 All E.R. 294.

[9] *Hochster* v. *De la Tour* (1853) 2 E. & B. 678; *Frost, supra*.

[10] *Universal Cargo Carriers Corpn.* v. *Citati* [1957] 2 Q.B. 401, 436.

[11] *Turnbull* v. *McLean* (1874) 1 R. 730; *Gilfillan* v. *Cadell & Grant* (1893) 21 R. 269.

damages for total non-performance.[1] But in this case the contract remains in being for the benefit of both parties and if the repudiating party is in fact able to perform when the due date comes he may do so without incurring any penalty, and if in the interval any event happens which discharges him or gives him an excuse for non-performance, he may take advantage of that event.[2] In each case the measure of damages is calculated as at the time when the repudiation is accepted and the contract rescinded, and it may be that in the latter case the innocent party's damages are increased or diminished according as prices have moved in the market in question since the date of repudiation.[3] But in some circumstances,[4] the duty to mitigate damages[5] may make it proper to accept the repudiation and make alternative arrangements at once rather than to await the due date of performance when alternative arrangements might be more difficult or expensive.

The innocent party is not obliged to accept a repudiation by the other party as terminating the contract and, at least where performance of the contract on his part is possible without need for the co-operation of the repudiating party, may perform his part of the contract, even if unwanted, and recover the full price thereof instead of merely claiming damages for the loss caused him by the repudiation.[6] But, though a contract cannot be terminated unilaterally or the innocent party compelled to accept the other's repudiation, the innocent party cannot insist on performing his part of the contract if the other's co-operation is requisite,[7] or if the court would not grant specific performance of the other's duties.

Breach at due date for performance

Breach may equally take place at the due date for performance, or during performance,[8] by express refusal to perform, or repudia-

---

[1] *Hochster, supra*; *Johnstone* v. *Milling* (1886) 16 Q.B.D. 460, 473; *Heyman* v. *Darwins* [1942] A.C. 356.

[2] *Hochster, supra*; *Avery* v. *Bowden* (1855) 5 E. & B. 714; (1856) 6 E. & B. 953 (outbreak of war).

[3] *Roper* v. *Johnson* (1873) L.R. 8 C.P. 167; *Michael* v. *Hart* [1902] 1 K.B. 482; *Melachrino* v. *Nickoll* [1920] 1 K.B. 693.

[4] e.g. if market prices are steadily rising or shortage in supply of the goods is in prospect.

[5] *Infra.*

[6] *White & Carter (Councils) Ltd.* v. *McGregor*, 1962 S.C. (H.L.) 1 overruling *Langford* v. *Dutch*, 1952 S.C. 15. *Sed quaere.* This decision seems to ignore the principle of mitigation of damages, on which see further, *infra*.

[7] e.g. contract of service, or probably where the repudiating party would have to accept goods or services.

[8] *O'Neil* v. *Armstrong* [1895] 2 Q.B. 418; *Ogdens, Ltd.* v. *Nelson* [1905] A.C. 109; *International Correspondence Schools* v. *Irving*, 1915 S.C. 28.

tion of the obligation,[1] or conduct implying repudiation,[2] or conduct leading reasonably to the conclusion that the party does not intend to perform[3] by a party disabling himself from completing performance,[4] by total failure to perform,[5] by defective performance,[6] or by delay in performance.[7] The effect of such a breach and the rights of the innocent party depends on the circumstances.

Excuses for non-performance

In general, unless a contracting party has protected himself by provisions in the contract habile to apply to the situation,[8] he is bound by his contract[9] and it is no defence to a claim of damages for non-performance that it was commercially impossible to perform,[10] or technically impracticable,[11] or that a strike hindered performance,[12] or that civil disturbance or the unwarrantable acts of port authorities have prevented performance,[13] or that there was apprehension that attempted performance would provoke a strike,[14] or that the contract proves more demanding than expected,[15] still less that the contract is proving more difficult than expected or less profitable. But it is a valid excuse that supervenient legislation or change in the law has rendered performance illegal,[16] that change of circumstances has made performance impossible,[17] that the contract has been frustrated,[18] that it was an

---

[1] *Thorneloe* v. *McDonald* (1892) 29 S.L.R. 409; *Dingwall* v. *Burnett*, 1912 S.C. 1097.

[2] *Turnbull* v. *McLean* (1874) 1 R. 730; *Gilfillan* v. *Cadell & Grant* (1893) 21 R. 269.

[3] *Forslind* v. *Bechely-Crundall*, 1922 S.C. (H.L.) 173.

[4] *N.B. Ry.* v. *Benhar Coal Co.* (1886) 14 R. 141; *Ross* v. *McFarlane* (1894) 21 R. 396.

[5] In special circumstances this may include refusal to accept goods, of equal quality to those ordered, but from a supplier other than the contracting party: *West Stockton Iron Co.* v. *Nielson & Maxwell* (1880) 7 R. 1055; *Johnson & Reay* v. *Nicoll* (1881) 8 R. 437.

[6] *Lord Polwarth* v. *N.B. Ry.*, 1908 S.C. 1275; *Dickson* v. *Hygienic Institute*, 1910 S.C. 352; *Sanderson* v. *Armour*, 1922 S.C. (H.L.) 117; *Pollock* v. *Macrae*, 1922 S.C. (H.L.) 192.

[7] *Grieve* v. *Konig* (1880) 7 R. 521; *Dorman Long* v. *Harrower* (1899) 1 F. 1109; *Shaw, Macfarlane & Co.* v. *Waddell* (1901) 2 F. 1070; *British Motor Body Co.* v. *Shaw*, 1914 S.C. 922.

[8] *Duncan & Co.* v. *Terrell*, 1918, 2 S.L.T. 340; *Blacklock & Macarthur* v. *Kirk*, 1919 S.C. 57.

[9] *Clark* v. *Glasgow Assce. Co.* (1854) 1 Macq. 668.

[10] *Hong Kong and Whampoa Dock Co.* v. *Netherton Shipping Co.*, 1909 S.C. 34.

[11] *Gillespie* v. *Howden* (1885) 12 R. 800.

[12] *Budgett* v. *Binnington* [1891] 1 Q.B. 35; *Forrester's Tr.* v. *McKelvie* (1895) 22 R. 437.

[13] *Jacobs* v. *Credit Lyonnais* (1884) 12 Q.B.D. 589; *Ashmore* v. *Cox* [1899] 1 Q.B. 436; *Matthey* v. *Curling* [1922] 2 A.C. 180.

[14] *Milligan* v. *Ayr Harbour Trs.*, 1915 S.C. 937.

[15] *Blacklock & Macarthur* v. *Kirk*, 1919 S.C. 57.

[16] *McMaster* v. *Cox, McEuen & Co.*, 1921 S.C. (H.L.) 24; cf. *Aurdal* v. *Estrella*, 1916 S.C. 882.

[17] Ch. 37, *infra*.   [18] Ch. 37, *infra*.

implied condition precedent to timeous performance that prior work should be completed in time,[1] or that an act of a third party has made implement impossible.[2]

Non-material breach

If the breach is in respect only of a less important and non-fundamental stipulation, not going to the root of the contract, the innocent party may not withhold performance of the obligations incumbent on him or rescind the contract but may only claim damages for the loss caused by the failure to implement the contract in the respect in question.[3] An innocent party who wrongly treats a breach as material and rescinds the contract thereby renders himself in material breach of contract.[4] Mere delay in payment, even repeatedly,[5] does not normally amount to fundamental breach.[6] Where a time is specified for performance damages are due for non-performance within that time,[7] but generally failure to perform on the due date is not material, though prolonged delay is.[8]

Material breach

If, on the other hand, the facts yield the inference that the party in breach does not intend to be bound by or implement his contract, or if the term or stipulation of the contract breached was one agreed to be, or is one held by the court to be, a warranty, or one material or fundamental or going to the root of the contract, the innocent party may withhold further performance of the obligations incumbent on him towards the party in breach, rescind the contract, and claim payment of the contract price for his services,[9] or damages for loss caused by the total failure of the contract,[10] unless the mutual undertakings of the parties can be held to be independent, in which case failure by one party does not

[1] *Duncanson* v. *Scottish County Investment Co.*, 1915 S.C. 1106.

[2] *McCormick* v. *Dalrymple* (1904) 12 S.L.T. 85; *Claddagh S.S. Co.* v. *Steven*, 1919 S.C. (H.L.) 132.

[3] *Wade* v. *Waldon*, 1909 S.C. 571; *Speirs, Ltd.* v. *Peterson*, 1924 S.C. 428.

[4] *Forbes* v. *Campbell* (1885) 12 R. 1065; *Wade, supra*; *Barr* v. *Lions, Ltd.*, 1956 S.C. 59.

[5] *Decro-Wall International S.A.* v. *Practitioners in Marketing* [1971] 1 W.L.R. 361.

[6] Sale of Goods Act, 1893, S. 10(1); *Forbes, supra*; *Somerville* v. *B.F. Goodrich Co.* (1904) 12 S.L.T. 188; cf. *Rodger (Builders) Ltd.* v. *Fawdry*, 1950 S.C. 483.

[7] *Macbride* v. *Hamilton* (1875) 2 R. 775.

[8] *Carswell* v. *Collard* (1893) 20 R. (H.L.) 47.

[9] *International Correspondence Schools* v. *Irving*, 1915 S.C. 28.

[10] *Turnbull* v. *McLean & Co.* (1874) 1 R. 730; *Charpentier & Bedex* v. *Dunn* (1878) 15 S.L.R. 726; *Gilfillan* v. *Cadell & Grant* (1893) 21 R. 269; *Wade* v. *Waldon*, 1909 S.C. 571; *Forslind* v. *Bechely-Crundall*, 1922 S.C. (H.L.) 173.

entitle the other to repudiate the obligations incumbent on him, but only to claim damages.[1] The mutual stipulations of a contract are presumed concurrent and the counterparts of one another[2] and it may be proved that even *ex facie* independent stipulations are in fact interdependent.[3] Conversely independent stipulations may be contained in one contract.[4]

Party in breach disabled from suing

In mutual contracts the stipulations are the counterparts of one another and failure to perform any material or substantial part of the contract on one part prevents that party from suing the other for performance.[5] The contract is generally to be treated as a unity so that one party cannot refuse to perform his part and yet insist on the other performing his part,[6] nor insist on the other performing if he is unable to perform his part.[7] Nor can a party in breach claim damages for the other party's alleged breach.[8] The only basis on which a party in breach can claim reward is that of recompense.[9]

Instalment contracts

In instalment contracts the question has arisen whether a failure in an early instalment justifies the inference of total repudiation in respect of future instalments. The chief considerations are the ratio which the breach bears to the contract as a whole, and the degree of probability or improbability that such a breach will be repeated.[10] The further performance has proceeded, the more

[1] *Pendreigh's Trs.* v. *Dewar* (1871) 9 M. 1037; *Sanderson* v. *Armour,* 1922 S.C. (H.L.) 117; *Dryburgh* v. *Caledonian Insce. Co.,* 1933 S.N. 85.

[2] Stair I, 10, 16; *Barclay* v. *Anderston Foundry Co.* (1856) 18 D. 1190; *Turnbull* v. *McLean* (1874) 1 R. 730; *Dingwall* v. *Burnett,* 1912 S.C. 1097.

[3] *Claddagh S.S. Co.* v. *Steven,* 1919 S.C. (H.L.) 132.

[4] *Penman* v. *Mackay,* 1922 S.C. 385.

[5] Ersk. III, 3, 86; Bell *Prin.* §70.71; *Barclay* v. *Anderson Foundry Co.* (1856) 18 D. 1190; *Johnston* v. *Robertson* (1861) 23 D. 646; *Turnbull* v. *McLean* (1874) 1 R. 730; *Ramsay* v. *Brand* (1898) 25 R. 1212; *Shaw, Macfarlane & Co.* v. *Waddell* (1900) 2 F. 1070; *Skinner* v. *Breslin* (1905) 13 S.L.T. 91; *Steel* v. *Young,* 1907 S.C. 360; *Dingwall* v. *Burnett,* 1912 S.C. 1097.

[6] *Turnbull, supra;* *Macbride* v. *Hamilton* (1875) 2 R. 775; cf. *Abrahams* v. *Campbell,* 1911 S.C. 353.

[7] *Todd* v. *McCarroll,* 1917, 2 S.L.T. 127.

[8] *Thorneloe* v. *McDonald* (1892) 29 S.L.R. 409; *Steel, supra;* *Graham* v. *U.T.R.,* 1922 S.C. 533.

[9] *Graham, supra.*

[10] *Simpson* v. *Crippin* (1872) L.R. 8 Q.B. 14; *Freeth* v. *Burr* (1874) L.R. 9 C.P. 208; *Honck* v. *Muller* (1881) 7 Q.B.D. 92; *Mersey Steel and Iron Co.* v. *Naylor* (1884) 9 App. Cas. 434; *Millar's Karri Co.* v. *Weddel* (1909) 100 L.T. 128; *Maple Flock* v. *Universal Furniture Products, Ltd.* [1934] 1 K.B. 148.

difficult it is to infer that a breach imports total repudiation of future liabilities.[1]

Indivisible contracts

Where on the other hand the contract is for a single service, even though to be performed by stages and to be paid for in instalments, each party's performance may be *unum quid* and indivisible, and either party may enforce full performance of the other party's undertaking.[2]

REMEDIES FOR BREACH OF CONTRACT

Rescission of contract

The innocent party may rescind the contract for the future or treat it as terminated, and also claim damages for the total loss of the contract only where the breach went to the root of the contract, or was in the circumstances material.[3] Rescission consists of intimation that the party rescinding considers the contract no longer binding and is effective from the date of intimation.[4] If not accepted rescission must be effected by an action of reduction of the contract. Breach of an unimportant stipulation does not justify rescission, and to rescind unjustifiably is itself a material breach of contract.[5] Parties may specify that any term of the contract is to be material,[6] but failing that, it is a question of fact depending on the terms of the contract and the circumstances of the breach.[7] Where a party justifiably rescinds a contract he is relieved of liability to perform, or further to perform, his own obligations under the contract,[8] but may recover payment or compensation for any obligations performed or liabilities entered into in connec-

---

[1] *Cornwall* v. *Henson* [1900] 2 Ch. 298, 304.

[2] *International Correspondence Schools* v. *Irving*, 1915 S.C. 28.

[3] *Wade* v. *Walden*, 1909 S.C. 571; *Llanelly Ry.* v. *L.N.W.R.* (1873) L.R. 8 Ch. 942; *Mersey Steel Co., supra*; *Johannesburg Corpn.* v. *Stewart*, 1909 S.C. (H.L.) 53; *Hagarty & Kelly* v. *Cosmopolitan Ins. Co.*, 1913 S.C. 377; *Sanderson* v. *Armour*, 1921 S.C. 18; *Forslind* v. *Bechely-Crundall*, 1922 S.C. (H.L.) 173.

[4] *Westville Shipping Co.* v. *Abram*, 1923 S.C. (H.L.) 68.

[5] *Forbes* v. *Campbell* (1885) 12 R. 1065; *Carswell* v. *Collard* (1893) 20 R. (H.L.) 47; *Wade, supra*.

[6] *Standard Life Assce. Co.* v. *Weems* (1884) 11 R. (H.L.) 48; *Dawsons Ltd.* v. *Bonnin*, 1922 S.C. (H.L.) 156.

[7] *Turnbull* v. *McLean* (1874) 1 R. 730; *Gilfillan* v. *Cadell & Grant* (1893) 21 R. 269; *Somerville* v. *B. F. Goodrich Co.* (1904) 12 S.L.T. 188; *Wade, supra; Graham* v. *U.T.R. Ltd.*, 1922 S.C. 533.

[8] *General Billposting Co.* v. *Atkinson* [1909] A.C. 118.

tion with the performance of the contract, and may also claim damages for loss caused by the total failure of the contract. If he unjustifiably rescinds the contract and fails to perform his part, he is himself in breach of contract and liable in damages.[1] It is too late to rescind a contract if innocent third parties have for onerous consideration acquired rights on the faith of the contract,[2] or if the contract has been assigned to a third party.[3]

Specific implement

By Scots law the innocent party has a general right to have performance of a contract judicially enforced in the terms in which it was undertaken,[4] by decree of specific implement if the contractual stipulations are positive,[5] by decree of interdict if they are negative. But either decree is competent only if the court can frame it precisely, thereby making clear to the party in breach what he must do or refrain from doing.[6] If such a decree is not complied with, the defaulter is in contempt of court and may be imprisoned until he complies.

Specific implement is an equitable remedy, so that the grant or refusal of it in a particular case is in the court's discretion, and the remedy will not be granted if it might work injustice.[7] An alternative conclusion for damages is accordingly customary and does not amount to an election to accept damages, failing voluntary performance, rather than implement under order of the court.[8] But a contract which cannot be enforced by specific implement so far as regards its form and substance is no contract at all and cannot form the ground of an action of damages.[9] Hence if a claim for implement falls to be dismissed, damages cannot be awarded in the alternative.[10]

Specific implement includes claims to have a thing sold handed over,[11] to remove buildings wrongfully erected,[12] to maintain a

[1] *Carswell* v. *Collard* (1893) 20 R. (H.L.) 47; *Wade, supra.*
[2] *Tennent* v. *City of Glasgow Bank* (1879) 6 R. (H.L.) 69.
[3] *Westville Shipping Co.* v. *Abram*, 1923 S.C. (H.L.) 68.
[4] *McArthur* v. *Lawson* (1877) 4 R. 1134; *Stewart* v. *Kennedy* (1890) 17 R. (H.L.) 1.
[5] e.g. *Union Electric Co.* v. *Holman*, 1913 S.C. 954.
[6] *Middleton* v. *Leslie* (1892) 19 R. 801.
[7] *Moore* v. *Paterson* (1881) 9 R. 337; *Grahame, supra*; *Cocker* v. *Crombie* (1893) 20 R. 954; *Aurdal* v. *Estrella*, 1916 S.C. 882; cf. *International Correspondence Schools* v. *Irving*, 1915 S.C. 28.
[8] *McKellar* v. *Dallas's, Ltd.*, 1928 S.C. 503.
[9] *McArthur* v. *Lawson* (1877) 4 R. 1134.
[10] *Harvey* v. *Smith* (1904) 6 F. 511.
[11] *Union Electric Co., supra.*
[12] *Grahame* v. *Kirkcaldy Mags.* (1882) 9 R. (H.L.) 91.

road,[1] to have a building constructed in accordance with the feu contract,[2] to have a building put up,[3] to have a building taken down,[4] to have heritable property conveyed.[5]

Where specific implement will not be granted

In certain classes of cases the court will not, at least normally, order specific implement: they are

(1) where the obligation is to pay money,[6] the remedy then appropriate being to take decree for payment and do diligence thereon. But specific implement of the undertaking to take up and pay for debentures in a company is competent,[7] and it may be ordered also where money has been ordered to be consigned in court.[8]

(2) where the contract involves a personal relationship, such as for services, or to enter into partnership, and enforced performance, if indeed possible, would be an undue restraint on personal liberty and doubtless be unsatisfactory.[9]

(3) where the contract cannot be performed, either physically or legally, and even if the failure is due to the defaulting party's own fault.[10]

(4) where the decree would be unenforceable by imprisonment, as where it is against a foreigner or a corporate body.[11]

(5) where there is no *pretium affectionis*, or special value attaching to the subject of contract beyond other things of the same kind.[12]

(6) where enforcement of the decree would cause exceptional hardship.[13]

---

[1] *Northern Lighthouses Commrs.* v. *Edmonston* (1908) 16 S.L.T. 439.

[2] *Waddell* v. *Campbell* (1898) 25 R. 456.

[3] *Middleton, supra*; *McKellar* v. *Dallas's, Ltd.*, 1928 S.C. 503.

[4] *Naismith* v. *Cairnduff* (1876) 3 R. 863.

[5] *Mackay* v. *Campbell*, 1966 S.C. 237.

[6] Because the sanction for non-implement is imprisonment, and imprisonment for non-payment of money is, in general, abolished.

[7] Companies Act, 1948, S. 92; *Beardmore* v. *Barry*, 1928 S.C. 101.

[8] *Mackenzie* v. *Balerno Paper Mill Co.* (1883) 10 R. 1147.

[9] *Cameron* v. *Fletcher* (1872) 10 M. 301; *Macarthur* v. *Lawson* (1877) 4 R. 1134; *Aitken* v. *Assoc. Carpenters* (1885) 12 R. 1206; *Skerret* v. *Oliver* (1896) 23 R. 468.

[10] *Macarthur, supra*; *Gillespie* v. *Howden* (1885) 12 R. 800; *Sinclair* v. *Caithness Flagstone Co.* (1898) 25 R. 703; *Leitch* v. *Edinburgh Ice and Cold Storage Co.* (1900) 2 F. 904; *Rudman* v. *Jay*, 1908 S.C. 552.

[11] *Gall* v *Loyal Glenbogie Lodge* (1900) 2 F. 1187.

[12] cf. *Union Electric Co., supra.*

[13] *Grahame* v. *Kirkcaldy Mags.* (1882) 9 R. (H.L.) 91; *Davidson* v. *Macpherson* (1889) 30 S.L.R. 2; *Mackay* v. *Campbell*, 1966 S.C. 237.

(7) where enforcement would thrust on the other party un-wanted goods or services,[1] as where a contract to perform work or render services has been repudiated.

It has been questioned whether in an appropriate case the court could order specific implement of an undertaking to execute a will.[2]

Interdict

Interdict is the appropriate remedy for the breach of a negative stipulation in contract,[3] or conduct in breach of an express or implied term of a contract.[4] It is similarly an equitable remedy and in the discretion of the court to grant or refuse it. Interdict will generally not be granted where the effect of granting would be the same as to grant degree of specific implement in a case where specific implement would not be granted.[5]

Damages

Where an innocent party has rescinded a contract for a breach by the other party, or a breach is not so material as to justify rescission of the contract, or the innocent party could justifiably, but elects not to, rescind the contract, though he might have done so, he is entitled to damages, as pecuniary compensation for the loss caused him by the breach. Damages is an award of money intended to put the innocent party in the same financial position as if the contract had been performed.[6] He may claim nominal damages for trouble and inconvenience caused him by the other's breach of contract, even though he sustains no actual pecuniary loss,[7] and substantial damages where actual loss has been sus-tained in consequence. Damages is a general remedy for breach of contract, and liability therefor in the event of breach can only be excluded by clear words in the contract.

[1] *White & Carter (Councils) Ltd.* v. *McGregor,* 1960 S.C. 275, 284 (revd. 1962 S.C. (H.L.) 1: *sed quaere*).
[2] *Rollo's Trs.* v. *Rollo,* 1940 S.C. 578.
[3] *Williams* v. *Fairbairn* (1899) 1 F. 944; *Dumbarton Steamboat Co.* v. *MacFarlane* (1899) 1 F. 993; *Mulvein* v. *Murray,* 1908 S.C. 528; *Randall* v. *Summers,* 1919 S.C. 396.
[4] *McCosh* v. *Crow* (1903) 5 F. 670; *Fraser* v. *Renwick* (1906) 14 S.L.T. 443.
[5] *Murray* v. *Dunbarton C.C.,* 1935 S.L.T. 239; contrast *Lumley* v. *Wagner* (1852) 1 De G.M. & G. 604.
[6] *Wertheim* v. *Chicoutimi Pulp Co.* [1911] A.C. 301, 307; *Duke of Portland* v. *Wood's Trs.,* 1927 S.C. (H.L.) 1.
[7] *Webster* v. *Cramond Iron Co.* (1875) 2 R. 752; cf. *Stiven* v. *Watson* (1874) 1 R. 412.

Exception

Damages are not, however, recoverable for the mere delay or refusal to pay money, the remedy for which is to take decree for the sum due, with interest thereon.[1] But damages may be given for non-payment where the breach impliedly conveys a discreditable imputation against credit, as where a bank wrongfully dishonours a customer's cheque.[2]

Nominal and compensatory damages

A small sum of nominal damages may be claimed, more in recognition of the breach of a binding obligation, than in compensation for loss sustained thereby though some loss, by way of inconvenience and trouble, necessarily results from a breach of contract.[3] Damages are usually, however, substantial and compensatory, intended as fair compensation for actual loss sustained. There is no warrant in Scotland for exemplary or punitive damages.

Whole loss to be recovered in one action

The whole loss, past and anticipated, resulting from a breach of contract must be recovered in one action.[4] A subsequent action is not allowed merely because the loss turns out to be greater than thought, or further loss emerges. But in the case of a continuing contract it is competent to claim for loss accrued to date, reserving claims for loss yet to be sustained.[5]

Causation and proof of loss

The party claiming damages must prove that he has sustained the alleged loss by reason of the breach of contract. If any loss sustained is not attributable to the breach the party in breach is not liable for that loss. Causal connection is entirely a question of fact.[6] Damages may, however, be given even if the breach of contract was not the sole cause of the loss, so long as it was one of the main co-operating causes.[7] He must also establish the extent

---

1 *Roissard* v. *Scott's Trs.* (1897) 24 R. 861.

2 *King* v. *B.L. Co.* (1899) 1 F. 928.

3 *Webster* v. *Cramond Iron Co.* (1875) 2 R. 752.

4 *Stevenson* v. *Pontifex and Wood* (1887) 15 R. 125.

5 *Jackson* v. *Cowie* (1872) 9 S.L.R. 617.

6 *Seton* v. *Paterson* (1880) 8 R. 236; *Wilson* v. *Carmichael* (1894) 21 R. 732; *Sutherland* v. *Hutton* (1896) 23 R. 718; *Millar* v. *Bellvale Chemical Co.* (1898) 1 F. 297; *Baird* v. *Banff District Lunacy Board*, 1914, 1 S.L.T. 284.

7 *Heskell* v. *Continental Express* [1950] 1 All E.R. 1033.

of the loss suffered; if no loss is proved to have resulted from the breach of contract he can recover nominal damages at most.[1]

Mitigation

The innocent party must take reasonable steps to mitigate or minimize his loss, and seek an alternative source of supply,[2] an alternative market,[3] alternative means of carriage,[4] of employment,[5] etc., as the case may be, and he can recover in damages only the loss not reasonably avoidable by promptly taking such measures.[6] The innocent party is not obliged to take extraordinary measures[7] or go to expense to mitigate damages, though it may be reasonable to accept an offer of modified terms[8] from the party in breach. He is not entitled to perform a contract unnecessarily and uselessly and charge the party in breach with the full cost.[9] The onus of proof that the alternative adopted by the innocent party was more costly than necessary is on the party in breach.[10]

Remoteness of damage

The party in breach is not necessarily liable for all loss occurring which can be shown to have resulted from the breach of contract, but only for such loss as is deemed to have been reasonably foreseeable by the defender at the time he made the contract, having regard to his then state of knowledge of the possible financial consequences of breach by him. His knowledge may be of two kinds, imputed knowledge, such as is attributed by law to all reasonable persons in such circumstances, comprehending foresight of the kinds of losses which arise naturally and in the ordinary course of things from breach of such a contract, and actual knowledge, which must have been communicated to the

---

[1] *Stiven* v. *Watson* (1874) 1 R. 412; *Webster* v. *Cramond Iron Co.* (1875) 2 R. 752; *Waugh* v. *More Nisbett* (1882) 19 S.L.R. 427; *Irving* v. *Burns*, 1915 S.C. 260.

[2] *British Westinghouse* v. *Underground Ry.* [1912] A.C. 673.

[3] *Warin & Craven* v. *Forrester* (1877) 4 R. (H.L.) 75; *Pommer & Thomsen* v. *Mowat* (1906) 14 S.L.T. 373.

[4] *Connal, Cotton & Co.* v. *Fisher, Renwick & Co.* (1883) 10 R. 824.

[5] *Ross* v. *Macfarlane* (1894) 21 R. 396.

[6] *Cazalet* v. *Morris*, 1916 S.C. 952; Walker, *Remedies*, 467.

[7] *Gunter* v. *Lauritzen* (1894) 31 S.L.R. 359; *Henderson* v. *Turnbull*, 1909 S.C. 510.

[8] *Payzu* v. *Saunders* [1919] 2 K.B. 581.

[9] *White & Carter (Councils) Ltd.* v. *McGregor*, 1962 S.C. (H.L.) 1, to the contrary effect, is, it is submitted, unsound.

[10] *Connal, Cotton & Co.*, *supra*.

defender in the actual circumstances of the case, comprehending foresight of other, further or exceptional losses which will or may arise in the event of breach in the particular circumstances of that case. Imputed knowledge imposes liability for all ordinary, natural and proximate losses; actual knowledge, if possessed by the defender, may impose liability for extraordinary, unusual and remote losses, if the possibility of their being incurred had been brought within his contemplation.[1] Loss not reasonably foreseeable by the defender at the time of contracting, having regard to his then state of knowledge, imputed and actual, is too remote in law to be recoverable in damages.

Ordinary losses, foresight of which is imputed to every reasonable person, have been held to include the loss on having to find another purchaser on a buyer's default;[2] the extra cost of obtaining elsewhere goods not supplied;[3] the extra cost of carriage by another means on the carrier's default;[4] the value of goods lost by a carrier, less the freight thereon;[5] the loss in value of goods delayed in delivery by seller or carrier;[6] loss of business by reason of the delayed delivery of a boiler;[7] loss of a sub-contract, if foreseeable in the circumstances;[8] loss of freight by a charterer not supplying a cargo;[9] the cost of transhipment when a carrier defaulted;[10] loss of profit on a transaction;[11] and possibly publication of the debtor's name in a 'black list'.[12]

Extraordinary losses, foresight of which was possessed in the circumstances by the defenders so as to make them liable therefor, have included loss of salvage rewards when a tug arrived too late;[13]

---

[1] Bell, *Comm.* I, 478–9; *Prin.* §33; M.P. Brown, *Sale*, 211; Walker, *Remedies*, 457; *Hadley* v. *Baxendale* (1854) 9 Ex. 341, 354; *Victoria Laundry* v. *Newman* [1949] 2 K.B. 528; *A/B Karlshamns Oljefabriker* v. *Monarch S.S. Co.*, 1949 S.C. (H.L.) 1; *Biggin, Ltd.* v. *Permanite* [1951] 1 K.B. 422.

[2] Sale of Goods Act, 1893, S. 50.

[3] Sale of Goods Act, 1893, S. 51; *Hinde* v. *Liddell* (1875) L.R. 10 Q.B. 265; *Patrick* v. *Russo-British Grain Export Co.* [1927] 2 K.B. 535.

[4] *Connal, Cotton & Co.* v. *Fisher, Renwick & Co.* (1883) 10 R. 824.

[5] *Rodocanachi* v. *Milburn* (1886) 18 Q.B.D. 67.

[6] *Wilson* v. *L. & Y. Ry.* (1861) 9 C.B. (N.S.) 632; *Schulze* v. *G.E. Ry.* (1887) 19 Q.B.D. 30.

[7] *Victoria Laundry, supra.*

[8] *Keddie, Gordon & Co.* v. *N.B. Ry.* (1886) 14 R. 233; *Stroms Bruks A/B* v. *Hutchison* (1905) 7 F. (H.L.) 131.

[9] *Dunford & Elliot* v. *Macleod* (1902) 4 F. 912.

[10] *A/B Karlshamns Oljefabriker* v. *Monarch S.S. Co.*, 1949 S.C. (H.L.) 1.

[11] *Duff* v. *Iron Buildings Co.* (1891) 19 R. 199; *Saint Line* v. *Richardson* [1940] 2 K.B. 99; *Rutherford* v. *Miln*, 1941 S.C. 125.

[12] *Gray* v. *Macintosh* (1906) 14 S.L.T. 403.

[13] *Mackenzie* v. *Liddell* (1883) 10 R. 705.

the expense of a ship delayed awaiting a replacement part of machinery.[1]

Losses held too remote to be recoverable, as being outwith the foresight, imputed and actual, of the defender in the circumstances, have included: loss of profit on a sub-sale;[2] loss of exceptional profits on a consignment of goods so delayed as to be rejected;[3] loss caused by the stoppage of a mill when a replacement part was delayed;[4] or the inability to start a mill by the loss of a part in transit.[5]

Interest on damages

The court may at common law give interest on damages from the date of decree till payment. Under the Interest on Damages (Scotland) Acts, 1958 and 1971, a court may give interest on damages from a date not earlier than the date when the right of action arose.

Damages assessed by parties

If parties have stipulated in their contract for liquidate damages[6] questions of liability for damages fall to be determined in the first place by the interpretation of the relevant part of the contract. Once liability has been determined the liquidate damages provision excludes the need to prove loss.

Defensive measures

Apart from active steps, such as rescission of contract or making a claim of damages, a breach of contract may in appropriate cases entitle the innocent party to take defensive measures against the party in breach, by exercising a right of retention or of lien as a compulsitor for performance or in security of a claim of damages. Appropriate cases include circumstances where the breach is not so material as to justify rescission, or where the innocent party does not desire to rescind, or where he wishes to put pressure on the other party to perform.

The terms retention and lien are used somewhat indifferently and clear distinction is difficult. Retention is properly the Scottish term and lien an importation from English law. The right covers three groups of cases:

[1] *Den of Ogil Co.* v. *Caledonian Ry.* (1902) 5 F. 99.
[2] *Williams Bros.* v. *Agius* [1914] A.C. 510.
[3] *Horne* v. *Midland Ry.* (1873) L.R. 8 C.P. 131.
[4] *Hadley, supra.*
[5] *British Columbia Sawmill Co.* v. *Nettleship* (1868) L.R. 3 C.P. 499.
[6] Ch. 34, *supra.*

(a) the right to withhold any subject of property, heritable or moveable, which the owner is under a personal obligation to convey to another, from that other in security for the payment of any debt or the performance of any obligation due to the owner. This right depends on property not on possession;

(b) the right of a debtor to refuse or delay payment of a debt, though liquid and presently due, in security of an illiquid claim against the creditor; and

(c) the right of a party having actual possession of property belong to the other party to withhold that property in security of claims by him against the other. This third species of retention is frequently, even in Scots law, called a lien.

(a) Retention on property title

Where a party has a right of property in any subject, heritable or moveable, and, whether or not he is in actual possession thereof, he is subject to a personal obligation to convey or transfer the subject to another, he may retain it in security for the payment of any debt or the performance of any obligation due to him by that other party, whether connected with the obligation to convey or not.[1] The commonest cases are of sales of heritage where the disposition has not been delivered to the buyer, sales of un-delivered moveables prior to 1893,[2] transfers, *ex facie* absolutely but truly in security, of land[3] or moveables held by written title,[4] subject to an obligation to reconvey usually contained in a back-bond, or an assignation of an incorporeal right in un-qualified terms,[5] or outright transfers, truly in trust.[6] The right

[1] Bell, *Comm.* I, 724.

[2] As to the effect of the Sale of Goods Act, 1893, on the time when property passes from seller to buyer see Ch. 103, *infra*. See *Main* v. *Boyle* (1828) 6 S. 360; *McEwan* v. *Smith* (1847) 9 D. 434; (1849) 6 Bell 340; *Melrose* v. *Hastie* (1850) 12 D. 655; (1851) 13 D. 880; *Robertson's Tr.* v. *Baird* (1852) 14 D. 1010; *Wyper* v. *Harveys* (1861) 23 D. 606; *Black* v. *Incorporation of Bakers* (1867) 6 M. 136; *Distillers Co.* v. *Russell's Tr.* (1889) 16 R. 479. By the Sale of Goods Act, 1893, Ss. 39, an unpaid seller, still in possession of undelivered goods, has a right of lien over them for the price, but if the passing of the property is postponed, the undivested owner still has his right of retention over them for any debt due by the buyer to him, as at common law.

[3] *Brough's Creditors* v. *Jollie* (1793) Mor. 2585; *National Bank* v. *Union Bank* (1885) 14 R. (H.L.) 1.

[4] *Hamilton* v. *Western Bank* (1856) 19 D. 152; *National Bank* v. *Forbes* (1858) 21 D. 79; *Nelson* v. *Gordon* (1874) 1 R. 1093; *McBain* v. *Wallace* (1881) 8 R. (H.L.) 106; *Darling* v. *Wilson's Tr.* (1887) 15 R. 180; *Robertson* v. *Hall's Tr.* (1896) 24 R. 120; *Hayman* v. *McLintock*, 1907 S.C. 936; *Gavin's Tr.* v. *Fraser*, 1920 S.C. 674.

[5] *Russell* v. *E. Breadalbane* (1831) 5 W. & S. 256; *Colquhoun's Tr.* v. *Diack* (1901) 4 F. 358; *Robertson's Tr.* v. *Riddell*, 1911 S.C. 14.

[6] *Robertson* v. *Duff* (1840) 2 D. 279, 293; see also *Smith* v. *Harrison & Co.'s Tr.* (1893) 21 R. 330; *Colquhoun's Tr.* v. *Diack* (1901) 4 F. 358.

of retention can be limited or excluded by a term in the back-bond and it possibly cannot be exercised in respect of debts prior to that for which the security was granted.[1] Nor can it be exercised against a party other than the original debtor, such as the trustee in the debtor's sequestration,[2] nor in breach of any conditions under which the absolute title was held.[3] It may also be held waived, as by the sellers failing to intimate their right of retention to sub-purchasers.[4] The property-holder's right to retain in security is limited to loans made prior to the receipt of intimation that the granter's reversionary right has been assigned to a third party, and he cannot retain in security of advances made subsequently thereto.[5]

(b) *Retention of debts*

By an equitable extension of the statutory principle of compensation,[6] whereby liquid claims can be set off against each other, a debtor having an illiquid claim, such as for performance or damages, against his creditor may retain in security thereof a liquid debt, ascertained in money, though presently due and payable, or though the cross-claims are of different substances. The underlying principle is that a person in breach of contract cannot himself claim implement from the other party.[7] The plea is an equitable one and will be sustained only when the court will not be doing injustice thereby.[8] The right to retain may be excluded by the contract.[9] Where parties are both solvent a right of retention can be claimed only where both claims arise out of the same contract, and not where the illiquid claim

---

[1] *Robertson, supra.*

[2] *Callum v. Goldie* (1885) 12 R. 1137.

[3] *Stewart v. Bisset* (1770) Mor. Compensation, Appx. 2; *Anderson's Tr. v. Somerville* (1899) 36 S.L.R. 833.

[4] *Robertson & Baxter v. McPherson Bros.* (1893) 1 S.L.T. 159; see also *Fleming v. Smith* (1881) 8 R. 548.

[5] *National Bank v. Union Bank* (1886) 14 R. (H.L.) 1; cf. *Deeley v. Lloyds Bank* [1912] A.C. 756.

[6] Compensation Act, 1592 (c. 61); see Ch. 37, *infra.*

[7] *Dick & Stevenson v. Woodside Steel Co.* (1889) 16 R. 242; *British Motor Body Co. v. Shaw*, 1914 S.C. 922; *Christie v. Birrells*, 1910 S.C. 986; *Smart v. Wilkinson*, 1928 S.C. 383, 387.

[8] *Graham v. Gordon* (1843) 5 D. 1207; *Ferguson & Stewart v. Grant* (1856) 18 D. 536; *Shepherd's Trs. v. Macdonald Fraser & Co.* (1898) 5 S.L.T. 296; *Garscadden v. Ardrossan Dry Dock Co.*, 1910 S.C. 178; *E. Galloway v. McConnell*, 1911 S.C. 846; *Fulton Clyde v. McCallum*, 1960 S.C. 78.

[9] *Skene v. Cameron*, 1942 S.C. 393.

arises from a different contract,[1] or from delict,[2] or has not yet materialized but is feared.[3] Nor can retention be claimed by virtue of a claim not yet exigible against a debt presently payable,[4] unless the claim can be readily verified.[5] The case of retention in mutual claims arising from one contract is illustrated by the right of a vassal to retain feu-duty in security of a claim for the superior's failure to implement an obligation to the vassal,[6] the right of a tenant to retain rent for the landlord's failure to give complete possession or otherwise to perform any material obligation of the lease,[7] though retention is not justified if the landlord's failure is not material;[8] the right of a landlord to retain in security of a claim against the tenant;[9] the right of a party to retain the price or freight or wages or other payment in security of a claim for delay or defective or damaged goods or bad work,[10] and the right of a party to retain a deposit paid by the other in security of his claim for damages for the latter's breach of contract.[11] A plea of reten-

---

[1] Ersk. III, 4, 15; Bell, *Prin.* §573; *Scottish N.E. Ry.* v. *Napier* (1859) 21 D. 700; *Burt* v. *Bell* (1861) 23 D. 13; *Mackie* v. *Riddell* (1874) 2 R. 115; *Brown* v. *Smith* (1893) 1 S.L.T. 158; *Sutherland* v. *Urquhart* (1895) 23 R. 284; *Grewar* v. *Cross* (1904) 12 S.L.T. 84; *Asphaltic Limestone Co.* v. *Glasgow Corpn.*, 1907 S.C. 463.

[2] *Christie* v. *Birrells*, 1910 S.C. 986; *Smart* v. *Wilkinson*, 1928 S.C. 383.

[3] *Paul & Thain* v. *Royal Bank* (1869) 7 M. 361.

[4] Ersk. III, 4, 15; Bell, *Comm.* II, 122.

[5] Ersk. III, 4, 16; *Munro* v. *Macdonald's Exors.* (1866) 4 M. 687; *Stuart* v. *S.* (1869) 7 M. 366; *Ross* v. *R.* (1895) 22 R. 461; *Lovie* v. *Baird's Tr.* (1895) 23 R. 1; contrast *Logan* v. *Stephen* (1850) 13 D. 262; *McConnell & Reid* v. *Muir* (1906) 14 S.L.T. 79; *Henderson & Co.* v. *Turnbull*, 1909 S.C. 510.

[6] *Hope* v. *Lumsdaine* (1871) 9 M. 865; *Arnott's Trs.* v. *Forbes* (1881) 9 R. 89; contrast *Cockburn* v. *Heriot's Hospital* (1826) 2 W. & S. 293. As to heritable creditor in possession see *Chamber's J.F.* v. *Vertue* (1893) 20 R. 257.

[7] e.g. *Kilmarnock Gas Light Co.* v. *Smith* (1872) 11 M. 58; *Guthrie* v. *Shearer* (1873) 1 R. 181; *Davie* v. *Stark* (1876) 3 R. 1114; *Critchley* v. *Campbell* (1884) 11 R. 475; *Muir* v. *McIntyres* (1887) 14 R. 470; *Munro* v. *McGeoghs* (1888) 16 R. 93; *Sivwright* v. *Lightbourne* (1890) 17 R. 917; *Duncan* v. *Brooks* (1894) 21 R. 760; *Macdonald* v. *Kydd* (1901) 3 F. 923; *Dougall* v. *Dunfermline Mags.*, 1908 S.C. 151; *Christie* v. *Birrells*, 1910 S.C. 986; *E. Galloway* v. *McConnell*, 1911 S.C. 846; *Haig* v. *Boswall-Preston*, 1915 S.C. 339; *Fingland & Mitchell* v. *Howie*, 1926 S.C. 319; *Marshall's Trs.* v. *Banks*, 1934 S.C. 405; *Stobbs* v. *Hislop*, 1948 S.C. 216; *Brodie* v. *Ker*, 1952 S.C. 216. *Drybrough* v. *D.* (1874) 1 R. 909 seems questionable.

[8] *Humphrey* v. *Mackay* (1883) 10 R. 647; *McLaughlan* v. *Reilly* (1892) 20 R. 41; *Sutherland* v. *Urquhart* (1895) 23 R. 284.

[9] *Lovie* v. *Baird's Trs.* (1895) 23 R. 1; *Jaffrey's Tr.* v. *Milne* (1897) 24 R. 602; *Craig's Tr.* v. *Malcolm* (1900) 2 F. 541; contrast *Sutherland, supra.*

[10] *Taylor* v. *Forbes* (1830) 9 S. 113; *Tait* v. *McIntosh* (1841) 13 Sc. Jur. 280; *Scottish N.E. Ry.* v. *Napier* (1859) 21 D. 700; *Gibson* v. *McNaughton* (1861) 23 D. 358; *Johnston* v. *Robertson* (1861) 23 D. 646; *Macbride* v. *Hamilton* (1875) 2 R. 775; *Gibson & Stewart* v. *Brown* (1876) 3 R. 328; *Sharp* v. *Rettie* (1884) 11 R. 745; *British Motor Body Co.* v. *Shaw*, 1914 S.C. 922.

[11] *Skinner* v. *Breslin* (1905) 13 S.L.T. 91; *Dingwall* v. *Burnett*, 1912 S.C. 1097.

tion implies an admission of liability.[1] The right secured by retention is postponed to any security right obtained by another party by prior diligence, such as arrestment.[2]

Where one party bankrupt—balancing accounts in bankruptcy

Where, however, one party is bankrupt the other is permitted a wider right of retention, and may withhold payment due by him by virtue of a claim against the bankrupt, though it is contingent, future or disputed,[3] but not a debt contracted after bankruptcy against a debt due to the bankrupt estate,[4] so long as the claim was acquired in good faith.[5] Otherwise the creditor would be obliged to pay in full and receive only a dividend on his claim against the bankrupt.

(c) Lien

The right of lien is the right of a person, having legitimate[6] possession of another's moveable[7] property, to withhold it from that other until his claims against that other are satisfied.[8] It has been called a pledge collateral to another contract of which it is an incident.[9] It may be justified on the ground of an implied term in a contract which results in the possession,[8] and hence cannot be claimed if the contract contains inconsistent provisions,[10] or impliedly contradicts lien.[11] It is also inconsistent with an express stipulation for security.[12] Or it may be justified on the basis of

---

[1] *Brodie, supra.*

[2] *Park, Dobson & Co.* v. *Taylor*, 1929 S.C. 571.

[3] Ersk. III, 4, 20; Bell, *Comm.* II, 122; *Mill* v. *Paul* (1825) 4 S. 219; *Anderson* v. *Mackinnon* (1876) 3 R. 608; *Hannay* v. *Armstrong* (1877) 4 R. (H.L.) 43; *Miller* v. *McIntosh* (1884) 11 R. 729; *Scott's Tr.* v. *S.* (1887) 14 R. 1043; *Taylor's Tr.* v. *Paul* (1888) 15 R. 313; *Davidson's Trs.* v. *Urquhart* (1892) 19 R. 808; *Ross* v. *R.* (1895) 22 R. 461.

[4] Bell, *Comm.* II, 123, corrected by *Booth* v. *Thomson*, 1972 S.L.T. (Notes) 18.

[5] *Reid* v. *Bell* (1884) 12 R. 178; *Middlemass* v. *Gibson*, 1910 S.C. 577.

[6] *Martinez y Gomez* v. *Allison* (1890) 17 R. 332; *Shepherd's Trs.* v. *Macdonald Fraser & Co.* (1898) 5 S.L.T. 296.

[7] *Turner* v. *T.* (1811) Hume 854; *Castle Douglas and Dumfries Ry.* v. *Lee, Son & Freeman* (1859) 22 D. 18.

[8] Bell, *Prin.* §1410; cf. *Meikle & Wilson* v. *Pollard* (1880) 8 R. 69; More's theory (Notes, cxxxi; *Lect.* I, 402) seems questionable.

[9] See generally *Miller* v. *Hutcheson & Dixon* (1881) 8 R. 489, 492; *Paton's Tr.* v. *Finlayson*, 1923 S.C. 872; *Lamonby* v. *Foulds*, 1928 S.C. 89; *Grand Empire Theatre Liqdr.* v. *Snodgrass*, 1932 S.C. (H.L.) 73, 76.

[10] Bell, *Prin.* §1439; *Borthwick* v. *Bremner* (1833) 12 S. 121; *Middlemass* v. *Gibson*, 1910 S.C. 577. See also *Robertson's Tr.* v. *Royal Bank* (1890) 18 R. 12; *Colquhoun's Tr.* v. *Diack* (1901) 4 F. 358.

[11] *Mackenzie* v. *Newall* (1824) 3 S. 206; *Drummond* v. *Muirhead & Guthrie Smith* (1900) 2 F. 585; *Lochee Sawmill Co. Liqr.* v. *Stevenson*, 1908 S.C. 559.

[12] *National Bank* v. *Forbes* (1858) 21 D. 79.

usage and common understanding in certain recognized cases where it is held to exist for reasons of commercial convenience.[1] Thus it may exist over goods entrusted for repair,[2] or for carriage,[3] title deeds,[4] business books,[5] the clothes of a guest at an inn,[6] but not over money deposited for a specified purpose only.[7] It is an equitable right and the court controls it[8] and may, exceptionally, refuse to give effect to it.[9] A solicitor's right of lien avails against everyone, but in other cases a lien avails against the creditor only.[10]

Possession necessary for lien

A right of lien requires actual[11] or constructive[12] possession of the other's property,[13] obtained lawfully[14] and not by mistake,[15] accident[16] or fraud,[17] and not merely the custody of the other's property acquired by virtue of employment under him.[18] It must have been acquired when acting in the capacity in which the security is claimed,[19] and before the other party's bankruptcy supervened[20] or possibly more than 60 days before such bank-

---

[1] Bell, *Prin.* §1410.

[2] *Garscadden* v. *Ardrossan Dry Dock Co.*, 1910 S.C. 178; *Lamonby* v. *Foulds*, 1928 S.C. 89.

[3] Bell, *Prin.* §1423–25; *Stevenson* v. *Likly* (1824) 3 S. 204; *Palmer* v. *Lee* (1880) 7 R. 651.

[4] *National Bank* v. *White & Park*, 1909 S.C. 1308; *Grand Empire Theatre, supra*.

[5] *Stuart* v. *Stevenson* (1828) 6 S. 591; *Bruce* v. *Edinburgh Trs.* (1835) 13 S. 437; *Reid* v. *Galbraith* (1893) 1 S.L.T. 273; *Barnton Hotel Co.* v. *Cook* (1899) 1 F. 1190; *Train & McIntyre* v. *Forbes*, 1925 S.L.T. 286.

[6] *McKichen* v. *Muir* (1849) J. Shaw 223; *McIntosh* v. *Chalmers* (1883) 11 R. 8.

[7] *Field & Allan* v. *Gordon* (1872) 11 M. 132; *McGregor* v. *Ally & McLellan* (1887) 14 R. 535; *Middlemas* v. *Gibson*, 1910 S.C. 577.

[8] *Ferguson & Stuart* v. *Grant* (1856) 18 D. 536; *Craig* v. *Howden* (1856) 18 D. 863; *Parker* v. *Brown* (1878) 5 R. 979.

[9] *Garscadden* v. *Ardrossan Dry Dock Co.*, 1910 S.C. 178, 181.

[10] *Macrae* v. *Leith*, 1913 S.C. 901.

[11] e.g. *Garscadden, supra*; *Findlay* v. *Waddell*, 1910 S.C. 670; *Paton's Tr.* v. *Finlayson*, 1923 S.C. 872.

[12] *Renny* v. *Rutherford* (1840) 2 D. 676; 3 D. 1134; *Gairdner* v. *Milne* (1858) 20 D. 565.

[13] Bell, *Prin.* §1412.

[14] *Shepherd's Trs.* v. *Macdonald, Fraser & Co.* (1898) 5 S.L.T. 296; cf. *Falconer* v. *Dickson's Tr.* (1903) 11 S.L.T. 16.

[15] *Glendinning's Trs.* v. *Montgomery* (1745) Mor. 2573; *Louson* v. *Craik* (1842) 4 D. 1452; *Patten* v. *Royal Bank* (1853) 15 D. 617.

[16] *National Bank* v. *White & Park*, 1909 S.C. 1308.

[17] *Martinez y Gomez* v. *Allison* (1890) 17 R. 332.

[18] *Burns* v. *Bruce & Baxter* (1799) Hume 29; *Dickson* v. *Nicholson* (1855) 17 D. 1011; *Martin* v. *Boyd* (1882) 19 S.L.R. 447; *Clift* v. *Portobello Pier Co.* (1877) 4 R. 462; *Gladstone* v. *McCallum* (1896) 23 R. 783; *Barnton Hotel Co.* v. *Cook* (1899) 1 F. 1190. Contrast *Robertson* v. *Ross* (1887) 15 R. 67; *Findlay* v. *Waddell*, 1910 S.C. 670.

[19] *National Bank* v. *White & Park*, 1909 S.C. 1308.

[20] Bell, *Comm.* II, 89; *Meldrum's Tr.* v. *Clark* (1826) 5 S. 122; *Dickson* v. *Nicholson* (1855) 17 D. 1011; *Jackson* v. *Fenwick's Tr.* (1898) 6 S.L.T. 319. See also *Stevenson, Lauder & Gilchrist* v. *Macbrayne* (1896) 23 R. 496.

ruptcy.[1] A maritime lien, so-called, is truly a hypothec, not a lien, in that possession of the security subject is not required.

Authority to create lien

The party claiming lien must show that the other, if not himself the owner, had the actual or ostensible authority of the owner to subject the goods to a lien.[2] Mere possession does not imply ostensible authority to subject to lien,[3] nor does ostensible authority to pledge,[4] but ostensible authority is conferred by statute[5] and may be by circumstances; thus a hirer may be held to have implied authority to have goods repaired and to give the repairer a lien.[6]

Loss of lien

The right of lien is lost if possession is surrendered,[7] unless obtained by fraud, or unless the redelivery is made under order of the court and under reservation of the right in security.[8] The court may, if the subject of security is likely to deteriorate, direct a sale, reserving a right in security over the price.[9] Lien may be maintained though the goods are entrusted to a third party[10] and part may be surrendered without relinquishing the lien over the rest.[11]

Special and general lien

Where it exists a right of lien is normally a special lien only, founded on the mutuality of obligations in contract, conferring a right to withhold in security only of claims arising from the particular transaction between parties which caused the transfer of possession.[12] The right secures primarily the charge for the

[1] *Anderson's Tr.* v. *Fleming* (1871) 9 M. 718.

[2] *Martinez y Gomez* v. *Allison* (1890) 17 R. 332; *Lamonby* v. *Foulds*, 1928 S.C. 89.

[3] *Mitchell* v. *Heys* (1894) 21 R. 600.

[4] *National Bank* v. *Dickie's Tr.* (1895) 22 R. 740; see also *Anderson* v. *N. of S. Bank* (1901) 4 F. 49.

[5] Factors (Sc.) Act, 1890; Sale of Goods Act, 1893, S. 25.

[6] *Lamonby* v. *Foulds*, 1928 S.C. 89.

[7] Bell, *Comm.* II, 89; *Morrison* v. *Fulwell's Tr.* (1901) 9 S.L.T. 34.

[8] *Reid* v. *Galbraith* (1893) 1 S.L.T. 273; *Donaldson's Liqr.* v. *White & Park*, 1908 S.C. 309; *Rorie* v. *Stevenson*, 1908 S.C. 559; *Liqr. of Scottish Workman's Assce. Co.* v. *Waddell* 1910 S.C. 670.

[9] *Parker* v. *Brown* (1878) 5 R. 979.

[10] Bell, *Prin.* §1424; *Renny* v. *Kemp* (1840) 3 D. 1134.

[11] *Bannatyne* v. *Malcolm*, 15 November 1814 F.C.; *Gray* v. *Wardrop's Trs.* (1851) 13 D. 963; (1855) 3 Macq. 435; *Mechan* v. *L.N.E. Ry.*, 1911 S.C. 1348.

[12] Stair I, 18, 7; Ersk. III, 4, 20; Bell, *Prin.* §1411, 1419; *Harper* v. *Faulds* (1791) Bell's Oct. Cas. 440; *Brown* v. *Sommerville* (1844) 6 D. 1267; *Miller* v. *Hutcheson* (1881) 8 R. 489.

work or service for which possession of the subject was trans-ferred,[1] including accounts for professional services.[2] An inn-keeper has a special lien founded on custom rather than implied contract, over a traveller's goods, animals and vehicles, in security of his charges for accommodating and feeding the traveller and his property.[3] So too the lien of a salvor of a ship, for his outlays and reward of salvage, is based on custom.[4] A right of lien exists also for claims of damages arising from the failure of the other party to carry out his part of the contract;[5] for the price where a seller has not been paid for goods still in his hands.[6]

General lien

A general lien, or claim to retain a subject in security of a balance due under all previous contracts of the same general character, and within the scope of the same business,[7] is recog-nized exceptionally, in some cases by virtue of express contract,[8] advertisement,[9] or custom and usage of trade.[10] Under the last head general lien has been recognized in cases of bankers,[11] brokers,[12] mercantile factors,[13] solicitors[14] and stockbrokers[15]

---

[1] e.g. *Harper* v. *Faulds* (1791) Bell's Oct. Cas. 440; *Stevenson* v. *Likly* (1824) 3 S. 291; *Laurie* v. *Denny's Tr.* (1853) 15 D. 404; *Anderson's Tr.* v. *Fleming* (1871) 9 M. 718; *Meikle & Wilson* v. *Pollard* (1880) 8 R. 69; *Ross & Duncan* v. *Baxter* (1885) 13 R. 185; *Findlay* v. *Waddell*, 1910 S.C. 178.

[2] *Robertson* v. *Ross* (1887) 15 R. 67.

[3] Ch. 38, *infra.*

[4] Ch. 53; *infra.*

[5] *Moore's Carving Machine Co.* v. *Austin* (1896) 4 S.L.T. 38; *Glendinning* v. *Hope*, 1911 S.C. (H.L.) 73.

[6] Sale of Goods Act, 1893, Ss. 41–43; *Black* v. *Bakers of Glasgow* (1867) 6 M. 136; *Distillers Co.* v. *Russell's Tr.* (1889) 16 R. 479; contrast *Fleming* v. *Smith* (1881) 8 R. 548; *Robertson & Baxter* v. *McPherson Bros.* (1893) 1 S.L.T. 159.

[7] Bell, *Comm.* II, 101; *Prin.* §143; *McCall* v. *Black* (1824) 2 Sh. App. 188; *Largue* v. *Urquhart* (1883) 10 R. 1229.

[8] *Scottish Central Ry.* v. *Ferguson* (1864) 2 M. 781. See also *Anderson's Trs.* v. *Fleming* (1871) 9 M. 718; *Mechan* v. *L.N.E. Ry.*, 1911 S.C. 1348.

[9] *Anderson's Trs.*, *supra.*

[10] Bell, *Comm.* II, 105; *Anderson's Trs.*, *supra*; *Strong* v. *Philips* (1878) 5 R. 770.

[11] *Robertson's Tr.* v. *Royal Bank* (1890) 18 R. 12; *Alston's Tr.* v. *Royal Bank* (1893) 20 R. 887.

[12] *Miller* v. *Hutcheson & Dixon* (1881) 8 R. 489.

[13] Ersk. III, 4, 21; Bell, *Comm.* II, 109; *Prin.* §1445; *Wilmot* v. *Wilson* (1841) 3 D. 815; *Millar & Paterson* v. *McNair* (1852) 14 D. 955; *Sibbald* v. *Gibson* (1852) 15 D. 217; *Miller* v. *Hutcheson* (1881) 8 R. 489; *Crockart's Tr.* v. *Hay*, 1913 S.C. 509; *Mackenzie* v. *Cormack*, 1950 S.C. 183.

[14] *Paul* v. *Meikle* (1868) 7 M. 235; *Grand Empire Theatre Liqdr.* v. *Snodgrass*, 1932 S.C. (H.L.) 73.

[15] *Glendinning* v. *Hope*, 1911 S.C. (H.L.) 73.

though not accountants,[1] nor commission agents,[2] and may be recognized in any case where there is proven custom of trade to that effect.[3] Even where a general lien exists it covers only debts incurred in the business relationship in issue, not in an unrelated one.[4] A solicitor's lien covers his business account and outlays, but not debts incurred on behalf of the client but not paid and for which he was not personally liable.[5]

Enforcement of lien

A lien is a right in security only and confers no right to sell,[6] unless express power is granted by contract or warrant obtained from the sheriff.[7] A mercantile agent or factor may however sell.[8] Titles and business books are probably not saleable in any case.[9] In case of bankruptcy they may be surrendered under reservation of the right of lien.[10]

---

[1] *Morrison* v. *Fulwell's Tr.* (1901) 9 S.L.T. 34; *Findlay* v. *Waddell,* 1910 S.C. 670; but see *Meikle & Wilson* v. *Pollard* (1880) 8 R. 69.

[2] *Murray* v. *Bernard* (1869) 6 S.L.R. 230.

[3] *Anderson's Trs., supra* (bleachers); *Strong* v. *Philips* (1878) 5 R. 770 (packers); *Mitchell* v. *Heys* (1894) 21 R. 600 (calico printers). Usage was not proved in *Laurie* v. *Denny's Tr.* (1853) 15 D. 404 (storekeepers) or *Smith* v. *Aikman* (1859) 22 D. 344 (scourers).

[4] *Christie* v. *Ruxton* (1862) 24 D. 1182; *Anderson's Trs., supra; Wylie's Exrx.* v. *McJannet* (1901) 4 F. 195.

[5] *Grand Empire Theatre, supra.*

[6] *Robertson's Tr.* v. *Royal Bank* (1890) 18 R. 12, 20.

[7] *Gibson & Stewart* v. *Brown* (1876) 3 R. 328; see also *Parker* v. *Brown* (1878) 5 R. 979. An unpaid seller has a statutory right to resell: Sale of Goods Act, 1893, Ss. 39, 47–48.

[8] Bell, *Comm.* II, 91.

[9] Bell, *Comm.* II, 108; *Ferguson & Stuart* v. *Grant* (1856) 18 D. 536; *Glendinning* v. *Hope,* 1911 S.C. (H.L.) 73.

[10] *Skinner* v. *Henderson* (1865) 3 M. 867; *Donaldson & Co.'s Liqr.* v. *White & Park,* 1908 S.C. 309.

CHAPTER 37

DISCHARGE OF CONTRACT

THE discharge of a contract terminates it and frees both parties from their contractual obligations. Discharge may be effected in various ways.

(a) PERFORMANCE

Where both parties duly perform their obligations the contract is discharged. What is required for performance depends on the interpretation of the contract, and in case of dispute the onus is on the party alleging performance to prove that he has made it, which may be done by parole evidence.[1] If a party alleges an excuse for non-performance, he must prove the facts raising the excuse.[2] In general the law requires strict and exact performance,[3] and partial performance or incorrect performance gives no right of action in contract for the price, though if such performance is accepted, a quasi-contractual claim lies for recompense *quantum meruit*.[4] If the obligation admits of performance in alternative ways the choice of which to adopt is for the debtor.[5] But if one of these is precluded, the debtor must perform the other.[6] Adherence to the time fixed for performance is essential, and delayed performance is a breach,[7] though some latitude is permitted in cases of sales of land.[8] If one party tenders performance and is prevented from completing by the conduct of the other party,

[1] Stair IV, 43, 4; Ersk. IV, 2, 20; *Taylor* v. *Nisbet* (1901) 4 F. 79; *Langlands* v. *McMaster*, 1907 S.C. 1090; *Owners of Chassie Maersk* v. *Love & Stuart*, 1916 S.C. (H.L.) 187.

[2] *Pyper* v. *Thomson* (1843) 5 D. 498; *Pullars* v. *Walker* (1858) 20 D. 1238; *McLean* v. *Warnock* (1883) 10 R. 1052; *Bain* v. *Strang* (1888) 16 R. 186; *Forrester's Tr.* v. *McKelvie* (1895) 22 R. 437; *Mustard* v. *Paterson*, 1923 S.C. 142; *Carruthers* v. *Macgregor*, 1927 S.C. 816.

[3] cf. buyer's rights of rejection if too much is delivered, or too little, or mixed goods, under Sale of Goods Act, 1893, S. 30; *Moore and Landauer & Co.* [1921] 2 K.B. 519; *Robertson* v. *Stewart*, 1928 S.N. 31.

[4] *Ramsay* v. *Brand* (1898) 25 R. 1212; *Steel* v. *Young*, 1907 S.C. 360; contrast *Forrest* v. *Scottish County Investment Co.*, 1916 S.C. (H.L.) 28; *Speirs* v. *Petersen*, 1924 S.C. 428; where performance was substantial though not exact.

[5] Stair I, 17, 20; Bankt. I, 23, 80; *Christie* v. *Wilson*, 1915 S.C. 645.

[6] More, *Notes*, cxxi.

[7] *Bowes* v. *Shand* (1877) 2 App. Cas. 455; *Reuter* v. *Sala* (1879) 4 C.P.D. 239; *Sharp* v. *Christmas* (1892) 8 T.L.R. 687; *Hartley* v. *Hymans* [1920] 3 K.B. 475.

[8] *Stickney* v. *Keeble* [1915] A.C. 386.

he is deemed to have performed[1] and is entitled to payment for what he has done. So, too, if he tenders performance and it is unjustifiably refused, he is entitled to damages, or possibly to the contract price.[2] If he is totally prevented from offering performance by the act of the other party, the other party is in breach of contract.[3]

(b) PAYMENT

A debtor must generally comply with any terms stipulated by the contract as to time, place or mode of payment,[4] though in sale of goods a stipulation as to time of payment is *prima facie* not deemed of the essence of the contract.[5] In the absence of contrary agreement a creditor is entitled to payment in legal tender.[6] A cheque is good payment conditional on its being honoured when presented, failing which the debt revives.[7] If not accepted it should be returned at once.[8] If a creditor objects to the tender of a cheque on any ground other than that it is not legal tender, he must be held to have waived the objection that payment was not made in money of legal tender.[9]

It is the duty of the debtor to tender payment, on the due date, at the creditor's residence, or place of business within business hours.[10] If payment be not then made the creditor may at once take legal proceedings or do diligence for recovery, and if thereafter tender of payment be made, it must include the expenses of

---

[1] *Startup* v. *Macdonald* (1843) 6 M. & G. 593; *Mackay* v. *Dick & Stevenson* (1881) 8 R. (H.L.) 37; cf. Sale of Goods Act, 1893, Ss. 29(4) and 37.

[2] cf. *White & Carter (Councils) Ltd.* v. *McGregor*, 1962 S.C. (H.L.) 1.

[3] cf. Sale of Goods Act, S. 50 (non-acceptance by buyer).

[4] cf. *International Sponge Importers* v. *Watt*, 1911 S.C. (H.L.) 57.

[5] Sale of Goods Act, 1893, S. 10(1).

[6] 'Legal tender' connotes the kinds of money which, if tendered, must be accepted as discharging the debt and in which alone the debtor may validly tender payment: see *Fraser* v. *Smith* (1899) 1 F. 487; *Glasgow Pavilion Ltd.* v. *Motherwell* (1903) 6 F. 116. Gold coins are legal tender to any amount, cupro-nickel or silver coins of more than 10p, up to £10, cupro-nickel or silver coins of not more than 10p, up to £5, bronze coins for not more than 20p, and other coins, if made current by proclamation, for payment of any amount not exceeding the amount specified in the proclamation: Coinage Act, 1971, S. 2. Bank of England notes for less than £5 are legal tender in Scotland: Currency and Bank Notes Act, 1954, S. 1(1) and (2); Scottish Bank notes are not legal tender anywhere, not even in Scotland. See also Decimal Currency Act, 1969, Ss. 2–13.

[7] *D. Buccleuch* v. *McTurk* (1845) 7 D. 927; *Walker & Watson* v. *Sturrock* (1897) 35 S.L.R. 26; *Leggat Bros.* v. *Gray*, 1908 S.C. 67; *McLaren's Tr.* v. *Argylls, Ltd.*, 1915, 2 S.L.T. 241. Cf. *Glasgow Pavilion, Ltd.*, *supra*.

[8] *Mintons* v. *Hawley* (1882) 20 S.L.R. 126; *Macdougall* v. *McNab* (1893) 21 R. 144.

[9] *Holt* v. *National Bank*, 1927 S.L.T. 484.

[10] *Haughhead Coal Co.* v. *Gallocher* (1903) 11 S.L.T. 156.

process or diligence incurred to date.[1] If the debtor tenders payment in some unusual, unbusinesslike or risky way he takes the risk of loss, theft or fraud.[2] If the creditor is pressing for payment, he is bound to accept payment on behalf of the debtor from any third party who has an interest to intervene.[3] He is not obliged to give change, nor to accept partial payment.[4] If partial payment be tendered, or other payment by way of compromise, it should be rejected at once, since, if accepted without protest, it will normally be presumed to have been accepted as payment in full.[5]

Payment is valid if made *bona fide* to a person honestly and reasonably believed to be the creditor, or to a partner of the creditor firm,[6] or to an agent who had actual or ostensible authority to receive payment.[7] A solicitor has been held to have ostensible authority to receive payment of a sum sued for,[8] or of the price of shares sold,[9] but not of the principal of a bond repaid.[10]

Ascription of payments

If the debtor owes the creditor on more than one account he may, when making a payment, ascribe it to any one account, and the creditor must abide by this appropriation, failing which the creditor may ascribe the payment to any account he chooses,[11] as to an unsecured debt rather than one secured,[12] but not to a prescribed or doubtful claim with the intention of excluding a challenge of its validity.[13] In the case of a continuing or current account between banker and customer, or parties in a similar

[1] *Pollock* v. *Goodwin's Trs.* (1898) 25 R. 1051; *Alexander* v. *Campbell's Trs.* (1903) 5 F. 634.

[2] *Robb* v. *Gow* (1905) 8 F. 90 (uncrossed bearer cheque).

[3] *Smith* v. *Gentle* (1844) 6 D. 1164; *Cunningham's Trs.* v. *Hutton* (1847) 10 D. 307; *Fleming* v. *Burgess* (1867) 5 M. 856.

[4] *Wilson's Tr.* v. *Watson* (1900) 2 F. 761.

[5] *Thew* v. *Sinclair* (1881) 8 R. 467; *Day* v. *McLea* (1889) 22 Q.B.D. 610; *Pollock* v. *Goodwin's Trs.* (1898) 25 R. 1051. See 1937 S.L.T. (News) 81.

[6] *Nicoll* v. *Reid* (1878) 6 R. 216.

[7] *International Sponge Importers* v. *Watt*, 1911 S.C. (H.L.) 57.

[8] *Smith* v. *N.B. Ry.* (1850) 12 D. 795.

[9] *Pearson* v. *Scott* (1878) 9 Ch. D. 198.

[10] *Richardson* v. *McGeoch's Trs.* (1898) 1 F. 145.

[11] Ersk. III, 4, 1; Bell, *Prin.* §563; *Allan* v. *A.* (1831) 9 S. 519; *Mitchell* v. *Cullen* (1852) 1 Macq. 190; *Semple* v. *Wilson* (1889) 16 R. 790; *Brenes* v. *Downie*, 1914 S.C. 97; intention to ascribe must be communicated: *Leeson* v. *L.* [1936] 2 K.B. 156; and may be express, implied or presumed: *Hay* v. *Torbet*, 1908 S.C. 781. See also *Jackson* v. *Nicoll* (1870) 8 M. 408; *Wilson's Tr.* v. *Watson* (1900) 2 F. 761.

[12] *Bremner* v. *Mabon* (1837) 16 S. 213; *Wauchope* v. *N.B. Ry.* (1863) 2 M. 326; *Buchanan* v. *Main* (1900) 3 F. 215; *Anderson* v. *N. of S. Bank*, 1909, 2 S.L.T. 262.

[13] *Dougall* v. *Lornie* (1899) 1 F. 1187.

relationship,[1] a rule, known as the rule in *Clayton's case*,[2] applies, to the effect that credit payments go to extinguish debits in chronological order.[3] This rule is important where a cautioner is liable for a fixed period only, as subsequent credits may extinguish all debits incurred during the material period and consequently extinguish his liability, even though there still remains a debit balance.[4] This rule does not apply to trust moneys paid into a trustee's private account[5] nor as between two separate accounts with a bank,[6] nor to a tradesman's account,[7] nor an account between farmer and auctioneer,[8] nor where a particular mode of dealing or express arrangement indicates a different intention of the parties.[9]

Proof of payment

In accordance with the maxim *unumquodque eodem modo dissolvitur quo colligatur*, proof of payment of a debt exceeding £100 Scots, if arising from an obligation constituted in writing,[10] or vouched by a document of debt such as a bill, is restricted to the creditor's writ[11] or admission on oath.[12] Hence a receipt or other discharge is normally the only admissible evidence of payment. A cheque bearing to have been paid by the drawer's bank is equivalent to a receipt.[13] But parole evidence is competent of a general settlement of accounts between the parties subsequent to the debt in issue,[14] that a creditor is not entitled to the document of debt

---

[1] *Royal Bank* v. *Christie* (1841) 2 Rob. 118; *McKinley* v. *Wilson* (1886) 13 R. 210; *Batchelor's Trs.* v. *Honeyman* (1892) 19 R. 903; *Cuthill* v. *Strachan* (1894) 21 R. 549; *Dougall, supra*; *Hay, supra*; *Deeley* v. *Lloyds Bank* [1912] A.C. 756.

[2] *Devaynes* v. *Noble (Clayton's Case)* (1816) 1 Mer. 529, 571; (1814–23) All E.R. Rep. 1.

[3] *Royal Bank* v. *Christie* (1841) 2 Rob. 118; *Lang* v. *Brown* (1859) 22 D. 113; *Jackson* v. *Nicoll* (1870) 8 M. 408; *McLaren* v. *Bradly* (1874) 2 R. 185; *Scott's Trs.* v. *Alexander's Tr.* (1884) 11 R. 407; *Cuthill* v. *Strachan* (1894) 21 R. 549.

[4] *Cuthill, supra*.

[5] *Macadam* v. *Martin's Tr.* (1872) 11 M. 33; *Jopp* v. *Johnston's Trs.* (1904) 6 F. 1028; *Hofford* v. *Gowans*, 1909, 1 S.L.T. 153.

[6] *Bradford Old Bank* v. *Sutcliffe* [1918] 2 K.B. 833; cf. *Beith* v. *Mackenzie* (1875) 3 R. 185.

[7] *Dougall* v. *Lornie* (1899) 1 F. 1187.

[8] *Hay* v. *Torbet*, 1908 S.C. 781.

[9] Bell, *Prin.* §563; *Macdonald Fraser & Co.* v. *Cairn's Exrx.*, 1932 S.C. 699.

[10] Bell, *Prin.* §564; *Keanie* v. *K.*, 1940 S.C. 549; *Nicol's Trs.* v. *Sutherland*, 1951 S.C. (H.L.) 21.

[11] On what is 'writ' see *Young* v. *Thomson*, 1909 S.C. 529, 536.

[12] *Patrick* v. *Watt* (1859) 21 D. 637; *Thiem's Trs.* v. *Collie* (1899) 1 F. 764; *Robertson* v. *Thomson* (1900) 3 F. 5; *Bishop* v. *Bryce*, 1910 S.C. 426; *Jackson* v. *Ogilvie's Exor.*, 1935 S.C. 154; *Nicol's Trs.* v. *Sutherland*, 1951 S.C. (H.L.) 21. This is so, notwithstanding the terms of the Bills of Exchange Act, 1882, S. 100.

[13] Cheques Act, 1957, S. 3.

[14] *Chrystal* v. *C.* (1900) 2 F. 373.

which he holds,[1] that bills did not relate to the debt in question,[2] and of facts and circumstances giving rise to an inevitable inference that the debt has been discharged.[3] If there is no document evidencing the debt parole proof of payment is competent.[4] If the debt arises from an oral contract parole proof of payment is competent of items not exceeding £100 Scots, but, if over that, it must be by writ or oath.[5] Payment for a cash purchase may be proved parole,[6] but only by writ or oath if the sale were on credit or delivery were postponed, even though the contract were oral.[7]

Inference of payment

Payment may also be inferred from facts and circumstances.[8] The possession by the debtor of the document of debt raises a presumption, expressed in the maxim *chirographum apud debitorem repertum praesumitur solutum*, rebuttable by parole evidence, that the debt has been paid.[9] The production by the debtor of receipts for the last three consecutive instalments of a termly payment, such as feu-duty, rent, wages or interest, raises a presumption, the *apocha trium annorum*, rebuttable by parole evidence, that all prior instalments have been duly paid.[10] The same inference is not justified by one receipt, even for three or more instalments.[11] Nor do receipts for three instalments justify an inference that a bill, granted for earlier arrears, has been paid.[12] The inability of the creditor to produce a document of debt on which he founds raises a presumption that the debt has been paid and the document handed over or destroyed.[13] Facts and circumstances inconsistent with the continued subsistence of a debt entitle the court to infer payment.[14]

---

[1] *Bishop* v. *Bryce,* 1910 S.C. 426; *McKenzie's Exors.* v. *Morrison's Trs.,* 1930 S.C. 830.

[2] *Gray* v. *Scott* (1868) 6 M. 197.

[3] *Campbell* v. *C's Exors.,* 1910, 2 S.L.T. 240; *McKenzie's Exors., supra.*

[4] *Newlands* v. *MacKinlay* (1885) 13 R. 353.

[5] *Brown* v. *Mason* (1856) 19 D. 137.

[6] *McDonald* v. *Callendar* (1786) Mor. 12366.

[7] Bell, *Prin.* §565; *Shaw* v. *Wright* (1877) 5 R. 245; *Young* v. *Thomson,* 1909 S.C. 529; *Kilpatrick* v. *Dunlop,* 1909, 2 S.L.T. 307.

[8] e.g. *Fairbairn* v. *F.* (1868) 6 M. 640; *Spence* v. *Paterson's Trs.* (1873) 1 R. 46; *Tosh* v. *Ogilvy* (1873) 1 R. 254; *Welsh* v. *W's Trs.* (1878) 5 R. 542; *Nicoll* v. *Reid* (1878) 6 R. 216; *Thiem's Trs.* v. *Collie* (1899) 1 F. 764; *Chrystal* v. *C.* (1900) 2 F. 373.

[9] Bell, *Prin.* §566; *Knox* v. *Crawford* (1862) 24 D. 1088; *Henry* v. *Miller* (1884) 11 R. 713.

[10] Stair I, 18, 2; IV, 40, 35; Ersk. III, 4, 10; Bell, *Prin.* §567; *Cameron* v. *Panton's Trs.* (1891) 18 R. 728; *Stenhouse* v. *S's Trs.* (1899) 6 S.L.T. 368.

[11] Dickson, §177.

[12] *Patrick* v. *Watt* (1859) 21 D. 637.

[13] cf. *Mackinnon's Tr.* v. *Bank of Scotland,* 1915 S.C. 411.

[14] *McKenzie's Exrx* v. *Morrison's Trs.,* 1930 S.C. 830.

Presumption of payment

A presumption of payment exists in the case of counsel's fees, which are not, in general, recoverable by action.[1] Where fellows of a college of physicians are prohibited by by-law from recovering their fees the same result follows.[2] Where a guest is permitted to leave a hotel his bill is presumed paid unless the hotelkeeper proves the contrary.[3]

(c) TERMINATION AT PLEASURE

A contract entered into for no specified term and enduring at the will of the parties may be terminated by either at his pleasure, at once or on giving reasonable notice to the other.[4]

(d) DISCHARGE OR ACCEPTILATION

The creditor in the obligation may unilaterally discharge or renounce his rights without performance or payment made by the other, and thereby release the other party.[5] If the contract were in writing, the discharge must be in writing, or proved by writ or oath of the creditor.[6] If the contract were oral, an oral discharge is probably adequate and it may be proved by parole evidence.[7] A discharge in general terms is normally interpreted as renouncing all claims known to the creditor,[8] but it may be reduced on the ground of error if a debt then unknown to the creditor emerges.[9] A general discharge, with an enumeration of debts, has been held limited by the *ejusdem generis* principle.[10] A statement of accounts between parties, if rendered by one and docqueted as correct by

[1] *Batchelor* v. *Pattison & Mackersy* (1876) 3 R. 914. But see *Ogilvie* v. *Simpson* (1837) 15 S. 746; *Cullen* v. *Buchanan* (1862) 24 D. 1132.

[2] Bell, *Prin.* §568; Medical Act, 1956, S. 27(2).

[3] *Barnet* v. *Colvil* (1840) 2 D. 337.

[4] *Fifeshire Road Trs.* v. *Cowdenbeath Coal Co.* (1883) 11 R. 18; *Neilson* v. *Mossend Iron Co.* (1886) 13 R. (H.L.) 50; *Welwood* v. *Midlothian C.C.* (1894) 22 R. 56; *Stewart* v. *Rendall* (1899) 1 F. 1002. See also *Galbraith & Moorhead* v. *Arethusa Co.* (1896) 23 R. 1011; *Bernards, Ltd.* v. *N.B. Ry.* (1897) 5 S.L.T. 116; cf. Partnership Act, 1890, S. 26.

[5] Stair I, 18, 5; Ersk. III, 4, 8.

[6] *Simpson's Trs.* v. *S.*, 1933 S.N. 22; *Keanie* v. *K.*, 1940 S.C. 549; cf. Bills of Exchange Act, 1882, S. 62: discharge must be in writing, or bill delivered to acceptor. Probative writ is not required to discharge a claim of damages: *Davies* v. *Hunter*, 1934 S.C. 10.

[7] Ersk. III, 4, 8; Dickson, §627; *Lavan* v. *Aird*, 1919 S.C. 345; *Edinburgh Entertainments Co.* v. *Stevenson*, 1926 S.C. 363.

[8] *B.L. Co.* v. *Esplin* (1849) 11 D. 1104; cf. *McAdam* v. *Scott*, 1913, 1 S.L.T. 12; *Davies* v. *City of Glasgow Friendly Socy.*, 1935 S.C. 224.

[9] *Dickson* v. *Halbert* (1854) 16 D. 586; *Purdon* v. *Rowat's Tr.* (1856) 19 D. 206.

[10] Bell, *Prin.* §583; *Greenock Banking Co.* v. *Smith* (1844) 6 D. 1340; *M. Tweeddale* v. *Hume* (1848) 10 D. 1053.

the other, raises a presumption that all mutual claims have been settled,[1] but this may be rebutted.[2]

A creditor may similarly discharge a claim though only partial performance or part-payment has been made.[3] Or he may accept an extra-judicial offer to make a payment in settlement of a claim: once accepted this cannot be resiled from even though the defender goes bankrupt.[4] Such a discharge may be reduced if impetrated by misrepresentation or concealment.[5]

Discharge may also be effected by bilateral agreement, whereby each party discharges the other from the contractual obligations so far as not implemented.

(e) COMPENSATION

At common law parties mutually indebted to each other under separate obligations had to bring cross-actions. The Compensation Act, 1592 (c. 61) made it possible to plead one in defence to an action for payment of the other, to the effect of extinguishing the lesser claim and *pro tanto* diminishing the greater.[6] The plea is competent only where there is *concursus debiti et crediti*, i.e. where each party is simultaneously, in the same legal capacity, indebted to the other under a separate obligation.[7] Except under special circumstances a debt due to or from several persons jointly cannot be set off against a debt from or to one of them separately.[8] The plea is not affected by the death of one party, as an executor is *eadem persona cum defuncto*.[9]

Compensation does not operate *ipso jure*,[10] but must be pleaded in defence, and may be pleaded in respect of an unsecured rather than a secured claim.[11] If sustained it is retrospective to the time when the mutual claims began to co-exist and prevents interest running on either,[12] and it interrupts prescription from the date of being pleaded. If not pleaded before decree passes, compensation

---

[1] *Glasgow R.I.* v. *Caldwell* (1857) 20 D. 1; *McLaren* v. *Liddell's Trs.* (1862) 24 D. 577; *Laing* v. *L.* (1862) 24 D. 1362; *Robb* v. *Gow* (1905) 8 F. 90; *Struthers* v. *Smith*, 1913 S.C. 1116.

[2] *Couper's Trs.* v. *National Bank* (1889) 16 R. 412.

[3] *Russell* v. *Farrell* (1900) 2 F. 892.   [4] *Davidson* v. *Whatmough*, 1930 S.L.T. 536.

[5] *Russell* v. *Farrell* (1900) 2 F. 892.

[6] On history see Bell, *Comm.* II, 120; *Fowler* v. *Brown*, 1916 S.C. 597.

[7] *Stuart* v. *S.* (1869) 7 M. 366; *Johnston* v. *J.* (1875) 2 R. 986.

[8] *Burrell* v. *B's Trs.*, 1916 S.C. 729.

[9] *Mitchell* v. *Mackersy* (1905) 8 F. 198.

[10] Ersk. III, 4, 12; Bell, *Comm.* II, 124; *Prin.* §575; *Cowan* v. *Gowans* (1878) 5 R. 581. *Contra*, Stair I, 18, 6.

[11] *Maxwell* v. *McCulloch's Crs.* (1738) Mor. 2550.

[12] *Cleland* v. *Stevenson* (1669) Mor. 2682; *Maxwell, supra*; but see Bell, *Comm.* II, 124.

is ineffective, and the debtor must satisfy the decree and raise a cross-action for his compensating claim.[1]

To be compensable mutual claims must be of the same kind, whether money or goods, though goods may by consent be converted into monetary terms, and not be earmarked or appropriated to any particular purpose;[2] they must be liquid, i.e. ascertained in amount,[3] and constituted against the debtor by decree or by writ or oath,[4] though this requisite has been extended to include claims which can readily be made liquid,[5] but not to claims which cannot be liquefied without inquiry or litigation;[6] and they must both be presently exigible, and not future or subject to unsatisfied condition.[7]

In case of bankruptcy, however, a liquid claim made by the trustee in bankruptcy may be opposed and compensated by a claim against the bankrupt estate, even though not liquid, but unascertained, future or contingent,[8] so long as it was acquired or constituted before notour bankruptcy.[9] There can be no compensation between a debt due before bankruptcy and a claim arising thereafter.[10]

(f) NOVATION

Novation is the substitution, by consent of parties, of a new obligation for that in existence,[11] such as the substitution of one

[1] Stair I, 18, 6; Ersk. III, 4, 19; *Paterson's Crs.* v. *McAulay* (1742) Mor. 2646.

[2] *Campbell* v. *C.* (1781) Mor. 2580; *Campbell* v. *Little* (1823) 2 S. 484; *Reid* v. *Bell* (1884) 12 R. 178; *Middlemas* v. *Gibson*, 1910 S.C. 577.

[3] Ersk. III, 4, 15; Bell, *Comm.* II, 122; *Blair Iron Co.* v. *Alison* (1855) 18 D. (H.L.) 49; *Sim* v. *Lundy* (1868) 41 Sc. Jur. 136; *Paul & Thain* v. *Royal Bank* (1869) 7 M. 361; *Gibson & Stuart* v. *Brown* (1876) 3 R. 328; *Mackie* v. *Riddell* (1874) 2 R. 115; *Pegler* v. *Northern Agric. Implement Co.* (1877) 4 R. 435; *Armour & Melvin* v. *Mitchell*, 1934 S.C. 94.

[4] Parole was allowed in *Seton* (1683) Mor. 2566; *Brown* v. *Elies* (1686) Mor. 2566; *Muir and Milliken* v. *Kennedy* (1697) Mor. 2567.

[5] *Ross* v. *Tain Mags.* (1711) Mor. 2568; *Logan* v. *Stephen* (1850) 13 D. 262; *Munro* v. *Macdonald's Exors.* (1866) 4 M. 687; *Macbride* v. *Hamilton* (1875) 2 R. 775; *Ross* v. *Ross* (1895) 22 R. 461; cf. *Henderson* v. *Turnbull*, 1909 S.C. 510.

[6] *Lawson* v. *Drysdale* (1844) 7 D. 153; *Scottish N.E. Ry.* v. *Napier* (1859) 21 D. 700. The court has sometimes allowed delay to enable the counter-claim to be ascertained: *Munro* v. *Macdonald's Exors.* (1866) 4 M. 687; *Ross* v. *R.*, *supra*; *Smart* v. *Wilkinson*, 1928 S.C. 383.

[7] *Paul & Thain* v. *Royal Bank* (1869) 7 M. 361; *Dorman Long & Co.* v. *Harrower* (1899) 1 F. 1109.

[8] *Fraser* v. *Robertson* (1881) 8 R. 347; see also *Taylor's Tr.* v. *Paul* (1888) 15 R. 313; *Smith* v. *Harrison & Co.'s Trs.* (1893) 21 R. 330.

[9] *Mill* v. *Paul* (1825) 4 S. 219; *Meldrum's Trs.* v. *Clark* (1826) 5 S. 112; *Maclean's Tr.* v. *Maclean of Coll's Tr.* (1850) 13 D. 90; *Davidson's Trs.* v. *Urquhart* (1892) 19 R. 808; *Jaffrey's Tr.* v. *Milne* (1897) 24 R. 602; *Forbes' Tr.* v. *Ogilvy* (1904) 6 F. 548.

[10] *Asphaltic Limestone Co.* v. *Glasgow Corpn.*, 1907 S.C. 463.

[11] Ersk. III, 4, 22.

form of indebtedness for another, as of a bond or bill for a number of unpaid accounts. It is always a question of interpretation whether an arrangement merely modifies an existing contract or supersedes it.[1] The presumption is that a new arrangement is in further security of, rather than in substitution for, an existing obligation[2] but it is competent to prove by parole evidence that the original claim was surrendered for the new one.[3] Where one document of debt is given in place of another, which is not surrendered, it is presumed that rights attaching to the old document still attach to the new one.[4] If an obligation is novated it is extinguished, cautioners thereon are liberated, and claims for damages or penalties thereon are discharged; claims lie only on the new obligation; thus if a bill is taken for preceding debts which are discharged, and is dishonoured, action lies on the bill, not on the debts.[5] Novation is also effected where a claim arising *ex lege*, as for reparation, is pursued to decree, or is compromised by agreement; the claim is thereby novated into a claim on the decree or on the agreement.[6] An alteration of the mode of performance, or a postponement of the time of performance, is not a novation and does not discharge but merely varies the obligation. If doubted, it must be proved by evidence competent to vary the contract.

(g) DELEGATION

Delegation is a species of novation; it is the substitution of one debtor for another, discharging the former but in other respects leaving the obligation unaltered.[7] The creditor's consent to this arrangement must be clearly proved, and the presumption is against delegation, but rather that any new debtor is a surety for

---

[1] *Hay & Kyd* v. *Powrie* (1886) 13 R. 777; *Jackson* v. *MacDiarmid* (1892) 19 R. 528; *Holmes* v. *Gardiner* (1904) 12 S.L.T. 668; *Hawthorns* v. *Whimster*, 1917, 2 S.L.T. 63; cf. *Morris* v. *Baron* [1918] A.C. 1.

[2] Stair I, 18, 8; Ersk. III, 4, 22; Bell, *Prin.* §577; *Pattie* v. *Thomson* (1843) 6 D. 350; *Fraser* v. *McLennan* (1849) 12 D. 208; *Anderson* v. *McDowal* (1865) 3 M. 727; *Hay & Kyd*, supra.

[3] *Hope Johnstone* v. *Cornwall* (1895) 22 R. 314.

[4] *Crow* v. *Weir* (1803) Hume 247; *Stevenson* v. *Campbell* (1806) Hume 247; contrast *Black* v. *Cuthbertson*, 15 Dec. 1814, F.C.; *Jackson* v. *McDiarmid* (1892) 19 R. 528; *Hope Johnstone* v. *Cornwall*, supra.

[5] Byles on *Bills*, 314; *Re Romer & Haslam* [1893] 2 Q.B. 286.

[6] *Dewar* v. *Ainslie* (1892) 20 R. 203.

[7] Ersk. III, 4, 22; Bell, *Prin.* §576; *Pearston* v. *Wilson* (1856) 17 D. 197; *McIntosh* v. *Ainslie* (1872) 10 M. 304; *Hay & Kyd* v. *Powrie* (1886) 13 R. 777; *Morton's Trs.* v. *Robertson's J.F.* (1892) 20 R. 72.

the original one and does not discharge him of liability.[1] Similarly acceptance of a new document of debt from the debtor does not imply abandonment of claims for interest under the old document.[2] Where the debtor transfers his business to another or a partnership is changed by the retiral of a partner, the undertaking of the new owner or firm to pay the outstanding debts, intimated to creditors and accepted by them, does not extinguish the former debtor's liability.[3]

(h) CONFUSIO

When the rights of both creditor and debtor come to be vested in the one person, in the same legal capacity, as by succession, gift or purchase, the obligation is extinguished,[4] unless the creditor has an interest to maintain the obligation in being[5] or the intention appears that confusio was not to operate.[6] Obligations are not necessarily extinguished *confusione* where there is a legal relationship, independent of the pecuniary incidents thereof, capable of revival by a subsequent separation of interests, as in the case of superior and vassal,[7] and dominant and servient tenements in relation to servitude.[8] Nor is the obligation extinguished where one person comes to be both creditor and cautioner for the debtor, or co-obligant with the debtor; in such a case the principal obligation still subsists.[9] Nor is it extinguished, but merely suspended, where a person is simultaneously creditor and debtor by virtue of different destinations which are both, for the time being vested in him, but which may subsequently diverge.[10]

[1] *Pearston, supra; McIntosh, supra; Hay & Kyd, supra.*

[2] *Hope Johnstone v. Cornwall* (1895) 22 R. 314.

[3] *Pollock v. Murray & Spence* (1863) 2 M. 14; see also *Morton's Tr. v. Robertson's J.F.* (1892) 20 R. 72; *Smith v. Patrick* (1901) 3 F. (H.L.) 14; Partnership Act, 1890, S. 17(3).

[4] Stair I, 18, 9; More, *Notes*, cxxxvi; Ersk. III, 4, 23; Bell, *Prin.* §580; *Dennison v. Fea's Trs.* (1873) 11 M. 392; *Murray v. Parlane's Tr.* (1890) 18 R. 287.

[5] *Fleming v. Imrie* (1868) 6 M. 363.

[6] *Murray, supra; Crichton's Trs. v. Clarke*, 1909, 1 S.L.T. 467; *Healy & Young's Tr. v. Mair's Trs.*, 1914 S.C. 893; *Sherry v. Sherry's Trs.*, 1918, 1 S.L.T. 31.

[7] *Motherwell v. Manwell* (1903) 5 F. 619; see also *Healy & Young's Tr., supra*, and contrast *King v. Johnston*, 1908 S.C. 684 (ground annual); *Colville's Trs. v. Marindin*, 1908 S.C. 911.

[8] *Walton Bros. v. Glasgow Mags.* (1876) 3 R. 1130; *Union Bank v. Daily Record (Glasgow)* (1902) 10 S.L.T. 71.

[9] Ersk. III, 4, 24; cf. *Fleming v. Imrie* (1868) 6 M. 363.

[10] Stair I, 18, 9; Ersk. III, 4, 27; *Cuninghame v. Cardross* (1680) Mor. 3038; *Cuming v. Irvine* (1726) Mor. 3042.

(j) RESOLUTIVE CONDITION

A contract is also discharged by the happening of any event such as one party's bankruptcy, which, by the terms of an express resolutive condition, is to determine the contract.

The three following grounds of discharge may be explained as cases of implied resolutive condition.

(k) SUPERVENING IMPOSSIBILITY

If a party undertakes an absolute and unconditional obligation he is *prima facie* liable if he fails to perform, even though performance has become impossible without his fault.[1] But even though there be no express condition exempting him, if without his fault performance becomes impossible, the court may in particular circumstances hold it to be an implied condition that he is excused and the contract discharged by impossibility in fact, by reason of circumstances arising, without the fault of either party, subsequent to the contract but before the date for performance, rendering performance impossible.[2] The clearest case is that of *rei interitus*, physical destruction of the subject of contract before performance or during the subsistence of the contract. This conclusion has been reached where the performance depended on the continued existence of a person or thing, parties contracted on that basis, and that person or thing has perished,[3] as where subjects let have been destroyed by fire,[4] or goods agreed to be sold have perished,[5] or a person employed died[6] or was otherwise wholly incapacitated from performance,[7] or vehicles on which advertisements were to be exhibited were withdrawn,[8] or a crop failed,[9] or a ship was seized.[10] The total destruction of the thing need not happen; it suffices if it ceases to be fit or available for the

---

[1] *Budgett* v. *Binnington* [1891] 1 Q.B. 35; cf. *Clark* v. *Glasgow Assce. Co.* (1854) 1 Macq. 668; *Gillespie* v. *Howden* (1885) 12 R. 800.

[2] Bell, *Prin.* §29; *Duncanson* v. *Scottish County Investment Co. Ltd.*, 1915 S.C. 1106, 1113.

[3] *Taylor* v. *Caldwell* (1863) 3 B. & S. 826.

[4] *Walker* v. *Bayne* (1815) 6 Paton 217; *Taylor, supra*; *Appleby* v. *Myers* (1867) L.R. 2 C.P. 651; *Allan* v. *Robertson's Trs.* (1891) 18 R. 932; *Leitch, infra*.

[5] Sale of Goods Act, 1893, S. 7; *Leitch* v. *Edinburgh Ice Co.* (1900) 2 F. 904; *Mertens* v. *Home Freeholds Co.* [1921] 2 K.B. 526.

[6] *Stubbs* v. *Holywell Ry.* (1867) L.R. 2 Ex. 311; cf. *Smith* v. *Riddell* (1886) 14 R. 95.

[7] *Robinson* v. *Davison* (1871) L.R. 6 Ex. 269; *Horlock* v. *Beal* [1916] 1 A.C. 486; *Marshall* v. *Glanville* [1917] 2 K.B. 87; *Morgan* v. *Manser* [1948] 1 K.B. 184.

[8] *Abrahams* v. *Campbell*, 1911 S.C. 353.

[9] *Howell* v. *Coupland* (1876) 1 Q.B.D. 258.

[10] *Tatem* v. *Gamboa* [1939] 1 K.B. 132.

contractual purpose.[1] In the case of premises leased the obligation is terminated only if the tenant is deprived of the major part or of essential parts of the subjects let.[2]

The contract is not, however, terminated nor a party discharged if the impossibility has been brought about or allowed to happen by the fault of the party bound to perform; he is in breach of contract.[3] If the creditor makes implement impossible he is in breach and the debtor is discharged.[4] This may be done by selling a business[5] or naming a loading port at which a ship could not be loaded.[6] If a third party makes implement by one of the contracting parties impossible the contract is to that extent discharged, unless the contract was in absolute terms.[7] Nor is a party discharged merely because performance has become more onerous,[8] or commercially impossible,[9] or unprofitable,[10] or has been delayed by strikes or other unforeseen circumstances, unless the delay was on the part of one who was, to the knowledge of the other party, supplying him.[11] Nor, probably, is he discharged by impossibility if the duty not implemented were one imposed by statute.[12]

(1) SUPERVENING ILLEGALITY OR LEGAL IMPOSSIBILITY

In the same way parties are discharged for the future if performance or further performance has become illegal, as by the outbreak of war,[13] or by change in the law of this country,[14] or of

[1] *Asfar* v. *Blundell* [1896] 1 Q.B. 123 (ship's cargo submerged and deteriorated); *Nickoll & Knight* v. *Ashton* [1901] 2 K.B. 126 (ship stranded); *Tay Salmon Fisheries* v. *Speedie*, 1929 S.C. 593 (statutory eviction); *Mackeson* v. *Boyd*, 1942 S.C. 56 (house requisitioned).

[2] *Kippen* v. *Oppenheim* (1847) 10 D. 242 (vermin infestation); *Duff* v. *Fleming* (1870) 8 M. 769 (house burned); *Allan* v. *Markland* (1882) 10 R. 383 (shop burned). Contrast *Hart's Trs.* v. *Arrol* (1903) 6 F. 36 (no *rei interitus* where licence not renewed).

[3] *Ross* v. *McFarlane* (1894) 21 R. 396; *Steel* v. *Bell* (1900) 3 F. 319.

[4] *N.B. Ry.* v. *Benhar Coal Co.* (1886) 14 R. 141; *Linton* v. *Sutherland* (1889) 17 R. 213.

[5] *Beckham* v. *Drake* (1849) 2 H.L.C. 579; *Emmens* v. *Elderton* (1853) 4 H.L.C. 624; *Hole* v. *Bradbury* (1879) L.R. 12 Ch. D. 886; *Ross* v. *McFarlane* (1894) 21 R. 396.

[6] *Charpentier & Bedex* v. *Dunn* (1878) 15 S.L.R. 726.

[7] *Maxwell's Trs.* v. *Warnock* (1900) 8 S.L.T. 144; *McCormick* v. *Dalrymple* (1904) 12 S.L.T. 85; *Duncanson* v. *Scottish County Investment Co., Ltd.*, 1915 S.C. 1106.

[8] *Blacklock & Macarthur* v. *Kirk*, 1919 S.C. 57; *Duncan* v. *Terrell*, 1918, 2 S.L.T. 340.

[9] *Hong Kong etc., Dock Co.* v. *Netherton Shipping Co.*, 1909 S.C. 34.

[10] *Blacklock, supra.*

[11] *Taylors* v. *Maclellans* (1891) 19 R. 10.

[12] *Milligan* v. *Ayr Harbour Trs.*, 1915 S.C. 937.

[13] *Davis & Primrose* v. *Clyde Shipbuilding Co.*, 1917, 1 S.L.T. 297; *Ertel Bieber* v. *Rio Tinto* [1918] A.C. 260; *Cantiere San Rocco* v. *Clyde Shipbuilding Co.*, 1923 S.C. (H.L.) 105.

[14] *In re Anglo-Russian Merchant Traders & Butt* [1917] 2 K.B. 679; *Scott* v. *Del Sel*, 1923 S.C. (H.L.) 37; cf. *McMaster* v. *Cox, McEuen & Co.*, 1921 S.C. (H.L.) 24.

the country of origin[1] or of performance.[2] The contract is not, however, discharged merely because change in the law has rendered performance more onerous or less profitable than had been contemplated,[3] or even worthless.

(m) FRUSTRATION

Where performance or further performance, though possibly not rendered wholly impossible, has been so affected by supervening circumstances for which neither party is to blame that it would differ fundamentally from the contract contemplated by the parties, the court may hold the contract frustrated and the parties discharged for the future.[4] The doctrine of frustration has developed from that of impossibility[5] and some of the cases are explicable under either head. 'The whole doctrine of frustration of contracts goes to this, that there is something which a *vis maior* (using that expression in the widest sense) has prevented the party from doing in the fulfilment of his contract.'[6] The doctrine has been held variously explained[7] as based on a judicially implied term that the occurrence of such an event as has happened would discharge the contract,[8] on the disappearance of the foundation of the contract,[9] on the basis that the court intervenes to impose what is in the circumstances the just and reasonable solution,[10] or on the basis that the obligation has been fundamentally changed by what has happened.[11]

The circumstances must be such as to render the adventure nugatory,[12] or destroy the identity of the work when resumed with

---

[1] *Scott* v. *Del Sel*, 1923 S.C. (H.L.) 37.

[2] *Ralli* v. *Compania Naviera* [1920] 2 K.B. 289; *Trinidad Shipping Co.* v. *Alston* [1920] A.C. 888; cf. *Aurdal* v. *Estrella*, 1916 S.C. 882.

[3] *Donald* v. *Leitch* (1886) 13 R. 790; *McMaster* v. *Cox, McEuen & Co.*, 1921 S.C. (H.L.) 24.

[4] The contract is neither void *ab initio* nor voidable, but discharged from the date of the frustrating event, neither party being liable for breach, nor liable to make further performance.

[5] *Tamplin* v. *Anglo-Mexican Petroleum Co. Ltd.* [1916] 2 A.C. 397, 404; *Constantine S.S. Line Ltd.* v. *Imperial Smelting Corpn. Ltd.* [1942] A.C. 154, 168.

[6] *McMaster* v. *Cox, McEuen & Co.*, 1921 S.C. (H.L.) 24, 28 per Lord Dunedin.

[7] *Metropolitan Water Board* v. *Dick Kerr & Co.* [1918] A.C. 119; *Tatem, infra*.

[8] *Tamplin, supra*.

[9] *Horlock* v. *Beal* [1916] 1 A.C. 486; *Tatem* v. *Gamboa* [1939] 1 K.B. 132. cf. *Trevalion* v. *Blanche*, 1919 S.C. 617.

[10] *Hirji Mulji* v. *Cheong Yue* [1926] A.C. 497; *Fraser* v. *Denny, Mott & Dickson, Ltd.*, 1944 S.C. (H.L.) 35.

[11] *Davis Contractors, Ltd.* v. *Fareham U.D.C.* [1956] A.C. 696.

[12] *Bensaude* v. *Thames & Mersey Marine Insce. Co.* [1897] A.C. 609.

that when interrupted,[1] or to put an end in a commercial sense to the undertaking,[2] or to make it unreasonable to require the parties to go on,[3] or to defeat the common intention of the parties,[4] and if the circumstances occurring be of such a character, they may be held to frustrate the contract, even though the frustrating event, though possibly of a less fundamental character, was foreseen and provided for in the contract.[5] If the circumstances impose delay on or interrupt performance it depends on the probable length of the delay whether the contract is frustrated or not.[6] The materiality of the delay, having regard to the nature of the contract is also relevant, and in some cases a delay of days may be enough to frustrate the contract.[7] Frustration may operate notwithstanding that the frustrating event should have been, or even was, foreseen and even provided against.[8]

The doctrine has been applied to quite exceptional delay,[9] as by ships stranding,[10] or war-time requisition,[11] to the cancellation of an event accepted as the basis and justification for the contract,[12] to the non-availability of premises,[13] or a person,[14] or a ship,[15] for the contractual purposes, and possibly to the closure of a route by which goods were to be carried,[16] but not to a mere uncontemplated turn of events.[17] It is questionable whether a feu-contract or

---

[1] *M.W.B.* v. *Dick, Kerr & Co.* [1918] A.C. 119; *Bank Line* v. *Capel* [1919] A.C. 435.
[2] *Jackson* v. *Union Marine Insce. Co.* (1874) L.R. 10 C.P. 125.
[3] *M.W.B., supra.*
[4] *Blackburn Bobbin Co.* v. *Allen* [1918] 2 K.B. 467.
[5] *M.W.B., supra; Tatem* v. *Gamboa* [1939] 1 K.B. 132.
[6] *Tamplin* v. *Anglo-Mexican Petroleum Co.* [1916] 2 A.C. 397; *Countess of Warwick S.S. Co.* v. *Le Nickel, S.A.* [1918] 1 K.B. 372; *M.W.B., supra; Nordman* v. *Rayner & Sturgess* (1916) 33 T.L.R. 87; *Unger* v. *Preston Corpn.* [1942] 1 All E.R. 200; *Morgan* v. *Manser* [1948] 1 K.B. 184.
[7] *Robinson* v. *Davison* (1871) L.R. 6 Ex. 269; *Poussard* v. *Spiers* (1876) 1 Q.B.D. 410.
[8] *Tatem, supra.*
[9] Lesser delay does not frustrate: *Davis Contractors, Ltd.* v. *Fareham U.D.C.* [1956] A.C. 696.
[10] *Jackson* v. *Union Marine Insce. Co.* (1874) L.R. 10 C.P. 125; *London & Edinburgh Shipping Co.* v. *Admiralty,* 1920 S.C. 309.
[11] *Tamplin, supra; Metropolitan Water Board* v. *Dick, Kerr & Co.* [1918] A.C. 119; *Bank Line* v. *Capel* [1919] A.C. 435; *Hirji Mulji* v. *Cheong Yue S.S. Co.* [1926] A.C. 497.
[12] *Krell* v. *Henry* [1903] 2 K.B. 740; contrast *Herne Bay Steamboat Co.* v. *Hutton* [1903] 2 K.B. 683.
[13] *Taylor* v. *Caldwell* (1863) 3 B. & S. 826; *Appleby* v. *Myers* (1867) L.R. 2 C.P. 651.
[14] *Morgan* v. *Manser* [1948] 1 K.B. 184; cf. *Nordman* v. *Rayner & Sturgess* (1916) 33 T.L.R. 87; *Unger* v. *Preston Corpn.* [1942] 1 All E.R. 200.
[15] *Nickoll & Knight* v. *Ashton* [1901] 2 K.B. 126.
[16] *Gaon* v. *Societe des Fluides Alimentaires* [1960] 2 Q.B. 348; *Tsakiroglou* v. *Noblee Thorl* [1962] A.C. 93, overruling *Carapanayoti* v. *Green* [1959] 1 Q.B. 131.
[17] *British Movietonews Ltd.* v. *London and District Cinemas* [1952] A.C. 166.

a long lease or a sale of land would necessarily be frustrated by requisition or destruction.[1]

A party cannot rely on a failure of the purpose of the contract brought about by himself as frustrating the contract; reliance cannot be placed on a self-induced frustration.[2] Nor can frustration operate if the parties are bound to perform notwithstanding a supervening event.[3]

Effect of frustration

Where frustration is held to have taken place, the contract is held discharged from that date, and both parties are released from any obligation to make further performance of the contract, and are not liable for breach in not doing so, but any rights accrued under the contract before its frustration are unaffected, and performance made to that date must be paid for.

Recovery of payments

Where a contract is held discharged on the ground of supervening impossibility, supervening illegality, or frustration, money paid in advance in consideration of performance of the contract is recoverable on the basis *condictio causa data causa non secuta*.[4] Payment must be made for the contract so far as performed, but, by settled maritime custom, advance freight is not returnable if the completion of the voyage is frustrated.[5] The contract may also provide expressly that part or the whole sum, if paid, is not recoverable even if full performance is frustrated.

(n) BREACH OF CONTRACT

Breach of contract by one party never by itself discharges the obligation[6] but, if fundamental or material in the circumstances, it amounts to a repudiation by that party, entitling but not requiring the other to treat the contract as at an end and to claim damages

---

[1] cf. *Cricklewood Property Trust* v. *Leighton's Investment Trust* [1945] A.C. 221; *Hillingdon Estates Co.* v. *Stonefield Estates, Ltd.* [1952] Ch. 627.

[2] *Bank Line* v. *Capel* [1919] A.C. 435; *Maritime National Fish Ltd.* v. *Ocean Trawlers, Ltd.* [1935] A.C. 524; *Ocean Tramp Tankers Corpn.* v. *Sovfracht* [1964] 2 Q.B. 226.

[3] *Constantine S.S. Co.* v. *Imperial Smelting Corpn.* [1942] A.C. 154.

[4] *Watson* v. *Shankland* (1872) 10 M. 142; (1873) 11 M. (H.L.) 51; *Davis & Primrose* v. *Clyde Shipbuilding Co.*, 1917, 1 S.L.T. 297; *Cantiere San Rocco* v. *Clyde Shipping Co.*, 1923 S.C. (H.L.) 105; cf. *Fibrosa* v. *Fairbairn* [1943] A.C. 32; and, as to contracts governed by English law, Law Reform (Frustrated Contracts) Act, 1943.

[5] *Byrne* v. *Schiller* (1871) L.R. 6 Ex. 319.

[6] *Heyman* v. *Darwins, Ltd.* [1942] A.C. 356; *White & Carter* v. *McGregor*, 1962 S.C. (H.L.) 1.

for a total failure in performance.[1] It is always a question of fact whether breach is so material as to justify the other party in treating it as a repudiation of the contract entitling him to rescind.[2] If he treats as a repudiation what did not amount to a fundamental breach, he is himself in breach thereby.[3] Whatever may have been the actual intention of the party in breach, if his conduct was such as to lead a reasonable person to the conclusion that he did not intend to fulfil his obligation, the other party is entitled to treat that as a repudiation.[4] Delay in payment only exceptionally justifies repudiation,[5] but delay in performance may more readily do so.[6] The bankruptcy of a party does not entitle the other to resile from or repudiate the agreement.[7]

The difficulty of deciding whether a breach amounts to a repudiation or not is particularly apparent in instalment contracts. It has been laid down[8] that the factors to be considered are the ratio which the breach bears to the contract as a whole, and the degree of probability or improbability that such a breach will be repeated. The further performance has proceeded the more difficult it will be to hold that breach in one instalment amounts to repudiation. One defective instalment may not justify repudiation while systematic defectiveness will.[9] An instalment contract may be expressed to be a series of separate contracts; then failure in one instalment will not justify repudiation for the future,[10] but *prima facie* an instalment contract is a unity, particularly where performance in one operation is impossible or very inconvenient.[11]

The other party is not obliged to accept a repudiation and treat the contract as discharged and claim damages. He may, where otherwise competent, obtain specific implement,[12] but not, unless he can do so without the repudiating party's cooperation, insist on tendering performance and exact the contract price.[13]

---

[1] *Wade* v. *Waldon*, 1909 S.C. 571; *Morrison* v. *Gray*, 1932 S.C. 712.
[2] *Grieve* v. *Konig* (1880) 7 R. 521; *Speirs, Ltd.* v. *Petersen*, 1924 S.C. 428.
[3] *Forbes* v. *Campbell* (1885) 12 R. 1065; *Wade, supra.*
[4] *Forslind* v. *Bechely-Crundall*, 1922 S.C. (H.L.) 173.
[5] *Barclay* v. *Anderston Foundry Co.* (1856) 18 D. 1190; *Rodger* v. *Fawdry*, 1950 S.C. 483.
[6] *Dunford & Elliot* v. *Macleod* (1902) 4 F. 912.
[7] *Davidson* v. *Whatmough*, 1930 S.L.T. 536.
[8] *Freeth* v. *Burr* (1874) L.R. 9 C.P. 208; *Mersey Steel & Iron Co.* v. *Naylor, Benzon & Co.* (1884) 9 App. Cas. 434; *Maple Flock Co.* v. *Universal Furniture Products Co.* [1934] 1 K.B. 148.
[9] *Govan Rope Co.* v. *Weir* (1897) 24 R. 368.
[10] *Higgins* v. *Oakbank Oil Co.* (1893) 20 R. 532.
[11] *Tancred, Arrol & Co.* v. *Steel Co. of Scotland* (1890) 17 R. (H.L.) 31.
[12] *Rodgers* v. *Fawdry*, 1950 S.C. 483, 492.
[13] *White & Carter (Councils) Ltd.* v. *McGregor*, 1962 S.C. (H.L.) 1; *sed quaere.*

(o) LAPSE OF TIME

A contract entered into for a fixed period comes to an end automatically on the expiry of that period.[1] But an exception arises in those contracts where, by the principle of tacit relocation, law, in the absence of contrary indication, implies a new contract.

In leases, if due notice of intent to terminate is necessary but is not given, or only ineffectual notice,[2] or notice not enforced,[3] law implies a renewal of the lease for a year, if originally for a year or longer, and for the same period as the former lease, if originally for a shorter period, the other terms and conditions of the former lease being held renewed.[4] But this implication is elided by contrary intention, such as an arrangement for a new lease, though not probative,[5] or continued possession after intimation of an increase of rent, despite refusal to pay the increase.[6] The implication of tacit relocation has been held inapplicable to seasonal lets, as of furnished houses, grass lands, shootings or fishings,[7] and the principle has no application to a service tenancy.[8]

In contracts of service of agricultural, domestic and similar employees[9] tacit relocation applies, and absence of notice implies renewal of the contract for the same period again, or at longest for a year, on the same terms and conditions as the former contract. It does not apply to appointments *ad vitam aut culpam*, till a retiring age, at will, or for a fixed period, nor to any contract on exceptional terms, nor to part-time employment,[10] nor, probably, to any employment for a period exceeding a year.[11] If services are rendered after the expiry of the contract period, a quasi-contractual claim lies for recompense.[10]

A partnership carried on after the expiry of the term fixed in the contract of copartnery is deemed a partnership at will, the

---

[1] cf. Partnership Act, 1890, S. 27; *Wallace* v. *W's Trs.* (1906) 8 F. 558.
[2] *Gates* v. *Blair*, 1923 S.C. 430. See also *Graham* v. *Stirling*, 1922 S.C. 90.
[3] *Taylor* v. *E. Moray* (1892) 19 R. 399.
[4] Stair II, 9, 23; Ersk. II, 6, 35 and 44; Bell, *Prin.* §1265; Rankine, *L.*, 598.
[5] *Sutherland's Trs.* v. *Miller's Trs.* (1888) 16 R. 10; *McFarlane* v. *Mitchell* (1900) 2 F. 901; *Buchanan* v. *Harris & Sheldon* (1900) 2 F. 935.
[6] *Macfarlane* v. *Mitchell* (1900) 2 F. 901.
[7] *Macharg* (1805) Mor. Removing, Appx. 4.
[8] *Dunbar's Trs.* v. *Bruce* (1900) 3 F. 137; *Sinclair* v. *Tod*, 1907 S.C. 1038.
[9] Bell, *Prin.* §187; *Campbell* v. *Fyfe* (1851) 13 D. 1041; *Cameron* v. *Scott* (1870) 9 M. 233; *Morrison* v. *Abernethy School Board* (1876) 3 R. 945; *Lennox* v. *Allan* (1880) 8 R. 38; *Stanley* v. *Hanway* (1911) 48 S.L.R. 757.
[10] *Lennox, supra.*
[11] *Brenan* v. *Campbell's Trs.* (1898) 25 R. 423.

remaining terms of the former contract remaining in force so far as consistent with a partnership at will.[1]

(p) PRESCRIPTION

A contractual obligation or claim arising therefrom is wholly extinguished by the running of the long negative prescription,[2] now of 20 years.[3] Thereafter not even admission or writ renders the claim exigible, and reference to oath is incompetent.[4] This applies to claims for payment,[5] for damages,[6] a claim to reduce a contract for fraud,[7] to recover property lent,[8] to recover money in bank on deposit receipt[9] or current account,[10] or money paid by mistake.[11] It does not, however, exclude the right to challenge a deed as a forgery or intrinsically null,[12] or to recover stolen property,[13] or property *extra commercium* but wrongly disposed of.[14]

Prescription does not, however, extinguish a right in the nature of *res merae facultatis*, exigible or not at the creditor's pleasure, such as the right to exact feu-duties (though the right to a particular termly payment will prescribe),[15] or a contractual right to open a doorway into a common stair.[16]

[1] Partnership Act, 1890, S. 27; *Neilson* v. *Mossend Iron Co.* (1886) 13 R. (H.L.) 50; *Browns* v. *Kilsyth Police Commrs.* (1886) 13 R. 515; *McGown* v. *Henderson*, 1914 S.C. 839.

[2] Prescription Acts, 1469, 1474 and 1617; Stair II, 10, 12; Ersk. III, 7, 7; Bell, *Prin.* §607; Napier, 542; *Kermack* v. *K.* (1874) 2 R. 156.

[3] Conveyancing (Sc.) Act, 1924, S. 17; *Sutherland C.C.* v. *Macdonald*, 1935 S.C. 915; *Marr's Exrx.* v. *Marr's Trs.*, 1936 S.C. 64; the period is still 40 years for extinction of servitudes, public rights of way or other public rights. With effect from 25th July 1976 the period is five years unless within that period a relevant claim has been made in relation to the obligation, or the subsistence of the obligation has been relevantly acknowledged: certain periods are excluded from account in computing the five years: Prescription and Limitation (Sc.) Act, 1973, S. 6 and Sch. 1. The period for servitudes, public rights of way, and other public rights is reduced to 20 years from the same date: 1973 Act, S. 8.

[4] *Napier* v. *Campbell* (1703) Mor. 10656; *Kermack, supra*.

[5] Bell, *Prin.* §608; *Sutherland C.C., supra*; *Marr's Exrx.* v. *Marr's Trs.*, 1936 S.C. 64 (bond); *Yuill's Trs.* v. *Maclachlan's Trs.*, 1939 S.C. (H.L.) 40 (bond of corroboration).

[6] *Cooke* v. *Falconer's Reps.* (1850) 13 D. 157.

[7] *Cubbison* v. *Hyslop* (1837) 16 S. 112, 119.

[8] *Aberscherder Kirk Session* v. *Gemrie Kirk Session* (1633) Mor. 10972.

[9] *Bertram Gardner & Co.'s Tr.* v. *King's Remembrancer*, 1920 S.C. 555.

[10] *Macdonald* v. *N. of S. Bank*, 1942 S.C. 369.

[11] *Edinburgh Mags.* v. *Heriot's Trust* (1900) 7 S.L.T. 371.

[12] *Kinloch* v. *Bell* (1867) 5 M. 360.

[13] Stair II, 12, 10; Prescription Act, 1973, Sch. 3.

[14] *Edinburgh Presbytery* v. *Edinburgh University* (1890) 28 S.L.R. 567; 1973 Act, Sch. 3.

[15] Ersk. III, 7, 10; Bell, *Prin.* §2017; *D. Buccleuch* v. *Officers of State* (1770) Mor. 10751; *Reid's Trs.* v. *Duchess of Sutherland* (1881) 8 R. 509; *Smith* v. *Stewart* (1884) 11 R. 921; 1973 Act, Sch. 3.

[16] *Gellatly* v. *Arrol* (1863) 1 M. 592.

The prescriptive period runs from the time when enforcement of the claim by action was first possible.[1] At common law periods during which the creditor was *non valens agere*, legally incapacitated from suing, by minority[2] or insanity,[3] were not counted, but since 1924[4] no deduction is allowed for the creditor's minority or legal disability.

Interruption of prescription

The running of prescription may be defeated at any time before it expires[5] by interruption, which may be effected judicially, by citation (which itself, however, prescribes in seven years unless renewed),[6] calling of an action in court (which itself prescribes in 20 years),[7] claiming in a sequestration[8] or multiplepoinding,[9] or doing diligence on a decree,[10] or extra-judicially, by actings, such as claiming principal or interest, or by a debtor's payment of interest on his debt,[11] or by acknowledgment of the existence of the debt,[12] or placing funds in dispute in neutral custody.[13]

Prescription after 1976

From 25 July 1976 obligations to pay money due as interest, an annuity, feuduty, ground annual, rent, payment for occupancy or use of land, periodical payment under a land obligation, under a bill of exchange or promisory note, and any other obligation arising from, or by reason of any breach of, a contract or promise, are extinguished by the lapse of five years.[14] An obligation constituted or evidenced by probative writ, not being a cautionary obligation nor one above-mentioned, subsists for twenty years and is then extinguished.[15] In each category if a 'relevant claim'[3] has been made in relation to the obligation, or its

[1] *Cooke, supra*; *Macdonald, supra*; see also *Simpson* v. *Marshall* (1900) 2 F. 447.

[2] Prescription Act, 1469, 1474, 1617; *Buchanan* v. *Bogle* (1847) 9 D. 686.

[3] Bell, *Prin.* §627.   [4] Conveyancing (Sc.) Act, 1924, S. 17(1).

[5] *Simpson* v. *Marshall* (1900) 2 F. 447.

[6] Prescription Act, 1669; *Cameron* v. *Macdonald* (1761) Mor. 11331.

[7] Bell, *Prin.* §615; *Pillans* v. *Sibbald* (1897) 5 S.L.T. 186; cf. *Bank of Scotland* v. *Fergusson* (1898) 1 F. 96.

[8] Bankruptcy (Sc.) Act, 1913, S. 105.

[9] *National Bank* v. *Hope* (1837) 16 S. 177.

[10] Bell, *Prin.* §621. Judicial interruption is defined by the Prescription Act, 1973, S. 4, but in relation to positive prescription only.

[11] *Kermack* v. *K.* (1874) 2 R. 156. The payment of interest is proveable only by writ.

[12] *Briggs* v. *Swan's Exors.* (1854) 16 D. 385; *Marr's Exrx.* v. *Marr's Trs.*, 1936 S.C. 64.

[13] *Simpson, supra*.

[14] Prescription and Limitation (Sc.) Act, 1973, S. 6 and Sch. 1(1).

[15] Ibid., S. 6 and Sch. 1(2) and S. 7.

[16] Defined, ibid., S. 9.

subsistence been 'relevantly acknowledged',[1] the prescriptive period is interrupted and recommences. Any period during which the creditor was induced to refrain from making a relevant claim by fraud on the part of the debtor or error induced by the debtor, or during which the original creditor was under legal disability, is not counted as part of the prescriptive period.[2]

(q) MORA

Lapse of time short of the prescriptive period does not extinguish a right,[3] but is a factor, particularly when coupled with failure to attempt to assert a right, or acquiescence, which may yield an inference that a claim is not insisted in or has been discharged.[4]

[1] Defined, ibid., S. 10.

[2] Ibid., S. 6(4).

[3] *Cuninghame* v. *Boswell* (1868) 6 M. 890; *Rankine* v. *Logie Den Land Co.* (1902) 4 F. 1074.

[4] *Cooke* v. *Falconer's Reps.* (1850) 13 D. 157, 166; *McKenzie's Exrx.* v. *Morrison's Trs.*, 1930 S.C. 830; *Smellie's Exrx.* v. *S.*, 1933 S.C. 725.

CHAPTER 38

MONOPOLIES, RESTRICTIVE TRADE PRACTICES AND FAIR TRADING

AGREEMENTS and contracts restrictive of competition and of the free working of economic forces in trade have been attacked by legislation since the sixteenth century.[1] Monopolies were commonly granted by the Crown until in England in 1623 the Statute of Monopolies declared all monopolies for the sole buying, selling, making or working of things were illegal, except letters patent for the sole working or making of any manner of new manufacture within the realm to the first true inventor of such manufactures, an exception which is the basis of the modern patents for inventions,[2] and the privileges of chartered corporations and companies. By the nineteenth century monopolies and near-monopolies existed again, but created by the agreements of traders seeking to corner the market in various commodities, to restrict or eliminate competition, and to regulate prices.

Such agreements were in restraint of trade and the courts developed the test of the validity of such contracts as being their reasonableness.[3] The modern test of validity of such an agreement at common law is that all restraints on freedom of trade, whether partial or general, are *prima facie* contrary to public policy and void, unless justifiable in the circumstances of particular cases if the restriction is reasonable in the interests both of the parties concerned and of the public.[4] If a contract in restraint of trade is *ex facie* unreasonable the court will not enforce it,[5] nor will it if satisfied of its unreasonableness be a party to the

---

[1] See generally Wilberforce, Campbell and Elles, *Restrictive Trade Practices and Monopolies*; Korah, *Monopolies and Restrictive Practices*; Hunter, *Competition and the Law*.

[2] On these see Ch. 108, *infra*.

[3] The leading cases were *Mitchel* v. *Reynolds* (1711) 1 P.Wms. 181; *Davies* v. *Mason* (1793) 5 T.R. 118; *Horner* v. *Graves* (1831) 7 Bing. 735; *Hilton* v. *Eckersley* (1856) 6 E. & B. 47; *Leather Cloth Co.* v. *Lorsont* (1869) L.R. 9 Eq. 345; *Mogul* v. *MacGregor* [1892] A.C. 25; *Evans* v. *Heathcote* [1918] 1 K.B. 418.

[4] *Nordenfelt* v. *Maxim Nordenfelt Guns and Ammunition Co.* [1894] A.C. 535, 565; *Mason* v. *Provident Clothing Co.* [1913] A.C. 724.

[5] *North Western Salt Co.* v. *Electrolytic Alkali Co.* [1914] A.C. 461.

contract.[1] Nevertheless the courts upheld many agreements providing for price-maintenance.[2]

They might also be attacked as being an actionable conspiracy to injure, if the predominant purpose of the combination was wilfully to injure a man in his trade,[3] or an indictable conspiracy.[4]

The invalidity of restraints on trade extends not only to contractual restraints but to involuntary restraints imposed by trade associations, professional bodies,[5] the rules of friendly societies,[6] and the like on members.

The Monopolies and Restrictive Practices (Inquiry and Control) Act, 1948,[7] established the Monopolies Commission[8] (now the Monopolies and Mergers Commission) to investigate on a reference to it whether monopoly conditions, as defined,[9] existed as respects the supply of goods of any description, the application of any process to goods, or exports of goods from the U.K., and to report on restrictive practices in industry.[10] Common restrictive practices found to exist are price-fixing agreements among manufacturers, regulation by trade associations of the terms on which members may deal with their customers, agreements regulating each producer's share of total output, or of sales, territory preservation agreements, agreements that members are to specialize in particular products, tendering agreements, trade mark protection agreements, resale price maintenance agreements,[11] agreements for rebates to particular buyers, exclusive dealing agreements, and patent agreements.

The Monopolies and Mergers Act, 1965, extended the scope of investigations to the supply of services of any description,

[1] *McEllistrim* v. *Ballymacelligot Co-operative Socy.* [1919] A.C. 548; *Esso Petroleum Co.* v. *Harper's Garage* [1968] A.C. 269.

[2] e.g. *English Hop Growers* v. *Dering* [1928] 2 K.B. 174; *Palmolive Co.* v. *Freedman* [1928] Ch. 264.

[3] *Mogul S.S. Co.* v. *McGregor* [1892] A.C. 25; *Allen* v. *Flood* [1897] A.C. 1; *Quinn* v. *Leathem* [1901] A.C. 495; *Crofter Co.* v. *Veitch*, 1942 S.C. (H.L.) 1.

[4] *Mulcahy* v. *R.* (1868) 3 H.L. 306, 317; *Crofter Co.*, *supra*.

[5] *Pharmaceutical Socy.* v. *Dickson* [1970] A.C. 403.

[6] *Swaine* v. *Wilson* (1889) 24 Q.B.D. 252.

[7] Amended by Monopolies and Restrictive Practices Commission Act, 1953, Restrictive Trade Practices Act, 1956, Part III, Monopolies and Mergers Act, 1965, Restrictive Trade Practices Act, 1968, and replaced by Fair Trading Act, 1973.

[8] Fair Trading Act, 1973, S. 4. See generally Guenault and Jackson, *Control of Monopoly in the U.K.*; Rowley, *The British Monopolies Commission*.

[9] 1973 Act, Ss. 6–11.

[10] 1973 Act, Ss. 6–11. The major report is the Report on Collective Discrimination (Cmd. 9504, 1955).

[11] Of this last the best known specimen is the Net Book Agreement, whereby all booksellers sell nearly all books at prices fixed by the publishers, on which see *Re Net Book Agreement* [1962] 3 All E.R. 751.

including both the rendering of services to order and the provision of services by making them available to potential users, but not the rendering of services under a contract of service.

The Director-General of Fair Trading has powers[1] to require information where he believes that a monopoly situation may exist in relation to the supply of goods or services of any description, or in relation to exports, and if he thinks that a monopoly situation exists or may exist in relation to supply of goods or services or export of goods, he may make a monopoly reference to the Commission.[2] Ministers may also make monopoly references.[3] The Commission must report thereon, and if it finds that a monopoly situation exists and specifies effects adverse to the public interest which the facts have or may be expected to have the Secretary of State may[4] make an order declaring it unlawful to make or carry out any specified agreement, requiring any party to terminate the agreement, declare it unlawful to withhold supplies or services or to impose conditions on the supply of goods or services, declare it unlawful to discriminate or to give preferences, to charge other than listed prices, to notify recommended resale prices, or may prohibit the acquisition by any person of the undertaking or assets of another.

The merger of newspapers or of other enterprises may be referred to the Commission.[5]

General references may be made to the Commission as to the effect on the public interest of specified practices or practices of a specified class which appear to be uncompetitive or may preserve monopoly situations.[6]

When the Commission has reported on a monopoly or a non-newspaper merger reference, that a monopoly situation exists or the merger may be against the public interest, the Director must consult the parties to try to obtain from them undertakings to take requisite action to remedy the defect or prevent the adverse effects specified. If undertakings are not obtained the Director may advise the Minister to make an order, and must keep the situation under review.[7]

---

[1] 1973 Act, Ss. 44–46.
[2] 1973 Act, Ss. 47–50.
[3] 1973 Act, S. 51.
[4] 1973 Act, S. 56 and Sch. 8. As to orders see also Ss. 90–93.
[5] 1973 Act, Ss. 57–77.
[6] 1973 Act, Ss. 78–80, 84.
[7] 1973 Act, S. 88.

Restrictive practices

The Restrictive Trade Practices Act, 1956, amended by the Fair Trading Act, 1973, established the Restrictive Practices Court,[1] and requires registration formerly with the Registrar of Restrictive Trading Agreements and now with the Director-General of Fair Trading of agreements between two or more persons carrying on business in the U.K. in the production or supply of goods,[2] or in the application to goods of any process of manufacture,[3] under which restrictions are accepted by two or more parties in respect of prices, terms or conditions subject to which goods are to be supplied or acquired or any such process to be applied, quantities or descriptions of goods, processes of manufacture to be applied to any goods, or the persons or classes of persons to, for, or from whom, or the places in or from which, goods are to be supplied or acquired, or any such process applied.[4] 'Agreement' includes any agreement or arrangement,[5] however informal, legally enforceable or not, and the Act applies to agreements made by a trade association as if made between all members and to recommendations by an association to its members.[6] Certain restrictions are to be disregarded and certain agreements are excepted,[7] certain agreements of importance to the national economy may be exempted from registration,[8] and agreements made at the request of certain government departments designed to prevent or restrict increases in prices are exempted from registration[9] but certain kinds of 'information agreements' are liable to registration.[10]

Judicial Investigation of registered agreements

Agreements registered under the Act are brought formerly by the Registrar and now by the Director General of Fair Trading

[1] Ss. 2–5. On the court see generally Stevens and Yamey, *The Restrictive Practices Court*.

[2] Defined: S. 36(1).

[3] *Re Scottish Monumental Sculptors* (1965) L.R. 5 R.P. 437.

[4] Non-registrable agreements remain subject to common law principles as to contracts in restraint of trade.

[5] Discussed in *Re Austin Motor Car Co. Ltd.'s Agreements* (1958) L.R. 1 R.P. 6; *Re British Basic Slag Ltd.'s Agreements* (1963) L.R. 4 R.P. 116.

[6] S. 6 amended 1973 Act, S. 95; *Re Electrical Installations at Exeter Hospital Agreement* [1970] 1 W.L.R. 1391. An industrial and provident society may be excepted from this section: 1973 Act, S. 98.

[7] Ss. 7–8, as amended by Restrictive Trade Practices Act, 1968, S. 4 and Fair Trading Act, 1973, Ss. 99–101.

[8] Restrictive Trade Practices Act, 1968, S. 1.

[9] 1968 Act, Ss. 2–3.

[10] Ibid., S. 5.

before the Restrictive Practices Court for it to declare whether or not any restrictions by virtue of which an agreement was registered are contrary to the public interest. If they are contrary, they are void, in which case the Court may make an order to restrain all persons party to the agreement from giving effect to or enforcing it, or making other agreements to the like effect.[1] There is a presumption that a restriction accepted in pursuance of a registered agreement is contrary to the public interest, and the onus is on the parties to the agreement to satisfy the court that a particular restriction is not contrary to the public interest, which may be done only by escaping through one or other of eight specified 'gateways' in, and also satisfying the concluding 'tailpiece' of, the section.[2]

The 'gateways' are, stated briefly: if the court is satisfied that

(a) the restriction is reasonably necessary to protect the public against injury;[3]

(b) removal of the restriction would deny to the public other specific and substantial benefits or advantages enjoyed or likely to be enjoyed by them;[4]

(c) the restriction is reasonably necessary to counteract measures taken by another to prevent or restrict competition;[5]

(d) the restriction is reasonably necessary to enable the parties to the agreement to negotiate fair terms with a party controlling a preponderant part of the trade;[6]

(e) removal of the restriction would have an adverse effect on the general level of unemployment in that industry;[7]

---

[1] 1956 Act, S. 20, extended by 1973 Act, S. 104; cf. *Re Black Bolt and Nut Association's Agreement* (No. 2) (1962) L.R. 3 R.P. 43; *Re Newspaper Proprietors Assocn. Ltd.* (1961) L.R. 2 R.P. 453; *Re Bolt and Nut Stockholders' Assocn.'s Agreement* (1966) L.R. 6 R.P. 126.

[2] S. 21. A recommendation from a retailers' federation to its members may be stopped by injunction, being equivalent to an agreement contrary to the public interest under S. 21: *Daily Mirror Newspapers* v. *Gardner* [1968] 2 All E.R. 163; *Brekkes* v. *Cattel* [1971] 1 All E.R. 1031.

[3] *Re Chemists' Federation Agreement* (1958) L.R. 1 R.P. 75; *Re Tyre Register Agreement* [1963] 1 All E.R. 890.

[4] *Wholesale and Retail Bakers of Scotland Association Agreement* (1960) L.R. 1 R.P. 347; 1960 S.L.T. 130; *Re Black Bolt and Nut Association's Agreement* (1960) L.R. 2 R.P. 50; *Re Net Book Agreement* (1962) L.R. 3 R.P. 246; *Re Distant Water Vessels Development Scheme* (1966) L.R. 6 R.P. 242.

[5] *Re National Sulphuric Acid Association's Agreement* (1963) L.R. 4 R.P. 169.

[6] *Re Water Tube Boilermakers' Agreement* (1959) L.R. 1 R.P. 285; *Re Associated Transformer Manufacturers' Agreement* (1961) L.R. 2 R.P. 295.

[7] *Re Yarn Spinners' Agreement* (1959) L.R. 1 R.P. 118; *Re British Jute Trade Council's Agreements* (1963) L.R. 4 R.P. 399.

(f) removal of the restriction would cause a reduction in exports;[1]

(g) the restriction is reasonably required for the maintenance of any other restriction accepted by the parties and not contrary to the public interest;[2]

(h)[3] the restriction does not directly or indirectly restrict or discourage competition to any material degree in any relevant trade or industry and is not likely to do so.

The 'tailpiece'[4] requires the court in any case to be satisfied in addition that the restriction is not unreasonable having regard to the balance between the circumstances and any detriment to the public resulting from the operation of the restriction.[5]

The court may discharge any previous declaration and order by it in respect of any restriction, and make another declaration and order.[6] It may also punish contempt of court[7] or breach of undertakings given to the court.[8]

The Director-General of Fair Trading may apply to the court for an interim order.[9]

Restrictive practices as to services

Part I of the 1956 Act may be extended to agreements as to the supply of services under which restrictions are accepted by two or more parties.[10]

Resale price maintenance

At common law, it was permissible for a seller to take the buyer bound not to resell below a stated price,[11] and to enforce such a provision in a contract by a clause providing for payment of

---

[1] *Re Water Tube Boilermakers' Agreement, supra*; *Re Associated Transformer Manufacturers' Agreement, supra.*

[2] *Re Black Bolt and Nut, supra*; *Re Standard Metal Window Companies' Agreements* (1962) L.R. 3 R.P. 198.

[3] Added by Restrictive Trade Practices Act, 1968, S. 10. This defence seem particularly appropriate for 'information agreements'.

[4] S. 21, at end.

[5] *Re Net Book Agreement, supra*; *Re National Sulphuric Acid Association's Agreement* (1963) L.R. 4 R.P. 169.

[6] S. 22; *Re British Paper and Board Makers' Association's Agreement* (1966) L.R. 6 R.P. 161.

[7] *Re A.G.'s application, A.G. v. Butterworth* (1962) L.R. 3 R.P. 327.

[8] *Re Galvanised Tank Mfrs. Agreement* (1965) L.R. 5 R.P. 315.

[9] 1973 Act, S. 105, adding S. 21A to 1956 Act.

[10] 1973 Act, Ss. 107–117.

[11] *Elliman v. Carrington* [1901] 2 Ch. 275; *Palmolive Co. v. Freedman* [1928] Ch. 264. On the subject in general see Yamey, *Resale Price Maintenance*; Pickering, *Resale Price Maintenance in Practice.*

liquidate damages if the buyer contravened,[1] or by the seller's trade association black-listing the buyer,[2] or demanding that he make a payment to it.[3]

The Restrictive Trade Practices Act, 1956, makes it unlawful for two or more persons to make or carry out any agreement or recommendation for enforcing conditions as to resale prices by withholding supplies, refusing trade terms, supplying only persons who will withhold supplies, or for imposing sanctions on suppliers who do not impose or enforce resale price maintenance conditions, or for the conduct of trade courts in connection therewith.[4] But where the goods are sold by a supplier subject to a condition as to resale price,[5] that condition may be enforced by the supplier against any person who subsequently acquires the goods with notice of the condition as if he had been a party thereto, except in respect of the resale of the goods by a person who acquires them otherwise than for the purpose of resale in the course of business,[6] or by any person who acquires them, whether immediately or not, from such a person, and in respect of resale of any goods under order of a court, or by any person who acquires them, after such resale.[7] In short S. 24 prohibits collective enforcement of resale price maintenance conditions in sale or hire-purchase, but S. 25 permits individual enforcement of such conditions, by interdict against a party in breach restraining him from reselling goods of the same or any other description.

The Resale Prices Act, 1964, declared void any term or condition of a contract for the sale of goods by a supplier to a dealer, or any agreement between a supplier and a dealer relating to such a sale, in so far as it purports to establish or provide for the establishment of minimum prices to be charged on the resale of the goods to a dealer, or to notify dealers of a price stated to be the minimum resale price of the goods in the U.K. But it is permissible to notify a price recommended as appropriate for the

---

[1] *Dunlop Tyre Co.* v. *New Garage Co.* [1915] A.C. 79.

[2] *Ware & de Freville* v. *M.T.A.* [1921] 3 K.B. 40.

[3] Held in *Thorne* v. *M.T.A.* [1936] A.C. 797 not to amount to blackmail.

[4] S. 24.

[5] Including a condition as to discount, S. 26.

[6] e.g. a user or consumer.

[7] Ibid., S. 25. This overrides such cases as *Dunlop* v. *Selfridge* [1915] A.C. 847, which held that a condition could not transmit with goods though it could with land. S. 25 is not repealed by the 1964 Act (next paragraph) and still applies to agreements exempted under the 1964 Act. On S. 25 see *Goodyear Tyre Co.* v. *Lancashire Batteries* [1958] 3 All E.R. 7; *Beecham Foods Ltd.* v. *North Supplies* [1959] 2 All E.R. 336; *Bulpitt* v. *Bellman* (1962) L.R. 3 R.P. 62.

resale of goods.[1] Indirect enforcement by withholding supplies from dealers on the ground of actual or apprehended price-cutting is unlawful, unless justifiable on some other ground,[2] but this does not apply where the dealer has supplied similar goods which have been used as loss leaders.[3] Compliance with these provisions is a duty, breach of which is actionable as a breach of statutory duty by any person affected by a contravention, and enforceable by civil proceedings on behalf of the Crown for interdict or declarator.[4]

Goods of certain classes may, on reference made by the Registrar of Restrictive Trading Agreements,[5] be exempted by the Restrictive Practices Court if it appears to that court that in default of a system of maintained resale prices applicable to those goods (a) the quality or variety of goods would be substantially reduced, or (b) the number of establishments selling the goods would be reduced, or (c) the prices would in general be increased, or (d) the goods would be sold by retail under conditions likely to cause danger to health in consequence of their misuse, or (e) any necessary services actually provided in connection with or after the sale of the goods by retail would cease to be so provided or would be substantially reduced to the detriment of the public. The onus of proof is on the supplier claiming exemption.[6] Until and unless the Court refuses to grant exemption in respect of a class of goods, a contractual term as to resale price is valid and enforceable under S. 25 of the 1956 Act.[7]

Fair trading

The Fair Trading Act, 1973, authorized the appointment of a Director-General of Fair Trading to keep under review the carrying on of commercial activities in the United Kingdom relating to supply of goods or services so as to discover practices which may adversely effect the economic interests of consumers.[8] Consumer

---

[1] 1964 Act, S. 1.
[2] Ibid., S. 2; *Oxford Printing Co.* v. *Letraset* [1970] 2 All E.R. 815.
[3] Ibid., S. 3.
[4] Ibid., S. 4.
[5] On the registrar's duty to register goods for which exemption has been claimed, and to refer them to the Court, see Ss. 6–8.
[6] Ibid., S. 5; *Re Chocolate and Sugar Confectionery Reference* (1967) L.R. 6 R.P. 338; *Re Footwear Reference* (1968) L.R. 6 R.P. 398. Ethical and proprietary drugs have been exempted: *Re Medicaments Reference* [1970] 1 W.L.R. 1339. The criteria of public interest are not the same as under the 1956 Act, S. 21.
[7] *E.M.I. Records, Ltd.* v. *Morris* [1965] 2 All E.R. 781.
[8] 1973 Act, Ss. 1–2.

trade practices as defined[1] may be referred by the Director to the Consumer Protection Advisory Committee for investigation and report and the Secretary of State may by order give effect to proposals contained in the report.[2] An order is enforceable by the local weights and measures authority.[3] He may also seek to make a person refrain from conduct in business which is detrimental to the interests of consumers in the U.K. and is to be regarded as unfair to consumers, and may take proceedings against such person before the Restrictive Practices Court or, in certain cases, an alternative court.[4]

Particular kinds of trading schemes are made subject to control.[5]

The Director-General of Fair Trading is also the authority supervising contracts of moneylending and pawnbroking, hiring, and hire-purchase.[6]

---

[1] 1973 Act, S. 13.

[2] 1973 Act, Ss. 13–32. As to procedure in references see Ss. 81–83. A contract for the supply of goods or services is not void or unenforceable by reason only of a contravention of an order under S. 22: S. 26. Orders are enforced by the local weights and measures authority: S. 27.

[3] 1973 Act, S. 27.

[4] 1973 Act, Ss. 34–43.

[5] 1973 Act, Ss. 118–123.

[6] Consumer Credit Act, 1974.

PART 2

THE PARTICULAR CONTRACTS

The chapters on the particular contracts deal with the specialties applicable to contracts of particular kinds or relating to particular subject-matter. Roman law divided contracts according to their mode of constitution, into contracts *re, verbis, literis* and *consensu,* constituted respectively by actual transfer of property, by solemn words, by writing, and by bare consent.[1] This classification has in general been adopted by Scots law[2] and the contracts within each class in Scots law resemble those of the Roman law. Real contracts required not only consent, which would create only a personal right to payment or performance, but that something should be actually paid or transferred by one party to constitute the obligation against the other; this category covered loan for consumption, loan for use, deposit and pledge. Scots law has adopted this category.[3] But in Scots law no contract need be constituted by particular solemn words so that the class of verbal obligations has come in Scots law to mean all contracts which may be entered into orally,[4] and the title of contracts *literis* is applied in Scots law to those which by statute and custom must be constituted by solemnly authenticated writing.[5] Apart from the case of contracts of service for longer than one year, these are all contracts relating to heritable property, and discussed in that context.[6] Consensual contracts in Scots, as in Roman law, are those perfected by consent alone, namely sale, hiring, partnership and mandate, and others which have developed since the Roman law, though this category is confined in Scots law to such contracts concerning moveables.[7] In the Scots law to sale, location, society and mandate, others have been added as recognized consensual contracts, such as insurance.

In modern practice, however, it is more satisfactory to depart from this classification and order of exposition and to categorize contracts differently. For one thing new kinds of contracts unknown to Roman law have developed, such as insurance and

---

[1] Inst. III, 13, 2; Dig. XIX, 5, 5; Buckland, 433.
[2] Stair I, 10, 11–12; Bankt. 1, 11, 20; Ersk. III, 1, 17–18; III, 2, 1; III, 3, 1; Bell, *Comm.* I, 335; *Prin.* §16–18.
[3] Stair I, 10, 11; Ersk. III, 1, 17; Chaps. 97, 98 and 100, *infra.*
[4] Stair, *supra*; Ersk. III, 1, 17; III, 2, 1.
[5] Stair, *supra*; Bankt. I, 11, 22; Ersk. III, 2, 2 and 5–6; *Paterson* v. *P.* (1897) 25 R. 144, 173.
[6] Book V, 2, *infra.*   [7] Stair, *supra*; Ersk. III, 3, 1.

hire-purchase; for another, some contracts, such as sale and transfer of property in security, have in Scots law developed very different rules in their applications to different kinds of property, and cannot properly be examined save in relation to the principles regulating each kind of property. A more convenient classification accordingly is into (a) contracts dealing with business relations and not essentially involving rights in any kind of property;[1] (b) contracts relating to transactions with corporeal heritable property, such as contracts of feu, sale of land, excambion, lease, creation of servitude rights, creation of rights in security over heritage, and related contracts;[2] (c) contracts relating to transactions with incorporeal heritable rights, such as with leases;[3] (d) contracts relating to transactions with corporeal moveable property or goods, such as loan, deposit, hiring, exchange, sale of goods, creation of rights in security over moveables, and similar contracts;[4] and (e) contracts relating to transactions with incorporeal moveable rights, such as to sell or transfer shares in companies or copyright.[5] In the four latter categories the contracts cannot be properly studied unrelated to the rights recognized in the kinds of property concerned. In relation to each of these four classes the contracts can be said generally to relate to temporary transfers of possession, e.g. loan, lease, to outright transfer of property in the subjects, e.g. sale, and to transfer of property or of possession in security of the repayment of money or the performance of some obligation, the property or possession to be re-transferred on repayment or performance being made. In addition to contracts falling within one or other of these categories there are instances of unclassifiable and innominate contracts, not assignable to any nominate category.[6]

It is a question of fact in each case, having regard to the substance of the transaction rather than its language, whether a transaction belongs to one category rather than another. Thus the transfer of goods without price or other consideration is gift;[7] if the consideration is the delivery of other goods, it is permutation or barter,[8] but if the consideration is money, or partly goods and partly money, or either goods or money, it is sale.[9] Again it may be a question whether a transaction is sale or an invitation to buy,[10]

---

[1] Chaps. 39–51, *infra*.   [2] Chaps. 76, 81–86, *infra*.
[3] Chaps. 90–92, *infra*.   [4] Chaps. 97–104, *infra*.
[5] Chaps. 109–110, *infra*.   [6] Chap. 51, *infra*.
[7] Ch. 101, *infra*.   [8] Ch. 102, *infra*.
[9] *Aldridge* v. *Thomson* (1857) 7 E. & B. 885; S. *Australian Ins. Co.* v. *Randell* (1869) L.R. 3 P.C. 101.
[10] *Pharmaceutical Socy.* v. *Boots* [1953] 1 Q.B. 401.

sale and return or agency,[1] sale and return or sale on approval,[2] sale or sale on commission,[3] sale or wager,[4] sale or work and materials,[5] sale or hire-purchase,[6] sale or hire,[7] sale or contract to do work as agent,[8] sale or pledge,[9] sale or option to buy,[10] sale or agency,[11] sale or loan,[12] sale or lease,[13] sale or joint adventure,[14] sale or donation of a business.[15]

[1] *Weiner* v. *Harris* [1910] 1 K.B. 285; *Michelin* v. *Macfarlane* (1917) 55 S.L.R. 35 (H.L.)

[2] *Brown* v. *Marr* (1880) 7 R. 427.   [3] *The Prinz Adalbert* [1917] A.C. 586.

[4] *Rourke* v. *Short* (1856) 5 E. & B. 904.

[5] *Clay* v. *Yates* (1856) 1 H. & N. 73; *Lee* v. *Griffin* (1861) 1 B. & S. 272; *Anglo-Egyptian Nav. Co.* v. *Rennie* (1875) L.R. 10 C.P. 271; *Robinson* v. *Graves* [1935] 1 K.B. 579; *Marcel* v. *Tapper* [1953] 1 All E.R. 15; *Newman* v. *Lipman* [1951] 1 K.B. 333.

[6] *Helby* v. *Matthews* [1895] A.C. 471; *Lee* v. *Butler* [1893] 2 Q.B. 318; *Muirhead & Turnbull* v. *Dickson* (1905) 7 F. 686.

[7] *Murdoch* v. *Greig* (1889) 16 R. 396; *Brechin Auction Co.* v. *Reid* (1895) 22 R. 711.

[8] *Lamb* v. *Goring Brick Co.* [1932] 1 K.B. 710.

[9] *The Orteric* [1920] A.C. 724; *Gavin's Trs.* v. *Fraser*, 1920 S.C. 674; *G. and C. Finance Corpn.* v. *Brown*, 1961 S.L.T. 408.

[10] *Marten* v. *Whale* [1917] 2 K.B. 480.

[11] *Brydon* v. *Muir* (1869) 7 M. 536.

[12] *Sproat's Factor* v. *McLellan* (1877) 14 S.L.R. 454 (H.L.); *Newbigging* v. *Ritchie's Tr.*, 1930 S.C. 273.

[13] *Ferguson* v. *Fyffe* (1868) 6 S.L.R. 68; *Clark* v. *Stewart* (1872) 10 S.L.R. 152.

[14] *Cunningham* v. *Maclachlan & Stewart's Tr.* (1891) 18 R. 460.

[15] *Lord Advocate* v. *McCourt* (1893) 20 R. 488.

CHAPTER 39

MEMBERSHIP OF ASSOCIATION, PARTNERSHIP OR COMPANY

ASSOCIATIONS

MEMBERSHIP of an association is constituted by contract, the main terms thereof being stated in the constitution and rules of the association. Membership may be open, or be restricted by rules of eligibility, and the admission of an ineligible person will be void.[1]

The member, once admitted, becomes bound by the rules[2]

[1] *Martin* v. *Scottish T. & G.W.U.*, 1952 S.C. (H.L.) 1; *Haggarty* v. *Scottish T. & G.W.U.*, 1955 S.C. 109. cf. *Boulting* v. *A.C.T.A.T.* [1963] 2 Q.B. 606; *Faramus* v. *Film Artistes Assocn.* [1964] A.C. 925.

[2] *Martin, supra*; *Bonsor* v. *Musicians Union* [1956] A.C. 104.

whether he reads them or not, and whether he agrees with them or not.

The contract may be rescinded if vitiated by misrepresentation.

The committee or a designated body of members may, if the rules provide for it and within those limits, exercise disciplinary powers over the member and censure, fine, or suspend him.

A member may normally resign at any time on giving notice to the secretary.[1] He cannot be expelled unless the rules provide power to expel,[2] and any procedure laid down is complied with.[3] To enforce his right to membership a member must show that by being expelled he is suffering patrimonial loss or invasion of a civil right.[4] The court will interfere to reinstate an expelled member only if the expulsion has not been carried out according to the rules, or the proceedings were not taken *bona fide* but fraudulently,[5] or the proceedings contravened the principles of natural justice.

PARTNERSHIPS

The relation of partnership[6] between individuals[7] is created by bilateral or multilateral consensual contract. The purpose is the joint conduct of some business, including every trade, occupation or profession,[8] for profit. Whether the relation established between persons is partnership or some other relationship is a question of fact, regard being had to the rules in the Partnership Act, 1890, S. 2.[9]

---

[1] *Finch* v. *Oake* [1896] 1 Ch. 409.

[2] *Dawkins* v. *Antrobus* (1881) 17 Ch. D. 615; *Luby* v. *Warwickshire Miners* [1912] 2 Ch. 371.

[3] *Young* v. *Ladies Imperial Club* [1920] 2 K.B. 523.

[4] *Rigby* v. *Connol* (1880) 14 Ch. D. 482; *Aitken* v. *Associated Carpenters* (1885) 12 R. 1206; *Murdison* v. *Scottish Football Union* (1896) 23 R. 449.

[5] *Labouchere* v. *Wharncliffe* (1879) 13 Ch. D. 346; *Dawkins* v. *Antrobus* (1881) 17 Ch. D. 615; *Cassel* v. *Inglis* [1916] 2 Ch. 211; *Weinberger* v. *Inglis* [1919] A.C. 606. cf. *Lee* v. *Showmen's Guild* [1952] 2 Q.B. 329.

[6] See generally Miller on *Partnership*; Lindley on *Partnership*.

[7] The status of the 'firm' constituted by a contract of copartnery and the position of it and of the partners thereof vis-à-vis third parties are discussed in Ch. 23, *supra*.

[8] Partnership Act, 1890, S. 45.

[9] See e.g. *Eaglesham* v. *Grant* (1875) 2 R. 960; *Stott* v. *Fender* (1878) 5 R. 1104; *Moore* v. *Dempster* (1879) 6 R. 930; *Morrison, supra*; *Kinnell* v. *Peebles* (1890) 17 R. 416; *Lawrie* v. *L's Trs.* (1892) 19 R. 675; *Gatherer* (1893) 1 S.L.T. 401; *Thomson* v. *Bell* (1894) 1 S.L.T. 433; *Laing Bros.* v. *Low* (1896) 23 R. 1105; *McCosh* v. *Brown & Co.'s Tr.* (1899) 1 F. (H.L.) 86; *Stewart* v. *Buchanan* (1903) 6 F. 15; *Allison* v. *A's Tr.* (1904) 6 F. 496; *Walker* v. *Reith* (1906) 8 F. 381; *Scott* v. *Dick*, 1909, 2 S.L.T. 118; *Eadie* v. *Crawford*, 1912, 2 S.L.T. 360; see also *Aitchison* v. *A.* (1877) 4 R. 899.

Any person, except an enemy alien, may become a partner. A minor may[1] but may rescind the contract on the ground of minority and lesion. A corporation may, if empowered by its constitution, become a partner with another corporation or an individual.[2]

In certain cases a contract of partnership is forbidden by professional etiquette.[3] The contract is illegal if it consists of more than twenty persons carrying on any business for gain,[4] except in the cases of firms of solicitors, accountants or stockbrokers,[5] or if one or more of the partners is unqualified to act in the profession in question,[6] or if the purpose of the partnership business is illegal or contrary to public policy.[7]

Formalities

The contract of partnership does not require any formalities for its constitution and though it is normally constituted in writing it may be constituted orally and proved *prout de jure*,[8] or be held established by a person holding himself out as a partner.[9] It must comply with the Registration of Business Names Act, 1916. The contract may be rescinded if induced by fraud or misrepresentation[10] or non-disclosure of material facts,[11] and may be a contract *uberrimae fidei*.[12] It involves *delectus personae*.[13]

Terms

The terms of the contract may be such as the parties may agree. Failing express provision on any matter, the Partnership Act, 1890, will supply terms on many matters.[14] The terms may

---

[1] *Hill* v. *City of Glasgow Bank* (1879) 6 R. 68, 75; *Lovell & Christmas* v. *Beauchamp* [1874] A.C. 607.

[2] Bell, *Comm.* II 514; *Stevenson* v. *A/G für Cartonnagen-Industrie* [1918] A.C. 239.

[3] The professions of advocate and of barrister.

[4] Companies Act, 1948, Ss. 429, 434, amd. Companies Act, 1967, Ss. 119–121.

[5] Companies Act, 1967, S. 120.

[6] *A.B.* v. *C.D.*, 1912, 1 S.L.T. 44.

[7] e.g. *Foster* v. *Driscoll* [1929] 1 K.B. 470.

[8] Ersk. III, 3, 18; Bell, *Prin.* §360; *Aitchison* v. *A.* (1877) 4 R. 899; *McArthur* v. *Lawson* (1877) 4 R. 1134; *Morrison* v. *Service* (1879) 6 R. 1158; *Gray* v. *Smith* (1889) 43 Ch. D. 208; *Lawrie* v. *L's Trs.* (1892) 19 R. 675.

[9] 1890 Act, S. 14(1); *Gardner* v. *Anderson* (1862) 24 D. 315.

[10] *Redgrave* v. *Hurd* (1881) 20 Ch. D. 1. As to rights of partners see Partnership Act, 1890, S. 41.

[11] *Adam* v. *Newbigging* (1888) 13 App. Cas. 308; *Manners* v, *Whitehead* (1898) 1 F. 171; *Ferguson* v. *Wilson* (1904) 6 F. 779; see also *Tennent* v. *T's Trs.* (1870) 8 M. (H.L.) 10.

[12] Bell, *Comm.* II, 508; *Ferguson, supra.*

[13] Bell, *Comm.* II, 509; *Beveridge* v. *B.* (1872) 10 M. (H.L.) 1.

[14] Ss. 20–31.

be varied by the consent of all the partners, either expressed or inferred from a course of dealing.[1] The interests and rights and duties of the partners *inter se* are determined by their co-partnery, failing which by the Partnership Act.[2] It is implied that each partner will show care and diligence in and about the partnership business, and good faith in dealing with his fellow-partners,[3] both while the firm exists and also during winding up after dissolution.[4]

Breach

The remedy for breach of an agreement to enter into partnership is damages and not specific implement,[5] and for breach of any of the duties owed by one partner to the others, is a dissolution of the partnership,[6] or petition for the appointment of a judicial factor.[7]

Duration

The duration of the partnership may be fixed by the co-partnery, failing which it will be deemed a partnership at will, which may be determined at any time by any partner giving notice of his intention to do so to all the other partners.[8] If it was originally entered into for a fixed term and is continued after that term has expired it will, in the absence of evidence as to an extended term, be deemed a partnership at will rather than be held renewed for another fixed term.[9] If it is entered into for a single adventure or undertaking it will be inferred that it is to last until the termination of such adventure or undertaking.[10]

Termination

The contract subsists till the end of the period stipulated for its duration,[11] or till the termination of the adventure or undertaking for which it was entered into,[12] or until any partner gives

---

[1] 1890 Act, S. 19.
[2] 1890 Act, S. 24.
[3] *Blisset* v. *Daniel* (1853) 10 Hare, 493, 522; 1890 Act, Ss. 29–30.
[4] 1890 Act, S. 29.
[5] *Scott* v. *Rayment* (1868) L.R. 7 Eq. 112.
[6] 1890 Act, S. 35(c)(d) and (f); *MacCredie's Trs.* v. *Lamond* (1886) 24 S.L.R. 348.
[7] *Macpherson* v *Richmond* (1867) 6 S.L.R. 348.
[8] 1890 Act, S. 26(1).
[9] S. 27; *Neilson* v. *Mossend Iron Co.* (1886) 13 R. (H.L.) 50.
[10] S. 32; *Reade* v. *Bentley* (1858) 4 K. & J. 656.
[11] S. 32; *Gracie* v. *Prentice* (1904) 12 S.L.T. 15.
[12] S. 32.

notice of withdrawal,[1] or till the death or sequestration of any partner,[2] or, in the option of the other partners, if any partner suffers his share of the partnership property to be charged under the Act for his separate debt,[3] or by the happening of any event which makes it unlawful for the business of the firm to be carried on or for the members of the firm to carry it on in partnership,[4] or until a conventional irritancy is incurred,[5] or until the partnership is dissolved by the court under and on any of the grounds stated in the Partnership Act, 1890, S. 35.[6]

COMPANIES

The contract to become a member of an incorporated company may be constituted by subscription of the Memorandum and Articles of Association of a nascent company and the agreement implied thereby to take such number of shares as the signatory has agreed to subscribe for;[7] neither allotment nor entry on the register of members is necessary.[8] The contract implied by subscription is doubtless voidable for misrepresentation, but whether *uberrima fides* is implied therein is uncertain. A subscriber cannot rescind for misrepresentation by a promoter because the company is not liable for his acts.[9] A contract to become a member is not constituted by a statement in a prospectus that a person has agreed to subscribe for shares; this is not an enforceable agreement.[10]

Membership of allotment of shares

It may also be constituted by an offer or application to take shares,[11] which may be made orally,[12] but in practice is invariably made in writing, and unless made irrevocably, may be withdrawn, orally or in writing, at any time before shares have been

---

[1] S. 32.

[2] S. 33(1); *Oswald's Trs.* v. *City of Glasgow Bank* (1879) 6 R. 461.

[3] S. 33(2).

[4] S. 34.

[5] *Hannan* v. *Henderson* (1879) 7 R. 380; cf. *Russell* v. *R.* (1880) 14 Ch. D. 471; *Green* v. *Howell* [1910] 1 Ch. 495.

[6] See *Thomson* (1893) 1 S.L.T. 59.

[7] Companies Act, 1948, S. 26(1).

[8] *Re London and Provincial Coal Co.* (1877) 5 Ch. D. 525; *Alexander* v. *Automatic Telephone Co.*, [1900] 2 Ch. 63.

[9] *Lord Lurgan's Case* [1902] 1 Ch. 707.

[10] *Todd* v. *Millen*, 1910 S.C. 868.

[11] cf. *Mason* v. *Benhar Coal Co.* (1882) 9 R. 883.

[12] *Re International Contract Co.*, *Levita's Case* (1867) L.R. 3 Ch. App. 36; *City of Glasgow Bank* v. *Nelson Mitchell* (1879) 6 R. 420.

allotted,[1] which has been accepted by the company, normally by allotting shares to the applicant. The contract may be conditional.[2] If the issue of shares of that class were *ultra vires* the contract to take shares is void.[3] So too if the company's objects disclosed in the Memorandum were materially different from those set out in the prospectus which induced the application.[4]

This contract at common law requires *uberrima fides* on the company's part, so that even innocent misrepresentation justifies resiling;[5] *a fortiori* negligent or fraudulent misrepresentation does so.[6] The common law requirements of full disclosure have been supplemented by statutory prescriptions of what must be disclosed.[7]

Apart from the common law remedy of rescission of the contract to take shares[8] together with, in the case of fraudulent misrepresentation, a claim of damages for loss caused thereby,[9] directors, promoters and persons who have authorized the issue of the prospectus are liable, subject to certain conditions, to pay compensation to all persons who subscribe for any shares on the faith of the prospectus for loss or damage they may have sustained by reason of any untrue statement included therein.[10] The statutory remedy is available whether the misrepresentations were fraudulent or not.

Membership by purchase and registration

Membership may also be effected by a purchase of shares in a company and being placed on the register of members. The contract to purchase may be made orally or in writing but must be completed by the execution of a stock transfer, or the instrument

---

[1] *Dunlop* v. *Higgins* (1848) 6 Bell, 195.

[2] *Fisher's Case* (1885) 31 Ch. D. 125; *Waverley Hydropathic Co.* v. *Barrowman* (1895) 23 R. 136; see also *Miln* v. *N.B. Fish Co.* (1887) 15 R. 21.

[3] *Waverley Hydropathic Co., supra*; *National House Property Co.* v. *Watson*, 1908 S.C. 888.

[4] *Downes* v. *Ship* (1868) L.R. 3 H.L. 343; *City of Edinburgh Brewery Co.* v. *Gibson's Tr.* (1869) 7 M. 886, 891; *Mair* v. *Rio Grande Rubber Estates*, 1913 S.C. 182, 190; revd. 1913 S.C. (H.L.) 74.

[5] *Central Ry. of Venezuela* v. *Kisch* (1867) L.R. 2 H.L. 99, 113; *Blakiston* v. *London and Scottish Banking Corpn.* (1894) 21 R. 417; *Lagunas Nitrate Co.* v. *Lagunas Syndicate* [1899] 2 Ch. 392.

[6] *Central Ry., supra*.

[7] Companies Act, 1948, Ss. 37–42 and Sched. IV. As to criminal liability for misstatements therein, see S. 44.

[8] Provided restitution can be made, which is precluded if the company has gone into liquidation: *Addie* v. *Western Bank* (1867) 5 M. (H.L.) 80; *Houldsworth* v. *City of Glasgow Bank* (1880) 7 R. (H.L.) 53; see also *Edinburgh Employers' Liability Co.* v. *Griffiths* (1892) 19 R. 550.

[9] *Houldsworth, supra*.

[10] Companies Act, 1948, S. 43.

of transfer required by the company's Articles, and registration of the transfer of ownership by the company's registrar. This contract is not one *uberrimae fidei* and it is voidable only for mis-representation, innocent, negligent or fraudulent, inducing the purchase. Rescission is conditional on restitution in integrum being possible,[1] and damages are recoverable only if fraud or negligence be established.[2] A purchaser cannot found on any misrepresentation made to original allottees of shares in a prospectus.[3] The contract binds the seller to put the buyer in the position to seek registration as a member[4] but not to secure the buyer's registration.[5] If the buyer does not take the steps to have himself registered the seller may apply to the company to register the transfer.[6]

Other modes of becoming a member

Other modes of becoming a member, such as taking shares on the holder's death or bankruptcy and becoming registered do not depend on contract.

Terms and conditions of the contract

The terms on which a person becomes and remains a member of a company depend on the Memorandum and Articles of Association of the company, which bind the company and the members as if signed by each member and containing covenants by each member to observe all the provisions of the Memorandum and Articles.[7] They also constitute an implied covenant with the other members,[8] but not with a third party, even such as a promoter.

Rectification of register of members

The register of members is prima facie evidence of any matters required to be inserted in it,[9] and if the name of any person is, without sufficient cause, entered in or omitted from the register,

---

[1] *Spence* v. *Crawford*, 1939 S.C. (H.L.) 52.

[2] *Spence, supra.*

[3] *Peek* v. *Gurney* (1873) L.R. 6 H.L. 377.

[4] *De Waal* v. *Alder* (1886) 12 App. Cas. 141.

[5] *London Founders Assocn.* v. *Clarke* (1888) 20 Q.B.D. 576; see also *Stevenson* v. *Wilson*, 1907 S.C. 445.

[6] *Skinner* v. *City of London Marine Ins. Corpn.* (1885) 14 Q.B.D. 882.

[7] Companies Act, 1948, S. 20(1); *Oakbank Oil Co.* v. *Crum* (1882) 10 R. (H.L.) 11; *Bradford Banking Co.* v. *Briggs* (1886) 12 App. Cas. 29; *Welton* v. *Saffery* [1897] A.C. 299.

[8] *Wood* v. *Odessa Waterworks Co.* (1889) 42 Ch. D. 636; *Welton, supra.*

1948 Act, S. 118.

or default or unnecessary delay takes place in entering on the register the fact of any person having ceased to be a member, the person aggrieved, or any member of the company, or the company, may apply to the court for rectification of the register.[1] The court may also order payment of damages to the person aggrieved.[1] This does not prevent the court altering the register in other cases where that is necessary.[2]

Disclosure of substantial shareholdings

The Companies Act, 1967, Ss. 33 and 34 require the disclosure of substantial individual shareholdings and the maintenance by the company of a register of shareholders holding ten per cent or more of the nominal value of the share capital of the company.

Termination of contract

The contract is terminated when the member transfers his shares to another person and the transferee becomes registered, or he dies, or is sequestrated (though his estate remains liable until a transfer is registered) or his shares are forfeited, or surrendered, or sold by the company under a power in the Articles and the purchaser is registered.

---

[1] S. 116.
[2] *Burns* v. *Siemens Bros.* [1919] 1 Ch. 225.

CHAPTER 40

MANDATE AND AGENCY

MANDATE[1] is a bilateral gratuitous consensual contract by which one empowers another to act in some respect on his behalf. It is a gratuitous obligation;[2] all commissions for the transaction of business where no reward is promised are presumed gratuitous and consequently proper mandates.[3] It is constituted by express or implied request,[4] completed by acceptance of the mandate, or by acting under it, and may be proved by any evidence.[5] Where granted in writing the mandate commonly takes the form of a factory and commission, or power of attorney.[6] If granted to enable another to represent the granter at a meeting, it is a proxy.[7] Ratification or homologation of actings on that party's behalf is equivalent to his having granted an express mandate.[8]

Mandatary's powers

The mandate may be general or special; if the latter, the powers granted are the limits of the authority; if general they will be more liberally construed according to the needs of the occasion, the ordinary or reasonable course of the transaction and the usage of

---

[1] Stair I, 12, 5; Ersk. III, 3, 31; Bell, *Comm.* I, 259; *Prin.* §216.

[2] Though an advocate, or physician debarred by etiquette from suing for his fees, may receive an honorarium for his services, the relation does not cease to be mandate. Ersk., *supra*; cf. *Macdonald* v. *Glasgow Western Hospitals*, 1954 S.C. 453, 485. On the advocate's mandate presumed from his appearance, see also *Ogston* v. *Turnbull* (1878) 13 S.L.R. 69; *Fischer* v. *Andersen* (1896) 23 R. 395; *Ferguson, Davidson & Co.* v. *Paterson and Dobbie* (1898) 1 F. 227; *Hendry's Trs.* v. *H.*, 1916, 2 S.L.T. 135; *Lauder* v. *National Bank*, 1918, 1 S.L.T. 43.

[3] Ersk. III, 3, 31; *Johnston's Trs.* v. *His Creditors* (1738) Mor. 13407.

[4] A wife, or other person *praeposita rebus domesticis*, acts under an implied mandate; cf. Ch. 16, *supra*.

[5] *Stevenson* v. *Manson* (1840) 2 D. 1204; *Anderson* v. *Buck & Holmes* (1841) 3 D. 975; *Clyde Trs.* v. *Duncan* (1853) 15 D. (H.L.) 36; *Swinburne* v. *Western Bank* (1856) 18 D. 1025; *Stewart* v. *Johnston* (1857) 19 D. 1071; *E. Galloway* v. *Grant* (1857) 19 D. 865; *Mackenzie* v. *Brodie* (1859) 21 D. 1048; *Woodrow* v. *Wright* (1861) 24 D. 31; *Annand's Trs.* v. *A.* (1869) 7 M. 526; *Grant* v. *Fleming* (1881) 9 R. 257; *Ross* v. *Cowie's Exor.* (1888) 16 R. 224; *Burt* v. *Laing*, 1925 S.C. 181.

[6] On proof of powers of attorney see Powers of Attorney Act, 1971, S. 3.

[7] The word 'proxy' is also applied to the person who represents the granter. The right to nominate a proxy exists only if conferred by statute or contract such as a company's Articles of Association.

[8] Ersk. III, 3, 47; Bell, *Comm.* I, 139.

trade.[1] Powers must be specially conferred to effect the more important transactions such as to buy or sell land[2] or moveables of value,[3] or to borrow money.[4] A general agent is assumed to have all the authority necessary to enable him to act as general agent, or general agent in a particular sphere.[5]

Mandatary's duties

By acceptance, or acting, the mandatary is bound to execute the mandate, and to follow the instructions of the mandant. He must account for his intromissions.

Duty of care

A mandatary is liable only for his actual intromissions and bound to show such diligence as a man of common prudence employs in his own affairs;[6] he must take reasonable care in the execution of his mandate and is liable for failure to do so, evidenced by the loss of or damage to the mandant's property without satisfactory exculpatory explanation.[7] If he delegates the mandate to another he does so at his peril.[8] If he has undertaken a duty involving professional skill he owes a similar duty of care to that of the person employed professionally,[9] though of rather lesser standard.

Mandatary exceeding powers

A mandatary who exceeds his powers will not bind the mandant, and may be liable to a party with whom he deals for breach of his implied warranty of authority.[10]

Mandant's duties

The mandant must reimburse the mandatary for all expenses reasonably and *bona fide* incurred in the execution of the mandate,

---

[1] Bell, *Comm.* I, 508; *Smith* v. *Harris* (1854) 16 D. 727.

[2] Stair I, 12, 15; Ersk. III, 3, 39; *Steuart* v. *Johnston* (1857) 19 D. 1071.

[3] Ersk., *supra*.

[4] *Sinclair, Moorhead & Co.* v. *Wallace* (1880) 7 R. 874.

[5] *Morrison* v. *Statter* (1895) 12 R. 1152.

[6] Ersk. III, 3, 36; Bell, *Prin.* §218; *Grierson* v. *Muir* (1802) Hume 329.

[7] *McDonald* v. *McDonald* (1807) Hume 344; *Gillies* v. *Smith* (1832) 10 S. 636; *Stiven* v. *Watson* (1873) 1 R. 412; *Copland* v. *Brogan*, 1916 S.C. 277; cf. *Grierson* v. *Muir* (1802) Hume 329 (theft); *Anderson* v. —— (1583) Mor. 10082 (shipwreck); *Mackaill* v. *Hamilton* (1724) Mor. 10091 (loss in post).

[8] *McNeil, Rowan & Co.* v. *Dawling* (1696) Mor. 10085.

[9] But by custom the advocate, though he may owe a duty of care, is not liable legally for breach thereof: *Batchelor* v. *Pattison and Mackersy* (1876) 3 R. 914.

[10] Bell, *Comm.* I, 543; *Morrison* v. *Statter* (1885) 12 R. 1152; *Anderson* v. *Croall* (1903) 6 F. 153.

relieve him of liabilities incurred and compensate him for loss sustained therein, even though the mandate has proved fruitless.[1]

Termination of mandate

The contract may be terminated at any time by either party, provided that the mandant indemnify the mandatary for trouble and expenses incurred.[2] It is impliedly terminated if the mandant grants the same powers to another. It also terminates on the expiry of any period for which it was granted, or on the completion of the task for which it was granted. It is also terminated by the death of either party, though the mandatary is entitled to act until he receive authentic news of the death of the mandant.[3] Insanity, at least of short duration, does not revoke a mandatary's authority.[4] Bankruptcy, at least of the mandatary, though not necessarily of the mandant, also terminates the mandate.[5]

AGENCY

Agency[6] is a bilateral onerous consensual contract whereby one party, the principal, authorizes another, the agent, to execute business on his behalf for reward.[7] The question whether a relationship is agency, employment, or *locatio operis faciendi* may sometimes be difficult,[8] though the choice may have material consequences.

Agency may be constituted expressly, in any mode, and proved by any evidence, whatever its duration,[9] or it may be implied by law,[10] or may be inferred from actings of parties which imply that the one has authority to act as agent of the other, or it may be constituted by the ratification by the principal of unauthorized actings of an ostensible agent, which ratification may be express, or by conduct implying approbation, in the full knowledge of all material facts,[11] or it may be assumed, without any grant of

---

[1] Ersk. III, 3, 38; *Smith* v. *Harding* (1877) 5 R. 147.

[2] Ersk. III, 3, 40; *Walker* v. *Somerville* (1837) 16 S. 217.

[3] *Campbell* v. *Anderson* (1826) 5 S. 86; 3 W. & S. 384; cf. *Kennedy* v. *K.* (1843) 6 D. 40.

[4] *Wink* v. *Mortimer* (1849) 11 D. 995; see also *Pollok* v. *Paterson*, 10 Dec. 1811, F.C.

[5] Bell, *Comm.* I, 525; *MacKenzie* v. *Campbell* (1894) 21 R. 904.

[6] See generally Bowstead on *Agency*; Fridman on *Agency*.

[7] Bell, *Comm.* I, 506; *Prin.* §216; cf. Ersk. III, 3, 35.

[8] *Smith* v. *Scott & Best* (1881) 18 S.L.R. 355; cf. *Mair* v. *Wood*, 1948 S.C. 83, 87.

[9] *Pickin* v. *Hawkes* (1878) 5 R. 676.

[10] e.g. partners (Partnership Act, 1890, Ss. 5, 8); company directors (cf. *Royal British Bank* v. *Turquand* (1856) 6 E. & B. 327).

[11] *Ballantine* v. *Stevenson* (1881) 8 R. 959; *Barnetson* v. *Petersen* (1902) 5 F. 86.

authority or prior actions, in circumstances of necessity or emergency.[1] Whether the relationship between two parties is that of agency or not is a question of fact.[2] So too it may be a matter of doubt for which of two parties an intermediary is acting.[3]

Capacity

Both principal and agent must be legally capable of acting in their respective capacities, and a principal cannot confer on an agent any authority which he could not himself exercise. Hence a nascent company, not yet incorporated, cannot as principal authorize an agent to act,[4] nor ratify an act done on its behalf.[5] Conversely a person may in general authorize an agent to do anything he could legally do himself.

Express creation of agency

Agency may be created expressly in any form, from the grant of a formal factory and commission or power of attorney[6] to oral instructions, and may be proved by parole evidence.[7] A deed conferring authority, such as a factory and commission, is strictly construed.[8]

Creation implied by law

In many cases a contract of another sort impliedly creates a person an agent. The creation of partnership impliedly makes every partner an agent of the firm and of the other partners for the purpose of the partnership business.[9] A director of a company is an agent of the company in all matters usually entrusted to a director, unless a party transacting with him actually knows that he does not have authority in that respect, or should know, having constructive notice of the Memorandum and Articles of Associa-

---

[1] *Sims* v. *Midland Ry.* [1913] 1 K.B. 103; *Prager* v. *Blatspiel* [1924] 1 K.B. 566.

[2] *Brydon* v. *Muir* (1869) 7 M. 536; *Athya* v. *Buchanan* (1872) 10 S.L.R. 18; *MacKessack* v. *Molleson* (1886) 13 R. 445; *Maffett* v. *Stewart* (1887) 14 R. 506; *Stewart, Brown & Co.* v. *Biggart & Fulton* (1893) 21 R. 293; *Wester Moffat Colliery Co.* v. *Jeffrey*, 1911 S.C. 346; *National Bank* v. *Shaw*, 1913 S.C. 133; *Michelin Tyre Co.* v. *Macfarlane*, 1917, 2 S.L.T. 205; *Boyd* v. *Millar*, 1934 S.N. 7.

[3] *Life and Health Assce. Assocn.* v. *Yule* (1904) 6 F. 437; *McMillan* v. *Accident Ins. Co.*, 1907 S.C. 484; *N.F.U. Mutual Ins. Socy.* v. *Tully*, 1935 S.L.T. 574; cf. *Equitable Life Assce. Socy.* v. *General Accident Assce. Corpn.* (1904) 12 S.L.T. 348.

[4] *Tinnevelley Sugar Co.* v. *Mirrlees Watson & Yaryan Co.* (1894) 21 R. 1009.

[5] *Kelner* v. *Baxter* (1866) L.R. 2 C.P. 174; *Newborne* v. *Sensolid (G.B.) Ltd.* [1954] 1 Q.B. 45.

[6] e.g. *Park* v. *Mood*, 1919, 1 S.L.T. 170.

[7] *Grant* v. *Fleming* (1881) 9 R. 257; *Ross* v. *Cowie's Exrx.* (1888) 16 R. 224.

[8] *Goodall* v. *Bilsland*, 1909 S.C. 1152; *Park* v. *Mood*, 1919, 1 S.L.T. 170.

[9] Partnership Act, 1890, S. 5.

tion of the company. Employment of a person in a supervisory or responsible capacity may be held to have impliedly conferred on him such authority as is customarily conferred on an employee of that grade,[1] but this does not apply to persons employed in a purely executive, clerical or working capacity.[2]

Creation inferred from actings

Where a course of conduct indicated that one party has been acting intentionally on behalf of another with the latter's assent, the latter may be held to have impliedly appointed the former his agent.[3]

Agency by ratification

Where a person, not having any authority to do so, acts on behalf of another, not in circumstances of emergency or necessity, the other may subsequently ratify the former's actings retrospectively to the same effect as if he had expressly or impliedly appointed the former as agent before the actings in question.[4] Ratification is possible only if the principal was in existence at the time of the actings and could have validly appointed the agent to act as such and to do what he did.[5] The agent must have purported to act as agent for an identified or identifiable principal, being the person who later ratifies, and not in his own name, nor as agent for anyone else.[6] At the time of ratification the principal must be legally capable of doing the act in question[7] and have had full knowledge of all facts material to the decision whether or not to adopt the transaction. He must also have had a choice whether to ratify or repudiate and is not held to ratify where he had no choice but to accept the benefit of the agent's contract.[8]

Where it is competent ratification may be effected by express words, or be implied by conduct on the principal's part indicating

[1] *Mackenzie* v. *Cluny Hill Hydro.*, 1908 S.C. 200 (hotel manager); *Finburgh* v. *Moss' Empires*, 1908 S.C. 928 (theatre manager); *Neville* v. *C. & A. Modes*, 1945 S.C. 175 (shop manager).

[2] *Agnew* v. *British Legal Life Assce. Co.* (1906) 8 F. 422; *Beaton* v. *Glasgow Corpn.*, 1908 S.C. 1010; *Riddell* v. *Glasgow Corpn.*, 1911 S.C. (H.L.) 35; *McAdam* v. *City and Suburban Dairies*, 1911 S.C. 430; *Jardine* v. *Lang*, 1911, 2 S.L.T. 494; *Cumming* v. *G.N.S. Ry.*, 1916, 1 S.L.T. 181; *Mandelston* v. *N.B. Ry.*, 1917 S.C. 442.

[3] See *Barnetson* v. *Petersen* (1902) 5 F. 86; *Bottomley* v. *Harrison* [1952] 1 All E.R. 368; *Sykes* v. *Millington* [1953] 1 Q.B. 770; *The Kirknes* [1957] P. 52.

[4] *Barnetson* v. *Petersen Bros.* (1902) 5 F. 86.

[5] *Kelner* v. *Baxter* (1866) L.R. 2 C.P. 174; *Tinnevelley Sugar Co.* v. *Mirrlees Watson* (1894) 21 R. 1009.

[6] *Wilson* v. *Tumman* (1843) 6 M. & G. 236; *Keighley, Maxted* v. *Durant* [1901] A.C. 240.

[7] *Goodall* v. *Bilsland*, 1909 S.C. 1152.

[8] *Forman* v. *The Liddesdale* [1900] A.C. 190.

clearly that he has adopted and approved the agent's actings on his behalf.[1] Silence does not justify an inference of ratification unless possibly it amounts to material delay in repudiating an unauthorized act. Where ratification has taken place it has the same effect as if agency had been duly created in advance.

Agency of necessity

In certain limited cases of emergency a person is deemed by law to have the authority to act as agent to the effect of binding his principal by his actings. The master of a ship has power, if the ship needs repairs, or the cargo is in danger of perishing, and the circumstances render it reasonably necessary, to sell or mortgage the ship, or sell the cargo at an intermediate port.[2] The master must act *bona fide* and for the benefit of the shipowners and cargo owners and must have been unable to communicate with them and obtain instructions or authority.[3] A similar principle has been applied in cases of carriage by land.[4] Such cases can equally be justified on the principle of *negotiorum gestio*.[5]

Different kinds of agents

Agents may act in many different circumstances and be persons of different kinds and qualifications. Their authority may, moreover, depend in part on the particular kind of agency undertaken.

The first distinction is between a general agent, who has authority to act as agent for his principal in all matters, or all of a particular nature, or all falling within the ordinary scope of his business or profession, and a special agent whose authority to act as agent is limited to a particular act or transaction.[6] Furthermore, various nominate kinds of agents are recognized as being vested with implied authority in various matters, in the absence of express contrary agreement.

(i) Factors or mercantile agents

A factor or mercantile agent is a person having in the customary course of his business as such agent authority to sell goods or to consign goods for the purpose of sale, or to buy goods,

1 *Ballantine* v. *Stevenson* (1881) 8 R. 959; *Barnetson* v. *Petersen* (1902) 5 F. 86.
2 Stair I, 12, 18; *Tronson* v. *Dent* (1853) 8 Moo. P.C. 419.
3 *The Australia* (1859) 13 Moo. P.C. 132.
4 *G.N. Ry.* v. *Swaffield* (1874) L.R. 9 Ex. 132; *Sims* v. *Midland Ry.* [1913] 1 K.B. 103.
5 Ch. 53, *infra*.
6 *Morrison* v. *Statter* (1885) 12 R. 1152; These species were formerly distinguished as factors and agents: see Bell, *Comm.* I, 507; *Prin.* §219.

or to raise money on the security of goods.[1] He has possession of the goods or of the document of title thereto, and normally[2] transacts in his own name. The category does not include persons having possession of goods as servants, or for custody, carriage or work thereon,[3] nor a commercial traveller, even though entrusted with goods,[4] nor a mere agent for forwarding goods.[5] A factor has implied authority to sell in the way he thinks best,[6] and to give credit[7] but not to pledge goods or barter them.[8] He has a general lien over the principal's property in his possession.[9]

(ii) Brokers

A broker is a mercantile agent employed to make contracts between persons in matters of trade, commerce and navigation, who has no possession of goods and may not contract in his own name.[10] He may act in accordance with the custom of the market in which he deals.[11] He has no right of lien. Contracts are normally made by bought and sold notes passing between the brokers for the parties.

(iii) Del credere agents

These also are mercantile agents who for an extra commission undertake to indemnify the principal if the third party with whom they deal fails to pay what is due.[12] Their liability is subsidiary only to that of the third party.[13]

---

[1] Factors Act, 1889, S. 1(1) applied to Sc. by Factors (Sc.) Act, 1890. See also Bell, *Prin.* §1317B; *Mackenzie* v. *Cormack*, 1950 S.C. 183.

[2] *Stevens* v. *Biller* (1883) 25 Ch. D. 31.

[3] *Hayman* v. *Flewker* (1863) 13 C.B. (N.S.) 519; *Weiner* v. *Harris* [1910] 1 K.B. 285; *Lowther* v. *Harris* [1927] 1 K.B. 393.

[4] *International Sponge Importers* v. *Watt*, 1909, 2 S.L.T. 24.

[5] *Martinez y Gomez* v. *Allison* (1890) 17 R. 332.

[6] *Smart* v. *Sanders* (1846) 3 C.B. 380.

[7] *Houghton* v. *Matthews* (1803) 3 B. & P. 485.

[8] *Guerriero* v. *Peile* (1820) 3 B. & Ald. 616.

[9] Bell, *Comm.* II, 87; *Glendinning* v. *Hope*, 1911 S.C. (H.L.) 73; *Mackenzie* v. *Cormack*, 1950 S.C. 183.

[10] Bell, *Comm.* I, 459, 506; *Prin.* §89, 219; *Fowler* v. *Hollins* (1872) L.R. 7 Q.B. 616, 623; among categories of brokers may be mentioned stockbrokers, insurance brokers and shipbrokers. See also *Gillies* v. *McLean* (1885) 13 R. 12; *Mackenzie & Aitken* v. *Robertson* (1886) 13 R. 494; *Maffett* v. *Stewart* (1887) 14 R. 506; *Universal Stock Exchange Co.* v. *Howat* (1891) 19 R. 128; *Clavering* v. *Hope* (1897) 24 R. 944; *Robb* v. *Gow Bros. & Gemmell* (1905) 8 F. 90; *Lamont, Nisbett & Co.* v. *Hamilton*, 1907 S.C. 628; *Newton's Exrx.* v. *Meiklejohn's J.F.*, 1959 S.L.T. 71.

[11] *Pollock* v. *Stables* (1848) 12 Q.B. 765.   [12] Bell, *Comm.* I, 395.

[13] *Morris* v. *Cleasby* (1816) 4 M. & S. 566; *Gabriel* v. *Churchill and Sim* [1914] 3 K.B. 1272; *Churchill and Sim* v. *Goddard* [1937] 1 K.B. 92: cf. *Lloyd's Exors.* v. *Wright* (1870) 7 S.L.R. 216.

(iv) *Commission agents*

The function of the commission agent is to secure orders for his principal's goods from retailers for resale to customers.[1] He has ostensible authority to accept orders for goods within his principal's line of business.[2]

(v) *Auctioneers*

Auctioneers are agents whose business is to sell other persons' goods or other property by public auction, at their saleroom or elsewhere; they act for both parties in negotiating sales and may or may not have possession of the things sold; if they have, they are mercantile agents within the Factors (Scotland) Act, 1890.[3] They have implied authority to contract for both parties,[4] but not to warrant goods sold,[5] give credit, or sell below a reserve price,[6] or sell except for payment in cash.[7] They have a lien over the goods, or the price therefor, for their charges and commission,[8] and may sue a successful bidder for the price of goods.[9] They incur no liability for implement or damages to a person claiming to be a purchaser,[10] save where they have sold by mistake, when they are liable for breach of warranty of authority.[11]

(vi) *House and estate agents*

These are agents who on behalf of the owners offer for sale houses and other heritable propery and seek to find a purchaser.[12] It is not normally part of their function to conclude an actual contract.

(vii) *House and estate factors*

These are agents employed to manage houses in multiple occupation or landed estates on behalf of the proprietors. An

---

[1] *Brydon* v. *Muir* (1869) 7 M. 536; *Lloyd & Co.* v. *Laurie* (1875) 2 R. (H.L.) 1.

[2] *Milne* v. *Harris* (1803) Mor. 8493; *Barry, Ostlere & Shepherd* v. *Edinburgh Cork Importing Co.*, 1909 S.C. 1113.

[3] *Manley* v. *Berkett* [1912] 2 K.B. 329; *Mackenzie* v. *Cormack*, 1950 S.C. 183.

[4] *Rosenbaum* v. *Belson* [1900] 2 Ch. 267.

[5] *Payne* v. *Leconfield* (1882) 51 L.J.Q.B. 642.

[6] *McManus* v. *Fortescue* [1907] 2 K.B. 1.

[7] *Williams* v. *Evans* (1866) L.R. 1 Q.B. 352.

[8] Bell, *Prin.* §1415; *Miller and Paterson* v. *McNair* (1852) 14 D. 955; *Miller* v. *Hutcheson & Dixon* (1881) 8 R. 489; *Crockart's Tr.* v. *Hay*, 1913 S.C. 509; *Mackenzie* v. *Cormack*, 1950 S.C. 183.

[9] *Couston, Thomson & Co.* v. *Chapman* (1871) 10 M. (H.L.) 74; *Macdonald & Fraser* v. *Henderson* (1882) 10 R. 95; *Mackenzie* v. *Cormack*, 1950 S.C. 183.

[10] *Fenwick* v. *Macdonald, Fraser & Co.* (1904) 6 F. 850.

[11] *Anderson* v. *Croall* (1903) 6 F. 153.

[12] e.g. *Dudley Bros.* v. *Barnet*, 1937 S.C. 632; *Luxor* v. *Cooper* [1941] A.C. 108.

estate factor has no implied authority to grant a servitude right,[1] or a lease.[2] He has no right of retention of the leases or other estate papers.[3] A house factor is the owner's agent for notice of defects in the premises and the owner is constructively affected by notice communicated to the factor.[4]

(viii) *Shipmasters*

These are both servants of the shipowner or charterer employed to manage the operation and navigation of a ship, and agents impliedly authorized to borrow money on the owner's credit and pledge the ship or cargo for repayment,[5] to render salvage services to other ships,[6] to accept salvage services and contract to pay salvage reward,[7] to pledge the owner's credit for repairs or stores necessarily obtained on credit,[8] but not to vary a contract made by the owners,[9] or to sign a bill of lading for goods not shipped.[10]

(ix) *Shipping or forwarding agents*

These are agents whose function is to arrange for the shipping and transport of goods.[11]

(x) *Solicitors*

Solicitors, formerly in Scotland called law agents, are agents employed to give legal advice and conduct legal business.[12] The extent of a solicitor's authority depends on the character of the work entrusted to him. Instructions to litigate do not include authority to appeal to the Court of Session,[13] nor to the House of

---

[1] *Macgregor* v. *Balfour* (1899) 2 F. 345; cf. *Gardner* v. *Findlay* (1892) 30 S.L.R. 248; *Macrae* v. *Leith,* 1913 S.C. 901. As to liability for negligence see *Williams' Trs.* v. *Macandrew and Jenkins,* 1960 S.L.T. 246.

[2] *Ballantine* v. *Stevenson* (1881) 8 R. 959; cf. *Steuart* v. *Johnston* (1857) 19 D. 1071. But if he has authority to grant a lease, he may modify its terms: *Grant* v. *Sinclair* (1861) 23 D. 796.

[3] *Macrae* v. *Leith,* 1913 S.C. 901.

[4] *McMartin* v. *Hannay* (1872) 10 M. 411.

[5] *Strickland* v. *Neilson and MacIntosh* (1869) 7 M. 400.

[6] *The Thetis* (1869) L.R. 2 A. & E. 365.

[7] *The Waverley* (1871) L.R. 3 A. & E. 369; *The Mariposa* [1896] P. 273.

[8] *Gunn* v. *Roberts* (1874) L.R. 9 C.P. 331.

[9] *Lindsay* v. *Scholefield* (1897) 24 R. 530.

[10] *Grant* v. *Norway* (1851) 10 C.B. 665.

[11] See e.g. *Marston Excelsior* v. *Arbuckle Smith & Co.* [1971] 1 Lloyd's Rep. 70; 115 Sol. Jo. 654; *Club Speciality Inc.* v. *United Marine* [1971] 1 Lloyd's Rep. 482.

[12] An advocate is a mandatary rather than an agent. As to handling client's money see *Brown* v. *Inland Revenue,* 1964 S.C. (H.L.) 180.

[13] *Stephen* v. *Skinner* (1863) 2 M. 287.

Lords,[1] nor to abandon an action without reference to the client,[2] nor to enter into a judicial reference,[3] nor submit to arbitration,[4] nor, probably, to compromise a claim.[5] They do authorize him to exercise some discretion[6] subject, where counsel is instructed, to the latter's directions.[7] He has no implied general authority to grant leases on behalf of the client,[8] nor to receive repayment of money lent by the client,[9] though he has ostensible authority to receive from a stockbroker the price of shares sold,[10] or the sum sued for in an action he conducted.[11] It is improper for a solicitor to represent two or more parties with conflicting interests.[12] He has a general lien on the client's papers, title-deeds and securities in his hands for his professional fees and outlays.[13]

(xi) *Retailers as agents of hire-purchase companies*

A retailer transferring goods to a customer by way of sale to a finance company which then lets the goods on hire-purchase terms to the customer is deemed to be the agent of the lessor or seller in respect of representations made as to the goods.[14] The retailer may also be the agent of the hire-purchase company for the receipt of offers to take goods on hire-purchase and of notices of withdrawal thereof,[15] of notices of cancellation,[16] and for receiving re-delivery of the goods.[17]

Other cases

An architect has been held to have implied authority to employ a surveyor,[18] but not to employ a measurer, at least before operations had been commenced.[19] A head shepherd had no implied

---

[1] *Robertson v. Foulds* (1860) 22 D. 714.

[2] *Urquhart v. Grigor* (1857) 19 D. 853; *Thoms v. Bain* (1888) 15 R. 613.

[3] *Livingston v. Johnson* (1830) 8 S. 594.

[4] *Livingston, supra*; *Black v. Laidlaw* (1844) 6 D. 1254.

[5] *Torbat v. T's Trs.* (1907) 14 S.L.T. 830.

[6] *Buchanan v. Davidson & Stevenson* (1877) 14 S.L.R. 233.

[7] *Batchelor v. Pattison & Mackersy* (1876) 3 R. 914.

[8] *Peden v. Graham* (1907) 15 S.L.T. 143; *Danish Dairy Co. v. Gillespie*, 1922 S.C. 656.

[9] *Richardson v. McGeoch's Trs.* (1898) 1 F. 145; *Peden, supra*; *Bowie's Trs. v. Watson*, 1913 S.C. 326; cf. *Clyde Trs. v. Duncan* (1853) 15 D. (H.L.) 36.

[10] *Pearson v. Scott* (1878) 9 Ch. D. 198.

[11] *Smith v. N.B. Ry.* (1850) 12 D. 795.

[12] *Ellis's Trs. v. E.* (1898) 1 F. 4; *Dunlop's Trs. v. Farquharson*, 1956 S.L.T. 16.

[13] *Richardson v. Merry* (1863) 1 M. 940; *Paul v. Meikle* (1868) 7 M. 235.

[14] Consumer Credit Act, 1974, S. 75.

[15] S. 56.

[16] S. 57.

[17] S. 72.

[18] *Black v. Cornelius* (1879) 6 R. 581.

[19] *Knox & Robb v. Scottish Garden Suburb Co.*, 1913 S.C. 872.

authority to buy sheep,[1] nor a stationmaster to pay for medical attendance on an injured employee beyond the first visit.[2]

AUTHORITY

Agent's authority

The nature and extent of the agent's authority defines the relations between principal and agent and those between either and a third party. Whether an agent has or has not particular authority is a question of fact in each case.[3]

An agent may exercise actual authority, which may be conferred expressly, be implied by the nature of the business, or be what is usual or customary in the circumstances; or apparent or ostensible authority, which the agent appears to have, whether in fact he had it or not; or presumed authority, which is presumed by law to exist and to be possessed by a person in particular circumstances.

Actual authority conferred expressly

The extent of the authority conferred is a question of fact, which falls to be ascertained by interpretation of any document constituting the agency,[4] or of the evidence relative to the creation of the agency relation.[5] A written mandate cannot be qualified by parole evidence.[6] The principle *expressio unius est exclusio alterius* may apply to exclude from authorization anything beyond what is expressly authorized.[7] An act within the scope of authority actually conferred does not cease to be authorized merely because the agent has acted with dishonest motive[8] as where an agent authorized to borrow misapplies the money borrowed.[9]

Actual authority conferred impliedly

An agent has implied authority to do anything necessary for, and ordinarily incidental to, the carrying out of his commission and the exercise of his express authority.[10] A person employed as a

[1] *Morrison* v. *Statter* (1885) 12 R. 1152.
[2] *Montgomery* v. *N.B. Ry.* (1878) 5 R. 796.
[3] *Laing* v. *Provincial Homes Investment Co.,* 1909 S.C. 813.
[4] *Sinclair, Moorhead & Co.* v. *Wallace* (1880) 7 R. 874.
[5] *Wylie & Lochhead* v. *Hornby* (1889) 16 R. 907.
[6] *Thompson* v. *Parochial Board of Inveresk* (1871) 10 M. 178.
[7] *Montgomery* v. *N.B. Ry.* (1878) 5 R. 796.
[8] *Dickson* v. *National Bank*, 1917 S.C. (H.L.) 50.
[9] *Craw* v. *Commercial Bank* (1840) 3 D. 193; *Union Bank* v. *Makin* (1873) 11 M. 499; *N. of S. Bank* v. *Behn, Moller & Co.* (1881) 8 R. 423; *Paterson's Trs.* v. *Caledonian Heritable Security Co.* (1885) 13 R. 369.
[10] e.g. *Park* v. *Mood*, 1919, 1 S.L.T. 170.

general agent is impliedly authorized to do what is usual in his business, trade or profession, for the purpose of carrying out his function,[1] and his exercise of the authority usual or customary in such cases will render the principal liable unless the principal has expressly limited the agent's authority and the third party had notice of the limitation.[2] An agent has been held not to have implied power to borrow money.[3] Express authority to open and operate on a bank account does not imply authority to overdraw.[4] An agent does not necessarily have implied authority to vary a contract[5] or compromise a claim,[6] or employ a solicitor on the principal's behalf.[7]

Apparent or ostensible authority

Ostensible authority is authority which has not in fact been conferred, but appears to exist from the conduct of the parties and the representation by the principal that the agent is authorized to act on his behalf, and is accordingly legally deemed to exist; in consequence the principal is held personally barred from denying that it does exist, unless the third party knew that the agent did not in fact have the authority which he appears to have.[8] Such authority may be deemed to exist where actual authority was conferred but has been withdrawn, or a limited authority has been given but exceeded. In the former case notice of withdrawal of authority must be given, specific notice in the case of parties who have previously had dealings with the agent,[9] and general notice, as by advertisement, in the case of parties who have not had such dealings. Failing such notice the principal will be liable on contracts made with the agent in the belief that the agent's authority still subsisted. In the case of a partner retiring from a firm this principle is now statutory.[10] In the latter case third parties may assume, failing contrary notice, that general agents have all the powers usually conferred in the case of that kind of general

---

[1] cf. *Molle* v. *Riddell* (1816) 6 Pat. 168; *Morrison* v. *Statter* (1885) 12 R. 1152.

[2] *Edmunds* v. *Bushell and Jones* (1865) L.R. 1 Q.B. 97; *Watteau* v. *Fenwick* [1893] 1 Q.B. 346.

[3] *Sinclair, Moorhead & Co.* v. *Wallace* (1880) 7 R. 874.

[4] *Royal Bank* v. *Skinner*, 1931 S.L.T. 382.

[5] *Lindsay* v. *Scholefield* (1897) 24 R. 530.

[6] *Broadhead* v. *Yule* (1871) 9 M. 921.

[7] *J. M. & J. H. Robertson* v. *Beatson, McLeod & Co.*, 1908 S.C. 921.

[8] *Hayman* v. *American Cotton Co.* (1907) 15 S.L.T. 606; *Barry, Ostlere & Shepherd* v. *Edinburgh Cork Co.*, 1909 S.C. 1113.

[9] Bell, *Prin.* §228; *N. of S. Bank* v. *Behn, Moller & Co.* (1881) 8 R. 423.

[10] Partnership Act, 1890, S. 36.

agent,[1] but they cannot assume that a special agent has any authority beyond that which he has been actually given.[2] Thus a partner in a trading firm has ostensible authority to borrow money,[3] to employ labout,[4] but not to grant a cautionary obligation,[5] or refer a question to arbitration,[6] a manager of a business has ostensible authority to order goods and receive payment of accounts,[7] but not to borrow money,[8] nor to draw or accept bills,[9] not to make representations about a party's credit;[10] a servant, or employed person of lower grade, has no ostensible authority to order goods on credit, unless there has been a course of dealing recognized by his employer.[11] But, except in cases covered by the Factors Act,[12] possession by an agent of documents normally indicative of ownership confers no ostensible authority to dispose of the property represented thereby, though a disposition in excess of an actual authority by a person having such possession may be binding on the principal.[13] Ostensible authority can probably never extend to acts known by the other party to be done by the agent when acting for his own interest rather than for behoof of the principal,[14] or known to be beyond the agent's authority,[15] or to the doing of anything illegal.[16]

---

[1] *Gemmell* v. *Annandale* (1899) 36 S.L.R. 658; cf. *International Sponge Importers* v. *Watt*, 1911 S.C. (H.L.) 57.

[2] Bell, *Prin.* §219.

[3] *Cameron* v. *Young* (1871) 9 M. 786; *Bryan* v. *Butters* (1892) 19 R. 490; *Paterson Bros.* v. *Gladstone* (1891) 18 R. 403.

[4] *Ciceri* v. *Hunter* (1904) 12 S.L.T. 293.

[5] *Shiell's Trs.* v. *Scottish Property Investment Socy.* (1884) 12 R. (H.L.) 14.

[6] *Lumsden* v. *Gordon* (1728) Mor. 14567.

[7] *Gemmell* v. *Annandale* (1899) 36 S.L.R. 658.

[8] *Ross, Skolfield & Co.* v. *State Line* (1875) 3 R. 134; *Sinclair, Moorhead & Co.* v. *Wallace* (1880) 7 R. 874; see also Bell, *Prin.* §231; *Craw* v. *Commercial Bank* (1840) 3 D. 193; *National Bank* v. *Martin* (1848) 11 D. 1; *Paterson's Trs.* v. *Caledonian Heritable Security Co.* (1885) 13 R. 369.

[9] *Swinburne* v. *Western Bank* (1856) 18 D. 1025; *Ross, Skolfield, supra.*

[10] *Hockey* v. *Clydesdale Bank* (1898) 1 F. 119.

[11] *Inches* v. *Elder* (1793) Hume, 322; *Mortimer* v. *Hamilton* (1868) 7 M. 158; *Morrison* v. *Statter* (1885) 12 R. 1152.

[12] See further *infra.*

[13] *Brocklesby* v. *Temperance Building Socy.* [1895] A.C. 173; *Bowie's Trs.* v. *Watson*, 1913 S.C. 326; but see *National Bank* v. *Dickie's Tr.* (1895) 22 R. 740; *London Joint Stock Bank* v. *Simmons* [1892] A.C. 201.

[14] *Colvin* v. *Dixon* (1867) 5 M. 603; *Hamilton* v. *Dixon* (1873) 1 R. 72; *Walker* v. *Smith* (1906) 8 F. 619.

[15] *Smith* v. *N.B. Ry.* (1850) 12 D. 795; *N. of S. Bank* v. *Behn, Moller & Co.* (1881) 8 R. 423; *Paterson Bros.* v. *Gladstone* (1891) 18 R. 403; *Hayman* v. *American Cotton Co.* (1907) 45 S.L.R. 207.

[16] *Finlayson* v. *Braidbar Quarry Co.* (1864) 2 M. 1297.

Ostensible authority of mercantile agents under Factors Acts

By the Factors Act, 1889,[1] the provisions of which are to be
construed in amplification of an agent's common law powers,[2] the
principle that possession of moveables evidences title to dispose of
them is admitted in certain cases. The principle is founded on
personal bar, that where the owner has given another apparent
authority to deal with goods, he is bound by those dealings as much
as if he had expressly authorized the dealing.[3] Section 2(1)
provides that where a mercantile agent[4] is, with the consent of the
owner, in possession of goods[5] or of the documents of title to
goods,[6] any sale, pledge[7] or other disposition of the goods,[8] made
by him when acting in the ordinary course of business of a
mercantile agent[9] shall, subject to the Act, be as valid as if he were
expressly authorized by the owner of the goods to make the same,[10]
provided that the person taking under the disposition acts in good
faith,[11] and has not at the time of the disposition notice that the
person making the disposition has not authority to make it.[12]
Furthermore,[13] where he has, with consent, been in possession of
goods or of the documents of title to goods, any disposition which
would have been valid if the consent had continued, is valid notwithstanding the determination of the consent, provided the person
taking has not at the time notice that the consent has been determined.[14] Possession of documents of title to goods by reason of

[1] Replacing Factors Acts, 1823–77, applied to Scotland by Factors (Sc.) Act, 1890, and
largely declaratory of Scottish common law: see *Vickers* v. *Hertz* (1871) 9 M. (H.L.) 65;
Bell, *Comm.* I, 518; *Prin.* (9 ed.) §824; (10 ed.) §229, 1317A–B.

[2] S. 13.

[3] See Bell, *Prin.* §1317A.

[4] Defined, S. 1(1); *Cole* v. *N.W. Bank* (1875) L.R. 10 C.P. 354; *Farquharson* v. *King*
[1902] A.C. 25; *Weiner* v. *Harris* [1910] 1 K.B. 285; *Lowther* v. *Harris* [1927] 1 K.B.
393.

[5] Defined S.1 (2) and (3); cf. *Martinez y Gomez* v. *Allison* (1890) 17 R. 332; *Astley
Industrial Trust* v. *Miller* [1968] 2 All E.R. 36. If the possession is under an illegal con-
tract, the illegality prevents a purchaser from relying on the owner's consent: *Belvoir
Finance Co.* v. *Cole* [1969] 2 All E.R. 904.

[6] Defined, S. 1(4); cf. *Vickers* v. *Hertz* (1871) 9 M. (H.L.) 65; *Browne* v. *Ainslie* (1893)
21 R. 173.

[7] Defined, S. 1(5).

[8] Not including a device to obtain temporary financial assistance: *Joblin* v. *Watkins and
Roseveare* [1949] 1 All E.R. 47.

[9] *Oppenheimer* v. *Attenborough* [1908] 1 K.B. 221; *Pearson* v. *Rose and Young* [1951]
1 K.B. 27.

[10] *Oppenheimer, supra.*

[11] *Oppenheimer* v. *Fraser* [1907] 2 K.B. 50.

[12] *Vickers, supra; Oppenheimer* v. *Frazer & Wyatt* [1907] 2 K.B. 50; *Folkes* v. *King* [1923]
1 K.B. 282.

[13] S. 2(2).

[14] *Moody* v. *Pall Mall Deposit Co.* (1917) 33 T.L.R. 306.

being or having been, with the owner's consent, in possession of
the goods represented thereby, or of any other document of title
to the goods, is deemed for the purposes of the Act to be with the
consent of the owner.[1] The owner's consent is to be presumed in
the absence of contrary evidence.[2]

A pledge of the documents of title to goods is to be deemed a
pledge of the goods.[3]

A pledge of goods as security for a debt or liability due from
pledgor to pledgee before the time of the pledge gives the pledgee
no further right to the goods than could have been enforced by the
pledgor at the time of the pledge.[4]

The validity of a sale, pledge or other disposition of goods in
pursuance of the Act depends on its being made for valuable
consideration; the pledgee's interest in anything pledged is
limited to the value of anything transferred in exchange.[5]

Where the owner of goods has given possession thereof to
another person for consignment or sale, or has shipped the goods
in the name of another person, and the consignee has not had
notice that such person is not the owner of the goods, the consignee has the same right of retention of the goods in respect of
advances made to or for the use of such person as if he were the
owner of the goods, and may transfer any such right of retention
to another person.[6]

Where a person, having sold goods, continues or is in possession of the goods or of the documents of title to the goods, the
delivery or transfer by that person, or by a mercantile agent acting
for him, of the goods or documents of title under any sale, pledge
or other disposition thereof,[7] to any person receiving them in good
faith and without notice of the previous sale, shall have the same
effect as if the person making the delivery or transfer were expressly authorized by the owner of the goods to make it.[8]

Where a person, having bought or agreed to buy goods, obtains with the consent of the seller possession[9] of the goods or the

[1] S. 2(3).

[2] S. 2(4).

[3] S. 3; cf. *Inglis* v. *Robertson & Baxter* (1898) 25 R. (H.L.) 70.

[4] S. 4; *Kaltenbach* v. *Lewis* (1885) 10 App. Cas. 617; *Martinez y Gomez* v. *Allison* (1890)
17 R. 332.

[5] S. 5; 1890 Act, S. 1(2).

[6] S. 7.

[7] cf. *Nicholson* v. *Harper* [1895] 2 Ch. 415; *City Fur Mfg. Co.* v. *Fureenbond (Brokers)
London, Ltd.* [1937] 1 All E.R. 799.

[8] S. 8; cf. Sale of Goods Act, 1893, S. 25(1) which is slightly narrower in terms.

[9] Even possession with consent obtained by fraud: *Du Jardin* v. *Beadman* [1952]
2 Q.B. 712.

documents of title to the goods,[1] the delivery or transfer, by that person or by a mercantile agent acting for him, of the goods or documents of title, under any sale, pledge, or other disposition thereof, or under any agreement for sale, pledge or other disposition thereof, to any person receiving the same in good faith and without notice of any right of retention or other right of the original seller in respect of the goods, has the same effect as if the person making the delivery or transfer were a mercantile agent in possession of the goods or documents of title with the consent of the owner.[2]

Where a document of title to goods has been lawfully transferred to a person as a buyer or owner of the goods, and that person transfers the document to a person who takes the document in good faith and for valuable consideration, the latter transfer has the same effect in defeating the seller's right of retention or of stoppage *in transitu* as has the transfer of a bill of lading.[3]

Presumed authority

Presumed authority is such as the law presumes the principal would have granted if he had been consulted and asked for authority in advance. Thus the agent of necessity is presumed to have authority to do what seems to him possible and necessary to save his ship, have it repaired, complete his voyage, prevent cargo becoming worthless, and so on as circumstances require. A wife or housekeeper has presumed authority to order household goods and pledge her husband or employer's credit therefor.[4]

PRINCIPAL'S LIABILITIES

Principal's liabilities to agent

When a principal appoints an agent, there is in general no obligation to furnish him with work whereby he may earn commission, and no breach if the principal transfer or discontinue his

---

[1] This does not cover possession under an agreement for sale or return: *Edwards* v. *Vaughan* (1910) 26 T.L.R. 545; nor under a hire-purchase contract with an option to buy: *Helby* v. *Matthews* [1895] A.C. 471; *Belsize Motor Co.* v. *Cox* [1914] 1 K.B. 244; but it does cover a conditional sale: *Marten* v. *Whale* [1917] 2 K.B. 480; and a credit sale: *Lee* v. *Butler* [1893] 2 Q.B. 318.

[2] S. 9; cf. Sale of Goods Act, 1893, S. 25(2), which is slightly narrower. See also *Browne* v. *Ainslie* (1893) 21 R. 173.

[3] S. 10: reproduced and developed in Sale of Goods Act, 1893, S. 47.

[4] Ch. 16, *supra*.

business.[1] If, however, the agent in any way pays for the agency it is presumed that the principal is impliedly bound not voluntarily to discontinue business,[2] and such may be implied where the contract contains an obligation to employ the agent[3] or to execute any orders he may be able to obtain.[4] A principal has been held impliedly bound not, by refusing to complete a contract negotiated by the agent, to prevent him from earning his commission.[5]

Remuneration

The principal is bound to pay his agent a fee or commission only if payment is an express or implied term of the contract.[6] Apart from express contract, the nature of the agency and the circumstances of the parties' relationship may indicate whether remuneration was intended or not. The general rule that a mercantile agent is entitled to some form of remuneration may be excluded by proof of a custom in the particular trade that agents rely exclusively on the security of goods entrusted to them.[7]

The duty to pay remuneration arises only when the agent has earned it; what the agent has to do to earn it is a question of interpretation of the contract, and whether he has done so is then a question of fact.[8] The question frequently is whether the result is fairly attributable to the agent's activities.[9] The amount of remuneration or commission may be fixed by express contract, or by what is customary in the particular branch of agency,[10] failing which it is implied that it will be fixed on the basis *quantum meruit*.[11]

---

[1] *London, etc. Shipping Co.* v. *Ferguson* (1850) 13 D. 51; *Rhodes* v. *Forwood* [1876] 1 App. Cas. 256; *Patmore* v. *Cannon* (1892) 19 R. 1004; *State of California Co.* v. *Moore* (1895) 22 R. 562; *French* v. *Leeston Shipping Co.* [1922] 1 A.C. 451.

[2] *Galbraith* v. *Arethusa Shipping Co.* (1896) 23 R. 1011; *Ogden* v. *Nelson* [1905] A.C. 109.

[3] *Turner* v. *Goldsmith* [1891] 1 Q.B. 544.

[4] *Reigate* v. *Union Mfg. Co.* [1918] 1 K.B. 592.

[5] *Dudley Bros.* v. *Barnet*, 1937 S.C. 632.

[6] *Moss* v. *Cunliffe & Dunlop* (1875) 2 R. 657; *Kennedy* v. *Glass* (1890) 17 R. 1085.

[7] *Dinesmann* v. *Mair*, 1912, 1 S.L.T. 217.

[8] *Menzies, Bruce Low & Thomson* v. *McLennan* (1895) 22 R. 299; *Van Laun* v. *Neilson, Reid & Co.* (1904) 6 F. 644; *Brett* v. *Bow's Emporium*, 1928 S.C. (H.L.) 19; *Dudley Bros.* v. *Barnet*, 1937 S.C. 632; *Luxor (Eastbourne) Ltd.* v. *Cooper* [1941] A.C. 108.

[9] *Moss, supra; White* v. *Munro* (1876) 3 R. 1011; *Walker, Donald & Co.* v. *Birrell, Stenhouse & Co.* (1883) 11 R. 369; *Kennedy* v. *Glass* (1890) 17 R. 1084; *Jacobs* v. *McMillan* (1894) 21 R. 623; *McCraig* v. *Broadley* (1897) 5 S.L.T. 163; *Robertson* v. *Burrell* (1899) 6 S.L.T. 368; *Gibb* v. *Bennett* (1906) 14 S.L.T. 64; *Walker, & Fraser & Steele* v. *Fraser's Trs.*, 1910 S.C. 222.

[10] *Gardner* v. *Findlay* (1892) 30 S.L.R. 248; *Stubbs* v. *Slater* [1910] 1 Ch. 632.

[11] *Bryant* v. *Flight* (1839) 5 M. & W. 114; *Kennedy* v. *Glass* (1890) 17 R. 1085. See also *Graham* v. *U.T.R.*, 1922 S.C. 533.

Relief

The principal must also relieve the agent of all liabilities, losses and outlays incurred in and directly and naturally following from the performance of the agency.[1] If not expressed,[2] this obligation is implied. This extends not only to liabilities on contracts made, but liability for expenses incurred defending an action brought against the agent arising out of his performance of his duties.[3] There is no duty to indemnify an agent who has acted illegally, carelessly or in breach of duty,[4] nor against casual personal misfortunes nor against expenses incurred in defending himself against an unfounded charge of having done what was not his duty to do, such not being an expense incurred in the discharge of his duties.[5]

Reimbursement of outlays

The principal must reimburse the agent for all outlays properly incurred in the performance of the agency,[6] but not pay interest thereon unless in accordance with the custom of trade.[7] Even a betting agent may recover disbursements.[8]

Lien

A mercantile agent[9] has a general lien over any property belonging to the principal in his possession in security of his claim for commission or for any debt incurred by him in the execution of the agency.[10] A solicitor also has a general lien.[11] Agents, other than mercantile agents and members of professions which have been recognized as having general rights of lien, have only a special lien.[12]

[1] Stevenson v. Duncan (1842) 5 D. 167; Robinson v. Middleton (1859) 21 D. 1089; Mackenzie v. Blakeney (1879) 6 R. 1329.

[2] cf. Tomlinson v. Liqdrs. of Scottish Amalgamated Silks, Ltd., 1934 S.C. 85.

[3] Re Famatina Dev. Corpn. Ltd. [1914] 2 Ch. 271.

[4] Duncan v. Hill (1873) L.R. 8 Ex. 242; Thacker v. Hardy (1878) 4 Q.B.D. 685.

[5] Tomlinson v. Liqdr. of Scottish Amalgamated Silks, Ltd., 1935 S.C. (H.L.) 1.

[6] Dinesmann v. Mair, 1912, 1 S.L.T. 217.

[7] Blair's Trs. v. Payne (1884) 12 R. 104; Somervell's Tr. v. Edinburgh Life Assce. Co., 1911 S.C. 1069.

[8] Knight v. Stott (1892) 19 R. 959.

[9] Including, for this purpose, an auctioneer: Miller v. Hutcheson (1881) 8 R. 489; and a stockbroker: Glendinning v. Hope, 1911 S.C. (H.L.) 73.

[10] Bell, Prin. §1445; Sibbald v. Gibson (1852) 15 D. 217; Gairdner v. Milne (1858) 20 D. 565; Glendinning, supra; Mackenzie v. Cormack, 1950 S.C. 183.

[11] Creditors of Hamilton of Provenhall (1781) Mor. 6253; Paul v. Meikle (1868) 7 M. 235; Richardson v. Merry (1863) 1 M. 940; McIntosh v. Chalmers (1883) 11 R. 8; Macrae, infra; Drummond v. Muirhead & Guthrie Smith (1900) 2 F. 585.

[12] Scott & Neill v. Smith (1883) 11 R. 316; Stevenson, Lauder & Gilchrist v. Dawson (1896) 23 R. 496; Macrae v. Leith, 1913 S.C. 901 (estate factor); Findlay v. Waddell, 1910 S.C. 670 (accountant).

Principal's liability to third parties

The principal is in general though personally innocent liable to third parties for loss caused to them by his agent's fraud in the performance of his agency, his knowledge being imputed to the principal, whether the principal benefits or not.[1] But this does not apply where the fraud was not committed in the course of the agency nor for the principal's benefit,[2] nor where the agent has a separate interest not to disclose these facts to his principal.[3] He may similarly be liable for wrongs of other kinds.[4]

Agent's liability to third parties

An agent may incur liabilities directly to third parties where he clearly incurs personal liability,[5] or does not disclose his principal,[6] or the fault resulting in the liability is his alone, as for causing harm in the execution of the agency,[7] or sells without authority, whereby the third party loses the bargain.[8]

AGENT'S LIABILITIES

Agent's responsibilities to principal

The agent's responsibilities are defined by the express or implied terms of the contract with him. He must perform what he has been instructed to do, and in so doing act in accordance with the authority conferred on him, with the general nature of his business, and with the customs and usages of the trade, business or profession.[9] If instructions are express, they must be complied with,[10] but if ambiguous, the agent is not liable for exceeding instructions if he honestly misinterprets them.[11] If there are no particular instructions the agent must act to the best of his judgment.

---

[1] *Lloyd* v. *Grace, Smith & Co.* [1912] A.C. 716.

[2] *Robb* v. *Gow Bros. & Gemmell* (1905) 8 F. 91.

[3] *Macarthur's Trs.* v. *Royal Bank,* 1933 S.N. 58.

[4] *Citizens Life Assce. Co.* v. *Brown* [1904] A.C. 423; *Agnew* v. *British Legal Life Assce. Co.* (1906) 8 F. 422.

[5] *Shiells* (1902) 10 S.L.T. 123.

[6] *Gibb* v. *Cunningham & Robertson,* 1925 S.L.T. 608; *Stone & Rolfe* v. *Kimber Coal Co.,* 1926 S.C. (H.L.) 45.

[7] *Taylor* v. *Rutherford* (1888) 15 R. 608.

[8] *Anderson* v. *Croall* (1903) 6 F. 153; *Rederi A/B Nordstjernan* v. *Salvesen* (1905) 7 F. (H.L.) 101.

[9] cf. *Maffett* v. *Stewart* (1887) 14 R. 506.

[10] Ersk. III, 3, 35; *Bank of Scotland* v. *Dominion Bank* (1891) 18 R. (H.L.) 21.

[11] *Ireland* v. *Livingston* (1872) L.R. 5 H.L. 395.

Skill and care

He must exercise due skill and care in acting such as an agent in his position would usually exercise;[1] where the agent is a professional man he must show the degree of skill and knowledge and exercise the care expected of a reasonably competent and careful member of the profession in question.[2] He must act honestly and without regard to personal interest,[3] and must make genuine transactions not unenforceable relations of the nature of gambles.[4]

Accounting

An agent is bound to keep accounts[5] and to make good any deficiency he cannot explain, even though no dishonesty be proved.[6] In accounting he must give credit for discounts received from third parties and not retain them as well as his own commission,[7] and for interest on his principal's moneys while in his hands.[8] Payment by a third party to an agent is good if the agent was in fact authorized to receive payment, or had ostensible authority to do so.[9]

Delegation

The relation of principal and agent is a confidential and fiduciary one, and unless permitted by the contract, an agent must act personally and not delegate: the presumption applies that *delegatus non potest delegare*.[10] But delegation is not a breach of duty if it is within the scope of the agent's authority, express, implied or usual, or is subsequently ratified, or justified by necessity.[11] Nor

[1] Bell, *Prin.* §221; *Simpson* v. *Duncan* (1849) 11 D. 1097; *Laing* v. *Darling* (1850) 12 D. 1279; *Hastie* v. *Campbell* (1857) 19 D. 557; cf. *Turnbull* v. *Cruickshank & Fairweather* (1905) 7 F. 791.

[2] *Purves* v. *Landell* (1845) 4 Bell 46; *Cooke* v. *Falconer's Reps.* (1850) 13 D. 157; *Simpson* v. *Kidstons*, 1913, 1 S.L.T. 74; but see *Free Church* v. *McKnight's Trs.*, 1916 S.C. 349.

[3] *Clavering, Son & Co.* v. *Hope* (1897) 24 R. 944; cf. *Cunningham* v. *Lee* (1874) 2 R. 83.

[4] *Gillies* v. *McLean* (1885) 13 R. 12; *Shaw* v. *Caledonian Ry.* (1890) 17 R. 466; *Universal Stock Exchange Co.* v. *Howat* (1891) 19 R. 128.

[5] *Robb* v. *Gowans* (1884) 11 R. 881; *Struthers* v. *Smith*, 1913 S.C. 1116; *Simpson* v. *Kidstons*, 1913, 1 S.L.T. 74; cf. *Russell's Trs.* v. *R.* (1885) 13 R. 331.

[6] *Tyler* v. *Logan* (1904) 7 F. 123.

[7] *Manners* v. *Raeburn & Verel* (1884) 11 R. 899.

[8] *Brown* v. *I.R.C.*, 1964 S.C. (H.L.) 180.

[9] *Pearson* v. *Scott* (1878) 9 Ch. D. 198; *Smith* v. *N.B. Ry.* (1850) 12 D. 795; contrast *Peden* v. *Graham* (1907) 15 S.L.T. 143.

[10] *Black* v. *Cornelius* (1879) 6 R. 581; *Robertson* v. *Beatson, Macleod & Co.*, 1908 S.C. 921; *Knox & Robb* v. *Scottish Garden Suburb Co.*, 1913 S.C. 872.

[11] *De Bussche* v. *Alt* (1878) 8 Ch. D. 286.

is it a breach, and consent to delegation is implied, where the employment of subordinates or sub-agents is usual and customary.[1] Where delegation is permissible principal and sub-agent are contractually bound and the principal must pay for the services and the sub-agent may not obtain any secret benefit for himself.[2] If the sub-agent fails in his duties, the main agent is liable for his default.[3]

Fiduciary duty

The agent should not permit conflict between his personal interest and his duties to his principal. In case of conflict he should disclose the circumstances to the principal, so that the latter may, if so advised, consent to the agent's actings. If full disclosure is not made the principal may, on discovering the facts, ratify the agent's actings, or rescind the transaction and claim from the agent any profit the latter may have made from it.[4] The fairness of the transaction is irrelevant. An agent instructed to buy may not, without the principal's knowledge, sell his own goods to the principal, who can repudiate any such offer;[5] such a practice is not justified by a custom of trade, if unknown to the principal.[6] If instructed to sell, he may not purchase himself,[7] though if not himself employed to sell he may do so, even unknown to the seller.[8] The agent also should not act for his principal and also for the third party, certainly not without making full disclosure to each of all relevant facts and obtaining the consent of both.[9] But under a contract of agency constituted in writing there is no implied condition that the agent will never, without the principal's permission act so as to bring his interests into conflict with those of the principal.[10]

Secret profits

The agent must not take a secret profit for himself from any transaction, beyond what he receives by way of commission or

[1] Thus the country agent may instruct an Edinburgh agent to handle Court of Session business; cf. *Robertson* v. *Foulds* (1860) 22 D. 714.

[2] *De Bussche, supra.*

[3] *McVicar* v. *McGregor* (1808) Hume 347; *Mackersy* v. *Ramsay, Bonar & Co.,* (1843) 2 Bell 30.

[4] *MacPherson's Trs.* v. *Watt* (1877) 5 R. (H.L.) 9; cf. *Henderson* v. *Huntingdon Copper Co.* (1877) 5 R. (H.L.) 1; *Pant-Mawr Quarry Co.* v. *Fleming* (1883) 10 R. 457.

[5] *G.N.S. Ry.* v. *Urquhart* (1884) 21 S.L.R. 377; *Maffett* v. *Stewart* (1887) 14 R. 506.

[6] *Robinson* v. *Mollett* (1874) L.R. 7 H.L. 802.

[7] *Macpherson's Trs., supra.*

[8] *Macpherson's Trs., supra,* 15–16.

[9] *N. & S. Trust Co.* v. *Berkeley* [1971] 1 All E.R. 980.

[10] *Lothian* v. *Jenolite, Ltd.* 1970 S.L.T. 31.

remuneration. If he does he is liable to be dismissed and forfeits his right to his remuneration,[1] and the principal may recover the commission from him.[2] The principal may recover damages from the third party for bribing his agent,[3] and may refuse to implement any contract made.[4] Secret profits cover not only bribes but the obtaining of any personal financial advantage from the exercise of the authority, as by buying at a discount, and any such advantage must be accounted for to the principal.[5] If, however, the principal knows about the agent's secret profits and consents thereto or takes no objection, the agent is entitled to keep his personal profit.[6] Consent may be presumed if no commission were being given and the work was such as is not normally done gratuitously.[7] A custom of trade unknown to the principal does not justify taking a secret commission.[8] The transaction between agent and third party is *pactum illicitum* and, whether the promise affected the agent's conduct or not, he cannot sue for the bribe.[9] It may also subject both parties to criminal penalties.[10]

Confidentiality

The agent must also maintain confidence as to all matters of the principal's business of which he may acquire knowledge in the course of executing the agency.[11]

Relief

When a principal is held liable on a transaction entered into by an agent exceeding his authority, or for a default by an agent, he is entitled to relief from the agent.[12]

---

[1] *Boston Deep Sea Fishing Co.* v. *Ansell* (1888) 39 Ch. D. 339; *Andrews* v. *Ramsay* [1903] 2 K.B. 635; *Graham* v. *Paton*, 1917 S.C. 203; cf. *Graham* v. *U.T.R. Ltd.*, 1922 S.C. 533.

[2] *Ronaldson* v. *Drummond & Reid* (1881) 8 R. 956; *Powell & Thomas* v. *Jones* [1905] 1 K.B. 11.

[3] *Mayor of Salford* v. *Lever* [1891] 1 Q.B. 168;

[4] *Cleland* v. *Morrison* (1878) 6 R. 156; *Shipway* v. *Broadwood* [1899] 1 Q.B. 369; *Alexander* v. *Webber* [1922] 1 K.B. 642.

[5] *Pender* v. *Henderson* (1864) 2 M. 1428; *Robertson* v. *Dennistoun* (1865) 3 M. 829; *De Bussche* v. *Alt* (1877) 8 Ch. D. 286; *Ronaldson* v. *Drummond & Reid* (1881) 8 R. 956; see also *Lister* v. *Stubbs* (1890) 45 Ch. D. 1.

[6] *Hippisley* v. *Knee* [1905] 1 K.B. 1.

[7] *G.W. Ins. Co.* v. *Cunliffe* (1874) L.R. 9 Ch. 525; *Baring* v. *Stanton* (1876) 3 Ch. D. 502.

[8] *Ronaldson*, *supra*.

[9] *Harrington* v. *Victoria Dock Graving Co.* (1878) 3 Q.B.D. 549.

[10] Prevention of Corruption Acts, 1906 and 1916.

[11] *Liverpool Victoria Friendly Socy.* v. *Houston* (1900) 3 F. 42; *Nordisk Insulinlaboratorium* v. *Gorgate Products* [1953] Ch. 430.

[12] *Milne* v. *Ritchie* (1882) 10 R. 365; *Barkley* v. *Simpson* (1897) 24 R. 346.

Liability of agent to principal

An agent is bound to indemnify the principal against all loss caused by his failure to act according to his instructions or loss due to his breach of duty.[1]

Principal's rights against third parties

A principal has a claim against a third party who has caused him loss by unjustified dealings with his agent, as by paying cheques payable to the principal to the agent when the latter was not held out as authorized to cash cheques.[2]

Agent's rights against third parties

Where an agent contracts as an individual he may sue the other contracting party direct.[3]

Agent's liabilities to third parties

If an agent employs a third party in excess of his authority he is personally, and his principal not at all, liable to the third party.[4]

OPERATION OF AGENCY

Operation of agency

Agency is created to enable the agent to effect legal relations between the principal and third parties. But particular issues arise with regard to the particular kind of legal relations involved.

Contract—principal named

Where a contract is entered into with a third party by an agent on behalf of a principal the effect of the contract may depend on whether the principal has been named, or his mere existence disclosed, or even his existence was undisclosed to the third party. Where an agent, having authority to do so, contracts on behalf of a named principal, in general the latter alone can sue and be sued on the contract and the agent is not a party to the contract.[5] But

---

[1] *Barkley* v. *Simpson* (1897) 24 R. 346; *Salvesen* v. *Rederi A/B Nordstjernan* (1905) 7 F. (H.L.) 101; *Turnbull* v. *Cruickshank & Fairweather* (1905) 7 F. 791.

[2] *Phillips* v. *Italian Bank*, 1934 S.L.T. 78.

[3] *Milne* v. *Ritchie* (1882) 10 R. 365; *Levy* v. *Thomsons* (1883) 10 R. 1134; *Graham* v. *Tait* (1885) 12 R. 588.

[4] *J. M. & J. H. Robertson* v. *Beatson, Macleod & Co.*, 1908 S.C. 921.

[5] Bell, *Comm.* I, 540, note. In *Hill S.S. Co.* v. *Stinnes*, 1941 S.C. 324, parties contracted 'as agents only'.

the principal cannot sue on and is not bound by a contract made by the agent outwith the scope of his actual or apparent authority.[1]

Exceptionally the agent for a named principal may be held personally liable. This arises where, in a contract in writing, he incurs liability *ex facie* personally, even though the other party knew of the fact of agency, and even knew the principal's name.[2] To avoid liability he must clearly indicate in the document that he contracts as agent only and undertakes no personal liability.[3] An agent may also incur personal liability when he contracts on behalf of an unincorporated body which cannot be sued as an entity,[4] or on behalf of a company not yet registered.[5] The agent may be sued if he declines to name his principal.[6] The custom of a particular trade may be that an agent, even when contracting as such, incurs personal liability.[7]

Principal disclosed

The same principles generally apply where the principal's existence is disclosed though he is not named.[8] It has been held that a principal was disclosed when it could readily have been discovered from a public register whether the contracting party was principal or agent.[9] In some markets it is customary for brokers to deal with others as principals. An auctioneer who warrants goods sold binds himself if he does not disclose the seller's name.[10] In some circumstances, however, the other party might be unwilling to rely on the credit of an unknown principal.[11]

---

[1] Bell, *Comm.* I, 536; *Millar* v. *Mitchell* (1860) 22 D. 833; *Livesey* v. *Purdom* (1894) 21 R. 911; *Fenwick* v. *Macdonald Fraser & Co.* (1904) 6 F. 850; *Comerford* v. *Britannic Assce. Co.* (1908) 24 T.L.R. 81.

[2] *Ransohoff & Wissler* v. *Burrell* (1897) 25 R. 284; *Stewart* v. *Shannessy* (1900) 2 F. 1288; *Lipton* v. *Ford* [1917] 2 K.B. 647; *Lindsay* v. *Craig*, 1919 S.C. 139. See also *Lamont, Nisbett & Co.* v. *Hamilton*, 1907 S.C. 628.

[3] *Universal S.N. Co.* v. *McKelvie* [1923] A.C. 492; *Stone & Rolfe* v. *Kimber Coal Co.*, 1926 S.C. (H.L.) 45. As to bills of exchange see Bills of Exchange Act, 1882, S. 26; *Chiene* v. *Western Bank* (1848) 10 D. 1523; *McMeekin* v. *Easton* (1889) 16 R. 363; *Brebner* v. *Henderson*, 1925 S.C. 643. See also *Brown* v. *Sutherland* (1875) 2 R. 615.

[4] *McMeekin, supra*; *Thomson* v. *Victoria Eighty Club* (1905) 43 S.L.R. 628.

[5] *Kelner* v. *Baxter* (1866) L.R. 2 C.P. 174.

[6] *Gibb* v. *Cunningham & Robertson*, 1925 S.L.T. 608.

[7] *Neill* v. *Hopkirk* (1850) 12 D. 618; *Fortune's Exors.* v. *Smith* (1864) 2 M. 1005.

[8] *Millar* v. *Mitchell* (1860) 22 D. 833, 845; *Fenwick* v. *Macdonald, Fraser & Co.* (1904) 6 F. 850; *Universal S.N. Co., supra.*

[9] *Armour* v. *Duff*, 1912 S.C. 120.

[10] *Ferrier* v. *Dods* (1865) 3 M. 561; contrast *Fenwick* v. *Macdonald, Fraser & Co.* (1904) 6 F. 850, where seller's name disclosed and only seller liable.

[11] cf. *Dores* v. *Horne & Rose* (1842) 4 D. 673; *Ferrier* v. *Dods* (1865) 3 M. 561.

Principal undisclosed

Where the agent acts for an undisclosed principal, the other party thinks that the agent is himself the principal and therefore looks to him for performance of the contract or for reparation for its breach,[1] but, provided the agent was acting within the scope of his authority, the principal may disclose himself and sue on the contract[2] and, once his identity is disclosed or discovered, may be sued thereon.[2] The third party must, when he discovers the principal's identity, elect whether to sue agent or principal on the contract; he cannot sue both,[3] and election, once made, is final. Election is not necessarily effected by debiting the agent[4] or raising an action against him,[5] but is by taking decree, even in absence and though it prove nugatory,[6] or by conduct, such as returning goods to the seller.[7] Similarly to claim in the bankruptcy of principal or agent,[8] unless, probably, a claim against the other be expressly reserved,[9] evidences election. If the agent seeks to evade liability by showing that the other party knew that he was contracting with an agent he may do so,[10] but if the contract is in writing and the agent's obligation *ex facie* unqualified he must prove that he was truly an agent and known to be such from the terms of the contract itself, and not from extrinsic evidence.[11]

---

[1] *Millar* v. *Mitchell* (1860) 22 D. 833, 845; *Athya* v. *Buchanan* (1872) 10 S.L.R. 18; cf. *Stewart* v. *Shannessy* (1900) 2 F. 1288; *Drughorn* v. *Rederi A/B Transatlantic* [1919] A.C. 203; *Hill S.S. Co.* v. *Stinnes*, 1941 S.C. 324, 331.

[2] *Armstrong* v. *Stokes* (1872) L.R. 7 Q.B. 598; *Lockhart* v. *Moodie* (1877) 4 R. 859; *Macphail* v. *Maclean's Tr.* (1887) 15 R. 47; *Bennett* v. *Inveresk Paper Co.* (1891) 18 R. 975, 983; *Girvin, Roper & Co.* v. *Monteith* (1895) 23 R. 129, 135; *Hill S.S. Co., supra; Laidlaw* v. *Griffin*, 1968 S.L.T. 278; Gloag, 128, submits that the undisclosed principal can sue only if the contract is assignable: Bell, *Comm.* I, 527; *Mabon* v. *Christie* (1844) 6 D. 619; see also *Salton* v. *Clydesdale Bank* (1898) 1 F. 110.

[3] *Ferrier* v. *Dods* (1865) 3 M. 561; *Lamont, Nisbett & Co.* v. *Hamilton*, 1907 S.C. 628.

[4] *Stevenson* v. *Campbell* (1836) 14 S. 562.

[5] *Meier* v. *Kuchenmeister* (1881) 8 R. 642; *Green, Holland & Son* v. *A/S City of Richmond* (1894) 1 S.L.T. 483; *Cory Bros.* v. *McLean* (1898) 6 S.L.T. 103.

[6] *Craig* v. *Blackater*, 1923 S.C. 472; *Morel* v. *E. Westmoreland* [1904] A.C. 11; *Moore* v. *Flanagan* [1920] 1 K.B. 919.

[7] *Ferrier, supra.*

[8] *Scarf* v. *Jardine* (1882) 7 App. Cas. 345; *Logan* v. *Schuldt* (1903) 10 S.L.T. 598.

[9] *Black* v. *Girdwood* (1885) 13 R. 243.

[10] *Nabonie* v. *Scott* (1815) Hume 353; *Struther's Patent Diamond Co.* v. *Clydesdale Bank* (1886) 13 R. 434; *Bank of Scotland* v. *Rorie* (1908) 16 S.L.T. 21.

[11] Bell, *Comm.* I, 527; *Edinburgh and Glasgow Bank* v. *Steele* (1853) 25 Sc. Jur. 245; *Stewart* v. *Shannessy* (1900) 2 F. 1288; *Muller* v. *Weber & Schaer* (1901) 3 F. 401; *Armour* v. *Duff*, 1912 S.C. 120; *Lindsay* v. *Craig*, 1919 S.C. 139; *Gibb* v. *Cunningham & Robertson*, 1925 S.L.T. 608.

Foreign principal

Where the agent acts for a foreign principal, who is not subject to the jurisdiction of the British courts, it was formerly presumed that he incurred personal liability but it is now regarded as a question of fact and circumstances whether this is so or not, the onus being on the party seeking to make the agent liable.[1] The presumption may be stronger when the agent is purchasing than when he is selling.[2] If a party is held out by a foreign principal as his agent, the principal is liable on contracts made by the agent, notwithstanding a private arrangement that the agent should transact as a principal.[3]

Agent unauthorized

If the agent, contracting as such, exceeded his authority the principal is not bound,[4] whether he was named or disclosed or not, unless the contract were within the agent's ostensible though beyond his actual authority,[5] or unless the principal in full knowledge of the facts, elects to ratify the agent's actings.[6] The agent is, however, personally liable. If the agent were wholly unauthorized but has purported to contract as agent, the principal is not bound, unless he adopts the agent's actings,[7] nor is the agent as an individual a party to the contract. If he purported fraudulently he is liable to the other contracting party in damages for fraud. If he did so innocently or mistakenly he is liable in damages to the other contracting party on the basis of breach of warranty of authority,[7] that he impliedly warranted his authority to contract and is liable to the other contracting party for the loss caused by the failure of the contract.[8] But there is no liability for breach of implied warranty of authority where the existence of the authority is a question of law and the other party has full means for ascertaining whether the authority asserted does in fact exist, as where it depends on the Articles of Association of a company.[9]

[1] *Millar* v. *Mitchell* (1860) 22 D. 833; *Bennett* v. *Inveresk Paper Co.* (1891) 18 R. 975; *Girvin Roper & Co.* v. *Monteith* (1895) 23 R. 129; *Miller, Gibb & Co.* v. *Smith & Tyrer* [1917] 2 K.B. 141; *Teheran-Europe Co.* v. *Belton* [1968] 2 All E.R. 886.

[2] *Millar, supra.*

[3] *Hayman* v. *American Cotton Co.* (1907) 15 S.L.T. 606.

[4] *Strickland* v. *Neilson and MacIntosh* (1869) 7 M. 400.

[5] Bell, *Prin.* §288; *Ferguson & Lillie* v. *Stephen* (1864) 2 M. 804; *Mann* v. *Sinclair* (1879) 6 R. 1078; *N. of S. Banking Co.* v. *Behn, Moller & Co.* (1881) 8 R. 423.

[6] *Keighley, Maxted* v. *Durant* [1901] A.C. 240.

[7] *Collen* v. *Wright* (1857) 8 E. & B. 647; *Firbank's Exors.* v. *Humphreys* (1886) 18 Q.B.D. 54.

[8] *Anderson* v. *Croall* (1903) 6 F. 153; *Salvesen* v. *Rederi A/B Nordstjernan* (1905) 7 F. (H.L.) 101; *Irving* v. *Burns,* 1915 S.C. 260.

[9] *Beattie* v. *Lord Ebury* (1874) L.R. 7 H.L. 102; *Firbank's Exors., supra.*

Liability of principal for agent's delicts

The principal is vicariously liable *ex delicto* to a third party for harm caused unjustifiably by his agent, while acting within the scope of the agent's authority, if he expressly authorized the harm,[1] or ratified the act,[2] or if the act were within the usual or ostensible authority of the agent,[3] whether it were done for the principal's[4] or the agent's[5] benefit, and even if it were expressly forbidden,[6] but not if the agent's act falls wholly outside the scope of his authority,[7] nor if the injured person were another agent of the same principal.[8] The agent is also normally personally liable, the principal's authority being no defence.[9]

Property

As between principal and agent possession by the latter is legally possession by the former, and the principal may obtain delivery by an action for delivery or for count, reckoning and payment. As against third parties the principal may recover property transferred by his agent without authority (unless in circumstances covered by the Factors Acts) so long as it is still identifiable and is not a negotiable instrument taken by a *bona fide* taker for value without notice of the agent's lack of authority.

Termination of agency

Agency terminates on the expiry of the period for which it was created,[10] or on the completion of the transaction,[11] on the death[12]

---

[1] *Monaghan* v. *Taylor* (1886) 2 T.L.R. 685; *Crawford* v. *Adams* (1900) 2 F. 987.

[2] *Buron* v. *Denman* (1848) 2 Ex. 167; *Eastern Counties Ry.* v. *Broom* (1851) 6 Ex. 314.

[3] *Makin* v. *Union Bank* (1873) 11 M. 499; *Beaton* v. *Glasgow Corpn.*, 1908 S.C. 1010; *Buchanan* v. *Glasgow Corpn.* (1905) 7 F. 1001; *McCormack* v. *Glasgow Corpn.*, 1910 S.C. 562; *Neville* v. *C. & A. Modes*, 1945 S.C. 175; *Ormrod* v. *Crosville Motor Services, Ltd.* [1953] 2 All E.R. 753.

[4] *Barwick* v. *English Joint Stock Bank* (1867) L.R. 2 Ex. 259.

[5] *Lloyd* v. *Grace Smith & Co.* [1912] A.C. 716; *United Africa Co.* v. *Saka Owoade* [1955] A.C. 130.

[6] *Bank of Scotland* v. *Watson* (1813) 1 Dow 40; *Limpus* v. *London G.O.C.* (1862) 1 H. & C. 526; *Yeo* v. *Wallace* (1867) 5 S.L.R. 253; *Sinclair, Moorhead & Co.* v. *Wallace* (1880) 7 R. 874; *Nicklas* v. *New Popular Cafe Co.* (1908) 15 S.L.T. 735.

[7] *Wardrope* v. *Hamilton* (1876) 3 R. 876; *Hockey* v. *Clydesdale Bank* (1898) 1 F. 119; *Beard* v. *London G.O.C.* [1900] 2 Q.B. 530; *Percy* v. *Glasgow Corpn.*, 1922 S.C. (H.L.) 144.

[8] *Mair* v. *Wood*, 1948 S.C. 83, 87.

[9] *Cameron* v. *Yeats* (1899) 1 F. 456.

[10] cf. *Dowling* v. *Henderson* (1890) 17 R. 921; *Brenan* v. *Campbell's Trs.* (1898) 25 R. 423; *Stevenson* v. *N.B. Ry.* (1905) 7 F. 1106.

[11] *Price* v. *Tennent* (1844) 6 D. 659; *Black* v. *Cullen* (1853) 15 D. 646; *Butler* v. *Knight* (1867) L.R. 2 Ex. 109; *Gillow* v. *Aberdare* (1893) 9 T.L.R. 12.

[12] Actings by the agent while ignorant of the death are good: Ersk. III, 3, 40; cf. *Kennedy* v. *K.* (1843) 6 D. 40; Bankt. I, 18, 1, 17.

or insanity[1] of either party, or the dissolution of a corporation,[2] or the principal's bankruptcy,[3] or by renunciation by the agent,[4] or revocation of authority by the principal,[5] or discontinuance of the principal's business.[6] Where the agent has been transacting with third parties, notice to them of revocation of the agent's authority is necessary to prevent them binding the principal by further transactions in reliance on the agent's ostensible agency.[7] An agency agreement may, however, in special circumstances not be terminable at pleasure.[8]

Accounting

On termination of the relation, the principal is entitled to an accounting from the agent for his intromissions; at least in the case of an agent acting under a factory and commission, the principal must either grant a discharge or state specific objections to the agent's accounts.[9] The agent is entitled to a formal discharge, not merely a receipt for the final balance paid over.[10]

---

[1] *Daily Telegraph Co.* v. *McLaughlin* [1904] A.C. 776; contrast *Wink* v. *Mortimer* (1849) 11 D. 995.

[2] *Salton* v. *New Beeston Cycle Co.* [1900] 1 Ch. 43.

[3] Bankt. I, 18, 1, 18; cf. *Re Pollitt* [1893] 1 Q.B. 455; *Re a debtor* [1937] Ch. 92.

[4] *Hochster* v. *de la Tour* (1853) 2 E. & B. 678.

[5] *Walker* v. *Somerville* (1837) 16 S. 217; *Galbraith & Moorhead* v. *Arethusa Co.* (1896) 23 R. 1011; *Re Hare and O'More's contract* [1901] 1 Ch. 93.

[6] *Patmore* v. *Cannon* (1892) 19 R. 1004; *S.S. State of California Co.* v. *Moore* (1895) 22 R. 562.

[7] *Ferguson & Lillie* v. *Stephen* (1864) 2 M. 804.

[8] *Galbraith & Moorhead, supra.*

[9] *Miln* v. *Short* (1879) 6 R. 800.

[10] *Johnstone's Trs.* v. *Smith Clark* (1896) 4 S.L.T. 180.

CHAPTER 41

HIRING OF SERVICE, OR EMPLOYMENT— *LOCATIO OPERARUM*

THE contract of hiring of service, or of employment (*locatio operarum*)[1] is that whereby one person, the servant or employee, lets out his services to another, the master or employer, for reward or benefit.[2] The main characteristic of the contract of service and the relationship of master and servant or employer and employee has traditionally been that the employer is entitled to control and direct the mode in which the work is done,[3] as distinct from the contract of agency,[4] or the contract for services, or for work (*locatio operis faciendi*),[5] in which the contractor is employed to perform a function or bring about a result in his own way, relying on his own skill and knowledge, and free of detailed control and direction from the employer.[6] The test of control and supervision is today incomplete,[7] and many persons are legally employees who theoretically might be, though are not and frequently cannot be in fact, controlled or directed in the detailed execution of their work.[8] Whether a

---

[1] Stair I, 15; Bankt. I, 2, 54; Ersk. III, 3, 16; Bell, *Prin.* §146–54; Fraser, *M. & S.*; Umpherston; Fridman, *Modern Law of Employment.*

[2] See also definitions in Employers and Workmen Act, 1875, S. 10; Industrial Courts Act, 1919, S. 8; Wages Councils Act, 1959, S. 24; and Contracts of Employment Act, 1972, S. 11. As to the position of an established civil servant see *I.R.C.* v. *Hambrook* [1956] 2 Q.B. 641.

[3] *Sc. Ins. Commrs.* v. *Ch. of Scotland*, 1914 S.C. 16; *Idem* v. *Edinburgh R.I.*, 1913 S.C. 751; *Idem* v. *McNaughton*, 1914 S.C. 826; *Ainslie* v. *Leith Dock Comms.*, 1919 S.C. 676; *Dow* v. *McNeill*, 1925 S.C. 50; *Walker* v. *Dept. of Health*, 1930 S.L.T. 506; *Robertson* v. *Secy. of State for Scotland*, 1943 S.C. 188; *Renfrewshire, etc. Cttee.* v. *Min. of National Ins.*, 1946 S.C. 83; *Gould* v. *Min. of National Ins.* [1951] 1 K.B. 731; *Stagecraft Ltd.* v. *Min. of National Ins.*, 1952 S.C. 288.

[4] Ch. 40, *supra.*

[5] Ch. 42, *infra.*

[6] *Stephen* v. *Thurso Police Commrs.* (1876) 3 R. 535; *Sweeney* v. *Duncan* (1892) 19 R. 870; *Foote* v. *Greenock Hospital*, 1912 S.C. 69; *Logan* v. *Shotts Iron Co.*, 1919 S.C. 131; *Lavelle* v. *Glasgow R.I.*, 1932 S.C. 245; *Reidford* v. *Aberdeen Mags.*, 1933 S.C. 276; cf. *P.R.S.* v. *Mitchell & Booker* [1924] 1 K.B. 762; *Park* v. *Wilsons & Clyde Coal Co.*, 1929 S.C. (H.L.) 38.

[7] *Short* v. *Henderson*, 1946 S.C. (H.L.) 24, 33; cf. *Stevenson Jordan and Harrison Ltd.* v. *MacDonald and Evans* [1952] 1 T.L.R. 101, 111; *Argent* v. *Minister of Social Security* [1968] 3 All E.R. 208.

[8] *Walker* v. *Crystal Palace F.C.* [1910] 1 K.B. 87; *Cassidy* v. *Ministry of Health* [1951] 2 K.B. 343; *Macdonald* v. *Glasgow Western Hospitals*, 1953 S.C. 453; *Roe* v. *Minister of Health* [1954] 2 Q.B. 66.

person is or is not an employee at a particular time is a question of fact, regard being paid to the contract, if any, and the work being done.[1] Other relevant factors are the mode of selection and employment, the type and manner of remuneration, and the power of dismissal,[2] and whether the person is part of the organization or not.[3] He may be an employee not of the principal but of a contractor employed by the principal.[4]

In relation to certain statutes an employee's rights may depend on whether he is a 'workman' or 'employee' as defined by the particular Act.[5]

The distinction between the relationship of service and of agency may be narrow, and an employee may in some circumstances act as an agent,[6] though an agent is *prima facie* not an employee but an independent party bringing two others into contractual relations.[7] The difference between the relationship of service and of partnership may also be narrow.[8]

A special class are 'office-holders', a very indefinite class who hold appointments regulated partly by common law and partly by statute and who cannot be dismissed without being informed of what is alleged against them and being heard in their own defence.[9]

Special problems arise in relation to Crown employees, whose position is regulated by regulations of the Civil Service Depart-

---

[1] *Conlon* v. *Glasgow Corpn.* (1899) 1 F. 869; *Littlejohn* v. *Brown*, 1909 S.C. 169; *McGeachy* v. *Dept. of Health for Sc.*, 1938 S.C. 282; *Morren* v. *Swinton B.C.* [1965] 2 All E.R. 349; *Ready Mixed Concrete Ltd.* v. *M.P.N.I.* [1968] 2 Q.B. 498.

[2] *P.R.S.* v. *Mitchell and Booker* [1925] 1 K.B. 762; *Park* v. *Wilsons & Clyde Coal Co.*, 1928 S.C. 121, 133.

[3] *Bank voor Handel* v. *Slatford* [1953] 1 Q.B. 248.

[4] *Sweeney* v. *Duncan* (1892) 19 R. 870; *Littlejohn* v. *Brown*, 1909 S.C. 169.

[5] See Truck Act, 1831, Ss. 1–4; Employers and Workmen Act, 1875, S. 10; Industrial Courts Act, 1919, S. 8; Contracts of Employment Act, 1972, S. 11; Redundancy Payments Act, 1965, S. 16.

[6] e.g. *Percy* v. *Glasgow Corpn.*, 1922 S.C. (H.L.) 144.

[7] See further *Pickin* v. *Hawkes* (1878) 5 R. 676; *Dowling* v. *Henderson* (1890) 17 R. 921; *Brenan* v. *Campbell's Trs.* (1898) 25 R. 423; *Stevenson* v. *N.B. Ry.* (1905) 7 F. 1106; *Neville* v. *C. & A. Modes*, 1945 S.C. 175.

[8] See Partnership Act, 1890, S. 2(3); *Redcliffe* v. *Rushworth* (1864) 33 Beav. 484; *Walker* v. *Reith* (1906) 8 F. 381; see also *Eaglesham* v. *Grant* (1875) 2 R. 960; *Stott* v. *Fender & Crombie* (1878) 5 R. 1104; *Laing's Tr.* v. *Low* (1896) 23 R. 1105; *Brown's Tr.* v. *McCosh* (1899) 1 F. (H.L.) 86; *Allison* v. *A's Trs.* (1904) 6 F. 496; *Clark* v. *Jamieson*, 1909 S.C. 132; *Dunbar's Trs.* v. *Bruce* (1900) 3 F. 137; *Philipps* v. *Humber* (1904) 6 F. 814; *Fife C.C.* v. *Minister of Nat. Ins.*, 1947 S.C. 629.

[9] This class includes a chief constable: *Ridge* v. *Baldwin* [1964] A.C. 40; a school teacher: *Malloch* v. *Aberdeen Corpn.*, 1971 S.L.T. 245. See also *Taylor* v. *N.U.S.* [1967] 1 All E.R. 767.

ment. They probably have a contract of employment.[1] Employees of local authorities and of National Health Service authorities are regulated largely by statutes and regulations. The police are not employees of anyone but all are holders of distinct public offices, though their conditions of service are regulated by statute and regulations. Dock workers work under statutory schemes at particular ports.

Problems may also arise in connection with employees lent, or let out, with or without equipment, to another employer,[2] with casual or temporary employees,[3] and with 'labour only' subcontracting.[4]

There is extensive statutory control of the employment of women, children, and young persons.[5]

Disabled Persons (Employment) Act, 1944

This Act requires undertakings employing a substantial number of employees (usually twenty) to take disabled persons as a prescribed quota of their work-force.

Race Relations Act, 1968

This Act makes it unlawful (S. 3) to discriminate on grounds of colour, race or ethnic or national origins[6] against a person seeking employment by refusing or deliberately omitting to employ him on any work of any description which is available and for which he is qualified.

Employment Agencies Act, 1973

This Act requires employment agencies and businesses to be licensed, regulates their conduct and imposes restrictions on charging persons seeking employment.

Constitution and proof

If the contract is to endure for more than a year it must be constituted by writing authenticated by both parties, or holo-

---

[1] *Brandy* v. *S.S. Raphael (Owners)* [1911] A.C. 413; *Sutton* v. *A.G.* (1923) 39 T.L.R. 294; *Reilly* v. *The King* [1934] A.C. 176; *A.G. for Guyana* v. *Nobrega* [1969] 3 All E.R. 1604.

[2] See e.g. *Mersey Docks and Harbour Board* v. *Coggins and Griffiths* [1947] A.C. 1.

[3] See e.g. *Market Investigations, Ltd.* v. *M. of Social Security* [1968] 3 All E.R. 732.

[4] See e.g. *Construction Industry Training Board* v. *Labour Force, Ltd.* [1970] 3 All E.R. 220.

[5] Children and Young Persons (Sc.) Act, 1937; Mines and Quarries Act, 1954; Factories Act, 1961.

[6] cf. *Ealing* v. *Race Relations Board* [1972] A.C. 342.

graph, or adopted as holograph.[1] Failing such writings *rei interventus* validates an improbative contract for the whole term,[2] and an oral contract for a year.[3] Failing *rei interventus* an oral contract for a longer period is possibly not valid even for a year.[4] Agreement to modification of a written contract for longer than a year can be established only by writ or oath.[5] A contract for the hire of a seaman as one of a crew requires to be in writing signed by the master and each seaman.[6]

If for a year or less the contract may be made orally and proved parole,[7] or inferred from actual service acquiesced in,[8] and the performance of services without express agreement raises an implied contract,[9] though if the defender stands *in loco parentis* to the pursuer, who resides with him, there is no presumption that services rendered are attributable to employment,[10] and there may be evidence of a custom to render services gratuitously.[11] Terms may be imported by notices if proved to have been brought to the notice of the employee.[12] The party founding on it must prove any term relied on.[13]

Duration of employment

The duration may be such as the parties determine; it is questionable whether a contract to serve for life is valid.[14] In appointments recognized by custom as being *munera publica*, which import duties to the public as well as to the employer, it is

[1] *Currie* v. *McLean* (1864) 2 M. 1076; *Thomson* v. *Fraser* (1868) 7 M. 39; *Stewart* v. *McCall* (1869) 7 M. 544; *Grant* v. *Ramage & Ferguson* (1897) 25 R. 35; *Nisbet* v. *Percy* 1951 S.C. 350; *Murray* v. *Roussel Labs.*, 1960 S.L.T. (Notes) 31; *Cook* v. *Grubb*, 1963 S.C. 1; cf. *Pickin* v. *Hawkes* (1878) 5 R. 676.

[2] *Campbell* v. *Baird* (1827) 5 S. 335.

[3] *Caddell* v. *Sinclair* (1749) Mor. 12416; *Napier* v. *Dick* (1805) Hume 388; *Reuter* v. *Douglas* (1902) 10 S.L.T. 294. But cf. *Brown* v. *Scottish Antarctic Expedition* (1902) 10 S.L.T. 433.

[4] Bell, *Prin.* §173; *Paterson* v. *Edington* (1830) 8 S. 931; *Currie* v. *McLean* (1864) 2 M. 1076; *Stewart & McDonald* v. *McCall* (1869) 7 M. 544.

[5] *Dumbarton Glass Co.* v. *Coatsworth* (1847) 9 D. 732; cf. *Ayr District Board of Control* v. *Lord Advocate*, 1926 S.L.T. 233.

[6] Merchant Shipping Act, 1970, S. 1.

[7] *Smellie* v. *Gillespie* (1833) 12 S. 125.

[8] *Anderson* v. *Halley* (1847) 9 D. 1222; *Thomson* v. *T's Trs.* (1889) 16 R. 333.

[9] *Anderson, supra*; but see *Gray* v. *Johnston*, 1928 S.C. 659.

[10] *Miller* v. *M.* (1898) 25 R. 995; *Urquhart* v. *U's Trs.* (1905) 8 F. 42; *Russell* v. *McClymont* (1906) 8 F. 821.

[11] *Corbin* v. *Stewart* (1911) 28 T.L.R. 99.

[12] *Wright* v. *Howard, Baker & Co.* (1893) 21 R. 25.

[13] *Cowan* v. *McMicking* (1849) 19 S. Jur. 91; *Robson* v. *Overend* (1878) 6 R. 213.

[14] *Mulcahy* v. *Herbert* (1898) 25 R. 1136; see also Ersk. I, 7, 62; *Allan* v. *Skene* (1728) Mor. 9454; *Wallis* v. *Dey* (1837) 2 M. & W. 273. As to 'permanent employment' see *Lawrie* v. *Brown*, 1908 S.C. 705; *Cook* v. *Grubb*, 1963 S.C. 1.

implied that the duration is *ad vitam aut culpam*,[1] and in any other case an appointment may expressly be given for life, in either case with liberty to resign earlier. Normally an appointment is for a term of years, or a period of a year,[2] or a month, or at will, in which case it runs on until terminated by either party giving reasonable notice to the other of intention to terminate. An inference as to the duration may be drawn from the provision for remuneration.[3] A contract of service with the Crown, unless statute provides otherwise,[4] is terminable at the Crown's pleasure without notice,[5] except in the case of purely civilian employment.[6]

Assignation

In view of its personal character a contract of service is not assignable by the employer,[7] nor is the duty of performance delegable.[8] But an employee may be lent or hired out with a machine he operates to another employer and may even be deemed to have become *pro hac vice* the employee of that other employer.[9]

Effect of illness or death

A temporary illness of the employee does not affect the contract,[10] unless it wholly prevents performance at some material time.[11] Disabling illness attributable to the employee's own fault

---

[1] *Munera publica* include judicial offices, benefices in the church: *Hastie* v. *McMurtrie* (1889) 16 R. 715; professorships in the universities: *Caird* v. *Sime* (1887) 14 R. (H.L.) 37; the office of session clerk: *Goldie* v. *Christie and Petrie* (1868) 6 M. 541; of parochial schoolmaster: *Morrison* v. *Abernethy School Board* (1876) 3 R. 945; of town clerk: *Rothesay Mags.* v. *Carse* (1902) 4 F. 641; *Sutherland* v. *Wick Mags.* (1904) 7 F. 374 and of notary public: *Finlay* v. *F's Trs.*, 1948 S.C. 16, 25; *Gorrie's Trs.* v. *Stiven*, 1952 S.C. 1, 13. But judges must now retire at 74: Judicial Pensions Act, 1959, S. 2; sheriffs at 72; Sheriff's Pensions (Sc.) Act, 1961, S. 71; and professors at the age fixed by the University Ordinances. See also *Lawrie* v. *Brown*, 1908 S.C. 705. For another kind of *munus publicum* see *Graham* v. *Cuthbert*, 1951 J.C. 25.

[2] *Bentinck* v. *Macpherson* (1869) 6 S.L.R. 376; contrast *Scott* v. *McMurdo* (1869) 6 S.L.R. 301,

[3] *Moffat* v. *Shedden* (1839) 1 D. 468; *Campbell* v. *Fyfe* (1851) 13 D. 1041.

[4] *Gould* v. *Stuart* [1896] A.C. 575.

[5] *Dunn* v. *R.* [1896] 1 Q.B. 116; *Denning* v. *Secy. for India* (1920) 37 T.L.R. 138; but see *Reilly* v. *R.* [1934] A.C. 176, 179.

[6] *Cameron* v. *Lord Advocate*, 1952 S.C. 165.

[7] *Ross* v. *McFarlane* (1894) 21 R. 396; cf. *Berlitz School* v. *Duchene* (1903) 6 F. 181; *Nokes* v. *Doncaster Amalgamated Collieries* [1940] A.C. 1014.

[8] *Campbell* v. *Price* (1831) 9 S. 264.

[9] *Malley* v. *L.M.S. Ry.*, 1944 S.C. 129.

[10] *Craig* v. *Graham* (1844) 6 D. 684; *Warburton* v. *C.W.S.* [1917] 1 K.B. 663; Contracts of Employment Act, 1972, Sched. 1, para. 5(1); *Tarbuck* v. *Wilson* (1967) 2 I.T.R. 157.

[11] *Robinson* v. *Davison* (1871) L.R. 6 Ex. 269; *Poussard* v. *Spiers and Pond* (1876) 1 Q.B.D. 410: cf. *Bettini* v. *Gye* (1876) 1 Q.B.D. 183; *Condor* v. *Barron Knights, Ltd.* [1966] 1 W.L.R. 87.

or misconduct may be held a breach of contract.[1] Illness of long duration may frustrate the contract or justify the employer in giving notice of dismissal,[2] particularly if due to the employee's own failure.[3] The employee's enforced absence on military service may also be held to frustrate the contract.[4] Illness not justifying rescission of the contract probably does not justify any deduction from wages.[5]

The death of either party[6] terminates the contract, in view of its personal character, though domestic servants are bound, if required, to remain with the family until the next term.[7] A deceased servant's executors are entitled to the proportion of salary earned down to the date of death.[7] The master's death is, however, not a breach of contract on his part.[8]

In the case of employment by a firm the contract is terminated by the death of a partner or a change in the constitution of the firm,[9] or if the firm is converted into a company[10] but such changes are not breaches of contract.[11]

Bankruptcy or liquidation of employer

The employer's bankruptcy is a breach of contract on his part justifying a claim of damages for wrongful dismissal against his estate.[12] Certain arrears of wages and salaries accrued before the date of sequestration are preferential claims against the bankrupt estate.[13] Similarly if a company goes into liquidation, that is a breach of contract[14] entitling employees to wages in lieu of notice,

---

[1] *McEwan* v. *Malcolm* (1867) 5 S.L.R. 62.

[2] *Manson* v. *Downie* (1885) 12 R. 1103; *Westwood* v. *S.M.T. Co.*, 1938 S.N. 8; *Orman* v. *Saville Sportswear, Ltd.* [1960] 1 W.L.R. 1055.

[3] *McEwan* v. *Malcolm* (1867) 5 S.L.R. 62.

[4] *Marshall* v. *Glanvill* [1917] 2 K.B. 87; *Morgan* v. *Manser* [1948] 1 K.B. 184; cf. *Unger* v. *Preston Corpn.* [1942] 1 All E.R. 200.

[5] Stair I, 15, 2; Ersk. III, 1, 16; *White* v. *Baillie* (1794) Mor. 10147.

[6] *Stubbs* v. *Holywell Ry.* (1867) L.R. 2 Ex. 311; *Farrow* v. *Wilson* (1869) L.R. 4 C.P. 744.

[7] Ersk. III, 3, 16; Bell, *Prin.* §179. As to service occupancy see *Torrance* v. *Traill's Trs.* (1897) 24 R. 837.

[8] *Hoey* v. *McEwan & Auld* (1867) 5 M. 814.

[9] *Harkins* v. *Smith* (1841) 13 Sc. Jur. 381; *Hoey, supra*; but see *Berlitz School, infra*, at 186; *Brace* v. *Calder* [1895] 2 Q.B. 253.

[10] *Berlitz School* v. *Duchene* (1903) 6 F. 181.

[11] *Hoey, supra*.

[12] *Hoey* v. *McEwan & Auld* (1867) 5 M. 814, 817; *Day* v. *Tait* (1900) 8 S.L.T. 40.

[13] Bankruptcy (Sc.) Act, 1913, S. 118, amd. Companies Act, 1947, S. 115.

[14] *Re General Rolling Stock Co., Chapman's Case* (1866) L.R. 1 Eq. 346; *Reid* v. *Explosives Co.* (1887) 19 Q.B.D. 264; *Day, supra*; *Laing* v. *Gowans* (1902) 10 S.L.T. 461; *Measures Bros.* v. *Measures* [1910] 2 Ch. 248; *Reigate* v. *Union Mfg. Co.* [1918] 1 K.B. 592.

and certain arrears of wages and salaries are preferential claims in the liquidation.[1]

Illegality

The contract may be vitiated by illegality in whole[2] or in part.[3]

Terms and conditions of contract

The express terms and conditions of the employment may be such as may be agreed. They may include conditions restrictive of the employee's liberty when he leaves the employment,[4] and the validity of which may be open to challenge as unreasonable in the circumstances. Terms may be imported by notice,[5] or by reference,[6] but many of the terms are implied by law or by the custom[7] of the business or trade in question. A provision in a circular issued by a government department has been held incorporated in a person's contract of employment.[8] An award made by the Industrial Court under the Terms and Conditions of Employment Act, 1959, S. 8, has effect as an implied term of a contract of employment.[9]

Variation of terms

After employment has commenced terms as to e.g. hours, wages, grading, or other factors may be varied by agreement, or by notice of termination of the contract and immediate re-employment,[10] but if sought to be made unilaterally by either party without notice of termination, it is a breach of contract.[11]

---

[1] Bell, *Prin.* §1404; Companies Act, 1948, S. 319.

[2] *Napier* v. *National Business Agency* [1951] 2 All E.R. 264.

[3] *Kearney* v. *Whitehaven Colliery* [1893] 1 Q.B. 700.

[4] e.g. *Mason* v. *Provident Clothing Co.* [1913] A.C. 724; *Morris* v. *Saxelby* [1916] 1 A.C. 688. See also *Eastham* v. *Newcastle United F.C.* [1964] Ch. 413.

[5] *Carus* v. *Eastwood* (1875) 32 L.T. 855.

[6] e.g. to a book of Works Rules: for specimen see Wedderburn: *Cases on Labour Law*, 62; or to a collective agreement between an employer or association of employers and a union or unions representing employees: for specimens, see Wedderburn, 312–30. Collective agreements are binding between employers and individual employees only so far as expressly, or by implication, incorporated in an individual contract of employment; cf. *Ayling* v. *London and India Docks Cttee.* (1893) 9 T.L.R. 409; contrast *Smithies* v. *N.A. Operative Plasterers* [1909] 1 K.B. 310; and see also *Rookes* v. *Barnard* [1963] 1 Q.B. 623; [1964] A.C. 1129.

[7] *Sagar* v. *Ridehalgh* [1931] 1 Ch. 310.

[8] *Palmer* v. *Inverness Hospitals Board*, 1963 S.C. 311.

[9] S. 8(4).

[10] e.g. *Spelman* v. *Garnham* (1968) 3 I.T.R. 370.

[11] e.g. *Cowey* v. *Liberian Operators, Ltd.* [1966] 2 Lloyd's Rep. 45; *Gresham Furniture Ltd.* v. *Wall* (1970) 5 I.T.R. 171.

Collective bargains and agreements

Collective bargains may be made by one or more unions with one or more employers to regulate the main conditions of employment of workers in a particular occupation or industry. They may be substantive agreements dealing with conditions or procedure agreements providing for the resolution of disputes or contain elements of both. Such agreements, made before the Industrial Relations Act, 1971, or made after the Act and containing a clause excluding the presumption enacted by that Act may not be contracts because not intended to be legally binding[1] but some may be contracts.

A collective agreement can be legally enforceable between the parties to an individual employment contract if the union were agent for the employee,[2] or the collective bargain is expressly incorporated in the contract,[3] or incorporated as implied terms,[4] or incorporated by custom of the trade.[5]

The Terms and Conditions of Employment Act, 1959, S. 8, provides that where terms and conditions of employment have been settled by agreement or award a trade union or employers' association may complain to the Minister about any employer who fails to comply with collectively agreed terms, and the Industrial Arbitration Board may make an award which is to have effect as an implied term of the contracts of employment of that employer's employees.

Code of Industrial Relations Practice

The Secretary of State for Trade and Industry must issue, with the approval of Parliament, a Code of Industrial Relations Practice.[6] A failure on the part of any person to observe any provision of the Code for the time being in force does not by itself render him liable to any proceedings, but in proceedings before the Industrial Court or an industrial tribunal under the 1974 Act the Code is admissible in evidence and any provision which appears to be relevant shall be taken into account in determining that question.[7]

---

[1] *Ford Motor Co.* v. *A.U.E.F.* [1969] 2 Q.B. 303. See now Trade Union and Labour Relations Act, 1974, S. 18.

[2] See *Holland* v. *London Compositors* (1924) 40 T.L.R. 440; *Rookes* v. *Barnard* [1963] 1 Q.B. 623, 675; Wedderburn, Cases and Materials on Labour Law, 286, 459.

[3] e.g. *N.C.B.* v. *Galley* [1958] 1 All E.R. 91; *Morris* v. *Bailey* [1969] 2 Lloyd's Rep. 215; *Stevenson* v. *Teesside Bridge Co.* [1971] 1 All E.R. 296.

[4] e.g. *Hill* v. *Levy* (1858) 3 H. & N. 7; *Joel* v. *Cammell Laird* (1968) 4 I.T.R. 206.

[5] e.g. *Maclea* v. *Essex Lines* (1933) 45 Ll.L.R. 25.

[6] Trade Union and Labour Relations Act, 1974, Sch. 1, paras 1–2.   [7] Ibid., para. 3.

Duties of employer

The employer must receive the employee into his employment, unless he has grounds for refusal such as would justify immediate dismissal. If he refuses *ab ante*[1] or at the date for commencement[2] he is in breach of contract and liable in damages.

Duties under Contracts of Employment Act, 1972

By the Contracts of Employment Act, 1972, S. 4, unless an employee has a contract in writing containing the requisite information, an employer must, not later than 13 weeks after the beginning of an employee's employment with that employer, give him a written statement identifying the parties, specifying the date when the employment began and giving particulars, as at a specified date nor more than one week before, of (a) the scale or rate of remuneration, or method of calculating it, (b) the intervals at which remuneration is paid; (c) any terms and conditions relating to hours of work;[3] (d) any terms and conditions relating to holidays and holiday pay, incapacity for work (including sick pay), pensions and pension schemes; and (e) the length of notice which the employee is obliged to give and entitled to receive to determine his contract of employment. If the contract is for a fixed term, the date of expiry shall be stated. The statement must also include a note indicating the nature of the employee's rights to join or not to join a union, specifying a person to whom he can apply for redress of grievances, and explaining the steps consequent on any such application. This statement is not the contract of employment but may bar either party from seeking to prove contradictory terms.[4] Changes in terms must be notified. The requirements do not apply to employment for less than 21 hours per week nor to categories excluded by S. 6. If a written statement is not furnished the employee may require a reference to an industrial tribunal to determine what particulars ought to have been included.[5]

---

[1] *Hochster* v. *De la Tour* (1853) 2 E. & B. 678.

[2] *Campbell* v. *Mackenzie* (1887) 24 S.L.R. 354.

[3] A notice furnished under the Act may by this clause import into the contract of employment of each man a collective agreement made between the employer and a trade union: *Camden Exhibition, Ltd.* v. *Lynott* [1965] 3 All E.R. 28.

[4] *Smith* v. *Blandford Gee Cementation Co.* [1970] 3 All E.R. 154.

[5] S. 8.

Duty to furnish work

There is no duty to furnish work[1] save where the remuneration is by piece-rates or commission, in which case work must be provided[2] or a fair reward paid. But in some classes of contracts the opportunity to work is of the essence of the contract and failure to provide work is a breach.[3]

Duty to pay wages

Where services are rendered the presumption is, in the absence of circumstances to exclude it, that the employer has to pay wages or other remuneration.[4] The amount may be determined by direct agreement,[5] by a prior course of dealing,[6] by agreement between the employer or an association of employers and a trade union or unions representing the employees,[7] by order made by a wages council established under the Wages Councils Act, 1959, or on the recommendation of a Joint Industrial Council. Failing any mode of fixing wages a fair recompense is due for the services rendered.[8] In contracts of service at will, wages accrue from day to day and are payable periodically. Remuneration at so much per year or per month may be held indivisible,[9] even though payments to account be made periodically.

An employee who receives less than he considers himself entitled to contractually may be held barred from objecting if he grants unqualified receipts, or fails to protest, or otherwise acquiesces in the payments made to him.[10] Conversely allegations of negligence made only after the service has terminated are not a relevant defence against a claim for wages.[11]

[1] *Turner* v. *Sawdon* [1901] 2 K.B. 653; *Browning* v. *Crumlin Valley Collieries, Ltd.* [1926] 1 K.B. 522; *Collier* v. *Sunday Referee Co.* [1940] 2 K.B. 647.

[2] Bell, *Prin.* §192; *Turner* v. *Goldsmith* [1891] 1 Q.B. 544; *Bauman* v. *Hulton Press* [1952] 2 All E.R. 1121.

[3] *Devonald* v. *Rosser* [1960] 2 K.B. 728; *Clayton* v. *Oliver* [1930] A.C. 209; *Collier* v. *Sunday Referee Pub. Co.* [1940] 2 K.B. 647.

[4] *Peter* v. *Rennie's Reps.* (1842) 14 Sc. Jur. 240; *Bell* v. *Ogilvie* (1863) 2 M. 336; *Landless* v. *Wilson* (1880) 8 R. 289; cf. *Wilkie* v. *Bethune* (1848) 11 D. 132.

[5] cf. *Eunson* v. *Johnson & Greig*, 1940 S.C. 49; *Paterson* v. *S.W.S. Electricity Board*, 1950 S.C. 582.

[6] *Stewart* v. *Clyne* (1835) 2 S. & McL. 45.

[7] Such an agreement is legally enforceable only insofar as its terms are incorporated in the contracts of employment of individual employees.

[8] *Sinclair* v. *Erskine* (1831) 9 S. 487; *Adam* v. *Peter* (1842) 4 D. 599; *Stuart* v. *McLeod* (1901) 9 S.L.T. 192.

[9] *Hoey* v. *McEwan & Auld* (1867) 5 M. 814; *Macgill* v. *Park* (1899) 2 F. 272.

[10] *Davies* v. *Glasgow Friendly Soc.*, 1935 S.C. 224; *Eunson* v. *Johnson & Greig*, 1940 S.C. 49.

[11] *Fraser* v. *Lang* (1831) 9 S. 418; *Tait* v. *Macintosh* (1841) 13 S. Jur. 280; see also *Logan* v. *Stephen* (1850) 13 D. 262.

Wages unpaid are recoverable as a civil debt and if the employer goes bankrupt an employee is to a limited extent a preferential creditor for salary or wages. Certain statutes provide particular remedies for the recovery of wages which have not, in breach of the Act, been paid to an employee. A failure to pay wages for a substantial period is a material breach of contract and in practice a failure, even on one occasion, would probably result in a strike.

Special cases—service by relative or neighbour

Where the employee is a close relative of the employer and there is no definite arrangement as to wages there is a slight presumption in favour of wages being due, which may be rebutted if the employee got board and lodging, clothing and pocket-money,[1] or there are indications that the service was intended to be gratuitous. Thus no wages have been held due where a niece lived with a lady as adopted daughter and nursed her,[2] or a son worked for his father for twelve years,[3] or a daughter worked in her father's house.[4] Similarly domestic services for a neighbour have been held not to justify wages in the absence of contract.[5]

Service occupancy of house

Wages may be partly satisfied by provision of a house or other accommodation, but occupation of an employer's house may be an ordinary tenancy rather than a service occupancy.[6]

Payment for extra work

Unless there is a relative arrangement extra remuneration is not due for extra work by employees paid a periodical or annual salary.[7] If there is a general increase in the duties of a post the claim is for increased salary rather than for extra payment.[8]

---

[1] *Thomson* v. *T's Tr.* (1889) 16 R. 333; *Urquhart* v. *U's Tr.* (1905) 8 F. 42; cf. *Shepherd* v. *Meldrum* (1812) Hume 394; *McNaughton* v. *McN.* (1813) Hume 396; *Anderson* v. *Halley* (1847) 9 D. 1222.

[2] *Russel* v. *McClymont* (1906) 8 F. 821.

[3] *Miller* v. *M.* (1898) 25 R. 995.

[4] *Macnaughton* v. *Finlayson's Trs.* (1902) 10 S.L.T. 322.

[5] *Ritchie* v. *Ferguson* (1849) 12 D. 119.

[6] *Dunbar's Trs.* v. *Bruce* (1900) 3 F. 137; *Philipps* v. *Humber* (1904) 6 F. 814; *MacGregor* v. *Dunnet*, 1949 S.C. 510; cf. *Stewart* v. *Robertson*, 1937 S.C. 701; *Pollock* v. *Inverness-shire Assessor*, 1923 S.C. 693; *Cairns* v. *Innes*, 1942 S.C. 164.

[7] *Latham* v. *Edinburgh & Glasgow Ry. Co.* (1866) 4 M. 1084; *Money* v. *Hannan & Kerr* (1867) 5 S.L.R. 32; *Mackenzie* v. *Baird's Trs.*, 1907 S.C. 838.

[8] *Mackison* v. *Dundee Burgh*, 1909 S.C. 571; 1910 S.C. (H.L.) 27.

Wages during sickness

Many contracts contain express provisions about sick pay, and particulars about it must be notified under the Contracts of Employment Act, 1972. Failing express provision a clause may be implied from the conduct of parties[1] or the custom of the trade.[2] In the absence of any such indication full wages must be paid during sickness.[3]

Suspension without wages

In the absence of contractual provision or proven trade practice an employer probably may not suspend from work as a disciplinary measure and withhold wages.[4]

Laying-off

The contract may include a term, including one imported by custom, that the employer may 'lay-off' employees without pay.[5]

Fair Wages Resolutions

The House of Commons has thrice[6] passed a resolution[7] that contractors employed on government contracts be required to observe such terms and conditions as have been established for the trade or industry in the district by representative joint machinery of negotiation or by arbitration, failing which terms and conditions which are not less favourable than the general level of wages, hours and conditions observed by other employers in comparable circumstances. The contractor must also observe fair conditions of work, recognize the freedom of his workers to be members of trade unions and be responsible for the observance of the resolution by any sub-contractors whom he may employ. The government has recommended that local authorities adopt this policy and this is general practice with such authorities and nationalized industries. Complaints of non-observance of the resolution may be settled by the Ministry of Labour or an independent tribunal, usually the Industrial Court.[8] The principle of

---

[1] O'Grady v. Saper [1940] 2 K.B. 469.

[2] Petrie v. Mac Fisheries [1940] 1 K.B. 258.

[3] Orman v. Saville Sportswear, Ltd. [1960] 3 All E.R. 105.

[4] Hanley v. Pease and Partners [1915] 1 K.B. 698; Marshall v. English Electric Co. (1945) 61 T.L.R. 379.

[5] cf. Puttick v. Wright [1972] I.C.R. 457.

[6] 1891, 1909 and 1946; see Ministry of Labour: Industrial Relations Handbook (1961), Ch. 9.

[7] It does not have statutory effect, and confers no actionable rights on an employee: Simpson v. Kodak, Ltd. [1948] 2 K.B. 184.

[8] See e.g. R. v. Industrial Court ex. p. A.S.S.E.T. [1965] 1 Q.B. 377.

the resolution has been embodied in various statutes which provide financial support to particular industries[1] or public authorities.

Statutory wage regulation

The Wages Councils Act, 1959,[2] empowers the Minister of Labour to establish wages councils in relation to particular trades, on his own initiative, on application by organizations of employers and workers, or after asking a Commission of Inquiry to consider whether establishment of a wages council is desirable. A wages council consists of members representing employers and workers in equal numbers, and independent members. It has power to submit proposals to the Minister for fixing minimum remuneration to workers in the trade concerned and fixing holidays and holiday remuneration and may make recommendations on matters relative to conditions in that industry. Wages regulation proposals are published and representations may be made after which the Minister makes a wages regulation order giving them legal effect. Wages regulation orders are enforced by wages inspectors of the Ministry of Labour and criminal sanctions. The wages of agricultural workers are determined by the Agricultural Wages Board under the Agricultural Wages (Sc.) Act, 1949.[3] Wages statutorily fixed may be sued for as being a statutorily implied term of the contract.[4]

Checkweighing

In mining provision has long existed[5] whereby workmen may appoint a checkweigher to check the weighing and measuring of the minerals extracted. This was extended by the Checkweighing in Various Industries Act, 1919 to various other industries in which payment depends on measurement of output.

Equal Pay Act, 1970

This Act provides for equal treatment as regards terms and conditions of employment for men and women employed on like work or rated as equivalent, and this equality is to be an implied term of every contract of employment. The requirement of equal

---

[1] e.g. Sugar Act, 1956, S. 24. See also Road Traffic Act, 1960, S. 152.
[2] Replacing Trade Boards Acts, 1909–18 and consolidating Acts of 1945 and 1948.
[3] cf. *Murray* v. *Burnet*, 1941 J.C. 53.
[4] *Macdonald* v. *Singer Mfg. Co.*, 1923 S.C. 551.
[5] Coal Mines Regulation Act, 1887, S. 13; Coal Mines (Check Weigher) Act, 1894, and Mines and Quarries Act, 1954; Coal Mines (Weighing of Minerals) Act, 1905.

treatment may give rise to a claim for arrears of remuneration or damages in respect of a failure to comply with an equal pay clause, which may be determined by an industrial tribunal. Collective agreements may be amended by the Industrial Arbitration Tribunal, as may wages regulation orders and agricultural wages orders. Equal treatment does not affect protective legislation affecting women's employment, and provision is made for equality of conditions between male and female members of the Services, except where based on different duties, and in police regulations. The Act comes into force at the end of 1975 but may be partially implemented earlier by order.

Payment of wages

By the Truck Acts, 1831 to 1940, a contract whereby wages payable to a workman[1] are paid otherwise than in current coin of the realm is illegal, void and an offence.[2] Nor may the contract contain any provision, direct or indirect, concerning the place where or the manner in which, or the person or persons with whom, the whole or any part of the wages shall be laid out or expended.[3] The entire amount of the wages must be actually paid to the worker in current coin and not otherwise.[4] It offends against the Act to supply goods and deduct the cost from wages,[5] or give an order on a shop in lieu of wages,[6] or sell drink on credit and deduct the cost from wages,[7] or deduct instalment payments for shares in the employing company,[8] or rent owed by the employee's father,[9] or deduct a sum due by the employee in respect

---

[1] The definition of 'workman' in the Employers and Workman Act, 1875, S. 10 is adopted by the Truck (Amdt.) Act, 1887, S. 2; thus the Acts have been held applicable to a potter's printer: *Grainger* v. *Aynsley* (1880) 6 Q.B.D. 182; a bus driver: *Smith* v. *Assoc. Omnibus Co.* [1907] 1 K.B. 916; a draper's packer: *Pratt* v. *Cook, Son & Co.* [1940] A.C. 437; a welder: *Duncan* v. *Motherwell Bridge Co.*, 1952 S.C. 131; but not to a foreman: *Phillips* v. *McInnes* (1874) 2 R. 224; a bus conductor: *Morgan* v. *L.G.O.C.* (1884) 13 Q.B.D. 832; tram driver: *Cook* v. *N. Metropolitan Tramways Co.* (1887) 18 Q.B.D. 683; grocer's assistant: *Bound* v. *Lawrence* [1892] 1 Q.B. 226; postman: *Pearce* v. *Lansdowne* (1893) 62 L.J. Q.B. 441; hospital mechanic: *Cameron* v. *Royal London Ophthalmic Hosp.* [1941] 1 K.B. 350.

The Truck Acts also apply to persons working at home or elsewhere for a shopkeeper, dealer or trader and as to articles valued under £5 of the kinds mentioned in the Truck (Amdt.) Act, 1887.

[2] Truck Act, 1831, S. 1.   [3] S. 2.

[4] S. 3. Similarly, Hosiery Manufacture (Wages) Act, 1874.

[5] *Wilson* v. *Cookson* (1863) 13 C.B. (N.S.) 496.

[6] *Athersmith* v. *Drury* (1858) 1 E. & E. 46; *Finlayson* v. *Braidbar Quarry Co.* (1864) 2 M. 1297.

[7] *Gould* v. *Haynes* (1889) 59 L.J.M.C. 9.

[8] *Kenyon* v. *Darwen Cotton Co.* [1936] 2 K.B. 193.

[9] *Penman* v. *Fife Coal Co.*, 1935 S.C. (H.L.) 39.

of an antecedent breach of his contract to work,[1] or deposit a monthly deduction in a bank at home while the employee worked abroad, in security of possible claims against the employee.[2] But deductions for bad work have been held in special circumstances to be a mode of ascertaining the true wages.[3] Any wages not paid as required by the Act may be recovered from the employer.[4]

By the Payment of Wages Act, 1960, it is nevertheless competent for an employee to request in writing that his wages be paid in whole or in part into an account at a bank, by postal order, money order or cheque, and for an employer to pay accordingly (S. 1). No deduction may be made for the payment and a written statement containing specific particulars must be given to the employee (S. 2). The request or the employer's agreement to pay may be cancelled by written notice (S. 3). In case of absence from the place of payment by duty or illness, payment of wages may be made by postal order or money order unless this mode is objected to (S. 4).

Where a workman is entitled to receive an advance on account of wages it is not lawful to withhold the advance or make a deduction for discount, interest or otherwise.[5] A contract with a servant in husbandry by which the latter receives food, drink, a cottage or other privileges in addition to money wages is competent.[6] If a workman sues the employer for wages the latter cannot counterclaim for goods supplied to the workman under an order or direction of the employer, nor can the employer sue the workman for goods so supplied unless they are those permitted by the Acts.[7]

The Payment of Wages in Public Houses Prohibition Act, 1883, prohibits the payment of wages to workmen in public houses or similar places or premises belonging thereto, except where the wages are paid by the resident owner or occupier to a workman employed by him.

Time of payment

Prima facie the wages for each period, week, month or year, fall to be paid at or shortly after the end of that period,[8] but there may be custom to pay wages at intervals.[9]

---

[1] *Williams* v. *North's Navigation Collieries, Ltd.* [1906] A.C. 136.   [2] *Duncan, supra.*
[3] *Hart* v. *Riversdale Mill Co.* [1928] 1 K.B. 176; *Sagar* v. *Ridehalgh* [1931] 1 Ch. 310.
[4] S. 4; *Pratt, supra; Duncan, supra.*   [5] Truck Amdt. Act, 1887, S. 3.
[6] Ibid., S. 4.
[7] Ibid., S. 5.
[8] *Sime* v. *Grimond,* 1920, 1 S.L.T. 270.
[9] *Macgill* v. *Park* (1899) 2 F. 272.

Proof of payment

Proof of payment is probably competent orally only where each term's payment does not exceed £10 Scots; if it exceeds that sum it must be proved by writ or oath.[1]

Deductions from wages

No deductions may be made from wages other than those permitted by the Truck Acts.[2] Permitted deductions may be made if the employer contracts to or does supply to his workman medicine or medical attendance, fuel, materials, tools or implements to be used by workmen employed in mines, hay, corn or provender to be consumed by a beast of burden; or he may let to his workmen the whole or any part of a tenement, or supply to his workmen food prepared and consumed on the premises. The deductions must not exceed the true value of the goods supplied or services rendered and in every case there must be a written agreement signed by the workman evidencing his consent to the deduction.[3] If deductions are made for medicine, medical attendance, tools or education of children the employer must prepare accounts and submit them to two auditors appointed by the workmen.[4] Thus deductions for monies payable under the Employers and Workmen Act, 1875,[5] for coals supplied,[6] for house rent and medical attendance,[7] and for rent due in respect of the workman's father's house,[8] have been held void and illegal. But the deduction of contributions to a benefit club, membership of which was a term of employment, was not struck at,[9] nor is it illegal to advance money to the employee to contribute to a friendly society or bank or for relief in sickness or for the education of his children and to deduct the advances from wages.[10]

The Truck Act, 1896, legalizes certain deductions by way of fines and for damaged goods. A contract, by notice constantly affixed and easily read or copied, or in writing, signed by the

---

[1] *Brown* v. *Mason* (1856) 19 D. 137.

[2] *Williams* v. *North's Navigation Collieries* [1906] A.C. 136; *Penman* v. *Fife Coal Co.*, 1935 S.C. (H.L.) 39.

[3] 1831 Act, S. 23; *Cutts* v. *Ward* (1867) L.R. 2 Q.B. 357; *Hynd* v. *Spowart* (1884) 22 S.L.R. 702; *Pratt* v. *Cook* [1940] A.C. 437.

[4] Truck Amdt. Act, 1887, S. 9.

[5] *Williams, supra.*

[6] *McLucas* v. *Campbell* (1892) 30 S.L.R. 226.

[7] *Hynd, supra.*

[8] *Penman, supra.*

[9] *Hewlett* v. *Allen* [1894] A.C. 383.

[10] 1831 Act, S. 24; see also 1887 Act, S. 7.

workman,[1] may provide for fines, fair and reasonable in the circumstances, for specified acts or omissions which cause or are likely to cause damage or loss to the employer, or interruption or hindrance to his business and of which written particulars are supplied to the workman (S. 1).[2] A similar contract may permit fair and reasonable deductions for the actual or estimated damage or loss occasioned to the employer by the act or omission of the workman,[3] or some person over whom he has control, or for whom he has by the contract agreed to be responsible (S. 2). A similar contract may permit deductions for the use or supply of materials, tools or machines, standing room, light, heat or any other thing to be done or provided by the employer in relation to the workman's work or labour (S. 3). Deductions made contrary to the Act are recoverable within six months; if the workman consented to the deduction he may recover only the excess over what was fair and reasonable. Every contract under the Act must be produced to an inspector of factories or of mines; a register of deductions must be kept and produced similarly (Ss. 5–6).

The Shop Clubs Act, 1902, makes it an offence for an employer to make it a condition of employment that a workman shall discontinue membership of any friendly society, or not become a member of one other than the shop club or thrift fund, or that a workman shall join a shop club or thrift fund unless it is registered under the Friendly Societies Acts, and certified by the assistant registrar, which he cannot do without being satisfied on various matters.

Retention or hypothec for wages

An employee cannot have a right of retention or lien over his employer's property for his wages because any property in his custody is held by him as custodier *qua* employee only, and he has not possession thereof.[4] But seamen have at common law[5] and under statute[6] a hypothec over the ship and freight for their wages, of which they cannot deprive themselves by contract. The

---

[1] The 1896 Act, S. 1, expressly applies to shop assistants also.

[2] e.g. indiscipline; see *Squire* v. *Bayer & Co.* [1901] 2 K.B. 299.

[3] e.g. *Pritchard* v. *Clay* [1926] 1 K.B. 238; cf. *Hart* v. *Riversdale Mill Co.* [1928] 1 K.B. 177; *Sagar* v. *Ridehalgh* [1931] 1 Ch. 310; *Bird* v. *British Celanese, Ltd.* [1945] K.B. 336.

[4] *Dickson* v. *Nicholson* (1855) 17 D. 1011; *Clift* v. *Portobello Pier Co.* (1877) 4 R. 462; *Gladstone* v. *McCallum* (1896) 23 R. 783; *Barnton Hotel Co.* v. *Cook* (1899) 1 F. 1190; contrast *Meikle & Wilson* v. *Pollard* (1880) 8 R. 69; *Findlay* v. *Waddell*, 1910 S.C. 670.

[5] Ersk. III, 1, 34.

[6] Merchant Shipping Act, 1894, S. 156.

master has a hypothec for his wages and disbursements.[1] The
hypothec gives security also for damages for wrongful dismissal.[2]

Arrestment of wages

A person holding a decree against an employee or an extract
recorded deed or bond containing a clause consenting to registration for execution, or an extract notarial protest of a bill, can
arrest his wages in the hands of the employer, but not merely on
the dependence of an action.[3] At common law wages are exempt
from this diligence so far as necessary for the employee's subsistence.[4] The Wages Arrestment Limitation (Sc.) Act, 1870,[5]
renders the wages of all labourers, farm servants, manufacturers,
artificers and workpeople[6] liable to arrestment for debt only to the
extent of half of the surplus of wages over four pounds per week,
and the expense of arrestment is not chargeable against the
debtor unless by virtue of the arrestment the creditor recovers a
sum larger than the amount of such expense or cost. The 1870
Act does not (S. 4) affect arrestments in virtue of decrees for
alimentary allowances or payments, or for rates and taxes imposed
by law, though to be effectual such arrestments must set forth the
nature of the debt for which it has been used. Salaries and wages
payable to Crown employees were formerly not arrestable[7] and
the salaries of holders of a *munus publicum*[8] are arrestable only so
far as they exceed what is considered a reasonable amount for the
debtor's maintenance. This principle may apply to any salary.[9]
The wages of any seaman or apprentice in the merchant service
are not arrestable.[10]

Pensions and superannuation

Contractual provision for pensions and superannuation is
common and in many employments membership of the super-

---

[1] S. 167.

[2] *Phillips* v. *Highland Ry. Co.* (1883) 8 App. Cas. 329; cf. *Moore's Carving Machine Co.* v. *Austin* (1890) 33 S.L.R. 613.

[3] Law Reform (Misc. Prov.) (Sc.) Act, 1966, S. 1(1).

[4] Bell, *Comm.* I, 127; *Prin.* §2276.

[5] Amd. Wages Arrestment Limitation (Amdt.) (Sc.) Act, 1960, S.1. The sum may be further amended by Order under Law Reform (Misc. Prov.) (Sc.) Act, 1966, S. 3.

[6] See *McMurchy* v. *Emslie and Guthrie* (1888) 15 R. 375.

[7] Bell, *Comm.* I, 123; *Prin.* §2276; *Mulvenna* v. *The Admiralty*, 1926 S.C. 842; altered by Law Reform (Misc. Prov.) (Sc.) Act, 1966, S. 2.

[8] *Laidlaw* v. *Wylde* (1801) Mor. Appx. Arrestment, 4; *Learmonth* v. *Paterson* (1858) 20 D. 418.

[9] *Caldwell* v. *Hamilton*, 1919 S.C. (H.L.) 100.

[10] Merchant Shipping Act, 1894, S. 163.

annuation fund is compulsory. Employments in the public service have statutory provision for superannuation. Under the National Insurance Acts, 1965 to 1974 contributions must be paid in respect of employed persons entitling them to benefits under those Acts.

Hours of work

The number of hours to be worked and the times at which they are to be worked is determined by agreement and custom. In many cases they are settled by collective bargaining with provision for extra time, or time worked at particular parts of the week, to be remunerated at special rates. In many cases statute imposes limits on the hours which may be worked.[1]

Holidays

Holidays are primarily a matter for agreement. The Banking and Financial Dealings Act, 1971, prescribes six days which banks must keep as holidays.[2] Collective agreements in industry normally provide for stated periods of holiday with pay, subject to conditions as to length of service, together with public holidays or days in lieu. All statutory wages regulation authorities are empowered to give directions for holidays with pay for the workers whom they cover,[3] and particular statutes make provision for holidays in particular cases.[4]

Early closing day

The Shops Act, 1950, S. 1, requires every shop, with certain exceptions, to close in the afternoon on one weekday every week, now chosen by the occupier of the shop,[5] and fixes general closing hours in the evening (S. 2).[6] Shop assistants are entitled (S. 17) to a free afternoon on at least one weekday in each week.[7]

---

[1] e.g. Employment of Women, Young Persons and Children Act, 1920; Hours of Employment (Conventions) Act, 1936; Young Persons (Employment) Act, 1938; Mines and Quarries Act, 1954, Ss. 125–132; Factories Act, 1961, Ss. 86–117; Shops Act, 1950, Ss. 24–36; Shops (Early Closing Days) Act, 1965.

[2] Sched. 1.

[3] Wages Councils Act, 1959, S. 11, replacing Holidays with Pay Act, 1938; Agricultural Wages (Sc.) Act, 1949.

[4] e.g. Factories Act, 1961, S. 94.

[5] Shops (Early Closing Days) Act, 1965, S. 1.

[6] The early closing provisions of the 1950 Act do not apply to shops at a designated airport: Shops (Airports) Act, 1962.

[7] For special cases, see S. 40.

Accommodation: medical attention

In domestic employment the employer must provide accommodation and sustenance of fair and reasonable quality, or pay board wages in lieu. In such employment the employer, though probably not bound to provide medical attention, must give reasonable thought to the employee's health and not negligently prejudice it.[1] The Factories Act, 1961, S. 151, requires the appointment of factory doctors for the purposes of the Act.

Rights as to trade union membership

As between himself and his employer every worker has the rights to be a member of any union he chooses, or of no union, or not of a particular union, and it is an unfair industrial practice for an employer to prevent or deter a worker from exercising any of these rights, or to penalise him for doing so, or to refuse to engage a man because he is or is not a union member.[2] It is unfair dismissal to dismiss a man because he was, or proposed to be, a member of a union or refused, or proposed to refuse, to become or remain a member.[3]

DUTIES OF CARE FOR EMPLOYEE'S SAFETY, HEALTH AND WELFARE

Employer's personal duty

At common law the employer is under a duty of care, personal to him and not discharged by delegation or instruction to a manager or foreman,[4] to take reasonable care for the safety of his employees.[5] The standard of care demanded is high, but is only reasonable care, not a duty of insurance nor a warranty of safety.[6] This duty has three main facets,[7] the provision of a competent staff of men, adequate materials, machinery, plant, appliances and works, and a proper system of working and effective supervision.

---

[1] *McKeating* v. *Frame,* 1921 S.C. 382; cf. *Jeffrey* v. *Donald* (1901) 9 S.L.T. 199.

[2] Trade Union and Labour Relations Act, 1974, S. 5.

[3] Ibid., Sch. 1, para. 6.

[4] *McKillop* v. *N.B. Ry.* (1896) 23 R. 768; *Bain* v. *Fife Coal Co.,* 1935 S.C. 681, 693.

[5] *Dixon* v. *Rankin* (1852) 14 D. 420; *Paterson* v. *Wallace* (1854) 1 Macq. 748; *Marshall* v. *Stewart* (1855) 2 Macq. 30; *Weems* v. *Mathieson* (1861) 4 Macq. 215; *English* v. *Wilsons & Clyde Coal Co.,* 1937 S.C. (H.L.) 46; Walker, *Delict,* 557.

[6] *Weems, supra; English, supra;* cf. *Paris* v. *Stepney B.C.* [1951] A.C. 367; *Cavanagh* v. *Ulster Weaving Co.* [1960] A.C. 145.

[7] *Brydon* v. *Stewart* (1855) 2 Macq. 30; *Wilson* v. *Merry & Cuninghame* (1868) 6 M. (H.L.) 84; *Bett* v. *Dalmeny Oil Co.* (1905) 7 F. 787; *Black* v. *Fife Coal Co.,* 1912 S.C. (H.L.) 33; *McMullen* v. *Lochgelly Iron Co.,* 1933 S.C. (H.L.) 64; *Bain* v. *Fife Coal Co.,* 1935 S.C. 681, 699; *English, supra.*

The duty to provide a competent staff is breached by the appointment of inexperienced staff,[1] a drunken workman,[2] an incompetent driver,[3] an inexperienced signalman,[4] a negligent foreman,[5] an unqualified fireman.[6] The duty of providing adequate materials, appliances, machinery and plant covers all kinds of machinery, tools, vehicles and working materials, protective equipment and safe premises in which to do the work.[7] There is no warranty of soundness. If the employer obtains tools or plant from a reputable supplier of goods of that kind and if, by reason of latent defect, not discoverable by any reasonable examination, the plant fails and causes injury to an employee the injury is deemed also attributable to fault on the part of the employer.[8] The duty is breached by failure to provide necessary plant,[9] or provision of inadequate or defective plant.[10] It includes a duty to repair and maintain, and to adopt improvements from time to time.[11] The duty of providing and enforcing a safe system of working covers defects of a relatively permanent and continuous kind, the practice and method of carrying on the business, the lay-out of the work, the prevention of horse-play,[12] and the provision of warnings, notices, and special instructions.[13] The employer is not responsible for casual departures from the system.[14] The employer's duty extends also to not exposing his employees to unnecessary risks, including risk of injury by criminals.[15]

---

[1] *Black, supra.*

[2] *Donald* v. *Brand* (1862) 24 D. 295.

[3] *McCarten* v. *McRobbie*, 1909 S.C. 1020.

[4] *Morton* v. *Edinburgh & Glasgow Ry.* (1864) 2 M. 589.

[5] *Flynn* v. *McGaw* (1891) 18 R. 554.

[6] *Ferguson* v. *N.B. Ry.*, 1915 S.C. 566.

[7] e.g. *Fraser* v. *Hood* (1887) 15 R. 178; *Moore* v. *Ross* (1890) 17 R. 796; *Harvey* v. *Singer Mfg. Co.*, 1960 S.C. 155.

[8] Employers Liability (Defective Equipment) Act, 1969, modifying *Davie* v. *New Merton Board Mills* [1959] A.C. 604.

[9] *Pratt* v. *Richards* [1951] 2 K.B. 208.

[10] *Gordon* v. *Pyper* (1892) 20 R. (H.L.) 23; *Tyrrell* v. *Paton & Hendry* (1905) 8 F. 112; *Richardson* v. *Beattie*, 1923 S.L.T. 440.

[11] *English, supra,* 65.

[12] *Hudson* v. *Ridge Mfg. Co.* [1957] 2 Q.B. 348.

[13] *Bain* v. *Fife Coal Co.*, 1935 S.C. 681, 692; *English* v. *Wilson & Clyde Coal Co.*, 1936 S.C. 883, 904; *Speed* v. *Swift* [1943] K.B. 557, 563; *Kerr* v. *Glasgow Corpn.*, 1945 S.C. 335, 350; *General Cleaning Contractors* v. *Christmas* [1953] A.C. 180; *Brown* v. *Rolls Royce*, 1960 S.C. (H.L.) 22.

[14] *Maguire* v. *Russell* (1885) 12 R. 1071; *Winter* v. *Cardiff R.D.C.* [1950] 1 All E.R. 819; *Grace* v. *Stephen*, 1952 S.C. 61.

[15] *Williams* v. *Grimshaw* (1967) 3 K.I.R. 610; *Houghton* v. *Hackney B.C.* (1967) 3 K.I.R. 615.

Vicarious liability

The employer is also vicariously liable for the fault of one employee who, while acting in the course of his employment, causes injury to a fellow-employee, as much as if he had caused injury to an outsider.[1] In this case the negligent employee is also liable and if the employer has to pay damages he has a right of relief against the negligent employee.[2]

Statutory duties

Numerous statutes and bodies of regulations made thereunder impose extensive and detailed duties of care on employers for the safety, health and welfare of their employees.[3] Breach of a duty is normally punishable criminally but in many cases has been held also to ground an action of damages by an employee injured by reason of a failure to implement the statutory duty of care.[4]

Employee's right of action

An employee injured by the breach of any of the employer's duties, personal or vicarious, common law or statutory, has a right of action against him for damages, either on the basis of breach of an implied term of the contract of employment, or of breach of a duty owed by law not to cause injury.[5] If the employee be killed certain surviving relatives have a right of action for the loss caused them by the death.[6]

[1] *Sword* v. *Cameron* (1839) 1 D. 493; *McNaughton* v. *Caledonian Ry.* (1857) 19 D. 271; *Cook* v. *Duncan* (1857) 20 D. 180; *Lindsay* v. *Connell*, 1951 S.C. 281; *Baxter* v. *Colvilles*, 1959 S.L.T. 325; *Mulholland* v. *Reid & Leys*, 1958 S.C. 290; *Bell* v. *Blackwood, Morton & Sons*, 1960 S.C. 11. Contrast *Kirby* v. *N.C.B.*, 1958 S.C. 514. Between 1858 (*Bartonshill Coal Co.* v. *Reid*) (1858) 3 Macq. 166; *Bartonshill Coal Co.* v. *McGuire* (1858) 3 Macq. 300) and 1948 (Law Reform (Personal Injuries) Act, 1948, S. 1), by the rule of common employment or collaborateur, the employer was held not vicariously liable for the fault of one employee causing injury to another with whom he was in common employment. Cases between 1858 and 1948 exempting the employer on this ground are now superseded. It is incompetent by contract to exclude or limit the master's vicarious liability: 1948 Act, S. 1(3).

[2] *Lister* v. *Romford Ice Co.* [1957] A.C. 555.

[3] Principally the Merchant Shipping Acts, 1894–1974; Railway Employment (Prevention of Accidents) Act, 1900; Shops Acts, 1950 and 1962; Mines and Quarries Act, 1954; Agriculture (Safety, Health and Welfare Provisions) Act, 1956; Factories Act, 1961; Offices, Shops and Railway Premises Act, 1963. See also Munkman, *Employer's Liability*; Samuels, *Factory Law*; Redgrave, *Factories Acts*; Redgrave, *Offices and Shops*; Fridman, *Modern Law of Employment*.

[4] e.g. *Millar* v. *Galashiels Gas Co.*, 1949 S.C. (H.L.) 31; *Latimer* v. *A.E.C.* [1953] A.C. 643; *Hamilton* v. *N.C.B.*, 1960 S.C. (H.L.) 1.

[5] *English* v. *Wilsons & Clyde Coal Co.*, 1937 S.C. (H.L.) 46; *Lister* v. *Romford Ice Co.* [1957] A.C. 555; *Davie* v. *New Merton Board Mills* [1959] A.C. 604; *Matthews* v. *Kuwait Bechtel Corpn.* [1959] 2 Q.B. 57. See generally Ch. 60, *infra*.

[6] Ch. 61, *infra*.

Duty to insure

The employer is bound to insure against liability for bodily injury or disease sustained by his employees arising out of and in the course of their employment in Great Britain in his business, trade or profession, subject to certain exceptions.[1]

Liability of third parties to employees

When a master's employees have to work on the premises of a third party, the third party owes duties of care directly to the employees to take reasonable care that they do not suffer injury or damage by reason of any danger due to the state of the premises or to anything done or omitted to be done on them for which the third party is liable as occupier thereof,[2] that any machinery, tackle or appliances provided for the employee's use by the third party are reasonably safe for the contemplated use,[3] that the place of working is reasonably safe,[4] and that the employee is not injured by any dangerous activity by the third party or his employees.

Employer's vicarious liability for employee

An employer is vicariously liable to third parties for injury or damage caused them by the fault of his employee, acting in the course of his employment.[5] The employee is also, or alternatively, personally liable.[6] The course of the employment includes doing an act authorized, but harmful, accidentally causing harm while doing the job the employee is paid to do,[7] doing carelessly or negligently the work the employee is employed to do,[8] doing authorized work in an unauthorized way,[9] causing harm by horse-play,[10] doing something incidental to the job,[11] causing harm

---

[1] Employers' Liability (Compulsory Insurance) Act, 1969.

[2] Occupiers Liability (Sc.) Act, 1960, S. 2; see Ch. 60, *infra*; cf. *Muirhead* v. *Watt & Wilson* (1895) 3 S.L.T. 71; *MacDonald* v. *Reid's Trs.*, 1947 S.C. 726; *Grant* v. *Sun Shipping Co.*, 1948 S.C. (H.L.) 73.

[3] *Oliver* v. *Saddler*, 1929 S.C. (H.L.) 94; cf. *Davison* v. *Henderson* (1895) 22 R. 448; *Traill* v. *Dalbeattie* (1904) 6 F. 798.

[4] *McLachlan* v. *Peveril S.S. Co.* (1896) 23 R. 753; *Chadwick* v. *Elderslie S.S. Co.* (1898) 25 R. 730; *Jordan* v. *Court Line*, 1947 S.C. 29; *Grant, supra*.

[5] *Baird* v. *Hamilton* (1826) 4 S. 790; *Duncan* v. *Findlater* (1839) MacL. & Rob. 911; *Gregory* v. *Hill* (1869) 8 M. 282.

[6] *Grieve* v. *Brown*, 1926 S.C. 787, 791; *Adler* v. *Dickson* [1955] 1 Q.B. 158.

[7] *Jefferson* v. *Derbyshire Farmers, Ltd.* [1921] 2 K.B. 281; *Century Ins. Co.* v. *N.I. Road Tpt. Board* [1942] A.C. 509.

[8] e.g. *Drew* v. *Western S.M.T. Co.*, 1947 S.C. 222.

[9] *Hanlon* v. *G.S.W. Ry.* (1899) 1 F. 559; *Kirby* v. *N.C.B.*, 1958 S.C. 514.

[10] *Hudson* v. *Ridge Mfg. Co.* [1957] 2 Q.B. 348.

[11] *Mulholland* v. *Reid & Leys*, 1958 S.C. 290.

while going to or leaving the place of employment,[1] or even deviating from the course of the employment, so long as not solely for the employee's private purposes.[2] It may include wholly wrongful acts, whether for the employer's benefit,[3] or for the employee's own benefit.[4] But he is not liable for the employee's wrongs while the latter was acting outwith the course of his employment, such as the employee's doing some act which he was wholly unauthorized to do[5] or an act outside the scope of his work, or using the employer's time or tools for his own purposes,[6] or deviating from the course of the employment to the extent of going off on a frolic of his own,[7] gratuitously assaulting a third party,[8] doing an illegal act,[9] making slanderous statements[10] or doing harm motivated by personal spite.[11] Whether conduct is within or outwith the course of the employment is a question of fact in each case.[12] The fact that conduct is prohibited does not automatically absolve the employer, but may take the conduct out of the scope of the employment.[13]

Employer's right of recourse

If an employer is held vicariously liable for the fault of an employee which has caused injury, either to a fellow employee or to a third party, the employer has a right of relief against the employee who was actually in fault, either on the basis that they are joint wrongdoers[14] or on the basis of an implied term of the employment not to subject the employer to liability for damages.[15]

---

[1] *Bell* v. *Blackwood, Morton & Sons,* 1960 S.C. 11.

[2] *Williams* v. *Hemphill,* 1966 S.C. (H.L.) 31.

[3] *Barwick* v. *English Joint Stock Bank* (1867) L.R. 2 Ex. 259; *Finburgh* v. *Moss' Empires, Ltd.,* 1908 S.C. 928.

[4] *Lloyd* v. *Grace, Smith & Co.* [1912] A.C. 716; *Central Motors (Glasgow) Ltd.* v. *Cessnock Garage Co.,* 1925 S.C. 796.

[5] *Gallagher* v. *Burrell* (1883) 11 R. 53; *Martin* v. *Wards* (1887) 14 R. 814.

[6] *Kirby* v. *N.C.B.,* 1958 S.C. 514.

[7] *Whatman* v. *Pearson* (1868) L.R. 3 C.P. 422; *Storey* v. *Ashton* (1869) L.R. 4 Q.B. 476; *Rayner* v. *Mitchell* (1877) 2 C.P.D. 357.

[8] *Warren* v. *Henly's* [1948] 2 All E.R. 935.

[9] *Wardrope* v. *D. Hamilton* (1876) 3 R. 876.

[10] *Cumming* v. *G.N.S. Ry.,* 1916, 1 S.L.T. 181; *Lurie* v. *N.B. Ry.,* 1917, 2 S.L.T. 59; *Mandelston* v. *N.B. Ry.,* 1917 S.C. 442.

[11] *Aiken* v. *Caledonian Ry.,* 1913 S.C. 66; *Power* v. *Central S.M.T. Co.,* 1949 S.C. 376.

[12] *Mulholland* v. *Reid & Leys,* 1958 S.C. 290; *Kirby* v. *N.C.B.,* 1958 S.C. 514.

[13] *Plumb* v. *Cobden Flour Mills Co.* [1914] A.C. 62, 67; *Donnelly* v. *Moore,* 1921 S.C. (H.L.) 41; *C.P. Ry.* v. *Lockhart* [1942] A.C. 591; *Conway* v. *Wimpey* [1951] 2 K.B. 266; *Alford* v. *N.C.B.,* 1952 S.C. (H.L.) 17.

[14] Law Reform (Misc. Prov.) (Sc.) Act, 1940, S. 3(2).

[15] *Semtex* v. *Gladstone* [1954] 2 All E.R. 206; *Lister* v. *Romford Ice Co.* [1957] A.C. 555.

Inducing breach of contract

The employer has an action against a third party who deliberately and without justification, in the knowledge of the contract between employer and employee,[1] seeks to, or does in fact, induce either to break his contract.[2] Thus it is actionable to induce an employee to desert his employment,[3] or to reveal confidential information.[4] Inducing breach may, in exceptional circumstances, be justifiable[5] and where the inducing party is a trade union it may invoke the statutory defence.[6]

Harbouring employee

It is a separate wrong to harbour an employee, giving him employment in the knowledge that he has wrongfully left his previous employment.[7]

Loss of services

An employer has no claim against a third party by whose fault he is deprived of the services of his employee.[8]

Indemnity

The employer must indemnify the employee against losses and liabilities properly incurred in the performance of the work.

EMPLOYEE'S DUTIES

Duties of employee

The employee must enter on the employment at the due date,[9] and continue therein for the period agreed, though a contract of service will not be enforced specifically. He must attend regularly and not, without leave, or in emergency, absent himself during working hours. He must comply with reasonable orders,[10] con-

---

[1] This is the commonest instance of the more general principle that it is a wrong to induce the breach of any lawful contract between two other parties; see Ch. 64, *infra*.

[2] *D.C. Thomson* v. *Deakin* [1952] Ch. 646.

[3] *Couper* v. *Macfarlane* (1879) 6 R. 683.

[4] *Rutherford* v. *Boak* (1836) 14 S. 732; *Roxburgh* v. *McArthur* (1841) 3 D. 556.

[5] *Brimelow* v. *Casson* [1924] 1 Ch. 302.

[6] Trade Unions and Labour Relations Act, 1974, S. 13.

[7] *Rose St. Foundry Co.* v. *Lewis*, 1917 S.C. 341.

[8] *Allan* v. *Barclay* (1864) 2 M. 873; *Reavis* v. *Clan Line*, 1925 S.C. 725; *Young* v. *Ormiston*, 1936 S.L.T. 79.

[9] *Wallace* v. *Wishart* (1800) Hume 383; *Tulk, Ley & Co.* v. *Anderson* (1843) 5 D. 1096.

[10] *Hamilton* v. *McLean* (1824) 3 S. 268; *Wilson* v. *Simson* (1844) 6 D. 1256; *Thomson* v. *Stewart* (1888) 15 R. 806; *Pepper* v. *Webb* [1969] 2 All E.R. 216. See also *Laws* v. *London Chronicle* [1959] 2 All E.R. 285.

duct himself decently, be honest[1] and diligent[2] in the master's service, take reasonable care of property entrusted to him, and refrain from misconduct[3] or immorality or competing occupation[4] inconsistent with the fair performance of his duties. He must not act contrary to his employer's interests[5] and keep confidence as to all secret knowledge which may come to his knowledge in the employment.[6] He may be under a duty to disclose personal defects, certainly if involving risk to himself and fellow workmen.[7] Dismissal is justified by substantial failure to implement these duties.[8]

Refusal to obey orders is justifiable if the order is to do what is illegal or immoral or outwith the scope of the employment[9] or would expose the employee to a danger not contemplated by the contract.[10]

The employee must apply himself to his work and do it to the best of his ability, exercise reasonable skill and care therein, and take reasonable care to avoid subjecting his employer to liability in damages.[11] He must not take time off to devote to his own purposes or carry on a competing business so as to injure his employer's interests.[12]

Standard of skill and care

Where the employee has held himself out to be and been engaged as a person of professional qualifications,[13] a tradesman[14] or skilled workman, he has impliedly undertaken to show the standard of knowledge and skill, and to take the care, reasonably

---

[1] *Sinclair* v. *Neighbour* [1967] 2 Q.B. 279.

[2] *Secy. of State for Employment* v. *A.S.L.E.F.* [1972] 2 Q.B. 455.

[3] *Watson* v. *Noble* (1885) 13 R. 347.

[4] *Whitwood Chemical Co.* v. *Hardman* [1891] 2 Ch. 416; *Warner Bros.* v. *Nelson* [1937] 1 K.B. 209.

[5] *Graham* v. *Paton*, 1917 S.C. 203; *Hivac* v. *Park Royal, Ltd.* [1946] Ch. 169.

[6] *Robb* v. *Green* [1895] 2 Q.B. 315; *Liverpool Victoria Fr. Soc.* v. *Houston* (1900) 3 F. 42; *Wessex Dairies, Ltd.* v. *Smith* [1935] 2 K.B. 80; *Bents Brewery* v. *Hogan* [1945] 2 All E.R. 570; *Cranleigh Engineering Co.* v. *Bryant* [1964] 3 All E.R. 289; *Technograph* v. *Chalwyn* (1967) R.P.C. 339.

[7] *Cork* v. *Kirby Maclean, Ltd.* [1952] 2 All E.R. 402.

[8] e.g. *Pearce* v. *Foster* (1886) 17 Q.B.D. 536; *Boston Deep Sea Fishing Co.* v. *Ansell* (1888) 39 Ch. D. 339; *Sinclair* v. *Neighbour* [1967] 2 Q.B. 279.

[9] *Thomson* v. *Douglas* (1807) Hume 392; *Wilson* v. *Simson* (1844) 6 D. 1256; *Cobban* v. *Lawson* (1868) 6 S.L.R. 60; *Moffat* v. *Boothby* (1884) 11 R. 501.

[10] *Sutherland* v. *Monkland Ry.* (1867) 19 D. 1004; *Lang* v. *St. Enoch Shipping Co.*, 1908 S.C. 103.

[11] *Lister* v. *Romford Ice Co.* [1957] A.C. 555.

[12] *Cameron* v. *Gibb* (1867) 3 S.L.R. 282.

[13] *Jameson* v. *Simon* (1899) 1 F. 1211; *Hunter* v. *Hanley*, 1955 S.C. 200; cf. *Dickson* v. *Hygienic Institute*, 1910 S.C. 352 (unregistered dentist).

[14] *Harmer* v. *Cornelius* (1858) 5 C.B. (N.S.) 236; *McIntyre* v. *Gallacher* (1883) 11 R. 64.

expected of a normally skilled and competent member of his profession, craft or trade: *spondet peritiam artis*.[1] Otherwise he must take reasonable care.[2] If the employee, by neglect of care, causes the employer to become liable in damages to a third party, he is liable to recompense the employer.[3] Alternatively employer and employee may in a claim by an injured third party be treated as joint wrongdoers and the employer may be entitled to contribution by the employee to the damages.[4]

Employee's authority

An employee may have conferred on him, expressly or by implication, an authority the exercise of which may bind or render liable his employer. Thus shop assistants have implied authority to act in protection of their employer's property,[5] and a manager of a shop has ostensible authority to order goods and receive payment of accounts.[6] But a domestic servant has been held to have had no implied authority to buy food and pledge the employer's credit,[7] nor a head shepherd to buy sheep,[8] nor a railway station-master to employ medical assistance following on an accident.[9] An employer may, by regularly employing an employee to make contracts of a particular kind, be held to have conferred on him ostensible authority to make contracts of that kind. In general an employee has no authority to make an admission of fault binding his employer.[10]

Employee's patents or copyright

An employee's invention or patent is his own and not automatically his employer's property; if the employer uses the invention the employee is entitled to a royalty therefor.[11] But if he makes it in the course of his employment, the invention and any patent

---

[1] Bell, *Comm.* I, 489; *Prin.* §153; cf. *Hamilton* v. *Emslie* (1869) 7 M. 173; *Blair* v. *Assets Co.* (1896) 23 R. (H.L.) 36; *Lister, supra.*

[2] *Gunn* v. *Ramsay* (1801) Hume 384.

[3] *Semtex* v. *Gladstone* [1954] 2 All E.R. 206; *Lister* v. *Romford Ice Co.* [1957] A.C. 555.

[4] Law Reform (Misc. Prov.) (Sc.) Act, 1940, S. 3; cf. *Jones* v. *Manchester Corpn.* [1959] 2 Q.B. 852; *Harvey* v. *O'Dell* [1958] 2 Q.B. 78.

[5] *Neville* v. *C. & A. Modes*, 1945 S.C. 175.

[6] *Gemmell* v. *Annandale* (1899) 36 S.L.R. 658.

[7] *Mortimer* v. *Hamilton* (1868) 7 M. 158.

[8] *Morrison* v. *Statter* (1885) 12 R. 1152.

[9] *Montgomery* v. *N.B. Ry.* (1878) 5 R. 796.

[10] *Scott* v. *Cormack*, 1942 S.C. 159; *Connachan* v. *S.M.T. Co.*, 1946 S.C. 428.

[11] *Mellor* v. *Beardmore*, 1927 S.C. 597.

therefor belong to the employer.[1] Where a literary, dramatic or musical work is made by an author in the course of his employment by the proprietor of a newspaper, magazine or similar periodical and for the purpose of publication therein, the proprietor is entitled to the copyright so far as it relates to publication in any newspaper, magazine or similar periodical or to reproduction for the purpose of its being so published, but in all other respects the author is entitled to any copyright therein.[2]

National Insurance

Persons employed under a contract of service or apprenticeship, including service on ships and aircraft, are in insurable employment and must pay contributions, as also must the employer, at the rates from time to time prescribed, by way of insurance stamps affixed to cards, into the National Insurance fund and the National Insurance (Industrial Injuries) fund.[3] By virtue of his contributions an employed person is entitled in case of need to claim National Insurance benefits, viz.: unemployment benefit, sickness benefit, maternity benefit (including maternity grant, and maternity allowance), widow's benefit (including widow's allowance, widowed mother's allowance and widow's pension), guardian's allowance, retirement pension, graduated retirement benefit, child's special allowance, and death grant.[4] Persons in insurable employment are also insured[5] against personal injury caused after 4 July 1948 by accident arising out of and in the course of such employment.[6] Employer and employee make weekly contributions to the Industrial Injuries Fund. The employee is entitled under the Act[7] to industrial injury benefit, industrial disablement benefit and industrial death benefit, payable to certain dependants. The rates of benefits are modified from time to time. An accident arising in the course of an insured person's employment is to be deemed, in the absence of evidence to the contrary, also to have arisen out of that employment.[8]

---

[1] *Triplex Safety Glass Co.* v. *Scorah* [1938] Ch. 211; *Sterling Engineering Co.* v. *Patchett* [1955] A.C. 534; *British Syphon Co.* v. *Homewood* [1956] 2 All E.R. 879; see also Patents Act, 1949, S. 56.

[2] Copyright Act, 1956, S. 4(2); *Stevenson, Jordan & Harrison* v. *Macdonald & Evans* [1952] 1 T.L.R. 101.

[3] Nat. Ins. Act, 1965, S. 1; Nat. Ins. (Industrial Injuries) Act, 1965, S. 1.

[4] Nat. Ins. Act, 1965, S. 17.

[5] National Insurance (Industrial Injuries) Act, 1965, S. 1.

[6] This phrase is taken over from the Workmen's Compensation Acts, 1897–1945, superseded by the N.I. (Ind. Inj.) Act, and has been interpreted in numerous cases under the Workmen's Compensation Acts.

[7] S. 5.   [8] S. 6.

Insured persons are insured also against prescribed diseases and prescribed personal injury not caused by accident, being a disease or injury due to the nature of that employment and developed after 4 July 1948.[1] The facilities provided under the National Health Service (Scotland) Act 1947 are financed in part by contributions collected with national insurance contributions and may be utilized by any contributor.

Interaction with common law claims

A claim of damages may be brought by an employee founded on common law fault and/or breach of statutory duty, and claims be made also under the National Insurance and Industrial Injuries Acts. But in assessing damages in an action for personal injuries there shall be taken into account, against any loss of earnings or profits, one half of the value of any rights which have accrued or probably will accrue to the pursuer in respect of industrial injury benefit, industrial disablement benefit, sickness or invalidity benefit for the five years beginning when the cause of action accrued, but disregarding any increase of industrial disablement pension in respect of the need of constant attendance, and also the possibility of avoiding any expenses incurred by taking advantage of facilities available under the National Health Service.[2] In assessing damages to a surviving relative in respect of a person's death at common law or under the Carriage by Air Act, 1932 (now 1961), no account is to be taken of any right to National Insurance benefit resulting from that person's death.[3]

Suspension

If there is an express term in the contract or a custom permitting it an employer may suspend an employee for misconduct less than would justify dismissal.[4]

---

[1] S. 56.

[2] Law Reform (Personal Injuries) Act, 1948, S. 2, and National Ins. Act, 1971, Sch. 5.

[3] Law Reform (Personal Injuries) Act, 1948, S. 5A, introduced by L.R. (Personal Injuries) Act, 1953, overruling *Adams* v. *Spencer*, 1951 S.C. 175; see also *Stott* v. *Arrol* [1953] 2 Q.B. 92; *Flowers* v. *Wimpey* [1956] 1 Q.B. 73.
Where the benefit is a lump-sum gratuity the court takes into account half of the proportion of the gratuity applicable to the five-year period as compared with the injured person's expectation of life or with the period, if shorter, for which the gratuity is granted: *Perez* v. *C.A.V. Ltd.* [1959] 1 W.L.R. 724; *Hulquist* v. *Universal Pattern Co.* [1960] 2 W.L.R. 886.

[4] *Marshall* v. *English Electric Co.* (1945) 61 T.L.R. 379; *Bird* v. *British Celanese Co.* [1945] K.B. 336.

Fines and deductions from wages

These are regulated by the Truck Act, 1896, and are permissible only if there is a term in the contract permitting it, expressly agreed to, or incorporated by adequate notice. But in the case of workmen not covered by the Truck Act disciplinary deductions may be made if agreed to in the contract, so long as they do not amount to a penalty but can be deemed liquidate damages.

DISPUTES BETWEEN EMPLOYERS AND EMPLOYEES

By the Employers and Workmen Act, 1875, the sheriff court is given additional jurisdiction (S. 3) in relation to any dispute between an employer and a workman[1] to adjust and set off mutual claims, whether liquidated or unliquidated, for wages, damages or otherwise, and to rescind any contract on such terms as it thinks just. This power entitles the sheriff to override arbitration clauses or awards under contracts which have terminated.[2]

Trade disputes

A strike,[3] or concerted cessation of work, in protest against some matter connected with the employment or to enforce some demand on the management, is a breach of contract justifying immediate dismissal, unless notice is given by or on behalf of all employees going to strike of intention to do so. The precise effect of a notice of intention depends on the words used, but notice by or on behalf of an employee of intention to take part in a strike is not, unless it otherwise expressly provides, to be construed as a notice to terminate his contract of employment or as a repudiation of that contract. Due notice is the same notice as the employee would have to give to terminate his contract. A strike without notice is a breach of contract.[4] A similar principle

---

[1] Defined, S. 10, as manual workers, excluding domestic or menial servants, and extended to seamen: Merchant Seamen Act, 1880, S. 11. It covers a tramway conductor: *Wilson* v. *Glasgow Tramways Co.* (1878) 5 R. 981; a packer: *Pratt* v. *Cook, Son & Co.* [1940] A.C. 437; but not shop assistants: *Bound* v. *Lawrence* [1892] 1 Q.B. 226. Whether a man is a workman depends on whether manual labour is the predominant part of his duties: *Anderson* v. *Duncan* (1906) 14 S.L.T. 575.

[2] *Wilson, supra.*

[3] See definitions of 'strike' and 'lockout' in Industrial Relations Act, 1971, S. 167 (repealed). Strikes are sometimes distinguished as official or unofficial according as they have or have not trade union authority and backing.

[4] cf. *Morgan* v. *Fry* [1968] 3 All E.R. 452; on damages see *N.C.B.* v. *Galley* [1958] 1 W.L.R. 16, 28.

applies to a lockout.[1] If continuous work has been guaranteed any strike or lockout is a breach of contract.[2] Men striking in furtherance of an industrial dispute do not commit crime, unless the object of their agreement or combination was the procuring or commission of an act which would constitute a crime if done by one person.[3] The malicious breach of a contract of service or hiring is criminal if the probable consequences will be to endanger human life, or cause serious bodily injury, or expose valuable property to destruction or serious injury.[4] A strike is unlawful if due notice is not given, or if the strike is in breach of a condition in the contracts of employment not to strike.[5] An unlawful strike justifies dismissal of the employees concerned, or an action for damages against some or all of them.

An agreement or combination by two or more to do or procure to be done any act in contemplation or furtherance of an industrial dispute is not indictable as a criminal conspiracy if such act committed by one person would not be punishable as a crime.[6]

Protection of parties to trade dispute

A 'trade dispute' is a dispute between employers and workers or workers and workers connected with one or more of (a) terms and conditions of employment, or the physical conditions in which any workers are required to work, (b) engagement or non-engagement or termination or suspension of employment or of the duties of employment of one or more workers, (c) allocation of work or the duties of employment as between workers or groups of workers, (d) matters of discipline, (e) membership or non-membership of a trade union by a worker, (f) facilities for officials of trade unions, (g) machinery for negotiation or consultation and other procedures.[7] An act done by a person in contemplation or furtherance of a trade dispute is not actionable as delict on the ground only[8] (a) that it induces another person to

---

[1] Cf. *Cummings* v. *Connell*, 1969 S.L.T. 25.

[2] *Cummings* v. *Connell*, 1969 S.L.T. 25.

[3] Conspiracy and Protection of Property Act, 1875, S. 3.

[4] 1875 Act, S. 5. These provisions do not prevent strikes after due notice.

[5] This occurred in *Rookes* v. *Barnard* [1964] A.C. 1129.

[6] Conspiracy and Protection of Property Act, 1875, S. 3; hence conspiracy to stop work is not criminal, but conspiracy to burn down the factory is.

[7] Trade Union and Labour Relations Act, 1974, S. 29. This excludes disputes between employers and employers, and between unions and workers: cf. *Larkin* v. *Long* [1915] A.C. 814; *Crofter Co.* v. *Veitch*, 1942 S.C. (H.L.) 1.

[8] But it may be actionable if it induces breach or prevents performance and causes some other harm.

break a contract of employment,[1] or (b) that it consists in his threatening that a contract of employment (whether one to which he is a party or not) will be broken or that he will induce another person to break a contract to which that other person is a party.[2]

Also an act done by a person in contemplation or furtherance of a trade dispute is not actionable as delict on the ground that it is an interference with the trade, business or employment of another person, or with the right of another person to dispose of his capital or his labour as he wills.[3]

An agreement or combination by two or more persons to do or procure the doing of any act in contemplation or furtherance of an industrial dispute shall not be actionable as delict, if the act is one which, if done without any such agreement or combination, would not be actionable as delict.[4]

Intimidation: picketing

It is actionable at common law to threaten or put pressure on a workman to his business injury, or to put pressure on his employer which results in injury to him.[5] It is criminal, with a view to compelling any other person to abstain from doing or to do any act which such other person has a legal right to do or abstain from doing, wrongfully and without legal authority, to use violence to or intimidate him, his wife or children, or injure his property, persistently to follow him about from place to place, hide any tools, clothes or other property or deprive or hinder him in the use thereof, watch or beset his residence, place of work or business, or the approach thereto, or follow him with two or more other persons in a disorderly manner in any street.[6] But it is neither criminal nor delictual for persons, acting in contemplation or furtherance of an industrial dispute, to attend at or near a place

---

[1] cf. *Rookes* v. *Barnard* [1964] A.C. 1129.

[2] 1974 Act, S. 13(7), replacing Trade Disputes Act, 1965, S. 1; *Cory Lighterage* v. *T.G.W.U.* [1973] 2 All E.R. 341.

[3] Ibid., S. 13(2) closely following (repealed) Trade Disputes Act, 1906, S. 3, held applicable in *Brimelow* v. *Casson* [1924] 1 Ch. 302, but inapplicable in *Conway* v. *Wade* [1909] A.C. 506; *Milligan* v. *Ayr Harbour Trs.*, 1915 S.C. 937; *Bents Brewery* v. *Hogan* [1945] 2 All E.R. 570, and *Rookes* v. *Barnard* [1964] A.C. 1129.

[4] Ibid., S. 13(4) closely following paragraph of Conspiracy and Protection of Property Act, 1875, S. 3, added by (repealed) Trade Disputes Act, 1906, S. 1.

[5] *Read* v. *Operative Stonemasons* [1902] 2 K.B. 732; *Hewit* v. *Edinburgh Lathsplitters* (1906) 14 S.L.T. 489.

[6] Conspiracy and Protection of Property Act, 1875, S. 7; *Agnew* v. *Munro* (1891) 18 R. (J). 22; *Gibson* v. *Lawson* [1891] 2 Q.B. 545; *Stuart* v. *Clarkson* (1894) 22 R. (J.) 5; *McKinlay* v. *Hart* (1897) 25 R. (J.) 7; *Lyons* v. *Wilkins* [1899] 1 Ch. 255; *Ward, Lock & Co.* v. *Operative Printers Assts. Assocn.* (1906) 22 T.L.R. 327; *Wilson* v. *Renton*, 1910 S.C. (J.) 32.

where a person works or carries on business or any other place where he happens to be, not being a place where he resides, if they so attend only for the purpose of peacefully obtaining or communicating information, or of peacefully persuading him to work or not to work.[1]

Prohibition of actions against trade unions and employers' associations

No action for delict lies in respect of any act alleged to have been done by or on behalf of a trade union which is not a special register body or by or on behalf of an unincorporated employers' association, or alleged to have been done, in connection with the regulation of relations between employers or their associations and workers or trade unions, by or on behalf of a special register trade union or an incorporated employers' association, or alleged to be threatened or intended to be done as mentioned above against the union or association in its own name, but certain actions not arising from trade disputes are excluded.[2]

Conspiracy to injure

The actings of unions and their officials in pursuance of their policies amount to actionable civil conspiracy to injure if a person can show injury arising from an agreement of two or more persons to do acts in themselves wrongful, such as to commit violence or to conduct a strike by means of conduct prohibited by the Trade Union Acts, or acts not wrongful but the predominant motive of which was to injure or gratify spite.[3] But the conspiracy is not actionable if the predominant motive is to further the conspirators' legitimate business or union interests.[4]

Inducing breach of contract

A person may be liable *ex delicto* for inducing another to break his contract with the complainer. Such inducement may be

---

[1] Trade Union and Labour Relations Act, 1974, S. 15, repeating with modifications Trade Disputes Act, 1906, S. 2; *Wilson, supra*; *Sloan* v. *Macmillan*, 1922 J.C. 1; cf. *Piddington* v. *Bates* [1960] 3 All E.R. 660; *Tynan* v. *Balmer* [1967] 1 Q.B. 91; *Hunt* v. *Broome* [1973] 2 All E.R. 1035.

[2] 1974 Act, S. 14; cf. Trade Disputes Act, 1906, S. 4(1). Whether this prevents the court granting interdict see *Ware and de Freville* v. *M.T.A.* [1921] 3 K.B. 40; *Boulting* v. *A.C.T.T.* [1963] 2 Q.B. 606; *Torquay Hotel Co.* v. *Cousins* [1969] 2 W.L.R. 289.

[3] *Quinn* v. *Leathem* [1901] A.C. 495; *Crofter Co.* v. *Veitch*, 1942 S.C. (H.L.) 1.

[4] *Mogul* v. *McGregor, Gow & Co.* [1892] A.C. 25; *White* v. *Riley* [1921] 1 Ch. 1; *Reynolds* v. *Shipping Federation* [1924] 1 Ch. 28; *Sorrell* v. *Smith* [1925] A.C. 700; *Crofter Co., supra*; *Huntley* v. *Thornton* [1957] 1 W.L.R. 321; *Scala Ballroom* v. *Ratcliffe* [1958] 3 All E.R. 220.

justifiable if motivated by an honest desire, reasonable in the circumstances, to improve the condition of the employees[1] but inducement is *prima facie* actionable.[2] To be liable the inducing party must know of the contract and directly intervene to persuade one party to break it, or commit a wrongful act to prevent a party performing his contract, or render performance impossible.[3]

Intimidation, threats or coercion

Intimidation is the wrong of causing harm to a person by threats directed against him, or against a third party who is thereby persuaded to act in a way harmful to the complainer, as by dismissing him.[4] The conduct alleged to amount to intimidation may be itself criminal,[5] or delictual,[6] or lawful but harmful, such as to withdraw services or to strike.[7]

Restriction on legal proceedings

No court may, by order of specific implement of a contract of employment or interdict restraining a breach or threatened breach of such a contract, compel an employee to do any work or attend at any place for the purpose of doing any work.[8]

Resolution of industrial disputes

Differences between employers and groups of workmen may be settled by arbitration or voluntary conciliation machinery. Statute provides for assistance to be available to prevent and settle disputes and Department of Employment officials may seek to assist when called on. Under the Conciliation Act, 1896, the Department of Employment may inquire into the causes and circumstances of an actual or apprehended difference between employers and workmen, take such steps as may seem expedient to enable the parties to meet, on the application of either side appoint a conciliator or board of conciliation, and on the application of both parties appoint an arbitrator. It may also register voluntary conciliation boards.

---

[1] *Brimelow* v. *Casson* [1924] 1 Ch. 302.

[2] *S. Wales Mines Federation* v. *Glamorgan Coal Co.* [1905] A.C. 239. *Denaby and Cadeby Main Collieries, Ltd.* v. *Yorkshire Miners Assocn.* [1906] A.C. 384.

[3] *D. C. Thomson & Co.* v. *Deakin* [1952] Ch. 646; *Stratford* v. *Lindley* [1965] A.C. 269; *Bowles* v. *Lindley* [1965] 1 Ll. Rep. 207; *Square Grip Reinforcement Co.* v. *Macdonald*, 1968 S.L.T. 65.

[4] *Rookes* v. *Barnard* [1964] A.C. 1129.

[5] e.g. threat of violence.

[6] e.g. threat to publish defamatory matter.

[7] *Cunard S.S. Co.* v. *Stacey* [1955] 2 Ll. Rep. 247; *Rookes, supra.*

[8] Trade Union and Labour Relations Act, 1974, S. 16.

The Industrial Courts Act, 1919, established the Industrial Court, renamed the Industrial Arbitration Board,[1] which is an independent tribunal though not a court of law, and its decisions are not legally enforceable. It may adjudicate on references made under voluntary agreements within an industry. Any trade dispute, present or apprehended, may be reported to the Ministry and if both parties consent be referred for settlement to the Industrial Court, or referred to the arbitration of one or more persons appointed by the Minister, or referred to a board of arbitration. A reference may be made only with the consent of both parties and only if any arrangements within the industry for settlement by conciliation or arbitration have failed. The Act also empowers the Minister to establish a court of inquiry to inquire into the causes and circumstances of a trade dispute. Its report must be published.

The Minister may seek to settle a claim reported to him under S. 8(1) of the Terms and Conditions of Employment Act, 1959, that a particular employer was failing to observe established terms and conditions of employment, and failing settlement, shall refer it to the Industrial Court, whose award shall have effect as an implied term of the contract of employment.

TERMINATION OF EMPLOYMENT

The contract of employment is terminated by expiry of the period set by the contract, by agreement, by the death of either party, the dissolution of a partnership, the winding up of a company,[2] by notice,[3] by the employer summarily dismissing the employee, by material breach by the employer which justifies the employee in treating the contract as repudiated, and by frustration.

Termination—lapse of time

When a contract of employment is entered into for a fixed period, it terminates automatically on the expiry of that period without need for notice. If it is to be continued it requires express renewal; if there is no renewal but it is in fact continued the inference is of a contract at will.

[1] Industrial Relations Act, 1971, Sch. 8.

[2] cf. *McEwan* v. *U.C.S.* [1972] I.T.R. 296.

[3] Where notice is necessary the obligation to give it is incumbent equally on a dismissing employer and a departing employee: *Hamilton* v. *Outram* (1855) 17 D. 798; *Morrison* v. *Abernethy School Board* (1876) 3 R. 945.

Termination—Tacit relocation

In the cases of agricultural, domestic and similar classes of workers,[1] and probably industrial employees, if due notice of intention to terminate the contract is not given by either party a reasonable time before expiry of the period of service, custom founded on presumed intention implies a renewal of the contract on the same terms for a further year, if the original contract were for a year, and, if for a shorter period, for the same period again. This principle does not apply to other classes of employees,[2] nor to part-time employment, nor any employment on exceptional terms[3] and possibly not to any employment longer than a year,[4] nor where the continued employment can be ascribed to another contract.[5] A uniform and notorious local custom to the contrary will dispense with the need for notice.[6]

Notice of termination of contract

Notice of termination by either party to the other is unnecessary where the contract is for a stated term,[7] or the employment not whole-time.[8] It is necessary where otherwise tacit relocation would operate to renew the contract,[9] or where the contract is a continuing one, at the will of the parties.[10] The employer may in such a case at any time terminate the contract by giving reasonable notice before the date of termination, or the end of a month or week as the case may be, or by paying wages (or, where customary, board wages) till the end of the period of due notice.[11] Notice may be given in any way, but must indicate the date of termination.

---

[1] Bell, *Prin.* §187; *McLean* v. *Fyfe*, 4 Feb. 1813, F.C.; *Morrison* v. *Allardyce* (1823) 2 S. 434; *E. Mansfield* v. *Scott* (1833) 6 W. & S. 277; *Tait* v. *Macintosh* (1841) 13 S. Jur. 280; *Campbell* v. *Fyfe* (1851) 13 D. 1041; *Cameron* v. *Scott* (1870) 9 M. 233; *Morrison* v. *Abernethy School Board* (1876) 3 R. 945; *Lennox* v. *Allan* (1880) 8 R. 38; *Moffat* v. *Boothby* (1884) 11 R. 501; *Stevenson* v. *N.B. Ry.* (1905) 7 F. 1106; *Stanley* v. *Hanway* (1911) 48 S.L.R. 757.

[2] *Stanley, supra*; but see *Houston* v. *C.P.A.* (1903) 10 S.L.T. 532; *Stevenson* v. *N.B. Ry.* (1905) 7 F. 1106.

[3] *Lennox, supra*.   [4] *Brenan* v. *Campbell's Trs.* (1898) 25 R. 423.

[5] *Sutherland's Trs.* v. *Miller's Tr.* (1888) 16 R. 10.

[6] *Morrison, supra*.

[7] *R.* v. *Secretary of State, ex parte Khan* [1973] 2 All E.R. 104.

[8] *Brenan* v. *Campbell's Trs.* (1898) 25 R. 423; cf. *Mollison* v. *Baillie* (1885) 22 S.L.R. 595; *Robson* v. *Hawick School Board* (1900) 2 F. 411.

[9] *Morrison* v. *Allardyce* (1823) 2 S. 434.

[10] *Morrison* v. *Abernethy School Board* (1876) 3 R. 945; *Robson* v. *Overend* (1878) 6 R. 213.

[11] *Graham* v. *Thomson* (1822) 1 S. 309; *Cooper* v. *Henderson* (1825) 3 S. 619; *Mollison* v. *Baillie* (1885) 22 S.L.R. 595. See also *Wallace* v. *Wishart* (1800) Hume 383.

The period of notice deemed reasonable is a question of fact;[1] it depends on custom and the status of the employee's post, the higher his grade the longer being the period deemed reasonable.[2] If the appointment is only a part-time one notice is probably not required.[3] By custom agricultural and domestic servants hired by the year or half-year are entitled to forty days' notice before the expiry of the period of service.[4] Once notice has been given it can be withdrawn only with the consent of the other party.

Under the Contracts of Employment Act, 1972, S. 1, the minimum periods of notice to be given by an employer if the employee has been continuously employed for 13 weeks or more are (a) continuous employment for less than two years: 1 week; (b) two years to five years: 2 weeks; (c) five years to ten years: four weeks; (d) ten years to fifteen years: six weeks; and fifteen years or more: eight weeks. An employee continuously employed for 13 weeks or more must give at least one week's notice. Either party may waive his rights or accept a payment in lieu of notice. Unless the notice to terminate is at least one week more than that required by S. 1, Sched. 2 states the rights of the employee during his period of notice (S. 2). If an employer fails to give the notice required by S. 1 the rights conferred by S. 2 and Sched. 2 are to be taken into account in assessing his liability for breach of the contract (S. 3). The calculation of a period of employment is governed by Sched. 1.[5]

Redundancy payments

Under the Redundancy Payments Act, 1965,[6] an employer must make payments, out of a fund to which contributions are made by employers (by way of addition to the employer's contributions under the National Insurance Acts) and the Treasury, to employees dismissed[7] by reason of redundancy,[8] with certain

---

[1] *Currie* v. *Glasgow Central Stores* (1905) 13 S.L.T. 38.

[2] *Morrison, supra* (teacher—3 mos.); *Robson* v. *Overend* (1878) 6 R. 213 (teacher—3 mos.); *Forsyth* v. *Heathery Knowe Coal Co.* (1880) 7 R. 887 (colliery manager—3 mos.); *Hinds* v. *Dunbar School Board* (1883) 10 R. 930 (teacher—3 mos.); *Currie* v. *Glasgow Central Stores* (1905) 13 S.L.T. 88 (clerk of works—4 weeks); *Wilson* v. *Anthony*, 1958 S.L.T. (Sh. Ct.) 13 (hotel manageress–4 weeks). See also *Adams* v. *Union Cinemas, Ltd.* [1939] 3 All E.R. 136, 142.

[3] *Cormack* v. *Keith & Murray* (1893) 20 R. 977; *Brenan, supra*.

[4] Removal Terms (Sc.) Amdt. Act, 1890, S. 2, altering *Cameron* v. *Scott* (1870) 9 M. 233; *Stewart* v. *Robertson*, 1937 S.C. 701.

[5] See *Fitzgerald* v. *Hall Russell & Co.*, 1970 S.C. (H.L.) 1.

[6] On this Act see Grunfeld, *Law of Redundancy*.

[7] As to 'dismissed' see S. 3.

[8] *Chapman* v. *Goonvean* [1973] 2 All E.R. 1062.

exceptions, or laid off or kept on short-time to specified extents (Ss. 5–7), but not to employees justifiably dismissed, except where the dismissal is as a result of a strike or lock-out. Before a redundancy payment can be claimed the employee must have been continuously employed[1] for 104 weeks since attaining the age of 18 (Ss. 1, 8).[2] The calculation of redundancy payments is based on the length of the employee's service and his weekly pay. No payment may be made unless agreed and paid, or claimed in writing, or any question as to its payment has been determined by a tribunal set up under the Industrial Training Act, 1964 (Ss. 7, 9). The onus is on the employer to rebut the presumption that dismissal is due to redundancy.[3] A demotion does, but a consensual variation of contract does not amount to dismissal.[4] There is no entitlement if the employer has offered to re-engage the employee or offered suitable alternative employment.[5] Redundancy payment may be claimed where the employment terminates through some act on the part of the employer or some event affecting him, including the death of the employer (Ss. 22–23). There is no redundancy if the employee leaves voluntarily, or is dismissed justifiably. Once a redundancy payment has been made an employee re-employed must requalify before receiving a further redundancy payment (S. 24). The amount of salary payable at common law on dismissal without notice cannot be reduced by the amount due under the 1965 Act.[6] Parties may contract out of the Act only in limited circumstances.[7]

Dismissal

A person employed at will, or during the employer's pleasure, may be dismissed at any time on reasonable notice, or on being paid a reasonable allowance in lieu of notice.[8] A person employed for a fixed period can be dismissed earlier only on cause shown.[9]

---

[1] Determined according to Contracts of Employment Act, 1963 (now 1972), Sch. 1.

[2] *Rencoule* v. *Hunt,* 1967 S.C. 131; *Kenmir* v. *Frizzell* [1968] 1 All E.R. 414; *Lloyd* v. *Brassey* [1969] 1 All E.R. 382.

[3] S. 9(2); *MacLaughlan* v. *Paterson,* 1968 S.L.T. 377; *Douglas* v. *Provident Clothing Co.* 1969 S.L.T. 57; *Hindle* v. *Percival Boats* [1969] 1 All E.R. 836.

[4] *Marriott* v. *Oxford and District Co-op Socy.* [1969] 3 All E.R. 1126; *Shields Furniture* v. *Goff* [1973] 2 All E.R. 653.

[5] *Carron Co.* v. *Robertson,* 1967 S.C. 273; *Paisley* v. *S.C.W.S.* (1967) I.T.R. 184; *Thomson & McIntyre* v. *McCreadie,* 1970 S.C. 235.

[6] *Hardy* v. *S.T.V. Ltd.,* 1968 S.L.T. 79.

[7] Ss. 11 and 15.

[8] *Morrison* v. *Abernethy School Board* (1876) 3 R. 945, 951; *Robson* v. *Overend* (1878) 6 R. 213; *Hastie* v. *McMurtrie* (1889) 16 R. 715.

[9] *Moffat* v. *Shedden* (1839) 1 D. 468.

An employer is entitled instantly to dismiss an employee before the expiry of his employment, and to claim damages, if the employee is in material breach of essential conditions of his contractual duties.[1] The employee also formerly forfeited his wages for the incomplete term of service.[2] Dismissal has been held justified for disobedience to orders,[3] insolence,[4] misconduct,[5] absence without leave,[6] drunkenness,[7] inefficiency.[8] It is a question of fact and degree whether the default justifies dismissal.[9] Reasons need not be given if the employee is employed during the employer's pleasure.[10] In some cases a statutory procedure must be followed before an employee is dismissed.[11] In such cases the person cannot be dismissed without stating what is alleged against him and hearing his defence.[12]

In others a collective agreement incorporated in contracts of employment may provide for a procedure in case of dismissal.[13] If the employee is an office-holder[14] the rules of natural justice must be complied with before his dismissal will be valid.[15]

The employee is bound to go, and cannot claim to remain on the ground that the dismissal was unjustified,[16] but he may challenge the justification for his dismissal by claiming damages for wrongful dismissal[17] or, if he holds *ad vitam aut culpam*, by

[1] cf. *Re Rubel Bronze & Metal Co. and Vos* [1918] 1 K.B. 315.
[2] *Gibson* v. *McNaughton* (1861) 23 D. 358; *Selby* v. *Baldry* (1867) 5 S.L.R. 64.
[3] *Hamilton* v. *McLean* (1824) 3 S. 379; *Wilson* v. *Simson* (1844) 6 D. 1256; *McKellar* v. *McFarlane* (1852) 15 D. 246; *A.* v. *B.* (1853) 16 D. 269; *Cobban* v. *Lawson* (1868) 6 S.L.R. 60; *Thomson* v. *Stewart* (1888) 15 R. 806; *Trotters* v. *Briggs* (1897) 5 S.L.T. 17; contrast *Moffat* v. *Boothby* (1884) 11 R. 501; *Laws* v. *London Chronicle, Ltd.* [1959] 2 All E.R. 285.
[4] *Scott* v. *McMurdo* (1869) 6 S.L.R. 301.
[5] *Greig* v. *Sanderson* (1864) 2 M. 1278; *Sharp* v. *Rettie* (1884) 11 R. 745; *Boston Fishing Co.* v. *Ansell* (1888) 39 Ch. D. 339; *Trotters* v. *Briggs* (1897) 5 S.L.T. 17; *Taylor* v. *Smith*, 1909, 1 S.L.T. 453.
[6] *Reid* v. *Lindsay Crawford* (1822) 1 Sh. App. 124.
[7] *Edwards* v. *Mackie* (1848) 11 D. 67.
[8] *Gunn* v. *Ramsay* (1801) Hume 384; *Sharp, supra.*
[9] cf. *Clouston* v. *Corry* [1906] A.C. 122; *Savage* v. *B.I.S.N. Co.* (1930) 46 T.L.R. 294.
[10] *Pollock's Trs.* v. *Commercial Banking Co.* (1829) 3 W. & S. 430; *Mitchell* v. *Smith* (1836) 14 S. 358; *Fosdick* v. *N.B. Ry.* (1850) 13 D. 281; *Morrison, supra*; *Ridge* v. *Baldwin* [1964] A.C. 40; *Malloch* v. *Aberdeen Corpn.*, 1971 S.L.T. 245.
[11] *Palmer* v. *Inverness Hospitals Management Board*, 1963 S.C. 311.
[12] *Palmer, supra: Ridge, supra.*
[13] *Tomlinson* v. *L.M.S. Ry.* [1944] 1 All E.R. 537.
[14] The criteria of, and extent of, this category of employee are uncertain.
[15] *Ridge* v. *Baldwin* [1964] A.C. 40, 65; *Malloch* v. *Aberdeen Corpn.* 1971 S.L.T. 245.
[16] *Ross* v. *Pender* (1874) 1 R. 352; *First Edinburgh, etc. Bldg. Soc.* v. *Munro* (1884) 21 S.L.R. 291; *Denmark* v. *Boscobel Productions, Ltd.* [1969] 1 Q.B. 699.
[17] *Craig* v. *Graham* (1844) 6 D. 684; *Bentinck* v. *Macpherson* (1869) 6 S.L.R. 376; *Cameron* v. *Fletcher* (1872) 10 M. 301; *Ross* v. *Pender* (1874) 1 R. 352. Redundancy payment is not deductible: *Yorkshire Eng. Co.* v. *Burnham* [1973] 3 All E.R. 1176.

declarator that he is still in office and for reduction of the resolution to dismiss him,[1] or, if the procedure for his dismissal were irregular, for reduction of the resolution to dismiss him.[2]

Unfair dismissal

In every employment, except those dealt with in paras. 9 to 14, an employee has the right not to be unfairly dismissed.[3] 'Dismissal' covers termination by the employer with or without notice, expiry of fixed term of employment without renewal under the same contract, and counter-notice by an employee in reply to notice of termination by the employer.[4] Complaints of unfair dismissal lie to an industrial tribunal. In determining whether dismissal was fair or unfair, it is for the employer to show the reason or principal reason for the dismissal, and that it related to the employee's capability or qualifications,[5] or conduct, or his redundancy, or the inability to continue to work without contravening a statutory duty or restriction, or was some other substantial reason of a kind such as to justify dismissal.[6] Dismissal by lockout is not unfair if re-engagement is offered.[7] Dismissal for participation in a strike is not unfair unless it is shown the other employees were not dismissed, or were re-engaged whereas the claimant was not.[8] An employee may be entitled both to a redundancy payment and to compensation for unfair dismissal.[9] It is unfair dismissal to dismiss an employee who has refused to be party to falsification of records[10] or to dismiss without giving an opportunity to explain.[11]

An employee unfairly dismissed may obtain an order determining the rights of the complainer and the employer as to the matter in dispute, and or an award of compensation not exceeding 104 weeks' pay or £5,200, whichever is the less, such award as

---

[1] *Goldie* v. *Christie & Petrie* (1868) 6 M. 541.

[2] *Palmer, supra*; *Malloch, supra*.

[3] Trade Union and Labour Relations Act, 1974, Sched. 1, para. 4. This is a statutory right additional to the common law right not to be dismissed wrongfully: *Norton Tool Co.* v. *Tewson* [1973] 1 All E.R. 183.

[4] Ibid., para. 5; see also *Lees* v. *Greaves* [1973] 2 All E.R. 21.

[5] Cf. *Davis* v. *Swift Automobiles* [1972] I.R.L.R. 54.

[6] Ibid., para. 6.

[7] Ibid., para. 7.

[8] Ibid., para. 8. See also para. 15.

[9] *Midland Foot Comfort Centre* v. *Richmond* [1973] 2 All E.R. 294.

[10] *Morrish* v. *Henlys* [1973] 2 All E.R. 137.

[11] *Earl* v. *Slater & Wheeler* [1973] 1 All E.R. 145.

the tribunal considers just and equitable in the circumstances, or it may make a recommendation for reinstatement.[1]

A tribunal may reduce compensation for unfair dismissal if the matters complained of were to any extent caused or contributed to by the claimant.[1]

Employer's material breach

If the employer is in material breach of duty, the employee may terminate the contract without notice and claim damages. If he has unjustifiably dismissed the employee, the latter's remedy is by action for damages.[2] He cannot insist on remaining in, or being restored to, a post from which he has been dismissed, even unjustifiably.[3] The measure of damages is the amount which the employee would have earned up to the natural termination of the contract,[4] but a dismissed employee is bound to minimize damages by seeking reasonable alternative employment and cannot recover loss in excess of that inevitably caused.[5] The damages are not aggravated by allegations of hurt feelings, or damage to reputation,[6] save in the case of employees to whom public reputation is of high importance.[7] If dismissed he has no longer a title to occupy any house occupied as part of his remuneration.[8] If the dismissal were justifiable the fact that the employer acted from oblique motive does not make it wrongful.[9] Normally an employee, and particularly a domestic servant, is not entitled to serve the full period and then bring up a catalogue of grievances, but should leave the employment and claim damages as soon as there is material breach by the employer.[10]

Frustration

A contract of employment may be determined by circumstances deemed to frustrate the contract, such as permanent incapacity,

---

[1] 1974 Act, Sch. 1, para. 20. On assessing compensation see *Norton Tool Co.*, *supra*.

[2] *Cameron* v. *Fletcher* (1872) 10 M. 301; *Caddies* v. *Holdsworth*, 1955 S.C. (H.L.) 27.

[3] *Ross* v. *Pender* (1874) 1 R. 352; *First Edinburgh Bldg. Socy.* v. *Munro* (1884) 21 S.L.R. 291.

[4] *Campbell* v. *Fyfe* (1851) 13 D. 1041; *Pollock* v. *Mair* (1901) 3 F. 332. The incidence of tax on earnings must be considered: *Stewart* v. *Glentaggart, Ltd.*, 1963 S.C. 300; *Parsons* v. *B.N.M. Laboratories, Ltd.* [1964] 1 Q.B. 95.

[5] *Hoey* v. *McEwan & Auld* (1867) 5 M. 814; *Ross, supra*; *Ross* v. *McFarlane* (1894) 21 R. 396; *Brace* v. *Calder* [1895] 2 Q.B. 253; *Yetton* v. *Eastwoods Froy, Ltd.* [1966] 3 All E.R. 353. [6] *Addis* v. *Gramophone Co.* [1909] A.C. 488.

[7] *Clayton & Waller* v. *Oliver* [1930] A.C. 209.

[8] *Sinclair* v. *Tod*, 1907 S.C. 1038; cf. *Clift* v. *Portobello Pier Co.* (1877) 4 R. 462.

[9] *Brown* v. *Edinburgh Mags.*, 1907 S.C. 256.

[10] *Fraser* v. *Laing* (1878) 5 R. 596; cf. *A.* v. *B.* (1853) 16 D. 269; *Maloy* v. *Macadam* (1885) 22 S.L.R. 790; *Davies* v. *City of Glasgow Friendly Socy.*, 1935 S.C. 224.

prolonged illness, or external circumstances which make the employee unavailable for a prolonged period.[1]

Testimonial as to character

An employer is not bound to give a departing employee a character,[2] or to answer inquiries about him; he may be obliged by custom of trade to give a certificate of the fact of service.[3] A seaman is entitled to such a certificate.[4] If an employer does give a character or answer enquiries he is entitled to give a true character, though prejudicial,[5] and his statements are entitled to qualified privilege,[6] though malice may be inferred;[7] he is similarly privileged in stating to one *in loco parentis* his reasons for dismissal,[8] in replying to a claim for wages,[9] in giving reasons for dismissal to an employment agency,[10] in reporting on an employee to an employer's organization.[11] A person receiving a character is under no duty to withhold its terms from the employee.[12]

APPRENTICESHIP

A contract of apprenticeship must in all cases be constituted in writing,[13] or, if informal, validated by *rei interventus*.[14] It is essential that the master oblige himself, expressly or impliedly, to instruct the apprentice in the profession or trade, personally or through qualified servants.[15] An apprentice's indenture may be assigned only with his consent.[16] The master may dismiss an apprentice for insolence and irregular attendance.[17] If inadequate instruction be given, the apprentice may recover damages for loss caused

---

[1] e.g. *Poussard* v. *Spiers and Pond* (1876) 1 Q.B.D. 410; *Marshall* v. *Glanvill* [1917]
[2] K.B. 87; *Morgan* v. *Manser* [1948] 1 K.B. 184; *Condor* v. *Barron Knights, Ltd.* [1966]
1 W.L.R. 87; *Marshall* v. *Harland & Wolff* [1972] 1 W.L.R. 899.
[2] *Fell* v. *Lord Ashburton*, 12 Dec. 1809, F.C.
[3] *Grant* v. *Ramage & Ferguson* (1897) 25 R. 35; *Royce* v. *Greig*, 1909, 2 S.L.T. 298.
[4] Merchant Shipping Act, 1894, S. 128.   [5] *Christian* v. *Kennedy* (1818) 1 Mur. 427.
[6] Bell, *Prin.* §188; *Anderson* v. *Wishart* (1818) 1 Mur. 429.
[7] *Macdonald* v. *McColl* (1901) 3 F. 1082.   [8] *Watson* v. *Burnet* (1862) 24 D. 494.
[9] *Laidlaw* v. *Gunn* (1890) 17 R. 394; *Sheriff* v. *Denholm* (1898) 5 S.L.T. 437.
[10] *Farquhar* v. *Neish* (1890) 17 R. 716.   [11] *Keith* v. *Lauder* (1905) 8 F. 356.
[12] *Mushets* v. *Mackenzie* (1899) 1 F. 756.
[13] *Murray* v. *McGilchrist* (1863) 4 Irv. 461; *Grant* v. *Ramage & Ferguson* (1897) 25 R. 35;
Eunson v. *Johnson & Greig*, 1940 S.C. 49.
[14] *Neil* v. *Vashon* (1807) Hume 20; cf. *Gow* v. *McEwan* (1901) 8 S.L.T. 484.
[15] *Gardner* v. *Smith* (1775) Mor. 593; *Ballantyne* v. *Kerr*, 21 Nov. 1811, F.C.; *Gordon* v. *Cran* (1904) 12 S.L.T. 471; *Royce* v. *Greig*, 1909, 2 S.L.T. 298; cf. *Fraser* v. *Min. of Nat. Ins.*, 1947 S.C. 594.
[16] *Edinburgh Glasshouse Co.* v. *Shaw* (1789) Mor. 597.
[17] *Stewart* v. *Crichton* (1847) 9 D. 1042.

thereby.[1] If any premium has been paid, a proportion is re-coverable if the master dies,[2] but if the apprentice die it is ir-recoverable.[3]

An apprentice deserting his master may at common law be imprisoned[4] or, if bound without premium or with a premium not exceeding £25, under the Employers and Workmen Act, 1875, Ss. 6 and 12. He may also be liable in damages for breach of indenture.[5]

The master may dismiss an apprentice who solicits business from the master's customers,[6] and, certainly in the case of mari-time apprenticeship, may chastise an apprentice without liability unless the conduct were wanton cruelty.[7] An apprentice wrong-fully dismissed may recover damages for loss of earnings and training, and for diminution of future prospects.[8]

[1] *Lyle* v. *Service* (1863) 2 M. 115.
[2] *Cutler* v. *Littleton* (1711) Mor. 583.
[3] *Shephard* v. *Innes* (1760) Mor. 589.
[4] *Cameron* v. *Murray & Hepburn* (1866) 4 M. 547; *McDermott* v. *Ramsay* (1876) 4 R. 217.
[5] *Ferguson* v. *Mackenzie* (1815) Hume 21; *Gunn* v. *Goodall* (1835) 13 S. 1142.
[6] *Malloch* v. *Duffy* (1882) 19 S.L.R. 697.
[7] *Wight* v. *Burns* (1883) 11 R. 217.
[8] *Dunk* v. *Waller* [1970] 2 All E.R. 630.

CHAPTER 42

CONTRACT FOR SERVICES, OR FOR LETTING WORK AND LABOUR— *LOCATIO OPERIS FACIENDI*

T H E contract of *locatio operis faciendi*, or contract for services, is that whereby one person lets out to another, frequently called the contractor, the doing, for a fee, of some piece of work, or the bringing about of some results, in the achievement of which the contractor is required to use his professional or technical skill and knowledge but is not subject to the detailed supervision, direction, or control of the client.[1] *Locatio operis faciendi* covers two main categories of contracts, many cases of the employment of trained and professional persons to render skilled services,[2] and the employment of contractors such as building, engineering and similar firms, to carry through construction or repair contracts.[3] The cardinal distinction between cases of this contract and cases of *locatio operarum* is that, in the present class of cases, the contractor is not subject to detailed direction or control as to the mode in which the desired result is achieved.[4] It is his responsibility to organize the manner in which the work is done, so as to achieve the result undertaken to be produced.[5] It may be a narrow question in particular cases whether a person is employed under *locatio operarum* or *locatio operis faciendi*.[6]

CONTRACTS FOR PROFESSIONAL SERVICES

The contract to employ a person to render skilled services within the scope of his profession or trade may be oral, written, or inferred from a consultation or the acceptance of instructions to undertake a particular commission. The work to be done must be

---

[1] Bell, *Comm.* I, 485; *Prin.* §153.

[2] An advocate (and, in England, a barrister) acts under a mandate, not a contract *locatio operis faciendi*, and a professional person, such as a solicitor or doctor, may be employed under a *locatio operarum*: see e.g. *Macdonald* v. *Glasgow Western Hospitals*, 1954 S.C. 453, 485.

[3] See also Hudson on *Building Contracts*; Emden and Watson: *Building Contracts and Practice*.

[4] Ch. 41, *supra*.

[5] cf. *Clayton* v. *Woodman & Son (Builders)* [1962] 2 Q.B. 533; *Clay* v. *Crump* [1964] 1 Q.B. 533.

[6] e.g. *Macdonald* v. *Glasgow Western Hospitals*, 1954 S.C. 453.

such as the professional person may, within the limits set by law[1] and professional etiquette and custom, undertake, and such as he impliedly professes to do.[2] He may generally decline to undertake work in an area of his professional field outside his specialty. But an advocate may not, save in very special circumstances, decline to act for any litigant requesting his aid and advice.[3]

Duty of care

By accepting a commission a professional or skilled person impliedly undertakes to bring to it and use a fair and reasonable standard of professional knowledge, skill and care, such as is possessed and used by the normally competent member of the profession or trade in question: *spondet peritiam artis*. He is liable in damages for loss caused by failure to show that degree of skill and care,[4] but not merely because his handling of the case fails,[5] or if his diagnosis is wrong,[6] nor because of an unforeseen accident in the course of dealing with the case,[7] nor for an error of judgment or a mistaken exercise of discretion,[8] nor for ignorance of a matter which an ordinarily competent person in his profession could not be expected to know,[9] nor where there is no settled

---

[1] e.g. a surgeon cannot be called on to perform an illegal operation, nor anyone other than an enrolled solicitor to prepare a conveyance.

[2] Thus a solicitor is not qualified to advise on the value or prospects of investment: *Johnstone* v. *Thorburn* (1901) 3 F. 497; *Wernham* v. *McLean, Baird & Neilson*, 1925 S.C. 407; but he may advise as to their legality: *Rae* v. *Meek* (1888) 15 R. 1033; *Johnstone* v. *Thorburn* (1901) 3 F. 497.

[3] *Batchelor* v. *Pattison and Mackersy* (1876) 3 R. 914, 918.

[4] Bell, *Comm.* I, 489; *Prin.* §153; *Hart* v. *Frame* (1839) McL. & Rob. 595 (solicitor); *Lanphier* v. *Phipos* (1838) 8 C. & P. 475 (surgeon); *Purves* v. *Landell* (1845) 4 Bell 46 (solicitor); *Cooke* v. *Falconer's Reps.* (1850) 13 D. 157 (solicitors); *Ritchie* v. *Macrosty* (1854) 16 D. 554 (solicitor); *Jenkins* v. *Betham* (1855) 15 C.B. 168 (surveyor); *McKechnie* v. *Halliday* (1856) 18 D. 659 (solicitor); *Anderson* v. *Torrie* (1857) 19 D. 356; *Urquhart* v. *Grigor* (1857) 19 D. 853; *Harmer* v. *Cornelius* (1858) 5 C.B. (N.S.) 236 (scene painter); *Bell* v. *Ogilvie* (1863) 2 M. 336 (solicitor); *Hay* v. *Baillie* (1868) 7 M. 32; *Hamilton* v. *Emslie* (1868) 7 M. 173 (solicitor); *Batchelor* v. *Pattison and Mackersy* (1876) 3 R. 914; *Jameson* v. *Simon* (1899) 1 F. 1211 (architect); *Blair* v. *Assets Co.* (1896) 23 R. (H.L.) 36 (solicitor); *Farquhar* v. *Murray* (1901) 3 F. 859 (doctor); *Dickson* v. *Hygienic Inst.*, 1910 S.C. 352 (dental practitioner); *McConnachie* v. *Macqueen's Trs.*, 1913, 1 S.L.T. 41 (solicitor); *Simpson* v. *Kidstons*, 1913, 1 S.L.T. 74 (solicitor); *R.* v. *Bateman* [1925] All E.R. Rep. 45 (doctor); *Shane* v. *Girvan*, 1927 S.L.T. 460 (solicitor); *Hunter* v. *Hanley*, 1955 S.C. 200 (doctor); *Bagot* v. *Stevens Scanlon & Co.* [1966] 1 Q.B. 197 (architect). See further Begg on *Law Agents*, Ch. 18.

[5] *Fish* v. *Kapur* [1948] 2 All E.R. 176; *Cassidy* v. *Min. of Health* [1951] 2 K.B. 343. *Hinshaw* v. *Adam* (1870) 8 M. 933 seems to be a case of express undertaking to do a job.

[6] *Hunter, supra.*

[7] *Roe* v. *Ministry of Health* [1954] 2 Q.B. 66.

[8] *Hart, supra,* 614.

[9] *Cooke, supra.*

rule or practice on the matter,[1] nor for failure to show the knowledge and skill a consultant or specialist or expert might be
expected to show, nor necessarily for failure to notice an English
decision relevant also in Scotland,[2] nor for inevitable loss, negligence or not.[3]

But there is liability for failure to do what any reasonably
competent practitioner would know to do, such as failure to
maintain instruments clean,[4] or forgetfulness of a well-settled
rule,[5] for defective workmanship,[6] for failure to warn a client on
matters within the advisor's knowledge,[7] for the unexplained
failure of a surveyor to detect woodworm.[8]

Deviation from standard practice

If the alleged breach of duty consists of deviation from ordinary
professional practice, this is not necessarily evidence of negligence, but it must be established that there was a usual and
normal practice in such circumstances, that it was not adopted by
the defender, and that the course in fact adopted was one which no
professional man of ordinary skill would have taken if acting with
ordinary care.[9]

A lesser standard of skill and care is demanded in emergency,
or in matters outwith the immediate scope of the practitioner's
profession.[10] A person not possessed of professional skill can be
expected to show only the skill of an ordinarily competent lay-
man doing a job of the kind in question.[11]

The duty of care is always owed *ex contractu* to the client, but
where personal injuries, damage to reputation or economic loss

---

[1] *Hamilton v. Emslie* (1868) 7 M. 173.

[2] *Free Church v. McKnight's Trs.*, 1916 S.C. 349.

[3] *Stuart v. Miller* (1840) 3 D. 255; *Stiven v. Watson* (1874) 1 R. 412; *Turnbull v. Cruikshank & Fairweather* (1905) 7 F. 791; *Wernham, supra,* 419; cf. *Stewart v. McLean, Baird & Neilson,* 1915 S.C. 13.

[4] *Hales v. Kerr* [1908] 2 K.B. 601.

[5] *Simpson v. Kidstons,* 1913, 1 S.L.T. 74; *Robertson v. Bannigan,* 1965 S.C. 20; contrast *Free Church v. McKnight's Trs.,* 1916 S.C. 349.

[6] *McIntyre v. Gallacher* (1883) 11 R. 64 (plumber).

[7] *William's Trs. v. Macandrew and Jenkins,* 1960 S.L.T. 246.

[8] *Stewart v. Brechin,* 1959 S.C. 306. cf. *Freeman v. Marshall* (1966) 200 E.G. 777; *Hardy v. Wamsley-Lewis* (1967) 203 E.G. 1039.

[9] *Hunter, supra;* cf. *Hart v. Frame* (1839) McL. & R. 595; *Clark v. Sim* (1833) 6 W. & S. 452; *Tully v. Ingram* (1891) 19 R. 65; *Fearn v. Gordon & Craig* (1893) 20 R. 352; *McConnachie v. Macqueen's Trs.,* 1913, 1 S.L.T. 41; contrast *Hamilton v. Emslie* (1868) 7 M. 173.

[10] *Banbury v. Bank of Montreal* [1918] A.C. 626; *Philips v. Whiteley* [1938] 1 All E.R. 566.

[11] *Wells v. Cooper* [1958] 2 Q.B. 265; cf. *Dickson v. Hygienic Institute,* 1910 S.C. 352.

may follow from failure to show adequate skill or take reasonable care a wider duty may also be owed *ex lege* to a person who might foreseeably be injured by the practitioner's failure to take care.[1]

Counsel, who do not act under *locatio operis faciendi*, by custom and on grounds of public policy, are not liable for professional negligence in any circumstances,[2] though they do owe a duty to exercise due and reasonable skill and care.[3]

Remuneration

The remuneration due is normally fixed within limits by the custom of the profession, or determined within limits by its approved scales of fees.[4] In the absence of proof that the services were gratuitous[5] a reasonable reward is due for services rendered.[6] A special agreement in lieu of ordinary professional charges is competent.[7] Counsel in Scotland and England, and Fellows of the Royal College of Physicians of London, the fellows of which are by by-law prohibited from doing so, may not sue for their fees.[8] A solicitor should not accept a benefit from a client unless the client has obtained independent advice or otherwise been free from reliance on the solicitor, and not do business with the client unless it can be justified as proper and fair.[9]

Termination of contract

The client may at any time discharge his professional adviser on paying the remuneration due for services performed to date,

[1] *Edgar* v. *Lamont*, 1914 S.C. 277; *Hedley Byrne & Co.* v. *Heller & Partners* [1964] A.C. 465; cf. *Smith* v. *Taylor* (1882) 10 R. 291; *Cook* v. *Wallace & Wilson* (1889) 16 R. 565; *Sturrock* v. *Welsh & Forbes* (1890) 18 R. 109; *MacRobbie* v. *McLellan's Trs.* (1891) 18 R. 470; *Macdougall* v. *McNab* (1893) 21 R. 144 (wrongful use of diligence); *Wilson* v. *Purvis* (1890) 18 R. 72 (slander); *Crawford* v. *Dunlop* (1900) 2 F. 987 (slander); as to skilled tradesmen see *Malcolm* v. *Dickson*, 1951 S.C. 542; *Gilmour* v. *Simpson*, 1958 S.C. 477 (painters); *Eccles* v. *Cross & McIlwham*, 1938 S.C. 697; *Waddell's C.B.* v. *Lindsay*, 1960 S.L.T. 189 (electricians); *McIntyre* v. *Gallacher* (1883) 11 R. 64; *McNamara* v. *Anderson Bros.* (1904) 11 S.L.T. 607 (plumbers).

[2] *Purves* v. *Landell* (1845) 4 Bell 46; *Burness* v. *Morris* (1849) 11 D. 1258; *Swinfen* v. *Lord Chelmsford* (1860) 5 H. & N. 890; *Batchelor* v. *Pattison and Mackersy* (1876) 3 R. 914, 918; *Rondel* v. *Worsley* [1969] 1 A.C. 191.

[3] The only sanction is probably a complaint to the Faculty of Advocates, or the barrister's Inn of Court. See *Re S.* [1969] 1 All E.R. 949.

[4] *Wilkie* v. *Scottish Aviation, Ltd.*, 1956 S.C. 198.

[5] *Mackersy's Exors.* v. *St. Giles Cathedral Board* (1904) 12 S.L.T. 391; *Campbell* v. *C's Exor.*, 1910, 2 S.L.T. 240.

[6] *Winton* v. *Airth* (1868) 6 M. 1095; *Landless* v. *Wilson* (1880) 8 R. 289; *Dunbar* v. *Wilson & Dunlop's Tr.* (1887) 15 R. 210.

[7] *Jacobs* v. *McMillan* (1899) 2 F. 79.

[8] *Kennedy* v. *Brown* (1863) 13 C.B. (N.S.) 677; *Batchelor* v. *Pattison and Mackersy* (1876) 3 R. 914, 918; Medical Act, 1956, S. 27(2); *Rondel* v. *Worsley, supra.*

[9] *Dick* v. *Alston*, 1913 S.C. (H.L.) 57.

including for work done but not yet utilized, such as for plans and calculations made. The adviser may not decline to continue to act unless the client is plainly refusing to comply with advice or instructions, or is requesting the execution of some work which is illegal, wrongful, dishonest, or dishonourable. An advocate, and probably also a solicitor in court business, owes a duty to the court and may refuse to act further for a client in a matter which he considers unstatable.[1]

BUILDING AND OTHER CONSTRUCTION CONTRACTS

A contract for the letting of a work of building or engineering construction, repair, installation or demolition may be entered into orally[2] but is normally entered into in writing, frequently incorporating standard conditions of contract formulated by a professional institution,[3] on the basis of contractors' tenders to do work as set out in architects' plans and surveyors' bills of quantities prepared for and provided by the client.[4] The terms of the contract are ascertainable from the invitation to tender,[5] plans or other documents incorporated therein, the contractor's tender and the acceptance thereof.[6] If a new contract to complete works is entered into between the same parties, necessary stipulations of the former contract may be impliedly included, but not special terms as to forfeiture or liquidate damages.[7]

The contract may be for the construction of the work for a lump sum, or to pay for work as it may be measured on completion, at rates agreed, or to pay the cost of work and materials plus a percentage profit, or to have no express agreement for payment,

---

[1] *Scott* v. *H.M.A.*, 1946 J.C. 68.

[2] There is no authority for regarding such a contract as one involving heritage so as to require probative writing; cf. *McManus* v. *Cooke* (1887) 35 Ch. D. 681.

[3] Standard forms of contract have been formulated by the Royal Incorporation of Architects in Scotland, the R.I.B.A., the Institution of Civil Engineers, and similar bodies. See e.g. *Morrison's Assoc. Companies, Ltd.* v. *Rome*, 1965 S.C. 160; *Harvey* v. *Cant*, 1970 S.L.T. (Sh. Ct.) 54 (General Conditions of Contract for Building Works in Scotland). Construction contracts with government departments incorporate the terms of the General conditions of Government Contracts for Building and Civil Engineering Works; cf. *Farr* v. *The Admiralty* [1953] 2 All E.R. 512.

[4] cf. *Murray* v. *Rennie & Angus* (1897) 24 R. 965. An architect has been held to have implied authority to employ a surveyor: *Black* v. *Cornelius* (1879) 6 R. 581; cf. *Knox & Robb* v. *Scottish Garden Suburb Co.*, 1913 S.C. 872.

[5] The employer in inviting tenders should disclose any exceptional difficulties of which he is aware: *Mackay* v. *L.A.*, 1914, 1 S.L.T. 33.

[6] *G.N. Ry.* v. *Witham* (1873) L.R. 9 C.P. 16; *Tancred Arrol & Co.* v. *Steel Co. of Scotland* (1890) 17 R. (H.L.) 31.

[7] *Barr* v. *Stirling and Dunfermline Ry.* (1855) 17 D. 582.

in which case there is an implied obligation to pay a reasonable price.

The contract may again be with a main contractor for the principal work and separate contracts with other contractors for work of particular trades, or a main contract, and sub-contracts between the main contractor and sub-contractors (who may be nominated by the architect[1] or by the main contractor) for particular work,[2] in which case the client has, save by arrangement, no direct claims against or liabilities to the sub-contractors,[3] though issues may arise between contractor and sub-contractor.[4]

Statutory regulation

Building or similar work is subject to the obtaining of planning permission for the execution of that work,[5] and to the obtaining of warrant from the local buildings authority,[6] and sometimes to the obtaining of a licence from the Ministry of Public Buildings and Works.[7] Failure to obtain planning permission may result in compulsory demolition or alteration of the unauthorized works,[8] failure to obtain a building warrant is an offence[9] and failure to obtain, or exceeding, a building licence renders the contract unlawful and void.[10] The building warrant requires the operations to be conducted in accordance with the building operations regulations[11] and the building to conform to the building standards regulations.[12]

Client's duties

Apart from express stipulations the client is impliedly bound to give the contractor free access to the site at the agreed time,[13] to permit such other access to or over his lands as may be necessary,

---

[1] e.g. *Bickerton* v. *N.W. Metropolitan Hospital Board* [1969] 1 All E.R. 977.

[2] e.g. *Chandler Bros.* v. *Boswell* [1936] 3 All E.R. 179.

[3] *Milestone* v. *Yates Castle Brewery Co.* [1938] 2 All E.R. 439.

[4] e.g. *McGlynn* v. *Rome*, 1968 S.L.T. (Notes) 16; *Holland & Hannan & Cubitts (Sc.) Ltd.* v. *Macdougall*, 1968 S.L.T. (Notes) 91.

[5] Town and Country Planning (Sc.) Act, 1972, S. 20.

[6] Building (Sc.) Act, 1959, Ss. 1–2 and Building (Sc.) Act, 1970; see also *Dumbarton C.C.* v. *Wimpey*, 1968 S.L.T. 246; *Williamson* v. *Purdie*, 1970 S.L.T. 350.

[7] Control of Office and Industrial Development Act, 1965; Building Control Act, 1966, S. 1.

[8] 1972 Act, S. 49.   [9] 1959 Act, S. 6; cf. S. 10.

[10] *Jamieson* v. *Watt's Tr.*, 1950 S.C. 265; *Designers and Decorators (Scotland)* v. *Ellis*, 1957 S.C. (H.L.) 69.

[11] 1959 Act, S. 5.   [12] 1959 Act, Ss. 3–4, 11.

[13] cf. *Roberts* v. *Bury Commrs.* (1870) L.R. 5 C.P. 310; *Mackay* v. *Leven Police Commrs.* (1893) 20 R. 1093.

to furnish plans and instructions as required[1] or as are customary,[2] to permit the contractor to carry out the work,[3] and not to interrupt, hinder or interfere with the progress of the work.[4] He may be expressly bound to further duties such as to supply materials to or carry out works for the convenience of the contractors. There is however, no implied obligation to indemnify the contractor against loss caused by a third party's interference.[5] Failure will justify a claim of damages or, in extreme cases, rescission of the contract,[6] and the client may be liable if other contractors employed by him cause delay to the main contractor.[7]

Contractor's duties

The contractor becomes bound impliedly, if not expressly, to bring about the result desired by the client within any time fixed or at all events within a reasonable time.[8] He is impliedly bound to employ competent workmen, to proceed diligently, and to execute the work in a tradesmanlike manner,[9] and impliedly warrants that materials used will be of sound quality and reasonably fit for the purpose,[10] unless they are directed or chosen by the client or the latter's architect. Unless expressly, he does not undertake to make an entity fit for any particular purpose, save that a dwelling-house is impliedly warranted fit for human habitation.[11] The contractor owes a contractual duty to his employer to adopt the usual and recognized standards and practices which a careful contractor would adopt in the trade concerned, e.g. in providing temporary support for a building undergoing alteration.[12]

[1] *McAlpine* v. *Lanarkshire and Ayrshire Ry.* (1889) 17 R. 113.

[2] *Kingdom* v. *Cox* (1848) 5 C.B. 522; *Stevens* v. *Taylor* (1860) 2 F. & F. 419; *Roberts, supra.*

[3] *Churchward* v. *R.* (1865) L.R. 1 Q.B. 173, 195; *Roberts, supra.*

[4] *Porter* v. *Tottenham U.D.C.* [1915] 1 K.B. 776.

[5] *Porter, supra.*

[6] *Roberts, supra*; *Wilson* v. *Northampton Ry.* (1874) 9 Ch. App. 279.

[7] cf. *Duncanson* v. *Scottish County Investment Co.,* 1915 S.C. 1106.

[8] *Lucas* v. *Godwin* (1837) 3 Bing. (N.C.) 737; *Startup* v. *Macdonald* (1843) 6 M. & G. 593; cf. *Hick* v. *Raymond and Reid* [1893] A.C. 22, 32; *Davis Contractors Ltd.* v. *Fareham U.D.C.* [1956] A.C. 696.

[9] *Halt* v. *Burke* (1886) 3 T.L.R. 165.

[10] *Myers* v. *Brent Cross Service Co.* [1934] 1 K.B. 46; *Prior* v. *McManus Childs* [1967] 3 All E.R. 451; *Gloucester C.C.* v. *Richardson* [1967] 3 All E.R. 458.

[11] *Jennings* v. *Tavener* [1955] 2 All E.R. 769; cf. *Miller* v. *Cannon Hill Estates* [1931] 2 K.B. 113; *Perry* v. *Sharon Developments Co.* [1937] 4 All E.R. 390; *Otto* v. *Bolton and Norris* [1936] 2 K.B. 46.

[12] *Morrison's Assoc. Companies Ltd.* v. *Rome,* 1964 S.C. 160, 178, 184.

The contractor owes duties of care to his own employees for their own safety,[1] and also duties to take care for the safety of members of the public who may in the circumstances be expected to come within the risk of danger from the contractor's operations,[2] and will also be liable if, by reason of negligent construction, a user of the premises constructed is injured.[3] He may be contractually bound to relieve the client of any claims to which the latter may become subject arising out of the operations.[4]

Joint and several liability

Where two or more contractors are in breach of separate but related contracts and harm results from the fault of both, they may competently be sued jointly and severally for breaches of their separate contracts.[5]

Time for completion

If no time is specified for completion it is implied that the work is to be completed within a time reasonable in the circumstances.[6] If a particular date is specified for completion, non-completion by then entitles the client to damages but not normally to rescind the contract;[7] the date of completion may be made of the essence of the contract, but only exceptionally in building contracts, and non-completion by then justifies rescission of the contract.[8] If a contractor has clearly bound himself to complete by a fixed date, it is no defence that delay was caused by alterations ordered by the client,[9] but this interpretation will not be adopted of ambiguous contracts.[10]

[1] e.g. *Davies* v. *A.C.D. Bridge Co.*, 1966 S.C. 211; *Price* v. *Claudgen*, 1967 S.C. (H.L.) 18; *O'Donnell* v. *Murdoch Mackenzie & Co.*, 1967 S.C. (H.L.) 63.

[2] *Mooney* v. *Lanarkshire C.C.*, 1954 S.C. 245; *Billings* v. *Riden* [1958] A.C. 240; cf. *Cuttress* v. *Scaffolding (G.B.) Ltd.* [1953] 2 All E.R. 1075.

[3] *Otto* v. *Bolton and Norris* [1936] 2 K.B. 46; *Gallagher* v. *McDowell* [1961] N.I. 26.

[4] *Hamilton* v. *Anderson*, 1953 S.C. 129; cf. *N. of S. Hydro-Electric Board* v. *Taylor*, 1956 S.C. 1; *McGill* v. *Pirie & Co. (Paisley) Ltd.*, 1967 S.L.T. 152; *Mackay* v. *Balfour Beatty & Co.*, 1967 S.L.T. (Notes) 15.

[5] *Grunwald* v. *Hughes*, 1965 S.L.T. 209.

[6] *Startup* v. *Macdonald* (1843) 6 M. & G. 593; *Hydraulic Eng. Co.* v. *McHaffie* (1878) 4 Q.B.D. 670.

[7] *Smith* v. *Johnson* (1899) 15 T.L.R. 179; *Port Glasgow Mags.* v. *Scottish Construction Co. Ltd.*, 1960 S.L.T. 319.

[8] *Rickards* v. *Oppenheim* [1950] 1 K.B. 616.

[9] *Steel* v. *Bell* (1900) 3 F. 319; cf. *Duncanson* v. *Baylis* (1869) 7 S.L.R. 139; *Jones* v. *St. John's College* (1870) L.R. 6 Q.B. 115.

[10] *Robertson* v. *Driver's Trs.* (1881) 8 R. 555.

Difficulties and frustration

If the contract is a lump sum one the contractor takes the risk of difficulties encountered in construction, such as more difficult excavation work,[1] but otherwise if it is a measure and value contract. In the absence of contractual provision for delays caused by bad weather, strikes or shortages of labour or materials, the contractor takes the risk of extra cost caused thereby.[2] If, however, difficulties and delays so affect the contract as fundamentally to change its character and to make completion, if possible at all, altogether different from what was contemplated by the parties, the contract may be held frustrated.[3]

Passing of property

The time or times at which the property passes to the client depends on the contract. In the case of building work on the client's land, *prima facie* the building passes to him as the materials are incorporated in it: *quicquid plantatur solo, solo cedit*; *accessorium sequitur principale*; and materials brought to the site may be deemed to have been constructively appropriated to the building and to pass with the land.[4] But this does not constitute acceptance of the materials and work thereon by the client as in full performance of the contract.[5] In the case of ships[6] the property may pass in stages as instalments of the price are paid, or on payment of a particular instalment;[7] nevertheless the client may reject the finished vessel before final acceptance if on completion it is defective or disconform to contract.[8]

Risk

Prima facie during construction the risk of damage or destruction is with the owner, provided the work, so far as done, had

[1] *Boyd and Forrest* v. *G.S.W. Ry.*, 1915 S.C. (H.L.) 20.

[2] *Mackay* v. *Leven Police Commrs.* (1893) 20 R. 1093; *Hick* v. *Raymond and Reid* [1893] A.C. 22; *Davis Contractors, Ltd.* v. *Fareham U.D.C.* [1956] A.C. 696; cf. *Union Totalisator Co.* v. *Scott*, 1951 S.L.T. (Notes) 5.

[3] *Metropolitan Water Board* v. *Dick Kerr & Co.* [1918] A.C. 119; contrast *Davis Contractors, Ltd., supra*; *Cantiere San Rocco* v. *Clyde Shipbuilding Co.*, 1923 S.C. (H.L.) 105.

[4] cf. Ersk. II, 2, 14; *Gordon* v. *G.* (1806) Hume 188; *Stewart* v. *Watson's Hospital* (1862) 24 D. 256; *Malloch* v. *McLean* (1867) 5 M. 335; *Appleby* v. *Myers* (1867) L.R. 2 C.P. 651; *Bank of Scotland* v. *White's Trs.* (1891) 29 S.L.R. 891.

[5] *Munro* v. *Butt* (1858) 8 E. & B. 738.

[6] Such a contract is legally a sale of goods, not a *locatio operis faciendi*: *Reid* v. *Macbeth & Gray* (1904) 6 F (H.L.) 25; *Nelson, infra*.

[7] *Appleby* v. *Myers* (1867) L.R. 2 C.P. 651, 660. As to ownership of materials on the shipbuilder's bankruptcy, see *Seath* v. *Moore* (1888) 13 R. (H.L.) 57; *Reid, supra*.

[8] *Nelson* v. *Chalmers*, 1913 S.C. 441; *McDougall* v. *Aeromarine Ltd.* [1958] 3 All E.R. 431.

been done conform to contract,[1] the builder having a claim for the value of the work and materials lost thereby, and after the works have been completed and handed over the loss falls on the owner. The owner also takes the risk of damage caused to adjacent property by the contractor's operations.[2] Where the thing damaged or destroyed is being constructed separately, e.g. in the contractor's workshop, and has not yet been handed over, the risk is on the contractor till he hands over the new thing.

Variation of contract

The contract usually contains power to the client or his architect to vary the works specified; if the variations ordered are so extensive as to amount to a new contract, the original contract may be held superseded and a new contract implied with provision for payment *quantum meruit*.[3] Short of that, the architect may sanction deviations in details of constructional arrangement, but not deviations from the contract,[4] such as the use of a particular substance in construction.[5] A variation made by the contractor for his own convenience does not justify a claim for extra payment in the absence of clear evidence of assent thereto by the client.[6]

Additions, omissions and extras

Additions and extras include all works not provided for in the original plans and specifications. Works and materials necessary for the completion of a lump sum contract are not extras even though not mentioned in plans or specifications,[7] but work necessary but in excess of quantities is extra,[8] even in a lump sum contract and, *a fortiori*, in a measure and value contract.[9]

Payment

The price may be a fixed lump sum for the whole works,[9] or a series of distinct payments for separate parts of the works,[10] or the

[1] *McIntyre* v. *Clow* (1875) 2 R. 278; *Richardson* v. *Dumfriesshire Road Trs.* (1890) 17 R. 805. If the work was disconform, the loss falls on the contractor.
[2] cf. *Gold* v. *Patman and Fotheringham* [1958] 2 All E.R. 497.
[3] *Parkinson* v. *Commrs. of Works* [1949] 2 K.B. 632; *Head Wrightson* v. *Aberdeen Harbour Commrs.*, 1958 S.L.T. (Notes) 12.
[4] *Forrest* v. *Sc. County Investment Co.*, 1916 S.C. (H.L.) 28.
[5] *Steel* v. *Young*, 1907 S.C. 360.
[6] *Tharsis Sulphur Co.* v. *McElroy* (1878) 5 R. (H.L.) 171.
[7] *Wilson* v. *Wallace* (1859) 21 D. 507; *Re Shell Transport and Trading Co.* (1904) 20 T.L.R. 517.
[8] *Bryant* v. *Birmingham Hospital Saturday Fund* [1938] 1 All E.R. 503.
[9] *Ramsay* v. *Brand* (1898) 25 R. 1212; *Speirs* v. *Petersen*, 1924 S.C. 428; *Mitchell* v. *Dalkeith Mags.*, 1930 S.L.T. 80.   [10] *Appleby* v. *Myers* (1867) L.R. 2 C.P. 651.

cost of the work and materials plus a percentage profit,[1] or be the sum to be ascertained according to the measurement of the work finally brought out, at values set for different classes of work,[2] or not fixed in any way, in which case the obligation is to pay a reasonable price for the work.[3] Where the client has been materially in breach, the contractor may be able to maintain that the contract is ended and that payment is due *quantum meruit*.[4] Provision is, however, normally made for payment by instalments, usually on certificates by the architect that the agreed stage of completion has been reached. Payment for additions and extras is recoverable where the client expressly or impliedly ordered them, or he or his architect authorized or ratified the extra works, or accepted them. There is no claim for payment for extras voluntarily done, or materials better than those stipulated.[5] When the whole work is completed in accordance with the contract, payment of the balance is then due, unless there is provision for the retention of part of the balance until the end of the contractor's maintenance period, to maintain the works or rectify defects on the contractor's failure to do so.[6] A client has been held entitled to retain, out of the sums due under the final certificate, a sum to meet the claim for liquidate damages for delayed performance,[7] and to counter-claim for damage done in the course of the work and not made good.[8]

Supervision and approval

It is commonly provided that work shall be done to the approval of the client's architect, such approval to be a condition precedent to payment for the work.[9] The architect's duty is to give such reasonable supervision as will enable him to certify whether or not

---

[1] *Parkinson v. Comm. of Works* [1949] 2 K.B. 632; cf. *N.B. Ry. Co. v. Wilson,* 1911 S.C. 730; *Johnston v. Greenock Corpn.,* 1951 S.L.T. (Notes) 57.

[2] *Jamieson v. McInnes* (1887) 15 R. 17; *Wilkie v. Hamilton Lodging House Co.* (1902) 4 F. 951.

[3] *Grafton v. Armitage* (1845) 2 C.B. 336; *Malloch v. Hodghton* (1849) 12 D. 215.

[4] *Thorn v. Mayor of London* (1876) 1 App. Cas. 120; *Lodder v. Slowey* [1904] A.C. 442; *Smellie v. Caledonian Ry.* (1916) 53 S.L.R. 336; cf. *Boyd & Forrest v. G.S.W. Ry.,* 1915 S.C. (H.L.) 20.

[5] *Grant v. Macleod* (1856) 19 D. 127; *Tharsis Sulphur Co. v. McElroy* (1878) 5 R. (H.L.) 171; *Forman v. The Liddesdale* [1900] A.C. 190. See also *Wilson v. Wallace* (1859) 21 D. 507.

[6] cf. *London, etc. Shipping Co. v. Duffus* (1841) 3 D. 929; *Speirs, supra.*

[7] *Port Glasgow Mags. v. Scottish Construction Co., Ltd.,* 1960 S.L.T. 319.

[8] *Laidlaw v. Griffin,* 1968 S.L.T. 278.

[9] cf. *Robertson v. Jarvie* (1907) 15 S.L.T. 703.

the work has been executed according to the contract.[1] The exercise of the architect's opinion may be challenged only on the ground of fraud or collusion.[2] But the architect's certificate is not always a condition precedent.[3] The architect or other supervisor is liable if he negligently permits deviations or passes defective work.[4] In the absence of clear contractual stipulation permitting arbitrary disapproval[5] it is implied that the client or his architect will not unreasonably refuse to approve work.[6] Even if not required to be reasonable, refusal to approve must be honest.[7] If the architect has no power to sanction deviations, the client is not bound by a certificate to accept work different from that contracted for by reason of deviations.[8] If the contractor has not performed his contract he cannot recover thereunder, but the client is barred from claiming damages if the work had proceeded without objection from the client's inspector.[9]

Acceptance

Acceptance is not to be inferred from payment of instalments of the price, still less from continuing in possession of the land or from the property in the thing being constructed having passed as it was built, or in stages, nor even from taking occupation of the premises.[10] If the client expressly or impliedly approved the completed work, he is held to have accepted it, but unless he knew of defects, and has waived any conditions as to contractual performance, acceptance does not imply acquiescence in defects, incomplete performance, or other non-compliance with contract.[11] After acceptance, no claim lies for patent defects.[12] Where the work has been subject to the approval of an architect or other third party, his approval precludes the client's objection to defects, patent or latent,[13] but otherwise if the party's approval is not final.[14] Acceptance does not preclude a claim of damages

---

[1] *Jameson* v. *Simon* (1899) 1 F. 1211.
[2] *Hickman* v. *Roberts* [1913] A.C. 229; cf. *Chapman* v. *Edinburgh Prison Board* (1844) 6 D. 1288; *Muldoon* v. *Pringle* (1882) 9 R. 915; *Ayr Road Trs.* v. *Adams* (1883) 11 R. 326.
[3] *Howden* v. *Powell Duffryn*, 1912 S.C. 920.
[4] *Gordon* v. *Millar* (1839) 1 D. 832.
[5] *Andrews* v. *Belfield* (1857) 2 C.B. (N.S.) 779.
[6] *Ranger* v. *G.W. Ry* (1854) 5 H.L. Cas. 72; *Stadhard* v. *Lee* (1863) 3 B. & S. 364.
[7] *Stadhard, supra; Roberts* v. *Bury Commrs.* (1870) L.R. 5 C.P. 310.
[8] *Ramsay* v. *Brand* (1898) 25 R. 1212.
[9] *Muldoon* v. *Pringle* (1882) 9 R. 915.
[10] *Munro* v. *Butt* (1858) 8 E. & B. 738; *Sumpter* v. *Hedges* [1898] 1 Q.B. 673.
[11] *Whitaker* v. *Dunn* (1887) 3 T.L.R. 602.
[12] *Bateman* v. *Thompson* (1875) 2 Hudson's Bldg. Contracts (4 ed.) 36.
[13] *Ayr Road Trs.* v. *Adams* (1883) 11 R. 326; *East Ham Corpn.* v. *Sunley* [1966] A.C. 406.
[14] *Bateman, supra; Muldoon* v. *Pringle* (1882) 9 R. 915.

for delay in performance.[1] Acceptance is normally subject to an obligation to make good defects appearing during a specified maintenance period.

Defective performance

The effect of defective performance depends partly on the nature of the contract. If the contract is a lump sum one, it falls to be performed entirely and if the contractor deviates substantially, he may not sue on the contract at all and is liable in damages for non-performance,[2] though if the client accepts the building he must pay for it *quantum lucratus*.[3] If, however, the deviation is not substantial or material, the contractor may sue and recover the lump sum, under deduction of the cost of making the building conform to the contract.[4] If the deviation is not material, but is irremediable, it may be that the contractor may recover the contract price under deduction of damages for the loss caused to the owner by the deviation.[5] If, on the other hand, the contract is by measure and value and the parts of it are separable the contractor may sue notwithstanding departure from the contract in some respects.[6] In the cases of contracts for repair or minor works the usual principle applies, that the contractor cannot sue if the work is disconform to contract.[7] Late completion, unless agreed to or acquiesced in, is a breach; a main contractor is not necessarily entitled to an extension of time because a sub-contractor's work has had to be remedied.[8]

Arbitration

The contract commonly provides for the settlement of disputes and differences by arbitration, frequently by the architect[9] or engineer. In exercising the arbitral function the architect must exercise his judgment impartially as between the parties, but is not

---

[1] *Sutherland* v. *Montrose Shipbuilding Co.* (1860) 22 D. 665.

[2] *Speirs* v. *Petersen*, 1924 S.C. 428.

[3] *Ramsay* v. *Brand* (1898) 25 R. 1212; cf. *Kerr* v. *Dundee Gas Co.* (1861) 23 D. 343.

[4] *Ramsay, supra*; *McMorran* v. *Morrison* (1906) 14 S.L.T. 578; *Steel* v. *Young*, 1907 S.C. 360; *Forrest* v. *Scottish County Investment Co.*, 1910 S.C. (H.L.) 28; *Speirs, supra.*

[5] *Forrest, supra*, commented on in *Graham* v. *U.T.R.*, 1922 S.C. 533; cf. *Dakin* v. *Lee* [1916] 1 K.B. 566.

[6] *Forrest, supra.*

[7] *Barclay* v. *Bruce's Trs.* (1904) 12 S.L.T. 100.

[8] *Westminster City Council* v. *Jarvis* [1970] 1 All E.R. 943.

[9] e.g. *Trowsdale* v. *Jopp* (1865) 4 M. 31; *Dickson* v. *Grant* (1870) 8 M. 566; *Mackay* v. *Barry Parochial Board* (1883) 10 R. 1046; *Beattie* v. *Macgregor* (1883) 10 R. 1094.

liable for negligence.[1] Whether a particular dispute is within the scope of the arbitration clause depends on its interpretation;[2] unless there is express provision the arbiter may not decide whether or not the client is in breach of contract.[3] If the architect has both the functions of certifying the work as it progresses and the task of arbitrating in the event of dispute between client and contractor, he is not disqualified from arbitrating by having expressed views as certifier,[4] but only if he has formed a view so strong as to debar him from acting fairly as arbiter.[5]

OTHER CONTRACTS WITH CONTRACTORS

Other contracts which are also cases of *locatio operis faciendi* are hiring a taxi, engaging a removal contractor to do a removal, hiring transport for persons or goods, mechanical equipment, and the like, with staff to operate them,[6] and many other similar contracts.[7]

---

[1] *Chambers* v. *Goldthorpe* [1901] 1 K.B. 624.

[2] cf. *Port Glasgow Mags.* v. *Scottish Construction Co., Ltd.*, 1960 S.L.T. 319; *Monmouth C.C.* v. *Costelloe & Kemble* (1965) 63 L.G.R. 429.

[3] *Levy* v. *Thomsons* (1883) 10 R. 1134.

[4] *Scott* v. *Carluke Corpn.* (1879) 6 R. 616; *Mackay* v. *Barry Parochial Board* (1883) 10 R. 1046; see also *Addie* v. *Henderson & Dimmack* (1879) 7 R. 79; *Halliday* v. *D. Hamilton's Trs.* (1903) 5 F. 800; *Low & Thomas* v. *Dunbarton C.C.* (1905) 13 S.L.T. 620; *Scott* v. *Gerrard*, 1916 S.C. 793; *Crawford* v. *Northern Lighthouses Commrs.*, 1925 S.C. (H.L.) 22.

[5] *Dickson* v. *Grant* (1870) 8 M. 566; *McLachlan & Brown* v. *Morrison* (1900) 8 S.I..T. 279.

[6] e.g. *White* v. *Tarmac Civil Engineering* [1967] 3 All E.R. 586.

[7] e.g. *Stevenson* v. *Maule*, 1920 S.C. 335.

CHAPTER 43

CONTRACT OF CARRIAGE—
LOCATIO OPERIS MERCIUM VEHENDARUM
(1) CARRIAGE BY LAND

T HIS contract, which also is a species of *locatio operis faciendi*, is one whereby one person hires another to convey his goods or himself from one place to another in the latter's vehicle, vessel or aircraft, operated by the latter or his employees. In modern law distinct bodies of rules have developed relating to carriage of goods and carriage of passengers, and in respect of carriage on land by road or rail, by sea,[1] and by air.[2] To a limited extent goods may also be conveyed by post.

CARRIAGE OF GOODS BY ROAD OR RAIL

Common carriers

At common law carriers by land[3] are distinguishable as common carriers and private carriers.[4] A common carrier makes a public and continuing offer to carry as a business, for hire,[5] the goods of anyone who chooses to employ him.[6] He may nevertheless limit the classes of goods which he is willing to carry,[7] or be willing to carry certain goods only on special conditions,[8] or to carry only from one place to another, or to any chosen terminus.[9] He is bound by a table of charges publicly advertised[10] and is in any event not entitled to charge more than a reasonable sum.[11]

---

[1] Ch. 44, *infra*.

[2] Ch. 45, *infra*.

[3] See generally Bell, *Prin.* §157–170; Macnamara on *Carriers*; Kahn-Freund on *Inland Transport*.

[4] Bell, *Prin.* §160; *Watkins* v. *Cottell* [1916] 1 K.B. 10; *Kemp* v. *Robertson*, 1967 S.C. 229; cf. *Ludditt* v. *Ginger Coote Airways* [1947] A.C. 233, 245.

[5] *Barr* v. *Caledonian Ry.* (1890) 18 R. 139; *Belfast Ropework Co.* v. *Bushell* [1918] 1 K.B. 210.

[6] *Nugent* v. *Smith* (1875) 1 C.P.D. 19; *Belfast, supra*; *G.N. Ry.* v. *L.E.P. Transport Ltd.* [1922] 2 K.B. 742; cf. *Clarke* v. *West Ham Corpn.* [1909] 2 K.B. 858.

[7] *Johnson* v. *Midland Ry.* (1849) 4 Ex. 367; *Dickson* v. *G.N. Ry.* (1886) 18 Q.B.D. 176.

[8] *Wood* v. *Burns* (1893) 20 R. 602; *Hunt & Winterbotham* v. *B.R.S. (Parcels) Ltd.* [1962] 1 All E.R. 111.

[9] *Liver Alkali Co.* v. *Johnson* (1874) L.R. 9 Ex. 338.

[10] *Campbell* v. *Ker*, 24 Feb. 1810, F.C.

[11] *G.W. Ry.* v. *Sutton* (1868) L.R. 4 H.L. 226, 237; *Crouch* v. *G.N. Ry.* (1856) 11 Exch. 742.

He may decline goods tendered to him for carriage only if they are of a class which he does not profess to carry,[1] or are dangerous,[2] or inadequately packed,[3] or are not tendered in reasonable time to be loaded,[4] or if he has no room in his vehicle,[5] or if his charges are not paid or tendered.[6] An unjustified refusal to carry is an actionable breach of duty.[7]

Whether a particular carrier is or is not a common carrier is a question of fact.[8] This may be inferred from his description of his own business, e.g. Glenmutchkin carrier. A carrier is still a common carrier though a terminus of his run is outwith the jurisdiction,[9] though he profess to carry only goods of a particular kind,[10] and a carrier not a common carrier may undertake the liabilities of a common carrier for a particular journey.[11] Railway companies were common carriers at common law and by statute,[12] but are not now common carriers.[13]

Consignor's duties

The consignor must pack the goods in a manner reasonably sufficient for the journey[14] and address them fully and distinctly.[15] Any loss resulting from failure in these respects falls on the consignor, though the carrier may be barred if he has accepted goods inadequately packed or labelled. The duty of stowage is on the carrier, who is not relieved merely by the consignor's presence[16] but only if the consignor himself stows the goods.[17] The

[1] *Johnson, supra.*   [2] *Bamfield* v. *Goole and Sheffield Tpt. Co.* [1910] 2 K.B. 94.
[3] *Munster* v. *S.E. Ry.* (1858) 4 C.B. (N.S.) 676; *Sutcliffe* v. *G.W. Ry.* [1910] 1 K.B. 478; *L.N.W. Ry.* v. *Hudson* [1920] A.C. 324.
[4] *Garton* v. *Bristol and Exeter Ry.* (1861) 30 L.J. Q.B. 273.
[5] *Riley* v. *Horne* (1828) 5 Bing. 217; *Spillers and Bakers, Ltd.* v. *G.W. Ry.* [1911] 1 K.B. 386.
[6] *Wyld* v. *Pickford* (1841) 8 M. & W. 443.
[7] Bell, *Prin.*, §159; *Johnson, supra*; *Crouch* v. *L.N.W. Ry.* (1854) 14 C.B. 255; *Allday* v. *G.W. Ry.* (1864) 5 B. & S. 903.
[8] *Belfast Co., supra.*
[9] *Crouch* v. *L.N.W. Ry.* (1854) 14 C.B. 255; *Pianciani* v. *L.S.W. Ry.* (1856) 18 C.B. 226.
[10] *Johnson* v. *Midland Ry.* (1849) 4 Ex. 367.
[11] *Tamvaco* v. *Timothy* (1882) Cab. & El. 1
[12] Railways Clauses Consolidation (Sc.) Act, 1845, S. 82; cf. *Johnson* v. *Midland Ry.* (1849) 4 Ex. 367; *Crouch* v. *L.N.W. Ry.* (1854) 14 C.B. 255; *Talley* v. *G.W. Ry.* (1870) L.R. 6 C.P. 44; *Dickson* v. *G.N. Ry.* (1886) 18 Q.B.D. 176; *G.W. Ry.* v. *Bunch* (1888) 13 App. Cas. 31; *Vosper* v. *G.W. Ry.* [1928] 1 K.B. 340.
[13] Transport Act, 1962, S. 43(6).
[14] Bell, *Prin.* §166; *Smith* v. *Bushell* [1919] 2 K.B. 362; *L.N.W. Ry.* v. *Hudson* [1920] A.C. 324.
[15] *Wilson* v. *Scott* (1797) Hume 302; *Campbell* v. *Caledonian Ry.* (1852) 14 D. 806; *Caledonian Ry.* v. *Hunter* (1858) 20 D. 1097.
[16] *Paxton* v. *N.B. Ry.* (1870) 9 M. 50.
[17] *Rain* v. *G.S.W. Ry.* (1869) 7 M. 439.

consignor must also deliver the goods to the carrier or to a person authorized to act for him, at his receiving office or other customary place.[1]

Consignor's warranty

The consignor impliedly warrants that the goods are fit to be carried and are not dangerous,[2] unless he has informed the carrier otherwise and the latter has accepted the goods, or the carrier was otherwise aware that they are dangerous.[3] Unless the contract excludes liability the consignor is liable for breach of this implied warranty.

Carrier's warranty

A common carrier by land must use a vehicle reasonably fit for the goods in question,[4] but he does not warrant the competency of his driver or the condition of his vehicle; his liability exists independently of such factors.

Loading

The carrier must load and stow the goods so that they can be carried safely,[5] and take reasonable precautions against damage from weather. He is not responsible if he can show that damage was due to exceptional circumstances,[6] or to the consignor's own fault.[7]

Duration of carrier's responsibility

The carrier's responsibility commences when he accepts the goods for carriage[8] and continues until he delivers safely at the destination, even though he is compelled to carry by a different or longer route.[9] Delivery should be made to the consignee's

---

[1] Bell, *Prin.* §162.

[2] This covers goods dangerous to life and limb: *Brass* v. *Maitland* (1856) 6 E. & B. 470; *Farrant* v. *Barnes* (1862) 11 C.B. (N.S.) 553; *Bamfield* v. *Goole and Sheffield Tpt. Co.* [1910] 2 K.B. 94; or liable to damage the carrier's vehicle: *Burley* v. *Stepney Corpn.* [1947] 1 All E.R. 507; or other goods carried by him: *G.N. Ry.* v. *L.E.P. Tpt.* [1922] 2 K.B. 742.

[3] The label may not be sufficient notice: *Cramb* v. *Caledonian Ry.* (1892) 19 R. 1054.

[4] Bell, *Prin.* §165; *Cargill* v. *Dundee and Perth Ry.* (1848) 11 D. 216; *Blower* v. *G.W. Ry.* (1872) L.R. 7 C.P. 655.

[5] *Paxton* v. *N.B. Ry.* (1870) 9 M. 50; *L.N.W. Ry.* v. *Hudson* [1920] A.C. 324; *Bastable* v. *N.B. Ry.*, 1912 S.C. 555.

[6] *Ralston* v. *Caledonian Ry.* (1878) 5 R. 671.

[7] *Rain* v. *G.S.W. Ry.* (1869) 7 M. 439; *L.N.W. Ry.* v. *Hudson, supra.*

[8] *Jenkyns* v. *Southampton S.P. Co.* [1919] 2 K.B. 135.

[9] *Mongaldai Tea Co.* v. *Ellerman Lines* [1920] W.N. 152.

business premises or home, or notice be given to the consignee to collect the goods from the carrier's premises. His responsibility as carrier ceases if the consignee cannot be found at the address given, or if the goods are refused,[1] but he then holds the goods as custodier.[2] He may incur delictual liability if he delivers the wrong goods and harm results.[3]

Charges

The carrier is entitled to a reasonable charge, and is not bound to charge all persons equally.[4] He has a special lien over the goods for the freight for that journey.[5]

Route: deviation

A common carrier is bound to carry by the usual and customary route (not necessarily the shortest route), and not to deviate unnecessarily therefrom.[6] If he deviates unjustifiably he loses the benefit of any contractual exemption from liability, whether the loss results from the deviation or not[7] or even was caused by the Queen's enemies.[8]

Delivery

The common carrier's duty is only to deliver within a reasonable time[9] and he is not liable for the consequences of delay not attributable to his fault,[10] but is for delay due to unnecessary deviation.[11] If delay is caused by factors beyond the carrier's control, he must take reasonable steps, but need not take extraordinary steps, nor incur extraordinary expense, to avoid the consequences of delay.[12] The carrier is not liable for delay in

---

[1] *Heugh* v. *L.N.W. Ry.* (1870) L.R. 5 Ex. 51.

[2] *Heugh, supra*; *Chapman* v. *G.W. Ry.* (1880) 5 Q.B.D. 278; *British Traders, Ltd.* v. *Ubique Transport, Ltd.* [1952] 2 Lloyd's Rep. 236.

[3] *Macdonald* v. *MacBrayne*, 1915 S.C. 716.

[4] *Branley* v. *S.E. Ry.* (1862) 31 L.J.C.P. 286.

[5] *Stevenson* v. *Likly* (1824) 3 S. 291; see also *Scottish Central Ry.* v. *Ferguson* (1864) 2 M. 781; *Peebles* v. *Caledonian Ry.* (1875) 2 R. 346.

[6] *Davis* v. *Garrett* (1830) 6 Bing. 716; *Hales* v. *L.N.W. Ry.* (1863) 4 B. & S. 66; *Myers* v. *L.S.W. Ry.* (1869) L.R. 5 C.P. 1.

[7] *Polwarth* v. *N.B. Ry.*, 1908 S.C. 1275; *L.N.W. Ry.* v. *Neilson* [1922] 2 A.C. 263.

[8] *Morrison* v. *Shaw, Savill and Albion Co.* [1916] 2 K.B. 783.

[9] *Taylor* v. *G.N. Ry.* (1866) L.R. 1 C.P. 385.

[10] *Taylor, supra*; *Sims* v. *Midland Ry.* [1913] 1 K.B. 103.

[11] *Mallet* v. *G.E. Ry.* [1899] 1 Q.B. 309.

[12] *Briddon* v. *G.N. Ry.* (1858) 28 L.J. Ex. 51.

delivery due to faulty addressing of the goods.[1] He is liable for misdelivery.[2]

The consignee on taking delivery should examine the goods; if he does not intimate objection without delay, the goods will be presumed delivered in good order.[3] A consignee is not bound to accept damaged goods with a sum for their repair, but may reject and claim the full value.[4] If the consignee refuses to accept or cannot be found the carrier must retain custody of the goods and redeliver them to, or to the order of, the consignor.[5] A consignee may give a carrier general instructions as to delivery of goods to him, or special directions superseding the address on the goods, such as that he will collect from the carrier's terminal himself.[6]

Delay in transit

A common carrier is not under special edictal liability for loss or injury caused by delay in transit. He is under an obligation to carry within a time reasonable in the circumstances, but is excused by circumstances beyond the carrier's control.[7] Goods known to be perishable should be expedited.[8] If the carrier is or becomes aware of circumstances likely to cause delay, he should warn the consignor.[9] If delay threatens damage to perishable goods the carrier may, as an agent of necessity, sell them, but must first, if reasonably practicable, communicate with the owner.[10]

A carrier may expressly, or impliedly, as by advertising a service to meet a particular market, undertake an obligation to deliver by a particular time, and be liable for loss of market if he causes delay by fault or negligence.[11] A railway has been held liable for damage to perishables for not giving them expedited transit when it was proved that it customarily did so.[12]

---

[1] *Wilson* v. *Scott* (1797) Hume 302; *Campbell* v. *Caledonian Ry.* (1852) 14 D. 806; *Caledonian Ry.* v. *Hunter* (1858) 20 D. 1097.

[2] *Gilmour* v. *Clark* (1853) 15 D. 478; *Caledonian Ry.* v. *Harrison* (1879) 7 R. 151.

[3] *Cruickshank, Fraser & Co.* v. *Caledonian Ry.* (1876) 3 R. 484; *Stewart* v. *N.B. Ry.* (1878) 5 R. 426; see also *Johnston* v. *Dove* (1875) 3 R. 202.

[4] *Dick* v. *East Coast Rys.* (1901) 4 F. 178.

[5] *Metzenburg* v. *Highland Ry.* (1869) 7 M. 919.

[6] *Wannan* v. *Scottish Central Ry.* (1864) 2 M. 1373; *Pickford* v. *Caledonian Ry.* (1866) 4 M. 755.

[7] *Anderson* v. *N.B. Ry.* (1875) 2 R. 443 (blockage on line not due to company's fault); *Sims* v. *Midland Ry.* [1913] 1 K.B. 103 (strike); *Crawford* v. *L.M.S. Ry.*, 1929 S.N. 66.

[8] *Macdonald* v. *Highland Ry.* (1873) 11 M. 614.

[9] *Jarvie* v. *C. Ry.* (1875) 2 R. 623; *McConnachie* v. *G.N.S. Ry.* (1875) 3 R. 79.

[10] *Springer* v. *G.W. Ry.* [1921] 1 K.B. 257.

[11] *Finlay* v. *N.B. Ry.* (1870) 8 M. 959.

[12] *Macdonald* v. *Highland Ry.* (1873) 11 M. 614.

Liability of common carrier for loss or damage

By common law, based on the praetorian edict, *nautae caupones stabularii*,[1] and independently of contract,[2] a common carrier is under a strict duty of care for the safety of goods accepted for carriage, and is liable, in substance as an insurer, without proof of fault, for their loss, or injury to them, while in transit, and even if they were stolen by a third party,[3] and also if damaged by accidental fire.[4] Failing contrary agreement, the carrier accepting goods may be liable for the whole transit, though it be known that he will carry only for part of it; but he may have relief if he show that a later carrier's fault was the cause of the loss or damage.[5] So too he is liable even if the loss or damage, while the goods are in his custody, was caused entirely by the fault of third parties over whom he had no control.[6]

Exceptions to edictal liability

The carrier is not, however, liable if the goods have been lost by reason of the sender's fault,[7] or fault of a third party brought about by the sender,[8] by act of God,[9] by act of the Queen's enemies,[10] or by reason of their inherent vice,[11] or defective packing.[12] But even in such cases the carrier remains liable if he has deviated from the agreed, or customary route, unless he can show that the loss would equally have happened had he not deviated,[13] or by his negligence has contributed to the loss.[14] The

---

[1] Dig. IV, 9, 1; Stair I, 13, 3; Ersk. III, 1, 29; Bell, *Prin.* §235. In Roman law this applied only to carriers by sea (*nautae*). For the history see Mackenzie Stuart (1926) 38 J.R. 205; Rodger (1968) 3 Ir. Jur. (N.S.) 175. It does not apply to gratuitous carriers, who need only take reasonable care in so doing: *Bullen* v. *Swan Electric Co.* (1907) 23 T.L.R. 258; *Copland* v. *Brogan*, 1916 S.C. 277.

[2] *L.N.W. Ry.* v. *Hudson* [1920] A.C. 324.

[3] Bell, *Prin.* §238. In England a similar liability attaches by custom of the realm.

[4] Mercantile Law Amdt. (Sc.) Act, 1856, S. 17; *Kemp* v. *Robertson*, 1967 S.C. 229.

[5] *Logan* v. *Highland Ry.* (1899) 2 F. 292; cf. *Aberdeen Grit Co.* v. *Ellerman's Wilson Line*, 1933 S.C. 9.

[6] *Laveroni* v. *Drury* (1852) 8 Ex. 166.

[7] *Caledonian Ry.* v. *Hunter* (1858) 20 D. 1097 (inadequate address); *L.N.W. Ry.* v. *Hudson* [1920] A.C. 324 (packing).

[8] *Briddon* v. *G.N. Ry.* (1858) 28 L.J. Ex. 51.

[9] *Nugent* v. *Smith* (1876) 1 C.P.D. 423; *Lloyd* v. *Guibert* (1865) L.R. 1 Q.B. 115.

[10] *Secy. for War* v. *M.G.W. Ry. of Ireland* [1923] 2 I.R. 102 (rebels); *Curtis* v. *Matthews* [1919] 1 K.B. 425 (mere riot insufficient).

[11] *Blower* v. *G.W. Ry.* (1872) L.R. 7 C.P. 655; *Kendall* v. *L.S.W. Ry.* (1872) L.R. 7 Ex. 373; *Ralston* v. *Caledonian Ry.* (1878) 5 R. 671; *Lister* v. *L. & Y. Ry.* [1903] 1 K.B. 878; *L.N.W. Ry.* v. *Hudson* [1920] A.C. 324; *G.N. Ry.* v. *L.E.P. Tpt.* [1922] 2 K.B. 742.

[12] *Baldwin* v. *L.C. & D. Ry.* (1882) 9 Q.B.D. 582; *Smith* v. *Buskell* [1919] 2 K.B. 362; *L.N.W. Ry.* v. *Hudson, supra.*

[13] *Blower, supra*; *Gill* v. *M.S. & L. Ry.* (1873) L.R. 8 Q.B. 186.

[14] *Blower, supra*; cf. *L.N.W. Ry.* v. *Hudson* [1920] A.C. 324.

carrier, moreover, must use reasonable care and diligence to avoid the consequences of even these excepted perils and is liable for loss due to breach of this duty.[1]

Limitation of liability

Prior to 1830 a common carrier by land might limit his liability by public notice. Under the Carriers Act, 1830, S. 4, he may no longer do so, but he may still (S. 6) make special contracts with individual consignors. It is a question of fact whether conditions limiting liability have been validly introduced into the contract.[2] If they have been, they are construed strictly.[3] Even if there are conditions limiting liability the carrier is not necessarily protected if he was in fundamental breach of contract and loss or damage occurred, whether or not it resulted from his conduct in breach of contract.[4] A common carrier is not protected by such a clause against liability for negligence unless negligence is mentioned or clearly implied therein,[5] whereas a private carrier, whose only liability is for negligence, will be protected against such liability by any provision excluding liability.[6]

By the Carriers Act, 1830, S. 1, no common carrier by land is liable for the loss of[7] or injury to any article of stated descriptions,[8] contained in any parcel or package[9] delivered to be carried

---

[1] *Gill* v. *M.S. & L. Ry.* (1873) L.R. 8 Q.B. 186.

[2] cf. *Henderson* v. *Stevenson* (1875) 2 R. (H.L.) 71; *Harris* v. *G.W. Ry.* (1876) 1 Q.B.D. 515; *Lightbody's Tr.* v. *Hutchison* (1886) 14 R. 4; *McCutcheon* v. *MacBrayne*, 1964 S.C. (H.L.) 28.

[3] *Sutton* v. *Ciceri* (1890) 17 R. (H.L.) 40; *Bastable* v. *N.B. Ry.*, 1912 S.C. 555; *L.N.W. Ry.* v. *Neilson* [1922] 2 A.C. 263; *Alexander* v. *Ry. Executive* [1951] 2 K.B. 882.

[4] *Bontex Knitting Works* v. *St. John's Garage* [1944] 1 All E.R. 381; *Alexander, supra.*

[5] *Sutton* v. *Ciceri* (1890) 17 R. (H.L.) 40; *Wood* v. *Burns* (1893) 20 R. 602; *Page* v. *L.M.S. Ry.* [1943] 1 All E.R. 455.

[6] *Turner* v. *Civil Service Supply Assocn.* [1926] 1 K.B. 50; *Fagan* v. *Green and Edwards* [1926] 1 K.B. 102; *Alderslade* v. *Hendon Laundry* [1945] K.B. 189.

[7] Including temporary loss, but the carrier is protected if he finds the goods and delivers within a reasonable time; *Millen* v. *Brasch* (1882) 10 Q.B.D. 142.

[8] Whether goods fall within the exceptions or not is a question of fact: *Jones* v. *Cheshire Lines Cttee.* (1901) 17 T.L.R. 443.

The descriptions of goods are: gold or silver coins (including cupro-nickel: Coinage Act, 1946, S. 5: Cupro-Nickel Coin (Carriers' Liability) Regs. 1951 (S.I. 1951, No. 1032)); gold or silver in a manufactured or unmanufactured state; precious stones, jewellery, watches, clocks or timepieces of any kind (including a ship's chronometer: *Le Conteur* v. *L.S.W. Ry.* (1865) L.R. 1 Q.B. 54); trinkets (*Bernstein* v. *Baxendale* (1859) 6 C.B. (N.S.) 251; *Jones* v. *Cheshire Lines Cttee.* (1901) 17 T.L.R. 443); bills (*Stoessiger* v. *S.E. Ry.* (1854) 3 E. & B. 549), bank notes, orders, notes, or securities for the payment of money; stamps, maps (including their case: *Wyld* v. *Pickford* (1841) 8 M. & W. 443), writings, title-deeds; paintings (*Woodward* v. *L.N.W. Ry.* (1878) 3 Ex. D. 121), engrav-

---

For note 9 see next page.

for hire or to accompany a passenger,[1] when the value of the articles in the package exceeds £10, unless at the time of delivery thereof at the carrier's receiving house,[2] or to his servant, the value and nature of such article has been declared by the consignor and an increased charge paid, if demanded.[3] The rates of increased charge must be notified by notice affixed in the office or receiving house, and consignors are bound by such notice (S. 2).[4] The carrier must give a receipt for the increased charge, and in the absence of notice and receipt, he is not entitled to the benefit of the Act (S. 3). Persons entitled to damages for loss of or damage to goods may recover the increased charges in addition to the value of the packet (S. 7).

Nothing in the Act protects any common carrier from liability for loss or injury arising from felonious acts by any servant, nor protects any such servant from personal liability (S. 8).[5] It is not necessary to prove that a particular servant of the carrier stole the goods[6] but it is not sufficient to show that it is more probable that a carrier's servant rather than a third party stole the goods.[7]

---

ings (*Boys* v. *Pink* (1838) 8 C. & P. 361), pictures (including frames: *Henderson* v. *L.N.W. Ry.* (1870) L.R. 5 Ex. 90), gold or silver plate or plated articles, glass (including a mirror: *Owen* v. *Burnett* (1834) 4 Tyr. 133; and smelling bottles: *Bernstein* v. *Baxendale* (1859) 6 C.B. (N.S.) 251; but not opera glasses or cameras: *Jones* v. *Cheshire Lines Cttee.* (1901) 17 T.L.R. 443); china; silks in a manufactured or unmanufactured state and whether wrought up or not wrought up with other materials (this category was excluded as to railways by the Railways Act, 1921, S. 56(1) and Sch. 6): (the category includes silk dresses: *Flowers* v. *S.E. Ry.* (1867) 16 L.T. 329; silk hose and tights; *Hart* v. *Baxendale* (1852) 6 Ex. 769; silk watch guards: *Bernstein* v. *Baxendale* (1859) 6 C.B. (N.S.) 251; and elastic silk webbing: *Brunt* v. *Midland Ry.* (1864) 2 H. & C. 889), furs (excluding felt: *Mayhew* v. *Nelson* (1833) 6 C. & P. 58) and lace (excluding machine-made lace: Carriers Act Amdt. Act, 1865; unless made wholly of silk: *Taylor* v. *Midland Ry.* (1877) 41 J.P. 504).

[9] This includes a parcel containing smaller parcels some of which were damaged: *Hartley* v. *G.N. Ry.* (1849) 14 L.T. 134; and an open wagon containing pictures and other goods: *Whaite* v. *L. & Y. Ry.* (1874) L.R. 9 Ex. 67.

[1] The Act applies to luggage carried without further charge: *Casswell* v. *Cheshire Lines Cttee.* [1907] 2 K.B. 499.

[2] Defined, S. 5.

[3] The declaration may be in any form but must be intended as a declaration under the Act and such as to indicate the intention to hold the carrier liable for a larger sum; (*Robinson* v. *L.S.W. Ry.* (1865) 19 C.B. (N.S.) 51; *Hirschel and Meyer* v. *G.E. Ry.* (1906) 12 Com. Cas. 11). If no declaration is made the carrier is protected even though he had failed to affix the statutory notice; *Hart* v. *Baxendale* (1852) 6 Ex. 769. If a declaration is made the carrier is under unlimited liability though he has not demanded any additional charge: *Behrens* v. *G.N. Ry.* (1861) 3 L.T. 863.

[4] The notice is a condition of increased charges only: *Rusk* v. *N.B. Ry.*, 1920, 2 S.L.T. 139.

[5] *Campbells* v. *N.B. Ry.* (1875) 2 R. 433; See also *Shaw* v. *G.W. Ry.* [1894] 1 Q.B. 373.

[6] *Vaughton* v. *L.N.W. Ry.* (1874) L.R. 9 Ex. 93.

[7] *Campbells* v. *N.B. Ry.* (1875) 2 R. 433; contrast *McQueen* v. *G.W. Ry.* (1875) L.R. 10 Q.B. 569.

Carriers are not bound by the declared value of goods but may require proof of the actual value, and are liable only to such damages as are proved, not exceeding the declared value and increased charges (S. 9).[1] The Act does not protect the carrier from liability for delay; if goods are mislaid and found again the carrier will be liable for damages for delay if he does not deliver within a reasonable time.[2]

The common law liability of a common carrier cannot be limited by public notice (S. 4), but nothing in the Act affects any special contract between carrier and consignor for the carriage of goods (S. 6) and such contract may be founded on a public notice. The carrier is then still entitled to the protection of the Act so far as the special contract is consistent with the Act.[3]

Variation of liability by contract

A common carrier may by contract vary or modify his liability. If the contract obliterates his character as a common carrier, he becomes a private carrier for the purposes of that contract, but if it merely limits his liability in certain respects, he remains subject to the common carriers' liability in other respects.[4] Contractual exemptions are strictly construed.[5] They must have been adequately brought to the consignor's notice so as to become part of the contract.[6] Any condition exempting the carrier is avoided if in the course of performance he commits a fundamental breach of contract.[7] An exemption clause will not be interpreted as relieving a common carrier from liability for negligence unless words expressly or impliedly give such protection.[8]

Extent of liability

The measure of damages for goods lost or destroyed is *prima facie* the full value thereof.[9] For delay in delivery the measure of damages is the loss arising from the carrier's default which was

---

[1] cf. *McCance* v. *L.N.W. Ry.* (1864) 3 H. & C. 343.

[2] *Hearn* v. *L.S.W. Ry.* (1855) 10 Ex. 793.

[3] *Baxendale* v. *G.E. Ry.* (1869) L.R. 4 Q.B. 244.

[4] *Scaife* v. *Farrant* (1875) L.R. 10 Ex. 358; *Sutton* v. *Ciceri* (1890) 17 R. (H.L.) 40; *Price* v. *Union Lighterage Co.* [1904] 1 K.B. 412; *G.N. Ry.* v. *L.E.P. Tpt. Ltd.* [1922] 2 K.B. 742.

[5] *Alexander* v. *Ry. Executive* [1951] 2 K.B. 882.

[6] cf. *Hood* v. *Anchor Line*, 1918 S.C. (H.L.) 143.

[7] *Mallet* v. *G.E. Ry.* [1899] 1 Q.B. 309; *Gunyon* v. *S.E. & C. Ry. Cttee.* [1915] 2 K.B. 370; *Hunt & Winterbotham* v. *B.R.S. (Parcels) Ltd.* [1962] 1 All E.R. 111.

[8] *Sutton, supra*; *Page* v. *L.M.S. Ry.* [1943] 1 All E.R. 455.

[9] *Crouch* v. *L.N.W. Ry.* (1849) 2 C. & K. 789; *O'Hanlan* v. *G.W. Ry.* (1865) 6 B. & S. 484; *Dick* v. *East Coast Railways* (1901) 4 F. 178.

foreseeable in the circumstances,[1] including depreciation, and possibly loss of market or of profits.

Private carriers

A private carrier of goods, such as a transport company or removal contractor,[2] makes no general public profession of willingness to carry for anyone, and is under no obligation to accept any offer of employment.[3] Each contract is an individual one, and the terms thereof a matter for negotiation.[4] The carrier is probably impliedly bound to supply a sufficient vehicle and trustworthy men,[5] but does not warrant either. The private carrier is not subject to edictal strict liability nor the Carriers Act, 1830, but is bound to take reasonable care of the goods carried, a rather lower standard of care being demanded if the carriage is gratuitous;[6] he is liable only for loss of or damage to goods carried which is attributable to his default or negligence.[7] He is also liable for damage by accidental fire.[8] Evidence of loss in transit or non-delivery is *prima facie* evidence of negligence.[9] Hauliers and drivers have a duty to plan their journeys to convey safely while complying with the law.[10] The contract may exempt the carrier from liability in stated circumstances. Since the private carrier's liability is only for negligence, any exclusion of liability for loss or damage must be understood as covering liability for loss or damage by negligence.[11]

---

[1] *Hadley* v. *Baxendale* (1854) 9 Ex. 341; *Den of Ogil Co.* v. *Caledonian Ry.* (1902) 5 F. 99; *Victoria Laundry* v. *Newman* [1949] 2 K.B. 528.

[2] *Pearcey* v. *Player* (1883) 10 R. 564; cf. *Turner* v. *Civil Service Sy. Assoc.* [1926] 1 K.B. 50; *Fagan* v. *Green and Edwards* [1926] 1 K.B. 102.

[3] *Belfast Ropework Co.* v. *Bushell* [1918] 1 K.B. 210.

[4] The contract may incorporate The Road Haulage Association's Conditions of Carriage: e.g. *Carter* v. *Hanson* [1965] 1 All E.R. 113; *Garnham, Ellis & Elton* v. *Ellis* [1967] 2 All E.R. 940.

[5] *Pearcey, supra,* 570; *Carter, supra.*

[6] *Copland* v. *Brogan,* 1916 S.C. 277.

[7] *Pearcey, supra;* cf. *Beal* v. *S. Devon Ry.* (1864) 3 H. & C. 337; *Richardson* v. *N.E. Ry.* (1872) L.R. 7 C.P. 75; *Searle* v. *Laverick* (1874) L.R. 9 Q.B. 122; *Garnham, supra;* B.R.S. v. *Crutchley* [1968] 1 All E.R. 811.

[8] Mercantile Law Amdt. (Sc.) Act, 1856, S. 17; *Kemp* v. *Robertson,* 1967 S.C. 229; *Anderson* v. *Jenkins,* 1967 S.C. 231.

[9] *Pearcey, supra,* 572; *Travers* v. *Cooper* [1915] 1 K.B. 73; *Brook's Wharf* v. *Goodman* [1937] 1 K.B. 534; *Presvale* v. *Sutch & Searle* [1967] 1 Lloyd's Rep. 131. cf. *Copland* v. *Brogan,* 1916 S.C. 277.

[10] *Lowenstein* v. *Poplar Motor Tpt,* [1968] 2 Lloyd's Rep. 233.

[11] *Travers* v. *Cooper* [1915] 1 K.B. 73; *Pyman S.S. Co.* v. *Hull and Barnsley Ry.* [1915] 2 K.B. 729; *Rutter* v. *Palmer* [1922] 2 K.B. 87; *Turner* v. *Civil Service Sy. Assocn.* [1926] 1 K.B. 50; *Fagan* v. *Green & Edwards* [1926] 1 K.B. 102; *Alderslade* v. *Hendon Laundry* [1945] K.B. 189; *Canada S.S. Lines* v. *The King* [1952] A.C. 192.

The National Freight Corporation

The National Freight Corporation has the function of carrying goods by road, or by rail, in co-operation with British Railways, and may also provide transport services by sea, store goods, and otherwise operate as a transport authority.[1] It is not to be regarded as a common carrier in respect of any of its activities.[2] Nor are its subsidiaries common carriers.[3]

Public control of road transport

Under the Road Traffic Act, 1960, Part IV, a carrier's licence is necessary for the carriage of goods in a motor vehicle for hire or reward, or for or in connection with a trade or business, but not for delivery by a tradesman of goods sold by him or in certain other cases.[4] 'A' or Public Carriers' licences permit the holder to use authorized vehicles only in connection with a carrier's business; 'B' or Limited Carriers' licences permit him to use authorized vehicles for the carriage of goods in connection with any business carried on by him, or, subject to any conditions of the licence, for the carriage of goods for hire or reward; and 'C' or Private Carriers' licences permit the holder to use authorized vehicles for the carriage of goods in connection with a business carried on by him but not for hire or reward.[5] These licences are issued by the chairman of the traffic commissioners for Scotland, as licensing authority for goods vehicles, and may be suspended, curtailed or revoked.[6] Though a prerequisite to acting as common or private carrier, such licences do not affect the conditions on which such carriers carry.

These requirements do not now apply to small vehicles or to medium vehicles for which an operator's licence is required.[7]

Under the Transport Act, 1968, Part V, carriage of goods for hire or reward, or for or in connection with a trade or business, but not for delivery by a tradesman of goods sold by him, or in certain other cases, may be done only under an operator's licence, authorizing the use of certain vehicles and trailers, issued by the licensing authority. Every operator's licence specifies a person

---

[1] Transport Act, 1968, Ss. 1–2. Subsidiaries of the Freight Corporation include British Road Services Ltd., Pickfords Ltd., and other companies.

[2] Ibid., S. 2(2).

[3] Ibid., S. 51(4).

[4] R.T.A., 1960, S. 164, amd. Transport Act, 1968, Ss. 60, 93.

[5] Ibid., S. 166. See also *Russell* v. *Road Services (Caledonian) Ltd.*, 1964 S.C. 334.

[6] Ibid., Ss. 165–182; 1968 Act, Ss. 62–70.

[7] Transport Act, 1968, S. 93.

who is to be responsible for the operation and maintenance of the authorized vehicles and who must hold a transport manager's licence.[1] Operator's licences are not required for small goods vehicles or vehicles of classes specified in regulations.[2]

Large goods vehicles must not be used to carry any goods on a controlled journey[3] or to carry more than 11 tons except under a special authorization from the licensing authority,[4] and no goods may be carried on a large goods vehicle unless a consignment note has been completed and is carried by the driver.[5]

International carriage by road

The Carriage of Goods by Road Act, 1965, gives effect to the Convention on the Contract for the International Carriage of Goods by Road of 1956 scheduled to the Act. It applies to every contract for the carriage of goods by road in vehicles for reward, where the place of taking over of the goods and the place for delivery are in different countries, of which at least one is a contracting country, irrespective of the residence and nationality of the parties.[6] It applies though part of the journey may be by rail, sea, canal or air, so long as the goods are not unloaded.

The contract must be confirmed by a consignment note which is prima facie evidence of the making of the contract, its conditions and the receipt of the goods.[7] The sender is normally liable for damage and expenses due to defective packing. He may dispose of the goods, by asking the carrier to stop them in transit, to change the place of delivery or to deliver to another consignee.[8] On arrival, if loss is established or the goods have not arrived after an agreed time or a reasonable time, the consignee may enforce in his own name any rights arising from the contract.[9]

The carrier is liable for total or partial loss of the goods and for damage between taking them over and delivery, and for delay; provision is made for calculating damages due.[10] The carrier

---

[1] Ibid., Ss. 59–70. Appeals lie to the Transport Tribunal.
[2] Ibid., S. 60.
[3] Over 100 miles or with loads of defined sizes.
[4] Transport Act, 1968, Ss. 71–80.
[5] Ibid., S. 81.
[6] 1965 Act, Sched., Art. 1. See also S.I. 1967, No. 1683; 1969, No. 385, specifying as parties the U.K., Austria, Belgium, Denmark, France, Germany, Italy, Luxembourg, Netherlands, and certain other countries. The Convention does not apply between the U.K. and Ireland.
[7] Sched., Arts. 4, 9.   [8] Ibid., Sch., Art. 12.   [9] Art. 13.
[10] Arts. 17–29; cf. *Tatton* v. *Ferrymasters* [1974] 1 Lloyd's Rep. 203.

cannot avail himself of provisions excluding or limiting his liability or shifting the burden of proof if the damage was caused by his wilful misconduct or equivalent default.[1]

The Convention makes provision for claims and actions; action must be brought within one year, or three years in case of wilful misconduct.[2] If there are successive carriers each is responsible for the whole carriage, but there is provision for contribution to liability.[3]

Carriage of goods by rail

The former independent railway companies, grouped in 1921,[4] were all taken into public ownership in 1947,[5] and are now[6] managed by the British Railways Board. The railways are not now common carriers[7] and the Carriers Act, 1830, no longer applies to them. The Board is no longer subject to control of its charges by the Transport Tribunal[8] and is no longer under the duty of providing reasonable facilities to the public for receiving, forwarding and delivering goods.[9]

Conditions of carriage

The Railways Board has complete freedom to use its services and facilities on such terms and conditions as it thinks fit.[10] It has settled General Conditions of Carriage for carriage by rail or road, and for carriage by water.[11]

British Railways' Conditions of Carriage

British Railways carry under contracts incorporating one or other of sets of General Conditions of Carriage,[12] applicable respectively to merchandise (other than dangerous goods and merchandise for which conditions are specially provided) carried at Board's risk, livestock, and coal. The merchandise conditions

---

[1] Art. 29.   [2] Art. 32.   [3] Arts. 34–40.

[4] Railways Act, 1921.

[5] Transport Act, 1947.

[6] Transport Act, 1962, replacing British Transport Commission established by 1947 Act.

[7] 1962 Act, S. 43(6).

[8] 1962 Act, S. 43(3). The Transport Tribunal replaced the former Railway Rates Tribunal.

[9] 1962 Act, S. 43(4).

[10] 1962 Act, S. 43(3). Fourteen sets of Standard Terms and Conditions were settled under the Railways Act, 1921, and between 1928 and 1962 regulated most cases of carriage.

[11] B.R. 18793 (1965).

[12] B.R. 18793 (1965).

apply to carriage by the Board by rail or road or by contractors employed by the Board, but not if the destination entails transfer to an independent carrier.[1] Every consignment must be accompanied by a consignment note and, if loaded at a private siding, labelled on each side of the wagon.[2] All merchandise is warranted fit to be carried and stored, and not to be dangerous.[3] The Board is liable for any loss or misdelivery of or damage to merchandise during transit unless the Board proves that it arose from (a) Act of God; (b) consequences of war, invasion, act of foreign enemy, hostilities (whether war be declared or not), civil war, rebellion, insurrection, military or usurped power or confiscation, requisition, destruction of or damage to property by or under the order of any government or public or local authority; (c) seizure under legal process; (d) act or omission of the trader, his servants or agents; (e) inherent liability to wastage in bulk or weight, latent defect or inherent defect, vice or natural deterioration of the merchandise; (f) casualty (including fire or explosion); provided that (i) where loss, misdelivery or damage arises and the Board have failed to prove that they used all reasonable foresight and care[4] in the carriage of the merchandise the Board shall not be relieved from liability for such loss, misdelivery or damage; (ii) the Board shall not incur liability of any kind in respect of merchandise where there has been fraud on the part of the trader.[5] The Board is not in any case liable for loss, damage or delay, proved by the Board to have been caused by or to have arisen from (a) insufficient or improper packing; (b) riots, civil commotions, strikes, lockouts, stoppage or restraint of labour from whatever cause, whether partial or general; or (c) consignee not taking or accepting delivery within a reasonable time.[6] The Board, subject to the Conditions, is liable for loss proved by the trader to have been caused by delay to, or detention of, or unreasonable deviation in the carriage of merchandise unless it proves that such delay or detention or unreasonable deviation has arisen without negligence on the part of the Board, their servants or agents.[7]

Subject to the Conditions the liability of the Board under the Conditions in respect of any one consignment is limited (i) where the monetary loss, however sustained, is in respect of the whole of the consignment to a sum at the rate of £800 per ton on the gross weight of the consignment; (ii) where the monetary loss however

[1] B.R. 18793/1, Cl. 2–3.
[2] Cl. 5–6.
[3] Cl. 7.   [4] *Hutchison* v. *B.R. Board*, 1971 S.L.T. 84.
[5] Cl. 8.   [6] Cl. 9.   [7] Cl. 10.

sustained is in respect of part of a consignment to the proportion of the sum ascertained in accordance with (i) above which the actual value of that part of the consignment bears to the actual value of the whole of the consignment. Provided that (a) nothing in this condition shall limit the Board's liability below the sum of £10 in respect of any one consignment; and (b) the Board shall be entitled to require proof of the value of the whole of the consignment. The Board is not in any case liable for indirect or consequential damages or for loss of a particular market whether held daily or at intervals.[1]

The conditions prescribe time limits for claims, provide for undelivered or unclaimed merchandise, and for merchandise being received and held by the Board subject to a lien for the cost of carriage and a general lien for charges due from the owners of such merchandise.[2] Merchandise may be carried at owner's risk or as damageable goods not properly protected by packing on these conditions with certain variations. The Conditions of Carriage of livestock and of coal are generally similar.

Delay in transit

In case of delay in delivery the railway is liable for such damages as arise in the ordinary course of things from the carriers' breach of duty, or such as may reasonably be supposed to have been in the contemplation of both parties as a probable consequence of the delay in circumstances known to both.[3] Damages for exceptional consequences of delay are recoverable only if the circumstances had been brought to the railway's notice at the time of the contract.[4] In the absence of notice of special circumstances the railway is not liable for exceptional loss caused by its delay.[5] The railway is not generally liable for delay in transit resulting in missing a market[6] unless the delay was or should have been foreseen and warned against,[7] or was the fault of the railways.[8]

---

[1] Cl. 13–14.

[2] Cl. 15, 17–18.

[3] *Hadley* v. *Baxendale* (1854) 9 Ex. 341; *Horne* v. *Midland Ry.* (1873) L.R. 8 C.P. 131; *Simpson* v. *L.N.W. Ry.* (1876) 1 Q.B.D. 274; *A/B Karlshamns Oljefabriker* v. *Monarch S.S. Co.*, 1949 S.C. (H.L.) 1.

[4] *Horne, supra*; *Simpson, supra*.

[5] *Den of Ogil Co.* v. *Caledonian Ry.* (1902) 5 F. 99.

[6] *Finlay* v. *N.B. Ry.* (1870) 8 M. 959; contrast *Macdonald* v. *Highland Ry.* (1873) 11 M. 614; *Anderson* v. *N.B. Ry.* (1875) 2 R. 443.

[7] *McConnachie* v. *G.N.S. Ry.* (1875) 3 R. 79.

[8] *Keddie, Gordon & Co.* v. *N.B. Ry.* (1886) 14 R. 273.

Damage in transit

If goods are delivered at the proper place and time the consignee should inspect them and if he does not intimate objection it will be presumed that they were delivered in good order.[1] It depends on the extent to which goods have been damaged whether the railways will be liable for the cost of a replacement or only for repairs to the damaged thing.[2] If goods are merely damaged the measure of damages is, *prima facie*, the diminution in value thereof, or in price realized therefor, by reason of the damage. Where repair is practicable, the cost thereof is a factor relevant to damages.

Loss in transit

If goods are wholly lost or destroyed damages are recoverable, measured *prima facie* by their market value at the place of delivery.[3] If there is no market, the damages are the cost price of the goods, plus freight and ordinary reasonable profit,[4] so long as the carrier knew the goods were intended for resale. If the consignor declared the value of the goods before transit began, he is bound thereby.[5]

Delivery and misdelivery

It depends on the contract whether delivery should be made to the consignee's premises, or at the terminus of carriage. The railway performs its contract if it delivers at the proper premises to the addressee, or one having ostensible authority to receive on his behalf.[6] Delivery elsewhere is at the carrier's risk. If the consignee cannot be found, or if he refuses the goods, the railway's liability as carrier is ended,[7] and thereafter it holds the goods as custodier only.[8] As such it must take reasonable care of the goods and may incur reasonable expenses in so doing.[9] If the railway

---

[1] *Stewart* v. *N.B. Ry.* (1878) 5 R. 426; *Cruickshank, Fraser & Co.* v. *Caledonian Ry.* (1876) 3 R. 484.

[2] *Dick* v. *East Coast Rys.* (1901) 4 F. 178.

[3] *Crouch* v. *L.N.W. Ry.* (1849) 2 C. & K. 789; *Rice* v. *Baxendale* (1861) 7 H. & N. 96; *Heskell* v. *Continental Express* [1950] 1 All E.R. 1033, 1049.

[4] *O'Hanlan* v. *G.W. Ry.* (1865) 6 B. & S. 484; *Heskell, supra.*

[5] *McCance* v. *L.N.W. Ry.* (1864) 3 H. & C. 343.

[6] *McKean* v. *McIvor* (1870) L.R. 6 Ex. 36; *Galbraith and Grant Ltd.* v. *Block* [1922] 2 K.B. 155.

[7] *Hudson* v. *Baxendale* (1857) 2 H. & N. 575; *G.W. Ry.* v. *Crouch* (1858) 3 H. & N. 183; *Heugh* v. *L.N.W. Ry.* (1870) L.R. 5 Ex. 51.

[8] *G.W. Ry., supra*; *Heugh, supra*; *Chapman* v. *G.W. Ry.* (1880) 5 Q.B.D. 278.

[9] *Mitchell* v. *L. & Y. Ry.* (1875) L.R. 10 Q.B. 256; *L.N.W. Ry.* v. *Crooke* (1904) 20 T.L.R. 506.

delivers to the wrong person, it, and the true owner, may recover the goods or their value from the person who received them. The railway may be liable for the direct consequences of delivering the wrong goods.[1]

Notices and times for claims

Notice of loss or damage should always be given as soon as possible and a claim therefor made. British Railways General Conditions of Carriage impose limits on the time within which claims must be made.[2]

CARRIAGE OF GOODS BY POST

Subject to the Post Office Act, 1969, and post office regulations packets of limited size and weight may be sent by post. No action for delict lies against the Post Office in respect of any loss or damage suffered by reason of anything done or not done in relation to the post, nor does liability attach to officers or servants of the Post Office,[3] but proceedings lie in respect of loss of or damage to a registered inland packet so far as due to any wrongful act or default of a servant or agent of the Post Office, if commenced within 12 months. Loss or damage is presumed due to neglect or default unless the contrary is proved. The amount recoverable is not to exceed the market value of the packet or the maximum amount under a statutory scheme for compensation.[4]

CARRIAGE OF PASSENGERS BY ROAD AND RAIL

Common carriers of passengers

While the common carrier of passengers, such as a bus operating company, is under a duty to carry anyone who offers himself for carriage, provided that he is in a reasonably fit state to be carried,[5] tenders the fare, presents himself at the departure point in time, and there is space for him,[6] it is not subject to strict edictal liability for injury to or death of passengers. The duty is only to take reasonable care for the safety of the passengers,

[1] *Macdonald* v. *Macbrayne*, 1915 S.C. 716.
[2] See B.R. 18793/1, Cl. 15.
[3] Post Office Act, 1969, S. 29.
[4] Ibid., S. 30.
[5] Bell, *Prin.* §159, 170.
[6] *Clarke* v. *West Ham Corpn.* [1909] 2 K.B. 858.

though the standard exacted is high[1] and is owed both *ex contractu* and *ex lege*.[2] Hence there is liability also to persons carried free.[3]

Contract of carriage

The contract is made by taking a ticket, or entering on the vehicle and paying the fare; the contract is to carry to the stated destination with due care and in a reasonable time.[4] The contract may include terms expressed on the ticket or incorporated by reference thereon, which are binding only if reasonable steps have been taken to bring them to the notice of the passenger.[5] Time-tables and general conditions incorporated in contracts may provide that carriers will not be responsible for delay, in which case no claim lies for loss or inconvenience caused thereby.[6]

Statutory control of carriage of passengers by road

Under Part III of the Road Traffic Act, 1960, public service vehicles (which comprises (a) express carriages, where no fare is less than five pence; (b) stage carriages carrying passengers at separate fares, not being express carriages; and (c) contract carriages, which carry eight or more passengers under a contract for the use of the vehicle as a whole) require a public service vehicle licence before they can be used for hire or reward on the road.[7] This is normally granted only if the vehicle complies with conditions of fitness, and may be refused, suspended or revoked if the Traffic Commissioners are of opinion that, having regard to the conduct of the applicant or holder, or to the manner in which the vehicle is being used, he is not a fit person to hold such a licence.[8] To use a vehicle as an express carriage or a stage carriage a road

[1] Bell, *Prin.* §170; *Pym* v. *G.N. Ry.* (1861) 2 F. & F. 619; *Readhead* v. *Midland Ry.* (1869) L.R. 4 Q.B. 379; *Gee* v. *Metropolitan Ry.* (1873) L.R. 8 Q.B. 161; *Allam* v. *Western S.M.T. Co.*, 1944 S.L.T. 100; *Barkway* v. *South Wales Tpt.* [1950] A.C. 185.

[2] *Hamilton* v. *Caledonian Ry.* (1857) 19 D. 457; *Little* v. *N.B. Ry.* (1877) 15 S.L.R. 12; *Foulkes* v. *Metropolitan Ry.* (1880) 5 C.P.D. 157; *G.T. Ry. of Canada* v. *Robinson* [1915] A.C. 740; Occupiers' Liability (Sc.) Act, 1960, Ss. 1(3) and 2.

[3] *G.N. Ry.* v. *Harrison* (1854) 10 Ex. 376; *Austin* v. *G.W. Ry.* (1867) L.R. 2 Q.B. 442.

[4] *Hurst* v. *G.W. Ry.* (1865) 19 C.B.N.S. 310.

[5] e.g. *Highland Ry.* v. *Menzies* (1878) 5 R. 887; *Lyons* v. *Caledonian Ry.*, 1909 S.C. 1185; *Gray* v. *L.N.E.R.*, 1930 S.C. 989; *Coyle* v. *L.M.S. Ry.*, 1930 S.L.T. 349; *Penton* v. *Southern Ry.* [1931] 2 K.B. 103.

[6] *Woodgate* v. *G.W. Ry.* (1884) 51 L.T. 826; *McCartan* v. *N.E. Ry.* (1885) 54 L.J.Q.B. 441; *Duckworth* v. *L. & Y. Ry.* (1901) 84 L.T. 774. Contrast *Le Blanche* v. *L.N.W. Ry.* (1876) 1 C.P.D. 286.

[7] cf. *Aitken* v. *Hamilton*, 1964 J.C. 28.

[8] R.T.A. 1960, S. 127; see also Transport Act, 1968, S. 35.

service licence is also required, the obtaining of which depends on satisfying the Traffic Commissioners of the need for the proposed service, having regard to existing services.[1] Conditions may be attached to the grant of a licence as to fares, exhibition of time-tables and fare-tables and points for taking up and setting down passengers.[2] Any contract for the conveyance of passengers in a public service vehicle is void in so far as it purports to restrict liability in respect of the death of or bodily injury to a passenger while being carried in, entering or alighting from the vehicle.[3]

Passenger Transport Authorities

A Passenger Transport Authority may be constituted in any area and a Passenger Transport Executive, the latter having powers to carry passengers by road or other land or water transport within, to and from the area, to let passenger vehicles, and perform related functions.[4] It may not carry passengers on terms or conditions which exclude or limit liability for death or injury of a passenger, or prescribe the time within which or the manner in which any such liability may be enforced.[5] In a passenger transport area local authority transport undertakings are to be transferred to the Executive.[6]

Scottish Transport Group

The Scottish Transport Group has power to carry passengers by road, subway, water or hovercraft in or outside Scotland and to carry goods by road, water or hovercraft within or to the islands.[7] The Group are not common carriers in respect of any of their activities concerned with carriage of goods.[8]

Duty as to vehicles

Carriers must maintain their vehicles in good order and make them as safe as reasonable skill and care can make them, and are liable for injury due to defects which reasonable examination

---

[1] Certain relaxations are permitted for small operators in rural areas by Transport Act, 1968, S. 30.

[2] R.T.A. 1960, S. 134. Drivers and conductors must also be licensed: S. 144. Regulations may be made as to the conduct of passengers in public service vehicles: S. 147.

[3] R.T.A. 1960, S. 151; see also *Wilkie* v. *L.P.T.B.* [1947] 1 All E.R. 258; *Gore* v. *Van der Lann* [1967] 1 All E.R. 360.

[4] Transport Act, 1968, Ss. 9–10.

[5] Ibid., S. 10(1)(xiii).

[6] Ibid., S. 17.

[7] Ibid., Ss. 24, 26, 28(2), 29(1).

[8] Ibid., S. 26(2).

would disclose.[1] There is a duty of regular inspection[2] and a breakdown is *prima facie* evidence of negligence.[3] There is no liability for latent defects which inspection and maintenance would not disclose.[4] A rebuttable inference of negligence may be drawn from a happening which would not have happened if all due care had been taken, as where a vehicle loses a wheel[5] or a tyre bursts.[6]

Duty as to operation of vehicles

The carrier is responsible for the adequacy of his servants in numbers, capacity and care.[7] The carrier's servants must take reasonable care in the operation of the vehicle to avoid causing injury to the passengers,[8] as by swerving violently,[9] or stopping suddenly,[10] or colliding with another vehicle.[11] Regard should be had to the fact, if known, that passengers are standing.[12] The conductor of a bus must take reasonable care that the bus does not move while passengers are still alighting or entering,[13] but may assume that passengers will not do so while the vehicle is moving.[14] If in his absence a passenger signals the driver to start and another passenger is injured the carrier is liable.[15] A passenger may be guilty of contributory negligence by travelling on the step or platform, or alighting while the vehicle is in motion.[16]

---

[1] *Hyman* v. *Nye* (1881) 6 Q.B.D. 685; *Fosbroke-Hobbes* v. *Airwork, Ltd.* [1937] 1 All E.R. 108; *Philippson* v. *Imperial Airways* [1939] A.C. 332; *Barkway* v. *S. Wales Tpt.* [1950] A.C. 185; R.T.A. 1960, S. 129.

[2] *Ritchie* v. *Western S.M.T. Co.*, 1935 S.L.T. 13; *Barkway, supra.*

[3] *Watson* v. *N.B. Ry.* (1876) 3 R. 637; *Barkway, supra.*

[4] *Readhead, supra*; *Ritchie, supra.*

[5] *Lilly* v. *Tilling* (1912) 57 Sol. Jo. 59.

[6] *Elliot* v. *Young's Bus Service*, 1945 S.C. 445; *Barkway, supra.*

[7] *Gray* v. *Caledonian Ry.*, 1912 S.C. 339; *Fowler* v. *N.B. Ry.*, 1914 S.C. 866.

[8] *Walker* v. *Pitlochry Motor Co.*, 1930 S.C. 565.

[9] *Mars* v. *Glasgow Corpn.*, 1940 S.C. 202; *O'Hara* v. *Central S.M.T. Co.*, 1941 S.C. 363; *Doonan* v. *S.M.T. Co.*, 1950 S.C. 136.

[10] *Ballingall* v. *Glasgow Corpn.*, 1948 S.C. 160; *Sutherland* v. *Glasgow Corpn.*, 1951 S.C. (H.L.) 1.

[11] *McKendrick* v. *Stewart & McDonald*, 1934 S.N. 4.

[12] *Allam* v. *Western S.M.T. Co.*, 1944 S.L.T. 100 (H.L.).

[13] *Davies* v. *Liverpool Corpn.* [1949] 2 All E.R. 175; *Prescott* v. *Lancashire United Tpt. Co.* [1953] 1 All E.R. 288.

[14] *Askew* v. *Bowtell* [1947] 1 All E.R. 883.

[15] *Hall* v. *London Tramways Co.* (1896) 12 T.L.R. 611; *Watt* v. *Glasgow Corpn.*, 1919 S.C. 300; *Gray* v. *Glasgow Corpn.*, 1926 S.C. 967; *Mottram* v. *South Lancashire Tpt. Co.* [1942] 2 All E.R. 452; *Davies, supra*; *Prescott, supra.*

[16] *Hall, supra*; *McSherry* v. *Glasgow Corpn.*, 1917 S.C. 156; *Watt, supra*; *Buchanan* v. *Glasgow Corpn.*, 1921 S.C. 658; *Gray, supra*; *Caldwell* v. *Glasgow Corpn.*, 1936 S.C. 490; *Jude* v. *Edinburgh Corpn.*, 1943 S.C. 399.

Liability for negligence only

Liability is only for negligence, but a *prima facie* inference of negligence may be drawn from the happening of an accident which would not have happened if proper care and skill had been exercised in vehicle management, as where a vehicle overturns,[1] or stops suddenly,[2] or mounts the pavement[3] or collides with a structure on the pavement,[4] or swerves violently.[5] In emergency, a driver owes a higher duty to his passengers than to avoid killing a small animal.[6] His conduct is judged by the action which a driver of ordinary skill and prudence would have taken in the circumstances.[7]

Liability for failure to carry to destination

The carrier is liable for failure to carry to the destination and must compensate the passenger for the reasonable expense of getting there by other means,[8] but not for remote consequences of such failure.[9]

Private carriers of passengers

A private carrier of passengers, such as a motor-hirer, is under no duty to provide transport for any person desirous of being carried[10] and, if he does contract, the terms and conditions on which he does so fall to be determined by the contract. It is an implied term of the contract that the hirer will take reasonable care to provide a safe and roadworthy vehicle and that the driver will take reasonable care for the safety of the passengers. Liability is for negligence only, though circumstances may raise a *prima facie* presumption of negligence.

---

[1] *Halliwell* v. *Venables* (1930) 99 L.J.K.B. 353.

[2] *Ballingall* v. *Glasgow Corpn.*, 1948 S.C. 160; *Sutherland* v. *Glasgow Corpn.*, 1951 S.C. (H.L.) 1; *Parkinson* v. *Liverpool Corpn.* [1950] 1 All E.R. 367.

[3] *Wing* v. *L.G.O.C.* [1909] 2 K.B. 652; *Barkway, supra.*

[4] *Walton* v. *Vanguard Motor Bus Co.* (1908) 25 T.L.R. 13.

[5] *Mars* v. *Glasgow Corpn.*, 1940 S.C. 202; *O'Hara* v. *Central S.M.T. Co.*, 1941 S.C. 363; *Doonan* v. *S.M.T. Co.*, 1950 S.C. 136.

[6] *Parkinson* v. *Liverpool Corpn.* [1950] 1 All E.R. 367; *Sutherland, supra.*

[7] *Mars, supra; O'Hara, supra; Parkinson, supra; Sutherland, supra.*

[8] *Le Blanche* v. *L.N.W. Ry.* (1876) L.R. 1 C.P.D. 286.

[9] *Hobbs* v. *L.S.W. Ry.* (1875) L.R. 10 Q.B. 111.

[10] A hackney carriage proprietor and its driver are under a statutory duty to carry passengers up to the number permitted by the licensing authority unless there is a reasonable excuse for refusal; see Burgh Police (Sc.) Act, 1892, S. 270; Sched. V, para 8; *Malloch* v. *Hunter* (1894) 21 R. (J.) 22.

Carriage of passengers by rail

The Railways Board is not a common carrier of passengers[1] but may be so on certain lines and to certain stations. The contract of carriage made by the passenger buying a ticket imports by reference the Board's general terms and conditions[2] but these may not purport, directly or indirectly, to exclude or limit their liability in respect of the death of, or bodily injury to any passenger other than a passenger travelling on a free pass, or purport to prescribe the time within which or the manner in which any such liability may be enforced.[3] There is no liability for failure to carry by a particular train,[4] for missing connections, or for delay so long as not unreasonable.[5] Railway servants are entitled to remove from a train a passenger who has not got a proper ticket, so long as no unnecessary force is used,[6] and to assign to passengers the seats which they are to occupy in the class of coaches for which they have tickets.[7]

Liability for injuries

The Board is under a duty to take all reasonable care to provide safe trains and to operate them safely. Liability to a passenger injured depends on fault but if the accident arises from a breakdown of the plant or the system the presumption is that it is the fault of the railway company.[8] Similarly, since the operation of trains is entirely under the control of railway servants the presumption is that an accident is attributable to fault on their part, as where two trains collide[9] or a train is derailed.[10] This may be rebutted by proof that the accident was attributable to a third party[11] or to an unforeseeable accident.[12]

---

[1] Transport Act, 1962, S. 43(6).

[2] See British Railways Board's Book of Regulations.

[3] Transport Act, 1962, S. 43(7).

[4] *Hurst* v. *G.N. Ry.* (1865) 19 C.B. (N.S.) 310.

[5] *Le Blanche* v. *L.N.W. Ry.* (1876) 1 C.P.D. 286.

[6] *Highland Ry.* v. *Menzies* (1878) 5 R. 887; *Brahan* v. *Caledonian Ry.* (1895) 2 S.L.T. 552; *MacRaild* v. *N.B. Ry.* (1902) 10 S.L.T. 348.

[7] *Scott* v. *G.N.S. Ry.* (1895) 22 R. 287.

[8] *Carpue* v. *London and Brighton Ry.* (1844) 5 Q.B. 747; *Watson* v. *N.B. Ry.* (1876) 3 R. 637.

[9] *Skinner* v. *L.B. & S.C. Ry.* (1850) 5 Ex. 787; *Ayles* v. *S.E. Ry.* (1868) L.R. 3 Ex. 146.

[10] *Dawson* v. *M.S. & L. Ry.* (1862) 5 L.T. 682.

[11] *McDowall* v. *G.W. Ry.* [1903] 2 K.B. 331.

[12] *Hart* v. *L. & Y. Ry.* (1869) 21 L.T. 261.

Safety of stations

Stations must be maintained reasonably safe for their intended purpose,[1] but no special duties are owed to persons suffering from disability.[2] Reasonable care must also be taken for the safety of persons coming to the station for any legitimate purpose, even if not travelling.[3] Ice or obstructions on a platform may evidence negligence.[4] Reasonable precautions should be taken to prevent accidental harm when crowds are expected, but there is no duty to protect against assaults by fellow-passengers.[5] Persons not travelling or otherwise entitled to enter stations may be excluded therefrom[6] and a lower standard of care may be owed to them.

Safety of rolling-stock

The Board is liable for any defect or insufficiency in their carriages which reasonable examination and maintenance would have revealed, but not for accidents due to latent defects not so discoverable.[7]

Safety of permanent way

The authority must take care that the line is maintained in safe condition[8] and is liable for running a train over line known, or reasonably suspected, to be defective or unsafe.[9] Line, bridges, embankments, etc., must be inspected and maintained and the collapse of a bridge or embankment is *prima facie* evidence of negligence,[10] but the authority is not liable for a collapse due to a defect which no care could detect or prevent.[11]

---

[1] *Foulkes* v. *Metropolitan Ry.* (1880) 5 C.P.D. 157; *McKeever* v. *Caledonian Ry.* (1900) 2 F. 1085; *Atherton* v. *L.N.W. Ry.* (1905) 21 T.L.R. 671; *Alexander* v. *City and S. London Ry.* (1928) 44 T.L.R. 450; *Protheroe* v. *Ry. Exec.* [1951] 1 K.B. 376; *Tomlinson* v. *Ry. Exec.* [1953] 1 All E.R. 1.

[2] *Henderson* v. *L.M.S. Ry.*, 1935 S.C. 734.

[3] Occupiers' Liability (Sc.) Act, 1960, S. 2; cf. *Stowell* v. *Ry. Exec.* [1949] 2 K.B. 519; *Bloomstein* v. *Ry. Exec.* [1952] 2 All E.R. 418; *Blackman* v. *Ry. Exec.* [1952] 1 All E.R. 4.

[4] *Tomlinson, supra; Blackman, supra.*

[5] *Hogan* v. *S.E. Ry.* (1873) 28 L.T. 271; *Pounder* v. *N.E. Ry.* [1892] 1 Q.B. 385.

[6] *Perth General Station Cttee.* v. *Ross* (1897) 24 R. (H.L.) 44; *Wood* v. *N.B. Ry.* (1899) 2 F. 1; cf. *N.B. Ry.* v. *Mackintosh* (1890) 17 R. 1065.

[7] *Readhead* v. *Midland Ry.* (1869) L.R. 4 Q.B. 379; *Holton* v. *L.S.W. Ry.* (1885) 1 Cab. & El. 542.

[8] *G.W. Ry. of Canada* v. *Fawcett* (1863) 8 L.T. 31.

[9] *Wyborn* v. *G.N. Ry.* (1858) 1 F. & F. 162; *Pym* v. *G.N. Ry.* (1861) 2 F. & F. 619.

[10] *G.W. Ry. of Canada, supra.*

[11] *Grote* v. *Chester and Holyhead Ry.* (1848) 2 Ex. 251.

Safety of level crossings

The Railway Board must take precautions for the safety of persons who have to cross rails on the level.[1] But much depends on the locality and the warning, if any, given by an approaching train.[2]

Carriage doors

It is negligence not to close carriage doors properly before a train starts,[3] but thereafter the fact that a door comes open is not by itself evidence of negligence.[4] If a door flies open it is not necessarily contributory negligence to have leaned on it,[5] but it may be to try to shut it again while the train is moving.[6] It may be evidence of negligence if a person on the platform has been struck by an open door of a moving train.[7] A window falling open is not evidence of negligence.[8] Whether it is negligence to close a carriage door, injuring a passenger's hand thereby, depends on the circumstances.[9]

Avoidance of overcrowding

The duty to provide reasonable accommodation[10] is breached by permitting overcrowding and damages may be given for injury directly caused by overcrowding[11] but no injuries indirectly caused.[12]

---

[1] *Cliff* v. *Midland Ry.* (1870) L.R. 5 Q.B. 258; cf. *Smith* v. *L.M.S. Ry.*, 1948 S.C. 125.

[2] *Davey* v. *L.S.W. Ry.* (1883) 12 Q.B.D. 70; *Coburn* v. *G.N. Ry.* (1891) 8 T.L.R. 31; *Lloyds Bank* v. *Railway Executive* [1952] 1 All E.R. 1248. See also *Ross* v. *Railway Exec.*, 1948 S.C. (H.L.) 58.

[3] *Gee* v. *Metropolitan Ry.* (1873) L.R. 8 Q.B. 161; *Inglis* v. *L.M.S. Ry.*, 1941 S.C. 551; *Brookes* v. *L.P.T.B.* [1947] 1 All E.R. 506.

[4] *Easson* v. *L.N.E. Ry.* [1944] 1 K.B. 421.

[5] *Gee, supra.*

[6] *Adams* v. *L. & Y. Ry.* (1869) L.R. 4 C.P. 739.

[7] *Toal* v. *N.B. Ry.*, 1908 S.C. (H.L.) 29; *Burns* v. *N.B. Ry.*, 1914 S.C. 754.

[8] *Murray* v. *Metropolitan Ry.* (1873) 27 L.T. 762.

[9] *Coleman* v. *S.E. Ry.* (1866) 4 H. & C. 699; *Fordham* v. *L.B. & S.C. Ry.* (1868) L.R. 3 C.P. 368; *Richardson* v. *Metropolitan Ry.*, ibid., 374; *Metropolitan Ry.* v. *Jackson* (1877) 3 App. Cas. 193; *Bullner* v. *L.C. & D. Ry.* (1885) 1 T.L.R. 534; *Drury* v. *N.E. Ry.* [1901] 2 K.B. 322; *Bird* v. *Ry. Executive* [1949] W.N. 196.

[10] *Jones* v. *G.N. Ry.* (1918) 34 T.L.R. 467.

[11] *Metropolitan Ry.* v. *Jackson* (1877) 3 App. Cas. 193; *Pounder* v. *N.E. Ry.* [1892] 1 Q.B. 385.

[12] *Pounder, supra*; *Cobb* v. *G.W. Ry.* [1894] A.C. 419.

Stopping short of or overshooting platform

To stop a train short of, or overshoot, the platform is not evidence of negligence,[1] but if passengers are allowed[2] or invited to alight[3] off the platform that may be negligence. A person who jumps down, knowing there is no platform, may be contributorily negligent.[4]

Operation of trains

The railway authority must take all reasonable care in the operation of trains to avoid causing injury. It is evidence of negligence if a train moves sharply while a passenger is entering or alighting,[5] or starts or stops suddenly,[6] or runs into the buffers,[7] or collides with another train.[8]

Damages for delay

A passenger who is inconvenienced by delay can recover for any substantial inconvenience, and loss resulting naturally therefrom.[9] He is entitled to recover the reasonable cost of completing his journey as soon as possible, or of expenses naturally resulting from the delay.[10]

Damages for personal injuries or death

Such damages are assessed in the same way as in other cases of injuries or death caused by delict.

Railway's liability under international Convention

The Carriage by Railway Act, 1972, gives the force of law in the United Kingdom to an international Convention scheduled to the Act, governing the liability of the railway for damage to passengers caused by accident on the territory of a convention

---

[1] *Bridges* v. *N. London Ry.* (1874) L.R. 7 H.L. 213; *Weller* v. *L.B. & S.C. Ry.* (1874) L.R. 9 C.P. 126; *Robson* v. *N.E. Ry.* (1876) 2 Q.B.D. 85; *Sharpe* v. *Southern Ry.* [1925] 2 K.B. 311.

[2] *Bridges, supra; Robson, supra.*

[3] *Cockle* v. *L. & S.E. Ry.* (1872) L.R. 7 C.P. 321; *Weller, supra; Bridges, supra; Robson, supra.*

[4] *Siner* v. *G.W. Ry.* (1869) L.R. 4 Ex. 117; *Owen* v. *G.W. Ry.* (1877) 46 L.J.Q.B. 486.

[5] *Metropolitan Ry.* v. *Delaney* (1921) 90 L.J.K.B. 721; *Goldberg* v. *G.S.W. Ry.*, 1907 S.C. 1035.

[6] *Angus* v. *L.T. & S. Ry.* (1906) 22 T.L.R. 222.

[7] *Burke* v. *M. S. & L. Ry.* (1870) 22 L.T. 442.

[8] *Skinner* v. *L.B. & S.C. Ry.* (1850) 5 Ex. 787; *Ayles* v. *S.E. Ry.* (1868) L.R. 3 Ex. 146.

[9] *Hamlin* v. *G.N. Ry.* (1856) 1 H. & N. 408; *Hobbs* v. *L.S.W. Ry.* (1875) L.R. 10 Q.B. 111; *Cooke* v. *Midland Ry.* (1892) 57 J.P. 388.

[10] *Le Blanche* v. *L.N.W. Ry.* (1876) 1 C.P.D. 286.

state. The railway is liable for damage resulting from death of or personal injury to a passenger caused by an accident arising out of the operation of the railway, and for damage to or total or partial loss of any articles which the passenger had with him such as hand luggage, including animals, unless the accident were caused by circumstances not connected with the operation of the railway and which the railway could not avoid or prevent, or the accident was due to the passenger's wrongful act or neglect, or a third party's behaviour.[1] The losses for which damages may be given are stated,[2] and limits are set for the amount of damages.[3] Conditions in the contract exempting the railway are valid.[4] Provision is made as to jurisdiction, the possible defenders, limitation of time for action, extinction of rights of action.[5] Failing provision in the Convention the national law of the state on whose territory the accident happens applies.[6] Provision is also made for procedure and diligence.[7]

Where by virtue of Art. 3, para. 2, any person has a right of action in respect of the death of a passenger by reason of being a person whom the passenger was under a legally enforceable duty to maintain no action may be brought at common law or under the corresponding English legislation.[8] A court dealing with proceedings limited by Art. 7 may take account of other proceedings relating to the same liability.[9] No action of any kind relating to a liability in respect of which provision is made by the Convention may be brought except in accordance with that Convention, and the rolling stock and other assets of a company cannot be attached by diligence.[10]

Carriage of passengers by road under international convention

The Carriage of Passengers by Road Act, 1974, gives effect to an international convention on the contract for international carriage of passengers and luggage by road. It applies where carriage is to take place in more than one state. A ticket must be issued and a luggage registration voucher. The carrier is liable for loss or damage resulting from injury or death caused as a result of an accident. The total damages are limited unless the carrier's principal place of business is in the U.K. There is also liability for total or partial loss of luggage.

---

[1] Sched. Art. 2.
[2] Arts. 3–5.
[3] Arts. 6–9.
[4] Art. 10.
[5] Arts. 13–17.
[6] Art. 18.
[7] Arts. 19–20.
[8] 1972 Act, S. 3.
[9] Ibid., S. 4.
[10] Ibid., S. 6.

CARRIAGE OF PASSENGERS' LUGGAGE

Carriers of passengers normally allow limited amounts of luggage to be carried without additional fare. Luggage comprises goods of a kind usually taken by a person away from home, for his personal use.[1] The liability of carriers for luggage is that of carriers of goods, common or private, not that of carriers of passengers,[2] save where the passenger takes personal charge of the luggage. The carrier is liable for the custody of the passenger's hand luggage, unless the passenger retained it in his sole charge and the loss was caused or contributed to by the passenger's fault.[3] The carrier becomes liable only if and when his servant accepts it for carriage,[4] and until the passenger has collected it within a reasonable time of the end of the journey.[5] Thereafter the carrier holds it as custodier only.[6]

Left luggage offices

In accepting luggage at left luggage offices the railways act as onerous custodiers; the conditions of the contract are normally set out or referred to on the ticket given for the luggage.[7]

But the railways may debar themselves from founding on any conditions limiting liability by themselves having acted in breach of contract.[8]

---

[1] *Macrow* v. *G.W. Ry.* (1871) L.R. 6 Q.B. 612; *Britten* v. *G.N. Ry.* [1899] 1 Q.B. 243; *Jenkyns* v. *Southampton S.P. Co.* [1919] 2 K.B. 135; *G.W. Ry.* v. *Evans* (1921) 38 T.L.R. 166.

[2] *Macrow, supra; Casswell* v. *Cheshire Lines Cttee.* [1907] 2 K.B. 499; *Houghland* v. *Low* [1962] 1 Q.B. 694.

[3] *Richards* v. *L.B. & S.C. Ry.* (1849) 7 C.B. 839; *Le Conteur* v. *L.S.W. Ry.* (1865) L.R. 1 Q.B. 54; *Talley* v. *G.W. Ry.* (1870) L.R. 6 C.P. 44; *Vosper* v. *G.W. Ry.* [1928] 1 K.B. 340.

[4] *G.W. Ry.* v. *Bunch* (1888) 13 App. Cas. 31; *Jenkyns, supra.*

[5] *Patscheider* v. *G.W. Ry.* (1878) 3 Ex. D. 153; *Parker* v. *L.M.S. Ry.*, 1930 S.C. 822.

[6] *Hodkinson* v. *L.N.W. Ry.* (1884) 14 Q.B.D. 228.

[7] *Lyons* v. *Caledonian Ry.*, 1909 S.C. 1185.

[8] *Handon* v. *Caledonian Ry.* (1880) 7 R. 966; *Alexander* v. *Railway Executive* [1951] 2 K.B. 882.

CHAPTER 44

CONTRACT OF CARRIAGE
(2) CARRIAGE BY SEA

CARRIAGE OF GOODS BY SEA

AT common law, apart from any express contract, a ship-owner undertaking to carry goods by sea for reward[1] comes under the edict *nautae caupones stabularii* and incurs the liabilities of a common carrier,[2] and is strictly responsible for delivering the goods entrusted to him in good order and condition. He can avoid liability for loss only by showing that the loss was due to act of God[3] or the Queen's enemies,[4] or inherent vice of the goods,[5] defective packing,[6] or voluntary jettison for the common safety.[7] But these exceptions do not apply if the loss has been caused by the shipowner's negligence,[8] deviation from the proper course of the voyage,[9] or if the ship was not in a seaworthy condition at the commencement of the voyage.[10]

In practice carriage by sea is invariably regulated by express contract.[11] Where the services of the whole, or substantially the whole, ship are let to one person, the contract is a charter-party. Where the ship is employed, by owner or charterers, as a general ship goods are normally carried under contracts embodied in bills of lading. If no bill of lading is used the contract must be ascertained from the shipowner's sailing bills and the terms actually agreed on.[12]

---

[1] See generally Bell, *Comm.* I, 550; *Prin.* §404–36; Abbott on Shipping (14 ed.); Carver on *Carriage of Goods by Sea* (12 ed.); Scrutton on *Charterparties and Bills of Lading* (17 ed.). The maritime law of Scotland has been said to be the same as that of England: *Currie* v. *McKnight* (1896) 24 R. (H.L.) 1; cf. *Blairmore Co.* v. *Macredie* (1897) 24 R. 893.

[2] Bell, *Comm.* I, 495; *Liver Alkali Co.* v. *Johnson* (1874) L.R. 7 Ex. 267; *Baxter's Leather Co.* v. *Royal Mail* [1908] 2 K.B. 626. But see *Consolidated Tea Co.* v. *Oliver's Wharf* [1910] 2 K.B. 395.

[3] *Nugent* v. *Smith* (1876) 1 C.P.D. 423.

[4] *Russell* v. *Niemann* (1864) 17 C.B. (N.S.) 163; *Liver Alkali Co.* v. *Johnson* (1874) L.R. 9 Ex. 338; *Paterson Steamships* v. *Canadian Wheat* [1934] A.C. 538.

[5] *The Barcore* [1896] P. 294; *Lindsay* v. *Scholefield* (1897) 24 R. 530.

[6] *L.N.W. Ry.* v. *Hudson* [1920] A.C. 324.

[7] *The Gratitudine* (1801) 3 C. Rob. 240; *Burton* v. *English* (1883) 12 Q.B.D. 218.

[8] *Notara* v. *Henderson* (1872) L.R. 5 Q.B. 346.

[9] *Morrison* v. *Shaw, Savill Co.* [1916] 2 K.B. 783.

[10] *Bank of Australasia* v. *Clan Line* [1916] 1 K.B. 39.

[11] Bell, *Comm.* I, 586; cf. *Watson* v. *Shankland* (1871) 10 M. 142; affd. 11 M. (H.L.) 51; *McCutcheon* v. *MacBrayne*, 1964 S.C. (H.L.) 28.

[12] *Harland and Wolff* v. *Burns and Laird Lines*, 1931 S.C. 722; *McCutcheon, supra.*

Contracts of affreightment generally

The contract for the carriage of goods by sea or contract of affreightment need not be in writing[1] but is usually embodied in either a charter-party or a bill of lading. A charter-party may contain what terms the parties agree on, though standard forms are commonly used; a bill of lading is sometimes subject to certain rules scheduled to the Carriage of Goods by Sea Act, 1924. Such contracts fall to be interpreted in accordance with any customary rules of the general maritime law.[2]

Contract by charter-party

In a contract by charter-party the charterer takes on hire an entire ship or some principal part thereof. It may be (a) a charter-party by demise,[3] in which case the ship, its master and crew, are transferred for the time being to the charterer, (b) a voyage charter, for the carriage of goods on one or more voyages,[4] or (c) a time charter, for a determinate period.[4] In the first case the charterer becomes owner for the time being, has possession of the ship, and master and crew are his servants.[5] In the latter two cases the charterer acquires only the temporary use of the ship and the services of the master and crew to convey his goods;[6] the owner retains ownership and possession, and the master and crew remain his servants.[7] Whether a charter-party operates by demise or not is a question of interpretation, the principal criterion being whether the master is servant of the owner or of the charterer.[6] Once a ship has been chartered her owners may not deal with her in a manner inconsistent with the charter, or they will be liable in damages.[8]

[1] *McCutcheon* v. *MacBrayne*, 1964 S.C. (H.L.) 28; the terms may be ascertained by reference to conversations, advertisements: *Phillips* v. *Edwards* (1858) 3 H. & N. 813; the usual course of business between the parties: *Lipton* v. *Jescott Steamers* (1895) 1 Com. Cas. 32; advice notes: *Armstrong* v. *Allan Bros.* (1892) 1 Com. Cas. 32; freight notes: *Lipton, supra*; mate's receipts: *Biddulph* v. *Bingham* (1874) 2 Asp. M.L.C. 225 or correspondence: *Harland & Wolff* v. *Burns & Laird Lines*, 1931 S.C. 722. It may be contained in correspondence though intended later to be contained in a charter-party: *A/B Nordstjernan* v. *Salvesen* (1903) 6 F. 64, 74.

[2] *Watson* v. *Shankland* (1871) 10 M. 142; affd. 11 M. (H.L.) 51.

[3] *locatio navis, vel locatio navis et operarum magistri et nauticorum.*

[4] *locatio operis mercium vehendarum*; *Omoa Coal Co.* v. *Huntley* (1877) 2 C.P.D. 464.

[5] *Colvin* v. *Newberry and Benson* (1832) 1 C. & Fin. 283; *Schuster* v. *McKellar* (1857) 7 E. & B. 704; *Meiklereid* v. *West* (1876) 1 Q.B.D. 428.

[6] *Sandeman* v. *Scurr* (1866) L.R. 2 Q.B. 86; *Baumwoll* v. *Furness* [1893] A.C. 8; *Weir* v. *Union S.S. Co.* [1900] A.C. 525.

[7] *Sandeman, supra.*

[8] *Sevin* v. *Deslandes* (1860) 30 L.J.Ch. 457; see also *Sorrentino* v. *Buerger* [1915] 3 K.B. 367; *Strathcona S.S. Co.* v. *Dominion Coal Co.* [1926] A.C. 108; *Port Line* v. *Ben Line Steamers* [1958] 2 Q.B. 146.

Under a charter-party by demise the charterer may, unless prohibited by its terms, use the ship to carry his own goods or those of others, and may sub-charter her.[1] In other cases, the extent of his right to have the ship carry goods of another depends on the contract,[2] and failing provision therefor he may not ship goods other than his own, unless the bill of lading is made out to himself.[3]

Form and interpretation of charter-parties

Charter-parties are usually made out on printed forms, the blanks being completed in writing to suit the circumstances. Such a contract is to be interpreted to give effect, so far as possible, to the intention of the parties as expressed therein. This may include meanings attaching to words by the usage of a particular trade or port. Parole evidence is inadmissible to vary the terms, but is admissible to explain ambiguous or technical terms.[4]

Charter-party by demise

This is in substance a hiring of the ship; the owner divests himself of control of the ship and its master and crew,[5] being entitled to receive the stipulated hire and to get back the ship when the charter-party expires.[6] During the charter-party the owner is under no liability to third parties who have supplied stores to the ship,[7] or whose goods are carried on the ship.[8] He is impliedly bound to deliver the ship in a seaworthy condition fit for the purpose of the charter.[9]

Usual clauses in voyage charter-party

A voyage charter-party usually includes provisions to the effect that:

(i) The shipowner agrees to provide a vessel, stating her name, location, capacity and class in Lloyds' register: such stipulations are treated as fundamental and, if not correct or not implemented, justify rescission.[10] The owner may be

---

[1] Abbott on Shipping, 340.   [2] *Smidt* v. *Tiden* (1874) L.R. 9 Q.B. 446.
[3] *Herman* v. *Royal Exchange Shipping Co.* (1884) Cab. & El. 413.
[4] *Leduc* v. *Ward* (1888) 20 Q.B.D. 475.   [5] *Baumwoll* v. *Furness* [1893] A.C. 8.
[6] *Meiklereid* v. *West* (1876) 1 Q.B.D. 428.
[7] *Reeve* v. *Davis* (1834) 1 Ad. & E. 312.
[8] *Baumwoll, supra.*
[9] *Schuster* v. *McKellar* (1857) 7 E. & B. 704.
[10] cf. *Behn* v. *Burness* (1863) 3 B. & S. 751; *Gifford* v. *Dishington* (1871) 9 M. 1045; *French* v. *Newgass* (1878) 3 C.P.D. 163; *Mackill* v. *Wright Bros.* (1888) 16 R. (H.L.) 1; *Bentsen* v. *Taylor* [1893] 2 Q.B. 274.

empowered or obliged to substitute another ship for the named one.

(ii) The ship will proceed with reasonable despatch to the port of loading;[1] delay, unless unreasonable, does not discharge the charterer, though it entitles him to damages;[2] unavoidable delay may be so fundamental as to frustrate the contract and liberate both parties,[3] or it may be covered by an exception clause.[4] If a loading port is named at which the ship cannot load a full cargo and the charterer will not pay dead freight, the owner may repudiate the charter.[5] There may be an absolute undertaking to sail for or arrive at the loading port by a fixed date; if this is not implemented the charterer may refuse to load.[6]

(iii) She is 'tight, staunch and in every way fitted for the voyage'; this condition relates to the time at which the contract is made, or the time of sailing for the loading port.[7]

(iv) The undertaking to carry the goods to the stated destination. Subject to the charter-party it is implied that the ship will proceed to the port of discharge by the usual route[8] and without unreasonable delay.[9] Voluntary departure from the usual route[10] or unreasonable delay, certainly if wilful,[11] is a deviation, which disentitles the shipowner from relying on any exception or stipulation in his favour in the charter-party and makes him liable for any loss of or damage to cargo, even though not due to the deviation, unless he can show that this would have occurred even if there had been no deviation.[12] Deviation is,

---

[1] *Forest Oak S.S. Co.* v. *Richard* (1899) 5 Com. Cas. 100; cf. *Nelson* v. *Dundee East Coast Shipping Co.*, 1907 S.C. 927.

[2] *MacAndrew* v. *Chapple* (1866) L.R. 1 C.P. 643; *Forest Oak, supra*; cf. *Nelson, supra*; *Connal, Cotton & Co.* v. *Fisher, Renwick & Co.* (1882) 10 R. 824.

[3] *Jackson* v. *Union Marine Insce. Co.* (1874) L.R. 10 C.P. 125; *Tamplin* v. *Anglo-Mexican Petroleum Co.* [1916] 2 A.C. 397; *Bank Line* v. *Capel* [1919] A.C. 435; *Universal Cargo Carriers* v. *Citati* [1957] 2 Q.B. 401.

[4] *Donaldson Bros.* v. *Little* (1882) 10 R. 413.

[5] *Charpentier & Bedex* v. *Dunn* (1878) 15 S.L.R. 726.

[6] *Glaholm* v. *Hays* (1841) 2 M. & G. 257.

[7] *Scott* v. *Foley* (1899) 5 Com. Cas. 53. The warranty of seaworthiness implied by law relates to the time of sailing from the loading port; cf. *Seville Sulphur Co.* v. *Colvils* (1888) 15 R. 616.

[8] *Leduc* v. *Ward* (1888) 20 Q.B.D. 475; *Reardon Smith Line* v. *Black Sea, etc. Co.* [1939] A.C. 562. See also *Allison* v. *Jacobsen* (1903) 11 S.L.T. 573.

[9] *Donaldson Bros.* v. *Little* (1882) 10 R. 413; *The Wilhelm* (1886) 14 L.T. 636.

[10] *Rio Tinto Co.* v. *Seed Shipping Co.* (1926) 17 Asp. M.L.C. 21; *Hain S.S. Co.* v. *Tate and Lyle* [1936] 2 All E.R. 597.

[11] *Scaramanga* v. *Stamp* (1880) 5 C.P.D. 295; *Wallems Rederi A/S* v. *Muller* [1927] 2 K.B. 99; *Cunard S.S. Co.* v. *Buerger* [1927] A.C. 1.

[12] *Thorley* v. *Orchis* [1907] 1 K.B. 660; *Morrison* v. *Shaw, Savill and Albion Co.* [1916] 2 K.B. 783.

however, excused and no breach of contract committed (i) where done for the purpose of saving life;[1] (ii) under stress of weather, or to avoid imminent danger;[2] (iii) if the charterer fails to load a full cargo, the shipowner may be justified in delaying while he obtains other cargo.[3]

Express provision is frequently made for deviation permitting it in such cases as (i) where the ship is given liberty to call at any ports in any order,[4] which involves liberty to remain to load or unload there;[5] (ii) liberty to tow and assist vessels in distress;[6] (iii) liberty to deviate to save property as well as life.[7]

The charterer may have the option of ordering the ship to various ports of discharge, in which case the risks of the voyage may be altered; in consequence the charter-party may specify conditions under which the option may be exercised.[8]

(v) The charterer undertakes to provide a full and complete cargo, which may be described generally or specifically. The cargo provided must at least substantially correspond with the description and be in a fit state for loading, and, if materially different, the shipowner may refuse to load it.[9] There may be an option to ship cargo of various kinds, possibly limited so as to limit the amount of less profitable cargo.[10] The obligation to load a full cargo must be complied with substantially,[11] so as to fill the whole cargo space in the ship.[12] The cargo must be prepared in the usual way for shipment but need not be packed in any special way.[13]

(vi) The charterer undertakes to pay freight: if payable as a

---

[1] Not property, unless expressly stipulated: *Scaramanga* v. *Stamp* (1880) 5 C.P.D. 295.

[2] *The Teutonia* (1872) L.R. 4 P.C. 171; *The San Roman* (1873) L.R. 5 P.C. 301. cf. *The Wilhelm Schmidt* (1871) 1 Asp. M.L.C. 82; *The Heinrich* (1871) L.R. 3 A. & E. 424; *Phelps James & Co.* v. *Hill* [1891] 1 Q.B. 605; *Kish* v. *Taylor* [1912] A.C. 604.

[3] *Wallems Rederi A/S* v. *Muller* [1927] 2 K.B. 99.

[4] So long only as substantially on the route: *Leduc* v. *Ward* (1888) 20 Q.B.D. 475; *Glynn* v. *Margetson* [1893] A.C. 351; *Reardon Smith Line* v. *Black Sea, etc., Co.* [1939] A.C. 562.

[5] *Leduc, supra.*

[6] *Potter* v. *Burrell* [1897] 1 Q.B. 97; *Stuart* v. *British and African S.N. Co.* (1875) 2 Asp. M.L.C. 497.

[7] *Kish* v. *Taylor* [1912] A.C. 604.   [8] cf. *Sully* v. *Duranty* (1864) 3 H. & C. 270.

[9] *Holman* v. *Dasnières* (1886) 2 T.L.R. 607.

[10] *Southampton Steam Colliery Co.* v. *Clarke* (1870) L.R. 6 Ex. 53; cf. *Reardon Smith Line* v. *Min. of Agriculture* [1961] 2 All E.R. 577.

[11] *Gifford* v. *Dishington* (1871) 9 M. 1045; *Harland and Wolff* v. *Burstall* (1901) 9 Asp. M.L.C. 184; cf. *Jardine, Matheson & Co.* v. *Clyde Shipping Co.* [1910] 1 K.B. 627; *Dreyfus* v. *Parnaso Cia Naviera S.A.* [1960] 2 Q.B. 49.

[12] *S.S. Heathfield Co.* v. *Rodenacher* (1896) 2 Com. Cas 53; *Mitcheson* v. *Nicol* (1852) 7 Ex. 929; *Neill* v. *Ridley* (1854) 9 Ex. 677.

[13] *Cuthbert* v. *Cumming* (1855) 11 Ex. 405; *S.S. Isis Co.* v. *Bahr* [1900] A.C. 340; *Anfartygs A/B Halfdan* v. *Price and Pierce* [1939] 3 All E.R. 672.

lump sum it is due irrespective of the quantity of cargo loaded;[1] otherwise it is payable at a stated rate per stated unit of weight or measurement. Freight is payable on the cargo as delivered and on delivery, but provision may be made for it to be payable on cargo as shipped and partly in advance.

(vii) Certain perils are listed as excepted: in the absence of excepted perils the shipowner's liability under a voyage charter is an absolute one for loss of or damage to the goods carried, excepting only loss or damage caused by act of God,[2] or of the Queen's enemies,[3] default of the shipper,[4] or inherent vice of the goods themselves.[5]

The charter-party normally lists various perils, other than those excepted by common law, as further exceptions to his absolute liability, in which cases the shipowner is accordingly not liable for loss or damage or for non-performance of the contract if prevented by an excepted peril. The perils usually expressly excepted are act of God,[6] the Queen's enemies,[7] restraints of princes and rulers,[8] perils of the seas,[9] fire,[10] barratry,[11] pirates,[12] collisions, strandings and accidents of navigation,[13] errors or negligence of navigation,[14] and sometimes leakage and breakage.[15] Such ex-

---

[1] *The Norway* (1865) 3 Moo. P.C. (N.S.) 245; *Thomas* v. *Harrowing S.S. Co.* [1915] A.C. 58. See also *Mackill* v. *Wright* (1888) 16 R. (H.L.) 1.

[2] *Nugent* v. *Smith* (1876) 1 C.P.D. 423.

[3] *Liver Alkali Co.* v. *Johnson* (1874) L.R. 9 Ex. 338.

[4] *The Helene* (1866) L.R. 1 P.C. 231.

[5] *The Barcore* [1896] P. 294; cf. *Lindsay* v. *Scholefield* (1897) 24 R. 530.

[6] *Liver Alkali Co.*, *supra*; *Nugent*, *supra*.

[7] *Avery* v. *Bowden* (1856) 6 E. & B. 953; *Russell* v. *Niemann* (1864) 17 C.B. (N.S.) 163.

[8] *Russell*, *supra*; *Geipel* v. *Smith* (1872) L.R. 7 Q.B. 404; *Cazalet* v. *Morris*, 1916 S.C. 952; *Tamplin* v. *Anglo-Mexican Petroleum Co.* [1916] 2 A.C. 397; *Watts, Watts & Co.* v. *Mitsui* [1917] A.C. 227; *Taylor* v. *John Lewis Ltd.*, 1927 S.C. 891.

[9] *Thames and Mersey Marine Insce. Co.* v. *Hamilton, Fraser & Co.* (1887) 12 App. Cas. 484; *Hamilton, Fraser & Co.* v. *Pandorf* (1887) 12 App. Cas. 518; *Hunter Craig* v. *Ropner* (1909) 1 S.L.T. 41.

[10] M.S.A., 1894, S. 502; 1958, S. 8(1); *The Diamond* [1906] P. 282. The fire must have happened without the shipowner's actual fault or privity.

[11] *Australasian Ins. Co.* v. *Jackson* (1875) 3 Asp. M.L.C. 26.

[12] *Republic of Bolivia* v. *Indemnity Mutual Marine Assce. Co.* [1909] 1 K.B. 785.

[13] *Letchford* v. *Oldham* (1880) 5 Q.B.D. 538; *Chartered Merc. Bank* v. *Netherlands India S.N. Co.* (1883) 10 Q.B.D. 521; *Garston Sailing Ship Co.* v. *Hickie Borman & Co.* (1886) 18 Q.B.D. 17; *Park* v. *Duncan* (1898) 25 R. 528.

[14] *Seville Sulphur Co.* v. *Colvils, Lowden & Co.* (1888) 15 R. 616; *Cunningham* v. *Colvils, Lowden & Co.* (1888) 16 R. 295; *Gilroy* v. *Price* (1892) 20 R. (H.L.) 1.

[15] *The Helene* (1866) L.R. 1 P.C. 231; *Moes, Moliere and Tromp* v. *Leith and Amsterdam Shipping Co.* (1867) 5 M. 988; cf. *Craig and Rose* v. *Delargy* (1879) 6 R. 1269; *Horsley* v. *Baxter* (1893) 20 R. 333; *Lindsay* v. *Scholefield* (1897) 24 R. 530.

ceptions are construed strictly and against the shipowner.[1] Unless clearly indicated, it will be assumed that the exceptions do not detract from the shipowner's implied duties to take reasonable care, to provide a seaworthy ship, and not to deviate, and the shipowner cannot rely on exception of a peril if it would not have caused loss or damage but for his failure in one or other of these fundamental duties.[2] In the event of loss or deterioration from accident covered by an exception the master must still take reasonable measures to minimize it.[3] The onus is primarily on the shipowner to bring himself within an excepted peril.[4] The excepted perils may cover the voyage to the port of loading as well as the main voyage,[5] unless it was a voyage under another charter.[6]

The charterers may also be entitled to be indemnified for loss caused by accidents of navigation even when caused by the master's negligence.[7] Such a provision is strictly construed, and must expressly cover negligence. It does not exclude the implied condition that the ship is to be seaworthy,[8] nor protect the shipowner against his personal default or negligence.[9]

(viii) Provision is made as to the manner of loading and discharge, the time allowed therefor, and the rate of demurrage. It is usually provided that cargo is to be brought to and taken from alongside the ship at charterer's expense and risk,[10] but it may be provided that the charterer is to provide for shipment, stowage or discharge of the cargo with indemnity against negligence, default or error of persons employed by him. Failing express provision loading and discharge are governed by the custom of the particular port.[11]

The charter-party usually stipulates that cargo is to be loaded within a specified number of days, 'lay days', which normally begin to run when notice is given to the charterer that

---

[1] *Adamastos Shipping Co.* v. *Anglo-Saxon Petroleum Co.* [1959] A.C. 133. On onus of proof see *The Xantho* (1887) 12 App. Cas. 503; *The Glendarroch* [1894] P. 226; cf. *Seville Sulphur Co.* v. *Colvils, Lowden & Co.* (1888) 15 R. 616.

[2] *The Glen Fruin* (1885) 10 P.D. 103; *McFadden* v. *Blue Star Line* [1905] 1 K.B. 697.

[3] *Adam* v. *Morris* (1890) 18 R. 153.

[4] *Williams* v. *Dobbie* (1884) 11 R. 982.

[5] *Harrison* v. *Garthorne* (1872) 26 L.T. 508.

[6] *Monroe Bros.* v. *Ryan* [1935] 2 K.B. 28; *Evera S.A. Commercial* v. *North Shipping Co. Ltd.* [1956] 2 Lloyd's Rep. 367.

[7] *Cunningham* v. *Colvils, Lowden & Co.* (1888) 16 R. 295; *Park* v. *Duncan* (1898) 25 R. 528.

[8] *Steel & Craig* v. *State Line* (1877) 4 R. (H.L.) 657; *Seville Sulphur Co.* v. *Colvils, Lowden & Co.* (1888) 15 R. 616; *Gilroy* v. *Price* (1892) 20 R. (H.L.) 1.

[9] *City of Lincoln* v. *Smith* [1904] A.C. 250.

[10] *Palgrave Brown & Son* v. *Turid (Owners)* [1922] 1 A.C. 397.

[11] *Brenda Steamship Co.* v. *Green* [1900] 1 Q.B. 518.

the ship is ready to receive cargo. Failure to tender a cargo within the specified period or within a reasonable time entitles the shipowner to treat the contract as repudiated. Failure to complete the loading within the specified period justifies damages only.

Similarly the time allowed for discharge may be stipulated, or it may be provided that a stated quantity of cargo is to be discharged per day.[1] If the period is exceeded the charterer is liable in damages,[2] unless the delay were caused by the ship-owner's fault,[3] or is covered by an express provision in the charter-party.[4] Alternatively the charter-party may provide for loading and discharge with customary despatch, or make no provision, in which case a reasonable time is allowed.[5]

Once the lay days have expired, the charterer may be al-lowed a stated further number of days in consideration of an additional payment, called demurrage,[6] or it may be provided that demurrage is payable for any delay beyond the lay days. It is important to define what is meant by 'day' in a charter-party.[7] *Prima facie* 'days' and 'running days' mean consecu-tive days,[8] but it is common to exclude Sundays and holidays, unless actually used for working;[9] 'working days' excludes Sundays and general holidays, but not days when it is im-possible to work by reason of the weather,[10] and 'weather working days' which are working days on which the weather does not directly prevent the operation of loading or unloading and from which must be deducted any time when work had to be suspended because of weather conditions.[11]

If no period of lay days is specified, demurrage becomes payable on the expiry of a reasonable time[12] and will continue payable so long as the ship is detained by the charterer,[13] unless the number of demurrage days is specified. Demurrage is only

---

[1] cf. *Horsley Line Ltd.* v. *Roechling Bros.*, 1908 S.C. 866.

[2] *Budgett* v. *Binnington* [1891] 1 Q.B. 35; *Kruuse* v. *Drynan* (1891) 18 R. 1110; *Granite City S.S. Co.* v. *Ireland* (1891) 19 R. 124; cf. *Wyllie* v. *Harrison* (1885) 13 R. 92.

[3] *Hansen* v. *Donaldson* (1874) 1 R. 1066; *Thorsen* v. *McDowall and Neilson* (1892) 19 R. 743; *Alexander* v. *A/B Dampskibet Hansa* [1920] A.C. 88.

[4] *Letricheux and David* v. *Dunlop* (1891) 19 R. 209.

[5] *Hick* v. *Raymond and Reid* [1893] A.C. 22; cf. *Rickinson* v. *S.C.W.S.*, 1918 S.C. 440.

[6] Demurrage is a form of liquidate damages: *Moor Line* v. *Distillers Co.*, 1912 S.C. 514.

[7] cf. *Hough* v. *Athya* (1879) 6 R. 961.   [8] *Niemann* v. *Moss* (1860) 6 Jur. N.S. 775.

[9] *Nelson* v. *Nelson Line (Liv.) Ltd.* [1908] A.C. 108.

[10] *Holman* v. *Peruvian Nitrate Co.* (1878) 5 R. 657.

[11] *Alvion S.S. Corpn. Panama* v. *Galban Lobo Trading Co.* [1955] 1 Q.B. 430; *Compania Crystal de Vapores* v. *Hermann and Mohatta* [1958] 2 Q.B. 196.

[12] *Hicks, supra*; *Hulthen* v. *Stewart* [1903] A.C. 389.

[13] *Lilly* v. *Stevenson* (1895) 22 R. 278; *A/S Reidar* v. *Arcos* [1927] 1 K.B. 352.

payable under an express stipulation therefor. Detention after the demurrage days, or, if none be specified, after the lapse of a reasonable time for loading or discharging, is a breach of contract rendering the charterer liable for any loss actually suffered by the shipowner in consequence of the delay,[1] but not to have the contract repudiated unless the detention is so long as to evidence an intention not to perform the contract.[2]

Liability for demurrage ceases when the charterer has completed loading or unloading, and he is not liable for further delay not caused by him.[3] Conversely, the charterer may be entitled to despatch money for time saved in loading or discharging. The charterer may not take into account any days saved at loading against demurrage due at discharge, unless the charter-party expressly permits it.[4]

(ix) exception clause relieving charterer: the charterer may be expressly protected against the consequence of delay in performing his undertakings necessarily brought about by specified events,[5] such as strikes and lockouts,[6] detention by railways,[7] civil commotions, accidents beyond the charterer's control,[8] storm or weather hazard, or outbreak of war.[9]

(x) cancelling clause: the charterer frequently has the option of cancelling if the ship is not ready to load by a specified time,[10] or on other stated grounds.[11] This clause does not limit the right to repudiate the contract for material breach,[12] nor does exercise of the option prejudice a claim for damages for delay in readiness to load.[13]

---

[1] *Lilly* v. *Stevenson* (1895) 22 R. 278; *A/S Reidar* v. *Arcos* [1927] 1 K.B. 352.

[2] *Inverkip S.S. Co.* v. *Bunge* [1917] 2 K.B. 193; see also *Chandris* v. *Isbrandtsen-Moller Co.* [1951] 1 K.B. 240.

[3] *Pringle* v. *Mollett* (1840) 6 M. & W. 80.

[4] *Avon Steamship Co.* v. *Leask* (1890) 18 R. 280; *Moliere S.S. Co.* v. *Naylor, Benzon Co.* (1897) 2 Com. Cas. 92; *Oakville S.S. Co.* v. *Holmes* (1899) 5 Com. Cas. 48; *Reardon Smith Line* v. *Min. of Agriculture* [1963] A.C. 691. Such a clause provides for 'reversible lay days'.

[5] *Granite City S.S. Co.* v. *Ireland* (1891) 19 R. 124; *Gardiner* v. *Macfarlane, McCrindell & Co.* (1893) 20 R. 414; *D/S Svendborg* v. *Love and Stewart*, 1915 S.C. 543; affd. 1916 S.C. (H.L.) 187; *Cazalet* v. *Morris*, 1916 S.C. 952.

[6] *Moor Line, Ltd.* v. *Distillers Co.*, 1912 S.C. 514; *D/S Svendborg, supra*; *Westoll* v. *Lindsay*, 1916 S.C. 782.

[7] *Letricheux and David* v. *Dunlop* (1891) 19 R. 209.

[8] *Abchurch S.S. Co.* v. *Stinnes*, 1911 S.C. 1010; cf. *Glasgow Navigation Co.* v. *Iron Ore Co.*, 1909 S.C. 1414; *Arden S.S. Co.* v. *Mathwin*, 1912 S.C. 211.

[9] *Avery* v. *Bowden* (1856) 6 E. & B. 953; *Esposito* v. *Bowden* (1857) 7 E. & B. 763.

[10] *Groves, Maclean & Co.* v. *Volkart* (1885) 1 T.L.R. 454; *Hick* v. *Tweedy* (1890) 6 Asp. M.L.C. 599; cf. *Dunford & Elliot* v. *Macleod* (1902) 4 F. 912.

[11] *Scottish Navigation Co.* v. *Souter* [1917] 1 K.B. 222.

[12] *Smith* v. *Dart* (1884) 14 Q.B.D. 105.

[13] *Nelson* v. *Dundee East Coast Shipping Co.*, 1907 S.C. 927.

(xi) 'general paramount clause', to incorporate the Hague Rules. It is common by this clause to embody in the charter-party the legislation of the place of contracting bringing into effect the Hague Rules (contained for the United Kingdom in the Carriage of Goods by Sea Act, 1924).[1] Such a clause does not exclude contractual stipulations or exceptions not inconsistent therewith.[2]

(xii) 'amended Jason clause': this is necessary in all voyages to and from the U.S.[3] and is a provision that the shipowner can recover for a general average loss even if due to the negligence of his servants, the validity of which was first upheld in *The Jason*,[4] and which has subsequently been amended.

(xiii) 'both-to-blame collision clause': if the ship is to call at a U.S. port this clause is desirable to counter the effect of certain U.S. decisions and free the carrying ship from liability to cargo owners for collision damage.[5]

(xiv) arbitration clause:[6]

(xv) clause providing for payment of commission to the shipbroker for negotiating the charter-party.[7]

(xvi) 'cesser' clause: This provides that the charterer's liability under the charter-party is to cease as soon as the cargo is shipped; this wholly excludes future liabilities,[8] but its effect on prior liabilities depends on its wording. If it clearly provides that prior liabilities are excluded, the charterer is exempted,[9] but otherwise his liability for prior breaches of the charter-party ceases only so far as the shipowner has acquired a remedy available against the consignee by way of lien over the cargo.[10] The cesser clause must be read along with the lien clause and they must, if possible, be taken to be co-extensive,[11]

---

[1] e.g. *Adamastos Shipping Co.* v. *Anglo-Saxon Petroleum Co.* [1959] A.C. 133.

[2] *Charlton & Bagshaw* v. *Law*, 1913 S.C. 317.

[3] To counter the effect of a contrary U.S. decision, which is not law in Scotland.

[4] (1912) 225 U.S. 32.

[5] See *The Atlas* (1876) 93 U.S. 302; *The Beaconsfield* (1894) 158 U.S. 303; *U.S.A.* v. *Atlantic Mutual Ins. Co.* [1952] 1 T.L.R. 1237.

[6] *The Swindon* (1902) 18 T.L.R. 681; *The Dawlish* [1910] P. 339; *Mauritzen* v. *Baltic Shipping Co.*, 1948 S.C. 646.

[7] See *Manners* v. *Raeburn and Verel* (1884) 11 R. 899; *Williamson* v. *Hine* [1891] 1 Ch. 390; *Moor Line* v. *Dreyfus* [1918] 1 K.B. 89; cf. *Sibson and Kerr* v. *Barcraig Co.* (1896) 24 R. 91.

[8] *Oglesby* v. *Yglesias* (1858) E. B. & E. 930; *Gray* v. *Carr* (1871) L.R. 6 Q.B. 522. But see *Hill S.S. Co.* v. *Stinnes*, 1941 S.C. 324.

[9] *Salvesen* v. *Guy* (1885) 13 R. 85.

[10] *Clink* v. *Radford* [1891] 1 Q.B. 625.

[11] *Clink, supra*; *Dunlop, Williamson & Co.* [1892] 1 Q.B. 507; *Hansen* v. *Harrold Bros.* [1894] 1 Q.B. 612.

no right being elided by the cesser clause unless recreated by the lien clause.[1]

(xvii) lien clause: This usually confers on the shipowner a lien over the cargo[2] for freight, advance freight,[3] dead freight,[4] demurrage[5] and general average and possibly other liens.

(xviii) penalty clause: A penalty clause is usually included, to come into operation if either party fails to perform the contract. Common forms of this clause, such as, Penalty for non-performance of this agreement estimated amount of freight, is unenforceable, and the aggrieved party can recover only the damages actually suffered.[6]

Implied undertakings by shipowner

In a voyage charter-party, unless expressly excluded or varied, the owner impliedly undertakes to provide a seaworthy ship, that she will proceed to the port of loading with reasonable dispatch and that she will proceed on the voyage without unjustifiable deviation.

(i) *seaworthiness*: The implied undertaking is that the ship shall be seaworthy, when the voyage begins,[7] for that voyage and for the cargo carried.[8] Seaworthiness is warranted, not merely due care to make the vessel seaworthy, and there is breach of the undertaking even if the owner were ignorant of the defect.[9]

But it is seaworthiness to withstand the ordinary perils of the sea only, not necessarily exceptionally heavy weather. Unseaworthiness includes defect in design, structure or condition,[10] inadequate instructions to the master,[11] lack of fuel,[12] an uncased pipe,[13] muddy water in the boilers,[14] defective boilers.[15] The onus

---

[1] *Clink, supra*; *Christoffersen* v. *Hansen* (1872) L.R. 7 Q.B. 509.

[2] Liens for freight and general average exist at common law, but the other liens must be created by special contract: see *McLean* v. *Fleming* (1871) 9 M. (H.L.) 38.

[3] *Tamvaco* v. *Simpson* (1866) L.R. 1 C.P. 363.

[4] *McLean, supra*; *Gray* v. *Carr* (1871) L.R. 6 Q.B. 522; *Rederi A/B Superior* v. *Dewar and Webb* [1909] 2 K.B. 998; *Kish* v. *Taylor* [1912] A.C. 604.

[5] *Birley* v. *Gladstone* (1814) 3 M. & S. 205.

[6] *Wall* v. *Rederi A/B Luggude* [1915] 3 K.B. 66; *Watts, Watts & Co.* v. *Mitsui* [1917] A.C. 227.

[7] This is not displaced by the express undertaking that the ship is in every way fitted for the voyage, which relates to the voyage to the port of loading: cf. *Cunningham* v. *Colvils, Lowden & Co.* (1888) 16 R. 295.

[8] *Stanton* v. *Richardson* (1874) L.R. 9 C.P. 390.

[9] *The Glenfruin* (1885) 10 P.D. 103.

[10] *Stanton* v. *Richardson* (1874) L.R. 9 C.P. 390.

[11] *Standard Oil Co. of N.Y.* v. *Clan Line*, 1924 S.C. (H.L.) 1.

[12] *The Vortigern* [1899] P. 140.   [13] *Gilroy* v. *Price* (1892) 20 R. (H.L.) 1.

[14] *Seville Sulphur Co.* v. *Colvils* (1888) 15 R. 616; but see 16 R. 295.

[15] *A/B Karlshamns Oljefabriker* v. *Monarch S.S. Co.*, 1949 S.C. (H.L.) 1.

of proof of unseaworthiness is on those asserting this and it is not presumed from an accident or even loss of the ship, but may sometimes be inferred from the facts.[1] The ship must also be seaworthy with respect to the cargo to be carried, and is unseaworthy if unfit to receive or handle the particular cargo.[2] If the charterer discovers that the ship is unseaworthy before the voyage begins and the defect is not readily remediable he may rescind the contract.[3] Thereafter he may only claim damages for loss due to the unseaworthiness. In a time charter, unlike a voyage charter, it has been held that there is no warranty that the vessel would be seaworthy at the commencement of each particular voyage during the charter.[4]

(ii) *reasonable despatch*: It is also implied that the vessel shall proceed on the voyage with reasonable despatch. Failure gives the shipper a claim of damages,[5] or in serious cases entitles him to rescind the contract.[6]

(iii) *no deviation*: It is further implied that the ship shall proceed without deviation from the prescribed course, or if not prescribed the ordinary trade route.[7] It is not deviation to be driven from one's course by weather. Deviation is, however, justifiable, if expressly permitted by the charter and, in any event, if necessary for the safe prosecution of the voyage, as for repairs[8] or the avoidance of grave peril,[9] and even if necessitated by the ship's initial unseaworthiness,[10] or to save life,[11] but not property, unless expressly provided for. An express clause may give liberty to deviate to tow or assist other ships, or in compliance with government orders. An unjustifiable deviation entitles the charterer to repudiate the contract, though he may treat it as still binding;[12] it prevents the shipowner from relying on exception clauses in the charter-party, so that he can rely only on the exceptions of act of God, or of the Queen's enemies, and that only if the loss would have occurred even if no deviation had taken place;[13] it

[1] *Klein* v. *Lindsay*, 1911 S.C. (H.L.) 9; *Fiumana Societa di Navigacione* v. *Bunge* [1930] 2 K.B. 47; cf. *Scott* v. *Kalning* (1877) 14 S.L.R. 260.
[2] cf. *Adam* v. *Morris* (1890) 18 R. 153.
[3] *Stanton* v. *Richardson* (1874) L.R. 9 C.P. 390.
[4] *Giertsen* v. *Turnbull*, 1908 S.C. 1101.
[5] *Barker* v. *McAndrew* (1865) 18 C.B.N.S. 759.
[6] *Freeman* v. *Taylor* (1831) 1 L.J.C.P. 26.
[7] *Reardon Smith Lines* v. *Black Sea and Baltic General Insce. Co.* [1939] A.C. 562.
[8] *Phelps, James & Co.* v. *Hill* [1891] 1 Q.B. 605.
[9] *The Teutonia* (1872) L.R. 4 P.C. 171.
[10] *Kish* v. *Taylor* [1912] A.C. 604.
[11] *Scaramanga* v. *Stamp* (1880) 5 C.P.D. 295.
[12] *Hain S.S. Co.* v. *Tate & Lyle Ltd.* [1936] 2 All E.R. 597.
[13] *Morrison* v. *Shaw, Savill & Albion Co. Ltd.* [1916] 2 K.B. 783.

prevents him recovering the freight payable, though he may be entitled to recompense if the goods reach their destination; and it prevents him from recovering a general average contribution from the charterer.[1]

Statutory exceptions for fire and theft

The Merchant Shipping Act, 1894, S. 502, imports protection for owners and charterers against liability for any loss or damage happening without their actual fault or privity,[2] for goods, merchandise or other things lost or damaged by reason of fire on board, or where specified valuables, the true nature and value of which have not at the time of shipment been declared by the shipper in writing, are lost or damaged by any robbery, embezzlement, making away with or secreting thereof.

Section 503, amended by the Merchant Shipping (Liability of Shipowners and Others) Act, 1958, limits liability for, *inter alia*, any damage or loss caused to any goods, merchandise, or other things whatsoever on board the ship, so long as without the actual fault or privity[2] of the owner or charterer.

Implied undertakings by charterer

The charterer impliedly undertakes not to ship dangerous goods, and he will be liable, even if they are accepted on board, if they cause loss or damage.[3] The charter-party may expressly prohibit dangerous goods, or permit them to be loaded on due notice to the master. By the Merchant Shipping Act, 1894, Ss. 446–450, the consignor of dangerous goods must indicate the nature thereof on the packages and give notice to the owner or master at or before the time of shipment.[4]

Usual clauses in time charter-party

Most time charter-parties include provisions on the following matters:

(i) The shipowner agrees to provide a named vessel for a stated period, stating her size, speed, fuel consumption and the amount of fuel on board:

---

[1] *Hain S.S. Co., supra.*

[2] See *Lennard's Carrying Co.* v. *Asiatic Petroleum Co.* [1915] A.C. 705; *Standard Oil Co.* v. *Clan Line*, 1924 S.C. (H.L.) 1; *The Empire Jamaica* [1956] 2 Lloyd's Rep. 119; *The Norman* [1960] 1 Lloyd's Rep. 1.

[3] *Chandris* v. *Isbrandtsen-Moller* [1951] 1 K.B. 240.

[4] See also Explosive Substances Act, 1883, S. 8; Merchant Shipping (Safety Convention) Act, 1949, S. 23.

(ii) The port of delivery and time of delivery of the vessel to the charterer: it may be a breach of contract not to put the vessel at the charterer's disposal at the earliest moment of the first day of the charter.[1]

(iii) The period for which the charter-party is to be in force.[2] There may be an option to renew it for a further period, and the shipowner frequently has the right to withdraw the ship if the hire is not duly paid.[3]

(iv) The charterer agrees to engage only in lawful trades, carry lawful merchandise and use only good and safe ports: if the charterer sends the vessel to an unsafe port and she is damaged in consequence, he must indemnify the owner,[4] unless the master acted unreasonably in so doing.[5] A safe port is one which that vessel can enter and leave, and lay at and discharge, always afloat.[6]

(v) The shipowner undertakes to pay for the crew's wages, the vessel's insurance and her stores, and undertakes to maintain her in a thoroughly efficient state: under the last clause the ship-owner is not bound to see that the ship is absolutely fit at all times, but must take reasonable steps to rectify defects as soon as notified to him.[7] Failure normally justifies damages only.[8]

(vi) The charterer undertakes to provide and pay for fuel, pay dock and harbour dues, and arrange and pay for loading and discharge.[9]

(vii) The charterer undertakes to pay a stated sum for the hire of the vessel, normally per month, and usually payable in advance, failing which the owner may withdraw the ship.[10] It is usually also provided that if the ship be lost, freight paid in advance and not earned is, as from the date of loss, returnable to the charterer.[11] It is further usually provided that the shipowner may withdraw the ship and determine the charter-party for non-payment of hire,

---

[1] *Mackenzie* v. *Liddell* (1883) 10 R. 705; cf. *Carswell* v. *Collard* (1893) 20 R. (H.L.) 47.

[2] There is usually provision for an extension to enable the last voyage to be completed: e.g. *Bucknall* v. *Murray* (1900) 5 Com. Cas. 312; *Hector* v. *Sovfracht* [1945] K.B. 343.

[3] *Re Tyrer & Co. and Hessler & Co.* (1902) 9 Asp. M.L.C. 292.

[4] *Lensen Shipping Co.* v. *Anglo-Soviet Shipping Co.* (1935) 40 Com. Cas. 320; *Grace* v. *General S.N. Co.* [1950] 2 K.B. 383.

[5] *Grace, supra*; cf. *Reardon Smith Line* v. *Australian Wheat Board* [1956] A.C. 266.

[6] *Hall Bros.* v. *Paul* (1914) 111 L.T. 811, 812; *Limerick S.S. Co.* v. *Stott* [1921] 2 K.B. 613.

[7] *Tynedale S.S. Co.* v. *Anglo-Soviet Shipping Co.* [1936] 1 All E.R. 389.

[8] *Hong Kong Fir Shipping Co. Ltd.* v. *Kawasaki Kisen Kaisha* [1962] 2 Q.B. 26.

[9] cf. *Giertsen* v. *Turnbull*, 1908 S.C. 1101.

[10] *Wehner* v. *Dean S.S. Co.* [1905] 2 K.B. 92; see also *A/S Tankexpress* v. *Compagnie Financiere Belge* [1949] A.C. 76.

[11] *Stewart* v. *Van Ommeren* [1918] 2 K.B. 560.

which right should, if necessary, be exercised promptly.[1] The right to withdraw may be waived by accepting hire late[2] or allowing the charterer to load[3] or otherwise.[4]

(viii) Provision is made for redelivery of the vessel at the expiry of the period of charter in as good condition as when delivered, fair wear and tear excepted.[5]

(ix) Provision is made for hire to cease to be payable in certain events, such as that no hire is to be paid in respect of time lost by the necessary dry-docking of the ship, deficiency of men[6] or stores, breakdown of machinery,[7] damage to hull or other causes preventing the working of the vessel for a period.[8]

(x) The master is to be under the orders of the charterer,[9] as regards employment, agency or other arrangements; but the charterer must normally indemnify the owner against the consequences of the master's actings while complying with such orders.[10]

(xi) The charterer undertakes to indemnify the shipowner from loss or damage to the vessel by careless loading or discharge.

(xii) Cancelling clause, whereby the charterer is entitled, or bound, to terminate the charter in stated circumstances.

(xiii) Clause incorporating the York-Antwerp Rules, 1950, relative to the payment of general average.

(xiv) Arbitration clause.

(xv) Clause providing for commission payable to the ship-broker for negotiating the charter-party.

Implied undertakings by shipowner in time charter-parties

The shipowner impliedly undertakes that the vessel is seaworthy at the commencement of the period of charter,[11] and that he will maintain her in that condition, but there is no implied warranty that she will be seaworthy at the commencement of each

---

[1] *Nova Scotia Steel Co.* v. *Sutherland S.S. Co.* (1899) 5 Com. Cas. 106.
[2] *Langford* v. *Canadian Forwarding Co.* (1907) 10 Asp. M.L.C. 414.
[3] *Nova Scotia Steel Co.* v. *Sutherland S.S. Co.* (1899) 5 Com. Cas. 106.
[4] *Modern Transport Co., Ltd.* v. *Duneric S.S. Co.* [1917] 1 K.B. 370.
[5] *Omoa Coal Co.* v. *Huntley* (1877) 2 C.P.D. 464; *Wye Shipping Co.* v. *Compagnie Paris-Orleans* [1922] 1 K.B. 617; *Chellew Navigation Co.* v. *A.R. Appelquist Kolimport A.G.* (1933) 38 Com. Cas. 218.
[6] *Greek Govt.* v. *Minister of Transport* [1949] 1 K.B. 525.
[7] *Giertsen* v. *Turnbull*, 1908 S.C. 1101.
[8] *Hogarth* v. *Miller Bros.* (1890) 18 R. (H.L.) 10; *A/S Lina* v. *Turnbull*, 1907 S.C. 507.
[9] Except in matters of navigation: *Larrinaga S.S. Co.* v. *R.* [1945] A.C. 246.
[10] *Milburn* v. *Jamaica Fruit Co. of London* [1900] 2 Q.B. 540.
[11] *Giertsen* v. *Turnbull*, 1908 S.C. 1101; *Hong Kong Fir Shipping Co.* v. *Kawasaki Kisen Kaisha Ltd.* [1962] 1 All E.R. 474.

particular voyage or stage of a voyage during the charter.[1] Unseaworthiness justifies repudiation of the contract only if the delay in remedying the defects is such as to defeat the purpose of the charter.

Implied undertakings by charterer

He undertakes impliedly that he will use the vessel only between good and safe ports, and that he will not ship dangerous goods.

Statutory exclusion and limitation of liability

The statutory exclusions of and limitations on liability[2] apply equally to time charters.

Breach of contract and frustration

In both voyage and time charters the charterer may normally rescind the contract for breach of such fundamental terms as the ship's position at the date of the charter,[3] nationality,[4] class on the register,[5] time of sailing,[6] capacity for the particular cargo,[7] date when she should be ready to load,[8] the vessel's seaworthiness at the commencement of the voyage,[9] reasonable despatch in proceeding,[10] and non-deviation.[11] Breaches in other respects normally justify damages only.

A charter-party may be frustrated in the same way as other contracts, by inordinate delay without the fault of either party,[12] but not necessarily by the blockage of the normal route.[13]

Bill of lading

A bill of lading is a document, usually in printed form, completed in writing,[14] stating that goods described therein have been

---

[1] Giertsen, supra.   [2] Vide supra.   [3] Behn v. Burness (1863) 3 B. & S. 751.
[4] Lothian v. Henderson (1803) 3 Bos. & P. 499.
[5] Routh v. Macmillan (1863) 2 H. & C. 750.
[6] Glaholm v. Hays (1841) 2 M. & G. 257.
[7] Dreyfus v. Parnasa Cia Naviera S.A. [1960] 2 Q.B. 49.
[8] Sanday v. Keighley, Maxted & Co. (1922) 91 L.J.K.B. 624.
[9] Stanton v. Richardson (1874) L.R. 9 C.P. 390.
[10] Freeman v. Taylor (1831) 1 L.J.C.P. 26.
[11] Reardon Smith Lines Ltd. v. Black Sea and Baltic Ins. Co. [1939] A.C. 562.
[12] Jackson v. Union Marine Ins. Co. (1874) L.R. 10 C.P. 125; Bank Line v. Capel [1919] A.C. 435; Constantine S.S. Line v. Imperial Smelting Corpn. [1942] A.C. 154; Port Line v. Ben Line Steamers [1958] 2 Q.B. 146; Hong Kong Fir Shipping Co. v. Kawasaki Kisen Kaisha [1962] 2 Q.B. 26.
[13] Tsakiroglou v. Noblee Thorl [1962] A.C. 93; contrast Société Franco Tunisienne v. Sidermar [1961] 2 Q.B. 278.
[14] Cowdenbeath Coal Co. v. Clydesdale Bank (1895) 22 R, 682,

shipped in good order and condition in a particular ship and setting out the terms on which they have been delivered to and accepted by the ship. Usually the ship is permitted to deviate, stated perils are excepted, and there is a negligence clause.[1] If there is a charter-party, it is usually incorporated to a greater or lesser extent in the bill, and there is provision for general average. A bill of lading authorizing the master to sign it without prejudice to the charter-party operates as a receipt or document of title only.[2] Bills are usually drawn in a set of two, three or four, numbered, with the stipulation that, any one being accomplished, the others are to be void.[3] The master usually retains one and delivers the others to the shipper.

A bill may perform one or more of several functions; it does not constitute, but is good though not conclusive evidence of the terms of, a contract under which the goods are carried;[4] it may serve as a receipt for goods received on board ship; and it serves as a document of title to the goods, and as a symbol of them is transferable. The shipowner has no right to alter the contract after the goods have been loaded, and must give a bill according to the terms agreed.[5] The contract is that the shipper will, subject to the excepted perils, deliver the goods at their destination in the same good order and condition as they were shipped.[6] The shipowner's responsibility as carrier commences when the goods are delivered to him for loading.[7]

Usual clauses in bill of lading

Usual provisions in a bill of lading include:

(i) the name of the ship, port of shipment, port of delivery, and consignee:

(ii) the number of goods shipped, their apparent order and condition, and their leading marks:

(iii) a 'general paramount clause' incorporating the Hague Rules:[8]

---

[1] cf. *Steel & Craig v. State Line S.S. Co.* (1877) 4 R. (H.L.) 103.

[2] *President of India v. Metcalfe Shipping Co.* [1970] 1 Q.B. 289.

[3] *Barber v. Meyerstein* (1870) L.R. 4 H.L. 317.

[4] *Crooks v. Allan* (1879) 5 Q.B.D. 38; *Sewell v. Burdick* (1884) 10 App. Cas. 74; *Ardennes v. Ardennes (Owners)* [1951] 1 K.B. 55. The actual contract may be made by booking shipping space for goods, or even by sending forward goods for loading: cf. *Heskell v. Continental Express* [1950] 1 All E.R. 1033.

[5] *Peek v. Larsen* (1871) L.R. 12 Eq. 378; *Jones v. Hough* (1879) 5 Ex. D. 115.

[6] *Bradley v. Federal S.N. Co.* (1927) 27 Ll. L.R. 395.

[7] *British Columbia Saw Mill Co. v. Nettleship* (1868) L.R. 3 C.P. 499.

[8] On these see *infra*. See further *Adamastos Shipping Co. v. Anglo-Saxon Petroleum Co.* [1959] A.C. 133.

(iv) list of 'excepted perils': the burden of proof that a loss was due to an excepted peril is on the shipowner.[1]

(v) deviation clause: express liberty to deviate to ports off the ordinary route may be conferred.[2]

(vi) the amount of freight payable:

(vii) the extent of the shipowner's lien over the goods:

(viii) the mode of delivery:

(ix) incorporation of the York Antwerp Rules, 1950, as to general average.[3]

(x) 'both-to-blame' collision clause:[4]

(xi) choice of law to govern the contract: such a declared choice is valid, certainly if the intention is *bona fide* and there is no ground of public policy for avoiding the parties' choice.[5]

Implied undertakings in bills of lading

The shipowner impliedly undertakes at common law

(1) that his ship is seaworthy; as in a voyage charter-party a ship must be seaworthy and cargo worthy;[6] this undertaking is absolute and not qualified or excluded save by clear terms.[7] Hence the shipowner is responsible for loss of or damage to the goods if his ship was not seaworthy at the outset of the voyage and the loss or damage was caused thereby.[8] But where the Carriage of Goods by Sea Act, 1924, applies, there is no absolute undertaking of seaworthiness but only an obligation to exercise due diligence to make the ship seaworthy, and in other stated respects.[9]

(2) that she will proceed on the voyage with reasonable dispatch.[10]

(3) that she shall proceed without unjustifiable deviation, such as for the purposes necessary for the prosecution of the voyage, or to save life.

[1] *Smith* v. *Bedouin S.N. Co.* [1896] A.C. 70.

[2] cf. *Leduc* v. *Ward* (1888) 20 Q.B.D. 475; *Connolly Shaw, Ltd.* v. *Nordenfjeldske S.S. Co.* (1934) 50 T.L.R. 418; *Renton* v. *Palmyra* [1957] A.C. 149.

[3] *infra.*   [4] *supra.*

[5] *Vita Food Products Inc.* v. *Unus Shipping Co. Ltd.* [1939] A.C. 277; *The Metamorphosis* [1953] 1 All E.R. 723; *The Assunzione* [1954] P. 150.

[6] *Stanton* v. *Richardson* (1874) L.R. 7 C.P. 421; *Steel* v. *State Line* (1877) 4 R. (H.L.) 103; *Cargo per Maori King* v. *Hughes* [1895] 2 Q.B. 550.

[7] *Tattersall* v. *National Steamship Co.* (1884) 12 Q.B.D. 297; *Ingram* v. *Services Maritime du Treport* [1914] 1 K.B. 541; *Atlantic Co.* v. *Dreyfus* [1922] 2 A.C. 250.

[8] *Baumwoll* v. *Gilchrest* [1893] 1 Q.B. 253; *The Europa* [1908] P. 84; *Kish* v. *Taylor* [1912] A.C. 604.

[9] See further *infra.*

[10] The 1924 Act, *infra*, does not refer to this undertaking so that it forms part of the contract even where that Act applies.

Statutory exceptions from and limitations of liability

The statutory exceptions from liability for loss or damage by fire, so long as happening without the owner or charterer's actual fault or privity may apply to protect him against the shipper.[1] So too the statutory limitation of liability[2] applies.

Implied undertakings by shipper

The shipper of the goods impliedly undertakes that the goods shipped are not to his knowledge dangerous when carried in the ordinary way, unless he expressly notifies the shipowner to the contrary, or the latter knows, or ought to know, that they are dangerous.[3] 'Dangerous' goods includes goods liable to cause the detention of forfeiture of the ship under the law of a foreign port.[4] The shipper does not impliedly undertake that the cargo can be loaded expeditiously.[5]

Bill of lading as receipt for goods

As a receipt for goods shipped, a bill is not conclusive, except against the person actually signing it,[6] and may be overcome by evidence that the goods were not in fact shipped;[7] so too, a shipowner may show that the quantities specified in the bill of lading are incorrect and that he has delivered all that was in fact loaded,[8] unless the bill of lading is expressly made conclusive evidence of the quantity shipped, in which case the shipowner cannot escape liability by proving that some of the goods were not in fact shipped,[9] or had been lost before shipment by an excepted peril.[10] If the bill of lading states 'weight and quantity unknown' it is not

---

[1] M.S.A. 1894, S. 503.

[2] M.S.A. 1894, S. 503, amd. by M.S. (Liability of Shipowners and others) Act, 1958: This limitation is not excluded from operation in cases governed by the Carriage of Goods by Sea Act, 1924.

[3] *Brass v. Maitland* (1856) 6 E. & B. 470; *Bamfield v. Goole Transport Co.* [1910] 2 K.B. 94; *Sebastian S.S. Owners v. De Vizcaya* [1920] 1 K.B. 332.

[4] *Mitchell, Cotts & Co. v. Steel Bros.* [1916] 2 K.B. 610.

[5] *Transoceanica Italiana v. Shipton* [1923] 1 K.B. 31.

[6] Bills of Lading Act, 1855, S. 3; but such person may show that the goods shipped were differently marked from those stated, unless the marks are material to the description of the goods: *Parsons v. N.Z. Shipping Co.* [1901] 1 K.B. 548.

[7] *Grant v. Norway* (1851) 10 C.B. 665; *Thorman v. Burt* (1886) 5 Asp. M.L.C. 563; *Immanuel (Owners) v. Denholm* (1887) 15 R. 152; *Leduc v. Ward* (1888) 20 Q.B.D. 475; *Smith v. Bedouin S.N. Co.* [1896] A.C. 70.

[8] *McLean and Hope v. Fleming* (1871) 9 M. (H.L.) 38; *British Columbia Sawmill Co. v. Nettleship* (1868) L.R. 3 C.P. 499; *Brown v. Powell Coal Co.* (1875) L.R. 10 C.P. 562; *Immanuel v. Denholm* (1887) 15 R. 152.

[9] *Lishman v. Christie* (1887) 19 Q.B.D. 333; *Mediterranean and N.Y. S.S. Co. v. Mackay* [1903] 1 K.B. 297; *Crossfield v. Kyle* [1916] 2 K.B. 885.

[10] *Fisher, Renwick & Co. v. Calder* (1896) 1 Com. Cas. 456.

even *prima facie* evidence of the quantity shipped and the shipper must prove that the goods were in fact shipped.[1] If the leading marks on the goods are inserted in the bill of lading it is *prima facie* evidence of the receipt of the goods therein described.

Similarly an admission in the bill of lading that goods were 'shipped in good order and condition' is *prima facie* evidence thereof,[2] but not conclusive of fault on the shipowner's part.[3] As against an endorsee for value of the bill of lading the shipowner is personally barred from denying the admission in the bill[4] unless the endorsee did not act to his detriment on the faith of the bill.[5]

An admission as to condition binds the shipowner only as to defects which should have been apparent on reasonable inspection.[6]

A description in the bill of lading of the quality of the goods does not generally bind the shipowners, and they may prove that goods of the stated quality were not in fact shipped.[7]

Bill of lading as evidence of contract

Where there is a bill of lading relating to goods, the terms are *prima facie* evidence of the terms of the contract of affreightment[8] but not, save in cases covered by statute,[9] conclusive evidence thereof.[10] The taker thereof is not necessarily bound by all its stipulations and may repudiate them if he did not know and could not reasonably be expected to know of their existence.[11] As between the shipowner and an endorsee of the bill of lading it constitutes the contract[12] and it may constitute the contract between shipowner and shipper.[13]

[1] *New Chinese Co.* v. *Ocean S.S. Co.* [1917] 2 K.B. 664; *Craig Line* v. *N.B. Storage Co.*, 1921 S.C. 114; *A.G. of Ceylon* v. *Scindia S.N. Co.* [1962] A.C. 60.

[2] *The Peter der Grosse* (1875) 1 P.D. 414; *Crawford and Law* v. *Allan Line*, 1912 S.C. (H.L.) 56; *The Tromp* [1921] P. 337.

[3] *The Ida* (1875) 32 L.T. 541.

[4] *Craig* v. *Delargy* (1879) 6 R. 1269; *Silver* v. *Ocean S.S. Co.* [1930] 1 K.B. 416; cf. *Brown, Jenkinson & Co.* v. *Dalton* [1957] 2 Q.B. 621.

[5] *The Skarp* [1935] P. 134.

[6] *The Peter der Grosse* (1875) 1 P.D. 414; *Compania Naviera Vazcongada* v. *Churchill* [1906] 1 K.B. 237.

[7] *Cox* v. *Bruce* (1886) 18 Q.B.D. 147.

[8] *Crooks* v. *Allan* (1879) 5 Q.B.D. 38; *Leduc* v. *Ward* (1888) 20 Q.B.D. 475; *Glyn, Mills & Co.* v. *E. & W. India Dock Co.* (1882) 7 App. Cas. 591.

[9] Bills of Lading Act, 1855, S. 3: bill in hands of consignee or endorsee for value is conclusive evidence that goods have been shipped as against the master or person signing them, unless such holder had actual notice that goods not in fact loaded.

[10] *Sewell* v. *Burdick* (1884) 10 App. Cas. 74; *The Ardennes* v. *The Ardennes (Owners)* [1951] 1 K.B. 55.

[11] *Crooks* v. *Allan* (1879) 5 Q.B.D. 38.

[12] *Glyn, Mills & Co.*, *supra*; *Bank of Australasia* v. *Clan Line* [1916] 1 K.B. 39.

[13] *Glyn, Mills & Co.*, *supra*; *Chartered Mercantile Bank of India* v. *Netherlands India S.N. Co.* (1883) 10 Q.B.D. 521.

Even where there is also a charter-party, the bill of lading is *prima facie*, as between shipowner and endorsee, the contract of carriage,[1] particularly when the endorsee is ignorant of the terms of the charter-party and possibly even if he knows of its terms.[2] As between shipowner and charterer, though in general the charter-party prevails and the bill operates only as a receipt,[3] the bill may sometimes have the effect of modifying the contract contained in the charter-party.[4]

Bill of lading as document of title to the goods

The bill also serves as a symbol of the right of property in the goods therein described,[5] and it may, by mercantile custom,[6] be transferred as symbolical delivery of the goods[7] to the same effect as actual delivery thereof.[8] Accordingly transfer of the bill, outright or in security, passes the property in the goods, provided the transferor was competent to transact with the goods,[9] and defeats the claims of the former owner.[10] But a bill of lading is not a negotiable instrument *stricto sensu* and the transferor's title to the bill and his competency to dispose of the goods therein are important factors in the validity of the transaction. The holder of a bill of lading is entitled on production of it to delivery of the goods by the shipowner[11] and, even if he is not entitled to the goods, this discharges the shipowner, so long as delivery is made in good faith and without notice of any defect in the holder's title.[12] The shipowner is not discharged by making delivery to a person without requiring production of the bill of lading.[13]

A bill of lading is not a negotiable instrument, but resembles one in that the contract evidenced thereby may be assigned by the delivery, or endorsement and delivery, of the bill, without

[1] *Fry* v. *Chartered Mercantile Bank of India* (1866) L.R. 1 C.P. 689; *Leduc* v. *Ward* (1888) 20 Q.B.D. 475.

[2] *Fry, supra.*

[3] *Rodocanachi* v. *Milburn* (1886) 18 Q.B.D. 67.

[4] *Davidson* v. *Bisset* (1878) 5 R. 706; *Gullischen* v. *Stewart Bros.* (1884) 13 Q.B.D. 317.

[5] *Barber* v. *Meyerstein* (1870) L.R. 4 H.L. 317; *Sanders* v. *Maclean* (1883) 11 Q.B.D. 327.

[6] *Lickbarrow* v. *Mason* (1794) 5 T.R. 683.

[7] *Sanders, supra; Sewell* v. *Burdick* (1884) 10 App. Cas. 74.

[8] *Cole* v. *N.W. Bank* (1875) L.R. 10 C.P. 345; *Sewell, supra;* even if signed by the master blank as to the amount of cargo: *Cowdenbeath Coal Co.* v. *Clydesdale Bank* (1895) 22 R. 682.

[9] Under the law of sale of goods.

[10] *Leask* v. *Scott* (1877) 2 Q.B.D. 376; *Kemp* v. *Falk* (1882) 7 App. Cas. 573.

[11] *Barber* v. *Meyerstein* (1870) L.R. 4 H.L. 317.

[12] *Glyn Mills & Co.* v. *E. & W. India Dock Co.* (1882) 7 App. Cas. 591.

[13] *Pirie* v. *Warden* (1871) 9 M. 523; *The Stettin* (1889) 14 P.D. 142.

separate assignation or intimation to the person liable thereunder;[1] the transferee may sue and be sued thereunder in his own name,[2] may in some cases acquire greater rights than the transferor by virtue of the transfer,[3] and, even though his own title be defective, may give a good discharge to the person liable.[4] But if the transferor has no title, or no authority to transfer on behalf of the owner, the transferee, even though taking in good faith, for value, and in ignorance of the defect, acquires no title as against the true owner.[5]

Transfer of bill of lading

A bill of lading, or one of a set,[6] containing the name of a consignee and providing for delivery to his order or to his assigns,[7] may be transferred by endorsement and delivery.[8] The endorsement may be special to a named transferee, or the endorsement may be in blank, in which case the goods are deliverable to the bearer of the bill.[9] If the bill does not name a consignee but makes the goods deliverable to bearer, or to order or assigns, it may be transferred by delivery without endorsement.[10] A specially endorsed bill may, if the endorsement permits, be endorsed and delivered to a subsequent endorsee; a bill endorsed in blank is further transferable by bare delivery.[11] A bill endorsed in blank may be specially endorsed by inserting a consignee's name.[12] The goods must be in transit and the delivery of the bill must have been made with intention to transfer the property,[13] as distinct from transfer to an agent to enable him to take delivery.

Notwithstanding delivery of the bill of lading the shipper's right to stop the goods *in transitu* is preserved,[14] unless the buyer

[1] *Barber* v. *Meyerstein* (1870) L.R. 4 H.L. 317.

[2] Bills of Lading Act, 1855, S. 1; *Sewell* v. *Burdick* (1884) 10 App. Cas. 74. See also *Delaurier* v. *Wyllie* (1889) 17 R. 167; *Cunningham* v. *Guthrie* (1888) 26 S.L.R. 208.

[3] *Dracachi* v. *Anglo-Egyptian Navigation Co.* (1868) L.R. 3 C.P. 190.

[4] *Glyn Mills & Co.* v. *E. & W. India Dock Co.* (1882) 7 App. Cas. 591.

[5] *Gurney* v. *Behrend* (1854) 3 E. & B. 622; *Barber* v. *Meyerstein* (1870) L.R. 4 H.L. 317; *Gilbert* v. *Guignon* (1872) 8 Ch. App. 16.

[6] Different bills of one set cannot be transferred to different persons: *Glyn Mills & Co.* v. *E. & W. India Dock Co.* (1882) 7 App. Cas. 591.

[7] If there is no reference to the named consignee's orders or assigns, it appears not to be transferable; *Henderson* v. *Comptoir d'Escompte de Paris* (1873) L.R. 5 P.C. 253.

[8] *Lickbarrow* v. *Mason* (1794) 5 T.R. 683.

[9] *Sewell* v. *Burdick* (1884) 10 App. Cas. 74.

[10] *Sewell, supra.*

[11] *Sewell* v. *Burdick* (1884) 10 App. Cas. 74.

[12] *Lickbarrow* v. *Mason* (1794) 5 T.R. 683.

[13] *Sewell, supra.*

[14] Bills of Lading Act, 1855, S. 2; Sale of Goods Act, 1893, S. 44.

takes delivery under the bill of lading,[1] or resells the goods and transfers the bill of lading.[2]

Transfer of a bill of lading passes no property in the goods if the transferee knew of circumstances which made the transfer inoperative,[3] or if the transferor had only a void title to the goods,[4] or the transferor had no property in the goods and no authority to transfer property in them.[5]

Effect of transfer of bill

On delivery of a bill of lading to the consignee named therein, or, duly endorsed, to an endorsee, with intent to pass the property therein specified, the rights and liabilities under the contract contained in the bill of lading are transferred to the consignee or endorsee as if the contract had been made with himself.[6] He can therefore on presenting the bill, claim delivery of the goods[7] and the shipowner can avoid liability for non-delivery only by proving that the goods were never in fact shipped[8] or that non-delivery is attributable to an excepted peril.[9] Unless similarly excepted he is liable for delivery in damaged condition.[10]

The consignee or endorsee is bound to take delivery[11] and pay the freight and any demurrage due,[12] though endorsement does not prevent the shipowner claiming the freight from the original consignor.[13] A consignee or endorsee who has endorsed the bill to a third party with intent to pass the property ceases to be liable on the contract evidenced by the bill, but a mere sale of the goods without endorsement of the bill does not thus affect the consignee or endorsee's position.[14]

The Bills of Lading Act, 1855, does not affect any liability of the consignee or endorsee which arises by reason of being such, or of receipt of the goods by reason or in consequence thereof. Apart

---

[1] *Re McLaren* (1879) 11 Ch. D. 68.

[2] *The Argentina* (1867) L.R. 1 A. & E. 370.

[3] *Pease* v. *Gloahec* (1866) L.R. 1 P.C. 219.

[4] *The Argentina* (1867) L.R. 1 A. & E. 370.

[5] *Gurney* v. *Behrend* (1854) 3 E. & B. 622; *Barber* v. *Meyerstein* (1870) L.R. 4 H.L. 317; *London Joint Stock Bank* v. *British Amsterdam Agency* (1910) 11 Asp. M.L.C. 571.

[6] Bills of Lading Act, 1855, S. 1.

[7] *Short* v. *Simpson* (1866) L.R. 1 C.P. 248.

[8] *Grant* v. *Norway* (1851) 10 C.B. 665; *McLean and Hope* v. *Fleming* (1871) 9 M. (H.L.) 38.

[9] *Steamship Calcutta Co.* v. *Weir* [1910] 1 K.B. 759.

[10] *Diederichsen* v. *Farquharson Bros.* [1898] 1 Q.B. 150.

[11] *Fowler* v. *Knoop* (1878) 4 Q.B.D. 299.

[12] *Wastwaster* v. *Neale* (1902) 9 Asp. M.L.C. 282.

[13] Bills of Lading Act, 1855, S. 2.

[14] *Fowler, supra.*

from this, liabilities not arising from the contract contained in the bill, such as terms of the contract between shipowner and shipper not incorporated in the bill, do not pass to him merely by reason of the consignment or endorsation.[1] The transfer of endorsed bills to an endorsee in security confers a good security as against the borrower's trustee in bankruptcy.[2]

Carriage of Goods by Sea Act, 1924

This Act gives statutory force to rules, known as The Hague Rules, set out in the Schedule to the Act, adopted by an international conference in 1923, which, where they apply, make important changes in the common law rights and liabilities of shipowners; so far as not expressly modified by the Act the common law remains applicable.[3] The Rules apply to goods, other than live animals and cargo stated as being carried and actually carried on deck,[4] carried from a port in Great Britain or Northern Ireland to any other port in or outside these places.[5] They do not apply to goods shipped in the British coasting trade,[6] nor to shipments of particular goods not made in the ordinary course of trade, when a special agreement is competent, provided that there is no stipulation as to seaworthiness which is contrary to public policy,[7] that no bill of lading is issued, and that the terms of contract are embodied in a receipt which is non-negotiable and marked as such.[8] They apply only from loading to discharge, and only where there is a contract covered by a bill of lading or any similar document of title. They do not apply to charter-parties, but they do to bills issued under charter-parties.[9] Every bill of lading to which the Act applies must contain an express statement that it is subject to the Hague Rules.[10] Article II makes the carrier under every contract of carriage by sea, in relation to the loading, handling, stowage, carriage, custody, care and discharge of such goods subject to the responsibilities and entitled to the rights and immunities thereafter set forth, though Art. VI preserves a limited right to make special contracts in regard to any particular goods.

[1] *The Helene* (1866) L.R. 1 P.C. 231; *Leduc* v. *Ward* (1888) 20 Q.B.D. 475.
[2] *Hayman* v. *McLintock*, 1907 S.C. 936.
[3] *Stag Line* v. *Foscolo Mango* [1932] A.C. 328.
[4] *Svenska Tractor* v. *Maritime Agencies* [1953] 2 Q.B. 295.
[5] Act, S. 1; *Stag Line, supra.*
[6] *Harland and Wolff* v. *Burns and Laird Lines, Ltd.,* 1931 S.C. 722.
[7] *Mack* v. *Burns and Laird Lines* (1944) 77 Ll.L.Rep. 377.
[8] Act, S. 4: Rules, Art. VI.   [9] Rules, Art. V.
[10] Act, S. 3. This is the 'general paramount clause'. Failure to comply with S. 3 does not by itself make the contract illegal: *Vita Food Products* v. *Unus Shipping Co.* [1939] A.C. 277.

Responsibilities and liabilities: Article III

Under Art. III, the carrier is bound,[1] before and at the beginning of the voyage,[2] to exercise due diligence to—(a) make the ship seaworthy;[3] (b) properly man, equip and supply the ship;[4] (c) make the holds, refrigerating and cool chambers, and all other parts of the ship in which goods are carried, fit and safe for their reception, carriage and preservation.[4] Subject to Art. IV, the carrier must properly and carefully load, handle, stow, carry, keep, care for and discharge the goods carried.[5] But the part each party is to play in the loading may be determined by contract.[6] After receiving the goods into his charge the master must, on demand, issue a bill of lading showing specified particulars.[7] Such a bill of lading is *prima facie* evidence of the receipt by the carrier of the goods as described therein.[8]

The shipper is deemed to have guaranteed to the carrier the accuracy of the marks, number, quantity, and weight as furnished by him and must indemnify the carrier against loss resulting from inaccuracies.[9]

Unless notice of loss or damage and the general nature thereof be given in writing to the carrier before or at the time of the removal of the goods, or, if the damage is not apparent, within three days, removal is *prima facie* evidence of the delivery by the carrier of the goods as described in the bill of lading. In any event the carrier is discharged unless suit is brought within one year after delivery or the date when the goods should have been delivered.[10]

After the goods are loaded, if the shipper so demands, the bill of

---

[1] Art. III, 1.

[2] This differs from the common law duty to make the ship seaworthy at any later stage of the voyage. See *Riverstone Meat Co.* v. *Lancashire Shipping Co.* [1961] A.C. 807.

[3] This replaces the absolute obligation at common law to provide a seaworthy ship, but the statutory obligation is incumbent on the shipowner, his servants and agents. See e.g. *Standard Oil Co. of N.Y.* v. *Clan Line*, 1924 S.C. (H.L.) 1.

[4] *Adamastos Shipping Co.* v. *Anglo-Saxon Petroleum Co.* [1959] A.C. 133.

[5] Art. III, 2; *International Packers, Ltd.* v. *Ocean Steamship Co.* [1955] 2 Lloyd's Rep. 218; *Renton* v. *Palmyra Trading Corpn. of Panama* [1957] A.C. 149; *Albacora S.R.L.* v. *Westcott & Laurence Line*, 1966 S.C. (H.L.) 19. This seems to be the same duty as at common law.

[6] *Pyrene Co.* v. *Scindia Nav. Co.* [1954] 2 Q.B. 402; *Renton, supra.*

[7] Art. III, 3.

[8] Art. III, 4; *Canada and Dominion Sugar Co.* v. *Canadian National (West Indies) Steamships Ltd.* [1947] A.C. 46.

[9] Art. III, 5.

[10] Art. III, 6; but see *Goulandris Bros.* v. *Goldman* [1958] 1 Q.B. 74. Most British shipowners and insurers have agreed, by the British Maritime Law Association Agreement, 1950, to extend the period to two years, but this is probably not legally enforceable.

lading issued must be a 'shipped' bill, and any document of title to the goods already taken must be exchanged therefor.[1]

Any clause or agreement in a contract of carriage relieving the carrier or ship from liability for loss or damage to or in connection with goods arising from negligence, fault or failure in the duties provided in Article III or lessening such liability otherwise than as provided in the Rules themselves is null, void and of no effect.[2]

Rights and Immunities: Article IV

Under Art. IV neither the carrier nor the ship is liable for loss or damage resulting from unseaworthiness unless caused by want of due diligence on the part of the carrier to make the ship seaworthy, to secure that the ship is properly manned and to make the holds fit and safe for the goods in accordance with Art. III, para. 1. The burden of proof of due diligence is on the person claiming exemption.[3]

Neither the carrier nor the ship is responsible[4] for loss or damage arising or resulting from:

(a) Act, neglect or default of the master, mariner, pilot or the servants of the carrier[5] in the navigation or in the management[6] of the ship:

(b) Fire, unless caused by the actual fault or privity of the carrier:

(c) Perils, dangers and accidents of the sea or other navigable waters:

(d) Act of God:

(e) Act of War:[7]

(f) Act of public enemies:

(g) Arrest or restraint of princes, rulers or people, or seizure under legal process:

(h) Quarantine restrictions:

(i) Act or omission of the shipper or owner of the goods, his agent or representative:

---

[1] Art. III, 7.

[2] Art. III, 8; a benefit of insurance or similar clause is deemed to be a clause relieving the carrier from liability. See also *Renton* v. *Palmyra Trading Corpn.* [1957] A.C. 149.

[3] Art. IV, 1; *Adamastos Shipping Co.* v. *Anglo-Saxon Petroleum Co.* [1959] A.C. 133.

[4] If the overriding duties, stated in Art. III, para. 1, are not implemented and damage results therefrom, the exceptions in Art. IV, 2, cannot be relied on: *Maxime Footwear Co.* v. *Canadian Govt. Merchant Marine, Ltd.* [1959] A.C. 589.

[5] There is no protection for personal neglects or defaults of the shipowner: cf. *Lennard's Carrying Co.* v. *Asiatic Petroleum Co.* [1915] A.C. 705.

[6] *Gosse Millerd* v. *Canadian Govt. Merchant Marine* [1929] A.C. 223.

[7] cf. *Kawasaki Kisen Kabushiki Kaisha of Kobe* v. *Bantham S.S. Co.* [1939] 2 K.B. 544.

(j) Strikes or lockouts or stoppage or restraint of labour from whatever cause, whether partial or general.

(k) Riots and civil commotions:

(l) Saving or attempting to save life or property at sea:

(m) Wastage in bulk or weight or any other loss or damage arising from inherent defect, quality or vice of the goods:[1]

(n) Insufficiency of packing:

(o) Insufficiency or inadequacy of marks:

(p) Latent defects not discoverable by due diligence:

(q) Any other cause arising without the actual fault or privity of the carrier, or without the fault or neglect of the agents or servants of the carrier, but the burden of proof shall be on the person claiming the benefit of this exception to show that neither the actual fault or privity of the carrier nor the fault or neglect of the agents or servants of the carrier contributed to the loss or damage.[2]

Shipper's immunities

The shipper is not responsible for loss or damage sustained by the carrier or ship resulting from any cause without the act, fault or neglect of the shipper, his agents or servants.[3]

Permissible deviation

Any deviation in saving or attempting to save life or property at sea, or any reasonable deviation is not to be deemed an infringement or breach of the Rules or of the contract of carriage, and the carrier is not liable for any loss or damage resulting therefrom.[4]

Limitation of liability

Neither carrier nor ship is in any event liable for loss or damage to or in connection with goods to an amount exceeding £100 per package or unit,[5] or its equivalent, unless the nature and value of such goods has been declared by the shipper and inserted in the bill of lading. Such a declaration is *prima facie* evidence, but not binding or conclusive on the carrier. By agreement a higher maximum may be fixed. There is no liability if the nature or

---

[1] *Albacora S.R.L.* v. *Westcott & Laurence Line*, 1966 S.C. (H.L.) 19.

[2] Art. IV, 2.

[3] Art. IV, 3.

[4] Art. IV, 4. See *Stag Line* v. *Foscolo Mango* [1932] A.C. 328; *Renton* v. *Palmyra Trading Corpn.* [1957] A.C. 149.

[5] This figure does not affect the limitation of liability under M.S.A., 1894, S. 503, and M.S. (Liability of Shipowners and Others) Act, 1958. The limit has been raised by the British Maritime Association Agreement, 1950, to £200.

value of the goods has been knowingly misstated by the shipper in the bill of lading.[1]

Dangerous goods

Goods of an inflammable, explosive or dangerous nature, if the carrier has not, knowing their nature and character, consented to their being carried, may be landed anywhere or destroyed or rendered innocuous by the carrier without compensation, and the shipper is liable for all damages and expenses resulting from such shipment. Goods of the like nature shipped with knowledge and consent, if becoming dangerous to ship or cargo, may similarly be unloaded or destroyed without liability except to general average if any.[2]

Right to limit or extend liability

The carrier's immunity cannot, in general, be extended by contract[3] but he may, by express provision, surrender any immunity or increase his liabilities.[4] This does not apply to charter-parties, but it does to bills of lading issued in the case of a ship under charter-party. Nor does it prevent the insertion of any lawful provision regarding general average.[5]

Other provisions

A special agreement is competent within limits provided no bill of lading is issued,[6] and as to the goods prior to loading and subsequent to discharge.[7] The provisions of the Hague Rules do not affect the rights and obligations of the carrier under any statute for the time being in force relating to the limitation of the liability of owners of ships.[8]

Relation of charter-party and bill of lading

Where the shipper is also the charterer the contract of carriage is in the charter-party alone and the bill of lading is, failing contrary indication,[9] only an acknowledgment of receipt of the goods.[10] But parties may, by the bill, expressly agree[11] to vary the

---

[1] Art. IV, 5.   [2] Art. IV, 6.   [3] Art. III, 8.

[4] Art. V; *The Touraine* [1928] P. 58.

[5] Art. V.

[6] Art. VI: *Harland and Wolff* v. *Burns and Laird Lines*, 1931 S.C. 722.

[7] Art. VII.

[8] Art. VIII, referring to M.S.A., 1894, S. 503 as amd.

[9] *Rodocanachi* v. *Milburn* (1886) 18 Q.B.D. 67; *Hill S.S. Co.* v. *Stinnes*, 1941 S.C. 324.

[10] *Sewell* v. *Burdick* (1884) 10 App. Cas. 74.

[11] Oral evidence of intention to vary is admissible: *Davidson* v. *Bisset* (1878) 5 R. 706.

charter-party in which case the bill prevails over the charter-party.[1] If the shipper is not also the charterer it depends on the circumstances whether the contract evidenced by the bill of lading is with the shipowner or the charterer,[2] but as a rule the shipper's claims lie against the shipowner and conversely.[3] As between shipowner and charterer, the contract is *prima facie* contained in the charter-party, though it may be modified by the bill of lading,[4] and as regards other parties *prima facie* in the bill of lading.

The terms of the charter-party may be incorporated in the bill of lading by express reference, in which case they become terms of the contract evidenced by the bill, enforceable by or against any party thereto.[5] A term *ex facie* inconsistent with an express term of the bill of lading cannot be held incorporated,[6] and conditions inapplicable must be disregarded as incapable of application.[7] Any reference to the charter-party is construed strictly,[8] and the terms incorporated are generally only those to be performed by the holders of the bill of lading.

Mate's receipt; delivery of bill of lading

When goods are delivered to the ship for loading the shipper is normally given a mate's receipt as acknowledgment of their receipt; it is *prima facie* but not conclusive evidence that the goods have been delivered to and received by the ship,[9] and may be a clear receipt or contain qualifications as to the condition of the goods at shipment.[10] A mate's receipt is not transferable to the effect of passing property in the goods mentioned therein,[11] but if there is no bill of lading and the mate's receipt mentions a consignee to whom the property is intended to pass, delivery must be made to him.[12] Possession of the mate's receipt is *prima facie*

[1] *Rodocanachi, supra*; *Hill S.S. Co. v. Stinnes*, 1941 S.C. 324, 333.

[2] Unless the charter is a charter by demise where the contract is clearly with the charterer: *Samuel, Samuel & Co. v. West Hartlepool S.N. Co.* (1906) 11 Com. Cas. 115; *Wilston S.N. Co. v. Weir* (1925) 31 Com. Cas. 111.

[3] *Manchester Trust, Ltd. v. Furness* [1895] 2 Q.B. 539.

[4] *Davidson v. Bisset* (1878) 5 R. 706; *Gullischen v. Stewart* (1884) 13 Q.B.D. 317; *Rodocanchi v. Milburn* (1886) 18 Q.B.D. 67; *President of India v. Metcalfe Shipping Co.* [1970] 1 Q.B. 289.

[5] *Porteous v. Watney* (1878) 3 Q.B.D. 534; *Arrospe v. Barr* (1881) 8 R. 602; *Delaurier v. Wylie* (1889) 17 R. 167.

[6] *Gardner v. Trechmann* (1884) 15 Q.B.D. 154.   [7] *Porteous, supra*.

[8] *The Modena* (1911) 16 Com. Cas. 292.

[9] *Biddulph v. Bingham* (1874) 2 Asp. M.L.C. 225.

[10] *Armstrong v. Allan Bros* (1892) 7 Asp. M.L.C. 293.

[11] *Hathesing v. Laing, Laing v. Zeden* (1873) L.R. 17 Eq. 92.

[12] *Evans v. Nichol* (1841) 3 M. & G. 614.

evidence of ownership. Transfer of the mate's receipt does not by itself pass the property in the goods, but sale of the goods entitles the transferee to receive the bill of lading, whether or not the mate's receipt is transferred.[1]

The person who is owner of the goods at the time of shipment is entitled to receive a bill of lading made out according to his instructions.[2] He may demand redelivery of the goods if he is refused a bill of lading, or if its terms differ from those which he is entitled to require, or if his instructions are not complied with.[3] Possession of the mate's receipt is *prima facie* evidence of ownership, entitling the holder to receive a bill of lading[4] and the shipowner is justified, in the absence of notice that the holder is not the owner, in signing a bill of lading and delivering it in exchange for the mate's receipt.[5] If he does not require delivery of the mate's receipt he must satisfy himself that the goods have been loaded and that the person to whom he delivers the bill of lading was entitled thereto, failing which he remains liable to the true owner.[6]

Voyage to the loading port

The shipowner's undertaking to bring his ship to the port of loading may be an absolute undertaking to arrive there by a fixed date, or merely an undertaking to proceed there with all convenient dispatch. In the latter case delay gives rise only to a claim of damages,[7] unless it has been such as to frustrate the object of the contract.[8] The excepted perils clauses may apply to the voyage to the loading port.[9]

Loading

The shipowner must have his ship at the port of loading in time to load for the voyage;[10] she must be ready to receive cargo,[11] and notice of readiness must be given to the charterer.[12] It is an implied

---

[1] *Cowas-Jee* v. *Thompson* (1845) 5 Moo. P.C. 165.

[2] *Falk* v. *Fletcher* (1865) 18 C.B. (N.S.) 403.

[3] *Armstrong* v. *Allan Bros.* (1892) 7 Asp. M.L.C. 277.

[4] *Schuster* v. *McKellar* (1857) 7 E. & B. 704; *Nippon Yusen Kaisha* v. *Ramjiban Serowgee* [1938] A.C. 429.

[5] *Craven* v. *Ryder* (1816) 6 Taunt. 433.   [6] *Schuster, supra.*

[7] *Forest Oak* v. *Richard* (1899) 5 Com. Cas. 100; *Nelson* v. *Dundee Shipping Co.*, 1907 S.C. 927.

[8] *Freeman* v. *Taylor* (1831) 1 L.J.C.P. 26; cf. *Jackson* v. *Union Marine Ins. Co.* (1874) L.R. 10 C.P. 125.

[9] *Harrison* v. *Garthorne* (1872) 26 L.T. 508; contrast *Monroe Bros.* v. *Ryan* [1935] 2 K.B. 28.

[10] *Gifford* v. *Dishington* (1871) 9 M. 1045; *Dahl* v. *Nelson* (1881) 6 App. Cas. 38.

[11] *Noemijulia Steamship Co.* v. *Minister of Food* [1951] 1 K.B. 223.

[12] *Stanton* v. *Austin* (1872) L.R. 7 C.P. 651; *Nelson* v. *Dahl* (1879) 12 Ch. D. 568.

term of all contracts of affreightment that the ship shall be sea-worthy when the loading begins;[1] if not the consignor may refuse to load and recover damages for breach of the condition.[2] This condition is absolute and it matters not that the defect was latent.[3]

Once the charterer has been notified, he must provide the stipulated cargo within the time specified, or a reasonable time.[4] If the cargo is not ready and the ship delayed the charterer is liable in damages,[5] and if the delay continues the shipowner may rescind the contract.[6] The charterer is excused if there is express provision in the charter-party relieving him,[7] if the contract is frustrated, or events have made loading illegal,[8] or the shipowner is in breach of a fundamental term, such as seaworthiness,[9] or failure to load is due to unexcused fault on the shipowner's part.[10]

Unless inconsistent with the contract the customs of the port as to loading are presumed applicable and binding on the parties.[11] The charterer cannot rely on an excepted peril unless it actually interferes with loading.[12] Unless contrary provision be made it is the ship's duty to receive and stow the goods properly, even though the work be done by stevedores appointed by the charterers.[13]

The charterer's undertaking is to load a full and complete cargo, not merely one equal to the ship's burden stated in the charter-party.[14] If he fails to do so, the charterer must pay dead freight for space not occupied by cargo. If the charter-party permits the loading of several kinds of cargo, the charterer may

---

[1] *Cohn* v. *Davidson* (1877) 2 Q.B.D. 455; *McFadden* v. *Blue Star Line* [1905] 1 K.B. 697.

[2] *Steel & Craig* v. *State Line S.S. Co.* (1877) 4 R. (H.L.) 103; cf. *Stanton* v. *Richardson* (1875) 3 Asp. M.L.C. 23.

[3] *The Glenfruin* (1885) 10 P.D. 103.

[4] *Ardan S.S. Co.* v. *Weir* (1905) 7 F. (H.L.) 126.

[5] *Grant* v. *Coverdale, Todd & Co.* (1884) 9 App. Cas. 470.

[6] *Stanton, supra*; *Universal Cargo Carriers* v. *Citati* [1957] 2 Q.B. 401.

[7] *Fenwick* v. *Schmalz* (1868) L.R. 3 C.P. 313; *Letricheux* v. *Dunlop* (1891) 19 R. 209; *Gardiner* v. *Macfarlane* (1893) 20 R. 414; *Turnbull, Scott* v. *Cruickshank* (1904) 7 F. 265; *Gordon S.S. Co.* v. *Moxey* (1913) 18 Com. Cas. 170; *D/S Denmark* v. *Poulsen*, 1913 S.C. 1043; *S.S. Matheos* v. *Dreyfus* [1925] A.C. 654. See also *Krog* v. *Burns* (1903) 5 F. 1189.

[8] *Esposito* v. *Bowden* (1857) 7 E. & B. 763; *Ralli Bros.* v. *Compania Naviera Sota y Aznar* [1920] 2 K.B. 287.

[9] *Stanton* v. *Richardson* (1874) L.R. 9 C.P. 390.

[10] *Seeger* v. *Duthie* (1860) 8 C.B. (N.S.) 45; *Phosphate Co.* v. *Rankin Co.* (1916) 86 L.J.K.B. 358.

[11] *The Nifa* [1892] P. 411.

[12] *Grant* v. *Coverdale* (1884) 9 App. Cas. 470; *S.S. Matheos* v. *Dreyfus* [1925] A.C. 654. cf. *Hudson* v. *Ede* (1868) L.R. 3 Q.B. 412.

[13] *Glengarnock Iron Co.* v. *Cooper* (1895) 22 R. 672; *Canadian Tpt. Co.* v. *Court Line, Ltd.* [1940] A.C. 934.

[14] *Hunter* v. *Fry* (1819) 2 B. & Ald. 421; *Windle* v. *Barker* (1852) 25 L.J.Q.B. 349; *Morris* v. *Levison* (1876) 1 C.P.D. 155; *Carlton S.S. Co.* v. *Castle Co.* [1898] A.C. 486.

load a full cargo of any one or more kinds[1] but may not load goods which leave storage spaces unfilled,[2] except where this is permitted by the custom of the port.[3] It is commonly provided that only 'lawful merchandise' may be loaded, that is, such goods as are ordinarily shipped from that port, and such as can be lawfully loaded, carried and discharged.[4]

The shipowner is bound to take, just as the charterer is to supply a full cargo, failing which he is liable in damages.[5] He impliedly undertakes that he will not ship goods involving unusual danger without notifying the owner.[6]

Time for loading

The loading must be completed in the stipulated time or within a reasonable time;[7] the 'lay days' allowed for loading usually commence to run when the ship is an 'arrived ship'[8] and is ready to load[9] and that fact has been notified to the charterer. The charterer is excused if delay is caused by the shipowner's fault or that of his servants,[10] or if it falls within an exceptions clause in his favour.[11] If loading is not completed[12] within the lay days, or a reasonable time, damages are due for the detention of the ship[13] or demurrage may be provided by the charter-party. In the absence of express stipulation time saved when loading or unloading cannot exclude liability for delay in the other operation.[14] By stipulation dispatch money may be paid for each day saved in loading.[15]

---

[1] *Moorsom* v. *Page* (1814) 4 Camp. 103.

[2] *Cliff* v. *Meek* (1804) 33 L.J.C.P. 183.

[3] *Cuthbert* v. *Cumming* (1855) 11 Ex. 405; cf. *Anfartygs* v. *Price and Pierce, Ltd.* [1939] 3 All E.R. 672.

[4] *Leolga Compania de Navigacion* v. *Glynn* [1953] 2 All E.R. 327.

[5] *Gifford* v. *Dishington* (1871) 9 M. 1045.

[6] *Brass* v. *Maitland* (1856) 6 E. & B. 471; *Mitchell, Cotts & Co.* v. *Steel* [1916] 2 K.B. 610; see also M.S.A., 1894, Ss. 446–50.

[7] *Hick* v. *Raymond & Reid* [1893] A.C. 22.

[8] As to this see *Leonis S.S. Co.* v. *Rank* [1908] 1 K.B. 499; *Stag Line* v. *Board of Trade* [1950] 2 K.B. 194.

[9] *Armement Adolf Deppe* v. *Robinson* [1917] 2 K.B. 204; a ship is not ready to load if delayed by quarantine restrictions: *White* v. *Winchester S.S. Co.* (1886) 13 R. 524; cf. *Reardon Smith Line* v. *Ministry of Agriculture* [1962] 1 Q.B. 42.

[10] *Houlder* v. *Weir* [1905] 2 K.B. 267.

[11] *Induna Co.* v. *British Phosphate Commrs.* [1949] 2 K.B. 430; *The Amstelmolen* [1961] 2 Lloyd's Rep. 1.

[12] Questions may arise as to when loading is completed, as where the cargo must be stowed: *Argonaut Navigation Co.* v. *Ministry of Food* [1949] 1 K.B. 572.

[13] *Inverkip S.S. Co.* v. *Bunge* [1917] 2 K.B. 193; *A/S Reidar* v. *Arcos* [1927] 1 K.B. 352.

[14] *Avon Steamship Co.* v. *Leask* (1890) 18 R. 280.

[15] *Rowtor Steamship Co.* v. *Love & Stewart*, 1916 S.C. (H.L.) 199.

Stowage

The shipowner must load and stow the goods with due skill and care. If they are destroyed or damaged by reason of improper stowage the shipowner is not protected, unless the exception clause covers negligent stowage, merely by an exception covering the cause of the damage.[1] If there is no relevant exception, the shipowner is strictly liable for loss or damage to the goods, apart from inherent vice. The goods must be stowed in the proper place.[2] The shipowner is not entitled to carry goods on deck, unless this is permitted by usage of trade,[3] or the shipper has consented.[4]

The Voyage

In cases not covered by the Hague Rules, the shipowner is impliedly absolutely bound to ensure that the ship is seaworthy at the commencement of the contract voyage,[5] that is, in all respects fit to encounter the ordinary perils of the voyage at that season.[6] A vessel may be unseaworthy if by reason of latent defect existing at the time she will become unfit for the due completion of the voyage,[7] if she be overloaded[8] or the cargo be improperly stowed.[9] The fact that the ship subsequently becomes unseaworthy is not a breach of that condition. If the voyage is divided into stages the condition as to seaworthiness need be satisfied only as to the stage on which the ship is entering.[10]

If the ship is unseaworthy, the shipowner is liable for any loss or damage caused thereby and is not protected by any contractual provision;[11] nor is it relevant that there are other co-operating causes of loss for which the shipowner is not to blame.[12] It is

---

[1] *The Helene* (1866) L.R. 1 P.C. 231; *Moes, Moliere and Tromp* v. *Leith, etc. Shipping Co.* (1867) 5 M. 988; *Horsley* v. *Baxter* (1893) 20 R. 333.

[2] *Wills* v. *Burrell* (1894) 21 R. 527.

[3] *Merrow & Fell* v. *Hutchison & Brown* (1873) 10 S.L.R. 338; *Royal Exchange Shipping Co.* v. *Dixon* (1886) 12 App. Cas. 11.

[4] *Burton* v. *English* (1883) 12 Q.B.D. 218.

[5] *Steel* v. *State Line S.S. Co.* (1877) 4 R. (H.L.) 103; *Gilroy* v. *Price* (1892) 20 R. (H.L.) 1; *McFadden* v. *Blue Star Line* [1905] 1 K.B. 697; *Nelson Line* v. *Nelson* [1908] A.C. 16.

[6] *Hedley* v. *Pinkney* [1894] A.C. 222.

[7] *Cohn* v. *Davidson* (1877) 2 Q.B.D. 455; *Seville Sulphur Co.* v. *Colvils, Lowden & Co.* (1888) 15 R. 616; *Cunningham* v. *Colvils, Lowden & Co.* (1888) 16 R. 295; *Northumbrian S.S. Co.* v. *Timm* [1939] A.C. 397.

[8] *Steel, supra.*   [9] *Kopitoff* v. *Wilson* (1876) 1 Q.B.D. 377.

[10] *Cunningham* v. *Colvils, Lowden & Co.* (1888) 16 R. 295; *The Vortigern* [1899] P. 140; *Reed* v. *Page, Son & East* [1927] 1 K.B. 743.

[11] *Steel* v. *State Line S.S. Co.* (1877) 4 R. (H.L.) 103; *The Glenfruin* (1885) 10 P.D. 103; *Gilroy* v. *Price* (1893) 20 R. (H.L.) 1; *The Vortigern* [1899] P. 140.

[12] *Smith Hogg & Co.* v. *Black Sea and Baltic Ins. Co.* [1940] A.C. 997; *A/B Karlshamns Oljefabriker* v. *Monarch S.S. Co.*, 1949 S.C. (H.L.) 1.

competent for the shipowner in cases regulated by common law to qualify or exclude the implied condition, but this can only be done by clear language.[1]

Once loaded, the master should obtain clearance and commence the voyage without delay. Liability for delay is on the shipowner. Thereafter the master, unless he has adequate excuse, must proceed without delay to the port of discharge.[2] The ship should take the most direct, safe, course to her destination.[3] At common law deviation to avoid danger[4] or to save life is justifiable, but not to save property only.[5] The charter-party may give liberty to deviate, such as to call at any ports.[6] An unwarranted deviation ends the contract, unless the shipper waives it.[7] If the ship becomes unseaworthy during the voyage the master must make necessary repairs,[8] failing which he is negligent and the shipowner is not protected unless by express provision in the contract.

Preservation of cargo

The master must on the shipowner's behalf take reasonable care of the cargo, to preserve it from damage or loss. The shipowner cannot rely on a contractual exception covering the actual cause of the loss or damage if the loss or damage were attributable to the master's failure to take proper care,[9] but may if the master took all reasonable precautions possible in the circumstances.[10] The master must also take reasonable steps to prevent deterioration or destruction through accidents.[11]

Master's authority in case of necessity

The master has implied authority in case of emergency to deal with the cargo on the owner's behalf, to jettison it,[12] have it made

---

[1] *The Laertes* (1887) 12 P.D. 187; *The Northumbria* [1906] P. 292.

[2] *Reardon Smith Line* v. *Black Sea and Baltic Ins. Co.* [1939] A.C. 562.

[3] *Reardon Smith Line, supra.*

[4] *The Teutonia* (1872) L.R. 4 P.C. 171; *The San Roman* (1872) L.R. 5 P.C. 301.

[5] *Scaramanga* v. *Stamp* (1880) 5 C.P.D. 295.

[6] *Leduc* v. *Ward* (1888) 20 Q.B.D. 475; *Glyn* v. *Margetson* [1893] A.C. 351; *Stag Line* v. *Foscolo Mango* [1932] A.C. 328.

[7] *Thorley* v. *Orchis S.S. Co.* [1907] 1 K.B. 660; *Morrison* v. *Shaw Savill* [1916] 2 K.B. 783.

[8] *The Rona* (1884) 5 Asp. M.L.C. 259; *Kish* v. *Taylor* [1912] A.C. 604.

[9] *The Helene* (1866) L.R. 1 P.C. 231; *Ministry of Food* v. *Lamport and Holt Line* [1952] 2 Lloyd's Rep. 371.

[10] *Moes, Moliere and Tromp* v. *Leith, etc. Shipping Co.* (1867) 5 M. 988; *Craig & Rose* v. *Delargy* (1879) 6 R. 1269; *Williams* v. *Dobbie* (1884) 11 R. 982; *Horsley* v. *Baxter Bros.* (1893) 20 R. 333: *The Glendarroch* [1894] P. 226.

[11] *Notara* v. *Henderson* (1872) L.R. 7 Q.B. 225; *Adam* v. *Morris* (1890) 18 R. 153.

[12] *Strang, Steel & Co.* v. *Scott* (1889) 14 App. Cas. 601.

fit to be carried further,[1] warehouse it,[2] or sell it.[3] To entitle him to do so, it must be reasonably necessary in the circumstances for him so to act, what he does must be reasonable and proper, and it must be impossible to communicate with the owner and obtain his instructions.[4] The master has no implied authority where it is possible to communicate with the cargo-owner.[5] If he exercises implied authority rightly, he is entitled to charge the owner with expenses reasonably incurred in so doing.[6] He may also hypothecate the cargo at an intermediate port to raise money to complete the voyage, or to forward the goods to their destination, if that is reasonably necessary in the interest of the cargo as well as of the ship, if he cannot procure funds in any other way, and he has been unable to communicate with the cargo-owner.[7]

Unloading at the destination

If a port is named the shipowner is under an absolute obligation to reach it and deliver there; if no port is named the charterer must nominate a safe port,[8] failing which the shipowner will perform his contract by delivering at the nearest safe port.[9] The obligation is frequently qualified by 'or so near thereto as she may safely get' which excuses failure to enter the port if this is prevented by a permanent obstacle.[10] He must not direct the ship to a place in the port where discharge is impracticable.[11] If the charterer nominates an unsafe port he is liable for damage sustained by the ship if she goes there.[12] The consignee must use

---

[1] *Tronson* v. *Dent* (1853) 8 Moo. P.C. 419; *Notara, supra*; *Acatos* v. *Burns* (1878) 3 Ex. D. 282.

[2] *Tronson, supra*.

[3] *Tronson, supra*; *Acatos, supra*; *Atlantic, infra*.

[4] *Atlantic Mutual Ins. Co.* v. *Huth* (1880) 16 Ch. D. 474; *Gemmill* v. *Somerville* (1905) 12 S.L.T. 674.

[5] *Garriock* v. *Walker* (1873) 1 R. 100; *Dymond* v. *Scott* (1877) 5 R. 196.

[6] *The Argos* (1873) L.R. 5 P.C. 134; *Garriock, supra*.

[7] *The Gratitudine* (1801) 3 Ch. Rob. 240; *The Onward* (1873) L.R. 4 A. & E. 38.

[8] i.e. a port to which the vessel can get laden, and at which she can lie and discharge, always afloat: *Hall Bros.* v. *Paull* (1914–15) All E.R. Rep. 234; cf. *Torkildsen* v. *Park, Dobson*, 1916, 2 S.L.T. 312; *Limerick S.S. Co.* v. *Stott* [1921] 2 K.B. 613; *Axel Brostrom* v. *Dreyfus* (1932) 38 Com. Cas. 79; *Grace* v. *General S.N. Co.* [1950] 1 All E.R. 201.

[9] *The Alhambra* (1881) 6 P.D. 68.

[10] *Metcalfe* v. *Britannia Ironworks* (1877) 2 Q.B.D. 423; *Dahl* v. *Nelson* (1881) 6 App. Cas. 38; *Knutsford* v. *Tillmanns* [1908] A.C. 406; *The Varing* [1931] P. 79. But see *Hillstrom* v. *Gibson* (1870) 8 M. 463; *La Cour* v. *Donaldson* (1874) 1 R. 912; *Dickinson* v. *Martin* (1874) 1 R. 1185; *Bremner* v. *Burrell* (1877) 4 R. 934.

[11] *Thorsen* v. *McDowall* (1892) 19 R. 743.

[12] *Compânia Naviera Maropan* v. *Bowaters* [1955] 2 Q.B. 68; *Reardon Smith Line* v. *Australian Wheat Board* [1956] A.C. 266; *Leeds Shipping Co.* v. *Société Française Bunge* [1958] 2 Lloyd's Rep. 127.

due diligence to discover when the ship arrives with the cargo,[1] and the time for unloading begins to run as soon as the ship is ready to unload.[2]

The person entitled to claim delivery is the holder of the bill of lading, whether as named consignee or as assignee.[3] If the shipowner delivers to another person he is liable to the true owner for the value of the cargo.[4] He is not bound to deliver unless the bill of lading is produced,[5] and any liens satisfied. Delivery to a dock authority or warehouse is not sufficient, unless contract or custom permit this.[6]

It is the duty of the shipowner to have the cargo unloaded, and of the consignee to accept delivery thereof.[7] The consignee must accordingly provide lighters, trucks, stowage facilities and relative labour, as required to receive and remove the cargo,[8] but these duties may be modified by contract or the custom of the port.[9] The general rule is that delivery is complete when each piece of cargo is passed over the ship's rail into the consignee's hands.[10] If there is a discrepancy between the quantity stated in the bill of lading and that delivered the onus of proving that the quantity stated in the bill was not loaded lies on the shipowner.[11]

The ship must not be kept waiting

The consignee must take delivery within the period fixed by the contract or ascertainable therefrom[12] or, at all events, a

---

[1] *Houlder* v. *General S.N. Co.* (1862) 3 F. & F. 170.

[2] *Houlder, supra.*

[3] *Glyn Mills & Co.* v. *E. & W. India Dock Co.* (1882) 7 App. Cas. 591; *J. & J. Cunningham* v. *Guthrie* (1888) 26 S.L.R. 208.

[4] *Strathlorne S.S. Co.* v. *Weir* (1934) 40 Com. Cas. 168.

[5] *The Stettin* (1889) 14 P.D. 142.

[6] *Borrowman, Phillips & Co.* v. *Wilson* (1891) 7 T.L.R. 416; *Grange* v. *Taylor* (1904) 9 Asp. M.L.C. 559.

[7] *The Clan Macdonald* (1883) 8 P.D. 178.

[8] *Dahl* v. *Nelson, Donkin & Co.* (1881) 6 App. Cas. 38; *Budgett* v. *Binnington* [1891] 1 Q.B. 35; *Crown Steamship Co.* v. *Leitch,* 1908 S.C. 506.

[9] *Wylie* v. *Harrison* (1885) 13 R. 92; *Holman* v. *Harrison* (1887) 29 S.L.R. 47; *Thorsen* v. *McDowall & Neilson* (1892) 19 R. 743; *Ballantyne* v. *Paton and Hendry,* 1912 S.C. 246; *Strathlorne S.S. Co.* v. *Baird,* 1916 S.C. (H.L.) 134; see also *Clacevich* v. *Hutcheson* (1887) 15 R. 11; *Hogarth* v. *Leith Cotton Seed Oil Co.,* 1909 S.C. 955; *Cazalet* v. *Morris,* 1916 S.C. 952.

[10] *British Shipowners Co.* v. *Grimond* (1876) 3 R. 968; *Knight Steamship Co.* v. *Fleming, Douglas & Co.* (1898) 25 R. 1070; see also *Avon Steamship Co.* v. *Leask* (1890) 18 R. 280.

[11] *Horsley* v. *Grimond* (1894) 21 R. 410; *Smith* v. *Bedouin S.N. Co.* (1895) 23 R. (H.L.) 1; *Langlands* v. *McMaster,* 1907 S.C. 1090; *Tyzack & Branfoot Steamship Co.* v. *Sandeman,* 1913 S.C. (H.L.) 84; *D/S Svenborg* v. *Love & Stewart,* 1916 S.C. (H.L.) 187; *Spalding & Valentine* v. *B.I.S.N. Co.,* 1927 S.C. 103. Contrast *Craig Line S.S. Co.* v. *N.B. Storage Co.,* 1921 S.C. 114.

[12] *Postlethwaite* v. *Freeland* (1880) 5 App. Cas. 599.

reasonable time;[1] this duty is absolute.[2] If he fails to do so, the shipowner may land and warehouse the cargo,[3] and if delay exceeds the fixed period or a reasonable period he may claim demurrage or damages for detention.[4] Delay is excusable only if it is attributable to the fault of the shipowner or of persons for whom he is responsible,[5] or is covered by an exception in the contract.[6] The shipowner may take steps which minimize the delay in discharging and recover from the charterers outlays thereon to the extent of the amount of demurrage thereby saved.[7]

Where cargo not claimed

If the consignee does not claim the cargo, the master may be entitled by contract or custom of the port[8] to land and warehouse the cargo at the consignee's risk and expense;[9] in any case he may land the cargo after a reasonable time.[10] If he does so, his liability, at common law, ceases as carrier but commences as custodier; if he lands cargo into a third party's warehouse he loses his lien, save under statute,[11] but may confer a lien on the warehouseman.[12]

Freight

Where the ship is under charter, the liability to pay the freight reserved by the charter-party is on the charterer in the first

[1] *Hick* v. *Raymond and Reid* [1893] A.C. 22.

[2] *Budgett* v. *Binnington* [1891] 1 Q.B. 35; *Houlder* v. *Weir* [1905] 2 K.B. 267; cf. *Hansen* v. *Donaldson* (1874) 1 R. 1066.

[3] *Hick, supra*; see also M.S.A., 1894, S. 493–501.

[4] e.g. *Dall Orso* v. *Mason* (1876) 3 R. 419; *Stephens, Mawson & Goss* v. *Macleod* (1891) 19 R. 38.

[5] *Hansen* v. *Donaldson* (1874) 1 R. 1066; *Budgett* v. *Binnington* [1891] 1 Q.B. 35; *Thorsen* v. *McDowall & Neilson* (1892) 19 R. 743; *Readhead* v. *Roesler*, 1914, 1 S.L.T. 281; *Carlberg* v. *Wemyss Coal Co.*, 1915 S.C. 616; *Rickinson* v. *S.C.W.S.*, 1918 S.C. 440.

[6] e.g. Strike: *Kruuse* v. *Drynan* (1891) 18 R. 1110; *Granite City S.S. Co.* v. *Ireland* (1891) 19 R. 124; *Letricheux & David* v. *Dunlop* (1891) 19 R. 209; *Gardiner* v. *Macfarlane, McCrindell & Co.* (1893) 20 R. 414; *Lilly* v. *Stevenson* (1895) 22 R. 278; *Mein* v. *Ottman* (1903) 6 F. 276; *Turnbull, Scott & Co.* v. *Cruickshank* (1904) 7 F. 265; *Elswick S.S. Co.* v. *Montaldi* [1907] 1 K.B. 626; *Horsley Line Ltd.* v. *Roechling Bros.*, 1908 S.C. 866; *Glasgow Navigation Co.* v. *Iron Ore Co.*, 1909 S.C. 1414; *Abchurch Steamship Co.* v. *Stinnes*, 1911 S.C. 1010; *Arden S.S. Co.* v. *Mathwin*, 1912 S.C. 211; *Moor Line* v. *Distillers Co.*, 1912 S.C. 514; *Schele* v. *Lumsden*, 1916 S.C. 709; *A/S Hansa* v. *Alexander*, 1919 S.C. (H.L.) 122; cf. *Westoll* v. *Lindsay*, 1916 S.C. 782. Such an exception may be excluded by charterers' failure to take reasonable measures to take delivery timeously: *D/S Danmark* v. *Poulsen*, 1913 S.C. 1043.

[7] *Cazelet* v. *Morris*, 1916 S.C. 952.

[8] *Aste, Son and Kercheval* v. *Stumore, Weston & Co.* (1884) Cab. & El. 319; *Dennis* v. *Cork S.S. Co.* [1913] 2 K.B. 393.

[9] *Hick* v. *Raymond & Reid* [1893] A.C. 22.

[10] *Howard* v. *Shepherd* (1850) 9 C.B. 297; cf. *Carlberg* v. *Wemyss Coal Co.*, 1915 S.C. 616.

[11] M.S.A. 1894, Ss. 492–501.

[12] *Mors-le-Blanch* v. *Wilson* (1873) L.R. 8 C.P. 227.

instance. If there is a cesser clause his liability should cease when the prescribed cargo has been shipped, but he is not necessarily discharged from all liability.[1] An undertaking to pay freight is implied from loading goods for carriage[2] under a bill of lading and is usually expressed. The person primarily liable is the shipper,[3] independently of ownership of the goods, and is liable even if he has transferred ownership before freight is payable.[4] The consignee is not, as such, liable for freight,[5] but if holder of a bill of lading as consignee or endorsee he is bound by statute to pay freight if the property in the goods has passed to him,[6] but if not, he is not liable for freight merely by virtue of the endorsement. A consignor who stops goods *in transitu* is liable for freight on re-delivery of the goods to him, or for damages in lieu.[7]

Prima facie the freight is payable to the shipowner; if the goods have been carried under a bill of lading the holder thereof should pay the shipowner if the contract was with him rather than with a charterer;[8] if the charter were by demise the charterer is entitled to the freight.[9] As between shipowner and charterer their rights depend on the charter-party.[10]

When freight payable

By legal implication freight is due on delivery[11] and delivery need not be made till freight is paid.[12] The shipowner is accordingly not entitled to demand payment of freight unless he is able to deliver the goods to the consignee at their destination.[13] If the shipowner fails to carry to the destination, as in cases of loss, seizures, capture or sale at an intermediate port,[14] or to deliver,[15]

---

[1] *Jenneson, Taylor & Co.* v. *Secy. of State for India* [1916] 2 K.B. 702.

[2] *Fox* v. *Nott* (1861) 6 H. & N. 630.

[3] *Fox, supra*; *Sewell* v. *Burdick* (1884) 10 App. Cas. 74.

[4] *Fox, supra*.

[5] *Sanders* v. *Vanzeller* (1843) 4 Q.B. 260.

[6] Bills of Lading Act, 1855, S. 1; *Sewell, supra*.

[7] *Booth S.S. Co.* v. *Cargo Fleet Iron Co.* [1916] 2 K.B. 570.

[8] *Mitchell* v. *Burn* (1874) 1 R. 900; *Wastwater S.S. Co.* v. *Neale* (1902) 9 Asp. M.L.C. 282.

[9] *Marquand* v. *Banner* (1856) 6 E. & B. 232; *Wehner* v. *Dene S.S. Co.* [1905] 2 K.B. 92.

[10] *Broadhead* v. *Yule* (1871) 9 M. 921.

[11] *Allison* v. *Bristol Marine Ins. Co.* (1876) 1 App. Cas. 209; *London Tpt. Co.* v. *Trechmann Bros.* [1904] 1 K.B. 635.

[12] *Paynter* v. *James* (1867) L.R. 2 C.P. 348; *The Energie* (1875) L.R. 6 P.C. 306.

[13] *Dakin* v. *Oxley* (1864) 15 C.B. (N.S.) 646; *St. Enoch Shipping Co.* v. *Phosphate Mining Co.* [1916] 2 K.B. 624.

[14] *Liddard* v. *Lopes* (1809) 10 East 526; *Hill* v. *Wilson* (1879) 4 C.P.D. 329; cf. *Dickson* v. *Buchanan* (1876) 13 S.L.R. 401.

[15] *Duthie* v. *Hilton* (1868) L.R. 4 C.P. 138; *Sandeman* v. *Tyzack and Branfoot S.S. Co.* [1913] A.C. 680.

he cannot, unless by express stipulation, recover any freight;[1] loss by an excepted peril is an excuse for non-delivery but gives no claim for freight;[2] if only part reach the destination freight can be claimed only for the part.[3]

Freight may be made payable in whole or in part in advance, usually on the signing of bills of lading or a stated period after sailing.[4] Advance freight may be retained, or payment exacted, even if the goods are lost by excepted perils during the voyage.[5] If the voyage cannot be accomplished the amount paid is recoverable.[6]

If the goods are delivered to the consignee short of the contractual destination the shipowner is entitled to freight *pro rata itineris* if there is an express or implied contract to that effect,[7] but not merely because the consignee has taken delivery at an intermediate port where the master insisted on leaving them,[8] nor because he has accepted the proceeds of sale where the master in the exercise of his discretion has sold the cargo.[9]

Amount payable

The amount payable, unless the contract provides for lump sum freight,[10] depends on the quantity delivered, without deduction for the damaged condition of any,[11] so long as the goods are still deliverable *in specie*.[12] The contract usually provides the rate per unit carried, failing which the rate is the ordinary rate ruling at the time the goods were loaded.[13] The weight or measurement of goods for the purposes of freight is, failing express provision, the lesser of the quantities loaded and that delivered.[14] If the contract is for lump freight[10] full freight is payable if any of the

[1] *The Cito* (1881) 7 P.D. 5; *Metcalfe v. Britannia Ironworks Co.* (1877) 2 Q.B.D. 423; *A/S Heimdal v. Noble*, 1907 S.C. 249.

[2] *Hunter v. Prinsep* (1808) 10 East 378.

[3] *Spaight v. Farnworth* (1880) 5 Q.B.D. 115; *Pacific S.N. Co. v. Thomson, Aikman & Co.*, 1920 S.C. (H.L.) 159.

[4] *Oriental S.S. Co. v. Tylor* [1893] 2 Q.B. 518.

[5] *Carr v. Wallachian Petroleum Co.* (1867) L.R. 2 C.P. 468; *Leitch v. Wilson* (1868) 7 M. 150; *Watson v. Shankland* (1873) 11 M. (H.L.) 51.

[6] *Watson v. Shankland, supra.*

[7] *St. Enoch Shipping Co., supra*; see also *Christy v. Row* (1808) 1 Taunt. 300.

[8] *Metcalfe, supra.*   [9] *Hunter, supra.*

[10] *Immanuel v. Denholm* (1887) 15 R. 152; *Thomas v. Harrowing S.S. Co.* [1915] A.C. 58; see also *Wills v. Burrell* (1894) 21 R. 527.

[11] But a counterclaim will lie for the damage: *The Norway* (1865) 3 Moo. P.C. (N.S.) 245.

[12] *Dakin v. Oxley* (1864) 15 C.B. (N.S.) 646; *Asfar v. Blundell* [1896] 1 Q.B. 123.

[13] *Keith v. Burrows* (1877) 2 App. Cas. 636.

[14] *Beynon v. Kenneth* (1881) 8 R. 594; *D/S Svendborg v. Love and Stewart*, 1916 S.C. (H.L.) 187; *Pacific S.N. Co. v. Thomson, Aikman & Co.*, 1920 S.C. (H.L.) 159; cf. *New Line S.S. Co. v. Bryson*, 1910 S.C. 409.

goods are delivered, and if it provides for freight 'lost or not lost' freight is payable even if none of the goods are delivered.[1] Where the goods are delivered short of the due destination, the shipowner is not entitled to freight in proportion to the distance carried, but by contract freight *pro rata itineris* may be payable;[2] such a contract is not inferred from the consignee's acceptance of delivery.[3] When dead freight is payable for cargo not furnished it is *prima facie* at the same rate as if cargo had been furnished.[4]

Claim of lien

The shipowner may withhold delivery by virtue of a claim of lien, which exists at common law for freight,[5] for general average contributions[6] and expenses incurred in the interests of the cargo at a port of refuge,[7] and may exist by express contract, for such claims as for dead freight, demurrage,[8] damages for detention[9] or other charges. The lien is lost if the shipowner lands and warehouses the goods, unless in his own warehouse,[10] or otherwise yields possession of the goods. It is discharged by payment of the sum due,[11] or tender thereof, or under statute, where imported goods are warehoused.[12]

Damages for non-delivery or delayed delivery

The shipowner is liable in damages for breach of contract by failure to arrive within the time contemplated by the contract[13] or failure to deliver the whole or part of the goods,[14] or delivery of the goods damaged by some cause for which he is responsible.[15]

[1] *Pacific S.N. Co.* v. *Thomson, Aikman & Co.*, 1920 S.C. (H.L.) 159.

[2] *St. Enoch Shipping Co.* v. *Phosphate Mining Co.* [1916] 2 K.B. 624; cf. *Hunter* v. *Prinsep* (1808) 10 East 378; *Vlierbloom* v. *Chapman* (1844) 13 M. & W. 230.

[3] *Metcalfe* v. *Britannia Ironworks Co.* (1877) 2 Q.B.D. 423.

[4] *McLean* v. *Fleming* (1891) 9 M. (H.L.) 38; *Henderson* v. *Turnbull*, 1909 S.C. 510.

[5] *Black* v. *Rose* (1864) 2 Moo. P.C. (N.S.) 277; *Youle* v. *Cochran* (1868) 6 M. 427; *Lamb* v. *Laselack, Alsen & Co.* (1882) 9 R. 482; there is no lien if freight is payable before delivery: *Nelson* v. *Protection of Property Assocn.* (1874) 43 L.J. C.P. 218; or after delivery: *Thorsen* v. *McDowall and Neilson* (1892) 19 R. 743; or payable 'lost or not lost': *Nelson, supra.*

[6] *Crooks* v. *Allan* (1879) 5 Q.B.D. 38; *Huth* v. *Lamport* (1886) 16 Q.B.D. 735.

[7] *Hingston* v. *Wendt* (1876) 1 Q.B.D. 367.

[8] *Birley* v. *Gladstone* (1814) 3 M. & S. 205.

[9] *Dunlop* v. *Balfour, Williamson & Co.* [1892] 1 Q.B. 507.

[10] *Mors-le-Blanch* v. *Wilson* (1873) L.R. 8 C.P. 227.

[11] *The Energie* (1875) L.R. 6 P.C. 306.   [12] M.S.A. 1894, Ss. 495–6.

[13] *Dunn* v. *Bucknall Bros.* [1902] 2 K.B. 614; *The Ardennes (Cargo Owners)* v. *The Ardennes (Owners)* [1951] 1 K.B. 55; *Koufos* v. *Czarnikow* [1969] 1 A.C. 350.

[14] *Rodocanach* v. *Milburn* (1886) 18 Q.B.D. 67; *Watts, Watts & Co.* v. *Mitsui* [1917] A.C. 227. As to delivery short of destination see *A/B Karlshamns Ohjefabriker* v. *Monarch S.S. Co.*, 1949 S.C. (H.L.) 1.

[15] *Martineaus* v. *R.M.S.P. Co.* (1912) 12 Asp. M.L.C. 190.

Exclusion or limitation of liability

A shipowner or other person to whom the exemption applies is not liable to make good any loss or damage, happening without his actual fault or privity, where goods, merchandise or other things on board the ship are lost or damaged by fire on board,[1] nor where any gold, silver, diamonds, watches, jewels or precious stones taken on board are lost or damaged by any robbery, embezzlement, making away with or secreting thereof, provided that the true nature and value of the articles was not declared to the owner or master at the time of shipment in the bills of lading or otherwise in writing.[2] In cases to which the Carriage of Goods by Sea Act, 1924, applies dangerous goods shipped without the carrier's consent may be landed at any place, destroyed or rendered innocuous without compensation.[3]

The owners and other persons to whom the exemption applies may have their liability to pay damages limited where, without their actual fault or privity, any damage or loss is caused to any goods, merchandise or other things whatsoever on board the ship,[4] or any loss or damage is caused to any other property or any rights are infringed through the act or omission of any person, on board the ship or not, in the navigation or management of the ship or in the loading, carriage or disembarkation of its passengers or through any other act or omission of any person on board the ship.[5] The occurrence must have happened without the actual fault or privity of the owner or person claiming exclusion or limitation of liability, i.e. without fault personal to the owner or directors of the owning company.[6]

Liability is limited to 1000 gold francs[7] per ton of the ship's tonnage in respect of loss, damage or infringement, whether or not accompanied by loss of life or personal injury.[8] Where claims exceeding the limited amount are anticipated, a petition is

---

[1] M.S.A., 1894, S. 502; M.S. (Liability of Shipowners and Others) Act, 1958, S. 3.

[2] M.S.A., 1894, S. 502.

[3] 1924 Act, Sched. Art. IV, 6.

[4] Including passengers' luggage: *The Stella* [1900] P. 161.

[5] M.S.A. 1894, S. 503; M.S. (Liability of Shipowners and Others) Act, 1958, S. 2; *Clifton Steam Trawlers* v. *MacIver*, 1953 S.L.T. 230; *Hamilton* v. *B.T.C.*, 1957 S.C. 300.

[6] e.g. *Kidston* v. *McArthur* (1878) 5 R. 936; *Lennard's Carrying Co.* v. *Asiatic Petroleum Co.* [1915] A.C. 705; *Standard Oil Co. of N.Y.* v. *Clan Line*, 1924 S.C. (H.L.) 1; *The Thames* [1940] P. 143; *Beauchamp* v. *Turrell* [1952] 2 Q.B. 207; *The Truculent* [1952] P. 1; *The Norman* [1960] 1 Lloyd's Rep. 1.

[7] £27.6396: S.I. 1974, No. 536.

[8] 1894 Act, S. 503; 1958 Act, Ss. 1, 2.

brought to have the limit declared.[1] Claims settled out of court are taken into account in distributing the limited fund.[2] In cases to which the Carriage of Goods by Sea Act, 1924, applies the limit is £100 per package or unit unless the nature and value of the goods were declared before shipment and inserted in the bill of lading.[3]

CARRIAGE OF PASSENGERS BY SEA

The relations between a shipowner, or a charterer who has control of the ship and is entitled to carry passengers,[4] and the passengers depends on the contract between them. The owner may hold himself out as a common carrier of passengers,[5] but the owner is not an insurer and bound only to take all due care to carry the passenger in safety.[6] This implies a duty to provide a fit and seaworthy ship, as far as reasonable skill and care can render it, and liability for discoverable but not for latent defects.[7] The owner must also make reasonable provision for the accommodation, food and comfort of the passengers,[8] reasonable facilities for carriage of their luggage,[9] and take reasonable care for their safety during the voyage.[10] The owner's liability for injuries to passengers depends on negligence,[11] and includes liability to passengers in another ship injured by the negligent management of his ship.[12]

---

[1] *Flensburg S.S. Co.* v. *Seligmann* (1871) 9 M. 1011; *Miller* v. *Powell* (1875) 2 R. 976; *Van Eijck & Zoon* v. *Somerville* (1906) 8 F. (H.L.) 22; *Kennedy* v. *Clyde Shipping Co.*, 1908 S.C. 895.

See also *Leadbetter* v. *Dublin and Glasgow S.P. Co.*, 1907 S.C. 538; *Hay* v. *Jackson*, 1911 S.C. 876.   [2] *Rankine* v. *Raschen* (1877) 4 R. 225.

[3] 1924 Act, Sched. Art. IV, 5. Sum raised to £200 by parties to British Maritime Law Assocn. Agreement, 1950.

[4] An owner may carry passengers, notwithstanding a charter to carry goods, if he can do so consistently with the charter and is not prohibited, expressly or impliedly, from doing so: *Sociedad Louis Dreyfus* v. *National Steamship Co.* [1935] 2 K.B. 313.

[5] *Henderson* v. *Stevenson* (1875) 2 R. (H.L.) 71; *Clarke* v. *West Ham Corpn.* [1909] 2 K.B. 858.

[6] cf. *Lyon* v. *Lamb* (1838) 16 S. 1188; *Readhead* v. *Midland Ry.* (1869) L.R. 4 Q.B. 379.

[7] Occupier's Liability (Sc.) Act, 1960, S. 1(3) and 2; cf. *Taylor* v. *P. & O. S.N. Co.* (1869) 21 L.T. 442.

[8] *Young* v. *Fewson* (1837) 8 C. & P. 55; *Andrews* v. *Little* (1887) 3 T.L.R. 544.

[9] *Upperton* v. *Union Castle Mail S.S. Co.* (1903) 19 T.L.R. 687.

[10] The Merchant Shipping Acts make detailed provisions as to safety and health, life-saving appliances, etc.

[11] Occupier's Liability (Sc.) Act, 1960, Ss. 1(3) and 2; cf. *Monaghan* v. *Buchanan* (1886) 13 R. 860.

[12] cf. *MacLean* v. *Clan Line*, 1925 S.C. 256; *Reavis* v. *Clan Line*, 1925 S.C. 725; *Lewis* v. *Laird Line*, 1925 S.L.T. 316; *McNamara* v. *Laird Line* (1925) 1948 S.C. 265. Passengers are not so identified with their ship as to be barred by its fault: *The Bernina* (1888) 13 App. Cas. 1.

Conditions in the contract of carriage, if validly imported into the contract,[1] may exempt the shipowner in whole or in part from liability for injury, loss or damage to the passenger[2] or his luggage,[3] but such provisions do not necessarily protect the shipowner's agents or servants.[4] All passenger steamers must be surveyed and have in force a certificate.[5]

Fare

The fare must be paid at the customary time. The master has a lien on the passenger's luggage for unpaid passage money, but not on his person or clothes.

Master's disciplinary powers

The master of a home-trade passenger steamer may refuse to take on board a passenger misconducting himself or in such a state as to annoy or injure passengers, and may land such a person at any convenient place.[6] He may also detain without warrant and take before a magistrate a person whose name and address are unknown who commits any of various offences in relation to the ship.[7] He has also at common law disciplinary powers to ensure the safe and proper conduct of the vessel.[8]

Delay

In the absence of any contractual stipulation, a passenger cannot insist on a voyage commencing at the advertised or any other time, but he has a claim if the sailing is unreasonably delayed[9] or the voyage unduly prolonged and may recover damages for the natural consequences of unreasonable delay in arrival.[10]

---

[1] *Henderson* v. *Stevenson* (1875) 2 R. (H.L.) 71; *Richardson* v. *Rowntree* [1894] A.C. 217; *Grieve* v. *Turbine Steamers, Ltd.* (1903) 11 S.L.T. 379; *Williamson* v. *N. of S.S.N. Co.*, 1916 S.C. 554; *Hood* v. *Anchor Line*, 1918 S.C. (H.L.) 143.

[2] Including liability for death: *Haigh* v. *R.M.S.P. Co.* (1883) 5 Asp. M.L.C. 189; *Beaumont-Thomas* v. *Blue Star Line* [1939] 3 All E.R. 127.

[3] *infra.*

[4] *Adler* v. *Dickson* [1955] 1 Q.B. 158; it is otherwise in carriage of goods by sea: *Elder Dempster* v. *Paterson, Zochonis* [1924] A.C. 522.

[5] M.S.A., 1894, Ss. 271–284; cf. *Yeudall* v. *Sweeney*, 1922 J.C. 32; *Young* v. *Docherty*, 1929 J.C. 57; *Duncan* v. *Graham* [1951] 1 K.B. 68.

[6] M.S.A., 1894, S. 288.

[7] M.S.A., 1894, S. 287; cf. *Lundie* v. *MacBrayne* (1894) 21 R. 1085.

[8] *King* v. *Franklin* (1858) 1 F. & F. 360; *Aldworth* v. *Stewart* (1866) 4 F. & F. 957; *Noden* v. *Johnson* (1850) 16 Q.B. 218.

[9] *Yates* v. *Duff* (1832) 5 C. & P. 369; *Cranston* v. *Marshall* (1850) 5 Ex. 395; *Crane* v. *Tyne Shipping Co. Ltd.* (1897) 13 T.L.R. 172.

[10] *Cranston, supra*; *The Rhine* (1853) 7 L.T. 533; *Bright* v. *P. & O. S.N. Co.* (1897) 2 Com. Cas. 106.

Limitation of liability

By statute,[1] a shipowner or charterer may limit his liability in damages for loss of life or personal injury caused to any person carried in the ship,[2] or another ship, by the act or omission of any person in the navigation or management of the ship,[3] to 3100 gold francs[4] per ton of the ship's registered tonnage, if the loss or damage has occurred without his actual fault or privity.[5] Where there are claims, both for loss of life or injury and for loss of or damage to goods, the personal claims fall first on the fund of 2100 francs per ton and if this is inadequate they rank against the further 1000 francs per ton *pari passu* with claims for damage to goods.[6]

Passenger's luggage

A passenger's ticket normally permits him to bring a stated quantity of luggage[7] with him. If the ship is a common carrier, edictal liability exists, unless excluded, for luggage.[8] In other cases there is a duty to convey it with reasonable care.[9] Contractual conditions may limit or exclude liability for loss of luggage.[10]

[1] M.S.A. 1894, S. 503, amd. M.S. (Liability of Shipowners and Others) Act, 1958.
[2] Including members of the crew: *Innes* v. *Ross*, 1956 S.C. 468.
[3] *The Warkworth* (1884) 9 P.D. 145; *The Athelvictor* [1946] P. 42.
[4] £85.6823: S.I. 1967, No. 1725.
[5] cf. *supra*.
[6] *The Victoria* (1888) 13 P.D. 125.
[7] On what is luggage see *Jenkyns* v. *Southampton Royal Mail Co.* (1919) 24 Com. Cas. 143.
[8] *Upperton* v. *Union Castle S.S. Co.* (1903) 19 T.L.R. 687; *Jenkyns, supra.*
[9] cf. *Upperton, supra*. See also *Ogilvie, Crichton & Walker* v. *Taylor* (1828) 6 S. 691.
[10] *Wilton* v. *Atlantic Royal Mail Steam Co.* (1861) 10 C.B.N.S. 453; *P. & O.S.N. Co.* v. *Shand* (1865) 2 Mar. L.C. 244; *Taubman v. Pacific S.N. Co.* (1872) 1 Asp. M.L.C. 336; *Thompson* v. *R.M.S.P. Co.* (1875) 5 Asp. M.L.C. 190; *The Stella* [1900] P. 161.

CHAPTER 45

CONTRACT OF CARRIAGE
(3) CARRIAGE BY AIR

CARRIAGE BY AIR GENERALLY

SERVICES for the carriage of goods and passengers by air are provided by the national airways corporation, British Airways Board,[1] by other airlines licensed by the Civil Aviation Authority[2] and, in respect of international carriage also by some foreign airlines. Detailed statutory provisions govern airports, registration of aircraft, airworthiness and safety, radio requirements, traffic control and flight rules, the licensing of crews and aerial navigation.[3]

A carrier of goods by air might in theory be a common carrier but in practice air carriers are all private carriers. An aircraft may be chartered for a flight or flights, or for a time, and in either case may be a 'bare-hull charter' whereby the charterer becomes owner of the aircraft and the crew his servants, or a charter conferring the use of the aircraft's carrying-space for goods or passengers. In the former case the owner probably warrants impliedly that the aircraft let is as fit for the purpose of the charter as reasonable care and skill can make it,[4] and that any crew are reasonably skilful and competent. In the latter case the owner probably warrants impliedly that the aircraft is as fit for the purpose of charter as reasonable skill and care can make it, that the crew are qualified and reasonably skilful and competent, and that reasonable care and skill will be exercised in the carriage of the goods or passengers.[5] Normally, however, a person hires space for the carriage of cargo, or of himself and his baggage, on such conditions as the carrier offers.

Warsaw Convention

Almost all carriage by air,[6] other than in chartered aircraft, if international, is regulated by the international rules contained in

---

[1] See Air Corporations Act, 1967; Civil Aviation Act, 1971, Part III.

[2] Civil Aviation Act, 1971, Part II; see generally Shawcross and Beaumont on *Air Law*.

[3] Civil Aviation Act, 1949, and orders thereunder.

[4] cf. *Reed* v. *Dean* [1949] 1 K.B. 188; *Aslan* v. *Imperial Airways* (1933) 149 L.T. 276.

[5] cf. *Aslan, supra*; *Fosbroke-Hobbes* v. *Airwork, Ltd.* [1937] 1 All E.R. 108.

[6] The only exceptions seem to be gratuitous carriage not by an air transport undertaking, carriage on experimental routes or in exceptional circumstances, and carriage under an international postal convention.

the Warsaw Convention, 1929, as amended at the Hague, 1955, enacted as United Kingdom law by the Carriage by Air Act, formerly 1932, now 1961,[1] and if non-international, by similar rules applied to non-international carriage.[2] The Convention has the force of law in the U.K. in relation to any carriage by air to which it applies, irrespective of the nationality of the aircraft and despite any attempt to exclude its operation or substitute other rules.[3] It applies to all international carriage[4] of persons, baggage or cargo for reward and to gratuitous carriage by an air transport undertaking.[5] A convention supplementary thereto, for the unification of rules relating to international carriage by air performed by a person other than the contracting carrier also has the force of law in the United Kingdom.[6]

The provisions of the Convention have been applied with modifications to all carriage by air not covered by the Convention.[7] Any provision contained in a contract of carriage and all special agreements by which the parties purport to infringe the rules by deciding the law to be applied are null and void,[8] but contractual provisions not conflicting with the rules are competent.[9]

CARRIAGE OF GOODS BY AIR

International carriage[10]

The consignor must make out and the carrier accept an air consignment note in three parts, for the carrier, the consignee, and the consignor, as receipt for the goods.[11] It must state specified particulars.[12] The consignor is responsible for the correctness of the particulars, and for any damage suffered by the carrier or

[1] Text of the Convention is contained in the Schedule to the Act. Some countries have not acceded to the Hague Protocol, and in the case of a journey to such a country the unamended Warsaw Convention applies.

[2] Carriage by Air Acts (Application of Provisions) Order, 1967 (S.I. 1967, No. 480).

[3] 1961 Act, S. 1; *Grein* v. *Imperial Airways* [1937] 1 K.B. 50; *Rotterdamsche Bank N.V.* v. *B.O.A.C.* [1953] 1 All E.R. 675.

[4] Defined, 1961 Act, Sched. I, art. 1(2).   [5] 1961 Act, Sched. I, art. 1(1).

[6] Carriage by Air (Supplementary Provisions) Act, 1962.

[7] Carriage by Air Acts (Application of Provisions) Order, 1967 (S.I. 1967, No. 480).

[8] 1967 Order, Sched. 3, art. 32.

[9] 1967 Order, Sched. 3, art. 33. B.E.A., B.O.A.C. and many other airlines have adopted the General Conditions of Carriage for Passengers, Baggage and Cargo settled by the International Air Traffic Association.

[10] Defined: 1961 Act, Sched. I, art. 1; see also arts. 2(1) and 34.

[11] 1961 Act, Sched. I, arts. 5–6.

[12] Ibid., art. 8; *Westminster Bank* v. *Imperial Airways* [1936] 2 All E.R. 890; see also *Philippson* v. *Imperial Airways* [1939] A.C. 332; *Montagu* v. *Swiss Air Transport* [1966] 1 All E.R. 814.

another person by reason of the incorrectness of the particulars.[1] If the carrier accepts goods without an air consignment note, or if it does not contain commercially useful particulars the carrier cannot rely on the Convention to exclude or limit his liability.[2] It is *prima facie* evidence of the conclusion of the contract, the receipt of the goods, their weight and other particulars.[3] The consignor may dispose of the goods, by withdrawing them, stopping them in transit at any landing, requiring them to be delivered to someone other than the consignee or returned to the consignor, but he must not do so so as to prejudice the carrier and must repay expenses caused thereby.[4]

The consignee is entitled, on receiving notice of their arrival, to require the carrier to hand over the air consignment note and deliver the goods on payment of any charges due.[5] If the carrier admits loss of the goods, or if they have not arrived seven days after they ought to have arrived the consignee is entitled to put into force against the carrier the rights which flow from the contract of carriage.[6] Consignor and consignee can respectively enforce all the rights given them by articles 12 and 13, each in his own name, provided he carries out the obligations imposed by the contract.[6]

The carrier is liable for damage occasioned by delay in the carriage of baggage or cargo,[7] or for destruction or loss of or damage to baggage or cargo, if the occurrence which caused the damage so sustained took place during the carriage by air.[8] Receipt of goods without complaint is *prima facie* evidence that they have been delivered in good condition and in accordance with the document of carriage.[9]

Contracting-out of the convention is prohibited,[10] but arbitration clauses are permitted, subject to the Convention, if to take place within one of the jurisdictions in which action must be brought. The carrier is not prevented from making regulations which do not conflict with the Convention.[11]

Exclusion and limitation of liability

The carrier may escape from his liabilities under the Convention by proving that he and his servants and agents have taken all necessary measures to avoid the damage or that it was impossible

---

[1] Ibid., art. 10; see also art. 16.
[2] Ibid., art. 9; *Corocraft Ltd.* v. *Pan American Airways* [1969] 1 All E.R. 82.
[3] Ibid., art. 11.   [4] Ibid., art. 12   [5] Ibid., art. 13.   [6] Ibid., art. 14.
[7] Ibid., art. 19: as to damages see *Romulus Films* v. *Dempster* [1952] 2 Lloyd's Rep. 535.
[8] Ibid., art. 18.   [9] Ibid., art. 26.   [10] Ibid., art. 32.   [11] Ibid., art. 33.

for him or them to take such measures.[1] The contributory negligence of the injured person may exonerate the carrier in whole or in part.[2]

The liability of the carrier for registered baggage or cargo is limited to 250 francs per kilogram, unless, at the time the package was handed over, the carrier made a special declaration of interest in delivery and paid a supplementary sum if required, in which case the carrier will be liable to pay a sum not exceeding the declared sum, unless he proves that the sum is greater than the actual interest in delivery to the consignor. In the case of objects of which the passenger takes charge himself, the carriers' liability is limited to 5000 francs per passenger.[3]

The limits of liability shall not apply if it is proved that the damage resulted from an act or omission of the carrier, his servants or agents, done with intent to cause damage or recklessly and with knowledge that damage would probably result,[4] provided that a servant or agent was acting within the scope of his employment.[5]

Complaints of damage to baggage or cargo must be made in writing within seven days in the case of baggage and fourteen days in the case of cargo; complaints of delay must be made within fourteen days from the date when the luggage or goods have been placed at his disposal.[6]

The right to damages is extinguished if action is not brought within two years from the date of arrival, or from the date when the aircraft ought to have arrived or when the carriage stopped.[7]

Non-international carriage

In non-international carriage rules generally similar to those of the Convention apply, and similar rules apply to liability for delay, or loss of or damage to goods, and for exclusion or limitation of liability.[8] Contracting-out of the rules is prohibited, but arbitration clauses are permitted and the carrier may make stipulations which do not conflict with the rules.[9] The carrier may exclude or limit liability in the same way as in international carriage.

---

[1] Ibid., art. 20; cf. *Grein* v. *Imperial Airways* [1937] 1 K.B. 50.

[2] Ibid., art. 21.

[3] Ibid., art. 22; *Westminster Bank* v. *Imperial Airways* [1936] 2 All E.R. 890. See also Carriage by Air (Sterling Equivalents) Order, 1973 (S.I. 1973, No. 1189).

[4] cf. *Horabin* v. *B.O.A.C.* [1952] 2 All E.R. 1016.

[5] 1961 Act, Sched. I, art. 25.　　[6] Ibid., art. 26.　　[7] Ibid., art. 29.

[8] Carriage by Air Acts (Application of Provisions) Order, 1967 (S.I. 1967, No. 480).

[9] 1961 Act, Sched. I, arts. 32–33.

CARRIAGE OF PASSENGERS BY AIR

International carriage

International carriage is governed by the Warsaw Convention as amended at The Hague. The carrier must deliver a passenger ticket containing stated particulars;[1] it is *prima facie* evidence of the conclusion and conditions of the contract of carriage;[2] while loss or irregularity of the ticket does not affect the contract a carrier who accepts a passenger without a ticket having been delivered is disentitled from availing himself of the Convention to exclude or limit his liability.[2]

A baggage check containing stated particulars must be issued in duplicate; it is *prima facie* evidence of the conditions of the contract of carriage; its irregularity or loss does not affect the contract, but if the carrier accepts luggage without a ticket having been delivered, or if it does not contain certain of the particulars the carrier is not protected by the Convention.[3] The carrier is liable for damage occasioned by delay in the carriage of passengers or their baggage.[4]

The carrier is liable for damage in case of the death of or injury to a passenger by accident on board the aircraft or while embarking or disembarking.[5] This statutory liability in case of death supersedes any common law liability;[6] it is enforceable by those relatives of the deceased who are entitled at common law to sue the carrier for patrimonial loss or solatium or both in respect of the death.[7]

The carrier is liable for damage sustained by destruction or loss of, or damage to, any registered baggage if the occurrence causing the damage took place during the carriage by air.[8] Receipt of the baggage without complaint is *prima facie* evidence that it has been delivered in good condition.[9]

Exclusion and limitation of liability

The carrier is not liable if he proves that he and his servants or agents have taken all necessary measures to avoid the damage or

---

[1] 1961 Act, Sched. I, art. 3; cf. *Lisi* v. *Alitalia-Linee Aeree Italiane* [1966] 2 Lloyd's Rep. 328.

[2] Ibid., art. 3(2); cf. *Preston* v. *Hunting Air Transport, Ltd.* [1956] 1 Q.B. 454.

[3] Ibid., art. 4.   [4] Ibid., art. 19.

[5] Ibid., art. 17; cf. *Preston* v. *Hunting Air Transport Ltd.* [1956] 1 Q.B. 454.

[6] 1961 Act, S. 11(b); it replaces claims competent in ordinary cases of fatal accidents under the principle of *Eisten* v. *N.B. Ry.* (1870) 8 M. 980. Damages will be assessed as at common law in Scotland.

[7] 1961 Act, S. 11(b).   [8] Sched. I, art. 18(1).   [9] Ibid., art. 26(1).

that it was impossible for him or them to take such measures.[1] The contributory negligence of the injured person may be a partial or total defence.[2]

The liability of the carrier for each passenger for death, injury or delay is limited to 250,000 francs,[3] but by special contract a higher limit of liability may be agreed.[3] Any provision tending to relieve the carrier of liability or to fix a lower limit is null and void.[4] The liability for baggage is the same as for cargo.[5] The limit of liability specified in Art. 22 does not apply if it is proved that the damage resulted from an act or omission of the carrier, his servants or agents, done with intent to cause damage or recklessly and with knowledge that damage would probably result, provided that any servant or agent was acting within the scope of his employment.[6]

Action to recover damages must be brought within two years from the date of arrival, or from the date when the aircraft should have arrived or from the date when the carriage stopped.[7]

Non-international carriage

There are no provisions in non-international carriage corresponding to those of the amended Warsaw Convention requiring carriers to deliver passenger or luggage tickets, but in other respects the modified rules similar to the Convention rules apply.[8] The rules as to liability for delay or death of or injury to passengers correspond to those imposed by the Convention.[9]

Carriage by hovercraft

The Hovercraft Act, 1968, S. 1, provides for the application by Order in Council to the carriage of persons and their baggage by hovercraft of the Carriage by Air Act, 1961 and the Carriage by Air (Supplementary Provisions) Act, 1962, to the carriage of

---

[1] 1961 Act, Sched. I, art. 20; Civil Aviation Act, 1949, S. 54; cf. *Grein* v. *Imperial Airways Ltd.* [1937] 1 K.B. 50.

[2] 1961 Act, Sched. I, art. 21.

[3] Ibid., art. 22(1). For conversion see Carriage by Air (Sterling Equivalents) Order, 1974 (S.I. 1974, No. 528). Higher limits have been accepted by most airlines for journeys from and to U.S.A., and for all non-international carriage.

[4] Ibid., art. 23.

[5] Ibid., art. 22(2).

[6] Ibid., art. 25; cf. *Horabin* v. *B.O.A.C.* [1952] 2 All E.R. 1016; see also *Westminster Bank* v. *Imperial Airways Ltd.* [1936] 2 All E.R. 890; *Philippson* v. *Imperial Airways, Ltd.* [1939] A.C. 332.

[7] 1961 Act, Sched. I, art. 29.

[8] Carriage by Air Acts (Application of Provisions) Order, 1967 (S.I. 1967, No. 480).

[9] Contrast *McKay* v. *Scottish Airways*, 1948 S.C. 254 (prior to Order).

property by hovercraft of the Carriage of Goods by Sea Act, 1924 and Part VIII of the Merchant Shipping Act, 1894, and in relation to loss of life or injury connected with a hovercraft to persons not carried by it, to loss or damage connected with a hovercraft caused to property not covered thereby and in relation to infringements of rights through acts or omissions connected with a hovercraft, to the said Part VIII.[1]

[1] See Hovercraft (Civil Liability) Order, 1971 (S.I. 1971, No. 720), which applies these Acts with modifications to hovercraft, and Hovercraft (Application of Enactments) Order, 1972 (S.I. 1972, No. 971).

CHAPTER 46

CONTRACTS OF INSURANCE

INSURANCE[1] is a consensual contract, but one not derived from the Roman law. It developed from maritime adventures, attended by chance of great profit or great loss, and is believed to have been introduced into England by the Lombards in the Middle Ages. The contract was developed largely by mercantile usage, incorporated into common law with the law merchant. By it one party, the insurer[2] or, in marine practice, the underwriter, undertakes, in consideration of a single or periodical payment of premium, to indemnify the insured or assured against stated possible losses, or to make him a payment in the case of the occurrence of a stated uncertain event,[3] or provide other benefit to him.[4] Insurance may be effected against the risk of any kind of happening and against the loss likely from the occurrence or non-occurrence of any kind of event.

Marine and non-marine insurance

The main division of insurance contracts is into those dealing with marine and with non-marine risks; the former alone is regulated by statute, and there are material differences between the two classes, though the latter class owes much to the former, and the general principles of insurance law are more illustrated by marine than by non-marine cases. The latter class includes life, fire, accident, and liability insurance.

Personal, property and liability insurance

Insurances may also be distinguished, according to the nature of the interest affected, into personal insurance (life, personal accident, sickness), property insurance (marine, fire, burglary, accident, solvency, fidelity, etc.) and liability insurance (employer's liability, third party liability). One insurance may cover various risks, of different classes.

---

[1] See generally Bell, *Comm.* I. 598, *Prin.* §457; Preston and Colinvaux on *Insurance*; Ivamy on *General Principles of Insurance Law*.

[2] The liberty to carry on business as an insurer is limited by the Insurance Companies Act, 1974.

[3] *Scottish Amicable Assocn., Ltd.* v. *Northern Assce. Co.* (1883) 11 R. 287; *Castellain* v. *Preston* (1883) 11 Q.B.D. 380; *Prudential Ins. Co.* v. *I.R.C.* [1904] 2 K.B. 658.

[4] *D.T.I.* v. *St. Christopher Motorists' Assocn.* [1974] 1 All E.R. 395.

Indemnity

Most contracts of insurance are contracts of indemnity in that the insurers' undertaking is to indemnify against loss, and their liability is limited to proven loss within the limit of the sum assured.[1] There is no liability merely on the happening of the event insured against. The policy may, however, be a valued one, containing an agreement as to the value of the thing insured, and thereby fixing the value recoverable if a loss occurs.[2] Contracts of life insurance,[3] personal accident,[4] and sickness insurance, and some cases of contingency insurance are not contracts of indemnity. The assured's estimate of his possible loss in the contingency happening is accepted, and he need not prove loss to the extent of the sum assured, or loss at all.[5] Hence life insurance is commonly largely an investment and a provision for dependants.

Insurance and rights of action

The assured is not bound to seek compensation, by action or otherwise, from a party who has caused him the loss before claiming from his insurers, unless the policy so provides; he may claim under his policy leaving it to the insurers to utilize their right of subrogation.[6] Nor is he precluded from claiming damages from the third party because he is insured,[7] nor because he has been paid by his own insurers under an agreement between them and the third party's insurers under which each insurer pays for damage to its own assured,[8] but if successful he must account to the insurers for any money recovered in respect of a loss for which they have paid him.[9]

Formation of contract—Insurable interest

It is a statutory prerequisite of validity that the person seeking to insure shall have an insurable interest in the life of the person assured, or on the other event or events against which insurance

---

[1] *Castellain, supra*; *Westminster Fire Office* v. *Glasgow Provident Ins. Soc.* (1888) 15 R. (H.L.) 89.

[2] e.g. Marine Ins. Act, 1906, S. 27; *N.B. and Mercantile Ins. Co.* v. *London, Liverpool & Globe Ins. Co.* (1877) 5 Ch. D. 569; *City Tailors, Ltd.* v. *Evans* (1921) 38 T.L.R. 230; *Elcock* v. *Thomson* [1949] 2 K.B. 755 (non-marine cases).

[3] *Dalby* v. *India and London Life Assce. Co.* (1854) 15 C.B. 365; *Gould* v. *Curtis* [1913] 3 K.B. 84.

[4] *Theobald* v. *Ry. Passengers Assce. Co.* (1854) 10 Ex. 45.

[5] *Dalby, supra*; *Gould* v. *Curtis* [1913] 3 K.B. 84.

[6] *West of England Fire Ins. Co.* v. *Isaacs* [1897] 1 Q.B. 226.

[7] *Port Glasgow and Newark Sailcloth Co.* v. *Caledonian Ry.* (1892) 19 R. 608.

[8] i.e. the 'knock-for-knock' agreement: *Morley* v. *Moore* [1936] 2 K.B. 359.

[9] *Morley, supra*.

is sought, failing which any policy is void.[1] This applies to every form of insurance, except marine.[2] The question of what amounts to an insurable interest depends on the kind of insurance in question, but the fundamental idea is that the insured must stand to gain if the event does not happen and to suffer a loss if it does.[3] The defence of lack of insurable interest may be waived.[4] Different persons may simultaneously have different insurable interests in one subject-matter.[5] A person has an insurable interest in property not merely if owner, but if possessor, trustee, depositary, or otherwise, and may have an insurable interest in the life of a person, such as his employer or employee.[6] One person may have an insurable interest in the life of another.[7] If there is no insurable interest, the policy is void and unenforceable, and gives rise to no claim of any kind.[8] The court may *ex proprio motu* take the objection of lack of interest.[9]

In general it is not necessary to specify in the contract of insurance the nature or extent of the insured's interest in the subject matter of insurance. Description of the interest is, however, required where the insurers expressly provide that the insured shall disclose his interest, where the interest is, by reason of its precarious nature, material to the risk,[10] or where the insurance is on prospective profits or against consequential loss.[11] The insurable interest must exist at the time of the loss, and may, in at least some cases, have to exist at the date of the insurance also.[12]

Formation—Formalities and proof

At common law the contract to indemnify might possibly be concluded orally but had to be evidenced by delivery of a policy,

---

[1] Life Assurance Act, 1774, S. 1; *MacDonald* v. *National Mutual Life Assocn. of Australasia* (1906) 14 S.L.T. 249.

[2] S. 4; *Castellain* v. *Preston* (1883) 11 Q.B.D. 380.

[3] *Lucena* v. *Crawford* (1806) 2 B. & P.N.R. 269; *Wilson* v. *Jones* (1867) L.R. 2 Ex. 139; cf. Marine Ins. Act, 1906, S. 5(2).

[4] *Hadden* v. *Bryden* (1899) 1 F. 710.

[5] Sc. *Amicable Assoc.* v. *Northern Assce. Co.* (1883) 11 R. 287; *Westminster Fire Office* v. *Glasgow Provident Inv. Socy.* (1888) 15 R. (H.L.) 89.

[6] *Turnbull* v. *Scottish Provident Inst.* (1896) 34 S.L.R. 146.

[7] *Carmichael* v. *C's Exrx.*, 1919 S.C. 636.

[8] *Cheshire* v. *Vaughan* [1920] 3 K.B. 240.

[9] *Gedge* v. *Royal Exchange Assce. Co.* [1900] 2 Q.B. 214.

[10] *Anderson* v. *Commercial Union Assce. Co.* (1885) 55 L.J.Q.B. 146.

[11] *Menzies* v. *N.B. Ins. Co.* (1847) 9 D. 694; *Mackenzie* v. *Whitworth* (1875) 1 Ex. D. 36; *Inman S.S. Co.* v. *Bischoff* (1882) 7 App. Cas. 670.

[12] Marine Ins. Act, 1906, S. 6.

or some informal writing followed by *rei interventus*, as by acceptance of a premium.[1] In practice the contract is invariably made in writing and evidenced by the policy issued by the insurer.

Formation—Offer and acceptance

The contract is made by offer and acceptance in the usual way, arriving at agreement on definite terms, and may remain inchoate if any material term is not agreed.[2] An undertaking to pay benefits, but excluding contractual liability, is not a contract of insurance.[3] The offer is normally made by completing a proposal form, supplied by the insurers, and setting out the proposed risk. The accuracy of answers is frequently made the basis of the contract.[4] A fair and reasonable construction must be given to questions in the proposal form and the answers thereto.[5]

In marine insurance a proposal for insurance is made on a slip containing brief particulars of the risk, marked by an accepting underwriter with the amount he is willing to take and his initials.[6] This constitutes a contract to issue a policy,[7] but binding in honour only until a stamped policy is issued.[8] The contract is deemed to be concluded when the assured's proposal is accepted by the insurer, whether the policy be then issued or not, and to show when it was accepted reference may be made to the slip, though unstamped.[9] The contract is inadmissible in evidence unless embodied in a marine policy in accordance with the Act, executed and issued at the time when the contract is concluded or afterwards.[10]

Formation—Duty of disclosure

Every kind of insurance is within the category of contracts *uberrimae fidei* so that each party[11] must not only refrain from misrepresentation or concealment but must positively disclose

---

[1] Ersk. III, 3, 17; *Christie* v. *N.B. Ins. Co.* (1825) 3 S. 519; *McElroy* v. *London Assce. Corpn.* (1897) 24 R. 287; *Parker* v. *Western Assce. Co.*, 1925 S.L.T. 131.

[2] *Christie* v. *N.B. Ins. Co.* (1825) 3 S. 519; *Rose* v. *Medical Invalid Life Assce. Socy.* (1848) 11 D. 151; cf. *Star Fire Ins. Co.* v. *Davidson* (1902) 5 F. 83; *Came* v. *City of Glasgow Friendly Socy.*, 1933 S.C. 69.

[3] *Woods* v. *Co-operative Ins. Socy.*, 1924 S.C. 692.

[4] *McCartney* v. *Laverty*, 1968 S.C. 207.

[5] *Condogianis* v. *Guardian Assce. Co.* [1921] 2 A.C. 125.

[6] *Thompson* v. *Adams* (1889) 23 Q.B.D. 361; *Haase* v. *Evans* (1934) 48 Ll.L.R. 131.

[7] *Thompson, supra*; *Grover* v. *Mathews* [1910] 2 K.B. 401.

[8] Marine Ins. Act, 1906, S. 22; *Clyde Marine Ins. Co.* v. *Renwick*, 1924 S.C. 113.

[9] M.I.A., 1906, S. 21.

[10] S. 22.

[11] cf. Marine Ins. Act, 1906, S. 17; *Brown* v. *National Fire Ins. Co.* (1885) 22 S.L.R. 679.

all facts known or which should have been known, which might be material[1] to the undertaking of the risk or the premium to be charged.[2] Non-disclosure and, *a fortiori*, misrepresentation or concealment of or about material facts, even though honest, render the contract voidable.[3] The question is whether the non-disclosure would influence a prudent or reasonable insurer, not whether it did influence the particular insurer.[4]

Any fact may in particular circumstances be material,[5] particularly any fact relevant to the risk, but it is no defence to repudiation of liability that the undisclosed risk did not result in the loss.[6] Facts which do not affect the risk are *prima facie* not material. Expert evidence may be led as to materiality.[7] Facts known to, or discoverable by, the insurers are normally immaterial.[8]

Insurers may competently stipulate that the accuracy of the answers to any question in a proposal form for insurance shall be material,[9] and a fact is not immaterial merely because no question relates to it,[10] but if a question is left unanswered without objection thereto, that fact may be deemed immaterial.[11]

---

[1] The definition of 'material' in M.I.A., 1906, S. 18(2), as 'every circumstance . . . which would influence the judgment of a prudent insurer in fixing the premium, or determining whether he will take the risk' is applicable to all forms of insurance: *Locker and Wolff, Ltd.* v. *Western Australian Ins. Co. Ltd.* [1936] 1 K.B. 308. Materiality is a question of fact: *Zurich Gen. Accident Co.* v. *Leven*, 1940 S.C. 406; see also *McCartney* v. *Laverty*, 1968 S.C. 207.

[2] Bell, *Comm.* I, 665; *Pri...* §474, 522.

[3] *London Assce.* v. *Mansel* (1879) 11 Ch. D. 363; *Brownlie* v. *Miller* (1880) 7 R. (H.L.) 66.

[4] *British and Foreign Marine Ins. Co.* v. *Sanday* [1916] 1 A.C. 650; *Assoc. Oil Carriers* v. *Union Ins. Socy. of Canton* [1917] 2 K.B. 184; *Mutual Life Assce. Co.* v. *Ontario Metals* [1925] A.C. 344.

[5] e.g. *Life Assoc.* v. *Foster* (1873) 11 M. 351 (fact unknown); *Hutchinson* v. *Aberdeen Sea Ins. Co.* (1876) 3 R. 682 (ship's nationality); *Scottish Widows Fund* v. *Buist* (1876) 3 R. 1078 (health); *Buist* v. *Sc. Equitable Life Assce. Soc.* (1878) 5 R. (H.L.) 64 (life and health); *Harvey* v. *Seligmann* (1883) 10 R. 680 (voyage); *Standard Life Assce. Co.* v. *Weems* (1884) 11 R. (H.L.) 48 (temperate habits); *Stuart* v. *Horse Ins. Co.* (1893) 1 S.L.T. 91 (use of horse); *Craig* v. *Palatine Ins. Co.* (1894) 1 S.L.T. 646 (previous proposals); *Cruickshank* v. *Northern Accident Ins. Co.* (1895) 23 R. 147 (disability); *Reid* v. *Employers' Accident and Live Stock Ins. Co.* (1899) 1 F. 1031 (number of claims); *Life and Health Assce. Assoc.* v. *Yale* (1904) 6 F. 437 (previous accidents); *Equitable Life Assce. Soc.* v. *General Accident Assce. Corpn.* (1904) 12 S.L.T. 348 (occupation); *Gunford Ship Co.* v. *Thames and Mersey Marine Ins. Co.*, 1911 S.C. (H.L.) 84 (shipmaster's history); *Dawsons, Ltd.* v. *Bonnin*, 1922 S.C. (H.L.) 156 (place where vehicle kept); *The Spathari*, 1925 S.C. (H.L.) 6 (insured's nationality).

[6] *Seaman* v. *Fonereau* (1743) 2 Stra. 1183.

[7] e.g. *Godfrey* v. *Britannic Assce. Co.* [1963] 2 Lloyd's Rep. 515.

[8] cf. M.I.A., 1906, S. 18(3).

[9] *Joel* v. *Law Union Ins. Co.* [1908] 2 K.B. 863.

[10] *Life Assoc. of Sc.* v. *Foster* (1873) 11 M. 351; *Dawsons Ltd.* v. *Bonnin*, 1922 S.C. (H.L.) 156.

[11] *Joel* v. *Law Union Ins. Co.* [1908] 2 K.B. 863.

The duty of full disclosure continues so long as negotiations are in progress,[1] but ends when the contract is concluded; material facts occurring thereafter or only thereafter coming to the proposer's notice need not be disclosed.[2] Insurers may, however, bar themselves from repudiating liability by conduct, such as taking over the defence in an action against the insured.[3]

Disclosure by agent

An insured has attributed to him knowledge of every material fact known to his agent, and which the agent, with reasonable diligence, could have communicated,[4] unless the agent is employed only for the purpose of effecting insurance.[5] An agent employed to insure is presumed to know every fact which in the ordinary course of business ought to be known to him, and is bound to disclose every material circumstance which the insured would be bound to disclose, unless it came to his knowledge too late to communicate it to his agent.[6] The insured is responsible for the accuracy of representations made by his agent.[7]

Acceptance

The contract is complete only when the insurers make an unqualified acceptance of the proposal.[8] There is no contract until and unless the proposer agrees to the premium asked by the insurers,[9] nor so long as any terms of the insurance are under discussion.[10] The issue of a policy is normally[10] clear intimation of acceptance, as is acceptance of the premium.[11] Sometimes the contract is made by acceptance by the insured of a general offer by the insurers contained in a coupon, by his doing of any acts stated therein as necessary to amount to acceptance of the offer.[12]

---

[1] *Canning* v. *Farquhar* (1886) 16 Q.B.D. 727; *Allis-Chalmers Co.* v. *Maryland Fidelity Co.* (1916) 32 T.L.R. 263; *Looker* v. *Law Union and Rock Ins. Co.* [1928] 1 K.B. 554.

[2] *Whitwell* v. *Autocar Fire and Accident Ins. Co.* (1927) 27 Ll.L.R. 418.

[3] *Nairn* v. *S.E. Lancashire Ins. Co.*, 1930 S.C. 606; *Neil* v. *S.E. Lancashire Ins. Co.*, 1930 S.C. 629.

[4] *Blackburn* v. *Vigors* (1887) 12 App. Cas. 531.

[5] *Blackburn* v. *Haslam* (1881) 21 Q.B.D. 144.

[6] Marine Ins. Act, 1906, S. 19.

[7] *McMillan* v. *Accident Ins. Co.*, 1907 S.C. 484; contrast *Cruickshank* v. *Northern Accident Ins. Co.* (1895) 23 R. 147.

[8] Cf. *Star Fire Insce. Co.* v. *Davidson* (1902) 5 F. 83.

[9] *Christie* v. *N.B. Ins. Co.* (1825) 3 S. 519.

[10] *Sickness and Accident Assce. Assocn.* v. *General Accident Corpn.* (1892) 19 R. 977.

[11] *McElroy* v. *London Assce. Corpn.* (1897) 24 R. 287.

[12] *Shanks* v. *Sun Life Assce. Co.* (1896) 4 S.L.T. 65; *Hunter* v. *General Accident Assce. Corpn.*, 1909 S.C. (H.L.) 30.

Where a risk accrued after a temporary cover note had been issued but before the policy had been issued, it has been held that the insurers' liability was determined by the former, even though it referred to 'the usual terms of the company's policy'.[1] But the terms of a cover note have been held effectual to import a clause in the policy referring disputes to arbitration.[2]

The premium

The premium is the price for the insurers' undertaking to pay the sum insured if the risk happens. The insurer is entitled to recover the premium in whole if the insured has no insurable interest, or the policy is illegal, or void, or avoided, or the subject-matter of the insurance had already been lost or is incapable of identification, or to recover in part if there has been over-insurance, or the policy provides therefor. There is no right to recover the premium if there has been no failure of consideration, or it was attributable to the conduct of the insured, or if the policy so provides.

The policy

Insurers are now bound by statute, in non-marine insurance, to issue a stamped policy within a month after receiving the premium;[3] failure subjects to a penalty but does not affect the validity or enforceability of the contract. Prior to the issue of a formal policy insurers may conclude a provisional contract evidenced by a 'cover note',[4] which may expressly or by reference incorporate the conditions of the policy to be issued,[5] and which normally is effective for a limited time only or until a policy be issued or the insurers intimate that they decline the assured's proposal for insurance.[6]

In marine insurance the Marine Insurance Act, 1906, prescribes the minimum particulars to be contained in a policy; in non-marine insurance there are no corresponding requirements. A policy is normally a unilateral undertaking by the insurers, in consideration of a certain premium, to pay to the assured the loss

---

[1] *Neil* v. *S.E. Lancashire Ins. Co.*, 1932 S.C. 35.

[2] *Cunningham* v. *Anglian Ins. Co.*, 1934 S.L.T. 273.

[3] Stamp Act, 1891, Ss. 100, 191 and Sched. I, amd. Finance Act, 1959, S. 30.

[4] *Thompson* v. *Adams* (1889) 23 Q.B.D. 361; *Re Yager and Guardian* (1912) 108 L.T. 38; *Praet* v. *Poland* [1960] 1 Lloyd's Rep. 420.

[5] *Re Coleman's Depositaries* [1907] 2 K.B. 298.

[6] *Mackie* v. *European Assce. Co.* (1869) 21 L.T. 102; *Levy* v. *Scottish Employers' Insce. Co.* (1901) 17 T.L.R. 229; *Neil* v. *S.E. Lancashire Ins. Co.*, 1932 S.C. 35; *Cunningham* v. *Anglian Ins. Co.*, 1934 S.L.T. 273.

sustained by specified events up to a stated limit, or to pay the insured a sum on the happening of a specified event. It may incorporate by reference the proposal form. It may be a valued policy fixing the amount recoverable on the event happening,[1] or an unvalued policy, where the sum payable is to be ascertained within the limit of the sum insured after the loss has happened.

It falls to be interpreted as a commercial document and effect given, so far as possible, to the intention of the parties; since it is framed by the insurers ambiguities fall to be construed *contra proferentem*. It must describe the subject-matter assured sufficiently to make it identifiable. It must state the perils insured against, and any perils excepted from the risk; it is a question of fact whether an event which happens falls within one category or the other.[2] It frequently also imposes conditions as to claims, notice thereof, and evidence in support of a claim, rights of cancellation and other matters. The interpretation of the policy is a question of law, the primary quest being for the intention of the parties as disclosed in the policy.[3]

If the policy is ambiguous the court may consider other documents, such as the proposal, or the back of the policy,[4] if not incorporated therein, and favours a construction *contra proferentem*.[5]

The policy should state when it comes into force and its duration.[6] It may be terminated earlier by agreement, by payment of the full sum insured, by the insurers going into liquidation, or by breach of a fundamental stipulation of the policy. On its expiry the policy may by agreement be renewed on payment of a renewal premium. The contract is commonly for one year only, renewable from year to year rather than a continuing contract, with an obligation on the insured to disclose prior to each renewal any material change in circumstances.[7] Alternatively it may be allowed to lapse, in which case it is unenforceable as to any claim

---

[1] This includes all personal accident policies.

[2] e.g. *Morrison and Mason* v. *Scottish Employers' Assce. Co.* (1888) 16 R. 212; *Harris* v. *Poland* [1941] 1 K.B. 462. Exceptions from liability should be clearly expressed: *Sangster's Trs.* v. *General Accident Corpn.* (1896) 24 R. 56. If there are two causes of loss, one within the exception, the insurers may rely on the exception: *Wayne Tank Co.* v. *Employer's Assce. Corpn.* [1973] 3 All E.R. 825.

[3] cf. *Hamilton's Trs.* v. *Fleming* (1870) 9 M. 329.

[4] *Scott* v. *Scottish Accident Ins. Co.* (1889) 16 R. 630.

[5] *Kelly* v. *Cornhill Ins. Co.*, 1964 S.C. (H.L.) 46.

[6] *Sickness and Accident Assce. Assocn.* v. *General Accident Corpn.* (1892) 19 R. 977; *Murfitt* v. *Royal Ins. Co.* (1922) 38 T.L.R. 334; cf. *Kelly* v. *Cornhill Ins. Co.*, 1964 S.C. (H.L.) 46.

[7] *Law Accident Ins. Socy.* v. *Boyd*, 1942 S.C. 384.

arising thereafter.[1] Despite lapse it may, by consent, be revived, possibly without prejudice to liability during the period of lapse.[2]

An insurance policy does not transmit automatically with the subject-matter insured,[3] but may be assigned with the consent of the insurers. It passes on the insured's death or bankruptcy to his executor or trustee.[4] A marine policy may be assigned unless that is expressly prohibited.[5]

Claims under policy

To entitle the insured to make a valid claim under the policy the peril, or one of the perils, insured against must have happened, and have caused him loss.[6] The loss must have been caused by the peril, not by some other factor,[7] and the peril must have been the proximate or immediate cause of the loss, rather than the remote or initial cause.[8] Whether a happening is a peril insured against, or an excepted peril which does not render the insurer liable, is a question of interpretation;[9] whether the peril was the proximate cause of the loss or not is a question of fact.

The insured is normally required to make a claim, and furnish particulars and proof of the loss sustained, sufficient to satisfy reasonable men.[10] The onus of proof is on the insured,[11] who must make at least a *prima facie* case.[12] If a claim is fraudulent the in-

---

[1] cf. *Employers' Ins. of G.B.* v. *Benton* (1897) 24 R. 908.

[2] *Kirkpatrick* v. *S. Australian Ins. Co.* (1886) 11 App. Cas. 177.

[3] *Rayner* v. *Preston* (1881) 18 Ch. D. 1; but see *Kelly* v. *Cornhill Ins. Co.*, 1964 S.C. (H.L.) 46.

[4] *Re Carr & Sun Fire Ins. Co.* (1897) 13 T.L.R. 186.

[5] Marine Ins. Act, 1906, S. 50.

[6] *Young* v. *Trustee, etc. Ins. Co.* (1893) 21 R. 222; *Laird* v. *Securities Ins. Co.* (1895) 22 R. 452.

[7] *McKechnie's Trs.* v. *Scottish Accident Ins. Co.* (1889) 17 R. 6; *Clidero* v. *Scottish Accident Ins. Co.* (1892) 19 R. 355; cf. *Morrison & Mason* v. *Scottish Employers' Ins. Co.* (1888) 16 R. 212.

[8] *Becker, Gray & Co.* v. *London Assce. Corpn.* [1918] A.C. 101.

[9] A negligent act by the insured frequently makes the insurer liable: *Shaw* v. *Robberds* (1837) 6 A. & E. 75; but a wilful act, if amounting to misconduct, exempts the insurer from liability: *Trinder Anderson & Co.* v. *N. Queensland Ins. Co.* (1897) 2 Com. Cas. 216; *Gray* v. *Barr* [1970] 2 All E.R. 702.

[10] *Macdonald* v. *Refuge Assce. Co.* (1890) 17 R. 955; *Ballantine* v. *Employers' Ins. Co. of G.B.* (1893) 21 R. 305.

[11] *A.B.* v. *Northern Accident Ins. Co.* (1896) 24 R. 258; *Regina Fur Co.* v. *Bossom* [1958] 2 Lloyd's Rep. 425.

[12] *McKechnie's Trs.* v. *Scottish Accident Ins. Co.* (1889) 17 R. 6; *Macdonald, supra*; *Ballantine, supra*; *Nobel's Explosive Co.* v. *British Dominions General Ins. Co.*, 1918 S.C. 373.

sured forfeits all benefit under the policy.[1] Questions of liability may, by the policy, be referred to arbitration.[2]

Settlement of claim

If the policy is a valued one, the valuation is conclusive as to sum due as indemnity.[3] In an unvalued policy the sum stated in the policy is the maximum,[4] and the amount payable is that proved to be necessary to give full indemnity.

Only a lesser sum may, however, be payable if the policy contains a contribution clause, requiring liability to be limited to a rateable proportion from each policy covering any of the loss sustained,[5] or an average clause whereby, if the sum insured is less than the value of the subject-matter the insured must bear a rateable proportion of the loss himself,[6] or an excess clause, whereby the insured must himself bear the liability of losses up to a stated sum.[7] If there is a franchise clause, any loss not exceeding a specified percentage of the whole value, must be met by the insured himself.[8]

Reinstatement

The insurers cannot in general without the insured's consent insist in making good the loss by reinstatement,[9] nor can they, in general, insist on the insured expending the money on reinstating the damaged property.[10] Policies insuring property may confer on the insurers the option of making good the loss by reinstatement. They must elect which course to adopt within a reasonable time and may be barred by their conduct.[11] The duty to reinstate from the proceeds of insurance may be incumbent on an insured under his feu-contract or lease.

---

1 *McKirby* v. *N.B. Ins. Co.* (1858) 20 D. 463; see also *Reid* v. *Employers' etc., Ins. Co.* (1899) 1 F. 1031; *Dryburgh* v. *Caledonian Ins. Co.*, 1933 S.N. 85.

2 *Palmer* v. *S.E. Lancashire Ins. Co.*, 1932 S.L.T. 68; *Cant* v. *Eagle Star Ins. Co.*, 1937 S.L.T. 444.

3 *Burnand* v. *Rodocanachi* (1882) 7 App. Cas. 333.

4 *Hercules Ins. Co.* v. *Hunter* (1836) 14 S. 1137; *Westminster Fire Office* v. *Glasgow Provident Inv. Socy.* (1888) 15 R. (H.L.) 89.

5 e.g. *N.B. and Mercantile Ins. Co.* v. *Liverpool, London & Globe Ins. Co.* (1877) 5 Ch. D. 569.

6 *Buchanan* v. *Liverpool, London & Globe Ins. Co.* (1884) 11 R. 1032; *Carreras* v. *Cunard Steamship Co.* [1918] 1 K.B. 118.

7 *Beacon Ins. Co.* v. *Langdale* [1939] 4 All E.R. 204.

8 *Stewart* v. *Merchants' Marine Ins. Co.* (1885) 16 Q.B.D. 619.

9 *Anderson* v. *Commercial Union Assce. Co.* (1885) 55 L.J.Q.B. 146.

10 *Re Law Guarantee Trust Socy. Ltd.* [1914] 2 Ch. 617.

11 *Scottish Amicable Assocn. Ltd.* v. *Northern Assce. Co.* (1883) 11 R. 287; cf. *Sutherland* v. *Sun Fire Office* (1852) 14 D. 775.

Subrogation

There follows from the principle of indemnity, in all cases where it applies,[1] that insurers have a right of subrogation,[2] entitling them, on admitting liability and indemnifying the assured,[3] to be put in the position of the assured and to exercise all claims and remedies competent to him against third parties in respect of the subject matter.[4] Thus where a third party has by breach of contract,[5] or by delict,[6] caused the assured loss, the latter's insurers are entitled, on compensating him, to enforce his claims against the third party.

The insurers must sue the third party in the assured's name, unless his rights are formally assigned to them,[7] and he is obliged, on being given an indemnity against expenses, to allow his name to be used.[8] The third party may utilize against the insurers any defence competent against the assured.[9] The insurers may recover damages not limited to the sum paid to the assured; they are entitled to the damages so far as needed to compensate for what they have paid the assured; any surplus belongs to the assured.[10]

The assured must not do anything to prejudice the insurers' right of subrogation, such as without their consent to settle with the third party,[11] and must assist the insurers to enforce his claims against the third party.[12]

If the assured's loss exceeds the amount paid under the policy, there is partial subrogation only and the assured is not deprived of any right against the third party, but must act for the benefit of the insurers as well as himself.

Contribution

Where two or more policies are effected by one assured in respect of one interest, and the total of the sums assured exceeds

---

[1] *Castellain* v. *Preston* (1883) 11 Q.B.D. 380 (fire); *Horse, Carriage and General Ins. Co.* (1916) 33 T.L.R. 131 (vehicle); *Edwards* v. *Motor Union Ins. Co.* [1922] 2 K.B. 249; *Meacock* v. *Bryant* [1942] 2 All E.R. 661 (contingency—non-payment of money). Subrogation does not apply to life or personal accident insurance.

[2] On history of the doctrine see *Edwards, supra.*　　　[3] *Edwards, supra.*

[4] *Castellain, supra*; *Page* v. *Scottish Ins. Corpn.* (1929) 45 T.L.R. 250.

[5] *Darrell* v. *Tibbitts* (1880) 5 Q.B.D. 560; *Castellain, supra.*

[6] *London Guarantee Co.* v. *Fearnley* (1880) 5 App. Cas. 911; *Horse, Carriage and General Ins. Co., supra*; *Lister* v. *Romford Ice Co.* [1957] A.C. 555.

[7] e.g. *King* v. *Victoria Ins. Co.* [1896] A.C. 250.

[8] *Dane* v. *Mortgage Ins. Corpn.* [1894] 1 Q.B. 54.

[9] *Phoenix Assce. Co.* v. *Spooner* [1905] 2 K.B. 753.　　　[10] *Castellain, supra.*

[11] *Phoenix Assce. Co., supra*; *Horse, Carriage and General Ins. Co., supra.*

[12] *London Guarantee Co., supra*; *Dane* v. *Mortgage Ins. Corpn.* [1894] 1 Q.B. 54.

what is necessary to give him full indemnity, there is double insurance. The assured, subject to policy conditions to the contrary, may effect more than one insurance but, where the contract is one of indemnity, he cannot recover more than the total amount of his loss.[1] Each insurer is liable only for a rateable proportion of the loss, and most policies so provide, by a contribution clause;[1] failing such provision, the assured can recover in full under any policy, leaving to the insurers to recover contribution from other insurers. Contribution is recoverable only where each policy covers the loss against the peril which caused it,[2] covers the same insurable interest in the same subject matter,[3] is legally binding,[4] and is in force at the time of the loss.[5]

MARINE INSURANCE

The law of marine insurance[6] is codified[7] by the Marine Insurance Act, 1906 but the common law, including the law merchant, still applies except in so far as inconsistent with the express provisions of the Act.[8] Moreover where any right, duty or liability would arise under a contract of marine insurance by implication of law, including the Act, it may be negatived or varied by express agreement or by usage, if the usage be such as to bind both parties to the contract.[9] The contract of marine insurance is one whereby an insurer or underwriter undertakes to indemnify the assured, in manner and to the extent thereby agreed, against marine losses.[10] A contract of marine insurance may by express terms or by usage of trade be extended to protect the assured against any land risk incidental to a sea voyage,[11] or to a ship in course of building, or the launch of a ship, or any adventure analogous to a marine adventure. Every lawful marine adventure may be insured, particularly where any

[1] *Scottish Amicable Assoc.* v. *Northern Assce. Co.* (1883) 11 R. 287.

[2] *N.B. and Mercantile Ins. Co.* v. *London, etc. Ins. Co.* (1877) 5 Ch. D. 569.

[3] *Scottish Amicable Assoc.*, *supra*; *Nichols* v. *Scottish Union and National Ins. Co.* (1885) 14 R. 1094; 2 T.L.R. 190.

[4] *Woods* v. *Co-operative Ins. Socy.*, 1924 S.C. 692.

[5] *Sickness and Accident Assce. Assoc.* v. *General Accident Assce. Corpn.* (1892) 19 R. 977.

[6] See generally Arnould on *Marine Insurance*; Chalmers' *Marine Insurance Act*; Ivamy, *Marine Insurance*.

[7] Only in case of doubt, accordingly, is resort to previous law legitimate: *Vagliano* v. *Bank of England* [1891] A.C. 107, 145; though the tendency is to interpret the Act as declaratory: *British & Foreign Mar. Ins. Co.* v. *Sanday* [1916] 1 A.C. 650, 672.

[8] M.I.A., 1906, S. 91(2).

[9] M.I.A., 1906, S. 87.

[10] M.I.A., 1906, S. 1.

[11] S. 2; *British and Foreign Marine Ins. Co.* v. *Gaunt* [1921] 2 A.C. 41.

insurable property, ship, goods or other moveables is exposed to maritime perils or where the earning of freight or profits is endangered thereby.[1] A contract of marine insurance by way of gaming or wagering is void, and is deemed to be by way of gaming or wagering where the insured has not an insurable interest and the contract is entered into with no expectation of acquiring such an interest, or where the policy is made 'interest or no interest' or 'without further proof of interest than the policy' or 'without benefit of salvage to the insurer' or subject to any other like term, though where there is no possibility of salvage a policy may be effected without benefit of salvage to the insurer.[2]

Insurable interest

Subject to the Act,[3] every person has an insurable interest who is interested in a marine adventure[4] particularly if he stands in any legal or equitable relation to the adventure or to any insurable property at risk therein, in consequence of which he may benefit by the safety or due arrival of insurable property, or may be prejudiced by its loss or by damage thereto, or by the detention thereof, or may incur liability in respect thereof.[5]

The interest must exist at the time of the loss but not necessarily when the insurance was effected,[6] save that when a subject is insured 'lost or not lost' the insured may recover though he did not acquire his interest till after the loss unless at the time of the insurance the assured was aware of the loss and the insurer was not.[7] Where he has no interest at the time of the loss, he cannot acquire interest by any act of election after he is aware of the loss.[8]

A defeasible interest, a contingent interest, and a partial interest are all insurable.[9] The insurer has an insurable interest in his risk and may reinsure in respect of it but, unless the policy otherwise provides, the original assured has no right or interest in respect of such reinsurance.[10] The lender of money on bottomry or respondentia has an insurable interest in respect of the loan, the master or

---

[1] S. 3; *N.Z. Shipping Co.* v. *Duke* [1914] 2 K.B. 682; 'marine adventure' and 'maritime perils' are defined in S. 3(2).

[2] S. 4.   [3] Ss. 6–15.

[4] *Wilson* v. *Jones* (1867) L.R. 2 Ex. 139.

[5] S. 5; cf. *Lucena* v. *Craufurd* (1806) 2 B. & P.N.R. 269; *Moran Galloway & Co.* v. *Uzielli* [1905] 2 K.B. 555; *Macaura* v. *Northern Assce. Co.* [1925] A.C. 619; *Papadimitriou* v. *Henderson* [1939] 3 All E.R. 908.

[6] *Anderson* v. *Morice* (1876) 1 App. Cas. 713; *Colonial Ins. Co.* v. *Adelaide Mar. Ins. Co.* (1886) 12 App. Cas. 128.

[7] *Sutherland* v. *Pratt* (1843) 11 M. & W. 296.

[8] S. 6.   [9] Ss. 7, 8.

[10] S. 9; *Uzielli* v. *Boston Mar. Ins. Co.* (1884) 15 Q.B.D. 11.

any member of the crew in respect of his wages, and the person advancing freight, in so far as advance freight is not repayable in case of loss.[1] The assured has an insurable interest in the charges of any insurance he may effect.[2] Where the subject-matter insured is mortgaged the mortgagor has an insurable interest in the full value thereof, and the mortgagee has an insurable interest in respect of any sum due or to become due under the mortgage.[3] A mortgagee, consignee or other person having an interest in the subject matter insured may insure on behalf and for the benefit of other persons interested as well as for his own benefit.[4] The owner of insurable property has an insurable interest in respect of the full value thereof, notwithstanding that some third person may have agreed, or be liable, to indemnify him in case of loss.[5] Where the assured assigns or otherwise parts with his interest in the subject matter assured, he does not thereby transfer to the assignee his rights under the contract of insurance, unless there be an express or implied agreement with the assignee to that effect. The provisions of the section do not affect a transmission of interest by operation of law.[6]

Insurable value

Clear settlement of insurable value is necessary to fix the measure of indemnity in an unvalued policy, and to give an approximate standard for fixing the value in a valued policy. The Act provides[7] subject to any express provision or valuation in the policy for the ascertainment of the insurable value of the subject matter as follows: in insurance on ship, the insurable value is the value at the commencement of the risk, of the ship, including her outfit, provisions and stores for the officers and crew, money advanced for seamen's wages and other disbursements, if any, incurred to make the ship fit for the voyage or adventure contemplated by the policy, plus the charges of insurance on the whole;[8] the insurable value in the case of a steamship includes also the machinery, boilers and coals and engine stores, if owned by the assured and in the case of a ship engaged in a

---

[1] Ss. 10–12.

[2] S. 13.

[3] N.B. Ins. Co. v. London Ins. Co. (1877) 5 Ch. D. 569.

[4] Castellain v. Preston (1883) 11 Q.B.D. 380.

[5] S. 14; Dufourcet v. Bishop (1886) 18 Q.B.D. 373.

[6] S. 15; N. of Eng. Oil Cake Co. v. Archangel Mar. Ins. Co. (1875) L.R. 10 Q.B. 249.

[7] S. 16.

[8] Moran Galloway & Co. v. Uzielli [1905] 2 K.B. 555.

special trade the ordinary fittings requisite for that trade;[1] in insurance on freight, whether paid in advance or otherwise, the insurable value is the gross amount of the freight at the risk of the assured, plus the charges of insurance;[2] in insurance on goods and merchandise the insurable value is the prime cost of the property insured plus the expenses of and incidental to shipping and the charges of insurance upon the whole;[3] in insurance on any other subject-matter, the insurable value is the amount at the risk of the assured when the policy attaches, plus the charges of insurance.

Disclosure and representations

The Act embodies the common law principles that the contract is one *uberrimae fidei* and, if the utmost good faith be not observed by either party, the other may avoid the contract.[4] Subject to S. 18 the assured must disclose to the insurer, before the contract is concluded, every material circumstance[5] which is known to the assured, and the assured is deemed to know every circumstance which, in the ordinary course of business, ought to be known by him. If he fails to make disclosure the insurer may avoid the contract.[6] Every circumstance is material which would influence the judgment of a prudent insurer in fixing the premium or determining whether he will take the risk.[7] In the absence of inquiry the following circumstances need not be disclosed,[8] namely (a) any circumstance which diminishes the risk;[9] any circumstance which is known or presumed to be known to the insurer; he is presumed to know matters of common notoriety or knowledge, and matters which an insurer in the ordinary course of his business, as such, ought to know;[10] any circumstance as to which information is waived by the insurer;[11] and any circumstance which it is superfluous to disclose by reason of any express or implied warranty.[12] Whether any particular circumstance,

---

[1] *Hogarth* v. *Walker* [1900] 2 Q.B. 283.

[2] *U.S. Shipping Co.* v. *Empress Assce. Corpn.* [1908] 1 K.B. 115.

[3] *Williams* v. *Atlantic Assce. Co.* [1933] 1 K.B. 81.

[4] S. 17; cf. *Brownlie* v. *Miller* (1880) 7 R. (H.L.) 66.

[5] Including communication made to, or information received by the assured: S. 18(5).

[6] S. 18(1); *Ionides* v. *Pender* (1874) L.R. 9 Q.B. 531.

[7] S. 18(2); *Rivaz* v. *Gerussi* (1880) 6 Q.B.D. 222; *Tate* v. *Hyslop* (1885) 15 Q.B.D. 368; *Gunford Ship Co.* v. *Thames and Mersey Marine Ins. Co.*, 1911 S.C. (H.L.) 84; *The Spathari*, 1925 S.C. (H.L.) 6.

[8] S. 18(3).   [9] *Carter* v. *Boehm* (1766) 3 Burr. 1905.

[10] *Carter*, *supra*; *Harrower* v. *Hutchinson* (1870) L.R. 5 Q.B. 584.

[11] *Carter*, *supra*; *Mann, McNeal & Co.* v. *General Marine Underwriters* [1921] 2 K.B. 300.

[12] *Gunford Ship Co.* v. *Thames and Mersey Marine Ins. Co.*, 1911 S.C. (H.L.) 84.

which is not disclosed, be material or not is, in each case, a question of fact.[1]

Disclosure by agent effecting insurance

Subject to S. 18, where an insurance is effected for the assured by an agent, the agent must disclose to the insurer (a) every material circumstance which is known to himself, and an agent to insure is deemed to know every circumstance which in the ordinary course of business ought to be known by or to have been communicated to him;[2] and (b) every material circumstance which the assured is bound to disclose, unless it come to his knowledge too late to communicate it to the agent.[3]

Representations

The Act[4] embodies the common law principle that a contract induced by material misrepresentation is voidable. Every material representation made by the assured or his agent to the insurer during the negotiations for the contract and before the contract is concluded must be true; if untrue, the insurer may avoid the contract.[5] A representation is material[6] which would influence the judgment of a prudent insurer in fixing the premium or determining whether he will take the risk. A representation may be as to a matter of fact, or as to a matter of expectation or belief; if as to a matter of fact it is true if it be substantially correct, i.e. if the difference between what is represented and what is actually correct would not be considered material by a prudent insurer; if as to a matter of expectation or belief it is true if made in good faith. A representation may be withdrawn or corrected before the contract is concluded.

When contract deemed concluded

A contract of marine insurance is deemed to be concluded when the proposal of the assured is accepted by the insurer whether the policy be then issued or not; and to show when the

---

[1] S. 18(4); *Ionides, supra.*

[2] *Blackburn* v. *Vigors* (1887) 12 App. Cas. 531; *Blackburn* v. *Haslam* (1888) 21 Q.B.D. 144.

[3] S. 19; *Blackburn* v. *Vigors, supra.*

[4] S. 20; cf. *Harvey* v. *Seligmann* (1883) 10 R. 680.

[5] *Anderson* v. *Pacific Marine Ins. Co.* (1872) L.R. 7 C.P. 65; *The Spathari*, 1925 S.C. (H.L.) 6.

[6] Whether it is material or not is in each case, a question of fact: S. 20(7); cf. *Rivaz* v. *Gerussi* (1880) 6 Q.B.D. 222; *Hutchinson* v. *Aberdeen Sea Ins. Co.* (1876) 3 R. 682; *Harvey, supra.*

proposal was accepted, reference may be made to the slip or covering note or other customary memorandum of the contract, although it be unstamped.[1]

Policy

A contract of marine insurance is inadmissible in evidence unless embodied in a marine policy in accordance with the Act, which may be executed and issued either when the contract is concluded or afterwards.[2] It must specify the name of the assured or of some person who effects the insurance on his behalf[3] and be signed by or on behalf of the insurer, or of each insurer, in which case each subscription constitutes a distinct contract with the assured.[4] An underwriter's 'slip'[5] and a contract note[6] are not policies.

A policy may be for a voyage, or for time, or for both.[7] The subject-matter insured must be designated in the policy with reasonable certainty, but the nature and extent of the assured's interest need not be specified. Where the policy designates the subject-matter insured in general terms, it has to be construed to apply to the interest intended by the assured to be covered. Regard has to be had to any usage regulating the designation of the subject-matter insured.[8] It may also be valued, or unvalued, according as the parties do or do not state a sum at which they agree to value the subject matter insured; the value fixed by the policy is, between underwriter and assured, conclusive of the value of the subject insured whether the loss is total or partial, but not for determining whether there has been a constructive total loss; in an unvalued policy the value of the subject matter insured is not admitted but has to be subsequently ascertained.[9] It may also be a floating policy, describing the insurance in general terms leaving the ship's name to be fixed by subsequent declaration.[10] It is always, however, open to the underwriter to show that

---

[1] S. 21; *Ionides* v. *Pacific Marine Ins. Co.* (1871) L.R. 6 Q.B. 674.

[2] S. 22; *Mead* v. *Davison* (1835) 3 A. & E. 303. But a policy cannot be issued after the insurers have gone into liquidation: *Clyde Marine Ins. Co.* v. *Renwick*, 1924 S.C. 113. A 'slip' evidencing an oral contract is inadmissible in evidence unless and until embodied in a policy: Bell, *Comm.* I, 649; *Clyde Marine, supra.*

[3] S. 23, amd. Finance Act, 1959, S. 30.

[4] S. 24; see also *Xenos* v. *Wickham* (1867) L.R. 2 H.L. 296; *Inverkeithing Marine etc., Assocn.* v. *Mackenzie* (1882) 9 R. 1043.

[5] *Clyde Marine Ins. Co.* v. *Renwick*, 1924 S.C. 113.

[6] *Mackay* v. *Scottish Boat Ins. Co.* (1903) 11 S.L.T. 91.

[7] S. 25(1); cf. *Hunter* v. *Northern Marine Ins. Co.* (1888) 15 R. (H.L.) 72.

[8] S. 26; *Mackenzie* v. *Whitworth* (1875) 1 Ex. D. 36.

[9] Ss. 27–28; see also *Muirhead* v. *Forth Mutual Ins. Assocn.* (1893) 21 R. (H.L.) 1.

[10] S. 29: *Union Ins. Socy. of Canton* v. *Wills* [1916] 1 A.C. 281.

part only of the subject intended to be valued in the policy was at risk.[1]

Most policies are based on the Lloyds policy, scheduled to the 1906 Act, frequently with special clauses inserted or incorporated by reference. It is interpreted in accordance with statutory rules of construction,[2] principles settled by decisions and evidence of general commercial usage.

Perils insured against

The perils insured against are those specified in the policy; in the Lloyd's policy these are perils of the seas, men-of-war, fire, enemies, pirates, rovers, thieves, jettisons, letters of mart and countermart, surprisals, taking at sea, arrests, restraints and detainments of all kings, princes and peoples of what nation, condition or quality soever, barratry of the master and mariners and of all other perils, losses and misfortunes that have or shall come to the hurt, detriment or damage of the said goods and merchandises and ship, etc. or any part thereof. In addition the policy frequently insures against such risks as war and collision risks, loss or damage caused by accidents in loading, discharging or shifting cargo or fuel, explosions, and latent defects in hull or machinery,[3] or others of the clauses settled by the Institute of London Underwriters.[4] Certain war risks are customarily excluded by a free of capture and seizure clause.[5] Most of these words have been interpreted by court decisions.

Onus of proof

The onus is on the assured to show that the loss is covered by his policy. Where the policy covers all risks and not merely risks of a specified class, it is sufficient to prove that the loss was caused by some event within the general expression, and not necessary to prove the exact cause of the loss.[6] It is fundamental that the underwriter is liable only for a loss proximately caused by a peril insured against, proximity being not in time but in causal efficacy,

---

[1] S. 75; *Tobin v. Harford* (1864) 17 C.B. (N.S.) 528; *The Main* [1894] P. 320.

[2] S. 30 and Sched. I. As to the *contra proferentem* rule see *Birrell* v. *Dyer* (1884) 11 R. (H.L.) 41.

[3] Introduced in consequence of the decision in *Thames and Mersey Marine Ins. Co.* v. *Hamilton, Fraser & Co.* (1887) 12 App.Cas. 484 and known in consequence as the *Inchmaree* clause.

[4] On these see Arnould, Appx. 2; Chalmers, *Marine Insurance*, Appx. 2.

[5] *Britain S.S. Co. Ltd.* v. *R.* [1921] 1 A.C. 99.

[6] *British and Foreign Marine Ins. Co.* v. *Gaunt* [1921] 2 A.C. 41; *Berk* v. *Style* [1956] 1 Q.B. 180.

and not liable for a loss not proximately caused.[1] Whether a peril insured against was the, or a, proximate cause of the loss is a question of fact to be determined on common-sense principles.[1] The insurer is not liable for loss caused by the assured's wilful misconduct, but is for loss caused by a peril insured against even though it would not have occurred but for the misconduct or negligence of the master or crew.[2]

Premium

Where an insurance is effected at a premium to be arranged and no arrangement is made, a reasonable premium is payable. Where an insurance is effected on the terms that an additional premium is to be arranged in a given event, and that event happens but no arrangement is made, then a reasonable additional premium is payable.[3]

Double Insurance

Where two or more policies are effected on the same adventure and interest or any part thereof and the sums insured exceed the indemnity allowed by the Act the assured is over-insured, and he may claim payment from the insurers in any order, but may not receive any sum in excess of indemnity.[4] If he claims under a valued policy, he may give credit against the valuation for any sum received under any other policy without regard to the actual value of the subject-matter insured; if under an unvalued policy, he must give credit, against the full insurable value, for any sum received by him under any other policy. Where the assured receives any sum in excess of the indemnity allowed by the act he is deemed to hold it in trust for the insurers according to their right of contribution among themselves.

Warranties

The contract may contain express or implied warranties;[5] an express warranty may be in any form of words disclosing the intention to warrant, and must be included in, written on, or be

---

[1] *Becker, Gray & Co.* v. *London Assce. Corpn.* [1918] A.C. 101; *Leyland Shipping Co.* v. *Norwich Union Fire Ins. Socy.* [1918] A.C. 350; *Smith, Hogg & Co.* v. *Black Sea and Baltic Co.* [1940] A.C. 997; *Boiler Inspection Co. of Canda* v. *Sherwin-Williams Co.* [1951] A.C. 319.

[2] S. 55 (2).   [3] S. 31.

[4] S. 32; cf. *N.B. and Mercantile Ins. Co.* v. *London Liverpool and Globe Ins. Co.* (1877) 5 Ch. D. 569.

[5] S. 33; 'warranty' as defined therein is as 'warranty' is understood in Scots law, or 'condition' in the English law of contract generally.

in a document incorporated by reference into the policy.[1] It does not exclude an implied warranty unless inconsistent therewith.[2] A warranty must be exactly complied with, whether material to the risk or not, failing which, unless the insurer waives the breach,[3] he is discharged from liability from the date of the breach without prejudice to liability incurred by him before that date.[4] It matters not that the warranty has been complied with before the loss,[5] nor that the breach was wholly unconnected with the loss.[6] Non-compliance with an express warranty is excused if the state of things contemplated by the warranty ceases, or when compliance is rendered unlawful by supervening law.[7]

Express warranties

An express warranty may be in any form of words from which the intention to warrant may be inferred.[8] It must be included in or written upon the policy, or contained in some document incorporated by reference into the policy.[9] Where insurable property is expressly warranted neutral, there is an implied condition that the property shall have a neutral character at the commencement of the risk and that, so far as the assured can control the matter its neutral character shall be preserved during the risk.[10] Where a ship is expressly warranted 'neutral' there is also an implied condition that, so far as the assured can control the matter, she shall be properly documented, i.e. carry the necessary papers to prove her neutrality, and shall not falsify or suppress her papers, or use simulated papers. If any loss occurs through breach of this condition, the insurer may avoid the contract.[11] Common express warranties include that the ship is 'well' or 'in good safety' on a particular day, in which case it is sufficient if it be safe at any time during that day,[12] or to sail on a given day[13] or of not carrying contraband.[14]

---

[1] S. 35(1) and (2); see e.g. *Andersen v. Marten* [1908] A.C. 334; *Leyland S.S. Co. v. Norwich Union* [1918] A.C. 350; *Britain S.S. Co. v. The King* [1921] 1 A.C. 100.

[2] S. 35(3); *Sleigh v. Tyser* [1900] 2 Q.B. 333.

[3] S. 34(3); *Provincial Ins. Co. v. Leduc* (1874) L.R. 6 P.C. 224.

[4] S. 33(3); *Birrell v. Dryer* (1884) 11 R. (H.L.) 41; *Fireman's Fund Ins. Co. v. W. Australian Ins. Co.* (1927) 33 Com. Cas. 36.

[5] S. 34(2).

[6] *Hibbert v. Pigou* (1783) 3 Doug. K.B. 224; *Newcastle Fire Ins. Co. v. Macmorran* (1815) 3 Dow 255.

[7] S. 34(1).   [8] S. 35(1).

[9] S. 35(2); *Bensaude v. Thames and Mersey Marine Ins.* [1897] A.C. 609; *Yorkshire Ins. Co. v. Campbell* [1917] A.C. 218.

[10] S. 36(1).   [11] S. 36(2).   [12] S. 38.

[13] *Cruickshank v. Janson* (1810) 2 Taunt. 301.

[14] *Seymour v. London and Provincial Marine Ins. Co.* (1872) 41 L.J.C.P. 193.

Implied warranties

There is no implied warranty as to the nationality of a ship, or that her nationality shall not be changed during the risk.[1] In a voyage policy there is an implied warranty that at the commencement of the voyage the ship shall be seaworthy[2] for the purposes of the adventure insured, i.e. reasonably fit in all respects to encounter the ordinary perils of the sea on such an adventure.[3] This may be excluded by an express term inconsistent therewith.[4] It is immaterial that the unseaworthiness was caused by acts of third parties or inevitable accident, or that the insured was ignorant of the fact.[5] A temporary defect is not a breach of warranty provided that the defect can be remedied or danger from it averted by due care during the voyage.[6] Seaworthiness includes possession of all necessary tackle and stores and having a competent master and adequate crew.[7] The warranty may be waived by a note on the policy[8] or by an act of the underwriter,[9] but otherwise breach of warranty discharges the underwriter from liability from the time of breach though the unseaworthiness were remedied before the loss and the loss was unconnected therewith.[10]

There is no warranty that a ship originally seaworthy shall continue to be so, or that master and crew will do their duty during the voyage, so that their negligence after the voyage has commenced is no defence, so long as the loss has been immediately caused by a peril insured against.[11] Where, however, the policy attaches when the ship is in port there is an implied warranty that the ship is reasonably fit to encounter the ordinary perils of the port,[12] but for the policy to continue in force to cover a subsequent voyage insured the ship must be seaworthy for that voyage.[13]

---

[1] S. 37; cf. *Hutchinson* v. *Aberdeen Sea Ins. Co.* (1876) 3 R. 682.

[2] Seaworthy means the same in this context as in a contract of carriage by sea: *Becker, Gray & Co.* v. *London Assce. Corpn.* [1918] A.C. 101; *Fireman's Fund Ins. Co.* v. *W. Australian Ins. Co.* (1927) 33 Com. Cas. 36.

[3] S. 39(1) and (4); *Stanton* v. *Richardson* (1874) L.R. 9 C.P. 390; 45 L.J.Q.B. 78 (H.L.); *Steel* v. *State Line S.S. Co.* (1877) 4 R. (H.L.) 103.

[4] S. 35(3); *Quebec Marine Ins. Co.* v. *Commercial Bank of Canada* (1870) L.R. 3 P.C. 234.

[5] *Quebec Marine Ins. Co., supra; The Glenfruin* (1885) 10 P.D. 103.

[6] *Steel, supra; Gilroy* v. *Price* [1893] A.C. 56.

[7] *Standard Oil Co.* v. *Clan Line,* 1924 S.C. (H.L.) 1.

[8] *Quebec Mar. Ins. Co.* v. *Commercial Bank of Canada* (1870) L.R. 3 P.C. 234.

[9] *Provincial Ins. Co. of Canada* v. *Leduc* (1874) L.R. 6 P.C. 224.

[10] *Quebec Marine Ins. Co., supra.*

[11] *Bermon* v. *Woodbridge* (1781) 2 Doug. K.B. 781; *Sadler* v. *Dixon* (1841) 8 M. & W. 895.

[12] S. 39(2).   [13] *Annen* v. *Woodman* (1810) 3 Taunt. 299.

Also, where the voyage is performed in different stages, during which the ship requires different kinds of or further preparation or equipment the implied warranty is that at the commencement of each stage she will be seaworthy for that stage.[1]

In a time policy there is no implied warranty that the ship shall be seaworthy at any stage of the adventure but where, with the privity of the assured, a ship is sent to sea in an unseaworthy state the insurer is not liable for any loss attributable to unseaworthiness.[2] The assured's privity, to defeat his claim, must have been in respect of the defect which caused the loss[3] and an omission to take precautions against unseaworthiness does not imply privity to unseaworthiness which such precautions might have disclosed.[4]

Warranty of cargoworthiness

In a voyage policy on goods there is an implied warranty that at the commencement of the voyage the ship is seaworthy and also reasonably fit to carry the goods to the destination contemplated,[5] but not that goods are seaworthy.[6]

Warranty of legality

There is an implied warranty that the adventure insured is lawful and, so far as within the assured's control will be carried through in a lawful manner.[7] The insurance on an illegal voyage is itself an illegal contract.[8] A voyage may be illegal by statute or by common law, or as contravening the laws of another country.[9]

The Voyage

Where the subject-matter is insured by a voyage policy 'at and from' or 'from' a particular place it is not necessary that the ship should be at that place when the contract is concluded, but there is an implied condition that the adventure should be commenced

---

[1] S. 39(3); *Bouillon* v. *Lupton* (1863) 15 C.B. (N.S.) 113; *The Vortigern* [1899] P. 140; *Greenock S.S. Co.* v. *Maritime Ins. Co.* [1903] 2 K.B. 657.

[2] S. 39(5); *Dudgeon* v. *Pembroke* (1877) 2 App. Cas. 284; *Kenneth* v. *Moore* (1883) 10 R. 547; *Mountain* v. *Whittle* [1921] 1 A.C. 615.

[3] *Thomas* v. *Tyne and Wear Steamship Ins. Assoc.* [1917] 1 K.B. 938.

[4] *Compania Naviera Vascongada* v. *British and Foreign Ins. Co.* (1936) 54 Ll.L.R. 35.

[5] S. 40(3); *Stanton* v. *Richardson* (1874) L.R. 9 C.P. 390; *Daniels* v. *Harris* (1874) L.R. 10 C.P. 1; *The Maori King* [1895] 2 Q.B. 550; *Sleigh* v. *Tyser* [1900] 2 Q.B. 333.

[6] S. 40(1); *Koebel* v. *Saunders* (1864) 33 L.J.C.P. 310.

[7] S. 41; *Dudgeon* v. *Pembroke* (1874) L.R. 9 Q.B.

[8] *Redmond* v. *Smith* (1844) 7 M. & G. 457.

[9] Cf. *Regazzoni* v. *Sethia* [1958] A.C. 301.

within a reasonable time,[1] failing which the insurer may avoid the contract, but such implied condition may be negatived by showing that the delay was caused by circumstances known to the insurer before the contract was concluded, or that he waived the condition.[2] Where the place of departure or of destination is specified in the policy and the ship sails from or for any other place, the risk does not attach.[3] Where after the commencement of the risk the destination of the ship is voluntarily changed from that contemplated by the policy, there is a change of voyage and, unless the policy otherwise provides, the insurer is discharged from liability from the time when the determination to change it is manifested, and it is immaterial that the ship may not in fact have left the course of voyage contemplated by the policy when the loss occurs.[4]

Deviation and delay

Where a ship without lawful excuse[5] deviates from the voyage contemplated by the policy, the insurer is discharged from liability as from the time of deviation, and it is immaterial that the ship may have regained her course before any loss occurs. There is deviation from the contemplated voyage where the course of the voyage is specifically designated by the policy and that course is departed from, or where the course is not specifically designated but the usual and customary course is departed from. The intention to deviate is immaterial; there must be a deviation in fact to discharge the insurer from his liability under the contract.[6] Notice of intention to deviate does not prevent the underwriter from being discharged though its receipt may evidence waiver of the condition of non-deviation.[7]

Where several ports of discharge are specified by the policy, the ship may proceed to all or any of them, but, in the absence of any usage or sufficient cause to the contrary, she must proceed to them, or such of them as she goes to, in the order designated by the policy, otherwise there is a deviation.[8] Where the policy is to 'ports of discharge' within a given area which are not named,

---

[1] This is a question of fact; S. 88.

[2] S. 42; *De Wolf* v. *Archangel Ins. Co.* (1874) L.R. 9 Q.B. 451; *Maritime Ins. Co.* v. *Stearns* [1901] 2 K.B. 912.

[3] Ss. 43–44.   [4] S. 45; *Tasker* v. *Cunningham* (1819) 1 Bligh 87.

[5] For excuses see S. 49.

[6] S. 46; evidence is admissible as to the, or a, usual route: *Reardon Smith Line* v. *Black Sea and Baltic General Ins. Co.* [1939] A.C. 562.

[7] *Redman* v. *Lowdon* (1814) 5 Taunt. 462.

[8] S. 47(1).

the ship must, in the absence of any usage or sufficient cause to the contrary, proceed to them, or such of them as she goes to, in their geographical order, otherwise there is a deviation.[1]

In the case of a voyage policy, the adventure insured must be prosecuted throughout its course with reasonable dispatch and if without lawful cause it is not so prosecuted the insurer is discharged from liability as from the time when the delay became unreasonable.[2]

Excuses for deviation or delay

Deviation or delay in prosecuting the contemplated voyage is excused[3] where authorized by any special term in the policy,[4] or where caused by circumstances beyond the control of the master and his employer,[5] or where reasonably necessary to comply with an express or implied warranty[6] or where reasonably necessary for the safety of the ship or subject-matter insured[7] or for the purpose of saving human life, or aiding a ship in distress where human life may be in danger,[8] or where reasonably necessary for the purpose of obtaining medical or surgical aid for any person on board the ship, or where caused by the barratrous conduct of the master or crew, if barratry be one of the perils insured against.[9] Where the cause excusing the deviation or delay ceases to operate the ship must resume her course and prosecute her voyage with reasonable dispatch.[10]

Assignation of policy

Unless it contains terms expressly prohibiting assignment a marine policy is assignable, either before or after loss, by indorsement thereon or in other customary manner; if assigned so as to pass the beneficial interest in the policy, the assignee may sue thereon in his own name and the defender may plead any defence arising out of the contract he could have if the action had been

---

[1] S. 47(2); *Marten* v. *Vestey Bros.* [1920] A.C. 307.
[2] S. 48; *Co. of African Merchants* v. *British Ins. Co.* (1873) L.R. 8 Ex. 154.
[3] S. 49(1).
[4] *Doyle* v. *Powell* (1832) 4 B. & Ad. 267; *Hyderabad Co.* v. *Willoughby* [1899] 2 Q.B. 530.
[5] *Richards* v. *Forestal Land Co.* [1942] A.C. 50.
[6] *Bouillon* v. *Lupton* (1863) 15 C.B. (N.S.) 113.
[7] *Phelps* v. *Hill* [1891] 1 Q.B. 605.
[8] *Scaramanga* v. *Stamp* (1880) 5 C.P.D. 295.
[9] *Ross* v. *Hunter* (1790) 4 T.R. 33.
[10] S. 49(2).

brought in the name of the person originally insured.[1] Where the assured has parted with or lost his interest in the subject-matter assured and has not, before or at the time of so doing, expressly or impliedly agreed to assign the policy, any subsequent assignment is inoperative; the section does not affect the assignment of a policy after loss.[2]

Premium

Unless otherwise agreed, the duty of the assured or his agent to pay the premium and the duty of the insurer to issue the policy to the assured or his agent are concurrent conditions and the insurer is not bound to issue the policy until payment or tender of the premium.[3] Failing contrary agreement, where a marine policy is effected for the assured by a broker, the latter is directly responsible to the insurer for the premium, and the insurer is directly responsible to the assured for the amount which may be payable in respect of losses or in respect of returnable premium. Unless otherwise agreed, the broker has, as against the assured, a lien on the policy for the amount of the premium and his charges for effecting the policy; and where he has dealt with the person who employs him as a principal he has also a lien on the policy in respect of any balance on any insurance account which may be due to him from such person, unless when the debt was incurred he had reason to believe that such person was only an agent.[4] Where a marine policy, effected on behalf of the assured by a broker, acknowledges the receipt of the premium, that is, in the absence of fraud, conclusive as between insurer and assured, but not as between insurer and broker.[5]

Liability for loss

Subject to the Act, and unless the policy otherwise provides, the insurer is liable for any loss proximately caused by a peril insured against but, subject to these qualifications, he is not liable for any loss which is not proximately caused by a peril

---

[1] S. 50; *Pickersgill* v. *London and Provincial Co.* [1912] 3 K.B. 614; see also *Graham Joint Stock Shipping Co.* v. *Merchants Marine Ins. Co.* [1924] A.C. 294; *Samuel* v. *Dumas* [1924] A.C. 431; *Williams* v. *Atlantic Assce. Co.* [1933] 1 K.B. 81.

[2] S. 51; *Lloyd* v. *Fleming* (1872) L.R. 7 Q.B. 299; *N. of England Oil Cake Co.* v. *Archangel Marine Ins. Co.* (1875) L.R. 10 Q.B. 249.

[3] S. 52; *Xenos* v. *Wickham* (1866) L.R. 2 H.L. 296; cf. *Clyde Marine Ins. Co.* v. *Renwick*, 1924 S.C. 113.

[4] S. 53; *Universo Ins. Co.* v. *Merchants' Marine Ins. Co.* [1897] 2 Q.B. 93.

[5] S. 54.

insured against.[1] In particular, the insurer is not liable for any loss attributable to the wilful misconduct of the assured, but, unless the policy otherwise provides, he is liable for any loss proximately caused by a peril insured against, even though the loss would not have happened but for the misconduct or negligence of the master or crew.[2] Unless the policy otherwise provides, the insurer on ship or goods is not liable for any loss proximately caused by delay, although the delay be caused by a peril insured against.[3] Also, unless the policy otherwise provides, the insurer is not liable for ordinary wear and tear, ordinary leakage and breakage, inherent vice or nature of the subject-matter insured, or for any loss proximately caused by rats or vermin, or for any injury to machinery not proximately caused by maritime perils.[4]

Losses

A loss may be an actual total loss, a constructive total loss, or a partial loss. Prima facie an insurance against actual, includes a constructive, total loss. Where the action is for a total loss and the evidence proves only a partial loss, the assured may, unless the policy provides otherwise, recover for a partial loss. Where goods reach their destination in specie, but by reason of obliteration of marks or otherwise are incapable of identification, the loss is partial and not total.[5]

Where the subject-matter insured is destroyed, or so damaged as to cease to be a thing of the kind insured, or where the assured is irretrievably deprived thereof, there is an actual total loss, and in that case no notice of abandonment need be given.[6] Where the ship concerned in the adventure is missing, and after the lapse of a reasonable time no news of her has been received, an actual total loss may be presumed.[7] Where by a peril insured against, the voyage is interrupted at an intermediate port or place, under such circumstances as, apart from any special stipulation in the

---

[1] S. 55(1); *Ionides* v. *Universal Mar. Ins. Assocn.* (1863) 32 L.J.C.P. 170; *Jackson* v. *Union Marine Ins. Co.* (1874) L.R. 10 C.P. 125; *Leyland Shipping Co.* v. *Norwich Union Ins. Co.* [1918] A.C. 350; *Samuel* v. *Dumas* [1924] A.C. 431; *Yorkshire Dale S.S. Co. Ltd.* v. *M.O.W.T.* [1942] A.C. 691; *Liverpool & London War Risks Ins. Assocn.* v. *Ocean S.S. Co.* [1948] A.C. 243.

[2] S. 55(2)(a); *Trinder* v. *Thames and Mersey Ins. Co.* [1898] 2 Q.B. 114.

[3] S. 55(2)(b); *Pink* v. *Fleming* (1890) 25 Q.B.D. 356.

[4] S. 55(2)(c); *Thames and Mersey Marine Ins. Co.* v. *Hamilton* (1887) 12 App. Cas. 484; *Stott (Baltic) Steamers* v. *Marten* [1916] 1 A.C. 304.

[5] S. 56; *Ship Blairmore* v. *Macredie* (1898) 25 R. (H.L.) 57.

[6] S. 57; *Cossman* v. *West* (1887) 13 App. Cas. 160; *Assoc. Oil Carriers* v. *Union Ins. Socy of Canton* [1917] 2 K.B. 184; *Marstrand Fishing Co.* v. *Beer* [1937] 1 All E.R. 158.

[7] S. 58; *Brice* v. *War Risks Assocn.* [1920] 3 K.B. 94.

contract of affreightment, to justify the master in landing and re-shipping the goods, or in transshipping them, and sending them on to their destination, the liability of the owner continues, notwithstanding the landing or transshipment.[1]

Subject to any express provision in the policy, there is a constructive total loss where the subject-matter insured is reasonably abandoned on account of its actual total loss appearing to be unavoidable or because it could not be preserved from actual total loss without an expenditure which would exceed its value when the expenditure has been incurred.[2] In particular there is a constructive total loss where the assured is deprived of the possession of his ship or goods by a peril insured against and either it is unlikely that he can recover the ship or goods or the cost of recovering would exceed their value when recovered; or, in the case of damage to a ship, where she is so damaged by a peril insured against, that the cost of repairing the damage would exceed the value of the ship when repaired; or, in the case of damage to goods, where the cost of repairing the damage and forwarding the goods to their destination would exceed their value on arrival.[3]

Where there is a constructive total loss the assured may either treat the loss as a partial loss, or abandon the subject-matter insured to the insurer and treat the loss as if it were an actual total loss.[4]

Subject to this section, where the assured elects to abandon the subject-matter insured to the insurer he must give notice of abandonment, failing which the loss can only be treated as a partial loss. Notice may be given in writing, or orally, or partly in each way, and in any terms which indicate the intention of the assured to abandon his insured interest in the subject-matter insured unconditionally to the insurer. Notice must be given with reasonable diligence after the receipt of reliable information of the loss, but where the information is of a doubtful character the assured is entitled to a reasonable time to make inquiry. Where notice is properly given, the rights of the assured are not prejudiced by the fact that the insurer refuses to accept the abandonment. Acceptance of the abandonment may be either express or

---

[1] S. 59; cf. *Hansen* v. *Dunn* (1906) 11 Com. Cas. 100.

[2] S. 60(1); *Shepherd* v. *Henderson* (1881) 9 R. (H.L.) 1; *Robertson* v. *Nomikos* [1939] 2 All E.R. 723.

[3] S. 60(2); *Scottish Maritime Ins. Co.* v. *Turner* (1853) 1 Macq. 334; *Court Line* v. *R.* [1945] 2 All E.R. 357.

[4] S. 61; *Fleming* v. *Smith* (1848) 1 H.L. Cas. 513; *Kaltenbach* v. *Mackenzie* (1878) 3 C.P.D. 467; *Robertson* v. *Royal Exchange Assce. Corpn.* 1925 S.C. 1.

implied from the conduct of the insurer; his mere silence after notice is not an acceptance. Where notice of abandonment is accepted the abandonment is irrevocable; the acceptance conclusively admits liability for the loss and' the sufficiency of the notice. Notice is unnecessary where at the time when the assured receives information of the loss there would be no possibility of benefit to the insurer if notice were given to him. Notice may be waived by the insurer. Where an insurer has reinsured his risk, no notice of abandonment need be given by him.[1]

Where there is a valid abandonment, the insurer is entitled to take over the interest of the assured in whatever may remain of the subject-matter insured and all proprietary rights incidental thereto. On the abandonment of a ship the insurer is entitled to any freight being earned, and earned by her subsequent to the casualty causing the loss, less the expenses of earning it incurred after the casualty; and where the ship is carrying the owner's goods the insurer is entitled to a reasonable remuneration for the carriage of them subsequent to the casualty causing the loss.[2]

Partial losses

A particular average loss is a partial loss caused by a peril insured against, and which is not a general average loss.[3] Particular charges are expenses incurred by or on behalf of the assured for the safety or preservation of the subject-matter insured, other than general average and salvage charges; they are not included in particular average.[4] Salvage charges, which are the charges recoverable under maritime law by a salvor independently of contract and do not include the expenses of services in the nature of salvage rendered by the assured or his agents, or any person employed for hire by them, for the purpose of averting a peril insured against, when properly incurred, may be recovered as particular charges or as a general average loss, according to the circumstances under which they were incurred.[5] If incurred in preventing a loss by perils insured against they may be recovered as a loss by those perils.[6]

---

[1] S. 62; *Currie* v. *Bombay Ins. Co.* (1869) L.R. 3 C.P. 72; *Kaltenbach, supra*; *Shepherd* v. *Henderson* (1881) 9 R. (H.L.) 1; *Ship Blairmore* v. *Macredie* (1898) 25 R. (H.L.) 57.

[2] S. 63; *Stewart* v. *Greenock Ins. Co.* (1848) 2 H.L. Cas. 159; *Scottish Marine Ins. Co.* v. *Turner* (1853) 1 Macq. 334.

[3] S. 64(1); e.g. where the ship is damaged or part of the goods lost; cf. *Kidston* v. *Empire Ins. Co.* (1867) L.R. 2 C.P. 357.

[4] S. 64(2).

[5] *Aitchison* v. *Lohre* (1879) 4 App. Cas. 755; *Dixon* v. *Sea Assce. Co.* (1880) 4 Asp. M.L.C. 457.   [6] S. 65.

General average loss

A general average loss is a loss caused by or directly consequential on a general average act and includes a general average
expenditure as well as a general average sacrifice. There is a
general average act where any extraordinary sacrifice or expenditure is voluntarily and reasonably made or incurred in time of
peril[1] for the purpose of preserving the property imperilled in
the common adventure.[2] Where there is a general average loss,
the party on whom it falls is entitled, subject to the conditions
imposed by maritime law,[3] to a rateable contribution from the
other parties interested, and such contribution is called a general
average contribution. Subject to any express provision in the
policy, where the assured has incurred a general average expenditure, he may recover from the insurer in respect of the proportion
of the loss which falls upon him; and in the case of a general
average sacrifice he may recover from the insurer in respect of
the whole loss without having enforced his right of contribution
from the other parties liable to contribute. Subject to any express
provision in the policy, where the assured has paid, or is liable to
pay, a general average contribution in respect of the subject
insured, he may recover therefor from the insurer. In the absence
of express stipulation, the insurer is not liable for any general
average loss or contribution where the loss was not incurred for
the purpose of avoiding, or in connection with the avoidance of, a
peril insured against. Where ship, freight and cargo, or any two
of those interests, are owned by the same assured, the liability of
the insurer in respect of general average losses or contribution
is to be determined as if those subjects were owned by different
persons.[4]

Measure of indemnity

The sum which the assured can recover in respect of a loss on a
policy by which he is insured, in the case of an unvalued policy,
to the full extent of the insurable value, or in the case of a valued
policy, to the full extent of the value fixed by the policy, is the

---

[1] *Watson* v. *Firemen's Fund Ins. Co.* [1922] 2 K.B. 355.

[2] See further Ch. 53, *infra*.

[3] These are that the claimant has no claim where the peril has been occasioned by the
fault of the claimant or his servant (see *The Carron Park* (1890) 15 P.D. 203) including
unseaworthiness: *Schloss* v. *Heriot* (1863) 14 C.B. (N.S.) 59; *Goulandris* v. *Goldman* [1957]
3 All E.R. 100; and that no contribution is recoverable for the jettison of deck cargo,
unless loading on deck is in accordance with the common usage of trade on such a voyage:
Wright v. *Marwood* (1881) 7 Q.B.D. 62; *Burton* v. *English* (1883) 12 Q.B.D. 218.

[4] S. 66; *Svendsen* v. *Wallace* (1885) 10 App. Cas. 404.

measure of indemnity. Where there is a loss recoverable under the policy, the insurer, or each insurer if more than one, is liable for such proportion of the measure of indemnity as the amount of his subscription bears to the value fixed by the policy in the case of a valued policy, or to the insurable value in the case of an unvalued policy [1]

Subject to the Act and to any express provision in the policy, where there is a total loss, if the policy be a valued policy the measure of indemnity is the sum fixed by the policy, and if an unvalued policy, the insurable value of the subject-matter insured.[2]

Partial loss of ship

Where a ship is damaged but not totally lost, the measure of indemnity, subject to any express provision in the policy, is as follows: where the ship has been repaired, the assured is entitled to the reasonable cost of the repairs, less customary deductions, but not exceeding the sum insured in respect of any one casualty; where the ship has been only partially repaired, the assured is entitled to the reasonable cost of such repairs, computed as above, and also to be indemnified for the reasonable depreciation, if any, arising from the unrepaired damage, provided that the aggregate amount shall not exceed the cost of repairing the whole damage, computed as above; where the ship has not been repaired, and has not been sold in her damaged state during the risk, the assured is entitled to be indemnified for the reasonable depreciation arising from the unrepaired damage, but not exceeding the reasonable cost of repairing such damage computed as above.[3] Unless the ship is a new one it is customary to deduct one-third of the expense of labour and materials of the repair because the repairs will make the ship better than before.[4]

Partial loss of freight

Subject to express provision in the policy, where there is a partial loss of freight, the measure of indemnity is such proportion of the sum fixed by the policy, in the case of a valued policy, or of the insurable value, in the case of an unvalued policy, as

---

[1] S. 67; cf. *Aitchison* v. *Lohre* (1879) 4 App. Cas. 759.
[2] S. 68; *Ship Blairmore* v. *Macredie* (1898) 25 R. (H.L.) 57; *Woodside* v. *Globe Marine Ins. Co.* [1896] 1 Q.B. 105.
[3] S. 69.
[4] cf. *Aitchison* v. *Lohre* (1879) 4 App. Cas. 755.

the proportion of freight lost by the assured bears to the whole freight at the risk of the assured under the policy.[1]

Partial loss of goods or other moveables

Where there is a partial loss of goods, merchandise, or other moveables, the measure of indemnity, subject to any express provision in the policy, is as follows: Where part of the goods, etc., insured by a valued policy is totally lost, the measure of indemnity is such proportion of the sum fixed by the policy as the insurable value of the part lost bears to the insurable value of the whole, ascertained as in the case of an unvalued policy; where part of the goods, etc., insured by an unvalued policy is totally lost, the measure of indemnity is the insurable value of the part lost, ascertained as in a case of total loss; where the whole or any part of the goods or merchandise insured has been delivered damaged at its destination, the measure of indemnity is such proportion of the sum fixed by the policy in the case of a valued policy, or of the insurable value in the case of an unvalued policy, as the difference between the gross sound and damaged values at the place of arrival bears to the gross sound value.[2]

Apportionment of valuation

Where different species of property are insured under a single valuation, the valuation must be apportioned over the different species in proportion to their respective insurable values, as in the case of an unvalued policy. The insured value of any part of a species is such proportion of the total insured value of the same as the insurable value of the part bears to the insurable value of the whole ascertained in both cases as provided by the Act. Where a valuation has to be apportioned, and particulars of the prime cost of each separate species, quality or description of goods cannot be ascertained, the division of the valuation may be made over the net arrived sound values of the different species, qualities, or descriptions of goods.[3]

General average contributions and salvage charges

Subject to any express provision in the policy, where the assured has paid, or is liable for, any general average contribution, the measure of indemnity is the full amount of such contribution

---

[1] S. 70; *The Main* [1894] P. 320.

[2] S. 71; S. 71(4) defines 'gross value' and 'gross proceeds'. See also *Spence* v. *Union Marine Ins. Co.* (1868) L.R. 3 C.P. 427; *Lysaght* v. *Coleman* [1895] 1 Q.B. 49.

[3] S. 72.

if the subject-matter liable to contribution is insured for its full contributory value; but if not, or if only part of it be insured, the indemnity payable by the insurer must be reduced in proportion to the under-insurance, and where there has been a particular average loss which constitutes a deduction from the contributory value and for which the insurer is liable, that amount must be deducted from the insured value to ascertain what the insurer is liable to contribute. Where the insurer is liable for salvage charges the extent of his liability is determined on the same principle.[1]

Liabilities to third parties

Where the assured has effected an insurance in express terms against any liability to a third party, the measure of indemnity, subject to any express provision in the policy, is the amount paid or payable by him to such third party in respect of such liability.[2]

Measure of indemnity generally

Where there has been a loss in respect of any subject-matter not expressly provided for in the foregoing provisions of the Act the measure of indemnity shall be ascertained, as nearly as may be, in accordance with those provisions, in so far as applicable to the particular case. Nothing in the Act relating to measure of indemnity affects the rules relating to double insurance, or prohibits the insurer from disproving interest in whole or in part, or from showing that at the time of the loss the whole or any part of the subject-matter insured was not at risk under the policy.[3]

Particular average warranties

Where the subject-matter insured is warranted free from particular average, the assured cannot recover for a loss of part, other than a loss incurred by a general average sacrifice, unless the contract contained in the policy be apportionable, in which case the assured may recover for a total loss of any apportionable part. Where so warranted, either wholly or under a certain percentage, the insurer is nevertheless liable for salvage charges and for particular charges and other expenses properly incurred pursuant to the suing and labouring clause to avert a loss insured against. Unless the policy otherwise provides, where the subject-matter

---

[1] S. 73; *Steamship Balmoral* v. *Marten* [1902] A.C. 511; see also *Robinows & Marjoribanks* v. *Ewing's Trs.* (1876) 3 R. 1134.
[2] S. 74; *Cunard S.S. Co.* v. *Marten* [1902] 2 K.B. 624.
[3] S. 75.

insured is warranted free from particular average under a specified
percentage, a general average loss cannot be added to a particular
average loss to make up the specified percentage. To ascertain
whether the specified percentage has been reached, regard shall
be had only to the actual loss suffered by the subject-matter
insured; particular charges and the expenses of and incidental
to ascertaining and proving the loss must be excluded.[1]

Successive losses

Unless the policy otherwise provides and subject to the Act,
the insurer is liable for successive losses, even though the total
amount thereof may exceed the sum insured. Where under the
same policy, a partial loss, which has not been repaired or otherwise made good, is followed by a total loss, the assured can only
recover in respect of the total loss. Nothing in that section affects
the liability of the insurer under the suing and labouring clause.[2]

Suing and labouring clause

The object of the suing and labouring clause contained in the
standard form of policy is to encourage the assured to take all
necessary steps for the preservation of the insured property. The
underwriters agree that any such action shall be without prejudice to the insurance or the notice of abandonment.[3]

Where the policy contains a suing and labouring clause, the
engagement thereby entered into is deemed to be supplementary
to the contract of insurance, and the assured may recover from
the insurer any expenses properly incurred pursuant to the clause,
notwithstanding that the insurer may have paid for a total loss,
or that the subject-matter may have been warranted free from
particular average, either wholly or under a certain percentage.
General average losses and contributions and salvage charges as
defined by the Act are not recoverable under the suing and labouring clause, nor are expenses incurred for the purpose of averting
or diminishing any loss not covered by the policy. It is the duty of
the assured and his agents in all cases to take such measures as
may be reasonable for the purpose of averting or minimizing a
loss.[4]

---

[1] S. 76.

[2] S. 77; *Woodside* v. *Globe Marine Ins. Co.* [1896] 1 Q.B. 105; *British and Foreign Ins.
Co.* v. *Wilson Shipping Co.* [1921] 1 A.C. 188.

[3] *Lohre* v. *Aitchison* (1878) 3 Q.B.D. 558; (1879) 4 App. Cas. 755.

[4] S. 78; see *Gaunt* v. *British and Foreign Ins. Co.* [1920] 1 K.B. 903; [1921] 2 A.C. 41;
Berk v. *Style* [1956] 1 Q.B. 180.

Right of subrogation

Where the insurer pays for a total loss, either of the whole, or in the case of goods of any apportionable part of the subject-matter insured, he thereupon becomes entitled to take over the interest of the assured in whatever may remain of the subject-matter so paid for, and he is thereby subrogated to all the rights and remedies of the assured in and in respect of that subject-matter as from the time of the casualty causing the loss. Subject thereto where the insurer pays for a partial loss, he acquires no title to the subject-matter insured, or such part of it as may remain, but he is thereupon subrogated to all rights and remedies of the assured in and in respect of the subject-matter insured from the time of the casualty causing the loss, in so far as the assured has been indemnified according to the Act by such payment for the loss.[1]

Right of contribution

Where the assured is overinsured by double insurance, each insurer is bound, as between himself and the other insurers, to contribute rateably to the loss in proportion to the amount for which he is liable under his contract. If any insurer pays more than his proportion of the loss he is entitled to maintain an action for contribution against the insurers, and is entitled to the like remedies of a surety who has paid more than his proportion of the debt.[2]

Effect of under-insurance

Where the assured is insured for an amount less than the insurable value or, in the case of a valued policy, for an amount less than the policy valuation, he is deemed to be his own insurer in respect of the uninsured balance.[3]

Enforcement of return of premium

Where the premium or a proportionate part thereof is by the Act declared to be returnable, if already paid, it may be recovered by the assured from the insurer, and if unpaid, may be retained by the assured or his agent.[4]

---

[1] S. 79; *Burnand* v. *Rodocanachi* (1882) 7 App. Cas. 333; see also *Simpson* v. *Thomson* (1877) 5 R. (H.L.) 40.

[2] S. 80; *Whitworth Bros.* v. *Shepherd* (1884) 12 R. 204; *American Surety Co.* v. *Wright-son* (1910) 16 Com. Cas. 37.

[3] S. 81; *Whitworth* v. *Shepherd* (1884) 12 R. 204.   [3] S. 82.

Where the policy contains a stipulation for the return of the premium, or a proportionate part thereof, on the happening of a certain event and that happens, the premium or as the case may be the proportionate part thereof is thereupon returnable to the assured.[1]

Return for failure of consideration

Where the consideration for the payment of the premium totally fails, and there has been no fraud or illegality on the part of the assured or his agents, the premium is thereupon returnable to the assured. Where the consideration is apportionable and there is a total failure of any apportionable part of the considera-tion, a proportionate part of the premium is, under the like conditions, thereupon returnable to the assured. In particular, where the policy is void, or is avoided by the insurer as from the commencement of the risk, the premium is returnable, provided that there has been no fraud or illegality on the part of the assured; but if the risk is not apportionable, and has once attached, the premium is not returnable. Also where the subject-matter insured or part thereof has never been imperilled, the premium, or, as the case may be, a proportionate part thereof, is returnable; but where the subject-matter has been insured 'lost or not lost' and has arrived in safety at the time when the contract is concluded, the premium is not returnable unless the insurer then knew of the safe arrival. Again where the assured has no insurable interest throughout the currency of the risk the prem-ium is returnable, provided that this rule does not apply to a policy effected by way of gaming or wagering. Again where the assured has a defeasible interest which is terminated during the currency of the risk, the premium is not returnable, and where the assured has over-insured under an unvalued policy, a pro-portionate part of the premium is returnable. Subject to these provisions, where the assured has over-insured by double insurance, a proportionate part of the several premiums is returnable; but if the policies are effected at different times, and any earlier policy has at any time borne the entire risk, or if a claim has been paid on the policy in respect of the full sum insured thereby, no premium is returnable in respect of that policy, and when the double insurance is effected knowingly by the assured no premium is returnable.[2]

[1] S. 83.
[2] S. 84; *Bradford* v. *Symondson* (1881) 7 Q.B.D. 456.

Mutual insurance

Where two or more persons mutually agree to insure each other against marine losses there is mutual insurance. The provisions of the Act relating to the premium do not apply to mutual insurance, but a guarantee or such other arrangement as may be agreed on may be substituted for the premium. The provisions of the Act, so far as they may be modified by the agreement of parties, may in the case of mutual insurance be modified by the terms of the policies issued by the association, or by its rules and regulations. Apart therefrom the Act applies to a mutual insurance.[1]

Ratification by assured

Where a contract of marine insurance is in good faith effected by one person on behalf of another, the person on whose behalf it is effected may ratify the contract even after he is aware of a loss.[2]

Memorandum to the policy

The memorandum appended to the ordinary form of policy deals with commodities naturally likely to be easily damaged and small losses which may have been caused by perils insured against or by inherent vice. Usage may assist to determine what is covered by the items listed. The words 'free from average, unless general' mean that the underwriter is not liable for a partial loss of or damage to the subject-matter insured, unless it is of the nature of general average, for losses of which kind the insurer is liable.[3]

The memorandum concludes 'unless the ship be stranded'. If the ship has stranded, the insurer is liable for the excepted losses, although the loss is not attributable to the stranding.[4] Stranding means taking the ground and remaining there.[5]

PERSONAL INSURANCE

Contracts of life insurance, personal accident, and sickness insurance are not strictly contracts of indemnity, and there is normally no need to prove a pecuniary loss; the insured may value

---

[1] S. 85; *British Marine Mutual Ins. Co.* v. *Jenkins* [1900] 1 Q.B. 299.

[2] *Williams* v. *North China Ins. Co.* (1876) 1 C.P.D. 757; this is an exception to the ordinary rule exemplified in *Keighley Maxted* v. *Durant* [1901] A.C. 240.

[3] 1906 Act, Sched., R. 13; *Price* v. *A.1. Ships' Ins. Assoc.* (1889) 22 Q.B.D. 580.

[4] 1906 Act, Sched., R. 14; *Thames and Mersey Marine Ins. Co.* v. *Pitts* [1893] 1 Q.B. 476.

[5] *Letchford* v. *Oldham* (1880) 5 Q.B.D. 538.

his life, or loss of a limb or health, at whatever figure he chooses and no one can foresee what at the date of death, or injury, his commitments to dependants may be.

Life insurance is a contract whereby the insurers undertake, in consideration of premiums being regularly paid throughout life, to pay a specified sum on a person's death,[1] or on a specified date if he survives so long.[2]

Insurable interest

By the Life Assurance Act, 1774, no insurance is to be made on the life or lives of any person or persons, or on any other event whatsoever wherein the person for whose benefit the policy is made has no interest, or by way of gaming or wagering, failing which it is void. The names of the persons interested in the policy have to be inserted, and no greater sum is to be recovered from the insurers than the amount or value of the interest of the assured in the life or event insured. The Act has been held to apply also to personal accident insurance and to insurance on events,[3] but not to apply to insurance by the assured on his own life for his own benefit, and insurances by spouses on each other's life.[4] The interest must be pecuniary and capable of monetary valuation.[5]

Spouses have insurable interest in each other's lives.[6] Relatives, other than spouses, are not presumed to have insurable interest[7] but pecuniary interest must be proved,[8] a legal obligation to pay for the funeral being sufficient.[9] Creditors have an insurable interest in the life of a debtor,[10] and employers and employees in each other's lives.[11] A policy by a husband on his wife's life is part of his moveable estate if he dies, survived by her.[12]

---

[1] The payer of the premiums is not necessarily the assured himself. Where the premiums are payable in small sums at short intervals to collectors, this is industrial assurance, which is regulated by the Industrial Assurance Acts, 1923–48.

[2] This is strictly endowment assurance, rather than life assurance.

[3] *Shilling* v. *Accidental Death Ins. Co.* (1857) 2 H. & N. 42; *Re London County Commercial Reinsurance Office* [1922] 2 Ch. 67.

[4] *MacFarlane* v. *Royal London Friendly Soc.* (1886) 2 T.L.R. 755; *Griffiths* v. *Fleming* [1909] 1 K.B. 805.

[5] *Simcock* v. *Scottish Imperial Ins. Co.* (1902) 10 S.L.T. 286; *Macaura* v. *Northern Assce. Co.* [1925] A.C. 619.

[6] *Griffiths, supra.*

[7] *Halford* v. *Kepner* (1830) 10 B. & C. 724.

[8] *Harse* v. *Pearl Life Assce. Co.* [1904] 1 K.B. 558; cf. *Came* v. *Glasgow Friendly Socy.*, 1933 S.C. 69.

[9] *Harse, supra;* cf. *Carmichael* v. *C's Exrx.*, 1919 S.C. 636.

[10] *Dalby* v. *India and London Life Assce. Co.* (1854) 15 C.B. 365.

[11] *Hebden* v. *West* (1863) 3 B. & S. 579.

[12] *Pringle's Trs.* v. *Hamilton* (1872) 10 M. 621.

Factors affecting risk

The assured's age, habits, occupation, health, and medical history are very relevant to the risk and information relative thereto is normally required from the proposer.[1] Similarly a contract of reinsurance has been held avoided by concealment of facts material to the risk.[2]

Event insured against

The event insured against is death; the cause of death is immaterial, save that death by suicide while of sound mind renders it contrary to public policy to pay the sum due,[3] and death from certain causes may be excepted.[4]

Assignation of life policies

A life policy is assignable by assignation and delivery, intimated to the insurers, to the effect of vesting in the assignee the rights of the assignor, but subject to pleas pleadable by the insurer against the assignor.[5] The assignation may be to trustees for stated purposes.[6] The form may be either the ordinary one provided by the Transmission of Moveable Property (Sc.) Act, 1862, or that provided by the Policies of Assurance Act, 1867.

By statute[7] an assignee may sue in his own name to recover monies due by insurers after written notice of the assignation has been given to the company concerned. Assignation may be by way of sale, gift, in security of money lent, or to a trustee for the benefit of creditors. Spouses domiciled in Scotland cannot assign a policy issued by an English company under the (English) Married Women's Property Act, 1882.[8] It is normally agreed that the assured will pay the premiums, or the assignee may do so, and add the amount to the assignor's debt. Custody of the policy by a third party, without assignation in his favour, confers no security right on the third party.[9]

---

[1] *Life Assocn.* v. *Foster* (1873) 11 M. 351; *Buist* v. *Scottish Equitable Life Assce. Socy.* (1878) 5 R. (H.L.) 64; *Standard Life Assce. Co.* v. *Weems* (1884) 11 R. (H.L.) 48; cf. *Adamson's Trs.* v. *Scottish Provincial Assce. Co.* (1868) 6 M. 442.

[2] *Equitable Life Assce. Socy.* v. *General Accident Assce. Corpn.* (1904) 12 S.L.T. 348.

[3] *Beresford* v. *Royal Ins. Co.* [1938] A.C. 586; cf. *Adamson's Trs.* v. *Scottish Provincial Assce. Co.* (1868) 6 M. 442; *Ballantyne's Trs.* v. *Scottish Amicable,* 1921, 2 S.L.T. 75.

[4] *Rowett, Leakey & Co.* v. *Scottish Provident Inst.* [1927] 1 Ch. 55.

[5] *Scottish Widows Fund* v. *Buist* (1876) 3 R. 1078; cf. *Buist* v. *Scottish Equitable* (1878) 5 R. (H.L.) 64.

[6] *Ballantyne's Trs.* v. *Scottish Amicable Life Assce. Socy.,* 1921, 2 S.L.T. 75.

[7] Policies of Assurance Act, 1867, S. 1.

[8] *Pender* v. *Commercial Bank,* 1940 S.L.T. 306.

[9] *Wylie's Exrx.* v. *McJannet* (1901) 4 F. 195.

On repayment of money lent, the assured is entitled to a retrocession and redelivery of the policy by the assignee, which also must be intimated to the insurers.

Payment under life policy

The amount payable is the sum insured with, if the contract so provides, bonuses, but without interest; it is due to the executor, assignee, or trustee in bankruptcy of the assured,[1] or if on the life of a third party, to the assured. If the policy were effected under the Married Women's Policies of Assurance (Sc.) Act, 1880, S. 2, it is payable to the trustee thereunder, or to the widow for whose benefit it was taken out.[2] Such a policy may be surrendered with the wife's concurrence,[3] but cannot be assigned to the husband's creditors,[4] nor may the wife deal with it *stante matrimonio*.[5] It is payable on proof of death, which may be difficult where the policy has been assigned.[6] If paid on false evidence of death, adduced bona fide, the policy may be revived and the sum repaid.[7]

Surrender

The value of a life policy at any time depends on the insured's expectation of life and the period during which it has been in force. If he allows the premiums to lapse, he loses the whole value of the policy. He may, if the contract so provides, have an option, on notice to the insurers, to surrender the policy and receive as its surrender value a modified sum, dependent on how long the policy had been in existence.[8] Alternatively the insured may sell his rights and assign the policy absolutely to the purchaser.

Endowment insurance

The contract of endowment insurance differs from life insurance in that the contingency is the duration of life to a

---

[1] cf. *Champion* v. *Duncan* (1867) 6 M. 17; *Muirhead* v. *M.'s Factor* (1867) 6 M. 95; *Ramsay's Trs.* v. *R.* (1899) 1 F. 495.

[2] cf. *Chrystal's Trs.* v. *C.*, 1912 S.C. 1003.

[3] *Schumann* v. *Scottish Widows' Fund Socy.* (1886) 13 R. 678.

[4] *Edinburgh Life Assce. Co.* v. *Balderston* (1909) 2 S.L.T. 323.

[5] *Scottish Life Assce. Co.* v. *Donald* (1901) 9 S.L.T. 200.

[6] The Presumption of Life Limitation (Sc.) Act, 1891, does not apply: *Murray* v. *Chalmers*, 1913, 1 S.L.T. 223.

[7] *N.B. and Mercantile Ins.* v. *Stewart* (1871) 9 M. 534.

[8] After election made, he is entitled only to the surrender value, even though he died before surrendering the policy: *Ingram-Johnson* v. *Century Ins. Co.*, 1909 S.C. 1032.

specified date rather than death.[1] The one policy may provide for both, life till a specified date or earlier death.[2] Where a parent takes out a policy for the benefit of a child, provision may be made for the child exercising various options on coming of age.[3]

Personal accident insurance

The object of personal accident insurance is to provide a sum of money in the event of the assured sustaining accidental injury; it is not a contract of indemnity but a contract to pay on a specified event.[4] By statute[5] an insurable interest is necessary; this is normally the potential pecuniary loss to the assured resulting from injury to himself or of a third party, if a third party is insured.

The event on which the sum is payable is normally described as 'accident' or 'an accident'. Injury by accident covers any unintended and undesired injury though not attributable to any distinct event;[6] injury from an accident covers physical harm resulting from a mishap or untoward occurrence.[7] Injury caused by the wilful act of a third party is injury by accident,[8] but injury by disease is not.[9] Injury caused by negligence may still be accidental injury.[10] In other cases it is a question of interpretation whether the event falls within the terms of the policy. The onus of proof thereof is on the claimant.[11] In the absence of contrary evidence it will be presumed that death arose from accident rather than suicide.[12]

The doctrine of proximate cause applies to personal accident insurance.[13]

---

[1] *Prudential Ins. Co.* v. *I.R.C.* [1904] 2 K.B. 658.

[2] *Gould* v. *Curtis* [1913] 3 K.B. 84.

[3] *Carmichael* v. *C.'s Exrx.*, 1920 S.C. (H.L.) 195.

[4] *Bradburn* v. *G.W. Ry.* (1874) L.R. 10 Ex. 1; *General Accident Assce. Corpn.* v. *I.R.C.* (1906) 8 F. 477; *Lloyds Bank, Ltd.* v. *Eagle Star Insce. Co.* [1951] 1 All E.R. 914.

[5] Life Assce. Act, 1774.

[6] *Macdonald* v. *Refuge Assce. Co.* (1890) 17 R. 955; *McInnes* v. *Dunsmuir and Jackson*, 1908 S.C. 1021 (cerebral haemorrhage); *Drylie* v. *Alloa Coal Co.*, 1913 S.C. 549 (pneumonia); *Aitken* v. *Finlayson, Bousfield & Co.*, 1914 S.C. 770 (apoplexy); *Brown* v. *Watson*, 1915 S.C. (H.L.) 44 (pneumonia); *Glasgow Coal Co.* v. *Welsh*, 1916 S.C. (H.L.) 141 (rheumatism).

[7] e.g. vehicle accident.

[8] *Nisbet* v. *Rayner and Burn* [1910] 2 K.B. 689.

[9] *Roberts* v. *Dorothea Slate Quarries Co.* [1948] 2 All E.R. 201.

[10] *Clidero* v. *Scottish Accident Ins. Co.* (1892) 19 R. 355.

[11] *A.B.* v. *Northern Accident Ins. Co.* (1896) 24 R. 258; cf. *Ballantine* v. *Employers' Ins. Co.* (1893) 21 R. 305; *Donnison* v. *Employers' Accident Co.* (1897) 24 R. 681.

[12] *Macdonald* v. *Refuge Assce. Co.* (1890) 17 R. 955.

[13] *McKechnie's Trs.* v. *Scottish Accident Ins. Co.* (1889) 17 R. 6; *Isitt* v. *Railway Passengers Assce. Co.* (1889) 22 Q.B.D. 504; *Hope's Trs.* v. *Scottish Accident Ins. Co.* (1896) 3 S.L.T. 252; *Smith* v. *Cornhill Ins. Co.* [1938] 3 All E.R. 145.

The policy may exclude certain risks, or accidents happening in certain circumstances, as while under the influence of drink,[1] or caused by the insured's exposing himself to obvious risks of injury.[2]

The policy may provide for a lump sum payment on the insured's death, or for periodical payments during disability. Pecuniary loss resulting from disability is too remote to be recoverable, unless expressly covered.[3] Similarly provisions may be made for insurance against disability by illness. Provision is normally made for payment to a specified relative on death.[4]

PROPERTY INSURANCE

Property insurance is a contract of indemnity against loss sustained by reason of stated contingencies, such as fire, theft, burglary, fraud, loss, death of live-stock, or other peril.

Insurable interest

The insured must have an insurable interest in the subject-matter of the insurance; this may be by virtue of ownership, or possession under any kind of legal title, even though temporary or defeasible. The existence of a contract which confers advantages which will be lost by the destruction of the property creates an insurable interest therein.[5] A custodier has an insurable interest in property left with him in respect of his charges,[6] a postponed bondholder in respect of his right in security.[7] Several persons may each have a distinct insurable interest in one subject, such as landlord and tenant, owner and bondholder, liferenter and fiar, and a composite policy may be effected for the benefit of the several interests of several parties.[8] A person not having an insurable interest in property may insure it for the benefit of one having an insurable interest, but the latter must

---

[1] *MacRobbie* v. *Accident Ins. Co.* (1886) 23 S.L.R. 391; cf. *Robertson* v. *London Guarantee Co.*, 1915, 1 S.L.T. 195.

[2] *Sangster's Trs.* v. *General Accident Ins. Corpn.* (1896) 24 R. 56.

[3] *Theobald* v. *Railway Passengers Assce. Co.* (1854) 10 Ex. 45.

[4] *Law* v. *Newnes* (1894) 21 R. 1027; *Hunter* v. *H.* (1904) 7 F. 136; *O'Reilly* v. *Prudential Assce. Co.* [1934] Ch. 519.

[5] *Collingridge* v. *Royal Exchange Assce. Corpn.* (1877) 3 Q.B.D. 173; *Phoenix Assce. Co.* v. *Spooner* [1905] 2 K.B. 753.

[6] *Dalgleish* v. *Buchanan* (1854) 16 D. 332.

[7] *Westminster Fire Office* v. *Glasgow Provident Inv. Socy.* (1888) 15 R. (H.L.) 89.

[8] *Nichols* v. *Scottish Union and National Ins. Co.* (1885) 14 R. 1094; 2 T.L.R. 190.

authorize or ratify the insurance before loss occurs.[1] The policy may require the interest to be described.[2] If the interest ceases, the insurance ceases to be effective unless assigned;[3] it does not transmit with property.[4]

The risk

The perils insured against are those stated in the policy, and it is a question of fact whether the event falls within the perils insured against.[5] The cause of a loss is immaterial, and insurance against fire covers fire caused negligently[6] or by fire deliberately lit getting out of control,[7] but not fire deliberately lit by the assured to destroy the property insured.[8]

Excepted perils

Liability is commonly excluded for loss caused by specified causes, such as riot, civil commotion, war, etc. Such words are construed in their ordinary legal meanings and it is a question of fact whether the happenings fall within them or not.[9]

Condition precedent

It may be made a prerequisite of liability that injury or damage be intimated and vouched by specified evidence.[10]

Proximate cause

It must be shown that the loss was proximately caused by a peril insured against, if not directly, at least as a necessary consequence thereof.[11] Losses which follow in the ordinary course of events from a peril are also proximately caused thereby,

---

[1] *Dalgleish* v. *Buchanan* (1854) 16 D. 332; *Ferguson* v. *Aberdeen Parish Council,* 1916 S.C. 715.

[2] *L.N.W. Ry.* v. *Glyn* (1859) 1 E. & E. 652.

[3] *N.B. and Mercantile Ins. Co.* v. *Moffatt* (1871) L.R. 7 C.P. 25; *Rogerson* v. *Scottish Automobile Ins. Co.* (1931) 48 T.L.R. 17.

[4] *Phoenix Assce. Co.* v. *Spooner* [1905] 2 K.B. 753.

[5] If the risks are described in legal terminology, e.g. housebreaking, such words are interpreted in their legal sense: *Re George and Goldsmiths, etc. Assocn.* [1899] 1 Q.B. 595; *Re Calf and Sun Insurance Office* [1920] 2 K.B. 366.

[6] *Shaw* v. *Robberds* (1837) 6 Ad. & El. 75; *Dixon* v. *Sadler* (1839) 5 M. & W. 405.

[7] *Dixon, supra; Harris* v. *Poland* [1941] 1 K.B. 462.

[8] *Upjohn* v. *Hitchens* [1918] 2 K.B. 48; *City Tailors, Ltd.* v. *Evans* (1921) 38 T.L.R. 230.

[9] *Curtis* v. *Mathews* [1919] 1 K.B. 425; *London & Lancs. Fire Ins. Co.* v. *Bolands* [1924] A.C. 836; *Munday* v. *Metropolitan Police District Receiver* [1949] 1 All E.R. 337; see also *Scottish Plate Glass Ins. Co.* v. *Edinburgh Corpn.,* 1941 S.C. 115.

[10] *Shields* v. *Scottish Assce. Corpn.* (1889) 16 R. 1014.

[11] *Johnston* v. *W. of Sc. Ins. Co.* (1828) 7 S. 52.

such as damage sustained from water used to extinguish a fire.[1] But the insurers are not liable for losses not proximately caused, but only indirectly or remotely caused, or consequential on the loss directly and proximately caused.[2] If the loss is proximately caused by an excepted peril the insurers are not liable, even if the excepted peril was itself initiated by a peril insured against.[3]

Amount recoverable

The sum insured is always specified in the policy, and is the maximum liability of the insurers. The assured is entitled only to full indemnity within that limit, and only on proof of loss. The amount recoverable is the diminution in value of the property by reason of the event.[4] In the case of total loss this is the full value of the property destroyed up to the limit of the sum insured, excluding sentimental value.[5] Prima facie this is market value, but where this is not adequate indemnity, the cost of reinstatement is the basis of indemnity.[6] In the case of partial loss the amount recoverable is normally based on the cost of repair or replacement.[7]

Reinstatement

The insurers may have the option to reinstate damaged property by rebuilding or repair rather than to pay money,[8] in which case the assured cannot require them to reinstate or prevent them from doing so;[9] their election, once made, is final,[10] and may be implied by their conduct.[11] If they elect to do so, their obligation is sufficiently performed if the property is put substantially into the same state as before the loss;[12] failure to do so is a breach of contract.[13]

---

[1] *Stanley* v. *Western Ins. Co.* (1868) L.R. 3 Ex. 71; *Canada Rice Mills Ltd.* v. *Union Marine Co.* [1941] A.C. 55.

[2] *Menzies* v. *N.B. Ins. Co.* (1847) 9 D. 694; *Westminster Fire Office* v. *Glasgow Provident Ins. Socy.* (1888) 15 R. (H.L.) 89.

[3] *Rogers* v. *Whittaker* [1917] 1 K.B. 942.

[4] *Westminster Fire Office* v. *Glasgow Provident Ins. Socy.* (1888) 15 R. (H.L.) 89.

[5] *Hercules Ins. Co.* v. *Hunter* (1836) 14 S. 1137; *Re Egmont's Trusts* [1908] 1 Ch. 821.

[6] *Castellain* v. *Preston* (1883) 11 Q.B.D. 380; *Westminster Fire Office, supra.*

[7] *Scottish Amicable Assoc.* v. *Northern Assce. Co.* (1883) 11 R. 287

[8] *Sutherland* v. *Sun Fire Office* (1852) 14 D. 775.

[9] *Bisset* v. *Royal Exchange Assce. Co.* (1821) 1 S. 174.

[10] *Sutherland, supra.*

[11] *Sutherland, supra; Scottish Amicable Assoc.* v. *Northern Assce. Co.* (1883) 11 R. 287.

[12] *Times Fire Assce. Co.* v. *Hawke* (1859) 28 L.J. Ex. 317.

[13] *Anderson* v. *Commercial Union Ins. Co.* (1885) 55 L.J.Q.B. 146.

Salvage

The insurers are entitled to take possession of any salvage recoverable from the damaged premises.[1]

LIABILITY INSURANCE

Persons may insure against loss arising from legal liability incurred to a third party for damages for breach of contract or delict. An insurance on property may be combined with, but does not automatically cover, liability arising incidentally from loss of or damage to the property.[2] Common cases are of insurance against liability in damages to employees[3] or third parties, or against liability for professional negligence,[4] or against liability to members of the public injured on the assured's premises or by reason of his operations.[5] Licensees of nuclear sites must by insurance or otherwise cover their liability under the Nuclear Installations Act, 1965.[6]

The contract is one of indemnity.[7] The risks insured against are those stated in the policy[8] and it is a question of interpretation whether the liability arises from a risk covered by the policy.[9] The liability must normally be a legal one.[10] The assured may defeat his own claim by breach of a condition of the policy.[11]

The insurers normally require the assured to intimate to them claims made against him, not to admit liability nor to settle a claim without their consent, and to allow them to assume the defence of any action brought against the assured.[12] Their liability under the policy may be limited by reference to any one accident,[13] or to the total claims in any one year.

---

[1] *Oldfield* v. *Price* (1860) 2 F. & F. 80.

[2] *De Vaux* v. *Salvador* (1836) 4 Ad. & El. 420.

[3] See Employer's Liability (Compulsory Insurance) Act, 1969.

[4] *Forney* v. *Dominion Ins. Co.* [1969] 3 All E.R. 831.

[5] *Weir* v. *Accident Ins. Co.* (1908) 16 S.L.T. 141; *Smellie* v. *British General Ins. Co.,* 1918, 2 S.L.T. 58.

[6] Nuclear Installations Act, 1965, S. 19.

[7] *British Cash and Parcels Conveyors, Ltd.* v. *Lamson Store Services Ltd.* [1908] 1 K.B. 1006.

[8] *Reid* v. *Employers' Accident Ins. Co.* (1899) 1 F. 1031; *Life and Health Assce. Assoc.* v. *Yule* (1904) 6 F. 437.

[9] *Morrison and Mason* v. *Scottish Employers' Assce. Co.* (1888) 16 R. 212; contrast *Hamilton* v. *Anderson,* 1953 S.C. 129; *Murray* v. *Scottish Automobile Ins. Co.,* 1929 S.C. 48.

[10] *Haseldine* v. *Hosken* [1933] 1 K.B. 822.

[11] *Stewart* v. *London and Midland Ins. Co.,* 1916, 2 S.L.T. 189.

[12] See *Lister* v. *Romford Ice Co.* [1957] A.C. 555.

[13] cf. *McKinlay* v. *Life and Health Ins. Assoc.* (1905) 13 S.L.T. 102.

Statutory subrogation of injured party

By the Third Parties (Rights against Insurers) Act, 1930, an injured person has a direct claim against the wrongdoer's insurers where the wrongdoer has become bankrupt or, if a company, has resolved to wind-up or a winding-up order has been made. It is necessary to obtain judgment against the assured,[1] and the Act then transfers to the third parties the claim the assured would have had against his insurers.

MOTOR VEHICLE AND AVIATION INSURANCE

In the case of motor vehicles and aircraft insurance is commonly effected against loss of or damage to the vehicle or aircraft, and against liability incurred by its operation.

By statute[2] it is an offence to use, or cause or permit another person to use, a motor vehicle on a road unless there is in force a policy of insurance, or a security, in respect of third party risks complying with the Act. Failure to implement the statutory duty involves also civil liability to a person injured by the uninsured vehicle.[3] The risks required to be insured are in respect of any liability which may be incurred by the persons covered by the policy in respect of the death of or bodily injury to any person caused by or arising out of the use of the vehicle on a road,[4] and of any liability which may be incurred under the provisions of the Act relating to payment for emergency treatment,[5] but not liability to passengers (except passengers carried for hire or reward) or liability arising by reason of a contract of employment or any contractual liability.[6] A policy is ineffective unless there is delivered to the assured a certificate of insurance in the prescribed form.[7] Certain exceptions to policies are statutorily avoided in respect of the compulsory liabilities.[8]

---

[1] *Post Office* v. *Norwich Union Fire Ins. Socy. Ltd.* [1967] 1 All E.R. 577.

[2] Road Traffic Act, 1972, S. 143.

[3] *Monk* v. *Warbey* [1935] 1 K.B. 75; *Houston* v. *Buchanan*, 1940 S.C. (H.L.) 17.

[4] Such liability is usually based on negligence.

[5] R.T.A., 1972, S. 145.

[6] R.T.A., 1972, S. 145. *Izzard* v. *Universal Ins. Co.* [1937] A.C. 773; *Bonham* v. *Zurich General Ins. Co.* [1945] K.B. 292.

[7] R.T.A., 1972, S. 147. The insurers can found on a breach of a condition in the policy even though it is not referred to in the certificate: *Martin* v. *Port of Manchester Ins. Co.* 1933 S.N. 32.

[8] Ibid., S. 148.

The Third Parties (Rights against Insurers) Act, 1930, enables a third party who has a claim against an assured to establish a direct right of action against the assured's insurers if the assured becomes insolvent.[1] Such a right of action is subject to all the conditions in the policy binding on the insured.[2]

The bankruptcy of an assured does not affect the liability on his part required to be covered by insurance under the Act.[3]

Also insurers who have delivered a certificate of insurance are bound, though entitled to avoid or cancel, or though they may have avoided or cancelled the policy, to pay to persons who have obtained a decree against an assured in respect of any liability required to be covered by the Act, any sum payable under the decree in respect of the liability, including expenses. No sum is payable unless the insurer had notice of the bringing of the proceedings within seven days of their commencement, or pending an appeal, or if before the event giving rise to the liability, the policy was cancelled by mutual consent and the certificate surrendered, nor if within three months of the commencement of the proceedings the insurer obtained a declaration that he is entitled to avoid the policy on the ground of non-disclosure or misrepresentation.[4]

Voluntary insurance

Apart from statute the user of a motor vehicle may insure against liability to a third party for injury or death, for damage to his property, against fire, theft, loss or damage, and personal accident to the assured while driving. The contract is one of indemnity, and it is not contrary to public policy because it will protect the user against the consequences of his own negligence,[5] even if serious, though it is otherwise if injury is caused by deliberate conduct.[6]

The policy normally describes the permitted uses of the vehicle and thereby defines the risks covered; if an accident happens while the vehicle is being used for another use the

---

[1] cf. *Rutherford* v. *Licences and General Ins. Co.*, 1934 S.L.T. 31; *Cunningham* v. *Anglian Ins. Co.*, 1934 S.L.T. 273.

[2] *Greenlees* v. *Port of Manchester Ins. Co.*, 1933 S.C. 383.

[3] R.T.A., 1972, S. 150.

[4] Ibid., S. 149; *Croxford* v. *Universal Ins. Co.* [1936] 2 K.B. 253; *Zurich General Accident Co.* v. *Livingston*, 1938 S.C. 582; *Zurich General Accident Co.* v. *Leven*, 1940 S.C. 406. See also *Robb* v. *McKechnie*, 1936 J.C. 25.

[5] *Tinline* v. *White Cross Ins. Co.* [1921] 3 K.B. 327.

[6] *Tinline, supra*; cf. *Beresford* v. *Royal Ins. Co.* [1938] A.C. 586.

assured cannot recover.[1] There may also be limitations on load, state of the vehicle, area of use or otherwise,[2] such as to use for social, domestic, and pleasure purposes.[3]

Motor Insurers' Bureau Agreement

Insurers transacting motor insurance in Great Britain entered into an agreement with the Minister of Transport in 1946[4] that, if judgment in respect of a liability compulsorily insurable is obtained in any court in Great Britain against any person, whether in fact insured or not, and is not satisfied in full within seven days from the date when it becomes enforceable, then the Bureau will pay to the holder of the decree any sum payable. Such sum may be recoverable from the assured. The Bureau's liability is conditional on notice being given of the bringing, or the intention to take, proceedings against the uninsured motorist before or within 21 days after their commencement and the claimant, if so required and subject to indemnity for expenses, taking all reasonable steps to obtain decree against all the wrongdoers responsible; and on any decree being assigned to the Bureau or its nominee. In some cases the Bureau may be sued direct.[5]

Voluntary aircraft insurance

Operators of aircraft may insure voluntarily against any liability which may be incurred to third parties, or against loss of or damage to their aircraft.

CONTINGENCY INSURANCE

Contingency insurance covers insurance against loss by a contingency other than those previously mentioned. The main kinds are fidelity insurance, debt insurance and consequential loss insurance. Such contracts are frequently, but not always, contracts of indemnity; sometimes they provide for the payment of a stipulated sum in the event of the contingency happening, e.g. if

---

[1] *Murray* v. *Sc. Automobile Ins. Co.*, 1929 S.C. 49; *A. Ins. Co. and B.*, 1938 S.L.T. 434; *A.* v. *B. Ins. Co.*, 1939 S.N. 51; *Houston* v. *Buchanan*, 1940 S.C. (H.L.) 17; cf. *Stuart* v. *Horse Ins. Co.* (1893) 1 S.L.T. 108; *Agnew* v. *Robertson*, 1956 S.L.T. (Sh. Ct.) 90; *Kelly* v. *Cornhill Ins. Co.*, 1964 S.C. (H.L.) 46.

[2] *Gray* v. *Blackmore* [1934] 1 K.B. 95; cf. *Dawsons Ltd.* v. *Bonnin*, 1922 S.C. (H.L.) 156.

[3] cf. *Wood* v. *General Accident Corpn.* (1948) 65 T.L.R. 53.

[4] Text in *Shawcross on Motor Insurance*, 364.

[5] *Lees* v. *Motor Insurers' Bureau* [1952] 2 All E.R. 511; *Buchanan* v. *Motor Insurers' Bureau* [1955] 1 All E.R. 607.

rain interferes with a cricket match.[1] The assured must have an insurable interest, as being likely to sustain loss if the contingency happens.

Fidelity insurance

A policy of fidelity insurance is intended to protect the assured against the contingency of a breach of fidelity by a trusted person, as by the fraud, embezzlement or other dishonesty of an employee.[2] The risk depends on the employee's duties and he must be employed on the same duties during the currency of the policy.[3] Change of duties imports alteration of the risk. Whether the loss falls within the perils insured against is a matter of interpretation; such words as fraud bear the same meaning as in criminal law.[4] It depends on the policy whether it covers losses actually sustained during its currency, or also losses discovered during that time but sustained earlier. It is a condition of liability that the employee's conduct is properly supervised.[5]

Debt insurance

Insurance is competent against the risk that a debtor will not pay his debt; the debt may be of any kind, secured or unsecured, a specific debt or a balance of indebtedness. The premium may be made payable by the debtor.[6] The creditor must disclose the debtor's financial position, including suspicions of his circumstances,[7] and not make any change in the terms of his relations with the debtor without the insurers' consent, unless it was contemplated when the contract was entered into.[8] The nature of the default giving rise to a claim depends on the terms of the policy.[9] On payment the insurers are subrogated to the creditors' rights and remedies against the debtor and any securities he has granted.[10]

---

[1] *Leon* v. *Casey* [1932] 2 K.B. 576.

[2] *Re Norwich Provident Ins. Socy., Bath's Case* (1878) 8 Ch. D. 334; *Ravenscroft* v. *Provident Clerks' Assoc.* (1888) 5 T.L.R. 3.

[3] *Haworth* v. *Sickness and Accident Ins. Co.* (1891) 28 S.L.R. 394.

[4] *Debenhams, Ltd.* v. *Excess Ins. Co.* (1912) 28 T.L.R. 505.

[5] *Dundee and Newcastle S.S. Co.* v. *National Guarantee Assocn.* (1881) 18 S.L.R. 685; *Haworth, supra*; *Snaddon* v. *London, etc. Assce. Co.* (1902) 5 F. 182; contrast *Bonthrone* v. *Patterson* (1898) 25 R. 391.

[6] *Employers' Ins. Co.* v. *Benton* (1897) 24 R. 908.

[7] *Seaton* v. *Burnand* [1900] A.C. 135.

[8] *Laird* v. *Securities Ins. Co.* (1895) 22 R. 452.

[9] *Young* v. *Assets Ins. Co.'s Tr.* (1893) 21 R. 222; *Laird* v. *Securities Ins. Co.* (1895) 22 R. 452; *Employers' Ins. Co., supra*.

[10] *Laird, supra*; *Dane* v. *Mortgage Ins. Corpn.* [1894] 1 Q.B. 54.

Consequential loss insurance

Consequential loss insurance protects against losses not recoverable under an ordinary policy, such as loss of business or profits consequential on fire, or overheads continuing despite interruption of business.

1 cf. *Dean* v. *Scottish Licences Mutual Ins. Assoc.* (1906) 14 S.L.T. 87.

CHAPTER 47

CAUTIONARY OBLIGATIONS

A CAUTIONARY obligation or obligation of guarantee or of personal security is an accessory engagement, as surety for another, that if the principal obligant does not pay the debt or perform the act for which he has engaged, the cautioner shall pay or otherwise fulfil the obligation.[1] The principles of Scots law are largely founded on the Roman law contract of *fidejussio*,[2] and correspond generally to those of suretyship in English law.[3]

The obligation is accessory to and presupposes a principal obligation which is legal, valid and enforceable against the principal debtor;[4] if there is none, or it be invalid, *pactum illicitum*, or unenforceable, the cautioner is not liable.[5] If the principal obligation were morally, though not legally, binding the cautioner may be bound.[6] A person who undertakes a cautionary obligation, knowing of the invalidity of the principal obligation, may be personally barred from founding on the invalidity.[7] The principal obligation may have been already constituted, or be only in contemplation and be constituted after the accessory obligation.[8]

Nature of undertaking

The guarantee may be of the payment of a debt already incurred, or of a debt to be incurred or obligation to be undertaken,[9] for the due execution of a contract, the faithful performance of a contract of service,[10] or that the principal debtor will perform some act.

---

[1] Stair I, 17, 3; Ersk. III, 3, 21 and 61; Bell, *Comm.* I, 364; *Prin.* §245; Gloag and Irvine, *Rights in Security and Cautionary Obligations*, Chs. 19–26.

[2] Dig. 46, 1.

[3] *Grant* v. *Campbell* (1818) 6 Dow 239, 252; *Aitken's Trs.* v. *Bank of Scotland*, 1944 S.C. 270, 279.

[4] Ersk. III, 3, 64; Bell, *Prin.* §245.

[5] Stair I, 17, 11; *Crighton* (1612) Mor. 2074; unless, possibly, the illegality were merely technical: *Garrard* v. *James* [1925] 1 Ch. 616.

[6] Stair I, 17, 10; Ersk. III, 3, 64; Bell, *Prin.* §251; *Crighton* (1612) Mor. 2074; *Shaw* v. *Maxwell* (1623) Mor. 2874; *Nimmo* v. *Brown* (1700) Mor. 2076; *Taylor* v. *Braco* (1748) Mor. 16813; *Buchanan* v. *Dickie* (1828) 6 S. 986.

[7] *Stevenson* v. *Adair* (1872) 10 M. 919; *Yorkshire Railway Waggon Co.* v. *McClure* (1881) 19 Ch. D. 478.

[8] Inst. III, 21, 3; Dig. 46, 1, 62.

[9] *Fortune* v. *Young*, 1918 S.C. 1. [10] *French* v. *Cameron* (1893) 20 R. 966.

Whether obligation cautionary or independent

It is a question of circumstances whether an obligation is an independent one, such as a promise for the benefit of a third party, or subsidiary to that of another;[1] if it be held to be the latter the question of proof arises.[2] Thus where a builder became unable to get materials and the defender carried on the work, promising to see the pursuer paid for materials supplied to the builder's order, it was held that the pursuer had a claim against the defender not as cautioner but as buyer of the materials.[3] A contrast of insurance against a debtor's default is similarly an independent obligation.[4] Agency *del credere*, it has been held, is not to be regarded as a guarantee so far as requiring proof of the contract in writing.[5]

Whether writing guarantee or representation

It is a question of interpretation whether a writing is a guarantee for another, or merely a representation as to the other's credit or capacity.[6] If it is the former, the granter may be liable directly for the other's default;[7] but if the latter the granter incurs no liability on the other's default if, even though mistaken, his representations were honest and of an opinion truly held, and consequently an innocent misrepresentation, though he may be liable in damages for loss caused if his representations were fraudulent,[8] or were made carelessly in circumstances where care or greater care should have been exercised,[9] or where there was a fiduciary relationship,[10] or such reasons may justify the reduction of an obligation induced thereby.[11] Oral representations are of no effect even if averred to be fraudulent.[12] It has been questioned whether

---

[1] *Woodside* v. *Cuthbertson* (1848) 10 D. 604; *Blackwood* v. *Forbes* (1848) 10 D. 920; *Mollison's Trs.* v. *Crawford* (1851) 13 D. 1075; *Grant* v. *Fenton* (1853) 15 D. 424; *Morrison* v. *Harkness* (1870) 9 M. 35; *Lakeman* v. *Mountstephen* (1874) L.R. 7 H.L. 17; *Aitken* v. *Pyper* (1900) 8 S.L.T. 258.

[2] *Milne* v. *Kidd* (1869) 8 M. 250; *Morrison* v. *Harkness* (1870) 9 M. 35; *Reid* v. *Reid Bros.* (1887) 14 R. 789; *Aitken* v. *Pyper* (1900) 8 S.L.T. 258; *Kirkcaldy Ry.* v. *Caledonian Ry.* (1901) 38 S.L.R. 579; *Sheldon & Ackhoff* v. *Milligan* (1907) 14 S.L.T. 703; *Roughead* v. *White*, 1913 S.C. 162.

[3] *Stevenson's Tr.* v. *Campbell* (1896) 23 R. 711; cf. *Milne, supra*; *Lakeman, supra*.

[4] *Laird* v. *Securities Ins. Co.* (1895) 22 R. 452.

[5] *Sutton* v. *Grey* [1894] 1 Q.B. 285.

[6] *Union Bank* v. *Taylor*, 1925 S.C. 835.

[7] e.g. *Fortune* v. *Young*, 1918 S.C. 1.

[8] *Thin & Sinclair* v. *Arrol* (1896) 24 R. 198.

[9] *Robinson* v. *National Bank*, 1916 S.C. (H.L.) 154; *Hedley Byrne* v. *Heller & Partners* [1964] A.C. 465.

[10] *Nocton* v. *Ashburton* [1914] A.C. 932; *Banbury* v. *Bank of Montreal* [1918] A.C. 626.

[11] *Union Bank* v. *Taylor*, 1925 S.C. 835.

[12] *Clydesdale Bank* v. *Paton* (1896) 23 R. (H.L.) 22; *Irving* v. *Burns*, 1915 S.C. 260.

the requirement of writing applies to representations by a bank agent to an intending guarantor of the account of one of the bank's customers.[1] A representation, unless otherwise expressed, relates to credit at the time it is made and does not give rise to an action in respect of advances made some months later.[2]

A representation as to a trader's credit is personal to the representee and will not found an action of damages by any other person who relies on it,[3] unless it could have been foreseen that such a person would see and might rely on it.[4] So too a guarantee not addressed to anyone may be founded on when it was signed in the knowledge that it would be seen by the person who acted in reliance on it.[5]

Caution distinct from delegation

It is also essential that the cautioner does not, by undertaking liability, release the principal debtor and merely assume his liability; such is delegation, not caution.[6] The presumption is against delegation, and for corroboration of the existing obligation.[7]

Kinds of cautionary obligations

There are three classes:[8] agreements between creditor, principal debtor and cautioner,[9] agreements between principal debtor and cautioner only, in which the creditor, so long as ignorant of the agreement, has none of the rights of a creditor in a true cautionary obligation,[10] and agreements whereby there exists a primary and secondary obligation for what is, among themselves, the debt of one only, as in the case of partners being sureties for the firm's debts,[11] or the acceptor of a bill of exchange and the drawer and indorsers thereof.[12]

[1] *Royal Bank* v. *Greenshields*, 1914 S.C. 259.

[2] *Salton* v. *Clydesdale Bank* (1898) 1 F. 110; see also *Hockey* v. *Clydesdale Bank* (1898) 1 F. 119.

[3] *Salton* v. *Clydesdale Bank* (1898) 1 F. 110; cf. *Hockey* v. *Clydesdale Bank* (1898) 1 F. 119; *Schmidt* v. *Duncan* (1902) 10 S.L.T. 55.

[4] *Robinson* v. *National Bank*, 1916 S.C. (H.L.) 154; *Hedley Byrne* v. *Heller & Partners* [1964] A.C. 465.

[5] *Fortune* v. *Young*, 1918 S.C. 1.

[6] Dig. 46, 1; Ersk. III, 3, 61; cf. *Jackson* v. *McDiarmid* (1892) 19 R. 528.

[7] cf. *Morrison* v. *Harkness* (1870) 9 M. 35.

[8] *Fox* v. *North and S. Wales Bank* (1880) 6 App. Cas. 1, 11.

[9] These alone are true cautionary obligations.

[10] *Morton's Trs.* v. *Robertson's J.F.* (1892) 20 R. 72; *Thow's Tr.* v. *Young*, 1910 S.C. 588.

[11] Bell, *Comm.* II, 506; *Prin.* §351.

[12] *Oriental Financial Corpn.* v. *Cleveland, Gurney & Co* (1874) L.R. 7 H.L. 348; *Fox*, supra; *Walker's Trs.* v. *McKinlay* (1880) 7 R. (H.L.) 85.

Constitution

A cautionary obligation may be constituted by an offer by the prospective cautioner to a creditor to guarantee the actings of a third party or a particular undertaking, which may be sufficiently accepted by the creditor giving credit to the third party on the faith of the other,[1] or by an offer to the principal debtor to guarantee his dealings or transactions, not in reference to a particular creditor, but enforceable by any creditor within the class, if any, of creditors envisaged, who has given credit in reliance thereon,[2] or by a unilateral undertaking by the cautioner to the creditor guaranteeing the debtor's debt generally, or to a stated extent.[3] There is no duty on a bank to give information to a proposed cautioner for a customer as to the state of the latter's account unless it is requested,[4] but a cautioner is not bound if his undertaking is induced by misrepresentations by the debtor and failure by the creditor to disclose material facts,[5] or by circumvention of a facile person.[6] A cautionary undertaking may be gratuitous or onerous.[7] A cautionary obligation is voidable if entered into under error induced by misrepresentation.[8]

Form

The undertaking may be in any form; it is not void merely because the creditors are not named,[9] or it is not addressed to anyone.[10] Receipts acknowledging receipt of money on the same terms as a prior receipt which admittedly instructed a cautionary obligation have themselves been held to instruct cautionary obligations.[11] Letters may be held to amount to a guarantee.[12]

---

[1] *Wallace* v. *Gibson* (1895) 22 R. (H.L.) 56.

[2] *Fortune* v. *Young*, 1918 S.C. 1; cf. *Clapperton, Paton & Co.* v. *Anderson* (1881) 8 R. 1004.

[3] *Aitken's Trs.* v. *Bank of Scotland*, 1944 S.C. 270.

[4] *Hamilton* v. *Watson* (1845) 4 Bell 67; *Young* v. *Clydesdale Bank* (1889) 17 R. 231; *Royal Bank* v. *Greenshields*, 1914 S.C. 259; see also *Clydesdale Bank* v. *Paton* (1896) 23 R. (H.L.) 22.

[5] *French* v. *Cameron* (1893) 20 R. 966; contrast *Wallace's J.F.* v. *McKissock* (1898) 25 R. 642.

[6] *Sutherland* v. *Low* (1901) 3 F. 972.

[7] Bell, *Prin.* §246. Thus an insurance company will, for a single premium, act as cautioner for an executor-dative.

[8] *N. of Scotland Bank* v. *Mackenzie*, 1925 S.L.T. 236; cf. *Union Bank* v. *Taylor*, 1925 S.C. 835.

[9] *Clapperton, Paton & Co.* v. *Anderson* (1881) 8 R. 1004.

[10] *Fortune* v. *Young*, 1918 S.C. 1.

[11] *Field* v. *Thomson* (1902) 10 S.L.T. 261.

[12] *Wallace* v. *Gibson* (1895) 22 R. (H.L.) 56.

Proof

At common law cautionary obligations, though they might be created by consent, could probably be proved only by probative or privileged writing,[1] or writing of which the subscription was acknowledged,[2] or by improbative writ or admission on oath followed by *rei interventus*, the creditor having, with the cautioner's knowledge, given credit in reliance on his undertaking.[12]

By the Mercantile Law Amendment (Scotland) Act, 1856, S. 6, 'all guarantees, securities, or cautionary obligations made or granted by any person for any other person, and all representations and assurances as to the character, conduct, credit, ability,[4] trade or dealings of any person, made or granted to the effect or for the purpose of enabling such person to obtain credit, money, goods, or postponement of payment of debt, or of any other obligation demandable from him, shall be in writing, and shall be subscribed by the person undertaking or by some person duly authorized by him or them, otherwise the same shall have no effect'. This provision precludes action based on an oral guarantee or representation as to credit, even though made fraudulently.[5] It is undecided whether this section requires probative writing, but almost certainly not;[6] an improbative writing is valid certainly if advances have been made in reliance thereon,[7] and in the case of a guarantee *in re mercatoria*.[8] A written undertaking to give a guarantee when required satisfies the Act.[9] A signature in the firm name binds the partner who signs.[10] It is doubtful whether a letter of guarantee is a writing *in re mercatoria*.[11] The section

---

[1] Bell, *Prin.* §248. But see *Park v. Gould* (1851) 13 D. 1049; *Church of England Assce. Co. v. Hodges* (1857) 19 D. 414; see also *Paterson v. P.* (1897) 25 R. 144, 167.

[2] Bell, *Prin.* §249.

[3] Ibid.; *Ballantyne v. Carter* (1842) 4 D. 419; *Johnston v. Grant* (1844) 6 D. 875; *National Bank v. Campbell* (1892) 19 R. 885.

[4] i.e. ability to pay: *Irving v. Burns*, 1915 S.C. 260.

[5] *Clydesdale Bank v. Paton* (1896) 23 R. (H.L.) 22; *Irving, supra*; *Union Bank v. Taylor*, 1925 S.C. 835.

[6] Bell, *Prin.* §249A says that in ordinary cases the writing must be probative or holograph; see also *Clapperton, Paton & Co. v. Anderson* (1881) 8 R. 1004; *Wylie & Lochhead v. Hornsby* (1889) 16 R. 907; *Gibson v. Alston's Trs.* (1893) 1 S.L.T. 62; *Snaddon v. London, etc. Assce. Co.* (1902) 5 F. 182. In *Fortune v. Young*, 1918 S.C. 1, it was holograph and signed in the firm name by a partner.

[7] Ersk. III, 2, 3; Bell, *Prin.* §249A; *Johnston v. Grant* (1844) 6 D. 875; *Ch. of England Life Assce. Co. v. Wink* (1857) 19 D. 1079; *National Bank v. Campbell* (1892) 19 R. 885.

[8] *Paterson v. Wright* (1814) 6 Pat. 38; *Johnston v. Grant* (1844) 6 D. 875; *National Bank v. Campbell* (1892) 19 R. 885.

[9] *Wallace v. Gibson* (1895) 22 R. (H.L.) 56.

[10] *Fortune v. Young*, 1918 S.C. 1.   [11] *National Bank, supra*.

applies whether the representations are founded on as the basis of action,[1] or in defence,[2] but probably not where the obligation of a party to a bill of exchange, though in substance a cautionary obligation, is that which the law merchant infers from the mere signatures appearing *ex facie* of the bill.[3] It has been doubted[4] whether it applies to representations by a bank agent to an intending guarantor of the account of a customer of the bank.

Ancillary agreements

Ancillary agreements, or modifications of the written agreement, must in the usual way themselves be in writing and parole evidence of some such arrangement is incompetent.[5] Any such agreement must also be made with the knowledge and consent of all parties.[5] But where a cautioner had obtained from the creditor a special security over part of the debtor's estate he was held entitled to prove by parole evidence that his co-cautioners had agreed to this and that to their knowledge it was only on such terms that he had agreed to be a cautioner only on condition of having this security.[6]

Who may rely on guarantee or representation

The creditor for whose benefit a guarantee is given may rely on it and enforce it, but where an association of underwriters required a guarantee for obligations to be contracted by a new member, this was held to confer a *jus quaesitum* on any person subsequently assured by him,[7] and a person has been held entitled to found on a guarantee not addressed to any one when it had been contemplated that it would be shown to the person who in fact relied on it.[8] But representations as to credit have been held personal to the representee and not entitling anyone else to found thereon,[9] or at least personal to persons including, in the circumstances, the person who relied thereon.[10]

---

[1] e.g. *Clydesdale Bank* v. *Paton* (1896) 23 R. (H.L.) 22; *Irving, supra*.
[2] *Union Bank* v. *Taylor*, 1925 S.C. 835.
[3] *Walker's Trs.* v. *McKinlay* (1880) 7 R. (H.L.) 85.
[4] *Royal Bank* v. *Greenshields*, 1914 S.C. 259. See also *Devlin* v. *McKelvie*, 1915 S.C. 180.
[5] *McPhersons* v. *Haggarts* (1881) 9 R. 306; *Devlin* v. *McKelvie*, 1915 S.C. 180.
[6] *Hamilton* v. *Freeth* (1889) 16 R. 1022.
[7] *Rose, Murison & Thomson* v. *Wingate, Birrell & Co.'s Tr.* (1889) 16 R. 1132.
[8] *Fortune* v. *Young*, 1918 S.C. 1.
[9] *Salton* v. *Clydesdale Bank* (1898) 1 F. 110; *Schmidt* v. *Duncan* (1902) 10 S.L.T. 55.
[10] *Robinson* v. *National Bank*, 1916 S.C. (H.L.) 154.

Conditional obligations

An obligation may be conditional, such as to be cautioner for a composition to creditors, where the consent of all concerned is an implied condition,[1] or on the terms that the principal debtor or his wife would relieve the cautioner if financial circumstances allowed.[2]

Obligations by several cautioners

Where there are to be several cautioners each signs under the implied condition that all the others are to be bound also and is not liable if this condition is not satisfied,[3] unless the signatures of later signing cautioners be not apparently a condition and the creditor has acted in reliance on the signatures obtained.[4] It is the creditor's duty to ensure that all are taken bound, except in the case of judicial cautionry, when a bond must be lodged to satisfy the court's requirements; in this case there is no duty to ensure that the signatures of all obligants are obtained.[5]

Revocation

A cautionary obligation is revocable so long as no creditor has acted in reliance on it. Thereafter it is not revocable without the creditor's knowledge or consent. A continuing guarantee or cautionary obligation given to a firm or to a third party in respect of the transactions of a firm is, in the absence of contrary agreement, revoked as to future transactions by any change in the constitution of the firm[6] to which, or in respect of whose transactions, the guarantee or obligation was given.[7]

Proper and improper caution

A cautionary obligation may be proper or improper: in proper caution the parties bind themselves, the one as principal debtor and the other or others as cautioner(s) 'but that *subsidiarie* and as proper cautioner only'; in improper caution the principal

---

[1] Bell, *Prin.* §250; *Culcreuch Cotton Co.* v. *Mathie* (1823) 2 S. 513.

[2] *Williamson* v. *Foulds*, 1927 S.N. 164.

[3] *Scottish Provincial Assce. Co.* v. *Pringle* (1858) 20 D. 465.

[4] *Blair* v. *Taylor* (1836) 14 S. 1069; cf. *Paterson* v. *Bonar* (1844) 6 D. 987; *B.L. Co.* v. *Thomson* (1853) 15 D. 314; *Craig* v. *Paton* (1865) 4 M. 192.

[5] *Simpson* v. *Fleming* (1860) 22 D. 679.

[6] e.g. retirement of partner: *Royal Bank* v. *Christie* (1841) 2 Rob. 118; admission of partner: *Speirs* v. *Houston's Exors.* (1829) 3 W. & S. 392; registration as a company: *Hay* v. *Torbet*, 1908 S.C. 781.

[7] Partnership Act, 1890, S. 18, superseding Mercantile Law Amdt. (Sc.) Act, 1856, S. 7.

obligant and the cautioners are all, *ex facie* of the bond, bound as principals, jointly and severally, the cautioner(s) thereby impliedly renouncing as regards the creditor the rights of a cautioner,[1] though retaining them as regards the principal obligant. Whether a particular party is bound as cautioner, or as a principal debtor, depends on the terms and interpretation of the bond in question.[2]

Extent of cautioner's liability

A cautionary obligation or guarantee may be in respect of one advance only,[3] or a continuing guarantee for the balance of continuous transactions.[4] There is no presumption either way, and the question is one of the fair interpretation of the terms of the obligation in the light of its subject-matter and the surrounding circumstances,[5] but where the guarantee is in respect of a current account or cash-credit bond there may be a presumption for a continuing guarantee.[6] In interpreting a guarantee in a form prepared by the creditor any ambiguity must be construed *contra proferentem*.[7]

A cautioner's liability may also be limited in time or amount. The general rule of construction is that the obligation is construed as narrowly as the words used will reasonably bear.[8] It can never be greater than the liability of the principal debtor,[9] and may be less extensive. It may be more strict, in that a natural obligation, void as against the principal, may be enforced against the cautioner.[10] A cautioner has been held liable for a deficiency caused by actings prior to the date of his bond,[11] but not for deficiencies outwith the true scope of the guarantee.[12] His liability may even extend to the debtor's liabilities as cautioner as well as his individual liabilities.[13]

If there is no limitation on amount a cautioner called on to pay

---

[1] viz., the *beneficium ordinis*; see further, *infra*.

[2] e.g. *Morton's Trs.* v. *Robertson's J.F.* (1892) 20 R. 72.

[3] e.g. *Scott* v. *Mitchell* (1866) 4 M. 551.

[4] e.g. *Forbes* v. *Dundas* (1829) 8 S. 865.

[5] *Caledonian Banking Co.* v. *Kennedy's Trs.* (1870) 8 M. 862.

[6] Ibid., 868.

[7] Gloag & Irvine, 734; Gloag, 401; *Aitken's Trs.*, *supra*, 277.

[8] *Houston* v. *Spiers* (1821) 3 W. & S. 392; *Sime* v. *Duncan* (1824) 2 S. 604; *Veitch* v. *National Bank*, 1907 S.C. 554; *Aberdeen Harbour Commrs.* v. *Adam*, 1910 S.C. 1009; *Harmer* v. *Gibb*, 1911 S.C. 1341; *Aitken's Trs.* v. *Bank of Scotland*, 1944 S.C. 270.

[9] *Jackson* v. *McIver* (1875) 2 R. 882.

[10] Ersk. III, 3, 64; Bell, *Prin.* §251; *Stevenson* v. *Adair* (1872) 10 M. 919.

[11] *Wallace's Factor* v. *McKissock* (1898) 25 R. 642.

[12] *N. of Scotland Bank* v. *Fleming* (1882) 10 R. 217; *Ayr C.C.* v. *Wylie*, 1935 S.C. 836.

[13] *Anderson* v. *Mackinnon* (1876) 3 R. 608; *Reid* v. *Lord Ruthven*, 1918, 2 S.L.T. 8.

is liable for the whole loss resulting from the principal debtor's failure to pay, including the capital sum owed, interest unpaid thereon, and expenses reasonably incurred in seeking to enforce payment against the principal debtor.[1]

If there is a limitation on amount the question arises whether the guarantor has accepted a liability for a limited amount of the debtor's debt, or liability for the debtor's whole debt, but not to have to pay more than a limited sum.[2] This depends entirely on the terms of the obligation. The difference is that in the former case the guarantor is not liable for any advances in excess of the limited amount; in the latter case he is liable for the full debt but cannot be called on to pay more than the sum undertaken.[3]

If the obligation is limited in time the cautioner can, on expiry of the time, claim to be relieved by the debtor of all liability to the creditor under the obligation, and to receive a discharge from the creditor.[4] He will also be relieved if the debtor continues to operate the account guaranteed and credit payments after the end of the cautioner's liability extinguish the debt as at that date, though subsequent debits restore an ultimate debit balance.[5]

If there is no limitation on time the guarantee may be held a continuing one;[6] the cautioner may, at any time before he is called on to implement his obligation to the creditor, give reasonable notice to the creditor withdrawing his guarantee, and may, on giving reasonable notice, require the principal debtor to relieve him of all liabilities he may have incurred, in which case the principal debtor must obtain from the creditor and deliver to the cautioner a discharge of the latter's liabilities.[7]

Default

Whether the principal debtor. is in default is a question of fact.[8] The creditor is not in general[9] bound to give notice to the cautioner that the principal debtor has defaulted.[10]

---

[1] *Struthers* v. *Dykes* (1847) 9 D. 1437.

[2] *Veitch* v. *National Bank,* 1907 S.C. 554; *Harmer* v. *Gibb,* 1911 S.C. 1341; cf. *Buchanan* v. *Main* (1900) 3 F. 215.

[3] The difference materially affects the questions of who can rank, and for how much, in the debtor's bankruptcy.

[4] *Doig* v. *Lawrie* (1903) 5 F. 295 (until recalled in writing).

[5] *Cuthill* v. *Strachan* (1894) 21 R. 549.

[6] *Caledonian Banking Co.* v. *Kennedy's Trs.* (1870) 8 M. 862.

[7] *Nicolsons* v. *Burt* (1882) 10 R. 121; *Doig* v. *Lawrie* (1903) 5 F. 295.

[8] *Ewart* v. *Latta* (1865) 3 M. (H.L.) 36; *Laird* v. *Securities Ins. Co.* (1895) 22 R. 452, 461; *Willison* v. *Ferguson* (1901) 9 S.L.T. 169.

[9] For an exception see *Clydebank Water Trs.* v. *Fidelity Co. of Maryland,* 1916 S.C. (H.L.) 69.

[10] *Britannic Steamship Ins. Assocn.* v. *Duff,* 1909 S.C. 1261, 1270.

Enforcement

In a case of proper cautionry the creditor had formerly, on the debtor's default, to take proceedings and no diligence against him before claiming from the cautioner.[1] He may now proceed against principal debtor or cautioner.[2] In a case of improper cautionry he may, on the debtor's default, take proceedings against any one or more of the cautioners (co-obligants in the bond), leaving the cautioners who pay to obtain what relief they can from the debtor. Enforcement may always be by action for payment. A formal bond of caution normally contains a clause of consent to registration for preservation and execution. In this event if the principal debtor defaults the creditor may record the bond in the Books of Council and Session or Sheriff Court books, obtain an extract and do diligence thereon on a charge of six days.[3] A cautioner is entitled to plead any defence against the creditor on which the principal debtor could rely.[4]

Benefit of discussion (beneficium ordinis)

In proper cautionry the cautioner had at common law, unless it were expressly renounced in the bond, the *beneficium ordinis*, whereby he could not be called on until the creditor had first discussed, i.e. pursued and done diligence against, the principal debtor.[5] The Mercantile Law Amdt. (Sc.) Act, 1856, S. 8, renders it unnecessary first to discuss or do diligence against the principal debtor, though it may be expressly stipulated in the bond that the creditor must first do diligence against the principal debtor. In the absence of any such stipulation the creditor may take action direct against the cautioner.[6] Even where a cautioner has stipulated for the benefit of discussion the creditor need not first discuss the principal debtor if his estates have been sequestrated,[7] or if he is furth of Scotland and has no estate subject to Scottish jurisdiction,[8] but he must first discuss the principal debtor's estate if he has merely died, unless he was then insolvent.[9]

[1] Stair I, 17, 4; Ersk. III, 3, 61; Bell, *Comm.* I, 364; *Prin.* §252–3.
[2] Mercantile Law Amdt. (Sc.) Act, 1856, S. 8.
[3] Titles to Land Consolidation Act, 1868, S. 138.
[4] Bell, *Prin.* §251.
[5] Stair I, 17, 5; Ersk. III, 3, 61; Bell, *Prin.* §252; as to sufficiency of diligence, see *Macfarlane* v. *Anstruther* (1870) 9 M. 117.
[6] *Ewart* v. *Latta* (1865) 3 M. (H.L.) 36; *Morrison* v. *Harkness* (1870) 9 M. 35; *Sheldon & Ackhoff* v. *Milligan* (1907) 14 S.L.T. 703; *Johannesburg Municipal Council* v. *Stewart*, 1909 S.C. (H.L.) 53.
[7] *Buchanan* v. *Dennistouns* (1831) 9 S. 557.
[8] *Elams* v. *Fisher* (1757) Mor. 2110.
[9] *Wishart* v. *W.* (1837) 2 S. & Macl. 564.

The *beneficium ordinis* had and has no place in improper cautionry, and the creditor can proceed direct against any one or more of the *ex facie* co-obligants for the whole sum due.[1]

Benefit of division (beneficium divisionis)

Where more than one cautioner is bound, expressly as such, for an obligation naturally divisible, as to pay money, each is liable only for his *pro rata* share of the obligation, unless he has expressly renounced his privilege. Any cautioner who is insolvent is ignored in fixing the *pro rata* share.[2]

This principle has no application in improper cautionry where all cautioners are in a question with the creditor jointly and severally liable along with the principal debtor, and where accordingly any one may be sued for the whole sum due.[3]

Rights of relief against principal debtor

A cautioner is entitled to be relieved by the principal debtor and repaid anything he has had to pay to the creditor under his obligation,[4] and in a proper cautionary obligation the debtor frequently binds himself expressly to do this.[5] In improper caution parole evidence that one or more co-obligants are truly only cautioners for the other or others is competent.[6] The right of relief may be excluded by the terms of the obligation.[7] The cautioner may seek relief by suing the principal debtor in security if he be *vergens ad inopiam*,[8] or having paid the debt,[9] or on having legal action against him by the creditor.[10] He has no right of relief if he has paid the debt prematurely[11] or paid when the principal debtor had a valid defence,[12] or the payment was truly for the cautioner's benefit,[13] and his right of relief is restricted

[1] *Blackwood* v. *Forbes* (1848) 10 D. 920; *Morrison, supra.*

[2] Ersk. III, 3, 63; Bell, *Pr.* §267; *Anderson* v. *Dayton* (1884) 21 S.L.R. 787; *Buchanan* v. *Main* (1900) 3 F. 215.

[3] *Richmond* v. *Grahame* (1847) 9 D. 633.

[4] Stair I, 17, 4; Ersk. III, 3, 61; Bell, *Prin.* §245; *Doig* v. *Lawrie* (1903) 5 F. 295.

[5] *Gray* v. *Phillips* (1905) 13 S.L.T. 145; see also *Jamieson* v. *Forrest* (1875) 2 R. 701.

[6] *Thorburn* v. *Howie* (1863) 1 M. 1169; *Hamilton* v. *Freeth* (1889) 16 R. 1022; *Crosbie* v. *Brown* (1900) 3 F. 83.

[7] *Murray* v. *McFarlane* (1894) 1 S.L.T. 577.

[8] *Kinloch* v. *Mackintosh* (1822) 1 S. 491; *Spence* v. *Brownlee* (1834) 13 S. 199; *Brodie* v. *Wilson* (1837) 15 S. 1195; *McPherson* v. *Wright* (1885) 12 R. 942.

[9] Ersk. III, 3, 65; *Craigie* v. *Graham* (1710) Mor. 14649.

[10] Ersk., *supra.*

[11] *Owen* v. *Bryson* (1833) 12 S. 130.

[12] *Maxwell* v. *Nithsdale* (1632) Mor. 2115.

[13] *Erskine* v. *Cormack* (1842) 4 D. 1478.

in the case of a merely natural obligation to the amount profitably used by the debtor.[1]

Right to assignation (beneficium cedendarum actionum)

The cautioner is entitled, on making payment in full,[2] to obtain from the creditor an assignation of the debt, of any security held for it, and any diligence done on it, to enable him to exact relief from the debtor or co-cautioners.[3] The creditor may in exceptional cases be permitted to refuse to assign the debt where that would conflict with some legitimate interest of his own,[4] but he cannot refuse to assign securities on the ground of wishing to retain them against another debt subsequently incurred.[5]

Relief against co-cautioners

A cautioner is also entitled, in the absence of express renunciation of the claim, if he has paid more than his *pro rata* share, without any assignation from the creditor,[6] to claim relief from his co-cautioners, excluding any who are insolvent, to the extent of the excess over his *pro rata* share.[7] This applies even if the co-cautioners are bound by different deeds.[8] If the cautioner gets any abatement from the creditor he must share it with the co-cautioners.[9] There can be no claim for relief *inter se* if each cautioner is bound up to a specified sum and the whole debt is exacted, but if a lesser sum is exacted, one who has paid more than his proportion may claim relief, unless the cautioners were taken bound in separate contracts for specific sums, in which case there is no right of relief.[10] It is competent for parties to

---

[1] Ersk. III, 3, 67.

[2] *Ewart* v. *Latta* (1865) 3 M. (H.L.) 36; see also *Fleming* v. *Burgess* (1867) 5 M. 856.

[3] Bell, *Pr.* §268; *Lowe* v. *Greig* (1825) 3 S. 543; *Sligo* v. *Menzies* (1840) 2 D. 1478; *Gray* v. *Thomson* (1847) 10 D. 145; *Anderson* v. *Dayton* (1884) 21 S.L.R. 787; *Thow's Tr.* v. *Young*, 1910 S.C. 588.

[4] Bell, *Prin.* §557; *Mitchell* v. *McKinlay* (1842) 4 D. 634; *Graham* v. *Gordon* (1842) 4 D. 903; *Fraser* v. *Carruthers* (1875) 2 R. 595; see also *Guthrie & McConnachy* v. *Smith* (1880) 8 R. 107.

[5] *Fleming* v. *Burgess* (1867) 5 M. 856; see also *Scott* v. *Fotheringham* (1859) 21 D. 737; *Veitch* v. *National Bank*, 1907 S.C. 554.

[6] *Finlayson* v. *Smith* (1827) 6 S. 264.

[7] Stair I, 8, 9; Bell, *Comm.* I, 368; *Anderson* v. *Dayton* [1884] 21 S.L.R. 787; *Stenhouse* v. *Tod* (1890) 27 S.L.R. 261; *Buchanan* v. *Main* (1900) 3 F. 215; *Marshall* v. *Pennycock*, 1908 S.C. 276; *Thow's Tr.* v. *Young*, 1910 S.C. 588; *Union Bank* v. *Taylor*, 1925 S.C. 835. cf. *Robinson* v. *National Bank*, 1916 S.C. (H.L.) 154.

[8] *Stirling* v. *Forrester* (1821) 1 Sh. App. 37; *Duncan, Fox & Co.* v. *N. & S. Wales Bank* (1888) 6 App. Cas. 1. See also *Thorburn* v. *Howie* (1863) 1 M. 1169.

[9] *Milligan* v. *Glen* (1802) Mor. 2140.

[10] *Morgan* v. *Smart* (1872) 10 M. 610.

arrange that among themselves one cautioner is entitled to total relief from another or others.[1]

Benefit of securities

A cautioner is also entitled, in the absence of contrary agreement, to share in the benefit of any securities granted to any co-cautioner over the estate of the principal debtor,[2] probably even if the claiming cautioner had bound himself without obtaining any security. But it is competent for one cautioner, on agreeing to be bound, to obtain a security of which he is to have the sole benefit, and the agreement of the other cautioners to this may be proved by parole evidence.[3] And the principle does not apply where each cautioner is bound for a separate sum,[4] nor where the security was given by a third party,[5] nor where the security held by the cautioner is applicable to other debts also, in which case it cannot be shared so far as applicable thereto.[6]

Ranking on debtor's bankruptcy

If the principal debtor goes bankrupt, the creditor is entitled to rank for his claim, receive a dividend, and recover the balance of his claim from the cautioner. The cautioner may not, however, rank in the debtor's sequestration for his payment, as this would be double ranking.[7] Alternatively, the cautioner may pay the creditor in full, take an assignation of the debt, and rank for that in full in the debtor's sequestration.[8] If the bond is a guarantee of the whole debt, though the sum for which the cautioner is liable is limited, the creditor may rank in the debtor's sequestration for the whole sum, and recover from the cautioner the balance required to indemnify him, up to the limit of the cautioner's liability.[9]

If, however, the cautioner's liability is limited to a fixed sum, and the principal debt is greater, the bond may be held to be a guarantee of part of the debt, in which case the creditor may rank in the sequestration and recover from the cautioner the

---

[1] *McPhersons* v. *Haggarts* (1881) 9 R. 306.
[2] Ersk. III, 3, 70; Bell, *Comm.* I, 367; *Prin.* §270; *Humble* v. *Lyon* (1792) Hume 83.
[3] *Hamilton* v. *Freeth* (1889) 16 R. 1022; *Scott* v. *Young*, 1909, 1 S.L.T. 47.
[4] *Lawrie* v. *Stewart* (1823) 2 S. 368.
[5] Bell, *Comm.* I, 368; *Coventry* v. *Hutchison* (1830) 8 S. 924.
[6] *Campbell* v. *C.* (1775) Mor. 2132.
[7] *Anderson* v. *Mackinnon* (1876) 3 R. 608; *Mackinnon* v. *Monkhouse* (1881) 9 R. 393.
[8] *Veitch* v. *National Bank*, 1907 S.C. 554.
[9] *Mein* v. *Sanders* (1824) 2 S. 778; *Harvie's Trs.* v. *Bank of Scotland* (1885) 12 R. 1141.

balance due after deduction of the dividend recovered in the sequestration, or the cautioner may make payment of the fixed sum due and rank in the creditor's stead in the sequestration.[1]

Discharge and liberation of cautioner

The creditor may always expressly discharge the cautioner and free him of liability while the principal debtor remains bound.[2]

Satisfaction or extinction of principal obligation

If the principal obligation is paid or otherwise satisfied and extinguished the cautioner is discharged as well as the principal.[3] If a debtor owing more than one sum to the creditor does not appropriate a payment to one debt rather than another, the creditor may do so without regard to the existence of the cautionary obligation.[4]

Novation or assignation of debt

The cautioner is also liberated if, without his assent, the principal debt is discharged and a new one substituted therefor.[5] Assignation to a new creditor has no such effect.[6]

Compensation

If the debtor's debt is extinguished on a plea of compensation the cautioner is liberated. But he is not liberated merely because the debt could have been extinguished on a plea of compensation, though, if sued, he may plead any plea of compensation which would have been available to the principal debtor.[7]

Where there is a continuing account between creditor and debtor, as between banker and customer,[8] and this is continued without a break after a date when the cautioner's liability is terminated, rather than a fresh account opened, the cautioner's liability may be diminished or excluded by the rule in *Clayton's Case*, that credit payments extinguish debts in order of date,

---

[1] *Hamilton v. Cuthbertson* (1841) 3 D. 494; *Mackinnon's Tr. v. Bank of Scotland*, 1915 S.C. 411.

[2] Bell, *Prin.* §257.

[3] Bell, *Prin.* §258.

[4] *Love v. Carmichael*, 1953 S.L.T. (Sh. Ct.) 46.

[5] *Commercial Bank of Tasmania v. Jones* [1893] A.C. 313; cf. *Hay & Kyd v. Powrie* (1886) 13 R. 777.

[6] *Bradford Old Bank v. Sutcliffe* [1918] 2 K.B. 833.

[7] *Bechervaise v. Lewis* (1872) L. R. 7 C.P. 372.

[8] *Hay v. Torbet*, 1908 S.C. 781.

notwithstanding the continuing existence of a debit on the running balance.[1]

Prescription

If the principal debt is allowed to prescribe and thereby cease to be exigible, the cautioner is thereby liberated.[2]

Change of firm

A cautionary obligation to a firm, or to a third person in respect of the transactions of a firm, is, failing contrary agreement, revoked for the future by a change in the constitution of the firm.[3]

Liberation of cautioner—discharge of principal debtor

Cautionry being an accessory obligation, the cautioner is discharged if the principal debtor is discharged without the cautioner's consent,[4] or unless the discharge reserves his claim of relief,[5] except in the case of the discharge of the bankrupt in sequestration proceedings.[6] The discharge may, however, be a mere *pactum de non petendo*, whereby the creditor relinquishes his rights against the principal, reserving claims against the cautioner,[7] in which case the cautioner is not discharged but, if called on to make payment, may demand an assignation of the debt and sue the debtor thereon.[8]

Liberation by discharge of co-cautioners

The discharge of any one of several cautioners without the consent of the others liberates all of them, except in the case of the discharge of one who has become bankrupt,[9] and possibly not if the rights of the remaining cautioners are expressly reserved.[10] This applies only if all cautioners are bound jointly and severally for the whole debt, and not where each was liable only for a specific sum,[11] and may not apply if the creditor merely undertakes not to sue one cautioner.[12]

---

[1] *Royal Bank* v. *Christie* (1841) 2 Rob. 118; *Cuthill* v. *Strachan* (1894) 21 R. 549.

[2] Ersk. III, 3, 66; *Halyburtons* v. *Graham* (1735) Mor. 2073.

[3] Partnership Act, 1890, S. 18, replacing Mercantile Law Amdt. (Sc.) Act, 1856, S. 7.

[4] *Fleming* v. *Wilson* (1823) 2 S. 336.

[5] Bell, *Prin.* §260; *Aitken's Trs.* v. *Bank of Scotland*, 1944 S.C. 270.

[6] Bankruptcy (Sc.) Act, 1913, S. 52 (not applicable to trust deeds for creditors).

[7] Bell, *Prin.* §258.

[8] *Muir* v. *Crawford* (1875) 2 R. (H.L.) 148.

[9] Mercantile Law Amdt. (Sc.) Act, 1856, S. 9.

[10] *B.L. Co.* v. *Thomson* (1853) 15 D. 314; *Bateson* v. *Gosling* (1871) L.R. 7 C.P. 9.

[11] *Morgan* v. *Smart* (1872) 10 M. 610; *Union Bank* v. *Taylor*, 1925 S.C. 835, 841.

[12] *Lewis* v. *Anstruther* (1852) 15 D. 260; *Church of England Assce. Co.* v. *Wink* (1857) 19 D. 1079; *Muir* v. *Crawford* (1875) 2 R. (H.L.) 148; *Morton's Trs.* v. *Robertson's J.F.* (1892) 20 R. 72.

Liberation by time given to principal debtor

If the creditor by agreement gives time to the principal debtor, as by delaying to enforce the claim, undertaking not to sue him,[1] or taking a bill payable at a future date for the debt,[2] or by agreeing to payment by instalments,[3] or disregarding the guarantee for years and receiving payments from the guarantor's trustees, who were ignorant of it,[4] or otherwise making an arrangement which debars the creditor from suing the debtor for payment, the cautioner is held liberated because the creditor has thereby prejudiced, or possibly prejudiced, the cautioner by preventing him also from suing the debtor. The cautioner need not prove any prejudice suffered,[5] and may even have already repudiated liability on other grounds.[6]

The principle of liberation by giving time does not extend to mere failure or delay by the creditor to sue the debtor or claim in his sequestration, because in such a case the cautioner can settle with the creditor and himself claim against the debtor.[7] Nor does it apply where the creditor has, subsequently to the cautionary obligation, allowed the debtor an ordinary period of credit on a transaction, or taken a bill of ordinary duration for the price;[8] nor where the creditor, in giving time, expressly reserves the rights of the cautioner;[9] nor where the creditor, before giving time to the principal debtor, has taken decree against the cautioner.[10]

Liberation by modification of contract

If the creditor and principal debtor modify their contract in a way which affects the cautioner's position without his knowledge or consent he is liberated.[11] Thus where creditors in a composition contract took a trust deed from the debtor they were held to have liberated the cautioner.[12] In a case of a fidelity guarantee,

---

[1] *Hay & Kyd* v. *Powrie* (1886) 13 R. 777.

[2] *Richardson* v. *Harvey* (1852) 15 D. 628; *Bowe & Christie* v. *Hutchison* (1868) 6 M. 642; *Stewart, Moir and Muir* v. *Brown* (1871) 9 M. 763; *Johnstone* v. *Duthie* (1892) 19 R. 624.

[3] *Wilson* v. *Lloyd* (1873) L.R. 16 Eq. 60.

[4] *Caledonian Banking Co.* v. *Kennedy's Trs.* (1870) 8 M. 862. See also *Forsyth* v. *Wishart* (1859) 21 D. 449; *Warne* v. *Lillie* (1867) 5 M. 283; *Nicolsons* v. *Burt* (1882) 10 R. 121.

[5] *Johnstone, supra.*   [6] *Johnstone, supra.*

[7] *Hay & Kyd* v. *Powrie* (1886) 13 R. 777; *Hamilton's Exor.* v. *Bank of Scotland*, 1913 S.C. 743.

[8] *Calder* v. *Cruikshank's Tr.* (1889) 17 R. 74.

[9] *Crawford* v. *Muir* (1875) 2 R. (H.L.) 148.

[10] *Aikman* v. *Fisher* (1835) 14 S. 56.

[11] Bell, *Prin.* §259; Gloag & Irvine, 873, 886; *Bonar* v. *Macdonald* (1850) 7 Bell 379; *Stewart, Moir & Muir* v. *Brown* (1871) 9 M. 763; *Napier* v. *Crosbie*, 1964 S.C. 129.

[12] *Allan, Allan & Milne* v. *Pattison* (1893) 21 R. 195.

the cautioner is liberated if the creditor does not undertake checks on the conduct of the officer guaranteed which were provided for in the contract, whether or not equivalent checks were in force and whether or not the checks agreed upon would have been effective,[1] or if the officer's duties were made known to the cautioner when he undertook the obligation and are subsequently changed,[2] even where the change is necessitated by statute,[3] though not if the officer's duties were not known to the cautioner and he undertook generally unless the change were material.[4] The cautioner is also liberated if the creditor discovers defalcations and fails to notify the cautioner, whether or not the information would have benefited the cautioner,[5] or if the debtor materially increases his liability without the cautioner's consent.[6]

But a creditor has been held to be under no duty to disclose to a cautioner his suspicions that the debtor had committed forgery.[7] Nor is the creditor in a fidelity guarantee under a duty to take special precautions beyond any provided for by the contract, and the cautioner is not liberated because greater precautions would have avoided the loss.[8]

Liberation by giving up securities

Since a cautioner is entitled, on payment, to have assigned to him any security the creditor may hold for the debt, he will be prejudiced if the creditor, without his consent, relinquishes any security, and if the creditor voluntarily does so he is deemed thereby to liberate the cautioner,[9] to the extent only of the value of the security surrendered,[10] unless it had been expressly agreed that the creditor should resort to a particular security before calling on the cautioner, in which case the surrender of that security liberates the cautioner completely.[11] The same consequence follows where the creditor has failed to take steps necessary to make his security effectual, such as to complete his title thereto, and has thereby lost the benefit thereof.[12]

[1] *Haworth v. Sickness, etc. Ins. Co.* (1891) 18 R. 563; *Clydebank Water Trs. v. Fidelity Co.*, 1916 S.C. (H.L.) 69.
[2] *Bonar v. Macdonald* (1850) 7 Bell 379.   [3] *Pybus v. Gibb* (1856) 6 E. & B. 902.
[4] *Nicolsons v. Burt* (1882) 10 R. 121.
[5] *Sneddon v. London, etc. Ins. Co.* (1902) 5 F. 182.
[6] *Napier v. Crosbie*, 1964 S.C. 129.   [7] *Bank of Scotland v. Morrison*, 1911 S.C. 593.
[8] *Mactaggart v. Watson* (1835) 1 S. & McL. 553; *Mayor of Kingston v. Harding* [1892] 2 Q.B. 494. But in the case of banking the cautioner is probably entitled to rely on such checks as are usual in banking practice: *Falconer v. Lothian* (1843) 5 D. 866, 870.
[9] *Sligo v. Menzies* (1840) 2 D. 1478.   [10] *Wright's Trs. v. Hamilton* (1835) 13 S. 380.
[11] *Drummond v. Rannie* (1836) 14 S. 437.
[12] *Fleming v. Thomson* (1826) 2 W. & S. 277.

Liberation by creditor's neglect

The cautioner is also liberated by the creditor's serious neglect of legal proceedings against the principal debtor,[1] or breach of a term of the cautionary obligation,[2] or failure to intimate the principal's criminal conduct,[3] but not by mere delay to take proceedings or forbearance in enforcing a right,[4] nor by failing to inform the cautioner of suspicions about the principal debtor's honesty.[5]

Creditor's refusal of payment

A cautioner is also liberated if the creditor refuses an unconditional offer of payment when payment is due,[6] or if the creditor has entered into some illegal agreement to the cautioner's prejudice.[7]

Termination of obligation

An obligation may be terminated by the cautioner on giving reasonable notice to the creditor and the principal debtor, to enable the principal debtor to reduce or extinguish his liability to the creditor so as to obtain from the creditor a discharge of the cautioner's liability.[8]

Death of a party

The death of the creditor does not affect the cautioner's liability for an existing debt, though in fidelity guarantees the employer's death terminates the guarantee, even though the employment is continued.[9] But it terminates the liability for the future.[10]

[1] Ersk. III, 3, 66; Bell, *Prin.* §263; *Macfarlane* v. *Anstruther* (1870) 9 M. 117.

[2] *Murray* v. *Lee* (1882) 9 R. 1040; *Haworth* v. *Sickness, etc. Assce. Corpn.* (1891) 18 R. 563; cf. *Dundee and Newcastle S.S. Co.* v. *National Guarantee Assocn.* (1881) 18 S.L.R. 685; *London and Midland Bank* v. *Forrest* (1899) 2 F. 179; *Clydebank Water Trs.* v. *Fidelity Co. of Maryland*, 1916 S.C. (H.L.) 69.

[3] *Snaddon* v. *London, etc. Assce. Co.* (1902) 5 F. 182; cf. *Waugh* v. *Clark* (1876) 14 S.L.R. 125.

[4] *Clapperton, Paton & Co.* v. *Anderson* (1881) 8 R. 1004; cf. *Britannia S.S. Ins. Assocn.* v. *Duff*, 1909 S.C. 1261.

[5] *Bank of Scotland* v. *Morrison*, 1911 S.C. 593; cf. *Bonthrone* v. *Patterson* (1898) 25 R. 391.

[6] *Cooper* v. *Blakemore* (1834) 12 S. 834.

[7] *Lawson* v. *Coldstream* (1837) 15 S. 930.

[8] *Doig* v. *Lawrie* (1903) 5 F. 295; *Gray* v. *Phillips* (1905) 13 S.L.T. 145.

[9] *Stewart* v. *Scot* (1834) 7 W. & S. 211.

[10] *Reddie* v. *Williamson* (1863) 1 M. 228.

The debtor's death will generally fix the cautioner's liability as at that date and exclude his liability for any debt not then due.[1]

The cautioner's death does not affect his liability at that date, which is enforceable against his estate, and if the obligation were a continuing guarantee, the estate will remain liable for debts incurred after his death unless his personal representatives withdraw the guarantee. They are liable even if they were unaware of the obligation, and the creditor is under no duty to apprise them of it.[2]

Prescription

By the Cautioners Act, 1695, a cautioner's obligation is totally extinguished if not enforced within seven years from the date when it was undertaken.[3] The Act cannot be excluded by any provision in the original deed.[4] The Act applies only where principal debtor and cautioner are taken bound in the same deed as such parties,[5] and where they are taken bound in the same deed *ex facie* as co-obligants but the cautioner has obtained a separate bond of relief and this has been intimated to the creditor, his private knowledge being ignored.[6] The bond must be for a sum of money. It does not apply where the cautionry has been undertaken for a term of payment more than seven years ahead,[7] or where the term's arrival depends on a condition not purified within seven years,[8] nor if undertaken by accepting a bill, even though expressly as cautioner,[9] nor to a cautionary obligation undertaken separately, as for an existing debt,[10] nor a fidelity guarantee for an official,[11] nor any judicial cautionry,[12] nor in a composition contract in bankruptcy.[13]

[1] *Woodfield Finance Trust* v. *Morgan*, 1958 S.L.T. (Sh. Ct.) 14; but contrast *Wilson* v. *Ewing* (1836) 14 S. 262 where obligation intended to continue.

[2] *British Linen Co.* v. *Monteith* (1858) 20 D. 557; *Caledonian Banking Co.* v. *Kennedy's Trs.* (1870) 8 M. 862.

[3] *Carrick* v. *Carse* (1778) Mor. 2931; *Cochrane* v. *Ferguson* (1831) 9 S. 501; *Stocks* v. *McLagan* (1890) 17 R. 1122.

[4] *Norie* v. *Porterfield* (1724) Mor. 11013.

[5] *Stocks* v. *McLagan* (1890) 17 R. 1122.

[6] *Bell* v. *Herdman* (1727) Mor. 11039; *Burnet* v. *Middleton* (1742) Mor. 11018; *Drysdale* v. *Johnstone* (1839) 1 D. 409; *Monteith* v. *Pattison* (1841) 4 D. 161; contrast *Smith* v. *Ogilvies* (1825) 1 W. & S. 315; *Wilson* v. *Tait* (1840) 1 Rob. 137.

[7] *Millers* v. *Short* (1762) Mor. 11027.

[8] *Balvaird* v. *Watson* (1709) Mor. 11005; *Borthwick* v. *Crawford* (1715) Mor. 11008; *Millers* v. *Short* (1762) Mor. 11027; see also *Molleson* v. *Hutchison* (1892) 19 R. 581.

[9] *Sharp* v. *Harvey* (1808) Mor. Appx. Bill, 22.

[10] *Scott* v. *Rutherford* (1715) Mor. 11012.

[11] *Strang* v. *Fleet* (1707) Mor. 11005.

[12] *Kerr* v. *Bremner* (1842) 1 Bell 280.

[13] *Cuthbertson* v. *Lyon* (1823) 2 S. 330.

The Act applies only where the debt was exigible in full throughout the period and enforceable, not where the cautioner was liable only for interest.[1]

After expiry of the septennium the obligation against the cautioner cannot be enforced, but the principal debtor remains bound and any claim the cautioner may have to relief against the principal debtor or a co-cautioner is unaffected.[2] Even payment of interest by the cautioner does not extend his liability and such payment is recoverable if made in error.[3]

If diligence is done or action raised against the cautioner within the septennium[4] it will preserve the creditor's rights for any debt covered by the diligence, but not make the creditor liable for debts subsequently incurred.[5] The cautioner's liability will also continue if he has renewed his undertaking to pay, outwith the septennium,[6] and he may be personally barred from founding on the Act if he induced the creditor to delay enforcement.[7]

The Act does not affect rights of relief among cautioners *inter se*,[8] nor cautioners in a bond of relief,[9] nor cautioners in an obligation *ad factum praestandum*,[10] nor granters of bonds of corroboration[11] nor cautioners for an annuity,[12] in a marriage-contract,[13] for, the discharge of an office,[14] in a judicial bond of caution,[15] or for a composition in bankruptcy.[16]

As from 1976 a cautionary obligation will be wholly extinguished by the lapse of five years.[17]

Special instances of cautionry

Judicial factors,[18] trustees in bankruptcy,[19] and executors dative[20] must find caution for their intromissions with the estates

---

[1] *Molleson* v. *Hutchinson* (1892) 19 R. 581.
[2] *Forbes* v. *Dunbar* (1726) Mor. 11014.
[3] *Carrick* v. *Carse* (1778) Mor. 2931; *Yuille* v. *Scott* (1831) 5 W. & S. 436.
[4] *Clark* v. *Stuart* (1779) Mor. 11043; *Reid* v. *Maxwell* (1780) Mor. 11043.
[5] Bell, *Prin.* §603; *Douglas, Heron & Co.* v. *Riddick* (1800) 4 Pat. 133.
[6] *McGregor's Exors.* v. *Anderson's Trs.* (1893) 21 R. 7.
[7] *Stocks* v. *McLagan* (1890) 17 R. 1122; *McGregor's Exors., supra.*
[8] *Park's Crs.* v. *Maxwell* (1785) Mor. 11031.
[9] *Bruce* v. *Stein's Reps.* (1793) Mor. 11033.
[10] *Stewart* v. *Campbell* (1726) Mor. 11010.
[11] *Tait* v. *Wilson* (1840) 1 Rob. 137.   [12] *Alexander* v. *Badenach* (1843) 6 D. 322.
[13] *Stewart, supra.*   [14] *Strang* v. *Fleet* (1709) Mor. 11005.
[15] *Gallie* v. *Ross* (1836) 14 S. 647.   [16] Bankruptcy (Sc.) Act, 1913, S. 141.
[17] Prescription and Limitation (Sc.) Act, 1973, S. 6 and Sch. 1(1)(g) and (2)(c).
[18] Judicial Factors (Sc.) Acts, 1849, Ss. 26, 27; 1880, Ss. 4, 5.
[19] Bankruptcy (Sc.) Act, 1913, S. 69.
[20] Confirmation of Executors (Sc.) Act, 1823, S. 2.

in their charge, normally by single premium policies granted by insurance companies or guarantee associations. A sheriff officer must find caution for loss caused by wrongful actings.[1]

Judicial caution

Cautionary obligations are employed also for various purposes in judicial proceedings.

Caution judicio sisti

This is caution found to await judgment within the jurisdiction of the court.[2] It may be demanded if the defender seems likely to flee the country, and the cautioner's obligation is to make the defender appear to answer before a court in Scotland. The obligation is discharged by presentment of the debtor on the creditor's demand, by the debtor's death, by notice to the creditor and presentment of the debtor's person in court, and by decree extracted without requisition to present the debtor.[3] In criminal proceedings the corresponding concept is that of bail.

Caution judicatum solvi

This is caution found to implement a decree or pay the sum due thereunder.[4] The cautioner's obligation is for the full amount due by the principal, including interest and expenses. If necessary for the conduct of the case, he may sist himself as a party. He is entitled to the benefit of discussion, but not to liberation under the septennial prescription.

Caution for violent profits

In an action of removing from heritable property, the defender may be ordered to find caution for violent profits,[5] i.e. for the full profits which the landlord could have made by personal possession of the lands, and all damage which the subjects may suffer during the defender's possession.[6]

---

[1] *Ayr C.C.* v. *Wyllie*, 1935 S.C. 836.

[2] Bell, *Comm.* I, 398; *Prin.* §274; *Douglas* v. *Wallace* (1842) 5 D. 338; *Muir* v. *Collett* (1866) 5 M. 47; *Cheyne* v. *Macdonald* (1863) 1 M. 960.

[3] Bell, *Prin., supra.*

[4] Bell, *Comm.* I, 401; *Prin.* §275.

[5] Sheriff Courts (Sc.) Act, 1907, Sch., R. 121, amended by 1913 Act; *Inglis's Trs.* v. *Macpherson*, 1910 S.C. 46.

[6] *Gardner* v. *Beresford's Trs.* (1877) 4 R. 1091.

Caution in lawburrows

Lawburrows is the process whereby anyone who has reason to apprehend danger from another can have the other obliged to find caution not to molest him. A sheriff, sheriff substitute, or J.P., if satisfied of the grounds for apprehension, may order a party complained against to find caution to an amount in the judge's discretion, or to grant his own bond without caution, not to molest the complainer.[1] If caution be not found or the bond not granted, the defender may be imprisoned for not more than six months. In the event of contravention the complainer brings an action craving forfeiture of the caution, and calling the cautioner as a defender.

Caution for expenses

A court may, in its discretion, ordain a party to find caution for expenses as a condition of being permitted to proceed with his claim or defence.[2]

Caution in criminal proceedings

In summary criminal proceedings a person convicted may be ordained to find caution for good behaviour for not longer than 12 months and for not more than £150, in lieu of or in addition to fine or imprisonment.[3] A criminal court may also, on making a probation order, require the offender or, if he is a young person, his parent or guardian, to give security for the offender's good behaviour.[4]

Agreements to indemnify

Akin to cautionary obligations are undertakings to indemnify one party if he incurs legal liability to and has to make some payment to another party, as where a contractor undertakes to indemnify his employer against claims by third parties, arising out of his operations under the contract.[5] Whether the right to indemnify arises in particular circumstances depends on the true interpretation of the words used.

---

[1] Lawburrows Act, 1597; Civil Imprisonment (Sc.) Act, 1882, S. 6; *Mackenzie* v. *Maclennan*, 1916 S.C. 617.

[2] *Harvey* v. *Farquhar* (1870) 8 M. 971; *Ritchie* v. *McIntosh* (1881) 8 R. 747; *Thom* v. *Andrew* (1888) 15 R. 780.

[3] Summary Jurisdiction (Sc.) Act, 1954, Ss. 7, 51.

[4] Children and Young Persons (Sc.) Act, 1937, S. 59(2); Criminal Justice (Sc.) Act, 1949, S. 8(1).

[5] e.g. *Hamilton* v. *Anderson*, 1953 S.C. 129; *N. of S. Hydro-Electric Board* v. *Taylor*, 1956 S.C. 1. See also *McGill* v. *Pirie & Co. (Paisley) Ltd.*, 1967 S.L.T. 152.

CHAPTER 48

OBLIGATIONS OF DEBT

AN obligation of debt arises where there has been an expressed intention to make a voluntary payment, or a contract undertaken, as where money is lent, or goods or services supplied on credit, and it raises an express or implied promise to pay at the due date. The creditor's right is to obtain payment of the sum due when the agreed time arrives, with interest, if need be by action and diligence, or by sequestration of the debtor. The debtor's duty is to pay the sum due, with interest.

In most cases the obligation is implied, as a legal consequence of promise of gift, or of loan, sale, or other contract which has not been discharged by payment, but in some cases, particularly of loan or voluntary payment the obligation may be formally expressed. If the obligation is to repay a loan of money in excess of £8.33,[1] or is voluntary and gratuitous,[2] it must be provable against the debtor by his writ or oath. Obligations to pay which are mere elements of onerous contracts, such as of hiring, sale, or otherwise, may be proved *prout de jure*.

Interest

Interest on money due but unpaid may be payable by law,[3] or by express stipulation, and is impliedly due on money lent[4] but on other debts only where there is a course of dealing or custom of trade implying an obligation for interest.[5] Apart from law or express or implied contract interest is due only where money has been wrongfully withheld and not paid when it ought to have been paid.[6] A demand for payment is, apart from contract, a condition precedent to a demand for interest. On illiquid claims interest is recoverable only from the date of decree constituting the debt.[7]

---

[1] Bell, *Prin.* §2257; *Bryan v. Butters* (1892) 19 R. 490; *Paterson v. P.* (1897) 25 R. 144.

[2] Ersk. IV, 2, 20; *Millar v. Tremamondo* (1771) Mor. 12395; *Mackenzie v. Brodie* (1859) 21 D. 1048; *Smith v. Oliver*, 1911 S.C. 103.

[3] e.g. on bills of exchange; Bills of Exchange Act, 1882, Ss. 9, 57.

[4] *Garthland's Trs. v. McDowall*, 26 May, 1820, F.C.; *Cunninghame v. Boswell* (1868) 6 M. 890; *Hope Johnstone v. Cornwall* (1895) 22 R. 314.

[5] Bell, *Comm.* I, 690; *Blair's Trs. v. Payne* (1884) 12 R. 104, 108.

[6] *Carmichael v. Caledonian Ry.* (1870) 8 M. (H.L.) 131; approved *Blair's Trs., supra*; *Durie's Trs. v. Ayton* (1894) 22 R. 34; cf. *Edinburgh and Glasgow Union Canal Co. v. Carmichael* (1842) 1 Bell 316; *Kearon v. Thomson's Trs.*, 1949 S.C. 287.

[7] *Wallace v. Geddes* (1821) 1 Sh. App. 42.

Exceptions

Save by express agreement interest does not run on unpaid feu-duties,[1] ground-annuals and rents.[2]

INSTRUMENTS OF DEBT

Undertaking not amounting to bill of exchange

An order on a debtor to pay, not complying with the definition of a bill of exchange, if accepted, may yet amount to an undertaking by him to pay, or an acknowledgment of debt.[3] So too a prescribed bill, supported by holograph admissions of the debt, amounts to an acknowledgment of debt.[4] Similarly a mere acknowledgment of indebtedness, as in a letter, may be valuable evidence of a debt, but does not bind the granter to pay, nor can it be sued on alone.[5]

I.O.U.

An I.O.U. is a mere acknowledgment of debt with an implied undertaking to pay on demand,[6] and, though valuable as evidence, does not constitute a debt or bind the granter to pay.[7] It is enforceable by the holder though it does not bear to be addressed to anyone.[8] It is not a promissory note or negotiable instrument,[9] need not be addressed to anyone, nor should it contain any promise to repay. If it does, it may be a promissory note rather than an I.O.U.[10]

Bill of exchange

A bill of exchange[11] drawn by and payable to the creditor and accepted by the debtor may be used to constitute an obligation to pay or repay money at a future date. Similarly a post-dated cheque granted by the debtor constitutes his obligation to pay at

---

[1] *Napier* v. *Spiers' Trs.* (1831) 9 S. 655; *Wallace* v. *Eglinton* (1835) 13 S. 564; *Wallace* v. *Crawford's Exors.* (1838) 1 D. 162; *Blair's Trs., supra*; *Maxwell's Trs.* v. *Bothwell School Board* (1893) 20 R. 958.

[2] *Advocate-General* v. *Sinclair's Trs.* (1855) 17 D. 290.

[3] *Fair* v. *Cranston* (1801) Mor. 1677; *Macdonald's Trs.* v. *Rankin*, 13 June 1817, F.C.; *Lawson's Exors.* v. *Watson*, 1907 S.C. 1353; *Paris* v. *P.*, 1913, 2 S.L.T. 209.

[4] *Elder* v. *Marshall* (1930) 9 S. 133.

[5] *Neilson's Trs.* v. *N's Trs.* (1883) 11 R. 119.

[6] *Black* v. *Gibb*, 1940 S.C. 24.

[7] Bell, *Prin.* §310; *Neilson's Trs.* v. *N's Trs.* (1883) 11 R. 119; *Black, supra*.

[8] *Macpherson* v. *Munro* (1854) 16 D. 612.

[9] cf. *Welsh's Trs.* v. *Forbes* (1885) 12 R. 851; *Todd* v. *Wood* (1897) 24 R. 1104.

[10] See Bills of Exchange Act, 1882, Ss. 83–89.

[11] See Ch. 49, *infra*.

maturity. A bill, but not a cheque,[1] may form the basis of summary diligence.[2]

Promissory note

A promissory note is an unconditional promise in writing made by one person to another, signed by the maker, engaging to pay on demand, or at a fixed or determinable future time, a sum certain in money, to or to the order of, a specified person or to bearer.[3] The promise may be express or implied;[4] a mere acknowledgment of debt is not a promissory note.[5] It may contain a pledge of security with authority to sell, but must not be so expressed as to be truly a bond and disposition in security.[6] Summary diligence is competent on a promissory note.

Personal bond

A personal bond[7] is a probative or holograph deed, usually narrating the receipt of money by the granter, and obliging the granter and, usually, his heirs, executors and representatives, jointly and severally, without the necessity of discussing them in their order, to pay or repay to the grantee, his heirs and executors, the principal sum, at a specified date and place, usually with a fifth part more of liquidate penalty in case of failure and interest at a stated rate from the date of granting till the date of payment, payable usually at Whitsunday and Martinmas each year. The creditor may resort, after the debtor's death, to his successors both in heritage and in moveables, but, unless the benefit of discussion is renounced in the bond, must, when going against the heirs in heritage, do so in the order (i) the heir specially bound or taking the property relative to which the obligation was granted; (ii) the heir of line; (iii) the heir male; (iv) other heirs of provision.[8] An heir subsidiarily liable but paying the debt has a claim for relief against the heir primarily liable. It has been suggested that the words 'heirs and executors, jointly and severally,' implies an

[1] *Glickman* v. *Linda*, 1950 S.C. 18.

[2] Bills of Exchange (Sc.) Act, 1772, S. 42.

[3] Bills of Exchange Act, 1882, S. 83(1).

[4] *McCubbin* v. *Stephen* (1856) 18 D. 1224; *McKinney* v. *Van Heek* (1863) 1 M. 1115; *Vallance* v. *Forbes* (1879) 6 R. 1099; *Blyth* v. *Forbes* (1879) 6 R. 1102.

[5] *Bankier* v. *Robertson* (1864) 2 M. 1153; *Morgan* v. *M.* (1866) 4 M. 321; *Tennent* v. *Crawford* (1878) 5 R. 433.

[6] *Macfarlane* v. *Johnston* (1864) 2 M. 1210.

[7] Bell, *Comm.* I, 352; *Prin.* §67–69; Ross, *Lect.* I, 1; Bell, *Convg.* I, 244; Menzies, 216; Wood, 459, 595; Craigie, *Mov.* 191. A bond may also be entered into *ad factum praestandum.*

[8] Bell, *Prin.* §1935; Bell, *Convg.* I, 247; Menzies, 223; McLaren, 1320.

exclusion of the benefit of discussion, because persons bound jointly and severally cannot plead the *beneficium ordinis*.[1]

The bond must be in favour of a grantee or grantees, named or adequately described,[2] failing which the bond is void.[3]

The stipulation for liquidate penalty covers only the expenses necessarily caused to the grantee in recovering his debt.[4]

The rate of interest should be specified and this is essential for summary diligence;[5] 'legal interest' has usually been interpreted as 5 per cent.[6]

The bond usually also includes a clause of consent to registration for preservation and execution, which enables it to be recorded in the Books of Council and Session and warrants summary diligence thereon on a charge of six days.[7]

Failing contrary provision[8] the debtor may repay at any time after the term of payment, without notice, and the creditor may call for payment at any time and raise an action, or record the bond and do diligence thereon.

A bond formally executed subsists as a document of debt for forty years from the date of payment,[9] and if holograph and unattested falls under the vicennial prescription, counted from the date of the bond.[10]

Bond of corroboration

A bond of corroboration is frequently used when it is desired to accumulate a debt and arrears of interest into one sum, or a new loan with a former debt and interest, or when a new obligant is introduced. The bond narrates the circumstances, obliges the granter, in corroboration of the bond, deed or debt narrated and without prejudice thereto or to diligence which has followed thereon, to make payment, and contains a clause of registration for preservation and execution. Such a bond constitutes a sub-

---

[1] *Burns* v. *Martin* (1887) 14 R. (H.L.) 20, 25.

[2] Ersk. III, 2, 6; *Duncan's Trs.* v. *Shand* (1872) 10 M. 984; *Clapperton, Paton & Co.* v. *Anderson* (1881) 8 R. 1004.

[3] Blank Bonds and Trusts Act, 1696 (c. 25).

[4] Craigie, *Mov.* 203; Bell, *Comm.* I, 701; *Gordon* v. *Maitland* (1761) Mor. 10050; *Young* v. *Sinclair* (1796) Mor. 10053; *Orr* v. *Mackenzie* (1839) 1 D. 1046; *Bruce* v. *Scottish Amicable Life Assce. Socy.*, 1907 S.C. 637; see also *Jameson* v. *Beilby* (1835) 13 S. 865.

[5] *Alston* v. *Nellfield Co.*, 1915 S.C. 912.

[6] *Kinloch, Petr.*, 1920, 2 S.L.T. 79; but see *Kearon* v. *Thomson's Trs.*, 1949 S.C. 287; *Prestwick Cinema Co.* v. *Gardiner*, 1951 S.C. 98.

[7] Titles to Land Consolidation Act, 1868, S. 138.

[8] cf. *Ashburton* v. *Escombe* (1892) 20 R. 187.

[9] Bell, *Prin.* §607.

[10] Bell, *Prin.* §590.

stantive obligation, supporting an action or diligence without reference to the former documents of debt.[1] It may be extinguished by prescription though the principal bond is unaffected.[2] The septennial limitation of cautionary obligations does not apply even to express cautioners in bonds of corroboration.[3]

Bond for cash-credit

A bond for cash-credit is a probative deed containing an obligation in favour of a bank for repayment of advances made by it to the granter as its customer, or for repayment of the debit balance due on a fluctuating cash account.[4] It narrates the credit granted to the customer and its maximum extent, obliges the granter to repay on demand, with penalty and interest, provides for the lender making changes in the rate of interest, the mode of fixing the balance due at any time,[5] and contains a clause of consent to registration for preservation and execution.[6] Frequently the creditor will insist on such a bond being granted by the debtor and by a cautioner,[7] or on being supported by an assignation or disposition in security.[8] A floating charge granted in respect of advances on cash-credit bond covers interest to the date of payment.[9]

Bond of annuity

A bond of annuity creates an obligation to pay the grantee a stated sum annually during the granter's[10] or grantee's lifetime, or for a stated period of years or for a period otherwise defined, payable usually at Whitsunday and Martinmas, with provision for penalty in the case of non-payment and for interest,[11] and with a clause of consent to registration for preservation and execution.

[1] *Beg* v. *Brown* (1663) Mor. 16091; *Johnston* v. *Orchardtown* (1676) Mor. 15798.

[2] *Yuill's Trs.* v. *Maclachlan's Trs.*, 1939 S.C. (H.L.) 40.

[3] *Gordon* v. *Tyrie* (1748) Mor. 11025.

[4] Bell, *Prin.* §299–304; cf. *Reddie* v. *Williamson* (1863) 1 M. 228; *Gilmour* v. *Bank of Scotland* (1880) 7 R. 734; *Commercial Bank* v. *Pattison's Trs.* (1891) 18 R. 476; *Buchanan* v. *Main* (1900) 3 F. 215; *Veitch* v. *National Bank*, 1907 S.C. 554.

[5] A stated account certified by the bank is normally stated to be the mode of fixing the sum due, and is admitted in practice, but a stipulation that a charge for this amount will not be suspended without consignation is not binding: *Forrester* v. *Walker*, 27 June, 1815, F.C. The balance stated as due may be challenged: *Smith* v. *Drummond* (1829) 7 S. 792.

[6] cf. *Fisher* v. *Stewart* (1825) 3 S. 607.

[7] As to the position of a cautioner, see Bell, *Prin.* §301; *Hamilton* v. *Watson* (1842) 5 D. 280; (1845) 4 Bell 67; *Falconer* v. *N. of S. Banking Co.* (1863) 1 M. 704; *Young* v. *Clydesdale Bank* (1889) 17 R. 231; *Veitch*, *supra*.

[8] e.g. *Thow's Tr.* v. *Young*, 1910 S.C. 588.

[9] *National Commercial Bank* v. *Liqdrs. of Telford Grier Mackay, Ltd.*, 1969 S.L.T. 306.

[10] e.g. *Reid's Exrx.* v. *R.*, 1944 S.C. (H.L.) 25.

[11] Bell, *Comm.*, I, 353; *Prin.* §68.

If no duration is stated the annuity is presumed payable for the life of the annuitant.[1] The sum must be certain and is not related to a particular capital sum or principal. Annuities are deemed heritable in succession[2] and fall to be paid out of heritage, if it is sufficient and failing contrary provision,[3] and primarily from income thereof.

The annuity, whether charged on heritage or on moveables, may be declared alimentary, in which case there must be a continuing trust;[4] if so made it cannot be assigned, nor can it be attached by the diligence of the annuitant's creditors, except for alimentary debts[5] or unless the court permits it to be the subject of diligence so far as it exceeds a reasonable sum,[6] though arrears of an alimentary fund may be arrested.[7] An alimentary provision in one's own favour can be created only by a married woman in her antenuptial marriage contract.[8] If no trust be created the annuitant may claim the capital sum needed to furnish the annuity.

If not declared alimentary, or even if so declared but not protected by a trust,[9] the annuity may be renounced,[10] though a wife cannot, so long as the marriage lasts, renounce an annuity provided under her marriage contract and protected by a trust.[11]

An annuity may be given with power to the donee to burden or dispose of it, in which case he may claim the capitalized value from the donor,[12] unless it is declared alimentary.[13]

---

[1] *Reid's Exrx.*, *supra*.

[2] Stair II, 1, 4; III, 5, 6; Ersk. II, 2, 6; Bell, *Comm.* II, 4; *Prin.* §1480; *Reid* v. *McWalter* (1878) 5 R. 630.

[3] *Breadalbane's Trs.* v. *Jamieson* (1873) 11 M. 912; *Mackintosh* v. *M's Trs.* (1873) 11 M. (H.L.) 28; *Moon's Trs.* v. *M.* (1899) 2 F. 201.

[4] *White's Trs.* v. *Whyte* (1877) 4 R. 786; *Murray* v. *Macfarlane's Trs.* (1895) 22 R. 927; *Kennedy's Trs.* v. *Warren* (1901) 3 F. 1087; *Turner's Trs.* v. *Fernie*, 1908 S.C. 883; *Brown's Trs.* v. *Thom*, 1916 S.C. 32; *Dunsmure's Trs.* v. *D.*, 1920 S.C. 147; *McDougal's Trs.* v. *McD.*, 1918 S.C. (H.L.) 6; *Dempster's Trs.* v. *D.*, 1921 S.C. 332; *Branford's Trs.* v. *B.*, 1924 S.C. 439; *Forbes' Trs.* v. *Tennant*, 1926 S.C. 294.

[5] *Moneypenny* v. *Earl of Buchan* (1835) 13 S. 1112; *Harvey* v. *Calder* (1840) 2 D. 1095; *Lewis* v. *Anstruther* (1852) 14 D. 857; (1853) 15 D. 263.

[6] *Livingstone* v. *L.* (1886) 14 R. 43.   [7] Bell, *Comm.* I, 127.

[8] Ersk. III, 6, 7; Bell, *Comm.* I, 124; *White's Trs.* v. *W.* (1877) 4 R. 786; *Reid* v. *Bell* (1884) 12 R. 178; *Elliott* v. *Purdom* (1895) 22 R. (H.L.) 26; *Douglas Gardiner & Mill* v. *Mackintosh's Trs.*, 1916 S.C. 125. Such a provision does not cease to be alimentary on the husband's death; *Sutherland*, 1968 S.L.T. (Notes) 40.

[9] *Forbes's Trs.*, *supra*.

[10] *Standard Property Investment Co.* v. *Cowe* (1877) 4 R. 695; *Christie's J.F.* v. *Hardie* (1899) 1 F. 703.

[11] *Ker's Trs.* v. *K.* (1895) 23 R. 317.

[12] *Tod* v. *T's Trs.* (1871) 9 M. 728; *Kippen* v. *K's Trs.* (1871) 10 M. 134; *Dow* v. *Kilgour's Trs.* (1877) 4 R. 403.

[13] *Smith* v. *Campbell* (1873) 11 M. 639; *Cosens* v. *Stevenson* (1873) 11 M. 761; *White's Trs.* v. *W.* (1877) 4 R. 786; *Branford's Trs.* v. *Powell*, 1924 S.C. 439.

If it is necessary to sue, or to record and do diligence on the bond, the annuitant may claim such a capital sum as would, if invested, produce the annual amount of the annuity, the capital to revert to the debtor on the termination of the annuity.[1] It is no defence to an action on a bond that the money is being wasted.[2]

Bond of relief

A bond may also be granted, as by debtor to a cautioner, to free and relieve the latter of liabilities undertaken on behalf of the granter. This fortifies and facilitates the grantee's recovery of payments he has had to make on behalf of the granter.[3]

[1] Bell, *Comm.* I, 355; cf. *Buchanan* v. *Eaton*, 1911, 1 S.L.T. 422; revd. on another ground, 1911 S.C. (H.L.) 40.
[2] *Weir* v. *W.*, 1968 S.C. 241.
[3] *Gray* v. *Phillips* (1905) 13 S.L.T. 145.

CHAPTER 49

CONTRACTS EVIDENCED BY BILLS OF EXCHANGE, CHEQUES AND PROMISSORY NOTES

Bills and cheques are convenient means of evidencing an undertaking to pay money, and for effecting payment without transfer of cash. Where one person is creditor of a second person but also debtor to a third person he may, instead of recovering from the second and paying the third, give the second person an order to pay the third person direct. If the second person accepts the order he incurs direct liability to the third, and by paying as ordered thereby diminishes the first's indebtedness to the third.[1] By custom long recognized legally the third party may treat the order to pay in his hands as the equivalent of money and transfer it by delivery, or endorsement and delivery, to a fourth party in settlement of his indebtedness to the fourth party, and so on.[2] If the second party fails to accept the order and to pay the third or fourth party or whoever holds the bill at the date of demand for payment, the first party is still liable to the holder. If he has accepted he is the principal debtor, but the drawer and after him, the indorsers in their order are subsidiary liable. Furthermore such an order confers on a *bona fide* holder for value a valid right notwithstanding any defect in the title of an earlier holder. Bills, cheques and notes are accordingly the principal examples of negotiable instruments.[3]

Bills of exchange were developed in the middle ages and used in foreign trade; the rights and liabilities of parties were developed and recognized by the customary law merchant and incorporated by judicial decisions into Scottish and English law.[4] Cheques developed with the modern system of banking and the validity of promissory notes was not established till the eighteenth century. The law was built up largely by judicial recognition of mercantile customs and usages from the seventeenth century

---

[1] *Goodwin* v. *Ronarts* (1875) L.R. 10 Ex. 346.

[2] Recognition of this custom is a settled exception to the general rule that assignation of an obligation to pay requires intimation to the debtor.

[3] On negotiable instruments in general see also Ch. 110, *infra*.

[4] Milnes Holden, *History of Negotiable Instruments in English Law*; Forbes, *Bills of Exchange*; See also Beawes, *Lex Mercatoria*; Marius, *Advice concerning Bills of Exchange*; Schmitthoff, *The Export Trade*.

onwards.[1] It was substantially codified by the Bills of Exchange Act, 1882, but the rules of common law, including the law merchant, save in so far as inconsistent with the express provisions of that Act, continue to apply to bills, cheques and promissory notes,[2] and the Act does not deal with bankruptcy, summary diligence or prescription. It does not apply to negotiable instruments other than bills, cheques and promissory notes.

BILLS OF EXCHANGE—GENERAL

Definition

A bill of exchange[3] is an unconditional[4] order[5] in writing, signed[6] and addressed by one person, the drawer, to another, the drawee,[7] requiring the drawee to pay[8] on demand,[9] or at a fixed or determinable future time,[10] a sum certain in money[11] to, or to the order[12] of, a specified payee,[13] or to bearer.[14] An instrument not complying with these conditions, or which orders any act to be

---

[1] Generally Stair I, 12, 1; Ersk. III, 2, 25; Bell, *Comm.* I, 411; *Prin.* §305; Forbes, *Bills of Exchange*; Hamilton, *Bills of Exchange*; Byles, *Bills*; Chalmers, *Bills of Exchange Act.*

[2] 1882 Act, S. 97(2).

[3] Defined in Bills of Exchange Act, 1882, S. 3(1).

[4] Excluding an order to pay out of a particular fund, but including an order with an indication of the funds out of which the drawee is to reimburse himself or a particular account to be debited or a statement of the transaction which gives rise to the bill: 1882 Act, S. 3(3). See *Isles* v. *Gill* (1836) 14 S. 996; *Chiene* v. *Western Bank* (1848) 10 D. 1523; *Macfarlane* v. *Johnston* (1864) 2 M. 1210; *Bank of Scotland* v. *Faulds* (1870) 42 Sc. Jur. 557; *Guaranty Trust* v. *Hannay* [1918] 2 K.B. 623.

[5] It must be an order, not a request nor an agreement.

[6] It may be signed per procuration: *Union Bank* v. *Makin* (1873) 11 M. 499; or by a person authorized to do so: S. 91(1); or by initials or mark: Bell, *Prin.* §323.

[7] The drawee must be named or otherwise indicated in the bill with reasonable certainty: S. 6(1): see *Watt's Trs.* v. *Pinkney* (1853) 16 D. 279; *Douglas* v. *Douglas Trs.* (1864) 2 M. 1389.

[8] A request to do anything other than to pay money is not a bill: *Pirie's Reps.* v. *Smith's Exrx.* (1833) 11 S. 473; *Martin* v. *Brash* (1833) 11 S. 782; *Dixon* v. *Bovill* (1854) 16 D. 619; 3 Macq. 1.

[9] Explained: S. 10.

[10] Explained: S. 11; cf. *Haddin* v. *McEwan* (1838) 16 S. 331; *Macfarlane* v. *Johnston* (1864) 2 M. 1210; *Morgan* v. *M.* (1866) 4 M. 321.

[11] A sum is certain though required to be paid with interest, by stated instalments, with or without a provision that on default in payment of an instalment the whole becomes due, (e.g. *Bartsch* v. *Poole* (1895) 23 R. 328; *Gordon* v. *Kerr* (1898) 25 R. 570) or according to an indicated rate of exchange: S. 9(1); see also *Morgan* v. *M.* (1866) 4 M. 321; *Vallance* v. *Forbes* (1879) 6 R. 1099; *Lamberton* v. *Aiken* (1899) 1 F. 189, *sed quaere*.

[12] Explained: S. 8(4) and (5).

[13] The payee must be named or otherwise indicated with reasonable certainty: S. 7(1): *Fraser* v. *Bannerman* (1853) 15 D. 756. A bill may be payable to payees jointly, or alternatively to one of two, or one of several payees, or to the holder of an office for the time being. Where the payee is a fictitious or non-existing person the bill may be treated as payable to bearer: S. 7(2) and (3); see *Bank of England* v. *Vagliano* [1891] A.C. 107.

[14] Explained S. 8(3).

done in addition to the payment of money, is not a bill of exchange.[1]

Parties

A bill may be drawn payable to, or to the order of, the drawer or the drawee.[2] Where drawer and drawee are the same person, or where the drawer is a fictitious person or a person not having capacity to contract, the holder may treat the instrument as a bill of exchange or a promissory note.[3] The drawee must be indicated with reasonable certainty. A bill may be addressed to two or more drawees, but an order to two drawees in the alternative, or in succession, is not a bill of exchange.[4] If a bill is not payable to bearer, the payee must be indicated with reasonable certainty. A bill may be made payable to two or more payees jointly, or to one of two, or one or some of several payees or to the holder of an office for the time being. If payable to a fictitious or non-existent person the bill may be treated as payable to bearer.[5]

Form of bill

A bill may be printed or written on any substance, except metal,[6] and in any form of words.[7] It must be signed by the drawer,[8] and formerly had to be stamped.[9] Witnesses, and the designations of parties, are unnecessary.[10] Where the sum payable is expressed in words and in figures and there is a discrepancy, the sum denoted by the words is the amount payable.[11] A bill is not invalid by reason that it is not dated, or does not specify the value given, or that any value has been given therefor, or that it does not specify the place of drawing or of payment,[12] nor because it is ante-dated, post-dated or dated on a Sunday.[13] The date of drawing, acceptance or any indorsement on a bill is presumed to be the

---

[1] S. 3(2); but an incomplete instrument may be evidence of indebtedness; see *Macdonald's Trs.* v. *Rankin*, 13 June, 1817, F.C.; *Lawson's Exors.* v. *Watson*, 1907 S.C. 1353; *Paris* v. *P.*, 1913, 2 S.L.T. 209.

[2] S. 5(1); *Chamberlain* v. *Young* [1893] 2 Q.B. 206.   [3] S. 5(2).

[4] S. 6.   [5] S. 7.   [6] Coinage Act, 1971, S. 9.

[7] It need not be in English: *Re Marseilles Extension Ry.* (1885) 30 Ch. D. 598.

[8] S. 23; *McCall* v. *Taylor* (1865) 34 L.J.C.P. 365; *S. Wales Coal Co.* v. *Underwood* (1899) 15 T.L.R. 157; *Lawson's Exors.* v. *Watson*, 1907 S.C. 1353. It may be signed on the drawer's behalf: S. 91(1). It may be notarially executed if the drawer is blind or cannot write.

[9] Formerly *ad valorem*; later a fixed duty of 2d.; abolished 1970.

[10] Bell, *Comm.* I, 342, 413; *Prin.* §21, 305; *King* v. *Creichton* (1843) 2 Bell 81; *Watt's Trs.* v. *Pinkney* (1853) 16 D. 279.

[11] S. 9(2).

[12] 1882 Act, S. 3(4).

[13] Ibid., S. 13(2).

true date,[1] but if undated, any holder may insert the true date of issue or acceptance; if the wrong date is inserted the bill operates as if that were the true date.[2] A bill must be payable on demand,[3] or at a fixed or determinable future date.[4] It must be payable in money.[5] By the Bank Notes (Sc.) Act, 1845, Ss. 16 and 20, negotiable bills and notes for less than twenty shillings are void in Scotland and subject to penalty, except in the case of drafts on a banker for money held to the use of the drawer. If expressed to be payable with interest, unless the instrument otherwise provides, interest runs from the date of the bill or, if undated, from the issue thereof.[6]

Inland and foreign bills

An inland bill is or purports to be drawn and payable within the British Isles, or drawn there upon a person resident therein. Unless the contrary appears on the face of the bill the holder may treat it as an inland bill. Any other bill is a foreign bill.[7] The distinction is that a foreign bill, if dishonoured, must be protested, while an inland bill need not.[8] Foreign bills are sometimes drawn in a set of two or more, each part being numbered, the whole constituting one bill[9] and each part being payable only so long as the others remain unpaid.

What bills are negotiable

When a bill contains words prohibiting transfer,[10] or indicating an intention that it should not be transferable, it is valid as between the parties thereto, but is not negotiable. A negotiable bill may be payable to order or to bearer. A bill is payable to order which is expressed to be so payable, or expressed to be payable to a particular person, and does not contain words prohibiting transfer or indicating an intention that it should not be transferable;[11] it is payable to bearer if expressed to be so payable, or on

---

[1] Ibid., S. 13(1); The stamp may assist to determine the date: *Speirs & Knox* v. *Semple*, (1901) 9 S.L.T. 153.

[2] Ibid., S. 12.

[3] Ibid., S. 10: including cases where no time for payment is expressed.

[4] Ibid., S. 11: if payable on a contingency it is not a bill, even if the contingency happens; cf. *Alexander* v. *Thomas* (1851) 16 Q.B. 333.

[5] *Dixon* v. *Bovill* (1856) 3 Macq. 1.

[6] Ibid., S. 9(3).

[7] S. 4.

[8] S. 51.

[9] S. 71.

[10] *National Bank* v. *Silke* [1891] 1 Q.B. 435; *Meyer* v. *Decroix* [1891] A.C. 520.

[11] *Glen* v. *Semple* (1901) 3 F. 1134.

which the only or last indorsement is in blank. A bill expressed, originally or by indorsement, to be payable to the order of a specified person, and not to him or his order, is nevertheless payable to him or his order at his option.[1]

Time of payment

The bill is payable on demand if expressed to be payable on demand or at sight or on presentation; if no time is expressed it is payable on demand.[2] It is deemed payable on demand as regards the acceptor or indorser, if accepted or indorsed when it is overdue.[3] Alternatively it is payable at a determinable future time if it is expressed to be payable so many months or days after date or sight, or on, or at a fixed period after, the occurrence of a specified event which is certain to happen, though the time of happening may be uncertain.[4] An instrument expressed to be payable on a contingency is not a bill, even if the event happens.[4]

Where a bill is not payable on demand, three days of grace were formerly added to the time of payment and the bill was due and payable on the last day of grace,[5] but it is now due and payable on the last day of the time of payment as fixed by the bill or if that is a non-business day, on the succeeding business day.[6] If payable at a fixed period after date, or sight, or a specified event, the time of payment excludes that day and includes the day of payment.[7] If payable at a fixed period after sight, time runs from the date of acceptance if the bill be accepted and from the date of noting or protest if the bill be noted or protested for non-acceptance or non-delivery.[8] In a bill a 'month' means a calendar month.[9]

Referee in case of need

The drawer and any indorser may insert in a bill the name of a person to whom the holder may resort in case of need, if the bill is dishonoured by non-acceptance or non-payment. The holder may resort to the referee in case of need in his option as he thinks fit.[10]

---

[1] S. 8.
[2] S. 10(1).
[3] S. 10(2).
[4] S. 11. As to computation of time see S. 14(2)–(4).
[5] cf. *Brown* v. *Bain* (1864) 2 M. 1143.
[6] S. 14(1), replaced by Banking and Financial Dealings Act, 1971, S. 3(2).
[7] S. 14(2).
[8] S. 14(3).
[9] S. 14(4).
[10] S. 15.

Optional stipulations

The drawer and any indorser may insert in a bill an express stipulation negativing or limiting his own liability to the holder, or waiving as regards himself some or all of the holder's duties.[1]

Acceptance

A bill may be accepted by the drawee, by writing words of acceptance on the bill and signing it, or signing it alone. This signifies that the drawee assents to the drawer's order to pay when due. The acceptance must not express that the drawee will perform his promise by any other means than the payment of money.[2] It may be accepted before signature by the drawer, or while otherwise incomplete, when it is overdue, or after dishonour by a previous refusal to accept, or by non-payment; if accepted after a refusal to accept, the holder is entitled to have the bill accepted as of the date of first presentment for acceptance.[3] An acceptance may be general, including an acceptance to pay at a particular place, or qualified, if in express terms it varies the effect of the bill as drawn, particularly if it is conditional, partial, local, i.e. an acceptance to pay only at a particular specified place, qualified as to time, or is the acceptance of one or more but not all of the drawees.[4] The holder may refuse to take a qualified acceptance and if he does not obtain an unqualified acceptance may treat the bill as dishonoured by non-acceptance.[5] Where a qualified acceptance is taken, and the drawer or an indorser has not expressly or impliedly authorized the holder to take a qualified acceptance, or does not subsequently assent thereto, such drawer or endorser is discharged from his liability on the bill, except in the case of a partial acceptance whereof due notice has been given. Where a foreign bill has been accepted as to part it must be protested as to the balance. When the drawer or indorser of a bill receives notice of a qualified acceptance and does not within a reasonable time express his dissent to the holder he shall be deemed to have assented thereto.[6]

---

[1] S. 16. cf. *Castrique* v. *Buttigieg* (1855) 10 Moo. P.C. 94. A drawee cannot alter his liability under this section: see Bell, *Comm.* I, 424; *Walker's Trs.* v. *McKinlay* (1880) 7 R. (H.L.) 85.

[2] S. 17; *Russell* v. *Phillips* (1850) 14 Q.B. 891; only the drawee can undertake the obligations of an acceptor: *Walker's Trs.* v. *McKinlay* (1880) 7 R. (H.L.) 85. See also *McDowall & Neilson's Tr.* v. *Snowball* (1904) 7 F. 35.

[3] S. 18.

[4] S. 19; *Russell, supra*; *Decroix* v. *Meyer* [1891] A.C. 520; *Bank Polski* v. *Mulder* [1942] 1 K.B. 497.

[5] S. 44(1).   [6] S. 44.

Inchoate instruments

If a signed blank stamped paper is delivered by the signer to be converted into a bill it may be completed for any amount using the signature for that of drawer, acceptor or indorser, and when a bill is wanting in any material particular, the person in possession has *prima facie* authority to fill up the omission in any way he thinks fit. To be enforceable against any person who became a party thereto prior to its completion, it must be filled up within a reasonable time[1] and in accordance with the authority given. Hence a person receiving a blank acceptance cannot fill it up after the giver's sequestration.[2] The onus of proof that the bill has not been completed in accordance with the authority given is on the party who signed and delivered it.[3] There is implied authority, failing contrary agreement, to insert the name of a third party as drawer,[4] or, if the bill is payable to the drawer's order, for the drawer to insert his name as payee.[5] But if such an instrument after completion is negotiated to a holder in due course it is valid and effectual for all purposes in his hands, and he may enforce it as if it had been filled up within a reasonable time and strictly in accordance with the authority given.[6]

Need for delivery

Every contract on a bill, the drawer's, acceptor's, or an indorser's, is incomplete and revocable until delivery[7] of the instrument to give effect thereto, save that where an acceptance is written on the bill and the drawee gives notice to or according to the directions of the person entitled to the bill that he has accepted it, the acceptance becomes complete and irrevocable.[8] As between immediate parties, and as regards a remote party other than a holder in due course, delivery, in order to be effectual must be made either by or under the authority of the party drawing, accepting or endorsing, as the case may be, and may be shown to have been conditional or for a special purpose only, and not for the

---

[1] *Anderson* v. *Somerville, Murray & Co.* (1898) 1 F. 90; *Maclean* v. *McEwen & Son* (1899) 1 F. 381.

[2] *McMeekin* v. *Russell* (1881) 8 R. 587.

[3] *Anderson, supra.*

[4] *Russell* v. *Banknock Coal Co.* (1897) 24 R. 1009.

[5] *Macdonald* v. *Nash* [1924] A.C. 625.

[6] S. 20; cf. *Russell* v. *Banknock Coal Co.* (1897) 24 R. 1009; *Lawson's Exors.* v. *Watson*, 1907 S.C. 1353.

[7] Delivery means transfer of possession, actual or constructive, from one person to another: S. 2.

[8] S. 21(1); cf. *Martini and Co.* v. *Steel and Craig* (1878) 6 R. 342.

purpose of transferring the property in the bill. But if the bill be in the hands of a holder in due course a valid delivery of the bill by all parties prior to him so as to make them liable to him is conclusively presumed.[1] Where a bill is no longer in the possession of a party who has signed it as drawer, acceptor or indorser, a valid and unconditional delivery by him is presumed unless the contrary is proved.[2] By delivering the bill to the payee the drawer issues it and puts the bill into circulation.

Capacity and authority of parties

Capacity to incur liability on a bill is co-extensive with capacity to contract.[3] Where a bill is drawn or indorsed by a minor, or corporation having no power to incur liability on a bill, the drawing or indorsement entitles the holder to receive payment of the bill and to enforce it against any party thereto.[4] A signature as an agent is binding only if the agent had authority to sign bills,[5] and signature as a partner binds the firm only if in the course of the firm's business and not exceeding any authority enjoyed by the partner.[6] No person is liable as drawer, indorser, or acceptor who has not signed as such. Where a person signs in a trade or assumed name, he is liable thereon as if he had signed in his own name.[7] The signature of a firm is equivalent to the signature of all the partners.[8]

Forged bills

Subject to the Act, where a signature on a bill is forged or placed thereon without the authority of the person whose signature it purports to be, the forged or unauthorized signature is wholly inoperative and no right to retain the bill or to give a discharge therefor or to enforce payment thereof against any party thereto can be acquired through or under that signature, unless the party against whom it is sought to retain or enforce payment of

---

[1] S. 21(2). [2] S. 21(3).

[3] S. 22(1); cf. *Pollok* v. *Burns* (1875) 2 R. 497; *McLean* v. *Angus* (1887) 1448; 4 R. *Mitchell & Baxter* v. *Cheyne* (1891) 19 R. 324; *Tyler* v. *Maxwell* (1892) 30 S.L.R. 583.

[4] S. 22(2).

[5] *Strickland* v. *Neilson & MacIntosh* (1869) 7 M. 400; cf. *N. of S. Bank* v. *Behn, Moller & Co.* (1881) 8 R. 423.

[6] *Cameron* v. *Young* (1871) 9 M. 786; *Paterson Bros.* v. *Gladstone* (1891) 18 R. 403; *Rosslund Cycle Co.* v. *McCreadie*, 1907 S.C. 1208; cf. *Goodwin* v. *Industrial and General Trust* (1890) 18 R. 193.

[7] *McMeekin* v. *Easton* (1889) 16 R. 363.

[8] S. 23. By the Companies Act, 1948, S. 108, any officer of a company who fails to have a bill executed in proper form by the company is personally liable: *Scottish and Newcastle Breweries* v. *Blair*, 1967 S.L.T. 72.

the bill is precluded from setting up the forgery or want of authority.[1] Even a *bona fide* holder for value has in general no right to sue on a bill where his title thereto had necessarily been made through a forgery.[2] A forged signature cannot be ratified, but may be adopted, in which case the party is fully liable.[3] An unauthorized signature not amounting to a forgery may be ratified.[4] The party whose signature was forged will be personally barred from repudiating liability if after discovery of the forgery he has deliberately refrained from notifying the fact and challenging the bill,[5] but not by mere delay unless prejudice has resulted,[6] nor if disclosure thereof is made with due diligence, though too late to prevent loss.[6] The onus of proving that a signature is genuine is on the holder of the bill.[7] Payment of a cheque forged as to the payee's name does not entitle the bank to debit the drawer's account.[8]

Procuration signature

A signature by procuration operates as notice that the agent has but a limited authority to sign, and the principal is only bound by such signature if the agent in so signing was acting within the actual limits of his authority.[9]

Person signing as agent or in a representative capacity

Where a person signs as drawer, indorser or acceptor and adds words to his signature, indicating that he signs for or on behalf of a principal, or in a representative character, he is not personally liable hereon; but the mere addition to his signature of words describing him as an agent, or as filling a representative character, does not exempt him from personal liability. In determining whether a signature on a bill is that of the principal or that of the agent by whose hand it is written, the construction most favourable to the validity of the instrument has to be adopted.[10] Where

---

[1] S. 24; Bell, *Prin.* §323; *Brewer* v. *Westminster Bank Ltd.* [1952] 2 All E.R. 650.

[2] *Kreditbank Cassel* v. *Schenkers* [1927] 1 K.B. 826.

[3] *McKenzie* v. *B.L. Co.* (1881) 8 R. (H.L.) 8; *B.L. Co.* v. *Cowan* (1906) 8 F. 704; cf. *Powrie* v. *Louis* (1881) 18 S.L.R. 533.

[4] S. 24.   [5] *Greenwood* v. *Martins Bank* [1933] A.C. 51.   [6] *McKenzie, supra.*

[7] *B.L. Co.* v. *Cowan* (1906) 8 F. 704; *McIntyre* v. *National Bank*, 1910 S.C. 150.

[8] *Dickson* v. *Clydesdale Bank*, 1937 S.L.T. 585.

[9] S. 25; *N. of S. Bank* v. *Behn, Moller & Co.* (1881) 8 R. 423; *Bryant Powis & Co.* v. *La Banque du Peuple* [1893] A.C. 170; *Midland Bank* v. *Reckitt* [1933] A.C. 1.

[10] S. 26; Bell, *Prin.* §312; *Brown* v. *Sutherland* (1875) 2 R. 615; *McMeekin* v. *Easton* (1889) 16 R. 363; *Brebner* v. *Henderson*, 1925 S.C. 643; as to agent exceeding his powers see *Strickland* v. *Neilson & MacIntosh* (1869) 7 M. 400; *Goodwin* v. *Industrial and General Trust* (1890) 18 R. 193; *Paterson Bros.* v. *Gladstone* (1891) 18 R. 403.

all the partners of a firm grant a bill the presumption is that it is granted for the firm's purposes, but the contrary may be proved.[1]

Consideration

The contract to pay, evidenced by a bill, being in writing, is enforceable though gratuitous.[2] In any event the Act provides[3] that valuable consideration for a bill may be constituted by any consideration sufficient to support a simple contract,[4] or any antecedent debt or liability, whether the bill is payable on demand or at a future time. Where value has at any time been given for a bill the holder is deemed to be a holder for value as regards the acceptor and all parties to the bill who became parties prior to such time. Where the holder of a bill has a lien on it, he is deemed to be a holder for value to the extent of the sum for which he has a lien.[5] A moral obligation to pay is good consideration,[6] but a bill granted in pursuance of a contract not implemented could not be enforced, there having been a failure of consideration.[7] If the consideration is immoral or illegal, the bill is invalid.[8] Formerly if it were alleged that the bill was not onerous or for value, this could be proved only by writ or oath,[9] but S. 100 now allows any fact relevant to liability to be proved by parole evidence and this may permit challenge of onerosity by parole evidence.[10]

Accommodation bill or party

An accommodation party to a bill is one who has signed a bill as drawer, acceptor or indorser without receiving value therefor and for the purpose of lending his name to some other person. Such a party is liable on the bill to a holder for value, whether or not the

---

[1] *Rosslund Cycle Co.* v. *McCreadie,* 1907 S.C. 1208.

[2] Bell, *Prin.* §333B; *L.A.* v. *McNeill* (1866) 4 M. (H.L.) 20; cf. *Law* v. *Humphrey* (1875) 3 R. 1192, laying down that in Scotland onerosity of a bill is to be assumed.

[3] S. 27.

[4] This is a concept of English law. See also *Stiell* v. *Holmes* (1868) 6 M. 994; *Hay & Kyd* v. *Powrie* (1886) 13 R. 777; *Byers* v. *Lindsay* (1886) 23 S.L.R. 306.

[5] S. 27.

[6] *Clark* v. *C.* (1869) 7 M. 335.

[7] *Wallace & Brown* v. *Robinson, Fleming & Co.* (1885) 22 S.L.R. 830.

[8] *Kennedy* v. *Cameron* (1823) 2 S. 192; *Hamilton* v. *Main* (1823) 2 S. 356; *Maitland* v. *Rattray* (1848) 11 D. 71; *Don* v. *Richardson* (1858) 20 D. 1138; *Young* v. *Gordon* (1896) 23 R. 419.

[9] Bell, *Prin.* §333B; *Little* v. *Smith* (1845) 8 D. 265; *Blackwood* v. *Hay* (1858) 20 D. 631; *Brock* v. *Newlands* (1863) 2 M. 71; *Gray* v. *Scott* (1868) 6 M. 197; *Mercer* v. *Livingstone* (1864) 3 M. 300; *Swanson* v. *Gallie* (1870) 9 M. 208; *Wilson* v. *Scott* (1874) 1 R. 1003; *Alexander* v. *Stewart* (1877) 4 R. 366; *Ferguson, Davidson & Co.* v. *Jolly's Trs.* (1880) 7 R. 500.

[10] cf. Bell, *supra.*

holder knew such party to be an accommodation party or not.[1] Evidence that a party, such as an acceptor, signed for the drawers' accommodation only was restricted to writ or oath,[2] but may now be proved by parole evidence,[3] but background facts relevant to the question whether a bill were granted for accommodation or not may be proved by parole.[4] An acceptor has been held entitled, under S. 100, to proof by parole that a bill was for the accommodation of the indorser.[5] A person who draws a bill for his own accommodation may not plead against an onerous indorsee that the bill was not duly presented for payment.[6]

Holder in due course

A holder in due course is a holder who has taken a bill, complete and regular on the face of it, under the conditions that he became the holder of it before it was overdue and without notice that it had been previously dishonoured, if such was the fact; and that he took the bill in good faith and for value, and that at the time the bill was negotiated to him he had no notice of any defect in the title of the person who negotiated it.[7] The title of a person who negotiates a bill is defective in particular when he obtained the bill, or its acceptance, by fraud, duress, or force and fear, or other unlawful means, or for an illegal consideration, or when he negotiates it in breach of faith or under such circumstances as amount to a fraud. A holder (whether for value or not) who derives his title to a bill through a holder in due course, and who is not himself a party to any fraud or illegality affecting it has all the rights of that holder in due course as regards the acceptor and all parties to the bill prior to that holder.[8]

---

[1] S. 28; *Downie* v. *Saunder's Trs.* (1898) 6 S.L.T. 134; *McMeekin* v. *Russell & Tudhope* (1881) 8 R. 587; *Russell* v. *Banknock Coal Co.* (1897) 24 R. 1009.

[2] *Catto, Thomson & Co.* v. *Thomson* (1867) 6 M. 54; *Thoms* v. *T.* (1867) 6 M. 174; *Swanson* v. *Gallie* (1870) 9 M. 208; *Baker Incorporation of Aberdeen* v. *Reid* (1873) 1 R. 196.

[3] S. 100.

[4] *Fraser* v. *F's Exors.* (1871) 9 M. 497.

[5] *Viani* v. *Gunn* (1904) 6 F. 989.

[6] *Shepherd* v. *Reddie* (1870) 8 M. 619.

[7] S. 29(1); *Lloyds Bank* v. *Cooke* [1907] 1 K.B. 794; *Hornby* v. *McLaren* (1908) 24 T.L.R. 494; *Jones* v. *Waring & Gillow* [1926] A.C. 670.

[8] S. 29(2)–(3); *Wright* v. *Guild & Wyllie* (1893) 30 S.L.R. 785; contrast *Fowlie* v. *Barnett* (1867) 5 S.L.R. 134; *Bank of Scotland* v. *Faulds* (1870) 7 S.L.R. 619; *Jones* v. *Gordon* (1877) 2 App. Cas. 616; *Martini* v. *Steel & Craig* (1878) 6 R. 342; *Tyler* v. *Maxwell* (1892) 30 S.L.R. 583; *Clark* v. *Davidson* (1893) 1 S.L.T. 141; *Semple* v. *Kyle* (1902) 4 F. 421; *Nelson* v. *Easdale Slate Quarries Co.* 1910, 1 S.L.T. 21; *Arab Bank* v. *Ross* [1952] 2 Q.B. 216.

Presumption of value and good faith

Every party whose signature appears on a bill is *prima facie* deemed to have become a party thereto for value,[1] and every holder is *prima facie* deemed to be a holder in due course;[2] but if in an action on a bill it is admitted or proved that the acceptance, issue or subsequent negotiation of the bill is affected with fraud, duress or force and fear, or illegality, the burden of proof is shifted, unless and until the holder proves that, subsequent to the alleged fraud or illegality, value has in good faith been given for the bill.[2]

NEGOTIATION OF BILLS

Transfer and negotiation

Every bill, cheque and note is in origin not only transferable but negotiable, in that it may be transferred by indorsement and delivery or, if payable to bearer, by delivery alone, to the effect of conferring a valid title on the transferee, notwithstanding any defect of title in the person of the transferor, provided the transferee has taken it in good faith, for value, and without notice of the defect in the transferor's title. Where a bill is negotiable in origin, it continues to be negotiable until it has been restrictively indorsed or discharged by payment or otherwise.[3] A restrictive indorsement does not necessarily prohibit further transfer of the bill, but though valid between the parties, it ceases to be negotiable if it contains words prohibiting transfer or indicating an intention that it should not be transferable.[4]

Negotiation

Bills, cheques and promissory notes are negotiated by transfer from one person to another in such a manner as to constitute the transferee the holder of the bill, if payable to bearer, by delivery, like money, or, if the bill is to order, by indorsement and delivery.[5] Delivery means transfer of possession, actual or constructive, from one person to another.[6] Where the holder of a bill payable to

---

[1] S. 30(1); see also *Wilson* v. *Loder* (1848) 10 D. 560.

[2] S. 30(2); *McLean* v. *Clydesdale Bank* (1883) 11 R. (H.L.) 1; a banker discounting a bill becomes holder of it: *Morton* v. *National Bank* (1882) 19 S.L.R. 611.

[3] S. 36(1).

[4] S. 8(1).

[5] S. 31(1)–(3). But it does not transfer any diligence raised on the bill: Bell, *Prin.* §331.

[6] S. 2.

order transfers it for value without indorsing it, the transfer gives the transferee such title as the transferor had in the bill and the transferee in addition acquires the right to have the indorsement of the transferor.[1] Where any person is under an obligation to indorse a bill in a representative capacity, he may indorse the bill in such terms as to negative personal liability.[2]

Requisites of indorsement

For an indorsement[3] to operate as a negotiation it must be written on the bill[4] and be signed by the indorser; the signature itself is enough;[5] it must be of the entire bill;[6] it must be indorsed by all payees or indorsers to whose order it is payable unless one indorsing has authority to indorse for the others.[7] If, in a bill payable to order, the payee or indorsee is wrongly designated, or his name misspelt, he may indorse the bill as therein described, adding, if thought fit, his proper signature.[8] Each indorsement is deemed to have been made in the order in which it appears on the bill until the contrary is proved.[9] Where a bill purports to be indorsed conditionally the condition may be disregarded by the payer and payment to the indorsee is valid whether the condition has been fulfilled or not.[10]

Blank, special and restrictive indorsements

An indorsement may be in blank or special, and may contain terms making it restrictive.[11] An indorsement in blank specifies no indorsee, and a bill so indorsed becomes payable to bearer.[12] A special indorsement specifies the person to whom, or to whose order, the bill is to be payable.[13] When a bill has been indorsed in blank, any holder may convert the blank indorsement into a special indorsement by writing above the indorser's signature a direction

---

[1] S. 31(4); *Hood* v. *Stewart* (1890) 17 R. 749.

[2] S. 31(5).

[3] An indorsement means an indorsement completed by delivery: S. 2; cf. S. 21.

[4] Including on an allonge, or additional piece of paper attached to the bill to give more room for indorsements, or on a copy of the bill issued or negotiated in a country where copies are recognized: S. 32(1).

[5] S. 32(1).

[6] S. 32(2).

[7] S. 32(3).

[8] S. 32(4).

[9] S. 32(5). See e.g. *Lombard Banking* v. *Central Garage* [1963] 1 Q.B. 220; *Yeoman Credit* v. *Gregory* [1963] 1 All E.R. 245.

[10] S. 33.   [11] S. 32(6).   [12] S. 34(1).

[13] S. 34(2): provisions as to a payee apply to a special indorsee: S. 34(3).

to pay the bill to or to the order of himself or some other person.[1] An indorsement is restrictive which prohibits the further negotiation of the bill or which expresses that it is a mere authority to deal with the bill as thereby directed and not a transfer of the ownership thereof.[2] A restrictive indorsement gives the indorsee the right to receive payment of the bill and to sue any party thereto that his indorser could have sued, but gives him no power to transfer his rights as indorsee unless it expressly authorizes him to do so.[3] Where it authorizes further transfer, all subsequent indorsees take the bill with the same rights and subject to the same liabilities as the first indorsee under the restrictive indorsement.[4]

Negotiation of overdue or dishonoured bill

Where a bill is negotiable in its origin it continues to be negotiable until it has been restrictively indorsed or discharged by payment or otherwise.[5] Where an overdue bill[6] is negotiated, it can only be negotiated subject to any defect of title affecting it at its maturity, and thenceforward no person who takes it can acquire or give a better title than that which the person from whom he took it had.[7] Except where an indorsement bears date after the maturity of the bill, every negotiation is *prima facie* deemed to have been effected before the bill was overdue.[8] Where a bill which is not overdue has been dishonoured any person who takes it with notice of the dishonour takes it subject to any defect of title attaching thereto at the time of dishonour, but nothing in the subsection affects the rights of a holder in due course.[9]

Negotiation to party already liable thereon

Where a bill is negotiated back to the drawer, or to a prior indorser, or to the acceptor, that party may, subject to the Act, re-issue and further negotiate the bill, but he is not entitled to enforce payment of the bill against any intervening party to whom he was previously liable.[10]

---

[1] S. 34(4).
[2] S. 35(1), instancing 'Pay D only', 'Pay D for the account of X', or 'Pay D or order for collection'. See *Stiells* v. *Holmes* (1868) 6 M. 994; *Bute* v. *Barclays Bank* [1955] 1 Q.B. 202.
[3] S. 35(2).   [4] S. 35(3).
[5] S. 36(1).
[6] S. 36(3) provides that a bill payable on demand is deemed overdue when it appears to have been in circulation for an unreasonable length of time, which is a question of fact.
[7] S. 36(2).   [8] S. 36(4).   [9] S. 36(5).
[10] S. 37; cf. *Wilkinson* v. *Unwin* (1881) 7 Q.B.D. 636.

Rights of holder of a bill

The holder of a bill is the payee or indorsee of a bill or note who is in possession of it, or the bearer thereof.[1] The holder's rights and powers are:[2] (1) to sue on the bill in his own name;[3] (2) where he is a holder in due course,[4] he holds the bill free from any defect of title of prior parties, as well as from mere personal defences available to prior parties among themselves, and may enforce payment against all parties liable on the bill; (3) where his title is defective, if he negotiates the bill to a holder in due course, that holder obtains a good and complete title to the bill, and if he obtains payment of the bill the person who pays him in due course gets a valid discharge for the bill. But a person fraudulently induced to sign a bill believing that it was a different deed is not liable even to a holder in due course.[5]

Transfer of bills otherwise than by negotiation

The 1882 Act does not deal with voluntary transfer of bill otherwise than by negotiation, as by gift[6] or sale, effected by written assignation,[7] nor with involuntary transfer on death, bankruptcy or under diligence.

GENERAL DUTIES OF THE HOLDER

Presentment for acceptance

Presentment for acceptance is necessary, in the case of a bill payable after sight, to fix the maturity of the bill, or where the bill expressly states that it shall be presented for acceptance, or is drawn payable elsewhere than at the residence or place of business of the drawee. In no other case is it necessary to render liable any party to the bill.[8] But it is always desirable to present for acceptance; if accepted the holder obtains the additional security of the acceptor; if refused prior parties become liable immediately. Where

---

[1] S. 2.

[2] S. 38.

[3] *Waterston* v. *Edinburgh and Glasgow Bank* (1858) 20 D. 642; *Agra and Masterman's Bank* v. *Leighton* (1866) L.R. 2 Ex. 56; *Agnew* v. *White* (1899) 1 F. 1026; *Crosbie* v. *Brown* (1900) 3 F. 83.

[4] Defined: S. 29.

[5] *Foster* v. *Mackinnan* (1869) L.R. 4 C.P. 704; *Lewis* v. *Clay* (1897) 14 T.L.R. 149.

[6] e.g. by delivery as donation *mortis causa*.

[7] cf. *Embiricos* v. *Anglo-Austrian Bank* [1905] 1 K.B. 677; *Bence* v. *Shearman* [1898] 2 Ch. 582; *Hibernian Bank* v. *Gysin and Hanson* [1939] 1 K.B. 483.

[8] S. 39(1)–(3).

the holder of a bill, drawn payable elsewhere than at the place of business or residence of the drawee, has not time with reasonable diligence, to present the bill for acceptance before presenting it for payment on the day that it falls due, the delay caused by presenting the bill for acceptance before presenting it for payment on the day that it falls due, the delay caused by presenting the bill for acceptance before presenting it for payment is excused, and does not discharge the drawer and indorsers.[1]

Time for presenting bill payable after sight

Subject to the Act, when a bill payable after sight is negotiated, the holder must either present it for acceptance or negotiate it within a reasonable time. If he does not do so, the drawer and all indorsers prior to the holder are discharged.[2]

Rules as to presentment for acceptance

Presentment to be duly made must be made by or on behalf of the holder to the drawee or someone authorized on his behalf at a reasonable hour on a business day and before the bill is overdue; if there are several drawees presentment must be made to them all unless one has authority to accept for all; if the drawee is dead, it may be made to his executor; if bankrupt, to him or his trustee; and, where authorized by agreement or usage, presentment by post is sufficient.[3] Presentment is excused and the bill may be treated as dishonoured by non-acceptance where the drawee is dead or bankrupt, or is a fictitious person, or one not having capacity to contract by bill; where after the exercise of reasonable diligence, presentment cannot be effected; and where although the presentment has been irregular, acceptance has been refused on some other ground. The fact that the holder has reason to believe that the bill, on presentment, will be dishonoured does not excuse presentment.[4]

Dishonour by non-acceptance

By custom a drawee may demand twenty-four hours to consider whether or not to accept a bill.[5] If a bill is duly presented and not

---

[1] S. 39(4).

[2] S. 40; 'reasonable time' is defined by S. 40(3). See also *Straker* v. *Graham* (1839) 4 M. & W. 721.

[3] S. 41(1); *Neilson* v. *Leighton* (1844) 6 D. 622.

[4] S. 41(2) and (3).

[5] Bell, *Prin.* §336; *Bank of Van Diemen's Land* v. *Bank of Victoria* (1871) L.R. 3 P.C. 526.

accepted within the customary time, the person presenting must treat it as dishonoured by non-acceptance. If he does not, the holder loses his right of recourse against the drawer and indorsers.[1] A bill is also dishonoured by non-acceptance when it is duly presented for acceptance and acceptance prescribed by the Act is refused or cannot be obtained, or when presentment for acceptance is excused and the bill is not accepted. Subject to the Act, when a bill is dishonoured by non-acceptance an immediate right of recourse against the drawer and indorsers accrues to the holder and no presentment for payment is necessary.[2]

Qualified acceptances

The holder of a bill may refuse to take a qualified acceptance, and if he does not obtain an unqualified acceptance, may treat the bill as dishonoured by non-acceptance. Where a qualified acceptance is taken, and the drawer or an indorser has not expressly or impliedly authorized the holder to take a qualified acceptance, or does not subsequently assent thereto, that drawer or indorser is discharged from his liability on the bill, but this does not apply to a partial acceptance, of which due notice has been given. Where a foreign bill has been accepted in part, it must be protested as to the balance. When the drawer or indorser of a bill receives notice of a qualified acceptance, and does not within a reasonable time express his dissent to the holder he shall be deemed to have assented thereto.[3]

Action on dishonour

The action necessary on dishonour by non-acceptance is the same as that necessary on dishonour by non-payment.[4]

Presentment for payment

Subject to the Act a bill must be duly presented for payment, failing which the drawer and indorsers are discharged.[5] When a bill is accepted generally presentment for payment is not necessary to render the acceptor liable. When by the terms of a qualified acceptance presentment for payment is required, the acceptor, failing an express stipulation to that effect, is discharged by the omission to present the bill for payment on the day that it matures.[6] If the bill is not payable on demand, it must be pre-

---

[1] S. 42; *Martini & Co.* v. *Steel and Craig* (1878) 6 R. 342.
[2] S. 43.
[3] S. 44.   [4] See *infra*.   [5] S. 45.
[6] S. 52; cf. *Bank of Scotland* v. *Lamont* (1889) 16 R. 769.

sented on the day it falls due.[1] In every case where the bill does not otherwise provide, three days of grace were added to the time of payment, and the bill is due and payable on the last day of grace.[2] Where a bill is payable at a fixed period after date, after sight, or after the happening of a specified event, the time of payment is determined by excluding the day from which the time is to begin to run and by including the day of payment. Where a bill is payable at a fixed period after sight, the time begins to run from the date of the acceptance if the bill be accepted, and from the date of noting or protest if the bill be noted or protested for non-acceptance or for non-delivery.[3] If a bill is payable on demand, then, subject to the Act, presentment must be made within a reasonable time after its issue to render the drawer liable,[4] and within a reasonable time after its indorsement, to render the indorser liable. In determining a reasonable time, regard must be had to the nature of the bill, the usage of trade with regard to similar bills and the facts of the particular case.[5]

Time and place of presentment

Presentment must be made by the holder or some person authorized to receive payment on his behalf at a reasonable hour on a business day[6] to the person designated in the bill as payer or to some person authorized to pay or refuse payment on his behalf if with the exercise of reasonable diligence such person can be found.[7] The proper place for presentment is the place, if any, specified in the bill as the place of payment, failing which, the address of the drawee or acceptor given in the bill, failing which, the drawee's or acceptor's place of business, or his ordinary residence; in any other case presentment may be made to the drawee or acceptor wherever he can be found or at his last known place of business or residence.[8] Where a bill is presented at the proper place and after the exercise of reasonable diligence no person authorized to pay or refuse payment can be found there, no

---

[1] S. 45(1).

[2] S. 14(1); this section contains provisions as to days of grace on Sundays, bank holidays, etc. See now Banking and Financial Dealings Act, 1971, S. 3(2).

[3] S. 14(2).

[4] *Nelson* v. *Easdale Slate Quarries Co.*, 1910, 1 S.L.T. 21.

[5] S. 45(2).

[6] Defined, S. 92, amd. Banking and Financial Dealings Act, 1971, S. 3(1).

[7] S. 45(3).

[8] S. 45(4); *Robertson* v. *Burdekin* (1843) 6 D. 17; *Gordon* v. *Stephen* (1845) 8 D. 146; see also *Sommerville* v. *Aaronson* (1898) 25 R. 524; *Neill* v. *Dobson, Molle and Co.* (1902) 4 F. 625.

further presentment is required.[1] Presentment must be made to all of several drawees if they are not partners and no place of payment is specified.[2] If the drawee or acceptor is dead and no place of payment is specified, presentment must be made to a personal representative, if any and if with reasonable diligence he can be found.[3] Where authorized by agreement or usage presentment by post is sufficient.[4]

Excuses for delay or non-presentment

Delay in presenting for payment is excused when caused by circumstances beyond the holder's control and not imputable to his default, misconduct or negligence. When the cause of delay ceases to operate presentment must be made with reasonable diligence.[5] Presentment for payment is dispensed with (a) where, after the exercise of reasonable diligence, presentment as required by the Act, cannot be effected. The fact that the holder has reason to believe that the bill will, on presentment, be dishonoured, does not dispense with the necessity for presentment; (b) where the drawee is a fictitious person; (c) as regards the drawer where the drawee or acceptor is not bound, as between himself and the drawer, to accept or pay the bill, and the drawer has no reason to believe that the bill would be paid if presented; (d) as regards an indorser where the bill was accepted or made for the accommodation of that indorser, and he has no reason to expect that the bill would be paid if presented; (e) by waiver of presentment, express or implied.[6]

Dishonour by non-payment

A bill is dishonoured by non-payment when it is duly presented for payment and payment is refused or cannot be obtained, or when presentment is excused and the bill is overdue and unpaid. Subject to the Act,[7] when a bill is dishonoured by non-payment, an immediate right of recourse against the drawer and indorsers accrues to the holder.[8]

---

[1] S. 45(5).   [2] S. 45(6).
[3] S. 45(7).   [4] S. 45(8).
[5] S. 46(1). cf. *Rouquette* v. *Overmann* (1875) L.R. 10 Q.B. 525; *Re Francke and Rasch* [1918] 1 Ch. 470.
[6] S. 46(2); cf. *Gordon* v. *Stephen* (1845) 8 D. 146; *Wirth* v. *Austin* (1875) L.R. 10 C.P. 689; *Allhusen* v. *Mitchell* (1870) 8 M. 600; *Bank of Scotland* v. *Lamont* (1889) 16 R. 769; *MacTavish's J.F.* v. *Michael's Trs.*, 1912 S.C. 425.
[7] Ss. 48, 51, 65–68.
[8] S. 47; *Kennedy* v. *Thomas* [1894] 2 Q.B. 759.

Notice of dishonour

Subject to the Act, when a bill has been dishonoured by non-acceptance or by non-payment, notice of dishonour must be given[1] to the drawer and each indorser, and any drawer or indorser to whom such notice is not given is discharged.[2] But where a bill is dishonoured by non-acceptance and notice of dishonour is not given, the rights of a holder in due course subsequent to the omission are not prejudiced thereby; and where a bill is dishonoured by non-acceptance and due notice of dishonour is given, it is not necessary to give notice of a subsequent dishonour by non-payment unless the bill has in the meantime been accepted.[3] Notice means actual notification; no particular form of notice is prescribed, but the bill must be sufficiently described to be identifiable; it is normally effected by post. It does not suffice that the drawer or indorser knows that it has been dishonoured.

Rules as to notice

To be valid and effectual notice of dishonour must be given in accordance with the rules of S. 49, viz.:

(1) The notice must be given by or on behalf of the holder, or by or on behalf of an indorser who, at the time of giving it, is himself liable on the bill.

(2) Notice of dishonour may be given by an agent either in his own name, or in the name of any party entitled to give notice whether that party be his principal or not.

(3) Where the notice is given by or on behalf of the holder, it enures for the benefit of all subsequent holders and all prior indorsers who have a right of recourse against the party to whom it is given.

(4) Where notice is given by or on behalf of an indorser entitled to give notice as hereinbefore provided, it enures for the benefit of the holder and all indorsers subsequent to the party to whom notice is given.

(5) The notice may be given in writing or by personal communication, and may be given in any terms which sufficiently identify the bill, and intimate that the bill has been dishonoured by non-acceptance or non-payment.[4]

---

[1] Even where presentment for acceptance was unnecessary, but was made.

[2] *Berridge* v. *Fitzgerald* (1869) L.R. 4 Q.B. 639. For form of Notice see Hamilton, *Bills*, 277.

[3] S. 48.

[4] *Thomson, Still & Co.* v. *McRuer*, 20 Jan. 1808, F.C.; *Calder* v. *Lyall*, 22 Dec. 1808, F.C.

(6) The return of a dishonoured bill to the drawer or an indorser is, in point of form, deemed a sufficient notice of dishonour.[1]

(7) A written notice need not be signed, and an insufficient written notice may be supplemented and validated by verbal communication. A misdescription of the bill shall not vitiate the notice unless the party to whom the notice is given is in fact misled thereby.

(8) Where notice of dishonour is required to be given to any person, it may be given either to the party himself, or to his agent in that behalf.[2]

(9) Where the drawer or indorser is dead, and the party giving notice knows it, the notice must be given to a personal representative if such there be, and with the exercise of reasonable diligence he can be found.

(10) Where the drawer or indorser is bankrupt, notice may be given either to the party himself, or to the trustee.

(11) Where there are two or more drawers or indorsers who are not partners, notice must be given to each of them, unless one of them has authority to receive such notice for the others.

(12) The notice may be given as soon as the bill is dishonoured and must be given within a reasonable time thereafter. In the absence of special circumstances notice is not deemed to have been given within a reasonable time, unless—

(a) where the person giving and the person to receive notice reside in the same place, the notice is given or sent off in time to reach the latter on the day after the dishonour of the bill.[3]

(b) where the person giving and the person to receive notice reside in different places, the notice is sent off on the day after the dishonour of the bill, if there be a post at a convenient hour on that day, and if there be no such post on that day then by the next post thereafter.

(13) Where a bill is dishonoured in the hands of an agent, he may either himself give notice to the parties liable on the bill, or he may give notice to his principal. If he give notice to his principal, he must do so within the same time as if he were the holder, and the principal upon receipt of such notice has himself

---

[1] Return of the bill does not alter the rights of the parties: *Cohn* v. *Werner* (1891) 8 T.L.R. 11.

[2] Notice left at the drawer's house may suffice: *McCartney* v. *Hannah* (1817) Hume 76; notice at his place of business will generally suffice: *Berridge* v. *Fitzgerald* (1869) L.R. 4 Q.B. 639.

[3] *Mackenzie* v. *Dott* (1861) 23 D. 1310.

the same time for giving notice as if the agent had been an independent holder.[1]

(14) Where a party to a bill receives due notice of dishonour, he has after the receipt of such notice the same period of time for giving notice to antecedent parties that the holder has after the dishonour.

(15) Where a notice of dishonour is duly addressed and posted, the sender is deemed to have given due notice of dishonour, notwithstanding any miscarriage by the post office.[2]

Excuses for delay in notice

Delay in giving notice of dishonour is excused where the delay is caused by circumstances beyond the control of the party giving notice, and not imputable to his default, misconduct or negligence. When the cause of delay ceases to operate the notice must be given with reasonable diligence.[3]

When notice of dishonour dispensed with

Notice of dishonour is dispensed with[4] (a) when, after the exercise of reasonable diligence, notice as required by the Act cannot be given to or does not reach the drawer or indorser sought to be charged: (b) by waiver express or implied. Notice of dishonour may be waived before the time of giving notice has arrived, or after the omission to give due notice:[5] (c) as regards the drawer (1) where drawer and drawee are the same person, (2) where the drawee is a fictitious person or a person not having capacity to contract, (3) where the drawer is the person to whom the bill is presented for payment, (4) where the drawee or acceptor is as between himself and the drawer under no obligation to accept or pay the bill, (5) where the drawer has countermanded payment: (d) as regards the indorser (1) where the drawee is a fictitious person or a person not having capacity to contract and the indorser was aware of the fact at the time he indorsed the bill, (2) where the indorser is the person to whom the bill is presented for

---

[1] cf. *Lombard Banking* v. *Central Garage* [1963] 1 Q.B. 220.

[2] The onus is on the sender: *Robertson* v. *Gamack* (1835) 14 S. 139; *Stock* v. *Aitken* (1846) 9 D. 75; see also *Milligan* v. *Barbour* (1829) 7 S. 489; *Burmester* v. *Barron* (1852) 17 Q.B. 828.

[3] S. 50(1).

[4] S. 50(2) Notice is not dispensed with merely because the drawer or indorser believed that the bill when presented, would be dishonoured: *Carew* v. *Duckworth* (1869) L.R. 4 Ex. 313.

[5] *Watt* v. *Fullerton* (1816) Hume 74; *Campbell* v. *Patten* (1833) 12 S. 269; *Allhusen* v. *Mitchell* (1870) 8 M. 600; *McTavish* v. *McMichael's Trs.*, 1912 S.C. 425; *Lombard Banking* v. *Central Garage* [1963] 1 Q.B. 220.

payment, (3) where the bill was accepted or made for his accommodation.[1]

Noting or protest of bill

Where an inland bill has been dishonoured it may, if the holder thinks fit, be noted for non-acceptance or non-payment, but it is not necessary to note or protest any such bill in order to preserve the recourse against the drawer or indorser.[2]

Where a foreign bill has been dishonoured by non-acceptance it must be duly protested for non-acceptance and where such a bill, which has not been previously dishonoured by non-acceptance, is dishonoured by non-payment it must be duly protested for non-payment. If it be not so protested the drawer and indorsers are discharged. Where a bill does not appear on the face of it to be a foreign bill, protest thereof in case of dishonour is unnecessary.[3] A bill which has been protested for non-acceptance may be subsequently protested for non-payment.[4]

Subject to the Act, when a bill is noted or protested, it may be noted on the day of its dishonour and must be noted not later than the next succeeding business day. When a bill has been duly noted, the protest may be subsequently extended as of the date of the noting.[5]

Where the acceptor of the bill becomes bankrupt or insolvent or suspends payment before it matures, the holder may cause the bill to be protested for better security against the drawer and indorsers.[6]

A bill must be protested at the place where it is dishonoured; provided that where a bill is presented through the post office and returned by post dishonoured, it may be protested at the place to which it is returned and on the day of its return if received during business hours, and if not received during business hours, then not later than the next business day; and when a bill payable at

---

[1] A person who has given a guarantee for the payment of the bill by the acceptor is not entitled to notice of dishonour: *Walton* v. *Mascall* (1844) 13 M. & W. 72.

[2] S. 51(1). Recourse is preserved by S. 43(2) (non-acceptance) and S. 47(2) (non-payment). 'Noting' is the note made by a notary public on the bill at the time of its dishonour; 'protesting' is the granting of a notarial certificate attesting the dishonour. A bill must be protested if it is to found summary diligence: S. 98.

[3] S. 51(2).

[4] S. 51(3).

[5] S. 51(4), amd. Bills of Exchange (Time of Noting) Act, 1917, S. 1. Notwithstanding this it is not necessary to found summary diligence that a bill be noted on the due date: *Carmont* v. *Cinema Trust Co.*, 1916, 2 S.L.T. 350.

[6] S. 51(5).

the place of business or residence of some person other than the drawee has been dishonoured by non-acceptance, it must be protested for non-payment at the place where it is expressed to be payable and no further presentment for payment to, or demand on, the drawee is necessary.[1]

A protest must contain a copy of the bill and must be signed by the notary making it, and must specify the person at whose request the bill is protested, the place and date of protest, the cause or reason for protesting the bill, the demand made and the answer given, if any, or the fact that the drawee or acceptor could not be found.[2] Where a bill is lost or destroyed, or is wrongly detained from the person entitled to hold it, protest may be made on a copy or written particulars thereof.[3]

The protest should be made by a notary public[4] who marks on the bill the date of dishonour, his initials and designation N.P.; there is subsequently extended a notarial protest narrating the facts, which is registered in the Books of Council and Session or Sheriff Court Books.[5] An extract thereof is a foundation for diligence. The protest must be conform to the actual noting of the bill.[6] If a notary is not available any householder or substantial resident of the place where the bill is dishonoured may, in the presence of two witnesses, give a certificate[7] signed by them, attesting the dishonour of the bill, to the same effect as a formal protest.[8]

Protest is dispensed with by any circumstance which would dispense with notice of dishonour.[9] Delay in noting or protesting is excused when the delay is caused by circumstances beyond the control of the holder, and not imputable to his default, misconduct or negligence. When the cause of delay ceases to operate the bill must be noted or protested with reasonable diligence.[10]

Duties of holder as regards drawee or acceptor

When a bill is accepted generally presentment for payment is not necessary to render the acceptor liable.[11] When by the terms of

---

[1] S. 51(6).

[2] S. 51(7); *Bartsch* v. *Poole & Co.* (1895) 23 R. 328.   [3] S. 51(8).

[4] Bell, *Prin.* §338. For form of protest see Hamilton, *Bills of Exchange Act*, 278.

[5] *Brown* v. *Dunbar* (1807) Mor. Bill, Appx. 21. A second protest is irregular: *Service* v. *Youngman* (1867) 6 M. 172.

[6] *McPherson* v. *Wright* (1885) 12 R. 942.   [7] 1882 Act, Sched. 1.

[8] S. 94; *Sommerville* v. *Aaronson* (1898) 25 R. 524. But it is doubtful if such a certificate warrants summary diligence.

[9] S. 50.   [10] S. 51(9).

[11] S. 52(1); *McNeill* v. *Innes Chambers & Co.*, 1917 S.C. 540; *Bank Polski* v. *Mulder* [1942] 1 K.B. 497.

a qualified acceptance presentment for payment is required, the acceptor, in the absence of an express stipulation to that effect, is not discharged by the omission to present the bill for payment on the day that it matures.[1] To render the acceptor of a bill liable it is not necessary to protest it, or that notice of dishonour be given to him. Where the holder of a bill presents it for payment, he must exhibit the bill to the person from whom he demands payment, and when a bill is paid the holder must forthwith deliver it up to the party paying it.[2]

Acceptance and payment for honour

Where a bill has been protested for dishonour by non-acceptance,[3] or protested for better security,[4] and is not overdue, any person, not being a party already liable thereon, may, with the consent of the holder, intervene and accept the bill supra protest, for the honour of any party liable thereon, or for the honour of the person for whose account the bill is drawn. It may be for part only of the sum for which the bill is drawn. Acceptance for honour is an undertaking by the acceptor to pay if the original drawee should persist in dishonouring the bill. To be valid it must be written on the bill and indicated that it is an acceptance for honour and signed by the acceptor for honour. When it does not expressly state for whose honour it is made, an acceptance for honour is deemed to be an acceptance for the honour of the drawer. Where a bill payable after sight is accepted for honour, its maturity is calculated from the date of its noting for non-acceptance, and not from the date of the acceptance for honour.[5] Acceptance for honour is thus an intervention to save the credit of the drawer or acceptor. The acceptor for honour should appear personally before the notary and declare that he accepts the protested bill for honour of the drawer or indorser and will satisfy it at the appointed time, and this 'act of honour' must be endorsed at the foot of the protest, and the acceptor for honour's acceptance then written on the bill.

Liability of acceptor for honour

The acceptor for honour of a bill engages that on due presentment he will pay the bill according to the tenor of his acceptance,

---

[1] S. 52(2); *Smith* v. *Vertue* (1860) 30 L.J.C.P. 56.
[2] S. 52(3)–(4).
[3] Under S. 51(1)–(4).
[4] Under S. 51(5).
[5] S. 65.

if it is not paid by the drawee, provided it has been duly presented for payment, and protested for non-payment, and that he receives notice of these facts. He is liable to the holder and all parties to the bill subsequent to the party for whose honour he has accepted.[1]

Presentment to acceptor for honour

Where a dishonoured bill has been accepted for honour supra protest, or contains a reference in case of need,[2] it must be protested for non-payment before it is presented for payment to the acceptor for honour, or referee in case of need. Where the address of the acceptor for honour is in the same place where the bill is protested for non-payment, the bill must be presented to him not later than the day following its maturity; and where his address is in some other place the bill must be forwarded not later than the date following its maturity for presentment to him. Delay in presentment, or non-presentment, is excused by any circumstance which would excuse delay in presentment for payment or non-presentment for payment.[3] When a bill is dishonoured by the acceptor for honour it must be protested for non-payment by him.[4]

Payment for honour supra protest

Where a bill has been protested for non-payment any person may intervene and pay it supra protest for the honour of any party liable thereon, or for the honour of the person for whose account the bill is drawn. Where two or more persons offer to pay a bill for the honour of different parties, the person whose payment will discharge most parties to the bill shall have preference. For payment for honour supra protest to operate as such and not as a mere voluntary payment, it must be attested by a notarial act of honour which may be appended to the protest or form an extension of it. This must be founded on a declaration made by the payer for honour, or his agent in that behalf, declaring his intention to pay the bill for honour, and for whose honour he pays.[5] Where a bill has been paid for honour, all parties subsequent to the party for whose honour it is paid are discharged, but the payer for honour is subrogated for, and succeeds to both the rights and duties of, the holder as regards the party for whose

---

[1] S. 66.
[2] Under S. 15.
[3] i.e. S. 46.
[4] S. 67.
[5] S. 68(1)–(4); see also *Grieve* v. *Lynn* (1882) 19 S.L.R. 736.

honour he pays, and all parties liable to that party. The payer for honour on paying to the holder the amount of the bill and the notarial expenses incidental to its dishonour is entitled to receive both the bill itself and the protest. If the holder do not on demand deliver them up he shall be liable to the payer for honour in damages. Where the holder of a bill refuses to receive payment supra protest he shall lose his right of recourse against any party who would have been discharged by such payment.[1]

LIABILITIES OF PARTIES

Funds in the hands of the drawee

In Scotland, where the drawee of a bill has in his hands funds available for the payment thereof, the bill operates as an assignment of the sum for which it is drawn in favour of the holder from the time when the bill is presented to the drawee.[2] This applies where the bill has been presented for acceptance and acceptance has been refused.[3] In the case of a cheque, if the credit balance is inadequate to enable the cheque to be met, it may be returned but the credit balance is assigned to the holder of the cheque and gives him a preference thereto in the event of the drawer's bankruptcy.[4] Presentment of a cheque does not effect assignation if, though the account on which it was drawn was in credit, the drawer was in debt to the bank over all his accounts,[5] nor when made by a person not the holder.[6]

Liability of acceptor

By accepting it, the acceptor engages that he will pay the bill according to the tenor of his acceptance. He is precluded from denying to a holder in due course (a) the existence of the drawer, the genuineness of his signature, and his capacity and authority to draw the bill; (b) in the case of a bill payable to drawer's order, the then capacity of the drawer to indorse, but not the genuineness, or validity of his indorsement, and (c) in the case of a bill payable to

---

[1] S. 68 (5)–(7).

[2] S. 53(2); cf. Bell, *Prin.* §315, 339; *B.L. Co.* v. *Carruthers* (1883) 10 R. 923; *B.L. Co.* v. *Rainey* (1885) 12 R. 825. It is otherwise in England. See also *Sutherland* v. *Commercial Bank* (1882) 20 S.L.R. 139. This does not apply to savings accounts or special investment accounts with a savings bank: Trustee Savings Bank Act, 1969, S. 20.

[3] *Watt's Trs.* v. *Pinkney* (1853) 16 D. 279; *Carter* v. *McIntosh* (1862) 24 D. 925. It matters not that presentment was irregular.

[4] *B.L. Co.* v. *Carruthers* (1883) 10 R. 923.

[5] *Kirkwood* v. *Clydesdale Bank*, 1908 S.C. 20.

[6] *Dickson* v. *Clydesdale Bank*, 1937 S.L.T. 585.

the order of a third person, the existence of the payee and his then capacity to indorse, but not the genuineness or validity of his indorsement.[1] The acceptor is the principal debtor, and the drawer and indorsers in a position analogous to guarantors for the acceptor.[2] It is competent to prove by parole the true relations between two acceptors.[3]

Liability of drawer

By drawing the bill the drawer (a) engages that on due presentment it will be accepted[4] and paid according to its tenor, and that if it be dishonoured he will compensate the holder or any indorser who is compelled to pay it, provided that the requisite proceedings on dishonour be taken; and (b) is precluded from denying to a holder in due course the existence of the payee and his then capacity to indorse.[5] The drawer and indorsers are jointly and severally responsible to the holder for the acceptance and payment of the bill.[6]

Liability of indorser

The indorser of a bill by indorsing it (a) engages that on due presentment it will be accepted and paid according to its tenor, and that if it be dishonoured he will compensate the holder or a subsequent indorser who is compelled to pay it, provided that the requisite proceedings on dishonour be duly taken; (b) is precluded from denying to a holder in due course the genuineness and regularity in all respects of the drawer's signature and all previous indorsements; and (c) is precluded from denying to his immediate or subsequent indorsee that the bill was at the time of his indorsement a valid and subsisting bill and that he had then a good title thereto.[7] Where a person signs a bill otherwise than as drawer or acceptor, he thereby incurs the liabilities of an indorser to a holder in due course.[8]

Action where bill dishonoured

Where a bill is dishonoured by non-payment the holder may, apart from giving notice of dishonour and having the bill noted

[1] S. 54.

[2] *Duncan, Fox & Co.* v. *N. &. S. Wales Bank* (1880) 6 App. Cas. 1.

[3] *Crosbie* v. *Brown* (1900) 3 F. 83.

[4] *National Bank of Australasia* v. *Turnbull* (1891) 18 R. 629.

[5] S. 55(1).

[6] *Rouquette* v. *Overmann* (1875) L.R. 10 Q.B. 525.

[7] S. 55(2); see *Speirs & Knox* v. *Semple* (1901) 9 S.L.T. 153.

[8] S. 56; *Macdonald* v. *Union Bank* (1864) 2 M. 963; *Walker's Trs.* v. *McKinlay* (1880) 7 R. (H.L.) 85.

and protested, bring an action against the acceptor, or the drawer or an indorser, or any or all of these, for damages.[1]

Damages where bill dishonoured

Where a bill is dishonoured by non-acceptance or non-payment the drawer's debt is not discharged. The Act provides[2] that the measure of damages, which shall be deemed to be liquidated damages, shall be as follows: (1) the holder may recover from any party liable on the bill,[3] and the drawer who has been compelled to pay the bill may recover from the acceptor, and an indorser who has been compelled to pay the bill may recover from the acceptor or from the drawer or from a prior indorser the amount of the bill, interest thereon from the time of presentment for payment if the bill is payable on demand and from the maturity of the bill in any other case and the expenses of noting or, when protest is necessary,[4] and the protest has been extended, the expenses of protest. (2) In the case of a bill which has been dishonoured abroad, in lieu of these damages, the holder may recover from the drawer or an indorser, and the latter, if he has been compelled to pay, may recover from any party liable to him the amount of the re-exchange[5] with interest thereon until the time of payment.[6] (3) Where by the Act interest may be recovered as damages, such interest may, if justice requires it, be withheld wholly or in part, and where a bill is expressed to be payable with interest at a given rate, interest as damages may or may not be given at the same rate as interest proper.

Summary diligence on bill

The 1882 Act, S. 98, preserves the existing practice of Scots law which permitted summary diligence, whereby payment might be enforced without the need to constitute the debt by action. By the Bills of Exchange Act, 1681, the Inland Bills Act, 1696, and the Bills of Exchange (Sc.) Act, 1772, summary diligence is competent where a bill[7] or note, but not a cheque,[8] is without

---

[1] e.g. *N.V. Ondix International* v. *Landay*, 1963 S.C. 270.

[2] S. 57. See *Ex p. Robarts* (1886) 18 Q.B.D. 286; *Re Commercial Bank of S. Australia* (1887) 36 Ch. D. 522.

[3] i.e. drawer, acceptor, or any indorser, Ss. 54–55.

[4] i.e. foreign bills only.

[5] Re-exchange is the difference in value of a bill resulting from its being dishonoured abroad; the existence and amount depends on the rate of exchange between the two countries.

[6] *Re Commercial Bank, supra.*

[7] Except a bill or note granted to or in favour of a moneylender: Moneylenders Act 1927, S. 18(h).   [8] *Glickman* v. *Linda*, 1950 S.C. 18.

alteration or vitiation in any essential part,[1] and where the liability of the person sought to be charged appears *ex facie* of the bill, without extrinsic evidence.[2] The party to be charged must be subject to the jurisdiction of the Scottish courts, and it is not enough that the bill is payable in Scotland.[3] If such a bill is dishonoured by non-acceptance or by non-payment, after regular presentment for payment has been made[4] or within six months of maturity,[5] the bill is protested for non-acceptance or non-payment,[6] and the protest registered within six months of the dishonour in the Books of Council and Session or Sheriff Court books of a sheriffdom having jurisdiction over the person to be charged. Once registered an extract may be obtained which is a warrant for arrestment, or for a charge for payment on an induciae of six days where the defender is resident in Scotland or fourteen days when resident in Orkney or Shetland or furth of Scotland, which may be followed by poinding and sale or by a petition for sequestration. Summary diligence extends only to the amount of the bill or note and interest; damages and expenses must be recovered by action.[7] It is not rendered incompetent by the statutory power to reopen a moneylending transaction.[8] Diligence may be suspended, usually on caution being found: the 1882 Act does not affect previous practice on this matter.[9]

Liability of transferor by delivery

A transferor by delivery, i.e. the holder of a bill payable to bearer who negotiates it by delivery without indorsing it, is not liable on the instrument, but he thereby warrants to his immediate transferee, being a holder for value, that the bill is what it purports to be,[10] that he has a right to transfer it, and that at the time of

[1] *Thomson* v. *Bell* (1850) 12 D. 1184; *Dominion Bank* v. *Bank of Scotland* (1891) 18 R. (H.L.) 21; see also *Cameron* v. *Morrison* (1869) 7 M. 382.
[2] *Summers* v. *Marianski* (1843) 6 D. 286; see also *Rosslund Cycle Co.* v. *McCreadie*, 1907 S.C. 1208.
[3] *Charteris* v. *Clydesdale Bank* (1882) 19 S.L.R. 602; *Davis* v. *Cadman* (1897) 24 R. 297.
[4] *Neill* v. *Dobson* (1902) 4 F. 625.
[5] *McNeill & Son* v. *Innes, Chambers & Co.*, 1917 S.C. 540.
[6] It is questionable whether summary diligence can follow on a householder's certificate of protest under S. 94, or only on a notarial protest: *Sommerville* v. *Aaronson* (1898) 25 R. 524.
[7] Ersk. III, 2, 36.
[8] *Inglis* v. *Rothfield*, 1920 S.C. 650; but see Moneylenders Act, 1927, S. 18(h).
[9] *Simpson* v. *Brown* (1888) 15 R. 716; see also *Kinloch Campbell & Co.* v. *Cowan* (1890) 27 S.L.R. 870; *Renwick* v. *Stamford, etc. Banking Co.* (1891) 19 R. 163; *Kechans* v. *Barr* (1893) 21 R. 75.
[10] *Gompertz* v. *Bartlett* (1853) 23 L.J.Q.B. 65.

transfer he is not aware of any fact which renders it valueless.[1]
When the transferee discovers any defect in the bill, he should
repudiate the transaction without delay.[2]

Proof of facts relevant to liability

At common law facts relevant to liability could be proved only
by writ or oath,[3] save where fraud or suspicious circumstances
were alleged.[4] By S. 100 of the Act any fact relating to a bill
relevant to any question of liability may be proved by parole
evidence,[5] except in the case of bills which have suffered the
sexennial prescription. Despite this it has been held incompetent
by parole to contradict liability appearing on the face of the bill,[6]
or modify a written agreement,[7] or to prove payment of the bill.[8]

DISCHARGE OF BILL

Discharge of bill

A bill is discharged by payment in due course[9] by or on behalf
of the drawee or acceptor, but not if paid by the drawer or an
indorser; if paid by the drawer, he may enforce payment against
the acceptor, but may not reissue the bill; if paid by an indorser, or
where a bill payable to drawer's order is paid by the drawer, the
paying party is remitted to his former rights as regards the
acceptor or antecedent parties and may, if he thinks fit, strike out
his own and subsequent indorsements and again negotiate the
bill.[10] Where an accommodation bill is paid in due course by the
party accommodated the bill is discharged.[11] So also when the
acceptor is or becomes holder of it at or after maturity, in his own

---

[1] S. 58.

[2] *Pooley* v. *Brown* (1862) 31 L.J.C.P. 134.

[3] e.g. *Wilson* v. *Scott* (1874) 1 R. 1003.

[4] e.g. *Ferguson, Davidson & Co.* v. *Jolly's Tr.* (1880) 7 R. 500.

[5] e.g. *Semple* v. *Kyle* (1902) 4 F. 421; *Drybrough* v. *Roy* (1903) 5 F. 665 (doubted in *Nicol's Trs., infra*); *Adam's Trs.* v. *Young* (1905) 13 S.L.T. 113; *Harker* v. *Pottage*, 1909, 1 S.L.T. 153; *Pert* v. *Bruce*, 1937 S.N. 81.

[6] *National Bank of Australasia* v. *Turnbull* (1891) 18 R. 629; *Gibson's Trs.* v. *Galloway* (1896) 23 R. 414; See also *Manchester and Liverpool District Banking Co.* v. *Ferguson* (1905) 7 F. 865.

[7] *Stagg & Robson* v. *Stirling*, 1908 S.C. 675.

[8] *Robertson* v. *Thomson* (1900) 3 F. 5; *Jackson* v. *Ogilvie's Exor.*, 1935 S.C. 154; *Nicol's Trs.* v. *Sutherland*, 1951 S.C. (H.L.) 21.

[9] Explained as being payment at or after the maturity of the bill to the holder thereof in good faith and without notice that his title to the bill is defective.

[10] S. 59(1) and (2); *Coats* v. *Union Bank*, 1929 S.C. (H.L.) 114.

[11] S. 59(3).

right.[1] When the holder of a bill at or after its maturity absolutely and unconditionally renounces his rights against the acceptor the bill is discharged. The renunciation must be in writing, unless the bill is delivered up to the acceptor.[2] But if the holder discharges the acceptor but expressly reserves claims against other obligants, he may still claim against an indorser.[3] The liabilities of any party to a bill may similarly be renounced by the holder before, at, or after its maturity; but nothing in the section affects the rights of a holder in due course without notice of the renunciation.[4]

Cancellation

A bill is also discharged where it is intentionally cancelled by the holder or his agent, and the cancellation is apparent thereon;[5] so too any party liable on a bill may be discharged by the intentional[6] cancellation of his signature by the holder or his agent; in such case any indorser who would have had a right of recourse against the party whose signature is cancelled, is also discharged.[7] Cancellation made unintentionally, or by mistake, or without authority, is inoperative; the burden of proof is on the party alleging that it was so made.[8] The mere granting of a new note and surrender of an old do not discharge a claim for interest on the sum advanced under the note.[9]

Alteration

Where a bill or acceptance is materially altered[10] without the assent of all parties liable on the bill, the bill is avoided except as against a party who has himself made, authorized, or assented to the alteration, and subsequent indorsers, but where a bill has been materially altered but the alteration is not apparent, and the bill is in the hands of a holder in due course, that holder may

[1] S. 61; *Jenkins* v. *J.* [1928] 2 K.B. 501. This is really discharge *confusione*. See also *Hope Johnstone* v. *Cornwall* (1895) 22 R. 314.

[2] S. 62(1).

[3] *Muir* v. *Crawford* (1875) 2 R. (H.L.) 148; *Jones* v. *Whitaker* (1887) 3 T.L.R. 723.

[4] S. 62(2); *Macvean* v. *Maclean* (1873) 11 M. 764.

[5] S. 63(1).

[6] Unintentional cancellation is inoperative: S. 63(3); *Dominion Bank* v. *Anderson* (1888) 15 R. 408.

[7] S. 63(2); *Bank of Scotland* v. *Dominion Bank* (1891) 18 R. (H.L.) 21.

[8] S. 63(3).

[9] *Hope Johnstone* v. *Cornwall* (1895) 22 R. 314.

[10] As to what are material alterations, see S. 64(2); *King* v. *Creighton* (1843) 2 Bell 81; *McRostie* v. *Halley* (1850) 12 D. 816; *Speirs & Knox* v. *Semple* (1901) 9 S.L.T. 153.

avail himself of the bill as if it had not been altered, and may enforce payment of it according to its original tenor.[1]

Prescription

Under the Bills of Exchange (Scotland) Act, 1772, Ss. 37, 39 and 40, no bill or note, except bank-notes, gives rise to action or diligence unless action is commenced or diligence raised and executed within six years from the terms at which the sums in the bill or note became exigible, but thereafter it is competent to prove the debts contained in the bills or notes, and that they are resting-owing, by the debtor's writ or oath.[2] The sexennium runs from the date of the bill, if payable on demand,[3] from the last day of grace, if payable on a fixed day,[4] or from the last day of the month after the demand for payment, if payable so many months after notice.[5] The running of the sexennium destroys the bill as a document of debt[6] and thereafter the onus is on the holder of proving by writ or oath that the debt was constituted and was still unpaid.[7]

Interruption

Where action has been commenced or diligence used within the sexennium that excludes prescription and keeps the bill alive,[8] but this interpretation has been doubted.[9] The production of the bill in other judicial proceedings has been held equivalent to action.[10] Oral admissions of the debt during the sexennium do not interrupt

---

[1] S. 64(1); cf. *Leeds Bank* v. *Walker* (1883) 11 Q.B.D. 84; *Woollatt* v. *Stanley* (1928) 138 L.T. 620. Alteration of an instrument purporting to be a bill, but invalid, whereby it becomes a good bill, is not struck at by this section: *Foster* v. *Driscoll* [1929] 1 K.B. 470; *Koch* v. *Dicks* [1933] 1 K.B. 307.

[2] Bell, *Comm.* I, 418; *Prin.* §594. See also *Darnley* v. *Kirkwood* (1845) 7 D. 595, 600; *Hamilton* v. *H's Exrx.*, 1950 S.C. 39.

[3] *Stephenson* v. *S's Trs.* (1807) Mor. Bill, Appx. 20.

[4] *Douglas, Heron & Co.* v. *Grant's Trs.* (1793) Mor. 4602; 3 Paton 503.

[5] *Broddelius* v. *Grischotti* (1887) 14 R. 536.

[6] *McNeil* v. *Blair* (1825) 3 S. 459; *Denovan* v. *Cairns* (1845) 7 D. 378; *Darnley* v. *Kirkwood* (1845) 7 D. 595.

[7] *Wood* v. *Howden* (1843) 5 D. 507; *Noble* v. *Scott* (1843) 5 D. 723; *Simpson* v. *Stewart* (1875) 2 R. 673; *Kerr's Trs.* v. *Ker* (1883) 11 R. 108; *Jackson* v. *Ogilvie's Exor.*, 1935 S.C. 154.

[8] *McLachlan* v. *Henderson* (1831) 9 S. 753; *Denovan, supra*; *Roy* v. *Campbell* (1850) 12 D. 1028; *Paxton* v. *Forster* (1842) 4 D. 1515; *Cullen* v. *Smeal* (1853) 15 D. 868; *Bank of Scotland* v. *Fergusson* (1898) 1 F. 96.

[9] *Milne's Trs.* v. *Ormiston's Trs.* (1893) 20 R. 523.

[10] *McCallum & Dalgleish* v. *Christie* (1833) 11 S. 321; *Lindsay* v. *Earl of Buchan* (1854) 16 D. 600; *Ross* v. *Robertson* (1855) 17 D. 1144.

it,[1] nor a claim under a private trust.[2] Despite the prescription having run, the debt is unaffected and the bill may be produced and used as an adminicle of evidence.[3]

Proof after six years

When the sexennium has run the constitution and resting-owing of the debt must be proved by the writ or oath of the debtor.[4] The writ, if dated within the sexennium, is valueless unless it founds a distinct obligation.[5] Subsequent writings are needed to prove its constitution.[6] It is not necessary to prove that the debt existed prior to the granting of the bill or note in question.[7] The debtor's writ or oath does not revive the bill for a second sexennium,[8] but creates only a debt subsisting till cut off by the long negative prescription.[9] The writing need not be probative, nor need it disclose the value given for the bill[10] but it must refer to the debt in question.[11] Entries in the debtor's books have been held sufficient writ,[12] and even receipts for interest granted by the creditor but kept by the debtor,[13] or letters,[14] or an inventory signed by the debtor as executor,[15] or correspondence.[16] The bill, if in the creditor's hands, is an adminicle of evidence to prove the debt and that it is resting owing.[17] The debtor's oath must be an admission of the continuing subsistence of the debt. Any period

---

[1] *Easton* v. *Hinshaw* (1873) 1 R. 23.

[2] *Blair* v. *Horn* (1858) 21 D. 45, 1004.

[3] *Laidlaw* v. *Hamilton* (1826) 4 S. 636; *Christie* v. *Henderson* (1833) 11 S. 744; *Darnley* v. *Kirkwood* (1845) 7 D. 595; *Galloway* v. *Moffatt* (1845) 7 D. 1088; *Nisbet* v. *Neil's Tr.* (1869) 7 M. 1097; *Storeys* v. *Paxton* (1878) 6 R. 293; *Milne's Trs.* v. *Ormiston's Trs.* (1893) 20 R. 523; *MacBain* v. *MacB.*, 1930 S.C. (H.L.) 72.

[4] Bell, *Prin.* §599; *Wood* v. *Howden* (1843) 5 D. 507; *Darnley* v. *Kirkwood* (1845) 7 D. 595; *McGregor* v. *McG.* (1860) 22 D. 1264; *Hamilton* v. *H's Exrx.*, 1950 S.C. 39; on onus see also *Simpson* v. *Stewart* (1875) 2 R. 673; *Kerr's Trs.* v. *Ker* (1883) 11 R. 108.

[5] *McTavish* v. *Lady Saltoun* (1825) 3 S. 472; *Bank of Scotland* v. *Taylor's Trs.* (1859) 21 D. 1004.

[6] *Macdonald* v. *Crawford* (1834) 12 S. 533; *Drummond* v. *Lees* (1880) 7 R. 452.

[7] *Campbell's Trs.* v. *Hudson's Exor.* (1895) 22 R. 943.

[8] *McIndoe* v. *Frame* (1824) 3 S. 295; *Drummond* v. *Lees* (1880) 7 R. 452; contra *Ferguson* v. *Bethune*, 7 Mar. 1811, F.C.; *Storeys* v. *Paxton* (1878) 6 R. 293, 300.

[9] *McIndoe, supra*; *Drummond* v. *Lees* (1880) 7 R. 452.

[10] *McGregor* v. *McG.* (1860) 22 D. 1264.

[11] *Bank of Scotland, supra*; *Nisbet* v. *Neil's Tr.* (1869) 7 M. 1097; *Fullerton's Trs.* v. *McDowall* (1897) 5 S.L.T. 248.

[12] *Drummond* v. *Lees* (1880) 7 R. 452; *Muir* v. *Goldie's Trs.* (1898) 6 S.L.T. 188.

[13] *Campbell's Trs.* v. *Hudson's Exor.* (1895) 22 R. 943; partial payment during the sexennium will not suffice: *Darnley, supra*.

[14] *Rennie* v. *Urquhart* (1880) 7 R. 1030.

[15] *Jackson* v. *Ogilvie's Exor.*, 1935 S.C. 154.

[16] *MacBain* v. *MacB.*, 1930 S.C. (H.L.) 72.

[17] *Campbell's Trs.* v. *Hudson's Exor.* (1895) 22 R. 943; *MacBain, supra*.

during which the creditor[1] was in minority is not included in the sexennium.[2]

Prescription after 1976

From 1976 an obligation under a bill of exchange or promissory note is wholly extinguished after the lapse of five years.[3]

Lost bills

Where a bill has been lost before it is overdue, the holder may obtain from the drawer another bill of the same tenor on giving security, if required to indemnify against all persons in the event of the lost bill being found again.[4] In an action on the bill, the court may order that the loss need not be set up, if an indemnity be given against the claims of anyone on the instrument.[5]

CHEQUES

A cheque is a bill of exchange drawn on a banker payable on demand.[6] With certain exceptions the provisions of the 1882 Act as to bills payable on demand apply to cheques.[7] Cheques are not normally presented for acceptance. A cheque granted for value and presented for payment operates as an assignation of the drawer's funds in the hands of the bank to its amount.[8]

PROMISSORY NOTES

A promissory note is an unconditional promise in writing made by one person to another,[9] signed by the maker, engaging to pay, on demand[10] or at a fixed or determinable future time, a sum certain in money,[11] to, or to the order of, a specified person or to

---

[1] *McNeil* v. *Blair* (1823) 2 S. 174. [2] *Patrick* v. *Watt* (1859) 21 D. 637.

[3] Prescription and Limitation (Sc.) Act, 1973, S. 6 and Sch. 1(1)(e).

[4] S. 69.

[5] S. 70; cf. *Enever* v. *Craig*, 1913, 2 S.L.T. 30.

[6] See further Ch. 50, *infra*.

[7] S. 73; cf. *McLean* v. *Clydesdale Bank* (1883) 11 R. (H.L.) 1; *Glen* v. *Semple* (1901) 3 F. 1134; *Bank of Scotland* v. *Rorie* (1908) 16 S.L.T. 21.

[8] S. 53(2); *B.L. Co.* v. *Carruthers* (1883) 10 R. 923; *B.L. Co.* v. *Rainey's Tr.* (1885) 12 R. 825; see also *Sutherland* v. *Commercial Bank* (1882) 20 S.L.R. 139; *Kirkwood* v. *Clydesdale Bank*, 1908 S.C. 20.

[9] *Macfarlane* v. *Johnston* (1864) 2 M. 1210; *Duncan's Trs.* v. *Shand* (1872) 10 M. 984; *Vallance* v. *Forbes* (1879) 6 R. 1099; *Blyth* v. *Forbes* (1879) 6 R. 1102; *Thomson* v. *Bell* (1894) 22 R. 16.

[10] On the obligations involved in this see *McAllister* v. *McGallagley*, 1911 S.C. 112.

[11] cf. S. 9(1); *Tennent* v. *Crawford* (1878) 5 R. 433; *Lamberton* v. *Aiken* (1899) 2 F. 189.

bearer.[1] It accordingly differs from a bill in that only two parties, promisor or maker, and promisee, are involved. It is essentially a unilateral obligation, effectual on delivery.[2] It may not include other terms.[3]

The provisions of the 1882 Act relating to bills apply to notes, the maker being deemed to correspond with the acceptor of a bill, and the first indorser of a note to correspond with the drawer of an accepted bill payable to drawer's order; but the provisions of the Act relating to presentment for acceptance, acceptance, acceptance supra protest and bills in a set do not apply to notes. Where a foreign note is dishonoured protest thereof is unnecessary.[4] No special words are necessary, provided that they amount in effect to an unconditional promise to pay and evidence the intention to make a promissory note.[5] An I.O.U. may be a promissory note.[6]

A note is inchoate and incomplete until delivery to the payee or bearer.[7] It may be made by two or more makers, and they may be liable thereon jointly, or jointly and severally according to its tenor; a note running 'I promise to pay' signed by two or more is deemed to be their joint and several note.[8]

Where a note payable on demand has been indorsed, it must be presented for payment within a reasonable time of the indorsement; if not the indorser is discharged. Where a note payable on demand is negotiated, it is not deemed to be overdue, for the purpose of affecting the holder with defects of title of which he had no notice, by reason that it appears that a reasonable time for presenting it for payment has elapsed since its issue.[9]

---

[1] S. 83(1); cf. *Thomson* v. *Black*, 1936 S.N. 78; *McTaggart* v. *MacEachern's J.F.*, 1949 S.C. 503; *Dickie* v. *Singh*, 1974 S.L.T. (Notes) 3. If payable to maker's order it is not a note unless and until indorsed by the maker: S. 83(2); it is not invalid by reason only that it contains also a pledge of collateral security with authority to sell or dispose thereof: S. 83(3). The distinction between inland and foreign notes exists: S. 83(4).

[2] *Vallance, supra*; *Thomson supra*; *McTaggart, supra*.

[3] *Dickie* v. *Singh*, 1974 S.L.T. (Notes) 3.

[4] S. 89.

[5] *Macfarlane* v. *Johnston* (1864) 2 M. 1210; *Vallance* v. *Forbes* (1879) 6 R. 1099; *Blyth* v. *Forbes* (1879) 6 R. 1102; *Watson* v. *Duncan* (1896) 4 S.L.T. 75; *Todd* v. *Wood* (1897) 24 R. 1104; contrast *Neilson's Trs.* v. *N's Trs.* (1883) 11 R. 119; *Welsh's Tr.* v. *Forbes* (1885) 12 R. 851; *Bell* v. *B.* (1897) 4 S.L.T. 214; *Lamberton* v. *Aiken* (1899) 2 F. 189; *Semple's Exors.* v. *S.*, 1912, 1 S.L.T. 382; *Cairney* v. *Macgregor's Trs.*, 1916, 1 S.L.T. 357; *Dick* v. *D.*, 1950 S.L.T. (Notes) 44.

[6] *Muir* v. *M.*, 1912, 1 S.L.T. 304.

[7] S. 84.

[8] S. 85; cf. *Smith's Exors.* v. *Johnston* (1901) 9 S.L.T. 240.

[9] S. 86; cf. *Glasscock* v. *Balls* (1889) 24 Q.B.D. 13; *Smith's Exors.* v. *Johnston* (1901) 9 S.L.T. 240.

Presentment for payment

Where a promissory note is in the body thereof made payable at a particular place, it must be presented for payment at that place in order to render the maker or an indorser liable.[1] In any other case presentment for payment is not necessary to render the maker liable, but is necessary to render the indorser of a note liable. When a place of payment is indicated on a note by way of memorandum only, presentment there is sufficient to render the indorser liable, but a presentment to the maker elsewhere, if sufficient in other respects, also suffices.[2]

Liability of maker

By making a promissory note the maker engages that he will pay it according to its tenor, and is precluded from denying to a holder in due course the existence of the payee and his then capacity to endorse.[3]

Bank notes

A bank note is a promissory note, made by a banker, payable to the bearer on demand, and intended to be negotiable by delivery like, and as, money. Bank of England notes of denominations less than £5 are legal tender in Scotland.[4] Notes of Scottish banks are not legal tender even in Scotland.

I.O.U.

An I.O.U., if containing a promise to pay, may be a promissory note,[5] but is normally only an acknowledgment of debt.[6] It is not a negotiable instrument.[7]

[1] Presentment on the day when payment is due is not necessary: *Gordon* v. *Kerr* (1898) 25 R. 570.

[2] S. 87.

[3] S. 88.

[4] Currency and Bank Notes Act, 1954.

[5] *Muir* v. *M.*, 1912, 1 S.L.T. 304.

[6] Bell, *Prin.* §310; see also *Woodrow* v. *Wright* (1861) 24 D. 31; *Bowe & Christie* v. *Hutchison* (1868) 6 M. 643; *Purvis* v. *Dowie* (1869) 7 M. 764; *Haldane* v. *Speirs* (1872) 10 M. 537; *Morgan* v. *M's Exors.* (1866) 4 M. 321; *McKenzie's Exrx.* v. *Morrison's Trs.* 1930 S.C. 830.

[7] *Horne* v. *Redfearn* (1838) 4 Bing. N.C. 433.

CHAPTER 50

BANKERS' CONTRACTS

THE principal part of the business of banking[1] is the receipt of money from customers and holding of it on current or on deposit account or on deposit receipt, the payment of cheques drawn by and the collection of cheques payable to and handed in for collection by the customer, and the making of advances to customers, but bankers undertake numerous other services for customers so that the relations between bankers and their customers, though normally contractual, are not always attributable to one, or always to the same, kind of contract.[2]

CUSTOMER AS CREDITOR OF BANKER

Credits with banker

When money is lodged with a banker the customer becomes the creditor and the banker the debtor in a transaction of loan.[3] If it is lodged on current account the banker is bound to account for it and to pay to the customer, or to a person authorized by him, the whole sum due, in a lump sum or in such portions as may be requested.[3] He is also bound to honour cheques drawn on him by his customer to the extent of the funds in his hands.[3] The customer is bound to take reasonable care not to mislead the bank or facilitate forgery of cheques and to inform the bank if he becomes aware that forged cheques are being presented.[3] So long as he can repay on demand, the banker may use the money deposited and his use cannot be questioned by the customer.[4] If money is lodged on deposit (or savings) account, the customer is allowed interest on his credit balance, but cannot draw cheques thereon; the banker's only obligation is to repay on demand.[5] If the money is lodged on deposit receipt, the banker's obligation is to repay the

---

[1] The business of banking dealt with in this chapter is the business of the clearing banks or joint stock banks. The Bank of England, as the central bank of the United Kingdom, merchant bankers, trustee savings banks and the National Savings Bank operate only in parts of this field of business. See also *Bank of Chettinad Ltd.* v. *I.R.C.* [1948] A.C. 378; *U.D.T.* v. *Kirkwood* [1966] 2 Q.B. 431; Companies Act, 1967, S. 123.

[2] See generally Paget, *Law of Banking*; Byles on *Bills*; Chalmers, *Bills of Exchange*.

[3] *Foley* v. *Hill* (1848) 2 H.L. Cas. 28; *London J.S. Bank* v. *Macmillan* [1918] A.C. 777.

[4] *Joachimson* v. *Swiss Bank Corpn.* [1921] 3 K.B. 110; cf. *Macdonald* v. *N. of S. Bank*, 1942 S.C. 369.

[5] *Macdonald, supra.*

money on demand to the person named in the deposit receipt, with interest from the date of lodgment to the date of payment at the rate then ruling. Money may be lodged on deposit receipt payable to another person.

A banker must observe any trust expressed or implied by the character in which the customer operates the account.[1] But if the contract on which the account is opened is adhered to, the banker has no concern with the way the money is applied.[2] He must also maintain the confidentiality of the relationship and not disclose the state of the account or transactions thereon unless justified or compelled by law.[3]

Where the customer operates more than one account, the banker is entitled to have regard to the overall position of all the accounts and may, on reasonable notice, decline to honour cheques drawn on an account in credit if there are countervailing debits on other accounts, even though secured.[4] Unless it has agreed not to do so, it may combine a customer's accounts and set one off against another.[5]

The sum shown on the counterfoil of a pay-in slip is *prima facie* evidence that such a sum was received by the banker, but it may be proved that this was incorrect.[6]

Money lodged on current or deposit account is liable to the ordinary incidents of a claim of debt; it may be arrested in the banker's hands for the customer's debt to another, assigned, in the case of current account, by the customer in part by drawing a cheque or, probably, as a whole by an assignation, passes on bankruptcy to the trustee under his Act and Warrant, may be bequeathed,[7] and passes on intestacy as moveable property. If no transactions take place for the period of the long negative prescription, the banker's obligation to repay is extinguished.[8]

Entries by the bank in a customer's pass-book or on a machined statement of the state of the customer's account are *prima facie* evidence thereof only and not conclusive, though they may become so if their accuracy is admitted by letter at the bank's annual

---

[1] e.g. a solicitor's clients account, or money banked as executor of X: *Re Gross, ex p. Kingston* (1871) 6 Ch. App. 632; cf. *Brown* v. *Inland Revenue,* 1964 S.C. (H.L.) 180.

[2] *Struthers Patent Co.* v. *Clydesdale Bank* (1886) 13 R. 434.

[3] *Tournier* v. *National Provincial Bank* [1924] 1 K.B. 461.

[4] *Kirkwood* v. *Clydesdale Bank,* 1908 S.C. 20; *Greenhalgh* v. *Union Bank of Manchester* [1924] 2 K.B. 153.

[5] *Halesowen* v. *Westminster Bank* [1970] 3 All E.R. 473.

[6] *Docherty* v. *Royal Bank,* 1963 S.L.T. (Notes) 43.

[7] cf. *Re Heilbronner* [1953] 2 All E.R. 1016.

[8] *MacDonald* v. *N. of S. Bank,* 1942 S.C. 369.

balance,[1] and the bank may be barred from disputing its own statement of the balance if the customer has altered his position in reliance thereon.[2]

The relationship subsists at the will of the parties and either party may at any time on reasonable notice ask for the account to be closed and require the debtor to pay the creditor the balance due him, provision being made for any cheques not yet presented.[3]

Current accounts—operations by cheques

A customer's operations on current account are largely effected by drawing and paying in cheques. A cheque is a bill of exchange drawn on a banker payable on demand,[4] and is a mandate to the banker to pay the payee the amount stated in the cheque.[5] It must conform to the requisites of a valid bill.[6] Like a bill it may pass by indorsement and delivery or, if payable to payee or bearer, by delivery alone. A cheque is not normally presented for acceptance,[7] but only for payment. A cheque for less than 20s. is void in Scotland and subject to penalty, except for drafts on a banker to pay money held to the use of the drawer.[8]

In drawing cheques the customer is bound to take reasonable care to avoid the banker being misled, and he is liable to the banker for loss arising naturally and directly from breach of this duty, as by drawing a cheque in a way which facilitates forgery or fraud.[9] He must notify the banker of any known forgery of his signature on any instrument likely to be presented for payment and will be barred from challenging the forgery if he does not do so.[10]

---

[1] *Commercial Bank* v. *Rhind* (1860) 3 Macq. 643; *Couper's Trs.* v. *National Bank* (1889) 16 R. 412; cf. *B.L. Bank* v. *Thomson* (1853) 15 D. 314; *British and North European Bank* v. *Zalzstein* [1927] 2 K.B. 92.

[2] *Holland* v. *Manchester and Liverpool District Banking Co.* (1909) 25 T.L.R. 386; *Holt* v. *Markham* [1923] 1 K.B. 504.

[3] *Buckingham* v. *London and Midland Bank* (1895) 12 T.L.R. 70; *Joachimson, supra*; *Prosperity, Ltd.* v. *Lloyds Bank* (1923) 39 T.L.R. 372.

[4] Bills of Exchange Act, 1882, S. 73; except as otherwise provided in Ss. 73–81, the whole provisions of the 1882 Act applicable to a bill of exchange payable on demand apply to a cheque; hence every holder of a cheque is presumed to be a holder in due course: S. 29; cf. *Glen* v. *Semple* (1901) 3 F. 1134; *Semple* v. *Kyle* (1902) 4 F. 421; *N. & S. Ins. Co.* v. *Nat. Prov. Bank* [1936] 1 K.B. 328.

[5] *B.L. Co.* v. *Carruthers* (1883) 10 R. 923; *London J.S. Bank* v. *Macmillan* [1918] A.C. 777.

[6] *Bank of Baroda Ltd.* v. *Punjab National Bank* [1944] A.C. 176.

[7] 1882 Act, Ss. 3–13; cf. *Henderson* v. *Wallace & Pennell* (1902) 5 F. 166; *Capital and Counties Bank* v. *Gordon* [1903] A.C. 240.

[8] Bank Notes (Sc.) Act, 1845, Ss. 16, 20.

[9] *B.L. Co.* v. *Carruthers* (1883) 10 R. 923; *London J.S. Bank* v. *Macmillan* [1918] A.C. 777.

[10] *Greenwood* v. *Martins Bank* [1933] A.C. 51.

A cheque is normally an order on the bank and branch thereof
where the customer keeps his account, but may be altered by the
customer to an order on another bank or branch where he has an
account,[1] but a branch other than that where he keeps an account
is not bound to honour his cheques without inquiry.[2]

Banker paying customer's cheques

By opening a current account the customer authorizes the
banker to pay cheques drawn by him on that banker, up to the
amount at credit of the account or within the limits of any overdrawing permitted by the banker. If the account is in credit the
banker is bound to honour cheques drawn.[3] The banker's duty
and authority to pay a customer's cheque are determined by
countermand of payment,[4] or notice of the customer's death,[5] and
probably also by notice of his insanity or of petition for his
sequestration, and certainly by his sequestration,[6] the appointment of a curator bonis on his estate,[7] or the arrestment of the sum
at credit of the account.[8]

The banker may refuse to pay a cheque which is invalid,[9] or
ambiguous, and may refuse to pay an undated cheque,[10] or a stale
cheque, i.e. one dated more than six months ago, or a post-dated
cheque before the date it bears,[11] or one drawn on a branch other
than that where the account is kept.[12] He must pay or refuse
payment at once; a request for delay is dishonour.[13] Since cheques
are not normally accepted for payment, the payee cannot enforce
payment from a bank which declines to pay.

A banker may not refuse to pay a cheque drawn on an account
in credit by reason of knowledge that sequestration is to be
applied for.[14] He may refuse to pay if there are insufficient funds

---

[1] *Burnett* v. *Westminster Bank* [1965] 3 All E.R. 81.
[2] *Woodland* v. *Fear* (1857) 7 E. & B. 519; *Clare* v. *Dresdner Bank* [1915] 2 K.B. 576.
[3] *London J.S. Bank* v. *Macmillan* [1918] A.C. 777.
[4] Bills of Exchange Act, 1882, S. 75; *McLean* v. *Clydesdale Bank* (1883) 11 R. (H.L.) 1;
Curtice v. *London City & Midland Bank, Ltd.* [1908] 1 K.B. 293; *Hilton* v. *Westminster Bank*
(1926) 43 T.L.R. 124.
[5] S. 75; *Kirkwood* v. *Clydesdale Bank*, 1908 S.C. 20.
[6] Bankruptcy (Sc.) Act, 1913, S. 107.
[7] *Mitchell & Baxter* v. *Cheyne* (1891) 19 R. 324.
[8] *Graham* v. *McFarlane* (1869) 7 M. 640.
[9] *Emanuel* v. *Robarts* (1868) 9 B. & S. 121.
[10] *Griffiths* v. *Dalton* [1940] 2 K.B. 264.
[11] *Royal Bank* v. *Tottenham* [1894] 2 Q.B. 715.
[12] *Clare* v. *Dresdner Bank* [1915] 2 K.B. 576.
[13] *Bank of England* v. *Vagliano* [1891] A.C. 107; *Bank of Baroda* v. *Punjab National Bank*
[1944] A.C. 176, 184.
[14] *Ireland* v. *N. of S. Bank* (1880) 8 R. 215.

at credit of the account; he is not obliged to permit overdrawing, even if he has done so in the past.[1] The banker must not pay a cheque if the customer stops the cheque, i.e. countermands his instructions, in time.[2] An unjustified refusal by a banker to pay a cheque is a serious imputation on the customer's credit and actionable.[3]

Apart from special instructions, the banker should pay his customer's cheques in the order in which they are presented for payment.[4] The cheque must be drawn by the customer or a person having express or implied authority from him to do so. A *per pro* signature gives the bank notice that the agent has only a limited authority to sign, and the principal is only bound if the agent in so signing was acting within the actual limits of his authority.[5] A forged or unauthorized signature is wholly inoperative and gives no right to payment,[6] so that a bank paying on a forged cheque is not entitled to debit the customer's account.

Cheque as an assignation

Where the drawee of a bill or cheque has in his hands funds available for the payment thereof,[7] the bill or cheque operates as an assignation of the sum for which it is drawn in favour of the holder, from the time when the bill is presented to the drawee.[8] Hence where the banker holds funds but insufficient to meet the cheque, he cannot pay the cheque but the sum at credit is deemed assigned in *pro tanto* satisfaction of the claim evidenced by presenting the cheque.[9] If the drawer is subsequently sequestrated the holder has accordingly a claim preferable to that of the trustee in sequestration.[9] A cheque does not operate assignation if presented by a person not the payee, nor by a person who by

---

[1] *Johnston* v. *Commercial Bank* (1858) 20 D. 790; *Ritchie* v. *Clydesdale Bank* (1886) 13 R. 866.

[2] *Waterston* v. *City of Glasgow Bank* (1874) 1 R. 470; *Westminster Bank* v. *Hilton* (1926) 43 T.L.R. 124.

[3] *Marzetti* v. *Williams* (1830) 1 B. & Ad. 415; *Summers* v. *City Bank* (1874) L.R. 9 C.P. 580; *King* v. *B.L. Co.* (1899) 1 F. 928; *Wilson* v. *United Counties Bank* [1920] A.C. 102; *Davidson* v. *Barclays Bank* [1940] 1 All E.R. 316; contrast *Frost* v. *London J.S. Bank* (1906) 22 T.L.R. 760. See also *Pyke* v. *Hibernian Bank* [1950] I.R. 195. These rules are not wholly applicable to deposit accounts with hire-purchase finance companies: *Gibb* v. *Lombank Scotland Ltd.*, 1962 S.L.T. 288.

[4] *Kilsby* v. *Williams* (1822) 5 B. & Ald. 815.   [5] Bills of Exchange Act, 1882, S. 25.

[6] Ibid., S. 24.   [7] *Kirkwood* v. *Clydesdale Bank*, 1908 S.C. 20.

[8] Bills of Exchange Act, 1882, S. 53(2). This does not apply to savings accounts or special investment accounts with a savings bank: Trustee Savings Bank Act, 1969, S. 20. Presentment need not be in accordance with the Act.

[9] *Sutherland* v. *Commercial Bank* (1882) 20 S.L.R. 139; *B.L. Co.* v. *Carruthers* (1883) 10 R. 923; *B.L. Co.* v. *Rainey* (1885) 12 R. 825.

forgery is named as payee.[1] But a cheque payable after death is neither effectual as a donation nor as a legacy.[2]

Overdue cheque

A cheque is deemed overdue when it appears to have been in circulation for an unreasonable length of time.[3] Where an overdue cheque is negotiated, it can only be negotiated subject to any defect of title affecting it at its maturity, and no person who takes it can acquire or give a better title than that had by the person from whom he took it.[4] Bankers commonly refuse to pay a cheque six months old without reference to the customer.

Presentment for payment

Presentment must be made to the banker at his place of business on a business day within banking hours by the holder or some person[5] authorized by him to receive payment on his behalf.[6]

Delay in presentment for payment

Where a cheque is not presented for payment within a reasonable time[7] of its issue, and the drawer or person on whose account it is drawn had the right at the time of such presentment as between him and the banker to have the cheque paid and suffers actual damage through the delay, he is discharged to the extent of such damage, to the extent to which such drawer is a creditor of such banker to a larger amount than he would have been had such cheque been paid.[8] The holder of such cheque shall be a creditor, in lieu of the drawer, of such banker to the extent of such discharge, and entitled to recover the amount from him.[9]

Action on dishonour

If a cheque is dishonoured the payee may seek to recover his debt by action and diligence against the drawer, but not by summary diligence,[10] or may petition for sequestration.

---

[1] *Dickson* v. *Clydesdale Bank*, 1937 S.L.T. 585.
[2] *Milne* v. *Grant's Exors.* (1884) 11 R. 887; *Stewart's Trs.*, 1953 S.L.T. (Notes) 26.
[3] 1882 Act, S. 36(3); a cheque may become overdue sooner than a bill: *London and County Bank* v. *Groome* (1881) 8 Q.B.D. 288.
[4] S. 36(2).
[5] Who normally is the payee's own banker, authorized to collect.
[6] 1882 Act, S. 45(3).
[7] As to determining reasonable time, see S. 74(2); *King* v. *Porter* [1925] N.I. 107.
[8] Bills of Exchange Act, 1882, S. 74(1).
[9] Ibid., S. 74(3).
[10] *Glickman* v. *Linda*, 1950 S.C. 18.

Indorsement when presenting cheque

Until the Cheques Act, 1957, a person presenting a cheque to a banker for payment was required to indorse it on the back, if a bearer cheque, as a means of identifying the presenter,[1] and if an order cheque, to connect its presentment with the person named as payee or indorsee. The banker was bound to pay, if he had funds in his hands to do so, if the indorsement was *ex facie* regular and in the absence of reasonable grounds for thinking that the indorsement was a forgery. If the signature of the indorsement did not match the name of the payee or indorsee, he might refuse payment. A forged or unauthorized indorsement extinguishes the debt due to such indorsee by the indorser from whom he received the cheque.[2]

Altered cheques

Where a cheque has been fraudulently altered the banker may debit the customer with the full sum in the cheque, only if the customer has been guilty of such carelessness as has been the proximate cause of the banker being misled.[3]

Where drawer's signature forged

Where a banker pays a cheque, the drawer's signature on which was forged or adhibited without authority, he is liable to repay the drawer, unless in the circumstances the drawer has contributed to the fraud so materially as to bar him from pleading the forgery or lack of authority. The drawer's silence, after the knowledge of the cheque's existence, does not alone bar him, nor does his carelessness in the custody of his cheque book.[4] Silence, or delay, with other circumstances, may bar him.[5]

Where payee's indorsement forged

Where the indorsement of the payee of a cheque is forged by a thief, the drawer, whose account has been debited, may recover

---

[1] It was doubted in *Haldane* v. *Speirs* (1872) 10 M. 537, whether the banker was entitled to require indorsement.

[2] Bills of Exchange Act, 1882, S. 24.

[3] *Young* v. *Grote* (1827) 4 Bing. 253; *Robarts* v. *Tucker* (1851) L.R. 16 Q.B. 560; *Orr & Barber* v. *Union Bank* (1854) 1 Macq. 513; *London Joint Stock Bank* v. *MacMillan* [1918] A.C. 777; contrast *Slingsby* v. *District Bank* [1932] 1 K.B. 544.

[4] *Bank of Ireland* v. *Evans' Charities* (1855) 5 H.L.C. 389.

[5] *Meicklem* v. *Walker* (1833) 12 S. 53; *Warden* v. *B.L. Co.* (1863) 1 M. 402; *McKenzie* v. *B.L. Co.* (1881) 8 R. (H.L.) 8; cf. *Freeman* v. *Cooke* (1847) 2 Ex. 654; *Findlay* v. *Currie* (1850) 13 D. 278; *Boyd* v. *Union Bank* (1854) 17 D. 159; *Brown* v. *B.L. Co.* (1863) 1 M. 793; *Urquhart* v. *Bank of Scotland* (1872) 9 S.L.R. 508; *B.L. Co.* v. *Cowan* (1906) 8 F. 704.

from the thief or from a third party who has facilitated the loss by adding his indorsement and receiving cash for the cheque.[1]

Protection of bankers paying cheques drawn to bearer

A banker who in good faith and without negligence pays a bearer cheque to the presenter is not liable to his customer and may debit the latter's account, even though the bearer had no title or only a defective title to the cheque.[2] Such a payment discharges the customer (drawer of the cheque) completely, even if the bearer were not the person truly entitled to the money.

Protection of bankers paying drafts or orders drawn to order

If a draft or order for a sum of money,[3] drawn payable to order on demand, is presented for payment, purporting to be indorsed by the person to whom it was drawn payable, it is sufficient authority to the banker to pay the bearer; and it is not incumbent on the banker to prove that the indorsement, or any subsequent indorsement was made by or under the direction or authority of the person to whom the draft was made payable by the drawer or any indorser thereof.[4]

Protection of bankers paying cheques drawn to order

A similar provision for bills and cheques payable to order on demand drawn on a banker is made by the Bills of Exchange Act.[5] It protects the paying banker only, and its object is to protect him against forged or unauthorized indorsements.[6] A banker is accordingly justified in paying a draft, order, bill or cheque which purports to be indorsed by the payee, or by or with his authority, though it should subsequently appear that the indorsement was forged, so long as the payment was made without negligence, in good faith, and in the ordinary course of business.[7] He is not protected if he pays uncrossed cheques not properly endorsed by the payee.[8]

---

[1] *Beith* v. *Allan,* 1961 S.L.T. (Notes) 80.

[2] *Charles* v. *Blackwell* (1877) 2 C.P.D. 151; Bills of Exchange Act, 1882, S. 59.

[3] This provision applies to drafts or orders which are not bills of exchange: *Capital and Counties Bank* v. *Gordon* [1903] A.C. 240.

[4] Stamp Act, 1853, S. 19; *Charles* v. *Blackwell* (1877) 2 C.P.D. 151.

[5] S. 60; *Slingsby* v. *District Bank* [1932] 1 K.B. 544.

[6] cf. *Charles, supra.*

[7] *Ogden* v. *Benas* (1874) L.R. 9 C.P. 513. Negligence is a question of fact in each case: *Bissell* v. *Fox* (1885) 53 L.T. 193.

[8] *Slingsby, supra; Phillips* v. *Italian Bank,* 1934 S.L.T. 78.

Protection of paying bankers since 1957

In 1957 the need for the payee or indorsee of a cheque to indorse it on presenting it for payment was removed. Since then a banker who, in good faith and in the ordinary course of business, pays a cheque drawn on him which is not indorsed or is irregularly indorsed, does not incur any liability by reason only thereof and is deemed to have paid it in due course. Where a banker in good faith and in the ordinary course of business pays such an instrument as a document issued by a customer which, though not a bill of exchange, is intended to enable a person to obtain payment from him of the sum mentioned therein, or a draft payable on demand drawn on him by himself, he does not thereby incur any liability by reason only of the absence of, or irregularity in, indorsement, and the payment discharges the instrument.[1]

Crossed cheques

Where a cheque bears across its face an addition of (a) the words 'and company' or any abbreviation thereof between two parallel transverse lines, either with or without the words 'not negotiable' or (b) two parallel transverse lines simply, either with or without the words 'not negotiable', that addition constitutes a crossing and the cheque is crossed generally. Where a cheque bears across its face an addition of the name of a banker, either with or without the words 'not negotiable', the cheque is crossed specially and to that banker.[2] A cheque may be crossed generally or specially by the drawer. If it is uncrossed, the holder may cross it generally or specially; if crossed generally, he may cross it specially; if crossed generally or specially, he may add the words 'not negotiable'; if crossed specially, the banker to whom it is crossed may again cross it specially to another banker for collection; and where an uncrossed cheque or a cheque crossed generally is sent to a banker for collection, he may cross it specially to himself.[3] A crossing authorized by the Act is a material part of the cheque, and it is not lawful for any person to obliterate or, except as authorized by the Act, add to or alter the crossing.[4]

Where a person takes a crossed cheque which bears on it the words 'not negotiable' he does not have, and is not capable of

---

[1] Cheques Act, 1957, S. 1. By practice indorsement remains necessary for cheques cashed across the counter. The protection of this section is additional to that of the 1853 and 1882 Acts.

[2] Bills of Exchange Act, 1882, S. 76. On the origin of crossing cheques see *Bellamy* v. *Marjoribanks* (1852) 7 Ex. 389, 402; *Smith* v. *Union Bank* (1875) 1 Q.B.D. 31, 33.

[3] Ibid., S. 77.

[4] Ibid., S. 78.

giving, a better title to the cheque than that had by the person from whom he took it.[1] Such a cheque is transferable but its negotiable quality is limited, and if the transferor's title is defective, a subsequent holder for value does not enjoy the privileges of a holder in due course.[2] None of the other forms of crossing has any effect on the negotiability of the cheque.

The words 'Account payee' are sometimes added to a crossing, but have no legal effect and do not prevent the cheque being transferred.[3] They are merely a direction to the paying banker but disregard by him of the words, without explanation, is negligence on his part.[4]

Duties of banker as to crossed cheques

Where a cheque is crossed specially to more than one banker, except when crossed to a banker as an agent for collection, the banker on whom it is drawn must refuse payment thereof.[5] Where the banker on whom a cheque is drawn which is so crossed nevertheless pays it, or if crossed specially otherwise than to the banker to whom it is crossed, or a banker who is his agent for collection, he is liable to the true owner[6] of the cheque for any loss he may sustain owing to the cheque having been so paid. But when a cheque is presented for payment which does not at the time of presentment appear to be crossed, or to have had a crossing which has been obliterated, or to have been added to or altered otherwise than as authorized by the Act, the banker paying the cheque in good faith and without negligence is not responsible nor incurs any liability, nor is the payment to be questioned by reason of the cheque having been crossed, or of the crossing having been obliterated or having been added to or altered otherwise than as authorized by the Act, and of payment having been made otherwise than to a banker or to the banker to whom the cheque is or was crossed, or to a banker who is his agent for collection, as the case may be.[7] Thus bankers have been held liable for paying cash on crossed cheques to a person not held out as having

---

[1] Ibid., S. 81. The words 'not negotiable' have no statutory effect unless combined with one of the normal crossings.

[2] *G. W. Ry.* v. *London and County Bank* [1901] A.C. 414.

[3] *National Bank* v. *Silke* [1891] 1 Q.B. 435; *House Property Co.* v. *London, etc. Bank* (1915) 84 L.J.K.B. 1846; *Importers Co.* v. *Westminster Bank* [1927] 2 K.B. 297.

[4] *Ladbroke* v. *Todd* [1914–15] All E.R. Rep. 1134; *Ross* v. *London County and Westminster Bank* [1919] 1 K.B. 678; *Underwood* v. *Bank of Liverpool and Martins* [1924] 1 K.B. 775.

[5] Bills of Exchange Act, 1882, S. 79(1).

[6] cf. *M. Bute* v. *Barclays Bank* [1955] 1 Q.B. 202.

[7] Ibid., S. 79(2).

authority to cash cheques in favour of the named payee.[1] Save under S. 79(1) a banker is not prohibited from paying in contravention of the crossing but if he does so he is liable to the true owner for any loss the latter sustains thereby.[2]

Protection of banker and drawer where cheque crossed

Where a banker, on whom a crossed cheque is drawn, in good faith and without negligence[3] pays it, if crossed generally, to a banker, and if crossed specially, to the banker to whom it is crossed, or to a banker who is his agent for collection, the banker paying the cheque and, if the cheque has come into the hands of the payee, the drawer, are respectively entitled to the same rights and be placed in the same position as if payment of the cheque had been made to the true owner thereof.[4] In respect that the payment must be made without negligence the protection under this section is narrower than under S. 60. The banker is not protected if the body of the cheque, as distinct from the crossing, has been materially altered.[5]

Banker collecting customer's cheques

A person normally does not present cheques held by him for payment personally but gives them to his own banker for collection. When a customer pays in cheques payable to him the banker becomes his agent to collect payment from the banker on whom the cheque is drawn and to hold the sum at the credit of the customer's account.[6] The banker must exercise due diligence in presenting cheques for payment and is liable to his customer for loss caused by delay.[7] Presentment for payment is normally made through the bankers' clearing-house, but may be by post, and normally the day after receipt.[8] When cheques are collected the collecting banker is allowed a reasonable time in which to credit his customer's account. A banker may allow his customer to draw on current account against cheques paid in but not yet cleared; if in such circumstances the collecting banker presents

---

[1] *Phillips* v. *Italian Bank*, 1934 S.L.T. 78.

[2] *Meyer* v. *Sze Hai Tong Banking Co.* [1913] A.C. 847; see also *Smith* v. *Union Bank of London* (1875) 1 Q.B.D. 31.

[3] *Slingsby* v. *District Bank* [1932] 1 K.B. 544.

[4] Bills of Exchange Act, 1882, S. 80.   [5] *Slingsby, supra.*

[6] *Capital and Counties Bank* v. *Gordon* [1903] A.C. 240; *Importers Co.* v. *Westminster Bank* [1927] 2 K.B. 297.

[7] *Lubbock* v. *Tribe* (1838) 3 M. & W. 607; *Forman* v. *Bank of England* (1902) 18 T.L.R. 339. Bills of Exchange Act, 1882, S. 74.

[8] *Heywood* v. *Pickering* (1874) L.R. 9 Q.B. 428; *Forman* v. *Bank of England* (1902) 18 T.L.R. 339.

the cheques and they are dishonoured, he may claim against the drawer as a holder in due course.[1] If the cheque is dishonoured on presentment, the collecting banker must give his customer or the drawer due notice of dishonour and, if he has already credited his customer's account, may debit it with the amount of the dishonoured cheque.[2]

Customer's defective title to cheque

A banker collecting an uncrossed cheque is unprotected if the customer had no title, or only a defective title, to the cheque, and is liable to the true owner for the face value of the cheque.[3] The banker is a holder of the cheque and may cross it generally or specially, or specially to himself.[4]

Crossed cheques

A banker to whom a cheque is crossed specially may again cross it specially to another banker for collection. If a cheque uncrossed, or crossed generally, is sent to a banker for collection, he may cross it specially to himself.[5]

Protection of collecting banker

Where a banker, in good faith and without negligence, receives payment for a customer[6] of an instrument to which the section applies, or, having credited a customer's account with the amount of such an instrument, receives payment thereof for himself, and the customer has no title, or a defective title thereto, the banker does not incur any liability to the true owner of the cheque by reason only of having received such payment. A banker is not to be treated as having been negligent by reason only of his failure to concern himself with absence of, or irregularity in, indorsement of an instrument.[7]

Unless the banker can bring himself within this section he may be liable for misappropriation of the money if the person from

---

[1] *Royal Bank* v. *Tottenham* [1894] 2 Q.B. 715; *Midland Bank* v. *Harris* [1963] 2 All E.R. 685.

[2] *Capital and Counties Bank, supra.*

[3] *Capital and Counties Bank* v. *Gordon* [1903] A.C. 240; *Morison* v. *London County & Westminster Bank* [1914] 3 K.B. 356; *Midland Bank* v. *Reckitt* [1933] A.C. 1.

[4] Bills of Exchange Act, 1882, S. 77.

[5] Bills of Exchange Act, 1882, S. 77(5)(6).

[6] Not for the banker himself, as where the banker has at once credited the customer's account. As to 'customer' see *Commrs. of Taxation* v. *English, Scottish & Australian Bank Ltd.* [1920] A.C. 683.

[7] Cheques Act, 1957, S. 4, replacing Bills of Exchange Act, 1882, S. 82. The instruments to which the section applies are defined in S. 4(2).

whom he takes the cheque had no title or only a defective title thereto. The onus is on the banker to disprove negligence.[1] It is negligence to collect for a private account a cheque bearing to be for the benefit of a company or firm and tendered by an official,[2] or otherwise to collect where the transaction was in the circumstances out of the ordinary course and such as should have aroused doubt and inquiry.[3]

Rights of bankers collecting cheques not indorsed

A banker who gives value for, or has a lien on, a cheque payable to order which the holder delivers to him for collection without indorsing it, has such, if any, rights as he would have had if, upon delivery, the holder had indorsed it in blank.[4] A banker is not deprived of any rights he would otherwise have had as holder of a cheque merely because it is not indorsed. Thus a bank which received unindorsed cheques from a customer for collection, which were not paid, could sue the drawers as a holder in due course.[5]

Cheque as payment of debt

A creditor is not bound to accept a cheque in payment, and a debtor who pays by an uncrossed cheque payable to X or bearer, sent by post, remains liable if the cheque is stolen.[6] A cheque is valid payment of a debt only if it is honoured; if it is stopped or dishonoured the debt subsists.[7] If the cheque is received by the payee and is stolen from or lost by him, and cashed, the loss falls on him and the debt is extinguished.[8]

---

[1] *Lloyds Bank* v. *Savory* [1933] A.C. 201; *Orbit Mining Co.* v. *Westminster Bank* [1963] 1 Q.B. 794; *Marfani* v. *Midland Bank* [1968] 2 All E.R. 573. It has been said to be conclusive evidence of negligence to take a cheque crossed 'account payee' and credit an account other than that designated: *Bevan* v. *National Bank* (1906) 23 T.L.R. 65; *Morison, supra,* 374.

[2] *Lloyds Bank, supra*; *M. Bute* v. *Barclays Bank, Ltd.* [1955] 1 Q.B. 202; *Baker* v. *Barclays Bank* [1955] 2 All E.R. 571.

[3] *Commrs. of Taxation* v. *English, Scottish and Australian Bank* [1920] A.C. 683; see also *G.W. Ry.* v. *London and County Banking Co.* [1901] A.C. 414; *Ladbroke* v. *Todd* [1914–15] All E.R. Rep. 1134; *Lloyds Bank* v. *Savory* [1933] A.C. 201; *Midland Bank* v. *Reckitt* [1933] A.C. 1; *Orbit Mining Co.* v. *Westminster Bank* [1963] 1 Q.B. 794.

[4] Cheques Act, 1957, S. 2.

[5] *Midland Bank* v. *Harris* [1963] 2 All E.R. 685; *Westminster Bank* v. *Zang* [1964] 3 All E.R. 683.

[6] *Robb* v. *Gow Bros. & Gemmell* (1905) 8 F. 90.

[7] *Cohen* v. *Hale* (1878) 3 Q.B.D. 371; *Leggat Bros.* v. *Gray,* 1908 S.C. 67.

[8] *Charles* v. *Blackwell* (1877) 2 C.P.D. 151.

Paid cheque as receipt

An unindorsed cheque which appears to have been paid by the banker on whom it is drawn is evidence of the receipt by the payee of the sum payable by the cheque.[1] It is accordingly equivalent to a signed receipt for the money paid.

Discharge of cheque

A cheque is discharged by payment in due course when the proceeds are applied to the holder's credit.[2]

Collection of other payable instruments

A banker is frequently employed also to collect for a customer other instruments payable to the latter, such as bills of exchange, interest warrants, dividend warrants, money orders and postal orders. A banker collecting bills must present them for acceptance and payment and give notice to the customer if they are dishonoured.[3] Such bills remain assets of the holder and the banker has, at most, a right of lien over them.[4] The crossed cheques provisions of the Bills of Exchange Act, 1882, apply to dividend warrants though they are not cheques,[5] and a collecting banker's rights and duties are the same as for a cheque. Money orders and postal orders are not cheques, nor negotiable, but may be crossed generally or specially and are payable only in accordance with such a crossing. A banker collecting postal orders for a customer is absolutely protected, whether they be crossed or not.[6]

Deposit or savings accounts

A deposit or savings account differs from a current account in that cheques may not be drawn on it, and interest is allowed on the credit balance. The banker's obligation is to repay the customer on demand the whole sum at credit of the account, with interest.[7]

---

[1] Cheques Act, 1957, S. 3.
[2] 1882 Act, S. 59(1); *Coats* v. *Union Bank*, 1929 S.C. (H.L.) 114.
[3] *Bank of Scotland* v. *Dominion Bank* (1891) 18 R. (H.L.) 21.
[4] *Clydesdale Bank* v. *Liqdrs. of Allan & Son*, 1926 S.C. 235.
[5] 1882 Act, S. 95; *Slingsby* v. *Westminster Bank* [1931] 1 K.B. 173.
[6] Post Office Act, 1953, S. 21(3), amd. Post Office Act, 1969, Sch. 4.
[7] *Macdonald* v. *N. of S. Bank*, 1942 S.C. 369.

Deposit receipts

A deposit receipt is an acknowledgment by a bank of receipt of a sum of money repayable in terms thereof. It is not a deed of trust.[1] Interest is payable thereon. The money is repayable on re-delivery of the receipt, indorsed by the depositor or payee. Payment cannot be refused on the ground that a payee is indebted to the bank in a greater sum.[2] An indorsed deposit receipt is not a negotiable instrument, and possession thereof by a third party merely implies a mandate to him to uplift the money on behalf of the depositor.[3] But the sum in the deposit receipt may be transferred by assignation written on or attached to the receipt and intimated to the bank. Nor is it a document of title and the terms in which it is taken justify no inference as to the ownership of the money.[4] The banker is liable if he pays to a wrongful holder, unless the depositor caused the loss by his fraud or negligence.[5]

By depositing money on deposit receipt in the joint names of parties, the money is placed in neutral custody and does not bear interest as being wrongfully withheld. If settlement of the purchase of heritage is delayed after entry has been taken, the purchase price is commonly consigned in the joint names of purchaser and seller, the purchaser indorsing and delivering the receipt on receiving a disposition of the lands bought, thereby enabling the seller to uplift the price.[6]

A deposit receipt payable to another person, or to two persons or the survivor, and delivered to that other, or at least known to him, has frequently been used to effect a donation *mortis causa*.[7]

A deposit receipt is discharged by indorsement and redelivery in return for payment; indorsement must be by the payee, or one of alternative payees, or by the payee's confirmed executor. But a

---

[1] *Cairns v. Davidson*, 1913 S.C. 1054.

[2] *Anderson v. N. of S. Bank* (1901) 4 F. 49.

[3] *Barstow v. Inglis & Hay* (1857) 20 D. 230; *Re Dillon* (1890) 44 Ch. D. 76.

[4] *Allan's Exor. v. Union Bank*, 1909 S.C. 206.

[5] *Forbes' Exor. v. Western Bank* (1854) 16 D. 807; *Wood v. Clydesdale Bank*, 1914 S.C. 397.

[6] *Prestwick Cinema Co. v. Gardiner*, 1951 S.C. 98.

[7] *B.L. Co. v. Martin* (1849) 11 D. 1004; *Ross v. Mellis* (1871) 10 M. 197; *Gibson v. Hutchison* (1872) 10 M. 923; *Crosbie's Trs. v. Wright* (1880) 7 R. 823; *McConnell's Trs. v. M's Trs.* (1886) 13 R. 1175; *Macdonald v. M.* (1889) 16 R. 758; *Dinwoodie's Exor. v. Carruthers' Exor.* (1895) 23 R. 234; *Brownlee's Exor. v. B.*, 1908 S.C. 232; *Hutchieson's Exor. v. Shearer*, 1909 S.C. 15.

banker may, despite indorsement by one of alternative payees, retain the sum against the other.[1]

CUSTOMER AS DEBTOR TO BANKER

Banker's advances

Where a banker advances money to his customer he becomes the creditor and the customer becomes the debtor in a loan relationship. This relationship may be established by discounting bills held by the customer, by the grant of a personal loan to the customer, or by permitting him to overdraw his current account to a specified extent; it may be evidenced by a personal bond, cash-credit bond, or supported by a cautionary obligation or guarantee.[2] An overdraft may be granted without security or on the security of any form of security competent in respect of particular assets.[3] Money advanced on loan to persons jointly renders them liable each for his share only.[4] It is customary to charge the customer interest on his overdraft or loan.[5] A person is personally liable for an overdraft only if he had individually contracted with the bank and not if he were in a representative capacity.[6]

The contract subsists at the will of the parties and may be terminated by either at any time by requiring or making payment of the balance due. The banker may, without giving any reason, call on the customer to liquidate his debt.[7] If overdrawing against security has been permitted the banker may be liable in damages if he, without reasonable notice, subsequently refuses to honour a cheque.[8]

Authority to an agent to open and operate a current account does not automatically include authority to overdraw, but such authority, if granted, need not be written.[9] In such a case the

---

[1] *Anderson* v. *N. of S. Bank* (1901) 4 F. 49.

[2] As to banker's duty of disclosure to cautioner see *Young* v. *Clydesdale Bank* (1889) 17 R. 231; *Royal Bank* v. *Greenshields*, 1914 S.C. 259. As to essential error, see *N. of S. Bank* v. *Mackenzie*, 1925 S.L.T. 236; and as to representations to cautioner see *Union Bank* v. *Taylor*, 1925 S.C. 835; cf. *Aitken's Trs.* v. *Bank of Scotland*, 1944 S.C. 270.

[3] cf. *Nelson* v. *National Bank*, 1936 S.C. 570.

[4] *Coats* v. *Union Bank*, 1929 S.C. (H.L.) 114.

[5] cf. *Reddie* v. *Williamson* (1863) 1 M. 228.

[6] *National Bank* v. *Shaw*, 1913 S.C. 133.

[7] *Johnston* v. *Commercial Bank* (1858) 20 D. 790; *Ritchie* v. *Clydesdale Bank* (1886) 13 R. 866.

[8] *Johnston, supra*; *Buckingham* v. *London and Midland Bank* (1895) 12 T.L.R. 70; *Forman* v. *Bank of England* (1902) 18 T.L.R. 339.

[9] *Royal Bank* v. *Skinner*, 1931 S.L.T. 382; see also *Commercial Bank* v. *Biggar*, 1958 S.L.T. (Notes) 46.

banker should warn the principal of the existence of the overdraft. The agent is not personally liable for such an overdraft.[1]

If there is a cautioner the banker is not generally bound to inform him of any fact affecting the customer's credit.[2]

Appropriation of payments

A customer paying in money may, expressly or impliedly, appropriate it to any account which he has with that banker.[3] A payment unappropriated may be appropriated by the banker towards any particular debt which the banker has requested him to pay off,[4] or to any debt he pleases,[5] to an unsecured rather than a secured debt.[6] Where no special appropriation is made, by the rule in *Clayton's Case*[7] the credits are deemed to extinguish the debits on the account in order of date.

Retention of negotiable instruments

A banker may, unless the right is excluded by agreement, retain all of a customer's negotiable instruments in his possession for securing a debtor balance on general account.[8]

OTHER RELATIONS BETWEEN BANKER AND CUSTOMER

Banker as depositary or custodier

Bankers frequently accept for safe custody boxes containing jewellery, deeds, securities, etc. In doing so they act as and have the obligations of gratuitous depositaries or onerous custodiers as the case may be. Greater care is required when the banker charges for the service, but the fact that the banker profits from keeping the credit balance in the same customer's account does not make him an onerous custodier.[9] In general a banker has no right of retention over goods or securities deposited with him for safe custody, but he may if it appears that the deposit was essentially in security of an overdraft.[10]

---

[1] *Royal Bank, supra.*   [2] *Bank of Scotland* v. *Morrison*, 1911 S.C. 593.

[3] *Deeley* v. *Lloyds Bank* [1912] A.C. 756.

[4] *Peters* v. *Anderson* (1814) 5 Taunt. 596.

[5] *Hay* v. *Torbet*, 1908 S.C. 781.

[6] *London and County Bank* v. *Terry* (1884) 25 Ch. D. 692.

[7] *Devaynes* v. *Noble (Clayton's Case)* (1816) 1 Mer. 608; see also *London and County Bank, supra*; *London and County Bank* v. *Radcliffe* (1881) 6 App. Cas. 722; *Lang* v. *Brown* (1859) 22 D. 113; *Cuthill* v. *Strachan* (1894) 21 R. 549; *Deeley* v. *Lloyds Bank* (1912) 29 T.L.R. 1; see also *N.W. Bank* v. *Poynter, Son & Macdonalds* (1894) 22 R. (H.L.) 1.

[8] *Robertson's Tr.* v. *Royal Bank* (1890) 18 R. 12.

[9] *Giblin* v. *McMullen* (1869) L.R. 2 P.C. 317.

[10] *Robertson's Tr.* v. *Royal Bank* (1890) 18 R. 12.

Banker as executor or trustee

Bankers may act as executor under a will or as trustee under a private trust disposition and settlement, as trustee for debenture holders, or under a unit trust scheme. They may charge reasonable fees for their services and provision should be made in the trust deed for their doing so.

Banker as adviser or manager of investments

It is a question of circumstances whether bankers hold themselves out as advisers on investments or financial matters.[1] If they do not their only duty when asked is to advise honestly, and to the best of their knowledge and belief.[2] If they do they owe a duty of care to a person who seeks advice to give it not only honestly but with reasonable skill and care, and will be liable for loss resulting from not having taken reasonable care, or advising without reasonable grounds for so doing.[3]

Banker as referee

The knowledge which a banker acquires of any particular customer's financial standing, credit-worthiness and business abilities makes him a suitable referee when such qualities are in issue. A banker giving a financial reference must not only answer honestly but, if he knows that the reference is to be or may be acted upon by a third party, must take reasonable care that he does not mislead that third party.[4]

Banker's lien

A banker has a judicially recognized general lien over all money, bills, notes and negotiable securities put into his hands, in security of any balance due to him by his customer,[5] but excepting instruments held by the banker as depositary, not as financial agent.[6] It does not extend over non-negotiable instruments, nor where there is a contract inconsistent with the lien. The holding of securities as depositary may not exclude the lien if the receipt therefor does not exclude lien, and advances have been made in

---

1 *Woods* v. *Martins Bank, Ltd.* [1959] 1 Q.B. 55; contrast *Banbury* v. *Bank of Montreal* [1918] A.C. 626.

2 *Woods, supra.*   3 *Dougall* v. *National Bank* (1892) 20 R. 8.

4 *Hedley Byrne* v. *Heller & Partners* [1964] A.C. 465. See also *Salton* v. *Clydesdale Bank* (1898) 1 F. 110; *Hockey* v. *Clydesdale Bank* (1898) 1 F. 119; *Midland Bank* v. *Seymour*, [1955] 2 Lloyd's Rep. 147.

5 Bell, *Comm.* II, 113; *Prin.* §1451; *Brandao* v. *Burnett* (1846) 12 Cl. & F. 787; *Misa* v. *Currie* (1876) 1 App. Cas. 554; *Clydesdale Bank* v. *Liqdrs. of Allan & Son*, 1926 S.C. 235.

6 *Brandao* v. *Burnett* (1846) 12 Cl. & F. 787.

reliance on those securities.[1] No lien exists if the banker has reason to believe that the securities are not the property of the customer nor are being deposited with their owner's authority,[2] nor to money or securities known by the banker to be held in trust. The lien does not give any right to realize the securities, but only to retain them.[3]

Banker's cards

A Banker's Card is a card issued by certain bankers to approved customers, authorizing the holder to obtain cash for his cheque to a limited sum at any branch of the participating banks and not merely at the branch where his account is kept. The issuing banker thereby undertakes unconditionally to pay the banker cashing the cheque. The banker further undertakes unconditionally that any payee accepting a cheque for up to the limited sum from the holder of the banker's card will be paid; he thereby guarantees payment of all cheques so drawn, and eliminates the risk to the payee that the cheque will be dishonoured on presentment.

Credit cards

Certain bankers and other companies[4] issue credit cards[5] which enable the holders to obtain goods and services on credit from establishments which have arranged with the issuing company to honour its cards. The accounts are sent to the issuing company which pays them and submits a consolidated account to the card holder periodically. The issuing company is thereby guaranteeing payment to the parties providing goods or services on credit to the cardholder and granting to the cardholder credit to the limit which it has permitted him to have outstanding at any time. The issuing company alone takes the risk and has recourse against the cardholder. A banker's credit card may also perform the functions of a banker's card.

Bank notes

Bank notes are promissory notes for fixed denominations issued by a banker payable on demand to the bearer, passing by delivery and commonly circulating like money, so long as the

[1] *Robertson's Tr.* v. *Royal Bank* (1890) 18 R. 12.
[2] *National Bank* v. *Dickie's Tr.* (1895) 22 R. 740 (stockbroker).
[3] *Robertson's Tr., supra.*
[4] e.g. Diner's Club, American Express.
[5] e.g. Barclaycard, Access.

issuing bank continues of good repute.[1] If its reputation is shaken, its notes would cease to be acceptable in settlement of debts. A bank note is exempted from sexennial prescription,[2] but is a warrant for summary diligence.[3]

Letters of credit

A letter of credit is a mandate by bankers to a third party recommending their customer to him, or authorizing him to furnish goods or pay money to the customer on the issuing bankers' credit and their undertaking to pay.[4] The letters may be addressed to a specific addressee or generally. Any restriction as to mandatary,[5] person to be credited,[6] transaction[7] or time[8] must be strictly adhered to. A letter of credit is not negotiable.[9] It may be difficult to distinguish a mere letter of introduction, a letter testifying to the customer's credit, and a guarantee of his obligations.

COMMERCIAL LETTERS OF CREDIT

Commercial letters of credit or documentary credits have developed as valuable machinery for the finance of international trading transactions.[10] To give a seller a greater assurance of payment than merely the buyer's undertaking, and to bridge the gap between despatch and payment on delivery, the buyer requests his banker, in respect of a particular transaction with the seller, to open a credit for a stated time with a correspondent banker in the seller's area for the benefit of the seller, which may be drawn upon by the seller by bills of exchange, on his presenting to the correspondent banker bills of lading, invoices or other specified evidence of despatch of the goods sold to the buyer. The correspondent banker may confirm the credit, thereby

---

[1] cf. *Miller* v. *Race* (1758) 1 Sm. L.C. 525. The issue of bank notes is regulated by statute.

[2] Bills of Exchange (Sc.) Act, 1772, S. 39; Prescription and Limitation (Sc.) Act, 1973, Sch. 1, para. 2(b). [3] Bank Notes (Sc.) Act, 1765.

[4] Bell, *Comm.* I, 389; *Prin.* §279.

[5] *Stewart* v. *Scott* (1803) Hume 91; *Philip* v. *Melville*, 21 Feb., 1809, F.C.

[6] *Douglas, Wilson & McAulay* v. *Gordon*, 24 Dec., 1814, F.C.

[7] *Crichton, Strachan, Bell & Co.* v. *Jack* (1797) Mor. 8229; *Ranken* v. *Murray*, 15 May, 1812, F.C.; *Scott* v. *Mitchell* (1866) 4 M. 551.

[8] *Tennant* v. *Bunten* (1859) 21 D. 631.

[9] *Struthers* v. *Commercial Bank* (1842) 4 D. 460; *Orr* v. *Union Bank* (1854) 17 D. (H.L.) 24; 1 Macq. 513.

[10] See generally Gutteridge and Megrah, *Law of Bankers' Commercial Credits*; Davis, *Commercial Letters of Credit*; Schmitthoff, *The Export Trade*; *Guaranty Trust* v. *Hannay* [1918] 2 K.B. 623; *Pavia* v. *Thurman-Nielsen* [1952] 2 Q.B. 84; *Trans Trust S.P.R.L.* v. *Danubian Trading Co.* [1952] 2 Q.B. 297.

adding his undertaking to pay. The seller may, by discounting the bill of exchange for the price, obtain immediate payment and the originating banker may hold the bill of lading for the goods until reimbursed by the buyer.

The opening of a confirmed letter of credit constitutes a bargain between the buyer's bankers and the sellers imposing on the former an absolute obligation to pay the latter, if goods answering the contract description are despatched in due time, irrespective of any dispute which there may be between the parties as to whether the goods satisfy the contract or not; the seller may accordingly tender delivery with the assurance that he will receive the price.[1]

A credit may be revocable or irrevocable; the former gives the seller little or no assurance of payment.[2] A correspondent banker will confirm only an irrevocable credit. There is no duty on a correspondent banker to inform the seller of the revocation of a credit.[3] Even if irrevocable the credit is normally open only for the period during which the seller must, to comply with his contract, despatch the goods and tender the documents therefor. A credit may also be transferable, or transferable and divisible, where the seller is in fact acting for one or more suppliers to whom he must transfer the whole or part of the credit.[4]

Apart from express provision,[5] the credit should be available within a reasonable time, and normally at least from the beginning of the period of despatch.[6] If it is a term of the contract that a credit will be opened, the seller may rescind the contract if it is not opened in time, or in appropriate form.[7] If no time is specified it must be done within a reasonable time.[8]

Relations between buyer and issuing bankers

The buyer who instructs his bankers to open a credit undertakes to pay them, if they pay the seller or his bankers on docu-

[1] Malas v. British Imex Industries, Ltd. [1958] 1 All E.R. 262; British Imex v. Midland Bank [1958] 1 All E.R. 264.
[2] Giddens v. Anglo-African Produce Co. Ltd. (1923) 14 Ll.L. Rep. 230.
[3] Cape Asbestos Co. v. Lloyds Bank [1921] W.N. 274.
[4] See Nicolene v. Simmonds [1952] 2 Lloyd's Rep. 419; Pavia v. Thurmann-Nielsen [1952] 2 Q.B. 84; Stach v. Baker Bosley [1958] 2 Q.B. 130.
[5] Knotz v. Fairclough, Dodd & Jones Ltd. [1952] 1 Lloyd's Rep. 226.
[6] Pavia v. Thurmann-Nielsen [1952] 2 Q.B. 84; Stach v. Baker Bosley [1958] 2 Q.B. 130.
[7] Panoutsos v. Raymond Hadley Corpn. [1917] 2 K.B. 473; Dix v. Grainger (1922) 10 Ll.L. Rep. 496; Giddens v. Anglo-African Produce Co. (1923) 14 Ll.L. Rep. 230; Plasticmoda v. Davidsons [1952] 1 Lloyd's Rep. 527; Trans Trust S.P.R.L. v. Danubian Trading Co. [1952] 2 Q.B. 297; Sinason-Teicher Corpn. v. Oilcakes Co. [1954] 3 All E.R. 468.
[8] Kronman v. Steinberger (1922) 10 Ll.L. Rep. 39; Etablissement Chaimbaux v. Harbormaster Ltd. [1955] 1 Lloyd's Rep. 303.

ments which satisfy the contract, and for this purpose the banker may require to be put in funds immediately. Any such funds, if appropriated to that purpose,[1] may be used for that purpose alone, and if not so used, must be returned to the buyer.[2] If the buyer does not pay him, the banker may claim indemnity for sums paid, so long as he has complied with the buyer's instructions.[3] The buyer cannot by himself cancel the credit.[4] To be entitled to reimbursement the banker must have insisted on exact compliance with the contract.[5]

Relations between issuing banker and correspondent (paying) banker

Prima facie the correspondent or paying banker is the agent of the issuing banker.[6] The paying banker is not normally in any direct contractual relation with the buyer, but only with the latter's banker, and the buyer accordingly cannot normally sue the paying banker, even if he has suffered loss by the latter's actings.[7] As agent the paying banker must comply strictly with his instructions.

Relations between paying banker and seller of goods

Their relations depend on the terms of the promise to pay. The paying banker is bound to pay only if the documents tendered by the seller are exactly in accordance with what is required by the credit,[8] and he is not entitled to pay against documents describing goods differently from those stipulated in the credit.[9] The documents are usually those required under a c.i.f. contract, viz., bill of lading, invoice and insurance policy. Bills of lading must be clean bills,[10] bear that the goods were 'shipped',[11] and conform to the credit in respect of the description of the goods.[12] An in-

---

[1] *Re Broad* (1884) 13 Q.B.D. 740.

[2] *Farley v. Turner* (1857) 26 L.J. Ch. 710; *Re Barned's Bank* (1870) 39 L.J. Ch. 635.

[3] *Equitable Trust Co. of N.Y.* v. *Dawson Partners* (1926) 27 Ll.L. Rep. 49.

[4] *Malas* v. *British Imex Industries Ltd.* [1957] 2 Lloyd's Rep. 549.

[5] *Equitable Trust Co., supra; Soproma* v. *Marine By-products Corpn.* [1966] 1 Lloyd's Rep. 367.

[6] *Bank Melli Iran* v. *Barclays Bank* [1951] 2 Lloyd's Rep. 367.

[7] *C.P.A.* v. *Barclays Bank* (1930) 36 Com. Cas. 71.

[8] *English, Scottish & Australian Bank Ltd.* v. *Bank of S. Africa* (1922) 13 Ll.L. Rep. 21; *Equitable Trust Co. of N.Y.* v. *Dawson Partners* (1926) 27 Ll.L. Rep. 49.

[9] *Rayner* v. *Hambros Bank* [1943] K.B. 37; *Bank Melli Iran* v. *Barclays Bank* [1951] 2 Lloyds Rep. 367.

[10] *National Bank of Egypt* v. *Hannevig's Bank* (1919) 1 Ll.L. Rep. 69.

[11] *Scott* v. *Barclays Bank* [1923] 2 K.B. 1.

[12] *London & Foreign Trading Corpn.* v. *British & N. European Bank* (1921) 9 Ll.L. Rep. 116; *Rayner* v. *Hambros Bank* [1943] K.B. 37; *Bank Melli Iran* v. *Barclays Bank* [1951] 2 Lloyds Rep. 367.

surance policy must cover the goods contracted for and no others,[1] for the voyage contracted for,[2] and against any risks which should have been contemplated.[3]

Payment

Payment is normally obtained from the issuing banker by drawing bills on him and sending them with the documents. If the issuing banker does not accept the bill, he is not entitled to retain the other documents and no property in the goods passes to him.[4] On accepting the bill he acquires a lien over the goods and may if need be, reimburse himself by selling the goods.[5]

[1] *May and Hassell, Ltd.* v. *Exportles of Moscow* (1940) 45 Com. Cas. 128.
[2] *Landauer & Co.* v. *Craven and Speeding Bros.* [1912] 2 K.B. 94.
[3] *Yuill* v. *Robson* [1908] 1 K.B. 270.
[4] Sale of Goods Act, 1893, S. 19(3).
[5] *Banner* v. *Johnston* (1871) L.R. 5 H.L. 157.

CHAPTER 51

OTHER AND INNOMINATE CONTRACTS

THERE are numerous other kinds of specific contracts, each having specialities peculiar to it. They all differ from those already discussed in that they involve not merely a personal contractual relationship but also involve the transfer, temporarily or permanently, outright or in security only, of rights in and over various kinds of objects of property, particularly the rights of possession and of ownership. For this reason they cannot be considered separately from the rights and interests which are recognized as existing in the various kinds of property. Accordingly in the context of rights in corporeal heritable property are considered contracts to create interests in land, to transfer land temporarily, as by lease, or outright, as by sale, or in security.[1] In the context of rights in incorporeal heritable property are considered contracts to transfer such rights outright or in security.[2] In the context of rights in corporeal moveable property or goods are considered contracts to transfer goods temporarily, by loan, deposit, custody or hire, to transfer them outright, by barter or sale or hire-purchase, and to transfer them in security, by pledge or pawn,[3] and in the context of rights in incorporeal moveable property are considered contracted to create, transfer, or transfer in security rights in property of those kinds.[4] Contracts of these kinds have the further distinctive feature that it is frequently necessary for some kind of deed, such as a disposition or assignation or stock transfer, to be executed to give effect to the contract; in short, the contract commonly indicates agreement to transfer some rights in property, but a deed is necessary to make the actual transfer. Since such contracts are inseparable from the property rights with which they deal examination of them at this point is inappropriate. But they include many important kinds of contracts and contracts raising many and difficult legal issues.

INNOMINATE CONTRACTS

Apart from contracts which may be classified under one or other of the foregoing recognized heads of nominate contracts,

[1] Chaps. 72, 77–87, *infra*. [2] Chaps. 90–92, *infra*.
[3] Chaps. 95–106, *infra*. [4] Chaps. 107–112, *infra*.

the general liberty of contracting for any purpose which is possible and legal implies that some agreements between persons may not be so classifiable.[1] An innominate contract is one which is not one of the recognized types of contract, such as sale, agency, and so on, to which a technical legal name attaches and which have reasonably settled incidents and implied terms.

No specialties of constitution or proof affect a contract merely because it is innominate and not classifiable,[2] but an agreement, which is both innominate and also unusual, anomalous, and peculiar in its terms may be proved only by writ or oath.[3] It is for the court in each case to say whether an innominate contract is also unusual, so as to demand proof by these means.[4]

Contracts merely innominate

Among contracts held innominate only have been an alleged bargain to commute ladle-dues for a lump sum,[5] to stable horses free if the defender's vehicle would depart from the pursuer's inn,[6] that a solicitor would act without fee unless he were successful,[7] that a person was to manage his brother's business at a salary and a share in profits,[8] that a widow would take an increased liferent in lieu of *jus relictae*,[9] and to pay a bonus to an employee while serving with the Admiralty.[10]

Under the same head have fallen various arrangements and compromises for the avoidance or termination of litigation, such as for the acceptance of a payment in full of a claim or of the conclusions of an action,[11] and *pacta de non petendo*.[12] But if the

---

[1] cf. Ersk. III, 1, 35.

[2] *Thomson v. Fraser* (1868) 7 M. 39, 41; *Forbes v. Caird* (1877) 4 R. 1141, 1142; *Allison v. A's Trs.* (1904) 6 F. 496; *Smith v. Reekie*, 1920 S.C. 188, 192.

[3] Ersk. IV, 4, 20; Bell, *Prin.* §2257; *Smith, supra*; *Cook v. Grubb*, 1963 S.C. 1.

[4] *Cook, supra*; but see *Hallet v. Ryrie* (1907) 15 S.L.T. 367.

[5] *Craig v. Hill* (1830) 8 S. 833.

[6] *Forbes, supra.*

[7] *Moscrip v. O'Hara* (1880) 8 R. 36; *Jacobs v. McMillan* (1899) 2 F. 79; *Campbell v. C's Exors.*, 1910, 2 S.L.T. 240; but see *Taylor v. Forbes* (1853) 24 D. 19 note.

[8] *Allison, supra.*

[9] *Jack v. McGrouther* (1901) 38 S.L.R. 701.

[10] *Smith, supra*; see also *Kinninmont v. Paxton* (1892) 20 R. 128; *Moncrieff v. Seivwright* (1896) 33 S.L.R. 456; *Mungall v. Bowhill Colliery Co.* (1904) 12 S.L.T. 262; *Toby Mfg. Co. v. Black*, 1957 S.L.T. (Sh. Ct.) 45.

[11] *Jaffrey v. Simpson* (1835) 13 S. 1122; *Thomson v. Fraser* (1868) 7 M. 39; see e.g. *Love v. Marshall* (1872) 10 M. 795; *Downie v. Black* (1885) 13 R. 271; *McDonagh v. MacLellan* (1886) 13 R. 1000; *N.B. Ry. v. Wood* (1891) 18 R. (H.L.) 27; *Campbell v. Morrison* (1891) 19 R. 282; *Delaney v. Stirling* (1893) 20 R. 506; *Gow v. Henry* (1899) 2 F. 48; *Anderson v. Dick* (1901) 4 F. 68; *Douglas v. Hogarth* (1901) 4 F. 148; *Torbat v. T's Trs.* (1906) 14 S.L.T. 830, explained in *Cook v. Grubb*, 1963 S.C. 1; see also *Reid v. Gow* (1903) 10 S.L.T. 606; *Hylander's Exors. v. H. & K. Modes*, 1957 S.L.T. (Sh. Ct.) 69.

[12] *Muir v. Crawford* (1875) 2 R. (H.L.) 148.

compromise is of an action relating to heritage or to a right requiring writing for its constitution parole evidence of the arrangement is insufficient.[1] And there has been said to be no authority for the view that an obligation to pay money, not incidental to one of the well-known ordinary consensual contracts, is provable otherwise than by writ or oath.[2]

Innominate and unusual contracts

Among contracts held to be both innominate and unusual have been alleged agreements to leave all of a person's property to his brother on condition of his settling as a medical practitioner in the neighbourhood,[3] to leave to a pursuer's children a sum as great as the defender had got from his wife's father's estate,[4] that one person would pay a fourth share of the expenses of a shooting syndicate,[5] that if a tenant would remain the landlord would repay money lost in the course of the lease,[6] that a contract *ex facie* of sale was intended to create agency only,[7] to divide funds destined by statute to the survivor,[8] that one party had to pay the expenses of a proposed feu, completed or not,[9] that parties had agreed to pay a capital sum instead of weekly payments of compensation,[10] that the pursuer had been appointed to a post on very exceptional terms,[11] and that as a compromise of a claim a person was to be re-employed permanently.[12]

---

[1] *Cook* v. *Grubb*, 1963 S.C. 1, explaining *Love* v. *Marshall* (1872) 10 M. 795; see also *McLean* v. *Richardson* (1834) 12 S. 865; *Kinninmont* v. *Paxton* (1892) 20 R. 128; *Moncrieff* v. *Seivwright* (1896) 33 S.L.R. 456; *Mungall* v. *Bowhill Colliery Co.* (1904) 12 S.L.T. 262.

[2] *McFadzean's Exor.* v. *McAlpine*, 1907 S.C. 1269, 1273. See also *Cochrane* v. *Trail* (1900) 2 F. 794, 799; *Binning* v. *Easton* (1906) 8 F. 407, 415.

[3] *Edmondston* v. *E.* (1861) 23 D. 995; cf. *Gray* v. *Johnston*, 1928 S.C. 659.

[4] *Johnston* v. *Goodlet* (1868) 6 M. 1067.

[5] *Stewart and Craig* v. *Phillips* (1882) 9 R. 501, 506.

[6] *Garden* v. *E. Aberdeen* (1893) 20 R. 896.

[7] *Muller* v. *Weber & Schaer* (1901) 3 F. 401.

[8] *McMurrich's Trs.* v. *McM's Trs.* (1903) 6 F. 121.

[9] *Woddrop* v. *Speirs* (1906) 14 S.L.T. 319.

[10] *McFadzean's Exor.* v. *McAlpine*, 1907 S.C. 1269.

[11] *Copeland* v. *Lord Wimborne*, 1912 S.C. 355.

[12] *Cook* v. *Grubb*, 1963 S.C. 1.